$\tilde{r}_t$	Uncertain actual rate of return in period t
r_D	Rate of return on firm's debt
r_E	Expected rate of return on firm's equity
r_f	Risk-free increase rate (on debt)
r_z	Return on riskless equity
r_m	Expected rate of return on the market portfolio
r_S	Dollar rate of interest
r^*	Adjusted cost of capital
$s_{\text{SFr/\$}}$	Spot rate of exchange between Swiss francs and dollars
t	Time
T_c	Rate of corporate income tax
T_{pfed}	Rate of personal tax (federal portion)
T_{prov}	Provincial tax on personal income, as a porportion of federal tax
T_{p}	Rate of personal tax on interest and salary income: $T_{\text{p}} = T_{\text{pfed}}(1 + T_{\text{prov}})$
T_{pE}	Rate of personal tax on equity income (weighted average of the rate on dividends and the present value of the rate on capital gains)
T^*	Effective corporate tax rate for earning interest tax shields
UCC_t	Undepreciated capital cost for tax purposes, at the end of year t
V	Market value of firm: $V = D + E$
β	Beta: A measure of market risk
δ	Delta: hedge ratio
λ	Lambda: Market price of risk $= \dfrac{r_m - r_f}{\sigma_m^2}$
ρ_{12}	Rho: Correlation coefficient between investments 1 and 2
σ	Sigma: Standard deviation
σ_{12}	Sigma: Covariance of investment 1 with investment 2
σ^2	Sigma squared: Variance
Σ	Capital sigma: "The sum of"

From the reference
library of

_____

P·R·I·N·C·I·P·L·E·S

of CORPORATE

FINANCE

Second Canadian Edition

Finance Titles from McGraw-Hill Ryerson

P·R·I·N·C·I·P·L·E·S
of CORPORATE
FINANCE

Second Canadian Edition

RICHARD BREALEY
London Business School

STEWART MYERS
Massachusetts Institute of Technology

GORDON SICK
University of Calgary

RONALD GIAMMARINO
University of British Columbia

McGraw-Hill Ryerson Limited

Toronto   Montreal   New York   Auckland   Bogotá
Caracas   Lisbon   London   Madrid   Mexico
Milan   New Delhi   Paris   San Juan
Singapore   Sydney   Tokyo

PRINCIPLES OF CORPORATE FINANCE
Second Canadian Edition

ISBN: 0-07-549923-1

1 2 3 4 5 6 7 8 9 0   D   1 0 9 8 7 6 5 4 3 2

Senior Editor: Jennifer Mix
Senior Supervising Editor: Susan Calvert
Production Editor: Edie Franks
Cover and Text Design: Michelle Losier
Technical Artist: Patricia Code
Typesetting and Page Make-Up: Compeer Typographic Services Limited
Printing and Binding: John Deyell Company Limited
Text set in: Meridien

Printed and bound in Canada

Canadian Cataloguing in Publication Data

Main entry under title:

Principles of corporate finance

2nd Canadian ed.
ISBN 0-07-549923-1

1. Corporations – Finance.   I. Brealey, Richard A.

HG4026.P75 1990   658.15   C90-094501-X

To our wives, Diana, Maureen, Carmel, and Stephanie
with special thanks to Matt, Andrew, Jessie, Laura, Jacob, Jonathan, and Mark.

C·O·N·T·E·N·T·S

x

PART 3 PRACTICAL PROBLEMS IN CAPITAL BUDGETING

PART 5 DIVIDEND POLICY AND CAPITAL STRUCTURE 391

PART 10 MERGERS, INTERNATIONAL FINANCE, AND PENSIONS 855

ABOUT THE AUTHORS:

Richard A. Brealey

London Business School. Professor of Corporate Finance. Past President of European Finance Association and Director of the American Finance Association. Current research interests include portfolio theory and international finance. Member of editorial board of *Midland Corporate Finance Journal*. Other books include *Introduction to Risk and Return from Common Stocks*. Formerly with Sun Life Assurance Company of Canada and Keystone Custodian Funds of Boston.

Stewart C. Myers

Gordon Y. Billard Professor of Finance at the Massachusetts Institute of Technology's Sloan School of Management. Director of the International Financial Services Research Center at the Sloan School. Research Associate of the National Bureau of Economic Research and past President and Director of the American Finance Association. His research is primarily concerned with the valuation of real and financial assets, corporate financial policy, and financial aspects of government regulation of business. Member of the *Midland Corporate Finance Journal*. Coauthor of *Optimal Financing Decisions* (with A.A. Robichek) and editor of *Modern Developments in Financial Management*.

Gordon A. Sick

Chairman of the Finance Area at the University of Calgary's Faculty of Management. Associate Editor for the Finance Department of *Management Science*. Director of the Western Finance Association and Finance Program Chairperson for the Administrative Sciences Association of Canada. He currently serves as President of the Calgary Association for the Mentally Handicapped. His research interests include capital budgeting, taxation, and the analysis of real options.

Ronald M. Giammarino

Associate Professor of Finance and Chairperson of the Master's Program Committee at the University of British Columbia's Faculty of Commerce and Business Administration. Member of the curriculum review committee for the Certified General Accountants. He is involved in developing management education courses under the auspices of the United Nations in China. His research interests include corporate financial policy, mergers, take-overs, bank regulation, and the study of financial distress.

P·R·E·F·A·C·E

This book describes the theory and practice of corporate finance. We hardly need explain why financial managers should master the practical aspect of their job, but a word on the role of theory may be helpful.

Managers learn from experience how to cope with routine problems. But the best managers are also able to respond rationally to change. To do this you need more than time-honoured rules of thumb; you must understand *why* companies and financial managers behave the way they do. In other words, you need a *theory* of corporate finance.

Does that sound intimidating? It shouldn't. Good theory helps you understand what is going on in the word around you. It helps you ask the right questions when times change and new problems must be analyzed. It also tells you what things you do *not* need to worry about.

Throughout the book we show how to use financial theory to solve practical problems, and how to illuminate the facts and institutional material that students of corporate finance must absorb.

Of course the theory presented in this book is not perfect and complete — no theory is. There are some famous controversies in which financial economists cannot agree on what firms ought to do. We have not glossed over these controversies. We set out the main arguments for each side and tell you where we stand.

There are also a few cases where theory indicates that the practical rules of thumb employed by today's managers are leading to poor decisions. Where financial managers appear to be making mistakes, we say so, while admitting that there may be hidden reasons for their actions. In brief, we have tried to be fair but to pull no punches.

Once understood, good theory is common sense. Therefore, we have tried to present it at a common-sense level. We have avoided abstract proofs and heavy mathematics. However, parts of the book may require a significant intellectual effort for those unused to economic reasoning. We have marked the most difficult sections and problems with asterisks, and suggest that you skim these sections on the first reading.

There are no ironclad prerequisites for reading this book except algebra and the English language. An elementary knowledge of accounting, statistics, and microeconomics is helpful, however. The study guide for this book, *Study Guide to Accompany Principles of Corporate Finance*, McGraw-Hill Ryerson, Toronto, 1992 includes chapter summaries, additional illustrations, solved problems, and other useful material.

Each chapter of this book closes with a summary, an annotated list of suggestions for further reading, a quick and easy quiz, and several more challenging questions and problems. Answers to the quiz questions may be found at the end of the book, along with present value tables and a glossary.

We should mention two matters of style now to prevent confusion later. First, you will notice that the most important financial terms are set in **boldface** type the first time they appear. Second, most algebraic symbols representing dollar values are set in capital letters. Other symbols are lowercase letters. Thus, the symbol for a dividend payment is DIV; the symbol for a percentage of rate of return is r. We hope this will make our algebra easier to follow.

Readers of the first edition of this book may be interested to know what we have changed and added. First, we have added material on analyzing Canadian mortgages and updated all the material related to taxation. These changes mainly affect the chapters on capital budgeting, dividend policy, and capital structure. We have updated historical data tables and figures throughout the book and added many new and interesting problems at the end of chapters.

We have rearranged the chapters on risk and return for improved clarity. Chapter 7 discusses historical risk-return performance, diversification, and the need for a measure of systematic risk. Chapter 8 discusses the capital asset pricing model (CAPM), consumption capital asset pricing model, and arbitrage pricing theory (APT) with greater intuition and detail. The chapter discusses the traditional mean-variance exposition of the CAPM and relates this to a graphical exposition of APT. Chapter 9 discusses practical issues arising when one implements these risk-return theories to evaluate capital projects.

Chapter 19 updates the discussion of interest tax shields to incorporate recent developments in the theory of the joint impact of corporate and personal taxation.

We have expanded our discussion of options. Chapter 20 discusses the binomial option pricing model in greater and more practical detail. It also emphasizes how to use this model to determine when to exercise an option early. Chapter 21 discusses the application of option theory to real investment decisions.

Chapter 25 discusses how to use financial markets to reduce risk by hedging. It includes practical issues such as the determination of hedge ratios. We have also moved the material on bond duration to that chapter.

We have clarified the discussion of leasing to focus the analysis on discounting after-tax cash flows at the after-tax cost of debt. This technique is still related to the APV technique. We also provide formulas for analyzing leases with monthly payments.

We have substantially rewritten the chapters on mergers (Chapter 33) and corporate debt (Chapters 23 and 24) to include more discussion of hostile take-overs, LBOs, corporate restructuring, and junk bonds. There is also some new interesting Canadian evidence on who wins in mergers.

We continue to illustrate the theory with examples drawn from a variety of countries to reflect the fact that Canadian businesses operate in an open economy.

Acknowledgements

The First Canadian Edition was co-authored with Bob Whaley, now at Duke University and many of his valuable insights remain in this Edition. We would also like to thank David Laughton and Bruce Rutherford at the University of Alberta; Sandra Betton, Chris Cumming, David Downie, Max Maksimovic, and Rex Thompson at the University of British Columbia; Mike Robinson at the University of Calgary; George Athanassakos at Wilfrid Laurier University; Paul Bishop at the University of Western Ontario; Alex Faseruk at Memorial University of Newfoundland; Swaminathan Sankaran at the University of Regina; and the 1990 Management Class at Shanghai Jiao Tong University. Finally, we would like to thank our sponsoring editor, Jennifer Mix, for her careful blend of cajoling and mentoring to get this book out of our minds and into print.

Richard A. Brealey
Stewart C. Myers
Gordon A. Sick
Ronald M. Giammarino

P·A·R·T

1

VALUE

C · H · A · P · T · E · R

1

WHY FINANCE MATTERS

This book is about financial decisions by corporations. We should start by saying what these decisions are and why they are important.

To carry on business a modern company needs an almost endless variety of **real assets**. Many of them are tangible assets, such as machinery, factories, and offices; others are intangible, such as technical expertise, trademarks, and patents. All of them unfortunately need to be paid for. To obtain the necessary money the company sells pieces of paper called **financial assets**, or securities. These pieces of paper have value because they are claims on the firm's real assets. Financial assets include not only shares of stock but also bonds, bank loans, lease obligations, and so on.

The financial manager faces two basic problems. First, how much should the firm invest, and what specific assets should the firm invest in? Second, how should the cash required for investment be raised? The answer to the first question is the firm's **investment**, or **capital budgeting**, **decision**. The answer to the second is its **financing decision**. The financial manager attempts to find the specific answers that make the firm's shareholders as well off as possible.

Success is usually judged by value: shareholders are made better off by any decision that increases the value of their stake in the firm. Thus, you might say that a good investment decision is one that results in purchase of a real asset that is worth more than it costs—an asset that makes a net contribution to value. The secret of success in financial management is to increase value. That is a simple statement, but not a very helpful one. It is like advising an investor in the stock market to "buy low, sell high." The problem is how to do it.

1-1 WHY FINANCE IS CHALLENGING AND INTERESTING

There may be a few activities in which one can read a textbook and then "do it," but financial management is not one of them. That is why finance is worth studying. Who wants to work in a field where there is no room for experience, creativity, judgement, and a pinch of luck? Although this book cannot supply any of these items, it does present the concepts and information on which good financial decisions are based.

There are many reasons that the financial manager's job is challenging and interesting. Here are four important ones.

**The
Importance of
Capital
Markets**

The first reason is that the financial manager must act as an intermediary, standing between the firm's operations and **capital markets**, where the firm's securities are traded. The financial manager's role is shown in Figure 1-1, which traces the flow of cash from investors to the firm and back to investors again. The flow starts when securities are issued to raise cash (arrow 1 in the figure). The cash is used to purchase real assets used in the firm's operations (arrow 2). (You can think of the firm's operations as a bundle of real assets.) Later, if the firm does well, the real assets generate cash inflows, which more than repay the initial investment (arrow 3). Finally, the cash is either reinvested (arrow 4a) or returned to the investors who purchased the original security issue (arrow 4b). Of course the choice between arrows 4a and 4b is not a completely free one. For example, if a bank loans the firm money at stage 1, the bank has to be repaid this money plus interest at stage 4b.

Figure 1-1 shows that the financial manager has to deal with capital markets as well as the firm's operations. Therefore, the financial manager must understand how capital markets work.

The financing decision always reflects some theory about capital markets. For example, suppose a firm chooses to finance a major expansion program by issuing

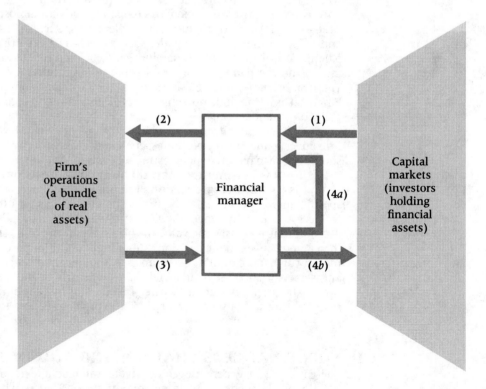

Figure 1-1   Flow of cash between capital markets and the firm's operations. Key: (1) cash raised by selling financial assets to investors; (2) cash invested in the firm's operations and used to purchase real assets; (3) cash generated by the firm's operations; (4a) cash reinvested; (4b) cash returned to investors.

Source: From *Modern Developments in Financial Management*, S.C. Myers, ed. Copyright © 1976 by Praeger Publishers, Inc., New York. Reprinted by permission of Holt, Rinehart and Winston.

bonds. The financial manager must have considered the terms of the issue and concluded that it was fairly priced. That required a theory of how bonds are priced. The financial manager must also have asked whether the firm's stockholders would be made better or worse off by the extra debt standing between them and the firm's real assets. That required a theory of how corporate borrowing affects the well-being of stockholders.

The investment decision cannot be separated from capital markets either. A firm that acts in its stockholders' interest should accept those investments that increase the value of their stake in the firm. But that requires a theory of how common stocks are valued.

Understanding Value

Understanding how capital markets work amounts to understanding how financial assets are valued. This is a subject on which there has been remarkable progress over the past ten to twenty years. New theories have been developed to explain the prices of bonds and stocks. And, when put to the test, these theories have worked well. We therefore devote a large part of this book to explaining these ideas and their implications.

Time and Uncertainty

The financial manager cannot avoid coping with time and uncertainty. Firms often have the opportunity to invest in assets that cannot pay their way in the short run and that expose the firm and its stockholders to considerable risk. The investment, if undertaken, may have to be financed by debt that cannot be fully repaid for many years. The firm cannot walk away from such choices—someone has to decide whether the opportunity is worth more than it costs and whether the additional debt burden can be safely borne.

Understanding People

The financial manager needs the opinions and cooperation of many people. For instance, many new investment ideas come from plant managers. The financial manager wants these ideas to be presented fairly; therefore, the proposers should have no personal incentives to be either overconfident or overcautious. Take another example. In some firms the plant manager needs permission from the head office to buy a company car but not to lease it, and the line of least resistance may be to lease the car. In other firms the plant manager needs permission from the head office to buy or lease, and the line of least resistance may be to travel everywhere by cab. The financial manager has to be aware of these effects and has to devise procedures that will avoid as far as possible any conflicts of interest.

These are not the only reasons that financial management is interesting and challenging. We think that as you read this book you will find many others.

1-2   WHO IS THE FINANCIAL MANAGER?

In this book we will use the term *financial manager* to refer to anyone responsible for a significant corporate investment or financing decision. But except in the smallest firms, no *single* person is responsible for all the decisions discussed in this book. Responsibility is dispersed throughout the firm. Top management is of course continuously involved in financial decisions. But the engineer who designs a new production facility is also involved: the design determines the kind of real asset the firm will hold. The advertising manager may also make important investment decisions in the course of his or her work. A major advertising campaign is really an investment in an intangible asset. If potential customers are aware of your product and convinced they should buy it, you have an asset that will pay off in future sales and earnings.

Nevertheless, there are some managers who specialize in finance. The **treasurer** is usually the person most directly responsible for obtaining financing, managing the firm's cash account and its relationships with banks and other financial institutions, and making sure the firm meets its obligations to the investors holding its securities. Typical responsibilities of the treasurer are listed in the left-hand column of Table 1-1.

For small firms, the treasurer is likely to be the only financial executive. However, larger corporations usually also have a **controller**. The right-hand column of Table 1-1 lists the typical controller's responsibilities. Notice that there is a conceptual difference between the two jobs. The treasurer's function is primarily custodial—he or she obtains and manages the company's capital. By contrast, the controller's function is primarily one of inspecting to see that the money is used efficiently. The controller manages budgeting, accounting, and auditing.

The largest firms usually appoint a financial vice-president, who acts as the chief financial officer, overseeing both the treasurer's and the controller's work. In addition, the financial vice-president is deeply involved in financial policy making and corporate planning. Often he or she will have general managerial responsibilities beyond strictly financial issues.

Major capital investment projects are so closely tied to plans for product development, production, and marketing that managers from these areas are inevitably drawn into planning and analyzing the projects. If the firm has staff members specializing in corporate planning, they are naturally involved in capital budgeting too. Usually the treasurer, controller, or financial vice-president is responsible for organizing and supervising the capital budgeting process.

Because of the importance of many financial issues, ultimate decisions often rest by law or by custom with the board of directors.[1] For example, only the board has the legal power to declare a dividend or to sanction a public issue of securities. Boards usually delegate decision-making authority for small- or medium-sized investment outlays. But the authority to approve large investments is almost never delegated.

Table 1-1
Some Typical Responsibilities of the Treasurer and Controller

Treasurer	Controller
Banking relationships	Accounting
Cash management	Preparation of financial statements
Obtaining financing	Internal auditing
Credit management	Payroll
Dividend disbursement	Custody of records
Insurance	Preparing budgets
Pensions management	Taxes

Note: This table is not an exhaustive list of tasks treasurers and controllers may undertake.

[1] Often, the firm's chief financial officer is also a member of its board of directors.

1-3 TOPICS COVERED IN THIS BOOK

This book covers investment decisions first, then financing decisions, and finally a series of topics in which investment and financing decisions interact and cannot be made separately.

In Parts 1, 2, and 3 we look at three different aspects of the investment decision. The first is the problem of how to value assets, the second is the link between risk and value, and the third is the management of the investment process. Our discussion of these topics occupies Chapters 2 to 12.

Eleven chapters devoted to the simple problem of "finding real assets that are worth more than they cost" may seem excessive, but that problem is not so simple in practice. Also, a conceptual base must be laid. So far, we only have asserted that increasing value is the appropriate financial objective for the firm. That assertion will have to be proved. Also, we will require a theory of how long-lived, risky assets are valued, and that requirement will lead us to basic questions about capital markets. For example:

- How are corporate bonds and stocks valued in capital markets?
- What risks are borne by investors in corporate securities? How can these risks be measured?
- What compensation do investors demand for bearing risk?
- What rate of return can investors in common stocks reasonably expect to receive?

Intelligent capital budgeting and financing decisions require answers to these and other questions about how capital markets work.

Financing decisions occupy Parts 4 through 7. We begin in Chapter 13 with another basic question about capital markets: "Do security prices reflect the fair value of the underlying assets?" The reason this question is so important is that the financial manager must know whether securities can be issued at a fair price. Exactly how and when securities should be issued are the subjects of the remaining chapters in Part 4.

Parts 5, 6, and 7 continue the analysis of the financing decision, covering dividend policy, debt policy, and the alternative forms of debt. Literally dozens of different financing instruments are described and analyzed, including debentures, convertibles, leases, eurobonds, financial futures, and many other exotic beasts. We will also describe what happens when firms find themselves in financial distress because of poor operating performance, excessive borrowing, or both. Furthermore, we will show how financing considerations sometimes affect capital budgeting decisions.

Part 8 covers financial planning. Decisions about investment, dividend policy, debt policy, and other financial issues cannot be reached independently. They have to add up to a sensible overall financial plan for the firm, one which increases the value of the shareholders' investment yet still retains enough flexibility for the firm to avoid financial distress and to pursue unexpected new opportunities.

Part 9 is devoted to decisions about the firm's short-term assets and liabilities. There are separate chapters on three topics: channels for short-term borrowing or investment, management of liquid assets (cash and marketable securities), and management of accounts receivable (money lent by the firm to its customers).

Part 10 covers three important problems that require decisions about both investment and financing. We first look at mergers and acquisitions. Then we consider international financial management. All the financial problems of doing business at home are present overseas, but the international financial manager faces the additional complications created by multiple currencies, different tax systems, and special regulations imposed by foreign institutions and governments.

The final chapter in Part 10 describes how pension plans are created and financed by corporations. Pension plan management is not a traditional subject in corporate finance texts, but we think it should be. Pensions represent an enormous liability for corporations in the United States and Canada.

Part 11 is our conclusion. It also discusses some of the things we *don't* know about finance. If you can be the first to solve any of these puzzles, you will be justifiably famous.

1-4 SUMMARY

In Chapter 2 we will begin with the most basic concepts of asset valuation. However, let us first sum up the principal points made in this introductory chapter.

The overall task of financial management can be broken down into (1) the investment, or capital budgeting, decision and (2) the financing decision. In other words, the firm has to decide (1) how much to invest and what assets to invest in and (2) how to raise the necessary cash. The objective is to increase the value of the shareholders' stake in the firm.

The financial manager's job is a challenging and interesting one. He or she acts as an intermediary between the firm and the capital markets. Good financial managers understand how capital markets work and how long-lived, risky assets are valued. They also work to devise procedures and incentives that encourage others in the firm to act sensibly when financial problems arise.

In small companies there is often only one financial executive. However, the larger corporation usually has both a treasurer and a controller. The treasurer's job is to obtain and manage the company's financing. By contrast, the controller's job is one of inspecting to see that the money is used correctly. In large firms there may also be a financial vice-president who acts as the firm's chief financial officer.

Of course all managers, not just finance specialists, face financial problems. In this book we will use the term *financial manager* to refer to any person confronted with a corporate financing or investment decision.

QUIZ

1. Read the following passage: "Companies usually buy (a) assets. These include both tangible assets such as (b) and intangible assets such as (c). In order to pay for these assets, they sell (d) assets such as (e). The decision regarding which assets to buy is usually termed the (f) or (g) decision. The decision regarding how to raise the money is usually termed the (h) decision." Now fit each of the following terms into the most appropriate space: *financing, real, bonds, investment, executive airplanes, financial, capital budgeting, brand names.*

2. Which of the following statements more accurately describes the treasurer rather than the controller?
   (a) Likely to be the only financial executive in small firms
   (b) Monitors capital expenditures to ensure they are not misappropriated
   (c) Responsible for investing the firm's spare cash

   (d) Responsible for arranging any issue of common stock
   (e) Responsible for the company's tax affairs
3.   Which of the following are real assets, and which are financial?
   (a) A share of stock
   (b) A personal IOU
   (c) A trademark
   (d) A truck
   (e) Undeveloped land
   (f) The balance in the firm's chequing account
   (g) An experienced and hardworking sales force
   (h) A corporate bond

C·H·A·P·T·E·R

2

PRESENT VALUE AND THE OPPORTUNITY COST OF CAPITAL

Companies invest in a variety of real assets. These include tangible assets, such as plants and machinery, and intangible assets, such as management contracts and patents. The object of the investment, or capital budgeting, decision is to find real assets that are worth more than they cost. In this chapter we will show what this objective means in a country with extensive and well-functioning capital markets. At the same time we will take the first, most basic steps toward understanding how assets are valued. It turns out that if there is a good market for an asset, its value is exactly the same as the market price.

There are a few cases in which it is not that difficult to estimate asset values. In real estate, for example, you can hire a professional appraiser to do it for you. Suppose you own an apartment building. The odds are that your appraiser's estimate of its value will be within a few percentage points of what the building would actually sell for.[1] After all, there is continuous activity in the real estate market, and the appraiser's stock-in-trade is knowledge of the prices at which similar properties have recently changed hands.

Thus the problem of valuing real estate is simplified by the existence of an active market in which all kinds of properties are bought and sold. For many purposes no formal theory of value is needed. We can take the market's word for it.

But we have to go deeper than that. First, it is important to know how asset values are reached in an active market. Even if you can take the appraiser's word for it, it is important to understand *why* that apartment building is worth, say, $250,000 and not a higher or lower figure. Second, the market for most corporate assets is pretty thin. Look in the classified advertisements in *The Financial Post* or *The Wall Street Journal*: it is not often that you see a blast furnace for sale.

---

[1] There are some kinds of properties that appraisers find really difficult to value — for example, nobody knows the potential selling price of the Taj Mahal or the Parthenon or Niagara Falls. If you own such a property, we congratulate you. But we assume that your apartment building is a standard property.

Companies are always searching for assets that are worth more to them than to others. That apartment house is worth more to you if you can manage it better than others. But in that case, looking at the price of similar buildings will not tell you what your apartment house is worth under your management. You need to know how asset prices are determined. In other words, you need a theory of value.

We start to build that theory in this chapter. We will stick to the simplest problems and examples to make basic ideas clear. Readers with a taste for more complication will find plenty to satisfy them in later chapters.

2-1   INTRODUCTION TO PRESENT VALUE

Later in this chapter we will prove why the concept of present value is useful. However, that concept will go down more easily if we first acquire an intuitive understanding of it.

Suppose your apartment house burns down, leaving you with a vacant lot worth $50,000 and a cheque for $200,000 from the fire insurance company. You consider rebuilding, but your real estate adviser suggests putting up an office building instead. The construction cost would be $300,000, and there would also be the cost of the land, which might otherwise be sold for $50,000. On the other hand, your adviser foresees a shortage of office space and predicts that a year from now the new building would fetch $400,000 if you sold it. Thus you would be investing $350,000 now in the expectation of realizing $400,000 a year hence. You should go ahead if the **present value** of the expected $400,000 payoff is greater than the investment of $350,000. Therefore, you need to ask yourself, "What is the value today of $400,000 one year from now, and is that present value greater than $350,000?"

Calculating Present Value   The present value of $400,000 one year from now must be less than $400,000. The reason for this is summed up by the following principle: *a dollar today is worth more than a dollar tomorrow*, because the dollar today can be invested to start earning interest immediately.

Thus, the present value of a delayed payoff may be found by multiplying the payoff by a **discount factor** that is less than one. (If the discount factor were more than one, a dollar today would be worth *less* than a dollar tomorrow.) If C_1 denotes the expected payoff at time period 1 (one year hence), then

$$\text{Present value (PV)} = \text{discount factor} \times C_1$$

This discount factor is expressed as the reciprocal of one plus a **rate of return:**

$$\text{Discount factor} = \frac{1}{1 + r}$$

The rate of return r is the reward investors demand for accepting delayed payment.

Let us consider the real estate investment, assuming for the moment that the $400,000 payoff is a sure thing. The office building is not the only way to obtain $400,000 a year from now. You could invest in federal government securities maturing in a year. Suppose these securities yield 7% interest. How much would you have to invest in them to receive $400,000 at the end of the year? That is an easy question. You would have to invest $400,000/1.07, which is $373,832.

Therefore at an interest rate of 7%, the present value of $400,000 one year from now is $373,832.

Let's assume that, as soon as you've committed the land and begun construction on the building, you decide to sell your project. How much could you sell it for? That's another easy question. Since the property produces $400,000, investors would be willing to pay $373,832 for it. That's what it would cost them to get a $400,000 payoff from investing in government securities. Of course you could always sell your property for less, but why sell for less than the market will bear? The $373,832 present value is the only feasible price that satisfies both buyer and seller. Therefore, the present value of the property is also its market price.

To calculate present value, we discount expected future payoffs by the rate of return offered by comparable investment alternatives. This rate of return is often referred to as the **discount rate, hurdle rate,** or **opportunity cost of capital**. It is called the *opportunity cost* because it is the return forgone by investing in the project rather than investing in securities. In our example the opportunity cost was 7%. Present value was obtained by dividing $400,000 by 1.07:

$$\text{PV} = \text{discount factor} \times C_1 = \frac{1}{1 + r}C_1 = \frac{\$400,000}{1.07} = \$373,832$$

Net Present Value The building is worth $373,832, but this does not mean that you are $373,832 better off. You committed $350,000, and therefore your **net present value** is $23,832. Net present value (**NPV**) is found by subtracting the required investment:

$$\text{NPV} = \text{PV} - \text{required investment} = \$373,832 - \$350,000 = \$23,832$$

In other words, your office development is worth more than it costs—it makes a *net* contribution to value. The formula for calculating NPV can be written as

$$\text{NPV} = C_0 + \frac{C_1}{1 + r}$$

remembering that C_0, the cash flow at time period 0 (that is, today) will usually be a negative number. In other words, C_0 is an investment and therefore a cash *outflow*. In our example, $C_0 = -\$350,000$.

A Comment on Risk and Present Value We made one unrealistic assumption in our discussion of the office development: your real estate adviser cannot be *certain* about future values of office buildings. The $400,000 figure represents the best *forecast*, but it is not a sure thing.

Therefore, our conclusion about how much investors would pay for the building is wrong. Since they could achieve $400,000 with certainty by buying $373,832 worth of federal government securities, they would not buy your building for that amount. You would have to cut your asking price to attract investors' interest.

Here we can invoke a second basic financial principle: *a safe dollar is worth more than a risky one*. Most investors avoid risk when they can do so without sacrificing return. However, the concepts of present value and the opportunity cost of capital still make sense for risky investments. It is still proper to discount the payoff by the rate of return offered by a comparable investment. But we have to think of *expected* payoffs and the *expected* rates of return on other investments.

Not all investments are equally risky. The office development is riskier than a government security but is probably less risky than drilling a wildcat oil well. Suppose you believe the project is as risky as investment in the stock market and that you forecast a 12% rate of return for stock market investments. Then 12% becomes the appropriate opportunity cost of capital. That is what you are giving up by not investing in comparable securities. You can now recompute NPV:

$$PV = \frac{400,000}{1.12} = \$357,143$$

$$NPV = PV - 350,000 = \$7,143$$

If other investors agree with your forecast of a $400,000 payoff and with your assessment of a 12% opportunity cost of capital, then your property ought to be worth $357,143 once construction is under way. If you tried to sell it for more than that, there would be no takers, because the property would then offer an expected rate of return lower than the 12% available in the stock market. The office building still makes a net contribution to value, but it is much smaller than our earlier calculations indicated.

In Chapter 1 we said that the financial manager must be concerned with time and uncertainty and their effects on value. This is clearly so in our example. The $400,000 payoff would be worth exactly that if it could be realized instantaneously. If the office building is as risk-free as government securities, the one-year delay reduces value to $373,832. If the office building is as risky as investment in the stock market, then uncertainty reduces value by a further $16,689 to $357,143.

Unfortunately, adjusting asset values for time and uncertainty is often more complicated than our example suggests. Therefore, we will take the two effects separately. For the most part, we will dodge the problem of risk in Chapters 2 through 6, either treating all payoffs as if they were known with certainty or talking about expected cash flows and expected rates of return without worrying how risk is defined or measured. Then in Chapters 7, 8, and 9 we will turn to the problem of understanding how capital markets cope with risk.

Present Values and Rates of Return

We have decided that construction of the office building is a smart thing to do, since it is worth more than it costs—it has a positive net present value. To calculate how much it is worth, we worked out how much one would have to pay to achieve the same income by investing directly in securities. The project's present value is equal to its future income discounted at the rate of return offered by these securities.

We can re-express our criterion by saying that our property venture is worth undertaking because the return exceeds the cost of capital. The return on the capital invested is simply the profit as a proportion of the initial outlay:

$$Return = \frac{profit}{investment} = \frac{400,000 - 350,000}{350,000} \approx 14\%$$

The cost of capital invested is once again just the return forgone by *not* investing in securities. In our present case, if the office building is about as risky as investing in the stock market, the return forgone is 12%. Since the 14% return on the office building exceeds the 12% cost, we should start digging the foundations of the building.

Here then we have two equivalent decision rules for capital investment.[2]

---

[2] You might check for yourself that these are equivalent rules. In other words, if the return 50,000/350,000 is greater than r, then the net present value $-350,000 + [400,000/(1 + r)]$ must be greater than zero.

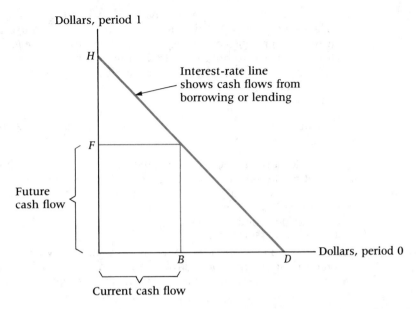

Figure 2-1   Notice how borrowing and lending enlarge the individual's choice. By borrowing against future cash flow *F*, an individual can consume an extra *BD* today; by lending current cash flow *B*, the individual can consume an extra *FH* tomorrow.

1. *Net present value rule.* Accept investments that have positive net present values.
2. *Rate-of-return rule.* Accept investments that offer rates of return in excess of their opportunity costs of capital.[3]

*2-2   FOUNDATIONS OF THE NET PRESENT VALUE RULE[4]

So far our discussion of net present value has been rather casual. Increasing NPV *sounds* like a sensible objective for a company, but it is more than just a rule of thumb. We need to understand why the NPV rule makes sense and why we look to the bond and stock markets to find the opportunity cost of capital.

Figure 2-1 illustrates the problem of choosing between spending today and spending in the future. Assume that you have a cash inflow of *B* today and *F* in a year's time. Unless you have some way of storing or anticipating income, you will be compelled to consume it as it arrives. This could be inconvenient or worse. If the bulk of your cash flow is received next year, the result could be hunger now and gluttony later. This is where the capital market comes in. It allows the transfer of wealth across time, so that you can eat moderately both this year and next.

The capital market is simply a market where people trade between dollars today and dollars in the future. The downward-sloping line in Figure 2-1 represents the

---

[3] The two rules can conflict when there are cash flows in more than two periods. We address this problem in Chapter 5.

[4] Sections marked with an asterisk contain more difficult material and may be skipped on a first reading.

rate of exchange in the capital market between today's dollars and next year's dollars; its slope is $1 + r$, where r denotes the one-year rate of interest. By lending all of your present cash flow, you could increase your *future* consumption by $(1 + r)B$ or FH. Alternatively, by borrowing against your future cash flow, you could increase your *present* consumption by $F/(1 + r)$ or BD.

Let us put some numbers into our example. Suppose that your prospects are as follows:

- Cash on hand: $B = \$20,000$
- Cash to be received one year from now: $F = \$25,000$

If you do not want to consume anything today, you can invest \$20,000 in the capital market at, say, 7%. The rate of exchange between dollars next year and dollars today is 1.07; this is the slope of the line in Figure 2-1. If you invest \$20,000 at 7%, you will obtain $\$20,000 \times 1.07 = \$21,400$. Of course, you also have \$25,000 coming in a year from now, so you will end up with \$46,400. This is point H in Figure 2-1.

What if you want to cash in the \$25,000 future payment and spend everything today on some ephemeral frolic? You can do so by borrowing in the capital market. The present value formula tells us how much investors would give you today in return for the promise of \$25,000 next year:

$$PV = \frac{C_1}{1 + r} = \frac{\$25,000}{1.07} = \$23,364$$

This is the distance BD. The total present value of the current and future cash flows (point D in the figure) is found by adding this year's flow.

$$C_0 + \frac{C_1}{1 + r} = \$20,000 + \frac{\$25,000}{1.07} = \$43,364$$

This is the formula that we used before to calculate net present value (except that in this case C_0 is positive).

What if you cash in but then change your mind and want to consume next year? Can you get back to point H? Of course—just invest the net present value at 7%.

$$\text{Future value} = \$43,364 \times 1.07 = \$46,400$$

As a matter of fact, you can end up anywhere on the straight line connecting D and H depending on how much of the \$43,364 current wealth you choose to invest. Figure 2-1 is actually a graphical representation of the link between present and future value.

*How the Capital Market Helps to Smooth Consumption Patterns

Few of us save all our current cash flow or borrow fully against our future cash flow. We try to achieve a balance between present and future consumption. But there is no reason to expect that the best balance for one person is best for another.

Suppose, for example, that you are of a prodigal disposition and favour present over future consumption. Your preferred pattern might be indicated by Figure 2-2.

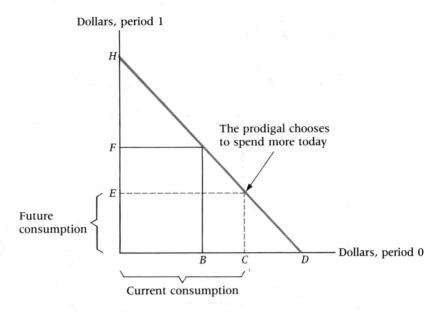

Figure 2-2   The prodigal chooses to borrow *BC* against tomorrow's cash flow, in order to consume *C* today and *E* tomorrow.

You choose to borrow *BC* against future cash flow and consume *C* today. Next year you are obliged to repay *EF* and, therefore, can consume only *E*. By contrast, if you have a more miserly streak, you might prefer the policy shown in Figure 2-3: you consume *A* today and lend the balance *AB*. In a year's time you receive a repayment of *FG* and are therefore able to indulge in consumption of *G*.[5]

    Both the miser and the prodigal *can* choose to spend cash only as it is received, but in these examples both prefer to do otherwise. By opening up borrowing and lending opportunities, the capital market removes the obligation to match consumption and cash flow.

*Now We Introduce Productive Opportunities   In practice, individuals are not limited to investing in capital market securities: they may also acquire plant, machinery, and other real assets. Thus, in addition to plotting the returns from buying securities, we can also plot an investment-opportunities line, which shows the returns from buying real assets. The return on the "best" project may well be substantially higher than returns in the capital market, so that the investment-opportunities line may be initially very steep. But, unless the individual is a bottomless pit of inspiration, the line will become

---

[5] The exact balance between present and future consumption that each individual will choose depends on personal taste. Readers who are familiar with economic theory will recognize that the choice can be represented by superimposing an "indifference map" for each individual. The preferred combination is the point of tangency between the interest-rate line and the individual's indifference curve. In other words, each individual will borrow or lend until one plus the interest rate equals the marginal rate of time preference (i.e., the slope of the indifference curve).

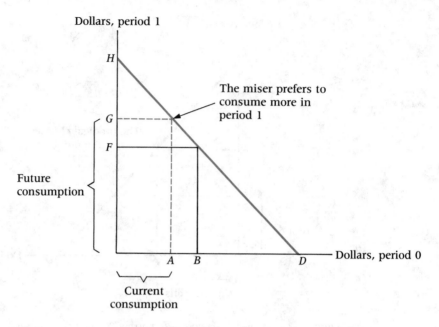

Figure 2-3   The miser chooses to lend *AB*, in order to consume *A* today and *G* tomorrow.

progressively flatter. This is illustrated in Figure 2-4, where the first $10,000 of investment, ranked in terms of return, produces a subsequent cash flow of $20,000, whereas the next $10,000 offers a cash flow of only $15,000. In the jargon of economics, there is a declining marginal return on capital.

We can now return to our hypothetical example and inquire how your welfare would be affected by the possibility of investing in real assets. The solution is illustrated in Figure 2-5. To keep our diagram simple, we shall assume that you have maximum initial resources of *D*. Part of this may come from borrowing against future cash flow; but we do not have to worry about that, because, as we have seen, the amount *D* can always be deployed into future income. If you choose to invest any part of this sum in the capital market, you can attain any point along the line *DH*.

Now let us introduce investment in *real assets* by supposing that you retain *J* of your initial resources and invest the balance *JD* in plant and machinery. We can see from the curved investment-opportunities line that such an investment would produce a future cash flow of *G*. This is all very well, but maybe you do not want to consume *J* today and *G* tomorrow. Fortunately you can use the capital market to adjust your spending pattern as you choose. By investing the whole of *J* in the capital market, you can increase *future* income by *GM*. Alternatively, by borrowing against your entire future earnings of *G*, you can increase *present* income by *JK*. In other words, by *both* investing *JD* in *real assets* and borrowing or lending in the capital market, you can obtain any point along the line *KM*. Regardless of whether you are a prodigal or a miser, you have more to spend either today or next year than if you invest *only* in the capital market (that is, choose a point along the line *DH*). You also have more to spend either today or next year than if you invest *only* in real assets (that is, choose a point along the curve *DL*).

Let us look more closely at the investment in *real assets*. The maximum sum that could be realized today from the investment's future cash flow is *JK. This is*

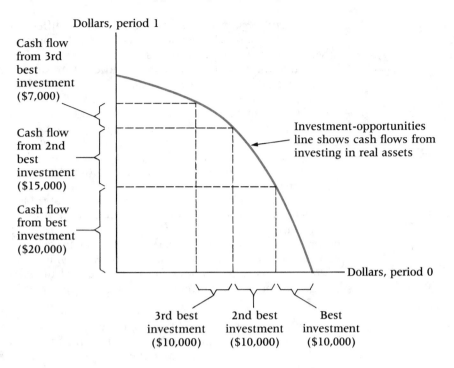

Figure 2-4   The effect of investment in real assets on cash flows in periods 0 and 1. Notice the diminishing returns on additional units of investment.

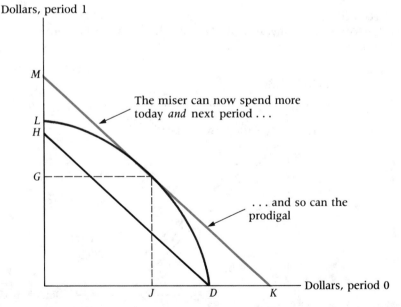

Figure 2-5   Both the prodigal and the miser have initial wealth of *D*. They are better off if they invest *JD* in real assets and then borrow or lend in the capital market. If they could invest *only* in the capital market, they would be obliged to choose a point along *DH*; if they could invest *only* in real assets, they would be obliged to choose a point along *DL*.

the investment's present value. Its cost is *JD*, and the difference between its present value and its cost is *DK*. *This is its net present value*. Net present value is the addition to your resources from investing in *real assets*.

Investing the amount *JD* is a smart move—it makes you better off. In fact it is the smartest possible move. We can see why if we look at Figure 2-6. If you invest *JD* in real assets, the net present value is *DK*. If you invest, say, *ND* in real assets, the net present value declines to *DP*. In fact investing either more or less than *JD* in real assets *must* reduce net present value.

Notice also that by investing *JD*, you have invested up to the point at which the investment-opportunities line just touches and has the same slope as the interest-rate line. Now the slope of the investment-opportunities line represents the return on the marginal investment, so that *JD* is the point at which the return on the marginal investment is exactly equal to the rate of interest. In other words, you will maximize your wealth if you invest in *real* assets until the marginal return on investment falls to the rate of interest. Having done that, you will borrow or lend in the capital market until you have achieved the desired balance between consumption today and consumption tomorrow.

We now have a logical basis for the two equivalent rules that we proposed so casually at the end of Section 2-1. We can restate the rules as follows:

1. *Net present value rule*. Invest so as to maximize the net present value of the investment. This is the difference between the discounted, or present, value of the future income and the amount of the initial investment.
2. *Rate-of-return rule*. Invest up to the point at which the marginal return on the investment is equal to the rate of return on equivalent investments in the capital market. This is the point of tangency between the interest-rate line and the investment-opportunities line.

*A Crucial Assumption   In our examples, the miser and the prodigal placed an identical value on the firm's investment. This would not have been the case if they had not faced

Figure 2-6   If the prodigal or the miser invests *ND* in real assets, the NPV of the investment would be only *DP*. The investor would have less to spend both today and tomorrow.

identical borrowing and lending opportunities. Whenever firms discount cash flows at capital market rates, they are implicitly making some assumptions about their shareholders' opportunities to borrow and lend. Strictly speaking, they are assuming:

1. that there are no barriers preventing access to the capital market and that no participant is sufficiently dominant as to have a significant effect on price;
2. that access to the capital market is costless and that there are no "frictions" preventing the free trading of securities;
3. that relevant information about the price and quality of each security is widely and freely available;
4. that there are no distorting taxes.

In sum, they are assuming a perfectly competitive capital market. Clearly, this is at best an approximation, but it may not be too bad a one. There are 1.5 million stockholders in Canada. Even a large institution like Royal Trust controls only about 3% of publicly traded Canadian stocks. Second, the costs of trading in securities are generally small, both in absolute terms and relative to the costs of trading in real assets like office buildings and blast furnaces. Finally, though there are obviously cases in which investors have possessed privileged information, the federal and provincial corporations acts and the provincial securities commissions (as well as the United States Securities and Exchange Commission, if the securities are traded in the United States) ensure that potentially profitable information seldom remains the property of one individual for long.[6]

Even though our conditions are not fully satisfied, there is considerable evidence that security prices behave almost as if they were. This evidence is presented and discussed in Chapter 13.

*Imperfect Capital Markets

Suppose that we did not have such a well-functioning capital market. How would this damage our net present value rule?

As an example, Figure 2-7 shows what happens if the borrowing rate is substantially higher than the lending rate. This means that when you want to turn period 0 dollars into period 1 dollars (that is, lend), you move *up* a relatively flat line; when you want to turn period 1 dollars into period 0 dollars (that is, borrow), you move *down* a relatively steep line. You can see that would-be borrowers (who must move *down* the steep line) prefer the company to invest only *BD*. In contrast, would-be lenders (who must move *up* the relatively flat line) prefer the company to invest *AD*. In this case the two groups of shareholders want the manager to use different discount rates. The manager has no simple way to reconcile their differing objectives.

No one believes that the competitive market assumption is fully satisfied. Later in this book we will discuss several cases in which differences in taxation, transaction costs, and other imperfections must be taken into account in financial decision making. However, we will also discuss research that indicates that, in general, capital markets function fairly well. That is one good reason for relying on net present value as a corporate objective. Another good reason is that net present value makes common sense; we will see that it gives obviously silly

---

[6] Avarice helps because any other individual who can obtain this information can use it to make trading profits.

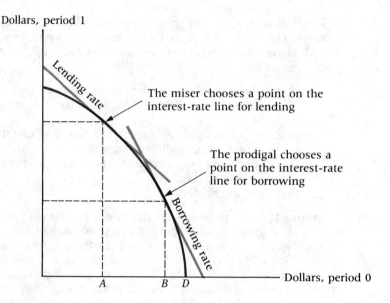

Dollars, period 1

Lending rate

The miser chooses a point on the interest-rate line for lending

The prodigal chooses a point on the interest-rate line for borrowing

Borrowing rate

Dollars, period 0

A   B D

Figure 2-7   Here there are separate borrowing and lending rates. The steep line represents the interest rate for a borrower; the flatter line represents the rate for a lender. In this case the prodigal and the miser prefer different levels of capital investment.

answers less frequently than its major competitors. But for now, having glimpsed the problems of imperfect markets, we shall, like an economist in a shipwreck, simply *assume* our life jacket and swim safely to shore.

2-3   A FUNDAMENTAL RESULT

The present value rule really dates back to the work of the great American economist Irving Fisher. What was so exciting about Fisher's analysis was his discovery, in 1930, that the capital investment criterion has nothing to do with the individual's preferences for current versus future consumption.[7] The prodigal and the miser are unanimous in the amount that they want to invest in real assets. Because they have the same investment criterion, they can cooperate in the same enterprise and can safely delegate the operation of that enterprise to a professional manager. Managers do not need to know anything about the personal tastes of their shareholders and should not consult their own tastes. Their task is to maximize net present value. If they succeed, they can rest assured that they have acted in the best interests of their shareholders.

Our justification of the net present value rule has been restricted to two periods and to certain cash flows. However, the rule also makes sense for cases in which the cash flows extend beyond the next period. The argument goes like this:

1.   A financial manager should act in the interest of the firm's stockholders.

---

[7] I. Fisher, *The Theory of Interest*, Augustus M. Kelley, Publishers, New York, 1965 (reprinted from the 1930 edition). Our graphical illustration closely follows the exposition in E.F. Fama and M.H. Miller, *The Theory of Finance*, Holt, Rinehart and Winston, New York, 1972.

2.   Each stockholder wants three things:
      (a) to be as rich as possible, that is, to maximize current wealth;
      (b) to transform that wealth into whatever time pattern of consumption he
          or she most desires;
      (c) to choose the risk characteristics of that consumption plan.
3.   But stockholders do not need the financial manager's help to reach the best
      time pattern of consumption. They can do that on their own, providing they
      have free access to competitive capital markets. They can also choose the
      risk characteristics of their consumption plan by investing in more or less
      risky securities.
4.   How then can the financial manager help the firm's stockholders? By increas-
      ing the market value of each stockholder's stake in the firm. The way to do
      that is to seize all investment opportunities that have a positive net present
      value.

This gives us the fundamental condition for the successful operation of a
capitalist economy. Separation of ownership and management is a practical
necessity for large organizations. Many corporations have hundreds of thousands
of shareholders, no two with the same tastes, wealth, or personal opportunities.
There is no way for all the firm's owners to be actively involved in management:
it would be like running Metropolitan Toronto through a series of town meetings
for all its citizens. Therefore, authority has to be delegated. The remarkable thing
is that managers of firms can all be given one simple instruction: maximize net
present value.

Other Corporate Goals

Do real managers really follow this simple instruction? Some idealists say that
managers should not be obliged to act in the selfish interests of their stockholders.
Some realists argue that, regardless of what managers ought to do, they in fact
look after themselves.

Let us respond to the idealists first. We do not know how energetically managers seek to maximize net present value, but we are reminded of a survey of
businesspeople that inquired whether they attempted to maximize profits. They
indignantly rejected the notion, protesting that they were responsible, God-
fearing, and so on: Their responsibilities went far beyond the narrow profit
objective. But when the question was reformulated and they were asked whether
they could increase profits by raising or lowering their selling price, they replied
that neither policy would do so.[8] In a rather similar vein, we suspect that many
managers do not have an explicit objective of maximizing net present value and
yet can think of no action that would do other than to reduce it.

Suppose, however, that we do believe that management should have these
wider responsibilities. Management still must be able to analyze a decision from
the shareholders' point of view if it is to strike a proper balance between their
interests and those of consumers, employees, and society at large. The net present
value calculation tells them how much a particular decision helps or hinders
stockholders.

Now, how about the realists who say that managers look after their own
interests rather than those of their shareholders? We agree that managers do

---

[8] Cited in G.J. Stigler, *The Theory of Price*, 3rd ed., The Macmillan Company, New York, 1966.

look to their own interests. But shareholders would not hand over their capital if they believed that their managers would dissipate it in luxury and leisure. What is it that prevents such dissipation—or at least keeps it down to acceptable proportions?

First, compensation packages can be designed to align managers' and stockholders' interests. For example, top managers are usually given options to buy stock in the business; the options pay off only if the business does well. Second, managers who are successful in increasing shareholder wealth will find that they can move on to better jobs and higher salaries. Managers who ignore shareholder wealth may find their companies taken over by some other firm more concerned with profitability. After the takeover, they may also find themselves out on the street.

No compensation plan can ensure that a manager always tries to increase shareholders' wealth, but a good manager knows that it is in his or her long-run interest to demonstrate that the shareholders' pockets are close to the manager's heart.

2-4 SUMMARY

In this chapter we have introduced the concept of present value as a way of valuing assets. Calculating present value is easy. Just discount future cash flow by an appropriate rate, usually called the *opportunity cost of capital*, or *hurdle rate*.

$$\text{Present value (PV)} = \frac{C_1}{1 + r}$$

Net present value is present value plus any immediate cash flow:

$$\text{Net present value (NPV)} = C_0 + \frac{C_1}{1 + r}$$

Remember that C_0 is negative if the immediate cash flow is an investment, that is, if it is a cash outflow.

The discount rate is determined by rates of return prevailing in capital markets. If the future cash flow is absolutely safe, then the discount rate is the interest rate on safe securities like federal government debt. If the size of the future cash flow is uncertain, then the expected cash flow should be discounted at the expected rate of return offered by equivalent-risk securities. We will talk more about this in Chapter 7.

Cash flows are discounted for two simple reasons: first, because a dollar today is worth more than a dollar tomorrow; and second, because a risky dollar is worth less than a safe one. Formulas for PV and NPV are numerical expressions of these ideas. We look to rates of return prevailing in capital markets to determine how much to discount for time and for risk. By calculating the present value of an asset, we are in effect estimating how much people will pay for it if they have the alternative of investing in the capital markets.

The concept of net present value allows efficient separation of ownership and management of the corporation. A manager who invests only in assets with positive net present values serves the best interests of each one of the firm's owners—regardless of differences in their wealth and tastes. This is made possible by the existence of the capital market, which allows each shareholder to construct a personal investment plan that is custom-tailored to his or her own needs. For example, there is no need for the firm to arrange its investment policy to obtain a sequence of cash flows that matches shareholders' preferred time patterns of consumption. The shareholders can shift funds forward or back over time perfectly well on their own, provided they have free access to competitive capital markets. In fact, their plan for consumption over time is constrained by only two things: their personal wealth (or lack of it) and the interest rate at which they can borrow and lend. The financial manager cannot affect the interest rate but can increase stockholders' wealth. The way to do so is to invest in assets having positive net present values.

FURTHER READING

The pioneering works on the net present value rule are:

I. Fisher, *The Theory of Interest*, Augustus M. Kelley, Publishers, New York, 1965. Reprinted from the 1930 edition.
J. Hirschleifer, "On the Theory of Optimal Investment Decision," *Journal of Political Economy*, **66**: 329–352 (August 1958).

For a more rigorous textbook treatment of the subject, we suggest:

E.F. Fama and M.H. Miller, *The Theory of Finance*, Holt, Rinehart and Winston, New York, 1972.

If you would like to dig deeper into the question of how managers may be motivated to maximize shareholder wealth, we suggest:

E.F. Fama; "Agency Problems and the Theory of the Firm," *Journal of Political Economy*, **88**: 288–307 (April 1980).
M.C. Jensen and W.H. Meckling: "Theory of the Firm: Managerial Behavior, Agency Costs, and Ownership Structure," *Journal of Financial Economics*, **3**: 305–360 (October 1976).

QUIZ

1. C_0 is the initial cash flow on an investment, and C_1 is the cash flow at the end of one year. The symbol r is the discount rate.
   (a) Is C_0 usually positive or negative?
   (b) What is the formula for the present value of the investment?
   (c) What is the formula for the net present value?
   (d) The symbol r is often termed the *opportunity cost of capital*. Why?
   (e) If the investment is risk-free, what is the appropriate measure of r?
2. If the present value of $150 paid at the end of one year is $130, what is the one-year discount factor? What is the discount rate?
3. Calculate the one-year discount factor DF_1 for discount rates of (a) 10%, (b) 20%, and (c) 30%.
4. A merchant pays $100,000 for a load of grain and is certain that it can be resold at the end of one year for $132,000.
   (a) What is the return on this investment?
   (b) If this return is *lower* than the rate of interest, does the investment have a positive or a negative net present value?
   (c) If the rate of interest is 10%, what is the present value of the investment?
   (d) What is the net present value?
5. What is the net present value rule? What is the rate-of-return rule? Do the two rules give the same answer?

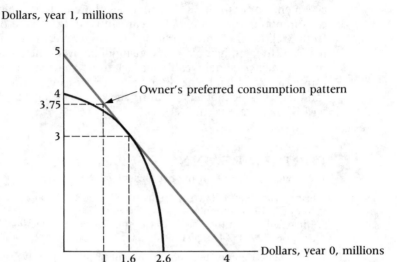

Figure 2-8   See Quiz, question 6.

*6. In Figure 2-8, the sloping line represents the opportunities for investment in the capital market and the solid curved line represents the opportunities for investment in plant and machinery. The company's only asset at present is $2.6 million in cash.
  (a) What is the interest rate?
  (b) How much should the company invest in plant?
  (c) How much will this investment be worth next year?
  (d) What is the average rate of return on the investment in plant?
  (e) What is the marginal rate of return?
  (f) What is the present value of this investment?
  (g) What is the net present value of this investment?
  (h) What is the total present value of the company?
  (i) How much will the individual consume today?
  (j) How much will he or she consume tomorrow?

7. We can imagine the financial manager doing several things on behalf of the firm's stockholders. For example, the manager might:
  (a) Make shareholders as wealthy as possible by investing in real assets with positive net present values.
  (b) Modify the firm's investment plan to help shareholders achieve a particular time pattern of consumption.
  (c) Choose high- or low-risk assets to match shareholders' risk preferences.
  (d) Help balance shareholders' cheque books.
  But in well-functioning capital markets, shareholders will vote for *only one* of these goals. Which one? Why?

---

* Problems marked with an asterisk are more difficult.

QUESTIONS AND PROBLEMS

1. In Section 2-1, we analyzed the possible construction of an office building on a plot of land appraised at $50,000. We concluded that this investment had a positive NPV of $7,143.

    Suppose E. Coli Associates, the genetic consultants, offer to purchase the land for $60,000, $30,000 paid immediately and $30,000 after one year. Government securities maturing in one year yield 7%.

    (a) Assume E. Coli is sure to pay the second $30,000 instalment. Should you take their offer or start on the office building? Explain.

    (b) Suppose you are *not* sure E. Coli will pay. You observe that other investors demand a 10% return on their loans to E. Coli to compensate for risk. Assume that the other investors have correctly assessed the risks that E. Coli will not be able to pay. Should you accept E. Coli's offer?

2. Write down the formulas for an investment's net present value and rate of return. Prove that NPV is positive *only* if the rate of return exceeds the opportunity cost of capital.

3. What is the net present value of a *firm's* investment in a government treasury security yielding 15% and maturing in one year? *Hint*: what is the opportunity cost of capital? Ignore taxes.

4. Calculate the NPV and rate of return for each of the following investments. The opportunity cost of capital is 20% for all four investments.

Investment	Initial Cash Flow, C_0	Cash Flow in Year 1, C_1
1	− 10,000	+ 20,000
2	− 5,000	+ 12,000
3	− 5,000	+ 5,500
4	− 2,000	+ 5,000

    (a) Which investment is most valuable?

    (b) Suppose each investment would require use of the same parcel of land. Therefore you can take only one. Which one? *Hint*: What is the firm's objective? To earn a high rate of return? Or to increase firm value?

*5. Redraw Figure 2-5 to scale to represent the following situation:

    (a) A firm starts out with $10 million in cash.

    (b) The rate of interest r is 10%.

    (c) To maximize NPV the firm invests today $6 million in real assets ($C_0 = -6$ million). This leaves $4 million, which can be paid out to the shareholders.

    (d) The NPV of the investment is $2 million.

    When you have finished, answer the following questions:

    (e) How much cash is the firm going to receive in year 1 from its investment?

    (f) What is the marginal return from the firm's investment?

    (g) What is the present value of the shareholders' investment after the firm has announced its investment plan?

    (h) Suppose shareholders want to spend $6 million today. How can they do this?

(i) How much will they then have to spend next year? Show this on your drawing.

*6. Redraw Figure 2-5 to show how the firm's investment plan should be affected by a decline in the interest rate. Mark the NPV of the revised investment plan. Show whether the miser or the prodigal would be better off.

*7. Look again at Figure 2-5. Suppose the firm decides to invest *more* than *JD* in real assets. Redraw the interest-rate line to show the NPV of the revised investment plan. Show that both the miser *and* the prodigal are worse off.

*8. The interest-rate line in our diagrams always has a slope greater than one. Why?

9. "The discount rate is the rate at which the company will be able to reinvest its cash flows." Is that right? Discuss.

10. Respond to the following comment: "It's all very well telling companies to maximize net present value, but 'net present value' is just an abstract notion. What I tell my managers is that profits are what matters and it's profits that we're going to maximize."

11. Respond to the following comment: "It's no good just telling me to maximize my stock price. I can easily take a short view and maximize today's price. What I would prefer is to keep it on a gently rising trend."

12. Here's a harder question. It is sometimes argued that the net present value criterion is appropriate for corporations but not for governments. First, governments must consider the time preferences of the community as a whole rather than those of a few wealthy investors. Second, governments must have a longer horizon than individuals, for governments are the guardians of future generations. What do you think?

13. Give examples of potential conflicts of interest between managers and shareholders. Why do managers generally work hard to make the firm successful?

C · H · A · P · T · E · R

3

HOW TO CALCULATE
PRESENT VALUES

In Chapter 2 we learned how to work out the value of an asset that produces cash exactly one year from now. But we did not explain how to value assets that produce cash two years from now or in several future years. That is the first thing that we must do in this chapter. We will then have a look at some short-cut methods for calculating present values and at some specialized present value formulas.

By then you will deserve some payoff for the mental investment you have made in learning about present values. In Chapter 4 we will try out the concept on common stocks, and after that we will tackle the firm's capital investment decisions at a practical level of detail.

3-1 VALUING LONG-LIVED ASSETS

Do you remember how to calculate the present value (PV) of an asset that produces a cash flow (C_1) one year from now?

$$PV = DF_1 \times C_1 = \frac{C_1}{1 + r_1}$$

The discount factor for year 1 cash flows is DF_1, and r_1 is the opportunity cost of investing your money for one year. Thus suppose you will receive a certain cash inflow of $100 next year $(C_1 = 100)$ and the rate of interest on one-year Canadian government Treasury bills is 7% $(r_1 = 0.07)$. Then present value equals

$$PV = \frac{C_1}{1 + r_1} = \frac{\$100}{1.07} = \$93.46$$

The present value of a cash flow two years hence can be written in a similar way as

$$PV = DF_2 \times C_2 = \frac{C_2}{(1 + r_2)^2}$$

C_2 is the year 2 cash flow, DF_2 is the discount factor for year 2 cash flows, and r_2 is the annual rate of interest on money invested for two years. Continuing with our example, suppose you get another cash flow of $100 in year 2 ($C_2 = 100$). The rate of interest on two-year Government of Canada bonds is 7.7% a year ($r_2 = 0.077$); this means that a dollar invested in two-year bonds will grow to 1.077^2 or $1.16 by the end of two years. The present value of your year-2 cash flow equals

$$PV = \frac{C_2}{(1 + r_2)^2} = \frac{\$100}{(1.077)^2} = \$86.21$$

Valuing Cash Flows in Several Periods

One of the nice things about present values is that they are all expressed in current dollars—so that you can *add* them up. In other words, the present value of cash flow $A + B$ is equal to the present value of cash flow A plus the present value of cash flow B. This happy result has important implications for investments that produce cash flows in several periods.

We calculated above the value of an asset that produces a cash flow of C_1 in year 1, and we calculated the value of another asset that produces a cash flow of C_2 in year 2. Following our additivity rule, we can write down the value of an asset that produces cash flows in *each* year. It is simply

$$PV = \frac{C_1}{1 + r_1} + \frac{C_2}{(1 + r_2)^2}$$

We can obviously continue in this way and find the present value of an extended stream of cash flows:

$$PV = \frac{C_1}{1 + r_1} + \frac{C_2}{(1 + r_2)^2} + \frac{C_3}{(1 + r_3)^3} + \cdots$$

This is sometimes called the **discounted cash flow** (or **DCF**) formula. A shorthand way to write it is

$$PV = \sum \frac{C_t}{(1 + r_t)^t}$$

where Σ refers to the sum of the series. To find the *net* present value we add the (usually negative) initial cash flow just as in the period 1 case:

$$NPV = C_0 + PV = C_0 + \sum \frac{C_t}{(1 + r_t)^t}$$

*Why the Discount Factor Declines as Futurity Increases— And a Digression on Money Machines

If a dollar tomorrow is worth less than a dollar today, one might suspect that a dollar the day after tomorrow should be worth even less. In other words, the discount factor DF_2 should be less than the discount factor DF_1. But is this *necessarily* so, when there is a different interest rate r_t for each period?

Suppose r_1 is 20% and r_2 is 7%. Then

$$DF_1 = \frac{1}{1.20} = 0.83$$

$$DF_2 = \frac{1}{(1.07)^2} = 0.87$$

Apparently the dollar received the day after tomorrow is *not* necessarily worth less than the dollar received tomorrow.

But there is something wrong with this example. Anyone who could borrow and lend at these interest rates could become a millionaire overnight. Let us see how such a "money machine" would work.

Suppose the first person to spot the opportunity is Hermione Kraft. Ms. Kraft first lends $1,000 for one year at 20%. That is an attractive enough return, but she notices that there is a way to earn an *immediate* profit on her investment and be ready to play the game again. She reasons as follows. Next year she will have $1,200, which can be reinvested for a further year. Although she does not know what interest rates will be at that time, she does know that she can always put the money in a chequing account and be sure of having $1,200 at the end of year 2. Her next step, therefore, is to go to her bank and borrow the present value of this $1,200. At 7% interest this present value is

$$PV = \frac{\$1,200}{(1.07)^2} = \$1,048$$

Thus Ms. Kraft invests $1,000, borrows back $1,048, and walks away with a profit of $48. If that does not sound like very much, remember that the game can be played again immediately, this time with $1,048. In fact it would take Ms. Kraft only 147 plays to become a millionaire (before taxes).[1]

Of course this story is completely fanciful. Such an opportunity would not last long in capital markets like ours. Any bank that would allow you to lend for one year at 20% and borrow for two years at 7% would soon be wiped out by a rush of small investors hoping to become millionaires and a rush of millionaires hoping to become billionaires. There are, however, two lessons to our story. The first is that a dollar tomorrow *cannot* be worth less than a dollar the day after tomorrow. In other words, the value of a dollar received at the end of one year (DF_1) must be greater than the value of a dollar received at the end of two years (DF_2). There must be some extra gain[2] from lending for two periods rather than one: $(1 + r_2)^2$ must be greater than $1 + r_1$.

Our second lesson is a more general one and can be summed up by the precept "There is no such thing as a money machine."[3] In well-functioning capital markets, any potential money machine will be eliminated almost instantaneously by investors who try to take advantage of it. Therefore, beware of self-styled experts who offer you a chance to participate in a "sure thing."

Later in the book we will invoke the *absence* of money machines to prove several useful properties about security prices. That is, we will make statements like "The prices of securities X and Y must be in the following relationship — otherwise there would be a money machine and capital markets would not be in equilibrium."

---

[1] That is, $\$1,000 \times (1.04813)^{147} = \$1,002,000$.

[2] The extra return for lending two years rather than one is often referred to as a *forward rate of return*. Our rule says that the forward rate must be positive.

[3] The technical term for money machine is **arbitrage**. There are no opportunities for arbitrage in well-functioning capital markets.

In principle there can be a different interest rate for each future period. This relationship between the interest rate and the maturity of the cash flow is called the **term structure of interest rates**. We are going to look at term structure in Chapter 21, but for now we will finesse the issue by assuming that the term structure is "flat"—in other words, the interest rate is the same regardless of the date of the cash flow. This means that we can replace the series of interest rates $r_1, r_2, \ldots, r_t$, and so on, with a single rate r and that we can write the present value formula as

$$PV = \frac{C_1}{1 + r} + \frac{C_2}{(1 + r)^2} + \ldots$$

So far all our examples can be worked out fairly easily by hand. Real problems are often much more complicated and require the use of an electronic calculator that is specifically programmed for present-value calculations, a computer spreadsheet, or the use of present value tables. Here is a somewhat complex example that illustrates how such tables are used.

You have some bad news about your office building venture (the one described at the start of Chapter 2): the contractor says that construction will take two years instead of one and requests payment on the following schedule:

1. A $100,000 down payment now. (Note that the land, worth $50,000, must also be committed now.)
2. A $100,000 progress payment after one year.
3. A final payment of $100,000 when the building is ready for occupancy at the end of the second year.

Your real estate adviser maintains that despite the delay the building will be worth $400,000 when completed.

All this yields a new set of cash-flow forecasts:

Period	$t = 0$	$t = 1$	$t = 2$
Land	− 50,000		
Construction	− 100,000	− 100,000	− 100,000
Payoff			+400,000
Total	$C_0 = -150,000$	$C_1 = -100,000$	$C_2 = +300,000$

If the interest rate is 7%, then NPV is

$$NPV = C_0 + \frac{C_1}{1 + r} + \frac{C_2}{(1 + r)^2}$$

$$= -150,000 - \frac{100,000}{1.07} + \frac{300,000}{(1.07)^2}$$

Table 3-1 shows how to set up the calculations and how to get NPV. The discount factors can be found in Appendix Table 1 at the end of the book. Look at the first two entries in the column headed 7%. The top one is 0.935 and the second is 0.873. Thus you do not have to compute 1/1.07 or 1/(1.07)²—you can pull the figures from the present-value table. (Notice that the other entries in the 7% column give discount factors out to 30 years and the other columns cover a range of discount rates from 1% to 30%.)

Table 3-1
Present Value Worksheet

Period	Discount Factor	Cash Flow ($)	Present Value ($)
0	1.0	−150,000	−150,000
1	$\dfrac{1}{1.07} = 0.935$	−100,000	−93,500
2	$\dfrac{1}{(1.07)^2} = 0.873$	+300,000	+261,900
			Total = NPV = 18,400

Fortunately the news about your office venture is not all bad. The contractor will accept a delayed payment so the PV of his fee is less than before. This partly offsets the delay in the payoff. Table 3-1 shows the NPV is $18,400—not a substantial decrease from the $23,800 calculated in Chapter 2. Since the NPV is positive, go ahead.

3-2　LOOKING FOR SHORTCUTS—PERPETUITIES AND ANNUITIES

Sometimes there are shortcuts that make it very easy to calculate the present value of an asset that pays off in different periods. Let us look at some examples.

Among the securities that have been issued by the British and Canadian governments are so-called **perpetuities**. These are bonds that the government is under no obligation to repay but that offer a fixed income for each year to perpetuity.[4] The rate of return on a perpetuity is equal to the promised annual payment divided by the present value:[5]

---

[4] In a fit of generosity, the Canadian government has indicated it will redeem its perpetuities in 1996 (they only have a 3% coupon payment).

[5] You can check this by writing down the present value formula.

$$PV = \frac{C}{1 + r} + \frac{C}{(1 + r)^2} + \frac{C}{(1 + r)^3} + \ldots$$

Now let $C/(1 + r) = a$ and $1/(1 + r) = x$. Then we have

$$PV = a(1 + x + x^2 + \ldots) \tag{1}$$

Multiplying both sides by x, we have

$$PVx = a(x + x^2 + \ldots) \tag{2}$$

Subtracting (2) from (1) gives us

$$PV(1 - x) = a$$

Therefore, substituting for a and x,

$$PV\left(1 - \frac{1}{1 + r}\right) = \frac{C}{1 + r}$$

Multiplying both sides by $(1 + r)$ and rearranging gives

$$r = \frac{C}{PV}$$

$$\text{Return} = \frac{\text{cash flow}}{\text{present value}}$$

$$r = \frac{C}{PV}$$

We can obviously twist this around and find the present value of a perpetuity given the discount rate r and the cash payment C. For example, suppose that some worthy person wishes to endow a chair in finance at a business school. If the rate of interest is 10% and if the aim is to provide $50,000 a year in perpetuity, the amount that must be set aside today is

$$\text{Present value of perpetuity} = \frac{C}{r} = \frac{\$50,000}{0.10} = \$500,000$$

How to Value Growing Perpetuities

Suppose now that our benefactor suddenly recollects that no allowance has been made for growth in salaries, which will probably average about 4% a year. Therefore, instead of providing $50,000 a year in perpetuity, the benefactor must provide $50,000 in year 1, $1.04 \times \$50,000$ in year 2, and so on. If we call the growth rate in salaries g, we can write down the present value of this stream of cash flows as follows:

$$PV = \frac{C_1}{1 + r} + \frac{C_2}{(1 + r)^2} + \frac{C_3}{(1 + r)^3} + \cdots$$

$$= \frac{C_1}{1 + r} + \frac{C_1(1 + g)}{(1 + r)^2} + \frac{C_1(1 + g)^2}{(1 + r)^3} + \cdots$$

Fortunately, there is a simple formula for the sum of this geometric series.[6] If we assume that r is greater than g, our clumsy-looking calculation simplifies to

$$\text{Present value of growing perpetuity} = \frac{C_1}{r - g}$$

Therefore, if our benefactor wants to provide perpetually an annual sum that keeps pace with the growth rate in salaries, the amount that must be set aside today is

$$PV = \frac{C_1}{r - g} = \frac{\$50,000}{0.10 - 0.04} = \$833,333$$

How to Value Annuities

An **annuity** is an asset that pays a fixed sum each year for a specified number of years. The equal-payment house mortgage or instalment credit agreement are common examples of annuities. In each case the bank or trust company receives the series of payments, and so it *owns* the annuity. You promise to make the series of payments, and so you have *issued* the annuity.

---

[6] We need to calculate the sum of an infinite geometric series $PV = a(1 + x + x^2 + \cdots)$ where $a = C_1/(1 + r)$ and $x = (1 + g)/(1 + r)$. In footnote 5, we showed that the sum of such a series is $a/(1 - x)$. Substituting for a and x in this formula we find that

$$PV = \frac{C_1}{r - g}$$

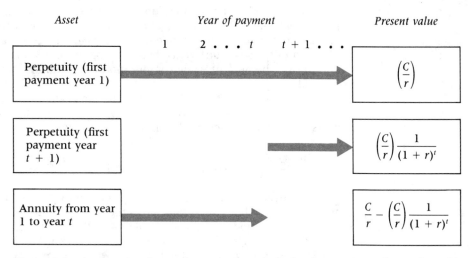

Figure 3-1 An annuity that makes payments in each of years 1 to t is equal to the difference between two perpetuities.

Figure 3-1 illustrates a simple trick for valuing annuities. The first row represents a *perpetuity* that produces a cash flow of C in each year *beginning in year 1*. It has a present value of

$$\text{PV} = \frac{C}{r}$$

The second row represents a second *perpetuity* that produces a cash flow of C in each year *beginning in year $t + 1$*. It *will* have a present value of C/r in year t and it therefore has a present value today of

$$\text{PV} = \frac{C}{r}\left[\frac{1}{(1 + r)^t}\right]$$

Both perpetuities provide a cash flow from year $t + 1$ onward. The only difference between the two perpetuities is that the first one *also* provides a cash flow in each of the years 1 through t. In other words, the difference between the two perpetuities is an annuity of C for t years. The present value of this annuity is, therefore, the difference between the values of the two perpetuities:

$$\text{Present value of annuity} = C\left[\frac{1}{r} - \frac{1}{r(1 + r)^t}\right] = \frac{C}{r}\left[1 - \frac{1}{(1 + r)^t}\right]$$

Note that two formulas for the present value of an annuity are given.[7] The first formula is provided to assist in the computation of present value when annuity

---

[7] Again we can work this out from first principles. We need to calculate the sum of the finite geometric series

$$\text{PV} = a(1 + x + x^2 + \ldots + x^{t-1}) \qquad (1)$$

where $a = C/(1 + r)$ and $x = 1/(1 + r)$. Multiplying both sides by x, we have

$$\text{PV}x = a(x + x^2 + \ldots + x^t) \qquad (2)$$

tables are provided. The expression in brackets is the *annuity factor*, which is the present value at discount rate r of an annuity of \$1 paid at the end of t periods. The second formula is provided to facilitate the interpretation of the present value of an annuity as the difference between the present values of two perpetuities and to ease the present value computation when annuity tables are not handily available.

Suppose, for example, that our benefactor begins to vacillate and wonders what it would cost to endow the chair by providing \$50,000 a year for only 20 years. The answer calculated from our formula is

$$PV = \$50,000 \left[\frac{1}{0.10} - \frac{1}{0.10(1.10)^{20}} \right] = \$50,000 \times 8.514 = \$425,700$$

Alternatively, we can simply look up the annuity factor in Appendix Table 3 at the end of the book. This table gives the present value of a dollar to be received in each of t periods. In our example $t = 20$, the interest rate $r = 0.10$, and therefore we look at the twentieth number from the top in the 10% column. It is 8.514. Multiply 8.514 by \$50,000, and we have our answer, \$425,700.

You should always be on the lookout for ways in which you can use these formulas to make life easier. For example, we sometimes need to calculate how much a series of annual payments earning a fixed annual interest would amass to by the end of t periods. In this case it is easiest to calculate the *present* value and then multiply it by $(1 + r)^t$ to find the future value. Thus suppose our benefactor wished to know how much wealth \$50,000 would produce if it were invested each year instead of being given to those no-good academics. The answer would be

$$\text{Future value} = PV \times 1.10^{20} = \$425,700 \times 6.727 = \$2.86 \text{ million}$$

How did we know that 1.10^{20} was 6.727? Easy—we just looked it up in Appendix Table 2 at the end of the book: "Future Value of \$1 at the End of t Periods."[8]

Subtracting (2) from (1) gives us

$$PV(1 - x) = a(1 - x^t)$$

Therefore, substituting for a and x,

$$PV \left(1 - \frac{1}{1 + r} \right) = C \left[\frac{1}{1 + r} - \frac{1}{(1 + r)^{t + 1}} \right]$$

Multiplying both sides by $(1 + r)$ and rearranging gives

$$PV = C \left[\frac{1}{r} - \frac{1}{r(1 + r)^t} \right] = \frac{C}{r} \left[1 - \frac{1}{(1 + r)^t} \right]$$

[8] For example, suppose you receive a cash flow of C in year 6. If you invest this cash flow at an interest rate of r, you will have by year 10 an investment worth $C(1 + r)^4$. You can get the same answer by calculating the *present value* of the cash flow $PV = C/(1 + r)^6$ and then working out how much you would have by year 10 if you invested this sum today.

$$\text{Future value} = PV(1 + r)^{10} = \frac{C}{(1 + r)^6}(1 + r)^{10} = C(1 + r)^4$$

3-3   COMPOUND INTEREST AND PRESENT VALUES

There is an important distinction between **compound interest** and **simple interest**. When money is invested at compound interest, each interest payment is reinvested to earn more interest in subsequent periods. In contrast, the opportunity to earn interest on interest is not provided by an investment that pays only simple interest.

TABLE 3-2
Value of $100 Invested at 10% Simple and Compound Interest

	Simple Interest			Compound Interest			
Year	Starting Balance	+ Interest	= Ending Balance	Starting Balance	+	Interest	= Ending Balance
1	100	+ 10	= 110	100	+	10	= 110
2	110	+ 10	= 120	110	+	11	= 121
3	120	+ 10	= 130	121	+	12.1	= 133.1
4	130	+ 10	= 140	133.1	+	13.3	= 146.4
10	190	+ 10	= 200	236	+	24	= 259
20	290	+ 10	= 300	612	+	61	= 673
50	590	+ 10	= 600	10,672	+	1,067	= 11,739
100	1,090	+ 10	= 1,100	1,252,783	+	125,278	= 1,378,061
120	1,290	+ 10	= 1,300	8,428,097	+	842,810	= 9,270,907
200	2,090	+ 10	= 2,100	17,264,116,020	+ 1,726,411,602		= 18,990,527,622

Table 3-2 compares the growth of $100 invested at compound versus simple interest. Notice that in the simple interest case, *the interest is paid only on the initial investment of $100*. Your wealth therefore increases by just $10 a year. In the compound interest case, you earn 10% on your initial investment in the first year, which gives you a balance at the end of the year of $100 × 1.10 = $110. In year 2 you earn 10% on this $110, which gives you a balance at the end of the second year of $100 × 1.10² = $121.

Table 3-2 shows that the difference between simple and compound interest is nil for a one-period investment, trivial for a two-period investment, but overwhelming for an investment of 20 years or more. A sum of $100 invested at the time of Confederation and earning compound interest of 10% a year would now be worth over $9.3 million. Don't you wish your ancestors had shown rather more foresight?

The two top lines in Figure 3-2 compare the results of investing $100 at 10% simple interest and at 10% compound interest. It looks as if the rate of growth is constant under simple interest and accelerates under compound interest. However, this is an optical illusion. We know that under compound interest our wealth grows at a *constant* rate of 10%. Figure 3-3 is in fact a more useful presentation. Here the numbers are plotted on a semilogarithmic scale and the constant compound growth rates show up as straight lines.

Problems in finance generally involve compound interest rather than simple interest, and therefore financial people always assume that you are talking about compound interest unless you specify otherwise. Discounting is a process of

Figure 3-2 Compound interest versus simple interest. The top two ascending lines show the growth of $100 invested at simple and compound interest. The longer the funds are invested, the greater the advantage with compound interest. The bottom line shows that $38.55 must be invested now to obtain $100 after ten periods. Conversely, the present value of $100 to be received after ten years is $38.55.

Figure 3-3 The same story as Figure 3-2, except that the vertical scale is logarithmic. A constant compound rate of growth means a straight ascending line. This graph makes clear that the growth rate of funds invested at simple interest actually *declines* as time passes.

compound interest. Some people find it intuitively helpful to replace the question "What is the present value of $100 to be received ten years from now, if the opportunity cost of capital is 10%?" with the question "How much would I have to invest now in order to receive $100 after ten years, given an interest rate of 10%?" The answer to the first question is

$$PV = \frac{\$100}{(1.10)^{10}} = \$38.55$$

And the answer to the second question is

$$Investment \times (1.10)^{10} = \$100$$

$$Investment = \frac{\$100}{(1.10)^{10}} = \$38.55$$

The bottom lines in Figures 3-2 and 3-3 show the growth path of an initial investment of $38.55 to its terminal value of $100. One can think of discounting as traveling *back* along the bottom line, from future value to present value.

*A Note on Compounding Intervals   So far we have implicitly assumed that each cash flow occurs at the end of the year. This is sometimes the case. For example, in France and Germany most corporations pay interest on their bonds annually. However, in Canada, the United States and Britain, most pay interest semiannually. In these countries, the investor will be able to earn an additional six months' interest on the first payment, so that an investment of $100 in a bond that paid interest of 10% per annum compounded semiannually would amount to $105 after the first six months, and by the end of the year it would amount to $1.05^2 \times \$100 = \$110.25$. In other words, 10% compounded semiannually is equivalent to 10.25% compounded annually. More generally, an investment of one dollar, at a rate of r per annum compounded m times a year, amounts by the end of the year to $\$[1 + (r/m)]^m$, and the **equivalent annually compounded rate of interest** is $[1 + (r/m)]^m - 1$.

The attractions to the investor of more frequent payments did not escape the attention of American savings and loan companies. Their rate of interest on deposits was traditionally stated as an annually compounded rate. The government, however, stipulated a maximum annual rate of interest that could be paid but made no mention of the compounding interval. When interest ceilings became effective, savings and loan companies changed progressively to semiannual and then to monthly compounding. Thus the equivalent annually compounded rate of interest increased first to $[1 + (r/2)]^2 - 1$ and then to $[1 + (r/12)]^{12} - 1$.

Eventually one company quoted a **continuously compounded rate**, so that payments were assumed to be spread evenly and continuously throughout the year. In terms of our formula, this is equivalent to letting m approach infinity.[9] This might seem like a lot of calculations for our savings and loan companies. Fortunately, however, someone remembered high school algebra and pointed out

---

[9] When we talk about *continuous* payments, we are pretending that money can be dispensed in a continuous stream like a liquid. One can never quite do this. For example, instead of paying out $50,000 every year, our benefactor could pay out $100 every $17^1/_2$ hours or $1 every $10^1/_2$ minutes or 1¢ every $6^1/_3$ seconds but could not pay it out *continuously*. Financial managers *pretend* that payments are continuous rather than hourly, daily, or weekly because (1) it simplifies the calculations, and (2) it gives a *very* close approximation to the NPV of frequent payments.

that as m approaches infinity $[1 + (r/m)]^m$ approaches $(2.718)^r$. The figure $2.718 -$ or e, as it is called — is simply the base for natural logarithms.

The sum $1 invested at a continuously compounded rate of r will, therefore, grow to $e^r = (2.718)^r$ by the end of the first year. By the end of t years it will grow to $e^{rt} = (2.718)^{rt}$. Appendix Table 4 at the end of the book is a table of values of e^{rt}. Let us practise using it.

EXAMPLE 1   Suppose you invest one dollar at a continuously compounded rate of 10% ($r = 0.10$) for one year ($t = 1$). The end-year value is simply $e^{0.10}$, which you can see from the second row of Appendix Table 4 is $1.105. In other words, investing at 10% a year *continuously* compounded is exactly the same as investing at 10.5% a year *annually* compounded.

EXAMPLE 2   Now suppose you invest one dollar at a continuously compounded rate of 11% ($r = 0.11$) for one year ($t = 1$). The end-year value is now $e^{0.11}$, which you can see from the second row of Appendix Table 4 is $1.116. In other words, investing at 11% a year *continuously* compounded is exactly the same as investing at 11.6% a year *annually* compounded.

EXAMPLE 3   Finally, suppose you invest one dollar at a continuously compounded rate of 11% ($r = 0.11$) for two years ($t = 2$). The final value of the investment is $e^{rt} = e^{0.22}$. You can see from the third row of Appendix Table 4 that $e^{0.22}$ is $1.246.

There is a particular value to continuous compounding in capital budgeting, where it may often be more reasonable to assume that a cash flow is spread evenly over the year than that it occurs at the year's end. It is very easy to adapt our previous formulas to handle this. For example, suppose that we wish to compute the present value of a perpetuity of C dollars a year. We already know that if the payment is made at the end of the year, we divide the payment by the *annually* compounded rate of r:

$$PV = \frac{C}{r}$$

If the same total payment is made in an even stream throughout the year, we use the same formula but substitute the *continuously* compounded rate.

For any other continuous payments, we can always use our formula for valuing annuities. For instance, suppose that our philanthropist has thought more seriously and decided to found a home for elderly donkeys, which will cost $50,000 a year, starting immediately, and spread evenly over 20 years. Previously, we used the annually compounded rate of 10%; now we must use the continuously compounded rate of $r = 9.53\%$ ($e^{0.0953} = 1.10$). To cover such an expenditure, then, our philanthropist needs to set aside the following sum:[10]

---

[10] To understand this formula it may help to remember that an annuity is simply the difference between a perpetuity received today and a perpetuity received in year t. A continuous stream of C dollars a year in perpetuity is worth C/r where r is the continuously compounded rate. Our annuity, then, is worth

$$PV = \frac{C}{r} - \text{present value of } \frac{C}{r} \text{ received in year } t$$

$$PV = C\left(\frac{1}{r} - \frac{1}{r} \times \frac{1}{e^{rt}}\right)$$

$$= \$50,000\left(\frac{1}{0.0953} - \frac{1}{0.0953} \times \frac{1}{6.727}\right) = \$50,000 \times 8.932 = \$446,600$$

Alternatively, we could have cut these calculations short by using Appendix Table 5. This shows that, if the annually compounded return is 10%, then one dollar a year spread over 20 years is worth $8.932.

If you look back at our earlier discussion of annuities, you will notice that the present value of $50,000 paid at the *end* of each of the 20 years was $425,700. Therefore, it costs the philanthropist $21,900 — or 5% — more to provide a continuous payment stream.

Often in finance we need only a ballpark estimate of present value. An error of 5% in a present value calculation may be perfectly acceptable. In such cases it doesn't usually matter whether we assume that cash flows occur at the end of the year or in a continuous stream. At other times precision matters, and we do need to worry about the exact frequency of the cash flows.

*3-4   A PRACTICAL EXAMPLE: CANADIAN MORTGAGES

A **mortgage** is a bond used to finance the purchase of real estate. We have now assembled enough tools to analyze a common, but complicated, financial asset — the Canadian mortgage. Canadian mortgages have two special features. First, interest is compounded semiannually, even though payments are made monthly. Second, the mortgage terms are re-negotiated before the mortgage is fully paid up. We will see how to calculate monthly payments on the mortgage and determine the unpaid balance when the mortgage is re-negotiated.

First we need a bit of background on mortgages. The simplest mortgage to understand is an American mortgage. Suppose Mary Bush, an American, borrows $100,000 from a bank in order to buy a house. She arranges to pay the mortgage loan off in equal monthly instalments over two years at a rate of 12% per year. Now, the stated interest rate on American mortgages is compounded monthly, so she really makes equal payments over $12 \times 2 = 24$ months at an interest rate of $12/12 = 1\%$ per month. At the end of the 24-month period, she will have paid off the loan and owes nothing more. Thus, Mary is paying a 24-month annuity.

How much are her payments? In order to persuade the bank to give up $100,000 in return for an annuity, the present value of the annuity of payments must be $100,000. Let's call the monthly payment PMT. This means that

$$\$100,000 = PMT \times \frac{1}{0.01}\left[1 - \frac{1}{(1.01)^{24}}\right]$$

Since r is the continuously compounded rate, C/r received in year t is worth $(C/r) \times (1/e^{rt})$ today. Our annuity formula is therefore

$$PV = \frac{C}{r} - \frac{C}{r} \times \frac{1}{e^{rt}}$$

sometimes written as

$$PV = \frac{C}{r}\left[1 - \frac{1}{e^{rt}}\right]$$

Or, using Appendix Table 3 to get the annuity factor for a 24-period annuity at 1%,

$$\$100,000 = \text{PMT} \times 21.24$$

Thus, Mary's monthly payment is PMT = 100,000/21.24 = \$4,708.10.

Mary feels that this payment is too high for her budget, so she decides to pay the loan off over the longer term of 25 years or 25 × 12 = 300 months. Unfortunately this means we can't use our Appendix Table 3 to find the annuity factor. In the mortgage business, there are too many combinations of term and interest rates to present annuity factors in small tables. If you had such tables you would likely lose them (if you are like us), so you will need to either use our formula to calculate the annuity factor or a financial calculator. Remember that mortgage brokers use sharp pencils and fancy calculators. The annuity factor for 300 periods at 1% per period is 94.9466, so Mary's payment under the new mortgage is a more affordable \$100,000/94.9466 = \$1,053.22 per month.

Mary has a cousin, Brian Turner, who is taking out a similar mortgage in Canada. Since the 10% interest is compounded semiannually, Brian must calculate the equivalent monthly rate of interest. If we let r_m be this monthly interest rate, then compounding the monthly rate 12 times must give the same result as compounding the semiannual rate of 10/2 = 5% two times:

$$(1 + r_m)^{12} = (1 + 0.10/2)^2$$

Taking the twelfth root and solving:

$$r_m = 1.05^{1/6} - 1 = 1.008165 - 1$$
$$= 0.008165 \text{ or } 0.8165\%$$

(Yes, we use a financial calculator.)

Brian's next step is to calculate his monthly payment. He uses his monthly interest rate in the same annuity formula as Mary:

$$100,000 = \text{PMT} \times \frac{1}{0.008165} \left[1 - \frac{1}{1.008165^{300}} \right]$$

$$100,000 = \text{PMT} \times 111.7959$$

Thus, Brian's payment is \$100,000/111.7959 = \$894.49 per month—somewhat less than Mary's.

So far we have only used the semiannual compounding feature of Canadian mortgages. the other important feature is that the mortgage payment is determined over a projected life or **amortization period** that is longer than the **term to maturity** (or simply the **term**) of the loan. At the end of the term, the loan is not completely paid off and Brian must make a final payment of the **unpaid balance** or **principal**. Equivalently, he can negotiate a new loan for that amount.[11]

Let's suppose that Brian negotiates a 5-year (60-month) mortgage with a 25-year (300-month) amortization period at 10% per year. His payments are \$894.49

---

[11] Typically, the new loan retains the same final payoff date as before, but the payment changes to reflect the interest rate that holds in the market at the renegotiation date. That is, Brian may buy a house and take a 5-year mortgage with a 25-year amortization period. After 5 years he negotiates a new loan that typically has a 20-year amortization, and so on.

per month, as we calculated earlier. Now he wants to know how much unpaid balance he will owe at the end of the 60-month term. Denote this unpaid principal or balance by BAL. We will discuss two methods of calculating BAL. The first method is easy to understand, but often tedious to work out, while the second method is harder to understand, but easy to work out.

Brian makes a stream of 60 monthly payments, PMT, plus a single payment at the end of the 60-month term of BAL. The present value of this stream must be the original amount of the loan:

$$100{,}000 = 894.49 \times \frac{1}{0.008165}\left[1 - \frac{1}{1.008165^{60}}\right] + \frac{BAL}{1.008165^{60}}$$

$$100{,}000 = 894.49 \times 47.2865 + BAL \times 0.6139$$

The final balance owing after 5 years is BAL = \$93,991.66. (We have kept more digits of accuracy in our calculator than we report here.) Some calculators let you calculate BAL easily and call it FV for future value, while PV is the initial amount of the loan (\$100,000 here).

Let's discuss the other way to calculate BAL. We know that the initial loan amount of \$100,000 equals the present value of a 300-period annuity of an amount PMT. We can regard this 300-month period annuity as a succession of two annuities. The first annuity goes from periods 1 to 60 and the second goes from 61 to 300. We can discount the second annuity in two stages: first discount the payments from period 61 to 300 to period 60 with the ordinary formula and then discount this result back to period 0. Thus, we have

$$100{,}000 = \text{PV of first 60 payments} + \text{PV of second 240 payments}$$

$$100{,}000 = PMT \times \frac{1}{0.008165}\left[1 - \frac{1}{1.008165^{60}}\right]$$

$$+ \frac{1}{1.008165^{60}} \times PMT \times \frac{1}{0.008165}\left[1 - \frac{1}{1.008165^{240}}\right]$$

But the first part of this looks very much like the first formula we used earlier to calculate the same unpaid balance, so the second parts must be the same as well:

$$BAL = PMT \times \frac{1}{0.008165}\left[1 - \frac{1}{1.008165^{240}}\right]$$

$$= 894.49 \times 105.0791 = \$93{,}992.17$$

The answer is the same as before, except for round-off error. This formula for the remaining balance is the present value of an annuity consisting of the extra monthly payments that would have to be made if one wanted to extend the term of the loan out to the full amortization period.

Summary of Canandian Mortgage Formulas

Let P denote the original principal that is borrowed, r the stated annual interest rate, t the term of the mortgage in months, and T the number of months to amortize the mortgage. The amortization period must be at least as long as the term of the mortgage, so $t \leq T$. The equivalent monthly interest rate is

$$r_m = (1 + r/2)^{1/6} - 1$$

The monthly payment is

$$\text{PMT} = \frac{P}{\dfrac{1}{r_m}\left[1 - \dfrac{1}{(1+r_m)^T}\right]} = \frac{P}{T\text{-period annuity factor}}$$

The balance owing at the end of the amortization period is[12]

$$\text{BAL} = \text{PMT} \times \frac{1}{r_m}\left[1 - \frac{1}{(1+r_m)^{T-t}}\right]$$

3-5 SUMMARY

The difficult thing in any present value exercise is to set up the problem correctly. Once you have done that, you must be able to do the calculations, but they are not difficult. Now that you have worked through this chapter, all you should need is a little practice.

The basic present value formula for an asset that pays off in several periods is the following obvious extension of our one-period formula:

$$\text{PV} = \frac{C_1}{1+r_1} + \frac{C_2}{(1+r_2)^2} + \ldots$$

You can always work out any present value using this formula, but when the interest rates are the same for each maturity, there may be some short cuts that can reduce the tedium. We looked at three such cases. First, there was the case of an asset that pays C dollars a year in perpetuity. Its present value is simply

$$\text{PV} = \frac{C}{r}$$

Second, there was the case of an asset whose payments increase at a steady rate g in perpetuity. Its present value is

$$\text{PV} = \frac{C}{r-g}$$

---

[12] We can also get this formula from our first definition of the balance outstanding:

$$P = \text{PMT} \times \frac{1}{r_m}\left[1 - \frac{1}{(1+r_m)^t}\right] + \frac{\text{BAL}}{(1+r_m)^t}$$

Substituting for P from our formula for the monthly payment

$$\text{PMT} \times \frac{1}{r_m}\left[1 - \frac{1}{(1+r_m)^T}\right] = \text{PMT} \times \frac{1}{r_m}\left[1 - \frac{1}{(1+r_m)^t}\right] + \frac{\text{BAL}}{(1+r_m)^t}$$

Rearranging and simplifying

$$\frac{\text{BAL}}{(1+r_m)^t} = \text{PMT} \times \frac{1}{r_m}\left[\frac{1}{(1+r_m)^t} - \frac{1}{(1+r_m)^T}\right]$$

Multiplying both sides by $(1+r_m)^t$ gives

$$\text{BAL} = \text{PMT} \times \frac{1}{r_m}\left[1 - \frac{1}{(1+r_m)^{T-t}}\right]$$

Third, there was the case of an annuity that pays C dollars a year for t years. To find its present value we take the difference between the values of two perpetuities:

$$PV = \frac{C}{r}\left[1 - \frac{1}{(1 + r)^t}\right]$$

Our next step was to show that discounting is a process of compound interest. It is the amount that we would have to invest now at compound interest r in order to produce the cash flows C_1, C_2, and so on. When someone offers to lend us a dollar at an annual rate of r, we should always check how frequently the interest is to be compounded. If the compounding interval is annual, we will have to repay $(1 + r)^t$ dollars; on the other hand, if the compounding is continuous, we will have to repay 2.718^{rt} (or, as it is often called, e^{rt}) dollars. Very often in capital budgeting we are willing to assume that the cash flows occur at the end of each year, and therefore we discount them at an annually compounded rate of interest. Sometimes, however, it may be fairer to assume that they are spread evenly over the year; in this case we must make use of continuous compounding.

Present value tables will help us to perform many of these calculations. You have been introduced now to tables that show:

1. Present value of one dollar received at the end of year t;
2. Future value of one dollar by the end of year t;
3. Present value of one dollar received at the end of each year until year t;
4. Future value of one dollar invested at a continuously compounded rate of interest;
5. Present value of one dollar received continuously for t years when the annually compounded interest rate is r.

We have shown you how to apply these techniques to analyze a Canadian mortgage, which is a monthly annuity plus a final payment at the end of the term of unpaid principal. Interest is compounded semiannually, even though payments are made monthly.

Finally, we introduced in this chapter two very important ideas that we will come across several times again. The first is that you can add present values: if your formula for the present value of $A + B$ is not the same as your formula for the present value of A plus the present value of B, you have made a mistake. The second is the notion that there is no such thing as a money machine: if you think you have found one, go back and check your calculations.

FURTHER READING

The material in this chapter should cover all you need to know about the mathematics of discounting; but if you wish to dig deeper, there are a number of books on the subject. Try, for example:

R. Cissell, H. Cissell, and D.C. Flaspohler: *The Mathematics of Finance,* 6th ed., Houghton Mifflin Company, Boston, 1982.

P. Zima and R.L. Brown, *Mathematics of Finance*, 3rd ed., McGraw-Hill Ryerson, Toronto, 1983.

QUIZ

1. At an interest rate of 12%, the six-year discount factor is 0.507. How many dollars is $0.507 worth in six years if invested at 12%?
2. If the present value of $139 is $125, what is the discount factor?
3. If the eight-year discount factor is 0.285, what is the present value of $596 received in eight years?
4. If the cost of capital is 9%, what is the present value of $374 paid in year nine?
5. A project produces the following cash flows:

Year	Flow
1	432
2	137
3	797

If the cost of capital is 15%, what is the project's present value?
6. If you invest $100 at an interest rate of 15%, how much will you have at the end of eight years?
7. An investment of $232 will produce $312.18 in two years. What is the annual interest rate?
8. An investment costs $1,548 and pays $138 in perpetuity. If the interest rate is 9%, what is the net present value?
9. It costs $2,590 to insulate your home. Next year's fuel saving will be $220. If the interest rate is 12%, what percentage growth rate in fuel prices is needed to justify insulation? Assume fuel prices will grow in perpetuity at the rate g.
10. A common stock will pay a cash dividend of $4 next year. After that, the dividends are expected to increase indefinitely at 4% per year. If the discount rate is 14%, what is the present value of the steam of dividend payments?
11. If you invest $502 at the end of each of the next nine years at an interest rate of 13%, how much will you have at the end?
12. Harold Filbert is 30 years of age and his salary next year will be $20,000. Harold forecasts that his salary will increase at a steady rate of 5% per annum until his retirement at age 60.
    (a) If the discount rate is 8%, what is the present value of these future salary payments?
    (b) If Harold saves 5% of his salary each year and invests these savings at an interest rate of 8%, how much will he have saved by age 60?
    (c) If Harold plans to spend these savings in even amounts over the subsequent 20 years, how much can he spend each year?
13. A factory costs $400,000. You reckon that it will produce an inflow after operating costs of $100,000 in year 1, $200,000 in year 2, and $300,000 in year 3. The opportunity cost of capital is 12%. Draw up a worksheet like that shown in Table 3-1 and use tables to calculate the net present value.
14. Do not use tables for these questions. The interest rate is 10%.
    (a) What is the present value of an asset that pays one dollar a year in perpetuity?
    (b) The value of an asset that appreciates at 10% per annum approximately doubles in seven years. What is the approximate present value of an asset that pays one dollar a year in perpetuity beginning in year 8?

(c) What is the approximate present value of an asset that pays one dollar a year for each of the next seven years?

(d) A piece of land produces an income that grows by 5% per annum. If the first year's flow is $10,000, what is the value of the land?

15. What are the monthly payments for a $50,000 American mortgage at 24% per year that is amortized over 30 months? What is the unpaid balance on the mortgage after 2 years?

*16. You will need a financial calculator for this. You are negotiating for a $75,000 Canadian mortgage to be amortized over 30 years, with the interest rate of 11% per year.

(a) What is the equivalent monthly compounded rate of interest?

(b) What are your monthly payments?

(c) What is the principal remaining after a 5-year term?

17. Use the tables at the end of the book for each of the following calculations:

(a) The cost of a new automobile is $10,000. If the interest rate is 5%, how much would you have to set aside now to provide this sum in five years?

(b) You have to pay $1200 a year in school fees at the end of each of the next six years. If the interest rate is 8%, how much do you need to set aside today to cover these bills?

(c) You have invested $6,048 at 8%. After paying the above school fees, how much would remain at the end of the six years?

*(d) You have borrowed $1,000 and in return have agreed to pay back $1,762 in five years. What is the *annually* compounded rate of interest on the loan? What is the *continuously* compounded rate of interest?

QUESTIONS AND PROBLEMS

1. Use the *discount factors* shown in Appendix Table 1 at the end of the book to calculate the present value of $100 received in:

(a) Year 10 (at a discount rate of 1%)

(b) Year 10 (at a discount rate of 13%)

(c) Year 15 (at a discount rate of 25%)

(d) Each of years 1 through 3 (at a discount rate of 12%)

2. Use the *annuity factors* shown in Appendix Table 3 to calculate the present value of $100 in each of:

(a) Years 1 through 20 (at a discount rate of 23%)

(b) Years 1 through 5 (at a discount rate of 3%)

(c) Years 3 through 12 (at a discount rate of 9%)

3. (a) If the one-year discount factor is 0.88, what is the one-year interest rate?

(b) If the two-year interest rate of 10.5%, what is the two-year discount factor?

(c) Given these one- and two-year discount factors, calculate the two-year annuity factor.

(d) If the present value of $10 a year for three years is $24.49, what is the three-year annuity factor?

(e) From your answers to (c) and (d), calculate the three-year discount factor.

4.   A factory costs $800,000. You reckon that it will produce an inflow after operating costs of $170,000 a year for ten years. If the opportunity cost of capital is 14%, what is the net present value of the factory? What will the factory be worth at the end of five years?

5.   Halcyon Lines is considering the purchase of a new bulk carrier for $8 million. The forecast revenues are $5 million a year and operating costs are $4 million. A major refit costing $2 million will be required after both the fifth and tenth years. After 15 years, the ship is expected to be sold for scrap at $1.5 million. If the discount rate is 8%, what is the ship's NPV?

6.   As winner of a breakfast cereal competition, you can choose one of the following prizes:
(a) $100,000 now;
(b) $180,000 at the end of five years;
(c) $11,400 a year forever;
(d) $19,000 for each of ten years;
(e) $6,500 next year and increasing thereafter by 5% a year forever.
     If the interest rate is 12%, which is the most valuable prize?

7.   Refer back to the story of Ms. Kraft in Section 3-1.
(a) If the one-year interest rate were 25%, how many plays would Ms. Kraft require to become a millionaire? (*Hint*: you may find it easier to use a calculator and a little trial and error.)
(b) What does the story of Ms. Kraft imply about the relationship between the one-year discount factor, DF_1, and the two-year discount factor, DF_2?

8.   Siegfried Basset is 65 years of age and has a life expectancy of 12 years. He wishes to invest $20,000 in an annuity that will make a level payment at the end of each year until his death. If the interest rate is 8%, what income can Mr. Basset expect to receive each year?

9.   James and Helen Turnip are saving to buy a boat at the end of five years. If the boat costs $20,000 and they can earn 10% a year on their savings, how much do they need to put aside at the end of years one through five?

10. Kangaroo Autos is offering free credit on a new $10,000 car. You pay $1,000 down and then $300 a month for the next 30 months. Turtle Motors next door does not offer free credit but will give you $1,000 off the list price. If the rate of interest is 10% a year, which company is offering the better deal?

11. Recalculate the net present value of the office building venture in Section 3-1 at interest rates of 5%, 10%, and 15%. Plot the points on a graph with NPV on the vertical axis and the discount rates on the horizontal axis. At what discount rate (approximately) would the project have zero NPV? Check your answer.

12. (a) How much will an investment of $100 be worth at the end of ten years if invested at 15% a year simple interest?
(b) How much will it be worth if invested at 15% a year compound interest?
(c) How long will it take your investment to double its value at 15% compound interest?

13. You own an oil pipeline which will generate a $2 million cash return over the coming year. The pipeline's operating costs are negligible and it is expected to last for a very long time. Unfortunately, the volume of oil shipped is declining, and cash flows are expected to decline by 4% per year. The discount rate is 10%.
(a) What is the present value of the pipeline's cash flows if its cash flows are assumed to last forever?

(b) What is the present value of the cash flows if the pipeline is scrapped after 20 years?

[*Hint* for part (b): Start with your answer to part (a), then subtract the present value of a declining perpetuity starting in year 21. Note that the forecasted cash flow for year 21 will be much less than the cash flow for year 1.]

14. You will need a financial calculator for this. Ted is negotiating with a Canadian bank for a $60,000 mortgage. The bank wants 10% per year and will allow him a 1-year term with amortization over 20 or 25 years. Ted would like to know how much his payments would be reduced by increasing the amortization period from 20 to 25 years. He is also concerned about how much his payments might rise if he takes the 1-year mortgage with 20-year amortization and has to renew the mortgage when interest rates are 14%. Answer these questions for Ted.

*15. If the interest rate is 7%, what is the value of the following three investments?

(a) an investment that offers you $100 a year in perpetuity with the payment at the *end* of each year;

(b) a similar investment with the payment at the *beginning* of each year;

(c) a similar investment with the payment spread evenly over each year.

*16. Refer back to Section 3-2. If the rate of interest is 8% rather than 10%, how much would our benefactor need to set aside to provide each of the following?

(a) $50,000 at the end of each year in perpetuity;

(b) a perpetuity that pays $50,000 at the end of the first year and that grows at 4% a year;

(c) $50,000 at the end of each year for 20 years;

(d) $50,000 a year spread evenly over 20 years.

*17. For an investment of $1,000 today, the Tiburon Finance Company is offering to pay you $1,600 at the end of eight years. What is the annually compounded rate of interest? What is the continuously compounded rate of interest?

*18. How much will you have at the end of 20 years if you invest $100 today at 15% *annually* compounded? How much will you have if you invest at 15% *continuously* compounded?

*19. You have just read an advertisement reading, "Pay us $100 a year for ten years and we will pay you $100 a year thereafter in perpetuity." If this is a fair deal, what is the rate of interest?

C·H·A·P·T·E·R

4

PRESENT VALUE OF BONDS
AND STOCKS

We should warn you that being a financial expert has its occupational hazards. One is that you are liable to be cornered at cocktail parties by people who are eager to explain their system for investing in stocks and bonds. Fortunately, these bores go into temporary hibernation whenever the market goes down: during these times you can enjoy your parties.

We may exaggerate the perils of the trade. The point is that there is no easy way to ensure superior investment performance. Later in the book we will show that changes in security prices are fundamentally unpredictable and that this result is a natural consequence of well-functioning capital markets. Therefore, when we say that we propose in this chapter to use the concept of present value to price common stocks and bonds, we are not promising you a key to investment success; we simply believe that the idea can help you to understand why some investments are priced higher than others.

We begin the chapter with a brief review of how bonds are valued. It is brief because we shall be considering some of the refinements of bond valuation in Chapter 23. After our discussion of bonds we will look at the valuation of common stocks. We will explain the real difference between growth stocks and income stocks and the significance of earnings-per-share and price-earnings multiples. Finally, in the appendix to this chapter, we discuss some of the special problems managers and investors encounter when they calculate the present values of entire businesses.

A final word of caution. Everybody knows that common stocks are risky and that some are more risky than others. Investors, therefore, will not commit funds to stocks unless the expected rates of return are commensurate with the risks. The present value formulas we have discussed so far can take account of the effects of risk on value, but they do not tell us exactly *how* to do so. Recognize, therefore, that risk comes into the following discussion in a loose and intuitive way. A more careful treatment of risk starts in Chapter 7.

4-1   A QUICK LOOK AT HOW BONDS ARE VALUED

When you own a bond, you receive a fixed set of cash payoffs. Each year until the bond matures you get an interest payment and then at maturity you also get back the face value of the bond.

Suppose that in May 1989 you invest in a 13¾% 1994 Government of Canada bond, often called a "Canada 13¾ of 1994." The bond has a coupon rate of 13¾% and a face value of $1,000.[1] This means that each year until 1994 you receive an interest payment of 0.1375 × $1,000 = $137.50. The bond matures in 1994: in that year, the government pays you the final $137.50 interest, plus the $1,000 face value. The cash flows from owning the bond are therefore as follows:

Cash Flows (dollars)				
1990	1991	1992	1993	1994
137.5	137.5	137.5	137.5	1,137.5

What is the market value in 1989 of this stream of cash flows? To determine that, we need to look at the return provided by similar bonds. Short-term Government of Canada bonds in May 1989 offered a return of about 10.2%. This is what investors were giving up when they bought the 13¾% bonds. Therefore, to value the 13¾% bonds of 1994, we need to discount the prospective stream of cash flows at 10.2%.

$$
\begin{aligned}
PV &= \sum_{t=1}^{5} \frac{C_t}{(1+r)^t} \\
&= \frac{137.5}{1+r} + \frac{137.5}{(1+r)^2} + \frac{137.5}{(1+r)^3} + \frac{137.5}{(1+r)^4} + \frac{1137.5}{(1+r)^5} \\
&= \frac{137.5}{1.102} + \frac{137.5}{(1.102)^2} + \frac{137.5}{(1.102)^3} + \frac{137.5}{(1.102)^4} + \frac{1,137.5}{(1.102)^5} \\
&= \$1,133.89
\end{aligned}
$$

Bond prices are usually expressed as a percentage of face value. Thus, we can say that our 13¾% Canada bond is worth $1,133.89, or 113.39%.

We could have phrased our question the other way around and asked, "If the price of the bond is $1,133.89, what return do investors expect?" In that case, we would need to find the value of r that satisfies the following equation:

$$
1,133.89 = \frac{137.50}{1+r} + \frac{137.50}{(1+r)^2} + \frac{137.50}{(1+r)^3} + \frac{137.50}{(1+r)^4} + \frac{1,137.50}{(1+r)^5}
$$

The value of r is often called the bond's **yield to maturity** or **internal rate of return**. In our case, r is 10.2%. If you discount the cash flows at 10.2%, you arrive at the bond's price of $1,133.89. As we shall see in Chapter 5, the only *general* procedure for calculating r is by trial and error. But financial electronic calculators can be used to calculate r, or you can use a book of bond tables that show values of r for different coupon levels and different maturities.

---

[1] The face value of the bond is known as the *principal*. Therefore, when the bond matures, the government pays you principal and interest.

In calculating the value of the Canada 13¾s we made two approximations. First, we assumed that interest payments occur annually. In practice, most bonds make coupon payments *semiannually*. Therefore, instead of receiving $137.50 every year, an investor who held Canada 13¾s would receive $68.75 every *half* year. Second, we treated the 10.2% yield as an annually compounded rate. Bond yields are usually quoted as semiannually compounded rates.

You may have noticed that the formula we used for calculating the present value of Canada 13¾s was slightly different from the general present value formula that we developed in Section 3-1. In the latter case, we allowed for the fact that r_1, the rate of return offered by the capital market on one-year investments, may be different from r_2, the rate of return offered on two-year investments. Later in Chapter 3 we finessed this problem by assuming that r_1 is the same as r_2. In this chapter we again assume that investors use the same rate to discount cash flows occurring in different years. That does not matter as long as short-term rates are approximately the same as long-term rates. But often when we value bonds we must discount each cash flow at a different rate. There will be more about that in Chapter 23.

4-2 HOW COMMON STOCKS ARE VALUED

Today's Price
The cash payoff to owners of common stocks comes in two forms: (1) cash dividends and (2) capital gains or losses. Usually investors expect to get some of each. Suppose that the current price of a share is P_0, that the expected price at the end of a year is P_1, and that the expected dividend per share is DIV_1. The rate of return investors expect from this share over the next year is defined as the expected dividend per share DIV_1 plus the expected price appreciation per share $P_1 - P_0$, all divided by the price at the start of the year P_0:

$$\text{Expected return} = r = \frac{DIV_1 + P_1 - P_0}{P_0}$$

This return expected by investors is often called the **market capitalization rate**.

Let us now see how our formula works. Suppose Fledgling Electronics stock is selling for $100 a share ($P_0 = 100$). Investors expect a $5 cash dividend over the next year ($DIV_1 = 5$). They also expect the stock to sell for $110 a year hence ($P_1 = 110$). Then the expected return to the stockholders is 15%:

$$r = \frac{5 + 110 - 100}{100} = 0.15, \text{ or } 15\%$$

Correspondingly, if you are given investors' forecasts of dividend and price and the expected return offered by other equally risky stocks, you can predict today's price:

$$\text{Price} = P_0 = \frac{DIV_1 + P_1}{1 + r}$$

For Fledgling Electronics $DIV_1 = 5$ and $P_1 = 110$. If r, the expected return on securities in the same "risk class" as Fledgling, is 15%, then today's price should be $100:

$$P_0 = \frac{5 + 110}{1.15} = 100$$

How do we know that $100 is the right price? Because no other price could survive in competitive capital markets. What if P_0 were more than $100? Then Fledgling stock would offer an expected rate of return that was *lower* than other securities of equivalent risk. Investors would, therefore, shift their capital to the other securities and in the process would force down the price of Fledgling stock. If P_0 were less than $100, the process would reverse. Fledgling's stock would offer a *higher* rate of return than comparable securities. In that case, investors would rush to buy, forcing the price up to $100.

The general conclusion is that at each point in time *all securities in an equivalent risk class are priced to offer the same expected return*. This is a condition for equilibrium in well-functioning capital markets. It is also common sense.

But What Determines Next Year's Price?

We have managed to explain today's stock price P_0 in terms of the dividend DIV_1 and the expected price next year P_1. Future stock prices are not easy things to forecast directly. But think about what determines next year's price. If our price formula holds now, it ought to hold then as well:

$$P_1 = \frac{DIV_2 + P_2}{1 + r}$$

That is, a year from now investors will be looking out at dividends in year 2 and price at the end of year 2. Thus we can forecast P_1 by forecasting DIV_2 and P_2 and we can express P_0 in terms of DIV_1, DIV_2 and P_2:

$$P_0 = \frac{1}{1 + r}(DIV_1 + P_1) = \frac{1}{1 + r}\left(DIV_1 + \frac{DIV_2 + P_2}{1 + r}\right) = \frac{DIV_1}{1 + r} + \frac{DIV_2 + P_2}{(1 + r)^2}$$

Take Fledgling Electronics. A plausible way to explain why investors expect its stock price to rise by the end of the first year is that they expect higher dividends and still more capital gains in the second. For example, suppose that they are looking today for dividends of $5.50 in year 2 and a subsequent price of $121. That would imply a price at the end of year 1 of

$$P_1 = \frac{5.50 + 121}{1.15} = 110$$

Today's price can then be computed either from our original formula

$$P_0 = \frac{DIV_1 + P_1}{1 + r} = \frac{5.00 + 110}{1.15} = 100$$

or from our expanded formula

$$P_0 = \frac{DIV_1}{1 + r} + \frac{DIV_2 + P_2}{(1 + r)^2} = \frac{5.00}{1.15} + \frac{5.50 + 121}{(1.15)^2} = 100$$

We have succeeded in relating today's price to the forecasted dividends for two years (DIV_1 and DIV_2) plus the forecasted price at the end of the *second* year (P_2). You will probably not be surprised to learn that we could go on to replace P_2 by $(DIV_3 + P_3)/(1 + r)$ and relate today's price to the forecasted dividends for three years (DIV_1, DIV_2, and DIV_3) plus the forecasted price at the end of the *third* year

(P_3). In fact, we can look as far out into the future as we like, removing Ps as we go. Let us call this final period H. This gives us a general stock-price formula

$$P_0 = \frac{DIV_1}{1 + r} + \frac{DIV_2}{(1 + r)^2} + \ldots + \frac{DIV_H + P_H}{(1 + r)^H}$$

$$= \sum_{t = 1}^{H} \frac{DIV_t}{(1 + r)^t} + \frac{P_H}{(1 + r)^H}$$

The expression $\sum_{t = 1}^{H}$ simply means the sum of the discounted dividends from year 1 to year H.

Table 4-1 continued the Fledgling Electronics example for various time horizons, assuming that the dividends are expected to increase at a steady 10% compound rate. The expected price P_t increases at the same rate each year. Each line in the table represents an application of our general formula for a different value of H. Figure 4-1 provides a graphical representation of the table. Each column shows the present value of the dividends up to the time horizon and the present value of the price at the horizon. As the horizon recedes, the dividend stream accounts for an increasing proportion of present value, but the *total* present value of dividends plus terminal price always equals $100.

Table 4-1
Applying the Stock Valuation Formula to Fledgling Electronics

| | Expected Future Values | | Present Values | | |
Horizon Period (H)	Dividend (Div_t)	Price (P_t)	Cumulative Dividends	Future Price	Total
0	—	100	—	100.00	100
1	5.00	110	4.35	95.65	100
2	5.50	121	8.51	91.49	100
3	6.05	133.10	12.48	87.52	100
4	6.66	146.41	16.29	83.71	100
10	11.79	259.37	35.89	64.11	100
20	30.58	672.75	58.89	41.11	100
50	533.59	11,739.09	89.17	10.83	100
100	62,639.15	1,378,061.23	98.83	1.17	100

Assumptions:
1. Dividends increase at 10% per year, compounded.
2. Capitalization rate is 15%.

How far out could we look? In principle, the horizon period H could be infinitely distant. Common stocks do not expire of old age. Barring such corporate hazards as bankruptcy or acquisition, they are immortal. As H approaches infinity, the present value of the terminal price ought to approach zero, as it does in the final column of Figure 4-1. We can, therefore, forget about the terminal price entirely and express today's price as the present value of a perpetual stream of cash dividends. This is usually written as

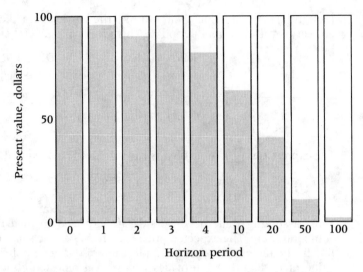

Figure 4-1 As your horizon recedes, the present value of the future price (shaded area) declines but the present value of the stream of dividends (unshaded area) increases. The *total* present value (future price and dividends) remains the same.

$$P_0 = \sum_{t=1}^{\infty} \frac{\text{DIV}_t}{(1 + r)^t}$$

where the sign ∞ is used to indicate infinity. This discounted cash flow (DCF) formula for the present value of a stock is just the same as it is for the present value of any other asset. We just discount the cash flows — in this case the dividend stream — by the return that can be earned in the capital market on securities of comparable risk. Some find the DCF formula implausible because it seems to ignore capital gains. But we know the formula was *derived* from the assumption that price in any period is determined by expected dividends and capital gains over the next period.

Remembering our rule about adding present values, we might be tempted to conclude that the *total* value of a company's common stock must be equal to the discounted stream of *all* future dividends paid by the company. But we need to be a little careful here. We must only include the dividends that will be paid on *existing* stock. The company may at some future date decide to sell more stock and this will be entitled to its share of the subsequent dividend stream. The total value of a company's existing common stock is, therefore, equal to the discounted value of that *portion* of the total dividend stream that will be paid to the stock outstanding today. It sounds obvious but it is surprising how often people forget.

4-3   A SIMPLE WAY TO ESTIMATE THE CAPITALIZATION RATE

In Chapter 3 we encountered some simplified versions of the basic present value formula. Let us see whether they offer any insights into stock values. Suppose, for example, that we forecast a constant-growth trend in a company's dividends. This does not preclude year-to-year deviations from the trend: it means only that *expected* dividends grow at a constant rate. Such an investment would be just another example of the growing perpetuity that we helped our fickle philanthropist to evaluate in the last chapter. To find its present value we must divide the annual cash payment by the difference between the discount rate and the growth rate:

$$P_0 = \frac{\text{DIV}_1}{r - g}$$

Remember, however, that we can use this formula only when g, the anticipated growth rate, is less than r, the discount rate. As g approaches r, the stock price becomes infinite. Obviously r must be greater than g if growth really is perpetual.

Our growing perpetuity formula explains P_0 in terms of next year's expected dividend DIV_1, the projected growth trend g, and the expected rate of return on other securities of comparable risk r. Alternatively, the formula can be used to obtain an estimate of r from DIV_1, P_0, and g:

$$r = \frac{\text{DIV}_1}{P_0} + g$$

The market capitalization rate equals the **dividend yield** (DIV_1/P_0) plus the expected rate of growth in dividends (g).

These two formulas are much easier to work with than the general statement that "price equals the present value of expected future dividends."[2] For instance, imagine that we are analyzing Brascan Ltd. late in 1988 when its stock is selling for about $25.75 a share. Dividend payments for 1989 are expected to be $0.96 a share. Now we can calculate the first half of our formula:

$$\text{Dividend yield} = \frac{\text{DIV}_1}{P_0} = \frac{0.96}{25.75} = 0.04$$

The hard part is to estimate g. One line of reasoning starts with Brascan's **payout ratio**, the ratio of dividends to earnings per share (EPS). This has generally been around 35%. In other words, each year Brascan plows back into the business about 65% of earnings per share:

$$\text{Plowback ratio} = 1 - \text{payout ratio} = 1 - \frac{\text{DIV}_1}{\text{EPS}_1} = 1 - 0.35 = 0.65$$

Also, Brascan's ratio of earnings per share to book equity per share is about 17%. This is its *return on equity* or ROE:

$$\text{Return on equity} = \text{ROE} = \frac{\text{EPS}_1}{\text{Book equity per share}} = 0.17$$

---

[2] These formulas were first developed in 1938 by J.B. Williams and were rediscovered by M.J. Gordon and E. Shapiro. See J.B. Williams, *The Theory of Investment Value*, Harvard University Press, Cambridge, Mass., 1938; and M.J. Gordon and E. Shapiro, "Capital Equipment Analysis: The Required Rate of Profit," *Management Science*, **3**:102–110 (October 1956).

Brascan has been a stable company, and it may not be too unreasonable to assume that these relationships will continue to hold. Suppose we forecast that Brascan will earn 17% of book equity and reinvest 65% of that, and therefore book equity will increase by $0.65 \times 0.17 = 0.11$. Since we assumed that the return on equity and the payout ratio are constant, earnings and dividends per share will also increase by 11%:

$$\text{Dividend growth rate} = g = \text{plowback ratio} \times \text{ROE}$$
$$= 0.65 \times 0.17 = 0.11$$

Now you have your estimate of the market capitalization rate (that is, the rate of return that investors use to discount Brascan's future dividends):

$$r = \frac{\text{DIV}_1}{P_0} + g = 0.04 + 0.11 = 0.15 \text{ or } 15\%$$

Using the DCF Model to Set Electricity Prices

Although our estimate of the market capitalization rate for Brascan stock seems reasonable enough, there are obvious dangers in analyzing any single firm's stock with such simple rules of thumb as the constant-growth DCF formula. First, the underlying assumption of regular future growth is at best an approximation. Second, even if it is an acceptable approximation, errors inevitably creep into the estimate of g. Remember, however, that r is not the personal property of Brascan: in well-functioning markets, investors must capitalize the dividends of *all* securities in Brascan's risk class at exactly the same rate. This means that we may do better to take a large sample of securities of equivalent risk, estimate r for each, and use the average of our estimates. Here is a practical example.

One task of the United States Federal Energy Regulatory Commission (FERC) is to set prices for interstate sales of electric power. These are almost always wholesale transactions. That is, an electric utility with surplus generating capacity will sell power to a utility in a neighbouring state. The buyer may have a shortage of capacity or it may not be able to produce electricity as cheaply as the seller.

The sale price is supposed to cover all costs of producing and transporting the electricity, including interest and tax payments, *and* to provide a reasonable profit for the seller. What is "reasonable"? It is the profit that provides a fair rate of return to the seller on its equity investment in generating equipment, transmission lines, and so on. What is a "fair" rate of return? It is usually interpreted as r, the market capitalization rate for the selling firm's common stock. That is, the expected rate of return on investments made by electric utilities ought to be the same rate offered by securities having risks equivalent to the utility's common stock.[3]

Thus, FERC's problem of determining fair profits boils down to estimating r for the common stock of electric utilities it regulates. This is done case by case, as each utility appears before FERC to justify its prices for interstate sales. The case-by-case analyses typically rely on DCF formulas.

---

[3] This is the accepted interpretation of the U.S. Supreme Court's directive in 1944 that ". . . the returns to the equity owner [of a regulated business] should be commensurate with returns on investments in other enterprises having corresponding risks." *Federal Power Commission v. Hope Natural Gas Company,* 302 U.S. 591 at 603. Canadian utilities are regulated in a similar fashion, although there is no single legislative ruling, since most utilities are regulated provincially rather than federally.

FERC also calculates quarterly a "generic" or "benchmark" estimate of r for the electric utility industry. In July 1986, for example, the benchmark was

$$r = \frac{DIV_1}{P_0} + g$$
$$= 0.0764 + 0.0454 = 0.1218, \text{ or about } 12\%^4$$

Some Warnings About Constant-Growth Formulas

These simple, constant-growth DCF formulas are extremely useful rules of thumb, but they are no more than that. Naive trust in the formulas has led many financial analysts to silly conclusions.

First, remember the difficulty of estimating r by analysis of one stock only. Try to work with a large sample of equivalent-risk securities. Even that may not work, but at least it gives the analyst a fighting chance, because the inevitable errors in estimating r for a single security tend to balance out across a broad sample.

Second, resist the temptation to apply the formula to firms having high current rates of growth. Such growth can rarely be sustained indefinitely, but the constant-growth DCF formula assumes it can. This erroneous assumption leads to an overestimate of r.

Consider Growth-Tech, Inc., a firm with $DIV_1 = \$0.50$ and $P_0 = \$50$. That firm has plowed back 80% of earnings and has had a return on equity (ROE) of 25%. This means that *in the past*

Dividend growth rate = plowback ratio × ROE = 0.80 × 0.25 = 0.20

The temptation is to assume that the future long-term growth rate (g) also equals 0.20. This would imply

$$r = \frac{0.50}{50.00} + 0.20 = 0.21$$

But this is silly. No firm can continue growing at 20% per year forever, except possibly under extreme inflationary conditions. Eventually, profitability will fall and the firm will respond by investing less.

In real life the return on investment will decline *gradually* over time, but for simplicity let's assume it suddenly drops to 16% at year 3 and the firm responds by plowing back only 50% of earnings. Then g drops to $0.50(0.16) = 0.08$.

Table 4-2 shows what's going on. Growth-Tech starts year 1 with assets of $10.00. It earns $2.50, pays out 50¢ as dividends, and plows back $2. Thus it starts year 2 with $10 + 2 = \$12$. After another year at the same ROE and payout, it starts year 3 with equity of $14.40. However ROE drops to 0.16 and the firm earns only $2.30. Dividends go up to $1.15, because the payout ratio increases, but the firm has only $1.15 to plow back. Therefore subsequent growth in earnings and dividends drops to 8%.

---

[4] We say "about 12%" because it's pointless to pretend that expected returns can be estimated to four decimal places. Utilities and regulators find themselves arguing about these decimal places, however. If a utility has a $1 billion equity investment, that 0.18% amounts to $0.0018 × 1,000,000,000 = \$1,800,000$ or $1.8 million *per year*.

The 12.18% estimate of r was published by FERC in "Notice of Benchmark Rate of Return on Common Equity for Public Utilities," July 16, 1986. The estimate was based on dividend yields and forecasted dividend growth rates for a sample of 99 electric utility common stocks.

Table 4-2
Forecasted earnings and dividends for Growth-Tech. Note the changes in year 3: ROE and earnings drop, but payout ratio increases, causing a big jump in dividends. However, subsequent growth in earnings and dividends falls to 8% per year. Note that the increase in equity equals the earnings not paid out as dividends.

Year	1	2	3	4
Book equity	10.00	12.00	14.40	15.55
Earnings per share, EPS	2.50	3.00	2.30	2.49
Return on equity, ROE	0.25	0.25	0.16	0.16
Payout ratio	0.20	0.20	0.50	0.50
Dividends per share, DIV	0.50	0.60	1.15	1.24
Growth rate of dividends	—	0.20	0.92	0.08

Now we can use our general DCF formula to find the capitalization rate r:

$$P_0 = \frac{DIV_1}{1 + r} + \frac{DIV_2}{(1 + r)^2} + \frac{DIV_3 + P_3}{(1 + r)^3}$$

Investors in year 3 will view Growth-Tech as offering 8% per year dividend growth. We will apply the constant-growth formula:

$$P_3 = \frac{DIV_4}{r - 0.08}$$

$$P_0 = \frac{DIV_1}{1 + r} + \frac{DIV_2}{(1 + r)^2} + \frac{DIV_3}{(1 + r)^3} + \frac{1}{(1 + r)^3}\frac{DIV_4}{(r - 0.08)}$$

$$= \frac{0.50}{1 + r} + \frac{0.60}{(1 + r)^2} + \frac{1.15}{(1 + r)^3} + \frac{1}{(1 + r)^3}\frac{1.24}{(r - 0.08)}$$

We have to use trial and error to find the value of r that makes P_0 equal $50. It turns out that the r implicit in these more realistic forecasts is approximately 0.099, quite a difference from our "constant-growth" estimate of 0.21.

A final warning. Do not use the simple constant-growth formula to test whether the market is correct in its assessment of a stock's value. If your estimate of the value is different from that of the market, it is probably because you have used poor dividend forecasts. Remember what we said at the beginning of this chapter about simple ways of making money on the stock market. There aren't any.

4-4   THE LINK BETWEEN STOCK PRICE AND EARNINGS PER SHARE

Investors often use the terms *growth stocks* and *income stocks*. They seem to buy growth stocks primarily for the expectation of capital gains, and they are interested in the future growth of earnings rather than in next year's dividends. On the other hand, they buy income stocks primarily for the cash dividends. Let us see whether these distinctions make sense.

Imagine first the case of a company that does not grow at all. It does not plow back any earnings and simply produces a constant stream of dividends. Its stock would be rather like the perpetual bond described in the last chapter. Remember that the return on a perpetuity is equal to the yearly cash flow divided by the present value. The expected return on our share would thus be equal to the yearly dividend divided by the share price (that is, the dividend yield). Since all the earnings are paid out as dividends, the expected return is also equal to the earnings per share divided by the share price (that is, the earnings-price ratio). For example, if the dividend is $10 a share and the stock price is $100, we have

$$\text{Expected return} = \text{dividend yield} = \text{earnings-price ratio}$$
$$= \frac{\text{DIV}_1}{P_0} \qquad = \frac{\text{EPS}_1}{P_0}$$
$$= \frac{10.00}{100} \qquad = 0.10$$

The price equals

$$P_0 = \frac{\text{DIV}_1}{r} = \frac{\text{EPS}_1}{r} = \frac{10.00}{0.10} = \$100$$

The expected return for growing firms can also equal the earnings-price ratio. The key is whether earnings are reinvested to provide a return greater or less than the market capitalization rate. For example, suppose our monotonous company suddenly hears of an opportunity to invest $10 a share next year. This would mean no dividend at $t = 1$. However, the company expects that in each subsequent year the project would earn $1 per share, so that the dividend could be increased to $11 a share.

Let us assume that this investment opportunity has about the same risk as the existing business. Then we can discount its cash flow at the 10% rate to find its net present value at year 1:

$$\text{Net present value per share at year 1} = -10 + \frac{1}{0.10} = 0$$

Thus the investment opportunity will make no contribution to the company's value; to put it another way, its prospective return is equal to the opportunity cost of capital.

What effect will the decision to undertake the project have on the company's share price? Clearly none. The reduction in value caused by the nil dividend in year 1 is exactly offset by the increase in value caused by the extra dividends in later years. Therefore, once again the market capitalization rate equals the earnings-price ratio:

$$r = \frac{\text{EPS}_1}{P_0} = \frac{10}{100} = 0.10$$

Table 4-3 repeats our example for different assumptions about the cash flow generated by the new project. Note that the earnings-price ratio, measured in terms of EPS_1, next year's expected earnings, equals the market capitalization rate (r) *only* when the new project's NPV = 0. This is an extremely important point — business people frequently make poor financial decisions because they confuse earnings-price ratios with the market capitalization rate.

Table 4-3
Effect on stock price of investing an additional $10 in year 1 at different rates of return. Notice that the earnings-price ratio overestimates r when the project has negative NPV and underestimates it when the project has positive NPV.

Project Rate of Return	Incremental Cash Flow, C	Project NPV in Year 1[a]	Project's Impact on Share Price in Year 0[b]	Share Price in Year 0, P_0	$\dfrac{EPS_1}{P_0}$	r
0.05	$ .50	− $5.00	− $4.55	$ 95.45	0.105	0.10
0.10	1.00	0	0	100.00	0.10	0.10
0.15	1.50	+ 5.00	+ 4.55	104.55	0.096	0.10
0.20	2.00	+ 10.00	+ 9.09	109.09	0.092	0.10
0.25	2.50	+ 15.00	+ 13.64	113.64	0.088	0.10

[a] Project costs $10.00 per share. NPV $= -10 + C/r$, where $r = 0.10$.
[b] NPV is calculated at year 1. To find the impact on P_0, discount for one year at $r = 0.10$.

In general, we can think of stock price as the capitalized value of average earnings under a no-growth policy, plus PVGO, the **present value of growth opportunities**:

$$P_0 = \frac{EPS_1}{r} + PVGO$$

The earnings-price ratio, therefore, equals

$$\frac{EPS_1}{P_0} = r\left(1 - \frac{PVGO}{P_0}\right)$$

It will underestimate r if PVGO is positive and overestimate it if PVGO is negative. (The latter case is less likely, since firms are rarely *forced* to take projects with negative net present values.)

*Calculating the Present Value of Growth Opportunities for Fledgling Electronics

Although in our last example both dividends and earnings were expected to grow, this growth made no net contribution to the share price. The stock was in this sense an "income stock." Now let us compare this case with that well-known "growth stock," Fledgling Electronics. You may remember that Fledgling's market capitalization rate, r, is 15%. The company is expected to pay a dividend of $5 in the first year, and thereafter the dividend is predicted to increase indefinitely by 10% a year. We can, therefore, use the simplified constant-growth formula to work out Fledgling's price:

$$P_0 = \frac{DIV_1}{r - g} = \frac{\$5}{0.15 - 0.10} = \$100$$

Suppose that Fledgling has earnings per share of $8.33. Its payout ratio is then

$$\text{Payout ratio} = \frac{DIV_1}{EPS_1} = \frac{5.00}{8.33} = 0.6$$

In other words, the company is plowing back $1 - 0.6$, or 40% of earnings. Suppose also that Fledgling's ratio of earnings to book equity is ROE = 0.25. This explains the growth rate of 10%:

$$\text{Growth rate} = g = \text{plowback ratio} \times \text{ROE} = 0.4 \times 0.25 = 0.10$$

The capitalized value of Fledgling's earnings per share if it had a no-growth policy would be

$$\frac{EPS_1}{r} = \frac{\$8.33}{0.15} = \$55.56$$

But we know that the value of Fledgling stock is $100. The difference of $44.44 must be the amount that investors are paying for growth opportunities. Let's see if we can explain that figure.

Each year Fledgling plows back 40% of its earnings into new assets. In the first year Fledgling invests $3.33 at a permanent 25% return on equity. Thus the cash generated by this investment is $0.25 \times \$3.33 = \$0.83$ per year starting at $t = 2$. The net present value of the investment as of $t = 1$ is

$$NPV_1 = -\$3.33 + \frac{\$0.83}{0.15} = \$2.22$$

Everything is the same in year 2 except that Fledgling will invest $3.67, 10% more than in year 1 (remember $g = 0.10$). Therefore at $t = 2$ an investment is made with a net present value of

$$NPV_2 = -\$3.33 \times 1.10 + \frac{\$0.83 \times 1.10}{0.15} = \$2.44$$

Thus the payoff to the owners of Fledgling Electronics stock can be represented as the sum of (1) a level stream of earnings, which could be paid out as cash dividends if the firm did not grow, and (2) a set of tickets, one for each future year, representing the opportunity to make investments having positive NPVs. We know that the first component of the value of the share is

$$\text{Present value of level stream of earnings} = \frac{EPS_1}{r} = \frac{\$8.33}{0.15} = \$55.56$$

The first ticket is worth $2.22 in $t = 1$; the second is worth $2.22 \times 1.10 = \$2.44$ in $t = 2$; the third is worth $2.44 \times 1.10 = \$2.69$ in $t = 3$. These are the forecasted cash values of the tickets. We know how to value a stream of future cash values that grows at 10% per year: use the simplified DCF formula, replacing the forecasted dividends with forecasted ticket values:

$$\text{Present value of growth opportunities} = \text{PVGO} = \frac{NPV_1}{r - g} = \frac{\$2.22}{0.15 - 0.10}$$
$$= \$44.44$$

Now everything checks:

$$\text{Share price} = \text{present value of level stream of earnings}$$
$$+ \text{ present value of growth opportunities}$$
$$= \frac{\text{EPS}_1}{r} + \text{PVGO}$$
$$= \$55.56 + \$44.44$$
$$= \$100$$

Why is Fledgling Electronics a growth stock? Not because it is expanding at 10% per year. It is a growth stock because the net present value of its future investments accounts for a significant fraction (about 44%) of the stock's price.

Stock prices today reflect investors' expectations of future operating *and investment* performance. Growth stocks sell at high price-earnings ratios because investors are willing to pay now for expected superior returns on investments that have not yet been made.[5]

A General Expression Linking Dividends and Growth Opportunities

Zeus made a habit of appearing in unusual disguises to unsuspecting maidens. The general DCF formula for valuing stocks is rather like that: it keeps cropping up in different forms. Here is another useful version of the formula. Cash not retained and reinvested in the business is often known as **free cash flow**:

$$\text{Free cash flow} = \text{revenue} - \text{costs} - \text{investment}$$

But cash that is not reinvested in the business is paid out as dividends. So dividends per share are the same as free cash flow per share, and the general DCF formula can be written in terms of per share revenues, costs, and investment:

$$P_0 = \sum_{t=1}^{\infty} \frac{(\text{Free cash flow per share})_t}{(1 + r)^t}$$

Notice that it is *not* correct to say that a share's value is equal to the discounted stream of its future earnings per share. That would recognize the *rewards* of investment (in the form of increased revenues) but not the *sacrifice* (in the form of investment). The correct formulation states that share value is equal to the discounted stream of free cash flow per share.

To summarize, we can think of a stock's value as representing either (1) the present value of the stream of expected future dividends, or (2) the present value of free cash flow, or (3) the present value of average future earnings under a no-growth policy plus the present value of growth opportunities.

Some companies have such extensive growth opportunities that they prefer to pay no dividends for long periods of time. PWA Corp., the parent of Canadian Airlines International, has not paid a dividend on its stock since it reorganized in December 1983. That was the start of a growth spurt that took if from a regional airline to become one of Canada's two major national airlines. It didn't pay dividends because any cash paid out to investors would have meant slower growth. Investors were evidently happy with management's decision to reinvest earnings. How else can we explain PWA's $300 million market value? Investors

---

[5] Michael Eisner, the chairman of Walt Disney Productions, made the point this way: "In school you had to take the test and then be graded. Now we're getting graded, and we haven't taken the test." This was in late 1985, when Disney stock was selling at nearly 20 times earnings. See Kathleen K. Wiegner, "The Tinker Bell Principle," *Forbes*, December 2, 1985, p. 102.

were willing to forgo cash dividends today in exchange for higher earnings and the expectation of high dividends sometime in the future. Thus PWA's common stock is not really a counterexample to the statement that stock price equals the present value of expected future dividends. PWA's dividends may continue to be zero for many years, but they are likely to be positive sooner or later. The company cannot continue to grow at the same rate forever. Eventually growth must slow down, releasing funds that can be paid to the stockholders. It is that prospect that makes PWA shares valuable today.

The inevitable deceleration of rapid growth is illustrated by the history of IBM, the most famous growth stock of the period after World War II. IBM has paid dividends since the 1930s, but most IBM stockholders bought the stock for growth, not dividends. Throughout the 1950s and 1960s the dividend yield (dividend per share as a percent of stock price) was very low—usually between 1 and 2%. Sales, earnings, and dividends grew at compound annual rates of roughly 20%.

That kind of growth cannot continue forever. By the mid-1970s IBM lacked investment opportunities attractive enough to justify continued growth at that rate. Yet its existing businesses remained healthy and profitable. Consequently, the firm accumulated cash at an embarrassing rate. It had $6.1 *billion* in cash and marketable securities at the end of 1976 and $5.4 billion at year-end 1977. It was therefore not surprising to find IBM paying more and more generous dividends: in 1978 it paid $2.88 per share on earnings per share of $5.32, a 54% payout ratio. Also, IBM spent about $1.4 billion in 1977 and 1978 to repurchase its own shares. That is, IBM distributed cash to its shareholders by buying shares from them. As Chapter 16 explains, this is essentially equivalent to paying a cash dividend.

What Do Price-Earnings Ratios Mean?

The **price-earnings ratio** is part of the everyday vocabulary of investors in the stock market. People casually refer to PWA stock as "selling at a high *P/E*." You can look up *P/E*s in stock quotations given in the newspaper. (However, the newspaper gives the ratio of current price to the more recent earnings. Investors are more concerned with price relative to *future* earnings.) Unfortunately, some financial analysts are confused about what price-earnings ratios really signify and often use the ratios in odd ways.

Should the financial manager celebrate if the firm's stock sells at a high *P/E*? The answer is usually yes. The high *P/E* shows that investors think that the firm has good growth opportunities (high PVGO), that its earnings are relatively safe and deserve a low capitalization rate (low r), or both. However, firms can have high price-earnings ratios not because price is high but because earnings are low. A firm that earns *nothing* (EPS = 0) in a particular period will have an *infinite* *P/E* as long as its shares retain any value at all.

Are relative *P/E*s helpful in evaluating stocks? Sometimes. Suppose you own stock in a family corporation whose shares are not actively traded. What are those shares worth? A decent estimate is possible if you can find a traded firm that has the same profitability, risks, and growth opportunities as those of your firm. Multiply your firm's earnings per share by the *P/E* of the counterpart firm.

Does a high *P/E* indicate a low market capitalization rate? No. There is *no* reliable association between a stock's price-earnings ratio and the capitalization rate r. The ratio of EPS to P_0 measures r only if PVGO = 0, and only if EPS is the average future earnings the firm could generate under a no-growth policy.

What Do Earnings Mean?

Another reason *P/E*s are hard to interpret is the difficulty of interpreting and comparing earnings per share, the denominator of the price-earnings ratio. What do earnings per share mean? They mean different things for different firms. For some firms they mean more than for others.

The problem is that the earnings that firms report are book, or accounting, figures, and as such reflect a series of more or less arbitrary choices of accounting methods. Almost any firm's reported earnings are changed substantially by the adoption of more or less "conservative" accounting procedures. A switch in the depreciation method used for reporting purposes directly affects EPS, for example. Yet it has *no* effect on cash flow, since depreciation is a noncash charge. (The depreciation method used for tax purposes, called **capital cost allowance**, *does* affect cash flow.) Other accounting choices that affect reported earnings are the valuation of inventory, the procedures by which the accounts of two merging firms are combined, the choice between expensing or capitalizing research and development, and the way the tax liabilities of the firm are reported. The list could go on and on.

We shall discuss the biases in accounting income and profitability measures in Chapter 12, after we have used present value concepts to develop measures of true, economic income. For the moment, we just want you to remember that accounting earnings are slippery animals.

4-5 SUMMARY

In this chapter we have used our new-found knowledge of present values to examine the market price of bonds and common stocks. In each case the value of the security is just like that of any other asset: it is equal to the stream of cash payments discounted at the rate of return that investors expect to receive on comparable securities.

The cash payments on a bond consist of the regular interest payments together with the final payment of the bond's face value. The rate of interest that makes the discounted value of these cash flows equal to the bond's market price is known as the bond's *yield to maturity* or *internal rate of return*.

Common stocks do not have a fixed maturity; their cash payments consist of an indefinite stream of dividends. Therefore, the present value of a common stock is

$$PV = \sum_{t=1}^{\infty} \frac{DIV_t}{(1 + r)^t}$$

However, we did not *derive* our DCF formula just by substituting DIV_t for C_t. We did not *assume* that the investors purchase common stocks solely for dividends. In fact, we began with the assumption that investors have relatively short horizons and invest for both dividends and capital gains. Our fundamental valuation formula is, therefore,

$$P_0 = \frac{DIV_1 + P_1}{1 + r}$$

This is a condition of market equilibrium: if it did not hold, the share would be overpriced or underpriced, and investors would rush to sell or buy it. The flood of sellers or buyers would force the price to adjust so that the fundamental valuation formula holds.

This formula will hold in each future period as well as the present. That allowed us to express next year's forecasted price in terms of the subsequent stream of dividends DIV_1, DIV_2, ...

We also made use of the formula for a growing perpetuity presented in Chapter 3. If dividends are expected to grow forever at a constant compound rate of g, then

$$P_0 = \frac{DIV_1}{r - g}$$

We showed how it is often helpful to twist this formula around and use it to estimate the capitalization rate r, given P_0 and estimates of DIV_1 and g.

Finally we transformed the general DCF formula into a statement about earnings and growth opportunities:

$$P_0 = \frac{EPS_1}{r} + PVGO$$

The ratio EPS_1/r is the capitalized value of the earnings per share that the firm would generate under a no-growth policy. PVGO is the net present value of the investments that the firm will make in order to grow. A "growth" stock is one for which PVGO is large relative to the capitalized value of EPS. Most growth stocks are stocks of rapidly expanding firms, but expansion alone does not create a high PVGO. What matters is the profitability of the new investments.

One thing we did *not* discuss is how an entire business is valued. (We looked only at present value *per share* of common stock.) Applying our present value formulas to a firm or line of business is easy in principle, but messy in application. Take a look at the appendix to this chapter: you may find the messy parts interesting.

In earlier chapters, you should have acquired—we hope painlessly—a knowledge of the basic principles of valuing assets and a facility with the mechanics of discounting. Now you know something of how common stocks are valued and market capitalization rates estimated. In Chapter 5 we can begin to apply all this knowledge in a more specific analysis of capital-budgeting decisions.

FURTHER READING

There are a number of discussions of the valuation of common stocks in investment texts. We suggest:

R.A. Brealey, *An Introduction to Risk and Return for Common Stocks*, 2nd ed., The MIT Press, 1983.

J.C. Francis and E. Kirzner, *Investments*, McGraw-Hill Ryerson, Toronto, 1988.

J.H. Lorie, P. Dodd and M. Hamilton Kimpton: *The Stock Market: Theories and Evidence*, 2nd ed., Richard D. Irwin, Inc., Homewood, Ill., 1985.

W.F. Sharp and G.J. Alexander: *Investments*, 4th ed., Prentice-Hall., Englewood Cliffs, N.J., 1989.

J.B. Williams's original work remains very readable. See particularly Chapter V of:

J.B. Williams, *The Theory of Investment Value*, Harvard University Press, Cambridge, Mass., 1938.

The following articles provide important developments of Williams's early work. We suggest, however, that you leave the third article until you have read Chapter 16:

D. Durand, "Growth Stocks and the Petersburg Paradox," *Journal of Finance*, **12**: 348–363 (September 1957).

M.J. Gordon and E. Shapiro, "Capital Equipment Analysis: The Required Rate of Profit," *Management Science*, **3**: 102–110 (October 1956).

M.H. Miller and F. Modigliani, "Dividend Policy, Growth and the Valuation of Shares," *Journal of Business*, **34**: 411–433 (October 1961).

There have also been many applications of the present value model. Two good examples are:

R.C. Higgins, "Growth, Dividend Policy and Capital Costs in the Electric Utility Industry," *Journal of Finance*, **29**: 1189–1201 (September 1974).

B.G. Malkiel, "Equity Yields, Growth and the Structure of Share Prices," *American Economic Review*, **53**: 467–494 (December 1963).

APPENDIX 4-1   VALUING A BUSINESS BY DISCOUNTED CASH FLOW

Investors routinely buy and sell shares of common stock. Companies frequently buy and sell entire businesses — as, for example, when Amoco Canada purchased Dome Petroleum for $5.2 billion in 1987, or when Polysar sold its latex division to BASF for $382.5 million in 1988.

Do the discounted cash flow formulas we presented in this chapter work for entire businesses as well as shares of common stock? Sure: it doesn't matter whether you forecast dividends per share or the total free cash flow of a business. Value today always equals future cash flow discounted at the opportunity cost of capital.

Of course things are never as easy in practice as they seem in principle. We have included this appendix to show some of the practical challenges that managers who value businesses often run into. This appendix walks you through the mechanics of valuing businesses. It also shows how smart application of some basic financial concepts can make discounted cash flow less mechanical and more trustworthy.

Forecasting Free Cash Flow for a Business

Rumour has it that Establishment Industries is interested in buying your company's concatenator manufacturing operation. Your company is willing to sell if it can get the full value of this rapidly growing business. The problem is to figure out what its true present value is.

Table 4-4 gives a forecast of free cash flow. The table is similar to Table 4-2, which forecasted earnings and dividends per share for Growth-Tech, based on assumptions about Growth-Tech's assets per share, return on equity, and the growth of its business. For the concatenator business, we also have assumptions about assets, profitability — in this case, after-tax operating earnings relative to assets — and growth. Growth starts out a a rapid 20% per year, then falls in two steps to a moderate 6% rate for the long run. The growth rate determines the net additional investment required to expand assets, the profitability rate determines the earnings thrown off by the business.[6]

---

[6] Table 4-4 shows *net* investment, which is total investment less depreciation. We are assuming that the investment for replacement of existing assets is covered by depreciation, and that net investment is devoted to growth.

  We could have reported gross investment in Table 4-4. However, that would have required adding depreciation back to earnings to get operating cash flow. The bottom line, free cash flow, would be the same.

Table 4-4
Forecasts of free cash flow, in millions of dollars, for the Concatenator manufacturing division. Rapid expansion in years 1–6 means that free cash flow is negative, because required additional investment outstrips earnings. Free cash flow turns positive when growth slows down after year 6.

Year	1	2	3	4	5	6	7	8	9	10
Asset value	10.00	12.00	14.40	17.28	20.74	23.43	26.47	28.05	29.73	31.51
Earnings	1.20	1.44	1.73	2.07	2.49	2.81	3.18	3.36	3.57	3.78
Investment	2.00	2.40	2.88	3.46	2.69	3.04	1.59	1.68	1.78	1.89
Free cash flow	−0.80	−0.96	−1.15	−1.39	−0.20	−0.23	1.59	1.68	1.79	1.89
Earnings growth from previous period (percent)	20	20	20	20	20	13	13	6	6	6

Notes:
1. Starting asset value is $10 million. Assets required for the business grow at 20% per year to year 4, at 13% in years 5 and 6, and at 6% afterward.
2. Profitability is constant at 12%.
3. Free cash flow equals earnings minus net investment. Net investment equals total capital expenditures less depreciation. Note that earnings are also calculated net of depreciation.

It turns out that free cash flow, the bottom line in Table 4-4, is negative in years 1 through 6. The concatenator business is paying a negative dividend to the parent company; it is absorbing more cash than it is throwing off.

Is that a bad sign? Not really; the business is not running a cash deficit because it is unprofitable, but only because it is growing so fast. Rapid growth is good news, not bad, as long as the business is earning more than the opportunity cost of capital. Your company, or Establishment Industries, will be happy to invest an extra $800,000 in the concatenator business next year, as long as the business offers a superior rate of return.

Valuation Format

The value of a business is usually computed as the discounted value of free cash flows out to a **valuation horizon** (*H*), plus the forecasted value of the business at the horizon, also discounted back to present value. That is,

$$PV = \underbrace{\frac{FCF_1}{1+r} + \frac{FCF_2}{(1+r)^2} + \cdots + \frac{FCF_H}{(1+r)^H}}_{PV \text{ (free cash flow)}} + \underbrace{\frac{PV_H}{(1+r)^H}}_{PV \text{ (horizon value)}}$$

Of course, the concatenator business will continue after the horizon, but it's not practical to forecast free cash flow year by year to infinity. PV_H stands in for free cash flow in periods $H+1$, $H+2$, etc.

Valuation horizons are often chosen arbitrarily. Sometimes the boss tells everybody to use 10 years because that's a round number. We will try year 6, because growth ofthe concatenator business seems to settle down to a long-run trend in year 7.

Estimating Horizon Value

There are several common formulas or rules of thumb for estimating horizon value. First, let us try the constant-growth formula. This requires free cash flow for year 7, which we have from Table 4-4, a long-run growth rate, which appears to be 6%, and a discount rate, which some high-priced consultant has told us is 10%. Therefore,

$$PV(\text{horizon value}) = \frac{1}{(1.1)^6}\left[\frac{1.59}{0.10 - 0.06}\right] = 22.4$$

The present value of the near-term free cash flows is:

$$PV(\text{cash flows}) = -\frac{0.80}{1.1} - \frac{0.96}{(1.1)^2} - \frac{1.15}{(1.1)^3} - \frac{1.39}{(1.1)^4} - \frac{0.20}{(1.1)^5} - \frac{0.23}{(1.1)^6}$$
$$= -3.6$$

and therefore, the present value of the business is:

$$PV(\text{business}) = PV(\text{free cash flow}) + PV(\text{horizon value})$$
$$= -3.6 \qquad\qquad + 22.4$$
$$= \$18.8 \text{ million}$$

Now, are we done? Well, the mechanics of this calculation are perfect. But doesn't it make you just a little nervous to find that 119% of the value of the business rests of the horizon value? Moreover, a little checking shows that the horizon value can change dramatically in response to apparently minor changes in assumptions. For example, if the long-run growth rate is 8, rather than 6%, the value of the business increases from $18.8 to $26.3 million.[7]

In other words, it's easy for a discounted cash flow business valuation to be mechanically perfect and practically wrong. Smart financial managers try to check their results by calculating horizon value in several different ways.

Suppose you can observe stock prices for mature manufacturing companies whose scale, risk, and growth prospects today roughly match those projected for the concatenator business in year 6. Suppose further that these companies tend to sell at price-earnings ratios of about 11. Then you could reasonably guess that the price-earnings ratio of a mature concatenator operation will likewise be 11. That implies:

$$PV(\text{horizon value}) = \frac{1}{(1.1)^6}(11 \times 3.18) = 19.7$$
$$PV(\text{business}) = -3.6 + 19.7 = \$16.1 \text{ million}$$

Suppose also that the market-book ratios of the sample of mature manufacturing companies tend to cluster around 1.4. (The market-book ratio is just the ratio of stock price to book value per share.) If the concatenator business's market-book ratio is 1.4 in year 6:

---

[7] If long-run growth is 8 rather than 6%, an extra 2% of period 7 assets will have to be plowed back into the concatenator business. This reduces free cash flow by $.53 to $1.06 million. So,

$$PV(\text{horizon value}) = \frac{1}{(1.1)^6}\left(\frac{1.06}{0.10 - 0.08}\right) = \$29.9$$
$$PV(\text{business}) = -3.6 + 29.9 = \$26.3 \text{ million}$$

$$\text{PV(horizon value)} = \frac{1}{(1.1)^6}(1.4 \times 23.43) = 18.5$$
$$\text{PV(business)} = -3.6 + 18.5 = \$14.9\,\text{million}$$

It's easy to poke holes in these last two calculations. Book value, for example, often is a poor measure of the true value of a company's assets. It can fall far behind actual asset values when there is rapid inflation, and it often entirely misses important intagible assets, such as your patents for concatenator design. Earnings may also be biased by inflation and a long list of arbitrary accounting choices. Finally, you never know when you have found a sample of truly similar companies.

But remember, the purpose of discounted cash flow is to estimate market value—to estimate what investors would pay for a stock or business. When you can *observe* what they actually pay for similar companies, that's valuable evidence. Try to figure out a way to use it. One way to use it is through valuation rules of thumb, based on price-earnings or market-book ratios. A rule of thumb, artfully employed, sometimes beats a complex discounted cash flow calculation hands down.

A Further Reality Check

Here is another approach to valuing a business. It is based on what you have learned about price-earnings ratios and the present value of growth opportunities.

Suppose the valuation horizon is set not by looking for the first year of stable growth, but by asking when the industry is likely to settle into competitive equilibrium. You might go to the operating manager most familiar with the concatenator business and ask:

> Sooner or later you and your competitors will be on an equal footing when it comes to major new investments. You may still be earning a superior return on your core business, but you will find that introductions of new products of attempts to expand sales of existing products trigger intense resistance from competitors who are just about as smart and efficient as you are. Give a realistic assessment of when that time will come.

"That time" is the horizon after which PVGO, the net present value of subsequent growth opportunities, is zero. After all, PVGO is positive only when investments can be expected to earn more than the cost of capital. When you competition catches up, the happy prospect disappears.[8]

We know that present value in any period equals the capitalized value of next period's earnings, plus PVGO:

$$\text{PV}_t = \frac{\text{earnings}_{t+1}}{r} + \text{PVGO}$$

But what if PVGO = 0? At the horizon period H, then:

$$\text{PV}_H = \frac{\text{earnings}_{H+1}}{r}$$

---

[8] We cover this point in more detail in Chapter 11.

In other words, when the competition catches up, the price-earnings ratio equals $1/r$, because PVGO disappears.

Suppose competition is expected to catch up by period 8. We can recalculate the value of the concatenator business as follows:

$$PV(\text{horizon value}) = \frac{1}{(1+r)^8}\left(\frac{\text{earnings in period 9}}{r}\right)$$

$$= \frac{1}{(1.1)^8}\left(\frac{3.57}{0.10}\right)$$

$$= \$16.7 \text{ million}$$

$$PV(\text{business}) = -3.6 + 16.7 = \$13.1 \text{ million}$$

Conclusion   We now have four estimates of what Establishment Industries ought to pay for the concatenator business. The estimates reflect four different methods of estimating horizon value. There is no "best" method, although in many cases we put most weight on the last method, which sets the horizon date at the point when management expects PVGO to disappear. The last method forces managers to remember that sooner or later competition catches up.

Our calculated values for the concatenator business range from $13.1 to $18.8 million, a difference of almost $6 million. The width of the range may be disquieting, but it is not unusual. Discounted cash flow formulas only estimate market value, and the estimates change as forecasts and assumptions change. Managers cannot know market value until an actual transaction takes place.

QUIZ

1.   Calculate the present value of each of the following bonds, assuming a yield to maturity of 8%:

Bond	Annual Coupon, %	Maturity
A	6	1
B	6	2
C	6	4
D	10	2
E	10	4

2.   Recalculate the present value of the bonds in question 1 assuming the yield to maturity changes to 10%. Does a rise in the return that investors require have a larger effect on the price of long-term bonds or short-term bonds?

3.   Company X is expected to pay an end-of-year dividend of $10 a share. After the dividend its stock is expected to sell at $110. If the market capitalization rate is 10%, what is the current stock price?

4.   Company Y does not plow back any earnings and is expected to produce a level dividend stream of $5 a share. If the current stock price is $40, what is the market capitalization rate?

5.   Company Z's dividends per share are expected to grow indefinitely by 5% a year. If next year's dividend is $10 and the market capitalization rate is 8%, what is the current stock price?

6. If company Z (see question 5) were to distribute all its earnings, it could maintain a level dividend stream of $15 a share. How much, therefore, is the market actually paying per share for growth opportunities?

7. Which of the following statements are correct?
   (a) The value of a share equals the discounted stream of future earnings per share.
   (b) The value of a share equals the present value of earnings per share assuming the firm does not grow, plus the net present value of future growth opportunities.
   (c) The value of a share equals the discounted stream of future dividends per share.

8. Under what conditions does r, a stock's market capitalization rate, equal its earnings-price ratio, EPS_1/P_0?

QUESTIONS AND PROBLEMS

1. What would happen to the value of the Canada 13¾s of 1994 (see Section 4-1) if the market rate of interest (a) fell to 9% and (b) rose to 12%? (Assume annual coupon payments.)

2. Calculate the value in 1989 of the following Government of Canada bonds, assuming that the rate of interest is 10%:
   (a) 8¾%, 1996.
   (b) 13½%, 1999.
   (c) 12%, 2005.
   (In your calculations recognize the fact that coupon payments occur semiannually.)

3. Rework Table 4-1 under the assumption that the dividend on Fledgling Electronics is $10 next year and that it is expected to grow by 5% a year. The capitalization rate is 15%.

4. (a) Look in *The Financial Post*. Can you find the dividend yield on the Toronto Stock Exchange 300 Composite Index?
   (b) Assume that the expected return on common stocks is 8% higher than on short-term Government of Canada bonds. Use the constant growth model to estimate the expected dividend growth for the TSE 300.
   (c) Estimate the change in the TSE 300 Index if investors reduce their forecast of the dividend growth by 2%.

5. Look in a recent issue of *The Financial Post* at the Stock Prices section.
   (a) What is the latest price of Northern Telecom stock?
   (b) What is the annual dividend payment and the dividend yield on Northern Telecom stock?
   (c) What would the yield be if Northern raised its yearly dividend to $0.50?
   (d) What is the *P/E* ratio on Northern Telecom stock?
   (e) Use the *P/E* ratio to calculate Northern's earnings per share.
   (f) Is Northern's *P/E* higher or lower than that of Imperial Oil?
   (g) What are the possible reasons for the difference in *P/E*?

6. Look up Canadian Pacific's current stock price and yearly dividend payment. Assume that the payment is expected to grow at a constant rate g.
   (a) What expected rate of return is indicated by (i) $g = 0.02$, (ii) $g = 0.05$, or (iii) $g = 0.10$?
   (b) Make an estimate of g from the company's plowback rate and return on equity. What expected rate of return is indicated by your estimate?

7. You believe that next year the Dong Lumination Company will pay a dividend of $2 on its common stock. Thereafter you expect dividends to grow at a rate of 4% a year in perpetuity. If you require a return of 12% on your investment, how much should you be prepared to pay for the stock?

*8. Rework the analysis of the present value of the growth opportunities for Fledgling Electronics, assuming (i) that the dividend is $10 next year, (ii) that it is expected to grow by 5% a year, and (iii) that it plows back a constant 20% of earnings.

(a) What is next year's expected earnings per share (EPS_1)?

(b) What is the return on book equity (ROE)?

(c) What is PVGO?

9. Explain carefully why different stocks may have different P/Es. Show how the price-earnings ratio is related to growth, dividend payout, and the required return.

10. Suppose that there is a general increase in the rates of return that investors require. Show what effect this would have on the prices of short-term bonds (for example, one-year bonds), long-term bonds (for example, perpetuities), income stocks, and growth stocks.

11. Each of the following formulas for determining shareholders' required rate of return can be right or wrong depending on the circumstances:

(a) $r = \dfrac{DIV_1}{P_0} + g$

(b) $r = \dfrac{EPS_1}{P_0}$

For each formula construct a *simple* numerical example showing that the formula can give wrong answers and explain why the error occurs. Then construct another simple numerical example for which the formula gives the right answer.

12. Phoenix Motor Corporation has pulled off a miraculous recovery. Four years ago, it was near bankruptcy. Now its charismatic leader, a corporate folk hero, may run for president.

Phoenix has just announced a $1 per share dividend, the first since the crisis hit. Analysts expect an increase to a "normal" $3 as the company completes its recovery over the next 3 years. After that, dividend growth is expected to settle down to a moderate long-term growth rate of 6%.

Phoenix stock is selling at $50 per share. What is the expected long-run rate of return from buying the stock at this price? Assume dividends of $1, $2, and $3 for years 1, 2, 3. A little trial and error will be necessary to find r.

*13 Look again at the financial forecasts for Growth-Tech given in Table 4-2. This time assume you *know* that the opportunity cost of capital is $r = 0.12$. (Discard the 0.099 figure calculated in the text.) Assume you do *not* know Growth-Tech's stock value. Otherwise, follow the assumptions given in the text.

(a) Calculate the value of Growth-Tech stock.

(b) What part of that value reflects the discounted value of P_3, the price forecasted for year 3?

(c) What part of P_3 reflects the present value of growth opportunities (PVGO) after year 3?

(d) Suppose that competition will catch up with Growth-Tech by year 4, so that it can only earn its cost of capital on any investments made in year 4 or subsequently. What is Growth-Tech stock worth now under this assumption? (Make additional assumptions if necessary.)

14. Consider a firm with existing assets that generate an EPS of $5. If the firm does not invest except to maintain existing assets, EPS is expected to remain constant at $5 a year. However, starting next year the firm has the chance to invest $3 per share each year in developing a newly discovered geothermal steam source for electricity generation. These investments are expected to generate a permanent 20% return. However, the source will be fully developed by the fifth year. What will be the stock price and earnings-price ratio assuming investors require a 12% rate of return? Show that the earnings-price ratio is 0.20 if the required rate of return is 20%.

15. Compost Science, Inc. (CSI) is in the business of converting Boston's sewage sludge into fertilizer. The business is not in itself very profitable. However, to induce CSI to remain in business, the Metropolitan District Commission (MDC) has agreed to pay whatever amount is necessary to yield CSI a 10% book return on equity. At the end of the year CSI is expected to pay a $4 dividend. It has been reinvesting 40% of earnings and growing at 4% a year.

    (a) Suppose CSI continues on this growth trend. What is the expected long-run rate of return from purchasing the stock at $100? What part of the $100 price is attributable to the present value of growth opportunities?

    (b) Now the MDC announces a plan for CSI to treat Cambridge sewage. CSI's plant will, therefore, be expanded gradually over five years. This means that CSI will have to reinvest 80% of its earnings for five years. Starting in year 6, however, it will again be able to pay out 60% of earnings. What will be CSI's stock price once this announcement is made and its consequences for CSI are known?

C · H · A · P · T · E · R

5

WHY NET PRESENT VALUE LEADS TO BETTER INVESTMENT DECISIONS THAN OTHER CRITERIA

In the first four chapters we have introduced, at times surreptitiously, most of the basic principles of the investment decision. In this chapter we consolidate that knowledge. We also take a critical look at other criteria that companies sometimes use to make investment decisions.

5-1 A REVIEW OF THE BASICS

Vegetron's financial manager is wondering how to analyze a proposed $1 million investment in a new venture called project X. He asks what you think.

Your response should be as follows: "First, forecast the cash flows generated by project X over its economic life. Second, determine the appropriate opportunity cost of capital. This should reflect both the time value of money and the risk involved in project X. Third, use this opportunity cost of capital to discount the future cash flows of project X. The sum of the discounted cash flows is called present value (PV). Fourth, calculate *net* present value (NPV) by subtracting the $1 million investment from PV. Invest in project X if its NPV is greater than zero."

However, Vegetron's financial manager is unmoved by your sagacity. He asks why NPV is so important.

Your reply: "Let us look at what is best for Vegetron stockholders. They want you to make their Vegetron shares as valuable as possible.

"Right now Vegetron's total market value (price per share times the number of shares outstanding) is $10 million. That includes $1 million cash we can invest in project X. The value of Vegetron's other assets and opportunities must therefore be $9 million. We have to decide whether it is better to keep the $1 million cash and reject project X or to spend the cash and accept project X. Let us call the value of the new project PV. Then the choice is as follows:

	Market Value (millions of dollars)	
Asset	Reject Project X	Accept Project X
Cash	1	0
Other assets	9	9
Project X	0	PV
	10	9 + PV

Clearly project X is worthwhile if its present value, PV, is greater than $1 million — that is, if net present value is positive."

Financial manager: "How do I know that the PV of project X will actually show up in Vegetron's market value?"

Your reply: "Suppose we set up a new, independent firm X, whose only asset is project X. What would be the market value of firm X?

"Investors would forecast the dividends firm X would pay and discount those dividends by the expected rate of return of securities having risks comparable to firm X. We know that stock prices are equal to the present value of forecasted dividends.

"Since project X is firm X's only asset, the dividend payments we would expect firm X to pay are exactly the cash flows we have forecasted for project X. Moreover, the rate investors would use to discount firm X's dividends is exactly the rate we should use to discount project X's cash flows.

"I agree that firm X is entirely hypothetical. But if project X is accepted, investors holding Vegetron stock will really hold a portfolio of project X and the firm's other assets. We know the other assets are worth $9 million considered as a separate venture. Since asset values are additive we can easily figure out the portfolio value once we calculate the value of project X as a separate venture.

"By calculating the present value of project X, we are replicating the process by which the common stock of firm X would be valued in capital markets."

Financial manager: "I don't understand where the discount rate comes from."

Your reply: "I agree that the discount rate is difficult to measure precisely. But it is easy to see what we are *trying* to measure. The discount rate is the opportunity cost of investing in the project rather than in the capital market. In other words, instead of accepting a project, the firm can always give the cash to shareholders and let them invest it in financial assets.

"Figure 5-1 shows the trade-off. The opportunity cost of taking the project is the return shareholders could have earned had they invested the funds on their own. When we discount the project's cash flows by the expected rates of return on comparable financial assets, we are measuring how much investors would be prepared to pay for your project.

"But which financial asset? The fact that investors expect only 12% on Bell Canada Enterprises stock does not mean that a firm should purchase Fly-by-Night Electronics Company if it offers 13%. The opportunity-cost concept makes sense only if assets of equivalent risk are compared. In general, you should identify financial assets with risks equivalent to the project under consideration, estimate the expected rate of return on these assets, and use this rate as the opportunity cost."

5-2 COMPETITORS OF NET PRESENT VALUE

Let us hope the financial manager is by now convinced of the correctness of the net present value rule. But it is possible that the manager has also heard of

Figure 5-1   The firm can either keep and reinvest cash or return it to investors. (Arrows represent possible cash flows or transfers.) If cash is reinvested, the opportunity cost is the expected rate of return that shareholders could have obtained by investing in financial assets.

some alternative investment criteria and would like to know why you do not recommend any of them. Just so that you are prepared, we will now look at the four most popular alternatives to the NPV rule. These are:

1. Payback
2. Average return on book value
3. Internal rate of return
4. Profitability index

As we look at these alternative criteria, it is worth keeping in mind the following key features of the net present value rule. First, the NPV rule recognizes that *a dollar today is worth more than a dollar tomorrow*, because the dollar today can be invested to start earning interest immediately. Any investment rule that does not recognize the time value of money cannot be sensible. Second, net present value depends solely on the *forecasted cash flows* from the project and the *opportunity cost of capital*. Any investment rule that is affected by the manager's tastes, the company's choice of accounting method, the profitability of the company's existing business, or the profitability of other independent projects will lead to inferior decisions. Third, *because present values are all measured in today's dollars, you can add them up*. Therefore, if you have two projects, A and B, the net present value of the combined investment is

$$NPV(A + B) = NPV(A) + NPV(B)$$

This additivity property has important implications. Suppose project B has a negative NPV. If you tack it onto project A, the joint project (A + B) will have a lower NPV than A on its own. Therefore, you are unlikely to be misled into accepting a poor project (B) just because it is packaged with a good one (A). As we shall see, the alternative measures do not have this additivity property. If you are not careful, you may be tricked into deciding that a package of a good and a bad project is better than the good project on its own.

5-3   PAYBACK

Companies frequently require that the initial outlay on any project should be recoverable within some specified cutoff period. The **payback period** of a project is found by counting the number of years it takes before cumulative forecasted cash flows equal the initial investment. Consider projects A and B:

	Cash Flows (dollars)				Payback	
Project	C_0	C_1	C_2	C_3	Period (years)	NPV at 10%
A	−2,000	+2,000	0	0	1	− 182
B	−2,000	+1,000	+1,000	+5,000	2	+3,492

Project A involves an initial investment of $2,000 ($C_0 = -2,000$) followed by a single cash inflow of $2,000 in year 1. Suppose the opportunity cost of capital is 10%. Then project A has an NPV of −$182:

$$NPV(A) = -\$2,000 + \frac{\$2,000}{1.10} = -\$182$$

Project B also requires an initial investment of $2,000 but produces a cash inflow of $1,000 in years 1 and 2 and $5,000 in year 3. At a 10% opportunity cost of capital project B has an NPV of +$3,492:

$$NPV(B) = -2,000 + \frac{1,000}{1.10} + \frac{1,000}{(1.10)^2} + \frac{5,000}{(1.10)^3} = +\$3,492$$

Thus the net present value rule tells us to reject project A and accept project B.

The Payback Rule   Now let us look at how rapidly each project pays back its initial investment. With project A you take one year to recover your $2,000; with project B you take two years. If the firm used the *payback rule* with a cutoff period of one year, it would accept only project A; if it used the payback rule with a cutoff period of two or more years, it would accept both A and B. Therefore, regardless of the choice of cutoff period, the payback rule gives a different answer from the net present value rule.

The reason for the difference is that payback gives equal weight to all cash flows before the payback date and no weight at all to subsequent flows. For example, the following three projects all have a payback period of two years:

	Cash Flow (dollars)					Payback
Project	C_0	C_1	C_2	C_3	NPV at 10%	Period (years)
B	−2,000	+1,000	+1,000	+5,000	3,492	2
C	−2,000	0	+2,000	+5,000	3,409	2
D	−2,000	+1,000	+1,000	+100,000	74,867	2

The payback rule says that these projects are all equally attractive. But project B has a higher NPV than project C for *any* positive interest rate ($1,000 in each of years 1 and 2 is more valuable than $2,000 in year 2). And project D has a higher NPV than either B or C.

To use the payback rule a firm has to decide on an appropriate cutoff date. If it uses the same cutoff regardless of project life, it will tend to accept too many short-lived projects and too few long-lived ones. If, on average, the cutoff periods are too long, it will accept some projects with negative NPVs; if, on average, they are too short, it will reject some projects that have positive NPVs.

Many firms that use payback choose the cutoff period essentially by guesswork. It is possible to do better than that. If you know the typical pattern of cash flows, then you can find the cutoff period that would come closest to maximizing net present value.[1] However, this "optimal" cutoff point works only for those projects that have "typical" patterns of cash flows. So it is still better to use the net present value rule.

Discounted Payback

Some companies discount the cash flows before they compute the payback period. The **discounted payback rule** asks, "How many periods does the project have to last in order to make sense in terms of net present value?" This modification to the payback rule surmounts the objection that equal weight is given to all flows before the cutoff date. However, the discounted payback rule still takes no account of any cash flows after the cutoff date.

Suppose there are two mutually exclusive investments, A and B. Each requires a $20,000 investment and is expected to generate a level stream of cash flows starting in year 1. The annual cash flow for investment A is $6,500 and lasts for six years. The annual cash flow for B is $6,000 but lasts for ten years. The appropriate discount rate for each project is 10%. Investment B is clearly a better investment on the basis of net present value:

$$NPV(A) = -20,000 + \sum_{t=1}^{6} \frac{6,500}{(1.10)^t} = +\$8,309$$

$$NPV(B) = -20,000 + \sum_{t=1}^{10} \frac{6,000}{(1.10)^t} = +\$16,867$$

Yet A has higher cash receipts than B in each year of its life, and so obviously it has the shorter discounted payback. The discounted payback of A is a bit less than four years, since the present value of $6,500 at 10% for four years is $20,604. The discounted payback of B is a bit more than four years, since the present value of $6,000 for four years is $19,019.

Discounted payback is a whisker better than undiscounted payback. It recognizes that a dollar at the beginning of the payback period is worth more than a dollar at the end of the payback period. This helps, but it may not help much. The discounted payback rule still depends on the choice of an arbitrary cutoff date and it still ignores all cash flows after that date.

5-4   AVERAGE RETURN ON BOOK VALUE

Some companies judge an investment project by looking at its **book rate of return**. To calculate book rate of return it is necessary to divide the average

---

[1] If the inflows are, on average, spread evenly over the life of the project, the optimal cutoff for the payback rule is

$$\text{Optimal cutoff period} = \frac{1}{r} - \frac{1}{r(1 + r)^n}$$

where n denotes the project life. This expression for the optimal payback was first noted in M.J. Gordon, "The Pay-Off Period and the Rate of Profit," *Journal of Business*, **28**: 253–260 (October 1955). Note that this is just the formula for the present value of an annuity. Can you see why?

forecasted profits of a project after depreciation and taxes by the average book value of the investment. This ratio is then measured against the book rate of return for the firm as a whole or against some external yardstick, such as the average book rate of return for the industry.

Table 5-1a
Computing the average book rate of return on an investment of $9,000 in project A.

	Cash Flow (dollars)		
Project A	Year 1	Year 2	Year 3
Revenue	12,000	10,000	8,000
Out-of-pocket cost	6,000	5,000	4,000
Cash flow	6,000	5,000	4,000
Depreciation	3,000	3,000	3,000
Net income	3,000	2,000	1,000

$$\text{Average book rate of return} = \frac{\text{average annual income}}{\text{average annual investment}} = \frac{2,000}{4,500} = 0.44$$

Table 5-1a shows projected income statements for project A over its three-year life. Its average net income is $2,000 per year (we assume for simplicity that there are no taxes). The required investment is $9,000 at $t = 0$. This amount is then depreciated at a constant rate of $3,000 per year. So the book value of the new investment will decline from $9,000 in year 0 to zero in year 3:

	Year 0	Year 1	Year 2	Year 3
Gross book value of investment	$9,000	$9,000	$9,000	$9,000
Accumulated depreciation	0	3,000	6,000	9,000
Net book value of investment	$9,000	$6,000	$3,000	$ 0

Average net book value = $4,500

The average net income is $2,000, and the average net investment is $4,500. Therefore, the average book rate of return is 2,000/4,500 = 0.44. Project A would be undertaken if the firm's target book rate of return is less than 44%.[2]

This criterion suffers from several serious defects. First, because it considers only the *average* return on book investment, there is no allowance for the fact that immediate receipts are more valuable than distant ones. Whereas payback gives no weight to the more distant flows, return on book gives them too much weight. Thus in Table 5-1b we can introduce two projects, B and C, which have the same average book investment, the same average book income, and the same average book profitability as project A. Yet A clearly has a higher NPV than B or C because a greater proportion of the cash flows for project A occur in the early years.

---

[2] There are many variants on this rule. For example, some companies measure the *accounting return on cost*; that is, the ratio of average profits before depreciation but after tax to the initial cost of the asset.

Table 5-1*b*
Projects A, B, and C all cost $9,000 and produce an average income of $2,000.
Therefore, they all have a 44% book rate of return.

Project	Cash Flow (dollars)		
	Year 1	Year 2	Year 3
A Cash flow	6,000	5,000	4,000
Net income	3,000	2,000	1,000
B Cash flow	5,000	5,000	5,000
Net income	2,000	2,000	2,000
C Cash flow	4,000	5,000	6,000
Net income	1,000	2,000	3,000

Notice also that the average return on book depends on accounting income; it is not based on the cash flows of a project. Cash flows and accounting income are often very different. For example, the accountant labels some cash outflows *capital investment* and others *operating expenses*. The operating expenses are, of course, deducted immediately from each year's income. The capital expenditures are depreciated according to an arbitrary schedule chosen by the accountant. Then the depreciation charge is deducted from each year's income. Thus the average return on book depends on which items the accountant treats as capital investments and how rapidly they are depreciated. However, the accountant's decisions have nothing to do with the cash flow[3] and therefore should not affect the decision to accept or reject.

A firm that uses average return on book has to decide on a yardstick for judging a project. This decision is also arbitrary. Sometimes the firm uses its current book return as a yardstick. In this case companies with high rates of return on their existing business may be led to reject good projects, and companies with low rates of return may be led to accept bad ones.

Payback is a bad rule. Average return on book is probably worse. It ignores the opportunity cost of money and is not based on the cash flows of a project, and the investment decision may be related to the profitability of the firm's existing business.

5-5 INTERNAL (OR DISCOUNTED CASH FLOW) RATE OF RETURN

Whereas payback and average return on book are ad hoc rules, internal rate of return has a much more respectable ancestry and is recommended in many finance texts. If, therefore, we dwell more on its deficiencies, it is not because they are more numerous but because they are less obvious.

In Chapter 2 we noted that net present value could also be expressed in terms of rate of return, which would lead to the following rule: "Accept investment opportunities offering rates of return in excess of their opportunity costs of capital." That statement, properly interpreted, is absolutely correct. However, interpretation is not always easy for long-lived investment projects.

There is no ambiguity in defining the true rate of return of an investment that generates a single payoff after one period:

---

[3] Of course, the depreciation method used for tax purposes does have cash consequences that should be taken into account in calculating NPV.

$$\text{Rate of return} = \frac{\text{payoff}}{\text{investment}} - 1$$

Alternatively, we could write down the NPV of the investment and find that discount rate which makes NPV = 0.

$$\text{NPV} = C_0 + \frac{C_1}{1 + \text{discount rate}} = 0$$

implies

$$\text{Discount rate} = \frac{C_1}{-C_0} - 1$$

Of course C_1 is the payoff and $-C_0$ the required investment, and so our two equations say exactly the same thing. *The discount rate that makes NPV = 0 is also the rate of return.*

Unfortunately, there is no wholly satisfactory way of defining the true rate of return of a long-lived asset. The best available concept is the so-called **discounted cash flow (DCF) rate of return** or **internal rate of return (IRR)**. The internal rate of return is used frequently in finance. It can be a handy measure, but, as we shall see, it can also be a misleading measure. You should, therefore, know how to calculate it and how to use it properly.

The internal rate of return is defined as the rate of discount that makes NPV = 0. This means that to find the IRR for an investment project lasting T years, we must solve for IRR in the following expression:

$$\text{NPV} = C_0 + \frac{C_1}{1 + \text{IRR}} + \frac{C_2}{(1 + \text{IRR})^2} + \cdots + \frac{C_T}{(1 + \text{IRR})^T} = 0$$

Actual calculation of IRR usually involves trial and error. For example, consider a project that produces the following flows:

Cash Flows (dollars)		
C_0	C_1	C_2
−4,000	+2,000	+4,000

The internal rate of return is IRR in the equation

$$\text{NPV} = 4,000 + \frac{2,000}{1 + \text{IRR}} + \frac{4,000}{(1 + \text{IRR})^2} = 0$$

Let us arbitrarily try a zero discount rate. In this case NPV is not zero but +\$2,000:

$$\text{NPV} = -4,000 + \frac{2,000}{1.0} + \frac{4,000}{(1.0)^2} = +\$2,000$$

The NPV is positive; therefore the IRR must be greater than zero. The next step might be to try a discount rate of 50%. In this case net present value is −\$889:

$$\text{NPV} = -4,000 + \frac{2,000}{1.50} + \frac{4,000}{(1.50)^2} = -\$889$$

Net present value, dollars

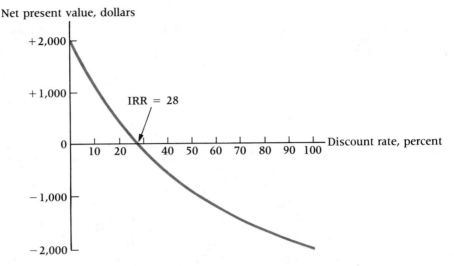

Figure 5-2 This project costs $4,000 and then produces cash inflows of $2,000 in year 1 and $4,000 in year 2. Its internal rate of return (IRR) is 28%, the discount rate at which NPV is zero.

The NPV is negative; therefore, the IRR must be less than 50%. In Figure 5-2 we have plotted the net present values implied by a range of discount rates. From this we can see that a discount rate of 28% gives the desired net present value of zero. Therefore IRR is 28%.

The easiest way to calculate IRR, if you have to do it by hand, is to plot three or four combinations of NPV and discount rate on a graph like Figure 5-2, connect the points with a smooth line, and read off the discount rate at which NPV = 0. It is of course quicker and more accurate to use a computer or a financial calculator, and this is what most companies do.

Now, the *rule* for capital budgeting on the basis of internal rate of return is to accept an investment project if the opportunity cost of capital is less than the internal rate of return. You can see the reasoning behind this idea if you look again at Figure 5-2. If the opportunity cost of capital is less than the 28% IRR, then the project has a *positive* NPV when discounted at the opportunity cost of capital. If it is equal to the IRR, the project has a *zero* NPV. And if it is greater than the IRR, the project has a *negative* NPV. Therefore, when we compare the opportunity cost of capital with the IRR on our project, we are effectively asking whether our project has a positive NPV. This is true not only for our example. The rule will give the same answer as the net present value rule *whenever the NPV of a project is a smoothly declining function of the discount rate.*[4]

Many firms use internal rate of return as a criterion in preference to net present value. We think that this is a pity. Although, properly stated, the two criteria are formally equivalent, the internal rate of return rule contains several pitfalls.

---

[4] Here is a word of caution. Some people confuse the internal rate of return and the opportunity cost of capital because both appear as discount rates in the NPV formula. The internal rate of return is a *profitability measure*, which depends solely on the amount and timing of the project cash flows. The opportunity cost of capital is a *standard of profitability* for the project, which we use to calculate how much the project is worth. The opportunity cost of capital is established in capital markets. It is the expected rate of return offered by other assets equivalent in risk to the project being evaluated.

Pitfall 1 — Lending or Borrowing?

Not all cash-flow streams have the property that NPV declines as the discount rate increases. Consider the following projects A and B:

	Cash Flows (dollars)			
Project	C_0	C_1	IRR, %	NPV at 10%
A	$-1,000$	$+1,500$	$+50$	$+364$
B	$+1,000$	$-1,500$	$+50$	-364

Each project has an IRR of 50%. (In other words, $-1,000 + 1,500/1.50 = 0$ and $+1,000 - 1,500/1.50 = 0$.)

Does this mean that they are equally attractive? Clearly not, for in the case of A, where we are initially paying out $1,000, we are *lending* money at 50%; in the case of B, where we are initially receiving $1,000, we are *borrowing* money at 50%. When we lend money, we want a *high* rate of return; when we borrow money, we want a *low* rate of return.

If you plot a graph like Figure 5-2 for project B, you will find that NPV increases as the discount rate increases. Obviously the internal rate of return rule, as we stated it above, won't work in this case; we have to look for an IRR *less* than the opportunity cost of capital.

This is straightforward enough, but now look at project C:

	Cash Flows (dollars)					
Project	C_0	C_1	C_2	C_3	IRR, %	NPV at 10%
C	$+1,000$	$-3,600$	$+4,320$	$-1,728$	$+20$	-0.75

It turns out that project C has zero NPV at a 20% discount rate. If the opportunity cost of capital is 10%, that means the project is a good one. Or does it? In part, project C is like borrowing money, because we receive money now and pay it out in the first period; it is also partly like lending money because we pay out money in period 1 and recover it in period 2. Should we accept or reject? The only way to find the answer is to look at the net present value. Figure 5-3 shows that the NPV of our project *increases* as the discount rate increases. If the opportunity cost of capital is 10% (that is, less than the IRR), the project has a very small negative NPV and we should reject.

Pitfall 2 — Multiple Internal Rates of Return

Project C had a unique IRR, but this will not always be the case when there is more than one change in the sign of the cash flows. Consider, for example, project D. It costs $4,000 and brings you in $25,000 in the first year. Then in year 2 you have to pay out $25,000. (There are many projects that have terminal cash outflows. For example, if you strip-mine coal, you may have to invest substantial amounts to reclaim the land after the coal is mined.)

	Cash Flows (dollars)				
Project	C_0	C_1	C_2	IRR, %	NPV at 10%
D	$-4,000$	$+25,000$	$-25,000$	25 *and* 400	-1934

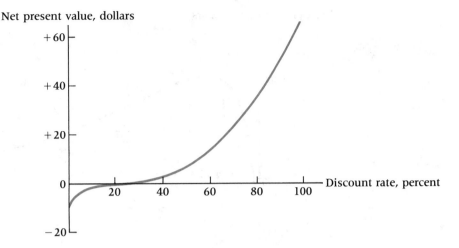

Figure 5-3   The net present value of project C increases as the discount rate increases.

Note there are *two* discount rates that make NPV = 0. That is, *each* of the following statements holds:

$$\text{NPV} = -4{,}000 + \frac{25{,}000}{1.25} - \frac{25{,}000}{(1.25)^2} = 0$$

and

$$\text{NPV} = -4{,}000 + \frac{25{,}000}{5} - \frac{25{,}000}{(5)^2} = 0$$

In other words, the investment has IRRs of both 25 and 400%. Figure 5-4 shows how this comes about. As the discount rate increases, NPV initially rises and then declines. The reason for this is the double change in the sign of the cash-flow stream. There can be as many different internal rates of return for a project as there are changes in the sign of the cash flows.[5]

As if this is not difficult enough, there are also cases in which *no* IRR exists. For example, project E has a positive net present value at all discount rates.

Project	Cash Flows (dollars)			IRR, %	NPV at 10%
	C_0	C_1	C_2		
E	+1,000	−3,000	+2,500	none	+339

A number of adaptations of the IRR rule have been devised for such cases. Not only are they inadequate, they are unnecessary, for the simple solution is to use NPV.

---

[5] By Descartes' "rule of signs" there can be as many different zeros (that is, zero values) to a polynomial as there are changes of sign and an internal rate of return is just a zero of a polynomial. For a discussion of the problem of multiple rates of return see J.H. Lorie and L.J. Savage, "Three Problems in Rationing Capital," *Journal of Business*, **28**: 229–239 (October 1955); and E. Solomon, "The Arithmetic of Capital Budgeting," *Journal of Business*, **29**: 124–129 (April 1956).

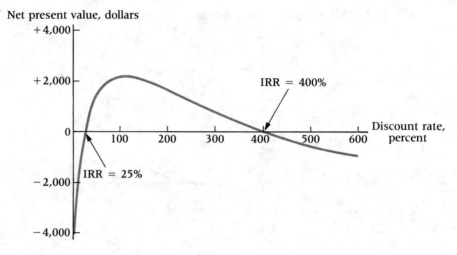

Net present value, dollars

Figure 5-4   Project D has two internal rates of return. NPV = 0 at discount rates of 25% and 400%.

Pitfall 3 —
Mutually
Exclusive
Projects

Firms often have to choose from among several alternative ways of doing the same job or using the same facility. In other words, they need to choose from among **mutually exclusive projects**. Here too the IRR rule can be misleading. Consider projects F and G:

| Project | Cash Flows (dollars) | | IRR, % | NPV at 10% |
	C_0	C_1		
F	− 100	+ 200	100	82
G	− 10,000	+ 15,000	50	3,636

Both are good projects, but G has the higher NPV and is, therefore, better. However, the IRR rule seems to indicate that if you have to choose, you should go for F since it has the higher IRR. If you follow the IRR rule, you have the satisfaction of earning a 100% rate of return; if you follow the NPV rule, you are $3,636 richer.

You can salvage the IRR rule in these cases by looking at the internal rate of return on the incremental flows. Here is how to do it. First, consider the smaller project (F in our example). It has an IRR of 100%, which is well in excess of the 10% opportunity cost of capital. You know, therefore, that F is acceptable. You now ask yourself whether it is worth making the additional $9,900 investment in G. The incremental flows from undertaking G rather than F are as follows:

| Project | Cash Flows (dollars) | | IRR, % | NPV at 10% |
	C_0	C_1		
G–F	− 9,900	+ 14,800	49	3,554

Net present value, dollars

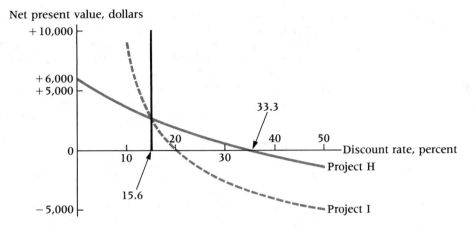

Figure 5-5   The IRR of project H exceeds that of project I, but the net present value of project I is higher *only* if the discount rate is less than 15.6%.

The IRR on the incremental investment is 49%, which is also well in excess of the 10% opportunity cost of capital. So you should prefer project G to project F.[6]

Unless you look at the incremental expenditure, IRR is unreliable in ranking projects of different scale. It is also unreliable in ranking projects that offer different patterns of cash flow over time. For example, suppose the firm can take project H *or* project I but not both (ignore J for the moment):

			Cash Flows (dollars)					IRR, %	NPV at 10%
Project	C_0	C_1	C_2	C_3	C_4	C_5	Etc.		
H	−9,000	+6,000	+5,000	+4,000	0	0	...	33	3,592
I	−9,000	+1,800	+1,800	+1,800	+1,800	+1,800	...	20	9,000
J		−6,000	+1,200	+1,200	+1,200	+1,200	...	20	6,000

Project H has a higher IRR, but project I has the higher NPV. Figure 5-5 shows why the two rules give different answers. The solid line gives the net present value of project H at different rates of discount. Since a discount rate of 33% produces a net present value of zero, this is the internal rate of return for project H. Similarly, the dashed line shows the net present value of project I at different discount rates. The IRR of project I is 20%. (We assume project I's cash flows continue indefinitely.) Note that project I has a higher NPV so long as the opportunity cost of capital is less than 15.6%.

The reason IRR is misleading is that the total cash inflow of project I is larger but tends to occur later. Therefore, when the discount rate is low, I has the higher NPV; when the discount rate is high, H has the higher NPV. (You can see from

[6] You may, however, find that you have jumped out of the frying pan into the fire. The series of incremental cash flows may involve several changes in sign. In this case there are likely to be multiple IRRs and you will be forced to use the NPV rule after all.

Figure 5-5 that the two projects have the *same* NPV when the discount rate is 15.6%.) The internal rates of return on the two projects tell us that at a discount rate of 20% I has a zero NPV (IRR = 20%) and H has a positive NPV. Thus if the opportunity cost of capital were 20%, investors would place a higher value on the shorter-lived project H. But in our example the opportunity cost of capital is not 20% but 10%. Investors are prepared to pay relatively high prices for longer-lived securities, and so they will pay a relatively high price for the longer-lived project. At a 10% cost of capital, an investment in I has an NPV of $9,000 and an investment in H has an NPV of only $3,592.[7]

This is a favourite example of ours. We have gotten many businesspeople's reaction to it. When asked to choose between H and I, many choose H. The reason seems to be the rapid payback generated by project H. In other words, they believe that if they take H, they will also be able to take a later project like J (note that J can be financed using the cash flows from H), whereas if they take I, they won't have money enough for J. In other words they implicitly assume that it is a *shortage of capital* that forces the choice between H and I. When this implicit assumption is brought out, they usually admit that I is better if there is no capital shortage.

But the introduction of capital constraints raises two further questions. The first stems from the fact that most of the executives preferring H to I work for firms that would have no difficulty raising more capital. Why would a manager at GM, say, choose H on the grounds of limited capital? GM can raise plenty of capital and can take project J regardless of whether H or I is chosen; therefore J should not affect the choice between H and I. The answer seems to be that large firms usually impose capital budgets on divisions and subdivisions as a part of the firm's planning and control system. Since the system is complicated and cumbersome, the budgets are not easily altered, and so they are perceived as real constraints by middle management.

The second question is this. If there is a capital constraint, either real or self-imposed, should IRR be used to rank projects? The answer is no. The problem in this case is to find that package of investment projects that satisfies the capital constraint and has the largest net present value. The IRR rule will not identify this package. As we will show in Chapter 6, the only practical way to do so is to use the technique of linear programming.

When we have to choose between projects H and I, it is easiest to compare the net present values. But if your heart is set on the IRR rule, you can use it as long as you look at the internal rate of return on the incremental flows. The procedure is exactly the same as we showed above. First, you check that project H has a satisfactory IRR. Then you look at the return on the additional investment in I.

Project	Cash Flows (dollars)							IRR, %	NPV at 10%
	C_0	C_1	C_2	C_3	C_4	C_5	Etc.		
I–H	0	−4,200	−3,200	−2,200	+1,800	+1,800	...	15.6	+5,408

[7] It is often suggested that the choice between the net present value rule and the internal rate of return rule should depend on the probable reinvestment rate. This is wrong. The prospective return on another independent investment should *never* be allowed to influence the investment decision. For a discussion of the reinvestment assumption see A.A. Alchian, "The Rate of Interest, Fisher's Rate of Return over Cost and Keynes' Internal Rate of Return," *American Economic Review*, **45**: 938–942 (December 1955).

The IRR on the incremental investment in I is 15.6%. Since this is greater than the opportunity cost of capital, you should undertake I rather than H.

Pitfall 4—What Happens When We Can't Finesse the Term Structure of Interest Rates?

We have simplified our discussion of capital budgeting by assuming that the opportunity cost of capital is the same for all the cash flows, C_1, C_2, C_3, and so on. Now this is not the right place to discuss the term structure of interest rates, but we must point out certain problems with the IRR rule that crop up when short-term interest rates are different from long-term rates.

Remember our most general formula for calculating net present value:

$$NPV = C_0 + \frac{C_1}{1 + r_1} + \frac{C_2}{(1 + r_2)^2} + \cdots$$

In other words, we discount C_1 at the opportunity cost of capital for one year, C_2 at the opportunity cost of capital for two years, and so on. The IRR rule tells us to accept a project if the IRR is greater than the opportunity cost of capital. But what do we do when we have several opportunity costs? Do we compare IRR with $r_1, r_2, r_3, \ldots$? Actually we would have to compute a complex weighted average of these rates to obtain a number comparable to IRR.

What does this mean for capital budgeting? It means trouble for the IRR rule whenever the term structure of interest rates becomes important.[8] In a situation where it is important, we have to compare the project IRR with the expected IRR (yield to maturity) offered by a traded security that (1) is equivalent in risk to the project and (2) offers the same time pattern of cash flows as the project. Such a comparison is easier said than done. It is much better to forget about IRR and just calculate NPV.

Many firms use the IRR, thereby implicitly assuming that there is no difference between short-term and long-term rates of interest. They do this for the same reason that we have so far finessed the term structure: simplicity.[9]

The Verdict on IRR

We have given four examples of things that can go wrong with IRR. We gave only one example of what could go wrong with payback or return on book. Does this mean that IRR is four times worse than the other two rules? Quite the contrary. There is little point in dwelling on the deficiencies of payback or return on book. They are clearly ad hoc rules that often lead to silly conclusions. The IRR rule has a much more respectable ancestry. It is a less easy rule to use than NPV, but, used properly, it gives the same answer. Now that you know the pitfalls, you should be able to use it properly.

5-6   PROFITABILITY INDEX OR BENEFIT-COST RATIO

The **profitability index** (or **benefit-cost ratio**) is the present value of forecasted future cash flows divided by the initial investment:

---

[8] The source of the difficulty is that the IRR is a derived figure without any simple economic interpretation. To define it, we can say only that it is the discount rate that, when applied to all cash flows, makes NPV = 0. The IRR is a complex average of the separate interest rates. The problem here is not that the IRR is a nuisance to calculate but that it is not a very useful number to have.

[9] In Chapter 9, we will look at some special cases in which it would be misleading to use the same discount rate for both short-term and long-term cash flows.

$$\text{Profitability index} = \frac{PV}{-C_0}$$

The profitability-index *rule* tells us to accept all projects with an index greater than one. If the profitability index is greater than one, the present value PV is greater than the initial investment $-C_0$ and so the project must have a positive net present value. The profitability index, therefore, leads to exactly the same decisions as net present value.[10]

However, like internal rate of return, the profitability index can be misleading when we are obliged to choose between two mutually exclusive investments. Consider the following two projects:

| | Cash Flows (dollars) | | | Profitability | |
Project	C_0	C_1	PV at 10%	Index	NPV at 10%
K	− 100	+ 200	182	1.82	82
L	− 10,000	+ 15,000	13,636	1.36	3,636

Both are good projects, as the profitability index correctly indicates. But suppose the projects are mutually exclusive. We *should* take L, the project with the higher NPV. Yet the profitability index gives K the higher ranking.

As with internal rate of return, you can always solve such problems by looking at the profitability index on the *incremental* investment. In other words, you first check that project K is worthwhile; then you calculate the profitability index on the $9,900 additional investment in L.

| | Cash Flows (dollars) | | | Profitability | |
Project	C_1	C_0	PV at 10%	Index	NPV at 10%
L–K	− 9,900	+ 14,800	13,454	1.36	3,554

The profitability index on the additional investment is greater than one, so you know that L is the better project.

Of our four rules, the profitability index most closely resembles net present value. In the next chapter we will encounter a rather special case in which the profitability index is the more useful rule. But for most purposes it is safer to work with net present values that add up, rather than with profitability indexes that do not.

5-7   SUMMARY

If you are going to persuade your company to use the net present value rule, you must be prepared to explain why other rules do *not* give correct decisions. That is why we have devoted this chapter to four alternative investment criteria.

Some companies use the payback method to make investment decisions. In other words, they accept only those projects that recover their initial investment within some specified period. Payback is an ad hoc rule. It ignores the order in which cash flows come within the payback period, and it ignores subsequent

---

[10] Some companies do not discount the benefits or costs before calculating the profitability index. The less said about these companies, the better.

cash flows entirely. It therefore takes no account of the opportunity cost of capital.

The simplicity of payback makes it an easy device for *describing* investment projects. Managers talk casually about "quick payback" projects in the same way that investors talk about "high *P/E*" common stocks. The fact that managers talk about the payback periods of projects does not mean that the payback rule governs their decisions. Some managers *do* use payback in judging capital investments. Why they rely on such a grossly oversimplified concept is a puzzle.

Some firms use average return on book value. In this case the company must decide which cash payments are capital expenditures and must pick appropriate depreciation schedules. It must then calculate the ratio of average income to the average book value of the investment and compare it with the company's target return. Average return on book is another ad hoc method. Since it ignores whether the income occurs next year or next century, it takes no account of the opportunity cost of money.

The internal rate of return (IRR) is defined as the rate of discount at which a project would have zero NPV. It is a handy measure and widely used in finance; you should therefore know how to calculate it. The IRR rule states that companies should accept any investment offering an IRR in excess of the opportunity cost of capital. The IRR rule is, like net present value, a technique based on discounted cash flows. It will, therefore, give the correct answer if properly used. The problem is that it is easily misapplied. There are four things to look out for:

1. *Lending or borrowing?* If a project offers positive cash flows followed by negative flows, NPV *rises* as the discount rate is increased. You should accept such projects if their IRR is *less* than the opportunity cost of capital.
2. *Multiple rates of return.* If there is more than one change in the sign of the cash flows, the project may have several IRRs or no IRR at all.
3. *Mutually exclusive projects.* Unlike NPVs, rates of return do not add up. If you tack a bad project onto a good project, the combined project may have a higher IRR than the good project on its own. You must make sure that you look at the IRR on each additional unit of investment. Also, the IRR rule may give the wrong ranking of mutually exclusive projects that differ in economic life or in scale of required investment.
4. *Short-term interest rates may be different from long-term rates.* The IRR rule requires you to compare the project's IRR with the opportunity cost of capital. But sometimes there is one opportunity cost of capital for one-year cash flows, a different cost of capital for two-year cash flows, and so on. In these cases there is no simple yardstick for evaluating the IRR of a project.

The fourth rule uses the profitability-index or benefit-cost ratio. It says that companies should accept projects only if the ratio of the discounted future cash flows to the initial investment is greater than one. This is just a roundabout way of saying that companies should accept projects with positive NPVs. The only drawback with using ratios is that you cannot add them up in the same way as you can add up values. Therefore you have to be careful when you are using this rule to choose between two projects.

This is a good point at which to stress political realities. Some people believe the earth is flat. It may be easier to persuade such people to accept the idea that the earth may be slightly curled at the corners than to convince them that it is completely round. You can therefore resolve that when you become president or treasurer, you will use net present value. But if the current management has an inalienable attachment to payback, you can still hope to make a substantial improvement by persuading them to use different cutoff periods for projects with different lives and to change to discounted payback.

If we are going to the expense of collecting forecasts, we might as well use them properly. Ad hoc criteria should therefore have no role in our firm's decisions, and the net present value rule should be employed in preference to other techniques using discounted cash flows. Having said that, we must be careful not to exaggerate the payoff of proper technique. Technique is important, but it is by no means the only determinant of the success of a capital-expenditure program. If the forecasts of cash flows are inadequate, even the most careful application of the net present value rule will fail.

FURTHER READING

Most capital budgeting texts contain a discussion of alternative budgeting criteria. See, for example:

H. Bierman, Jr. and S. Smidt, *The Capital Budgeting Decision*, 7th ed., The Macmillan Company, New York, 1988.

Classic articles on the internal rate of return rule include:

A.A. Alchian, "The Rate of Interest, Fisher's Rate of Return over Cost and Keynes' Internal Rate of Return," *American Economic Review*, **45**: 938–942 (December 1955).
J.H. Lorie and L.J. Savage, "Three Problems in Rationing Capital," *Journal of Business*, **28**: 229–239 (October 1955).
E. Solomon, "The Arithmetic of Capital Budgeting Decisions," *Journal of Business*, **29**: 124–129 (April 1956).

For a discussion of the profitability index, see:

B. Schwab and P. Lusztig, "A Comparative Analysis of the Net Present Value and the Benefit-Cost Ratios as Measures of the Economic Desirability of Investment," *Journal of Finance*, **24**: 507–516 (June 1969).

QUIZ

1. What is the opportunity cost of capital supposed to represent? Give a concise definition.
2. (a) What is the payback period on each of the following projects?

Project	Cash Flows (dollars)				
	C_0	C_1	C_2	C_3	C_4
A	−5,000	+1,000	+1,000	+3,000	0
B	−1,000	0	+1,000	+2,000	+3,000
C	−5,000	+1,000	+1,000	+3,000	+5,000

   (b) *Given* that you wish to use the payback rule with a cutoff period of two years, which projects would you accept?
   (c) If you use a cutoff period of three years, which projects would you accept?
   (d) If the opportunity cost of capital is 10%, which projects have positive NPVs?

(e) "Payback gives too much weight to cash flows that occur after the cutoff date." True or false?

(f) "If a firm uses a single cutoff period for all projects, it is likely to accept too many short-lived projects." True or false?

3. A machine costs $8,000 and is expected to produce profit before depreciation of $2,500 in each of years 1 and 2 and $3,500 in each of years 3 and 4. Assuming that the machine is depreciated at a constant rate of $2,000 a year and that there are no taxes, what is the average return on book?

4. True or false? Why?

(a) "The average return on book rule gives too much weight to the later cash flows."

(b) "If companies use their existing return on book as a measuringstick for new investments, successful companies will tend to undertake too much investment."

5. (a) Calculate the net present value of the following project for discount rates of 0%, 50%, and 100%.

Cash Flows (dollars)		
C_0	C_1	C_2
− 6,750	+ 4,500	+ 18,000

(b) What is the IRR of the project?

6. Consider projects A and B:

Project	Cash Flows (dollars)			IRR, %
	C_0	C_1	C_2	
A	− 4,000	+ 2,410	+ 2,930	21
B	− 2,000	+ 1,310	+ 1,720	31

(a) The opportunity cost of capital is less than 10%. Use the IRR rule to determine which project or projects you should accept (i) if you can undertake both, and (ii) if you can undertake only one.

(b) Suppose that project A has an NPV of $690 and project B has an NPV of $657. What is the NPV of the $2,000 incremental investment in A?

7. Consider the following projects:

Project	Cash Flow (dollars)		
	C_0	C_1	C_2
A	− 1,600	+ 1,200	+ 1,440
B	− 2,100	+ 1,440	+ 1,728

(a) Calculate the profitability index for A and B assuming a 20% opportunity cost of capital.

(b) Use the profitability-index rule to determine which project(s) you should accept (i) if you could undertake both, and (ii) if you could undertake only one.

8. Projects C and D both involve the same outlay and offer the same IRR, which exceeds the opportunity cost of capital. The cash flows generated by project C are larger than those of D but tend to occur later. Which project has the higher NPV?

9. You have the chance to participate in a project that produces the following cash flows:

Cash Flows (dollars)

C_0	C_1	C_2
+5,000	+4,000	−11,000

The internal rate of return is 13%. If the opportunity cost of capital is 10%, would you accept the offer?

QUESTIONS AND PROBLEMS

1. Consider the following projects:

Cash Flows (dollars)

Project	C_0	C_1	C_2	C_3	C_4	C_5
A	−1,000	+1,000	0	0	0	0
B	−2,000	+1,000	+1,000	+4,000	+1,000	+1,000
C	−3,000	+1,000	+1,000	0	+1,000	+1,000

(a) If the opportunity cost of capital is 10%, which projects have a positive NPV?

(b) Calculate the payback period for each project.

(c) Which projects would a firm using the payback rule accept if the cutoff period were three years?

2. Project A (shown in Table 5-1a) has undergone some revisions. The initial investment has been reduced to $6,000, and the firm proposes to depreciate this investment by $2,000 a year. Operating costs unfortunately have increased by $1,000 a year. If the opportunity cost of capital is 7%, how do these changes alter the NPV of the project? How do they affect the average return on book?

3. Consider a project with the following cash flows:

C_0	C_1	C_2
−100	+200	−75

(a) How many internal rates of return does this project have?

(b) The opportunity cost of capital is 20%. Is this an attractive project? Briefly explain.

4. Respond to the following comments:
    (a) "We like to use payback principally as a way of coping with risk."
    (b) "The great merit of the IRR rule is that one does not have to think about what is an appropriate discount rate."

5. The payback rule is still used by many firms despite its acknowledged theoretical shortcomings. Why do you think this is so?

6. Unfortunately, your chief executive officer refuses to accept any investments in plant expansion that do not return their original investment in 4 years or less. That is, he insists on a *payback rule* with a *cutoff period* of 4 years. As a result, attractive long-lived projects are being turned down.

    The CEO is willing to switch to a *discounted payback rule* with the same 4-year cutoff period. Would this be an improvement? Explain.

7. Consider the following two mutually exclusive projects:

| | Cash Flows (dollars) | | | |
Project	C_0	C_1	C_2	C_3
A	−100	+60	+60	0
B	−100	0	0	+140

    (a) Calculate the NPV of each project for discount rates of 0%, 10% and 20%. Plot these on a graph with NPV on the vertical axis and discount rate on the horizontal axis.
    (b) What is the approximate IRR for each project?
    (c) In what circumstances should the company accept project A?
    (d) Calculate the NPV of the incremental investment (B-A) for discount rates of 0%, 10%, and 20%. Plot these on your graph. Show that the circumstances in which you would accept A are also those in which the IRR on the incremental investment is less than the opportunity cost of capital.

8. Mr. Cyrus Clops, the president of Giant Enterprises, has to make a choice between two possible investments:

| | Cash Flows (thousands of dollars) | | | |
Project	C_0	C_1	C_2	IRR, %
A	−400	+241	+293	21
B	−200	+131	+172	31

    The opportunity cost of capital is 9%. Mr. Clops is tempted to take B, which has the higher IRR.
    (a) Explain to Mr. Clops why this is not the correct procedure.
    (b) Show him how to adapt the IRR rule to choose the best project.
    (c) Show him that this project also has the higher NPV.

9. The Titanic Shipbuilding Company has a non-cancellable contract to build a small cargo vessel. Construction involves a cash outlay of $250,000 at the end of each of the next two years. At the end of the third year the company will receive payment of $650,000. The company can speed up construction by working an extra shift. In this case there will be a cash outlay of $550,000

at the end of the first year followed by a cash payment of $650,000 at the end of the second year. Use the IRR rule to show the (approximate) range of opportunity costs of capital at which the company should work the extra

10.   Look again at projects A and B in Section 5-3. Assume that the projects are mutually exclusive and that the opportunity cost of capital is 20%.
   (a) Calculate the profitability index for each project.
   (b) Show how the profitability-index rule can be used to select the superior project.

C · H · A · P · T · E · R

6

MAKING INVESTMENT DECISIONS WITH THE NET PRESENT VALUE RULE

We hope that by now you are convinced that wise investment decisions are based on the net present value rule. In this chapter we can think about how to apply the rule to practical investment problems. Our task is threefold. The first issue is to decide what should be discounted. We know the answer in principle: discount cash flows. But useful forecasts of cash flows do not arrive on a silver platter. Often the financial manager has to make do with raw data supplied by specialists in product design, production, marketing, taxation and so on, and must check such information for relevance, completeness, consistency, and accuracy and then pull everything together into a usable forecast.

Our second task is to explain how the net present value rule should be used when there are project interactions. These occur when a decision about one project cannot be separated from a decision about another. Project interactions can be extremely complex. We will make no attempt to analyze every possible case. But we will work through most of the simple cases, as well as a few examples of medium complexity.

Our third task is to develop procedures for coping with capital rationing or other situations in which resources are strictly limited. There are two aspects to this problem. One is computational. Resource constraints often create problems of such complexity that a hunt-and-peck search for the right answer cannot cope with the vast number of alternatives. Linear programming can solve this problem and help the financial manager handle some project interactions at the same time. The other part of the problem is deciding whether capital rationing really exists and whether it invalidates net present value as a criterion for capital budgeting. Our discussion of these issues will take us back to the first principles outlined in Chapter 2.

6-1 WHAT TO DISCOUNT

Up to this point we have been concerned mainly with the mechanics of discounting and with the various methods of project appraisal. We have had almost nothing to say about the problem of *what* one should discount. When you are faced with this problem, you should always stick to three general rules:

1. Only cash flow is relevant.
2. Always estimate cash flows on an incremental basis.
3. Be consistent in your treatment of inflation.

We will discuss each of these rules in turn.

Only Cash Flow is Relevant

The first and most important point is that the net present value rule is stated in terms of cash flows. Cash flow is the simplest possible concept; it is just the difference between dollars received and dollars paid out. Many people nevertheless confuse cash flow with accounting profits.

Accountants *start* with "dollars in" and "dollars out," but to obtain accounting income they adjust these data in two important ways. First, they try to show profit as it is *earned* rather than when the company and the customer get around to paying their bills. Second, they sort cash outflows into two categories: current expenses and capital expenses. They deduct current expenses when calculating profit but do *not* deduct capital expenses. Instead they "depreciate" capital expenses over a number of years and deduct the annual depreciation charge from profits. As a result of these procedures, profits include some cash flows and exclude others, and are reduced by depreciation charges, which are not cash flows at all.

It is not always easy to translate the customary accounting data back into actual dollars—dollars you can buy beer with. If you are in doubt about what is a cash flow, simply count the dollars coming in and take away the dollars going out. Don't assume without checking that you can find cash flow by simple manipulation of accounting data.

You should always estimate cash flows on an after-tax basis. Some firms do not deduct tax payments. They try to offset this mistake by discounting the cash flows before taxes at a rate higher than the opportunity cost of capital. Unfortunately, there is no reliable formula for making such adjustments to the discount rate.

You should also make sure that cash flows are recorded *only when they occur* and not when the work is undertaken or the liability incurred. For example, taxes should be discounted from their actual payment date, not from the time when the tax liability is recorded in the firm's books.

Estimate Cash Flows on an Incremental Basis

The value of a project depends on *all* the additional cash flows that follow from project acceptance. Here are some things to watch for when you are deciding which cash flows should be included:

Do Not Confuse Average with Incremental Payoffs   Most managers naturally hesitate to throw good money after bad. For example, they are reluctant to invest more money in a losing division. But occasionally you will encounter "turnaround" opportunities in which the *incremental* NPV on investment in a loser is strongly positive.

Conversely, it does not always make sense to throw good money after good. A division with an outstanding past profitability record may have run out of good opportunities. You would not pay a large sum for a 20-year-old horse, sentiment aside, regardless of how many races that horse had won or how many champions it had sired.

Here is another example illustrating the difference between average and incremental returns. Suppose that a railroad bridge is in urgent need of repair. With the bridge the railroad can continue to operate; without the bridge it can't. In this case the payoff from the repair work consists of all the benefits of operating the railroad. The incremental NPV of the investment may be enormous. Of course, these benefits should be net of all other costs and all subsequent repairs; otherwise the company may be misled into rebuilding an unprofitable railroad piece by piece.

Include All Incidental Effects   It is important to include all incidental effects on the remainder of the business. For example, a branch line for a railroad may have a negative NPV when considered in isolation, but still be a worthwhile investment when one allows for the additional traffic that it brings to the main line.

Do Not Forget Working Capital Requirements   *Net working capital* (often referred to simply as *working capital*) is the difference between a company's short-term assets and liabilities. The principal short-term assets are cash, accounts receivable (customers' unpaid bills), and inventories of raw materials and finished goods. The principal short-term liabilities are accounts payable (bills that *you* have not paid). Most projects entail an additional investment in working capital. This investment should, therefore, be recognized in your cash-flow forecasts. By the same token, when the project comes to an end, you can usually recover some of the investment. This is treated as a cash inflow.

Forget Sunk Costs   Sunk costs are like spilt milk: they are past and irreversible outflows. Because sunk costs are bygones, they cannot be affected by the decision to accept or reject the project, and so they should be ignored.

This fact is often forgotten. For example, in 1971 Lockheed sought a United States government guarantee for a bank loan to continue development of the TriStar airplane. Lockheed and its supporters argued it would be foolish to abandon a project on which nearly $1 billion had already been spent. Some of Lockheed's critics countered that it would be equally foolish to continue with a project that offered no prospect of a satisfactory return on that $1 billion. Both groups were guilty of the so-called *sunk-cost fallacy*; the $1 billion was irrecoverable and, therefore, irrelevant.[1]

Include Opportunity Costs   The cost of a resource may be relevant to the investment decision even when no cash changes hands. For example, suppose a new manufacturing operation uses land that could otherwise be sold for $100,000. This resource is not free: it has an opportunity cost, which is the cash it could generate for the company if the project were rejected and the resource sold or put to some other productive use.

This example prompts us to warn you against judging projects on the basis of "before versus after." The proper comparison is "with or without." A manager comparing before versus after might not assign any value to the land because the firm owns it both before and after:

Before		After	
	Take Project		Cash Flow, Before
Firm owns land	$\longrightarrow$	Firm still owns land	versus After = 0

[1] U.E. Reinhardt provides an analysis of the values of the TriStar in 1971: "Break-even Analysis for Lockheed's TriStar: An Application of Financial Theory," *Journal of Finance*, **28**: 821–838 (September 1973). (Reinhardt does not fall into the sunk-cost fallacy.)

The proper comparison, which is with or without, is as follows:

Before	After	
	Take Project → Firm still owns land	Cash Flow, With Project = 0
Firm owns land	Do Not Take Project → Firm sells land for $100,000	Cash Flow, Without Project = $100,000

Comparing the two possible "afters," we see that the firm gives up $100,000 by undertaking the project. This reasoning still holds if the land will not be sold but is worth $100,000 to the firm in some other use.

Sometimes opportunity costs may be very difficult to estimate;[2] however, where the resource can be freely traded, its opportunity cost is simply equal to the market price. Why? It cannot be otherwise. If the value of a parcel of land to the firm is less than its market price, the firm will sell it. On the other hand the opportunity cost of using land in a particular project cannot exceed the cost of buying an equivalent parcel to replace it.

Beware of Allocated Overhead Costs   We have already mentioned that the accountant's objective in gathering data is not always the same as the investment analyst's. A case in point is the allocation of overhead costs. Overheads include such items as supervisory salaries, rent, heat, and light. These overheads may not be related to any particular project, but they have to be paid for somehow. Therefore, when the accountant assigns costs to the firm's projects, a charge for overhead is usually made. Now our principle of incremental cash flows says that in investment appraisal we should include only the *extra* expenses that would result from the project. A project may generate extra overhead expenses—and then again it may not. We should be cautious about assuming that the accountant's allocation of overheads represents the true extra expenses that would be incurred.

Treat Inflation Consistently   Interest rates are usually quoted in *nominal* rather than *real* terms. In other words, if you buy a Treasury bill the government promises to pay you so many dollars. It makes no promises about what that money will buy. Investors take that into account when they decide what is a fair rate of interest.

For example, suppose that the rate of interest on a one-year Government of Canada Treasury bill is 8% and that next year's inflation is expected to be 6%. If you buy the bill, you get back principal and interest in period-1 dollars, which are worth 6% less than current dollars:

Invest Current Dollars	Receive Period-1 Dollars	Result
$1,000 →	$1,080	8% *nominal* rate of return

[2] They may be so difficult to estimate that it is often preferable just to note their existence rather than attempt to quantify them.

How much actual purchasing power is represented by the $1,080 return? Let us measure units of purchasing power in terms of current dollars. We convert period-1 dollars into current dollars by dividing by 1.06 (one plus the expected inflation rate):[3]

$$\text{Purchasing power of } 1,080 \text{ period-1 dollars} = \text{number of current dollars having same purchasing power} = \frac{\$1,080}{1.06} = \$1,018.87$$

This is the *real* payoff to the bill holder:

Invest Current Dollars		Expected Real Value of Period-1 Receipts	Result
$1,000	$\longrightarrow$	$1,018.87	Expected real rate of return is 0.0187, or about 1.9%

Thus we could say "The bill offers an 8% nominal rate of return" *or* "It offers a 1.9% expected real rate of return." Note that the nominal rate is certain but the real rate is only expected. The actual real rate cannot be calculated until period 1 arrives and the inflation rate is known.

If the discount rate is stated in nominal terms, then consistency requires that cash flows be estimated in nominal terms, taking account of trends in selling price, labour and materials cost, and so on. This calls for more than simply applying a single assumed inflation rate to all components of cash flow. Labour cost per hour of work, for example, normally increases at a faster rate than the consumer price index because of improvements in productivity and increasing real wages throughout the economy. Tax shields on depreciation (capital cost allowance) do not increase with inflation; they are calculated in nominal terms because tax law allows only the original cost of assets to be depreciated.

Of course, there is nothing wrong with discounting real cash flows at a real discount rate, although this is not commonly done. Here is a simple example showing the equivalence of the two methods.

Suppose your firm usually forecasts cash flows in nominal terms and discounts at a 15% nominal rate. In this particular case, however, you are given project cash flows estimated in real terms, that is, current dollars:

Real Cash Flows (thousands of dollars)			
C_0	C_1	C_2	C_3
-100	$+35$	$+50$	$+30$

It would be inconsistent to discount these real cash flows at 15%. You have two alternatives: either restate the cash flows in nominal terms and discount at 15%,

---

[3] A 6% inflation rate means that $1.00 now has the same purchasing power as $1.06 next year. Thus, the real purchasing power of $1,080 next year is $1,080/1.06. Real purchasing power is measured in terms of today's dollars.

or restate the discount rate in real terms and use this to discount the real cash flows. We will now show you that both methods produce the same answer.

Assume that inflation is projected at 10% a year. Then the first cash flow for year 1, which is $35,000 in current dollars, will be $35,000 × 1.10 = $38,500 in year-1 dollars. Similarly the cash flow for year 2 will be $50,000 × (1.10)^2 = $60,500 in year-2 dollars, and so on. If we discount these nominal cash flows at the 15% nominal discount rate, we have

$$NPV = -100 + \frac{38.5}{1.15} + \frac{60.5}{(1.15)^2} + \frac{39.9}{(1.15)^3} = 5.5 \text{ or } \$5,500$$

Instead of converting the cash-flow forecasts into nominal terms, we could convert the discount rate into real terms by using the following relationship:

$$\text{Real discount rate} = \frac{1 + \text{nominal discount rate}}{1 + \text{inflation rate}} - 1$$

In our example this gives

$$\text{Real discount rate} = \frac{1.15}{1.10} - 1 = 0.045 \text{ or } 4.5\%$$

If we now discount the real cash flows by the real discount rate, we have an NPV of $5,500, just as before:

$$NPV = -100 + \frac{35}{1.045} + \frac{50}{(1.045)^2} + \frac{30}{(1.045)^3} = 5.5 \text{ or } \$5,500$$

Note that the real discount rate is approximately equal to the *difference* between the nominal discount rate of 15% and the inflation rate of 10%. Discounting at 5% would give NPV = $4,600 — not exactly right, but close.

The message of all this is quite simple. Discount nominal cash flows at a nominal discount rate. Discount real cash flows at a real rate. Obvious as this rule is, it is sometimes violated. For example, in 1974 there was a political storm in Ireland over the government's acquisition of a stake in Bula Mines. The price paid by the government reflected an assessment of £40 million as the value of Bula Mines; however, one group of consultants thought that the company's value was only £8 million and others thought that it was as high as £104 million. Although these valuations used different cash-flow projections, a significant part of the difference in views seemed to reflect confusion about real and nominal discount rates.[4]

6-2   CORPORATE TAXES IN CANADA — THE BASICS

Businesses have many dealings with governments. They pay out money in the form of income taxes, property taxes, license fees, and stumpage charges, and they get some of it back as government grants and subsidies. The most important of these cash flows is the corporate income tax and you must know how it is calculated.

Income tax is paid at both the federal and provincial levels. Each province has

[4] In some cases it is unclear what procedure was used. At least one expert seems to have discounted nominal cash flows at a real rate. For a review of the Bula Mines controversy see E. Dimson and P.R. Marsh, *Cases in Corporate Finance*, Wiley International, London, 1987.

its own tax laws. Since provincial laws are generally similar to the federal law, we will concentrate on federal law.[5]

Federal and provincial income taxes currently total about 36% of a company's taxable income.[6] However, when calculating taxable income, the firm is allowed to make a deduction for depreciation. In Canada this depreciation is called **capital cost allowance (CCA)**. Thus

$$\text{Taxable income} = \text{revenues} - \text{expenses} - \text{CCA}$$

$$\text{Tax} = 0.36 \times \text{taxable income}$$

Notice that CCA is not itself a cash flow, though it does affect the cash flow by reducing the tax paid by $0.36 \times$ CCA. This tax saving is sometimes called the **CCA tax shield** or **depreciation tax shield**. Also, CCA is not necessarily the same as the depreciation figure shown in the company's profit statement: Revenue Canada allows the company to keep one set of books for the tax collector and a different set for stockholders.

The Asset Class System

A few assets, such as land or securities, cannot be depreciated at all. The others are divided by Revenue Canada into different CCA **asset classes**. Some classes of assets can be depreciated much more rapidly than other classes.

Most industrial buildings acquired after 1987 fall into Class 1. Class 1 assets can be depreciated each year by 4% of the undepreciated balance. For example, suppose you start up a new business by investing $10 million in a new factory. In the first year you are entitled to a CCA deduction of 4% of this capital cost:

$$\text{CCA} = 0.04 \times 10 = \$0.4 \text{ million}$$

In the next year the undepreciated balance (known as the **undepreciated capital cost** or **UCC**) declines to $10 - 0.4 = \$9.6$ million. Therefore, in the second year you are entitled to a CCA deduction of $0.04 \times \$9.6 = \$0.384$ million, and so on.

A great deal of machinery falls into Class 8. Class 8 assets can be depreciated at a 20% rate. Thus, if you invested that $10 million in machinery, you would be entitled to a CCA deduction in the first year of $0.2 \times \$10 = \$2$ million. In the second year the UCC would decline to $10 - \$2 = \$8$ million and you would be entitled to a deduction of $0.2 \times \$8 = \$1.6$ million, and so on.

All assets within a particular CCA class are depreciated as if they were one asset. For example, suppose that after the first year you acquire a second machine for $10 million. Your UCC of Class 8 assets would rise to $8 + \$10 = \$18$ million, and the CCA deduction in the next year would be $0.2 \times \$18 = \$3.6$ million.

The Disposition of Assets

The tax laws provide a complex set of rules that arise when an asset is sold. The procedure is as follows:

A. When a depreciable asset is sold, the lower of the sale price or the initial cost is deducted from the undepreciated capital cost of its asset class.

---

[5] The province of Quebec deviates the most sharply from the federal tax law.

[6] Appendix 6-1 discusses these tax rates in more detail. They vary according to province, size of the business, as well as whether it is a manufacturing or processing firm. Typically, a large firm in general industry pays tax at approximately 40% while a small firm pays at 22%. If a large firm is in a manufacturing or processing business, the rate is reduced to about 36% in many provinces.

B. If Step A leaves a negative balance, this amount is called **recaptured depreciation** and is added to taxable income. The undepreciated capital cost of the asset class is then set to zero.

C. If Step A leaves a positive balance and *there are no other assets remaining* in the class, this remaining balance is called a **terminal loss**, and is deducted from taxable income. Also, the undepreciated capital cost is set to zero, so that the class ceases to generate CCA tax shields. But if Step A leaves a positive balance and *there are other assets remaining* in the class, this balance becomes the new UCC of the class and it continues to generate CCA tax shields.[7]

D. When an asset is sold for more than its initial cost, the difference between the sale price and initial cost is called a **capital gain**.[8] Three-quarters of the capital gain is taxable and therefore is added to the year's taxable income.[9]

EXAMPLE 1   Suppose you start a new business by purchasing a Class 8 machine for $10 million. After taking two years of CCA, the undepreciated capital cost of that machine is $6.4 million. At that point you sell the machine for $12 million. Because the sale price is higher than the asset cost, the machine has appreciated in value, not depreciated. Thus the tax authorities calculate that you have taken $10 − $6.4 = $3.6 million of depreciation to which you were (in an economic sense) not entitled. This $3.6 million of depreciation is, therefore "recaptured" and added to your income. In addition, you have also made a capital gain of $12 − $10 = $2 million. Three quarters of this gain is taxable, and is added to your taxable income.

Now, we have assumed that the machine is your only Class 8 asset. Suppose instead that there are other items in Class 8, and just before you dispose of the machine, Class 8 has a UCC greater than $10 million. Then there is no recaptured depreciation, but there is still the $2 million capital gain and a reduction of the UCC of Class 8 by $10 million.

EXAMPLE 2   Again, suppose you buy a Class 8 machine for $10 million. But now suppose you sell the machine for $4 million after taking two years of CCA tax shields. If it is the only asset you have in Class 8, the UCC of the class is again $6.4 million at the time of sale, and you are allowed to deduct $6.4 − $4 = $2.4 million from your income as a terminal loss. In reality, the machine suffered economic depreciation to a value of $4 million, but the tax laws only allowed you to depreciate it to $6.4 million. The terminal loss can thus be regarded as an extra depreciation tax shield that brings the total tax depreciation into line with the economic depreciation.

You already know what happens in this example if there are other Class 8 assets: if the UCC of Class 8 exceeds $4 million at the time of sale, you simply deduct $4 million from the UCC and nothing else happens, but if the UCC is less than $4 million, you have recaptured depreciation.

---

[7] Many classes contain a large number of assets, so this CCA treatment of the sale of an asset is very common.

[8] Capital gains or losses also arise from the sale of non-depreciable assets such as land and financial securities. However, you never get a capital loss with a depreciable asset: Steps A, B, and C apply instead.

[9] The 75% rate at which capital gains are included in taxable income applies for 1990 onward. Prior to 1988, the inclusion rate was 50% and for 1988 and 1989 it is a transitional 66⅔%.

Present Values of CCA Tax Shields

Our two examples illustrate a peculiar feature of the asset class system embodied in Canadian tax law: an asset can still generate CCA tax shields for the firm even after it is sold, provided there are other assets remaining in its class. To calculate the PV of a project, you must know how to calculate the PV of a perpetual CCA tax shield.

Suppose you start a new asset class by buying an asset. We'll use this notation to describe the asset and your firm:

C = capital cost of an asset acquired in year 0
d = CCA rate for the asset class
T_c = corporate tax rate
r = discount rate
UCC_t = undepreciated capital cost in year t after deducting CCA for the year

For simplicity, we'll assume you get your first CCA tax shield from the asset in year 1.[10] The UCC of the class starts out at $UCC_0 = C$, so the CCA you get for year 1 is $d \times UCC_0 = Cd$.

After deducting the CCA, the UCC for year 1 becomes:

$$UCC_1 = UCC_0 - CCA$$
$$= C - Cd$$
$$= C(1 - d)$$

Similarly, the CCA taken for year 2 is

$$d \times UCC_1 = Cd(1 - d)$$

In year t, you will have taken $t-1$ previous CCA tax shields, so the UCC at the start of the year is $UCC_{t-1} = C(1-d)^{t-1}$. Thus, your CCA for year t will be

$$d \times UCC_{t-1} = Cd(1-d)^{t-1}$$

There are two ways you can handle CCA tax shields when computing the net present value of a project. On the one hand, you can compute the taxable income every year from the revenues, expenses, and CCA, and multiply by the tax rate to get the annual tax cash flow. Don't forget to include any recaptured depreciation or terminal loss when the project is salvaged. You must also account for any perpetual CCA tax shields left in the class after salvaging the project's assets. This approach is illustrated in Section 6-3. It is cumbersome unless you have access to a spreadsheet program on a personal computer.[11]

On the other hand, you can apply the tricks you learned in Chapter 3 to get simple formulas for the present value of the CCA tax shields themselves. Then you can add the PV of the CCA tax shields to the PV of the annual "after-tax" revenues and expenses to get the overall PV of the project. The after-tax revenues and expenses are simply revenues and expenses multiplied by $(1 - T_c)$. This

---

[10] This simplifies two aspects of Canadian tax law. First, there is the "half-year rule" which says that half of the asset cost C is added to the class in year 0 and the other half is added in year 1. Second, CCA is based on the UCC of the asset class at the tax year-end. Thus, you actually get half of the first year's CCA tax shield in year 0 and half in year 1. We'll get a simple formula that is not too far from the truth if we assume that all of the first year's CCA tax shield occurs in year 1. For a more precise analysis, see Appendix 6-1.

[11] But you *must* use this approach if your firm is likely to have tax losses at some time in the future. These are carried back and forward against other years' income, as discussed in Appendix 6-1. This means that any benefit from CCA tax shields may be deferred until the firm has taxable income.

approach gives the overall PV of the project because of the additivity property of present values discussed in Section 5-2. That is, if we let ATCF stand for the annual after-tax cash flow and Rev and Exp stand for revenues and expenses, respectively, then after-tax cash flow equals after-tax revenues net of expenses plus the CCA tax shield:

$$\text{ATCF} = (1 - T_c) \times (\text{Rev} - \text{Exp}) + T_c \times \text{CCA}$$

Because present values are additive, the PV of after-tax cash flows equals the PV of the after-tax revenues net of expenses plus the PV of the CCA tax shield:

$$\text{PV (ATCF)} = \text{PV} ((1 - T_c) \times (\text{Rev} - \text{Exp})) + \text{PV}(T_c \times \text{CCA})$$

Thus we have two equivalent approaches to calculating present values in the presence of taxes, and we shall use both in this text. They give the same answers.

Let's see how to calculate the PV of a CCA tax shield. First, let's suppose you never sell the asset. The project generates the following CCA tax shields.

Year	1	2	3	...	t	...
CCA tax shield	CdT_c	$CdT_c (1 - d)$	$CdT_c (1 - d)^2$	...	$CdT_c (1 - d)^{t-1}$	...

This forms a perpetuity in the amount CdT_c that is growing (really declining) at the rate $-d$. From Section 3-2 we know that the present value of this is:[12]

$$\text{PV of perpetual CCA tax shield} = \frac{CdT_c}{r + d}$$

What happens if you sell the asset after using it for a few years? We use the same type of trick you saw in Section 3-2: we combine the present value of two declining perpetuities to calculate the present value of a declining annuity. Let's look at some examples showing how to combine tax principles and present value principles to get the PV of the tax shields. You can sharpen your understanding of these principles by doing some of the problems at the end of the chapter.

While going through these examples, remember that we always analyze the *incremental* cash flows created by the project in order to calculate its present value. In particular, we are looking for incremental changes in CCA and UCC that arise because of the purchase (or sale) of assets for the project. Fortunately the formula given above for the PV of a perpetual CCA tax shield still works if the firm already has other assets in the class to which the assets of the project are to be added. In this case the formula gives the PV of the incremental perpetual tax shields generated by the purchase of the asset for an amount C. This is exactly what we need in calculating the PV of the project.

EXAMPLE 3   Suppose you buy an airplane hangar for C ($1 million) in year 0 (Class 6, CCA rate $d = 0.10$). You will sell the hangar in year 10 for S ($200,000), at which time you will still have other assets in the class (which includes your

---

[12] To see this, use the formula for a growing perpetuity with $C_t = CdT_c(1-d)^{t-1}$ and $g = -d$. Thus, $C_1 = CdT_c$. We have

$$\text{PV} = \frac{C_1}{1 + r} + \frac{C_1 (1 - d)}{(1 + r)^2} + \frac{C_1 (1 - d)^2}{(1 + r)^3} + \cdots$$
$$= \frac{C_1}{r - (-d)}$$
$$= \frac{CdT_c}{r + d}$$

fences and wharves) and a UCC in excess of $200,000. Your tax rate is 36% and your discount rate is 15%. You want to know the present value of the incremental tax shields generated by the ownership and sale of the asset. Since you have other assets in the class and a UCC in excess of the sale price, you will have neither recaptured depreciation nor a terminal loss. The only tax effect of the sale of the asset will arise from the reduction of the UCC of Class 6 by $200,000 in year 10. You have:[13]

PV of CCA tax shields
= PV of perpetual tax shield on $1 million in year 0
  − PV of perpetual tax shield on $200,000 in year 10

$$= \frac{CdT_c}{r + d} - \frac{1}{(1 + r)^{10}} \frac{SdT_c}{r + d}$$

$$= \frac{1,000,000 \times 0.1 \times 0.36}{0.15 + 0.1} - \frac{1}{(1.15)^{10}} \times \frac{200,000 \times 0.1 \times 0.36}{0.15 + 0.1}$$

$$= \$136,886$$

Note that the UCC generated by the hanger after ten years of CCA tax shields is $UCC_{10} = (1 - 0.1)^{10} \times \$1,000,000 = \$348,678$. Even *after* selling the hanger assets in year 10, you will continue to depreciate $348,678 − $200,000 = $148,678 of it because of the special features in Canadian tax law.

The calculations in Example 3 are easy, since you do not need to know UCC_{10} to calculate an amount of recaptured depreciation or terminal loss. Most asset classes are very broadly defined and include many assets; the situation described in Example 3 is quite common. However, the Income Tax Regulations also specify many situations where an asset must be in a class by itself,[14] so the disposition of such an asset will always generate a terminal loss or recaptured depreciation.

EXAMPLE 4   Suppose you have the same situation as in Example 3, except that the hanger is the only Class 6 asset you have from years 0 through 10. You get a terminal loss of $UCC_{10} - S = \$148,678$, but you must also subtract UCC_{10} from the class balance to close it out when the asset is sold. You have:

PV of ten years of CCA tax shields and terminal loss
= PV of perpetual tax shield on $1,000,000 in year 0
  + PV of terminal loss tax shield on $148,678 in year 10
  − PV of perpetual tax shield on $348,678 in year 10

$$= \frac{CdT_c}{r + d} + \frac{T_c}{(1 + r)^{10}} (UCC_{10} - S) - \frac{1}{(1 + r)^{10}} \frac{UCC_{10}dT_c}{r + d}$$

$$= \frac{1,000,000 \times 0.1 \times 0.36}{0.15 + 0.1} + \frac{0.36}{(1.15)^{10}} (348,678 - 200,000)$$

$$- \frac{1}{(1.15)^{10}} \frac{348,678 \times 0.1 \times 0.36}{0.15 + 0.1}$$

$$= \$144,819$$

---

[13] Here we assume, for simplicity, that the first CCA tax shield lost due to the sale occurs in year 11, or the year after the sale. The $SdT_c/(r + d)$ formula has already discounted the effect of the lost tax shields back to one year before the first lost tax shield, year 10, so you must discount it back another ten years. In reality, half of the first lost tax shield will be in year 10 and the other half will be in year 11, because the half-year rule effectively applies to asset dispositions as well. See Appendix 6-1.

[14] Separate classes are required for rental properties worth more than $50,000, for many types of ships, for telecommunication spacecraft, and for assets associated with different "businesses."

Some Asset Classes Give Straight-Line Depreciation

Not all asset classes in Canada's tax system have the declining balance feature you have just seen. For example, a "two-year writeoff" (that is, straight-line depreciation over two years) is allowed for some pollution control and energy conservation equipment. Also patents, franchises, and improvements to leasehold interests (for example, redecoration of a store you have leased) generate straight-line capital cost allowances. The CCA tax shield is just an annuity in these cases.

The Investment Tax Credit

In addition to allowing a company to deduct CCA from taxable income, Canadian tax laws sometimes allow an **investment tax credit** (ITC). A **tax credit** is a reduction of taxes owing, while an **allowance** (such as CCA) is only a reduction of taxable income. One type of ITC applies to acquistions of *new depreciable* property in the manufacturing and processing, farming, fishing, logging, or mineral processing industries. Another type of ITC applies to qualified expenditures in scientific research and experimental development (R&D). For property acquisitions, the ITC is only available in Atlantic Canada, where it is 15% of the cost of the property. For R&D, the ITC is 30% of the R&D expenditure in Atlantic Canada and 20% elsewhere in Canada. For small business (with income less than $200,000 in the previous year), the ITC rate for R&D is 35% throughout Canada. The depreciable cost of the property is reduced by the amount of the ITC. If the ITC exceeds 75% of the federal tax payable, there is a complicated set of rules that may limit how much ITC you can claim for the year, and how much can be applied against other years.

For example, suppose your Newfoundland division invests $10 million is a fish processing plant. If you owe more than $2 million in federal tax, your tax bill for the year is reduced by 0.15 × $10 million or $1.5 million. However, you are only allowed to claim CCA on a net capital cost of $(10–1.5) million or $8.5 million. Now consider a more complicated case and suppose you are paying only $1 million in tax for the year. You can apply the ITC against only 75% of $1 million or $0.75 million of income for the year.[15] Then you are allowed to apply the unused $(1.5–0.75) million or $0.75 million ITC against income in any of the previous three years (and receive a retroactive refund) – this is called a **carry-back.** Suppose your income for the previous three years totalled only $0.4 million. They you still have an unused credit of $(0.75–0.4) million or $0.35 million. In the year you acquire the asset, the federal government will give you a refund of up to 40% of this unused amount, or 0.4 × $0.35 million = $0.14 million.[16] Now you have an unused credit of $(0.35 − 0.14) million or $0.21 million that you can **carry-forward** for up to ten years against future taxes.

That sounds a little complicated, doesn't it? Here is a summary of what you do:

1. Apply the ITC against as much as 75% of current income.
2. Apply any unused ITC against the three prior years of income.
3. Apply for a refund of 40% of the amount not used to this point.

---

[15] Actually, the situation is even more complicated; you can apply the ITC against 100% of the tax on your first $200,000 of income and against 75% of the income above that. The difference between this and what we describe in the text will be almost eaten up by your tax accountant's fees.

[16] Actually, if your taxable income for the previous year was less than $200,000, you get a 100% refund, rather than a 40% refund. The refund is paid as a cheque to you, if you pay no other tax.

4.   Carry the remainder forward for up to ten years.

5.   Sit back and relax with your favourite beverage.

6-3   ANOTHER EXAMPLE—IM&C PROJECT

As the newly appointed financial manager of International Mulch and Compost Company (IM&C), you are about to analyze a proposal for marketing guano as a garden fertilizer. (IM&C's planned advertising campaign features a rustic gentleman who steps out of a vegetable patch singing, "All my troubles have guano way.")[17]

You are given the forecasts shown in Table 6-1. The project requires an investment of $10 million in plant and machinery (line 1), which is in Asset Class 10 (30%). This machinery can be dismantled and sold for net proceeds estimated at $1 million in period 7 (line 1, column 7). This amount is the plant's *salvage value*. IM&C always has many assets and a positive balance in Class 10.

Table 6-1 shows the incremental effects of accepting the project. For example, the undepreciated capital costs and the tax cash flows are incremental. Thus, a negative tax means a reduction in taxes paid by IM&C on its other projects. The raw data for a project are often presented in a "massaged form" like this to reflect the book value of the investment and estimated annual profits. Indeed, the pro forma depreciation figures that are usually given are those that would appear on annual financial statements. But we know they do not represent cash flows, so we have presented the capital cost allowances instead, which generate tax shields.[18]

Lines 5 to 11 in Table 6-1 show a simplified income statement for the guano project. This might be taken as a starting point for estimating cash flow. However, you discover that all figures submitted to you are based on costs and selling prices prevailing in year 0. IM&C's production managers realize there will be inflation, but they have assumed that prices can be raised to cover increasing costs. Thus they claim that inflation won't affect the real value of the project.

Though this line of argument sounds plausible, it will get you into trouble. First, opportunity costs of capital are usually expressed as *nominal* rates. You cannot use a nominal rate to discount real cash flows. Second, not all prices and costs increase at the same rate. For example, the tax savings provided by capital cost allowances are unaffected by inflation, since tax law allows you to depreciate only the original cost of the equipment, regardless of what happens to prices after the investment is made. On the other hand, wages generally increase faster than the inflation rate. Labour cost per tonne of guano will rise in real terms unless technological advances allow more efficient use of labour.

Assume that future inflation is forecasted at 10% a year. Table 6-2 restates Table 6-1 in nominal terms, assuming, just for simplicity, that sales, investment, operating costs, and required working capital appreciate at this general rate. You can see, however, that CCA is not affected by inflation.

Table 6-3 derives cash-flow forecasts from the investment and income data given in Table 6-2. Cash flow from operations is defined as sales less operating

---

[17] Sorry.

[18] This presents a problem if you are a financial analyst outside the firm. You may have access to audited financial statements for shareholders, but will not have access to the information on the tax return.

Table 6-1
IM&C's Guano Project—Initial Projections (figures in thousands of dollars)

Period	0	1	2	3	4	5	6	7
1. Capital investment	10,000							-1,000[a]
2. Undepreciated capital cost at year end	10,000	7,000	4,900	3,430	2,401	1,681	1,177	-176[b]
3. Working capital		500	1,065	2,450	3,340	2,225	1,130	0
4. Total book value[c] (2 + 3)	10,000	7,500	5,965	5,880	5,741	3,906	2,306	-176
5. Sales		475	10,650	24,500	33,400	22,250	11,130	
6. Operating costs		761	6,388	14,690	20,043	13,345	6,678	
7. Other costs	4,000	2,000						
8. Capital cost allowance (30% for Class 10)		3,000	2,100	1,470	1,029	720	504	353
9. Taxable income (5 − 6 − 7 − 8)	-4,000	-5,286	2,162	8,340	12,328	8,185	3,948	-353
10. Tax at 36%	-1,440	-1,903	778	3,002	4,438	2,947	1,421	-127
11. Profit after tax[c] (9 − 10)	-2,560	-3,383	1,384	5,338	7,890	5,238	2,527	-50[d]

[a] Salvage value.
[b] UCC of $824 in period 7 less salvage value. Since this is negative, it gives a reduction in future CCA tax shields on IM&C's other Class 10 assets.
[c] Based on depreciation charges being equal to CCA.
[d] This includes the $176 profit on salvage: −353 − (−127) + 176 = −50.

Table 6-2
IM&C's Guano Project—Revised Projections Reflecting Inflation (figures in thousands of dollars)

Period	0	1	2	3	4	5	6	7
1. Capital investment	10,000							-1,949[a]
2. Undepreciated capital cost at year end	10,000	7,000	4,900	3,430	2,401	1,681	1,177	-1,125[b]
3. Working capital		550	1,289	3,261	4,890	3,583	2,002	0
4. Sales		523	12,887	32,610	48,901	35,834	19,717	
5. Operating costs		837	7,729	19,552	29,345	21,492	11,830	
6. Other costs	4,000	2,200						
7. Capital cost allowances (30% for Class 10)		3,000	2,100	1,470	1,029	720	504	353
8. Taxable income (4 − 5 − 6 − 7)	-4,000	-5,514	3,058	11,588	18,527	13,622	7,383	-353
9. Tax at 36%	-1,440	-1,985	1,101	4,172	6,670	4,904	2,658	-127
10. Profit after tax (8 − 9)	-2,560	-3,529	1,957	7,416	11,857	8,718	4,725	-899[c]

[a] Salvage value.
[b] UCC of $824 in period 7 less salvage value.
[c] Includes $1,125 profit on salvage.

Table 6-3
IM&C's Guano Project—Cash Flow Analysis (figures in thousands of dollars)

Period	0	1	2	3	4	5	6	7
1. Sales		523	12,887	32,610	48,901	35,834	19,717	
2. Operating and other costs	4,000	3,037	7,729	19,552	29,345	21,492	11,830	
3. Tax on operations	−1,440	−1,985	1,101	4,172	6,670	4,904	2,658	−127
4. Cash flow from operations (1 − 2 − 3)	−2,560	−529	4,057	8,886	12,886	9,438	5,229	127
5. Change in working capital		−550	−739	−1,972	−1,629	1,307	1,581	2,002
6. Capital investment and disposal	−10,000							1,949
7. PV of CCA tax shields lost on other projects								−243[a]
8. Net cash flow and lost tax shield (4 + 5 + 6 + 7)	−12,560	−1,079	3,318	6,914	11,257	10,745	6,810	3,835
9. Present value at 20%	−12,560	−899	2,303	4,003	5,426	4,319	2,281	1,070

Net present value = $5,943

[a] Salvage value exceeds UCC (Table 6-2, line 2, column 7) by 1,125, so PV of lost CCA tax shields on other projects = $\dfrac{1,125 \times 0.3 \times 0.36}{0.2 + 0.3} = 243$

costs, other costs, and taxes.[19] The remaining cash flows include the changes in working capital, the initial capital investment, and the final recovery of salvage value. The salvage value exceeds the undepreciated capital cost of the assets at the time of disposal. Since IM&C has other assets in the same class, this will not result in recaptured depreciation. However, it will reduce the UCC of those other assets at the time of disposal. The item in line 7, column 7 reflects the loss of the present value of the associated tax shields.

IM&C estimates the nominal opportunity cost of capital for projects of this type as 20%. (We have already used this discount rate to calculate the PV of lost CCA on salvage.)[20] When all cash flows are added up and discounted, the guano project is seen to offer a net present value of $5.9 million:

$$NPV = -12,560 - \frac{1,079}{1.20} + \frac{3,318}{(1.20)^2} + \frac{6,914}{(1.20)^3} + \frac{11,257}{(1.20)^4} + \frac{10,745}{(1.20)^5} + \frac{6,810}{(1.20)^6}$$
$$+ \frac{3,835}{(1.20)^7} = 5,943 \text{ or } \$5,943,000$$

Separating Investment and Financing Decisions

Our analysis of the guano project takes no notice of how that project is financed. It may be that IM&C would decide to finance partly by debt, but, if it did, we would not subtract the debt proceeds from the required investment, nor would we recognize interest and principal payments as cash outflows. We would treat the project as if it were all equity-financed, treating all cash outflows as coming from stockholders and all cash inflows as going to them.

We approach the problem in this way so that we can separate the analysis of the investment decision from the financing decision. Then, when we have calculated NPV, we can undertake a separate analysis of financing. Financing decisions and their possible interaction with investment decisions are covered later in the book.

*A Further Note on Estimating Cash Flow

Now here is an important point. You can see from line 5 of Table 6-3 that working capital increases in the early and middle years of the project. Why is this? There are several possibilities.

1. Sales recorded on the income statement overstate actual cash receipts from guano shipments because customers are slow to pay their bills. Therefore, accounts receivable increase.
2. Projected operating costs understate cash outlays for raw materials and production. Therefore inventory increases.
3. An offsetting effect occurs if payments for materials and services used in guano production are delayed. In this case accounts payable will increase.

Thus a detailed cash-flow forecast for, say, year 3 might look like Table 6-4. In practice you may find, for example, that the accounts receivable and payable are

---

[19] Sales revenue may not represent actual cash inflow. Costs and taxes may not represent cash outflows. This is why change in working capital must be taken into account, as it is in Table 6-3. The "Further Note on Estimating Cash Flow" in this section discusses the relationship between operating cash flow and change in working capital in more detail.

[20] By discounting the depreciation tax shields at 20%, we implicitly assume that they are as risky as the other cash flows. Since they depend only on tax rates, depreciation method, and IM&C's ability to generate taxable income, they may well be less risky. In some contexts—the analysis of financial leases, for example—depreciation tax shields are treated as safe, nominal cash flows and discounted at an after-tax borrowing or lending rate. See Chapter 26.

proportional to forecasted sales for the year, while inventories are proportional to forecasted sales for the same or the next year. The constants of proportionality could be determined by analyzing an existing operation, and we have made assumptions about typical values to get the data in Table 6-4. Since these sales represent real cash flows, working capital is also real.

Table 6-4
Details of Cash-flow Forecast for IM&C's Guano Project in Year 3 (figures in thousands of dollars)

Cash Flows		Data From Forecasted Income Statement	Working Capital Changes	
Cash inflow	=	Sales	−	Increase in accounts receivable
$31,110	=	32,610	−	1,500
Cash outflow	=	Operating costs and taxes	+	Increase in inventory net of increase in accounts payable
$24,196	=	(19,552 + 4,172)	+	(972 − 500)
Net cash flow	=	Cash inflow	−	Cash outflow
$6,914	=	31,110	−	24,196

Instead of worrying about changes in working capital, you could estimate cash flow directly by counting up the dollars coming in and taking away the dollars going out. But you would still need to put together a projected income statement to estimate taxes. In Chapter 28 we discuss techniques for modelling cash flows in more detail.

A Final Comment on Project Analysis

Let's review. A few pages ago, you embarked on an analysis of IM&C's guano project. It appeared, at first, that you had all the facts you needed in Table 6-1, but many of those numbers had to be thrown away because they didn't reflect expected inflation. So you worked out revised projections and calculated project net present value.

You were lucky to get away with just one NPV calculation. In real situations, it often takes several tries to purge all inconsistencies and mistakes. Then there are "what if" questions. For example: what if inflation rages at 15% per year, rather than 10%? What if technical problems delay startup to year 2? What if gardeners prefer chemical fertilizers to your natural product?

You won't truly understand the guano project until these questions are answered. *Project analysis* is more than one or two NPV calculations, as we will see in Chapter 10.

However, before you become too deeply immersed in guano, we should now turn to the subject of project interactions.

6-4   PROJECT INTERACTIONS

Almost all decisions about capital expenditure involve either-or choices. The firm can build either a 9,000-square-metre warehouse or a 10,000-square-metre warehouse in one of several locations. It can heat it either by oil or by natural gas, and so on. These mutually exclusive options are simple examples of *project interactions*.

Project interactions can arise in countless ways. The literature of operations research and industrial engineering sometimes addresses cases of extreme complexity and difficulty. We will concentrate on five simple but important cases.

Case 1 — Optimal Timing of Investment

The fact that a project has a positive NPV does not mean that it is best undertaken now. It might be even more valuable if undertaken in the future. Similarly, a project with a currently negative NPV might become a valuable opportunity if we wait a bit. Thus *any* project has two mutually exclusive alternatives: do it now, or wait and invest later.

The question of optimal timing of investment is not difficult under conditions of certainty. We first examine alternative dates (*t*) for making the investment and calculate its net *future* value as of each date. Then, to find which of the alternatives would add most to the firm's *current* value, we must work out

$$\frac{\text{Net future value as of date } t}{(1 + r)^t}$$

For example, suppose you own a large tract of inaccessible timber. To harvest it, you have to invest a substantial amount in access roads and other facilities. The longer you wait, the higher the investment required. On the other hand, lumber prices will rise as you wait, and the trees will keep growing, although at a gradually decreasing rate.

Let us suppose that the net value of the harvest at different future dates is as follows:

Year of Harvest	0	1	2	3	4	5
Net *future* value (thousands of dollars)	50	64.4	77.5	89.4	100	109.4
Change in value from previous year, %		+28.8	+20.3	+15.4	+11.9	+9.4

As you can see, the longer you defer cutting the timber, the more money you will make. However, your concern is with the date that maximizes the net *present* value of your investment. You therefore need to discount the net future value of the harvest back to the present. Suppose the appropriate discount rate is 10%. Then if you harvest the timber in year 1, it has a net *present value of* $58,500:

$$\text{NPV if harvested in year 1} = \frac{64.4}{1.10} = 58.5 \text{ or } \$58,500$$

The net present value (at *t* = 0) for other harvest dates is as follows:

Year of Harvest	0	1	2	3	4	5
Net present value (thousands of dollars)	50	58.5	64.0	67.2	68.3	67.9

The optimal point to harvest the timber is year 4 because this is the point that maximizes NPV.

Notice that before year 4 the net future value of the timber increases by more than 10% a year: the gain in value is greater than the cost of the capital that is tied up in the project. After year 4 the gain in value is still positive but less than the cost of capital. You maximize the net present value of your investment if you harvest your timber as soon as the rate of increase in value drops below the cost of capital.[21]

The problem of optimal timing of investment under uncertainty is, of course, much more complicated. An opportunity not taken at $t = 0$ might be either more or less attractive at $t = 1$; there is rarely any way of knowing for sure. Perhaps it is better to strike while the iron is hot even if there is a chance it will become hotter. On the other hand, if you wait a bit you might obtain more information and avoid a bad mistake.[22]

Case 2—Choosing Between Long- and Short-Lived Equipment

Suppose the firm is forced to choose between two machines, A and B. The two machines are designed differently, but have identical capacity and do exactly the same job. Machine A costs $15,000, and will last three years. It costs $4,000 per year to run. Machine B is an "economy" model costing only $10,000, but it will last only two years, and costs $6,000 per year to run. These are real cash flows: The costs are forecasted in dollars of constant purchasing power.[23]

Because the two machines produce exactly the same product, the only way to choose between them is on the basis of cost. Suppose we compute the present value of cost:

	Costs (thousands of dollars)				Present Value at 6% (thousands of dollars)
Machine	C_0	C_1	C_2	C_3	
A	+15	+4	+4	+4	25.69
B	+10	+6	+6		21.00

Should we take machine B, the one with the lower present value of costs? Not necessarily, because B will have to be replaced a year earlier than A. In other words, there is a future investment decision contingent on today's choice of A or B.

So, a machine with total PV (costs) of $21,000 spread over three years (0, 1, and 2) is not necessarily better than a competing machine with PV (costs) of

---

[21] Our timber-cutting example conveys the right idea about investment timing, but it misses an important practical point: the sooner you cut the first crop of trees, the sooner the second crop can start growing. Thus, the value of the second crop depends on when you cut the first. This more complex and realistic problem might be solved in one of two ways:
1. Find the cutting dates that maximize the present value of a series of harvests, taking account of the different growth rates of young and old trees.
2. Repeat our calculations, counting the future market value of cut-over land as part of the payoff to the first harvest. The value of cut-over land includes the present value of all subsequent harvests.
The second solution is far simpler if you can figure out what cut-over land will be worth.

[22] H. Bierman and S. Smidt discuss the tree-cutting problem in *The Capital Budgeting Decision*, 7th ed., New York: The Macmillan Company, 1988, pp. 281–286.

[23] The following calculations are best done in real terms. Of course we must be consistent and use a real discount rate. We will assume it is 6%.

$25,690 spread over four years (0 to 3). Somehow we have to convert total PV (costs) to a cost *per year*.

Suppose the financial manager is asked to *rent* machine A to the plant manager actually in charge of production. There will be three equal rental payments starting in year 1. Obviously the financial manager has to make sure that the rental payments are worth $25,690, the total PV (costs) of machine A. This fair rental payment, which is usually called the *equivalent annual cost,* turns out to be 9.61 or $9,610 per year:

	Cash Flows (thousands of dollars)				NPV at 6% (thousands of dollars)
	C_0	C_1	C_2	C_3	
Machine A	+15	+4	+4	+4	25.69
Equivalent annual cost		+9.61	+9.61	+9.61	25.69

The fair rental payment, or equivalent annual cost, is the annuity that has exactly the same life and present value as machine A. How did we know that the right cash flow from the annuity is 9.61? It was easy! We set the NPV of the annuity equal to the present value of A and solved for the payment of the annuity:

$$\text{PV of annuity} = \text{PV of cash outflows of A} = 25.69$$
$$= \text{annuity payment} \times \text{three-year annuity factor}$$

Therefore the annuity payment equals the present value divided by the annuity factor, which is 2.673 for three years and a 6% cost of capital.[24]

$$\text{Annuity payment} = \frac{25.69}{2.673} = 9.61$$

If we make a similar calculation for machine B, we get:

	Costs (thousands of dollars)			Present Value at 6% (thousands of dollars)
	C_0	C_1	C_2	
Machine B	+10	+6	+6	21.00
Equivalent two-year annuity		+11.45	+11.45	21.00

We see that machine A is better, because its equivalent annual cost is less ($9,610 versus $11,450 for machine B). In other words, machine A could be rented to the production manager for less than machine B.

Our rule for comparing assets of different lives is, therefore, as follows. Select the machine that has the lowest equivalent annual cost. The equivalent annual cost is simply the net present value of the cost divided by the annuity factor.

Now any rule this simple cannot be completely general. The rule implicitly assumes that like will be replaced with like—that no cheaper machine will come along in year 2 or 3. Suppose, for example, that machine C will arrive in year 2

---

[24] This factor can be obtained from a PV table or from the annuity formula given in Section 3-2.

with equivalent annual cost of only $5,000. We would then have to consider scrapping or selling machine A at year 2 (more on this decision below). The financial manager could not choose between machines A and B in year 0 without taking a detailed look at what each machine could be replaced with.

Finally, remember why equivalent annual costs are necessary in the first place. The reason is tht A and B will be replaced at different future dates. The choice between them therefore affects future investment decisions. If subsequent decisions are not affected by the initial choice — for example, because neither machine will be replaced — then we do *not need to take future decisions into account.*[25]

Case 3 — Deciding When to Replace an Existing Machine

The previous example took the life of each machine as fixed. In practice the point at which equipment is replaced reflects economic considerations rather than total physical collapse. *We* must decide when to replace. The machine will rarely decide for us.

Here is a common problem. You are operating an elderly machine that is expected to produce a net cash *inflow* of $4,000 in the coming year and $4,000 next year. After that it will give up the ghost. You can replace it now with a new machine, which costs $15,000 but is much more efficient and will provide a cash inflow of $8,000 a year for three years. You want to know whether you should replace your equipment now or wait a year.

We can calculate the NPV of the new machine and also its equivalent annual cash flow, that is, the three-year annuity that has the same net present value:

	Cash Flows (thousands of dollars)				NPV at 6% (thousands of dollars)
	C_0	C_1	C_2	C_3	
New machine	−15	+8	+8	+8	6.38
Equivalent three-year annuity		+2.387	+2.387	+2.387	6.38

In other words, the cash flows of the new machine are equivalent to an annuity of $2,387 per year. So we can equally well ask at what point we would want to replace our old machine with a new one producing $2,387 a year. When the question is put this way, the answer is obvious. As long as your old machine can generate a cash flow of $4,000 a year, who wants to put in its place a new one that generates only $2,387 a year?

It is a simple matter to incorporate salvage values into this calculation. Suppose the current salvage value is $8,000 and next year's value is $7,000. Let's see where you come out next year if you wait and then sell. On the one hand you gain $7,000, but you lose today's salvage value *plus* a year's return on that money. That is, $8,000 × 1.06 = $8,480. Your net loss is $8,480 − $7,000 = $1,480, which only partly offsets the operating gain. You should not replace yet.

Remember: the logic of such comparisons requires that the new machines should be the best of the available alternatives and that it, in turn, will be replaced at the optimal point.

---

[25] However, if neither machine will be replaced, then we would have to consider the extra revenue generated by machine A in its third year, when it will be operating but B will not.

Case 4—Cost of Excess Capacity

Any firm with a computer encounters many proposals for using it. Recently installed computers tend to have excess capacity, and, since the immediate marginal cost of using such computers seems to be negligible, management often encourages new uses. Sooner or later, however, the load on the machine will increase to a point at which management must either terminate the uses they originally encouraged or invest in another computer several years earlier than they had planned. Such problems can be avoided if a proper charge is made for the use of spare capacity.

Suppose we have a new investment project that requires heavy use of the computer. The effect of adopting the project is to bring the purchase date of a new computer forward from year 4 to year 3. This new computer has a life of five years, and at a discount rate of 6% the present value of the cost of buying and operating it is $500,000.

We begin by converting the $500,000 present value of cost of the computer to an equivalent annual cost of $118,700 for each of five years.[26] Of course, when the new computer in turn wears out, we will replace it with another. So we face the prospect of computing expenses of $118,700 a year. If we undertake the new project, the series of expenses begins in year 4; if we do not undertake it, the series begins in year 5. The new project, therefore, results in an *additional* computing cost of $118,700 in year 4. This has a present value of $118,700/(1.06)^4$, or $94,010. This cost is properly charged against the new project. When we recognize it, the NPV of the project may prove to be negative. If so, we still need to check whether it is worthwhile undertaking the project now and abandoning it later when the excess capacity of the present computer disappears.

Case 5— Fluctuating Load Factors

Although a $10 million warehouse may have a positive net present value, it should be built only if it has a higher NPV than a $9 million alternative. In other words, the NPV of the $1 million *marginal* investment required to buy the more expensive warehouse must be positive.

One case in which this is easily forgotten occurs when equipment is needed to meet fluctuating demand. Consider the following problem. A widget manufacturer operates two machines, each of which has a capacity of 1,000 units a year. They have an indefinite life and no salvage value, and so the only costs are the operating expenses of $2 per widget. Widget manufacture, as everyone knows, is a seasonal business, and widgets are perishable. During the fall and winter, when demand is high, each machine produces at capacity. During the spring and summer, each machine works at 50% of capacity. If the discount rate is 10% and the machines are kept indefinitely, the present value of the costs is $30,000:

	Two Old Machines
Annual output per machine	750 units
Operating cost per machine	2 × 750 = $1,500
PV operating cost per machine	1500/0.10 = $15,000
PV operating cost of two machines	2 × 15,000 = $30,000

---

[26] The present value of $118,700 for five years discounted at 6% is $500,000.

The company is considering whether to replace these machines with newer equipment. The new machines have a similar capacity, and so two would still be needed to meet peak demand. Each new machine costs $6,000 and lasts indefinitely. Operating expenses are only one dollar per unit. On this basis the company calculates that the present value of the costs of two new machines would be $27,000:

	Two New Machines
Annual output per machine	750 units
Capital cost per machine	$6,000
Operating cost per machine	$1 \times 750 = \$750$
PV total cost per machine	$6,000 + 750/0.10 = \$13,500$
PV total cost of two machines	$2 \times 13,500 = \$27,000$

Therefore, it scraps both old machines and buys two new ones.

The company was quite right in thinking that two new machines are better than two old ones, but unfortunately it forgot to investigate a third alternative: to replace just one of the old machines. Since the new machine has low operating costs, it would pay to operate it at capacity all year. The remaining old machine could then be kept simply to meet peak demand. The present value of the costs under this strategy is $26,000:

	One Old Machine	One New Machine
Annual output per machine	500 units	1,000 units
Capital cost per machine	0	$6,000
Operating cost per machine	$2 \times 500 = \$1,000$	$1 \times 1000 = \$1000$
PV total cost per machine	$1,000/0.10 = \$10,000$	$6,000 + 1000/0.10 = \$16,000$
PV total cost of both machines	$26,000	

Replacing one machine saves $4,000; replacing two machines saves only $3,000. The net present value of the *marginal* investment in the second machine is $-\$1,000$.

6-5   CHOOSING THE CAPITAL EXPENDITURE PROGRAM WHEN RESOURCES ARE LIMITED

The entire discussion of methods of capital budgeting rests on the proposition that the wealth of a firm's shareholders is highest if the firm accepts *every* project that has a positive net present value. Suppose, however, that there are limitations on the investment program that prevent the company from undertaking all such projects. If this is the case, we need a method of selecting the package of projects that is within the company's resources yet gives the highest possible net present value.

Profitability Index Under Capital Rationing

Let us start with a very simple example. Suppose that there is a 10% opportunity cost of capital, that our company has total resources of $10 million, and that it has the following opportunities:

Project	Cash Flows (millions of dollars)			NPV at 10% (millions of dollars)	Profitability Index
	C_0	C_1	C_2		
A	−10	+30	+5	21	3.1
B	−5	+5	+20	16	4.2
C	−5	+5	+15	12	3.4

The firm has sufficient resources to invest either in project A or in projects B and C. Although individually B and C have lower net present values than project A, when taken together they have the higher net present value. It is clear, therefore, that we cannot choose between projects solely on the basis of individual net present values. When funds are limited, we need to concentrate on getting the biggest bang for our buck. In other words, we much pick the projects that offer the highest ratio of present value to initial outlay. This ratio is simply the profitability index, or benefit-cost ratio, that we described in Chapter 5:

$$\text{Profitability index} = \frac{\text{present value}}{\text{investment}}$$

Of our three projects, B has the highest profitability index and C the next highest. Therefore, if our budget limit is $10 million, we should accept these two projects.

Unfortunately, there are some limitations to these simple ranking methods. One of the most serious is that they break down whenever more than one resource is rationed. For example, suppose that a $10 million budget limit applies to cash flows in *each* of years 0 and 1 and that our menu is expanded as follows:

Project	Cash Flows (millions of dollars)			NPV at 10% (millions of dollars)	Profitability Index
	C_0	C_1	C_2		
A	−10	+30	+5	21	3.1
B	−5	+5	+20	16	4.2
C	−5	+5	+15	12	3.4
D	0	−40	+60	13	1.4

One strategy is to accept projects B and C; however, if we do this, we cannot also accept D, which costs more than our budget limit for period 1. An alternative is to accept project A in period 0. Although this has a lower net present value than the combination of B and C, it provides a $30 million positive cash flow in period 1. With that added to the $10 million budget we can also afford to undertake D. A and D have *lower* profitability indexes than B and C, but they have a *higher* total net present value.

The reason that ranking on the profitability index fails in this example is that resources are constrained in each of two periods. In fact, this ranking method is inadequate whenever there is *any* other constraint on the choice of projects. This means that it cannot cope with cases in which two projects are mutually exclusive or in which one project is dependent on another.

*Some More Elaborate Capital Rationing Models

The simplicity of the profitability-index method may sometimes outweigh its limitations. For example, it may not pay to worry about expenditures in subsequent years if you have only a hazy notion of future capital availability or investment opportunities. But there are also circumstances in which the limitations of the profitability-index method are intolerable. For such occasions we need a more general method for solving the capital rationing problem.

We begin by restating the problem just described. Suppose that we were to accept proportion x_A of project A in our example. Then the net present value of our investment in the project would be $21x_A$. Similarly the net present value of our investment in project B can be expressed as $16x_B$, and so on. Our objective is to select the set of projects with the highest *total* net present value. In other words we wish to find the values of x that maximize

$$\text{NPV} = 21x_A + 16x_B + 12x_C + 13x_D$$

Our choice of projects is subject to several constraints. First, total cash outflow in period 0 must not be greater than \$10 million. In other words,

$$10x_A + 5x_B + 5x_C + 0x_D \leq 10$$

Similarly, total outflow in period 1 must not be greater than \$10 million.

$$-30x_A - 5x_B - 5x_C + 40x_D \leq 10$$

Finally, we cannot invest a negative amount in a project and we cannot purchase more than one of each. Therefore we have

$$0 \leq x_A \leq 1, 0 \leq x_B \leq 1, \ldots$$

Collecting all these conditions, we can summarize the problem as follows:

$$\text{Maximize } 21x_A + 16x_B + 12x_C + 13x_D$$

Subject to

$$10x_A + 5x_B + 5x_C + 0x_D \leq 10$$

$$-30x_A - 5x_B - 5x_C + 40x_D \leq 10$$

$$0 \leq x_A \leq 1, 0 \leq x_B \leq 1, \ldots$$

One way to tackle such a problem is to keep selecting different values for $x_A, \ldots, x_D$, noting which combination both satisfies the constraints and gives the highest net present value. But it's smarter to recognize that the equations above constitute a linear programming (LP) problem. It can be handed to a computer equipped to solve LPs.

The answer given by the LP method is somewhat different from the one we obtained earlier. Instead of investing in one unit of project A and one of project D, we are told to take half of project A, all of project B, and three-quarters of D. The reason is simple. The computer is a dumb, but obedient, pet, and since we did not tell it that $x_A, \ldots, x_D$ had to be whole numbers, it saw no reason to make them so. By accepting "fractional" projects, it is possible to increase NPV by \$2.25 million. For many purposes this is quite appropriate. If project A represents an investment in 1,000 square metres of warehouse space or in 1,000 tonnes of steel plate, it might be feasible to accept 500 square metres or 500 tonnes, and quite reasonable to assume that cash flow would be reduced proportionately. If, however, project A is a single crane or oil well, such fractional investments make little sense.

When fractional projects are not feasible, we can use a form of linear programming known as *integer* (or *zero-one*) programming, which limits the variables to being integers. Unfortunately, integer programs are less common and more awkward to use.

Uses of Capital Rationing Models

Linear programming models seem tailor-made for solving capital budgeting problems when resources are limited. Why then are they not universally accepted either in theory or in practice? One reason is that these models are often not cheap to use. We know of an oil company that spent more than $4 million in one year on an investment planning model using integer programming. While linear programming is considerably cheaper in terms of computer time, it cannot be used when large, indivisible projects are involved.

Second, as with any sophisticated long-range planning tool, there is the general problem of getting good data. It is just not worth applying costly, sophisticated methods to poor data. Furthermore, these models are based on the assumption that all future investment opportunities are known. In reality, the discovery of investment ideas is an unfolding process.

Our most serious misgivings centre on the basic assumption that capital is limited. When we come to discuss company financing, we shall see that most firms do not face capital rationing and can raise very large sums of money on fair terms. Why then do many company presidents tell their subordinates that capital is limited? If they are right, the capital market is seriously imperfect. What then are they doing maximizing NPV?[27] We might be tempted to suppose that if capital is not rationed, they do not need to use the LP model and, if it is rationed, then surely they *ought* not to use it. But that would be too quick a judgement. Let us look at this problem more deliberately.

Soft Rationing   Many firms' capital constraints are "soft." They reflect no imperfections in capital markets. Instead they are provisional limits adopted by management as an aid to financial control.

Some ambitious divisional managers habitually overstate their investment opportunities. Rather than trying to distinguish which projects really are worthwhile, headquarters may find it simpler to impose an upper limit on divisional expenditures and thereby force the divisions to set their own priorities. In such instances budget limits are a rough but effective way of dealing with biased cash-flow forecasts. In other cases management may believe that very rapid corporate growth could impose intolerable strains on management and the organization. Since it is difficult to quantify such constraints explicitly, the budget limit may be used as a proxy.

Because such budget limits have nothing to do with any inefficiency in the capital market, there is no contradiction in using an LP model in the division to maximize net present value subject to the budget constraint. On the other hand, there is not much point in elaborate selection procedures if the cash-flow forecasts of the division are seriously biased.

Even if capital is not rationed, other resources may be. The availability of management time, skilled labour, or even other capital equipment often constitutes an important constraint on a company's growth. In Appendix 6-2 we show you how the programming model we have described can be extended to incorporate such constraints. And we also show how they may be used to cope with project interactions.

---

[27] Don't forget that we had to assume perfect capital markets to derive the NPV rule.

Hard Rationing   Soft rationing should never cost the firm anything. If capital constraints become tight enough to hurt—in the sense that projects with significant positive NPVs are passed up—then the firm raises more money and loosens the constraint. But what if it *can't* raise more money—what if it faces *hard* rationing?

Hard rationing implies market imperfections, but that does not necessarily mean we have to throw away net present value as a criterion for capital budgeting. It depends on the nature of the imperfection.

Sunshine Coast Aquaculture (SCA) borrows as much as the banks will lend it, yet it still has good investment opportunities. This is not hard rationing as long as SCA can issue stock. But perhaps it can't. Perhaps the founder and majority shareholder vetoes the idea from fear of losing control of the firm, or perhaps a stock issue would bring costly red tape or legal complications.[28]

This does not invalidate the NPV rule. SCA's *shareholders* can borrow or lend, sell their shares, or buy more. They have free access to security markets. The type of portfolio they hold is independent of SCA's financing or investment decisions. The only way SCA can help its shareholders is to make them richer. Thus SCA should invest its available cash in the package of projects having the largest aggregate net present value.

A barrier between the firm and capital markets does not undermine net present value so long as the barrier is the *only* market imperfection. The important thing is that the firm's *shareholders* have free access to well-functioning capital markets.

The method of net present value *is* undermined when imperfections restrict shareholders' portfolio choice. Suppose that Beachcomber Aquaculture, Inc. (BAI) is solely owned by its founder, Alexander Turbot. Mr. Turbot has no cash or credit remaining, but he is convinced that expansion of his operation is a high-NPV investment. He has tried to sell stock but has found that prospective investors, skeptical of prospects for fish farming in the desert, offer him much less than he thinks his firm is worth. For Mr. Turbot capital markets hardly exist. It makes little sense for him to discount the prospective cash flows at a market opportunity cost of capital.

6-6   SUMMARY

By now, present value calculations should be a matter of routine. However, forecasting cash flows will never be routine. It will always be a skilled, hazardous occupation. Mistakes can be minimized by following three rules.

1. Concentrate on cash flows after taxes. Be wary of accounting data masquerading as cash-flow data.
2. Always judge investments on an incremental basis. Tirelessly track down all cash-flow consequences of your decision.
3. Treat inflation consistently. Discount nominal cash-flow forecasts at nominal rates and real forecasts at real rates.

We might add a fourth rule: recognize project interactions. Decisions involving only a choice of accepting or rejecting a project rarely exist, since capital projects can rarely be isolated from other projects or alternatives. The simplest decision normally encountered is accept or reject or delay. A project having a positive NPV if undertaken today may have a still higher NPV if undertaken tomorrow.

Another kind of project interaction stems from *capital rationing*. If capital is strictly limited, then acceptance of project A may preclude acceptance

---

[28] A majority owner who is "locked in" and has much personal wealth tied up in SCA may be effectively cut off from capital markets. The NPV rule may not make sense to such an owner, though it will to the other shareholders.

of B. If capital is limited in only one period, the objective of the firm shifts from maximizing NPV to maximizing NPV *per dollar of capital*. Projects can be ranked by their profitability index, and top-ranked projects chosen until funds are exhausted. This procedure fails when capital is rationed in more than one period or when there are other constraints on project choice. The only general solution is linear or integer programming.

"Hard" capital rationing always reflects a market imperfection—a barrier between the firm and capital markets. If that barrier also implies that the firm's shareholders lack free access to a well-functioning capital market, the very foundations of net present value crumble. Fortunately, hard rationing is rare for corporations in the United States and Canada. Many firms do use "soft" capital rationing, however. That is, they set up self-imposed limits as a means of financial planning and control.

This chapter is concerned with the mechanics of applying the net present value rule in practical situations. All our analysis boils down to two simple themes. First, be careful about the definition of alternative projects. Make sure you are comparing like with like. Second, make sure that your calculations include all incremental cash flows.

FURTHER READING

Canadian income tax law is consolidated in:

H.H. Stikeman, *Income Tax Act: Annotated*, 20th ed., Richard DeBoo, Don Mills, 1990.

A more readable but less comprehensive source of tax information is:

Canadian Master Tax Guide, 46th ed., CCH Canadian Limited, Don Mills, 1991.

The tax act and extensive editorial comment is provided in ten volumes, updated on a weekly subscription basis:

Canadian Tax Reporter, CCH Canadian Limited, Don Mills, 1991.

There are several good general texts on capital budgeting that cover project interactions. Two examples are:

H. Bierman and S. Smidt, *The Capital Budgeting Decision*, 7th ed., The Macmillan Company, New York, 1988.

E.L. Grant, W.G. Ireson, and R.S. Leavenworth, *Principles of Engineering Economy*, 7th ed., Ronald Press, New York, 1982.

Terborgh treats decisions involving machine replacement in detail.

G.W. Terborgh, *Business Investment Management*, Machinery and Allied Products Institute and Council for Technological Advancement, 1967.

The classic treatment of linear programming applied to capital budgeting is:

H.M. Weingartner, *Mathematical Programming and the Analysis of Capital Budgeting Problems*, Prentice-Hall, Inc., Englewood Cliffs, N.J., 1963.

There is a long scholarly controversy on whether capital constraints invalidate the NPV rule. Weingartner has reviewed this literature.

H.M. Weingartner, "Capital Rationing: *n* Authors in Search of a Plot," *Journal of Finance*, **32**: 1403–1432 (December, 1977).

Reinhardt provides an interesting case study of a capital investment decision in:

U.E. Reinhardt, "Break-Even Analysis for Lockheed's TriStar: An Application of Financial Theory," *Journal of Finance*, **32**: 821–838 (September 1973).

APPENDIX 6-1   CORPORATE INCOME TAXES IN CANADA

In this appendix we will discuss some more complicated issues in Canadian tax law, particularly as they relate to capital budgeting.

Corporate Tax Rates

The basic Canadian corporate tax rate is 38%, although this is reduced for manufacturing and processing (M&P) business and for small business. Starting in 1991, the M&P tax rate will be 33%, a result of a phased-in reduction from 36% in 1988. The *small business deduction* reduces the rate on first $200,000 of taxable income for all businesses to 22%.

The federal government allows a further 10% deduction from corporate taxes to allow for provincial taxes. The provinces often used the federal definition of taxable income, but they each charge taxes at their own rates. In 1988, provincial tax rates for general business varied from 13% to 17%, the rates for M&P business varied from 5.9% to 14.5% and the rates for small business varied from 0% to 10%.

From time to time, the federal government also imposes a surtax or allows an abatement to help implement short-term fiscal policy. Starting in 1987, the surtax was 3% of federal tax paid. Some overall tax rates are illustrated in Table 6-5.

Table 6-5
Calculation of 1988 Corporate Tax Rates for a Manufacturing and Processing Business

| | British Columbia | | Québec | |
	Small Business	Ordinary Business	Small Business	Ordinary Business
Federal tax	22%	36%	22%	36%
Less: provincial tax credit	10%	10%	10%	10%
	12%	26%	12%	26%
Plus surtax (3% of federal tax)	0.36%	0.78%	0.36%	0.78%
	12.36%	26.78%	12.36%	26.78%
Plus provincial tax	9%	14%	3.22%	5.90%
Net income tax rate	21.36%	40.78%	15.58%	32.68%

Loss Carry-forward and Carry-back

Recall that capital losses can only occur on the sale of non-depreciable assets, like land or securities. However, capital gains can occur on the sale of depreciable and non-depreciable assets. Taxpayers are allowed to:

1. deduct capital losses from capital gains in the same year;
2. **carry-back** capital losses for up to three years to be applied against previous capital gains; and
3. **carry-forward** capital losses against any future capital gains.

Ordinary losses (that is, non-capital losses) may be carried back up to three years or carried forward up to seven years, to be applied against taxable income.

Clearly you should carry losses back before you carry them forward, because you can benefit from their tax shields as they occur. However, the government only rebates excess taxes paid under a carry-back. It does not pay any interest on these taxes.

*The "Half-Year Rule" for Capital Cost Allowance and the Timing of Tax Payments

We made two simplifying assumptions in our analysis of CCA tax shields in Section 6-2. Fortunately, the formula we gave there for the PV of CCA tax shields is quite accurate because the two simplifications generally create errors that offset each other. The first simplification was to ignore a feature of tax law called the "half-year rule." This rule requires that, when depreciable assets are purchased, only half of the value of asset purchases (net of dispositions) are added to the asset class balance. The other half is added to the asset class balance in the next year. The second issue we have simplified is the relative timing of asset purchase and the receipt of the tax benefit from the CCA. Now we want to discuss these issues more carefully because they often lead to some confusion.

Let's use the same notation as in Section 6-2:

C = capital cost of an asset (year 0)
S = salvage value of asset (year n)
d = CCA depreciation rate
T_c = corporate tax rate
r = discount rate
UCC_t = undepreciated capital cost after deducting CCA tax shield for year t

The incremental effect of purchasing the asset is to start depreciating half of it in year 0 and the other half in year 1, as follows:

Year	0	1	2	...	t	...
CCA on first half of asset	$Cd/2$	$Cd(1-d)/2$	$Cd(1-d)^2/2$	...	$Cd(1-d)^t/2$	...
CCA on second half of asset	0	$Cd/2$	$Cd(1-d)/2$	...	$Cd(1-d)^{t-1}/2$	...

We can multiply by T_c and discount these tax shields to get:[29]
PV of perpetual CCA tax shields

$$= \frac{1}{2}\left(CdT_c + \frac{CdT_c(1-d)}{1+r} + \frac{CdT_c(1-d)^2}{(1+r)^2} + \cdots\right)$$

$$+ \frac{1}{2}\left(\frac{CdT_c}{1+r} + \frac{CdT_c(1-d)}{(1+r)^2} + \cdots\right)$$

$$= \frac{1}{2}\frac{CdT_c}{r+d}(1+r) + \frac{1}{2}\frac{CdT_c}{r+d}$$

$$= \frac{CdT_c}{r+d}(1+r/2)$$

Compared to the formula in Section 6-2, this formula gives a PV of a perpetual CCA tax shield that is larger by a half-year of interest.[30] Clearly this is not a significant difference in many situations, but it could be important in evaluating

---

[29] To see this, you could grind out the sums of geometric series, as in Section 3-2, or simply note that the formula in Section 6-2 gives the PV of the tax shields (if they start in year 1) as $CdT_c/(r+d)$. If the tax shields start in year 0, there is one less year of discounting, so they would have a PV of $(1+r)CdT_c/(r+d)$.

[30] Some textbooks suggest that the PV of a perpetual CCA tax shield under the half-year rule is $\frac{CdT_c}{r+d}\left(\frac{1+r/2}{1+r}\right)$ because the tax shields on half of the asset start in year 1 and the tax shields on the other half don't start until year 2. This is analogous to taking tax shields in year 2 for cash expenses that occur in year 1, although these texts generally do not split the timing of

projects (like leases) where competitive market forces drive the NPV of the project close to zero.

Now suppose the asset is in a class that has many other assets and a substantial UCC. We'll also assume that in the salvage year n other assets are added to the same class (for example, a replacement asset) with a cost greater than S. Since the half-year rule works on acquisitions *net* of dispositions, the *incremental* effect of selling the asset for S in year n is to deduct $S/2$ from the UCC of the class in each of years n and $n + 1$. Thus we have:

PV of incremental CCA tax shields

$$= \frac{CdT_c}{r + d}\left(1 + \frac{r}{2}\right) - \frac{1}{(1 + r)^n}\frac{SdT_c}{r + d}\left(1 + \frac{r}{2}\right)$$

On the other hand, suppose the asset is always in a class by itself. Then

$$\text{UCC}_t = \frac{C}{2}((1 - d)^{t + 1} + (1 - d)^t) = C(1 - d)^t\left(1 - \frac{d}{2}\right)$$

A little algebra shows that the recapture and terminal loss cases can be combined to give:

PV of CCA tax shield and tax effect of recaptured depreciation or terminal loss

$$= \frac{CdT_c}{r + d}\left(1 + \frac{r}{2}\right) - \frac{1}{(1 + r)^n}\text{UCC}_n\frac{dT_c}{r + d} + \frac{T_c}{(1 + r)^n}(\text{UCC}_n - S)$$

This analysis assumes the owner gets the CCA tax shield for year n. But the tax shield is lost immediately because of the recapture. Thus we could get the same results by re-working the formulas for lost PV of CCA and UCC to reflect the assumption that no CCA tax shield is taken in year n.

*Project Interactions Arising From Recaptured Depreciation

Since Canadian tax law often groups the assets of many projects together in a single class, interactions can arise amongst projects regarding recaptured depreciation and terminal losses. For example, if you are about to face recaptured depreciation from the disposal of assets of an existing project, any project requiring new assets in the same class will effectively get a "fast write-off" of the new assets. On the other hand, if the existing project is about to get a terminal loss benefit, acquiring other assets in the same class will generate an onerous tax liability that should be avoided. Let's look at two examples of this. In both cases, we are evaluating a project that entails:

$$C = \$100{,}000 \text{ of assets}$$
$$d = 0.1 \text{ (Class 6)}$$
$$T_c = 0.4$$
$$r = 0.15$$
$$S = \$20{,}000, \text{ salvage in year 6}$$

We'll ignore the half-year rule, and use the simple formulas of Section 6-2.

---

expenses and their tax shields in this way. Even though there can be complicated schemes of tax-instalment payments under various circumstances, taking expenses and their tax shields in the same year gives the most accurate PV calculations. Thus, it is best to treat the CCA tax shields as starting in year 0, as we do here. See G.A. Sick and G.A. Mumey, "The Timing of Cash Flows and Related Taxes," *Administrative Sciences Association of Canada, Finance Proceedings,* **11**: 151–158 (1990), and a related note with the same title and authors: "The Timing of Cash Flows and Related Taxes," *Financial Management,* **19**, No. 4: 14–15 (December 1990).

EXAMPLE 1   Suppose your firm is planning to liquidate some assets in year 0, generating recaptured depreciation of $150,000. By accepting the new project and putting $100,000 back into Class 6 before the end of the tax year, your firm can avoid immediate recapture of $100,000. In effect, all of the incremental CCA tax shield will be realized in year 0, as though there were a one-year tax write-off for the project. However, Class 6 will have a UCC of $0 for years 1 to 5 and the salvage in year 6 will generate a recapture. The overall effect is:

$$\begin{aligned} &\text{PV of incremental CCA tax shield and recapture} \\ &= T_c \times \text{recapture avoided in year 0} \\ &\quad - \text{PV of } T_c \times \text{recapture in year 6} \\ &= 0.4 \times 100,000 - \frac{0.4}{(1.15)^6} \times 20,000 \\ &= \$36,541 \end{aligned}$$

EXAMPLE 2   Suppose your firm is planning to liquidate all of its Class 6 assets in year 0, generating a terminal loss of $130,000. If you add the new assets to Class 6 before the tax year-end, you cannot close out the asset class and hence you will be ineligible for the terminal loss. Instead, the UCC of Class 6 will rise to $230,000 (the original $130,000 plus the new $100,000). Salvage of the asset in year 6 will generate a terminal loss based on a UCC of $230,000 \times (1 - 0.1)^6 = \$122,231$. In effect, the terminal loss on the old assets is deferred from year 0 to year 6, so we have

$$\begin{aligned} &\text{PV of deferred terminal loss and incremental CCA tax shields} \\ &= -0.4 \times 130,000 + \frac{230,000 \times 0.1 \times 0.4}{0.15 + 0.1} - \frac{1}{(1.15)^6} \frac{122,231 \times 0.1 \times 0.4}{0.15 + 0.1} \\ &\quad + \frac{1}{(1.15)^6} \times 0.4 \times (122,231 - 20,000) = -\$5,976 \end{aligned}$$

Note that this is actually negative. You should try to avoid this situation by incorporating the project as a separate firm for tax purposes, by delaying the purchase of the asset until year 1, or by leasing the asset.

APPENDIX 6-2   SOME EMBELLISHMENTS TO THE CAPITAL RATIONING MODEL

In Section 6-5 we showed that when capital is rationed you can set up the investment decision as a linear programming problem. In this appendix we describe some embellishments to these models, and we show how you can use them to cope with other resource constraints and project interactions.

Cash Carry-forward   A plant manager who is forced to return the unspent part of an annual capital allocation may be goaded into a substantial year-end investment in pink carpeting for the foundry floor or other equally silly assets. (How can you argue for a high budget next year if there's money left over this year?) Headquarters can alleviate this problem by permitting the manager to carry forward any unspent balance. (Then the manager could at least wait until January and get a better selection of carpet colours.) Let us take the sample problem that we described in Section 6-5. To incorporate the possibility of cash carry-forward, we simply need to add another term to our spending constraint. Let s denote funds transferred from year 0 to year 1 and let them earn interest at the rate of r. Then we can rewrite our constraint for year zero as

$$10x_A + 5x_B + 5x_C + 0x_D + s = 10$$

Similarly, the constraint for year 1 becomes

$$-30x_A - 5x_B - 5x_C + 40x_D \leq 10 + (1 + r)s$$

Since carrying forward a negative amount is equivalent to borrowing, we will probably wish to add the constraint $s \geq 0$.

Mutually Exclusive Projects   Suppose now that projects B and C are mutually exclusive. We can take care of this in an *integer* program by specifying that our *total* investment in the two projects cannot be greater than one.

$$x_B + x_C \leq 1, x_B, x_C = 0 \text{ or } 1$$

In other words, if x_B is 1, x_C must be 0; if x_C is 1, x_B must be 0.

Contingent Projects   Suppose next that project D is an attachment to project A, and we cannot accept D *unless* we also accept A. In this case we need to add

$$x_D - x_A \leq 0; x_D, x_A = 0 \text{ or } 1$$

In other words, if x_A is 1, x_D can be 0 or 1; but if x_A is 0, x_D must likewise be 0.

Constraints on Nonfinancial Resources   Money may not be the only scarce resource. Each of our projects may require services from a 12-person technical design department. If project A would employ three designers, project B two, and so on, we would need to add a constraint like

$$3x_A + 2x_B + 8x_C + 3x_D \leq 12$$

Constraints on Nonfinancial Output   Sometimes it is appropriate to place constraints on the total increase in physical capacity. Suppose that projects A and C produce four and three units, respectively, of the same product. If the company is unable to sell more than five units, it is necessary to add

$$4x_A + 3x_C \leq 5$$

We could go on—but you get the idea.

QUIZ

1. Which of the following should be treated as incremental cash flows when deciding whether to invest in a new manufacturing plant? The site is already owned by the company, but existing buildings would need to be demolished.
    (a) The market value of the site and existing buildings
    (b) Demolition costs and site clearance
    (c) The cost of a new access road put in last year
    (d) Lost earnings on other products due to executive time spent on the new facility

(e) A proportion of the cost of leasing the president's jet airplane

(f) Future depreciation of the new plant

(g) The reduction in the corporation's tax bill resulting from the investment tax credit

(h) The initial investment in inventories of raw materials

(i) Money already spent on engineering design of the new plant

2. M. Loup Garou will be paid 100,000 French francs one year hence. This is a nominal flow, which he discounts at a 15% nominal discount rate:

$$PV = \frac{100,000}{1.15} = 86,957 \text{ francs}$$

The inflation rate is 10%.

Calculate the present value of M. Garou's payment using the equivalent *real* cash flow and *real* discount rate. (You should get exactly the same answer as he did.)

3. Machines A and B are mutually exclusive and are expected to produce the following cash flows:

	Cash Flows (thousands of dollars)			
Machine	C_0	C_1	C_2	C_3
A	−100	+110	+121	−
B	−120	+110	+121	+133

The opportunity cost of capital is 10%.

(a) Calculate the NPV of each machine.

(b) Use present value tables to calculate the equivalent annual cash flow from each machine.

(c) Which machine should you buy?

4. Machine C was purchased five years ago for $200,000 and produces an annual cash flow of $80,000. It has no salvage value but is expected to last another five years. The company can replace machine C with machine B (see question 3, above) *either* now *or* at the end of five years. Which should it do?

5. Suppose you have the following investment opportunities, but only $100,000 available for investment. Which projects should you take?

Project	NPV	Investment
1	5,000	10,000
2	5,000	5,000
3	10,000	90,000
4	15,000	60,000
5	15,000	75,000
6	3,000	15,000

6. What is the difference between "hard" and "soft" capital rationing? Does soft rationing mean the manager should stop trying to maximize NPV? How about hard rationing?

7. You are considering whether to undertake a project that will generate revenues of $50,000 a year and expenses of $20,000 a year for eight years. To undertake the project you must invest $150,000 in machinery in Class 8 (20%). The corporate tax rate is 40% and your discount rate for the project is

12%. Calculate the NPV of the project under each of the following scenarios:

(a) You always have other assets and a positive UCC in Class 8, and you can salvage the machinery in nine years for:
   (i) $20,000
   (ii) $200,000

(b) The machine will always be in its own asset class and you can salvage the machinery in nine years for:
   (i) $20,000
   (ii) $30,000
   (iii) $200,000

(c) The machinery can be lumped in with other Class 8 assets, on which you are about to immediately realize recaptured depreciation of $100,000, and you can salvage the new machinery in nine years for $20,000. You do not plan any other purchases or sales of Class 8 assets for the next nine years.

8. You are planning to purchase a low-rise apartment building in Class 1 (4%) for $250,000 (net of the cost of land). Under Canadian tax law, this building must be in its own asset class, so you may have recaptured depreciation when you sell it. Indeed, you expect to sell the building in six years for $220,000, even though the UCC, after five years of CCA, would then be only $203,843. A friend has pointed out that the 10% CCA rate for Class 32 is only a *maximum* CCA rate, and you may take CCA at a lower rate if you wish. He recommends that you avoid recapture by taking CCA at a reduced rate so that the UCC in six years is exactly $220,000. What do you think?

9. A project requires an investment of $10,000 in Class 8 (20%) production equipment. It will generate real pretax revenues of $3,000 per year for five years. You can liquidate the equipment in year 6. Currently, six-year-old production equipment of that type sells for $1,500. You feel that both of these figures are likely to keep pace with inflation. Your tax rate is 36%, you expect an inflation rate of 5% over the next six years, and the real opportunity cost of capital is 3%. Round off the nominal rate of interest so you can read PV factors from the Appendix tables.

(a) You always have assets and a positive balance in the production equipment class. What is the NPV of the project?

(b) The production equipment is in a class by itself, resulting in recapture or terminal loss when it is liquidated. What is the NPV of the project?

QUESTIONS AND PROBLEMS

1. When appraising mutually exclusive projects, many companies calculate the projects' equivalent annual costs and rank the projects on this basis. Why is this necessary? Why not just compare the projects' NPVs?

2. Calculate the NPV of some personal investment decision, such as buying a washing machine instead of using the laundromat, insulating the attic, or replacing the car. Ignore the extra convenience of the new asset. Just focus on the cash costs and benefits.

3. Discuss the following statement: "We don't want individual plant managers to get involved in the firm's tax position. So instead of telling them to discount after-tax cash flows at 10%, we just tell them to take the pretax cash flows and discount at 15%. With a 36% tax rate, 15% pretax generates approximately 10% after tax."

4. Discuss the following statement: "We like to do all our capital budgeting calculations in real terms. It saves making any forecasts of the inflation rate."

5. A project requires use of spare computer capacity. If the project is not terminated, the company will need to buy an additional disk at the end of year 2. If it is terminated, the disk will not be required until the end of year 4. If disks cost $10,000 and become filled with data every five years, and if the opportunity cost of capital is 10%, what is the present value of the cost of this extra usage if the project is terminated at the end of year 2? What if the project continues indefinitely?

6. Mrs. T. Potts, the treasurer of Ideal China, has a problem. The company has just ordered a new kiln for $400,000. Of this sum, $50,000 is described by the supplier as "installation cost." Mrs. Potts does not know whether Revenue Canada will permit the company to treat this cost as a current expense or as a capital investment. In the latter case, the company could claim a 15% investment tax credit on the $50,000 and put it in Class 8 (20%). If the tax rate is 36% and the opportunity cost of capital is 5%, what is the present value of the tax shield in either case?

7. You own 500 hectares of timberland, with young timber worth $40,000 if logged now. This represents 1,000 cords of wood worth $40 per cord net of costs of cutting and hauling. A paper company has offered to purchase your tract for $140,000. Should you accept the offer? You have the following information:

    (a)

Years	Yearly Growth Rate of Cords Per Hectare
1–4	16%
5–8	11
9–13	4
14 and subsequent years	1

    (b) You expect price per cord to increase at 4% per year indefinitely.
    (c) The cost of capital is 9%. Ignore taxes.
    (d) The market value of your land would be $100 per hectare if you cut and removed the timber this year. The value of cut-over land is also expected to grow at 4% per year indefinitely.

8. The Borstal Company has to choose between two machines that do the same job but have different lives. The two machines have the following costs:

Year	Machine A	Machine B
0	$40,000	$50,000
1	10,000	8,000
2	10,000	8,000
3	10,000 + replace	8,000
4		8,000 + replace

These costs are expressed in real terms.

(a) Suppose you are Borstal's financial manager. If you had to buy one or the other machine, and rent it to the production manager for that machine's economic life, what annual rental payment would you have to charge? Assume a 6% real discount rate and ignore taxes.

(b) Which machine should Borstal buy?

(c) Usually the rental payments you derived in part (a) are just hypothetical—a way of calculating and interpreting equivalent annual cost. Suppose you actually do buy one of the machines and rent it to the production manager. How much would you actually have to charge in each future year if there is steady 8% per year inflation? (*Note:* The rental payments calculated in part (a) are real cash flows. You would have to mark those payments up to cover inflation.)

9. What biases or errors might be introduced by using nominal cash flows and discount rates to calculate equivalent annual costs? Think of situations like that described in problem 8 above.

10. Borghia Pharmaceuticals has $1 million allocated for capital expenditures. Which of the following projects should the company accept to stay within the $1 million budget? How much does the budget limit cost the company in terms of its market value? The opportunity cost of capital for each project is 11%.

Project	Investment (thousands of dollars)	NPV (thousands of dollars)	IRR, %
1	300	66	17.2
2	200	−4	10.7
3	250	43	16.6
4	100	14	12.1
5	100	7	11.8
6	350	63	18.0
7	400	48	13.5

11. The *Financial Analysts Journal* currently offers the following subscription options: one year, $48; two years, $84; three years, $108. These rates are expected to increase at the general rate of inflation. What is your optimal strategy, assuming you intend to be a permanent subscriber? Make other assumptions as appropriate.

12. The president's executive jet is not fully utilized. You judge that its use by other officers would increase direct operating costs by only $20,000 a year and would save $100,000 a year in airline bills. On the other hand, you believe that with the increased use the company will need to buy another jet at the end of three years rather than four. A new jet costs $1.1 million. The corporate fleet is generally expanded by one jet every six years. Assume that the company does not pay taxes and that the opportunity cost of capital is 12%. Should you try to persuade the president to allow other officers to use the plane?

13. A project requires an initial investment of $100,000 and is expected to produce a cash inflow before tax of $26,000 per year for five years. Company A has substantial accumulated tax losses and is unlikely to pay taxes in the foreseeable future. Company B pays corporate taxes at a rate of 36% and can depreciate the investment for tax purposes in Class 8 (20%), which

has many other assets and a substantial UCC. The asset will have no salvage value after five years.

Suppose the opportunity cost of capital is 8%.

(a) Calculate project NPV for each company.

(b) What is the IRR of the after-tax cash flows for each company? What does comparison of the IRRs suggest is the effective corporate tax rate?

14. A widget manufacturer currently produces 200,000 units a year. It buys widget lids from an outside supplier at a price of $2 a lid. The plant manager believes that it would be cheaper to make these lids rather than buy them. Direct production costs are estimated to be only $1.50 a lid. The necessary machinery would cost $150,000. This investment would be placed in Class 10 (30%). The plant manager estimates that the operation would require additional working capital of $30,000 but argues that this sum can be ignored since it is recoverable at the end of the ten years. If the company pays tax at a rate of 36%, and the opportunity cost of capital is 15%, would you support the plant manager's proposal? State clearly any additional assumptions that you need to make.

15. Reliable Electric is considering a proposal to manufacture a new type of industrial electric motor, which would replace most of its existing product line. A research breakthrough has given Reliable a two-year lead on its competitors. The project proposal is summarized in Table 6-6.

(a) Read the notes to the table carefully. Which entries make sense? Which do not? Why or why not?

(b) What additional information would you need to construct a version of Table 6-6 that makes sense?

(c) Construct such a table and recalculate NPV. Make additional assumptions as necessary.

16. Suppose the IM&C guano project will be incorporated as a separate firm for income tax purposes, and the capital assets are eligible for a 15% investment tax credit. How does this change its NPV?

17. Your firm is planning to produce and sell a new type of widget, called a "midget" (a male widget). You already have a building on some land, but would require $5 million of Class 8 (20%) machinery. You paid $200,000 for the land five years ago and the building is in a class by itself—Class 1 (4%)—with an undepreciated capital cost of $150,000. Right now the land could be sold for $300,000 and the building for $100,000, but in 11 years they could be sold for $500,000 and $100,000 respectively. You can sell $2 million worth of midgets per year for ten years, with annual production costs of $1 million. The machinery can be salvaged in 11 years for $1.2 million. You always have many assets in Class 8, with a large UCC. There is no investment tax credit for this project. Your corporate tax rate is 36% and your opportunity cost of capital is 10%. What is the NPV of the project?

18. Recalculate your answer to problem 17 by assuming that the 10% nominal opportunity cost of capital consists of a real 6% return and expected inflation of 4%. The salvage values for land, buildings, and machinery are real.

Table 6-6
**Cash Flows and Present Value of Reliable Electric's Proposed Investment
(see problem 15) (annual cash flows in thousands of dollars)**

	1990	1991	1992	1993–2000
1. Capital expenditure	− 10,400			
2. Research and development	− 2,000			
3. Working capital	− 4,000			
4. Revenue		8,000	16,000	40,000
5. Operating costs		− 4,000	− 8,000	− 20,000
6. Overhead		− 800	− 1,600	− 4,000
7. Depreciation		− 1,040	− 1,040	− 1,040
8. Interest		− 2,160	− 2,160	− 2,160
9. Income	− 2,000	0	3,200	12,800
10. Tax	0	0	432	4,608
11. Net cash flow	− 16,400	0	2,768	8,192

Net present value = + 13,489

Notes:

1. *Capital expenditure*: $8 million for new machinery and $2.4 million for a warehouse extension. The full cost of the extension has been charged to this project, although only about half of the space is currently needed. Since the new machinery will be housed in an existing factory building, no charge has been made for land and building.

2. *Research and development*: $1.82 million spent in 1989. This figure was corrected for 10% inflation from the time of expenditure to date. Thus 1.82 × 1.1 = $2 million.

3. *Working capital*: Initial investment in inventories.

4. *Revenue*: These figures assume sales of 2,000 motors in 1991, 4,000 in 1992, and 10,000 per year from 1993 through 2000. The initial unit price of $4,000 is forecasted to remain constant in real terms.

5. *Operating costs*: These include all direct and indirect costs. Indirect costs (heat, light, power, fringe benefits, and so on) are assumed to be 200% of direct labour costs. Operating costs per unit are forecasted to remain constant in real terms at $2,000.

6. *Overhead*: Marketing and administrative costs, assumed equal to 10% of revenue.

7. *Depreciation*: Straight-line for ten years.

8. *Interest*: Charged on capital expenditure and working capital at Reliable's current borrowing rate of 15%.

9. *Income*: Revenue less the sum of research and development, operating costs, overhead, depreciation, and interest.

10. *Tax*: 36% of income. However, income is negative in 1990. This loss is carried forward and deducted from taxable income in 1992.

11. *Net cash flow*: Assumed equal to income less tax.

12. *Net present value*: NPV of net cash flow at a 15% discount rate.

P · A · R · T

2

RISK

C · H · A · P · T · E · R

7

INTRODUCTION TO RISK, RETURN, AND THE OPPORTUNITY COST OF CAPITAL

We have managed six chapters without directly addressing the problem of risk, but now the jig is up. We can no longer be satisfied with vague statements like: "The opportunity cost of capital depends on the risk of the project." We need to know how risk is defined, what the links are between risk and the opportunity cost of capital, and how the financial manager can cope with risk in practical situations.

In this chapter we will concentrate on the first of these issues and leave the other two to Chapters 8 and 9. We start by summarizing more than 60 years of evidence on rates of return in capital markets. We will then take a first look at investment risks and show how they can be reduced by portfolio diversification. We will introduce you to **beta**, the standard risk measure for individual securities.

The themes of this chapter, then, are portfolio risk, security risk, and diversification. For the most part we will take the view of the individual investor. But at the end of the chapter we will turn the problem around and ask whether diversification makes sense as a *corporate* objective.

7-1 SIXTY-THREE YEARS OF CAPITAL MARKET HISTORY IN ONE EASY LESSON

Studies by Ibbotson Associates and the Canadian Institute of Actuaries

Financial analysts are blessed with an enormous quantity of data on American security prices and returns and a somewhat less bountiful quantity of data on Canadian security prices and returns. For example, University of Chicago's Center for Research in Security Prices (CRSP) has developed a file of prices and dividends for each month since 1926 for every stock that has been listed on the New York Stock Exchange (NYSE). Other American files give data for stocks that are traded on the American Stock Exchange and the over-the-counter market: data for bonds, for options, and so on. The Toronto Stock Exchange and the University of Western Ontario maintain a file of Toronto Stock Exchange (TSE) stocks starting in 1950, and Université Laval has a file of monthly returns on TSE stocks starting in 1963. There are also other files of Canadian security returns.

But this is supposed to be one easy lesson. We will, therefore, concentrate on an American study by Ibbotson Associates and a Canadian study by Boyle, Panjer, and Sharp.[1] These studies measure, among other things, the historical performance of four American and four Canadian portfolios of securities:

1. A portfolio of Treasury bills — United States or Canadian government securities maturing in less than one year.[2]
2. A portfolio of long-term government bonds.
3. A portfolio of long-term corporate bonds.[3]
4. A stock market index — the Standard and Poor's Composite Index (S&P) in the United States and the Toronto Stock Exchange Composite Index (TSE) in Canada. These are portfolios of 500 and 300 common stocks, respectively.[4]

These portfolios offer different degrees of risk. Treasury bills are about as safe an investment as you can get. There is no risk of default and their short maturity means that the prices of Treasury bills are relatively stable. In fact, an investor who wishes to lend money for, say, six months can achieve a perfectly certain payoff by purchasing a Treasury bill maturing in six months. However, the investor cannot lock in a *real* rate of return: there is still uncertainty about inflation.

By switching to long-term government bonds, the investor acquires an asset whose price fluctuates as interest rates vary. (Bond prices fall when interest rates rise, and rise when interest rates fall.) An investor who switches from government to corporate bonds accepts an additional *default* risk. An investor who shifts from corporate bonds to common stocks has a direct share in the risks of the enterprise.

These studies have calculated a rate of return for each of their portfolios for each year from 1926 to 1988. This rate of return reflects both cash receipts — dividends or interest — and the capital gain or loss realized during the year. Averages of the annual rates of return for each portfolio are shown in Table 7-1.[5]

---

[1] The studies are: *Stocks, Bonds, Bills and Inflation: 1989 Yearbook*, Ibbotson Associates, Chicago, 1989, and P.P. Boyle, H.H. Panjer, and K.P. Sharp, "Report on Canadian Economic Statistics 1924–1988," Canadian Institute of Actuaries, Ottawa, 1989.

[2] Canada did not have Treasury bills prior to 1933, and Boyle, Panjer, and Sharp use only Treasury bill data that start at 1946. Thus, to get a series for the whole period, we used the Ibbotson Associates Treasury bill for 1926-1933 and annual averages of three-month Canadian Treasury bill monthly auction rates, compounded annually for 1934-1945. The monthly Canadian treasury bill data are from the Statistics Canada CANSIM series B14007. CANSIM is a registered mark of Statistics Canada.

[3] The two bond portfolios were revised in each year to maintain a constant maturity.

[4] Actually, data for the TSE 300 Index in Canada are only available for periods starting in 1956, so the TSE Industrial Index was used for 1935-1956, and an index by Urquhart and Buckley for 1925-1934. (See Urquhart, M.C. and Buckley, K.A.H., *Historical Statistics of Canada*, Macmillan Company, Toronto, 1965.) Naturally, this raises questions as to whether these three indices are really comparable in terms of risk. Of course, the structure of the S & P Index has changed over time, as well.

[5] These are arithmetic averages. They are obtained by simply adding up the annual returns and dividing by the number of years. The arithmetic average return is higher than the compound annual return over the period. For example, suppose the market doubles in value one year and halves the next. Since you are back where you started, the compound annual return is zero. But the arithmetic average return is $(+100 - 50)/2 = +25\%$. When estimating discount rates, you are interested in the arithmetic average return.

Table 7-1
Average rates of return on Treasury bills, government bonds, corporate bonds, and common stocks, 1926–1988 (figures in percent per year). (Canadian corporate bond data are for 1949–1988.)

Portfolio	Average Annual Rate of Return (Nominal)		Average Annual Rate of Return (Real)		Average Risk Premium (Extra Return versus Treasury Bills)	
	Canada	United States	Canada	United States	Canada	United States
Treasury bills	4.4	3.6	1.1	0.5	0.0	0.0
Government bonds	5.2	4.7	2.0	1.7	0.8	1.1
Corporate bonds	6.5	5.3	1.9	2.4	0.3	1.7
Common stocks	11.9	12.1	8.3	8.8	7.4	8.4

Sources: American results are calculated from data in *Stocks, Bonds, Bills and Inflation: 1989 Yearbook*, Ibbotson Associates, Chicago, 1989. Canadian results are from data provided in P.P. Boyle, H.H. Panjer, and K.P. Sharp, "Report on Canadian Economic Statistics 1924–1988," Canadian Institute of Actuaries, Ottawa, 1989, Footnotes 2, 4, and 5 discuss details of the calculations.

You can see that these returns coincide with our intuitive risk ranking. The safest Canadian investment, Treasury bills, also gave the lowest rate of return—4.4% a year in *nominal* terms and 1.1% in *real* terms.

In other words, the average rate of inflation over this period was about 3½% per year. Long-term Canadian government bonds ("long Canadas") gave a slightly higher nominal return than Treasury bills, and corporate bonds gave still higher returns. Common stocks were in a class by themselves. Investors who accepted the extra risk of common stocks received on average a premium of 7.4% a year (8.5% in the United States) more than Treasury bills.

You may ask why we look back over such a long period to measure average rates of return. The reason is that annual rates of return for common stocks fluctuate so much that averages taken over short periods are meaningless. Our only hope of gaining insights from historical rates of return is to look at a very long period.[6]

The annual real returns are calculated as $(1 + \text{nominal return})/(1 + \text{inflation rate}) - 1$, and then averaged. The risk premia are the average nominal returns minus the average nominal Treasury bill returns. Ibbotson Associates calculate risk premia in the same way as they calculate real returns, so our analysis is based on their raw data.

[6] Even with 63 years of data we cannot be sure that this period is truly representative and that the average is not distorted by a few unusually high or low returns. The reliability of an estimate of the average is usually measured by its *standard error*. For example, the standard error of our estimate of the average risk premium on common stocks is 2.5%. There is a 95% chance that the *true* average is within plus or minus 2 standard errors of the 11.9% estimate. In other words, if you were to say that the true average was between 6.9% and 16.9%, you would have a 95% chance of being right. [Technical note: The standard error of the mean is equal to the standard deviation divided by the square root of the number of observations. In our case, standard deviation is 19.5%; therefore, the standard error is $19.5/\sqrt{63} = 2.5$.]

Using
Historical
Evidence to
Evaluate
Today's Cost of
Capital

Suppose there is a capital-investment project which you know — don't ask how — has the same risk as the Toronto Stock Exchange 300 Composite Index. We will say that it has the same degree of risk as the *market portfolio*, although this is speaking loosely, because the index does not include all risky securities. What rate should you use to discount this project's forecasted cash flows?

Clearly you should use the currently expected rate of return on the market portfolio: that is the return investors would forgo by investing in the proposed project. Let us call it r_m. One way to estimate r_m is to assume that the future will be like the past and that today investors expect to receive the same "normal" rates of return revealed by the averages shown in Table 7-1. In this case you would set r_m at 11.9%, the average of past market returns.

Unfortunately, this is not the way to do it. The normal value of r_m is not likely to be stable over time. Remember that it is the sum of the risk-free interest rate r_f and a premium for risk. We know r_f varies over time. For example, as we finish this chapter in early 1991, Treasury bills yield 9.4%, or 5% above the average return of our Treasury bill portfolio.

What if you were called upon to estimate r_m in 1991? Would you have said 11.9%? That would have squeezed the risk premium to 2.5%. A much more sensible procedure would have been to take the current interest rate on Treasury bills and add 7.4%, the average *risk premium* shown in Table 7-1. With a rate of 9.4% for Treasury bills, that would have given

$$r_m(1991) = r_f(1991) + \text{normal risk premium}$$
$$= 0.094 + 0.074 = 0.168 \text{ or } 16.8\%$$

The crucial assumption here is that there is a normal, stable risk premium on the market portfolio, so that the expected *future* risk premium can be measured by the average past risk premium. One could quarrel with this assumption, but at least it yields estimates of r_m that seem sensible.[7]

7-2   MEASURING PORTFOLIO RISK

You now have a couple of benchmarks. You know the discount rate for safe projects and you know the rate for "average-risk" projects. But you *don't* know yet how to estimate discount rates for assets that do not fit these simple cases. In order to do that you have to learn (1) how to measure risk and (2) the relationship between risks borne and risk premiums demanded.

Figure 7-1 shows the annual rates of return calculated by Ibbotson and Associates and by Boyle, Panjer, and Sharp for the American (S&P) and Canadian (TSE) stock market indices, respectively. The fluctuations in year-to-year returns are remarkably wide. The highest annual return on the TSE index was 51.6% in 1933 and 51.7% in 1950. On the other hand, there were losses exceeding 25% in three years, the worst being the −33.0% return in 1931.

Another way of presenting these data is by a histogram or frequency distribution. This is done in Figure 7-2, where the variability of year-to-year returns on the market portfolios shows up in the wide "spread" of outcomes. (Note that the 22.6% market crash of October 1987 did not even cause the overall return for 1987 to be negative, since the market had risen strongly in the months preceding October.)

---

[7] For example, estimates of r_m by this procedure are consistent with long-run average rates of return actually earned in the nonfinancial sector of the United States economy. See D.M. Holland and S.C. Myers, "Trends in Corporate Profitability and Capital Costs in the United States," in D.M. Holland (ed.), *Measuring Profitability and Capital Costs*, Lexington Books, Mass., 1984.

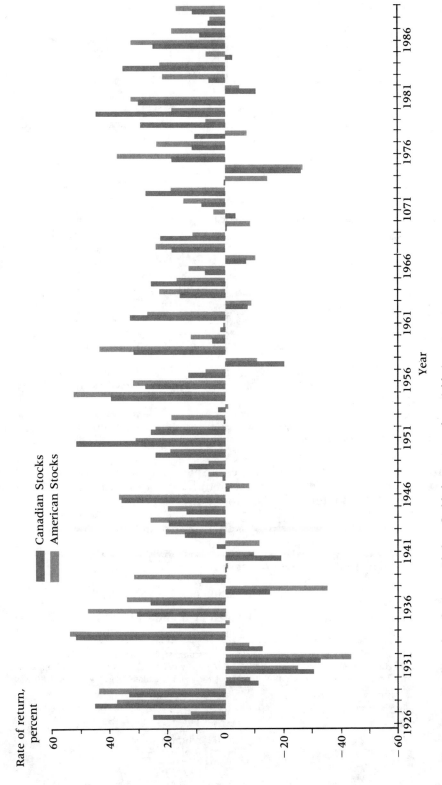

Figure 7-1   Stock markets have provided profitable but extremely variable investments.
Sources: Stocks, Bonds, Bills and Inflation: 1989 Yearbook, Ibbotson Associates, Chicago, 1989 and P.P. Boyle, H.H. Panjer, and K.P. Sharp, "Report on Canadian Economic Statistics 1924–1988," Canadian Institute of Actuaries, Ottawa, 1989.

Figure 7-2   Histograms of the annual rates of return from stock markets in Canada and the United States, 1926–1988, showing the wide spreads of returns from investment in common stocks.

Sources: P.P. Boyle, H.H. Panjer, and K.P. Sharp, "Report on Canadian Economic Statistics 1924–1988," Canadian Institute of Actuaries, Ottawa, July 1989; R.G. Ibbotson and R.A. Sinquefield, *Stocks, Bonds, Bills and Inflation: 1989 Yearbook*, Chicago, 1989.

Variance and Standard Deviation

The standard statistical measures of spread are **variance** and **standard deviation**. The variance of the market return is the expected squared deviation from the expected return. In other words,

$$\text{Variance } (\tilde{r}_m) = \text{the expected value of } (\tilde{r}_m - r_m)^2$$

where $\tilde{r}_m$ is the actual return and r_m is the expected return.[8] The standard deviation is simply the square root of the variance:

$$\text{Standard deviation of } \tilde{r}_m = \sqrt{\text{variance } (\tilde{r}_m)}$$

Standard deviation is often denoted by σ and variance by σ^2.

---

[8] Here is a technical point. When variance is estimated from a sample of *observed* returns, we add up the squared deviations and divide by $N - 1$, where N is the number of observations. We divide by $N - 1$, rather than N, to correct for what is called *the loss of a degree of freedom*. The formula is

$$\text{Variance } (\tilde{r}_m) = \frac{1}{N-1} \sum_{t=1}^{N} (\tilde{r}_{mt} - r_m)^2$$

where

$$\tilde{r}_{mt} = \text{market return in period } t$$

$$r_m = \text{mean of the values of } \tilde{r}_{mt}$$

Example   Here is a very simple example showing how variance and standard deviation are calculated. Suppose you are offered the chance to play the following game. You start by investing $100. Then two coins are flipped. For each head that comes up you get back your starting balance *plus* 20%, and for each tail that comes up you get back your starting balance *less* 10%. Clearly there are four equally likely outcomes:

- Head + head: you gain 40%
- Head + tail: you gain 10%
- Tail + head: you gain 10%
- Tail + tail: you lose 20%

There is a chance of one in four, or 0.25, that you will make 40%; a chance of two in four, or 0.5, that you will make 10%; and a chance of one in four, or 0.25, that you will lose 20%. The game's expected return is, therefore, a weighted average of the possible outcomes:

$$\text{Expected return} = (0.25 \times 40) + (0.5 \times 10) + (0.25 \times -20) = +10\%$$

Table 7-2 shows that the variance of percentage returns is 450. Standard deviation is the square root of 450, or 21. This figure is in the same units as the rate of return, so that we can say that the game's variability is 21%.

Table 7-2
The coin-tossing game: calculating variance and standard deviation

(1) % Rate of Return $\bar{r}$	(2) Deviation From Expected Return $\bar{r} - r$	(3) Squared Deviation $(\bar{r} - r)^2$	(4) Probability	(5) Probability $\times$ Squared Deviation
+40	+30	900	0.25	225
+10	0	0	0.5	0
−20	−30	900	0.25	225
		Variance = expected value of $(\bar{r} - r)^2$ = 450		
		Standard deviation = $\sqrt{\text{variance}}$ = $\sqrt{450}$ = 21		

One way of defining uncertainty is to say that more things can happen than will happen. The risk of an asset can be completely expressed, as we first did for the coin-tossing game, by writing all possible outcomes and the probability of each one. For real assets this is cumbersome and often impossible. Therefore, we use variance or standard deviation to summarize the spread of possible outcomes.[9]

These measures are natural indexes of risk.[10] If the outcome of the coin-tossing game had been certain, the standard deviation would have been zero. The actual standard deviation is positive because we *don't* know what will happen.

---

[9] Which of the two we use is solely a matter of convenience. Since standard deviation is in the same units as the rate of return, it is generally more convenient to use standard deviation. However, when we are talking about the *proportion* of risk that is due to some factor, it is usually less confusing to work in terms of the variance.

[10] As we explain in Chapter 8, standard deviation and variance are the correct measures of risk if the returns on stocks are normally distributed.

Or think of a second game, the same as the first except that each head means a 35% gain and each tail means a 25% loss. Again, there are four equally likely outcomes:

- Head + head: you gain 70%
- Head + tail: you gain 10%
- Tail + head: you gain 10%
- Tail + tail: you lose 50%

For this game the expected return is 10%, the same as the first game's. But its standard deviation is double that of the first game, 42% versus 21%. By this measure the second game is twice as risky as the first.

Measuring Variability

In principle you could estimate the variability of any portfolio of stocks or bonds by the procedure we have just described. You would identify the possible outcomes, assign a probability to each outcome, and grind through the calculations. But where do the probabilities come from? You can't look them up in the newspaper; newspapers seem to go out of their way to avoid definite statements about prospects for securities. We once saw an article headlined "BOND PRICES POSSIBLY SET TO MOVE SHARPLY EITHER WAY." Stockbrokers are much the same. Yours may respond to your query about possible market outcomes with a statement like this:

> "The market currently appears to be undergoing a period of consolidation. For the intermediate term, we would take a constructive view provided economic recovery continues. The market could be up 20% a year from now, perhaps more if inflation moderates. On the other hand . . ."

The Delphic oracle gave advice, but no probabilities.

Most financial analysts start by observing past variability. Of course, there is no risk in hindsight, but it is reasonable to assume that portfolios with histories of high variability also have the least predictable future performance.

The annual standard deviations and variances observed for our four American and four Canadian portfolios were:[11]

Portfolio	Standard deviation σ		Variance σ^2	
	Canadian Market	American Market	Canadian Market	American Market
Treasury bills	4.3	3.3	18.6	10.9
Long-term government bonds	8.3	8.5	68.6	72.3
Corporate bonds	9.1	8.4	83.6	70.6
Common stocks	19.5	20.9	379.2	436.8

[11] Ibbotson Associates, *op. cit.*, and calculations based on Boyle, Panjer, and Sharp, *op. cit.*, and the Treasury-bill data discussed in footnote 2. Notice that in discussing the riskiness of *bonds* we must be careful to specify the time period and whether we are speaking in real or nominal terms. The *nominal* return on a long-term government bond is absolutely certain to an investor who holds on until maturity; in other words, it is risk free if you forget about inflation. After all, the government can always print money to pay off its debts. However, the real return on Treasury securities is uncertain because no one knows how much future dollars will buy.

The returns were measured annually. The bond returns reflect year-to-year changes in prices as well as interest received. The *one-year* returns on long-term bonds are risky in *both* real and nominal terms.

As expected, Treasury bills were the least variable security and common stocks the most. Government and corporate bonds hold the middle ground.[12]

You may find it interesting to compare the coin-tossing game and the stock market as alternative investments. The Canadian stock market generated an average annual return of 11.9%, with a standard deviation of 19.5%. The game offers 10% and 21%, respectively—slightly lower return, and about the same variability. Your gambling friends may have come up with a crude representation of the stock market.

Of course there is no reason the market's variability should stay the same over more than 60 years. For example, it is less now than in the boom-and-bust cycles of the last 1920s and early 1930s. Here are standard deviations of the returns on Boyle, Panjer, and Sharp's, and on Ibbotson Associates' market portfolios, respectively:

| Period | Market standard deviation σ_m | |
	Canadian Market	American Market
1926–1939	27.3	31.9
1940–1949	15.2	16.5
1950–1959	21.5	19.8
1960–1969	14.1	14.4
1970–1979	19.7	19.2
1980–1988	15.2	12.5

We should be cautious about reading too much into standard deviations calculated from ten or so annual returns. However, these figures do not support the widespread impression of especially volatile stock prices during the 1980s. Overall, the 1980s were below average on the volatility front.

However, there were brief episodes of extremely high volatility. On Black Monday, October 19, 1987, the U.S. market index fell by 23% *on a single day*. (The TSE 300 dropped only 11% that day.) The standard deviation of the index for the week surrounding Black Monday was equivalent to 89% per year. Fortunately, volatility dropped back to normal levels within a few weeks after the crash.

How Diversification Reduces Risk

We can calculate our measures of variability just as well for individual securities as for portfolios of securities. Of course, the level of variability over 63 years is less interesting for specific companies than for the market portfolio—it is a rare company that faces the same business risks today as it did in 1926.

---

[12] You may have noticed that U.S. corporates come in just ahead of U.S. governments in terms of low variability. You shouldn't get excited about this. The problem is that it is difficult to get two sets of bonds that are alike in all other respects. For example, most corporate bonds are callable (that is, the company has an option to repurchase them for their face value). Government bonds are not callable. Also, interest payments are higher on corporate bonds. Therefore, the investor in corporate bonds gets their money sooner. As we will see in Chapter 25, this also reduces the bond's variability. Finally, note that the Canadian corporate bond data are for a shorter period than the other data, so their variability shouldn't be directly compared to the others.

Table 7-3
Standard deviations for selected common stocks, 1985–1990 (figures in percent per year)

Stock	Standard Deviation	Stock	Standard Deviation
Abitibi-Price	39.3	Imperial Oil	24.9
Alberta Energy Company	30.2	Molson Companies	21.5
Alcan	28.9	Northern Telecom	28.4
Bell Canada Enterprises	11.6	Power Corporation	26.8
Bombardier	35.0	PWA Corporation	32.1
Denison Mines	39.3	Spar Aerospace	32.1

Derived from monthly returns reported on the Toronto Stock Exchange/University of Western Ontario data file for February 1985 to January 1990.

Table 7-3 presents estimated standard deviations for 10 well-known common stocks for a recent 5-year period.[13] Do these standard deviations look high to you? They should. Remember that the market portfolio's standard deviation was about 20% over the entire 1926–1988 and somewhat less in the later years. Of our individual stocks only Bell Canada Enterprises had a standard deviation of less than 20%. Most stocks are substantially more variable than the market portfolio; only a handful are less variable.

This raises an important question: "The market portfolio is made up of individual stocks, so why doesn't its variability reflect the average variability of its components?" The answer is that *diversification reduces variability*.

Even a little diversification can provide a substantial reduction in variability. Suppose you calculate and compare the standard deviations of randomly chosen one-stock portfolios, two-stock portfolios, five-stock portfolios, etc. You can see from Figure 7-3 that diversification can cut the variability of returns about in half.

 Portfolio
standard deviation

1   5   10   15   Number of securities

Figure 7-3   Diversification reduces risk (standard deviation) rapidly at first, then more slowly.

[13] These estimates are derived from *monthly* rates of return. Five annual observations are insufficient for estimating variability. We converted the monthly variance into an annual variance by multiplying by 12. That is, the variance of the monthly return is about one-twelfth of the annual variance. The longer you hold a security or portfolio, the more risk you have to bear.

This conversion assumes that successive monthly returns are statistically independent. This is, in fact, a good assumption, as we will show in Chapter 13.

Because variance is approximately proportional to the length of time interval during which a security or portfolio return is measured, *standard deviation* is about proportional to the square root of the interval.

But you can get most of this benefit with relatively few stocks: The improvement is slight when the number of securities is increased beyond, say, 20 or 30.

Diversification works because prices of different stocks do not move exactly together. Statisticians make the same point when they say that stock price changes are less than perfectly correlated. Look, for example, at Figure 7-4. You can see that an investment in *either* the holding company shares of Imasco *or* the Teck B mining shares would have been very variable. But there were many occasions on which a decline in the value of one stock was cancelled out by a rise in the price of the other.[14] Therefore, there was an opportunity to reduce your risk by diversification. Figure 7-4 shows that if you had divided your funds evenly between the two stocks, the variability of your portfolio would have been substantially less than the average variability of the two stocks.[15]

The risk that can potentially be eliminated by diversification is called unique risk.[16] Unique risk stems from the fact that many of the perils that surround an individual company are peculiar to that company and perhaps its immediate competitors. But there is also some risk that you can't avoid however much you diversify. This risk is generally known as market risk.[17] Market risk stems from the fact that there are other economy-wide perils which threaten all businesses. That is why stocks have a tendency to move together. And that is why investors are exposed to "market uncertainties" no matter how many stocks they hold.

In Figure 7–5 we have divided the risk into its two parts—unique risk and market risk. If you have only a single stock, unique risk is very important, but once you have a portfolio of 20 or more stocks, diversification has done the bulk of its work. For a reasonably well-diversified portfolio, only market risk matters. Therefore, the predominant source of uncertainty for a diversified investor is that the market will rise or plummet, carrying the investor's portfolio with it.

*7–3   CALCULATING PORTFOLIO RISK

We have given you an intuitive idea of how diversification reduces risk, but in order to understand fully the effect of diversification you need to know how the risk of a portfolio depends on the risk of the individual shares.

Suppose that 60% of your portfolio is invested in the shares of Imasco and the remainder in Teck Corp. You expect that over the coming year the shares of Imasco will give a return of 15% and those of Teck will return 21%. The expected return on your portfolio is simply a weighted average of the expected returns on the individual stocks:[18]

$$\text{Expected portfolio return} = (0.60 \times 15\%) + (0.40 \times 21\%) = 17.4\%$$

Calculating the expected portfolio return is easy. The hard part is to work out the risk of your portfolio. In the past the standard deviation of returns was about

---

[14] Over this period the correlation between the returns on the two stocks was 0.36.

[15] For the five years from February 1985 to January 1990 the standard deviations of Imasco and Teck were 25.3% and 33.0% respectively. The standard deviation of a portfolio half invested in each was 24.5%.

[16] Unique risk may be called *unsystematic risk, residual risk, specific risk,* or *diversifiable risk.*

[17] Market risk may be called *systematic risk* or *undiversifiable risk.*

[18] Let's check this. Suppose you invest $60 in Imasco and $40 in Teck. The expected dollar return on your Imasco holding is 0.15(60) = $9.00 and on Teck it is 0.21(40) = $8.40. The expected dollar return on your portfolio is $9.00 + $8.40 = $17.40. The portfolio *rate* of return is 17.40/100 = 0.174 or 17.4%.

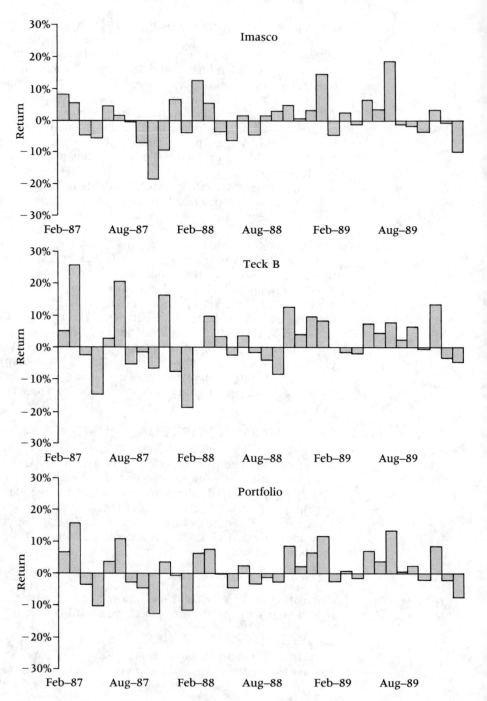

Figure 7-4   The variability of a portfolio with equal holdings in Imasco and Teck B would have been less than the average variability of the individual stocks.

Portfolio
standard deviation

Unique risk

Market risk

Number of
securities

1   5   10   15

Figure 7-5 Diversification eliminates unique risk. But there is some risk that diversification *cannot* eliminate. This is called *market risk*.

25% for Imasco and 33% for Teck. You believe that these figures are a fair measure of the spread of possible *future* outcomes. Your first inclination may be to assume that the standard deviation of the returns on your portfolio is a weighted average of the standard deviations on the individual holdings—that is, $(0.60 \times 25) + (0.40 \times 33) = 28.2\%$. That would be correct *only* if the prices of the two stocks moved in perfect lockstep. In any other case diversification would reduce the risk below this figure.

	Stock 1	Stock 2
Stock 1	$x_1^2\sigma_1^2$	$x_1x_2\sigma_{12}$ $= x_1x_2\rho_{12}\sigma_1\sigma_2$
Stock 2	$x_1x_2\sigma_{12}$ $= x_1x_2\rho_{12}\sigma_1\sigma_2$	$x_2^2\sigma_2^2$

Figure 7-6 The variance of a two-stock portfolio is the sum of these four boxes. x_j = proportion invested in stock j; σ_i^2 = variance of return on stock i; σ_{ij} = covariance of returns on stock i and j ($\rho_{ij}\sigma_i\sigma_j$); ρ_{ij} = correlation between returns on stocks i and j.

The exact procedure for calculating the risk of a two-stock portfolio is given in Figure 7–6. You need to fill in four boxes. To complete the top left box, you weight the variance of the returns on stock 1 (σ_1^2) by the *square* of the proportion invested in it (x_1^2). Similarly, to complete the bottom right box, you weight the variance of the returns on stock 2 (σ_2^2) by the square of the proportion invested in stock 2 (x_2^2).

The entries in these diagonal boxes depend on the variances of stocks 1 and 2; the entries in the other two boxes depend on their *covariance*. As you might guess, the covariance is a measure of the degree to which the two stocks "covary." The covariance can be expressed as the product of the correlation coefficient ρ_{12} and the two standard deviations:[19]

---

[19] Another way to define the covariance is as follows:

Covariance between stocks 1 and 2 = σ_{12} = expected value of $(\tilde{r}_1 - r_1) \times (\tilde{r}_2 - r_2)$

Note that any security's covariance with itself is just its variance:

σ_{11} = expected value of $(\tilde{r}_1 - r_1) \times (\tilde{r}_1 - r_1)$ = expected value of $(\tilde{r}_1 - r_1)^2$ = variance of stock 1

Covariance between stocks 1 and 2 $= \sigma_{12} = \rho_{12}\sigma_1\sigma_2$

For the most part, stocks tend to move together. In this case the correlation coefficient ρ_{12} is positive and therefore the covariance σ_{12} is also positive. If the prospects of the stocks were wholly unrelated, both the correlation coefficient and the covariance would be zero; if the stocks tended to move in opposite directions, the correlation coefficient and the covariance would be negative. Just as you weighted the variances by the square of the proportion invested, so you must weight the covariance by the *product* of the two proportionate holdings x_1 and x_2.

Once you have completed these four boxes, you simply add up the entries in order to obtain the portfolio variance:

$$\text{Portfolio variance} = (x_1^2\sigma_1^2) + (x_2^2\sigma_2^2) + 2(x_1x_2\rho_{12}\sigma_1\sigma_2)$$

The portfolio standard deviation is, of course, the square root of the variance.

Now you can try putting in some figures for Imasco and Teck. We said earlier that if the two stocks were perfectly correlated, the standard deviation of the portfolio would lie 40% of the way between the standard deviations of the two stocks. Let us check this out by filling in the boxes with $\rho_{12} = +1$.

	Imasco	Teck
Imasco	$x_1^2\sigma_1^2 = (0.60)^2 \times (25)^2$	$x_1x_2\rho_{12}\sigma_1\sigma_2 =$ $0.60 \times 0.40 \times 1 \times 25 \times 33$
Teck	$x_1x_2\rho_{12}\sigma_1\sigma_2 =$ $0.60 \times 0.40 \times 1 \times 25 \times 33$	$x_2^2\sigma_2^2 = (0.40)^2 \times (33)^2$

The variance of your portfolio would be the sum of these entries:

$$\begin{aligned}\text{Portfolio variance} &= [(0.60)^2 \times (25)^2] + [(0.40)^2 \times (33)^2] \\ &\quad + 2[0.60 \times 0.40 \times 1 \times 25 \times 33] \\ &= 795\end{aligned}$$

The standard deviation would be $\sqrt{795} = 28.2\%$, 40% of the way between 25% and 33%.

Imasco and Teck do not move in perfect lockstep. If past experience is any guide, the correlation between the two stocks is about 0.4. If we go through the same exercise again with $\rho_{12} = +0.4$, we find:

$$\begin{aligned}\text{Portfolio variance} &= [(0.60)^2 \times (25)^2] + [(0.40)^2 \times (33)^2] \\ &\quad + 2[0.60 \times 0.40 \times 0.4 \times 25 \times 33] \\ &= 558\end{aligned}$$

The standard deviation is $\sqrt{558} = 23.6\%$. The risk is now less than 40% of the way between 25 and 33—in fact, it is slightly less than investing in Imasco alone.

The greatest payoff to diversification comes when the two stocks are *negatively* correlated. Unfortunately, this almost never occurs with real stocks but, just for illustration, let us assume it for Imasco and Teck. And, as long as we are being unrealistic, we might as well go whole hog and assume perfect negative correlation ($\rho_{12} = -1$). In this case,

$$\begin{aligned}\text{Portfolio variance} &= [(0.60)^2 \times (25)^2 + [(0.40)^2 \times (33)^2] \\ &\quad + 2[0.60 \times 0.40 \times (-1) \times 25 \times 33] \\ &= 1.7\end{aligned}$$

Figure 7-7   To find the variance of an N-stock portfolio we must add up a matrix like this. The diagonal boxes contain variance terms $(x_i^2 \sigma_i^2)$ and the off-diagonal boxes contain covariance terms $(x_i x_j \sigma_{ij})$.

When there is perfect negative correlation, there is always a portfolio strategy (represented by a particular set of portfolio weights) that will completely elimi-nate risk.[20] It's unfortunate that perfect negative correlation doesn't really occur between common stocks.

*General Formula for Computing Portfolio Risk

The method for calculating portfolio risk can easily be extended to portfolios of three or more securities. We just have to fill in a larger number of boxes. Each of those down the diagonal—the shaded boxes in Figure 7–7—contains the variance weighted by the square of the proportion invested. Each of the other boxes contains the covariance between that pair of securities, weighted by the product of the proportions invested.[21]

*Limits to Diversification

Did you notice in Figure 7–7 how much more important the covariances become as we add more securities to the portfolio? When there are just two securities, there are an equal number of variance boxes and covariance boxes. When there are many securities, the number of covariances is much larger than the number of variances. Thus, the variability of a well-diversified portfolio reflects mainly the covariances.

Suppose we are dealing with portfolios in which equal investment are made in each of N stocks. The proportion invested in each stock is, therefore, $1/N$. So in each variance box we have $(1/N)^2$ times the variance and in each covariance box we have $(1/N)^2$ times the covariance. There are N variance boxes and $N^2 - N$ covariance boxes. Therefore,

---

[20] Since the standard deviation of Teck is $33/25 = 1.32$ times that of Imasco, you need to invest 1.32 times as much in Imasco to eliminate risk in this two-stock portfolio. You can check that if you invest $1.32/(1 + 1.32) = 0.569$ or 56.9% in Imasco and 43.1% in Teck, the variance of your portfolio is zero.

[21] The formal equivalent to "add up all the boxes" is

$$\text{Portfolio variance} = \sum_{i=1}^{N} \sum_{j=1}^{N} x_i x_j \sigma_{ij}$$

Notice that when $i = j$, σ_{ij} is just the variance of stock i.

$$\text{Portfolio variance} = N\left(\frac{1}{N}\right)^2 \times \text{average variance}$$

$$+ (N^2 - N)\left(\frac{1}{N}\right)^2 \times \text{average covariance}$$

$$= \frac{1}{N} \times \text{average variance} + \left(1 - \frac{1}{N}\right) \times \text{average covariance}$$

Notice that as N increases, the portfolio variance steadily approaches the average covariance. If the average covariance were zero, it would be possible to eliminate *all* risk by holding a sufficient number of securities. Unfortunately, common stocks move together, not independently. Thus, most of the stocks that the investor can actually buy are tied together in a web of positive covariances which set the limit to the benefits of diversification. Now we can understand the precise meaning of the market risk portrayed in Figure 7–5. It is the average covariance that constitutes the bedrock of risk remaining after diversification has done its work.

7–4   HOW INDIVIDUAL SECURITIES AFFECT PORTFOLIO RISK

We presented earlier some data on the variability of 12 individual securities. Abitibi-Price and Denison Mines each had the highest standard deviation and Bell Canada Enterprises (BCE) the lowest. If you had held Abitibi-Price on its own, the spread of possible returns would have been almost four times greater than if you had held BCE on its own. But that is not a very interesting fact. Wise investors don't put all their eggs into just one basket: They reduce their risk by diversification. They are interested, therefore, in the effect that each stock will have on the risk of their portfolio.

This brings us to one of the principal themes of this chapter:

> The risk of a well-diversified portfolio depends on the market risk of the securities included in the portfolio.

Tattoo that statement on your forehead if you can't remember it any other way. It is one of the most important ideas in this book.

Market Risk Is Measured by Beta

If you want to know the contribution of an individual security to the risk of a well-diversified portfolio, it is no good thinking about how risky that security is if held in isolation—you need to measure its market risk, and that boils down to measuring how sensitive it is to market movements. This sensitivity is called **beta(β)**.

Stocks with betas greater than 1.0 tend to amplify the overall market's movements. Stocks with betas between zero and 1.0 tend to move in the same direction as the market but not as far. Of course, the market is the portfolio of all stocks, so the "average" stock has a beta of 1.0. Table 7–4 reports betas for the 12 well-known common stocks we referred to earlier.

Alcan had a beta of 1.22 over the five years from February 1985 to January 1990. If the future resembles the past, this means that on average, when the market rises an extra 1%, Alcan's stock price will rise by an extra 1.22%. When the market falls an extra 10%, Alcan will tend to fall an extra 12.2%, and so on.

Table 7-4
Betas for selected common stocks, 1985–1990

Stock	Beta	Stock	Beta
Abitibi-Price	0.91	Imperial Oil	0.88
Alberta Energy Company	0.94	Molson Companies	0.73
Alcan	1.22	Northern Telecom	0.98
Bell Canada Enterprises	0.38	Power Corporation	1.21
Bombardier	1.08	PWA Corporation	1.32
Denison Mines	1.33	Spar Aerospace	0.88

Measured against the TSE 300 Total Return Index from monthly returns reported on the Toronto Stock Exchange/University of Western Ontario data file for February 1985 to January 1990.

Thus, a line fitted to a plot of expected Alcan returns against expected market returns has a slope of 1.22. See Figure 7–8.[22]

Of course, Alcan's stock returns are not perfectly correlated with market returns. The company is also subject to unique risk, so the actual returns will be scattered about the fitted line in Figure 7–8. This is illustrated in Figure 7–9. Sometimes Alcan will head south while the market goes north, or vice versa.[23]

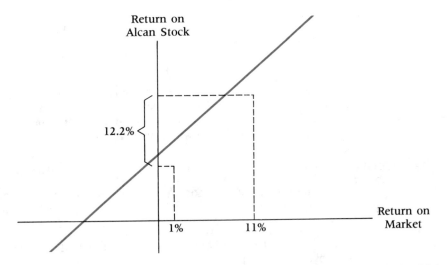

Figure 7-8   The return on Alcan stock changes on average by 1.22% for each additional 1% change in the market return. Beta is therefore 1.22. This is not drawn to scale, in order to emphasize some features.

---

[22] Note that we said that an *extra* market return of 1% is associated with an *extra* Alcan return of 1.22%. This does not force the line to go through the origin or zero point. The intercept on the vertical axis is called *alpha* (α). Thus, if the market is unchanged, we would expect Alcan's stock to change by α%. The equation of the line is

$$r_{\text{Alcan}} = \alpha_{\text{Alcan}} + \beta_{\text{Alcan}} \times r_{\text{m}}.$$

We have more to say about alpha in Chapters 9 and 13. Alcan's alpha is 0.2%, on an annual basis, which is almost zero in Figure 7–8.

[23] The circled point in Figure 7–9 corresponds to the market crash of October 1987 when Alcan fell by 29% and the market fell by 22.5%. This is often called an *outlier* by statisticians, and there is some debate as to whether outliers should be deleted when calculating betas. If we delete October 1987 from the data sample, our estimate of Alcan's beta is 1.16. This is essentially identical to the estimate using the full sample.

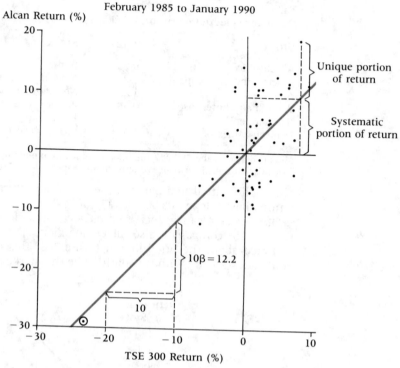

February 1985 to January 1990

Figure 7-9   Alcan stock returns and TSE 300 market index returns. The slope of the line is β = 1.22. The circled point is for October 1987 when Alcan lost 29.0% and the TSE 300 lost 22.5%. Each stock return consists of a systematic portion determined by the line and a unique portion determined by the deviation from the line.

Why Security Betas Determine Portfolio Risk

Let's review the two crucial points about security risk and portfolio risk:

• Market risk accounts for most of the risk of a well-diversified portfolio.
• An individual security's beta measures its sensitivity to market movements.

It's easy to see where we hare headed: in a portfolio context a security's risk is measured by beta. Perhaps we could just jump to that conclusion, but we'd rather explain it. In fact, we'll offer two explanations.

Explanation 1: Where's bedrock?   Look back to Figure 7–5 which shows how the standard deviation of portfolio return depends on the number of securities in the portfolio. With more securities, and therefore better diversification, portfolio risk declines until all unique risk is eliminated and only the bedrock of market risk remains.

Where's bedrock? It depends on the average beta of the securities selected.

Suppose we constructed a portfolio containing a large number of stocks — 500, say — drawn randomly from the whole market. What would we get? The market itself, or a portfolio *very* close to it. The portfolio beta would be 1.0 and the correlation with the market would be 1.0. If the standard deviation of the market is 20% (roughly its average for 1926-88), then the portfolio standard deviation will also be 20%.

But suppose we constructed the portfolio from a large group of stocks with an average beta of 1.5. Again, we end up with a 500-stock portfolio with virtually no unique risk — a portfolio that moves almost in lockstep with the market.

However, *this* portfolio's standard deviation will be 30%, 1.5 times the market's.[24] A well-diversified portfolio with a beta of 1.5 will amplify every market move by 50%, and end up with 150% of the market's risk.

Of course, we could repeat the same experiment with stocks with a beta of 0.5 and end up with a well-diversified portfolio half as risky as the market. Figures 7-10(*a*), 7–10(*b*), and 7–10(*c*) show these three cases.

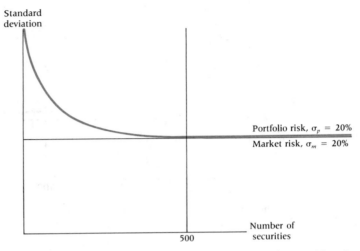

Figure 7-10(*a*)   A randomly selected 500-stock portfolio ends up with a β = 1 and a standard deviation equal to the market's—in this case, 20%.

* pt : individual security affects the whole portfolio

Figure 7-10(*b*)   A 500-stock portfolio constructed with stocks with average β = 1.5 has a standard deviation of about 30% or 150% of the market's standard deviation.

---

[24] A 500-stock portfolio with β = 1.5 would still have some unique risk because it would be unduly concentrated in high-beta industries. Its actual standard deviation would be a bit higher than 30%. If that worries you, relax; we will show you in Chapter 8 how you can construct a fully-diversified portfolio with a beta of 1.5 by borrowing and investing in the market portfolio.

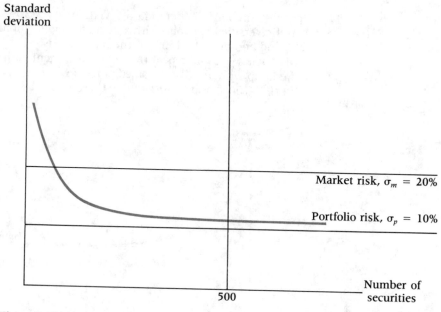

Figure 7-10(c) A 500-stock portfolio constructed with stocks with average β = 0.5 has a standard deviation of about 10%—half the market's.

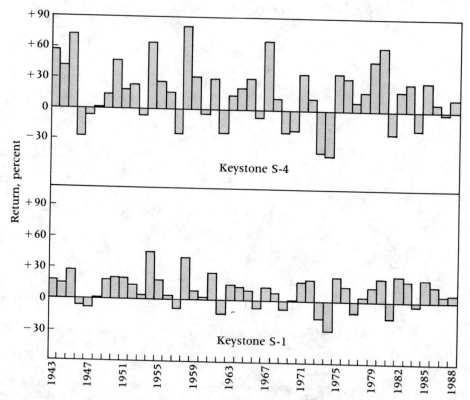

Figure 7-11 These two mutual funds are both well-diversified, but the S-4 Fund is about twice as variable as S-1. This is because it is more sensitive to market movements.

The general point is this: the risk of a well-diversified portfolio is proportional to the portfolio beta, which equals average beta of the securities included in the portfolio. This shows you how portfolio risk is driven by security betas.

Look, for example, at Figure 7–11 which shows the performance of two mutual funds — the Keystone S-1 Fund and the Keystone S-4 Fund. Both funds were well-diversified and therefore had little unique risk.[25] Yet the S-4 Fund was about twice as variable as the S-1 Fund. The reason was that the S-4 Fund held stocks that were particularly sensitive to market movements. The average beta of the stocks in the S-4 Fund was 1.56. By contrast, the more stable S-1 Fund held stocks that were relatively *insensitive* to market movements. On average, the beta of the stocks in the S-1 Fund was only 0.84.

Explanation 2: Betas and covariances   A statistician would define the beta of stock *i* as

$$\beta_i = \frac{\sigma_{im}}{\sigma_m^2}$$

where σ_{im} is the covariance between stock i's return and the market return, and σ_m^2 is the variance of the market return.

It turns out that this ratio of covariance to variance measures a stock's contribution to portfolio risk. You can see this by looking back at our calculations for the risk of the portfolio of Imasco and Teck.

Remember that the risk of this portfolio was the sum of the following boxes:

	Imasco	Teck
Imasco	$(0.60)^2 \times (25)^2$	$0.60 \times 0.40 \times 0.4 \times 25 \times 33$
Teck	$0.60 \times 0.40 \times 0.4 \times 25 \times 33$	$(0.40)^2 \times (33)^2$

If we add up each *row* of boxes, we can see how much of the portfolio's risk comes from Imasco and how much from Teck:

Stock	Contribution to risk
Imasco	$0.60 \times \{[0.60 \times (25)^2] + [0.40 \times 0.4 \times 25 \times 33]\} = 0.60 \times 507$
Teck	$0.40 \times \{[0.60 \times 0.4 \times 25 \times 33] + [0.40 \times (33)^2]\} = \underline{0.40 \times 634}$
Total portfolio	558

Imasco's contribution to portfolio risk depends on its relative importance in the portfolio (0.60) and its average covariance with the stocks in the portfolio (507). (Notice that the average covariance of Imasco with the portfolio includes its covariance with itself; i.e., its variance.) The *proportion* of the risk that comes from the Imasco holding is:

$$\text{Relative market value} \times \frac{\text{average covariance}}{\text{portfolio variance}}$$

$$= 0.60 \times \frac{507}{558} = 0.60 \times 0.91 = 0.55$$

---

[25] If the returns on the S-1 and S-4 Funds were perfectly correlated with the market returns, *all* the risk would be market risk and there would be no unique risk. In practice, neither fund was fully diversified. This shows up in the correlation coefficients which were 0.95 and 0.87 for the S-1 and S-4 Funds, respectively.

Similarly, Teck's contribution to portfolio risk depends on its relative importance in the portfolio (0.40) and its average covariance with the stocks in the portfolio (634). The *proportion* of the risk that comes from the Teck holding is 0.45:

$$0.40 \times \frac{634}{558} = 0.40 \times 1.14 = 0.45$$

In each case the proportion depends on two numbers—the relative size of the holding (0.60 or 0.40) and a measure of the effect of that holding on portfolio risk (0.91 or 1.14). The latter are the betas of Imasco and Teck *relative to that portfolio*. On average, an extra 1% change in the value of the portfolio would be associated with an extra 0.91% change in the value of Imasco and a 1.14% change in the value of Teck.

To calculate Imasco's beta relative to the portfolio, we simply take the covariance of Imasco with the portfolio and divide by portfolio variance. The idea is exactly the same if we wish to calculate the beta of Imasco *relative to the market portfolio*. We just have to calculate its covariance with the market portfolio and divide by the variance of the market.

$$\begin{matrix} \text{Beta relative to} \\ \text{market portfolio} \\ \text{(or, more simply, beta)} \end{matrix} = \frac{\text{Covariance with market}}{\text{Variance of market}} = \frac{\sigma_{im}}{\sigma_m^2}$$

7–5   DIVERSIFICATION AND VALUE ADDITIVITY

We have seen that diversification reduces risk and, therefore, makes sense for investors. But does it also make sense for the firm? Is a diversified firm more attractive to investors than an undiversified one? If it is, we have an *extremely* disturbing result. If diversification is an appropriate corporate objective, each project would have to be analyzed as a potential addition to the firm's portfolio of assets. The value of the diversified package would be greater than the sum of the parts. So present values would no longer add up.

Diversification is undoubtedly a good thing, but that does not mean that firms should practise it. If investors were *not* able to hold a large number of securities, then they might want firms to diversify for them. But investors *can* diversify.[26] In many ways they can do so more easily than firms. Individuals can invest in the steel industry this week and pull out the next week. A firm cannot do that. To be sure, the individual would have to pay brokerage fees on the purchase and sale of steel company shares, but think of the time and expense for a firm to acquire a steel company or to start up a new steel-making operation.

You can probably see where we are heading. If investors can diversify on their own account, they will not pay any *extra* for firms that diversify. And, if they have a sufficiently wide choice of securities, they will not pay any *less* because they are unable to invest separately in each factory. Therefore, in countries such as Canada and the United States with large and competitive capital markets, diversification does not add to a firm's value nor subtract from it. The total value is the sum of its parts.

This conclusion is important for corporate finance, because it justifies adding present values. The concept of value additivity is so important that we will give

---

[26] One of the simplest ways for an individual to diversify is to buy shares in a mutual fund which holds a diversified portfolio.

a formal definition of it. If the capital market establishes a value PV(A) for asset A and PV(B) for asset B, then the market value of a firm that holds only these two assets is:

$$PV(AB) = PV(A) + PV(B)$$

A three-asset firm combining assets A, B, and C would be worth PV(ABC) = PV(A) + PV(B) + PV(C), and so on for any number of assets.

We have relied on intuitive arguments for value additivity. But the concept is a general one that can be proved formally by several different routes.[27] The concept of value additivity seems to be widely accepted as evidenced by thousands of managers who add thousands of present values daily, usually without thinking about it.

7–6 SUMMARY

Our review of capital market history showed that the returns to investors have varied according to the risks they have borne. At one extreme, very safe securities such as Treasury bills have provided an average return over more than half a century of only 4.4% a year. The riskiest securities that we looked at were common stocks. They have provided an average return of 11.9%, a premium of more than 7% over the safe rate of interest.

This gives us two benchmarks for the opportunity cost of capital. If we are evaluating a safe project, we discount at the current risk-free rate of interest. If we are evaluating a project of average risk, we discount at the expected return on the average common stock, which historical evidence suggests is about 7.4% above the risk-free rate. That still leaves us with a lot of assets that don't fit these simple cases. Before we can deal with them, we need to learn how to measure risk.

Risk is best judged in a portfolio context. Most investors do not put all their eggs in one basket: they diversify. Thus, the effective risk of any security cannot be judged by an examination of that security alone. Part of the uncertainty about the security's return is diversified away when the security is grouped with others in a portfolio.

Risk in investment means that future returns are unpredictable. This spread of possible outcomes is usually measured by standard deviation. The standard deviation of the *market portfolio* — generally represented by the Toronto Stock Exchange 300 Composite Index — is around 20% a year.

Most individual stocks have higher standard deviations than this, but much of their variability represents *unique* risk that can be eliminated by diversification. Diversification cannot eliminate *market* risk. Diversified portfolios are exposed to variations in the general level of the market.

A security's contribution to the risk of a well-diversified portfolio depends on how much the security will be affected by a general market decline. This sensitivity to market movements is known as *beta* (β). Beta measures the amount that investors expect the stock price to change for each additional 1% change in the market. The average beta of all stocks is 1.0. A stock with a beta greater than 1 is unusually sensitive to market movements; a stock with a beta below 1 is unusually insensitive to market movements. The standard deviation of a well-

---

[27] You may wish to refer to the Appendix to Chapter 33, which discusses diversification and value additivity in the context of mergers.

diversified portfolio is proportional to its beta. Thus, a diversified portfolio invested in stocks with a beta of 2.0 will have twice the risk of a diversified portfolio with a beta of 1.0.

One theme of this chapter is that diversification is a good thing *for the investor*. This does not imply that *firms* should diversify. Corporate diversification is redundant if investors can diversify on their own account. Since diversification does not affect firm value, present values add even when risk is explicitly considered. Thanks to *value additivity* the net present value rule for capital budgeting works even under uncertainty.

FURTHER READING

There are several valuable records of the performance of North American securities. The classic reference is Ibbotson and Associates, which covers the U.S. market since 1926. Boyle, Panjer, and Sharp covers the Canadian market since 1924, while Hatch and White covers the Canadian market since 1950:

P.P. Boyle, H.H. Panjer, and K.P. Sharp, "Report on Canadian Economic Statistics 1924–1988," Canadian Institute of Actuaries, Ottawa (July 1989).
J.E. Hatch and R.W. White, *Canadian Stocks, Bonds, Bills and Inflation: 1950–1987*, The Institute of Chartered Financial Analysts, Charlottesville Virginia (1988).
Ibbotson Associates: *Stocks, Bonds, Bills and Inflation: 1989 Yearbook*, Ibbotson Associates, Chicago, 1989.

Merton discusses the problems encountered in measuring average returns from historical data:

R.C. Merton, "On Estimating the Expected Return on the Market: An Exploratory Investigation," *Journal of Financial Economics*, **8**: 323–361 (December 1980).

Most investment texts devote a chapter or two to the distinction between market and unique risk and to the effect of diversification on risk. See, for example:

J.C. Francis and E. Kirzner, *Investments: Analysis and Management*, 1st Cdn ed., McGraw-Hill Ryerson, Toronto, 1988.
J.E. Hatch and M.J. Robinson, *Investment Management in Canada*, 2nd ed., Prentice Hall, Scarborough, 1989.
W.F. Sharpe and G.J. Alexander, *Investments*, 4th ed., Prentice-Hall, Englewood Cliffs, N.J., 1989.

An important analysis of the degree to which stocks move together is:

B.F. King, "Market and Industry Factors in Stock Price Behavior," *Journal of Business, Security Prices: A Supplementary*, **39**: 179–190 (January 1966).

There have been several studies of the way that standard deviation is reduced by diversification. Here are two:

M. Statman, "How Many Stocks Make a Diversified Portfolio?" *Journal of Financial and Quantitative Analysis*, **22**: 353–364 (September 1987).
W.H. Wagner and S.C. Lau, "The Effect of Diversification on Risk," *Financial Analysts Journal*, **27**: 48–53 (November-December 1971).

Formal proofs of the value additivity principle can be found in:

S.C. Myers, "Procedures for Capital Budgeting under Uncertainty," *Industrial Management Review*, **9**: 1-20 (Spring 1968).
L.D. Schall, "Asset Valuation, Firm Investment and Firm Diversification," *Journal of Business*, **45**: 11-28 (January 1972).

QUIZ

1. (a) What was the average annual return on Canadian common stocks from 1926 to 1988 (approximately)?
    (b) What was the average difference between this return and the return on Treasury bills?
    (c) What was the average return on Treasury bills in real terms?
    (d) What was the standard deviation of annual returns on the market index?
    (e) Was this market standard deviation more or less than that on most individual stocks?

2. Fill in the missing words:
    Risk is usually measured by the variance of returns or the _____, which is simply the square root of the variance. As long as the stock price changes are not perfectly _____ the risk of a diversified portfolio is _____ than the risk of the individual stocks.
    The risk that can be eliminated by diversification is known as _____ risk. But diversification cannot remove all risk; the risk that it cannot eliminate is known as _____ risk.

3. True or false?
    (a) Investors prefer diversified companies because they are less risky.
    (b) If stocks were perfectly positively correlated, diversification would not reduce risk.
    (c) The contribution of a stock to the risk of a well-diversified portfolio depends on its market risk.
    (d) A well-diversified portfolio with a beta of 2.0 is twice as risky as the market portfolio.
    (e) An undiversified portfolio with a beta of 2.0 is less than twice as risky as the market portfolio.

4. What is the beta of each of the stocks shown in Table 7–5?

Table 7-5
See quiz, question 4

Stock	Expected Stock Return if Market Return is −10%	Expected Stock Return if Market Return is +10%
A	0	+20
B	−20	+20
C	−30	0
D	+15	+15
E	+10	−10

5. Suppose the standard deviation of the market return is 20%.
    (a) What is the standard deviation of returns on a well-diversified portfolio with a beta of 1.3?
    (b) What is the standard deviation of returns on a well-diversified portfolio with a beta of 0?
    (c) A well-diversified portfolio has a standard deviation of 15%. What is its beta?
    (d) A poorly diversified portfolio has a standard deviation of 20%. What can you say about its beta?

6. A portfolio contains equal investments in 10 stocks. Five have a beta of 1.2; the remainder have a beta of 1.4. The portfolio beta is which of the following?
(a) 1.3.
(b) greater than 1.3 because the portfolio is not completely diversified.
(c) less than 1.3 because diversification reduces beta.

7. During the past 5 years, the stock of Great American Fish (GAF) has moved as follows:

Year	1	2	3	4	15
Price change, %	+20	−10	−30	+5	+15

Calculate the variance and standard deviation of the returns of GAF.

8. In which of the following situations would you get the largest reduction in risk by spreading your investment across two stocks?
(a) When the two shares are perfectly correlated.
(b) When there is no correlation.
(c) When there is modest negative correlation.
(d) When there is perfect negative correlation.

9. To calculate the variance of a three-stock portfolio you need to add nine boxes:

Use the same symbols that we used in this chapter; e.g., x_1 = proportion invested in stock 1 and σ_{12} = covariance between stocks 1 and 2. Now complete the nine boxes.

QUESTIONS AND PROBLEMS

1. There are few if any real companies with negative betas. But suppose you found one with $\beta = -0.25$.
(a) How would you expect this stock's price to change if the overall market rises by an extra 5%? What if the market falls by an extra 5%?
(b) You have $1 million invested in a well-diversified portfolio of stocks. Now you receive an additional $20,000 bequest. Which of the following actions will yield the safest overall portfolio return?
(i) Invest $20,000 in Treasury bills (which have $\beta = 0$).
(ii) Invest $20,000 in stocks with $\beta = 1$.
(iii) Invest $20,000 in stocks with $\beta = -0.25$.
Explain your answer.

2. Lonesome Gulch Mines has a standard deviation of 42% per year and a beta of +0.10. Amalgamated Copper has a standard deviation of 31% a year and a beta of +0.66. Explain why Lonesome Gulch is the safer investment for a diversified investor.

*3. Table 7–6 shows standard deviations and correlation coefficients for seven stocks. Calculate the variance of a portfolio invested 40% in Provigo, 40% in TransAlta Utilities, and 20% in Teck.

Table 7-6
Standard deviations and correlation coefficients for a sample of seven stocks

	Standard Deviation (%)	Correlation						
		Acklands	BP Canada	Imasco	Provigo	Power Corp	Trans-Alta	Teck B
Acklands	15	1.00						
BP Canada	31	0.19	1.00					
Imasco	25	0.29	0.25	1.00				
Provigo	26	0.30	0.11	0.41	1.00			
Power Corp.	27	0.21	0.22	0.56	0.37	1.00		
TransAlta	11	0.08	0.16	0.35	0.23	0.31	1.00	
Teck B	33	0.19	0.49	0.40	0.10	0.29	0.22	1.00

*4. Look back at your calculations for question 3. Calculate each stock's contribution to overall portfolio variance. What is each stock's beta relative to the three-stock portfolio?

*5. Your eccentric Aunt Claudia has left you $50,000 in Acklands shares plus $50,000 cash. Unfortunately, her will requires that the Acklands stock cannot be sold for one year, and the $50,000 cash must be entirely invested in *one* of the stocks shown in Table 7–6. What is the safest attainable portfolio under these restrictions?

6. (a) List four common stocks that are likely to have very high standard deviations and four stocks that are likely to have very low standard deviations.

   (b) List four pairs of securities that are likely to be highly correlation and four pairs that are likely to be relatively uncorrelated.

7. "There's upside risk and downside risk. Standard deviation doesn't distinguish between them." Do you think the speaker has a fair point?

8. Respond to the following comments:

   (a) "Risk is not variability. If I know a stock is going to fluctuate between $10 and $20, I can make myself a bundle."

   (b) "There are all sorts of risk in addition to beta risk. There's the risk that we'll have a downturn in demand, there's the risk that my best plant manager will drop dead, there's the risk of a hike in steel prices. You've got to take all these things into consideration."

   (c) "Risk to me is the probability of loss."

   (d) "Those guys who suggest beta is a measure of risk make the big assumption that betas don't change."

*9. Here are some historical data on the risk characteristics of Provigo and TransAlta Utilities:

	Provigo	TransAlta
β (beta)	0.78	0.28
Yearly standard deviation of return	26	11

Assume that the standard deviation of the return on the market was 20%.

The correlation coefficient of Provigo's return versus TransAlta's is 0.23.

(a) What is the standard deviation of a portfolio half invested in Provigo and half in TransAlta?

(b) What is the standard deviation of a portfolio one-third invested in Provigo, one-third in TransAlta, and one-third in Treasury bills?

(c) What is the standard deviation if the portfolio is split evenly between Provigo and TransAlta and financed at 50% margin — that is, the investor puts up only 50% of the total amount and borrows the balance from the broker?

(d) What is the *approximate* standard deviation of a portfolio composed of 100 stocks with β's of 0.78 like Provigo? How about 100 stocks like Trans Alta? (*Hint*: Part (d) should not require anything but the simplest arithmetic to answer.)

*10. You believe that there is a 40% chance that stock A will decline by 10% and a 60% chance that it will rise by 20%. Correspondingly, there is a 30% chance that stock B will decline by 10% and a 70% chance that it will rise by 20%. The correlation coefficient between the two stocks is 0.7. Calculate the expected return, the variance, and the standard deviation for each stock. Then calculate the covariance between their returns.

*11. An individual invests 60% of his funds in stock I and the balance in stock J. The standard deviation of returns on I is 10% and on J it is 20%. Calculate the variance of portfolio returns assuming

(a) The correlation between the returns is 1.0.

(b) The correlation is 0.5.

(c) The correlation is 0.

*12. (a) How many variance terms and how many covariance terms do you need to calculate the risk of a 100-share portfolio?

(b) Suppose all stocks had a standard deviation of 30% and a correlation with each other of 0.4. What is the standard deviation of the returns on a portfolio that has equal holdings in 50 stocks?

(c) What is the standard deviation of a fully diversified portfolio of such stocks?

*13. Suppose that the standard deviation of returns from a typical share is about 0.40 (or 40%) a year. The correlation between the returns of each pair of shares is about 0.3. Calculate the variance and standard deviation of the returns on a portfolio that has equal investments in two shares, three shares, and so on up to ten shares.

(a) Use your estimates to draw two graphs like Figure 7–5 (one for variance, the other for standard deviation). How large is the underlying market risk that cannot be diversified away?

(b) Now repeat the exercise assuming that the correlation between each pair of stocks is zero.

*14. The market portfolio has a standard deviation of 20% and the covariance between the returns on the market and those on stock Z is 800.

(a) What is the beta of stock Z?

(b) What is the standard deviation of a fully diversified portfolio of such stocks?

(c) What is the average beta of all stocks?

(d) If the market portfolio gave an extra return of 5%, how much extra return can you expect from stock Z?

*15. It is often useful to know how well your portfolio is diversified. Two measures have been suggested:

(a) The variance of the returns on a fully diversified portfolio as a proportion of the variance of returns on *your* portfolio.

(b) The number of shares in a portfolio that (i) has the same risk as yours, (ii) is invested in "typical" shares, and (iii) has equal amounts invested in each share.

Suppose that you hold eight stocks. All are fairly typical—they have a standard deviation of 0.40 a year and the correlation between each pair is 0.3. Of your fund, 20% is invested in one stock, 20% in a second, and the remaining 60% is spread evenly over a further six stocks.

Calculate each of the above two measures of portfolio diversification.

C · H · A · P · T · E · R

8

RISK AND RETURN

In order to estimate the net present value of a risky investment the financial manager needs to know how much investors expect to be paid for taking risk. That is why in Chapter 7 we began to come to grips with the problem of measuring risk. Here is the story so far.

The stock market is risky because there is a spread of possible outcomes. The usual measure of this spread is the standard deviation or variance. The risk of any stock can be broken down into two parts. There is the *unique risk* that is peculiar to that stock, and there is the *market risk* that is associated with market-wide variations. Investors can eliminate unique risk by holding a well-diversified portfolio, but they cannot eliminate market risk. *All* the risk of a fully diversified portfolio is market risk.

A stock's contribution to the risk of a fully diversified portfolio depends on its sensitivity to market changes. This sensitivity is generally known as *beta*. A security with a beta of 1.0 has average market risk—a well-diversified portfolio of such securities has the same standard deviation as the market index. A security with a beta of 0.5 has below-average market risk—a well-diversified portfolio of these securities tends to move half as far as the market moves and has half the market's standard deviation.

In this chapter we shall use this new-found knowledge to develop some theories linking risk and return in a competitive economy and we shall show you how to use these theories to estimate the return that investors require in different stock market investments. Then in Chapter 9 we look at how these ideas can help the financial manager cope with risk in practical capital-budgeting situations.

8-1 HARRY MARKOWITZ AND THE BIRTH OF PORTFOLIO THEORY

Most of the ideas in Chapter 7 date back to an article written in 1952 by Harry Markowitz.[1] Markowitz drew attention to the common practice of portfolio diversification and showed exactly how an investor can reduce the standard deviation of portfolio returns by choosing stocks that do not move exactly together. But Markowitz did not stop there—he went on to work out the basic principles of

---

[1] H.M. Markowitz, "Portfolio Selection," *Journal of Finance*, **7**: 77–91 (March 1952).

Figure 8-1   Daily price changes of Norcen stock from 1987 to 1989 are approximately normally distributed.

portfolio construction. These principles are the foundation for much of what has been written about the relationship between risk and return.

We begin with Figure 8–1, which shows a histogram of the daily returns on Norcen stock from 1987 to 1989. On this histogram we have superimposed a bell-shaped normal distribution. The result is typical: When measured over some fairly short interval, the past rates of return on any stock conform closely to a normal distribution.[2]

One important feature of a normal distribution is that it can be completely defined by two numbers. One is the average or "expected" return; the other is the variance or standard deviation. Now you can see why in Chapter 7 we discussed the calculation of expected return and standard deviation. They are not just arbitrary measures: if returns are normally distributed, they are the *only* two measures that an investor need consider.

Figure 8–2 pictures the distribution of possible returns from two investments. Both offer an expected return of 10% but A has much the wider spread of possible outcomes. Its standard deviation is 30%; the standard deviation of B is 15%. Most investors dislike uncertainty and would therefore prefer B to A.

Figure 8–3 pictures the distribution of returns from two other investments. This time both have the *same* standard deviation but the expected return is 20% from stock C and only 10% from stock D. Most investors like high expected return and would therefore prefer C to D.

_____

[2] If you were to measure returns over a *long* interval, the distribution would be skewed. For example, you would encounter returns greater than 100% but none *less* than −100%. The distribution of returns over a period of, say, one year would be better approximated by a *lognormal* distribution. The lognormal distribution, like the normal, is completely specified by its mean and standard deviation.

Probability

Investment A

Return, percent (*r*)

−20   +10   +40

Probability

Investment B

Return, percent (*r*)

−5 +10 +25

Figure 8-2   These two investments both have an *expected* return of 10%; but because investment A has the greater spread of *possible* returns, it is more risky than B. We can measure this spread by the standard deviation. Investment A has a standard deviation of 30%; B, 15%. Most investors would prefer B to A.

Combining Stocks into Portfolios   Suppose that you are wondering whether to invest in the shares of Imasco or Teck Corp. You decide that Imasco offers an expected return of 15% and Teck an expected return of 21%. After looking back at the past variability of the two

Probability

Investment C

Return, percent (*r*)

+5 +20 +35

Probability

Investment D

Return, percent (*r*)

−5 +10 +25

Figure 8-3   The standard deviation of possible returns is 15% for both these investments, but the expected return from C is 20% compared with an expected return from D of only 10%. Most investors would prefer C to D.

Expected return (%), r

Figure 8-4   The curved line illustrates how expected return and standard deviation change as you hold different combinations of two stocks. For example, if you invest 40% of your money in Teck and the remainder in Imasco, your expected return is 17.4%, which is 40% of the way between the expected returns on the two stocks. The standard deviation is 28.1%, which is *much less* than 40% of the way between the standard deviations on the two stocks. This is because diversification reduces risk.

stocks, you also decide that the standard deviation of returns is 25% for Imasco and 33% for Teck. Figure 8–4 illustrates the choice that you face. Teck offers the higher expected return but it is considerably more risky.

Now there is no reason to restrict yourself to holding only one stock. For example, in Section 7–3 we analyzed what would happen if you invested 60% of your money in Imasco and 40% in Teck. The expected return on this portfolio is 17.4%, which is simply a weighted average of the expected returns on the two holdings. What about the risk of such a portfolio? We know that thanks to diversification portfolio risk is less than the average of risks of the separate stocks. In fact, on the basis of past experience the standard deviation of this portfolio is 23.6%.[3]

---

[3] We pointed out in Section 7–3 that the correlation between the returns of Imasco and Teck has been about 0.4.

The variance of a portfolio that is invested 60% in Imasco and 40% in Teck is:

$$
\begin{aligned}
\text{Variance} &= x_1^2\sigma_1^2 + x_2^2\sigma_2^2 + 2x_1x_2\rho_{12}\sigma_1\sigma_2 \\
&= [(0.60)^2 \times (25)^2] + [(0.40)^2 \times (33)^2] + 2[0.60 \times 0.40 \times 0.4 \times 25 \times 33] \\
&= 558
\end{aligned}
$$

The portfolio standard deviation is $\sqrt{558} = 23.6\%$

Expected return, percent (r)

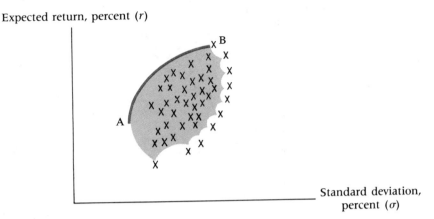

Standard deviation,
percent (σ)

Figure 8-5   Each cross shows the expected return and standard deviation from investing in a single stock. The broken-egg-shaped area shows the possible combinations of expected return and standard deviation if you invest in a *mixture* of stocks. If you like high expected returns and dislike high standard deviations, you will prefer portfolios along the heavy line. These are *efficient* portfolios.

In Figure 8–4 we have plotted the expected return and risk that you could achieve by different combinations of the two stocks. Which of these combinations is best? That depends on your stomach. If you want to stake all on getting rich quickly, you would do best to put all your money in Teck. If you want a more peaceful life, you should invest most of your money in Imasco—to minimize risk you should keep a small investment in Teck.[4]

In practice you are unlikely to be limited to investing in only two stocks. Figure 8–5 shows what happens when you have a larger choice of securities. Each cross represents the combination of risk and return offered by a different individual security. By mixing these securities in different proportions you can obtain an even wider selection of risk and expected return. For example, the range of attainable combinations might look something like the broken-egg-shaped area in Figure 8–5. Since you wish to increase expected return and reduce standard deviation, you will be interested only in those portfolios that lie along the heavy solid line. Markowitz called them **efficient portfolios**. Once again, whether you want to choose the minimum-risk portfolio (portfolio A) or the maximum expected return portfolio (portfolio B) or some other efficient portfolio depends on how much you dislike taking risk.

The problem of finding these efficient portfolios is rather similar to a problem that we encountered in Section 6–5. There we wanted to deploy a limited amount of capital in a mixture of projects to give the highest total NPV. Here we want to deploy a limited amount of capital to give the highest expected return for a given standard deviation. In principle both problems can be solved by a hunt-and-peck procedure—but only in principle. To solve the capital-rationing problem in practice, we can employ linear programming techniques; to solve the portfolio problem, we can employ a variant of linear programming known as *quadratic programming*. If we estimate the expected return and standard deviation for each stock in Figure 8–5, and also the correlation between each pair of stocks, then we can use a standard computer quadratic program to calculate the set of efficient portfolios.

---

[4] The portfolio with the minimum risk has 28.0% in Teck.

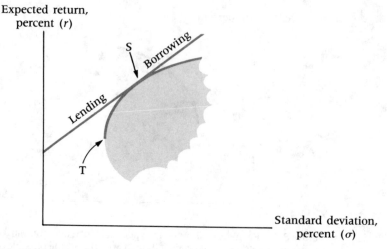

Expected return, percent (r)

Standard deviation, percent (σ)

Figure 8-6 Lending and borrowing extend the range of investment possibilities. If you invest in portfolio S and lend or borrow at the risk-free interest rate, r_f, you can achieve any point along the straight line from r_f through S. This gives you a higher expected return for any level of risk than if you just invest in common stocks.

We Now Introduce Borrowing and Lending

Now we can introduce yet another possibility. Suppose that you can also lend and borrow money at some risk-free rate of interest r_f. If you invest some of your money in Treasury bills (i.e., lend money) and place the remainder in common stock portfolio S, you can obtain any combination of expected return and risk along the straight line joining r_f and S in Figure 8-6.[5] Since borrowing is merely negative lending, you can extend the range of possibilities to the right of S by borrowing funds at an interest rate of r_f and investing them as well as your own money in portfolio S.

Let us put some numbers on this. Suppose that portfolio S has an expected return of 15% and a standard deviation of 16%. Treasury bills offer an interest rate (r_f) of 5% and are risk-free (i.e., standard deviation is zero). If you invest half your money in portfolio S and lend the remainder at 5%, the expected return on your investment would be halfway between the expected return on S and the interest rate on Treasury bills:

$$r = (1/2 \times \text{expected return on S}) + (1/2 \times \text{interest rate})$$
$$= 10\%$$

And the standard deviation would be halfway between the standard deviation of S and the standard deviation of Treasury bills:

$$\sigma = (1/2 \times \text{standard deviation of S}) + (1/2 \times \text{standard deviation of bills})$$
$$= 8\%$$

Or suppose that you decide to go for the big time: you borrow at the Treasury bill rate an amount equal to your initial wealth and invest everything in portfolio S.

---

[5] If you want to check this, write down the formula for the standard deviation of a two-stock portfolio:

$$\text{Standard deviation} = \sqrt{x_1^2\sigma_1^2 + x_2^2\sigma_2^2 + 2x_1x_2\rho_{12}\sigma_1\sigma_2}$$

Now see what happens when security 2 is riskless—that is, when $\sigma_2 = 0$.

You have twice your own money invested in S but you have to *pay* interest on the loan. Therefore, your expected return is:

$$r = (2 \times \text{expected return on S}) - (1 \times \text{interest rate})$$
$$= 25\%$$

And the standard deviation of your investment is:

$$\sigma = (2 \times \text{standard deviation of S}) - (1 \times \text{standard deviation of bills})$$
$$= 32\%$$

You can see from Figure 8–6 that when you lend a portion of your money you end up partway between r_f and S; if you can borrow money at the risk-free rate, you can extend your possibilities beyond S. You can also see that regardless of what level of risk you choose, you can get the highest expected return by a mixture of portfolio S and borrowing or lending. There is no reason ever to hold, say, portfolio T.

This means that we can separate the investor's job into two stages. First, the "best" portfolio of common stocks must be selected—S, in our example.[6] Second, this portfolio must be blended with borrowing or lending to obtain an exposure to risk that suits the particular investor's taste. Each investor, therefore, should put money into just two benchmark investments—a risky portfolio S and a risk-free loan (borrowing or lending).[7]

What does portfolio S look like? If you have better information than your rivals, you will want it to include relatively large investments in the stocks you think are undervalued. But in a competitive market you are unlikely to have a monopoly on good ideas. In that case there is no reason to hold a different portfolio of common stocks from anybody else. In other words, you might just as well hold the market portfolio. That is why many professional investors invest in a market-index portfolio and why most others hold well-diversified portfolios.

8–2   THE RELATIONSHIP BETWEEN RISK AND RETURN

In Chapter 7 we looked at the returns on selected investments. The least risky investment was Treasury bills. Since the return on Treasury bills is fixed, it is unaffected by what happens to the market. In other words, Treasury bills have a beta of zero. The *most* risky investment that we considered was the market portfolio of common stocks. This has average market risk: its beta is 1.0.

Wise investors don't take risks just for fun. They are playing with real money. Therefore, they require a higher return from the market portfolio than from Treasury bills. The difference between the return on the market and the interest rate is termed the *market risk premium.* Over a period of 63 years the Canadian market risk premium ($r_m - r_f$) has averaged 7.4% a year.

In Figure 8–7 we have plotted the risk and expected return from Treasury bills and the market portfolio. You can see that Treasury bills have a beta of zero and a risk premium of zero.[8] The market portfolio has a beta of 1.0 and a risk premium

---

[6] Portfolio S is the point of tangency to the set of efficient portfolios. It offers the highest expected risk premium ($r - r_f$) per unit of standard deviation (σ).

[7] This so-called *separation theorem* was first pointed out by J. Tobin in "Liquidity Preference as Behavior toward Risk," *Review of Economic Studies,* **25**: 65–86 (February 1958).

[8] Remember that the risk premium is the difference between the investment's expected return and the risk-free rate. For Treasury bills, the difference is zero.

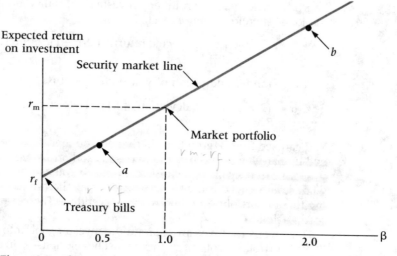

Figure 8-7 The capital asset pricing model states that the expected risk premium on each investment is proportional to its beta. This means that each investment should lie on the sloping security market line connecting Treasury bills and the market portfolio.

of $r_m - r_f$. This gives us two benchmarks for the expected risk premium. But what is the expected risk premium when beta is not zero or one?

In the mid-1960s three economists—William Sharpe, John Lintner, and Jack Treynor—produced an answer to this question.[9] Their answer is known as the **capital asset pricing model** or **CAPM**. The model's message is both startling and simple. In a competitive market, the expected risk premium varies in direct proportion to beta. This means that in Figure 8–7, all investments must plot along the sloping line, known as the **security market line**. The expected risk premium on an investment with a beta of 0.5 is, therefore, *half* the expected risk premium on the market; and the expected risk premium on an investment with a beta of 2.0 is *twice* the expected risk premium on the market. We can write this relationship as:

Expected risk premium on stock = beta × expected risk premium on market
$$r - r_f = \beta (r_m - r_f)$$

Some estimates of expected returns

Before we tell you where this formula comes from, let us use it to figure out what returns investors are looking for from particular stocks. To do this we need three numbers—r_f, $(r_m - r_f)$, and β. In early 1991 the interest rate on Treasury bills was about 9.4%. From past evidence we would judge that $r_m - r_f$ is about 7.4%. Finally, in Table 7–4 we gave you estimates of the betas of 12 stocks. Table 8–1 puts these numbers together to give an estimate of the expected return on each

---

[9] See W.F.Sharpe, "Capital Asset Prices: A Theory of Market Equilibrium Under Conditions of Risk," *Journal of Finance,* **19**: 425–442 (September 1964); J. Lintner, "The Valuation of Risk Assets and the Selection of Risky Investments in Stock Portfolios and Capital Budgets," *Review of Economics and Statistics,* **47**: 13–37 (February 1965); Treynor's article has not been published.

Table 8-1
These estimates of the returns *expected* by investors in early 1991 were based on the capital asset pricing model. We assumed that the interest rate $r_f = 9.4\%$ and the expected market premium $r_m - r_f = 7.4\%$.

Stock	Beta	Expected return (%) $r_f + \beta(r_m - r_f)$
Abitibi-Price	0.91	16.1
Alberta Energy Company	0.94	16.4
Alcan	1.22	18.4
Bell Canada Enterprises	0.38	12.2
Bombardier	1.08	17.4
Denison Mines	1.33	19.2
Imperial Oil	0.88	15.9
Molson Companies	0.73	14.8
Northern Telecom	0.98	16.7
Power Corporation	1.21	18.4
PWA Corporation	1.32	19.2
Spar Aerospace	0.88	15.9

stock. The least risky stock in our sample is Bell Canada Enterprises. Our estimate for the expected return from BCE is 12.2%. The *most* risky stock is Denison Mines. Our estimate of the expected return from Denison is 19.2%, 9.8% more than the interest rate on Treasury bills.

You can also use the capital asset pricing model to find the discount rate for a new capital investment. For example, suppose that you are analyzing a proposal by Spar Aerospace to expand its capacity. At what rate should you discount the expected cash flows? According to Table 8–1 investors are looking for a return of 15.9% from businesses with the risk of Spar. So, the cost of capital for a further investment in the same business is 15.9%.[10]

In practice, choosing a discount rate is seldom so easy. (After all, you can't expect to be paid a fat salary just for plugging numbers into a formula.) For example, you must learn how to adjust for the extra risk caused by company borrowing and how to estimate the discount rate for projects that do not have the same risk as the company's existing business. There are also tax issues. But these refinements can wait until later.[11]

A proof of the capital asset pricing model

Let's review four basic principles of portfolio selection:

1. Investors like high expected return and low standard deviation. Common stock portfolios that offer the highest expected return for a given standard deviation are known as *efficient portfolios*.

---

[10] Remember that instead of investing in plant and machinery, the firm could return the money to the shareholders. The opportunity cost of investing is the return that shareholders could expect to earn by buying financial assets. This expected return depends on the market risk of the assets.

[11] Tax issues arise because a corporation must pay tax on income from an investment in Treasury bills or other interest-paying securities. It turns out that the correct discount rate for risk-free investments is the *after-tax* Treasury bill rate. We come back to this point in Chapters 19 and 26.
Various other points on the practical use of betas and the capital asset pricing model are covered in Chapter 9.

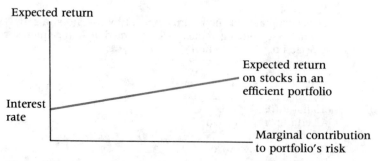

Figure 8-8 If a portfolio is efficient, each stock should lie along a straight line linking the stock's expected return with its marginal contribution to the portfolio's risk.

2.   If you want to know the marginal impact of a stock on the risk of a portfolio, you must look not at the risk of that stock in isolation, but at its contribution to portfolio risk. That contribution depends on the stock's sensitivity to changes in the value of the portfolio.

3.   A stock's sensitivity to changes in the value of the *market* portfolio is known as *beta*. Beta, therefore, measures the marginal contribution of a stock to the risk of the market portfolio.

4.   If investors can borrow and lend at the risk-free rate of interest, then they should always hold a mixture of the risk-free investment and one particular common stock portfolio. The composition of this stock portfolio depends only on investors' assessment of the prospects for each stock and not on their attitude to risk. If they have no superior information, they should hold the same stock portfolio as everybody else—in other words, they should hold the market portfolio.

Now if everyone holds the market portfolio, and if beta measures each security's contribution to the market portfolio risk, then it's no surprise that the risk premium demanded by investors is proportional to beta.

Risk premiums always reflect contribution to portfolio risk. Suppose you are constructing a portfolio. Some stocks will add to the risk of the portfolio and you will, therefore, buy them only if they also increase the expected return. Others will reduce portfolio risk and you may, therefore, be prepared to buy them even if they also reduce the portfolio's expected return. If the portfolio you have chosen is efficient, each of your investments must be working equally hard for you. So, if one stock has a greater marginal effect on portfolio risk than another stock, it must also have proportionately greater expected return. This means that if you plot each stock's expected return against its marginal contribution to the risk of your efficient portfolio, you will find that the stocks lie along a straight line, as in Figure 8–8. This is *always* the case: if a portfolio is efficient, there must be a straight-line relationship between each stock's expected return and its marginal contribution to portfolio risk. The converse is also true: if there is not a straight-line relationship, the portfolio is not efficient.

Now you can see that Figures 8–7 and 8–8 are identical *if* the efficient portfolio in Figure 8–8 is the market portfolio. (Remember that the beta of a stock measures its marginal contribution to the risk of the market portfolio.) So, the capital asset pricing model boils down to the statement that the market portfolio is efficient. As we have already seen, this will be so if each investor has the same information and faces the same opportunities as everyone else. In these circumstances, each investor should hold the same portfolio as everyone else—in other words, each should hold the market portfolio.

What Would Happen if a Stock Did *Not* Lie on the Security Market Line?

Imagine that you encounter stock A in Figure 8–9(a). Would you buy it? We hope not[12]—if you want an investment with a beta of 0.5, you could get a higher expected return by investing half your money in Treasury bills and half in the market portfolio. If everybody shares your view of the stock's prospects, the price of A will have to fall until the expected return rises up to what you could get elsewhere. (Remember: if the stock price falls, its expected *future* return rises, just as a falling bond price increases its yield or future return.)

What about stock B in Figure 8–9(b)? Would you be tempted by its high return? You wouldn't if you are smart. You could get a higher expected return for the same beta by borrowing 50 cents for every dollar of your own money and investing in the market portfolio. Again, if everybody agrees with your assessment, the price of stock B cannot hold. It will have to fall until the expected return on B is equal to the expected return on the combination of borrowing and investment in the market portfolio.

We think we have made our point. An investor can always obtain an expected risk premium of $\beta (r_m - r_f)$ by holding a mixture of the market portfolio and a risk-free loan. So, in well-functioning markets nobody will hold a stock that offers an expected risk premium of *less* than $\beta (r_m - r_f)$. But what about the other possibility? Are there stocks that offer a higher expected risk premium? In other words, can there by a stock like C that lies above the security market line in Figure 8–9? If we take all stocks together, we have the market portfolio. Therefore, we know that stocks *on average* lie on the line. Since none lies *below* the line, then there also can't be any that lie *above* the line. Thus, each and every stock must lie on the security market line and offer an expected risk premium of:

$$r - r_f = \beta(r_m - r_f)$$

8–3 VALIDITY AND ROLE OF THE CAPITAL ASSET PRICING MODEL

Any economic model is a simplified statement of reality. We need to simplify in order to interpret what is going on around us. But we also need to know how much faith we can place in our model.

Let us begin with some matters on which there is broad agreement. First, few people quarrel with the idea that investors require some extra return for taking on risk. That is why common stocks have given on average a higher return than Treasury bills. Who would want to invest in risky common stocks if they offered only the *same* expected return as bills? We wouldn't and we suspect you wouldn't either.

Second, investors do appear to be concerned principally with those risks that they cannot eliminate by diversification. If this were not so, we should find that stock prices increase whenever two companies merge to spread their risks. And we should find that investment companies that invest in the shares of other firms are more highly valued than the shares they hold. But we don't observe either phenomenon. Mergers undertaken just to spread risk don't increase stock prices, and investment companies are no more highly valued than the stocks they hold.

The capital asset pricing model captures these ideas in a simple way. That is why many financial managers find it the most convenient tool for coming to grips with the slippery notion of risk. And it is why economists often use the capital asset pricing model to demonstrate important ideas in finance even when

---

[12] Unless, of course, we were trying to sell it.

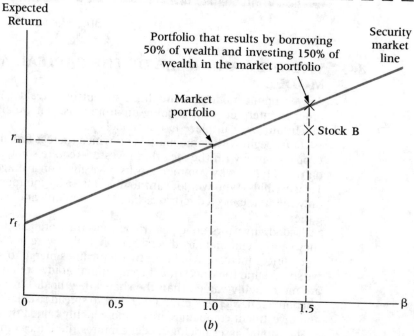

Figure 8-9 In equilibrium no stock can lie below the security market line. For example, instead of buying Stock A in Figure 8-9(a), investors would prefer to lend part of their money and put the balance in the market portfolio. This would give them a higher expected return on the security market line with the same beta risk. Instead of buying stock B in Figure 8-9(b), investors would prefer to borrow and invest in the market portfolio, obtaining a higher expected return on the security market line and the same beta.

there are other ways to prove these ideas. But that doesn't mean that the capital asset pricing model is ULTIMATE TRUTH. We will see later that it has several unsatisfactory features and we will also look at some alternative theories. Nobody knows whether one of these theories is eventually going to come out on top or whether there are other, better models of risk and return that have not yet seen the light of day.

Tests of the Capital Asset Pricing Model

The ultimate test of any model is whether it fits the facts. Unfortunately, there are two problems in testing the capital asset pricing model. First, it is concerned with *expected* returns, whereas we can observe only *actual* returns. Stock returns reflect expectations, but they also embody lots of "noise"—the steady flow of surprises that gives many stocks standard deviations of 30 or 40% per year. Second, the market portfolio should comprise all risky investments, including stocks, bonds, commodities, real estate—even human capital. Most market indexes contain only a sample of common stocks.[13]

No study has solved the second problem. However, a classic paper by Fama and MacBeth avoids the main pitfalls that come from having to work with actual rather than expected returns. Fama and MacBeth grouped all New York Stock Exchange Stocks into 20 portfolios. They then plotted the estimated beta of each portfolio in one 5-year period against the portfolio's average return over a subsequent 5-year period.[14] Figure 8–10 shows what they found. You can see that the estimated beta of each portfolio told investors quite a lot about its future return.

If the capital asset pricing model is correct, investors would not have expected any of these portfolios to perform better or worse than a comparable package of Treasury bills and the market portfolio. Therefore, the expected return on each portfolio, given the market return, should plot along the sloping lines in Figure 8–10. Notice that the *actual* returns on Fama and MacBeth's portfolios do plot *roughly* along these lines. That is encouraging, but we should like to know why the portfolios don't plot *exactly* along the lines. Is it because the capital asset pricing model is only a rough approximation to real markets? Or is it because the tests are not appropriate? (Remember that Fama and MacBeth are looking at *actual* returns, whereas the capital asset pricing model is concerned with expectations; also, Fama and MacBeth did not include *all* risky assets in their market index.) Unfortunately, nobody knows which explanation is correct. Betas that are calculated using a stock market index seem to tell us something about expected return, but we can't be sure what we would find if we were able to calculate betas using the full market portfolio of *all* risky assets.

---

[13] For example, see R. Roll, "A Critique of the Asset Pricing Theory's Tests; Part 1: On Past and Potential Testability of the Theory," *Journal of Financial Economics*, **4**: 129–176 (March 1977).

[14] Fama and MacBeth first estimated the beta of each stock during one period and then formed portfolios on the basis of these estimated betas. Next, they re-estimated the beta of each portfolio by using the returns in the subsequent period. This ensured that the estimated betas for each portfolio were largely unbiased and free from error. Finally, these portfolio betas were plotted against returns in an even later period. E.F. Fama and J.D. MacBeth, "Risk, Return and Equilibrium: Empirical Tests," *Journal of Political Economy*, **81**: 607–636 (May 1973).

The CAPM is tested for Canadian markets in R.A. Morin. "Market Line Theory and the Canadian Equity Market," *Journal of Business Administration*, **12** No.1: 57–76 (1980); A.L. Calvet and J. Lefoll, "Risk and Return on Canadian Capital Markets," *Canadian Journal of Administrative Sciences*, **5** No.1: 1–12 (1988); and M.J. Robinson, "Univariate CAPM Tests," Working Paper, Faculty of Management, University of Calgary (1991) to appear in M.J. Robinson and B.F. Smith: *Canadian Capital Markets*.

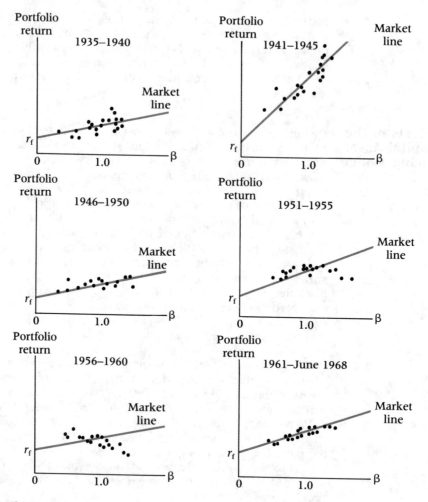

Figure 8-10 The capital asset pricing model states that the *expected* return from any investment should lie on the market line. The dots show the *actual* returns from portfolios with different betas.

Source: Results supplied by E.F. Fama and J.D. MacBeth. See their paper, "Risk Return and Equillibrium: Empirical Tests," *Journal of Political Economy*, **81**: 607–636 (May 1973).

There are other ways to test the capital asset pricing model. For example, remember that the model is equivalent to saying that the market portfolio is efficient. Efficient portfolios offer the highest expected return for their risk. That does not mean that they will always *with hindsight* provide the highest return but we can at least see whether any shortfall could simply have been due to bad luck. It turns out that the common stock market indexes were *not* efficient portfolios but we don't know whether a more comprehensive market index would have performed better.[15]

---

[15] See, for example, J.D. Jobson and B.M. Korkie, "Potential Performance and Tests of Portfolio Efficiency," *Journal of Financial Economics*, **10**: 433–466 (1982), and S. Kandel and R.F. Stambaugh, "On Correlations and Inferences about Mean-Variance Efficiency," *Journal of Financial Economics*, **18**: 61–90 (March 1987).

The capital asset pricing model also predicts that beta is the *only* reason that expected returns differ. But we shall present some evidence in Chapter 13 that the average return on small-firm stocks has been substantially larger than predicted by the capital asset pricing model.[16] If investors *expected* the returns to depend on firm size, then the simple version of the capital asset pricing model cannot be the whole truth.

*What Market Index Should Be Used in Canada?

We have stressed the notion that the market index must include *all* risky assets. Does that mean we should use an international index that is weighted more heavily toward American stocks than Canadian stocks, simply because the American market is so much larger than the Canadian market? Should we include European and Asian stocks in the index? Or, should we note that Canadians, on the whole, own more Canadian stocks than foreign stocks,[17] and take an index that is more heavily weighted with Canadian stocks? Or does it matter which index we use?

Certainly, the American and Canadian market indexes are highly correlated with each other. But they are not *perfectly* correlated, and Roll has shown that this can be enough to create substantially different estimates of expected return, depending on which index is used to calculate beta.[18] Several authors have approached the problem from an empirical perspective. In general, they provide evidence that a "made-in-Canada" capital asset pricing model is appropriate for Canadians. Canadian stocks seem to be accurately priced by the capital asset pricing model using an index of Canadian stocks, without having to include foreign securities in the index.

For example, Jorion and Schwartz[19] estimated a two-market-factor model for Canadian stocks. One factor was the U.S. value-weighted market index (as in the Fama-MacBeth study, for example) and the other factor was the Canadian market index. Essentially, they found that the Canadian market index had a risk premium, but the U.S. value-weighted index did not. This suggests that, in Canada, it is inappropriate to use a U.S.-based market index alone. It also provides evidence that it is appropriate to use a Canadian-based index alone. Mittoo[20] also studies this latter question by estimating the single-factor CAPM for 35 large-capitalization TSE stocks, of which 18 are interlisted on foreign exchange and 17 are not. She finds that the CAPM explains security returns better for both sets of stocks when the index is a Canadian stock index rather than when it is an "integrated index" consisting of a value-weighted combination of U.S. and Canadian stocks.

Suret and Chrisman[21] ask whether the Canadian market index is efficient like

---

[16] Of course, this could be because small-firm stocks have higher betas. This is the case but the difference in betas does not appear to be nearly sufficient to explain the difference in returns.

[17] One reason Canadians concentrate on domestic stocks is that Canadian stocks expose Canadian investors to lower personal taxes (see Chapter 16). Another reason may be that Canadians find it more awkward to transact in American security markets than in Canadian security markets.

[18] See R. Roll, *op cit.*

[19] See P. Jorion and E. Schwartz, "Integration vs. Segmentation in the Canadian Stock Market," *Journal of Finance*, **41:** 603–604 (July 1986).

[20] See U.R. Mittoo, "International Listing and Market Segmentation: Additional Evidence in the Canadian Stock Market," *Finance Proceedings, Administrative Sciences Association of Canada*, **12** Part 1: 59–68 (1991).

[21] See J-M Suret and H.H. Chrisman, "Some Evidence on the Gains to International Diversification for Canadian Investors," *Asia Pacific Journal of Management*, **7:** 109–131 (December 1990).

portfolio S in Figure 8–6 when investors are also allowed to invest in 22 national index portfolios, such as Australia, Belgium, England, France, Germany, Hong Kong, Japan, Mexico, South Africa, and the United States. If the Canadian market index is not efficient, then Canadian investors will always want to diversify the Canadian index with these international portfolios, and it would not be correct to measure systematic risk against the Canadian index only. Their results are consistent with the Canadian index being efficient, again suggesting that it is adequate for use by Canadians in the capital asset pricing model. However, they used daily data over a short time period (1986–1989), so their tests may not be sufficiently powerful to prove the inefficiency of the Canadian market portfolio in a global context.

Overall, the evidence is that the Canadian market is unique, in a risk-return sense. Moreover, unless further evidence is gathered to the contrary, it seems appropriate to use a Canadian market index for the capital asset pricing model rather than a global market index when estimating returns on Canadian stocks.

Assumptions behind the Capital Asset Pricing Model

The capital asset pricing model rests on several assumptions that we did not fully spell out. For example, we assumed that investment in Treasury bills is risk-free. It is true that there is little chance of default but they don't guarantee a *real* return. There is still some uncertainty about inflation. Another assumption was that investors can *borrow* money at the same rate of interest that they can lend. Generally, borrowing rates are higher than lending rates.

It turns out that many of these assumptions are not crucial and with a little pushing and pulling it is possible to modify the capital asset pricing model to handle them. The really important idea is that investors are content to invest their money in a limited number of benchmark portfolios. (In the basic CAPM these benchmarks are Treasury bills and the market portfolio.) In these modified CAPMs expected return still depends on market risk but the definition of market risk depends on the nature of the benchmark portfolios.[22] In practice none of these alternative capital asset pricing models is as widely used as the standard version.

*8–4 Consumption Betas versus Market Betas

SOME ALTERNATIVE THEORIES

The capital asset pricing model pictures investors as solely concerned with the level and uncertainty of their future wealth. But for most people wealth is not an end in itself. What good is wealth if you can't spend it? People invest now to provide future consumption for themselves, or for their families and heirs. The most important risks are those which might force a cutback of future consumption.

Douglas Breeden has developed a model in which a security's risk is measured by its sensitivity to changes in investors' consumption. If he is right, a stock's expected return should move in line with its *consumption beta* rather than its market beta. Figures 8–11(*a*) and 8–11(*b*) summarize the chief differences between the standard and consumption CAPMs.[23] In the standard model invest-

---

[22] For example, see M.C. Jensen (ed.), *Studies in the Theory of Capital Markets*, Frederick A. Praeger, Inc., New York, 1972. In the introduction to his book, Jensen provides a very useful summary of some of these variations on the capital asset pricing model.

[23] The consumption CAPM is compared empirically to the traditional CAPM in D. Breeden, M. Gibbons, and R. Litzenberger, "Empirical Tests of the Consumption-Oriented CAPM," *Journal of Finance*, **44**: 231–262 (1989).

Figure 8-11(*a*)   The standard CAPM concentrates on how stocks contribute to the level and uncertainty of investors' wealth. Consumption is outside the model.

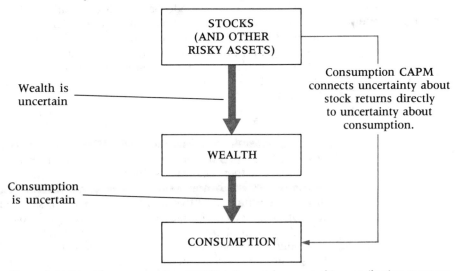

Figure 8-11(*b*)   The consumption CAPM defines risk as a stock's contribution to uncertainty about consumption. Wealth (the intermediate step between stock returns and consumption) drops out of the model.

ors are concerned exclusively with the amount and uncertainty of their future wealth. Each investor's wealth ends up perfectly correlated with the return on the market portfolio; the demand for stocks and other risky assets is thus determined by their market risk. The deeper motive for investing—to provide for consumption—is outside the model.

In the consumption CAPM, uncertainty about stock returns is connected directly to uncertainty about consumption. Of course, consumption depends on wealth (portfolio value), but wealth does not appear explicitly in the model.

The consumption CAPM has several appealing features. For example, you don't have to identify the market or any other benchmark portfolio. You don't have to worry that the TSE or Standard and Poor's composite index doesn't track returns on bonds, commodities, and real estate.

On the other hand, you do have to be able to measure consumption. *Quick*: how much did you consume last month? It's easy to count up the hamburgers and movie tickets—but what about the depreciation on your car or washing machine or the daily cost of your homeowner's insurance policy? We suspect that your estimate of total consumption will rest on rough or arbitrary allocations and assumptions. And if it's hard for you to put a dollar value on your total consumption, think of the task facing a government statistician asked to estimate month-by-month consumption for all of us.

Compared to stock prices, estimated aggregate consumption changes smoothly and gradually over time. Changes in consumption often seem to be out of phase with the stock market. Individual stocks seem to have low or erratic consumption betas. Moreover, the volatility of consumption appears too low to explain the past average rates of return on common stocks unless one assumes unreasonably high investor risk aversion.[24] These problems may reflect our poor measures of consumption, or perhaps poor models of how individuals distribute consumption over time. It seems too early for the consumption CAPM to aspire to practical use.

Arbitrage Pricing Theory

The capital asset pricing model begins with an analysis of how investors construct efficient portfolios. Stephen Ross's **arbitrage pricing theory (APT)** comes from a different family. It does not ask which portfolios are efficient. Instead, it starts by *assuming* that each stock's return depends partly on pervasive macroeconomic influences or "factors" and partly on "noise" — events that are unique to that company. Moreover, the return is assumed to obey the following simple relationship:

$$\text{Return} = a + b_1(r_{\text{factor 1}}) + b_2(r_{\text{factor 2}}) + b_3(r_{\text{factor 3}}) + \cdots + \text{"noise"}$$

The theory doesn't say what the factors are: there could be an oil price factor, an interest rate factor, and so on. The return on the market portfolio *might* serve as one factor, but then again it might not.

Some stocks will be more sensitive to a particular factor than others. Imperial Oil would be more sensitive to an oil factor than, say, Bombardier. If factor 1 picks up unexpected changes in oil prices, the beta for factor $1 (b_1)$ would be higher for Imperial Oil.

For any individual stock there are two sources of risk. First is the risk that stems from the pervasive macroeconomic factors and that cannot be eliminated by diversification. Second is the risk arising from possible events that are unique to the company. Diversification *does* eliminate unique risk and diversified investors can therefore ignore it when deciding whether to buy or sell a stock. The expected risk premium on a stock is affected by "factor" or "macroeconomic" risk: it is *not* affected by unique risk.

Arbitrage pricing theory states that the expected risk premium on a stock should depend on the expected risk premium associated with each factor and the stock's sensitivity to each of the factors (b_1, b_2, b_3, etc.). Thus, the formula is[25]

$$\begin{aligned} \text{Expected risk premium} \\ \text{on investment} \end{aligned} \begin{aligned} &= r - r_{\text{f}} \\ &= b_1(r_{\text{factor 1}} - r_{\text{f}}) + b_2(r_{\text{factor 2}} - r_{\text{f}}) + \cdots \end{aligned}$$

---

[24] See R. Mehra and E.C. Prescott, "The Equity Risk Premium: A Puzzle," *Journal of Monetary Economics*, **15**: 145–161 (1985).

[25] There may be some macroeconomic factors that investors are simply not worried about. (For example, some macroeconomists believe that money supply doesn't matter and therefore investors are not worried about inflation.) Such factors would not command a risk premium. They would drop out of the APT formula for expected return.

Notice that this formula makes two statements:

1. If you plug in a value of zero for each of the b's in the formula, the expected risk premium is zero. A diversified portfolio that is constructed to have zero sensitivity to each macro factor is essentially risk-free and therefore must be priced to offer the risk-free rate of interest. If the portfolio offered a higher return, investors could make a risk-free (or "arbitrage") profit by borrowing to buy the portfolio. If it offered a lower return, you could make an arbitrage profit by running the strategy in reverse—in other words, you would *sell* the diversified "zero-sensitivity" portfolio and *invest* the proceeds in Treasury bills.

2. A diversified portfolio that is constructed to have exposure only to, say, factor 1, will offer a risk premium that will vary in direct proportion to the portfolio's sensitivity to that factor. For example, imagine that you construct two portfolios—A and B—that are affected only by factor 1. If portfolio B is twice as sensitive to factor 1 as portfolio A, it must offer twice the risk premium. Therefore, if your divide your money equally between Treasury bills and portfolio B, your combined portfolio would have exactly the same sensitivity to factor 1 as portfolio A and it would offer the same risk premium.

Suppose that the arbitrage pricing formula did *not* hold. For example, suppose that the combination of Treasury bills and portfolio B offered a higher return. In that case investors could make an arbitrage profit by selling portfolio A and investing the proceeds in the mixture of bills and portfolio B.

The arbitrage that we have described applies to well-diversified portfolios where the unique risk has been diversified away. But, if the arbitrage pricing relationship holds for all diversified portfolios, it must hold generally for the individual stocks. Each stock must offer an expected return commensurate with its contribution to portfolio risk. In the APT, this contribution depends on the sensitivity of the stock's return to unexpected changes in the macroeconomic factors.

Does this argument sound familiar? It should, because it is the explanation we just gave for why all stocks lie on the security market line in the capital asset pricing model. Just replace stock A in Figure 8–9(a) with portfolio A and the market portfolio with portfolio B. The intuition behind the two theories is very similar.[26]

Figure 8–12 illustrates the arbitrage argument for the situation where you must borrow rather than lend at the riskless rate. This time, we will look directly at stocks, rather than portfolios. Again, for simplicity, we suppose that only one factor is important, so we can focus on stock returns and the stock sensitivities to this factor. Suppose stock C lies above the line through the riskless interest rate and stock D, which is twice as sensitive to the factor as C. You could borrow $100 and invest $200 in stock C for a net cost of $100. Call this portfolio P. Like stock D, portfolio P is twice as sensitive to the factor as stock C. Portfolio P lies on the line through the riskless interest rate and stock C, so it has a higher expected return than stock D. You finance the $100 cost of portfolio P by selling short $100 of stock D. Your overall investment costs $0 and has no sensitivity to the factor. But you expect to earn a profit of $100 times the difference between the expected return on P and the expected return on short position in D, or $100 $(r_P - r_D)$.

---

[26] You might find an early version of our CAPM "proof" in S.A. Ross, "Return, Risk and Arbitrage," which appears in I. Friend and J. Bicksler, eds. *Risk and Return in Finance, Volume I,* Cambridge, Mass.: Ballinger, 1977. Well, first you must find the book—it is a bit of a collector's item. If you find the book, you'll find the proof.

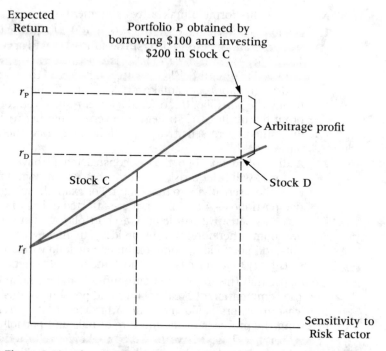

Figure 8-12   If stock C lies above the security market line, you could earn an arbitrage profit of $100 ($r_P - r_D$) by going short on $100 of stock D and long on portfolio P, which consists of $200 of stock C and $100 of borrowing. Since both portfolio P and stock D have the same sensitivity to the systematic risk factor, the resulting portfolio has no systematic risk. You can diversify away any remaining unique risk because the investments are so small.

What have you done to earn this profit? Your investment is costless and has no systematic risk. The profit is almost an arbitrage profit, except that you might still be exposed to unique risk. This is because stock C's unique risk probably won't be perfectly correlated with D's unique risk. But, you have only taken a small position in C and D, so the unique risk will be diversified away in the context of your whole portfolio.[27] Thus you have made an essentially riskless, costless investment, but earned a profit. This is a money machine. As long as you don't take too large an arbitrage position, you are exposed to negligible risk. But, other people could make similar small arbitrage profits. The popularity of the money machine would drive up the price of C and drive down the price of D. Stock C's future expected return would fall and stock D's future expected return would rise, until the two stocks fall onto a single line through the riskless interest rate. By repeating the process for all possible stocks, we find that they must all lie on the same risk-return line in this single-factor world. It is the absence of arbitrage that guarantees the risk-return relationship of arbitrage pricing theory.

---

[27] We can be confident that, as a successful business student, your whole portfolio is worth substantially more than $100. Right?

A Comparison of the Capital Asset Pricing Model and Arbitrage Pricing Theory

Like the capital asset pricing model, arbitrage pricing theory stresses that expected return depends on the risk that stems from economy-wide influences and is not affected by unique risk. You can think of the factors in arbitrage pricing as representing special portfolios of stocks that tend to be subject to a common influence. If the expected risk premium on each of these portfolios is proportional to the portfolio's market beta, then the arbitrage pricing theory and the capital asset pricing model will give the same answer. In any other case they won't.

How do the two theories stack up? Arbitrage pricing has some attractive features. For example, the market portfolio that plays such a central role in the capital asset pricing model does not feature in arbitrage pricing theory.[28] So we don't have to worry about the problem of measuring the market portfolio and we can in principle test the arbitrage pricing theory even if we have data on only a sample of risky assets.

Unfortunately, you win some, you lose some. Arbitrage pricing theory doesn't tell us what the underlying factors are—unlike the capital asset pricing model, which collapses *all* macroeconomic risks into a well-defined *single* factor: the return on the market portfolio. Arbitrage pricing theory will provide a good handle on expected returns only if we can (1) identify a reasonably short list of macroeconomic factors, (2) measure the expected risk premium on each of these factors, and (3) measure the sensitivity of each stock to these factors.

Research is proceeding on all three issues. For example, Chen, Roll, and Ross have argued that there are four principal pervasive influences on stock prices.[29] These are unanticipated changes in

- the level of industrial activity
- the rate of inflation
- the spread between short- and long-term interest rates, and
- the spread between the yields of low- and high-risk corporate bonds.

Others are not so sure that this list is comprehensive: they point out that the more stocks you look at, the more factors you need to take into account.[30]

So far, we are not at the stage where the arbitrage pricing theory is used to estimate the company's cost of capital in everyday situations.[31] For the immediate future financial managers are likely to continue to rely on the capital asset pricing model as the dominant theory of risk and return.

---

[28] Of course, the market portfolio *may* turn out to be one of the factors but that is not a necessary implication of arbitrage pricing theory.

[29] See N-F. Chen, R. Roll, and S.A. Ross, "Economic Forces and the Stock Market: Testing the APT and Alternative Pricing Theories," *Journal of Business*, **59**: 383–403 (July 1986). E. Otuteye, "On the Specification of the Arbitrage Pricing Theory," *Finance Proceedings, Administrative Sciences Association of Canada*, **12** Part 1: 69–80 (1991) performs the same type of analysis on Canadian data.

[30] See, for example, P.J. Dhrymes, I. Friend, and N.B. Gultekin, "A Critical Reexamination of the Empirical Evidence on the Arbitrage Pricing Theory," *Journal of Finance*, **39**: 323–346 (June 1984). Some tests of the APT on Canadian data cannot find strong evidence that *any* factor is priced. See S. Abeysekera and A. Mahajan, "A Test of the APT in Pricing Canadian Stocks," *Canadian Journal of Administrative Sciences*, **4**: 113–124 (1987) and B.F. Smith, "A Study of the Arbitrage Pricing Theory Using Daily Returns of Canadian Stocks," Working Paper, School of Business, Wilfrid Laurier University (1991), forthcoming in M.J. Robinson and B.F. Smith: *Canadian Capital Markets*. Of course, it is unlikely that systematic risk does not command a risk premium in Canada, but the Canadian data sets are small, so it is hard to gather enough data to come to a definitive conclusion about the price of risk.

[31] However, in the next chapter we shall look at how one company has used the arbitrage pricing theory as well as the capital asset pricing model to estimate the expected stock return.

8–5   SUMMARY

The basic principles of portfolio selection boil down to a common-sense statement that investors try to increase the expected return on their portfolios and to reduce the standard deviation of that return. A portfolio that gives the highest expected return for a given standard deviation, or the lowest standard deviation for a given expected return, is known as an *efficient portfolio*. In order to work out which portfolios are efficient, an investor must be able to state the expected return and standard deviation of each stock and the degree of correlation between each pair of stocks.

Investors who are restricted to holding common stocks should choose an efficient portfolio that suits their attitude to risk. But investors who can also borrow and lend at the risk-free rate of interest should choose the "best" common stock portfolio *regardless* of their attitude to risk. Having done that, they can then set the risk of their overall portfolio by deciding what proportion of their money they are willing to invest in stocks. For an investor who has only the same opportunities and information as everybody else, the best stock portfolio is the same as the best stock portfolio for other investors. In other words, he or she should invest in a mixture of the market portfolio and a risk-free loan (i.e., borrowing or lending).

A stock's marginal contribution to portfolio risk is measured by its sensitivity to changes in the value of the portfolio. If a portfolio is efficient, there will be a straight-line relationship between each stock's expected return and its marginal contribution to the risk of the portfolio. The marginal contribution of a stock to the risk of the *market portfolio* is measured by *beta*. So, if the market portfolio is efficient, there will be a straight-line relationship between the expected return and beta of each stock. That is the fundamental idea behind the *capital asset pricing model* which concludes that each security's expected risk premium should increase in proportion to its beta:

$$\text{Expected risk premium} = \text{beta} \times (\text{market risk premium})$$
$$r - r_f = \beta (r_m - r_f)$$

The capital asset pricing theory is the best-known model of risk and return. A number of modifications have been proposed to cope with such complexities as different borrowing and lending rates, and a new theory called the *consumption capital asset pricing model* suggests that security risk reflects the sensitivity of returns to changes in investors' *consumption*. This theory calls for a consumption beta rather than a beta relative to the market portfolio.

The *arbitrage pricing theory* offers an alternative theory of risk and return. It states that the expected risk premium on a stock should depend on the stock's exposure to several pervasive macroeconomic factors that affect stock returns:

$$\text{Expected risk premium} = b_1(r_{\text{factor 1}} - r_f) + b_2(r_{\text{factor 2}} - r_f) + \cdots$$

Here the b's represent the individual security's sensitivities to the factors, and $(r_{\text{factor}} - r_f)$ is the risk premium demanded by investors who are exposed to this factor.

Arbitrage pricing theory does not say what these factors are. It asks for economists to hunt for unknown game with their statistical tool kits. The hunters have returned with several candidates including unanticipated changes in:

- the level of industrial activity
- the rate of inflation

- the spread between short- and long-term interest rates, and
- the spread between the yields of low- and high-risk corporate bonds.

Each of these different models of risk and return has its fan club. However, all financial economists agree on two basic ideas: (1) investors require extra expected return for taking on risk, and (2) they appear to be concerned predominantly with the risk that they cannot eliminate by diversification.

FURTHER READING

The pioneering article on portfolio selection is:

H.M. Markowitz, "Portfolio Selection," *Journal of Finance*, **7**: 77–91 (March 1952).

There is a number of textbooks on portfolio selection which explain both Markowitz's original theory and some ingenious simplified versions. See, for example:

E.J. Elton and M.J. Gruber, *Modern Portfolio Theory and Investment Analysis*, 2nd ed., John Wiley & Sons, New York, 1984.
H. Levy and M. Sarnat, *Portfolio and Investment Selection: Theory and Practice*, Prentice-Hall International, Englewood Cliffs, N.J., 1984.

Of the three pioneering articles on the capital asset pricing model, Jack Treynor's has never been published. The other two articles are:

J. Lintner, "The Valuation of Risk Assets and the Selection of Risky Investments in Stock Portfolios and Capital Budgets," *Review of Economics and Statistics*, **47**: 13–37 (February 1965).
W.F. Sharpe, "Capital Asset Prices: A Theory of Market Equilibrium under Conditions of Risk," *Journal of Finance*, **19**: 425–442 (September 1964).

The subsequent literature on the capital asset pricing model is enormous. The following book provides a collection of some of the more important articles plus a very useful survey by Jensen:

M.C. Jensen (ed.), *Studies in the Theory of Capital Markets*, Frederick A. Praeger, Inc., New York, 1972.

There has been a number of tests of the capital asset pricing model. Some of the more important tests are:

F. Black, M.C. Jensen, and M. Scholes, "The Capital Asset Pricing Model: Some Empirical Tests," in M.C. Jensen (ed.), *Studies in the Theory of Capital Markets*, Frederick A. Praeger, Inc., New York, 1972.
E.F. Fama and J.D. MacBeth, "Risk, Return and Equilibrium: Empirical Tests," *Journal of Political Economy*, **81**: 607–636 (May 1973).
M.R. Gibbons, "Multivariate Tests of Financial Models," *Journal of Financial Economics*, **10**: 3–27 (March 1982).

For a critique of empirical tests of the model, see:

R. Roll, "A Critique of the Asset Pricing Theory's Tests; Part I: On Past and Potential Testability of the Theory," *Journal of Financial Economics*, **14**: 129–176 (March 1977).

Breeden's 1979 article describes the consumption asset pricing model and the Breeden, Gibbons, and Litzenberger paper tests the model and compares it with the standard CAPM:

D.T. Breeden "An Intertemporal Asset Pricing Model with Stochastic Consumption and Investment Opportunities," *Journal of Financial Economics*, **7**: 265–296 (September 1979).
D.T. Breeden, M.R. Gibbons, and R.H. Litzenberger, "Empirical Tests of the Consumption-Oriented CAPM," *Journal of Finance*, **44**: 231–262 (June 1989).

Arbitrage pricing theory is described in Ross's 1976 and 1977 papers. (The 1976 paper is easier to find, but the 1977 paper is easier to read.) The other three papers are classic tests of the model:

N-F. Chen, "Some Empirical Tests of the Theory of Arbitrage Pricing," *Journal of Finance,* **38:** 1393–1414 (December 1983).

N-F. Chen, R. Roll, and S.A. Ross, "Economic Forces and the Stock Market: Testing the APT and Alternative Pricing Theories," *Journal of Business,* **59:** 383–403 (July 1986).

R. Roll and S.A. Ross, "An Empirical Investigation of the Arbitrage Pricing Theory," *Journal of Finance,* **35:** 1073–1103 (December 1983).

S.A. Ross: The Arbitrage Theory of Capital Asset Pricing," *Journal of Economic Theory,* **13:** 341–360 (December 1976).

S.A. Ross: "Return, Risk and Arbitrage," which appears in I. Friend and J. Bicksler (eds.), *Risk and Return in Finance, Volume I,* Cambridge, Mass.: Ballinger, 1977.

QUIZ

1. Figures 8–13 and 8–14 purport to show the range of attainable combinations of expected return and standard deviation.
   (a) Which diagram is incorrectly drawn and why?
   (b) Which is the efficient set of portfolios?
   (c) If r_f is the rate of interest, mark with an X the optimal stock portfolio.

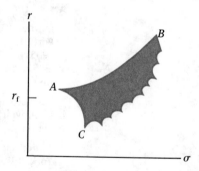

Figure 8-13   See Quiz, question 1.   Figure 8-14   See Quiz, question 1.

2. For each of the following pairs of investments, state which would always be preferred by a rational investor (assuming that these are the *only* investments that are available to the investor):
   (a) Portfolio A $r = 18\%$ $\sigma = 20\%$
       Portfolio B $r = 14\%$ $\sigma = 20\%$
   (b) Portfolio C $r = 15\%$ $\sigma = 18\%$
       Portfolio D $r = 13\%$ $\sigma = 8\%$
   (c) Portfolio E $r = 14\%$ $\sigma = 16\%$
       Portfolio F $r = 14\%$ $\sigma = 10\%$
3. Consider the following four portfolios:
   (a) 50% in Treasury bills, 50% in share W
   (b) 50% in share W, 50% in share X, where the returns are perfectly positively correlated.
   (c) 50% in share X, 50% in share Y, where the returns are uncorrelated.
   (d) 50% in share Y, 50% in share Z, where the returns are perfectly negatively correlated.

In which of these cases would the standard deviation of the portfolio lie exactly midway between that of the two securities?

4. (a) Plot the following risky portfolios on a graph:

Portfolio	A	B	C	D	E	F	G	H
Expected return, r, %	10	12.5	15	16	17	18	18	20
Standard deviation, σ, %	23	21	25	29	29	32	35	45

   (b) Five of these portfolios are efficient and three are not. Which are *inefficient* ones?
   (c) Suppose you can also borrow and lend at an interest rate of 12%. Which of the above portfolios is best?
   (d) Suppose you are prepared to tolerate a standard deviation of 25%. What is the maximum expected return that you can achieve if you cannot borrow or lend?
   (e) What is your optimal strategy, if you can borrow or lend at 12% and are prepared to tolerate a standard deviation of 25%? What is the maximum expected return that you can achieve?

5. True or false?
   (a) The capital asset pricing model implies that, if you could find an investment with a negative beta, its expected return would be less than the interest rate.
   (b) The expected return on an investment with a beta of 2.0 is twice as high as the expected return on the market.
   (c) If a stock lies below the security market line, it is undervalued.

6. Suppose that the Treasury bill rate is 4% and the expected return on the market is 10%. Using the information in Table 8–1:
   (a) Calculate the expected return from Spar Aerospace.
   (b) Find the highest expected return that is offered by one of these stocks.
   (c) Find the lowest expected return that is offered by one of these stocks.
   (d) Would PWA Corporation offer a higher or lower expected return if the interest rate was 6% rather than 4%? Assume that the expected return on the market stays at 10%.
   (e) Would Bell Canada Enterprises offer a higher or lower expected return if the interest rate was 6%?

7. The capital asset pricing model states that a stock has the same market risk and expected return as:
   (a) A portfolio with proportion β invested in Treasury bills and $1 - \beta$ in the market
   (b) A portfolio with β invested in the market and $1 - \beta$ in Treasury bills
   (c) A portfolio evenly divided between the market and Treasury bills
   Which is the correct answer?

QUESTIONS AND PROBLEMS

1. Enter in Figure 8–15 a line showing the relationship between the expected risk premium on the portfolio given the risk premium on the market index for (a) a portfolio that is evenly divided between Treasury bills and the market index, and (b) a portfolio that is financed half by borrowing and is entirely invested in the market index.

Figure 8-15   See Questions and Problems, 1.

2. Last week Prudence Puffin analyzed three common stock portfolios. She
    remembers that portfolio X offered an expected return of 10% and standard
    deviation of 10%, and that portfolio Y offered an expected return of 14%
    and standard deviation of 20%. Unfortunately, all that she can remember
    about portfolio Z is that it is the best of the three portfolios as long as the
    interest rate is between 5% and 9%. Otherwise, she would do better to
    invest in one of the other two portfolios and borrow or lend the balance of
    her money.
    (a) What are the expected return and standard deviation of portfolio Z?
    (b) When should Ms. Puffin invest in portfolio X and portfolio Y?
3. "There may be some truth in the capital asset pricing model, but over the
    past year many stocks gave a substantially higher return than the capital
    asset pricing model predicted and many others gave a substantially lower
    return." Is this a valid criticism of the model?
4. Sketch the efficient set of common stock portfolios. Show the combinations
    of expected return and risk that you could achieve if you could borrow and
    lend at the same risk-free rate of interest. Now show the combinations of
    expected return and risk that you could achieve if the rate of interest is
    higher for borrowing than for lending.
5. Look back at the calculation for Imasco and Teck Corp in Section 8–1. Using
    Table 7–3 data for Bell Canada Enterprises and Molson Companies, re-do
    the analysis. That is, calculate the expected portfolio return and standard
    deviation for different values of x_1 and x_2 assuming $\rho_{12} = 0$. Plot the range
    of possible combinations of expected return and standard deviation as in
    Figure 8–4. Repeat the exercise for $\rho_{12} = +1$ and for $\rho_{12} = -1$.
6. Mark Harrywitz proposes to invest in two shares, X and Y. He expects a
    return of 12% from X and 8% from Y. The standard deviation of returns is
    8% for X and 5% for Y. The correlation coefficient between the returns is
    0.2.
    (a) Compute the expected return and standard deviation of the following
        portfolios:

Portfolio	% in X	% in Y
1	50	50
2	25	75
3	75	25

(b) Sketch the set of portfolios composed of X and Y.

(c) Suppose that Mr. Harrywitz can also borrow or lend at an interest rate of 5%. Show on your sketch how this alters his opportunities. Given that he can borrow or lend, what proportions of the common stock portfolio should be invested in X and Y?

7. Hilda Hornbill has invested 60% of her money in share A and the remainder in share B. She assesses their prospects as follows:

	A	B
Expected return, %	15	20
Standard deviation, %	20	22

Correlation between returns 0.5

(a) What is the expected return and standard deviation of returns on her portfolio?

(b) How would your answer be changed if the correlation coefficient was 0 or −0.5?

(c) Is Ms. Hornbill's portfolio better or worse than one invested entirely in share A or is it not possible to say?

8. The Treasury bill rate is 4% and the expected return on the market portfolio is 12%. On the basis of the capital asset pricing model:

(a) Draw a graph similar to Figure 8–7 showing how expected return varies with beta.

(b) What is the risk premium on the market?

(c) What is the required return on an investment with a beta of 1.5?

(d) If an investment with a beta of 0.8 offers an expected return of 9.8%, does it have a positive NPV?

(e) If the market expects a return of 11.2% from stock X, what is the beta?

9. Estimate the returns expected by investors *today* for the 12 stocks in Table 8–1. Plot the expected returns against beta as in Figure 8–7.

10. A company is deciding whether to make a stock issue to raise money for an investment project which has the same risk as the market and an expected return of 20%. If the risk-free rate is 10% and the expected return on the market is 15%, the company should go ahead

(a) Unless the company's beta is greater than 2.0

(b) Unless the company's beta is less than 2.0

(c) Whatever the company's beta

Which answer is correct? Say briefly why.

11. The stock of United Merchants has a beta of 1.0 and very high unique risk. If the expected return on the market is 20%, the expected return on United will be

(a) 10% if the interest rate is 10%

(b) 20%

(c) More than 20% because of the high unique risk

(d) Indeterminate unless you also know the interest rate

Which is the right answer? Say *briefly* why.

12. The expected return on a stock is frequently written as $r = \alpha + \beta r_m$, where r_m is the expected return on the market. The capital asset pricing model says that in equilibrium

(a) $\alpha = 0$

(b) $\alpha = r_f$ (the risk-free rate of interest)

(c) $\alpha = (1 - \beta)r_f$

(d) $\alpha = (1 - r_f)$

Which is correct?

13. Estimate the expected return from the stock market in Canada over the next year. Subtract the current dividend yield to give you a rough estimate of the expected capital appreciation.

14. In footnote 4 we noted that the minimum risk portfolio contained an investment of 28.0% in Teck and 82.0% in Imasco. Prove it. *Hint*: You need a little calculus to do so.

*15. The following question illustrates the arbitrage pricing theory. Imagine that there are only two pervasive macroeconomic factors. Investments X, Y, and Z have the following sensitivities to these two factors:

	b_1	b_2
X	1.75	0.25
Y	−1.00	2.00
Z	2.00	1.00

We assume that the expected risk premium is 4% on factor 1 and 8% on factor 2. Treasury bills obviously offer zero risk premium.

(a) According to arbitrage pricing theory what is the risk premium on each of the three stocks?

(b) Suppose you buy $200 of X and $50 of Y and sell $150 of Z. What is the sensitivity of your portfolio to each of the two factors? What is the expected risk premium?

(c) Suppose you buy $80 of X and $60 of Y and sell $40 of Z. What is the sensitivity of your portfolio to each of the two factors? What is the expected risk premium?

(d) Finally, suppose you buy $160 of X and $20 of Y and sell $80 of Z. What is your portfolio's sensitivity now to each of the two factors? And what is the expected risk premium?

(e) Suggest two possible ways that you could construct a fund that had a sensitivity of 0.5 to factor 1 only. Now compare the expected risk premiums on each of these investments.

(f) Suppose that the arbitrage pricing relationship did *not* hold and that X offered a risk premium of 8%, Y offered a premium of 14% and Z a premium of 16%. Devise an investment that had zero sensitivity to each factor and that offered a risk premium.

C · H · A · P · T · E · R

9

CAPITAL BUDGETING AND RISK

Long before the development of modern theories linking risk and expected return, smart financial managers adjusted for risk in capital budgeting. They realized intuitively that, if other things are equal, risky projects are less desirable than safe ones. Therefore, they demanded a higher rate of return from risky projects or they based their decisions on conservative estimates of the cash flows.

Various rules of thumb are often used to make these risk adjustments. For example, many companies estimate the rate of return required by investors in their securities and use the company cost of capital to discount the cash flows on all new projects. Since investors require a higher rate of return from a very risky company, such a firm will have a higher company cost of capital and will set a higher discount rate for its new investment opportunities. For example, in Table 8–1 we estimated that investors expected a rate of return of 0.159 or about 16% from the stock of Spar Aerospace. Therefore, according to the company cost of capital rule, Spar should have been using a 16% discount rate to compute project net present values.[1]

This is a step in the right direction. Even though we can't measure risk or the expected return on risky securities with absolute precision, it is still reasonable to assert that Spar faced about the same risk as the average firm and, therefore, should have demanded about the same rate of return from its capital investments.

But the company cost of capital rule can also get a firm into trouble if the new projects are more or less risky than its existing business. Each project should be evaluated at its *own* opportunity cost of capital. This is a clear implication of the value-additivity principle introduced in Chapter 7. For a firm composed of assets A and B, firm value is

Firm value = PV(AB) = PV(A) + PV(B) = sum of separate asset values

Here, PV(A) and PV(B) are valued just as if they were mini-firms in which stockholders could invest directly. Note: investors would value A by discounting its forecasted cash flows at a rate reflecting the risk of A. They would value B by

---

[1] Spar did not use any significant amount of debt financing. Thus, its cost of capital is the rate of return investors expect on its common stock. The complications caused by debt are discussed later in this chapter.

Figure 9-1   A comparison between the company cost of capital rule and the required return under the capital asset pricing model. Spar's company cost of capital is about 16%. This is the correct discount rate only if the project beta is 0.88. In general, the correct discount rate increases as project beta increases. Spar should accept projects with rates of return above the security market line relating required return to beta.

discounting at a rate reflecting the risk of B. The two discount rates will, in general, be different.

If the firm considers investing in a third project C, it should also value C as if it were a mini-firm. That is, it should discount the cash flows of C at the expected rate of return that investors would demand to make a separate investment in C. *The true cost of capital depends on the use to which the capital is put.*

This means that Spar should accept any project that more than compensates for the *project's beta*. In other words, it should accept any project lying above the upward-sloping line that links expected return to risk in Figure 9–1. If the project has a high risk, Spar needs a higher prospective return than if the project has a low risk. Now contrast this with the company cost of capital rule, which is to accept any project *regardless of its risk* as long as it offers a higher return than the *company's* cost of capital. In terms of Figure 9–1, it tells Spar to accept any project above the horizontal cost-of-capital line — that is, any project offering a return of more than 16%.

It is clearly silly to suggest that Spar should demand the same rate of return from a very safe project as from a very risky one. If Spar used the company cost of capital rule, it would reject many good low-risk projects and accept many poor high-risk projects. It is also silly to suggest that, just because Bell Canada Enterprises has a low company cost of capital, it is justified in accepting projects that Spar would reject. If you followed such a rule to its seemingly logical conclusion, you would think it possible to enlarge the company's investment opportunities by investing a large sum in Treasury bills. That would make the common stock safe and create a low company cost of capital.[2]

The notion that each company has some individual discount rate or cost of capital is widespread, but far from universal. Many firms require different return from different categories of investment. Discount rates might be set, for example, as follows:

---

[2] If the present value of an asset depended on the identity of the company that bought it, present values would not add up. Remember that a good project is a good project is a good project.

Category	Discount Rate, %
Speculative ventures	30
New products	20
Expansion of existing business	15 (company cost of capital)
Cost improvement, known technology	10

The capital asset pricing model is widely used by large corporations to estimate the discount rate. It states

$$\text{Expected project return} = r = r_f + (\text{project beta}) (r_m - r_f)$$

In order to calculate this you have to figure out the project beta.

Before thinking about the betas of individual projects, we will first look at some problems you would encounter in using beta to estimate a company's cost of capital. It turns out that beta is difficult to measure accurately for an individual firm: much greater accuracy can be achieved by looking at an average of similar companies. But then we have to define *similar*. Among other things we will find that a firm's borrowing policy affects its stock beta. It would be misleading, for example, to average the betas of Chrysler, which is a heavy borrower, and General Motors, which is not.

The company cost of capital is the correct discount rate for projects that have the same risk as the company's existing business but *not* for those that are safer or riskier than the company's average. The problem is to judge the relative risks of the projects available to the firm. In order to handle that problem, we will need to dig a little deeper and look at those features that make some investments riskier than others. After you know *why* Bell Canada Enterprises stock has less market risk than, say, Bombardier, you will be in a better position to judge the relative risks of capital investment opportunities.

There is still another complication: project betas can shift over time. Some projects are safer in youth than in old age, others are riskier. In this case, what do we mean by *the* project beta? There may be a separate beta for each year of the project's life. To put it another way, can we jump from the capital asset pricing model, which looks out one period into the future, to the discounted-cash-flow formula that we developed in Chapters 2 to 6 for valuing long-lived assets? Most of the time it is safe to do so, but you should be able to recognize and deal with the exceptions.

9–1   MEASURING BETAS

Suppose that you are considering an across-the-board expansion by your firm. Such an investment would have about the same degree of risk as the existing business. Therefore, you should discount the projected flows at the company cost of capital. To estimate that, you could begin by estimating the beta of the company's stock.

An obvious way to measure the beta of the stock is to look at how its price has responded in the past to market movements. For example, in Figure 9–2 we have plotted monthly rates of return from British Columbia Telephone and Canadian Pacific against market returns for the same months. In each case we have fitted a line through the points. Beta is the slope of the line. It varied from one period to the other, but there is little doubt that CP's beta was greater than BC Tel's. If you had used the past beta of either stock to predict its future beta, you wouldn't have been too far off in most cases.

Figure 9-2(a) We can use data on past prices to obtain an estimate of British Columbia Telephone's beta. Notice that it is consistently less than 1.

Figure 9-2(b) Here is a similar exercise for Canadian Pacific. Notice that CP's beta is consistently greater than BC Tel's.

Stability of Betas over Time

We would not want you to go away with the idea that all betas are as stable as Canadian Pacific's. Nevertheless, betas do appear to be *reasonably* stable.

An extensive study of stability was provided by Sharpe and Cooper.[3] They divided stocks into ten classes according to the estimated beta in that period. Each class contained one-tenth of the stocks in the sample. The stocks with the lowest betas went into class 1. Class 2 contained stocks with slightly higher betas, and so on. They then looked at the frequency with which stocks jumped from one class to another. The more jumps, the less stability. You can see from Table 9–1 that there is a marked tendency for stocks with very high or low betas to stay that way. If you are willing to stretch the definition of *stable* to include a jump to an adjacent risk class, then from 40 to 70% of betas were stable over the subsequent five years.

Table 9-1
Sharpe and Cooper divided stocks into risk classes according to their betas in one 5-year period (class 10 contains high betas, class 1 contains low betas). They then looked at how many of these stocks were in the same risk class 5 years later.

Risk Class	Percent in Same Risk Class 5 Years Later	Percent within One Risk Class 5 Years Later
10	35	69
9	18	54
8	16	45
7	13	41
6	14	39
5	14	42
4	13	40
3	16	45
2	21	61
1	40	62

One reason that these estimates of beta are only imperfect guides to the future is that the stocks may genuinely change their market risk. However, a more important reason is that the betas in any one period are just estimates based on a limited number of observations. If good company news coincides by chance with high market returns, the stock's beta will appear higher than if the news coincides with low market returns. We can twist this the other way around. If a stock appears to have a high beta, it may be because it genuinely does have a high beta, or it may be because we have overestimated it.

This explains some of the observed fluctuations in betas. Suppose a company's true beta really is stable. Its apparent (estimated) beta will fluctuate from period to period due to random measurement errors. So the stability of true betas is probably better than Sharpe and Cooper's results seem to imply.

Using a Beta Book

Because of the investment community's interest in market risk, beta estimates of varying quality are regularly published by a number of brokerage and advisory services. Table 9–2 shows a sample page of the kind of information they often

---

[3] W.F. Sharpe and G.M. Cooper, "Risk-Return Classes of New York Stock Exchange Common Stocks, 1931–1967," *Financial Analysts Journal*, **28**: 46–54, 81 (March–April 1972).

Table 9-2

A sample page of a "beta book." The calculations are done by straight regression of monthly percentage security returns on the TSE 300 Total Return Index percentage returns for the period February 1985 to January 1990.

Ticker symbol	Security name	Beta	Std. error	Alpha	Std. error	R^2	Resid Std. dev.	Number of obs.
LDM.A	Laidlaw Transportation A	1.09	0.23	1.99	1.06	0.28	8.02	60
LDM.B	Laidlaw Transportation B	1.23	0.22	1.93	1.01	0.35	7.68	60
LMK	Landmark Corp.	0.82	0.58	−2.83	2.67	0.03	20.21	60
LTL	Lytton Minerals	0.85	0.63	−3.61	2.90	0.03	1.40	60
LUM	Lumonics Inc.	0.73	0.33	−1.87	1.61	0.09	11.32	52
MB	MacMillan Bloedel	1.49	0.22	0.36	1.01	0.45	7.64	60
MCL	Moore Corp.	0.84	0.14	0.15	0.63	0.39	4.80	60
MCS	McChip Resources	0.85	0.37	−0.76	1.71	0.08	12.96	60
MEC	Maritime Electric Company	0.39	0.11	0.87	0.49	0.19	3.70	60
MG.A	Magna International A	1.73	0.26	−2.70	1.22	0.42	9.26	60
MG.B	Maga International B	0.61	0.18	−0.89	0.83	0.17	6.30	60
MGI	Mavtech Holdings Inc.	0.81	0.51	−0.50	2.38	0.04	18.04	60
MHG.A	MDS Health Group A	0.64	0.15	0.32	0.71	0.23	5.40	60
MHG.B	MDS Health Group B	0.80	0.17	0.20	0.77	0.29	5.80	60
MHI	Morgan Hydrocarbons Inc.	1.33	0.36	0.31	1.66	0.19	12.54	60
MHR	McGraw-Hill Ryerson Ltd.	0.45	0.08	0.47	0.38	0.34	2.89	60
MIV	MICC Investments	1.17	0.33	2.89	1.53	0.18	11.61	60
MJC	Majestic Contractors	1.64	0.33	0.05	1.55	0.29	11.74	60
MKC	Mark Resources	1.13	0.26	−0.64	1.21	0.24	9.18	60
ML	Maple Leaf Gardens	0.31	0.23	2.77	1.05	0.03	7.92	60
MLT	Mitel Corp.	1.19	0.26	−2.82	1.22	0.26	9.27	60
MNN	Moneco Ltd.	0.57	0.28	−1.84	1.31	0.07	9.88	60
MOF	Moffat Communications	0.92	0.17	0.32	0.77	0.34	5.86	60
MOL.A	Molson Companies A	0.92	0.16	0.81	0.75	0.36	5.68	60
MOL.B	Molson Companies B	0.73	0.15	1.03	0.70	0.29	5.26	60

Source: Based on data contained in the Toronto Stock Exchange/University of Western Ontario data file.

provide. Look more closely at Laidlaw Transportation B (LDM.B), one of the stocks in Table 9–2. The table entries are based on 60 monthly returns (February 1985 to January 1990) for Laidlaw B stock and for the market (represented by the TSE 300 Composite Index). The rates of return consist of price changes, plus dividends, per dollar invested. Laidlaw B's beta of 1.23 was estimated by "straight" regression, that is, by using a standard least-squares regression program to find the line of "best fit."[4]

The other information in Table 9–2 is interesting.

Alpha.   Figure 9–3 shows the line that the regression program fitted to the plot of returns on Laidlaw B and the market. (It is similar to Figure 7–9, in which we showed Alcan returns.) Beta is the slope of the line and alpha (α) is the intercept. Laidlaw B's alpha was 1.93.

Alpha is a rate of price change. Its units are percent per period—in this case, percent per month since the line was fitted to monthly data. Laidlaw is in the

---

[4] Although it is easy in principle to find a line of best fit, there are some tricks to finding the best time period over which to measure returns, to dealing with stocks that trade only infrequently, and so on. Some "beta services" are much more careful than others.

Figure 9-3 Results of regressing Laidlaw B's returns on the market returns for 60 months ending in January 1990. The slope of the fitted line is beta. The intercept is alpha.

transportation and waste removal business. Concerns during the late 1980s about finding appropriate sanitary landfill sites helped Laidlaw stock, because the company would benefit from higher fees for transporting waste greater distances. Laidlaw was also the subject of a partial takeover by Canadian Pacific during the period, which helped to drive up its stock price. This is reflected in the alpha of 1.93, which is approximately equal to 12 × 1.93 or 23.2% per year. From Figure 9–3, we see that alpha was the average rate of price appreciation borne by Laidlaw B stockholders when investors in the market as a whole earned nothing. Investors in some other stocks in Table 9–2 were less fortunate. What about the future? Will Laidlaw B continue to perform so well? Possibly, but you should not bet on it. The most likely outcome is that the return will simply compensate for the market risk.

R-Squared and Residual Standard Deviation. The column headed R^2 shows the proportion of the total variance of Laidlaw B stock price changes that can be explained by market movements. That is, 35% of its risk is market risk, and 65% is unique risk.[5] The next column is the amount of unique or diversifiable risk, measured as a standard deviation: 7.68% per month for Laidlaw B, equivalent to 26.6% per year. This is the standard deviation of the unique price change, that part of the actual change that was not explained by the change in the market index.[6]

---

[5] All of the *R*-squared figures in Table 9–2 are below 50%. This does not mean that the regression models are "bad fits." It just means that the majority of the risk in these stocks is unique, rather than market risk. As an investor, you would be pleased to know this, because you can diversify away most of the risk in these stocks.

[6] From these two columns we can figure out the *total* risk of Laidlaw B stock. The unique variance is the square of the unique standard deviation: $(7.68)^2 = 59.0$ per month. We know this amounts to 35% of the total variance, so total variance must be 59.0/0.35, or 168.6 per month. The total variance per year is, therefore, 168.6 × 12 = 2,023 and the standard deviation is $\sqrt{2,023}$ or 45.0%.

Standard Errors of Alpha and Beta.   The betas in Table 9–2 are simply *estimates* based on 60 particular months. Therefore, we would like to have an idea of the extent of the possible error in these estimates. The column beside the beta column labeled "Std. error" provides this information. Statisticians set up a *confidence interval* of the estimated value plus or minus two standard errors. Thus, the confidence interval for Laidlaw B's beta is between 1.23 plus or minus (2 × 0.22). If you state that the *true* beta for Laidlaw B stock was between 0.79 and 1.67, you have a 95% chance of being right. You have to do the best you can when estimating risk, but never forget the huge margin for error when estimating beta for individual stocks.[7] Similarly, the standard error of alpha (in the column to the right of alpha) tells us to be cautious about inferring anything as to Laidlaw B's "true" or "normal" alpha. All we can say is that Laidlaw's stockholders did do quite well in this particular period.

Industry Betas and the Divisional Cost of Capital

That concludes our lesson on how to estimate and predict betas for individual stocks. You should now understand the basic idea of how to estimate a stock's beta by fitting a line to past data, and you should be able to read and understand a "beta book." Bear in mind that such estimates should enable you to pick up major differences in market risk, but they do not allow you to draw fine distinctions. The reason is that you are exposed to potentially large estimation errors when you estimate betas of individual stocks from a limited sample of data. Fortunately, these errors tend to cancel out when you estimate betas of *portfolios.* Suppose that you were to compute the average of the betas of 100 common stocks. The standard error of the average would be about one-tenth of the average standard error of the 100 individual betas.[8] That is why it often is easier to estimate *industry betas* than betas for individual firms.

If Spar Aerospace is contemplating an across-the-board expansion, it would be reasonable to discount the cash flows at the company cost of capital. To estimate this company cost of capital, Spar could use its stock beta or, better still, the average beta of several similar aerospace firms.[9] Suppose, however, that Spar proposed instead to invest in the production of computer-controlled machine tools. The company cost of capital is not likely to be the right discount rate for its new machine tool division. For such a venture the company needs an estimate of the division's cost of capital. This is where the notion of an industry beta comes into its own. Probably the best way to estimate the discount rate for such an expansion is to use the beta of a portfolio of firms in the machine tool industry.

Thus, we can think of *divisional* costs of capital as a way station between company and project costs of capital. Company costs of capital are nearly useless for diversified firms. If Spar's machine tool venture becomes at all significant, Spar's beta will not measure the risk of *either* the machine tool *or* the aerospace businesses. It will measure just the average risk of the two divisions. A company cost of capital based on Spar's beta will almost inevitably be too high for one division and too low for the other.

---

[7] The standard error of beta is a more useful measure of the "goodness of fit" of the regression model than the level of R^2. Some of the other stocks in Table 9–2 have a higher standard error of beta than does Laidlaw. This may be due to infrequent trading of those stocks. We will discuss this later in the chapter.

[8] If the observations are independent, the standard error of the estimated mean declines in proportion to the square root of the number of observations.

[9] But we would have to adjust the observed betas for differences in the debt policies of the firms. This is explained in section 9-3.

*9–2   INFREQUENT TRADING AND BETA ESTIMATION

In Table 9–2 there are several firms with both Class A and Class B shares. In many cases one of these classes has restricted voting privileges but the same or a slightly larger dividend payment compared to the other.[10] The two share prices often track each other closely, so we would expect them to have approximately the same beta. For example, on May 17, 1991, Laidlaw A and B shares both closed at $13.25. These two shares typically trade for the same price because they pay the same dividend, although Laidlaw B has restricted voting privileges. However, 236,430 shares of Laidlaw B changed hands during the preceding week while only 32,560 shares of Laidlaw A traded during the same week. Why, then, does Laidlaw B have a beta of 1.23, while Laidlaw A has a reported beta of only 1.09? Similarly, Magna International A has a much larger beta than Magna International B. A total of 35,980 shares of Magna A traded during the week ended May 17, but no shares of Magna B were traded between March 5 and May 17. The beta of Magna A in Table 9–2 is 1.73, while that of Magna B is reported to be only 0.61. In general, the beta of the infrequently traded class of shares is reported to be less than that of the heavily traded class.

Do restricted voting shares have that much more systematic risk than full voting shares? Not likely. Remember, that we are talking about sensitivity to systematic market risk when we look at beta. It is difficult to come up with an explanation of how the absence of a vote almost triples the *sensitivity* of Magna A's stock to systematic market forces. What we have here is an example of a *bias* or error that arises in estimating the betas of infrequently traded stocks. The least squares regression technique used in Table 9–2 systematically underestimates the betas of infrequently traded stocks. Thus, we can be reasonably confident that the beta of the heavily traded shares of Laidlaw B and Magna A are as reported in Table 9–2. But we should be suspicious of the reported betas of the thinly traded shares like Laidlaw A and Magna B. Their true betas are likely higher than those reported in Table 9–2.[11]

To see how this can affect beta estimates, suppose you use monthly rates of return on the stock and the securities in the market index to estimate beta. *Information* about these securities that is important to investors arrives on a regular basis, and this causes their prices to rise and fall when they are traded. (In Figure 8–1 we saw that the price of Norcen stock changes on most days, so that, for practical purposes, information about Norcen and many other firms arrives in the market continuously.)

The problem occurs when there are no stock trades recorded to reflect the impact of the most up-to-date information on the stock. This is illustrated in Figure 9–4. Suppose the last trade for the stock in May occurs on May 20 and the last trade in June occurs on June 15, because the stock is infrequently traded. These trades give the prices upon which the rate of return for June is calculated. This rate of return will be based partly on information that arrives in May and will ignore some information that arrives in June. For simplicity, let us assume all the stocks in the market index trade on May 31 and June 30, so the index

---

[10] We discuss restricted voting shares in Chapter 14.

[11] Fowler, Rorke, and Jog examined the 634 securities listed continuously on the Toronto Stock Exchange from 1970 to 1979 and found that only 38, or 6% of them, had a trade on the last day of every month; a further 328, or 51.7% of them, traded every month but not always on the last day; and 268, or 42.3% of them, failed to have any trade during *some* months of the study. Thus, the problem we are describing is common in Canada. See D.J. Fowler, C.H. Rorke, and V.M. Jog, "Thin Trading and Beta Estimation Problems on the Toronto Stock Exchange," *Journal of Business Administration*, **12**: 77–90 (Fall 1980).

Figure 9-4   Infrequent trading of a stock causes its return to be calculated over a different time interval than the return for the market index.

rate of return for June is based precisely on all the information that arrives in June.

When we regress monthly stock returns on market index returns to measure betas we are trying to measure the extent to which the information about market index securities that arrives in June (for example) also affects the stock value. That is, we want to relate June information about the market index to June information about the stock. But the rates of return we use for the stock will miss some of the June stock information and substitute May stock information in its place. As a result, the regression *understates* the strength of the joint relationship between the stock and the index. That is, *the use of standard regression techniques results in underestimation of the betas of infrequently traded stocks.*[12] This problem is often called a *Fisher effect*, after Lawrence Fisher, formerly of the University of Chicago, who first called attention to it.

*Can We Improve Canadian Beta Estimates?

Several statistical techniques have been proposed to reduce or eliminate the "bias" or tendency to underestimate the betas of infrequently traded stocks. The techniques fall into two basic categories.

The first category includes techniques proposed by Scholes and Williams, by Dimson, and by Fowler, Rorke, and Jog.[13] The basic idea is to measure the covariances of the stock return with the contemporaneous index return as well as with the index returns before and after the stock return, since the information involved in the reported stock return is associated with the information in the index returns in the months before (if the stock is subject to infrequent trading) and also the index returns in the months after (if the index is subject to infrequent trading). These covariances are all combined in an appropriate way to get an improved estimate of beta.

The advantage of these techniques is that they tend to eliminate all of the bias in the estimate of beta that results from infrequent trading. The problem is that they introduce a lot of new statistical "noise," or random variability, in the estimate of beta, so that the standard error of the estimates tends to be high. The extra noise arises because three noisy covariance estimates are used rather than one, as in the standard regression approach.

---

[12] In the extreme case of a stock that never trades, its reported rate of return will always be zero, which appears to be riskless. The measured beta of such a stock will be zero.

[13] See M. Scholes and J. Williams, "Estimating Betas from Nonsynchronous Data," *Journal of Financial Economics*, **5**: 309–327 (December 1977), E. Dimson, "Risk Measurement when Shares are Subject to Infrequent Trading," *Journal of Financial Economics*, **7**: 197–226 (June 1979), and Fowler, Rorke, and Jog, *op. cit.*

Fowler, Rorke, and Jog studied the question of which of the two evils (*bias* and *noise*) is worse by examining the (mean squared) estimation errors of all the techniques in this first category. They conclude that:

> It is quite clear from the results presented that for most circumstances OLS [that is, standard regression technique] provides the best overall estimates. Only for some extreme cases does the SW [Scholes-Williams] technique yield better estimates and its use in normal circumstances is unnecessary.[14]

In fact, an examination of their results indicates that in the cases where the complicated Scholes-Williams technique is better, the standard (OLS) regression approach is not far behind. Moreover, if you use the standard regression approach you know the direction of your potential error (underestimate), but with the Scholes-Williams approach the direction is random.

The second category of techniques to remove the bias towards underestimation of the betas of infrequently traded stocks involves estimating the bias of the standard (OLS) regression and then multiplying the estimated beta by a factor to eliminate the bias. This was proposed by Fowler, Rorke, and Jog.[15] The only problems with their technique are that it is computationally cumbersome and that it requires a lot of data. The data that are needed are the probabilities of the last trade of the month for a given stock occurring on the various days of the month. That is, they need to know the amount of overlap of the intervals over which stock return and the index return are calculated, as illustrated in Figure 9–4.

9–3   CAPITAL STRUCTURE AND THE COMPANY COST OF CAPITAL

The cost of capital is a hurdle rate for capital budgeting decisions. It depends on the *business risk* of the firm's investment opportunities. The risk of a common stock reflects the business risk of the real assets held by the firm. But shareholders also bear *financial risk* to the extent that the firm issues debt to finance its real investments. The more a firm relies on debt financing, the riskier its common stock is.

We did not have to worry about this in Spar's case, because Spar had essentially no debt. But Spar is unusual. For many companies, outstanding debt is worth more than their outstanding equity.

Borrowing is said to create **financial leverage** or **gearing**. Financial leverage does not affect the risk or the expected return on the firm's assets but it does push up the risk of the common stock and lead the stockholders to demand a correspondingly higher return.

How Changing Capital Structure Affects Expected Returns

Think again of what the *company* cost of capital is and what it is used for. We *define* it as the opportunity cost of capital for the firm's existing assets; we *use* it to value new assets which have the same risk as the old ones.

If you owned a portfolio of all the firm's securities — 100% of the debt and 100% of the equity — you would own the firm's assets lock, stock, and barrel. You wouldn't share the cash flows with anyone; every dollar of cash the firm pays out would be paid to you.

---

[14] Fowler, Rorke, and Jog, *op. cit.*, p. 88.

[15] See D.J. Fowler, C.H. Rorke, and V.M. Jog, "A Bias Correcting Procedure for Beta Estimation in the Presence of Thin Trading," Administrative Sciences Association of Canada, *Proceedings of 1981 Conference*, Halifax, **2**: 95–105.

You can think of the company cost of capital as the expected return on this hypothetical portfolio. In order to calculate it, you just take a weighted average of the expected returns on the debt and the equity:

$$\text{Company cost of capital} = r_{\text{assets}} = r_{\text{portfolio}}$$
$$= \frac{\text{debt}}{\text{debt + equity}} r_{\text{debt}} + \frac{\text{equity}}{\text{debt + equity}} r_{\text{equity}}$$

For example, suppose that the firm's market value balance sheet is as follows:

Asset value	100	Debt value (D)	40
		Equity value (E)	60
Asset value	100	Firm value (V)	100

Note that the values of debt and equity add up to firm value ($D + E = V$), and that firm value equals asset value. (These figures are *market* values not *book* values: the market value of the firm's equity is often substantially different from its book value.)

If investors expect a return of 8% on the debt and 15% on the equity, then the expected return on the assets is:

$$r_{\text{assets}} = \frac{D}{V} r_{\text{debt}} + \frac{E}{V} r_{\text{equity}}$$
$$= \left(\frac{40}{100} \times 8\right) + \left(\frac{60}{100} \times 15\right) = 12.2\%$$

If the firm is contemplating investment in a project that has the same risk as the firm's existing business, the opportunity cost of capital for this project is the same as the firm's cost of capital; in other words, it is 12.2%.

What would happen if the firm issued an additional 10% of equity and used the cash to repay 10% of its debt? The revised market value balance sheet is:

Asset value	100	Debt value (D)	30
		Equity value (E)	70
Asset value	100	Firm value (V)	100

The change in financial structure does not affect the amount or risk of the cash flows on the total package of the debt and the equity. Therefore, if investors require a return of 12.2% on the total package before the refinancing, they must require a 12.2% return on the firm's assets afterwards.

Although the required return on the *package* of the debt and equity is unaffected, the change in financial structure does affect the required return on the individual securities. Since the company has less debt than before, the debtholders are likely to be satisfied with a lower return. We will suppose that the expected return on the debt falls to 7.3%. Now you can write down the basic equation for the return on assets and solve for the return on equity:

$$r_{\text{assets}} = \frac{D}{V} r_{\text{debt}} + \frac{E}{V} r_{\text{equity}}$$
$$= \left(\frac{30}{100} \times 7.3\right) + \left(\frac{70}{100} \times r_{\text{equity}}\right) = 12.2\%$$

Therefore, $r_{\text{equity}} = 14.3\%$

Reducing the amount of debt reduced debtholder risk and led to a fall in the return that debtholders required (r_{debt} fell from 8% to 7.3%). The lower leverage also made the equity safer and reduced the return that shareholders required (r_{equity} fell from 15% to 14.3%). The weighted average return on debt and equity remained at 12.2%:

$$r_{assets} = (0.3 \times r_{debt}) + (0.7 \times r_{equity})$$
$$= (0.3 \times 7.3) + (0.7 \times 14.3) = 12.2\%$$

Suppose that the company issues enough equity to repay all the debt. In that case, all the cash flows would go to the equity holders. The firm cost of capital, r_{assets}, stays at 12.2% and r_{equity} is also 12.2%.

How Changing Capital Structure Affects Beta

We have looked at how changes in financial structure affect expected return. Let us now look at the effect on beta.

The stockholders and debtholders both receive a share of the firm's cash flows and both bear part of the risk. For example, if the firm's assets turn out to be worthless, there will be no cash to pay stockholders *or* debtholders. But debtholders bear much less risk than stockholders. Debt betas of large blue-chip firms are typically close to zero—close enough that for such companies many financial analysts just assume $\beta_{debt} = 0$.[16]

If you owned a portfolio of all the firm's securities, you wouldn't share the cash flows with anyone. You wouldn't share the risks with anyone either; you would bear them all. Thus, the firm's **asset beta** is equal to the beta of a portfolio of all the firm's debt and its equity.

The beta of this hypothetical portfolio is just a weighted average of the debt and equity betas:

$$\beta_{assets} = \beta_{portfolio} = \frac{D}{V}\beta_{debt} + \frac{E}{V}\beta_{equity}$$

Think back to our example. If the debt before the refinancing has a beta of 0.2 and the equity a beta of 1.2, then

$$\beta_{assets} = (0.4 \times 0.2) + (0.6 \times 1.2) = 0.8$$

What happens after the refinancing? The risk of the total package is unaffected but both the debt and the equity are now less risky. Suppose that debt beta falls to 0.1. We can work out the new equity beta:

$$\beta_{assets} = \frac{D}{V}\beta_{debt} + \frac{E}{V}\beta_{equity}$$
$$0.8 = (0.3 \times 0.1) + (0.7 \times \beta_{equity})$$
$$\beta_{equity} = 1.1$$

Figure 9–5 shows the expected return and beta of the firm's assets. It also shows how expected return and risk are shared between the debt and equity holders before the refinancing. Figure 9–6 shows what happens after the refinancing. Both debt and equity are less risky and therefore investors are satisfied with a lower expected return. But equity now accounts for a larger proportion of firm value than before. As a result the weighted average of both the expected return and beta on the two components is unchanged.

---

[16] This assumption should be challenged in periods of volatile interest rates, when prices of long-term corporate and government bonds can fluctuate dramatically. There were periods in the early 1980s when bond betas were as high as 0.3 to 0.4.

Figure 9-5 Expected returns and betas before refinancing. The expected return and beta of the firm's assets and weighted average of the expected return and betas of the debt and equity.

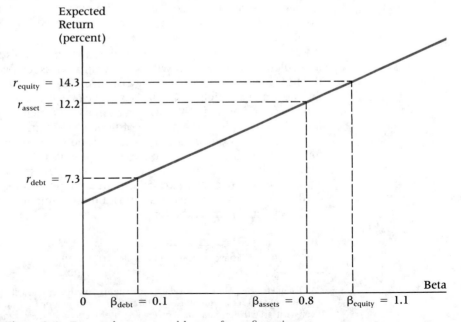

Figure 9-6 Expected returns and betas after refinancing.

**A Word of
Caution and
a Few
Observations**

In many ways we have given an oversimplified version of how financial leverage affects equity risks and returns. For example, later on we will need to amend our formula for r_{assets} to recognize the fact that interest can be deducted from taxable income. These finer points can wait.[17] For now, there are just a few points to remember:

- It is the company cost of capital that is relevant in capital budgeting decisions and not the expected return on the common stock.
- The company cost of capital is a weighted average of the returns that investors expect from the various debt and equity securities issued by the firm.
- The company cost of capital is related to the firm's asset beta and not to the beta of the common stock.
- The asset beta can be calculated as a weighted average of the betas of the various securities.
- When the firm changes its financial leverage, the risk and expected returns of the individual securities change. The asset beta and the company cost of capital do *not* change.

9–4   HOW TO ESTIMATE ALBERTA ENERGY COMPANY'S COST OF CAPITAL — AN EXAMPLE

Suppose that in early 1991 you were called on to estimate the company cost of capital of Alberta Energy Company (AEC). Remember the company cost of capital is the expected return on a portfolio of all the firm's securities. Thus, it can be calculated as a weighted average of the returns on the separate parts.

**The Expected
Return on AEC
Common Stock**

The difficult step is to estimate the expected return on AEC's common stock. It is the same problem that we encountered in Chapter 4 where we showed you how to use the constant-growth DCF formula to estimate the expected returns for a sample of utility stocks.[18] The constant-growth formula and the capital asset pricing model are two different ways of getting a handle on the same problem.[19]

Remember that we faced many of the same difficulties there as we do here. In particular, the constant-growth DCF formula is less reliable for an individual firm than for a sample of comparable-risk firms. We, therefore, suggested that the financial analyst might take a large sample of equivalent-risk securities, measure r for each, and average. We gave an example in which the constant-growth DCF formula was applied to a sample of large electric utilities.

Table 9–3 shows estimates of beta and the standard errors of these estimates for the common stocks of 11 oil and gas producers. Most of the standard errors are about the same as Alberta Energy's, and they are still large enough to preclude a precise estimate of any particular petroleum producer's beta (look at the standard error for Ocelot Industries' beta). But our confidence about the *average* beta of the 11 firms is much better.

---

[17] In fact, they will have to wait until Chapters 18 and 19.

[18] See Section 4–3.

[19] In Chapter 4 we pointed out that the constant-growth formula will not give you good estimates of the required return for stocks with rapid or unstable growth. But, in other cases, the constant-growth formula could give you a useful check on the estimate of r that you get from the capital asset pricing model.

Table 9-3
Betas for 11 oil and gas producers

Ticker	Firm	Beta	Standard error
AEC	Alberta Energy Company	0.94	0.22
BPC	BP Canada	1.04	0.21
CNW	Canada Northwest Energy	1.28	0.32
MKC	Mark Resources	1.14	0.26
NCN	Norcen Energy Resources	1.02	0.21
OIL.B	Ocelot Industries	0.99	0.45
OMH	Omega Hydrocarbons	0.89	0.33
RGO	Ranger Oil	0.88	0.28
SCR	Scurry-Rainbow Oil	0.86	0.16
SRL	Sceptre Resources Ltd.	1.19	0.23
ULP	Ulster Petroleums	1.43	0.25
	Average	1.06	

Are the stocks of these oil companies really equivalent-risk securities? Judging from Table 9–3, that appears to be a reasonable assumption. Much of the spread of estimated betas could be attributed to random measurement errors. It would be hard to reject the hypothesis that the "true" beta was the same for each of the firms.

You now have two clues to the true beta of Alberta Energy: the direct estimate of 0.94 and the average estimate for the industry of 1.06.[20] Fortunately, these two pieces of evidence are in broad agreement, so let us suppose that you take the easy way out and elect to use the figure of 0.94. In early 1991 the risk-free rate of interest r_f was about 9.4%. Therefore, if you accept our estimate of 7.4% for the risk premium on the market, you would conclude that the expected return on AEC's stock was about 16.4%:[21]

$$r_{equity} = r_f + \beta_{equity} (r_m - r_f)$$
$$= 0.094 + 0.94(0.074) = 0.164 \text{ or } 16.4\%$$

We have focused on using the capital asset pricing model to estimate the expected return on Alberta Energy's common stock. But it might be useful to get a check

---

[20] Using the average beta of petroleum producer stocks as a guide to the beta of AEC could be misleading if AEC had abnormally high or low leverage. In fact, the average degree of leverage for the companies in Table 9–4 was only slightly less than that of AEC.

[21] This is really a discount rate for near-term cash flows, since it rests on a risk-free rate measured by the yield on Treasury bills with maturities less than 1 year. Is this, you may ask, the right discount rate for cash flows from an asset with, say, a 10- or 20-year expected life? Well, now that you mention it, possibly not. In early 1991 longer-term government bonds yielded 9.8%, that is, about 0.4% above the Treasury bill rate.

The risk-free rate could be defined as a long-Canada bond yield. If you do this, however, you should subtract the risk premium of long-Canada bonds over bills, which we gave as 0.8% in Table 7–1. This gives a rough-and-ready estimate of the expected yield on short-term Treasury *bills* over the life of the bond:

$$\frac{\text{Expected average}}{\text{T-bill rate}} = \frac{\text{long-Canada}}{\text{bond yield}} - \frac{\text{premium of}}{\text{bonds over bills}}$$
$$= 9.8 - 0.8 = 9.0\%$$

This figure could be used as an expected average future r_f in the capital asset pricing model. For AEC:

$$r = r_f + \beta (r_m - r_f)$$
$$= 0.090 + 0.94(0.074) = 0.160 \text{ or } 16.0\%$$

on this figure. We have already mentioned one possibility: the constant-growth DCF formula. It states that for steady-growth companies the expected returr ⌐⌐ the stock is equal to the dividend yield plus the expected rate of growt' dividends. In spring 1991, AEC common stock yielded 2.3%. The company traditionally plowed back about 60% of its earnings and the return on comᵐᵒⁿ book equity (ROE) was about 5% in 1985–89. As explained in Section 4–3, this suggests that AEC's earnings and dividends will grow at $0.6 \times 5 = 3\%$. Putting this information together gives:

$$\text{Expected return on stock} = \text{Dividend yield} + \text{Expected dividend growth}$$
$$= 2.3 + 3.0 = 5.3\%.$$

This is *much* lower than the 16.4% we estimated for the cost of equity using the capital asset pricing model. What's going on? The accounting standards in the mining and petroleum industries give a great deal of latitude in earnings measurement. For example, there are many different ways to deal with depletion (depreciation of the mineral resource) and unsuccessful exploration efforts. As a result, analysts place little faith in earnings measures in the resource industries—they prefer to look at cash flow. We are likely understating AEC's true earnings and plowback ratio. Alternatively, AEC could have had an abnormally low ROE in 1991, as some analysts have suggested. In either case, we are far more confident in the CAPM estimate of the cost of equity than in the DCF estimate of the cost of equity. On the other hand, in the utility industry, for example, earnings are measured in a more reliable fashion and earnings are more stable, so you will find substantial agreement between the CAPM and DCF estimates of the cost of equity.

Estimating AEC's Company Cost of Capital

If AEC was financed only by common stock, the company cost of capital would be the same as the expected return on its stock. In early 1990 common stock accounted for about 61% of the market value of the company's securities. Debt accounted for 34% and preferred stock for the remaining 5%.[22] To keep matters simple we will lump the preferred stock in with the debt.

We estimated the expected return from AEC's common stock as 16.4%. The yield on the company's debt is about 10.6%.[23] To find the company cost of capital we simply calculate a weighted average of the expected returns on the different securities:

$$\text{Company cost of capital} = r_{\text{assets}} = \frac{D}{V} r_{\text{debt}} + \frac{E}{V} r_{\text{equity}}$$
$$= 0.39 (10.6) + 0.61 (16.4)$$
$$= 14.1\%[24]$$

---

[22] We will discuss preferred stock in Chapter 14. For now all you need to know is that it is less risky than common stock but more risky than debt.

[23] This is a *promised* yield—that is, it is the yield if AEC makes all the promised payments. Since there is some risk of default, the *expected* return is less than the promised yield. For a blue-chip company like AEC, the difference is small. But for a company that is hovering on the brink of bankruptcy, it can be important.

[24] Note you should get exactly the same result if you estimated the asset beta and then plugged this into the capital asset pricing model. Let's check.

$$r_{\text{debt}} = r_f + \beta_{\text{debt}} (r_m - r_f)$$
$$10.6 = 9.4 + \beta_{\text{debt}} (7.4)$$
$$\beta_{\text{debt}} = 0.16$$

Now calculate the beta of the firm's assets:

9–5   SETTING DISCOUNT RATES WHEN YOU CAN'T USE A BETA BOOK

Stock or industry betas provide a rough guide to the risk encountered in various lines of business. But an asset beta for, say, the steel industry, can take us only so far. Not all investments made in the steel industry are "typical." What other kinds of evidence about business risk might a financial manager examine?

In some cases the asset is publicly traded. If so, we can simply estimate its beta from past price data. For example, suppose a firm wants to analyze the risks of holding a large inventory of copper. Because copper is a standardized, widely traded commodity, it is possible to calculate rates of return from holding copper and to calculate a copper beta.

In other cases, you may have a lot of data on historic cash flows of similar projects or divisions of your firm. You could estimate the systematic risk of the cash flows directly instead of indirectly through the stock-market risk of the firm. There are extensions of the capital asset pricing model that allow you to use such a risk measure to determine the risk-adjusted present value of the project.[25] This approach can be useful if you want to consider expanding a division of your firm when there are no publicly traded firms that deal exclusively in that type of business.

What should a manager do if the asset has no such convenient price record? What if the proposed investment is not close enough to business as usual to justify using a company or divisional cost of capital?

These cases clearly call for judgement. For managers making that kind of judgement, we offer two pieces of advice:

1. *Avoid fudge factors.* Don't give in to the temptations to add fudge factors to the discount rate to offset things that could go wrong with the proposed investment. Adjust cash flow forecasts first.
2. *Think about the determinants of asset betas.* Often the characteristics of high- and low-beta assets can be observed when the beta itself cannot be.

Let us expand on each of these two points.

Avoiding Fudge Factors in Discount Rates

We have defined risk, from the investor's viewpoint, as the standard deviation of portfolio return or the beta of a common stock or other security. But in everyday usage "risk" simply equals "bad outcome." People think of the "risks" of a project as a list of the things that can go wrong. For example,

$$\beta_{assets} = \beta_{debt}\frac{D}{V} + \beta_{equity}\frac{E}{V}$$
$$= 0.39(0.16) + 0.61(0.94) = 0.64$$

Finally, use the capital asset pricing model to calculate r_{assets}:

$$r_{assets} = r_f + \beta_{assets}(r_m - r_f)$$
$$= 9.4 + 0.64(7.4) = 14.1\%$$

[25] Since participants in the stock market are always attempting to forecast future economic activity (or cash flow), you need to consider a sequence of risk measures—one for each time lag between the future project cash flow and the market factor that can be used to forecast it. The risk measures are called *cash-flow betas.* The risk-adjusted present value formulas are based on the certainty-equivalent version of the capital asset pricing model that is discussed in the Appendix to this chapter. See G.A. Sick, "A Certainty-equivalent Approach to Capital Budgeting," *Financial Management,* **15**: 23–32 (Winter 1986) and G.A. Sick, "Multi-period Risky Project Valuation: A Mean-covariance Certainty-equivalent Approach," *Advances in Financial Planning and Forecasting,* **3**: 1–36, ed. by C.F. Lee, JAI Press (1989).

- A geologist looking for oil worries about the "risk of a dry hole."
- A pharmaceutical manufacturer worries about the "risk" that a new drug which cures baldness may not be approved by the U.S. Food and Drug Administration.
- The owner of a hotel in a politically unstable part of the world worries about the "political risk" of expropriation.

Managers often add judge factors to discount rates to offset worries such as these.

This sort of adjustment makes us nervous. First, the bad outcomes we cited appear to reflect unique (that is, diversifiable) risks, which would not affect the expected rate of return demanded by investors. Second, the need for a discount rate adjustment usually arises because managers fail to give bad outcomes their due weight in cash-flow forecasts. The managers then try to offset that mistake by adding a fudge factor to the discount rate.

Example   Project Z will produce just one cash flow, forecasted at $1 million at year 1. It is regarded as average risk, suitable for discounting at a 10% company cost of capital:

$$PV = \frac{C_1}{1 + r} = \frac{1,000,000}{1.1} = \$909,100$$

But now you discover that the company's engineers are behind schedule in developing the technology required for the project. They're "confident" it will work, but admit to a small chance that it won't. You still see the *most likely* outcome as $1 million, but you also see some chance that project Z will generate *zero* cash flow next year.

Now the project's prospects are clouded by your new worry about technology. It must be worth less than the $909,100 you calculated before that worry arose. But how much less? There is *some* discount rate (10% plus a fudge factor) which will give the right value, but we don't know what that adjusted discount rate is.

We suggest you reconsider your original $1 million forecast for project Z's cash flow. Project cash flows are supposed to be *unbiased* forecasts, which give due weight to all possible outcomes, favourable and unfavourable. Managers making unbiased forecasts are correct on average. Sometimes their forecasts will turn out high, sometimes low, but their errors will average out over many projects.

If you forecast cash flow of $1 million for projects like Z, you will overestimate the average cash flow, because every now and then you will hit a zero. Those zeros should be "averaged in" to your forecasts.

For many projects, the most likely cash flow is also the unbiased forecast. If there are three possible outcomes, for example, with the probabilities shown below, the unbiased forecast is $1 million. (The unbiased forecast is the sum of the probability-weighted cash flows.)

Possible Cash Flow	Probability	Probability-Weighted Cash Flow	Unbiased Cash Flow
1.2	0.25	0.3	
1.0	0.50	0.5	1.0, or $1 million
0.8	0.25	0.2	

This might describe the initial prospects of project Z. But, if technological uncertainty introduces the chance of a zero cash flow, the unbiased forecast could drop to $833,300:

Possible Cash Flow	Probability	Probability-Weighted Cash Flow	Unbiased Cash Flow
1.2	0.25	0.3	
1.0	0.333	0.333	0.833, or $833,000
0.8	0.25	0.2	
0	0.167	0	

Present value is:

$$PV = \frac{0.833}{1.1} = 0.757, \text{ or } \$757,000$$

Now, of course, you can figure out the right fudge factor to add to the discount rate to apply to the original $1 million forecast to get the right answer. But you have to think through possible cash flows in order to get that fudge factor, and once you have thought through the cash flows you don't *need* the fudge factor.

Managers often work out a range of possible outcomes for major projects, sometimes with explicit probabilities attached. (We give more elaborate examples and further discussion in Chapter 10.) But even when a range of outcomes and probabilities is not explicitly written down, the manager can still consider the good and bad outcomes as well as the most likely one. When the bad outcomes outweigh the good, the cash-flow forecast should be reduced until balance is regained.

Step 1, then, is to do your best to make unbiased forecasts of a project's cash flows. Step 2 is to consider whether *investors* would regard the project as more or less risky than typical for a company or division. Here our advice is to search for characteristics of the asset that are associated with high or low betas. We wish we had a more fundamental scientific understanding of what these characteristics are. We see business risks surfacing in capital markets, but as yet there is no satisfactory theory describing how these risks are generated. Nevertheless, some things are known.

What Determines Asset Betas?

Cyclicality   Many people intuitively associate risk with the variability of book, or accounting, earnings. But much of this variability reflects unique or diversifiable risk. Lone prospectors in search of gold look forward to extremely uncertain future earnings, but whether or not they strike it rich is unlikely to depend on the performance of the market portfolio. Even if they do find gold, they do not bear much market risk. Therefore, an investment in gold has a high standard deviation but a relatively low beta.

What really counts is the strength of the relationship between the firm's earnings and the aggregate earnings on all real assets. We can measure this either by the *accounting beta* or by the *cash flow beta*. These are just like a real beta except that changes in book earnings or cash flow are used in place of rates of return on securities. We would predict that firms with high accounting or cash-flow betas should also have high stock betas — and the prediction is correct.[26]

This means that cyclical firms — firms whose revenues and earnings are strongly dependent on the state of the business cycle — tend to be high-beta firms. Thus, you should demand a higher rate of return from investments whose performance is strongly tied to the performance of the economy.

---

[26] For example, see W.H. Beaver and J. Manegold, "The Association between Market-Determined and Accounting-Determined Measures of Systematic Risk: Some Further Evidence," *Journal of Financial and Quantitative Analysis*, **10**: 231–284 (June 1975).

Operating Leverage   We have already seen that financial leverage—in other words, the commitment to fixed debt charges—increases the beta of an investor's portfolio. In just the same way, operating leverage—in other words, the commitment to fixed *production* charges—must add to the beta of a capital project. Let's see how this works.

The cash flows generated by any productive asset can be broken down into revenue, fixed costs, and variable costs:

$$\text{Cash flow} = \text{revenue} - \text{fixed cost} - \text{variable cost}$$

Costs are variable if they depend on the rate of output. Examples are raw materials, sales commissions, and some labour and maintenance costs. Fixed costs are cash outflows that occur regardless of whether the asset is active or idle—property taxes, for example, or the wages of workers under contract.

We can break down the asset's present value in the same way:

$$\text{PV(asset)} = \text{PV(revenue)} - \text{PV(fixed cost)} - \text{PV(variable cost)}$$

Or, equivalently:

$$\text{PV(revenue)} = \text{PV(fixed cost)} + \text{PV(variable cost)} + \text{PV(asset)}$$

Those who *receive* the fixed costs are like debtholders in the project—they simply get a fixed payment. Those who receive the net cash flows from the asset are like holders of common stock—they get whatever is left after payment of the fixed costs.

We can now figure out how the asset's beta is related to the betas of the values of revenue and costs. We just use our previous formula with the betas relabeled:

$$\beta_{\text{revenues}} = \beta_{\text{fixed cost}} \frac{\text{PV(fixed cost)}}{\text{PV(revenue)}} + \beta_{\text{variable cost}} \frac{\text{PV(variable cost)}}{\text{PV(revenue)}}$$
$$+ \beta_{\text{asset}} \frac{\text{PV(asset)}}{\text{PV(revenue)}}$$

In other words, the beta of the value of the revenues is simply a weighted average of the beta of its component parts. Now the fixed-cost beta is zero by definition: whoever receives the fixed costs holds a safe asset. The betas of the revenues and variable costs should be approximately the same, because they respond to the same underlying variable, the rate of output. Therefore, we can substitute $\beta_{\text{variable cost}}$ and solve for the asset beta. Remember that $\beta_{\text{fixed cost}} = 0$.

$$\beta_{\text{asset}} = \beta_{\text{revenue}} \frac{\text{PV(revenue)} - \text{PV(variable cost)}}{\text{PV(asset)}}$$
$$= \beta_{\text{revenue}} \left[1 + \frac{\text{PV(fixed cost)}}{\text{PV(asset)}} \right]$$

Thus, given the cyclicality of revenues (reflected in β_{revenues}), asset beta is proportional to the ratio of the present value of fixed costs to the present value of the project.

Now you have a rule of thumb for judging the relative risks of alternative designs or technologies for producing the same project. Other things being equal, the alternative with the higher ratio of fixed costs to project value will have the higher project beta.

Firms or assets whose costs are mostly fixed generally are said to have high **operating leverage**. The beta of the asset increases in proportion to the ratio of the value of the fixed costs to the value of the asset. Empirical tests confirm that companies with high operating leverage actually do have high betas.[27]

This is a somewhat oversimplified way of looking at operating leverage. Fixed costs and variable costs are not given to us on a silver platter, but are determined by the capital budgeting decision process. For example, in Chapters 10 and 21 we will show how you can adjust your production plans as information about sales opportunities arrives—if the market for your product is good, you produce and sell more, but if it is bad, you contract and produce less. This flexibility is valuable, and you have more of it when you have relatively more variable inputs than fixed inputs in your production process. You will take this into account, along with the information about the relative productivity of variable inputs and fixed inputs in making the capital budgeting decision about which technology to use to make your product.

For example, suppose the productivity of the variable input increases relative to that of the fixed input. You then choose a technology that relies more heavily on the variable input. But this increases your operating leverage, because you will produce more in good times and less in bad times, magnifying the natural swings of the business cycle. This means your beta tends to increase, even though your fixed costs have decreased.[28] Taking this into account, we would still expect companies with high operating leverage to have high betas. The surprise is that these companies get the high operating leverage despite a relatively *low* reliance on fixed inputs. The high operating leverage arises because these companies use their highly productive variable inputs to expand in good times and magnify the business cycle swings.

Searching for Clues

Recent research suggests a variety of other factors that affect an asset's beta.[29] But going through a long list of these possible determinants would take us too far afield.

You cannot hope to examine the relative risk of assets with any precision, but good managers examine any project from a variety of angles and look for clues as to its riskiness. They know that high market risk is a characteristic of cyclical ventures and of projects with high fixed costs. They think about the major uncertainties affecting the economy and consider how projects are affected by these uncertainties.[30]

---

[27] See B. Lev, "On the Association between Operating Leverage and Risk," *Journal of Financial and Quantitative Analysis*, **9**: 627–642 (September 1974), and G.N. Mandelker and S.G. Rhee, "The Impact of the Degrees of Operating and Financial Leverage on Systematic Risk of Common Stock," *Journal of Financial and Quantitative Analysis*, **19**: 45–57 (March 1984).

[28] This point is made in L. Booth, "The Influence of Production Technology on Risk and the Cost of Capital," *Journal of Financial and Quantitative Analysis*, **26**: 109–127 (March 1991).

[29] This work is reviewed in G. Foster, *Financial Statement Analysis*, 2nd ed., Prentice-Hall, Inc., Englewood Cliffs, N.J., 1986, Chapter 10.

[30] Sharpe's article on a "multi-beta" interpretation of market risk offers a useful way of thinking about these uncertainties and tracing out their impact on a firm's or project's risk. See W.F. Sharpe, "The Capital Asset Pricing Model: A 'Multi-Beta' Interpretation," in H. Levy and M. Sarnat (eds.), *Financial Decision Making Under Uncertainty*, New York, Academic Press, 1977.

*9–6   ANOTHER LOOK AT RISK AND DISCOUNTED CASH FLOW

In practical capital budgeting, a single discount rate is usually applied to all future cash flows. For example, an expected return may be calculated from the capital asset pricing model:

$$r = r_f + \beta (r_m - r_f)$$

The resulting r would be plugged directly into the standard discounted cash flow formula:

$$PV = \sum_{t=1}^{T} \frac{C_t}{(1 + r)^t}$$

Among other things, this procedure assumes that beta is constant over the project's entire life.[31] Here is an example which shows what that assumption really means.

Example   Project A is expected to produce a cash inflow of $100 million for each of three years. The risk-free interest rate is 6%, the market risk premium is 8%, and project A's beta is 0.75. You therefore calculate A's opportunity cost of capital as follows:

$$r = r_f + \beta (r_m - r_f)$$
$$= 6 + 0.75 (8) = 12\%$$

Discounting at 12% gives the following present value for each cash flow:

Project A

Year	Cash flow	PV at 12%
1	100	89.3
2	100	79.7
3	100	71.2
	Total PV	240.2

Now compare these figures with the cash flows of project B. Notice that B's cash flows are lower than A's, but B's flows are safe and therefore they are discounted at the risk-free interest rate. The *present value* of each year's cash flow is identical for the two projects.

Project B

Year	Cash flow	PV at 12%
1	94.6	89.3
2	89.6	79.7
3	84.8	71.2
	Total PV	240.2

In year 1 project A has a risky cash flow of 100. This has the same present value as the safe cash flow of 94.6 from project B. Economists would describe the 94.6 as the certainty equivalent of the risky expected flow of 100. Since the two cash

---

[31] See E.F. Fama, "Risk-Adjusted Discount Rates and Capital Budgeting under Uncertainty," *Journal of Financial Economics*, **5**: 3–24 (August 1977); or S.C. Myers and S.M. Turnbull, "Capital Budgeting and the Capital Asset Pricing Model: Good News and Bad News," *Journal of Finance*, **32**: 321–332 (May 1977).

flows have the same present value, investors are willing to give up $100 - 94.6$ or 5.4 in expected year 1 income in order to get rid of the uncertainty.

In year 2 project A has a risky cash flow of 100 and B has a safe cash flow of 89.6. Again both flows have the same present value. Thus, to eliminate the uncertainty in year 2, investors are prepared to give up $100 - 89.6$ or 10.4 of future income. And to eliminate uncertainty in year 3, they are willing to give up $100 - 84.8$ or 15.2 of future income.

To value project A, you discounted each cash flow at the same risk-adjusted discount rate of 12%. Now you can see what is implied when you did that. By using a constant rate you effectively made a larger deduction for risk from the later cash flows:

Year	Forecasted flow for project A	Certainty equivalent cash flow	Deduction for risk
1	100	94.6	5.4
2	100	89.6	10.4
3	100	84.8	15.2

The second cash flow is riskier than the first because it is exposed to *two* years of market risk. The third cash flow is riskier still because it is exposed to *three* years of market risk. You can see this increased risk reflected in the steadily declining certainty equivalents.

In the case of the first year, investors would be willing to accept a 5.4% lower cash flow if it were risk-free:

$$\text{Risky cash flow} \div 1.054 = \text{Certainty equivalent cash flow}$$
$$100 \div 1.054 = 94.6$$

In the case of the second year's cash flow, the deduction for risk is:

$$100 \div 1.054^2 = 89.6$$

And for the third year's flow, the deduction for risk is:

$$100 \div 1.054^3 = 84.8$$

There's no law of nature stating that certainty equivalents have to decrease in this smooth and regular way. In just a moment we'll sketch a real example in which they did not. But first let's formalize and review the concept of certainty equivalents.

Valuing Certainty Equivalent Flows

Let us start again with a single future cash flow C_1. If C_1 is certain, its present value is found by discounting at the risk-free rate r_f:

$$PV = \frac{C_1}{1 + r_f}$$

If the cash flow is risky, the normal procedure is to discount its forecasted (expected) value at a *risk-adjusted discount rate, r*, which is greater than r_f.[32] The risk-adjusted discount rate adjusts for both time and risk. This is illustrated by the northerly route in Figure 9-7.

---

[32] The quantity r can be less than r_f for assets with negative betas. But the betas of the assets which corporations hold are almost always positive.

Figure 9-7   Two ways to calculate present value.

The alternative approach is the certainty-equivalent method which makes separate adjustments for risk and time. This is illustrated by the southerly route in Figure 9–7. When we use this method, we ask, "What is the smallest *certain* payoff for which I would exchange the risky cash flow, C_1?" This is called the *certainty equivalent* of C_1, denoted by CEQ_1.[33]

Since CEQ_1 is the value-equivalent of a safe cash flow, it is discounted at the risk-free rate, r_f. Thus, we have two identical expressions for PV:

$$PV = \frac{C_1}{1 + r} = \frac{CEQ_1}{1 + r_f}$$

For cash flows two, three, or t years away:

$$PV = \frac{C_t}{(1 + r)^t} = \frac{CEQ_t}{(1 + r_f)^t}$$

But if we are to use the same discount rate for every future cash flow, then the certainty equivalents must decline steadily as a fraction of the cash flow. We saw this with project A, where the ratio of the certainty equivalent cash flow to the forecasted flow declined by 5.4% a year:

---

[33] CEQ_1 can be calculated directly from the capital asset pricing model. The formula is:

$$CEQ_1 = C_1 - \lambda \, cov(\tilde{C}_1, \tilde{r}_m)$$

where $cov(\tilde{C}_1, \tilde{r}_m)$ is the covariance between the dollar cash flow ($\tilde{C}_1$) and the return on the market portfolio ($\tilde{r}_m$), and

$$\lambda = \frac{r_m - r_f}{\sigma_m^{\,2}}$$

Here $r_m - r_f$ is the expected risk premium on the market portfolio; σ_m^2 is the variance of the market return. The quantity λ is often referred to as the *market price of risk*. In the Appendix to this chapter we show you where this formula for CEQ_1 comes from.

Year	Forecasted flow for project A (C_t)	Certainty equivalent cash flow (CEQ_t)	Ratio of CEQ_t to C_t
1	100	94.6	0.946
2	100	89.6	$0.896 = 0.946^2$
3	100	84.8	$0.848 = 0.946^3$

When You
Cannot **Use a**
Single Risk-
Adjusted
Discount Rate
for Long-Lived
Assets

Here is a disguised, simplified, and somewhat exaggerated version of an actual project proposal that one of the authors was asked to analyze. The scientists at Vegetron have come up with an electric mop, and the firm is ready to go ahead with pilot production and test marketing. The preliminary phase will take a year and cost $125,000. Management feels that there is only a 50% chance that pilot production and market tests will be successful. If they are, then Vegetron will build a $1 million plant which would generate an expected annual cash flow in perpetuity of $250,000 a year after taxes. If they are not successful, the project will have to be dropped.

The expected cash flows (in thousands of dollars) are:

$$C_0 = -125$$
$$C_1 = 50\% \text{ chance of } -1{,}000 \text{ and } 50\% \text{ chance of } 0$$
$$= 0.5(-1{,}000) + 0.5(0) = -500$$
$$C_t \text{ for } t = 2, 3, \ldots$$
$$= 50\% \text{ chance of } 250 \text{ and } 50\% \text{ chance of } 0$$
$$= +0.5(250) + 0.5(0) = 125$$

Management has little experience with consumer products and considers this a project of extremely high risk.[34] Therefore, they discount the cash flows at 25%, rather than Vegetron's normal 10% standard:

$$\text{NPV} = -125 - \frac{500}{1.25} + \sum_{t=2}^{\infty} \frac{125}{(1.25)^t} = -125, \text{ or } -\$125{,}000$$

This seems to show that the project is not worthwhile.

Management's analysis is open to criticism if the first year's experiment resolves a high proportion of the risk. If the test phase is a failure, then there's no risk at all—the project is *certain* to be worthless. If it is a success, there could well be only normal risk from there on. That means there is a 50% chance that in 1 year Vegetron will have the opportunity to invest in a project of *normal* risk, for which the *normal* discount rate of 10% would be appropriate. Thus, they have a 50% chance to invest $1 million in a project with a net present value of $1.5 million:

Pilot production and market tests

Success → $\text{NPV} = -1{,}000 + \dfrac{250}{0.10} = +1{,}500$ (50% chance)

Failure → $\text{NPV} = 0$ (50% chance)

---

[34] We will assume they mean high *market* risk, and that the difference between 25% and 10% is *not* a fudge factor introduced to offset optimistic cash-flow forecasts.

Thus, we could view the project as offering an expected payoff of $0.5(1,500) + 0.5(0) = 750$ or \$750,000 at $t = 1$ on a \$125,000 investment at $t = 0$. Of course, the certainty equivalent of the payoff is less than \$750,000 (to the extent that the risk of failure is systematic market risk rather than unique risk), but the difference would have to be very large to justify rejecting the project. For example, if the certainty equivalent is half the forecasted cash flow, and the risk-free rate is 7%, the project is worth \$225,500:

$$NPV = C_0 + \frac{CEQ_1}{1 + r_f}$$

$$= -125 + \frac{0.5(750)}{1.07} = 225.5, \text{ or } \$225,500$$

Not bad for a \$125,000 investment—and quite a change from the negative NPV that management got by discounting all future cash flows at 25%.

A Common Mistake   You sometimes hear people say that because distant cash flows are "riskier," they should be discounted at a higher rate than earlier cash flows. That is quite wrong: using the same risk-adjusted discount rate for each year's cash flow *implies* a larger deduction for risk from the later cash flows. The reason is that the discount rate compensates for the risk borne *per period*. The more distant the cash flows, the greater the number of periods and the larger the *total* risk adjustment.

It makes sense to use a single risk-adjusted discount rate as long as the project has the same market risk at each point in its life. But look out for exceptions like the electric mop project, where market risk changes as time passes.

9–7   SUMMARY

In Chapter 8 we set out some basic principles for valuing risky assets. In this chapter we have tried to show you how to apply these principles to practical situations.

The problem is easiest when you believe that the project has the same market risk as the company's existing assets. In this case, the required return would be equal to the required return on a portfolio of the company's securities. This is often called the *company's cost of capital*.

Capital asset pricing theory states that the required return on any asset depends on its beta:

$$r = r_f + \beta (r_m - r_f)$$

A good place to start is with the beta of the company's stock. The most common way to estimate the beta of a stock is to figure out how the stock price has responded to market changes in the past. Of course, this will only give you an estimate of the stock's true beta. You may get a more reliable figure if you take an average of the estimated betas for a group of similar companies.

Suppose that you now have an estimate of the stock's beta. Can you plug that into the capital asset pricing model to find the company cost of capital? No, the stock beta may reflect both business and financial risk. Whenever a company borrows money, it increases the beta (and the expected return) of its stock. Remember, the company cost of capital is the expected return on a portfolio of all the firm's securities, not just the common stock. You can calculate it by estimating the expected return on each of the securities and then taking a weighted average of these separate returns. Or you can do so by calculating the beta of the portfolio of securities and then plugging this *asset beta* into the capital asset pricing model.

The company cost of capital is the correct discount rate for projects that have the same risk as the company's existing business. Many firms, however, use the company cost of capital to discount the forecasted cash flows on all new projects. This is a dangerous procedure. Each project should be evaluated at its own opportunity cost of capital; the true cost of capital depends on the use to which the capital is put. If we wish to estimate the cost of capital for a particular project, it is *project risk* that counts.

We cannot give you a neat formula that will allow you to estimate project betas, but we can give you some clues. First, avoid adding fudge factors to discount rates to offset worries about bad project outcomes. Adjust cash-flow forecasts to give due weight to bad outcomes as well as good; *then* ask whether the chance of bad outcomes adds to the project's market risk. Second, you can often identify the characteristics of a high- or low- beta project even when project beta cannot be calculated directly. For example, you can try to figure out how far the cash flows are affected by the overall performance of the economy: cyclical investments are generally high-beta investments. Another thing you should look at is the project's operating leverage: fixed production charges work like fixed debt charges; that is, they increase beta.

There is one more fence to jump. Most projects produce cash flows for several years. Firms generally use the same risk-adjusted rate, r, to discount each of these cash flows. When they do this, they are implicitly assuming that cumulative risk increases at a constant rate as you look further into the future. That assumption is usually reasonable. It is precisely true when the project's future beta will be constant, that is, when risk *per period* is constant.

It is the exceptions that prove the rule. You, therefore, should be on the alert for projects where risk clearly does *not* increase steadily. In these cases, you should break the project into segments within which the same discount rate can be reasonably used. Or you should use the certainty-equivalent version of the DCF model which allows you to make separate risk adjustments to each period's cash flow.

Appendix 9–1 USING THE CAPITAL ASSET PRICING MODEL TO CALCULATE CERTAINTY EQUIVALENTS

When calculating present value you can take account of risk in either of two ways. You can discount the expected cash flow C_1 by the risk-adjusted discount rate r:

$$PV = \frac{C_1}{1 + r}$$

Alternatively, you can discount the certainty equivalent cash flow CEQ_1 by the risk-free rate of interest r_f:

$$PV = \frac{CEQ_1}{1 + r_f}$$

In this appendix we show how you can derive CEQ_1 from the capital asset pricing model.

We know from our present value formula that $1 + r$ equals the expected dollar payoff on the asset divided by its present value:

$$1 + r = \frac{C_1}{PV}$$

The capital asset pricing model also tells us that $1 + r$ equals

$$1 + r = 1 + r_f + \beta (r_m - r_f)$$

Therefore,

$$\frac{C_1}{PV} = 1 + r_f + \beta (r_m - r_f)$$

To find beta, we calculate the covariance between the asset return and the market return and divide by the market variance:

$$\beta = \frac{\text{cov}(\tilde{r}, \tilde{r}_m)}{\sigma_m^2} = \frac{\text{cov}[(\tilde{C}_1/PV - 1, \tilde{r}_m)]}{\sigma_m^2}$$

The quantity $\tilde{C}_1$ is the future cash flow and is, therefore, uncertain. But PV is the asset's present value: it is *not* unknown, and therefore, does not "covary" with $\tilde{r}_m$. Therefore, we can rewrite the expression for beta as

$$\beta = \frac{\text{cov}(C_1, \tilde{r}_m)}{PV\sigma_m^2}$$

Substituting this expression back into our equation for C_1/PV gives

$$\frac{C_1}{PV} = 1 + r_f + \frac{\text{cov}(\tilde{C}_1, \tilde{r}_m)}{PV} \times \frac{r_m - r_f}{\sigma_m^2}$$

The expression $(r_m - r_f)/\sigma_m^2$ is the expected risk premium on the market per unit of variance. It is often known as the *market price of risk* and is written as λ (lambda). Thus

$$\frac{C_1}{PV} = 1 + r_f + \frac{\lambda \, \text{cov}(\tilde{C}_1, \tilde{r}_m)}{PV}$$

Multiplying through by PV and rearranging, gives

$$PV = \frac{C_1 - \lambda \, \text{cov}(\tilde{C}_1, \tilde{r}_m)}{1 + r_f}$$

This is the certainty-equivalent form of the capital-asset pricing model. It tells us that, if the asset is risk-free, cov $(\tilde{C}_1, \tilde{r}_m)$ is zero and we simply discount C_1 by the risk-free rate. But, if the asset is risky, we must discount the certainty equivalent of C_1. The deduction that we make from C_1 depends on the market price of risk and on the covariance between the cash flows on the project and the return on the market.

FURTHER READING

There is a good review article by Rubinstein on the application of the capital asset pricing model to capital investment decisions:

M.E. Rubinstein, "A Mean-Variance Synthesis of Corporate Financial Theory," *Journal of Finance*, **28**: 167–182 (March 1973).

For evidence on the stability of betas estimated from past stock price data, see:

M.E. Blume, "On the Assessment of Risk," *Journal of Finance*, **26**: 1–10 (March 1971).
W.F. Sharpe and G.M. Cooper, "Risk-Return Classes of New York Stock Exchange Common Stocks, 1931–1967," *Financial Analysts Journal*, **28**: 46–54, 81 (March–April 1972).

There have been a number of studies of the relationship between accounting data and beta. Many of these are reviewed in:

G. Foster, *Financial Statement Analysis*, 2nd ed., Prentice-Hall, Inc., Englewood Cliffs, N.J. 1986.

For some ideas on how one might break down the problem of estimating beta, see:

W.F. Sharpe, "The Capital Asset Pricing Model: A 'Multi-Beta' Interpretation," in H. Levy and M. Sarnat (eds.), *Financial Decision Making Under Uncertainty*, New York, Academic Press, 1977.

The assumptions required for use of risk-adjusted discount rates are discussed in:

E.F. Fama, "Risk-Adjusted Discount Rates and Capital Budgeting under Uncertainty," *Journal of Financial Economics*, **5**: 3–24 (August 1977).
S.C. Myers and S.M. Turnbull, "Capital Budgeting and the Capital Asset Pricing Model: Good News and Bad News," *Journal of Finance*, **32**: 321–332 (May 1977).

The Fama and Myers-Turnbull approaches are difficult to implement. A more general approach to using the capital asset pricing model to measure cash-flow risk, which does not necessarily give risk-adjusted discount rates, is given in:

G.A. Sick, "A Certainty-equivalent Approach to Capital Budgeting," *Financial Management*, **15**: 23–32 (Winter 1986).

G.A. Sick, "Multi-period Risky Project Valuation: A Mean-covariance Certainty-equivalent Approach," *Advances in Financial Planning and Forecasting*, **3**: 1–36, ed. by C.F. Lee, JAI Press (1989).

The relationship between the certainty equivalent and risk-adjusted discount rate valuation formulas was first discussed by:

A.A. Robichek and S.C. Myers, "Conceptual Problems in the Use of Risk-Adjusted Discount Rates," *Journal of Finance*, **21**: 727–730 (December 1966).

QUIZ

1. Suppose a firm uses its company cost of capital to evaluate all capital projects. What kinds of mistakes will it make?
2. A project costs $100,000 and offers a single $150,000 cash flow 1 year hence. The project beta is 2.0 and the market risk premium $(r_m - r_f)$ is 8%. Look up current risk-free interest rates in *The Globe and Mail* or another newspaper. Use the capital asset pricing model to find the opportunity cost of capital and the present value of the project.

3. Look again at Table 9–2 and the row of statistics shown for Magna International A. Define and interpret each of these statistics.

4. A company is financed 40% by risk-free debt. The interest rate is 10%, the expected market return is 20%, and the stock's beta is 0.5. What is the company cost of capital?

5. The total market value of the common stock of the Okenfenokee Real Estate Company is $6 million and the total value of its debt is $4 million. The treasurer estimates that the beta of the stock is currently 1.5 and that the expected risk premium on the market is 10%. The Treasury bill rate is 8%.
   (a) What is the required return on Okenfenokee stock?
   (b) What is the beta of the company's existing portfolio of assets?
   (c) Estimate the company's cost of capital.
   (d) Estimate the discount rate for an expansion of the company's present business.
   (e) Suppose the company wants to diversify into the manufacture of rose-coloured spectacles. The beta of unleveraged optical manufacturers is 1.2. Estimate the required return on Okenfenokee's new venture.

6. A geologist fears that a new oil well will be a dry hole. He therefore discounts the well's forecasted cash flows at 30% rather than the oil company's 10% overall cost of capital. Is this good discounting practice? Can you suggest a better approach?

7. Which of these companies is likely to have the higher cost of capital?
   (a) A's sales force is paid a fixed annual rate; B's is paid on a commission basis.
   (b) C produces machine tools; D produces breakfast cereal.

8. Select the appropriate phrase from within each pair of brackets:
   "In calculating PV there are two ways to adjust for risk. One is to make a deduction from the expected cash flows. This is known as the *certainty-equivalent method*. It is usually written as

   $$PV = [CEQ_t/(1 + r_f)^t; CEQ_t/(1 + r_m)^t]$$

   The certainty-equivalent cash flow, CEQ_t, is always [more than; less than] the forecasted risky cash flow. Another way to allow for risk is to discount the expected cash flows at a rate of r. If we use the capital asset pricing model to calculate r, r is

   $$[r_f + \beta r_m; r_f + \beta (r_m - r_f); r_m + \beta (r_m - r_f)]$$

   This method is exact only if the ratio of the certainty equivalent cash flow to the forecasted risky cash flow [is constant; declines at a constant rate; increases at a constant rate]. For the majority of projects, the use of a single discount rate, r, is probably a perfectly acceptable approximation.

9. A project has a forecasted cash flow of $110 in year 1 and $121 in year 2. The interest rate is 5%, and the project has a beta of 0.5. If you use a constant risk-adjusted discount rate, what is
   (a) The present value of the project?
   (b) The certainty-equivalent cash flows in years 1 and 2?
   (c) The ratio of the certainty-equivalent cash flows to the expected cash flows in years 1 and 2?

QUESTIONS AND PROBLEMS

1. Look at Table 9–2.
    (a) How much did Moore Corporation's stock price tend to change in an unchanged market?
    (b) Which stock had price changes that were most closely related with the market? What proportion of the stock's risk was market risk, and what proportion was unique risk?
    (c) What is the confidence interval on Morgan Hydrocarbon's beta?
    (d) What is the total risk of Moffat Communications stock, *per year?*
2. Explain the estimate of alpha for Mitel Corporation stock in Table 9–2. Why is this not a good guide to the stock's future alpha? What is your best forecast of alpha?
3. (a) Nero Violins has the following capital structure:

Security	Beta	Total Market Value, Millions of Dollars
Debt	0	100
Preferred stock	0.20	40
Common stock	1.20	200

What is the firm's asset beta (that is, the beta of a portfolio of all the firm's securities)?
    (b) How would the asset beta change if Nero issued an additional $140 million of common stock and used the cash to repurchase all the debt and preferred stock?
    (c) Assume the capital asset pricing model is correct. What discount rate should Nero set for investments that expand the scale of its operations without changing its asset beta? Assume any new investment is all-equity financed. Plug in numbers that are reasonable today. Specify two discount rates, one real and one nominal.
4. Amalgamated Products has three operating divisions:

Division	Percent of Firm Value
Food	50
Electronics	30
Chemicals	20

In order to estimate the cost of capital for each division, Amalgamated has identified the following three principal competitors:

	Estimated Equity Beta	Debt/(Debt + Equity)
United Foods	0.8	0.3
General Electronics	1.6	0.2
Associated Chemicals	1.2	0.4

(a) Assuming that the debt of these firms is risk-free, estimate the asset beta for each of Amalgamated's divisions.

(b) Amalgamated's debt to debt plus equity ratio is 0.4. If your estimates of divisional betas are right, what is Amalgamated's equity beta?

(c) Assume that the risk-free interest rate is 7% and the expected return on the market index is 15%. Estimate the cost of capital for each of Amalgamated's divisions.

(d) How much would your estimates of each division's cost of capital change if you assumed that each company's debt had a beta of 0.2?

5. Calculate the financial leverage for any three companies in Table 9–2 (other than Spar) and estimate the opportunity cost of capital for a "typical" investment by each firm.

6. "The errors in estimating beta are so great that you might just as well assume that all betas are 1.0." Do you agree?

7. Mom and Pop Groceries has just dispatched a year's supply of groceries to the government of the Central Antarctic Republic. Payment of $250,000 will be made 1 year hence after the shipment arrives by snow train. Unfortunately, there is a good chance of a coup d'état, in which case the new government will not pay. Mom and Pop's controller therefore decides to discount the payment at 40%, rather than the company's 12% cost of capital.

(a) What's wrong with using a 40% rate to offset "political risk"?

(b) How much is the $250,000 payment really worth if the odds of a coup d'état are 25%?

8. Here is a more challenging problem involving cash-flow forecasts, discount rates, and fudge factors. An oil company executive is considering investing $10 million in one or both of two wells: *Well 1* is expected to produce oil worth $3 million a year for 10 years; *Well 2* is expected to produce $2 million for 15 years. These are *real* (inflation-adjusted) cash flows.

The beta for *producing wells* is 0.9. The market risk premium is 8%, the nominal risk-free interest rate is 6%, and expected inflation is 4%.

The two wells are intended to develop a previously discovered oil field. Unfortunately, there is still a 20% chance of a dry hole in each case. A dry hole means zero cash flows and a complete loss of the $10 million investment.

Ignore taxes and make further assumptions as necessary.

(a) What is the correct real discount rate for cash flows from developed wells?

(b) The oil company executive proposes to add 20 percentage points to the real discount rate to offset the risk of a dry hole. Calculate the NPV of each well with this adjusted discount rate.

(c) What do *you* say the NPV of the two wells are?

(d) Is there any *single* fudge factor that could be added to the discount rate for developed wells that would yield the correct NPV for both wells? Explain.

9. "For a high-beta project, you should use a high discount rate to value positive cash flows and a low discount rate to value negative cash flows." Is this statement correct? Should the sign of the cash flow affect the appropriate discount rate?

*10. A project has the following forecasted cash flows:

Cash Flows,
Thousands of Dollars

C_0	C_1	C_2	C_3
− 100	+ 40	+ 60	+ 50

The estimated project beta is 1.5. The market return r_m is 16%, and the risk-free rate r_f is 7%.
(a) Estimate the opportunity cost of capital and the project's present value (using the same rate to discount each cash flow).
(b) What are the certainty-equivalent cash flows in each year?
(c) What is the ratio of the certainty-equivalent cash flow to the expected cash flow in each year?
(d) Explain why this ratio declines.

*11. Look back at Project A in Section 9–5. Now assume that:
(a) Expected cash flow is $150 per year for 5 years.
(b) The risk-free rate of interest is 5%.
(c) The market risk premium is 9%.
(d) The estimated beta is 1.2.
   Recalculate the certainty-equivalent cash flows and show that the ratio of these certainty equivalent cash flows to the risky cash flows declines by a constant proportion each year.

*12. The McGregor Whisky Company is proposing to market diet scotch. The product will first be test-marketed for 2 years in Southern California at an initial cost of $500,000. This test launch is not expected to produce any profits but should reveal consumer preferences. There is a 60% chance that demand will be satisfactory. In this case, McGregor will spend $5 million to launch the scotch nationwide and will receive an expected annual profit of $700,000 in perpetuity. If demand is not satisfactory, diet scotch will be withdrawn.
   Once consumer preferences are known, the product will be subject to an average degree of risk and, therefore, McGregor requires a return of 12% on its investment. However, the initial test-market phase is viewed as much riskier, and McGregor demands a return of 40% on this initial expenditure.
   What is the NPV of the diet scotch project?

*13. The president of Amalgamated Blue Sky Resources, Ltd., a small mining company, says, "We will never use the capital asset pricing model to estimate our cost of capital because our beta is only 0.6 and we feel this is too low to reflect the true risk of our company." Discuss.

14. Find a monthly copy of the *Toronto Stock Exchange Review* in your library. In it, locate the following information:
(a) The value of the TSE 300 Composite Total Return Index. This is the TSE 300 Composite Index with dividends reinvested.
(b) The values of Total Return Indexes representing the performance of: oil and gas producers, forest products companies, steel producers, and gold mines.
(c) The closing stock prices of Northern Telecom, Stelco, and Canadian Pacific Ltd.

Now, collect a sequence of 25 issues of the *TSE Review* and calculate 24 monthly rates of return for each of these stocks and indexes. Since the *TSE Review* does not record dividend payment or ex dividend dates, you'll have to ignore dividends in calculating the stock rates of return. This will not affect beta estimates very much. (You can also find these data in a loose-leaf manual called the *Toronto Stock Exchange 300 Stock Price Index System*.) What are the betas of these stocks and indexes? You'll need a computer or calculator to perform the regressions.

P · A · R · T

3

PRACTICAL PROBLEMS IN CAPITAL BUDGETING

C · H · A · P · T · E · R

10

A PROJECT IS NOT A
BLACK BOX

A *black box* is something that we accept and use but do not understand. For most of us a computer is a black box. We may know what it is supposed to do, but we do not understand how it works and, if something breaks, we cannot repair it.

We have been treating capital projects as black boxes. In other words, we have talked as if managers are handed unbiased cash-flow forecasts and their only task is to assess risk, choose the right discount rate, and crank out net present value. Actual financial managers won't rest until they understand what makes the project tick and what could go wrong with it. Remember Murphy's law, "If anything can go wrong, it will," and O'Reilly's corollary, "at the worst possible time."

Even if the project's risk is wholly diversifiable, you still need to understand why the venture could fail. Once you know that, you can decide whether it is worth trying to resolve the uncertainty. Maybe further expenditure on market research would clear up these doubts about acceptance by consumers, maybe another drill hole would give you a better idea of the size of the ore body, and maybe some further work on the test bed would confirm the durability of those welds. If the project really has a negative NPV, the sooner you can identify it, the better. And even if you decide that it is worth going ahead on the basis of present information, you do not want to be caught by surprise if things subsequently go wrong. You want to know the danger signals and the actions you might take.

In short, managers avoid black boxes whenever they can, and they reward whoever can help them look inside. Consequently, consultants and academics have developed procedures for what we will call *project analysis*. We will discuss several of the procedures in this chapter, mainly sensitivity analysis, break-even analysis, Monte Carlo simulation, and decision trees. There is no magic in these techniques, just computer-assisted common sense. You don't need a licence to use them.

Some analysts have proposed these techniques not only for project analysis but also as a supplement or replacement for net present value. You can imagine our reaction to that. Their proposals seem to reflect a belief that net present value cannot cope with risk. But we have seen that it can cope.

10-1 SENSITIVITY ANALYSIS

Uncertainty means that more things can happen than will happen. Therefore, whenever you are confronted with a cash-flow forecast, you should try to discover what else can happen.

Put yourself in the well-heeled shoes of the treasurer of the Jalopy Motor Company. You are considering the introduction of a small electrically powered car for city use. Your staff members have prepared the cash-flow forecasts shown in Table 10-1. Since NPV is positive at 10% opportunity cost of capital, it appears to be worth going ahead.

Table 10-1
Preliminary cash-flow forecasts in millions of dollars for Jalopy Motor's electric car project

	Year 0	Years 1 to 10
Investment	150	
1. Revenue		375
2. Variable cost		300
3. Fixed cost		30
4. Depreciation for tax purposes		15
5. Pretax profit $(1 - 2 - 3 - 4)$		30
6. Tax		15
7. Net profit $(5 - 6)$		15
8. Operating cash flow $(4 + 7)$		30
Net cash flow	$-\$150$	$\$30$

Assumptions:
Investment is depreciated over ten years straight line.
Income is taxed at a rate of 50%.

$$\text{NPV} = -150 + \sum_{t=1}^{10} \frac{30}{(1.10)^t} = \$34.3 \text{ million}$$

Before you decide, you want to delve into these forecasts[1] and identify the key variables that determine whether the project succeeds or fails. It turns out that the marketing department has estimated revenue as follows:

Unit sales = new product's share of market × size of car market
= 0.01 × 10 million = 100,000 cars
Revenue = unit sales × price per unit
= 100,000 × 3,750 = $375 million

The production department has estimated variable costs per unit as $3,000. Since projected volume is 100,000 cars per year, *total* variable cost is $300 million. Fixed costs are $30 million per year. The initial investment can be depreciated on a straight-line basis over the ten-year period, and profits are taxed at a rate of 50%.

---

[1] Bear in mind, when you are working with cash-flow forecasts, the distinction between the expected value and the most likely (or modal) value. Present values are concerned with *expected* cash flows—that is, the weighted average of the possible cash flows. If the distribution of possible outcomes is skewed, the expected cash flow will not be the same as the most likely cash flow.

These seem to be the important things you need to know, but look out for unidentified variables. Perhaps there are patent problems, or perhaps you will need to invest in service stations that will recharge the car batteries. The greatest dangers often lie in these *unknown* unknowns, or "unk-unks," as scientists call them.

Having found no unk-unks (no doubt you'll find them later), you conduct a **sensitivity analysis** with respect to market size, market share, and so on. To do this, the marketing and production staffs are asked to give optimistic and pessimistic estimates for the underlying variables. These are set out in the left-hand columns of Table 10-2. The right-hand side shows what happens to the project's net present value if the variables are set *one at a time* to their optimistic and pessimistic values. Your project appears to be by no means a sure thing. The most dangerous variables appear to be market share and unit variable cost. If market share is only 0.004 (and all other variables are as expected), then the project has an NPV of − $104 million. If unit variable cost is $3,600 (and all other variables are as expected), then the project has an NPV of − $150 million.

Table 10-2
To undertake a sensitivity analysis of the electric car project, we set each variable *in turn* at its most pessimistic or optimistic value and recalculate the net present value of the project.

	Range			Net Present Value (millions of dollars)		
Variable	Pessimistic	Expected	Optimistic	Pessimistic	Expected	Optimistic
Market size	9 million	10 million	11 million	+11	+34	+57
Market share	0.004	0.01	0.016	−104	+34	+173
Unit price	$3,500	$3,750	$3,800	−42	+34	+50
Unit variable cost	$3,600	$3,000	$2,750	−150	+34	+111
Fixed cost	$40 million	$30 million	$20 million	+4	+34	+65

Value of Information

Now you can check whether an investment of time or money could resolve some of the uncertainty *before* your company parts with the $150 million investment. Suppose that the pessimistic value for unit variable cost partly reflects the production department's worry that a particular machine will not work as designed and that the operation will have to be performed by other methods at an extra cost of $200 per unit. The chance that this will occur is only one in ten. But, if it did occur, the extra $200 unit cost would reduce after-tax cash flow by

$$\text{Unit sales} \times \text{additional unit cost} \times (1 - \text{tax rate})$$
$$= 100,000 \times 200 \times 0.50 = \$10 \text{ million}$$

It would reduce the net present value of your project by

$$\sum_{t=1}^{10} \frac{10}{(1.10)^t} = \$61.4 \text{ million}$$

Suppose further that a $100,000 pretest of the machine will reveal whether it will work and allow you to clear up the problem. It clearly pays to invest $100,000 to avoid a 10% probability of $61.4 million loss. You are ahead by − 100,000 + 0.10 × 61,400,000 = 6,040,000.

On the other hand, the value of additional information about market size is small. Because the project is acceptable even under pessimistic assumptions about market size, you are unlikely to be in trouble if you have misestimated that variable.[2]

Limits to Sensitivity Analysis

Sensitivity analysis boils down to expressing cash flows in terms of unknown variables and then calculating the consequences of misestimating the variables. It forces the manager to identify the underlying variables, indicates where additional information would be most useful, and helps to expose confused or inappropriate forecasts.

One drawback to sensitivity analysis is that it always gives somewhat ambiguous results. For example, what exactly does *optimistic* or *pessimistic* mean? The marketing department may be interpreting the terms in a different way from the production department. Ten years from now, after hundreds of projects, hindsight may show that the marketing department's pessimistic limit was exceeded twice as often as the production department's; but what you may discover ten years hence is no help now. One solution is to ask the two departments for a *complete* description of the various odds. However, it is far from easy to extract a forecaster's subjective notion of the complete probability distribution of possible outcomes.[3]

Another problem with sensitivity analysis is that the underlying variables are likely to be interrelated. What sense does it make to look at the effect in isolation of an increase in market size? If market size exceeds expectations, it is likely that demand will be stronger than you anticipated and unit prices will be higher. And why look in isolation at the effect of an increase in price? If inflation pushes prices to the upper end of our range, it is quite probable that costs will also be inflated. And so on.

Sometimes the analyst can get around the problem by defining underlying variables so that they are roughly independent. But you cannot push *one-at-a-time* sensitivity analysis too far. It is impossible to obtain expected, optimistic, and pessimistic values for total *project* cash flows from the information in Table 10-2.

Examining the Project under Different Scenarios

If the variables are interrelated, it may help to consider some alternative plausible combinations. For example, perhaps the company economist is worried about the possibility of another sharp rise in world oil prices. The direct effect of this would be to encourage the use of electrically powered cars. The popularity of "compacts" after the oil price increases in the 1970s leads you to estimate that an immediate 20% price rise in oil would enable you to capture an extra 0.3% of the automobile market. On the other hand, the economist also believes that higher oil prices would prompt a world recession and at the same time stimulate inflation. In that case, market size might be in the region of 8 million cars and

---

[2] Of course, these are very simple examples. The derivation of optimal rules for investing in information is a well-developed part of Bayesian statistics. See H. Raiffa, *Decision Analysis: Introductory Lectures on Choices under Uncertainty*, Addison-Wesley Publishing Company, Inc., Reading, Mass., 1968; and H. Raiffa and R. Schlaifer, *Applied Statistical Decision Theory*, Division of Research, Graduate School of Business Administration, Harvard University, Boston, 1961.

[3] If you doubt this, try some simple experiments. Ask the person who repairs your television to state a numerical probability that your set will work for at least one more year. Or construct your own subjective probability distribution of the number of telephone calls you will receive next week. That ought to be easy. Try it.

both prices and costs might be 15% higher than your initial estimates. Table 10-3 shows that this scenario of higher oil prices and recession would on balance help your new venture. Its net present value would increase to $65 million.

Table 10-3
How the net present value of the electric car project would be affected by higher oil prices and a world recession.

	Cash Flows Years 1 to 10 (millions of dollars)	
	Base Case	**High Oil Prices and Recession Case**
1. Revenue	375	449
2. Variable cost	300	359
3. Fixed cost	30	35
4. Depreciation for tax return	15	15
5. Pretax profit (1 − 2 − 3 − 4)	30	40
6. Tax	15	20
7. Net profit (5 − 6)	15	20
8. Net cash flow (4 + 7)	+30	35
Present value of cash flows	+184	+215
Net present value	+34	+65

	Assumptions	
	Base Case	**High Oil Prices and Recession Case**
Market size	10 million	8 million
Market share	0.01	0.013
Unit price	$3,750	$4,313
Unit variable cost	$3,000	$3,450
Fixed cost	$30 million	$35 million

Managers often find it helpful to look at how their product would fare under different scenarios. It allows them to look at different but *consistent* combinations of variables. Forecasters generally prefer to give an estimate of revenues or costs under a particular scenario than to give some absolute optimistic or pessimistic value.

Break-Even Analysis   When we undertake a sensitivity analysis of a project or when we look at alternative scenarios, we are asking how serious it would be if sales or costs turn out to be worse than we forecasted. Managers sometimes prefer to rephrase this question and ask how bad sales can get before the project begins to lose money. This exercise is known as **break-even analysis**.

In the left-hand portion of Table 10-4 we set out the revenues and costs of the electric car project under different assumptions about annual sales.[4] In the right-hand portion of the table we discount these revenues and costs to give us the *present value* of the inflows and the *present value* of the outflows. *Net* present value is, of course, the difference between these numbers.

---

[4] Notice that if the project makes a loss, this loss can be used to reduce the tax bill on the rest of the company's business. In this case the project produces a tax saving—the tax outflow is negative.

Table 10-4
NPV in millions of dollars of electric car project under different assumptions about unit sales

Unit Sales (thousands of cars)	Inflows Revenue Years 1 to 10	Outflows Year 0 Invest-ment	Outflows Years 1 to 10 Variable Costs	Outflows Years 1 to 10 Fixed Costs	Outflows Years 1 to 10 Taxes	PV Inflows	PV Outflows	NPV
0	0	150	0	30	−22.5	0	196	−196
100	375	150	300	30	15	2,304	2,270	34
200	750	150	600	30	52.5	4,608	4,344	264

You can see that NPV is strongly negative if the company does not produce a single car. It is just positive if (as expected) the company sells 100,000 cars and is strongly positive if it sells 200,000 cars. Clearly the *zero*-NPV point occurs a little under 100,000 cars.

In Figure 10-1 we have plotted the present value of the inflows and outflows under different assumptions about annual sales. The two lines cross when sales are 85,000 cars. This is the point at which the project has zero NPV. As long as sales are greater than 85,000, the project has a positive NPV.

Instead of working with the present values of the inflows and outflows, we could work equally well with the equivalent annual revenues and costs. The annual cost of the project includes the recurring costs (variable costs, fixed costs, and taxes) *plus* the equivalent annual cost of the $150 million initial investment. To calculate the equivalent annual cost of the initial investment we divide the investment by the ten-year annuity factor:

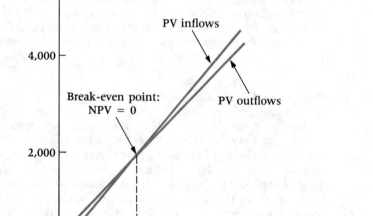

Figure 10-1   A break-even chart showing the present value of Jalopy's cash inflows and outflows under different assumptions about unit sales. NPV is zero when sales are 85,000.

$$\text{Equivalent annual cost of investment} = \frac{\text{Investment}}{\text{10-year annuity factor}}$$

$$= \frac{150}{6.145} = \$24.4 \text{ million}$$

In Table 10-5 we show the equivalent annual revenues and costs under our three assumptions about unit sales. The final column of this table shows the difference between the annual revenues and costs. As long as this is positive, the project has a positive NPV.

Table 10-5
Equivalent annual cash flow from the electric car project under different assumptions about unit sales (millions of dollars)

Unit Sales (thousands of cars)	Inflows Revenues	Equivalent Annual Outflow					Net Equivalent Annual Flow
		Initial Investment	Variable Costs	Fixed Costs	Taxes	Total	
0	0	24.4	0	30	−22.5	31.9	−31.9
100	375	24.4	300	30	15	369.4	5.6
200	750	24.4	600	30	52.5	706.9	43.1

In Figure 10-2 we have plotted the equivalent annual revenues and costs against different levels of sales. As you would expect, it tells exactly the same story as Figure 10-1. The two lines cross when sales are 85,000 cars. At this point, equivalent annual revenues equal equivalent annual costs and the project has zero NPV.

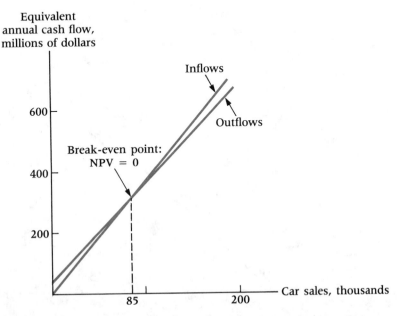

Figure 10-2 We can redraw our break-even chart in terms of Jalopy's equivalent annual revenues and costs. The net equivalent annual outflow is zero when sales are 85,000.

Table 10-6
Effect of the electric car project on accounting profit under different assumptions about unit sales (millions of dollars)

Unit Sales (thousands of cars)	Revenue	Variable Costs	Fixed Costs	Depreciation	Taxes	Total Costs	Profit After Tax
0	0	0	30	15	−22.5	22.5	−22.5
100	375	300	30	15	15	360	15
200	750	600	30	15	52.5	697.5	52.5

It really makes no difference whether we work with present values or equivalent annual revenues and costs. The two methods give identical answers. Very frequently, however, managers do not use either method: instead, they calculate the break-even points in terms of accounting profits. Table 10-6 shows the effect on Jalopy's after-tax profit of differences in electric car sales. Once again, in Figure 10-3 we have plotted revenues and costs against unit sales. But the story this time is different. Figure 10-3, which is based on accounting profits, shows a break-even point of 60,000 cars; Figures 10-1 and 10-2, which are based on present values and equivalent annual flows, both show a break-even point of 85,000 cars. Why the difference?

When we work in terms of accounting profit, we deduct depreciation of $15 million each year to cover the cost of the initial investment. If Jalopy sells 60,000 cars a year, revenues will be sufficient both to pay operating costs and to recover the initial outlay of $150 million. But they will *not* be sufficient to repay the *opportunity cost* of that $150 million. If we allow for the fact that the $150 million could have been invested elsewhere to earn 10%, the annual cost of the investment is not $15 million but $24.4 million.

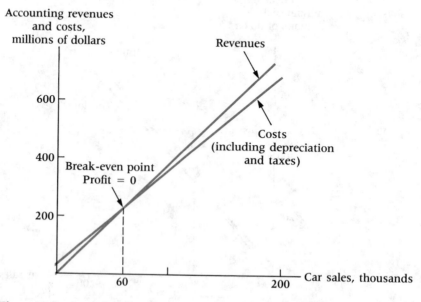

Figure 10-3   Sometimes break-even charts are constructed in terms of accounting numbers. After-tax profit is zero when sales are 60,000.

Companies that break even on an accounting basis are really making a loss—they are losing the opportunity cost of their investment. Reinhardt has described a dramatic example of this mistake.[5] In 1971 Lockheed managers found themselves having to give evidence to the United States Congress on the viability of the company's L-1011 TriStar program. They argued that the program appeared to be "commercially attractive" and that TriStar sales would eventually exceed the break-even point of about 200 aircraft. But in calculating this break-even point, Lockheed appears to have ignored the opportunity cost of the huge $1 billion capital investment on this project. Had it allowed for this cost, the break-even point would probably have been nearer to 500 aircraft.

10-2   MONTE CARLO SIMULATION

Sensitivity analysis allows you to consider the effect of changing one variable at a time. By looking at the project under alternative scenarios, you can consider the effect of a *limited number* of plausible combinations of variables. **Monte Carlo simulation** is a tool for considering *all* possible combinations. It therefore enables you to inspect the entire distribution of project outcomes. Its use in capital budgeting is principally associated with David Hertz[6] and McKinsey and Company, the management consultants. As we shall see, it is a controversial method.

Imagine that you are a gambler at Monte Carlo. You know nothing about the laws of probability (few gamblers do), but a friend has suggested to you a complicated strategy for playing roulette. Your friend has not actually tested the strategy but is confident that it will *on the average* give you a 2½ return for every 50 spins of the wheel. Your friend's optimistic estimate for any series of 50 spins is a profit of 55%; your friend's pessimistic estimate is a loss of 50%. How can you find out whether these really are the odds? An easy but possibly expensive way is to start playing and record the outcome at the end of each series of 50 spins. After, say, 100 series of 50 spins each, plot a frequency distribution of the outcomes and calculate the average and upper and lower limits. If things look good, you can then get down to some serious gambling.

An alternative is to tell a computer to simulate the roulette wheel and the strategy. In other words, you could instruct the computer to draw numbers out of its hat to determine the outcome of each spin of the wheel and then to calculate how much you would make or lose from the particular gambling strategy.

That would be an example of Monte Carlo simulation. In capital budgeting we replace the gambling strategy with a model of the project, and the roulette wheel with a model of the world in which the project operates. Let's see how this might work with our project for an electrically powered car.

Simulating the Electric Car Project

Step 1: Modeling the Project   The first step in any simulation is to give the computer a precise model of the project. For example, the sensitivity analysis of the car project was based on the following implicit model of cash flow:

$$\text{Cash flow} = (\text{revenues} - \text{costs} - \text{depreciation}) \times (1 - \text{tax rate}) + \text{depreciation}$$

[5] U.E. Reinhardt, "Break-Even for Lockheed's TriStar: An Application of Financial Theory," *Journal of Finance,* **28**: 821–838 (September 1973).

[6] See D.B. Hertz, "Investment Policies That Pay Off," *Harvard Business Review,* **46**: 96–108 (January–February 1968).

$$\text{Revenues} = \text{market size} \times \text{market share} \times \text{unit price}$$

$$\text{Costs} = (\text{market size} \times \text{market share} \times \text{variable unit cost}) + \text{fixed cost}$$

This model of the project was all you needed for the simple-minded sensitivity analysis we described above. But if you wish to simulate the whole project, you need to think about how the variables are interrelated.

For example, consider the first variable—market size. The marketing department has estimated a market size of 10 million cars in the first year of the project's life, but of course you do not *know* how things will work out. Actual market size will exceed or fall short of expectations by the amount of the department's error in the forecast:

$$\text{Market size, year 1} = \text{expected market size, year 1} \times \left(1 + \begin{array}{c} \text{proportionate} \\ \text{forecast error,} \\ \text{year 1} \end{array} \right)$$

You *expect* the forecast error to be zero but it could turn out to be positive or negative.

You can write the market size in the second year in exactly the same way:

$$\text{Market size, year 2} = \text{expected market size, year 2} \times \left(1 + \begin{array}{c} \text{proportionate} \\ \text{forecast error,} \\ \text{year 2} \end{array} \right)$$

But at this point you must consider how the expected market size in year 2 is affected by what happens in year 1. If car sales are below expectations in year 1, it is likely that they will continue to be below in subsequent years. Suppose that a shortfall in sales in year 1 would lead you to revise down your forecast of sales in year 2 by a like amount. Then

$$\text{Expected market size, year 2} = \text{actual market size, year 1}$$

Now you can rewrite the market size in year 2 in terms of the actual market size in the previous year plus a forecast error:

$$\text{Market size, year 2} = \text{market size, year 1} \times \left(1 + \begin{array}{c} \text{proportionate} \\ \text{forecast error,} \\ \text{year 2} \end{array} \right)$$

In the same way you can describe the expected market size in year 3 in terms of market size in year 2 and so on.

This set of equations illustrates how you can describe interdependence between different *periods*. But you also need to allow for interdependence between different *variables*. For example, the price of electrically powered cars is likely to increase with general inflation and with market size. Suppose that these are the only uncertainties and that a 10% shortfall in market size would lead you to predict a 3% reduction in price. Then you could model the first year's price as follows:

$$\text{Price, year 1} = \text{expected price, year 1} \times \left(1 + \begin{array}{c} \text{error in} \\ \text{inflation} \\ \text{forecast,} \\ \text{year 1} \end{array} + \begin{array}{c} 0.3 \times \text{error in} \\ \text{market size} \\ \text{forecast,} \\ \text{year 1} \end{array} \right)$$

Then, if these variations in the inflation rate and market size exert a permanent effect on price, you can define the second year's price as

$$\text{Price, year 2} = \text{expected price, year 2} \times \left(1 + \frac{\text{error in inflation forecast, year 2}}{} + \frac{0.3 \times \text{error in market size forecast, year 2}}{} \right)$$

$$= \text{actual price, year 1} \times \left(1 + \frac{\text{error in inflation forecast, year 2}}{} + \frac{0.3 \times \text{error in market size forecast, year 2}}{} \right)$$

The complete model of your project would include a set of equations for each of the variables—market size, price, market share, unit variable cost, and fixed cost. You can imagine that even if you allow for only a few interdependencies between variables and across time, the result would be quite a complex list of equations.[7] Perhaps that is not a bad thing if it forces you to understand what the project is all about. Model building is like spinach: you may not like the taste, but it is good for you.

Step 2: Specifying Probabilities   Remember the procedure for simulating the gambling strategy? The first step was to specify the strategy, the second was to specify the numbers on the roulette wheel, and the third was to tell the computer to select these numbers at random and calculate the results of the strategy:

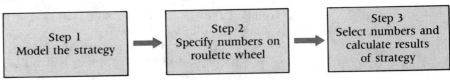

The steps are just the same for your car project:

Figure 10-4 illustrates how you might go about specifying your possible errors in forecasting market size. You *expect* market size to be 10 million cars. You obviously don't think that you are underestimating or overestimating market size; therefore your expected forecast error is zero. On the other hand, the marketing department has given you a range of possible estimates. Market size could be as low as 9 million cars or as high as 11 million cars. Thus the forecast error has an expected value of zero and a range of plus or minus 10%.

You need to draw up similar patterns of the possible forecast errors for each of the other variables that are in your model.[8]

---

[7] Specifying the interdependencies is the hardest and most important part of a simulation. If all components of project cash flows were unrelated, simulation would rarely be necessary.

[8] Figure 10-4 asserts that you are less likely to have made a large forecast error than a small forecast error. More precisely, it says that the probability of a possible error declines in proportion to the absolute size of the error. But forecast errors do not always fit this pattern.

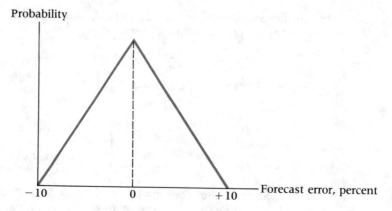

Figure 10-4 Distribution of errors in forecasting market size. The expected error is zero, but the error could be as large as plus or minus 10%.

Step 3: Simulate the Cash Flows   The computer now *samples* from the distribution of the forecast errors, calculates the resulting cash flows for each period, and records them. After many iterations you begin to get accurate estimates of the probability distributions of the project cash flows.[9]

Figure 10-5 shows the output of some actual simulations of the Jalopy Motor Company project. You can see that in the first year the expected cash flow is about $31 million and that there is a 95% chance that the cash flow will fall within the range $4 million to $57 million.

Have you noticed one slightly curious feature of this result? Our simulations tell us that the expected cash flow in each year is about $31 million, but the new products group told you that the expected cash flow was $30 million. They evidently arrived at this figure by taking the expected sales, multiplying by the expected profit per unit, and deducting the expected fixed cost and tax:

$$\text{Expected sales (units)} \times \left(\text{expected unit price} - \begin{array}{c} \text{expected} \\ \text{variable} \\ \text{unit cost} \end{array} \right)$$

$$- \text{ expected fixed costs} - \text{expected tax}$$

$$= 100{,}000 \ (3{,}750 - 3{,}000) - 30 \text{ million} - 15 \text{ million} = \$30 \text{ million}$$

Unfortunately, there was an error in the logic of the new products group. The expected revenues are *not* equal to the expected unit sales times the expected unit price unless sales and price are unrelated. If that sounds odd to you, consider the following example. Suppose a firm is equally likely to sell 100 items at a price of $1 each or 300 items at a price of $3 each. Its expected unit sales are (100 + 300)/2 = 200, and the expected price is (1 + 3)/2 = $2. The expected unit sales times the expected price is, therefore, 200 × 2 = $400. But the expected *revenue* is [(100 × 1) + (300 × 3)]/2 = $500.

For example, the marketing department may feel that it is equally likely that market size will fall anywhere within the 9 million to 11 million car range.

[9] Accurate only to the extent that your model and the probability distributions of the forecast errors are accurate. Remember the GIGO principle: "Garbage in, garbage out."

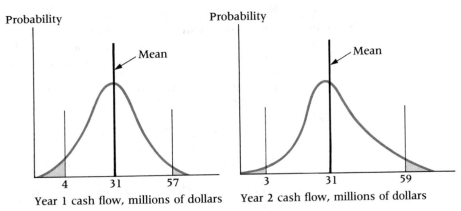

Figure 10-5   An example of the simulation output for the first two years of the electric car project. It provides cash-flow forecasts (that is, the means of the simulated distributions) as well as some idea of the predictability. The outer pairs of vertical lines include 95% of the simulated cash flows.

Similarly in the case of Jalopy Motors, price tends to go up and down with sales volume. Therefore the calculations of the new products group have *underestimated* the expected cash flow. Simulation therefore has given us one useful piece of information: project NPV is

$$- 150 + \sum_{t=1}^{10} \frac{31}{(1.10)^t} = \$40 \text{ million}$$

Assessing Simulation: You Pay for What You Get

Simulation, though costly and complicated, has the obvious merit of compelling the forecaster and the decision maker to face up to uncertainty and to interdependencies.

Once you have constructed your model, it is simple to analyze what would happen if you were able to narrow down the range of uncertainty about any of the variables. You may also be able to use it to explore the effect of modifications to the project.

All this makes simulation sound like a panacea for the world's ills. But, as usual, you pay for what you get. In fact you sometimes pay for *more* than you get.

It is not just a matter of the time and money spent in building the model. It is extremely difficult to estimate interrelationships between variables and the underlying probability distributions, even when you are trying to be honest. But in capital budgeting, forecasters are seldom impartial and the probability distributions on which the simulation is based can be highly biased.

In practice, a simulation that attempts to be realistic will also be very complex. That usually means the decision maker delegates the task of constructing the model to management scientists or consultants. The danger here is that, even if the builders understand their creation, the decision maker cannot and therefore does not rely on it. This is a common but ironic experience: the model that was intended to open up black boxes ends up creating another one.

Misusing Simulation

The financial manager, like a detective, must use every clue. Simulation should be regarded as one of several ways to obtain information about expected cash flows and risk. But the final investment decision involves only one number, net present value.

Some of the early champions of simulation made much greater claims for the method. They started with the premise that net present value cannot in itself reflect risk properly and, therefore, they bypassed that last crucial step.

In this alternative approach the financial manager is given distributions not of cash flows but of NPVs or internal rates of return. Now that may sound attractive—isn't a whole distribution of NPVs better than a single number? But we shall see that this "more is better" reasoning leads the financial manager into a trap.

First, we should explain what is meant by a distribution of NPVs. The cash flows for each iteration of the simulation model are translated into a net present value *by discounting at the risk-free rate*. Why are they not discounted at the opportunity cost of capital? Because, if you know what that is, you don't need a simulation model, except perhaps to help forecast cash flows. The risk-free rate is used to avoid prejudging risk.

Look at Figure 10-6, which shows the distribution of NPVs for the Jalopy Motor project. The "expected NPV" includes no allowance for risk. Risk is reflected in the dispersion of the NPV distribution. Thus the term *net present value* takes on a very different meaning from the usual one. If an asset has a number of possible "present values," it makes little sense to associate PV with *the* price the asset would sell at in a competitive capital market.[10]

The "risk" of this distribution ignores the investors' opportunity to diversify. Moreover, it is sensitive to the definition of the project. If two unrelated projects are combined, the "risk" of the NPV of the combined projects will be less than the average "risk" of the NPVs of the two separate projects. That not only offends the value additivity principle, but it also encourages sponsors of marginal projects to beat the system by submitting joint proposals.

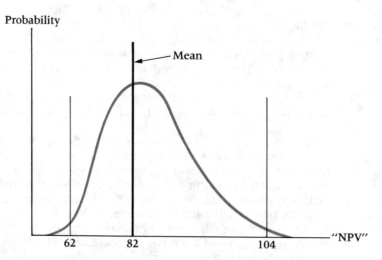

Figure 10-6   Some advocates of simulation propose that the financial manager should be presented with a distribution of "NPVs" like this one of the electric car project.

[10] The only interpretation we can put on these bastard NPVs is the following: suppose all uncertainty about the project's ultimate cash flows were resolved the day after the project is undertaken. On that day the project's opportunity cost of capital would fall to the risk-free rate. The distribution of NPVs represents the distribution of possible project values on that second day of the project's life.

Finally, it is very difficult to interpret a distribution of NPVs. Since the risk-free rate is not the opportunity cost of capital, there is no economic rationale for the discounting process. Because the whole edifice is arbitrary, managers can only be told to stare at the distribution until inspiration dawns. No one can tell them how to decide or what to do if inspiration never dawns.

Some of these difficulties can be dodged by presenting a distribution of internal rates of return. This avoids the arbitrary discount rate at the cost of introducing all the problems associated with the internal rate of return. Moreover, the manager is again left staring at the distribution with no guidance concerning the acceptable balance of expected return and variance of return.[11]

10-3 DECISION TREES AND SUBSEQUENT DECISIONS

If financial managers treat projects as black boxes, they may be tempted to think only of the first accept–reject decision and to ignore the subsequent investment decisions that may be tied to it. But if subsequent investment decisions depend on those made today, then today's decision may depend on what you plan to do tomorrow.

An Example: Vegetron

We have already solved in the last chapter a simple sequential decision problem, Vegetron's electric mop project. The problem was the following one:

> The scientists at Vegetron have come up with an electric mop and the firm is ready to go ahead with pilot production and test marketing. The preliminary phase will take a year and cost $125,000. Management feels that there is only a 50/50 chance that the pilot production and market tests will be successful. If they are, then Vegetron will build a $1 million plant, which will generate an expected annual cash flow in perpetuity of $250,000 a year after taxes. If they are not successful, Vegetron will not continue with the project.

Of course, Vegetron *could* go ahead even if the tests fail. Let's suppose that in that case the $1 million investment would generate only $75,000 per year.

Financial managers often use **decision trees** for analyzing projects involving sequential decisions. Figure 10-7 displays the electric mop problem as a decision tree. You can think of it as a game between Vegetron and fate. Each square represents a separate decision point for Vegetron; each circle represents a decision point for fate. Vegetron starts the play at the left-hand box. If Vegetron decides to test, then fate casts the enchanted dice and decides the result of the tests. If the tests are successful—there is a probability of ½ that they will be—then the firm faces a second decision: invest $1 million in a project offering a $1.5 million net present value or stop. If the tests fail, Vegetron has a similar choice but the investment yields a net present value of −$250,000.

It is obvious what the second-stage decisions will be: invest if the tests are successful and stop if they fail. The net present value of stopping is zero, so the decision tree boils down to a simple problem: should Vegetron invest $125,000 now to obtain a 50% chance of $1.5 million a year later?

[11] He or she might use the standard deviation of the IRR as a proxy for the relative risk of projects in the same line of business, however.

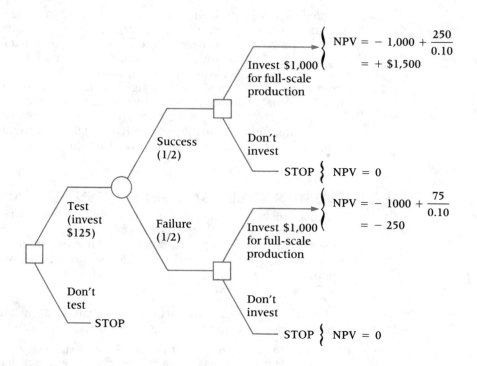

$$NPV = -1,000 + \frac{250}{0.10}$$
$$= +\$1,500$$

$$NPV = -1000 + \frac{75}{0.10}$$
$$= -250$$

Figure 10-7 The electric mop example from Chapter 9 expressed as a decision tree. This is a project involving sequential decisions. The investment in testing generates the opportunity to invest in full-scale production. (All figures are in thousands; probabilities are in parentheses.)

*A Tougher Example: Magna Charter

Magna Charter is a new corporation formed by Agnes Magna to provide an executive flying service for the Windsor–Québec City corridor. The founder thinks there will be a ready demand from businesses that cannot justify a full-time company plane but nevertheless need one from time to time. However, the venture is not a sure thing. There is a 40% chance that demand in the first year will be low. If it is low, there is a 70% chance that it will remain low in subsequent years. On the other hand, if the initial demand is high, there is an 80% chance that it will stay high.

The immediate problem is to decide what kind of plane to buy. A brand-new turboprop costs $400,000. A used piston-engine plane costs only $200,000 but has less capacity and customer appeal. Moreover, the piston-engine plane is an old design and likely to depreciate rapidly. Ms. Magna thinks that next year secondhand piston aircraft will be available for only $100,000.

That gives Ms. Magna an idea: why not start out with one piston plane and buy another if demand is still high? It will cost only $100,000 to expand. If demand is low, Magna Charter can sit tight with one small, relatively inexpensive aircraft.

Figure 10-8 displays these choices. The square on the left marks the company's initial decision to purchase a turboprop for $400,000 or a piston aircraft for $200,000. After the company has made its decision, fate decides on the first year's demand. You can see in parentheses the probability that demand will be high or

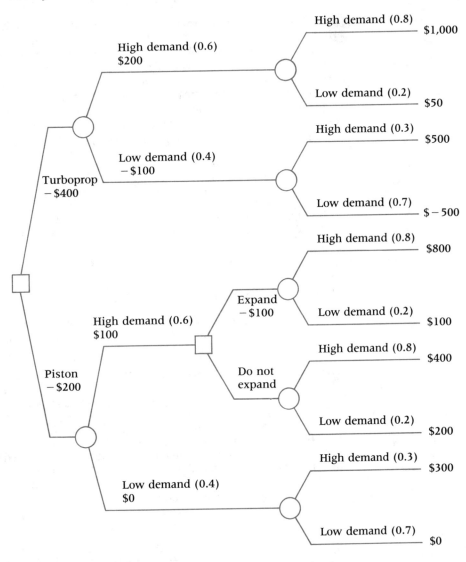

Figure 10-8 Decision tree for Magna Charter. Should it buy a new turboprop or a smaller, secondhand piston-engine plane? A second piston plane can be purchased in year 1 if demand turns out to be high. (All figures are in thousands.)

low, and you can see the expected cash flow for each combination of aircraft and demand level. At the end of the year the company has a second decision to make if it has a piston-engine aircraft: it can either expand or sit tight. This decision point is marked by the second square. Finally fate takes over again and selects the level of demand for year 2. Again you can see in parentheses the probability of high or low demand. Notice that the probabilities for the second year depend on the first-period outcomes. For example, if demand is high in the first period, then there is an 80% chance that it will also be high in the second. The chance of high demand in *both* the first and second periods is 0.6 × 0.8 = 0.48. After the parentheses we again show the profitability of the project for each combination of aircraft and demand level. You can interpret each of these figures as the present value at the end of year 2 of the cash flows for that and all subsequent years.

The problem for Ms. Magna is to decide what to do today. We solve that problem by thinking first what she would do next year. This means that we start at the right side of the tree and work backward to the beginning on the left.

The only decision that Ms. Magna needs to make next year is whether to expand if purchase of a piston-engine plane is succeeded by high demand. If she expands, she invests $100,000 and receives a payoff of $800,000 if demand continues to be high and $100,000 if demand falls. So her *expected* payoff is

$$\begin{array}{c} \text{(Probability high demand} \times \text{payoff with high demand)} \\ + \text{(probability low demand} \times \text{payoff with low demand)} \\ = (0.8 \times 800) + (0.2 \times 100) = \$660,000 \end{array}$$

If the opportunity cost of capital for this venture is 10%,[12] then the net present value of expanding, computed as of year 1, is

$$\text{NPV} = -100 + \frac{660}{1.10} = +500 \text{ or } \$500,000$$

If Ms. Magna does *not* expand, the expected payoff is

$$\begin{array}{c} \text{(Probability high demand} \times \text{payoff with high demand)} \\ + \text{(probability low demand} \times \text{payoff with low demand)} \\ = (0.8 \times 400) + (0.2 \times 200) = \$360,000 \end{array}$$

The net present value of *not* expanding, computed as of year 1, is

$$\text{NPV} = 0 + \frac{360}{1.10} = +327 \text{ or } \$327,000$$

Expansion obviously pays if market demand is high.

Now that we know what Magna Charter ought to do if faced with the expansion decision, we can "roll back" to today's decision. If the first piston-engine plane is bought, Magna can expect to receive cash worth $600,000 in year 1 if demand is high and cash worth $82,000 if it is low:

The net present value of the investment in the piston-engine plane is therefore $157,000:

$$NPV = -\ 200 + \frac{0.6(600) + 0.4(82)}{1.10} = +\$157,000$$

If Magna buys the turboprop, there are no future decisions to analyze, and so there is no need to roll back. We just calculate expected cash flows and discount:

$$
\begin{aligned}
NPV = -400 &+ \frac{0.6(200) + 0.4(-100)}{1.10} \\
&+ \frac{0.6[0.8(1,000) + 0.2(50)] + 0.4[0.3(500) + 0.7(-500)]}{(1.10)^2} \\
= -400 &+ \frac{80}{1.10} + \frac{406}{(1.10)^2} = +8, \text{ or } \$8,000
\end{aligned}
$$

Thus, the investment in the piston-engine plane has an NPV of $157,000; the investment in the turboprop has an NPV of $8,000. The piston-engine plane is the better bet. Note, however, that the choice would seem much closer if we forgot to take account of the option to expand. In that case the NPV of the piston-engine plane would drop from $157,000 to $63,000:

$$
\begin{aligned}
NPV = 200 &+ \frac{0.6(100) + 0.4(0)}{1.10} \\
&+ \frac{0.6[0.8(400) + 0.2(200)] + 0.4[0.3(300) + 0.7(0)]}{(1.10)^2} \\
= +63 &\text{ or } \$63,000
\end{aligned}
$$

The value of the *option to expand* is, therefore,

$$157 - 63 = +94, \text{ or } \$94,000$$

*Bailing Out   If the option to expand has value, how about the option to *contract* or to abandon the venture entirely?

We have assumed that Magna Charter can buy a secondhand piston-engine plane for $100,000 in year 1. We can also assume that it could sell one for the same amount. That is exactly what it should do if it buys the piston-engine plane and encounters low demand: $100,000 cash received from the sale of the plane now is obviously better than a 30% chance of a recovery in demand and $300,000 a year later.

Let's suppose that the turboprop could be sold for $300,000 in year 1. Again, it obviously makes sense to sell if demand is low.

But now we must think again about the decision to buy the piston-engine plane. If Magna Charter can "bail out" of either investment, why not take the turboprop and shoot for the big payoff?

Figure 10-9 represents Magna Charter's decision problem with the abandonment options included. First, we figure out the net present value of buying the turboprop. This reduces to a simple one-period problem:

Figure 10-9 Revised decision tree for Magna Charter, taking account of the possibility of abandoning the business if demand turns out to be low. (All figures are in thousands.)

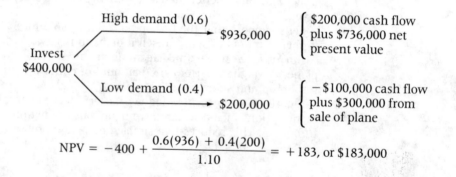

$$\text{NPV} = -400 + \frac{0.6(936) + 0.4(200)}{1.10} = +183, \text{ or } \$183,000$$

Thus, when we allow for the possibility of abandonment, the net present value of the turboprop investment increases from $8,000 to $183,000. The value of the *option to abandon* is

Value of abandonment option = NPV with abandonment − NPV without abandonment

= 183 − 8

= 175, or $175,000

Now we figure out the net present value of buying the piston-engine plane with the abandonment option included. The payoffs for this plane are as follows:

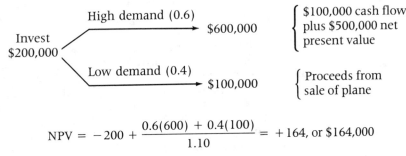

$$NPV = -200 + \frac{0.6(600) + 0.4(100)}{1.10} = +164, \text{ or } \$164,000$$

With the abandonment option the piston-engine plane is worth $164,000; without it, the plane is worth $157,000. Therefore the value of the abandonment option is

164 − 157 = 7, or $7,000

It is a good thing we remembered the possibility of reselling the aircraft. When we include the value of the abandonment option, the turboprop has an NPV of $183,000 and the piston-engine plane has an NPV of only $164,000.

Abandonment Value and Capital Budgeting

Abandonment value—the value of the option to bail out of a project—is a simple idea that has surprisingly broad practical implications. In a way it is just common sense; disaster, like a cat, is always waiting to pounce, and so you must always be prepared to cut and run.

Some assets are easier to bail out of than others. Tangible assets are usually easier to sell than intangible ones.[13] It helps to have active secondhand markets, which really only exist for standardized, widely used items. Real estate, airplanes, trucks, and certain machine tools are likely to be relatively easy to sell. The knowledge accumulated by Vegetron's research and development program, on the other hand, is a specialized intangible asset and probably would not have a significant abandonment value.

In the worst case a firm's stockholders can bail out by going bankrupt. It may sound strange to say that an investor is helped by the possibility of bankruptcy, but it is true. Investors in corporations have *limited liability*: they risk only the money they invest. From their point of view there is a limit to the money the firm can lose; they always have the option of walking away from the firm and leaving its problems in the hands of the creditors and the bankruptcy courts.[14]

---

[13] This is, of course, not always the case. Some tangible assets you have to pay to get rid of— worn out refrigerators, for instance.

[14] We will discuss bankruptcy in Chapters 18 and 30.

Expansion value can be just as important as abandonment value. When things turn out well, the quicker and easier the business can be expanded, the better. The best of all possible worlds occurs when good luck strikes and you find that you can expand quickly *but your competitors cannot.*

Pro and Con Decision Trees

Our examples of abandonment and expansion are extreme simplifications of the sequential decision problems that financial managers face. But they make an important general point. If today's decisions affect what you can do tomorrow, then tomorrow's decisions have to be analyzed before you can act rationally today.

Any cash-flow forecast rests on some assumption about the firm's future investment and operating strategy. Often that assumption is implicit. Decision trees force the underlying strategy into the open. By displaying the links between today's and tomorrow's decisions, they help the financial manager to find the strategy with the highest net present value.[15]

The trouble with decision trees is that they get so _____ complex so _____ quickly (insert your own expletives). What will Magna Charter do if demand is neither high nor low but just middling? In that event Ms. Magna might sell the turboprop and buy a piston-engine plane, or she might defer expansion and abandonment decisions until year 2. Perhaps middling demand requires a decision about a price cut or an intensified sales campaign.

There are other possibilities. Perhaps there is uncertainty about future prices of secondhand aircraft. If so, abandonment will depend not just on the level of demand but also on the level of secondhand prices. What is more, secondhand prices are likely to be depressed if demand is low and buoyant if demand is high.

We could draw a new decision tree covering this expanded set of events and decisions. Try it if you like: you'll see how fast the circles, squares, and branches accumulate.

Life is complex, and there is very little we can do about it. It is therefore unfair to criticize decision trees because they can become complex. Our criticism is reserved for analysts who let the complexity become overwhelming. The point of decision trees is to allow explicit analysis of possible future events and decisions. They should be judged not on their comprehensiveness but on whether they show the most important links between today's and tomorrow's decisions. Decision trees used in real life will be more complex than Figures 10-8 and 10-9, but they will nevertheless display only a small fraction of possible future events and decisions. Decision trees are like grapevines: they are productive only if they are vigorously pruned.

Our analysis of the Magna Charter project begged an important question. The option to expand enlarged the spread of possible outcomes and therefore increased the risk of investing in a piston aircraft. Conversely, the option to bail out narrowed the spread of possible outcomes. So it reduced the risk of investment. We should have used different discount rates to recognize these changes in risk, but decision trees do not tell us how to do this. In fact, decision trees don't tell us how to value options at all; they are just a convenient way to summarize cash-flow consequences. But the situation is not hopeless. Modern techniques of option valuation are beginning to help value these investment options. We will describe these techniques in Chapters 20 and 21.

---

[15] Some analysts go further than that. Like the early advocates of simulation models, they start with the premise that net present value cannot take account of risk. They therefore propose that the decision tree should be used to calculate a *distribution* of "NPVs" or internal rates of return for each possible sequence of company decisions. That may sound like a gingerbread house, but you should know by now that there is a witch inside.

**Decision Trees
and Monte
Carlo
Simulation**

We have said that any cash-flow forecast rests on assumptions about future investment and operating strategy. Think back to the Monte Carlo simulation model that we constructed for the Jalopy Motor Company. What strategy was that based on? We don't know. Inevitably Jalopy will face decisions about pricing, production, expansion, and abandonment, but the model builder's assumptions about these decisions are buried in the model's equations. At some point the model builder may have explicitly identified a future strategy for Jalopy, but it is clearly not the optimal one. There will be some runs of the model when nearly everything goes wrong and when in real life Jalopy would abandon to cut its losses. Yet the model goes on period after period, heedless of the drain on Jalopy's cash resources. The most unfavourable outcomes reported by the simulation model would never be encountered in real life.

On the other hand, the simulation model probably understates the project's potential value if nearly everything goes right: there is no provision for expanding to take advantage of good luck.

Most simulation models incorporate a "business as usual" strategy, which is fine as long as there are no major surprises. The greater the divergence from expected levels of market growth, market share, cost, and so on, the less realistic is the simulation. Therefore the extreme high and low simulated values—the "tails" of the simulated distributions—should be treated with extreme caution. Don't take the area under the tails as realistic probabilities of disaster or bonanza.

10-4   SUMMARY

There is more to capital budgeting than grinding out calculations of net present value. If you can identify the major uncertainties, you may find that it is worth undertaking some additional preliminary research that will *confirm* whether the project is worthwhile. And even if you decide that you have done all you can to resolve the uncertainties, you still want to be aware of the potential problems. You do not want to be caught by surprise if things go wrong: you want to be ready to take corrective action.

There are three ways in which companies try to identify the principal threats to a project's success. The simplest is to undertake a sensitivity analysis. In this case the manager considers in turn each of the determinants of the project's success and estimates how far the present value of the project would be altered by taking a very optimistic view or a very pessimistic view of that variable.

Sensitivity analysis of this kind is easy, but it is not always helpful. Variables do not usually change one at a time. If costs are higher than you expect, it is a good bet that prices will be higher also. And if prices are higher, it is a good bet that sales volume will be lower. If you don't allow for the dependencies between the swings and the merry-go-rounds, you may get a false idea of the hazards of the fairground business. Many companies try to cope with this problem by examining the effect on the project of alternative plausible combinations of variables. In other words, they will estimate the net present value of the project under different scenarios and compare this estimate with the base case.

In a sensitivity analysis you change variables one at a time: when you analyze scenarios, you look at a limited number of alternative combinations of variables. If you want to go whole hog and look at *all* possible combinations of variables, then you will probably need to use Monte Carlo simulation to cope with the complexity. In that case you must construct a complete model of the project and specify the probability distribution of each of the determinants of cash flow. You can then ask the computer to select a random number for each of these determinants and work out the cash flows that would result. After the computer has repeated this process a hundred or so times, you should have a fair idea of the expected cash flow in each year and the spread of possible cash flows.

Simulation can be a very useful tool. The discipline of building a model of the project can in itself lead you to a deeper understanding of the project. And once you have constructed your model, it is a simple matter to see how the outcomes would be affected by altering the scope of the project or the distribution of any of the variables. There are, of course, limits to what you can learn from simulations. A marine engineer uses a tank to simulate the performance of alternative hull designs but knows that it is impossible to fully replicate the conditions the ship will encounter. In the same way, the financial manager can learn a lot from "laboratory" tests but cannot hope to build a model that accurately captures all the uncertainties and interdependencies that really surround a project.

Books about capital budgeting sometimes create the impression that, once the manager has made an investment decision, there is nothing to do but sit back and watch the cash flows unfold. In practice, companies are constantly modifying their operations. If cash flows are better than anticipated, the project may be expanded; if they are worse, it may be contracted or abandoned altogether. Good managers take account of these options when they value a project. One convenient way to analyze them is by means of a decision tree. You identify the principal things that could happen to the project and the main counteractions that you might take. Then, working back from the future to the present, you can calculate which action you *should* take in each case. Once you know that, it is easy to work out how much the value of the project is increased by these opportunities to react to changing circumstances.

Many of the early articles on simulation and decision trees were written before we knew how to introduce risk into calculations of net present value. Their authors believed that these techniques might allow the manager to make investment decisions without estimating the opportunity cost of capital and calculating net present value. Today we know that simulation and decision analysis cannot save you from having to calculate net present value. The value of these techniques is to help the manager go behind the cash-flow forecast; they help the manager to understand what could go wrong and what opportunities are available to modify the project. That is why we described them as tools to open up black boxes.

FURTHER READING

For an excellent case study of break-even analysis, see:

U.E. Reinhardt, "Break-Even Analysis for Lockheed's TriStar: An Application of Financial Theory," *Journal of Finance*, **28**: 821–838 (September 1973).

The principal exponent of simulation in investment appraisal is David Hertz. See:

D.B. Hertz, "Investment Policies that Pay Off," *Harvard Business Review*, **46**: 96–108 (January–February 1968).

D.B. Hertz, "Risk Analysis in Capital Investment," *Harvard Business Review*, **42**: 95–106 (January–February 1964).

Lewellen and Long are generally against simulation. See, however, Myers's "Postscript."

W.G. Lewellen and M.S. Long, "Simulation vs. Single-Value Estimates in Capital Expenditure Analysis," *Decision Sciences*, **3**: (1972).

S.C. Myers, "Postscript: Using Simulation for Risk Analysis," in S.C. Myers, ed., *Modern Developments in Financial Management*, Praeger Publishers, Inc., New York, 1976.

The use of decision trees in investment appraisal is discussed in:

R.F. Hespos and P.A. Strassmann, "Stochastic Decision Trees for the Analysis of Investment Decisions," *Management Science*, **11**: 244–259 (August 1965).

J. Magee, "How to Use Decision Trees in Capital Investment," *Harvard Business Review*, **42**: 79–96 (September–October 1964).

Hax and Wiig discuss how Monte Carlo simulation and decision trees were used in an actual capital budgeting decision:

A.C. Hax and K.M. Wiig, "The Use of Decision Analysis in Capital Investment Problems," *Sloan Management Review*, **17**: 19–48 (Winter 1976).

The abandonment option in capital budgeting was first analyzed by:

A.A. Robichek and J.C. Van Horne, "Abandonment Value in Capital Budgeting," *Journal of Finance*, **22**: 577–590 (December 1967).

QUIZ

1. Define and briefly explain each of the following terms or procedures:
   (a) Project analysis
   (b) Sensitivity analysis
   (c) Break-even analysis
   (d) Monte Carlo simulation
   (e) Decision tree
   (f) Abandonment value
   (g) Expansion value
2. What is the NPV of the electric car project under the following *scenario*?

Market size	11 million
Market share	0.01
Unit price	$4,000
Unit variable cost	$3,600
Fixed cost	$20 million

3. Jalopy Motor is considering an alternative production method for its electric car. It would require an additional investment of $150 million but would reduce variable costs by $40 million a year.
   (a) What is the NPV of this alternative scheme?
   (b) Draw break-even charts for this alternative scheme along the lines of Figures 10-1 and 10-3.
   (c) Explain how you would interpret the break-even figures.
4. Summarize the problems a manager would encounter in interpreting a standard sensitivity analysis, such as the one shown in Table 10-2. Which of these problems are alleviated by examining the project under alternative scenarios?
5. True or false?
   (a) Project analysis is unnecessary for projects with asset betas that are equal to zero.
   (b) Sensitivity analysis can be used to identify the variables most crucial to a project's success.
   (c) Sensitivity analysis gives "optimistic" and "pessimistic" values for project cash flow and NPV.

(d) The break-even sales level of a project is higher when a *break-even* is defined in terms of NPV rather than accounting income.

(e) Monte Carlo simulation can be used to help forecast cash flows.

(f) Monte Carlo simulation eliminates the need to estimate a project's opportunity cost of capital.

(g) Decision trees are useful when future decisions may depend on today's decision.

(h) High abandonment value increases NPV, other things being equal.

6. Suppose a manager has already estimated a project's cash flows, calculated its NPV, and done a sensitivity analysis like the one shown in Table 10-2. List the additional steps required to carry out a Monte Carlo simulation of project cash flows.

7. Use a decision tree to show that it pays Jalopy Motor to conduct a pretest of the suspect machine (see Section 10-1).

8. Big Oil is wondering whether to drill for oil in West Pembina. The prospects are as follows:

Depth of Well (feet)	Total Cost (millions of dollars)	Cumulative Probability of Finding Oil	PV of Oil (if found) (millions of dollars)
10,000	2	0.5	5
15,000	2.5	0.6	4.5
20,000	3	0.7	4

Draw a decision tree showing the successive drilling decisions to be made by Big Oil. How deep should it be prepared to drill?

QUESTIONS AND PROBLEMS

1. Your staff has come up with the following revised estimates for the electric car project:

	Pessimistic	Expected	Optimistic
Market size	8 million	10 million	12 million
Market share	0.004	0.01	0.016
Unit price	$3,000	$3,750	$4,000
Unit variable cost	$3,500	$3,000	$2,750
Fixed cost	$50 million	$30 million	$10 million

Conduct a sensitivity analysis. What are the principal uncertainties in the project?

2. Amalgamated Boot is proposing to replace its old shoe-making machinery with more modern equipment. The new equipment costs $10 million and the company expects to sell its old equipment for $1 million. The attraction of the new machinery is that it is expected to cut manufacturing costs from their current level of $8 a pair to $4. However, as the following table shows, there is some uncertainty both about future sales and about the performance of the new machinery:

	Pessimistic	Expected	Optimistic
Sales (millions of pairs)	0.4	0.5	0.7
Manufacturing cost with new			
machinery (dollars per pair)	6	4	3
Economic life of new machinery (years)	7	10	13

Conduct a sensitivity analysis of the replacement decision assuming (a) a discount rate of 12%, and (b) that Amalgamated does not pay taxes.

3. Use a computer spreadsheet program to perform a sensitivity analysis of the IM&C guano project in Section 6-3. Examine the effect of differences in:
   (a) the inflation rate
   (b) the project life
   (c) working capital requirements
   (d) sales
   (e) operating costs
   (f) the discount rate

*4. Agnes Magna has found some errors in her data (see Section 10-3). The corrected figures are as follows:

   Price of turbo, year 0 = $350,000
   Price of piston, year 0 = $180,000
   Price of turbo, year 1 = $300,000
   Price of piston, year 1 = $150,000
   Discount rate = 8%

   Redraw the decision tree with the changed data. Calculate the value of the option to expand. Recalculate the value of the abandonment option. Which plane should Ms. Magna buy?

*5. Ms. Magna has thought of another idea. Perhaps she should buy a piston-engine plane now. Then, if demand is high in the first year, she can sell it and buy a turboprop. Redraw Figure 10-8 to incorporate this possibility. What should Ms. Magna do?

6. For what kinds of capital investment projects do you think Monte Carlo simulation would be most useful? For example, can you think of some industries in which this technique would be particularly attractive? Would it be more useful for large-scale investments than small ones? Discuss.

7. You own an unused gold mine that will cost $100,000 to reopen. If you open the mine, you expect to be able to extract 1,000 ounces of gold a year for each of three years. After that, the deposit will be exhausted. The gold price is currently $500 an ounce, and each year the price is equally likely to rise or fall by $50 from its level at the start of the year. The extraction cost is $460 an ounce and the discount rate is 10%.
   (a) Should you open the mine now or delay in the hope of a rise in the gold price?
   (b) What difference would it make to your decision if you could costlessly (but irreversibly) shut down the mine at any stage?

8. Read and criticize the Hax–Wiig article mentioned in the "Further Reading" for this chapter. Are all of their recommendations consistent with finance theory?

9. You are considering a new consulting service. There is a 60% chance that demand will be high in the first year. If it is high, there is an 80% chance

that it will continue high indefinitely. If demand is low in the first year, there is a 60% chance that it will continue low indefinitely.

If demand is high, forecasted revenue is $90,000 a year; if demand is low, forecasted revenue is $70,000 a year. You can cease to offer the service at any point, in which case, of course, revenues are zero. Costs other than computing are forecasted at $50,000 a year regardless of demand. These costs also can be terminated at any point. You have a choice on computing costs. One possibility is to buy your own minicomputer. This involves an initial outlay of $200,000 and no subsequent expenditure. It has an economic life of ten years and no salvage value. The alternative is to rent computer time as you need it. In this case computer costs are 40% of revenues.

Assume that the computing decision cannot be reversed (that is, if you buy a computer, you cannot resell it; if you do *not* buy it today, you cannot do so later). There are no taxes and the opportunity cost of capital is 10%.

Draw a decision tree showing the alternatives. Is it better to buy a computer or rent? State clearly any additional assumptions that you need to make.

C·H·A·P·T·E·R

11

WHERE POSITIVE
NET PRESENT VALUES
COME FROM

We have now spent several chapters explaining how to calculate exact net present values but we have had little to say about the forecasts that are the basis of every investment decision. But good investment decisions require good cash flow forecasts. If financial managers are to get the kind of forecasts that they need, they must understand how those forecasts are produced. What can financial managers do to ensure that everybody is acting consistently? It is impossible to make rational investment choices if each forecaster is employing different assumptions about the prospects for the economy. Also, how should financial managers cope with biased or exaggerated forecasts? It's easy if the biases can be identified before the fact, but that is rarely possible. Perhaps crude rules of thumb, like payback, can protect against forecasting disasters. Is there any way to distinguish NPVs that are truly positive from those that merely reflect overoptimism? We suggest that managers should ask some probing questions about the possible source of economic gains.

11-1 INCONSISTENT ATTITUDES AND ASSUMPTIONS

Inconsistent recommendations and forecasts can crop up in various ways. For example, some managers are more averse to risk than others and they may let their attitudes toward risk interfere with their judgement of what is a good project. Managers of divisions that have assured good performance are more likely to propose high risk projects than managers of faltering divisions with an uncertain future. Also a large division is more likely than a small division to risk a $1 million loss. Such a loss might merely dent the profits of the larger division, but it could throw the managers of the small division out of work.

A manager's attitude to risk will partly depend on the way his or her performance is measured and rewarded. A good measurement and reward system should have some tolerance for mistakes and should be able to discriminate between good decisions and lucky ones. Ideally, managers would be rewarded for good decisions thwarted by bad luck and penalized for bad decisions rescued by good luck.

Another danger is that investment proposals may be based on inconsistent assumptions. For example, suppose the manager of your furniture division is bullish on housing starts but the manager of your appliance division is bearish. This inconsistency makes the projects of the furniture division look better than those of the appliance division. Senior management ought to negotiate a consensus estimate and make sure that all NPVs are recomputed using that joint estimate. Then a rational decision can be made.

This is why many firms begin the capital budgeting process by establishing forecasts of economic indicators like inflation and the growth in national income, as well as forecasts of particular items that are important to the firm's business, such as housing starts or the price of raw materials. These forecasts can then be used as the basis for all project analyses.

11-2 THE PROBLEMS OF BIAS AND ERRORS

Overoptimism and exaggeration appear to be very common in financial forecasts. For example, a study by one company of 50 projects showed that the actual present value of "cost reduction" projects was 10% above the forecast, whereas for "sales expansion" projects the actual present value was 40% *below* the forecast, and for "new products" it was 90% *below*.[1] Perhaps these results were not typical, but it looks as if management was receiving grossly biased forecasts on any project that involved expansion.

You will probably never be able to eliminate bias completely, but if you are aware of why bias occurs, you are at least part of the way there. Project sponsors are likely to overstate their case deliberately only if you, the financial manager, encourage them to do so. For example, if they believe that success depends on having the largest division rather than the most profitable one, they will propose large expansion projects that they do not truly believe have positive NPVs. Or, if they believe you won't listen to them unless they paint a rosy picture, you will be presented with many rosy pictures. Or if you invite each division to compete for limited resources, you will find that each attempts to outbid the other for those resources. The fault in such cases is your own — it is only because you are holding up the hoop that others try to jump through it.

Our development of the net present value rule assumed implicitly that you are supplied with unbiased cash-flow forecasts. If the forecasts are biased, the net present value rule may lead to wrong decisions. If you are aware that a forecaster always doubles the original figures, you can correct for this bias. But what do you do when you do not know forecasters' idiosyncrasies or when they play games with you? In that case, you may find that ad hoc procedures sometimes provide better protection against the effects of bias than the net present value rule.

Suppose, for example, that a divisional manager is congenitally overoptimistic. Simple application of the net present value rule would lead to too much investment by that division: the company may, therefore, do better to pretend that capital is limited and confine the division's spending to some arbitrary amount. That *forces* the divisional manager to define priorities.[2] Or suppose that forecasters' biases are stronger for more distant cash flows — it's much easier to put on the

---

[1] Cited in J.L. Bower, *Managing the Resource Allocation Process*, Division of Research, Graduate School of Business Administration, Harvard University, Boston, 1970.

[2] Of course, it may also encourage divisions to compete even more strongly to get a large allocation of funds to invest.

rose-coloured glasses if you're forecasting 10 or 15 years into the future. The net present value rule will then give long-term forecasts more weight than they deserve. The financial manager might do better to use a payback criterion that places *no* weight on them.

These two examples illustrate that, unless the forecasts are corrected for bias, the ad hoc criterion can *sometimes* give the better result. The converse is also true: a company that uses an ad hoc criterion may *sometimes* find that it pays to use biased forecasts.[3] Two wrongs do not make a right, but they may come closer than a right and a wrong combined.

We should stress that we are *not* recommending the use of ad hoc criteria. The essential point is that improvements in one aspect of the decision-making process must take account of deficiencies in other areas.

Errors in Forecasting

Let us suppose that you have persuaded all your project sponsors to give honest forecasts. You have eliminated the problem of bias but the forecasts will still contain errors. Some errors will be positive and some negative; the average error will be zero. But that is little consolation because you want to accept only projects with *truly* superior profitability.

Think, for example, of what would happen if you were to jot down your estimates of the cash flows from operating various items of equipment. You would probably find that about half *appeared* to have positive net present values. This is not because you personally possess any superior skill in operating jumbo jets or running a chain of laundromats but because you have introduced a large amount of error into your estimates of the cash flows. The more projects you contemplate, the more likely you are to uncover projects that *appear* to be extremely worthwhile. Indeed, if you were to extend your activities to making cash-flow estimates of other companies, you would also find a number of *apparently* attractive merger candidates. In some of these cases you may have genuine information and the proposed investment really may have a positive NPV. But in many other cases the investment only looks good because you have made a forecasting error.

11-3 LOOK FIRST AT MARKET VALUES

What can you do to prevent forecast errors from swamping genuine information? We suggest that you begin by looking at market values.[4]

The following parable should help to illustrate what we mean by this. Your local Cadillac dealer is announcing a special offer. For $50,001 you not only get a brand new Cadillac, you also get the chance to shake hands with your favourite movie star. You wonder how much you are paying for that handshake. There are two possible approaches to the problem. You could evaluate the worth of the Cadillac's power steering, disappearing windshield wipers, and other features and conclude that the Cadillac is worth $51,000. This would seem to suggest that the dealership is willing to pay $999 to have a movie star shake hands with you.

---

[3] We stress the word *sometimes*. In very many circumstances use of an ad hoc criterion makes matters worse. For a discussion of the interactions between criterion, forecasting ability, and bias, see P. Marsh and R.A. Brealey, "The Use of Imperfect Forecasts in Capital Investment Decisions," *Proceedings of the European Finance Association, 1976*, North Holland, Amsterdam, 1976.

[4] Black also makes a similiar suggestion in a paper that outlines a number of general rules for investment decisions. See F. Black, "Corporate Investment and Discounting Rules," unpublished paper, Sloan School of Management, MIT, February 1983.

Alternatively, you might note that the market price for Cadillacs is $50,000, so that you are paying a dollar for the handshake. As long as there is a competitive market for Cadillacs, the latter approach is more appropriate.

Whenever security analysts value a company's stock, they are also faced with the task of valuing a package. They must evaluate all the information that is known to the market about a company *and* they must evaluate the information that is known only to them. The information that is known to the market is the Cadillac; the private information is the handshake with a movie star. Investors have already evaluated the information that is generally known. Security analysts do not need to evaluate this information again. They can *start* with the market price of the stock and concentrate on valuing their private information.

While lesser mortals would instinctively accept the Cadillac's market value of $50,000, the financial manager is trained to enumerate and value all the costs and benefits from an investment, and is therefore tempted to substitute his or her own opinion for the market's. Unfortunately this approach increases the chance of error. Many capital assets are traded in a competitive market and so it makes sense to *start* with the market price and then ask why these assets should earn more in your hands than in those of your rivals.

For example, we encountered a department store chain that estimated the present value of the expected cash flows from each proposed store, including the price at which it could eventually sell the store premises. Although the firm took considerable care with these estimates, it was disturbed to find that the conclusions were heavily influenced by the forecasted selling price of each store. Thus, despite the fact that the firm disclaimed any particular real estate expertise, it discovered that its investment decisions were unintentionally dominated by its assumptions about future real estate prices. Thereafter, whenever he was faced with a proposal to open a new store, the financial manager always checked the decision by asking the following question: "Let us assume that the property is fairly priced. What is the evidence that it is best suited to one of our department stores rather than to some other use?" In asking himself this question the financial manager was observing the eternal wisdom:

> If an asset is worth more to others than it is to you, then beware of bidding for the asset against them.

Let us take the department store problem a little further. Suppose that the new store costs $100 million and you forecast that it will generate income of $8 million a year for 10 years. Real estate prices are estimated to grow by 3% a year, so the expected value of the store at the end of 10 years is $100 \times (1.03)^{10} = \$134$ million. At a discount rate of 10%, your proposed department store has an NPV of $1 million:

$$\text{NPV} = -100 + \frac{8}{1.10} + \frac{8}{(1.10)^2} + \cdots + \frac{8 + 134}{(1.10)^{10}} = \$1 \text{ million}$$

It is helpful to imagine such a business as divided into two parts—a real estate subsidiary which buys the building and a retailing subsidiary that rents and operates it. Then figure out how much the real estate subsidiary would have to charge.

In some cases a fair rental can be estimated from real estate transactions. For example, we might observe that similar retail space recently rented for $10 million a year. In that case we would conclude that our department store was an unattractive use for the site. Once the site was acquired, it would be better to rent it out at $10 million than to use it for a store generating only $8 million.

You can also estimate a fair rent even if similar real estate transactions are not available. Suppose that the cost of capital for the $100 million invested in real estate is 10%. The real estate subsidiary expects to earn 3% in the form of capital appreciation and, therefore, the immediate rental yield must be 10 − 3 or 7%. Thus, for the first year the retailing subsidiary should pay a rent of 0.07 × 100 = $7 million; in the second year the rent should be 0.07 × 103 = $7.21 million; and so on. We can now calculate the NPV of the retailing subsidiary's new department store, remembering that it now rents the store instead of buying it:

$$NPV = \frac{8-7}{1.10} + \frac{8-7.21}{(1.10)^2} + \cdots + \frac{8-8.87}{(1.10)^9} + \frac{8-9.13}{(1.10)^{10}}$$

The answer's the same as before,[5] but we can now see that our forecasts don't stack up. During the last 5 years of the project's life the income from the store fails to cover the rental charge. If the forecasted income levels and growth in real estate prices are correct, we should terminate the project in year 5. But that brings us back to the key question: Do we believe that a department store will continue to be the best use for the site?[6] If we do, then we must be ignoring potential growth in income from the store. Another possibility is that real estate prices are expected to grow by less than 3% a year. But that would imply that initial rents are higher; if so, the store might not be a positive NPV investment for any project life.

Here is another example of how market prices can help you make better decisions. Kingsley Solomon is considering a proposal to open a new gold mine. He estimates that the mine will cost $200 million to develop and that in each of the next 10 years it will produce 0.1 million ounces of gold at a cost, after mining and refining, of $200 an ounce. Although the extraction costs can be predicted with reasonable accuracy, Mr. Solomon is much less confident about future gold prices. His best guess is that the price will rise by 5% per year from its current level of $400 an ounce. At a discount rate of 10%, this gives the mine an NPV of −$10.4 million.

$$NPV = -200 + \frac{0.1(420-200)}{1.10} + \frac{0.1(441-200)}{1.10^2} + \cdots + \frac{0.1(652-200)}{1.10^{10}}$$
$$= -\$10.4 \text{ million}$$

Therefore, the gold mine project is rejected.

Unfortunately, Mr. Solomon did not look at what the market was telling him. What is the present value of an ounce of gold? Clearly, if the gold market is functioning properly, it is the current price−$400 an ounce. Gold does not produce any income, so $400 is the discounted value of the expected future gold price.[7] Since the mine is expected to produce a total of 1 million ounces (0.1

---

[5] It has to be. Since the real estate subsidiary simply earns its cost of capital, all the NPV goes to the retailing subsidiary.

[6] It is possible but unlikely that the project is expected to terminate early because the real estate is expected to become too expensive for a department store. A more likely reason for shifting location is that the productivity of the initial site declines and the store is induced to move to a newer, more productive site.

[7] Investing in an ounce of gold is like investing in a stock that pays no dividends: the investor's return comes entirely as capital gains. Look back at Section 4-2, where we showed that P_0, the price of a stock today, depends on DIV_1 and P_1, the expected dividend and price for next year, and the opportunity cost of capital r:

$$P_0 = \frac{DIV_1 + P_1}{1+r}$$

million ounces per year for 10 years), the present value of the revenue stream is $1 \times 400 = \$400$ million.[8] We assume that 10% is an appropriate discount rate for the relatively certain extraction costs. Thus

$$\text{NPV} = -\text{ initial investment} + \text{PV revenues} - \text{PV costs}$$

$$= -200 + 400 - \sum_{t=1}^{10} \frac{0.1 \times 200}{1.10^t} = \$77 \text{ million}$$

It looks as if Kingsley Solomon's mine is not such a bad bet after all.

Mr. Solomon's gold was just like anyone else's gold. So there was no point in trying to value it separately. By taking the present value of the gold sales as given, Mr. Solomon was able to focus on the crucial issue: were the extraction costs sufficiently low to make the venture worthwhile?

Our example is somewhat special. Unlike gold, most commodities are not kept solely for investment purposes, and therefore you cannot automatically assume that today's price is equal to the present value of the future price.[9] But when you do have the market value of an asset, *use it*, at least as a starting point for your analysis.

One more example. Suppose that an oil company is contemplating an additional investment in tankers. Tankers are freely traded in a competitive market.

But for gold $\text{DIV}_1 = 0$, so

$$P_0 = \frac{P_1}{1+r}$$

In words, *today's price is the present value of next year's price.* Therefore, we don't have to know either P_1 or r to find the present value. *Today's price is also the present value of the year 2 price.* Since $\text{DIV}_2 = 0$,

$$P_1 = \frac{P_2}{1+r}$$

and we can express P_0 as

$$P_0 = \frac{P_1}{1+r} = \frac{1}{1+r}\left(\frac{P_2}{1+r}\right) = \frac{P_2}{(1+r)^2}$$

In general,

$$P_0 = \frac{P_t}{(1+r)^t}$$

This holds for any asset that pays no dividends, is traded in a competitive market, and costs nothing to store. Storage costs for gold or common stock are very small compared to asset value.

Storage costs would have to be treated as negative dividends. The owner of a warehouse full of butter would have to *pay* cash for use of the warehouse, refrigeration, and so on.

[8] We assume that the extraction rate does not vary with the gold price. If it does, you would need to read Chapters 20 and 21 before you could value the mine.

[9] However, Hotelling has pointed out that if there are constant returns to scale in mining any mineral, the expected rise in the price of the mineral *less* extraction costs should equal the cost of capital. If the expected growth were faster, everyone would want to postpone extraction; if it were slower, everyone would want to exploit the resource today. In this case the value of a mine would be independent of when it was exploited and you could value it by calculating the value of the mineral at today's price less the current cost of extraction. If (as is usually the case in practice), there are declining returns to scale, the expected price rise net of costs must be less than the cost of capital. For a review of Hotelling's principle, see S. Devarajan and A.C. Fisher, "Hotelling's Economics of Exhaustible Resources': Fifty Years Later," *Journal of Economic Literature,* **19:** 65–73 (March 1981). And for an application to the problem valuing mineral deposits, see M.H. Miller and C.W. Upton, "A Test of the Hotelling Valuation Principle," *Journal of Political Economy,"* **93:** 1–25 (1985).

Therefore the present value of a tanker to the oil company is equal to the tanker's market price *plus* any extra gains that are likely to come from having the oil company, rather than another owner, operate the vessel.

11-4 FORECASTING ECONOMIC RENTS

We recommend that financial managers ask themselves whether an asset is more valuable in their hands than another's. A bit of classical microeconomics can help to answer that question. When an industry settles into long-run competitive equilibrium, all its assets are expected to earn their opportunity costs of capital — no more and no less. If they earned more, firms in the industry would expand, or firms outside the industry would try to enter it.

Profits that *more* than cover the opportunity cost of capital are known as *economic rents*. These rents may be either temporary (in the case of an industry that is not in long-run equilibrium) or persistent (in the case of a firm with some degree of monopoly or market power).[10] The NPV of an investment is simply the discounted value of the economic rents it will produce. Therefore, when you are presented with a project that appears to have a positive NPV, don't just accept the calculations at face value. They may reflect simple estimate errors in forecasting cash flows. Probe behind the cash flow estimates and *try to identify the economic rents*. A positive NPV for a new project is only believable if *you* believe that your company has some special advantage.

Such advantages can arise in several ways. You may be smart or lucky enough to be first to the market with a new, improved product for which customers are prepared to pay premium prices (until your competitors enter and squeeze out excess profits). You may have a patent, proprietary technology, or production cost advantage that competitors cannot match, at least for several years. You may have some valuable contractual advantage, for example the distributorship for gargle blasters in France (see Section 11-5 below).

Thinking about competitive advantage can also help ferret out negative NPV calculations that are negative by mistake. If you are the lowest-cost producer of a profitable product in a growing market, then you should invest to expand along with the market. If your calculations show a negative NPV for such an expansion, then you have probably made a mistake.

*11-5 EXAMPLE—MARVIN ENTERPRISES DECIDES TO EXPLOIT A NEW TECHNOLOGY

To illustrate some of the problems involved in predicting economic rents, let us leap forward to the 21st century and look at the decision by Marvin Enterprises to exploit a new technology.[11]

One of the most unexpected developments of these years is the remarkable growth of a completely new industry. By 2013, annual sales of gargle blasters totalled $1.68 billion or 240 million units. Although it controlled only 10% of the market, Marvin Enterprises was among the most exciting growth companies of the decade. Marvin had come late into the business, but it had pioneered the use of integrated microcircuits to control the genetic engineering processes used to manufacture gargle blasters. This development had enabled producers to cut the

---

[10] Temporary rents are often called *quasi rents*.

[11] We thank Stewart Hodges for permission to adapt this example from a case prepared by him, and the BBC for permission to use the term *gargle blasters*.

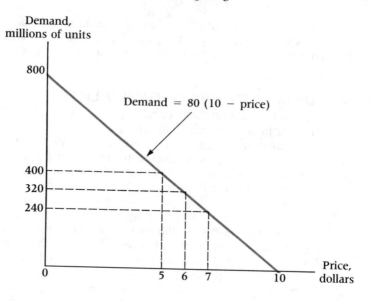

Figure 11-1   The demand "curve" for gargle blasters shows that for each $1 cut in price there is an increase in demand of 80 million units.

price of gargle blasters from $9 to $7 and had thereby contributed to the dramatic increase in the size of the market. The estimated demand curve in Figure 11-1 shows just how responsive demand is to such price reductions.

Table 11-1 summarizes the cost structure of the old and new technologies. While companies with the new technology were earning 20% on their initial investment, those with first generation equipment had been hit by the successive price cuts. Since all of Marvin's investment was in the 2009 technology, it had been particularly well placed during this period.

Rumours of new developments at Marvin had been circulating for some time and the total market value of Marvin's stock had risen to $460 million by January 2014. At that point Marvin called a press conference to announce another technological break-through. Management claimed that their new third-generation process involving mutant neurons enabled the firm to reduce capital costs to $10 and manufacturing costs to $3 a unit. Marvin proposed to capitalize on this invention by embarking on a huge $1 billion expansion program that would add 100 million units to capacity. The company expected to be in full operation within 12 months.

Before deciding to go ahead with this development, Marvin had undertaken extensive calculations on the effect of the new investment. The basic assumptions were as follows:

1. The cost of capital was 20%.
2. The production facilities had an indefinite physical life.
3. The demand curve and the costs of each technology would not change.
4. There was no chance of a fourth-generation technology in the foreseeable future.
5. The corporate income tax, which had been abolished in 2004, was not likely to be reintroduced.

Marvin's competitors greeted the news with varying degrees of concern. There was general agreement it would be five years before any of them would have

Table 11-1
Size and cost structure of the gargle blaster industry before Marvin announced its expansion plans.

	Capacity (millions of units)		Capital Cost per Unit (dollars)	Manufacturing Cost per Unit (dollars)	Salvage Value per Unit (dollars)
Technology	Industry	Marvin			
First generation (2001)	120	...	17.50	5.50	2.50
Second generation (2009)	120	24	17.50	3.50	2.50

Note: Selling price is $7 per unit. One "unit" means one gargle blaster.

access to the new technology. On the other hand, many consoled themselves with the reflection that Marvin's new plant could not compete with fully depreciated existing plant.

Suppose that you were Marvin's financial manager. Would you have agreed with the decision to expand? Do you think it would have been better to go for a larger or smaller expansion? How do you think Marvin's announcement is likely to affect the price of its stock?

You have a choice. You can go on *immediately* to read *our* solution to these questions. But you will learn much more if you stop and work out your own answer first. Try it.

*Forecasting Prices of Gargle Blasters

Up to this point in any capital budgeting problem we have always given you the set of cash flow forecasts. In the present case you have to *derive* those forecasts.

The first problem is to decide what is going to happen to the price of gargle blasters. Marvin's new venture will increase industry capacity to 340 million units. From the demand curve in Figure 11-1, you can see that the industry can sell this number of gargle blasters only if the price declines to $5.75:

$$\text{Demand} = 80(10 - \text{price})$$
$$= 80(10 - 5.75) = 340 \text{ million units}$$

If the price falls to $5.75, what will happen to companies with the 2001 technology? They also have to make an investment decision—should they stay in business or should they sell their equipment for its salvage value of $2.50 per unit? With a 20% opportunity cost of capital, the NPV of staying in business is

$$\text{NPV} = -\text{investment} + \text{PV}(\text{price} - \text{manufacturing cost})$$
$$= -2.50 + \frac{5.75 - 5.50}{0.20} = -\$1.25 \text{ per unit}$$

Smart companies with 2001 equipment will, therefore, see that it is better to sell off capacity. No matter what their equipment originally cost or how far it is depreciated, it is more profitable to sell the equipment for $2.50 per unit than to operate it and lose $1.25 per unit.

As capacity is sold off, the supply of gargle blasters will decline and the price will rise. An equilibrium is reached when the price gets to $6. At this point 2001 equipment has a zero NPV:

$$\text{NPV} = -2.50 + \frac{6.00 - 5.50}{0.20} = \$0 \text{ per unit}$$

How much capacity will have to be sold off before the price reaches $6? You can check that by going back to the demand curve:

$$\begin{aligned} \text{Demand} &= 80(10 - \text{price}) \\ &= 80(10 - 6) = 320 \text{ million units} \end{aligned}$$

Therefore Marvin's expansion will cause the price to settle down at $6 a unit and will induce first-generation producers to withdraw 20 million units of capacity.

But after five years Marvin's competitors will also be in a position to build third-generation plants. As long as these plants have positive NPVs, companies will increase their capacity and force prices down once again. A new equilibrium will be reached when the price reaches $5. At this point, the NPV of new third-generation plants is zero and there is no incentive for companies to expand further:

$$\text{NPV} = -10 + \frac{5.00 - 3.00}{0.20} = \$0 \text{ per unit}$$

Looking back once more at our demand curve, you can see that with a price of $5 the industry can sell a total of 400 million gargle blasters:

$$\text{Demand} = 80(10 - \text{price}) = 80(10 - 5) = 400 \text{ million units}$$

The effect of the third-generation technology is, therefore, to cause industry sales to expand from 240 million units in 2013 to 400 million five years later. But this rapid growth is no protection against failure. By the end of five years any company that has only first-generation equipment will no longer be able to cover its manufacturing costs and will be *forced* out of business.

*The Value of Marvin's New Expansion   We have shown that the introduction of third-generation technology is likely to cause gargle blaster prices to decline to $6 for the next five years and to $5 thereafter. We can now set down the expected cash flows from Marvin's new plant:

	Year 0 (Investment)	Years 1 to 5 (Revenue – Manufacturing Cost)	Years 6, 7, 8, … (Revenue – Manufacturing Cost)
Cash flow, per unit (dollars)	−10	6 − 3 = 3	5 − 3 = 2
Cash flow, 100 million units (millions of dollars)	−1,000	600 − 300 = 300	500 − 300 = 200

Discounting these cash flows at 20% gives us

$$\text{NPV} = -1,000 + \sum_{t=1}^{5} \frac{300}{(1.20)^t} + \frac{1}{(1.20)^5}\left(\frac{200}{0.20}\right) = \$299 \text{ million}$$

It looks as if Marvin's decision to go ahead was correct. But there is something we have forgotten. When we evaluate an investment, we must consider *all* incremental cash flows. One effect of Marvin's decision to expand is to reduce the value of its existing 2009 plant. If Marvin decided not to go ahead with the new technology, the $7 price of gargle blasters would hold until Marvin's competitors start to cut prices in five years' time. Marvin's decision, therefore, leads to an immediate $1 cut in price. This reduces the present value of its 2009 equipment by

$$24 \text{ million} \times \sum_{t=1}^{5} \frac{1.00}{(1.20)^t} = \$72 \text{ million}$$

Considered in isolation, Marvin's decision has an NPV of $299 million. But it also reduces the value of existing plant by $72 million. The net present value of Marvin's venture is, therefore, 299 − 72 = $227 million.

*Alternative Expansion Plans

Marvin's expansion has a positive NPV, but perhaps Marvin could do better to build a larger or smaller plant. You can check that by going through the same calculations as above. First you need to estimate how the additional capacity will affect gargle blaster prices. Then you can calculate the net present value of the new plant and the change in the present value of the existing plant. The total NPV of Marvin's expansion plan is

Total NPV = NPV of new plant + change in PV of existing plant

We have undertaken these calculations and plotted the results in Figure 11-2. You can see how total NPV would be affected by a smaller or larger expansion.

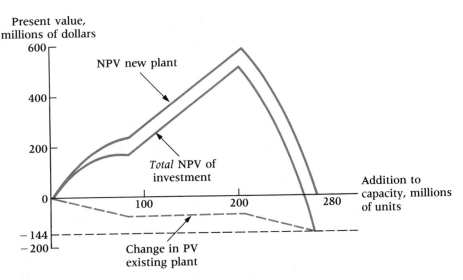

Figure 11-2   Effect on net present value of alternative expansion plans. Marvin's 100-million-unit expansion has a total NPV of $227 million (total NPV = NPV new plant + change in PV existing plant = 299 − 72 = 227). Total NPV is maximized if Marvin builds 200 million units of new capacity. If Marvin builds 280 million units of new capacity, total NPV is −$144 million.

When the new technology becomes generally available in 2019, firms will construct a total of 280 million units of new capacity.[12] But Figure 11-2 shows that it would be foolish for Marvin to go that far. If Marvin added 280 million units of new capacity in 2014, the discounted value of the cash flows from the new plant would be zero *and* the company would have reduced the value of its old plant by $144 million. To maximize NPV Marvin should construct 200 million units of new capacity and set the price just below $6 to drive out the 2001 manufacturers. Output is, therefore, less and price is higher than either would be under free competition.[13]

*The Value of Marvin Stock

Let us think about the effect of Marvin's announcement on the value of its common stock. Marvin has 24 million units of second-generation capacity. In the absence of any third generation technology, gargle blaster prices would hold at $7 and Marvin's existing plant would be worth

$$PV = 24 \text{ million} \times \frac{7.00 - 3.50}{0.20} = \$420 \text{ million}$$

Marvin's new technology reduces the price of gargle blasters initially to $6 and after five years to $5. Therefore the value of existing plant declines to

$$PV = 24 \text{ million} \times \left[\sum_{t=1}^{5} \frac{6.00 - 3.50}{(1.20)^t} + \frac{5.00 - 3.50}{0.20 \times 1.20^5} \right]$$
$$= \$252 \text{ million}$$

But the *new* plant makes a net addition to shareholders' wealth of $299 million. So after Marvin's announcement its stock will be worth[14]

$$252 + 299 = \$551 \text{ million}$$

Now here is an illustration of something we talked about in Chapter 4. Before the announcement, Marvin's stock was valued in the market at $460 million. The difference between this figure and the value of the existing plant represented the present value of Marvin's growth opportunities (PVGO). The market valued Marvin's ability to stay ahead of the game at $40 million even before the announcement. After the announcement PVGO rises to $299 million.[15]

---

[12] Total industry capacity in 2019 will be 400 million units. Of this, 120 million units is second-generation capacity, and the remaining 280 million units is third-generation capacity.

[13] Notice that we are assuming all customers have to pay the same price for their gargle blasters. If Marvin could charge each customer the maximum price that customer was willing to pay, output would be the same as under free competition. Such direct price discrimination is illegal and in any case difficult to enforce. But firms do search for indirect ways to differentiate between customers. For example, stores often offer free delivery, which is equivalent to a price discount for customers who live at an inconvenient distance. Publishers differentiate their product by selling hardback copies to libraries and paperbacks to impecunious students. In the early years of electronic calculators, manufacturers put a high price on their product. Although buyers knew that the price would be reduced in a year or two, the additional outlay was more than compensated by the convenience of having the machines for the extra time.

[14] To finance the expansion Marvin is going to have to sell $1,000 million of new stock. Therefore the *total* value of Marvin's stock will rise to $1,551 million. But investors who put up the new money will receive shares worth $1,000 million. The value of Marvin's old shares after the announcement is therefore $551 million.

[15] Notice that the market value of Marvin stock will be greater than $551 million if investors expect the company to expand again within the five-year period. In other words, PVGO after the expansion may still be positive. Investors may expect Marvin to *stay* one step ahead of its competitors, or to successfully apply its special technology in other areas.

The Lessons of Marvin Enterprises

Marvin Enterprises may be just a piece of science fiction, but the problems it confronts are very real. Whenever IBM considers a new generation of computers or Imperial Oil evaluates a new method of producing heavy oil or Polaroid thinks about developing a new camera, these firms must face up to exactly the same issues as Marvin. We have tried to illustrate the *kind* of questions you should be asking when presented with a set of cash flow forecasts. Of course no economic model is going to predict the future with accuracy. Perhaps Marvin can hold the price above $6. Perhaps competitors will not appreciate the rich pickings to be had in the year 2019. In that case, Marvin's expansion would be even more profitable. But would you want to *bet* $1 billion on such possibilities? We don't think so.

Investments often turn out to earn far more than the cost of capital because of a favourable surprise. This surprise may, in turn, create a temporary opportunity for further investments earning more than the cost of capital. But anticipated and more prolonged rents are less common. Unless there are substantial economies of scale, prospective rents will naturally lead to the entry of rival producers. That is why you should be suspicious of any investment proposal that predicts a stream of economic rents into the indefinite future. Try to estimate *when* competition will drive the NPV of new plants down to zero and think what that implies for the price of your product.

Many companies try to identify the major growth areas in the economy and then concentrate their investment in these areas. But the sad fate of first-generation gargle blaster manufacturers illustrates how rapidly existing plants can be made obsolete by changes in technology. It is fun being in a growth industry when you are at the forefront of the new technology, but a growth industry has no mercy on technological laggards.

You can expect to earn economic rents only if you have some superior resource such as management, sales force, design team, or production facilities. Therefore, rather than trying to move into growth areas, you would do better to identify your firm's comparative advantages and try to capitalize on them. Unfortunately, superior profits will still not accrue to the firm unless it can also avoid paying for them. For example, the Boeing 757 is a much more efficient plane to operate than older aircraft. But that does not mean the airlines that operate the 757 can expect to earn supernormal profits. The greater efficiency is likely to be reflected in the price Boeing charges for the 757. An airline will earn superior profits (that is, economic rents) only if the 757 is more valuable to it than to other operators.[16]

We do not wish to imply that good investment opportunities don't exist. For example, such opportunities frequently arise because the firm has invested money in the past that gives it the option to expand cheaply in the future. Perhaps the firm can increase its output just by adding an extra production line, whereas its rivals would need to construct an entire new factory. In such cases, you must take into account not only *whether* it is profitable to exercise your option, but also *when* it is best to do so.

Marvin also reminded us of project interactions, which we first discussed in Chapter 6. When you estimate the incremental cash flows from a project, you must remember to include the project's impact on the rest of the business. By introducing the new technology immediately, Marvin reduced the value of its

---

[16] The rent you earn because equipment worth more to you than to your rivals is known as "consumer surplus." If Boeing were able to charge each customer the maximum price it were prepared to pay, no airline could expect to earn a consumer surplus from operating the 757 and Boeing would capture all the benefits.

existing plant by $72 million. Sometimes the losses on existing plants may completely offset the gains from a new technology. That is why we sometimes see established, technologically advanced companies deliberately slowing down the rate at which they introduce new products.

Notice that Marvin's economic rents were equal to the difference between its costs and those of the marginal producer. The costs of the marginal 2001 generation plant consisted of the manufacturing costs plus the opportunity cost of not selling the equipment. Therefore, if the salvage value of the 2001 equipment were higher, Marvin's competitors would incur higher costs and Marvin could earn larger rents. We took the salvage value as given, but it in turn depends on the cost savings from substituting outdated gargle blaster equipment for some other asset. In a well-functioning economy, assets will be used so as to minimize the *total* cost of producing the chosen set of outputs. The economic rents earned by any asset are equal to the total extra costs that would be incurred if that asset were withdrawn.

Here's another point about salvage value which takes us back to our discussion of Magna Charter in the last chapter. A high salvage value gives the firm an option to abandon a project if things start to go wrong. However, if competitors *know* that you can bail out easily, they are more likely to enter your market. If it is clear that you have no alternative but to stay and fight, in which case your competitors will be more cautious about competing.

When Marvin announced its expansion plans, many owners of first-generation equipment took comfort in the belief that Marvin could not compete with their fully depreciated plant. Their comfort was misplaced. Regardless of past depreciation policy, it paid to scrap first-generation equipment rather than to keep it in production. Do not expect that numbers in your balance sheet can protect you from harsh economic reality.

11-6   SUMMARY

It helps to use net present value when making investment decisions, but that is not the whole story. Good investment decisions depend both on a sensible criterion and on sensible forecasts. In this chapter, we have looked at some of the things financial managers can do to get the forecasts they need.

One source of trouble is inconsistency in the macroeconomic assumptions that underlie the forecasts. If cash-flow forecasts for one project assume no inflation and those for another project are based on a 5% inflation rate, meaningful comparisons between these projects are impossible. The financial manager must therefore ensure that all forecasts within the company are based on a consistent view.

The net present value criterion is concerned with *expected* cash flows. But many of the cash flow forecasts the financial manager receives are likely to be biased. Companies employ a variety of ad hoc ways for limiting the worst effects of bias. For example, if the head office believes that each division is submitting overoptimistic forecasts, it can force the divisions to be more critical by imposing capital rationing. A financial manager who does away with these ad hoc rules without tackling the underlying problem may well bring about worse investment decisions. That is why the manager must think about how project sponsors can be encouraged to give fair and honest forecasts and how cases of overoptimism or exaggeration can be identified.

Projects may look attractive for two reasons: (1) there may be some errors in the sponsor's forecasts; (2) the company can genuinely expect to earn excess profit from the project. Good managers, therefore, try to ensure that the odds are stacked in their favour by expanding in areas in which the company has a comparative advantage. We like to put this another way by saying that good managers try to identify projects which will generate "economic rents."

Our story of Marvin Enterprises illustrates the origin of rents and how they determine a project's cash flows and net present value.

Any present value calculation, including our calculation for Marvin Enterprises, is subject to error. That's life: there's no other sensible way to value most capital investment projects. But some assets, such as gold, real estate, crude oil, ships, airplanes, and financial assets such as stocks and bonds, are traded in reasonably competitive markets. When you have the market value of such an asset, *use it*, at least as a starting point for your analysis.

FURTHER READING

Most microeconomics texts contain a discussion of the determinants of economic rent. See, for example,

S. Fisher, *et al., Introduction to Microeconomics,* 2nd ed., McGraw-Hill Book Company, New York, 1988.

For an interesting analysis of the likely effect of a new technology on the present value of existing assets, see

S.P. Sobotka and C. Schnabel, "Linear Programming as a Device for Predicting Market Value: Prices of Used Commerical Aircraft, 1959–65," *Journal of Business,* **34**: 10–30 (January 1961).

QUIZ

1. You have inherited 250 hectares of prime Saskatchewan farmland. There is an active market in land of this type, and similar properties are selling for $2,000 per hectare. Net cash returns per hectare are $150 per year. These cash returns are expected to remain constant in real terms. How much is the land worth? (A local banker has advised you to use a 12% discount rate.)

2. True or false?
   (a) A firm that earns the opportunity cost of capital is earning economic rents.
   (b) A firm that invests in positive NPV ventures expects to earn economic rent.
   (c) Financial managers should try to identify areas where their firm can earn economic rents, because it's there that positive NPV projects are likely to be found.
   (d) Economic rent is the equivalent annual cost of operating capital equipment.

3. Demand for concave utility meters is expanding rapidly, but the industry is highly competitive. A utility meter plant costs $50 million to set up and it has an annual capacity of 500,000 meters. The production cost is $5 per meter, and this cost is not expected to change. If the machines have an indefinite physical life and the cost of capital is 10%, what is the price of a utility meter?
   (a) $5
   (b) $10
   (c) $15

4. The following comment appeared in *Aviation Week and Space Technology*, July 25, 1966: "Alitalia has decided against ordering an advanced technology jet transport. The carrier's analysis, in common with some other airlines, indicates that it can operate fully depreciated Douglas DC-8s at fare levels competitive with a Boeing 747. This is because seat or ton-mile costs of a fully depreciated current generation subsonic jet may not differ greatly from the advanced technology jet." Discuss whether the low depreciation charge on a DC-8 justifies the continued use of that plane. Under what circumstances would it pay to operate 747s?

5. If a capital equipment producer brings out a new, more efficient product, who is likely to get the benefits? In what circumstances would purchase of the new equipment be a positive NPV investment?

QUESTIONS AND PROBLEMS

1. Suppose you are considering investing in an asset for which there is a reasonably good secondary market. Specifically, you're Canadian Airlines International and the asset is a Boeing 737—a very widely used airplane. How does the presence of a secondary market simplify your problem in principle? Do you think these simplifications could be realized in practice? Explain.

2. Photographic laboratories recover and recycle the silver used in photographic film. Stikine River Photo is considering purchase of improved equipment for their lab at Telegraph Creek. Here is the information they have:
(a) The equipment costs $100,000.
(b) It will cost $80,000 per year to run.
(c) It has an economic life of 10 years and would be in Asset Class 8 with a 20% CCA rate (see Section 6-2).
(d) It will recover an additional 5,000 ounces of silver per year.
(e) Silver is selling for $20 per ounce. Over the past 10 years, the price of silver has appreciated by 4.5% per year in real terms. Silver is traded in an active, competitive market.
(f) Stikine's marginal tax rate is 36%.
(g) Stikine's company cost of capital is 8% in real terms.
What is the NPV of the new equipment? Make additional assumptions as necessary.

3. Does it make any difference whether a capital equipment producer sells equipment or rents it out? Does it affect the producer's willingness to bring out new products?

4. The manufacture of polysyllabic acid is a competitive industry. Most plants have an annual output of 100,000 tonnes. Operating costs are 90 cents a tonne and the sales price is $1 a tonne. A 100,000-tonne plant costs $100,000, has an indefinite life, and a scrap value of $60,000.

   Phlogiston, Inc., proposes to invest $100,000 in a plant that employs a new low-cost process to manufacture polysyllabic acid. The plant has the same capacity as existing units, but operating costs are 85 cents a tonne. Phlogiston estimates that it has two years' lead over each of its rivals in use of the process but is unable to build any further plants itself before year 2. Also it believes that demand over the next two years is likely to be sluggish and that its new plant will therefore cause temporary overcapacity.

   You can assume that there are no taxes, and that the cost of capital is 10%.

(a) By the end of year 2 the prospective increase in acid demand will require the construction of several new plants using the Phlogiston process. What is the likely NPV of such plants?

(b) What would be the present value of each of these new plants?

(c) What does that imply for the price of polysyllabic acid in year 3 and beyond?

(d) Would you expect existing plant to be scrapped in year 2? How would your answer differ if scrap value were $40,000 or $80,000?

(e) The acid plants of United Alchemists, Inc. have been fully depreciated. Can it operate them profitably after year 2?

(f) Acidosis, Inc. purchased a new plant last year for $100,000 and is writing it down by $10,000 a year. Should it scrap this plant in year 2?

(g) What would be the present value of Phlogiston's venture?

5. The Cambridge Opera Association has come up with a unique door prize for its December (1991) fund-raising ball: 20 door prizes will be distributed, each one a ticket entitling the bearer to receive a cash award from the Association on December 30, 1992. The cash award is to be determined by calculating the ratio of the level of the Toronto Stock Exchange 300 Composite Stock Price Index[17] on December 30, 1992, to its level on June 30, 1992, and multiplying by $100. Thus, if the index turns out to be 125 on June 30, 1992, and 150 on December 30, 1992, the payoff will be 100 × (150/125) = $120.

After the ball, a black market springs up in which the tickets are traded. What will the tickets sell for on January 1, 1992? On June 30, 1992? Assume the risk free interest rate is 10% per year. Also, assume the Cambridge Opera Association will be solvent at year end 1992 and will in fact pay off on the tickets. Make other assumptions as necessary.

Would ticket values be different if the tickets' payoffs depended on the TSE Oil and Gas Producer Index rather than the TSE 300 Composite?

6. You are asked to value a large building in northern Ontario. The valuation is needed for a railroad bankruptcy settlement. Here are the facts:

(a) The settlement *requires* that the building's value equal the present value of the *net cash proceeds* the railroad would receive if it cleared the building and sold it for its highest and best nonrailroad use, which is as a warehouse.

(b) The building has been appraised at $1 million. This figure is based on actual recent selling prices of a sample of similar northern Ontario buildings used as, or available for use as, warehouses.

(c) If rented out today as a warehouse, the building could generate $60,000 per year. This cash flow is calculated *after* out-of-pocket operating expenses, and *after* real estate taxes of $50,000 per year:

Gross rents	$160,000
Operating expenses	50,000
Real estate taxes	50,000
Net	$ 60,000

Gross rents, operating expenses, and real estate taxes are uncertain but are expected to grow with inflation.

(d) However, it would take one year and $200,000 to clear out the railroad

---

[17] To be more precise, they will use the TSE 300 Total Return Index, which has dividends reinvested.

equipment and prepare the building for use as a warehouse. This expenditure would be spread evenly over the next year.

(e) The property will be put on the market when ready for use as a warehouse. Your real estate advisor says that properties of this type take, on average, one year to sell after they are put on the market. However, the railroad could rent out the building as a warehouse while waiting for it to sell.

(f) The opportunity cost of capital for investment in real estate is 8% in *real* terms.

(g) Your real estate advisor notes that selling prices of comparable buildings in northern Ontario have declined, in real terms, at an average rate of 2% per year over the last ten years.

(h) A 5% sales commission would be paid by the railroad at the time of the sale.

(i) The railroad pays no income taxes. It would have to pay property taxes.

7. The world airline system is composed of the routes X and Y, each of which requires ten aircraft. These routes can be serviced by three types of aircraft — A, B, and C. There are five A-type aircraft available, ten B-type, and ten C-type. These aircraft are identical except for their operating costs which are as follows:

Aircraft Type	Annual Operating Cost (thousands of dollars)	
	Route X	Route Y
A	15	15
B	25	20
C	45	35

The aircraft have a useful life of five years and a salvage value of $10,000. The aircraft owners do not operate the aircraft themselves but rent them out to the operators. Owners act competitively to maximize their rental income, and operators attempt to minimize their operating costs. Air fares are also competitively determined.

Assume the cost of capital is 10%.

(a) Which aircraft would be used on which route and how much would each aircraft be worth?

(b) What would happen to usage and prices of each aircraft if the number of A-type aircraft increased to 10?

(c) What would happen if the number of As increased to 15?

(d) What would happen if the number of As increased to 20?

State any additional assumptions you need to make.

*8. Taxes are a cost and, therefore, changes in tax rates can affect consumer prices, project lives, and the value of existing firms. The following (difficult) problem illustrates this. It also illustrates that tax changes that appear to be "good for business" do not always increase the value of existing firms. Indeed, unless new investment incentives increase consumer demand, they can only work by obsoleting existing equipment.

The manufacturer of bucolic acid is a competitive business. Demand is steadily expanding and new plants are constantly being opened. Expected cash flows from an investment in plant are a follows:

	0	1	2	3
1. Initial investment	100			
2. Revenues		100	100	100
3. Cash operating costs		50	50	50
4. Tax depreciation		33.33	33.33	33.33
5. Income pre-tax		16.67	16.67	16.67
6. Tax at 40%		6.67	6.67	6.67
7. Net income		10	10	10
8. After tax salvage				15
9. Cash flow (7+8+4−1)	−100	+ 43.33	+ 43.33	+ 58.33
NPV at 20% = 0				

Assumptions:
1. Tax depreciation is straight line over 3 years.
2. Pre-tax salvage value is 25 in year 3, and 50 if the asset is scrapped in year 2.
3. Tax on salvage value is 40% of the difference between salvage value and depreciated investment.
4. The cost of capital is 20%.

(a) What is the value of a 1-year-old plant? Of a 2-year-old plant?
(b) Suppose that the government now changes tax depreciation to allow a 100% write-off in year 1. How does this affect the value of existing 1- and 2-year-old plants? Existing plants must continue using the original tax depreciation schedule.
(c) Would it now make sense to scrap existing plants when they are 2 rather than 3 years old?
(d) How would your answers change if the corporate income tax were abolished entirely?

C·H·A·P·T·E·R

12

ORGANIZING CAPITAL EXPENDITURE AND EVALUATING PERFORMANCE AFTERWARDS

Our task up to this point has been to show how a firm *should* set its capital budget. In this chapter we discuss how this is done in practice. We give particular attention to how capital budgeting is organized and to the administrative problems that inevitably crop up.

A good capital budgeting system does more than just make accept–reject decisions on individual projects. It must tie into the firm's long-range planning process—the process that decides what lines of business the firm concentrates in and sets out plans for financing, production, marketing, research and development, and so on. It must also tie into a procedure for measurement of performance. Otherwise the firm has no way of knowing how its decisions about capital expenditure finally turn out. Measurement of performance occupies a substantial part of this chapter. The pitfalls in measuring profitability are serious but not as widely recognized as they should be.

12-1 CAPITAL BUDGETS AND PROJECT AUTHORIZATIONS

For most sizable firms the first step in the investment process is the preparation of an annual **capital budget**, which is a list of planned investment projects and a breakdown of planned investment outlays by plant and division. (In this chapter we will think of plants as building blocks for divisions, and divisions as building blocks for firms. That is arbitrary: there may be more than two layers. Also, divisions are often organized by product line, region, or some other business unit.) In principle, the capital budget should be a list of all positive NPV opportunities open to the firm.

Most firms let project proposals bubble up from plants for review by division management, and from divisions for review by senior management. The administrative process typically works as follows.

Plant managers identify "interesting" opportunities, analyze them, and decide which ones are really worthwhile. Proposed expenditures for these projects are then submitted to division managers for further review. Some of the proposals by the plants do not "make the cut" at the divisional level. But divisional management may add its own ideas, usually new, larger ventures, like manufacturing a new product, that plant managers could not be expected to initiate. The lists of the divisions are forwarded to the corporate controller, who prunes and consolidates them into a proposed company budget. For very large diversified firms there may be several intermediate review stages.

The resulting budget is a list of proposed new projects for the coming year and of any projects from former years that are incomplete. Supporting information is usually provided on standard forms, supplemented by descriptive memoranda for larger projects. Since approval of the budget rarely confers authority to spend money, backup information is not as detailed at this stage as it is later. Projects below a specified size are typically not even listed separately, but simply included under a blanket approval for a given division or plant. In many companies the budget also contains rough estimates of likely expenditures over a five-year period.

The suggested budget is then reviewed by senior management and staff specializing in planning and financial analysis. It may be considered initially by a committee that includes the president, treasurer, and controller. Usually there are negotiations between the firm's senior management and its divisional management, and perhaps there will also be special analyses of major outlays or ventures into new areas, before the budget is submitted to the board for approval. Once approved, the budget generally remains the basis for planning over the ensuing year. In a few firms, however, it is updated each quarter.

Because each proposal in the budget requires subsequent specific authorization, the use of a budget involves some duplication of effort. But it allows information exchange up and down the management hierarchy before attitudes have hardened and personal commitments have been made. The danger with the whole procedure is loss of flexibility. There is a tendency for most projects to appear for the first time in the annual budget, and in some companies it is difficult to initiate project ideas at any other time of year.

Project Authorizations

The approval of a capital budget rarely confers authority to undertake the expenditures listed in the budget. Most companies stipulate that formal **appropriation requests** should be prepared for each proposal. The requests are accompanied by more or less elaborate backup, depending on the project's size, novelty, and strategic importance. Also, the type of backup information required depends on project category. Some firms use a fourfold breakdown:

1. Safety or environmental outlays required by law or company policy—for example, for pollution control equipment
2. Maintenance or cost reduction—for example, machine replacement
3. Capacity expansion in existing businesses
4. Investment for new products or ventures

The information requirements for projects differ across these categories:

1. Pollution control does not have to pay its own way. The main issue is whether standards are met at minimum present value of cost. The decision is likely to hinge on engineering analyses of alternative technologies.

2. Engineering analysis is also important in machine replacement, but new machines have to pay their own way. In category 2 above, the firm faces the classical capital budgeting problems described in Chapter 6.

3. Projects in category 3 are less straightforward capital budgeting problems; these decisions may hinge on forecasts of demand, of possible shifts in technology, and of competitors' strategies.

4. Projects in category 4 are most likely to depend on intangibles. The first projects in a new area may not have positive NPVs if they are considered in isolation, yet the firm may go ahead in order to establish a position in a market and pave the way for profitable future projects. The first projects are not taken for their own sake, but because they give the firm a valuable *option* to undertake follow-on projects. Thus, for projects in category 4, cash-flow forecasts may be less important than the issue of whether the firm enjoys some technological or other advantage that promises to generate economic rents for the firm. That issue becomes the main focus of project analysis.

Most large companies have manuals providing check lists to make sure that all relevant costs and alternatives are considered. The manual may contain instructions showing how to forecast cash flows and how to compute NPV, internal rate of return, or other measures of project value. Sometimes the manual also specifies the opportunity cost of capital.

Though appropriation requests may be prepared by the project originator, the plant manager is usually responsible for submitting them. These requests come up through the ranks of operating management for approval at each succeeding level. If the project is large, the request may be checked at some stage by staff accountants, engineers, and economists. The number of hurdles the proposal must pass depends on the magnitude of the expenditure involved.

Because the investment decision is central to the development of the firm, authorization tends to be reserved for senior management. Almost all companies set ceilings on the size of capital projects that divisional managers can authorize without specific approval from their superiors. Moreover, the ceilings are surprisingly low. Scapens and Sale surveyed 203 larger firms, with average capital budgets of \$130 million per year, and found that the average ceiling for individual projects was only \$136,000.[1] When you consider that a large company may generate thousands of authorization requests each year, the limited extent of delegation is striking.

Bottom-Up versus Top-Down

We have pictured the capital investment process as if all proposals bubbled up from the bottom of the organization. That is never the whole story. The managers of plants A and B cannot be expected to see the potential economies of scale of closing their plants and consolidating production at a new plant C. We expect divisional management to propose plant C. Similarly, divisions 1 and 2 may not be eager to give up their own data processing operations to a large, central computer. That proposal would come from senior management.

The final capital budget must also reflect strategic choices made by senior management. Strategic planning attempts to identify the businesses in which the firm has a real competitive advantage. It also attempts to identify businesses to sell or liquidate as well as declining businesses that should be allowed to run down. Strategic planning is really capital budgeting on a grand scale.

---

[1] R.W. Scapens and J.T. Sale, "Performance Measurement and Formal Capital Expenditure Controls in Divisionalized Companies," *Journal of Business Finance and Accounting*, **8**: 389–420 (Autumn 1981).

In many firms, strategic plans impose a strong top-down input to capital-budgeting decisions. Projects that appear to have negative NPVs may be accepted if they help to establish the firm in a business with good long-run potential. Similarly, projects that appear to have positive NPVs may be rejected if the firm plans to run down this part of its business. Of course, if a "declining" business continually generates high NPV projects, the strategic planners ought to think again—perhaps the business isn't declining.

The Decision Criteria Firms Actually Use

We know that companies use a number of different criteria for project selection. Table 12-1 shows the results of a survey by Schall, Sundem, and Geijsbeek of the relative popularity of different techniques. Notice the popularity of theoretically inappropriate techniques like payback and book rate of return, usually in combination with IRR, NPV, or both. But comparison of this study with earlier ones confirms that the sophisticated techniques are gaining.[2]

Of course, the use of intelligent techniques does not guarantee intelligent decisions. You can have good techniques and poor judgement, or vice versa. Often operating managers display considerable conceptual confusion on financial issues. One encounters such statements as, "We do all three (book rate of return, payback, and internal rate of return) and may decide that one is more relevant than the other," or "We don't use present value because it can't handle uncertainty." Even when companies do impose theoretically justifiable criteria, their application is often imperfect. For example, a British survey noted that almost half of the companies producing cash-flow estimates treated depreciation as a cash outflow.[3] Many companies think they can ignore inflation in cash-flow forecasts because "on the average revenues increase to cover inflated costs."

There is ignorance in the world. But before we get too smug, let's stop and think of other explanations. There are, in fact, several.

The Role of Judgement   Businesspeople often act smarter than they talk. (For students and scholars it is the other way around.) They may make correct decisions but they may not be able to explain them in the language of finance and economics. Many decisions are fundamentally intuitive. If *intuitive* sounds capricious, replace the word with *informed judgement*. As we argued in Chapter 11: if a firm enjoys an advantage that promises to generate economic rents in a stable or growing business, it probably should press on regardless of calculated payback or present value. Experience helps in identifying such opportunities.

Of course, this is not a complete answer. Few decisions are totally judgemental. In principle, if *any* quantitative measure of project value affects a decision, it should be present value, not payback or return on book.

Communication   Payback is the easiest way to *communicate* an idea of project profitability. It is important to have one measure everyone can understand,

[2] An earlier survey of large Canadian firms produced similar results: while 35% of respondents used some method of discounted cash flow analysis in 1962, 79% did so in 1972. See C.G. Hoskins and M.J. Dunn, "The Evaluation of Capital Expenditure Proposals under Uncertainty: The Practice of Large Corporations in Canada," *Journal of Business Administration*, **6**: 45–55, Fall 1974. J.D. Blazouske, I. Carlin and S.H. Kim, "Current Capital Budgeting Practices in Canada," *CMA Magazine*, **67**: 51–54 (March 1988) surveyed 208 Canadian firms in 1985, and found that 36% were using NPV as either the primary or secondary evaluation technique while 53% used IRR as the primary or secondary technique.

[3] See L.E. Rockley, *Investment for Profitability: An Analysis of the Policies and Practices of UK and International Companies*, Business Books Ltd., London, 1973.

Table 12-1
This survey of capital investment procedures shows that many firms use more than one investment criterion and that they frequently employ theoretically inappropriate criteria.

Payback	Return on Book	IRR	NPV	% of Firms Using Each Combination of Criteria
X	X	X	X	17
X	X	X		14
X	X		X	9
X		X	X	9
	X	X	X	2
X	X			8
X		X		8
X			X	7
		X	X	7
	X		X	4
	X	X		2
		X		6
	X			4
			X	2
				2
X				2

Source: L.D. Schall, G.L. Sundem, and W.R. Geijsbeek, "Survey and Analysis of Capital Budgeting Methods," *Journal of Finance*, **33**:281–287 (March 1978), table 1, p. 282.

because capital budgeting is a process of discussion and negotiation involving people from all parts of the firm. Insisting that everyone commenting on a project do so in terms of NPV may cut off those who don't understand NPV, but who nevertheless can contribute useful information.

There is a law at work here that we can also observe working in television, publishing, and many other areas: a wider audience demands simpler concepts and language. Perhaps we could have sold more copies of this book by making it easier.

Rewards to Managers   Plant and divisional managers are concerned for their own futures. Sometimes their interests conflict with stockholders'. New plant managers, for example, naturally want to demonstrate good performance right away in order to move up the corporate ladder. Perhaps they will propose quick-payback projects even if NPV is sacrificed. If their performance is judged on book earnings, they will be attracted by projects whose accounting results look good. Even if managers propose the right (NPV-maximizing) projects, we can understand their concern for payback and book return.

The problem lies in the way many firms measure performance and reward managers. Don't expect them to concentrate only on NPV if you always demand quick results or if you will reward them later on the basis of book return. More on this later in the chapter.

12-2 PROBLEMS AND SOME SOLUTIONS

Problems of Cooperation Valuing capital investment opportunities is hard enough when you can do the entire job yourself. In real life it is a cooperative effort. Although cooperation brings more knowledge and intelligence to bear, it brings its own problems. Some are unavoidable—just another cost of doing business. Some can be alleviated by adding checks and balances to the capital investment process.

Many of the problems stem from sponsors' eagerness to obtain approval for their favourite projects. As the proposal proceeds up the organization, alliances are formed. Preparation of the request inevitably involves discussions and compromises, which limit subsequent freedom of action. Thus once a division has screened its plants' proposals, the plants unite in competing against "outsiders."

This competition among divisions can be put to good use if it forces division managers to develop better justifications for what they want to do. But the competition has its costs as well. Several thousand appropriation requests may reach the senior management level each year, all of them essentially sales documents presented by united fronts and designed to persuade. Alternative schemes have been filtered out at an earlier stage. The danger is that senior management cannot obtain (let alone absorb) the information to evaluate each project rationally.

The dangers are illustrated by the following practical question. "Should we establish a definite opportunity cost of capital for computing the NPV of projects in our furniture division?" The answer in theory is a clear yes, providing that the projects of the division are all in the same risk class. Remember that most project analysis is done at the plant or divisional level. Only a small proportion of project ideas analyzed survives for submission to top management. Plant and division managers cannot judge projects correctly unless they know the true opportunity cost of capital.

Suppose senior management settles on 12%. That helps plant managers make rational decisions. But it also tells them exactly how optimistic they have to be to get their pet project accepted. Brealey, Myers, Sick, and Giammarino's second law states that the proportion of proposed projects having a positive estimated NPV is independent of top management's estimate of the opportunity cost of capital.[4] If the law is true, top management is better off concealing its estimates of the cost of capital, asking instead for NPVs calculated for a range of different discount rates, and applying the right rate when the final decision is made.

A firm that accepts poor information at the top faces two consequences. First, senior management cannot evaluate individual projects. In a study by Bower of a large multidivisional company, projects that had the approval of a division general manager were seldom turned down by his or her group of divisions, and those reaching the executive committee were almost never rejected. Second, the only effective control available to management is to impose expenditure limits on individual plants or divisions. The effect is to force the subunits to choose among projects and to encourage the divisions to compete for funds. The firm ends up using capital rationing as a way of decentralizing decisions.

Of course, capital rationing is not the only solution. Firms can improve the quality of information flowing to the top by setting up corporate capital budgeting staffs to enforce consistency, uncover specified assumptions, and undertake sophisticated analyses of major projects.

These analysts may also have to ferret out local managers who are evading the controls in the capital investment process. For example, managers may be permitted to approve projects only up to a certain value. But this authority may become infinite if each project can be broken down into a large number of small parts. The following story illustrates this problem:

---

[4] There is no first law. We thought "second law" sounded better. There *is* a third law, but that is for another chapter.

Our [top managers] like to make all the major capital decisions. They think they do, but I've just seen one case where a division beat them.

I received for editing a capital request from the division for a large chimney. I couldn't see what anyone could do with just a chimney so I flew out for a visit. They've built and equipped a whole plant on plant expense orders. The chimney is the only indivisible item that exceeded the $50,000 limit we put on the expense orders. Apparently they learned informally that a new plant wouldn't be favourably received, and since they thought the business needed it, and the return would justify it, they built the damn thing.[5]

This embarrassment might have been avoided if the firm had imposed a limit on individual discretionary expenditures and *also* on the total amount of such expenditures by each manager in any one year.

A similar difficulty stems from the imprecise concept of a capital expenditure. It may not be material whether a firm purchases or leases a piece of equipment: the subsequent effect on operating cash flows is similar. Clearly management's interest is in controlling the acquisition of any important asset, whether it be leased or purchased. It also wants to control acquisition not only of tangible assets, but also of intangible ones such as a patent or a long-term contract. Authorization procedures should be broadly construed and should not encourage the inefficient substitution of one kind of asset for another.

Another problem is to ensure that the authorization request draws attention to all likely contingent expenditures. Too often, seemingly small and innocuous investments are the first step in a chain of economically dependent investments. Management should be aware of the full consequences of letting a plant or division get its foot in the door.

Some Partial Solutions

We risk overemphasizing the problems and underemphasizing the ability of organizations to cope with them. They cope because people are sensible and because informal communication and negotiation reinforce formal procedures. There are also formal solutions, most of them mentioned in passing as we discussed the problems. Now we will present them in a more organized way.

Corporate Staff   Corporate staff can be assigned to enforce consistency in project analyses, check the assumptions behind cash-flow forecasts, and undertake special analyses. Large corporations often have special staff departments devoted to these tasks.

Budgeting and Planning   The capital budget is a part of a broader budgeting and planning cycle. The firm has to set operating budgets for plants and divisions and also plan marketing, research, financing, and long-term growth. Capital investments have to make sense in terms of these other plans.

Strategic Choices   We referred to strategic planning as *capital budgeting on a grand scale*. It attempts to identify the businesses that offer the best long-run opportunities and to develop a plan for achieving success in those businesses.

Strategic planning deals in intangibles. Present values are rarely calculated explicitly. But the goal is clear: to identify areas where the firm has a competitive advantage. Firms that emphasize strategic planning are doing just what we recommended in Chapter 11: looking for the sources of economic rents as a check against bias and exaggeration in cash-flow forecasts.

---

[5] Cited in J.L. Bower, *Managing the Resource Allocation Process: A Study of Corporate Planning and Investment*, Division of Research, Graduate School of Business Administration, Harvard University, Boston, 1970, p. 15.

A firm's capital investment choices should reflect both "bottom-up" and "top-down" processes—capital budgeting and strategic planning, respectively. The two processes should complement one another. Plant and division managers, who do most of the work in bottom-up capital budgeting, may not see the forest for the trees. Strategic planners may have a mistaken view of the forest because they do not look at the trees one by one.

Strategic planning is more important in some industries than in others. It is not important for oil exploration companies, which have to analyze prospects one by one. It is important in industries where tomorrow's opportunities are created by today's investments and where success depends on intangible assets like technology, product design, and reputation, or on elaborate marketing and distribution systems. Intangible assets are hard to evaluate in a purely bottom-up process.

Decentralization   Most decisions on significant capital outlays are reserved for top management. At least that is the formal process. The real decisions may be made further down in the organization. Senior management may have limited effective control over project-by-project decisions because of lack of information at the top.

When this happens capital investment decisions are effectively decentralized regardless of what formal procedures specify. Many firms force divisions to set their own priorities by setting rigid constraints on the capital expenditures of the divisions. Other firms are less rigid: they accept decentralization; they relax and enjoy it, keeping control by budgeting, planning, and monitoring the overall operations of the divisions.

But decentralization can only work if plant and division managers are rewarded for doing the right things. The way performance is measured and rewarded affects the kinds of projects that are proposed. Capital tends to flow more easily to divisions that seem to perform well.

Therefore any discussion of the capital expenditure process has to consider what happens *after* the project is accepted. That is our next topic.

12-3   EVALUATING PERFORMANCE

Most firms have formal procedures for evaluating the performance of their capital investments. There are three aspects to performance measurement. First, companies need to monitor projects under construction to ensure that there are no serious delays or cost overruns. Second, companies generally conduct a postmortem on major projects shortly after they have begun to operate. These investigations are known as **postaudits**. They help to identify problems that need repairing, to check the accuracy of forecasts, and to suggest questions that should have been asked before the project was undertaken. Postaudits pay off mainly by helping managers do a better job when they come to analyze the next round of investment proposals. Finally, there is ongoing performance measurement, which is done through the firm's accounting and control system. We will explain how that system should work to support the capital investment process and why it sometimes fails.

Controlling Projects in Progress   Control over projects is an essential follow-up to a decision to authorize expenditure. The authorization usually specifies how much money may be spent and when. Control is established by accounting procedures for recording expenditures as they occur. Typically, companies will permit up to 10% expenditure overruns, but beyond that the sponsor is required to submit a supplemental appropriation request. To ensure that the money is not diverted to other uses, the sponsor is also required to submit a revised appropriation request if there is any significant change in the nature of the project.

To avoid delays, a few companies attempt to set limits to the length of time before construction begins. Almost all firms require the sponsor to submit a formal notice of completion, so that the accumulated costs can be transferred to the permanent accounts and any unspent cash can be recovered rather than kept in a hidden kitty for miscellaneous uses.

These procedures are necessary aspects of control. More general information on progress is usually contained in monthly or quarterly status reports.

Postaudits   Postaudits of capital expenditures are now undertaken in most large firms. Not all projects are audited, and those that are are usually audited only once. A few firms require further audits for "problem" projects. The most common time for audit is one year after construction or installation is completed.

The audit is usually the responsibility of the corporation's controller and is handled by the internal audit department. Because this department may be ill-equipped to assess technical issues, the task is sometimes jointly assigned to accounting and engineering departments. Sometimes the audit is delegated to plants, and not infrequently it is assigned to the project originator. The scope for conflicts of interest in such cases is obvious.

It is a sensible precaution to check on the progress of recent investments. Otherwise problems may go undetected and uncorrected. Postaudits can also provide useful insights to the next round of decision making on capital investments. After a postaudit the controller may say, "We should have anticipated the extra working capital needed to support the project." Next time working capital will get the attention it deserves.

The postaudit is sometimes also used to monitor the quality of forecasts made by project proposers. However, it is worth sounding a note of caution here. The audit is usually taken far too soon after installation to provide any clear assessment of the project's success. And, since the forecasters rarely specify the economic assumptions behind their forecasts, it is hard to measure if they really got it right or if they were bailed out by a buoyant economy. Finally, the number of audited projects is so small and their authorship so imprecise that it is difficult to associate forecasting ability with a particular type of project or proposer.

Of course, the mere threat of postaudit may spur the forecaster to greater accuracy. But it can work the other way around. Many managers make conservative forecasts in the belief that what matters is to beat one's forecasts. In other cases the threat of audit may cause risky projects to be suppressed altogether.

Problems in Measuring Incremental Cash Flows after the Fact   Often postaudits cannot measure all cash flows generated by a project. It may be impossible to split the project away from the rest of the business.

Suppose you have just taken over a trucking firm that operates a package delivery service for local stores. You decide to try to revitalize the business by cutting costs and improving service. This requires three investment projects:

1. Buy five new trucks
2. Construct two additional dispatching centres
3. Buy a small computer to keep track of packages and schedule trucks

A year later you try a postaudit of the computer. You verify that it is working properly and check actual costs of purchase, installation and training against projections. But how do you identify the incremental cash *inflows* generated by the computer? No one has kept records of the extra gas that *would have* been used, or the number of packages that *would* have been lost, had the computer not been installed. You may be able to verify that service is better, but how much of the improvement comes from the new trucks, how much from the dispatching centres, and how much from the computer? It is impossible to say. The only meaningful way to judge the success or failure of your revitalization program is to examine the delivery business as a whole.

Evaluating Operating Performance

Think again of your package delivery business. We could measure its performance in two ways:

1. *Actual versus projected.* We could compare actual operating earnings or cash flow with what you predicted.
2. *Actual profitability versus an absolute standard of profitability.* We could also compare actual profitability against an absolute standard of profitability. Ideally we would like to know the present value of that business's future cash flow relative to the parent firm's current investment in it. The current investment is the value of the assets now committed to the business if they were put to the best alternative use.

The first measure is easy to understand and implement. The second is full of pitfalls, as we will now see.

Accounting Rate of Return as a Performance Measure

Let us think for a moment about how profitability should be measured in principle. It is easy enough to compute the true or "economic" rate of return for a common stock that is continuously traded. We just record cash receipts (dividends) for the year, add the change in price over the year, and divide by the beginning price:

$$\text{Rate of return} = \frac{\text{cash receipts} + \text{change in price}}{\text{beginning price}} = \frac{C_1 + (P_1 - P_0)}{P_0}$$

The numerator of the expression for rate of return (cash flow plus change in value) is called **economic income**:

$$\text{Economic income} = \text{cash flow} + \text{change in present value}$$

Any reduction in present value represents **economic depreciation**; any increase in present value represents *negative* economic depreciation. Therefore

$$\text{Economic depreciation} = \text{reduction in present value}$$

and

$$\text{Economic income} = \text{cash flow} - \text{economic depreciation}$$

The concept works for any asset. Rate of return equals cash flow plus change in value divided by starting value. The return on the package delivery service for 1984 is

$$\text{Rate of return} = \frac{C_{1984} + (PV_{1984} - PV_{1983})}{PV_{1983}}$$

where PV_{1983} and PV_{1984} indicate the present values of the business at the ends of 1983 and 1984.

The only hard part in measuring economic income and return is calculating present value. You can observe market value if shares in the asset are actively traded, but few plants, divisions, or capital projects have *their own* shares traded in the stock market. You can observe the present market value of *all* the firm's assets but not of any one of them taken separately.

Accountants rarely even attempt to measure present value. Instead they give us net book value (BV), which is original cost less depreciation computed according to some arbitrary schedule. Many companies use the book value to calculate the book return on investment (ROI):

$$\text{Book income} = \text{cash flow} - \text{book depreciation}$$
$$= C_1 + (BV_1 - BV_0)$$

Therefore

$$\text{Book ROI} = \frac{C_1 + (BV_1 - BV_0)}{BV_0}$$

If book depreciation and economic depreciation are different (they are rarely the same), then the book profitability measures will be wrong; that is, they will not measure true profitability. (In fact, it is not clear that accountants should even *try* to measure true profitability. They could not do so without heavy reliance on subjective estimates of value. Perhaps they should stick to supplying objective information, and leave the estimation of value to managers and investors.)

12-4   EXAMPLE—MEASURING THE PROFITABILITY OF THE NODHEAD SUPERMARKET

Supermarket chains invest heavily in building and equipping new stores. The regional manager of a chain is about to propose investing $1 million in a new store in Nodhead. Projected cash flows are:

Year	1	2	3	4	5	6	After Year 6
Cash flow (thousands of dollars)	100	200	250	298	298	298	0

Of course real supermarkets last more than six years. But these numbers are realistic in one important sense: it may take two or three years for a new store to catch on—that is, to build up a substantial, habitual clientele. Thus cash flow is low for the first few years even in the best locations.

We will assume the opportunity cost of capital is 10%. The Nodhead store's NPV at 10% is zero. It is an acceptable project, but not an unusually good one:

$$NPV = -1{,}000 + \frac{100}{1.10} + \frac{200}{(1.10)^2} + \frac{250}{(1.10)^3} + \frac{298}{(1.10)^4} + \frac{298}{(1.10)^5} + \frac{298}{(1.10)^6} = 0$$

It is not hard to forecast economic income and the rate of return. Table 12-2 shows the calculations. From the cash-flow forecasts we can forecast present value at the start of periods 1 to 6. Cash flow plus *change* in present value equals economic income. Rate of return equals economic income divided by start-of-period value.

Table 12-2
Forecasted economic income and rate of return for the proposed Nodhead store. Economic income equals cash flow plus change in present value. Rate of return equals economic income divided by value at start of year.

	Year					
	1	2	3	4	5	6
Cash flow	100	200	250	298	298	298
Present value, at *start* of year, 10% discount rate	1,000	1,000	901	741	517	271
Present value at *end* of year, 10% discount rate	1,000	901	741	517	271	0
Change in value during year	0	−99	−160	−224	−246	−271
Economic income	100	101	90	74	52	27
Rate of return	0.10	0.10	0.10	0.10	0.10	0.10
Economic depreciation	0	99	160	224	246	271

Note: There are minor rounding errors in some annual figures.

Of course, these are forecasts. Actual future cash flows and values will be higher or lower. Table 12-2 shows that investors *expect* to earn 10% in each year of the store's six-year life. In other words, investors expect to earn the opportunity cost of capital each year from holding this asset.[6]

Table 12-3 shows the store's forecasted *book* profitability assuming straight-line depreciation over its six-year life. The book ROI is lower than the true return for the first two years and higher afterwards.[7] The error can be traced to the use of straight-line depreciation, which overstates economic depreciation at first and understates it later on. Note that any kind of accelerated depreciation would make the errors worse. Economic depreciation is *decelerated* in this case.

Book Earnings versus True Earnings

At this point the regional manager steps up on stage for the following soliloquy:

"The Nodhead store's a decent investment. I really should propose it. But if we go ahead, I won't look very good at next year's performance review. And what if I also go ahead with the new stores in Russet, Gravenstein, and Sheepnose? Their cash-flow patterns are pretty much the same. I could actually appear to lose money next year. The stores I've got won't earn enough to cover the initial losses on four new ones.

"Of course, everyone knows new supermarkets lose money at first. The loss would be in the budget. My boss will understand—I think. But what about her boss? What if the board of directors starts asking pointed questions about profitability in my region? I'm under a lot of pressure to generate better earnings. Pamela Quince, the upstate manager, got a bonus for generating a 40% increase in book ROI. *She* didn't spend much on expansion. . . . "

---

[6] This is a general result. Forecasted profitability always equals the discount rate used to calculate the estimated future present values.

[7] The errors in book ROI always catch up with you in the end. If the firm chooses a depreciation schedule that overstates a project's return in some years, it must also understate the return in other years. In fact, you can think of a project's IRR as a kind of average of the book returns. It is not a simple average, however. The weights are the project's book values discounted at the IRR. See J.A. Kay, "Accountants, Too, Could Be Happy in a Golden Age: The Accountant's Rate of Profit and the Internal Rate of Return," *Oxford Economic Papers,* **28**: 447–460 (1976).

Table 12-3
Forecasted book income and ROI for the proposed Nodhead store. Book ROI is lower than the economic rate of return for the first two years and higher thereafter.

	Year					
	1	2	3	4	5	6
Cash flow	100	200	250	298	298	298
Book value at *start* of year, straight-line depreciation	1,000	833	667	500	333	167
Book value at *end* of year, straight-line depreciation	833	667	500	333	167	0
Change in book value during year	−167	−167	−167	−167	−167	−167
Book income	−67	+33	+83	+131	+131	+131
Book ROI	−0.067	+0.04	+0.124	+0.262	+0.393	+0.784
Book depreciation	167	167	167	167	167	167

The regional manager is getting conflicting signals. On the one hand he is told to find and propose good investment projects. *Good* is defined by discounted cash flow. On the other hand, he is also urged to increase book earnings. But the two goals conflict because book earnings do not measure true earnings. The greater the pressure for immediate book profits, the more the regional manager is tempted to forgo good investments or to favour quick-payback projects over longer-lived projects, even if the latter have higher NPVs.

Does ROI Give the Right Answer in the Long Run?

Some people downplay the problem we have just described. Is a temporary dip in book profits a major problem? Don't the errors wash out in the long run, when the region settles down to a steady state with an even mix of old and new stores?

It turns out that the errors diminish but do *not* exactly offset. The simplest steady-state condition occurs when the firm does not grow, but reinvests just enough each year to maintain earnings and asset values. Table 12-4 shows steady-state book ROIs for a regional division that opens one store a year. For simplicity we assume the division starts from scratch and that each store's cash flows are carbon copies of the Nodhead store. The true rate of return on each store is, therefore, 10%. But, as Table 12-4 demonstrates, steady-state book ROI, at 12.6%, overstates the true rate of return. Therefore, you cannot assume that the errors in book ROI will wash out in the long run.

Thus we still have a problem even in the long run. The extent of error depends on how fast the business grows. We have just considered one steady state with a zero growth rate. Think of another firm with a 5% steady-state growth rate. Such a firm would invest $1,000 the first year, $1,050 the second, $1,102.50 the third, and so on. Clearly the faster growth means more new projects relative to old ones. The greater weight given to young projects, which have low book ROIs, the lower the business's apparent profitability. Figure 12-1 shows how this works out for a business composed of projects like the Nodhead store. Book ROI will either overestimate or underestimate the true rate of return unless the amount that the firm invests each year grows at the same rate as the true rate of return.[8]

---

[8] This also is a general result. Biases in steady-state book ROIs disappear when the growth rate equals the true rate of return. This was discovered by E. Solomon and J. Laya, "Measurement of Company Profitability: Some Systematic Errors in Accounting Rate of Return," in A.A. Robichek (ed.), *Financial Research and Management Decisions*, John Wiley & Sons, Inc., New York, 1967, pp. 152–183.

Table 12-4
**Book ROI for a group of stores like the Nodhead store. The steady-state book
ROI overstates the 10% *economic* rate of return.**

	Year					
	1	2	3	4	5	6
Book income for store						
1	−67	+33	+83	+131	+131	+131
2		−67	+33	+83	+131	+131
3			−67	+33	+83	+131
4				−67	+33	+83
5					−67	+33
6						−67
Total Book Income	−67	−34	+49	180	311	442
Book value for store						
1	1,000	833	667	500	333	167
2		1,000	833	667	500	333
3			1,000	833	667	500
4				1,000	833	667
5					1,000	833
6						1,000
Total Book Value	1,000	1,833	2,500	3,000	3,333	3,500
Book ROI for all stores = $\frac{\text{total book income}}{\text{total book value}}$	−0.067	−0.019	+0.02	+0.06	+0.093	+0.126[a]

[a]Steady-state book ROI.
Note: Book income = cash flow + change in book value during year.

Book measures of profitability can be wrong or misleading because:

1. Errors occur at different stages of project life. Book measures are likely to understate true profitability for new projects and overstate it for old ones.
2. Errors also occur when firms or divisions have a balanced mix of old and new projects. Our "steady-state" analysis shows this.
3. Errors occur because of inflation, basically because inflation shows up in revenue faster than it shows up in costs. For example, a firm owning a plant built in 1975 will, under standard accounting procedures, calculate depreciation in terms of the plant's original cost in 1975 dollars. The plant's output is sold for current dollars. This is why the United States Securities and Exchange Commission and the Canadian Institute of Chartered Accountants now require large corporations to report what their profits would be under replacement cost accounting. This procedure bases depreciation, not on the original cost of the firm's assets, but on what it would cost to replace its assets at current prices.
4. Book measures are often confused by "creative accounting." Some firms pick and choose among available accounting procedures, or even invent new ones, in order to make their income statements and balance sheets look good. This was done with particular imagination in the "go-go years" of the mid-1960s.

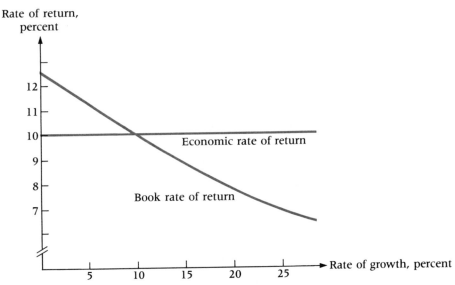

Figure 12-1   The faster a firm grows, the lower its book rate of return, providing true profitability is constant. This graph is drawn for a firm composed of identical projects all like the Nodhead store (Table 12-2), but growing at a constant compound rate.

Investors and financial managers, having been burned by inflation and creative accounting, have learned not to take accounting profitability at face value. Yet many people do not realize the depth of the problem. They think that if firms adopted inflation accounting and eschewed creative accounting, everything would be all right except perhaps for temporary problems with very old or very young projects. In other words, they worry about reasons 3 and 4, and a little about reason 1, but not at all about 2. We think reason 2 deserves more attention.

12-5   WHAT CAN WE DO ABOUT BIASES IN ACCOUNTING PROFITABILITY MEASURES?

The dangers in judging profitability by accounting measures are clear from this chapter's discussion and examples. To be forewarned is to be forearmed. But we can say something beyond just "be careful."

It is natural for firms to set an absolute standard of profitability for plants or divisions. Ideally that standard should be the opportunity cost of capital for investment in the plant or division. But if performance is measured by book ROI, then the standard should be adjusted to reflect accounting biases.

This is easier said than done, because accounting biases are notoriously hard to measure in complex practical situations. Thus, many firms end up asking not, "Did the widget division earn more than its cost of capital last year?" but, "Was the widget division's book ROI typical of a successful firm in the widget industry?" The underlying assumptions are (1) similar accounting procedures are used by other widget manufacturers and (2) successful widget companies earn their cost of capital.

There are some simple accounting changes that could reduce biases in book ROI. Remember that the biases all stem from *not* using economic depreciation. Therefore why not switch to economic depreciation? The main reason is that each asset's present value would have to be re-estimated every year. Imagine the confusion if this were attempted. You can understand why accountants set up a depreciation schedule when an investment is made and then stick to it apart from exceptional circumstances. But why restrict the choice of depreciation schedules to the old standbys, straight-line, double-declining balance, and sum-of-the-years' digits? Why not specify a depreciation pattern that at least matches *expected* economic depreciation? For example, the Nodhead store could be depreciated according to the expected economic depreciation schedule shown in Table 12-2. This would avoid any systematic biases.[9] It would break no law or accounting standard. This step seems so simple and effective that we are at a loss to explain why firms have not adopted it.[10]

Much of the pressure for good book earnings comes from the top management. Chief executives have good reasons to shoot for good short-run earnings. Probably their bonuses depend on it. The market watches current earnings per share (partly because it isn't allowed to look over top management's shoulder at the five-year plan). Is it surprising that top management does not always jump happily into high-NPV projects that will depress next year's earnings per share?

We do not mean to imply that chief executives typically sacrifice long-run value for immediate earnings. But they at least *worry* about earnings, and their worries affect attitudes and decisions down the line.

We think managers worry too much. They are uptight about book earnings. They often picture investors as mindless creatures who respond only to the latest earnings announcement. Investors are more sophisticated than that. Polaroid Corporation provides a good example. Its earnings dropped sharply in the early 1970s because of heavy development expenditures on the SX-70 instant camera, which was successfully introduced in 1973. If investors looked only at the latest earnings announcement they would have concluded that Polaroid was in big trouble in 1972. In fact they understood *why* earnings were low and acted accordingly.

Financial managers can help investors do better by *not* playing the earnings game. That is, they should not hire creative accountants or emphasize book earnings while downplaying more fundamental information about their firm's performance. The firm that brags only about its book earnings will be judged on its book earnings.

12-6   SUMMARY

We began this chapter by describing how capital budgeting is organized and ended by exposing serious biases in accounting measures of financial performance. Inevitably such discussions stress the mechanics of organization, control, and accounting. It is harder to talk about the informal procedures that reinforce the formal ones. But remember that it takes informal communication and personal initiative to make capital budgeting work. Also, the accounting biases are partly or wholly alleviated because managers and stockholders are smart enough to look behind reported book earnings.

Formal capital-budgeting systems usually have four stages:

---

[9] Using expected economic depreciation will not generate book ROIs that are exactly right unless realized cash flows exactly match forecasted flows. But we expect forecasts to be right on average.

[10] This procedure has been suggested by several authors, most recently by Zvi Bodie in "Compound Interest Depreciation in Capital Investment," *Harvard Business Review*, **60**: 58–60 (May–June 1982).

1. Preparation of a *capital budget* for the firm. This is a plan for capital expenditure by plant, division, or other business unit.
2. *Project authorizations* give authority to go ahead with specific projects.
3. Procedures for *control of projects under construction* warn if projects are behind schedule or costing more than planned.
4. *Postaudits* check on the progress of recent investments.

The formal criteria used in project evaluation are a mixture of modern rules like net present value and internal rate of return, and old-fashioned rules like payback and average return on book. The old rules survive partly because everyone understands them; they provide a common language for discussing the project. They also survive because of the way performance is evaluated and rewarded. If managers are expected to generate quick results, and results are measured as contribution to book earnings, then management is naturally interested in payback and book return.

Most specific project proposals originate at the plant of division level. If the project doesn't cost much, it may be approved by middle management. But the final say on major capital outlays belongs to top management. The desire of top management to retain control of capital budgeting is understandable. But the chief executive cannot undertake a detailed analysis of every project he or she approves. Information at the top is often limited; project proposals may be designed more to persuade than inform.

Top management copes by relying on staff financial analysts, by making capital budgeting part of a broader budgeting and planning process, and by keeping the capital budgeting process flexible and open to informal communication.

Capital budgeting is not entirely a bottom-up process. Strategic planners practice "capital budgeting on a grand scale" by attempting to identify those businesses in which the firm has a special advantage. Project proposals that support the firm's accepted overall strategy are much more likely to have clear sailing as they come up through the organization.

Usually the plant or division proposing a capital investment will be responsible for making the project work. A project's sponsors are naturally concerned that the project performs well, and also that it *appears* to perform well. Thus the way the firm evaluates operating performance can affect the kinds of projects that middle managers are willing to propose.

There are two approaches to performance measurement. The first and easier is to compare actual cash flow with projected cash flow. The second is to compare actual profitability with the opportunity cost of capital. Both approaches are needed.

The second approach is the difficult and dangerous one. Most firms measure performance in terms of accounting or book profitability. Unfortunately book income and ROI are often seriously biased measures of true profitability and thus should not be directly compared to the opportunity cost of capital.

In principle, true or economic income is easy to calculate: you just subtract economic depreciation from the asset's cash flow for the period you are interested in. Economic depreciation is simply the decrease in the asset's present value during the period. (If the asset's value increases, then economic depreciation is negative.)

Unfortunately we can't ask accountants to recalculate each asset's present value every time income is calculated. But it does seem fair to ask why they don't try at least to match book depreciation schedules to typical patterns of economic depreciation.

FURTHER READING

The most extensive study of the capital budgeting process is:

J.L. Bower, *Managing the Resource Allocation Process,* Division of Research, Graduate School of Business Administration, Harvard University, Boston, 1970.

Scapens and Sale's article is a more up-to-date survey of current practice.

R.W. Scapens and J.T. Sale, "Performance Measurement and Formal Capital Expenditure Controls in Divisionalized Companies," *Journal of Business Finance and Accounting*, **8**: 389–420 (Autumn 1981).

There are many surveys of the application of capital budgeting criteria, including:

C.G. Hoskins and M.J. Dunn, "The Evaluation of Capital Expenditure Proposals under Uncertainty: The Practice of Large Corporations in Canada," *Journal of Business Administration*, **6**: 45–55 (Fall 1974).

T. Klammer, "Empirical Evidence of the Adoption of Sophisticated Capital Budgeting Techniques," *Journal of Business*, **45**: 387–397 (July 1972).

L.D. Schall, G.L. Sundem, and W.R. Geijsbeek, "Survey and Analysis of Capital Budgeting Methods," *Journal of Finance*, **33**: 281–287 (March 1978).

Swalm and Weingartner discuss some of the incentive problems arising in corporations:

R.O. Swalm, "Utility Theory: Insights into Risk-taking," *Harvard Business Review*, **44**: 123–136 (November–December 1966).

H.M. Weingartner, "Some New Views on the Payback Period and Capital Budgeting," *Management Science*, **15**: B594–607 (August 1969).

Biases in book ROI and procedures for reducing the biases are discussed by:

Z. Bodie, "Compound Interest Depreciation in Capital Investment," *Harvard Business Review*, **60**: 58–60 (May–June 1982).

F.M. Fisher and J.I. McGowan, "On the Misuse of Accounting Rates of Return to Infer Monopoly Profits," *American Economic Review*, **73**: 82–97 (March 1983).

J.A. Kay, "Accountants, Too, Could Be Happy in a Golden Age: The Accountant's Rate of Profit and the Internal Rate of Return," *Oxford Economic Papers*, **28**: 447–460 (1976).

E. Solomon and J. Laya, "Measurement of Company Profitability: Some Systematic Errors in the Accounting Rate of Return," in A.A. Robichek (ed.), *Financial Research and Management Decisions*, John Wiley & Sons, Inc., New York, 1967, pp. 152–183.

QUIZ

1. True or false?
   (a) The approval of a capital budget allows managers to go ahead with any projects included in the budget.
   (b) In most companies the controller authorizes all appropriation requests for capital expenditures.
   (c) Typically, companies will permit up to 10% expenditure overruns, but beyond that the sponsor is required to submit a supplemental appropriation request.
   (d) Most firms use several criteria for project selection.
   (e) Postaudits are usually undertaken about five years after project completion.
   (f) Setting capital budgets and project authorizations is a bottom-up process. Strategic planning, insofar as it affects capital investment decisions, is a top-down process.
2. Fill in the blanks:
   A project's economic income for a given year equals the project's ____ less

its _____ depreciation. Book income is typically _____ than economic income early in the project's life and _____ than economic income later in its life.

3.   Consider the following project:

Year	0	1	2	3
New cash flow	−100	0	78.55	78.55

The internal rate of return is 20%. The NPV, assuming a 20% opportunity cost of capital, is exactly zero. Calculate the expected *economic* income and economic depreciation in each year.

4.   True or false?
   (a) Book profitability measures are biased measures of true profitablity for individual assets. However, these biases "wash out" when firms hold a balanced mix of old and new assets.
   (b) Accountants do not allow firms to pick and choose among accounting procedures to make their income statements look good.
   (c) The Canadian Institute of Chartered Accountants now requires large corporations to report what their profits would be under replacement cost accounting.
   (d) Systematic biases in book profitability would be avoided if companies used depreciation schedules which matched expected economic depreciation. However, few, if any, firms have done this.

QUESTIONS AND PROBLEMS

1.   Discuss the value of postaudits. Who should conduct them? When? Should they consider solely financial performance? Should they be confined to the larger projects?

2.   Rework Table 12-4 assuming that the firm's investment expands by 10% per year; that is, it invests $1 million in year 0, $1.10 million in year 1, and so on. Then rework the table assuming a 20% annual expansion. How does the bias in the steady-state book ROI vary with the rate of expansion?

3.   Suppose that the cash flows from Nodhead's new supermarket are as follows:

Year	0	1	2	3	4	5	6
Cash flows thousands of dollars	−1,000	+298	+298	+298	+138	+138	+138

   (a) Recalculate economic depreciation. Is it accelerated or decelerated?
   (b) Rework Tables 12-2 and 12-3 to show the relationship between the "true" rate of return and book ROI in each year of the project's life.
   (c) Redraw Figure 12-1 to show how the bias in steady-state ROI varies with the rate of firm growth.

Year	0	1	2	3
Cash flows (millions of dollars)	−12	+5.20	+4.80	+4.40

4. Consider an asset with the following cash flows:
   The firm uses straight-line book depreciation. Thus, for this project, it writes off $4 million per year in years 1, 2, and 3. The discount rate is 10%.
   (a) Show that economic depreciation equals book depreciation.
   (b) Show that the book rate of return is the same in each year.
   (c) Show that the project's book profitability is its true profitability.
   Notice that you've just illustrated an interesting theorem: if the book rate of return is the same in each year of a project's life, the book rate of return equals the IRR.

5. For internal accounting purposes, many firms charge each subsidiary or division for the cost of the capital that it uses. Income after deduction of this charge is usually known as *residual income*.
   What do you think are the advantages and disadvantages of such a system? How would you measure residual income?

6. Many accountants believe that instead of showing the written-down book value of the company's assets, the balance sheet should show the "written-down replacement cost." What is meant by this statement? Do you agree?

7. A project is expected to produce the following cash flows:

C_0	C_1	C_2	C_3
-900	$+300$	$+400$	$+500$

   (a) Find the IRR of the project.
   (b) Calculate the accounting return in each year assuming straight-line depreciation.
   (c) In footnote 7, we stated that the IRR is a weighted average of the accounting returns where the weights are equal to the book values (at start of year) discounted by the IRR. Show that this is true for the above project.

8. Here is a harder question. It is often said that book income is overstated when there is rapid inflation because book depreciation understates true depreciation.
   What definition of *true depreciation* is implicit in this statement? Does *true depreciation* equal *economic depreciation* as we have defined the latter term?

9. Instead of looking at past market returns for a guide to the cost of capital, some financial managers look at past accounting returns. What do you think are the advantages of doing this?

10. The following are extracts from two newsletters sent to a stockbroker's clients:
    Investment Letter—March 1990

    Kipper Parlours was founded earlier this year by its president, Mr. Albert Herring. It plans to open a chain of kipper parlours where young people can get together over a kipper and a glass of wine in a pleasant, intimate atmosphere. In addition to the traditional grilled kipper, the parlours serve such delicacies as Kipper Schnitzel, Kipper Grandemere, and (for dessert) Kipper Sorbet.
    The economics of the business are simple. Each new parlour requires an initial investment in fixtures and fittings of $200,000 (the property itself is rented). These fixtures and fittings have an estimated life of five years and are depreciated straight-line over that period. Each new parlour involves

significant start-up costs and is not expected to reach full profitability until its fifth year. Profits per parlour are estimated as follows:

	Year After Opening				
	1	2	3	4	5
Profit	0	40	80	120	170
Depreciation	40	40	40	40	40
Profit after depreciation	−40	0	40	80	130
Book value at start of year	200	160	120	80	40
Return on investment, %	−20	0	33	100	325

Kipper has just opened its first parlour and plans to open one new parlour each year. Despite the likely initial losses (which simply reflect start-up costs), our calculations show a dramatic profit growth and a long-term return on investment that is substantially higher than Kipper's 20% cost of capital.

The total market value of Kipper stock is currently only $250,000. In our opinion, this does not fully reflect the exciting growth prospects and we strongly recommend clients to buy.

Investment Letter—April 1990

Albert Herring, president of Kipper parlours, yesterday announced an ambitious new building plan. Kipper plans to open two new parlours next year, three the year after, and so on.

We have calculated the implications of this for Kipper's earnings per share and return on investment. The results are extremely disturbing and under the new plan, there seems to be no prospect of Kipper *ever* earning a satisfactory return on capital.

Since March, the value of Kipper's stock has fallen by 40%. Any investor who did not heed our earlier warnings should take the opportunity to sell the stock now.

Compare Kipper's accounting and economic income under the two expansion plans. How does the change in plan affect the company's return on investment? What is the present value of Kipper stock? Ignore taxes in your calculations.

P·A·R·T

4

FINANCING DECISIONS AND MARKET EFFICIENCY

C·H·A·P·T·E·R

13

CORPORATE FINANCING AND THE SIX LESSONS OF MARKET EFFICIENCY

Up to this point we have concentrated almost exclusively on the left-hand side of the balance sheet—the firm's capital expenditure decision. Now we move to the right-hand side and to the problems involved in providing finance for the capital expenditures. To put it crudely, you've learned how to spend money—now learn how to raise it.

Of course, we haven't totally ignored financing in our discussion of capital budgeting. But we made the simplest possible assumption: all-equity financing. That means we assumed that the firm raises its money by selling stock and then invests the proceeds in real assets. Later, when those assets generate cash flows, the cash is either returned to stockholders or invested in a second generation of real assets. Stockholders supply all of the firm's capital, bear all the business risks, and receive all the rewards.

Now we are turning the problem around. We take the firm's present portfolio of real assets and its future investment strategy as given, and then determine what the best financing strategy is. We will analyze trade-offs between different financing alternatives. For example,

- Should the firm reinvest most of its earnings in the business or should it pay them out as dividends?
- If the firm needs more money, should it issue more stock or should it borrow?
- Should it borrow short-term or long-term?
- Should it borrow by issuing a normal long-term bond or a convertible bond (that is, a bond that can be exchanged by the bondholders for common stock of the firm)?

There are countless other financing trade-offs, as you will see.

The purpose of holding the firm's capital budgeting decision constant is to separate those decisions from the financing decision. Strictly speaking, this assumes that capital budgeting and financing decisions are *independent*. In many circumstances this is a quite reasonable assumption. The firm is generally free to change its capital structure by repurchasing one security and issuing another. In that case there is no need to associate a particular investment project with a particular source of cash. The firm can think first about what projects to accept and second about how they should be financed.

Sometimes decisions about capital structure depend on project choice or vice versa, and in those cases the investment and financing decisions have to be considered jointly. However, we defer discussion of such interactions of financing and investment decisions until later in the book.

13-1   WE ALWAYS COME BACK TO NPV

Although it is helpful to separate investment and financing decisions, there are basic similarities in the criteria for making them. The decisions to purchase a machine tool or to sell a bond each involve valuation of a risky asset. The fact that one asset is real and the other financial doesn't matter. In both cases we end up computing net present value.

The phrase *net present value of borrowing* may seem odd to you. But the following example should help to explain what we mean. As part of its policy of encouraging small business, the government offers to lend your firm $100,000 for ten years at an interest rate of 3%. This means that the firm is liable for interest payments of $3,000 in each of the years 1 through 10 and that it is responsible for repaying the $100,000 in the final year. Should you accept the offer?

We can compute the NPV of the loan agreement in the usual way. The one difference is that the first cash flow is *positive* and the subsequent flows *negative*:

$$\text{NPV} = \text{amount borrowed} - \text{present value of interest payments}$$
$$- \text{present value of loan repayment}$$

$$= +100,000 - \left[\sum_{t=1}^{10} \frac{3,000}{(1+r)^t} \right] - \frac{100,000}{(1+r)^{10}}$$

The only missing variable is r, the opportunity cost of capital. You need that to value the liability created by the loan. We reason this way. The government's loan to you is a financial asset: a piece of paper representing your promise to pay $3,000 per year plus the final repayment of $100,000. How much would that paper sell for if freely traded in capital markets? It would sell for the present value of those cash flows, discounted at r, the rate of return offered by other securities of equivalent risk. Now, the class of equivalent-risk securities includes other bonds issued by your firm, so that all you have to do to determine r is to answer this question: "What interest rate would my firm have to pay to borrow money directly from the capital markets rather than from the government?" Suppose that this rate is 10%. Then

$$\text{NPV} = +100,000 - \left[\sum_{t=1}^{10} \frac{3,000}{(1.10)^t} \right] - \frac{100,000}{(1.10)^{10}}$$

$$= +100,000 - 56,988 = +\$43,012$$

Of course, you don't need any arithmetic to tell you that borrowing at 3% is a good deal when the fair rate is 10%. But the NPV calculation tells you just how much that opportunity is worth ($43,012).[1] It also brings out the essential similarity of investment and financing decisions.

---

[1] We ignore here any tax consequences of borrowing. We show in Chapter 19 how a taxpaying firm should value a subsidized loan.

Differences between Investment and Financing Decisions

In some ways investment decisions are simpler than financing decisions. The number of different financing instruments (that is, securities) is continually expanding. You will have to learn the major families, genera, and species. You should also be aware of the major financial institutions that provide financing for business firms. Finally, the vocabulary of financing has to be acquired. You will learn about *tombstones, red herrings, balloons, sinking funds*, and many other exotic beasts—behind each of these terms lies an interesting story.

There are also ways in which financing decisions are much easier than investment decisions. First, financing decisions do not have the same degree of finality as investment decisions. They are easier to reverse. In other words, their abandonment value is higher.

Second, it's harder to make or lose money by smart or stupid financing strategies. In other words, it is difficult to find financing schemes with NPVs significantly different from zero. That reflects the nature of the competition.

When the firm looks at capital investment decisions, it does *not* assume that it is facing perfect, competitive markets. It may have only a few competitors that specialize in the same line of business in the same geographical area. And it may own some unique assets that give it an edge over its competitors. Often these assets are intangible items, like patents, expertise, reputation, or market position. All this opens up the opportunity of making superior profits and of finding projects with positive NPVs. It also makes it difficult to tell whether any specific project has a positive NPV.

In financial markets your competition is all other corporations seeking funds, to say nothing of the provincial, local, and federal governments, financial institutions, individuals, and foreign firms and governments that also come to Bay Street for financing. The investors who supply financing are comparably numerous, and they are smart: money attracts brains. The financial amateur often views capital markets as *segmented*, that is, broken down into distinct sectors. But money moves between those sectors, and it moves fast.

Remember that a good financing decision generates a positive NPV. It is one in which the amount of cash raised exceeds the value of the liability created. But turn that statement around. If selling a security generates a positive NPV for you, it must generate a negative NPV for the buyer. Thus, the loan we discussed was a good deal for your firm, but a negative NPV investment from the government's point of view. By lending at 3% it offered a $43,012 subsidy.

What are the chances that your firm could consistently trick or persuade investors into purchasing securities with negative NPVs to them? Pretty low. In general, firms should assume that the securities they issue are fairly priced and therefore have NPV equal to zero.

Efficient Capital Markets

We are leading up to the fundamental financial concept of **efficient capital markets**. *If capital markets are efficient, then purchase or sale of any security at the prevailing market price is never a positive-NPV transaction.*

Does that sound like a sweeping statement? It is. That is why we have devoted all of the rest of this chapter to the history, logic, and tests of the efficient-market hypothesis.

You may ask why we start our discussion of financing issues with this conceptual point, before you have even the most basic knowledge about securities, issue procedures, and financial institutions. We do it this way because financing decisions seem overwhelmingly complex if you don't learn to ask the right questions. We are afraid you might flee from confusion to the myths that often dominate popular discussion of corporate financing.

You need to understand the efficient-market hypothesis, not because it is *universally* true and relevant, but because it leads you to ask the right questions.

13-2 WHAT IS AN EFFICIENT MARKET?

When economists say that the security market is efficient, they are not talking about whether the filing is up-to-date or whether desk tops are tidy. They mean that information is widely and cheaply available to investors and that all relevant and ascertainable information is already reflected in security prices. That is why purchases or sales in an efficient security market cannot be positive-NPV transactions.

A Startling Discovery: Price Changes Are Random

As is so often the case with important ideas, this concept of efficient markets was a by-product of a chance discovery. In 1953, the Royal Statistical Society met in London to discuss a rather unusual paper.[2] Its author, Maurice Kendall, was a distinguished statistician and its subject was the behaviour of stock and commodity prices. Kendall had been looking for regular price cycles but to his surprise he could not find them. Each series appeared to be "a 'wandering' one, almost as if once a week the Demon of Chance drew a random number . . . and added it to the current price to determine the next week's price." In other words, prices seemed to follow a *random walk*.

If you are not sure what we mean by "random walk," you might like to think of the following example. You are given $100 to play a game. At the end of each week a coin is tossed. If it comes up heads, you win 3% of your investment; if it is tails, you lose 2.5%. Therefore your capital at the end of the first week is either $103.00 or $97.50. At the end of the second week the coin is tossed again. Now the possible outcomes are:

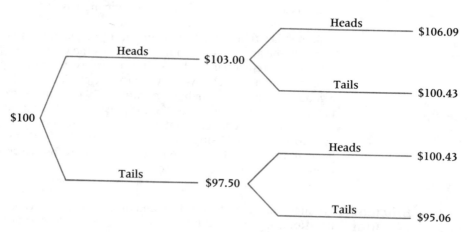

This process is a random walk with a positive drift of 0.25% per month.[3] It is a random walk because successive changes in value are independent. That is, the odds each month of winning are 50%, regardless of the value at the start of the week or of the pattern of heads and tails in the previous months.

---

[2] See M.G. Kendall, "The Analysis of Economic Time-Series, Part 1. Prices." *Journal of the Royal Statistical Society*, **96**:11–25 (1953).

[3] The drift is equal to the expected outcome:

$$\frac{1}{2}(3) + \frac{1}{2}(-2.5) = 0.25\%$$

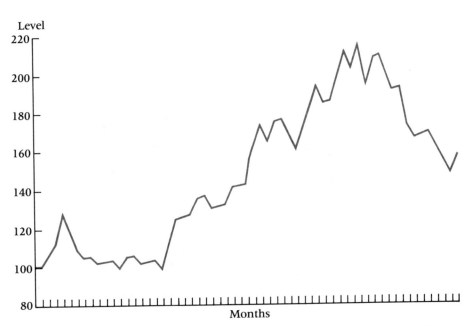

Figure 13-1   One of these charts shows the Toronto Stock Exchange Index for a 5-year period. The other shows the results of playing our coin-tossing game for 5 years. Can you tell which is which?

If you find it difficult to believe that there are no patterns in share price changes look at the two charts in Figure 13-1. One of these charts shows the outcome from playing our game for 5 years; the other shows the actual performance of the Standard and Poor's Index for a 5-year period. Can you tell which one is which?   Figure 13-1 shows the outcome from playing the game for one 60-month period. It is easy to imagine cycles in the value of the investment, but you know it was randomly generated. We will give you the answer in a moment.[4]

---

[4] A similar comparison between cumulated random numbers and actual price series was first suggested by H.V. Roberts, "Stock Market 'Patterns' and Financial Analysis: Methodological Suggestions," *Journal of Finance*, **14**: 1–10 (March 1959).

When Maurice Kendall suggested that stock prices follow a random walk, he was implying that the price changes are as independent of one another as the gains and losses in our game. To most economists this was a startling and bizarre idea. In fact the idea was *not* completely novel. It had been proposed in an almost forgotten doctoral thesis written 53 years earlier by a Frenchman, Louis Bachelier.[5] Bachelier's suggestion was original enough, but his accompanying development of the mathematical theory of random processes anticipated by five years Einstein's famous work on the random motion of gas molecules in collision.

Kendall's work did not suffer the neglect of Bachelier's. As computers and data became more readily available, economists and statisticians rapidly amassed a large volume of supporting evidence. Let us look very briefly at the kinds of tests they have used.

Suppose you wished to assess whether there is any tendency for price changes to persist from one day to the next. You might begin by drawing a scatter diagram of changes on successive days. Figure 13-2 is an example of such a diagram. Each cross shows the change in the price of Northern Telecom stock on successive

Figure 13-2 Each point shows a pair of returns for Northern Telecom stock on two successive days during 1984, 1985, or 1986. For example, the circled point records a return of 1.9% on January 7, 1986 and a −5.2% return on the following day. This scatter diagram shows no relationship between successive days. (There are no points near the axes because the minimum price change is $0.125.)

---

[5] See L. Bachelier, *Théorie de la Spéculation*, Gauthier-Villars, Paris, 1900. Reprinted in English (A.J. Boness, trans.) in P.H. Cootner (ed.), *The Random Character of Stock Market Prices*, M.I.T. Press, Cambridge, Mass., 1964, pp. 17–78. During the 1930s the food economist Holbrook Working had also noticed the random behaviour of commodity prices. See H. Working, "A Random Difference Series for Use in the Analysis of Time Series," *Journal of the American Statistical Association*, **29**: 11–24 (March 1934).

days. The percentage price change was 1.9% on January 7, 1986 and -5.2% the next day. This gives the circled point in the southeast quadrant of Figure 13-2. If there was a systematic tendency for a positive price change to be followed by another positive one, there would be many points in the northeast quadrant and few in the southeast quadrant. It is obvious from a glance that there is very little pattern in these price movements, but we can test this more precisely by calculating the coefficient of correlation between each day's price change and the next. If price movements persisted, the correlation would be strongly positive; if there were no relationship, it would be 0. In our example, the correlation was 0.04—there was a very faint tendency for a price rise to be followed by another price rise.

Figure 13-2 showed the behaviour of only one stock but our finding is typical. Researchers have looked at daily changes, weekly changes, monthly changes; they have looked at many different stocks in many different countries and for many different periods; they have calculated the coefficient of correlation between these price changes; they have looked for runs of positive or negative price changes; they have examined some of the so-called *technical rules* that have been used by some investors to exploit the "patterns" they claim to see in past stock prices. With remarkable unanimity researchers have concluded that there is no useful information in the sequence of past changes in stock price. As a result, many of the researchers have become famous. None has become rich.

Which Was the Real TSE Index?

The answer to the puzzle in Figure 13-1 is that the top chart shows the real Toronto Stock Exchange Index for the years 1985 through 1989; the lower chart is a series of cumulated random numbers. Of course, 50% of you will have guessed right, but we bet it was just a guess.

A Theory to Fit the Facts

We have mentioned that the initial reaction to the random walk finding was surprise. It was in fact several years before economists appreciated that this price behaviour is exactly what one should expect in any competitive market.

Suppose, for example, that you wish to sell an antique painting at an auction but you have no idea of its value. Can you be sure of receiving a fair price? The answer is that you can if the auction is sufficiently competitive. In other words, you need to satisfy yourself that it is to be fairly conducted,[6] that there is no substantial cost involved in submitting a bid, and that the auction is attended by a reasonable number of skilled potential bidders, each of whom has access to the available information. In this case, no matter how ignorant *you* may be, competition among experts will ensure that the price you realize fully reflects the value of the painting.

In just the same way, competition among investment analysts will lead to a stock market in which prices at all times reflect true value. But what do we mean by *true value*? It is potentially a slippery phrase. True value does not mean ultimate *future value*—we do not expect investors to be fortunetellers. It means an equilibrium price that incorporates *all* the information available to investors at that point in time. That was our definition of an efficient market.

Now you can begin to see why price changes in an efficient market are random. If prices always reflect all relevant information, then they will change only when new information arrives. But new information *by definition* cannot be predicted

---

[6] That includes no collusion among bidders.

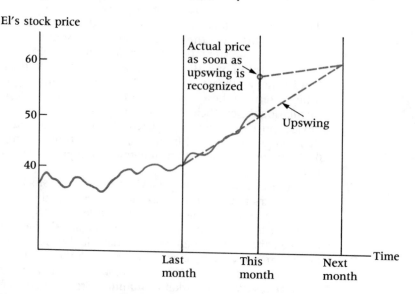

Figure 13-3   Cycles self-destruct as soon as they are recognized by investors. The stock price instantaneously jumps to the present value of the expected future price.

ahead of time (otherwise it would not be new information). Therefore price changes cannot be predicted ahead of time. To put it another way, if stock prices already reflect all that is predictable, then stock price *changes* must reflect only the unpredictable. The series of price changes must be random.[7]

Suppose, however, that competition among research analysts were not so strong and that there were predictable cycles in stock prices. Investors could then make superior profits by trading on the basis of these cycles. Figure 13-3, for example, shows a two-month upswing for Establishment Industries (EI). The upswing started last month, when EI's stock price was $40, and it is expected to carry the stock price to $60 next month. What will happen when investors perceive this bonanza? It will self-destruct. Since EI stock is a bargain at $50, investors will rush to buy. They will stop buying only when the stock offers a normal rate of return. Therefore, as soon as a cycle becomes apparent to investors, they immediately eliminate it by their trading.

Two types of investment analyst help to make price changes random. Many analysts study the company's business and try to uncover information about its profitability that will shed new light on the value of the stock. These analysts are often called *fundamental analysts.* Competition in fundamental research will tend to ensure that prices reflect *all* relevant information and that price changes are unpredictable. The other analysts study the past price record and look for cycles. These analysts are called *technical analysts.* Competition in technical research will tend to ensure that current prices reflect all information in the past sequence of prices and that future price changes cannot be predicted from past prices.

---

[7] When economists speak of stock prices as following a random walk, they are being a little imprecise. A statistician reserves the term *random walk* to describe a series that has a constant expected change each period and a constant degree of variability. But market efficiency does not imply that risks and expected returns cannot shift over time.

Three Forms of the Efficient-Market Theory

Harry Roberts has defined three levels of market efficiency.[8] The first is the case in which prices reflect all the information contained in the record of past prices. Roberts called this a *weak* form of efficiency. The random-walk research shows that the market is at *least* efficient in this weak sense.

The second level of efficiency is the case in which prices reflect not only past prices but all other published information. Roberts called this a *semistrong* form of efficiency. Researchers have tested this by looking at specific items of news, such as announcements of earnings and dividends, forecasts of company earnings, changes in accounting practices, and mergers.[9] Most of this information was rapidly and accurately impounded in the price of the stock.[10]

Finally, Harry Roberts envisaged a *strong* form of efficiency in which prices reflect not just public information but *all* the information that can be acquired by painstaking fundamental analysis of the company and economy. In such a case, the stock market would be like our ideal auction house: prices would *always* be fair and *no* investor would be able to make consistently superior forecasts of stock prices. Most tests of this view have involved an analysis of the performance of professionally managed portfolios. These studies have concluded that, after taking account of differences in risk, no group of institutions has been able to outperform the market consistently and that even the differences between the performance of individual funds are no greater than you would expect from chance.[11]

---

[8] See H.V. Roberts, "Statistical Versus Clinical Prediction of the Stock Market." Unpublished paper presented to the Seminar on the Analysis of Security Prices, University of Chicago, May 1967.

[9] See, for example, R. Ball and P. Brown, "An Empirical Evaluation of Accounting Income Numbers," *Journal of Accounting Research,* **6**: 159–178 (Autumn 1968); R.R. Pettit, "Dividend Announcements, Security Performance, and Capital Market Efficiency," *Journal of Finance,* **27**: 993–1007 (December 1972); G. Foster, "Stock Market Reaction to Estimates of Earnings Per Share by Company Officials," *Journal of Accounting Research,* **11**: 25–37 (Spring 1973); R.S. Kaplan and R. Roll, "Investor Evaluation of Accounting Information: Some Empirical Evidence," *Journal of Business,* **45**: 225–257 (April 1972); G. Mandelker, "Risk and Return: The Case of Merging Firms," *Journal of Financial Economics,* **1**: 303–335 (December 1974); and G. Charest, "Returns to Dividend Splitting Stocks on the Toronto Stock Exchange," *Journal of Business Administration,* **12**: 1–18 (Fall 1980).

[10] The price reaction to news appears to be almost immediate. For example, within 5 to 10 minutes of earnings or dividend announcements appearing on the broad tape, most of the price adjustment has occurred and any remaining gain from acting on the news is less than the transaction costs. See J.M. Patell and M.A. Wolfson, "The Intraday Speed of Adjustment of Stock Prices to Earnings and Dividend Announcements," *Journal of Financial Economics,* **13**: 223–252 (June 1984). The price reaction to the sale of a large block of stock seems to be equally rapid. See L. Dann, D. Mayers, and R. Raab, "Trading Rules, Large Blocks, and the Speed of Adjustment," *Journal of Financial Economics,* **4**: 3–22 (January 1977).

[11] The classic study was M.C. Jensen, "The Performance of Mutual Funds in the Period 1945–64," *Journal of Finance,* **23**: 389–416 (May 1968). More recent studies include D. Grant, "Investment Performance of Canadian Mutual Funds: 1960–1974," *Journal of Business Administration,* **8**: 1–10 (Fall 1976); T. Kim, "An Assessment of the Performance of Mutual Fund Management: 1969–1975," *Journal of Financial and Quantitative Analysis,* **13**: (September 1978); J.C. Bogle and J.M. Twardowski, "Institutional Investment Performance Compared: Banks, Investment Counselors, Insurance Companies, and Mutual Funds," *Financial Analysis Journal,* **36**: 33–41 (January–February 1980); S.J. Kon and F.C. Jen, "The Investment Performance of Mutual Funds: An Empirical Investigation of Timing, Selectivity and Market Efficiency," *Journal of Business,* **52**: 263–289 (1979); and A.L. Calvet and J. Lefoll, "The CAPM under Inflation and the Performance of Canadian Mutual Funds," *Journal of Business Administration,* 107–117 (Fall 1980).

Table 13-1

On average, the stocks of small companies have outperformed those of large companies.

				Average Annual Return		
	Small Canadian Stocks	Large Canadian Stocks			Small U.S. Stocks	Standard & Poor's Index (U.S.)
				1926–35	12.5%	10.8%
				1936–45	28.6	11.1
1950–59	13.7%	13.8%		1946–55	13.1	17.9
1960–69	21.4	10.4		1956–65	17.7	12.2
1970–79	23.1	13.5		1966–75	9.3	5.0
1980–87	12.5	12.1		1976–88	23.8	14.8
1950–87	17.9%	12.5%		1926–88	18.2%	12.1%

Note: these are arithmetic averages of annual data, as in Table 7-1.
Derived from: J.E. Hatch and R.W. White, *Canadian Stocks, Bonds, Bills, and Inflation: 1950–1987*, The Research Foundation of the Institute of Chartered Financial Analysts, Charlottesville, Virginia, 1988 and R.G. Ibbotson and R.A. Sinquefield, *Stocks, Bonds, Bills, and Inflation, 1989 Yearbook*, Ibbotson Associates, Chicago, 1989.

Although few simple economic ideas are as well supported by the evidence as the efficient-market theory, it would be wrong to pretend that there are no puzzles or apparent exceptions. For instance, New York Stock Exchange specialists seem to have made consistently superior profits; so do company managers when they deal in their own company's stock.[12] These are two cases that don't seem to square well with the strong form of the efficient-market theory.

It is not so surprising that insiders make superior profits, but there are other phenomena that take rather more explaining. For example, Table 13-1 shows the average returns of indices of small and large stocks in Canada and the United States. The Canadian small stock portfolio comprises the half of the firm's trading on the Toronto Stock Exchange that are smallest, while the large stock portfolio comprises the remaining firms' stocks. The U.S. small stock portfolio consists of approximately 20% of U.S. firms' stocks that are smallest. The Standard and Poor's Index consists mainly of the largest U.S. firms. The substantially higher returns of the small company stocks have far outweighed their extra risk. Also the magnitude of this size effect seems to differ both by months of the year and

---

[12] See V. Niederhoffer and M.F.M. Osborne, "Market Making and Reversal on the Stock Exchange," *Journal of the American Statistical Association*, **61**: 897–916 (December 1966); J. Jaffe, "The Effect of Regulation Changes on Insider Trading," *Bell Journal of Economics and Management Science*, **5**: 93–121 (Spring 1974); and H.N. Seyhun, "Insiders' Profits, Costs of Trading, and Market Efficiency," *Journal of Financial Economics*, **16**: 189–212 (June 1986).

Canadian stock exchanges have market makers or registered traders, but no specialists. Both stand ready to make a market as buy and sell orders come in from investors. However, each NYSE stock has only one specialist, while each Canadian stock may have several market makers. Thus, a specialist has monopolistic access to information about any imbalance between buy and sell orders, which may be used to earn superior profits. W.M. Lawson, "Market Efficiency: The Trading of Professionals on the Toronto Stock Exchange," *Journal of Business Administration*, **12**: 41–55 (Fall 1980) studied daily filter rules based on the trading activities of professional traders (market makers and persons affiliated with securities firms) on the Toronto Stock Exchange, and found no violation of market efficiency.

days of the week. In particular, much of the superior performance is concentrated during the first week of January.[13]

We believe that there is now widespread agreement that capital markets function well. So nowadays when economists come across instances where this apparently isn't true, they don't throw the efficient-market hypothesis onto the economic garbage heap. Instead they ask whether there isn't some missing ingredient that their theories ignore. Thus, despite the apparent superior performance of small company stocks, no economist has to our knowledge been tempted to make a king-size investment in such stocks. Instead economists have assumed that investors aren't stupid and have looked at whether small-firm stocks suffer from some other defect, such as a lack of easy marketability, that is not allowed for in our theories or tests.

Some Misconceptions

The efficient-market hypothesis is frequently misinterpreted. One common error is to think that it implies perfect forecasting ability. In fact it implies only that prices reflect all available information. In the same vein, some have suggested that prices cannot represent fair value because they go up and down. The answer, however, is that they would not represent fair value *unless* they went up and down. It is because the future is so uncertain and people are so often surprised that prices fluctuate. (Of course, when we look *back*, nothing seems quite so surprising: it is easy to convince ourselves that we really knew all along how prices were going to change.) A rather different temptation is to believe that the inability of institutions to achieve superior portfolio performance is an indication that portfolio managers are incompetent. This is incorrect. Market efficiency exists only because competition is keen and portfolio managers are doing their job.

Another error is to think that the random behaviour of stock prices implies that the market is irrational. *Randomness* and *irrationality* are not synonymous. Stock price changes are random because investors are rational and competitive. There is an important corollary to this. If the price of any risky asset does *not* vary randomly, then its price *cannot* represent competitive market value.

When we talk about an efficient market, we mean that the market is functioning well and the prices are fair.[14] For the financial manager the concept of market efficiency entails six main lessons. Let us consider them in turn and at the same time introduce briefly some of the issues with which we shall be concerned in subsequent chapters.

---

[13] A readable summary of these size and seasonal effects is given by D.B. Keim, "The CAPM and Equity Return Regularities," *Financial Analysts Journal,* **42**: 19–34 (May–June 1986). For Canadian evidence, see A. Berges, J.J. McConnell, and G. Schlarbaum, "The Turn-of-the-Year in Canada," *Journal of Finance,* **39**: 185–192 (March 1984) and S.M. Tinic, G. Barone-Adesi, and R.R. West, "Seasonality in Canadian Stock Prices: A Test of the 'Tax-Loss-Selling' Hypothesis," *Journal of Financial and Quantitative Analysis,* **22**: 51–63 (March 1987).

[14] Everyone thinks they know a duck when they see one, but it is hard to come up with a satisfactory definition. It is rather like that with efficient markets. We have talked about "well-functioning" markets and "fair" markets without ever saying what this means. Fama defined efficient markets in terms of the difference between the actual price and the price that investors expected given a particular set of information. An efficient market, Fama argues, is one in which the expected value of this difference is zero. [See E.F. Fama, "Efficient Capital Markets: A Review of Theory and Empirical Work," *Journal of Finance,* **25**: 383–417 (May 1970).] Rubinstein defines an efficient market as one in which prices would not be altered if everyone revealed all that they knew. [See M. Rubinstein, "Securities Market Efficiency in an Arrow-Debreu Economy," *American Economic Review,* **65**: 812–824 (December 1975).]

13-3   **THE FIRST LESSON OF MARKET EFFICIENCY: MARKETS HAVE NO MEMORY**

The weak form of the efficient-market hypothesis states that the sequence of past price changes contains no information about future changes. Economists express the same idea more concisely when they say that the market has no memory. Sometimes financial managers *seem* to act as if this were not the case. For example, they are often reluctant to issue stock after a fall in price. They are inclined to wait for a rebound. Similarly, managers favour equity rather than debt financing after an abnormal price rise. The idea is to "catch the market while it is high." But we know that the market has no memory and the cycles that financial managers seem to rely on do not exist.

Sometimes a financial manager will have inside information indicating that the firm's stock is overpriced or underpriced. Suppose, for example, that there is some good news the market does not know but you do. The stock price will rise sharply when the news is revealed. Therefore, if the company sold shares at the current price, it would be offering a bargain to new investors at the expense of present stockholders.

Naturally, managers are reluctant to sell new shares when they have favourable inside information. But such inside information has nothing to do with the history of the stock price. Your firm's stock could be selling now at half its price of a year ago and yet you could have special information suggesting that it is *still* grossly overvalued. Or it may be undervalued at twice last year's price.

13-4   **THE SECOND LESSON OF MARKET EFFICIENCY: TRUST MARKET PRICES**

In an efficient market you can trust prices. They impound all available information about the value of each security.

This means that in an efficient market there is no way for most investors to achieve consistently superior rates of return. To do so, you not only need to know more than *anyone* else; you need to know more than *everyone* else. This message is important for the financial manager who is responsible for the firm's exchange rate policy or for its purchases and sales of debt. If you operate on the basis that you are smarter than others at predicting currency changes or interest rate moves, you will trade a consistent financial policy for an elusive will-o'-the wisp.

The company's assets may also be directly affected by management's faith in its investment skills. For example, one company will often purchase another simply because its management thinks that the stock is undervalued. On approximately half the occasions the stock of the acquired firm really will be undervalued. But on the other half it will be overvalued. On average the value will be correct, so that the acquiring company is playing a fair game except for the costs of the acquisition.

Example: Northwestern Bell's Bond Repurchase Offer

Here is another instance in which the financial manager should trust market prices. In early 1977 four American Telephone and Telegraph, Inc. (AT&T) subsidiaries offered to repurchase outstanding bonds that had been issued in 1974 at a time of high interest rates. The bonds of one issue by Northwestern Bell carried a *coupon rate* of 10% and had a *maturity* of 40 years. In other words, Northwestern Bell had promised to pay the bondholder $100 a year for every $1,000 borrowed. These interest payments were to continue for 40 years, until 2014, at which time the original amount borrowed was to be repaid.

The bonds had a zero NPV *at the time of issue*. The fair interest rate at that time was 10%:

$$\text{NPV at time of issue} = +1,000 - \sum_{t=1}^{40} \frac{100}{(1.10)^t} - \frac{1,000}{(1.10)^{40}} = 0$$

$$= \text{amount borrowed} - \text{present value of interest payments}$$
$$- \text{present value of loan repayment}$$

By January 1977 interest rates on newly issued bonds had dropped to approximately 8.2%. As a result, the market value of the Northwestern Bell bonds on January 20 had risen to $1,130. Northwestern Bell would clearly have gained by handing back to each bondholder the original amount borrowed ($1,000 a bond) and cancelling the debt issue. But the company had no right to do so, at least not in 1977. The firm did have the option to repurchase or "call" the bonds in 1979 at a price of $1,085.70, but that option was no help in 1977.[15]

Northwestern Bell offered to repurchase the bonds for $1,160, in effect offering bondholders a bonus of $30 per bond for agreeing to retire the issue. Bondholders were naturally happy to accept the unexpected $30 bonus, and 80% of the issue was retired.

Why did Northwestern Bell do it? The stated reason was to reduce interest charges. These interest charges amounted to $15 million a year on the old bonds. Notice that the company could have financed the repurchase by issuing $1,160/1,000 \times $150 million or $174 million of fresh debt at an interest rate of 8.2%. Therefore instead of paying out $15 million as interest, it would have had to pay out only $0.082 \times 174 = $14.3 million, a saving of $700,000 per year.

But what was the NPV of this venture? The company was investing $1,160 per bond to eliminate a liability with a market value of $1,130. In an efficient market the price of the bonds must represent their true value. Therefore the NPV of the transaction was −$30 per bond.

Northwestern Bell was right. The bond repurchase did reduce interest charges. But our analysis shows that this was no justification for the transaction in an efficient market. Why didn't the firm wait and call the bonds in 1979 at the lower price of $1,085.70 stated in the bond contract? Northwestern Bell's managers are not stupid. Thus we suspect that there was some other reason for the repurchase.[16] Our point is that the *stated* reason was clearly wrong in an efficient bond market.

13-5   THE THIRD LESSON OF MARKET EFFICIENCY: THERE ARE NO FINANCIAL ILLUSIONS

In an efficient market there are no financial illusions. Investors are unromantically concerned with the firm's cash flows and the portion of those cash flows to which they are entitled.

---

[15] But the call option explains why the bonds sold at only $1,130 and not at the present value of $100 per year for 37 years followed by a final payment of $1,000. Investors anticipated that the bonds would be retired before maturity.

[16] Taxes are one possibility. If Northwestern Bell could claim the difference between $1,160 cost of repurchase and the $1,000 face value of each bond as a loss for tax purposes, the firm's income taxes for 1977 were reduced by 48% of $160. If so the effective repurchase cost was $1,083.20, not $1,160. For a discussion of the tax consequences of refunding debt, see J.D. Finnerty, "Refunding High-Coupon Debt," *Midland Corporate Finance Journal*, **3**: 59–74 (Winter, 1986).

**Stock Splits
and Dividends**

We can illustrate our third lesson by looking at the effect of stock splits and stock dividends. Every year many companies increase the number of shares in issue either by subdividing the stock that is already outstanding or by distributing more shares of stock as dividends. For a large company, the administrative costs of such action may exceed a million dollars. Yet it does not affect in any other way the company's cash flows nor the proportion of these cash flows attributable to each shareholder. You may think that you are better off, but that is an illusion.

Suppose the stock of Chaste Manhattan Finance Company is selling for $210 per share. A 3-for-1 split would replace each outstanding share with three new shares.[17] Chaste would probably arrange this by printing two new shares for each original share and distributing the new shares to its stockholders as a "free gift." After the split we would expect each share to sell for 210/3 = $70. Dividends per share, earnings per share, and all other "per share" variables would be one-third their previous levels.

A variety of justifications have been proposed for splits and stock dividends. One endorsement came from the president of a large American corporation, who observed that stock dividends "give shareholders a reasonable hedge against inflation and let them participate in the increase in book value. On the other hand," he warned, "it would be silly to declare [them] if not earned because that would just lower the book value." A further argument was proposed by the chairman of another company, who suggested that paying a stock dividend would provide investors with "a greater return while at the same time conserving cash to finance the company's anticipated growth."[18] A third and disarmingly simple explanation was offered by a textbook, which observed that stockholders like stock splits because they expect them to be followed by more stock splits. Claims such as these contrast strongly with the efficient-market notion that investors are concerned solely with their share of the company's cash flows.

Of course extremely high stock prices are inconvenient for small investors. In June 1987 shares in Nippon Telegraph and Telephone were trading at 2.85 million yen each, or about $20,000. That is a nuisance if you only have $1,000 to invest. A stock split by Nippon Telegraph and Telephone could therefore have significant convenience value. But convenience value does not justify the many companies that split their shares when they are selling for less than $100.[19]

**Calculating
Abnormal
Returns**

We can check whether investors are fooled by stock splits by looking at whether there were any abnormal changes in the stock price at the time of the split. First, however, we must explain how you can use some of the ideas in Chapter 9 to identify these abnormal price movements.[20] In Chapter 9 we introduced you to

---

[17] There are some confusing transatlantic differences in terminology. In the United Kingdom such increases usually take the form of a "scrip issue." A 2-for-1 scrip issue (that is, two new shares in addition to one old) is equivalent to a 3-for-1 stock split.

[18] Cited in J.E. Walter, *Dividend Policy and Enterprise Valuation,* Wadsworth Publishing Company, Inc., Belmont, Calif., 1967.

[19] Lakonishok and Lev provide some evidence that many companies do split their stock in order to keep the price in a desirable trading range. See J. Lakonishok and B. Lev, "Stock Splits and Stock Dividends: Why, Who and When," *Journal of Finance,* **42**: 913–932 (September 1987).

[20] There is more to being a good driver than knowing which way to turn the steering wheel. Similarly, if you want a good estimate of the abnormal return, you need to know more about how to calculate it than the brief overview that we provide. We suggest that you consult S.J. Brown and J.B. Warner, "Measuring Security Price Performance," *Journal of Financial Economics,* **8**: 205–258 (1980).

a "beta book." This contains two measures of each stock's performance. Alpha (α) describes how much, on average, the stock price moved when the market was unchanged. Beta (β) describes the average additional return for each 1% change in the market index. For example, Table 9-2 shows that MacMillan Bloedel's stock price rose on average by 0.36% when the market was unchanged ($\alpha = 0.36$), and it rose a further 1.49% for each 1% change in the market index ($\beta = 1.49$).[21] Now suppose you were interested in the performance of MacMillan Bloedel stock in January 1989 when the market rose 7.0%. On past evidence you would judge that the expected change in the stock price that month was

$$\text{Expected price change} = 0.36 + (1.49 \times \text{market change})$$
$$= 0.36 + (1.49 \times 7.0) = 10.8\%$$

In fact MacMillan Bloedel rose 12.5% in January 1989. Its abnormal price change was, therefore,

$$\text{Abnormal price change} = \text{actual change} - \text{expected change}$$
$$= 12.5 - 10.8 = 1.7\%$$

This 1.7% rise in MacMillan Bloedel's stock was over and above the normal rise in such market conditions.[22]

Now we can look at the abnormal price movements that generally take place around the time of a stock split. Figure 13-4 summarizes the results of an important study of splits during the period 1926–1960.[23] It shows the abnormal performance of stocks around the time of the split after adjusting for the increase in the number of shares.[24] Notice the rise in price before the split. The announcement of the split would have occurred in the last month or two of this period. That means the decision to split is both the consequence of a rise in price and the cause of a further rise. It looks as if shareholders are not as hard-headed as we have been making out: they do seem to care about form as well as substance.

---

[21] It is important when estimating α and β that you choose a period in which you believe the stock behaved normally. If its performance was abnormal, then estimates of α and β cannot be used to measure the return investors expected. As a precaution ask yourself whether your estimates of expected returns *look* sensible.

[22] You will generally get a fairly similar answer if you use the capital asset pricing model to measure abnormal returns. This states that the expected return for MacBloedel stock is

$$\text{Expected return} = r_f + \beta(r_m - r_f)$$

The market return (r_m) in January 1989 was equal to the 7.0%, including dividends, since we used the Total Return Index. The interest rate (r_f) was 12% per year, or about 1.0% per month. Therefore,

$$\text{Expected return} = 1.0 + 1.49(7.0 - 1.0) = 9.9\%$$

$$\text{Abnormal return} = 12.5 - 9.9 = 2.6\%$$

Note that since MacMillan Bloedel did not pay a dividend in January 1989, *return* and *price change* are identical.

[23] See E.F. Fama, L. Fisher, M. Jensen, and R. Roll, "The Adjustment of Stock Prices to New Information," *International Economic Review*, **10**: 1–21 (February 1969). Later researchers have discovered that shareholders make abnormal gains both when the split or stock dividend is announced and when it takes place. Nobody has offered a convincing explanation for latter phenomenon. See, for example, M.S. Grinblatt, R.W. Masulis, and S. Titman, "The Valuation Effects of Stock Splits and Stock Dividends," *Journal of Financial Economics*, **13**: 461–490 (December 1984).

[24] By this we mean that the study looked at the change in the shareholder's wealth. A decline in the price of Chaste Manhattan stock from $210 to $70 at the time of the split would not affect shareholder's wealth.

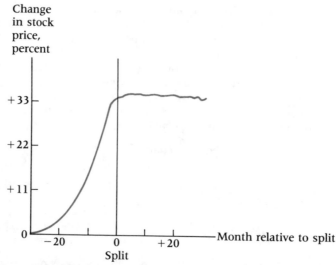

Figure 13-4 Changes in stock price at the time of a stock split. The changes are adjusted for both general market movements and the increase in the number of shares. Notice the rise before the split and the absence of abnormal changes after the split.

Source: E. Fama, L. Fisher, M. Jensen, and R. Roll, "The Adjustment of Stock Prices to New Information," *International Economic Review*, 10 (February 1969), fig. 2b, p. 13.

However during the subsequent year, two-thirds of the splitting companies announced above-average increases in cash dividends. Usually such an announcement would cause an unusual rise in the stock price, but in the case of the splitting companies there was no such occurrence at any time after the split. Indeed, the stocks of those companies that did *not* increase their dividends by an above-average amount declined in value to levels prevailing well before the split. The apparent explanation is that the split was accompanied by an explicit or implicit promise of a subsequent dividend increase, and the rise in price at the time of the split had nothing to do with a predilection for splits as such but with the information that it was thought to convey.[25] A stock split seems an expensive way to send the message, however.[26]

Accounting Changes

There are other occasions on which managers seem to assume that investors suffer from financial illusion. For example, some firms devote enormous ingenuity to the task of manipulating earnings reported to stockholders. This is done by "creative accounting"—that is, by choosing accounting methods that stabilize and increase reported earnings. Presumably firms go to this trouble because management believes that stockholders take the figures at face value. Leonard Spacek, one of America's leading accountants, echoes this belief in the following complaint.

---

[25] This does not imply that investors like high-dividend payouts for their own sake. It could be that dividend increases are valued only because they are a sign of company prosperity. We will discuss this point in Chapter 16.

[26] Guy Charest, in "Returns to Splitting Stocks on the Toronto Stock Exchange," *Journal of Business Administration*, **12**: 19–40 (Fall 1980), studied 177 Canadian stock splits that occurred between 1963 and 1975. He found that prices tend to *fall* significantly in the 24 months following a split, which suggests that investors may have ignored negative information associated with the split announcement. However, these anomalous results may be unreliable because of the small sample size.

Let us assume that you sincerely want to report the profits in the way you feel fairly presents the true results of your company's business. . . . This is an admirable and objective motive; but when you do this, you find that your competitor shows a relatively more favourable profit result than you do. This creates a demand for his stock, while yours lags behind. You put your analyst to work, and you find that if your competitor followed the same accounting practices you do, your results would be better than his. . . . You show this analysis to your complaining stockholders. Naturally they ask, "If this is true, and if your competitor's accounting practices are generally accepted, too, why not change your accounting practices and thus improve your profits?" At that point you try to explain why your accounting is much more factual and reliable than your competitor's. Your stockholders listen, but nothing you can say will convince them that they should give up a 20%, 50%, or 100% possible increase in the market values just because you like certain accounting practices better than others.[27]

Is Spacek right? Can the firm increase its market value by creative accounting? Or are the firm's shares traded in an efficient, well-functioning market, in which investors can see through such financial illusions?

A number of researchers have tried to resolve this question by looking at how the market reacts when companies change their accounting methods. For example, Kaplan and Roll have studied what happens to stock prices when companies boost their reported profits by switching from accelerated depreciation to straight-line depreciation.[28] This switch is purely cosmetic. It reduces the reported depreciation charge but it does not affect the company's tax bill — the tax authorities allow firms to use accelerated depreciation for tax purposes but straight-line depreciation for reporting purposes.

Figure 13-5 shows the results of Kaplan and Roll's study. The preliminary announcement of increased earnings seems to prompt a slight abnormal rise in the stock price but this could simply be because investors were not informed at that stage of the accounting change. Within three months of the earnings announcement investors appear to have concluded that the accounting cosmetics were a sign of weakness rather than strength.

This result not only suggests the futility of earnings manipulation. It also raises some more basic questions about the role of accounting conventions. Jack Treynor illustrates the problem with the fable of nail soup:

There was once a band of itinerant soldiers who, when they had difficulty persuading townsmen to feed them, hit upon the following solution. They set a large pot of water to boiling and then, when all the townsmen were watching curiously, dropped in a nail and announced with much licking of lips that they were making nail soup. The townsmen were assured that there would be enough soup for everybody. When one of the soldiers allowed that a few carrots actually improved the flavour of nail soup, a townsman dashed off to fetch some carrots. When it was observed that tomatoes made a wonderful garnish for nail soup, another townsman quickly produced some tomatoes. Soon the nail soup contained beef stock, turnips, and onions. Before the soup was served, the nail was removed. But the townsmen continued to regard the soup as nail soup.

---

[27] See L. Spacek, "Business Success Requires an Understanding of Unsolved Problems of Accounting and Financial Reporting." Address before the Financial Accounting Class, Graduate School of Business Administration, Harvard University, September 25, 1959.

[28] See R.S. Kaplan and R. Roll, "Investor Evaluation of Accounting Information: Some Empirical Evidence," *Journal of Business*, **45**: 225–257 (April 1972).

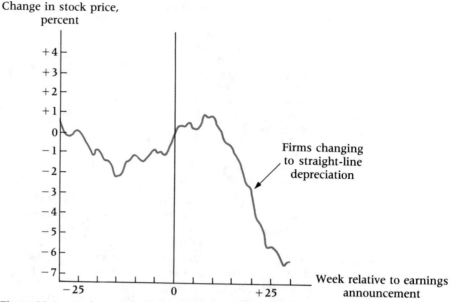

Figure 13-5   Kaplan and Roll's study shows that investors are not misled by accounting changes that are designed to inflate earnings. (Changes in price of the firms' stock are adjusted for general market movements.)

Source: R.S. Kaplan and R. Roll, "Investor Evaluation of Accounting Information: Some Empirical Evidence," *Journal of Business*, 45 (April 1972), fig. 1c, p. 239. © 1972 by the University of Chicago. All rights reserved.

Nail soup was nourishing, but not because of the nail. Earnings have information content, but not because of the ingredients that have been the main concern of the FASB and the AcSC.[29] Accountants painstakingly put the nail into the soup; analysts painstakingly take it out, all the while believing they are really supping on nail soup. The overall process may seem unnecessarily complicated since the same result could have been obtained without the nail.[30]

13-6   THE FOURTH LESSON OF MARKET EFFICIENCY: THE DO-IT-YOURSELF ALTERNATIVE

In an efficient market investors will not pay others for what they can do equally well themselves. As we shall see, many of the controversies in corporate financing centre on how well individuals can replicate corporate financial decisions. For example, companies often justify mergers on the grounds that they produce a more diversified and hence more stable firm. But if investors can hold the stocks of both companies, why should they thank the companies for diversifying? It is much easier and cheaper for them to diversify than it is for the firm.

The financial manager needs to ask the same question when considering whether it is better to issue debt or common stock. If the firm issues debt, it will

---

[29] FASB is the Financial Accounting Standards Board in the United States; AcSC is the Accounting Standards Committee of the Canadian Institute of Chartered Accountants.

[30] See J.L. Treynor, "Discussion: Changes in Accounting Techniques and Stock Prices," *Empirical Research in Accounting: Selected Studies*, 1972, Institute for Professional Accounting, Graduate School of Business, University of Chicago, Chicago, 1972, p. 43.

create financial leverage. As a result, the stock will be more risky and it will offer a higher expected return. But stockholders can obtain financial leverage without the firm's issuing debt. They can issue debt on their own account. The problem for the financial manager is, therefore, to decide whether it is cheaper for the company to issue debt than for the individual shareholder.

13-7   THE FIFTH LESSON OF MARKET EFFICIENCY: SEEN ONE STOCK, SEEN THEM ALL

The elasticity of demand for any article measures the percentage change in the quantity demanded for each percentage addition to the price. If the article has close substitutes, the elasticity will be strongly negative; if not, it will be near zero. For example, coffee, which is a staple commodity, has a demand elasticity of about -0.2. This means that a 5% increase in the price of coffee changes sales by $-0.2 \times 0.05 = 0.01$; in other words, it reduces demand by only 1%. Consumers are likely to regard different *brands* of coffee as much closer substitutes for each other. Therefore the demand elasticity for a particular brand could be in the region of, say, -2.0. A 5% increase in the price of Maxwell House relative to that of Nescafé would in this case reduce demand by 10%.

Investors don't buy a stock for its unique qualities; they buy it because it offers the prospect of a fair return for its risk. This means that stocks should be like very similar brands of coffee, almost perfect substitutes for each other. Therefore, the demand for one company's stock should be very elastic. If its prospective risk premium is lower relative to its risk than other stocks, *nobody* will want to hold that stock. If it is higher, *everybody* will want to hold it.

Suppose that you want to sell a large block of stock. Since demand is elastic, you naturally conclude that you need only cut the offering price very slightly to attract buyers. Unfortunately that doesn't necessarily follow. When you come to sell your stock, other investors may suspect that you want to get rid of it because you know something they don't. Therefore they will revise their assessment of the stock's value downward. Demand is still elastic but the whole demand curve moves down. Elastic demand does *not* imply that stock prices never change: it *does* imply that you can sell large blocks of stock at close to the market price *as long as you can convince other investors that you have no private information.*

Here is one case that supports this view. In June 1977 the Bank of England offered its holding of BP shares for sale at 845 pence each. The bank owned nearly 67 million shares of BP, so that the total value of the holding was £564 million, or about $970 million. It was a huge sum to ask the public to find, and the sale was by far the largest of its kind in history.

Anyone who wished to apply for BP stock had nearly two weeks within which to do so. Just before the bank's announcement the price of BP stock was 912 pence. Over the next two weeks the price drifted down to 898 pence, largely in line with the British equity market. Therefore by the final application date, the discount being offered by the bank was only 6%. In return for this discount, any applicant had to raise the necessary cash, taking the risk that the price of BP would decline before the result of the application was known, and had to pass over to the Bank of England the next dividend on BP.

If Maxwell House coffee is offered at a discount of 6%, the demand is unlikely to be overwhelming. But the discount on BP stock was enough to bring in applications for $4,600 million worth of stock,[31] 4.7 times the amount on offer.

---

[31] However, applicants were required to put up only £3 per share on application and the remainder at a later date.

We admit that this case was unusual in some respects, but an important study by Myron Scholes of a large sample of secondary offerings confirmed the ability of the market to absorb blocks of stock.[32] The average effect of the offerings was to reduce the stock price slightly, but the decline was almost independent of the amount offered. Scholes' estimate of the demand elasticity for a company's stock was −3,000. Of course, this figure was not meant to be precise, and some researchers have argued that demand is not as elastic as Scholes's study suggests.[33] However, there seems to be widespread agreement with the general point that you can sell large quantities of stock at close to the market price as long as other investors do not deduce that you have some private information.

Here again we encounter an apparent contradiction with practice. Many corporations seem to believe that the demand elasticity is not only low, but that it varies with the stock price, so that when the price is relatively low new stock can only be sold at a substantial discount. American state and federal regulatory commissions, which set the prices charged by telephone companies, electric companies, and other utilities, often allow 10% higher earnings to compensate the firm for price "pressure." This pressure is the decline in the firm's stock price that is supposed to occur when new shares are offered to investors. Yet, Paul Asquith and David Mullins, who searched for evidence of pressure, found that new stock issues by utilities resulted in a *temporary* decline in price of only about 0.9%.[34] We will come back to the subject of pressure when we discuss stock issues in Chapter 15.

13-8 THE SIXTH LESSON OF MARKET EFFICIENCY: READING THE ENTRAILS

If the market is efficient, prices impound all available information. Therefore, if only we can learn to read the entrails, security prices can tell us a lot about the future. For example, in Chapter 27 we will show how information in the company's accounts can help the financial manager to estimate the probability of bankruptcy. But of course these accounts are only one of many sources of information available to investors. The return offered by the company's bonds and the performance of its common stock are, therefore, just as good indicators of bankruptcy as accounting data.[35]

Here is another example. Statistics Canada and the United States National Bureau of Economic Research have identified series of leading indicators of

---

[32] See M. Scholes, "The Market for Securities: Substitution versus Price Pressure and the Effects of Information on Share Prices," *Journal of Business*, **45**: 179–211 (April 1972). A secondary distribution is a large block of stock sold off the floor of the exchange.

[33] For example, see W.H. Mikkelson and M.M. Partch, "Stock Prices Effects and Costs of Secondary Distributions," *Journal of Financial Economics*, **14**: 165–194 (1985). M.J. Robinson and R.W. White, "Block Trading Price Effects: An Inter-Market Comparison," School of Business Administration, University of Western Ontario, mimeo. (1989) use bid and ask quotations rather than transaction prices and find that there are not any significant price effects from block trades compared to ordinary trades. They also find that the price effects on the Toronto Stock Exchange are essentially the same as those on the New York and American Stock Exchanges.

[34] See P. Asquith and D.W. Mullins, "Equity Issues and Offering Dilution," *Journal of Financial Economics*, **15**: 61–89 (January-February 1986).

[35] See W.H. Beaver, "Market Prices, Financial Ratios and the Prediction of Failure," *Journal of Accounting Research*, **6**: 179–192 (Autumn 1968).

economic activity.[36] Since stock prices are heavily influenced by economic prospects, it is not surprising that they earn relatively high marks as leading indicators. In other words, the TSE 300 Index represents an informed consensus about Canada's economic prospects.

Suppose that investors are confident that interest rates are going to rise over the next year. In that case, they will prefer to wait before they enter into long-term loans. Any firm that wants to borrow long-term money today will have to offer the inducement of a higher rate of interest. In other words, the long-term rate of interest will have to be higher than the one-year rate. Differences between the long-term interest rate and the short-term rate tell you something about what investors expect to happen to short-term rates in the future.[37]

13-9   SUMMARY

The patron saint of the Bolsa (stock exchange) in Barcelona, Spain, is Nuestra Señora de la Esperanza — Our Lady of Hope. She is the perfect patron, for we all hope for superior returns when we invest. But competition between investors will tend to produce an efficient market. In such a market, prices will rapidly impound any new information, and it will be very difficult to make consistently superior returns. We may indeed *hope*, but all we can rationally *expect* in an efficient market is that we shall obtain a return that is just sufficient to compensate us for the time value of money and for the risks we bear.

The efficient-market hypothesis comes in three different flavours. The weak form of the hypothesis states that prices efficiently reflect all the information contained in the past series of stock prices. In this case it is impossible to earn superior returns simply by looking for patterns in stock prices — in other words, price changes are random. The semistrong form of the hypothesis states that prices reflect all published information. That means it is impossible to make consistently superior returns just by reading the newspaper, looking at the company's annual accounts, and so on. The strong form of the hypothesis states that stock prices effectively impound all available information. It tells us that inside information is hard to find because in pursuing it you are in competition with thousands, perhaps millions, of active, intelligent, and greedy investors. The best you can do in this case is to assume that securities are fairly priced and to hope that one day Nuestra Señora will reward your humility.

The concept of an efficient market is astonishingly simple and remarkably well-supported by the facts. Less than 20 years ago any suggestion that security investment is a fair game was generally regarded as bizarre. Today it is not only widely accepted in business schools, but it also permeates investment practice and government policy toward the security markets.

For the corporate treasurer who is concerned with issuing or purchasing securities the efficient-market theory has obvious implications. In one sense, however, it raises more questions than it answers. The existence of efficient markets does not mean that the financial manager can let financing "take care of itself." It only provides a starting point for analysis. It is time to get down to details about securities, issue procedures, and financial institutions. We start in Chapter 14.

---

[36] See G.H. Moore and J. Shiskin, *Indicators of Business Expansions and Contraction*, National Bureau of Economic Research, New York, 1967. However, you should be cautious about placing too much faith in any such leading indicators. We are reminded of Paul Samuelson's quip that stock prices have predicted 7 of the past 5 recessions.

[37] We will discuss the relationship between short-term and long-term interest rates in Chapter 23. Notice, however, that in an efficient market the difference between the prices of *any* short-term and long-term contracts always says something about how participants expect prices to move.

FURTHER READING

A good review article on market efficiency is:

E.F. Fama, "Efficient Capital Markets: A Review of Theory and Empirical Work," *Journal of Finance*, **25**: 383–417 (May 1970).

There are several books of readings that contain a selection of the classic articles on the subject. See, for example:

P.H. Cootner (ed.), *The Random Character of Stock Market Prices*, M.I.T. Press, Cambridge, Mass., 1964.

J.H. Lorie and R.A. Brealey (eds.), *Modern Developments in Investment Management*, 2nd ed., Dryden Press, Hinsdale, Ill., 1978.

A useful collection of recent work on possible exceptions to the efficient-market theory is contained in:

"Symposium on Some Anomalous Evidence on Capital Market Efficiency," a special issue of the *Journal of Financial Economics*, **6** (June 1977).

QUIZ

1. Stock prices appear to behave as though successive values
   (a) Are random numbers
   (b) Follow regular cycles
   (c) Differ by a random number
   Which (if any) of these statements are true?

2. Supply the missing words: "There are three forms of the efficient-market hypothesis. Tests of randomness in stock prices provide evidence for the _____ form of the hypothesis. Tests of stock price reaction to well-publicized news provide evidence for the _____ form and tests of the performance of professionally managed funds provide evidence for the _____ form. Market efficiency results from competition between investors. Many investors search for new results from competition between investors. Many investors search for new information about the company's business that would help them to value the stock more accurately. This is known as _____ research. Such research helps to ensure that prices reflect all available information: in other words, it helps to keep the market efficient in the _____ form. Other investors study past stock prices for recurrent patterns that would allow them to make superior profits. This is known as _____ research. Such research helps to ensure that prices reflect all the information contained in past stock prices: in other words, it helps to keep the market efficient in the _____ form.

3. Which of the following statements (if any) are true? The efficient-market hypothesis assumes:
   (a) That there are no taxes
   (b) That there is perfect foresight
   (c) That successive price changes are independent
   (d) That investors are irrational
   (e) That there are no transaction costs
   (f) That forecasts are unbiased

4. The stock of United Boot is priced at $400 and offers a dividend yield of 2%. The company has a 2-for-1 stock split.
   (a) Other things equal, what would you expect to happen to the stock price?
   (b) Other things equal, what would you expect to happen to the dividend yield?

    (c) In practice, would you expect the stock price to fall by more or less than this amount?

    (d) Suppose a few months later United Boot announces a rise in dividends that is exactly in line with that of other companies. Would you expect the announcement to lead to a slight abnormal rise in the stock price, a slight abnormal fall, or no change?

5. True or false?

    (a) Financing decisions are less easily reversed than investment decisions.

    (b) Financing decisions don't affect the total size of the cash flows; they just affect who receives the flows.

    (c) Tests have shown that there is almost perfect negative correlation between successive price changes.

    (d) The semistrong form of the efficient-market hypothesis states that prices reflect all publicly available information.

    (e) In efficient markets the expected return on each stock is the same.

    (f) Myron Schole's study of the effect of secondary distributions provided evidence that the demand for a single company's shares is highly elastic.

QUESTIONS AND PROBLEMS

1. How would you respond to the following comments?

    (a) "Efficient market, my eye! I know of lots of investors who do crazy things."

    (b) "Efficient market? Balderdash! I know at least a dozen people who have made a bundle in the stock market."

    (c) "The trouble with the efficient-market theory is that it ignores investors' psychology."

    (d) "Despite all the limitations, the best guide to a company's value is its written-down book value. It is much more stable than market value, which depends on temporary fashions."

2. Respond to the following comments:

    (a) "The random-walk theory with its implication that investing in stocks is like playing roulette is a powerful indictment of our capital markets."

    (b) "If everyone believes you can make money by charting stock prices, then price changes won't be random."

    (c) "The random-walk theory implies that events are random but many events are not random—if it rains today, there's a fair bet that it will rain again tomorrow."

3. Which of the following observations *appear* to indicate market inefficiency? Explain whether the inefficiency is weak, semistrong, or strong. (*Note:* if the market is not weak-form-efficient, it is said to be *weak-form-inefficient*; if it is not semistrong-form-efficient, it is *semistrong-form-inefficient*, and so on.)

    (a) American tax-exempt municipal bonds offer lower pretax returns than taxable government bonds.

    (b) Managers make superior returns on their purchases of their company's stock.

    (c) There is a positive relationship between the return on the market in one quarter and the change in aggregate corporate profits in the next quarter.

    (d) There is disputed evidence that stocks that have appreciated unusually in the recent past continue to do so in the future.

    (e) The stock of an acquired firm tends to appreciate in the period before the merger announcement.

    (f) Stocks of companies with unexpectedly high earnings *appear* to offer high returns for several months after the earnings announcement.

    (g) Very risky stocks on the average give higher returns than safe stocks.

4. Look again at Figure 13-4.

    (a) Is the steady rise in the stock price before the split evidence of market inefficiency?

    (b) How do you think those stocks performed that did *not* increase their dividends by an above-average amount?

5. Stock splits are important because they convey information. Can you suggest some other financial decisions that convey information?

6. Estimate the *abnormal* return in each of the past three months for one of the stocks shown in Table 9-2.

7. Select a small sample of mutual funds and estimate whether they have been able to achieve consistently abnormal returns. (*Hint*: funds may have different degrees of risk.)

8. It is sometimes suggested that low price-earnings stock are generally underpriced. Describe a possible test of this view. Be as precise as possible.

9. "If a project provides an unusually high rate of return in one year, it will probably do so again in the next year." Does this statement make sense if you use the definition of economic rate of return that we gave in Chapter 12?

10. "Long-term interest rates are at record highs. Most companies, therefore, find it cheaper to finance with common stock or relatively inexpensive short-term bank loans." Discuss.

11. "If the efficient-market hypothesis is true, then it makes no difference what securities a company issues. All are fairly priced." Does this follow?

12. "If the efficient-market hypothesis is true, the pension fund manager might as well select a portfolio with a pin." Explain why this is not so.

13. Bond dealers buy and sell bonds at very low spreads. Used car dealers buy and sell cars at very wide spreads. What has this got to do with the strong form of the efficient-market hypothesis?

14. In May 1987 Citicorp announced that it was bolstering its loan loss reserves by $3 billion in order to reflect its exposure to Third World borrowers. Consequently, second-quarter earnings were transformed from a $.5 billion profit to a $2.5 billion loss.

    In after-hour trading the price of Citicorp stock fell sharply from its closing level of $50 but next day when the market had had a chance to digest the news, the price recovered to $53. Other bank stocks fared less well and *The Wall Street Journal* reported that Citicorp's decision "triggered a big sell-off of international banking stocks that roiled stock markets around the world."

    Comment on the Citicorp action varied. The bank's chairman claimed that "it significantly strengthens the institution" and analysts and bankers suggested that it was a notable step toward realism. For example, one argued that it was the recognition of the problem that made the difference, while another observed that the action "is merely recognizing what the stock market has been saying for several months: that the value of the sovereign debt of the big U.S. money center banks is between 25% and 50% less than is carried in their books." The *London Financial Times* made the more cautionary comment that Citicorp had "simply rearranged its balance sheet not strengthened its capital base" and the Lex column described the move as an "outsize piece of cosmetic self-indulgence rather than a great stride towards the reconstruction of Third World debt." A lead article in same paper stated that "even if all this means that Citicorp shareholders are $3 billion poorer today, the group as a whole is better placed to absorb whatever shocks lie ahead."

There was also considerable discussion of the implications for other banks. As one analyst summed up. "There's no question that the market will put higher confidence in those institutions that can reserve more fully."

Discuss the general reaction to the Citicorp announcement. It is not often that a company announces a $2.5 billion loss in one quarter and its stock price rises. Do you think that the share price reaction was consistent with an efficient market?

C · H · A · P · T · E · R

14

AN OVERVIEW OF
CORPORATE FINANCING

This chapter begins our analysis of long-term financing decisions — a task we will not complete until Chapter 26. We will devote considerable space in these chapters to the classic finance problems of dividend policy and the use of debt versus equity financing. Yet to concentrate on these problems alone would miss the enormous *variety* of financing instruments that are used by companies today.

Look, for example, at Table 14-1. It shows the many long-term securities issued by Canadian Pacific. Yet CP has not come close to exhausting the different kinds of securities that exist.

This chapter introduces you to the principal families of securities, and it explains how they are used by corporations. We also draw attention to some interesting aspects of the behaviour of the firms issuing these securities.

Table 14-1
Large firms often use many different kinds of securities. Look at the long-term securities that have been issued by Canadian Pacific Limited and its subsidiaries. Note that there are several issues of most of these security types.

Stock:
    Ordinary (common) stock
    Cumulative redeemable preferred shares
    Noncumulative preferred shares
    Sterling perferred shares
Long-term debt:
    Collateral trust bonds
    Equipment trust certificates
    Bank loans
    Mortgages
    Notes
    Guaranteed notes
    Sinking fund bonds
    First mortgage sinking fund bonds
    Sinking fund debentures
    Floating-rate income debentures
Other liabilities:
    Perpetual 4% consolidated debenture stock (denominated in pounds sterling, U.S. dollars and Canadian dollars)

Table 14-2
Book value of common stockholders' equity of Canadian Pacific, December 31, 1988 (figures in thousands)

Common shares	1,182,300
Premium on stock and other paid-in surplus	1,467,700
Retained income	4,638,200
	$7,288,200

Note:
Shares

Authorized shares	Unlimited
Issued shares	316,858

Source: Canadian Pacific Limited 1988 Annual Report.

14-1   COMMON STOCK

Table 14-2 shows the common equity of Canadian Pacific as it was reported in the company's books at the end of 1988.

The maximum number of shares that can be issued is known as the *authorized share capital*—for CP, it is unlimited. This maximum is specified in the firm's articles of incorporation and can be changed only with the permission of the stockholders. CP has already issued 316,857,840 shares.

CP originally issued its shares with a par value of $1.67 per share. Then the Canada Business Corporations Act required firms to convert their par-value shares to shares of no par value because par value has no economic significance. The price of the shares CP sold to the public usually exceeded par value. Under the old par-value system, if CP sold 100,000 shares for $5.00, the common stock account would have increased by 100,000 × 1.67 = $167,000 and the paid-in capital account would have increased by 100,000 × (5.00 − 1.67) = $333,000. These distinctions are retained in CP's balance sheet, although the value of any new share issues will simply be added to the common share account.

Usually CP pays out less than half its earnings as dividends. The remainder is retained in the business and used to finance new investment. The cumulative amount of retained earnings is $4,638,200.

Stockholders' Rights

The common stockholders are the owners of the corporation. They therefore have a general *pre-emptive right* to anything of value that the company may wish to distribute. They also have the ultimate control of the company's affairs. In practice this control is limited to a right to vote, either in person or by proxy, on appointments to the board of directors and a number of other matters.

If the corporation's articles specify a *majority voting system*, each director is voted upon separately and stockholders can cast one vote for each share they own. If the articles permit *cumulative voting*, the directors are voted upon jointly and the stockholders can, if they want, allot all their votes to just one candidate.[1] Cumulative voting makes it easier for a minority group among the stockholders

---

[1] For example, suppose there are five directors to be elected and you own 100 shares. You therefore have a total of 5 × 100 = 500 votes. Under the majority voting system, you can cast a maximum of 100 votes for any one candidate. Under a cumulative voting system, you can cast all 500 votes for your favourite candidate.

to elect directors representing the group's interests. That is why minority groups devote so much of their efforts to campaigning for cumulative voting.

The issues on which stockholders are asked to vote are rarely contested, particularly in the case of large, publicly traded firms. Occasionally there are proxy contests in which the firm's existing management and directors compete with outsiders for control of the corporation. But the odds are stacked against the outsiders, for the insiders can get the firm to pay all the costs of presenting their case and obtaining votes.

Most companies issue just one class of common stock. Occasionally, however, a firm may have two classes outstanding, which differ in their right to vote and receive dividends. Suppose a firm needs fresh equity capital but its present stockholders do not want to relinquish their control of the firm. The existing shares could be labeled class A and class B shares issued to outside investors. The class B shares could have limited voting privileges, although they might sell for less as a result.[2] Several Canadian companies have such class B shares with restricted voting privileges. A spectacular example of the discount at which they can trade is provided by a recent case in which a group of independent Canadian Tire store dealers offered to purchase the Canadian Tire Class A voting shares for $160.24, while they made no such offer for the Class B nonvoting stock, which traded at about $14.50. Their offer would have given them 49% of the Class A stock, which would have given them control of the firm, since they already had 17% of the voting stock. The maneuver was ultimately stopped in court. Now the Ontario Securities Commission requires that new issues of nonvoting stock have a "coattail provision" that requires a takeover bid for the voting shares to be extended to the nonvoting shareholders.[3]

The New York Stock Exchange (NYSE) has traditionally stood for "one share, one vote." Unlike the Toronto Stock Exchange, the American Stock Exchange, and the over-the-counter market, the NYSE has turned down companies attempting to list two or more share classes with different voting rights. But the NYSE is under pressure from companies which want to deter hostile takeover bids by concentrating voting power in a class of stock which can be held in friendly hands. These companies feel they deserve protection against "corporate raiders" and "takeover pirates." On the other hand, perhaps these pirates capture only the slower ships; many investors believe that the takeover specialists prey mostly on entrenched management teams that are not doing a good job for their stockholders.

14-2   A FIRST LOOK AT CORPORATE DEBT

When they borrow money, companies promise to make regular interest payments and to repay the principal (that is, the original amount borrowed) according to

---

[2] R.C. Lease, J.J. McConnell, and W.H. Mikkleson have studied companies with two classes of publicly traded shares. They found that the class with superior voting rights almost always traded at the higher price. Typical premiums were on the order of 2 to 4%. See "The Market Value of Control in Publicly Traded Corporations," *Journal of Financial Economics,* **11**: 439–471 (April 1983), especially table 4, pp. 460–461. For evidence on the determinants of the discount accorded nonvoting shares, see C.M. Robinson and A.D. White, "Empirical Evidence on the Relative Valuation of Voting and Restricted Shares," *Canadian Journal of Administrative Science,* **7**: 9–18 (December 1990), and E. Maynes, "Takeover Rights and the Value of Restricted Shares," working paper, Faculty of Administrative Studies, York University (May 1989).

[3] For further information on the Canadian Tire case, see D. Toole, "A Subordinate Cause," *Moneywise,* Financial Post, 22–26 (August 1987).

an agreed schedule. However, this liability is limited. Stockholders have the right to default on any debt obligation, handing over the corporation's assets to the lenders. Clearly they will choose to do this only if the value of the assets is less than the amount of the debt.

Because lenders are not regarded as proprietors of the firm, they do not normally have any voting power. The company's payments of interest are regarded as a cost and are deducted from taxable income. Thus interest is paid from *before-tax* income. In contrast, dividends on common stock are paid out of *after-tax* income. Therefore the government provides a tax subsidy on the use of debt that it does not provide on equity.

Debt Comes in Many Forms

Some orderly scheme of classification is essential to cope with the almost infinite variety of corporate debt claims. We will spend several chapters examining the various features of corporate debt. But here is a preliminary guide to the major distinguishing characteristics.

Maturity   Long-term debt is an obligation repayable more than one year from the date of issue. Debt due in less than one year is carried on the balance sheet as a current liability. Clearly, however, it is artificial to call a 364-day note short-term and a 366-day note long-term (except on leap years).

There are corporate bonds of nearly every conceivable maturity. Canadian Pacific's **perpetuities** have no specified maturity. They may survive forever. At the other extreme, we find firms borrowing literally overnight. We describe how this is done in Chapter 32.

Repayment Provision   Long-term loans are commonly repaid in a steady, regular way, perhaps after an initial grace period. For publicly traded bonds this is done by means of a **sinking fund**. Each year the firm pays a sum of cash into a sinking fund which is then used to repurchase the bonds.

Most firms issuing debt to the public reserve the right to **call** the debt—that is, to repay and retire all the bonds in a given issue before the final maturity date. Call prices are specified when the debt is originally issued. Usually lenders are given at least five years of call protection. During this period the firm cannot call the bonds.

Seniority   Some debt instruments are **subordinated**. In the event of default the subordinated lender gets in line behind the firm's general creditors. The subordinated lender holds a junior claim and is paid after all senior creditors are satisfied.

When you lend money to a firm you can assume that you hold a senior claim unless the debt agreement says otherwise. However, this does not always put you at the front of the line, for the firm may have set aside some of its assets specifically for the protection of other creditors. That brings us to our next classification.

Security   We have used the word *bond* to refer to all kinds of corporate debt, but in some contexts it means **secured debt;** often bonds are secured by mortgages on plant and equipment, and unsecured long-term claims are usually called *debentures.*[4] In the event of default, the bondholders have a general claim on the mortgaged assets; investors holding debentures have a general claim on the unmortgaged assets but only a junior claim on the mortgaged assets.

---

[4] The terminology can be confusing. A *debenture* in the United States and Canada signifies unsecured debt; in Great Britain it usually refers to *secured* debt.

Floating versus Fixed Rates   The interest payment or *coupon* on most long-term debt is fixed at the time of issue. If a $1,000 bond is issued when long-term interest rates are 10%, the firm continues to pay $100 per year regardless of how interest rates fluctuate.

Loan agreements negotiated with banks usually incorporate a **floating rate**. For example, your firm may be offered a loan at "1% above prime." The **prime rate**, which is the interest rate the bank charges on loans to its most creditworthy customers, is adjusted up or down as interest rates on traded securities change. Therefore when the prime rate changes, the interest on your floating rate loan also changes.

Default Risk   Seniority and security do not guarantee payment. A bond can be senior and secured, but still as risky as a vertiginous tightrope walker — it depends on the value and the risk of the issuing firm's assets.

A debt security is **investment grade** if it qualifies for one of the top four ratings from the ratings services such as the Canadian Bond Rating Service, the Dominion Bond Rating Service, Moody's or Standard and Poor's. (We describe the rating criteria in Chapter 23.) Below-investment-grade debt is traded in the so-called **junk bond market.**

Some junk debt issues are "fallen angels," securities issues as investment grade later fell from grace. But in the late 1970s, a *new-issue* junk bond market was created. Companies discovered a pool of investors willing to accept unusually high default risk in exchange for high promised yields. New issues of junk bonds in the United States were about $1.5 billion in 1978 and $34.2 billion in 1986.[5] Many of these issues were made on short notice to finance mergers and acquisitions, such as Campeau Corporation's acquisition of Federated Stores.

Junk bonds combine the tax advantage of debt with the high risk and return characteristics of equity. In Chapter 18 we discuss the relative merits of debt and equity financing. The relative tax advantage of debt over equity is much stronger in the United States than in Canada, because Canada offers tax relief to equity holders with a dividend tax credit. Thus, the new-issue junk bond market is not nearly so significant in Canada as it is in the United States. For example, although Campeau Corporation is a Canadian firm, it issued its junk debt in the United States when it acquired the U.S.-based Federated Stores. The acquisition was so large that Campeau could not have quickly obtained equity or debt financing in Canada.

Country and Currency   Many large firms, particularly those having significant overseas operations, borrow abroad. If such a firm wants long-term debt, it will probably borrow by an issue of **eurobonds** sold simultaneously in several countries; if it wants short-term debt, it will probably obtain a **eurodollar** loan from a bank.

Corporations sometimes issue bonds denominated in foreign currencies. Often their overseas subsidiaries borrow directly from banks in the countries in which the subsidiaries are operating.

A Debt by Any Other Name   The word *debt* sounds straightforward, but companies enter into a number of financial arrangements that look suspiciously like debt but are treated differently in the accounts. Some of these obligations are easily identifiable. For example, accounts payable are simply obligations to pay for goods that have already been

---

[5] See E.I. Altman, "The Anatomy of the High-Yield Bond Market," *Financial Analysts Journal,* **45**: 12–25 (July-August 1987).

delivered. Other arrangements are not so easily detected. For example, instead of borrowing money to buy equipment, many companies **lease** or rent it on a long-term basis. As we will show in Chapter 26, such arrangements are economically equivalent to secured long-term debt.

14-3 PREFERRED STOCK

In the chapters that follow, we shall have much more to say about common stock and debt. **Preferred stock** will occupy less of our time later on. However, we shall see that it sometimes has tax advantages compared to debt and that it is a useful method of financing in mergers and certain other special situations.

Preferred stock is legally an equity security. Despite the fact, like debt, that it offers a fixed dividend, payment of the dividend is almost invariably within the complete discretion of the directors. The only stipulation is that no dividends may be paid on the common until after the preferred dividend has been paid. For some older issues the firm could pay common dividends *without* making up preferred dividends that had been skipped in previous years. This gave an opportunity for considerable abuse. Therefore, almost all new issues specifically provide that the obligation should be **cumulative** so that the firm must pay *all* past preferred dividends before common stockholders get a cent.

Like common stock, preferred stock does not have a final repayment date. However, roughly half the issues make some provision for periodic retirement and in many cases companies have an option to **redeem** or call preferred stock at a specified price. If the company goes out of business, the claim of the preferred stock is junior to that of any debt but senior to that of common stock.

The contract that sets out the terms of the preferred stock also imposes restrictions on the company, including some limits on payments to common stockholders either as dividends or through repurchase of the common stock. These restrictions may also stipulate that the company cannot make any payments to common stockholders unless it is able to maintain a minimum level of common equity and a minimum ratio of working capital to debt and preferred. Other clauses typically require that further issues of securities must have the consent of two-thirds of the preferred shareholders unless the ratio of equity to all debt and preferred stock exceeds a specified minimum.

Preferred stock rarely confers full voting privileges. However, almost always the consent of two-thirds of the preferred holders must be obtained on all matters affecting the seniority of their claim. Most issues also provide the holder with some voting power if the preferred dividend is skipped.

Unlike interest payments on debt, dividends are not an allowable deduction from taxable corporate income. Thus, the dividend is paid from after-tax income. However, dividend income is generally not taxed when received by Canadian corporations, and is taxed at reduced or even negative rates when received by individuals. (This is discussed more fully in Chapter 16.) Thus, preferred shares are a popular method of financing when the tax benefits in the hands of the investors are worth more than the tax burden imposed on the issuer.

For example, suppose a bank will lend at an interest rate of 10%. After paying tax on the interest at 36%, the bank will receive a net return of $(1 - 0.36) \times 10 = 6.4\%$. Alternatively, the bank can recover an equally high return by buying a preferred stock with a tax-free yield of 6.4%. On the other hand, if a corporation pays no taxes, for example, it is better off paying a 6.4% yield on preferred stock than 10% interest on a loan. Fearing an erosion of its tax base, Parliament made it harder for banks to buy preferred stock from other corporations with section 258 of the Income Tax Act in 1979.

Moreover, the dividend tax credit also makes preferred shares a popular financing vehicle in Canada. But, in the United States, preferred shares are relatively rare, since they are taxed at full personal rates. They are sometimes purchased by corporations, since U.S. corporations only have to count 20% of a dividend as taxable income. Also, regulated American public utilities, which can take tax payments into account when negotiating the rates they charge customers, can effectively pass the tax disadvantage of preferred stock on to the consumer. As a result, a large fraction of the dollar value of new American offerings of nonconvertible preferred stock consists of issues by utilities.

14-4   CONVERTIBLE SECURITIES

Corporations often issue securities with terms that can be altered subsequently at the option of the firm, the holder of the security, or both. We have already seen one example, the call option on corporate bonds, which allows the firm to retire a bond issue before its maturity date.

Options often have a substantial effect on value. The most dramatic example is provided by a **warrant** which is *nothing but* an option issued by a corporation. The owner of a warrant can purchase a set number of common shares at a set price on or before a set date. For example, in February 1990 you could have purchased a Cominco Resources International warrant for $0.11. The owner of 3 of those warrants had the right to purchase 1.02 common shares of Cominco Resources for $2.70 at any time up to and including May 26, 1990. Warrants are often sold as part of a package of other securities. Thus, the firm might make a "combination offer" of bonds and warrants.

A **convertible bond** is like a package of corporate bond and a warrant. There is one principal difference. When the owners of a convertible wish to exercise their option to buy shares, they do not pay cash—they just give up the bond. The bond is *converted* into a specific number of shares.[6]

These examples do not exhaust the options encountered by the financial manager. Far from it: we will see in Chapter 20 that *all* corporate securities can be analyzed in terms of options. In fact, once you read that chapter and learn how to analyze options, you will find that they are all around you.

14-5   VARIETY'S THE VERY SPICE OF LIFE

We have indicated several dimensions along which corporate securities can be classified. The financial manager has at least that many alternatives in designing corporate securities. As long as you can convince investors of its attractions, you can issue a convertible, callable, subordinated, floating-rate bond denominated in Deutschmarks. Rather than combining features of existing securities, you may create an entirely new one. Firms and countries that produce commodities like silver and oil have issued "commodity-linked" bonds, which pay off in either money or in the underlying commodity. For example, in 1980, the Sunshine Mining Company, operator of the largest American silver mine, issued $50 million in bonds backed by silver. Each $1,000 bond pays a coupon rate of $8\frac{1}{2}$%, and at maturity Sunshine Mining promises to pay either the $1,000 face value or the market value of 50 ounces of silver, whichever is greater.[7]

---

[6] Convertible preferred is also issued, often to finance mergers.

[7] This example is cited in Eduardo Schwartz, "The Pricing of Commodity-Linked Bonds," *Journal of Finance*, **37**: 525–539 (May 1982). Schwartz also describes how to determine the market value of such bonds using the Black-Scholes option pricing methodology of Chapter 20.

Variety is intrinsically good. People have different tastes, levels of wealth, rates of tax and so on. Why not offer them a choice? Of course the problem is that it may be expensive for the firm to design new securities. But if you can think of a new security that will appeal to investors, you may be able to increase the value of your company.

Financial market innovation in the 1980s has been usually fast and extensive. New varieties of debt seem to appear almost daily. In addition, there has been a remarkable growth in the use of *derivative instruments*. These securities are side bets on interest rates, commodity prices, and so on. Firms do not issue these securities to raise money; they buy or sell them to protect against adverse changes in various external factors.

Here are four types of side bets that have experienced rapid growth in the last decade.

Traded Options   An option gives the firm the right (but not the obligation) to buy or sell an asset in the future at a price tht is agreed upon today. We have already seen that the firm sometimes issues options either on their own or tacked on to other securities. But, in addition, there is a huge volume of dealing in options that is created by specialized options exchanges. Trading in stock options took off in 1973 when the Chicago Board Options Exchange was established. Now you can deal in options to buy or sell common stocks, bonds, currencies, and commodities. We describe options and their applications in Chapters 20 and 21.

Futures   A futures contract is an order that you place in advance to buy or sell an asset or commodity. The price is fixed when you place the order but you don't pay for the asset until the delivery date. Futures markets have existed for a long time in commodities such as wheat, soybeans, and copper. The major development of the 1970s occurred when the futures exchanges began to trade contracts on financial assets, such as bonds, currencies, and stock market indexes. Within 10 years, the worldwide volume of transactions in these financial futures increased from zero to more than $10 *trillion* a year.

Forwards   Futures contracts are standardized products bought and sold on organized exchanges. A forward contract is a tailor-made futures contract that is not traded on an organized exchange. For example, firms that need to protect themselves against a change in the exchange rate have usually bought or sold forward currency through a bank. Since 1983, banks have also been prepared to enter into forward contracts to borrow or lend money. If you buy a forward rate agreement (FRA), you agree to borrow in the future at a rate that is fixed today; if you sell an FRA, you agree to lend in the future at a preset rate.

Swaps   Suppose that you would like to swap your dollar debt for Deutschmark debt. In this case, you can arrange for a bank to pay you each year the dollars that are needed to service your dollar debt, and in exchange you agree to pay the bank the cost of servicing a Deutschmark loan. Such an agreement is known as a *currency swap*.

Companies also enter into *interest rate swaps*. For example, the bank might agree to pay you each year the cost of servicing a fixed-rate loan, and in return you agree to pay the bank the cost of servicing a similar floating-rate loan.

We discuss swaps, as well as forward and futures contracts, in Chapter 25.

The Process of Innovation

Developing a new financial instrument is like developing any other product. Initially, the emphasis is on creativity and experiment. Then, as the market develops, the focus switches to low-cost methods of volume production. Finally, it becomes economic to offer the customer optional extras.

For example, when swaps were invented, banks were unwilling to take one side of the swap for their own accounts. They acted solely as arrangers and looked about for another firm that was prepared to take on the other side of the bargain. No two swaps were alike, and they could take weeks to fix up. By 1986, banks were prepared to take on the risks of swaps themselves, documentation was standardized, and you could arrange a swap within hours. Banks were also beginning to work on the problem of making it easy for one party to resell his or her side of the swap to someone else. By the time you read this chapter, there probably will be a regular market for trading swaps. As swaps have become more standardized and cheaper to arrange, banks have also been able to offer extra features. For example, you can now buy a forward swap and even an option on a swap (or "swaption").

What are the causes of financial innovation? One answer is taxes and regulation. In the following chapters, we shall come across a number of cases where taxes and government regulation have in effect subsidized innovation. Buy why do many new instruments survive long after the initial government stimulus has been removed? And why has so much innovation occurred in the last 10 years? Taxes and regulation have been around for much longer than that.

A second important motive for innovation is to widen investor choice. In particular, the sharp recent fluctuations in exchange rates and interest rates have increased the demand by firms and investors for ways to hedge themselves against such hazards.

But this still cannot be the entire explanation. For example, firms have long been able to protect themselves against exchange rate changes by buying or selling forward currency through a bank. So why are traded currency futures needed as well? The answer is that many of these new financial instruments are low-cost ways to mass-produce a particular service. These low production costs reflect improvements in telecommunications and computing which make it possible to disseminate prices and execute orders rapidly throughout the world.

There have also been developments in the design of instruments and trading systems. For example, if you sell a commodity future and don't buy it back, you will eventually have to deliver that commodity to the buyer. This would not be possible with many financial futures (try delivering a stock market index to someone). The novel feature of these contracts is that instead of delivering the asset at maturity, you just settle up the profit or loss in cash.

That completes our tour of corporate securities and derivative instruments. You may feel like the tourist who has just emerged from 12 cathedrals in 5 days. But there will be plenty of time in later chapters for reflection and analysis.

14-6   PATTERNS OF CORPORATE FINANCING

Let us now turn to Table 14-3, which summarizes the relative importance of alternative sources of capital for corporations in Canada. The most striking aspect of this table is the dominance of internally generated cash (line 6), defined as

Table 14-3
Sources and Uses of Funds in Nonfinancial Corporations

	Sources and Uses (% of total)[a]												
	1962	1963	1964	1965	1966	1967	1968	1969	1970	1971	1972	1973	1974
Uses:													
1. Capital expenditures	66	67	64	57	68	68	68	75	77	61	69	58	56
2. Investment in inventories	7	8	10	13	10	0	5	8	5	3	7	9	14
3. Investment in liquid assets	11	11	13	16	16	24	22	3	8	24	14	18	12
4. Investment in accounts receivable	16	13	13	14	6	8	5	14	11	11	10	15	18
5. Total expenditures	100	100	100	100	100	100	100	100	100	100	100	100	100
Sources:													
6. Internally generated cash[b]	75	75	68	55	57	62	69	70	68	53	61	52	47
7. Financial deficit (5 − 6) = required external financing	25	25	32	45	43	38	31	30	32	47	39	48	53
Financial deficit covered by:													
8. Net stock issues	7	4	2	3	7	5	9	8	6	2	3	1	−2
9. Net increase in long-term debt	11	12	14	16	17	14	13	17	17	15	8	5	8
10. Net increase in short-term debt	17	6	8	10	10	8	5	13	9	18	15	20	25
11. Increase in accounts payable	8	12	8	14	5	7	3	3	3	8	12	15	19
12. Other liabilities	5	2	3	2	3	2	6	1	1	7	2	6	9
13. Discrepancy[c]	22	10	3	1	−1	−2	5	11	4	4	0	0	6
	Expenditure and Deficit (millions of dollars)												
Total expenditures	5,390	5,870	7,622	9,816	10,157	9,645	9,491	10,005	10,735	14,592	14,403	20,484	25,849
Financial deficit	1,356	1,468	2,469	4,383	4,322	3,689	2,938	3,042	3,430	6,812	5,659	9,772	13,679

Table 14-3 (continued)

Sources and Uses (% of total)[a]

	1975	1976	1977	1978	1979	1980	1981	1982	1983	1984	1985	1986	1987
Uses:													
1. Capital expenditures	66	72	66	56	55	71	80	121	85	67	82	84	69
2. Investment in inventories	3	7	7	1	8	−5	0	−37	−5	10	4	4	3
3. Investment in liquid assets	19	9	20	22	24	15	8	13	12	15	8	11	20
4. Investment in accounts receivable	12	11	7	21	13	18	12	3	8	9	7	1	8
5. Total expenditures	100	100	100	100	100	100	100	100	100	100	100	100	100
Sources:													
6. Internally generated cash[b]	58	71	65	51	47	58	44	64	84	74	79	73	68
7. Financial deficit (5−6) = required external financing	42	29	35	49	53	42	56	36	16	26	21	27	32
Financial deficit covered by:													
8. Net stock issues	3	1	6	7	−1	0	−11	5	9	6	1	10	7
9. Net increase in long-term debt	10	12	16	8	3	8	14	14	12	4	9	12	12
10. Net increase in short-term debt	14	23	14	12	29	29	46	22	−15	12	14	12	18
11. Increase in accounts payable	11	4	4	17	13	9	13	−3	10	8	4	1	5
12. Other liabilities	2	2	2	9	10	7	7	1	4	−1	−1	0	−5
13. Discrepancy[c]	−1	13	5	5	1	12	13	3	3	4	7	7	4
Expenditure and Deficit (millions of dollars)													
Total expenditures	23,395	23,925	26,114	36,129	48,982	46,542	50,654	29,421	37,196	51,843	51,800	54,062	72,030
Financial deficit	9,752	6,887	9,179	17,706	25,737	19,763	28,283	10,672	6,132	13,524	10,626	14,612	23,247

[a] Columns may not add to 100% because of rounding.

[b] Net income plus capital cost allowance and depletion less cash dividends paid to stockholders.

[c] As reported by Statistics Canada; the excess of external financing over the financial deficit.

Derived from: CANSIM Matrix 702. CANSIM is the registered trademark for Statistics Canada's machine-readable data base.

cash flow from operations less cash dividends paid to stockholders.[8] Internally generated cash normally covers a majority of firms' capital requirements: it fell below half of total expenditures in only five years.

Do Firms Rely Too Heavily on Internal Funds?

As we have already noted, retained earnings are additional capital invested by shareholders—they represent, in effect, a compulsory issue of shares. A firm which retains $1 million could have paid out the cash as dividends and then sold new common shares to raise additional capital. In the same way, any reinvestment of dollars labeled "depreciation" amounts to investing dollars that could have been paid to investors. The opportunity cost of capital ought not to depend on whether the project is financed by depreciation, retained earnings, or a new stock issue.

Some people have been distressed by the heavy reliance on internal funds. Gordon Donaldson, in a field survey of corporate debt policies, encountered several firms which acknowledged "that it was their long-term object to hold to a rate of growth which was consistent with their capacity to generate funds internally." A number of other firms appeared to apply more stringent criteria to expenditure proposals that might require outside finance. Donaldson pointed out that depending on retained earnings is the line of least resistance for most companies; it allows them to avoid "the glare of publicity and shareholder attention" which accompanies a public issue. His concern may well be justified, but there may be other, less sinister explanations.[9]

William Baumol has expressed a slightly different concern about the use of retained earnings. He argued as follows:

> ... A very substantial proportion of American business firms manage to avoid the *direct* disciplining influences of the securities market, or at least to evade the type of discipline which can be imposed by the provision of funds to inefficient firms only on extremely unfavourable terms. A company which makes no direct use of the stock market as a source of capital can, apparently, proceed to make its decisions confident in its immunity from this type of punishment by the impersonal mechanism of the stock exchange.[10]

In this passage, Baumol echoes a widespread belief that internal funds are allocated by management, whereas external funds are somehow allocated by investors. It is not obvious that this is true. For example, if the authorized capital is sufficient, a company can *always* raise money by the sale of shares as long as

---

[8] In Table 14-3, internally generated cash was calculated by adding CCA (or depreciation) and depletion to retained earnings for the year. CCA and depletion are noncash expenses. Thus retained earnings for the year understates the cash flow available for reinvestment.

[9] See G. Donaldson, *Corporate Debt Capacity*, Division of Research, Graduate School of Business Administration, Harvard University, Boston, 1961, Chap. 3, especially pp. 51–56. One less sinister explanation would be the following: as we suggested in Chapter 11, if management has to invest on the basis of severely biased cash-flow forecasts, it may well use such simple capital-rationing schemes as a crude guide to an appropriate rate of expansion.

[10] Reprinted by permission of the publisher from *The Stock Market and Economic Efficiency* by W.J. Baumol (New York, Fordham University Press, 1965), copyright © 1965 by Fordham University Press, p. 70. Another related concern is commonly expressed by left-wing politicians in Great Britain. They argue that since retained earnings provide the bulk of industry's capital needs, the securities markets serve little function. Of course, the individual shareholders are happy for the firm to plow back their money *only* because the securities markets allow them to sell their stock if they need liquidity.

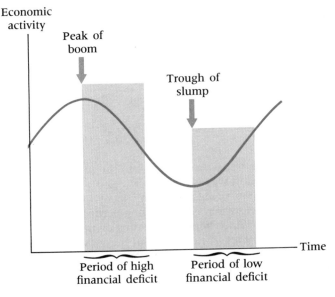

Figure 14-1   Companies are generally short of funds just after the peak of a boom. They need new funds least just after the bottom of a slump.

it sets the price sufficiently low. Any discipline, therefore, must exist solely in the mind of the manager.

The subject is not one on which we can take a strong stand. Donaldson's diagnosis of management's motives is by no means implausible, but equally we have no good reason to suppose that managers would invest more wisely if they were forced to use the capital market more frequently.[11]

When Do Firms Need External Finance?

Line 7 of Table 14-3 shows that corporations have incurred a financial deficit in every year since 1962. Thus they have been persistent sellers of financial assets.

The financial deficit is linked to the general level of economic activity. Figure 14-1 illustrates this. In general, the deficit is lowest when the economy is pulling out of a recession. At this point companies are operating well below capacity, and so even a small increase in sales can produce a sharp improvement in profits and retained earnings. But the *need* for funds does not increase so sharply. As long as companies have significant spare capacity, management is unlikely to authorize major investment in new plant. Furthermore, the pickup in sales may reduce inventories, which releases cash.

The financial deficit is usually largest when economic activity begins to turn down. The decline in sales brings about a fall in retained earnings but the high level of investment in plant and inventory continues until firms have managed to adjust their spending to the gathering recession.

It is natural to associate bad times with a shortage of funds. But for corporations as a whole the opposite relationship holds.

---

[11] Even if Donaldson is right, how do we know whether managers impose too high a standard for external capital or too low a one for retained earnings?

Timing Debt and Equity Issues

A further interesting aspect of Table 14-3 is the extent of the year-to-year variation in stock issues. Compare 1981 with 1983 (an extreme example but it illustrates the point):

Stock Issues	1981	1983
As % of total corporate sources of funds	−11	9
As % of financial deficit	−19	57
Absolute amount, in millions	−5,345	3,516

In 1981, stock issues were *negative* to the tune of $5.3 billion but, just two years later, $3.5 billion was issued.

Some companies did raise new money by stock issues in 1981. But this new supply was overwhelmed by the unprecedented scale of stock repurchases made by companies which bought back their own shares, or purchased and retired *other* companies' shares in the course of mergers and acquisitions.[12]

Now 1981 was clearly an exceptional year. What can we say about the behaviour of firms in the longer run?

Several things seem to be happening simultaneously: First, we would expect firms to seek a balance of debt and equity.

If debt weighs too heavily in their capital structure, they acquire equity by retaining earnings or issuing stock. If the debt ratio is too low, they favour debt over equity. But firms are never precisely on target. They are continually buffeted by changing business conditions. They always move toward the targets but they hardly ever get there. Because the adjustment process is slow, it does not preclude substantial short-term fluctuations in capital structure and in external financing by corporations.

Some of the fluctuations in stock issues can be explained by managers' attempts to time these issues. Studies by Taggart and others in the United States and by Marsh in Great Britain show that stock is more likely to be issued after stock prices have risen.[13] The rational explanation for this is that an increase in the stock price signals expanded investment opportunities, and the need to finance these investments really prompts the stock issues. Unfortunately the rational explanation doesn't explain all the facts. It tells us why firms raise more money in *total* when stock prices are historically high but it does not tell us why they only issue more equity and not more debt. If anything, a company should be even more ready to issue debt at such times, because the company's higher market value and enhanced prospects increase its "debt capacity." Yet Marsh finds exactly the opposite behaviour: debt issues do *not* respond to high stock prices, other things being equal. Firms in effect substitute equity for debt issues at precisely the time they should find it easier to borrow more.

Why should managers act in this way? Do they believe that equity is cheap when stock prices are historically high? As we pointed out in Chapter 13, in an efficient market buying or selling stock cannot be a positive-NPV transaction regardless of whether the price is historically high or historically low.

---

[12] We discuss share repurchases in Chapter 16, and mergers and acquisitions in Chapter 33.

[13] R.A. Taggart, "A Model of Corporate Financing Decisions," *Journal of Finance,* **32**: 1467–1484 (December 1977); P. Asquith and D.W. Mullins, Jr., "Equity Issues and Offering Dilution," *Journal of Financial Economics,* **15**: 16–89 (January-February 1986). P. Marsh, "The Choice Between Equity and Debt: An Empirical Study," *Journal of Finance,* **37**: 121–144, (March 1982.)

We don't know why managers tend to issue equity rather than debt after a rise in the stock price. It may reflect confused interpretations of price-earnings and market-book ratios. Some financial managers still think that a high P/E indicates a low rate of return demanded by stockholders and a good time to issue equity. Many of the same managers worry that selling stock at low prices relative to book value will "dilute" earnings per share. These managers defer issues when stock price is low, and their stored up demand for fresh equity is released after prices rise.

The Dilution Fallacy

The popular P/E fallacies were amply described in Chapter 4. But we haven't yet dissected the dilution fallacy.

The imagined dangers of dilution are dramatized by the sad tale of Quangle Hats. Quangle's profitability is as follows:

- Book net worth $100,000
- Number of shares   1,000
- Book value per share $100,000/1,000 = $100
- Net earnings $8,000
- Earnings per share $8,000/1,000 = $8.00
- Price-earnings ratio   10
- Stock price   10 × $8.00 = $80.00
- Total market value $80,000

The total amount of money that has been put up by Quangle's stockholders is $100,000 or $100 per share. But that investment is earning only $8 per share—an 8% book return. Investors evidently regard this return as inadequate, for they are willing to pay only $80 per share for Quangle stock.

Now, suppose that Quangle raises $10,000 by issuing 125 additional shares at the market price of $80 per share; suppose also that the $10,000 is invested to earn a return of 8%. In that case, we would expect investors to continue to pay $10 for each $1 of Quangle's earnings. Now we have:

	Before the Issue	After the Issue
Book net worth	$100,000	$110,000
Number of shares	1,000	1,125
Book value per share	$100,000/1,000 = $100	$110,000/1,125 = $97.78
Net earnings	$8,000	8% of book net worth = $8,800
Earnings per share	$8,000/1,000 = $8.00	$8,800/1,125 = $7.82
Price-earnings ratio	10	10
Stock price	10 × $8.00 = $80.00	10 × $7.82 = $78.20
Total market value	$80,000	$88,000

We note that selling stock below book *does* decrease book value per share and stock price as well.

But there are two things wrong with our example. First, we assumed investors could be tricked in paying $80 for shares shortly destined to be worth $78.20. Actually, if Quangle wishes to raise $10,000, it will have to offer shares *worth* $10,000. And since we know that aggregate market value after the stock issue is $88,000, the *original* 1,000 shares must end up with an aggregate value of $78,000. The price per share will therefore be $78,000/1,000 = $78 and the firm will have to issue $10,000/$78 = 128 shares to raise the capital it requires.

Many financial analysts would stop at this point, satisfied that they had "proved" the folly of selling stock for less than book value. But there is a second thing wrong with our example: We never questioned Quangle's decision to expand. It is raising $10,000 and getting only $8,000 in additional market value. In other words, the market's verdict is that expansion has an NPV of $-$2,000. Note that this is exactly the loss suffered by the original shareholders.

What if the investment earned a *10%* return? In that case the issue of shares would cause the firm's market value to increase by $10,000 to $90,000, and the earnings per share and stock price would be unchanged. Quangle could therefore raise $10,000 by selling only $10,000/$80 = 125 new shares.

The point is simple. There is no harm whatsoever in selling stock at prices below book value per share, as long as investors know that you can earn an adequate rate of return on the new money. If the firm has good projects and needs equity capital to finance them, then "dilution" should not bar it from going to the market.

Has Capital Structure Changed?

In 1974 *Business Week* devoted a special edition to "The Debt Economy," which described a United States in which everybody appeared to be a borrower and there was not a lender in sight. Prominent among these borrowers were American corporations, which, it was pointed out, had tripled their debt in the previous 15 years. With typical understatement, *Business Week* concluded that this debt imposed "an ominously heavy burden with the world as it is today—ravaged by inflation, threatened with economic depression, torn apart by the massive redistribution . . . "[14]

Is there really a trend to heavier reliance on debt financing? This is a hard question to answer in general, because financing policy varies so much from industry to industry and firm to firm. But a few statistics will do no harm as long as you keep these difficulties in mind.

Table 14-4 shows the aggregate balance sheets of all manufacturing corporations in Canada and the United States at the end of 1986. If all Canadian or American manufacturing corporations were merged into one gigantic firm, Table 14-4 would be their balance sheets.

The table shows that Canadian manufacturing corporations had total book assets of $179.0 million. On the "right-hand side" of the balance sheet, we find total long-term liabilities of $49.2 million and stockholders' equity of $87.8 million.

What was the debt ratio of manufacturing corporations in Canada in 1986? It depends on what you mean by "debt." If all liabilities are counted as debt, the debt ratio is 0.51:

$$\frac{\text{Debt}}{\text{Total assets}} = \frac{42.0 + 49.2}{179.0} = 0.51$$

This measure of debt includes both current liabilities and long-term obligations. Sometimes financial analysts look at the proportions of debt and equity in long-term financing. The proportion of debt in long-term financing is[15]

$$\frac{\text{Long-term debt}}{\text{Long-term debt} + \text{stockholders' equity}} = \frac{29.2}{29.2 + 87.8} = 0.25$$

---

[14] Reprinted from the October 12, 1974, issue of *Business Week*, p. 45, by special permission; © 1974 by McGraw-Hill, Inc., New York, N.Y. 10020. All rights reserved.

[15] For the American corporations the ratio of debt to total assets is 0.56 and the ratio of long-term debt to long-term financing is 0.32.

Table 14-4
Aggregate balance sheets for manufacturing corporations in Canada[a] and the United States, 1986 (figures in billions of domestic dollars)

	Canada		U.S.	
Current assets		$74.6		$808.4
Fixed assets[b]	$123.1		$1,320.1	
Less depreciation	50.1		587.0	
Net fixed assets		73.0		733.1
Other long-term assets		31.4		464.0
Total assets		179.0		2,005.5
Current liabilities		42.0		515.2
Long-term debt	29.2		410.9	
Other long-term liabilities[c]	20.0		188.3	
Total long-term liabilities		49.2		599.2
Stockholders' equity		87.8		891.1
Total liabilities and stockholders' equity		179.0		2,005.5

[a] Canadian data are only for firms having $10 million or more in total assets.

[b] Includes land, mineral rights, and construction in progress, as well as plant and equipment.

[c] Includes deferred taxes and several miscellaneous categories.

Sources: Statistics Canada, *Industrial Corporations, Financial Statistics*, Fourth Quarter, 1987, Table 9 and U.S. Federal Trade Commission, *Quarterly Financial Report for Manufacturing, Mining, and Trade Corporations*, Third Quarter, 1986, p. 56.

Figure 14-2 plots these two ratios from 1962 to 1989. There is a clear upward shift from the 1950s to the 1980s. By these measures corporations are "using more debt." We do not know whether the shift to more debt is permanent or why it has occurred. However, it is worth noting that the rate of inflation began to accelerate in the late 1960s, and remained high through the 1970s. Rapid inflation means that the *book* value of corporate assets falls behind the actual value of those assets. If corporations are borrowing against *actual* value, it would not be surprising to observe rising ratios of debt to book asset values.

To illustrate, suppose that you bought a house ten years ago for $30,000. You financed the purchase in part with a $15,000 mortgage, 50% of the purchase price. Today the house is worth $60,000. Suppose you repay the remaining balance of your original mortgage and take out a new mortgage for $30,000, which is again 50% of current market value. Your *book* debt ratio would be 100%. The reason is that the book value of the house is its *original* cost of $30,000 (we assume no depreciation). An analyst having only book values to work with would conclude that you had decided to "use more debt" — ten years ago your book debt ratio was only 50%. But you have no more debt relative to the actual value of your house.

Figure 14-3 shows debt as a fraction of the total inflation-adjusted value of assets held by United States corporations.[16] Since inflation-adjusted values exceed book values, we would expect these debt ratios to be lower than the ones in the top line of Figure 14-2, and so they are. But you can still see the same upward trend since the 1940s and 1950s.

---

[16] These debt ratios are estimates for all nonfinancial corporations, not just manufacturing corporations, as in Figure 14-2. Comparable figures for manufacturing are not readily available, but manufacturing corporations generally carry less debt than all nonfinancial corporations.

Figure 14-2 Average debt ratios for manufacturing corporations in Canada have increased in the postwar period. However, note that these ratios compare debt with the book value of total assets and total long-term financing. The actual value of corporate assets is higher as a result of inflation.

Source: CANSIM — Statistics Canada, matrices 4788 and 6639.

Should we be worried? It's true that higher debt ratios mean that more companies will fall into financial distress if a serious recession hits the economy. But all companies have to live with this risk to some degree, and it does not follow that less risk is better. Finding the optimal debt ratio is like finding the optimal speed limit: We can agree that accidents at 50 km/h are less dangerous, other things equal, than accidents at 100, but we do not therefore set the national speed limit at 50. Speed has benefits as well as risks. So does debt, as we will see in Chapter 18.

There is no God-given, correct debt ratio, and if there were it would change. It may be that the recent wave of financial innovation, by giving firms easier access to financial markets and the ability to hedge operating risks, has made higher debt ratios possible without increasing the risks or costs of financial distress. Note, too, that debt ratios in the 1980s, though higher than in the early postwar period, are still lower than in the first third of this century. They are also lower than in most other countries. Successful companies in Germany, for example, often operate at debt levels much higher than United States and Canadian companies are accustomed to.

14-7 SUMMARY

Financing is principally a marketing problem. The company tries to split the cash flows generated by its assets into different streams that will appeal to investors with different tastes, wealth, and tax rates. In this chapter we have introduced you to the principal sources of finance and outlined their relative importance.

The simplest and most important source of finance is shareholders' equity, raised either by stock issues or retained earnings.

Debt as fraction
of total inflation –
adjusted assets

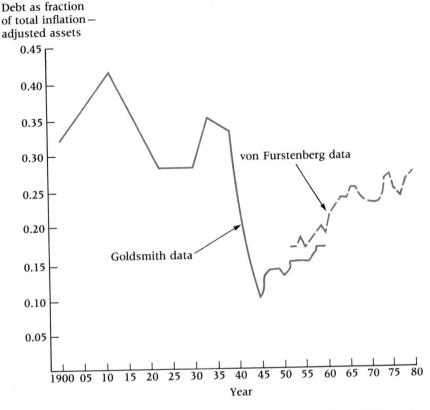

Figure 14-3 Debt as a fraction of total inflation-adjusted asset values of U.S. nonfinancial corporations. The 1900–1958 series was prepared by Raymond Goldsmith, the 1952–1978 series by George Von Furstenburg. Note the upward trend since the 1940s, and the high debt ratios in the early 1900s.

Source: R.A. Taggart, Jr., "Secular Patterns in the Financing of U.S. Corporations," in B.F. Friedman, ed., *Corporate Capital Structures in the United States,* University of Chicago Press, Chicago, 1985, fig. 1.3, p. 25.

The next most important source of finance is debt. Debtholders are entitled to a fixed regular payment of interest and the final repayment of principal. But the company's liability is not unlimited. If it cannot pay its debts, it can file for bankruptcy. The usual result is that the debtholders then take over and operate the company's assets.

Note that the tax authorities treat interest payments as a cost. That means the company can deduct interest when calculating its taxable income. Interest is paid from pretax income.

The third source of finance is preferred stock. Preferred is like debt in that it promises a fixed dividend payment, but payment of this dividend is within the discretion of the directors. They must, however, pay the dividend on the preferred before they are allowed to pay a dividend on the common stock. Lawyers and tax experts treat preferred as part of the company's equity. That means preferred dividends must be paid out of after-tax income. This is one reason that preferred is less popular than debt. The principal attraction of preferred stock is the softened tax treatment of dividends in the hands of Canadian investors.

The fourth source of finance consists of options. These are not recorded separately in the company's balance sheet. The simplest option is the warrant that gives its holder the right to buy a share at a set price by a set date. Warrants are often sold in combination with other securities and are merely recorded in a note to the accounts. Convertible bonds are securities that give their holder the right to convert the bond into shares. They are therefore like a mixture of straight debt and a warrant.

Table 14-3 summarized the ways in which companies raise and spend money. Have another look at it and try to get some feel for the numbers. Notice that:

1.   Internally generated cash is the principal source of funds. Some people worry about that: they think that if management does not have to go to the trouble of raising the money, it won't think so hard when it comes to spending it.
2.   Internally generated cash does not provide all the money companies need. The deficit is particularly large after a period of buoyant sales: this is the time when companies tend to come to the capital markets for more money.
3.   There are cycles in company financing. Sometimes companies prefer to issue debt, sometimes equity. In part this reflects their attempt to keep to a target debt-equity ratio. But it also looks as if companies try to make equity issues after a market rise. Nobody knows why they do this. There does not seem any reason to do so in an efficient market. An equity issue is never a positive-NPV transaction regardless of whether the stock price has just risen or fallen.

Table 14-4 and Figures 14-2 and 14-3 show the net effect of this fund raising on the aggregate balance sheet of corporations in Canada and the United States. Debt ratios have generally increased over the postwar period. Some find this cause for concern. But successful companies in many other countries, Germany for example, operate at debt ratios higher than Canadian companies would think prudent.

FURTHER READING

Donaldson describes a survey of corporate attitudes to different sources of finance in:

C. Donaldson, *Corporate Debt Capacity*, Division of Research, Graduate School of Business Administration, Harvard University, Boston, 1961.

Some common concerns about the role of the capital market in providing funds for industry are set out in:

W.J. Baumol, *The Stock Market and Economic Efficiency*, Fordham University Press, New York, 1965.

Taggart and Marsh provide some evidence on why and when companies use different sources of finance:

P. Marsh, "The Choice between Equity and Debt: An Empirical Study," *Journal of Finance*, **37**: 121–144 (March 1982).

R.A. Taggart, "A Model of Corporate Financing Decisions," *Journal of Finance*, **32**: 1467–1484 (December 1977).

Taggart describe long-term trends in corporate financing in:

R.A. Taggart: "Secular Patterns in the Financing of Corporations," in B.M. Friedman, ed., *Corporate Capital Structures in the United States*, University of Chicago Press, Chicago, 1985.

QUIZ

1. The authorized share capital of the Alfred Cake Company is 100,000 shares. The equity is currently down in the company's books as follows:

Common stock	$40,000
Additional paid-in capital	10,000
Retained earnings	30,000
Common equity	80,000

    Suppose that the company issues 10,000 shares at $2 a share. Which of the above figures would be changed?

2. If there are ten directors to be elected and a shareholder owns 80 shares, indicate the maximum number of votes that he or she can cast for a favourite candidate under:
    (a) Majority voting
    (b) Cumulative voting

3. Choose from the terms below the one that best fits each of the blanks.
    (a) Debt maturing in more than one year is often called _____ debt.
    (b) An issue of bonds that is sold simultaneously in several countries is called a _____ .
    (c) If a lender ranks behind the firm's general creditors in the event of default, his or her loan is said to be _____ .
    (d) Unsecured bonds are usually termed _____ bonds.
    (e) In many cases, a firm is obliged to make regular contributions to a _____ , which is then used to repurchase bonds.
    (f) Most bonds give the firm the right to repurchase or _____ the bonds at specified prices.
    (g) The rate that banks charge to their most creditworthy customers is generally termed the _____ .
    (h) The interest rate on bank loans is often tied to short-term interest rates. These loans are usually called _____ loans.
    (i) A long-term, noncancellable rental agreement is called a _____ .
    (j) A _____ bond can be exchanged for shares of the issuing corporation.
    (k) A _____ gives its owner the right to buy shares in the issuing company at a predetermined _____ .
    lease, funded, floating-rate, eurobond, exercise price, commercial paper, convertible, long-term loan, subordinated, call, sinking fund, prime rate, debentures, mortgage bond, senior, short term, eurodollar rate, warrant.

4. The figures in the following table are in the wrong order. Place them in their correct order.

	% of Total Sources in 1987
Internally generated cash	7
Financial deficit	12
New share issues	18
Long-term debt issues	68
Short-term debt issues	32

QUESTIONS AND PROBLEMS

1. "It is frequently held that the cost of funds on the security market falls whenever stock prices rise, just as the yield of a bond varies inversely with its price. One would think that it pays management to turn to the market for funds whenever the cost of stock market capital, thus interpreted, falls sufficiently."[17] Discuss.

2. It is sometimes suggested that since retained earnings provide the bulk of industry's capital needs, the securities markets are largely redundant. Do you agree?

3. Can you think of any new kinds of security that might appeal to investors? Why do you think they have not been issued?

4. Look back at Table 14-2.
   (a) Suppose that Canadian Pacific issues 15,000 shares at $25 a share. Rework Table 14-2 to show the company's equity after the issue.
   (b) Suppose CP subsequently repurchases and cancels 10,000 shares at $30 a share. Rework Table 14-2 to show the effect of the further change.

5. The shareholders of the Pickwick Paper Company need to elect five directors. There are 100,000 shares outstanding. How many shares do you need to own to *ensure* that you can elect at least one director if:
   (a) The company has majority voting.
   (b) It has cumulative voting.

6. Compare the yields on preferred stocks with those on corporate bonds. Can you explain the difference?

7. Who are the main holders and issuers of preferred stock? Explain why.

8. Briefly explain the chief difference between a forward and a futures contract.

9. Work out the financing proportions given in Table 14-3 for a particular industrial company—Bombardier, for example—for some recent year.

10. Here is recent financial data on Pisa Construction, Inc.

    - Stock price = $40
    - Number shares = 10,000
    - Book net worth = $500,000
    - Market value of firm = $400,000
    - Earnings per share = $4
    - Return on investment = 8%

    Pisa has not performed spectacularly to date. However, it wishes to issue new shares to obtain $80,000 to finance expansion into a promising market. Pisa's financial advisers think a stock issue is a poor choice because, among other reasons, "sale of stock at a price below book value per share can only depress the stock price and decrease shareholders' wealth." To prove the point they construct the following example: "Suppose 2,000 new shares are issued at $40 and the proceeds invested. (Neglect issue costs.) Suppose return on investment doesn't change, Then

    $$\text{Book net worth} = \$580,000$$
    $$\text{Total earnings} = 0.08\,(580,000) = \$46,400$$
    $$\text{Earnings per share} = \frac{46,400}{12,00} = \$3.87$$

---

[17] W.J. Baumol, *Stock Market and Economic Efficiency*, p. 71.

Thus, EPS declines, book value per share declines, and share price will decline proportionately to $38.70."
Evaluate this argument with particular attention to the assumptions implicit in the numerical example.

C·H·A·P·T·E·R

15

How Corporations Issue
Securities

In Chapter 11 we encountered Marvin Enterprises, one of the most remarkable growth companies of the twenty-first century. It was founded by George and Mildred Marvin, two high school dropouts, together with their chum Charles P. (Chip) Norton. To get the company off the ground the three entrepreneurs relied on their own savings together with personal loans from a bank. However, the company's rapid growth meant that they had soon borrowed to the hilt and needed more equity capital. Equity investment in young private companies is generally known as **venture capital**. Such venture capital may be provided by specialist venture capital partnerships, by investment institutions, or by wealthy individuals who are prepared to back an untried company in exchange for a piece of the action. In the first part of this chapter we will explain how companies like Marvin go about raising venture capital.

Venture capital companies aim to help growing firms over that awkward adolescent period before they are large enough to "go public." For a successful firm such as Marvin there is likely to come a time when it needs to tap a wider source of capital and therefore decides to make its first public issue of common stock. The first public issue of a security by a company is known as an **unseasoned issue.** We will describe in the next section of the chapter what is involved in an unseasoned issue of stock.

A company's first public offering is rarely also its last. In Chapter 14 we saw that corporations face a persistent financial deficit which they meet by selling securities. We will look therefore at how established public corporations go about raising more capital.

If a stock or bond is sold publicly, it can then be traded on the securities markets. But sometimes investors intend to hold on to their securities and are not concerned about whether they can sell them. In these cases there is little advantage to a public issue, and the firm may prefer to place the securities directly with one or two financial institutions. At the end of this chapter we will discuss the choice between a public offer and a private placement.

15–1 VENTURE CAPITAL

On April 1, 2003, George and Mildred Marvin met with Chip Norton in their research lab (which also doubled as a bicycle shed) to celebrate the incorporation of Marvin Enterprises. The three entrepreneurs had raised $100,000 from savings and personal bank loans and had purchased 1 million shares in the new company. At this *zero stage* investment, the company's assets were $90,000 in the bank ($10,000 had been spent for legal and other expenses of setting up the company), plus the *idea* for a new product, the household gargle blaster. George Marvin was the first to see that the gargle blaster, up to that point an expensive curiosity, could be commercially produced using microgenetic refenestrators.

Marvin Enterprises's bank account steadily drained away as design and testing proceeded. Local banks did not see Marvin's idea as adequate collateral, so a transfusion of equity capital was clearly needed. Preparation of a *business plan* was a necessary first step. The plan was a confidential document describing the proposed product, its potential market, the underlying technology, and the resources — time, money, employees, plant, and equipment — needed for success.

Most entrepreneurs are able to spin a plausible yarn about their company. But it is as hard to convince a venture capitalist that your business plan is sound as it is to get a first novel published. Marvin's management were able to point to the fact that they were prepared to put their money where their mouths were. Not only had they staked all their savings in the company but they were mortgaged to the hilt. This *signaled* their faith in the business.[1]

First Meriam Venture Partners were impressed with Marvin's presentation and agreed to buy 1 million new shares for $1 each. After this *first-stage* financing, the company's market value balance sheet looked like this:

Marvin Enterprises First-Stage Balance Sheet (market values in millions)

Cash from new equity	$1	$1	New equity from venture capital
Other assets, mostly intangible	1	1	Original equity held by entrepreneurs
Value	$2	$2	Value

By accepting a $2 million *after-the-money* valuation, First Meriam implicitly put a $1 million value on the entrepreneurs' idea and their commitment to the enterprise. They also handed the entrepreneurs a $900,000 paper gain over their original $100,000 investment. In exchange, the entrepreneurs gave up half their company and accepted First Meriam's representatives to the board of directors.[2]

The success of a new business depends critically on the effort put in by the managers. So venture capital firms try to structure a deal so that management has a strong incentive to work hard. For example, any entrepreneur who demands a water-tight employment contract and a fat salary is not going to find it easy to raise venture capital. The Marvin team agreed to put up with modest salaries and, therefore, they could cash in only from appreciation of their stock. If Marvin

---

[1] For a formal analysis of how management's investment in the business can provide a reliable signal of the company's value, see H.E. Leland and D.H. Pyle, "Informational Asymmetries, Financial Structure, and Financial Intermediation," *Journal of Financing*, **32**: 371–387 (May 1977).

[2] Venture capital investors do not necessarily demand a majority on the board of directors. Whether they do depends, for example, on how mature the business is and on what fraction of it they own. A common compromise gives an equal number of seats to the founders and to outside investors; the two parties then agree to one or more additional directors to serve as tie-breakers in case a conflict arises. Regardless of whether they have a majority of directors, venture capital companies are seldom silent partners; their judgement and contacts can often prove useful to a relatively inexperienced management team.

failed they would get nothing, because First Meriam actually bought *preferred* stock designed to convert automatically into common stock when and if Marvin Enterprises succeeded in an initial public offering or consistently generated more than a target level of earnings. This raised even further the stakes for the company's management.[3]

Venture capitalists rarely give a young company all the money it will need all at once. At each stage they give enough to reach the next major checkpoint. Thus in spring 2005, having designed and tested a prototype, Marvin Enterprises was back asking for more money for pilot production and test marketing. Its *second-stage* financing was $4 million, of which $1.5 million came from First Meriam, its original backers, and $2.5 million from two other venture capital partnerships and wealthy individual investors. The balance sheet just after the second stage was as follows:

Marvin Enterprises Second-Stage Balance Sheet (market values in millions)

Cash from new equity	$ 4	$ 4	New equity, second stage
Fixed assets	1	5	Equity from first stage
Other assets, mostly intangible	9	5	Original equity held by entrepreneurs
Value	$14	$14	Value

Now the after-the-money valuation was $14 million. First Meriam marked up its original investment to $5 million, and the founders noted an additional $4 million paper gain.

Does this begin to sound like a (paper) money machine? It was so only with hindsight. At stage one it wasn't clear whether Marvin would ever get to stage two: if the prototype hadn't worked, First Meriam could have refused to put up more funds and effectively closed the business down.[4] Or they could have advanced stage-two money in a smaller amount on less favourable terms. The board of directors also could have fired George, Mildred, and Chip and found someone else to try to develop the business.

For every 10 first-stage venture capital investments, only two or three may survive as successful, self-sufficient businesses, and one may pay off big as Marvin Enterprises did.[5] From these statistics come two rules for success in venture capital investment. First, don't shy away from uncertainty; accept a low

---

[3] Notice there is a trade-off here. Marvin's management is being asked to put all its eggs into one basket. That creates pressure for managers to work hard but it also means that they take on risk that they could have diversified away.

    The problem of ensuring that managers act in the interests of investors is sometimes referred to as an *agency* problem. For a discussion of these issues, see M.C. Jensen and W.H. Meckling, "Theory of the Firm: Managerial Behavior, Agency Costs and Capital Structure," *Journal of Financial Economics*, **3**: 305–360 (1976).

[4] If First Meriam had refused to invest at stage two, it would have been an exceptionally hard sell convincing another investor to step in in its place. The other outside investors knew they had less information about Marvin than First Meriam and would have read its refusal as a bad omen for Marvin's prospects.

[5] One study of venture capital investments between 1960 and 1975 found that about one in six were total failures. On the other hand, thanks to a few outstanding successes, the average return after costs was about 19% a year. See B. Huntsman and J.P. Hoban, Jr., "Investment in New Enterprise: Some Empirical Observations on Risk, Return, and Market Structure," *Financial Management*, **9**: 44–51 (Summer 1980).

probability of success. But don't buy into a business unless you can see the *chance* of a big, public company in a profitable market. There's no sense taking a long shot unless it pays off big if you win. Second, cut your losses; identify losers early, and if you can't fix the problem — by replacing management, for example — throw no good money after bad.

For Marvin, fortunately, everything went like clockwork. Third-stage financing was arranged,[6] full-scale production began on schedule, and gargle blasters were acclaimed by music critics worldwide. Marvin Enterprises "went public" on February 3, 2009. Once its shares were traded, the paper gains earned by First Meriam and the company's founders turned into fungible wealth.

Before we get on to this initial public offering, a word on the venture capital market.

Enterpreneurs have generated a continuous flow of successful new corporations for at least a century. Some of the new companies managed to grow by their own bootstraps, by borrowing and generating funds internally. Others sought out equity investment, often from wealthy families or established firms. So venture capital has been around for some time.

In the early 1980s, the U.S. venture capital market totalled $11 billion and the Canadian venture capital market totalled $1.2 billion. By 1988, the Canadian market had grown to $2.5 billion.[7] American venture capital companies are often syndicates composed of tax-exempt pension funds or insurance companies and taxable individuals or corporations. These syndicates are designed to be wound up after, say, 10 years. Canadian venture capital is often provided by corporations that have an indefinite life span.

Governments around the world seem to believe that, unless they intervene, profitable new ventures are likely to fail for lack of finance. They therefore look for ways to provide subsidized finance for young companies. In the United States, the government provides cheap loans to Small Business Investment Companies (SBICs) who then relend the money to deserving entrepreneurs. In Canada, government venture capital is usually provided by the provinces. For example, Alberta has Vencap Equities, which is the largest venture capital company in Canada, with $280 million available for investment.

15–2   THE INITIAL PUBLIC OFFERING

Very few new businesses make it big, but venture capitalists keep sane by forgetting about the many failures and reminding themselves of the success stories — the investors who got in on the ground floor of firms like DEC, MDI Mobile Data International, and Lotus Development Corporation.[8] When First Meriam invested in Marvin Enterprises, it was not looking for a high income stream from the investment; instead it was hoping for rapid growth that would allow Marvin to "go public" and give First Meriam an opportunity to cash in on some of its gains.

---

[6] Later-stage financing is often called *mezzanine financing*, in contrast to financing by those investors who get in on the "ground floor."

[7] These figures are cited in G. Fells, "Venture Capital in Canada — A Ten-Year Review," *Business Quarterly*, **52**: 57–63 (Spring 1988) and Venture Economics Canada, *Venture Capital in Canada: A Guide and Sources*, Department of Industry, Science and Technology, and Association of Canadian Venture Capital Companies, Ottawa (1989).

[8] The founder of Lotus took a finance class from one of the authors. Within 5 years he had become a multimillionaire. Perhaps that will make you feel better about the cost of this book.

By 2009 Marvin had grown to the point at which it needed substantial new capital to implement its second-generation production technology. At this point it decided to make an initial public offering of stock. This was to be partly a **primary** offering—that is, new shares were to be sold to raise additional cash for the company. It was also to be partly a **secondary** offering—that is, the venture capitalists and the company's founders were looking to sell some of their existing shares.

Often when companies go public, the issue is solely intended to raise new capital for the company. But there are also occasions when no new capital is raised and all the shares on offer are being sold by existing shareholders. In fact some of the biggest initial public offerings occur when governments sell off their shareholdings in companies. For example, the Canadian government made a secondary issue of $490 million when it divested Air Canada in 1989.[9]

Arranging a Public Issue[10]

Once Marvin had taken the decision to go public, the next task was to select the underwriters. Underwriters act as financial midwives to a new issue. Usually they play a triple role—first providing the company with procedural and financial advice, then buying the issue, and finally reselling it to the public. After some discussion Marvin settled on Klein Merrick as the lead underwriter. Klein Merrick would be responsible for forming and managing a syndicate of underwriters who would buy and resell the issue.

Together with Klein Merrick and firms of lawyers and accountants, Marvin prepared a **preliminary prospectus** for submission to the Securities Commission.[11] This is required for most public issues of securities[12] and is often called a *red herring* because of the statement printed in red ink denying that Marvin and Merrick are attempting to sell securities before the issue is approved. The preliminary prospectus contains financial statements as well as information about the proposed financing and Marvin's history, any existing business and plans for the future, but does not contain some details such as the offering price of the issue. In Appendix 15–2, we have reproduced the prospectus for Marvin's

---

[9] This issue looks tiny compared with the secondary offering by the Japanese government of $12.6 billion of the stock of Nippon Telegraph and Telephone or the $9 billion offering by the British government of British Gas.

[10] For an excellent case study of how one company went public, see B. Uttal, "Inside the Deal That Made Bill Gates $350,000,000," *Fortune* July 21, 1986.

[11] Each province has its own securities commission, but there is only one such commission in the United States, the federal Securities and Exchange Commission (SEC). Much of the legislation for these various jurisdictions is similar, partly because of leadership roles assumed by the SEC and the Ontario Securities Commission (OSC). A firm seeking a broadly based distribution of its securities in all ten provinces as well as the United States must obtain approval from 11 different securities commissions.

[12] Canadian resource companies or companies that are issuing more shares of a security that is already publicly traded can sometimes file a relatively simple **statement of material facts** instead of a full prospectus. In other circumstances, a firm can issue a **short form prospectus** that can incorporate by reference information filed with the securities commission, but not included in the prospectus.

   If the issue is to be sold in the United States, the preliminary prospectus forms a part of a larger file called the **registration statement**, which is submitted to the SEC. The registration statement is not needed for loans maturing within nine months or issues involving less than $1.5 million. The latter are known as *Regulation A* issues, and for these the SEC needs only a simple notification and an example of the offering circular that is to be sent to prospective buyers.

first public issue of stock. Most prospectuses would go into much more detail on each topic, but this example should serve to give you a feel for the mixture of valuable information and redundant qualification that characterizes these documents. The Marvin prospectus also illustrates how the securities commissions take care to ensure that investors' eyes are opened to the dangers of purchase (see "Certain Considerations" of the prospectus). Some investors have joked that if they read prospectuses carefully, they would never dare buy any new issue.

With the preliminary prospectus, Klein Merrick may attempt to "pre-sell" the issue or accept "indications of interest" from potential buyers.

After the securities commission has studied the preliminary prospectus, it notifies the company of any deficiencies and requests additions and changes. An amended prospectus is then filed, and so on, until the issue is approved.[13] The final prospectus must be sent to all purchasers of the securities.

Marvin had other tasks during the process of issuing a security. It had to appoint a **registrar** to record any issues of stock and to prevent any unauthorized issue. It appointed a **transfer agent** to look after the transfer of the newly issued securities.

Pricing a New Issue

During the pre-selling period Marvin and its underwriters began to firm up the issue price. First they looked at the price-earnings ratios of the shares of Marvin's principal competitors. Then they worked through a number of discounted cash-flow calculations like the ones we described in the appendix to Chapter 4 and in Chapter 11. Most of the evidence pointed to a market value of around $90 a share.

While Marvin's management were anxious to secure the highest possible price for their stock, the underwriters were more cautious. Not only would they be left with any unsold stock if they overestimated investor demand; they also argued that some degree of underpricing was needed to tempt investors to buy the stock.

Immediately after the company received clearance from the commissions, Marvin and the underwriters agreed on an issue price of $80 a share. On February 3, 2009, Marvin finally went public and the underwriters began to telephone interested buyers of the stock. The issue proved popular with investors; the underwriters had no difficulty selling the stock at the issue price. By the end of the first week, the shares were trading at a price of $95. The issue brought the Marvin management team $16 million in cash before their share of the costs, and the 800,000 shares that they retained were worth 800,000 × $95 = $76 million.

Costs of a Public Issue

Marvin's issue created substantial administrative costs. Preparation of the registration statement and prospectus involved management, legal counsel, and accountants, as well as the underwriters and their advisers. In addition, the firm had to pay fees for registering the new securities, printing and mailing costs, and so on. You can see from the first page of the Marvin prospectus (Appendix 15–2)

---

[13] In Canada, the securities can legally be sold as soon as each of the securities commissions issues a receipt for the final prospectus. The time between issuing receipts for the preliminary and final prospectuses must be at least ten days. In the United States, the registration statement becomes effective 20 days after it is accepted by the SEC, and then the securities can legally be sold. The securities commissions are concerned solely with disclosure, and they have no power to prevent an issue as long as there has been proper disclosure.

that these administrative and registration costs amounted in total to $820,000.

The second major cost of the Marvin issue was underwriting. Underwriters make their profit by buying the issue from the company at a discount from the price at which they resell it to the public. In Marvin's case this discount, or *spread*, amounted to $4.5 million, which was equivalent to 6.25% of the total amount of the issue.

Marvin's issue was costly in yet another way. Since the offering price was *less* than the true value of the issued securities, investors who bought the issue got a bargain at the expense of the firm's original stockholders.

These costs of *underpricing* are hidden but nevertheless real. For initial public offerings they generally exceed the other issue costs. Whenever any company goes public, it is very difficult for the underwriter to judge how much investors will be willing to pay for the stock. A number of researchers have tried to measure underwriters' success in gauging the value of such issues. With remarkable unanimity they have found that on average investors who buy at the issue price realize very high returns over the following weeks. For example, a study by Jay Ritter[14] of approximately 5,000 new issues from 1960 to 1982 indicated average underpricing of 19%.

This underpricing does not imply that any investor can expect to become wealthy by purchasing unseasoned stock from the underwriters, for if the issue is attractive, the underwriters will not have enough stock to go around. In order to get stock at the issue price investors would probably have to be prepared to pay for it indirectly, for example, by allocating more brokerage business to the underwriter than they otherwise would. Therefore underpricing helps underwriters. It reduces the risk of underwriting and gains them the gratitude of investors who buy the issue. Does that mean the underwriter earns excessive profits? Possibly, but not necessarily. If the business is sufficiently competitive, underwriters will take all these hidden benefits into account when they negotiate the spread.

Suppose that you could always be sure of getting your fair share of any issue that you applied for without having to ingratiate yourself with the investment banker. Does that mean that you could make handsome profits on average by applying for an equal amount of each issue? Unfortunately, no. If an issue is cheap, it is also likely to be oversubscribed; if it is dear, it is likely to be undersubscribed. So you will receive a small proportion of the cheap issues and a large proportion of the dear ones. If you are smart, you will play the game only if there is substantial underpricing on the average.[15]

Many investment bankers and institutional investors argue that underpricing is in the interests of the issuing firm. They say that a low offering price on the initial offer raises the price of the stock when it is subsequently traded in the market and enhances the firm's ability to raise further capital. At least one industrialist has accepted this argument, for writing some time after his company went public the president described the pricing decision as follows:

> Our underwriting group suggested a price of $15. The general market was strong . . . when our registration statement was filed and we felt that the public might well pay $17 or $18 for our stock rather than $15. Our underwriters were strong in their desire to have the stock sold at $15 a share on the basis that this was a proper price for the stock. They pointed out that the after-market was important and that the price could decline if the stock was overpriced. Having practiced law for many

---

[14] J. Ritter, "The 'Hot Issue' Market of 1980," *Journal of Business,* **57**: 215–240 (April 1984).
[15] For a discussion of this point, see K. Rock, "Why New Issues Are Underpriced," *Journal of Financial Economics,* **15**: 187–212 (January–February 1986).

years . . . , it was always my opinion that clients should not second-guess their counselors. I had to follow the same rules in accepting the advice of our investment bankers. And how right our underwriting group was! Within six months our stock rose from $15 a share to $50. Would the stock have had this dramatic increase if the initial price had been $17 or $18? There may have been some who felt that it was overpriced initially and would not have been in the market for our stock. Suffice it to say that the overall result was extremely good. It points out the importance of working with competent investment bankers who guide you in these matters.[16]

Contentment at selling an article for one-third of its ultimate worth is rarely achieved.

15–3 GENERAL CASH OFFERS BY PUBLIC COMPANIES

After its initial public offering, Marvin Enterprises continued to grow and, like most growing companies, from time to time it needed to make further issues of debt and equity. But at this point we will leave Marvin and review in general terms the procedures involved in these periodic security issues.

Any issue of securities needs to be formally approved by the firm's board of directors. If the stock issue requires an increase in the company's authorized capital, it also needs the consent of the stockholders.

Public companies can issue securities either by making a general cash offer to investors at large or by making a rights issue that is limited to existing stockholders. We will concentrate in this section on the mechanics of the general cash offer, which is used for virtually all debt issues and many equity issues. In Appendix 15–1, we describe rights issues.

International Security Issues

Well-established companies are not restricted to the capital market in Canada; they can also raise money in the United States and offshore capital markets. They often offer equity securities jointly on Canadian and foreign markets. The Canadian capital market cannot absorb large security issues, so Canadian firms are often *forced* to use international capital markets, especially for large debt issues. We saw in Chapter 14 that this can mean one of two things. Either the company makes a foreign bond issue in another country's market (in which case it is subject to the laws and customs of that country), or it makes an issue of eurobonds, which are offered internationally, but payable in domestic Canadian currency.

The procedures for making a eurobond issue are broadly similar to the procedures for a domestic bond issue. Here are two points to note:

1. As long as the bond is not publicly offered in Canada, it does not have to satisfy the requirements of all the provincial securities commissions. The foreign requirements may be simpler to satisfy.
2. Frequently a eurobond issue takes the form of a *bought deal*, in which case one or a few underwriters buy the entire issue. Bought deals allow companies to issue bonds at very short notice. In response, some Canadian underwriters are also offering bought deals.

---

[16] From E.L. Winter, *A Complete Guide to Making a Public Offering.* © 1962, published by Prentice-Hall, Inc., Englewood Cliffs, N.J. Here's another example. In 1987 the British company Sock Shop International went public at 125p a share. First-day dealings were at a price of 205p. The company's chairman was reported to be "ecstatic" about the market's reaction. She dismissed suggestions that the issue was underpriced by saying that had the shares been more expensive, the company would "quite justifiably" have been accused of overpricing. See *Financial Times,* May 15, 1987.

Table 15-1
Issue Costs as a Percent of Proceeds for Registered Issues of Common Stock during 1971–1975

Size of Issue (millions of dollars)	General Underwritten Cash Offers			Underwritten Rights Issues		
	Underwriters' Compensation %	Other Expenses %	Total Cost %	Underwriters' Compensation %	Other Expenses %	Total Cost %
0.50 to 0.99	7.0	6.8	13.7	3.4	4.8	8.2
1.00 to 1.99	10.4	4.9	15.3	6.4	4.2	10.5
2.00 to 4.99	6.6	2.9	9.5	5.2	2.9	8.1
5.00 to 9.99	5.5	1.5	7.0	3.9	2.2	6.1
10.00 to 19.99	4.8	0.7	5.6	4.1	1.2	5.4
20.00 to 49.99	4.3	0.4	4.7	3.8	0.9	4.7
50.00 to 99.99	4.0	0.2	4.2	4.0	0.7	4.7
100.00 to 500.00	3.8	0.1	4.0	3.5	0.5	4.0
Average	5.0	1.2	6.2	4.3	1.7	6.1

Source: C.W. Smith, "Alternative Methods for Raising Capital: Rights versus Underwritten Offerings," *Journal of Financial Economics*, **5**: 273–307 (December 1977), table 1, p. 277.

Table 15-2
Average Underwriting and Administrative Costs for Underwritten Public Issues of Bonds, 1960–1969

Size of Issue (millions of dollars)	Underwriters' Compensation, %	Other Expenses %
Under 0.50	13.6	6.2
0.50 to 0.99	7.7	5.2
1.00 to 1.99	6.4	3.0
2.00 to 4.99	4.6	1.7
5.00 to 9.99	1.6	0.9
10.00 to 19.99	1.2	0.6
20.00 to 49.99	1.1	0.4
50.00 and above	0.8	0.3

Source: R. Hillstrom and R. King (eds.), *1960–69: A Decade of Corporate and International Finance*, Investment Dealers Digest, Inc., New York, p. 18.

The Costs of the General Cash Offer

Whenever a firm makes a cash offer, it incurs substantial administrative costs. Also the firm needs to compensate the underwriters by selling them securities below the price that they expect to receive from investors. Tables 15–1 and 15–2 show the average underwriting and administrative costs for United States domestic stock and debt issues.[17] Two aspects of the data are of immediate interest. (Ignore for the moment the data on rights issues.)

First, it is more expensive to issue common stock than the same amount of debt. For example, a large issue of common stock might involve total expenses (administrative costs and underwriters' compensation) of 4%. A comparable debt issue would cost only about 1%. This difference partly reflects the greater administrative costs of stock issues, but it is chiefly because underwriters require compensation for the greater risks they bear in buying and reselling stock.

---

[17] The figures do not capture *all* administrative costs. For example, they do not include management time spent on the issue.

Second, a large part of the issue cost is fixed. Therefore there are economies of scale in issuing securities: Costs may absorb 15% of a $1 million underwritten stock issue but only 4% of a $500-million issue.

*Market Reaction to Stock Issues

Because stock issues usually throw a large additional supply of shares onto the market, it is widely believed that they must temporarily depress the stock price. If the proposed issue is very large, the price pressure may, it is thought, be so severe as to make it almost impossible to raise new money. If so, the firm effectively faces capital rationing.

This belief in price pressure implies that after the decline in price the company's shares can be bought for less than their true value. It is therefore inconsistent with market efficiency. The alternative view stresses that investors buy stocks because they offer a fair reward for their risk. If the stock price fell solely because of increased supply, then that stock would offer a reward which was *more* than the shares for less than the *offering price* at which the securities are sold on to investors. In the more risky cases the underwriter usually receives some extra noncash compensation, such as warrants to buy additional stock. Occasionally, where a new issue of common stock is regarded as particularly risky, the underwriter may be unwilling to enter into a fixed commitment and will handle the issue only on a "best efforts" or an "all-or-none" basis. *Best efforts* means that the underwriter promises to sell as much of the issue as possible but does not guarantee the sale of the entire issue. *All or none* means that if the entire issue cannot be sold at the offering price, the deal is called off and the issuing company receives nothing.

If the issue is large, a group of underwriters will usually get together to form a syndicate to handle the sale. In this case one underwriter acts as syndicate manager and for this job keeps about 20% of the spread. A further 20% to 30% of the spread is used to pay those members of the group who buy the issue. The remaining 50% to 60% goes to the larger number of firms that provide the sales force for the issue.

If the market price falls below the stated offering price, the underwriter is generally allowed to support the market by repurchasing shares at the market price.[18] (Look, for example, at the second page of the Marvin prospectus.) We have no information about the effects of such stabilizing transactions. But, if capital markets are efficient, then transactions affect prices only insofar as they are thought to convey information. In that case the underwriters' efforts at stabilization cannot have a lasting effect on prices.

In any case, if the issue obstinately remains unsold and the market price falls substantially below the offering price, the underwriters have no alternative but to break the syndicate. The members then dispose of their commitments individually as best they can.

Most companies raise new capital only occasionally, but underwriters are in the business all the time. Established underwriters are, therefore, careful of their reputation and will not handle a new issue unless they believe the facts have been presented fairly to investors. Thus, in addition to handling the sale of an issue, the underwriters in effect give their seal of approval to it. This implied endorsement may be worth quite a bit to a company that is coming to the market for the first time.

---

[18] In such cases, syndicate members could escape their obligation by selling their shares in the market to the principal underwriter. To prevent this, a record is kept so that syndicate members whose shares end up in the hands of the principal underwriter lose that portion of their selling concession.

Who Are the Underwriters? Since underwriters play such a crucial role in the general offer, we should look at who they are.[19] The market is dominated by a few firms that enjoy great prestige, experience, and financial resources. Table 15–3 lists some of the largest underwriting firms in Canada and the United States. Note that, since Canadian firms raise a lot of their capital in the United States, American firms like Goldman Sachs can make it into the top eight in Canada.

Table 15–3
Managing Underwriters Listed in Order of Total Value of Corporate Issues in which They Were the Lead Underwriter in 1988

Canada	United States
RBC Dominion	Merrill Lynch
Wood Gundy	Goldman Sachs
Merrill Lynch	Salomon Brothers
ScotiaMcLeod	First Boston
Union Bank	Shearson Lehman Hutton
Burns, Fry	Morgan Stanley
Nesbitt Thomson Deacon	Drexel Burnham Lambert
Goldman Sachs	Prudential-Bache
Salomon Brothers	Bear Stearns
Gordon Capital	Kidder Peabody

Sources: Barry Critchley and Jean Murphy, "Gundy Tops in Underwriter Ranking," *Financial Post*, p. 11 (July 10, 1989); and "The 1989 Corporate Sweepstakes," *Institutional Investor*, **21**: 141–151 (February 1989), based on data from IDD Information Services.

For each public issue a "tombstone" advertisement is published that lists the names of all the underwriters. In Figure 15–1 we reproduce the tombstone for an offering by Rogers Communications. The ordering of the names on the tombstone reflects a well-established hierarchy among underwriters. The most important underwriters are listed in alphabetical order at the top of the list. Then come the second-rankers, and so on.

Firms guard their rankings with a remarkable possessiveness. Those that struggle to attain a particular ranking often have to consent to being listed "out of order." But the old regime does change. Many Canadian underwriters have merged with each other or with subsidiaries of banks. Firms with strong sales forces, such as Merrill Lynch, have over the years increased their participation and improved their ranking. At the same time the large, traditional U.S. houses, such as Morgan Stanley, have responded to the need for greater distribution capacity by forming loose networks of regional firms.

Since a eurobond issue is marketed internationally, a eurobond underwriting syndicate is not restricted to domestic investment banks. As you can see from Table 15–4, foreign banks are major players in this market; among them, the Japanese have been increasing their share of the business very aggressively. Also, the London branches of Canadian and commercial banks are involved in underwriting eurobond issues, whereas their parents are prohibited from underwriting domestic bond issues.

Choosing an Underwriter Many companies develop a well-established relationship with a particular investment banker, who underwrites the firm's security issues and provides other

---

[19] In the United States, underwriters are usually called **investment bankers**, although they are usually called underwriters in Canada. In either case, they are security dealers or brokers.

These securities have been sold on a private placement basis.
This announcement appears as a matter of record only.

New Issue

Rogers Communications Inc.

$200,000,000

**Cumulative Redeemable Convertible
Auction Perpetual Preferred Shares, Series XV**

November 1989

Toronto Dominion Securities Inc.

**ScotiaMcLeod
Inc.**

**Gordon Capital
Corporation**

**Wood Gundy
Inc.**

**Lévesque Beaubien
Geoffrion Inc.**

**Trilon Securities
Corporation**

Figure 15-1 "Tombstone" advertisements such as this list the underwriters to a new issue.

Source: Courtesy Rogers Communication Inc.

Table 15–4
Managing Underwriters of Eurobonds in Order of Total Value Underwritten in 1988. (Note that rankings are based on issues from all countries.)

Nomura Securities
Credit Suisse First Boston
Deutsche Bank
Daiwa Securities
Yamaichi Securities
Nikko Securities
Merrill Lynch
Banque Paribas
J.P. Morgan Securities
Union Bank of Switzerland

Source: "The 1989 Corporate Sweepstakes," *Institutional Investor,* **21**: 141–151 (February 1989), based on data from IDD Information Services.

financial services. American utility holding companies are an exception, for they are generally required to choose underwriters by competitive bids (although sometimes, when a holding company faces "unsettled market conditions," the SEC relents and allows negotiation). Utilities that are not organized as holding companies can do as they like.

The competition is real. Utilities almost always get at least two bids. For smaller issues, where fewer firms are needed to form a syndicate, four or five bids may be made. But does the competition make a difference?

It does seem to reduce the spreads charged by underwriters. For example, a study by Bhagat and Frost of 479 utility stock issues between 1973 and 1980 found average spreads of 3.9% for negotiated issues and 3.1% for competitive ones.[20] Yet negotiated underwriting is used by almost all firms that have a choice. Why?

Underwriters argue that negotiated offerings allow them to allocate more time to marketing the issue—for example, identifying large buyers, and recruiting "salespeople" in brokers' local offices. This marketing is most effective if done well before the issue date. Under competitive bidding, a syndicate does not put the same effort into marketing because the investment is wasted if the syndicate does not win. Therefore it has to attract buyers by underpricing the issue rather than by sales expertise.

If the underwriters are right, we ought to observe that competitive offerings cause a larger temporary price decline around the offering date. There is less unanimity as to whether this is in fact the case. Bhagat and Frost's study found the reverse: There was on average *less* underpricing for competitive offerings, though there was a much greater variation in the degree of underpricing.[21]

This is a controversial issue and we suspect that Bhagat and Frost's study may not be the final word on it. There is no evidence that companies are on average

---

[20] S. Bhagat and P.A. Frost, "Issuing Costs to Existing Shareholders in Competitive and Negotiated Underwritten Public Utility Equity Offerings," *Journal of Financial Economics,* **15**: 233–259 (January–February 1986).

[21] Looking at an earlier period, Logue and Jarrow found a greater degree of underpricing for competitive issues, which almost offset the benefits of the lower underwriting spread. See D.E. Logue and R.A. Jarrow, "Negotiation vs. Competitive Bidding in the Sale of Securities by Public Utilities," *Financial Management,* **7**: 31–39 (Autumn 1978).

losing out from competitive bidding and, according to Bhagat and Frost's calculations, they may be reducing their costs substantially.

15–4   THE PRIVATE PLACEMENT

Whenever a company makes a public offering, it is required to obtain approval from the securities commissions for the jurisdictions in which it sells the issue. It can avoid this costly process if it is willing to sell the security privately. In Canada, this can be done if the purchasers are "exempt institutions," such as banks, trust companies, or insurance companies. A private placement can also be made to senior officers of the firm making the offering, or their close relatives, or to fewer than 25 sophisticated investors.

One of the disadvantages of a private placement is that the investor cannot easily resell the security. For the common stock investor this drawback looms large, so **letter stock**, as it is called,[22] is rarely issued except by small, closely held companies.

Liquidity is less important to institutions like life insurance companies, which invest huge amounts of money in corporate debt for the "long haul." Consequently, an active private placement mechanism has evolved for corporate debt. The size of this market is illustrated by Table 15–5, which shows the numbers of public and private offerings and the aggregate amounts raised through each channel from 1976 to 1980. You can see that private placements outnumbered public issues, although the public issues were generally larger. Also note that private placements were used more by industrial firms than by utilities.

Table 15-5
A Comparison of Debt Financing in Public and Private Markets, 1976–1980. In Some Years, the Total Amount of Private Placements Nearly Matches the Amount Raised by Public Issues (figures in billions, numbers of issues in parentheses).

	Utilities		Industrials		Total[a]	
	Private	Public	Private	Public	Private	Public
1976	$2.2	8.2	10.6	8.4	20.5	31.9
	(109)	(128)	(540)	(99)	(963)	(454)
1977	1.9	8.3	13.8	4.9	23.7	27.6
	(97)	(113)	(810)	(88)	(1,290)	(448)
1978	2.0	7.7	12.3	4.1	21.7	23.4
	(123)	(92)	(731)	(106)	(1,323)	(364)
1979	3.8	9.2	7.9	6.5	19.5	28.9
	(127)	(98)	(661)	(109)	(1,209)	(343)
1980	1.7	13.1	6.9	15.2	14.5	41.6
	(76)	(138)	(494)	(212)	(933)	(517)

[a] Includes issues by transportation, finance, and other companies in addition to issues by utilities and industrials.

Source: Compiled from issues listed in the *Investment Dealers Digest*, by G.D. Hawkins, "Essays on Non-Publicly Issued Debt: Revolving Credit Agreements and the Pricing of Privately Placed Debt," unpublished Ph.D. dissertation, MIT, 1982, table I, p. 57.

---

[22] So-called because it requires a letter from the buyer confirming that the stock is not bought for resale, or will not be sold within a specified period of time.

Often the privately placed debt is negotiated directly between the company and the lender. If the issue is too large to be absorbed by one institution, the company generally employs an investment banker to draw up the prospectus and identify possible buyers.

As you would expect, the costs of issuing private placements are less than for public issues. Unfortunately, we have no up-to-date statistics on issue costs for private placements, but we do know that underwriting costs are substantially lower than, say, the figures shown for public debt issues in Table 15–2. This is a particular advantage for companies making smaller issues.

Another advantage of the private placement is that the debt contract can be custom-tailored for firms with special problems or opportunities. The relationship between borrower and lender is much more intimate. Imagine a $20 million debt issue privately placed with an insurance company and compare it with an equivalent public issue held by 200 anonymous investors. The insurance company can justify a more thorough investigation of the company's prospects and therefore may be more willing to accept unusual terms or conditions.[23] Renegotiating the debt contract in response to unexpected developments is also extremely cumbersome for a public issue but relatively easy for a private placement.

Therefore, it is not surprising that private placements occupy a particular niche in the corporate debt market, namely loans to small-sized and medium-sized firms. These are the firms that face the highest issue costs in public issues, that require the most detailed investigation, and that may require specialized, flexible loan arrangements.[24]

Of course, these advantages are not free. Lenders in private placements have to be compensated for the risks they face and for the costs of research and negotiation. They also have to be compensated for holding an illiquid asset. All of these factors are rolled into the interest rate paid by the firm. It is difficult to generalize about the differences in interest rates between private placements and public issues, but a typical differential is on the order of 50 basis points or 0.50 percentage points.

15–5　SUMMARY

In this chapter we have summarized the various procedures for issuing corporate securities. We first looked at how infant companies raise venture capital to carry them through to the point where they can make their first public issue of stock. We then looked at how companies can make further public issues of securities by a general cash offer. Finally, we looked at the private placement. It is always difficult to summarize a summary. Instead, we will attempt to state the most important implications for the financial manager who must decide how to raise capital:

1. *Larger is cheaper.* There are always economies of scale in issuing securities. It is cheaper to go to the market once for $100 million than to make two trips for $50 million each. Consequently, firms "bunch" security issues. That may often mean relying on short-term financing until a large issue is justified. Or it may mean issuing more than is needed at the moment in order to avoid another issue later.

---

[23] Of course, debt with the same terms could be offered publicly, but then 200 separate investigations would be required—a much more expensive proposition.

[24] However, many large companies use private placements too. Gregory Hawkins examined a sample of large firms listed in the 1977 *Moody's Industrial Manual.* Eight percent of the firms that had made public debt issues had *also* borrowed privately. See G.D. Hawkins, "Essays on Non-Publicly Issued Debt: Revolving Credit Agreements and the Pricing of Privately Placed Debt," unpublished Ph.D. dissertation, MIT, 1982, table II, p. 62.

2. *There are no issue costs for retained earnings.* There are significant costs associated with any stock issue. But stock issues can be avoided to the extent that the firm can plow back its earnings. Why then do we observe firms paying generous cash dividends *and* issuing stock from time to time? Why don't they cut the dividend, reduce new issues, and avoid paying underwriters, lawyers, and accountants? This is a question to which we will return in Chapter 16.

3. *Private placements for the small, risky, and unusual.* We do not mean that large, safe, and conventional firms should rule out private placements. Enormous amounts of capital are sometimes raised by this method. For example, AT&T once borrowed $500 million in a single private placement. But the special advantages of private placement stem from avoiding registration expenses and a more direct relationship with the lender. These are not worth as much to blue-chip borrowers.

4. *Watch out for underpricing.* Underpricing is a hidden cost to the existing shareholders. Fortunately, it is usually serious only for companies who are selling stock to the public for the first time.

5. *New issues may depress the stock price.* The extent of this price pressure varies, but for industrial issues, the fall in the value of the existing stock may amount to a significant proportion of the money raised. We think that the likely explanation for this pressure is the information the market reads into the company's decision to issue stock.

APPENDIX 15–1   THE PRIVILEGED SUBSCRIPTION OR RIGHTS ISSUE

We have examined what happens when firms sell their securities to the public at large: now we must look at what happens when they restrict the offer to existing stockholders.

Firms' articles of incorporation often state that shareholders have a **pre-emptive right** to subscribe to new offerings. Such a provision simply reinforces the fact that shareholders, as owners of the business, are entitled under common law to anything of value that the company may distribute, including the potentially valuable opportunity to buy new issues of securities. A strict interpretation of pre-emptive rights would place intolerable restrictions on management's freedom of action, and so it is not surprising that these rights have been interpreted in a limited way. First, they usually apply to issues of common stock, to convertible securities, and to voting preferred stock, but not to issues of debt. Second, they do not apply to common stock that is issued as payment for a merger.

How Rights Issues Work

It is important to understand the mechanics of offering securities to existing shareholders. Let us look at an example. In September 1989, Nova Corp. issued over $445,000,000 of common stock by a rights issue. The preliminary stages of the issue were similar to those for any other public issue, although in this case, since a great deal of information about Nova is publicly available, the firm merely had to issue a short form prospectus[25] to buyers. The short form prospectus did not contain any financial statements, although these were filed with the

---

[25] Nova also filed a full registration statement for the rights offering with the SEC so that U.S. shareholders could exercise their rights. The same information was also filed with the International Stock Exchange of Great Britain and Northern Ireland, so that the U.K. shareholders could exercise their rights.

appropriate securities commissions. The major difference lay in selling procedures. Shareholders of record (that is, those listed on the company's books as
share owners) on August 24, 1989, were sent "rights certificates"[26] showing that
they owned one "right" for each share they held. Five of these rights entitled a
shareholder to buy one additional share[27] at a subscription or issue price of $8.75
at any time before September 14, 1989. To take advantage of the offer, the
shareholder simply had to **exercise** the right by completing the subscription
form on the rights certificate and forwarding it with payment to the firm's
subscription agent, National Trust.

Shareholders could either sell, exercise, or throw away these rights. The rights
were listed for trading on the Toronto, Montréal, Alberta, and New York stock
exchanges. Those who didn't sell should have postponed any exercise decision
until the expiry date. At that point, they should have taken advantage of the
opportunity to buy stock at $8.75 if, and only if, the stock price was higher than
$8.75.

To guard against the danger that the price might end up below the subscription
price, Nova arranged for the issue to be underwritten. Instead of actually buying
the issue as in the cash offer, the underwriters were paid a **management** or
standby fee of $9,100,000.[28] In return, they stood ready to buy any unsubscribed
or "residual" shares for the subscription price. (In other rights issues, the underwriter may be able to deduct a **take-up fee** from the subscription price, but there
was no such fee in this case.) The underwriters were protected by a **market-out**
clause, allowing them out of the standby arrangement if there were various types
of significant adverse changes in market conditions.

As it turned out, Nova shares closed at $9.75 on the September 14 expiry date.
Even though this was above the $8.75 subscription price, there were about 1.7
million shares that were unsubscribed, because the stockholders failed to exercise
or sell their rights. We must attribute this lapse to either ignorance or vacations.[29]

**How a Rights
Issue Affects
the Stock Price**

The left-hand portion of Table 15–6 shows the case of a stockholder who owned
five shares of Nova stock just prior to the rights issue. The price of the stock at
that time was about $10, and so this stockholder's holding was worth 5 × 10 or
$50. The Nova offer gave the opportunity to purchase one additional share for
$8.75. Put yourself in the stockholder's shoes. If you buy the new share immedi-
ately, your holding increases to six shares and, other things being equal, the

---

[26] Sometimes the rights certificate is called a **warrant**.

[27] A rights issue that gives the shareholder one right for each share held is known as a "New
York" right. In Canada and the United States, almost all issues are New York rights. But in
some countries, such as the United Kingdom, you need one right to purchase one new share.
This is known as a "Philadelphia right." If Nova were a company in the United Kingdom, the
shareholder would need to own 5 shares in order to receive one right and this right would be
correspondingly 5 times more valuable.

[28] You can think of standby underwriting as providing shareholders with an option. In return for
paying the standby fee, they can sell their stock to the underwriters at the issue price. We will
tell you how to value such options in Chapter 20.

[29] Despite this shortfall, Nova did not have to turn to its underwriters. Nova's shareholders had
been given an oversubscription privilege, which allowed them to buy unsubscribed shares at the
subscription price ($8.75). As it turned out, Nova had no trouble selling the unsubscribed
shares to shareholders who applied for extra shares. Of course, these shareholders profited at
the expense of the vacationers and *incognoscenti*.

Table 15–6
Issue Price in a Rights Offering Does Not Affect the Shareholder's Wealth

	1 for 5 at $8.75	1 for 2½ at $4.375
Before issue		
Number of shares held	5	5
Share price (cum-rights)	$10.00	$10.00
Value of holding	$50.00	$50.00
After issue		
Number of new shares	1	2
Amount of new investment	$8.75	2 × $4.375 = $8.75
Total value of holding	$58.75	$58.75
Total number of shares	6	7
New share price (ex-rights)	58.75/6 = $9.79	58.75/7 = $8.39
Value of a right	10.00 − 9.79 = $0.21	10.00 − 8.39 = $1.61

value of the 6 shares is $50 + 8.75 = \$58.75$. The price per share after the issue would no longer be $50, but $58.75/6 = \$9.79$.

The only difference between the old $10 shares and the new $9.79 shares was that the former carried the rights to subscribe to the issue. Therefore, the old shares are generally termed *cum-rights* or *rights-on* shares and the new shares are termed *ex-rights* shares. The 21-cent difference in price between the two shares represented the price of one right. We can confirm that this is the correct price of the right by imagining a second investor who had no stock in Nova, but wished to acquire some. One way to do this would be to buy five rights at 21 cents and then exercise them at a further cost of $8.75. The total cost of this investor's share would be $5 × 0.21 + \$8.75 = \$9.80$, which, save for rounding error, is the same outlay required to buy one of the new shares directly.

Inside the back cover of this book we have listed the formulas for calculating the value of a right and the corresponding ex-rights price.

Issue Price Is Irrelevant as long as the Rights Are Exercised

It should be clear on reflection that Nova could have raised the same amount of money on a variety of terms. For example, instead of a 1-for-5 at $8.75 it could have made a 1-for-2½ at $4.375. In this case it would have sold twice as many shares at half the price. If we now work through the arithmetic again in the right-hand portion of Table 15–6, we can see that the issue price is irrelevant in a rights offering. After all, it cannot affect the real plant and equipment owned by the company or the proportion of these assets to which each shareholder is entitled. Therefore, the only thing a firm ought to worry about in setting the terms of a rights issue is the possibility that the stock price will fall below the issue price. If that happens, shareholders will not take up their rights and the whole issue will be torpedoed. You can avoid this danger by arranging a standby agreement with the underwriter. But standby agreements tend to be expensive. It may be cheaper just to set the issue price low enough to foreclose the possibility of failure.

The Choice between the Cash Offer and the Rights Issue

You now know about the two principal forms of public issue—the cash offer to all investors and the rights issue to existing shareholders. The former method is used for almost all debt issues and unseasoned stock issues and many seasoned stock issues. Rights issues are largely restricted to seasoned stock issues.

One essential difference between the two methods is that in a rights offering the issue price is largely irrelevant. Shareholders can sell their new stock or their rights in a free market. Therefore, they can expect to receive a fair price. In a cash offer, however, the issue price may be important. If the company sells stock for less than the market would bear, the buyer has made a profit at the expense of existing shareholders. Although this danger creates a natural presumption in favour of the rights issue, it can be argued that underpricing is a serious problem only in the case of the unseasoned issue of stock in which a rights issue is not a feasible alternative.

Some firms whose stockholders have enjoyed preemptive rights have cajoled their stockholders into giving them up. For example, consider the following appeal made in 1976 by Consolidated Edison to its stockholders:

> Expenses involved in a pre-emptive Common Stock rights offering are significantly greater than expenses involved in a direct offering of Common Stock to the public due to additional printing and mailing costs, expenses associated with the handling of rights and the processing of subscriptions, higher underwriters' commissions and the longer time required for consummation of the financing. Thus, if the amendment is adopted, the Company will be able to obtain the amount of capital needed through the issuance of fewer shares. Over a period of time this will result in slightly less dilution, higher equity value per share, and better earnings per share.[30]

What are the major points in this argument?

1. *Higher expenses?* Take another look at Table 15–1. Rights issues seem no more expensive than general cash offers. Nova didn't think its offer was expensive.[31] Note also that underwriters' compensation is a major part of the costs of rights issues, and that rights issues don't have to be underwritten as long as the exercise price is set well below the stock price. *Nonunderwritten* rights issues might be significantly *cheaper* than general cash offers.[32]
2. *Longer time required?* Perhaps an extra month—rarely an important consideration.
3. *Fewer shares issued?* You should know the argument against that one by now.

In short, the arguments that firms make for avoiding rights issues don't make sense. We don't know why they use cash offers. Perhaps there are hidden reasons, but until they are uncovered we don't think you should rule out rights issues.

---

[30] We are indebted to Clifford Smith for finding the quotation from Consolidated Edison.

[31] Some financial executives dismiss rights offerings as expensive and cumbersome. American Electric, according to Gerald P. Maloney, senior vice president for finance, has found them to be neither.
  'The underwriting costs on the utility's last offering totaled $1.1 million,' Mr. Maloney said in an interview the other day, 'only six-tenths of one percent of the total amount of money involved.'
  'We think that's very inexpensive,' he continued. He estimated that underwriting costs would have amounted to '3 or 4 percent' if the company had bypassed shareholders and gone directly to the public."
  From Richard Phalon, "Personal Investing—American Electric's Rights Offering," *The New York Times*, July 9, 1977.

[32] Clifford Smith, who prepared Table 15–3, also calculated costs for a small sample of nonunderwritten rights issues, and found average issue costs of only 2.5%.

APPENDIX
15–2   MARVIN'S NEW ISSUE PROSPECTUS[33]

PROSPECTUS

900,000 Shares
Marvin Enterprises Inc.
Common Shares

Of the 900,000 shares of Common Stock offered hereby, 500,000 shares are being sold by the Company and 400,000 shares are being sold by the Selling Stockholders. See "Principal and Selling Stockholders." The Company will not receive any of the proceeds from the sale of shares by the Selling Stockholders.

Before this offering there has been no public market for the Common Shares. **These securities involve a high degree of risk. See "Certain Considerations."** In the opinion of counsel, the Common Shares will be eligible for investment under certain statutes. See "Eligibility for Investment."

	Price to Public	Underwriting Discount	Proceeds to Company (1)	Proceeds to Selling Stockholders (2)
Per share	$80.00	$5.00	$75.00	$75.00
Total (2)	$72,000,000	$4,500,000	$37,500,000	$30,000,000

(1) Before deducting expenses payable by the Company estimated at $820,000, of which $455,555 will be paid by the Company and $364,445 by the Selling Stockholders.
(2) The Company has granted to the Underwriters an option to purchase up to an additional 50,000 shares at the initial public offering price, less the underwriting discount, solely to cover over-allotment.

The Common Shares are offered subject to receipt and acceptance by the Underwriters, to prior sale, and to the Underwriters' right to reject any order in whole or in part and to withdraw, cancel, or modify the offer without notice.

Klein Merrick Inc.   **February 3, 2009**

---

[33] Most prospectuses have content similar to that of the Marvin prospects but go into considerably more detail. Also, we have omitted from Marvin prospectus the list of underwriters and Marvin's financial statements.

Prospectus Summary

The following summary information is qualified in its entirety by the detailed information and financial statements appearing elsewhere in this Prospectus.

The Offering

Common Stock offered by the Company .... 500,000 shares
Common Stock offered by the Selling Stockholders .... 400,000 shares
Common Stock to be outstanding after this offering .... 4,100,000 shares

Use of Proceeds

For the construction of new manufacturing facilities and to provide working capital.

The Company

Marvin Enterprises Inc. designs, manufactures, and markets gargle blasters for domestic use. Its manufacturing facilities employ integrated microcircuits to control the genetic engineering processes used to manufacture gargle blasters.

The Company was organized in Ottawa in 2003.

Use of Proceeds

The net proceeds of this offering are expected to be $37,044,445. Of the net proceeds, approximately $27.0 million will be used to finance expansion of the Company's principal manufacturing facilities. The balance will be used for working capital.

Certain Considerations

Investment in the Common Shares involves a high degree of risk. The following factors should be carefully considered in evaluating the Company:

Substantial Capital Needs   The Company will require additional financing to continue its expansion policy. The Company believes that its relations with its lenders are good, but there can be no assurance that additional financing will be available in the future.

Licensing   The expanded manufacturing facilities are to be used for the production of a new imploding gargle blaster. An advisory panel to the U.S. Food and Drug Administration (FDA) has recommended approval of this product for the U.S. market but no decision has yet been reached by the full FDA committee.

Dividend Policy

The company has not paid cash dividends on its Common Shares and does not anticipate that dividends will be paid on the Common Shares in the foreseeable future.

Eligibility for Investment

In the opinion of Thatcher, Kohl, and Lubbers, Montréal, and of Hawke and Mulroney, Toronto, the Common Shares offered hereby will qualify at the closing date as eligible investments only by resort to the so-called "basket" provisions for:

(i)   insurance companies regulated under the Canadian and British Insurance Companies Act;
(ii) loan companies regulated under the Loan Companies Act;
(iii) pension plans registered under the Pension Benefits Standards Act.

In the opinion of such counsel, under the current provisions of the Income Tax Act (Canada), the Common Shares are also qualified investments for registered retirement savings plans, registered retirement income funds, and deferred profit-sharing plans.

Management

The following table sets forth information regarding the Company's directors, executive officers, and key employees.

Name	Age	Position
George Marvin	32	President, Chief Executive Officer, & Director
Mildred Marvin	28	Treasurer & Director
Chip Norton	30	General Manager

George Marvin — George Marvin established the Company in 2003 and has been its Chief Executive Officer since that date. He is a past president of the Institute of Gargle Blasters.

Mildred Marvin — Mildred Marvin has been employed by the Company since 2003.

Chip Norton — Mr. Norton has been General Manager of the Company since 2003. He is a former vice president of Amalgamated Blasters, Inc.

Executive Compensation

The following table sets forth the cash compensation paid for services rendered for the year 2008 by the Executive officers:

Name	Capacity	Cash Compensation
George Marvin	President and Chief Executive Officer	$200,000
Mildred Marvin	Treasurer	$120,000
Chip Norton	General Manager	$120,000

Certain Transactions

At various times between 2005 and 2007 First Meriam Venture Partners invested a total of $8.5 million in the Company.

Principal and Selling Stockholders

The following table sets forth certain information regarding the beneficial ownership of the Company's voting Common Stock as of the date of this prospectus by (i) each person known by the Company to be the beneficial owner of more than 5% of its voting Common Stock, and (ii) each director of the Company who beneficially owns voting Common Stock. Unless otherwise indicated, each owner has sole voting and dispositive power over his shares.

	Common Stock				
Name of Beneficial Owner	Shares Beneficially Owned Prior to Offering		Shares to Be Sold	Shares Beneficially Owned After Offer (1)	
	Number	Percent		Number	Percent
George Marvin	337,500	9.4	60,000	277,500	6.8
Mildred Marvin	337,500	9.4	60,000	277,500	6.8
Chip Norton	250,000	6.9	80,000	170,000	4.1
First Meriam Venture Partners	1,700,000	47.2	—	1,700,000	41.5
TFS Investors	260,000	7.2	—	260,000	6.3
Centri-Venture Partnership	260,000	7.2	—	260,000	6.3
Henry Pobble	180,000	5.0	—	180,000	4.4
Georgina Sloberg	200,000	5.6	200,000	—	—

(1) Assuming no exercise of the Underwriters' over-allotment option.

Description of Capital Stock

The Company's authorized capital stock consists of 10,000,000 shares of voting Common Stock.

As of the date of this Prospectus, there are 10 holders of record of the Common Stock.

Under the terms of one of the Company's loan agreements, the Company may not pay cash dividends on Common Stock except from net profits without the written consent of the lender.

Underwriting

Subject to the terms and conditions set forth in the Underwriting Agreement, the Company has agreed to sell to each of the Underwriters named below, and each of the Underwriters, for whom Klein Merrick Inc. are acting as Representatives, has severally agreed to purchase from the Company, the number of shares set forth opposite its name below.

Underwriters   **Number of Shares to Be Purchased**

[Table of Underwriters omitted.]

In the Underwriting Agreement, the several Underwriters have agreed, subject to the terms and conditions set forth therein, to purchase all shares offered hereby if any such shares are purchased. In the event of a default by any Underwriter, the Underwriting Agreement provides that, in certain circumstances, purchase commitments of the nondefaulting Underwriters may be increased or the Underwriting Agreement may be terminated.

There is no public market for the Common Stock. The price to the public for the Common Shares was determined by negotiation between the Company and the Underwriters and was based on, among other things, the Company's financial and operating history and condition, its prospects and the prospects for its industry in general, the management of the Company, and the market prices of securities for companies in businesses similar to that of the Company.

Legal Matters

Certain legal matters in connection with this offering will be passed upon on behalf of the Company by Thatcher, Kohl, and Lubbers, Montréal, and on behalf of the Underwriters by Hawke and Mulroney, Toronto.

The validity of the shares of Common Stock offered by the Prospectus is being passed on for the Company by Thatcher, Kohl, and Lubbers, Montréal, and for the Underwriters by Hawke and Mulroney, Toronto.

Experts

The consolidated financial statements of the Company have been so included in reliance on the reports of Hopper Firebrand, independent accountants, given on the authority of that firm as experts in auditing and accounting.

Financial Statements

[*Text and tables omitted.*]

APPENDIX
15–3   SHELF REGISTRATION

In 1982 the SEC in the United States issued its Rule 415, which allows large companies to file a single registration statement covering financing plans for up to two years into the future. The actual issue, or issues, can be done with scant additional paperwork, whenever the firm needs the cash or thinks it can issue securities at an attractive price. This is called *shelf registration* — the registration statement is "put on the shelf," to be taken down and used as needed.

Think of how a financial manager might use shelf registration. As financial manager of Establishment Industries, you anticipate a need for up to $200 million of new long-term debt during the next year or so. You file a shelf registration for that amount. We will assume that Establishment Industries qualifies for shelf registration and that the SEC approves the filing.

Establishment now has prior approval to issue up to $200 million of debt, but it isn't obligated to issue a penny. Nor is it required to work through any particular underwriters — the registration statement may name one or more underwriters the firm thinks it may work with, but others can be added later.

Now you can sit back and issue debt as needed, in bits and pieces if you like. Suppose Merrill Lynch comes across an insurance company with $10 million ready to invest in blue-chip corporate bonds. Your phone rings. It's Merrill Lynch offering to buy $10 million of your bonds, priced to yield, say, 12$\frac{1}{2}$%. If you think that's a good price, you say "OK" and the deal is done, subject to only a little additional paperwork. Merrill Lynch then resells the bonds to the insurance company, it hopes, at a slightly higher price than it paid for them, thus earning a middleman's profit.

Here is another possible deal. Suppose you don't know, or don't believe, that capital markets are efficient, and you think you see a window of opportunity in which interest rates are "temporarily low." You invite bids for $100 million of bonds. Some bids may come from large investment bankers acting alone, others from ad hoc syndicates. But that's not your problem: if the price is right, you just take the best deal offered.

Thus shelf registration gives firms several different things that they did not have previously:

1. Securities can be issued in dribs and drabs in successive *tranches* without incurring excessive transaction costs.
2. Securities can be issued on short notice.
3. Security issues can be timed to take advantage of "market conditions" (although any financial manager who can *reliably* identify favourable market conditions could make a lot more money by quitting and becoming a bond or stock trader instead).
4. The issuing firm can make sure that underwriters compete for its business. It can, in effect, auction off securities.

Underwriters do compete. Although several large investment banking houses lobbied hard against Rule 415 when the SEC was considering it, once the rule was approved, they played the new game with gusto. As an attorney who works with them observed, "If the SEC passed a rule saying you had to do underwriting in Watertown, N.Y., in the snow stark naked, these guys would take the first plane up."[34]

---

[34] Quoted in Tim Carrington, "New Ball Game: Investment Bankers Enter a New Era," *The Wall Street Journal,* June 21, 1982, p. 10.

Not all companies eligible for shelf registration actually use it for all their public issues. Sometimes they believe they can get a better deal by making one large issue through traditional channels, especially when the security to be issued has some unusual feature or when the firm believes it needs the investment banker's counsel or stamp of approval on the issue. Shelf registration is thus less common for issues of common stock or convertible securities than for garden variety corporate bonds.

FURTHER READING

Two useful works on underwriting or investment banking are:

I. Friend, et al., *Investment Banking and the New Issues Market*, The World Publishing Company, Cleveland, 1967.

C.W. Smith, "Investment Banking and the Capital Acquisition Process," *Journal of Financial Economics*, **15**: 3–29 (January–February 1986).

For information on venture capital in Canada, see:

Department of Industry, Science and Technology and Association of Canadian Venture Capital Companies, *Venture Capital in Canada: A Guide and Sources*, Ottawa (1989).

There has been a number of studies of the market for unseasoned issues of common stock. Two good articles to start with are:

J.R. Ritter, "The 'Hot Issue' Market of 1980," *Journal of Business*, **57**: 215–240 (1984).

K. Rock, "Why New Issues Are Underpriced," *Journal of Financial Economics*, **15**: 187–212 (January–February 1986).

The first two articles both find a significant and permanent fall in price after an industrial stock issue in the United States. The Marsh paper, using data from the United Kingdom, finds only a negligible fall in price:

P. Asquith and D.W. Mullins, "Equity Issues and Offering Dilution," *Journal of Financial Economics*, **15**: 61–90 (January–February 1986).

P.R. Marsh, "Equity Rights Issues and the Efficiency of the UK Stock Market," *Journal of Finance*, **34**: 839–862 (September 1979).

R.W. Masulis and A.N. Korwar, "Seasoned Equity Offerings: An Empirical Investigation," *Journal of Financial Economics*, **15**: 91–118 (January–February 1986).

Smith, in the following article, argues that the cheapest way to issue stock is to offer it by a rights issue to existing stockholders. Hansen and Pinkerton disagree:

R.S. Hansen and J.M. Pinkerton, "Direct Equity Financing: A Resolution of a Paradox," *Journal of Finance*, **37**: 651–666 (June 1982).

C.W. Smith, "Alternative Methods for Raising Capital: Rights versus Underwritten Offerings," *Journal of Financial Economics*, **5**: 273–307 (December 1977).

A good analysis of the relative merits of negotiated underwriting and competitive bidding is given in:

S. Bhagat and P.A. Frost, "Issuing Costs to Existing Shareholders in Competitive and Negotiated Underwritten Public Utility Equity Offerings," *Journal of Financial Economics*, **15**: 213–232 (January–February 1986).

The following collection contains several articles on the issue of international securities:

A.M. George and I.H. Giddy (eds.), *International Finance Handbook*, Volume 1, John Wiley & Sons, New York, 1983.

For an analysis of the role of private placements see:

E. Shapiro and C.R. Wolf, *The Role of Private Placements in Corporate Finance*, Division of Research, Graduate School of Business Administration, Harvard University, Boston, 1972.

QUIZ

1. Beside each of the following issue methods we have listed two issues. Choose the one most likely to employ that method.
   (a) Rights issue (issue of seasoned stock/issue of unseasoned stock)
   (b) Competitive general cash offer (bond issue by industrial company/bond issue by utility holding company)
   (c) Private placement (issue of seasoned stock/bond issue by industrial company)
   (d) Shelf registration (issue of unseasoned stock/bond issue by a large industrial company)

2. Each of the following terms is associated with one of the events beneath. Can you match them up?
   (a) Company registrar
   (b) Best efforts
   (c) Tombstone
   (d) Red herring
   (e) Shelf registration
   (f) Letter stock
     (A) The company issues a preliminary prospectus.
     (B) Some issues are privately placed and exempted from issuing a prospectus.
     (C) An advertisement is published in the financial press listing members of the underwriting syndicate.
     (D) A trust company is appointed to ensure that no unauthorized shares are issued.
     (E) The underwriter accepts responsibility only to try to sell the issue.
     (F) Several tranches of the same security may be issued under one registration.

3. State for each of the following pairs of issues which you would expect to involve the lower proportionate underwriting and administrative costs, other things equal:
   (a) A large issue/a small issue
   (b) A bond issue/a common stock issue
   (c) A large negotiated bond issue/a large competitive bond issue
   (d) A small private placement of bonds/a small general cash offer of bonds

4. Look at Marvin's initial public offering in Appendix 15-2:
   (a) If there is unexpectedly heavy demand for the issue, how many extra shares can the underwriters buy?
   (b) How many shares are to be sold in the primary offering? How many will be sold in the secondary offering?
   (c) What with the benefit of hindsight was the degree of underpricing? How does that compare with the average degree of underpricing found by Ritter?
   (d) There are three kinds of cost to Marvin's new issue—underwriting expense, administrative costs, and underpricing. What was the *total* dollar cost of the Marvin issue?

5. You need to choose between issuing
   (A) *A public issue of $10 million face value of 10-year debt.* The interest rate on the debt would be 8.5% and the debt would be issued at face value. The underwriting spread would be 1.5% and other expenses would be $80,000.

(B) *A private placement of $10 million face value of 10-year debt.* The interest rate on the private placement would be 9% but the total issuing expenses would be only $30,000.
(a) What is the difference in the proceeds to the company net of expenses?
(b) Other things equal, which is the better deal?
(c) What other factors beyond the interest rate and issue costs would you wish to consider before deciding between the two offers?

6. Associated Breweries is planning to market unleaded beer. To finance the venture it proposes to make a rights issue at $10 of 1 new share for each 2 shares held. (The company currently has outstanding 100,000 shares priced at $40 a share.) Assuming that the new money is invested to earn a fair return, give values for the following using the analysis of Appendix 15-1:
(a) Number of rights needed to purchase one share
(b) Number of new shares
(c) Amount of new investment
(d) Total value of company after issue
(e) Total number of shares after issue
(f) Rights-on price
(g) Ex-rights price
(h) Price of a right

QUESTIONS AND PROBLEMS

1. In some countries initial public offerings of common stock are sold by auction. Another procedure is for the underwriter to advertise the issue publicly and invite orders for shares at the issue price. If the applications exceed the number of shares on offer, then they are scaled down in proportion; if there are too few applications, any unsold shares are left with the underwriters. Compare these procedures with the initial public offering in Canada. Can you think of any better ways to sell new shares?

2. (a) Why do venture capital companies prefer to advance money in stages? If you were the management of Marvin Enterprises, would you have been happy with such an arrangement? With the benefit of hindsight did First Meriam gain or lose by advancing money in stages?
(b) The price at which First Meriam would advance more money to Marvin was not fixed in advance. But Marvin could have given First Meriam an *option* to buy more shares at a preset price. Would this have been better?
(c) At the second stage Marvin could have raised money from another venture capital company in preference to First Meriam. To protect themselves against this, venture capital firms sometimes demand first refusal on new capital issues. Would you recommend this arrangement?

3. "For small issues of common stock, the costs of flotation amount to about 15% of the proceeds. This means that the opportunity cost of external equity capital is about 15 percentage points higher than that of retained earnings." Does this follow?

4. Do you think that there could be a shortage of finance for new ventures? Should the government help to provide such finance and, if so, how?

5. Get hold of a copy of the prospectus for a recent issue of securities. How do the issue costs compare with (a) those of the Marvin issue in Appendix 15-2, (b) those shown in Tables 15–1 and 15–2? Can you suggest reasons for the difference?

6. In 1991 Pandora, Inc. makes a rights issue at $5 a share of one new share for every four shares held. Before the issue there were 10 million shares outstanding and the share price was $6. Using the analysis of Appendix 15-1, answer the following questions:
   (a) What is the total amount of new money raised?
   (b) How many rights are needed to buy one new share?
   (c) What is the value of one right?
   (d) What is the prospective ex-rights price?
   (e) How far could the total value of the company fall before shareholders would be unwilling to take up their rights?

7. Problem 6 contains details of a rights offering by Pandora. Suppose that the company had decided to issue new stock at $4. How many new shares would it have needed to raise the same sum of money? Recalculate the answers to questions (b) to (e) in problem 6. Show that Pandora's shareholders are just as well off if it issues the shares at $4 a share rather than the $5 assumed in problem 6.

8. Construct a simple numerical example to show the following:
   (a) Existing shareholders are made worse off when a company makes a cash offer of new stock below the market price.
   (b) Existing shareholders are *not* made worse off when a company makes a rights issue of new stock below the market price even if the stockholders do not wish to take up their rights.

*9. There are three reasons that a common stock issue might cause a fall in price—(a) demand for the company's stock is inelastic, (b) the issue causes price pressure until it has been digested, and (c) management has information that stockholders do not have. Explain these reasons more fully. Which do you find most plausible? Is there any way that you could seek to test whether you are right?

10. (a) "A signal is credible only if a false signal is costly." Explain why management's willingness to invest in Marvin's equity rather than its debt was a credible signal. Was their willingness to accept only a part of the venture capital that would eventually be needed also a credible signal?
    (b) "When managers take their reward in the form of increased leisure or executive jets, the cost is borne by the shareholders." Explain how First Meriam's financing package avoided this problem.

P·A·R·T

5

DIVIDEND POLICY
AND CAPITAL
STRUCTURE

C · H · A · P · T · E · R

16

THE DIVIDEND CONTROVERSY

In this chapter we explain how companies set their dividend payments and we discuss the controversial question of how dividend policy affects value.

Why should you care about the answer to this question? Of course, if you are responsible for deciding on your company's dividend payment, you will want to know how it affects value. But there is a more general reason than that. We have up to this point assumed that the company's investment decision is independent of its financing policy. In that case a good project is a good project is a good project, no matter who undertakes it or how it is ultimately financed. If dividend policy does not affect value, that is still true. But perhaps it *does* affect value. In that case the attractiveness of a new project may depend on where the money is coming from. For example, if investors prefer companies with high payouts, companies might be reluctant to take on investments financed by retained earnings.

The first step toward understanding dividend policy is to recognize that the phrase means different things to different people. Therefore we must start by defining what we mean by it.

A firm's decisions about dividends are often mixed up with other financing and investment decisions. Some firms pay low dividends because management is optimistic about the firm's future and wishes to retain earnings for expansion. In this case the dividend is a by-product of the firm's capital budgeting decision. Suppose, however, that the future opportunities evaporate, that a dividend increase is announced, and that the stock price falls. How do we separate the impact of the dividend increase from the impact of investors' disappointment at the lost growth opportunities?

Another firm might finance capital expenditures largely by borrowing. This releases cash for dividends. In this case the firm's dividend is a by-product of the borrowing decision.

We must isolate dividend policy from other problems of financial management. The precise question we should ask is: "What is the effect of a change in cash dividends paid, *given the firm's capital budgeting and borrowing decisions*?" Of course the cash used to finance a dividend increase has to come from somewhere. If we fix the firm's investment outlays and borrowing, there is only one possible source—an issue of stock. Thus we define *dividend policy* as the trade-off between retaining earnings on the one hand and paying out cash and issuing new shares on the other.

This trade-off may seem artificial at first, for we do not observe firms scheduling a stock issue with every dividend payment. But there are many firms that pay dividends and also issue stock from time to time. They could avoid the stock issues by paying lower dividends. Many other firms restrict dividends so that they *do not* have to issue shares. They could issue stock occasionally and increase the dividend. Both groups of firms are facing the dividend policy trade-off.

16-1   HOW DIVIDENDS ARE PAID

The dividend is set or "declared" by the firm's board of directors. They make an announcement that the payment will be made to all those stockholders who are registered on a particular "record date," which is usually about one to four weeks after the date of the announcement. Dividend cheques are mailed to stockholders about two to four weeks after the record date.

Shares are normally bought and sold "with dividend" or "cum dividend" until four days before the record date. But investors who buy with dividend do not have to worry if their shares are not registered in time. The dividend must be paid over to them by the seller. Similarly, investors who buy a share "ex dividend" are obliged to return the dividend if they receive it.

Some Legal Limitations on Dividends

Suppose that an unscrupulous board decided to sell all the firm's assets and distribute the money as dividends. That would not leave anything in the kitty to pay the company's debts. Therefore, bondholders usually guard against this danger by placing a limit on dividend payments.

Federal and provincial law also helps to protect the company's creditors against excessive dividend payments. For example, for federally incorporated companies, the Canada Business Corporations Act prohibits payment of a dividend if there are "reasonable grounds for believing" that, after payment of the dividend, either, (a) the corporation would be "unable to pay its liabilities as they become due," or (b) "the realizable value of the corporation's assets would . . . be less than . . . its liabilities and stated capital . . ."[1] A company's *stated capital* is the total amount of stock issued. In effect, dividends must come out of the retained earnings and must not push the firm too close to insolvency.

If a firm decides to wholly or partially liquidate, it may repurchase its shares on the open market or by a tender offer, or pay a "liquidating dividend," but this may reduce the realizable value of its assets below its liabilities plus stated capital. In that case, the firm must, by a special resolution of the shareholders, reduce its stated capital.[2]

These laws give most corporations a large degree of flexibility in deciding what to pay out. Nevertheless, they do help prevent unscrupulous firms from escaping their creditors.

Par value of stock has little economic significance. It was often set arbitrarily at $1 per share. Now Canadian corporations issue stock with no par value.

---

[1] Section 40 of the Canada Business Corporations Act [1975].

[2] Canada Business Corporations Act, Section 36.

**Dividends
Come in
Many Forms**

Most dividends are paid in the form of cash. **Regular cash dividends** are usually paid quarterly, but a few companies declare them monthly, semiannually, or annually.[3] The term *regular* merely indicates that the company expects that it will be able to maintain the payment in the future. If the company does not want to give that kind of assurance, it usually declares both a regular and an **extra dividend**. Investors understand that the extra dividend may not be repeated. Finally, the term **special dividend** tends to be reserved specifically for payments that are unlikely to be repeated.

Paying a dividend reduces the amount of retained earnings shown on the firm's balance sheet. However, if all retained earnings are "used up," and if funds are not needed for the protection of creditors, the company may be permitted to pay a **liquidating dividend**. Because such payments are regarded as a return of capital, they are not taxed as income.

Dividends are not always paid in the form of cash. Frequently companies declare **stock dividends**. For example, in the United States, General Tire has paid a yearly stock dividend of 2% for more than a decade. That means it sends each shareholder two extra shares for every 100 shares that he or she currently owns. In Canada, many firms have allowed shareholders the option of receiving cash or stock dividends. A stock dividend is very much like a stock split. Both increase the number of shares, and both reduce value per share, other things equal. If the stock dividend or stock split is distributed among all shareholders, nobody is made better off. But if some shareholders can receive stock dividends and some can receive cash dividends, they may all be able to act to minimize personal taxes, as discussed in Section 16-5.

There are also other types of noncash dividends. For example, companies sometimes send shareholders a sample of their product. The British company Dominion International (formerly Dundee Crematorium) offers its more substantial shareholders a discount cremation. Needless to say, you are not *required* to receive this dividend.

**Share
Repurchase**

When a firm wants to pay cash to its shareholders, it usually declares a cash dividend. But an alternative and increasingly popular method is to repurchase its own stock. In the period 1973–1974, the United States government imposed a limit on dividends but it forgot to impose a limit on share repurchase. Many firms discovered share repurchase for the first time, and the total value of repurchases swelled to about a fifth of the value of dividend payments. IBM was one of the firms to repurchase its stock in 1974. As IBM's rapid expansion of the 1960s slowed down, the company found itself with more cash than it needed. Therefore in 1974 IBM gave back $1.4 billion to its stockholders by repurchasing shares. The Seagram Company has periodically bought back shares. For example, it bought back about five million shares, worth about $300 million, in the fall of 1987.

---

[3] Many companies have automatic dividend reinvestment plans. The usual procedure is for the corporation to send the dividends of the participating stockholders directly to a trust company, which then purchases stock on behalf of shareholders in the open market. However, some firms issue new shares directly to stockholders who wish to reinvest dividends. Often the new shares are issued at a 5% discount from market price; the firm offers this sweetener because it saves the underwriting costs of a regular share issue. Sometimes 10% or more of total dividends will be reinvested under such plans.

There are three principal methods of repurchase: (1) Shares are often acquired in the open market. (2) Shares can be acquired by a general tender offer either to all shareholders or just to small shareholders.[4] In this case the firm usually engages an investment banker to manage the tender and pays a special commission to brokers who persuade shareholders to accept the offer. (3) Finally, repurchase may take place by direct negotiation with a major shareholder. The most notorious instances are **greenmail** transactions, in which the target of a take-over attempt buys off the hostile bidder. Bidders accumulate shares in the target company in the course of the take-over battle. "Greenmail" means that these shares are repurchased by the target at a price which makes the bidder happy to agree to leave the target alone. The price does not always make the target's other shareholders happy, as we point out in Chapter 33.

The most important distinction between repurchase and dividends lies in their tax treatments. This is discussed in Section 16-5.

16-2   HOW DO COMPANIES DECIDE ON DIVIDEND PAYMENTS?

Lintner's Model

In the mid-1950s John Lintner conducted a classic series of interviews with corporate managers about their dividend policies.[5] His description of how dividends are determined can be summarized in four "stylized facts":[6]

1. Firms have long-run target dividend payout ratios.
2. Managers focus more on dividend changes than on absolute levels. Thus, paying a $2.00 dividend is an important financial decision if last year's dividend was $1.00, but no big deal if last year's dividend was $2.00.
3. Dividend changes follow shifts in long-run, sustainable earnings. Managers "smooth" dividends. Transitory earnings changes are unlikely to affect dividend payouts.
4. Managers are reluctant to make dividend changes that might have to be reversed. They are particulary worried about having to rescind a dividend increase.

Lintner developed a simple model which is consistent with these facts and explains dividend payments well. Here it is: Suppose that a firm always stuck to its target payout ratio. Then the dividend payment in the coming year (DIV_1) would equal a constant proportion of earnings per share (EPS_1):

$$DIV_1 = \text{target dividend}$$
$$= \text{target ratio} \times EPS_1$$

The dividend *change* would equal

$$DIV_1 - DIV_0 = \text{target change}$$
$$= \text{target ratio} \times EPS_1 - DIV_0$$

---

[4] The costs of printing and mailing annual reports, dividend cheques, and so on, are the same for small stockholders as for large ones. Firms often try to reduce these costs by buying out small holdings.

[5] J. Lintner, "Distribution of Incomes of Corporations among Dividends, Retained Earnings, and Taxes," *American Economic Review*, **46**: 97–113 (May 1956).

[6] The stylized facts are given by Terry A. Marsh and Robert C. Merton, "Dividend Behavior for the Aggregate Stock Market," *Journal of Business* **60**: 1–40 (January 1987). See pp. 5–6. We have paraphrased and embellished.

A firm that always stuck to its payout ratio would have to change its dividend whenever earnings changed. But the managers in Lintner's survey were reluctant to do this. They believed that shareholders prefer a steady progression in dividends. Therefore even if circumstances appeared to warrant a large increase in their company's dividend, they would move only partway toward their target payment. Their dividend changes therefore seemed to conform to the following model:

$$\text{DIV}_1 - \text{DIV}_0 = \text{adjustment rate} \times \text{target change}$$
$$= \text{adjustment rate} \times (\text{target ratio} \times \text{EPS}_1 - \text{DIV}_0)$$

The more conservative the company, the more slowly it would move toward its target and, therefore, the *lower* would be its adjustment rate.

Lintner's simple model suggests that the dividend depends in part on the firm's current earnings and in part on the dividend for the previous year, which in turn depends on that year's earnings and the dividend in the year before. Therefore if Lintner is correct, we should be able to describe dividends in terms of a weighted average of current and past earnings.[7] The probability of an increase in the dividend rate should be greatest when *current* earnings have increased; it should be somewhat less when only the earnings from the previous year have increased, and so on. An extensive study by Fama and Babiak confirmed the hypothesis.[8]

The Information Content of Dividends	We have suggested above that the dividend payment depends on both last year's dividend and this year's earnings. This simple model seems to provide a fairly good explanation of how companies decide on the dividend rate, but it is unlikely to be the whole story. For example, we would also expect managers to take future prospects into account when setting the payment. And that is what we find. When companies pay dividends lower than our simple model suggests, earnings on the average subsequently decline. When they pay dividends higher than the model suggests, earnings on the average subsequently rise by an abnormal amount.[9] Since dividends anticipate future earnings, it's no surprise to find that announcements of dividend increases are usually taken as good news (stock price

---

[7] This can be demonstrated as follows: Dividends per share in time t are

$$\text{DIV}_t = aT(\text{EPS}_t) + (1 - a)\text{DIV}_{t-1} \tag{1}$$

where a is the adjustment rate and T the target payout ratio. But the same relationship holds in $t - 1$:

$$\text{DIV}_{t-1} = aT(\text{EPS}_{t-1}) + (1 - a)\text{DIV}_{t-2} \tag{2}$$

Substitute for DIV_{t-1} in (1):

$$\text{DIV}_t = aT(\text{EPS}_t) + aT(1 - a)(\text{EPS}_{t-1}) + (1 - a)^2\text{DIV}_{t-2}$$

We can make similar substitutions for DIV_{t-2}, DIV_{t-3}, thereby obtaining

$$\text{DIV}_t = aT(\text{EPS}_t) + aT(1 - a)(\text{EPS}_{t-1}) + aT(1 - a)^2(\text{EPS}_{t-2}) + \cdots + aT(1 - a)^n(\text{EPS}_{t-n})$$

[8] E.F. Fama and H. Babiak, "Dividend Policy: An Empirical Analysis," *Journal of the American Statistical Association,* **63**: 1132–1161 (December 1968), p. 1134.

[9] See, for example, R. Watts, "The Information Content of Dividends," *Journal of Business,* **46**: 191–211 (April 1973); F. Adjouad, "The Information Content of Dividends: A Canadian Test," *Canadian Journal of Administrative Sciences,* **1**: 338–351 (December 1984); and G. Charest, "Returns to Dividend Changing Stocks on the Toronto Stock Exchange," *Journal of Business Adminstration,* **12**: 1–18 (Fall 1980).

typically rises), and that dividend cuts are bad news (stock price typically falls).[10] But the stock price changes don't prove that investors like higher dividends for their own sake. A dividend increase may be important only as a sign of higher earnings.

Do you remember from Chapter 13 that stock splits lead to stock price increases? That is not because splits create value, but because they signal future prosperity, specifically increased dividends. Now we see that dividend increases in turn may be important mostly as signals of future earnings. (Finally, we could say that *earnings* are important because they tell investors something about the *true* measures of corporate prosperity: cash flow and the extent of positive-NPV capital investment opportunities.)

Market efficiency means that all information available to investors is quickly and accurately impounded in stock prices. It does not imply that fundamental information about a company's operations or prospects is always cheaply or easily obtained. Investors therefore seize on any clue. That is why stock prices respond to stock splits, dividend changes, and other actions or announcements which reveal managements' optimism or pessimism about their firms' futures.

16-3   CONTROVERSY ABOUT DIVIDEND POLICY

Now we turn to the controversial question of how dividend policy affects value. One endearing feature of economics is that it can always accommodate not just two, but three opposing points of view. And so it is with the controversy about dividend policy. On the right there is a conservative group which believes that an increase in dividend payout increases firm value. On the left, there is a radical group which believes that an increase in payout reduces value. And in the centre there is a middle-of-the-road party, which claims that dividend policy makes no difference.

The middle-of-the-road party was founded in 1961 by Miller and Modigliani (always referred to as *MM* or *M and M*), when they published a theoretical paper showing the irrelevance of dividend policy in a world without taxes, transaction costs, or other market imperfections.[11] By the standards of 1961 MM were leftist radicals, because at that time most people believed that even under idealized assumptions increased dividends made shareholders better off.[12] But now MM's

---

[10] For example, Paul Asquith and David W. Mullins, who examined firms that paid cash dividends for the first time (or the first time in at least 10 years), found that stock price rose by 3.7% on average at the announcement. See "The Impact of Initiating Dividend Payments on Shareholders' Wealth," *Journal of Business,* **56**: 77–96 (January 1983). Similiar results are documented in S.D. Deshpande and V.M. Jog, "The Information Content of Dividend Resumptions: The Canadian Evidence," *Proceedings of the Finance Division of the Administrative Science Association of Canada,* **7**: 151–172 (1986).

Terry E. Dielman and Henry R. Oppenheimer examined a sample of firms that cut or omitted dividends. For firms that cut dividends by more than 25%, stock price fell by 7.7% on average. Stock price fell by 8.1% on average when dividends were omitted altogether. See "An Examination of Investor Behavior During Periods of Large Dividend Changes," *Journal of Financial and Quantitative Analysis,* **19**: 208 (June 1984), table 2.

Stock price changes in these studies were corrected for market movements by the methods explained in Chapter 13, Section 13-5. Dielman and Oppenheimer also tried more elaborate statistical procedures with essentially consistent results.

[11] M.H. Miller and F. Modigliani, "Dividend Policy, Growth and the Valuation of Shares," *Journal of Business,* **34**: 411–433 (October 1961).

[12] Not *everybody* believed dividends make shareholders better off. MM's arguments were anticipated in 1938 in J.B. Williams, *The Theory of Investment Value,* Harvard University Press, Cambridge, Mass., 1938. Also, a proof very similar to MM's was developed by J. Lintner in "Dividends, Earnings, Leverage, Stock Prices and the Supply of Capital to Corporations," *Review of Economics and Statistics,* **44**: 243–269 (August 1962).

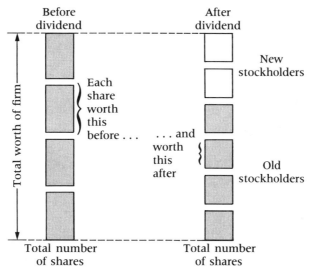

Figure 16-1   This firm pays out a third of its worth as a dividend and raises the money by selling new shares. The transfer of value to the new stockholders is equal to the dividend payment.

proof is generally accepted as correct, and the argument has shifted to whether taxes or other market imperfections alter the situation. In the process MM have been pushed toward the centre by a new leftist party, which argues for *low* dividends, particularly in the United States. The leftists' position is based on MM's argument modified to take account of taxes and costs of issuing securities. The conservatives are still with us, relying on essentially the same arguments as in 1961.

We begin our discussion of dividend policy with a presentation of MM's original argument. Then we will undertake a critical appraisal of the positions of the three parties. Perhaps we should warn you before we start that our own position is in the middle of the road.

Dividend Policy is Irrelevant in Perfect Capital Markets

In their classic 1961 article, MM argued as follows: suppose your firm has settled on its investment program. You have worked out how much of this program can be financed from borrowing, and you plan to meet the remaining funds requirement from retained earnings. Any surplus money is to be paid out as dividends.

Now think what happens if you want to increase the dividend payment without changing the investment and borrowing policy. The extra money must come from somewhere. If the firm fixes its borrowing, the only way it can finance the extra dividend is to print some more shares and sell them. The new stockholders are going to part with their money only if you can offer them shares that are worth as much as they cost. But how can the firm do this when its assets, earnings, investment opportunities and, therefore, market value are all unchanged? The answer is that there must be a *transfer of value* from the old to the new shareholders. The new ones get the newly printed shares, each one worth less than before the dividend change was announced, and the old ones suffer a capital loss on their shares. The capital loss borne by the old shareholders just offsets the extra cash dividend they receive.

Figure 16-1 shows how this transfer of value occurs. Our hypothetical company pays out a third of its total value as a dividend and it raises the money to do so

Figure 16-2   Two ways of raising cash for the firm's original shareholders. In each case the cash received is offset by a decline in the value of the old stockholders' claim on the firm. If the firm pays a dividend, each share is worth less because more shares have to be issued against the firm's assets. If the old stockholders sell some of their shares, each share is worth the same but the old stockholders have fewer shares.

by selling new shares. The capital loss suffered by the old stockholders is represented by the reduction in the size of the shaded boxes. But that capital loss is exactly offset by the fact that the new money raised (the white boxes) is paid over to them as dividends.

Does it make any difference to the old stockholders that they receive an extra dividend payment plus an offsetting capital loss? It might if that were the only way they could get their hands on cash. But as long as there are efficient capital markets, they can raise the cash by selling shares. Thus the old shareholders can "cash in" either by persuading the management to pay a higher dividend or by taking a "home-made dividend," by selling some of their shares. In either case there will be a transfer of value from old to new shareholders. The only difference is that in the former case this transfer is caused by a dilution in the value of each of the firm's shares, and in the latter case it is caused by a reduction in the number of shares held by the old shareholders. The two alternatives are compared in Figure 16-2.

Because investors do not need dividends to get their hands on cash, they will not pay higher prices for the shares of firms with high payouts. Therefore firms ought not to worry about dividend policy. They could let dividends fluctuate as a by-product of their investment and financing decisions.

Dividend Irrelevance— An Illustration

Consider the case of Rational Demiconductor, which at this moment has the following balance sheet:

Rational Demiconductor's Balance Sheet (market values)

Cash ($1,000 held for investment)	$1,000	$0	Debt
Fixed assets	$9,000	$10,000 + NPV	Equity
Investment opportunity ($1,000 investment required)	NPV		
Total asset value	$10,000 + NPV	$10,000 + NPV	Value of firm

Rational Demiconductor has $1,000 cash earmarked for a project requiring $1,000 investment. We do not know how attractive the project is, and so we enter it at

NPV; after the project is undertaken it will be worth $1,000 + NPV. Note that the balance sheet is constructed with market values; equity equals the market value of the firm's outstanding shares (price per share times number of shares outstanding). It is not necessarily equal to book net worth.

Now Rational Demiconductor uses the cash to pay a $1,000 dividend to its stockholders. The benefit to them is obvious: $1,000 of spendable cash. It is also obvious that there must be a cost. The cash is not free.

Where does the money for the dividend come from? Of course, the immediate source of funds is Rational Demiconductor's cash account. But this cash was earmarked for the investment project. Since we want to isolate the effects of dividend policy on shareholders' wealth, we assume that the company *continues* with the investment project. That means that $1,000 cash must be raised by new financing. This could consist of an issue of either debt or stock. Again, we just want to look at dividend policy for now, and we defer discussion of the debt–equity choice until Chapters 17 and 18. Thus Rational Demiconductor ends up financing the dividend with a $1,000 stock issue.

Now we examine the balance sheet after the dividend is paid, the new stock sold, and the investment undertaken. Because Rational Demiconductor's investment and borrowing policies are unaffected by the dividend payment, its *overall* market value must be unchanged at $10,000 + NPV.[13] We know also that if the new stockholders pay a fair price, their stock is worth $1,000. That leaves us with only one missing number—the value of the stock held by the original stockholders. It is easy to see that this must be

$$\text{Value of original stock} = \text{value of company} - \text{value of new stock}$$
$$= (10,000 + NPV) - 1,000$$
$$= \$9,000 + NPV$$

The old shareholders have received a $1,000 cash dividend and incurred a $1,000 capital loss. Dividend policy doesn't matter.

By paying out $1,000 with one hand and taking it back with the other, Rational Demiconductor is recycling cash. To suggest that this makes shareholders better off is like advising a cook to cool the kitchen by leaving the refrigerator door open.

Of course, our proof ignores taxes, issue costs, and a variety of other complications. We will turn to those items in a moment. The really crucial assumption in our proof is that the new shares are sold at a fair price. The shares sold to raise $1,000 must actually be *worth* $1,000.[14] In other words, we have assumed efficient capital markets.

Calculating Share Price

We have assumed that Rational Demiconductor's new shares can be sold at a fair price, but what is that price and how many new shares are issued?

Suppose that before this dividend payout the company had 1,000 shares outstanding and that the project had an NPV of $2,000. Then the old stock was worth in total 10,000 + NPV = $12,000, which works out at 12,000/1,000 = $12 per share. After the company has paid the dividend and completed the financing, this old stock is worth 9,000 + NPV = $11,000. That works out at 11,000/1,000

---

[13] All other factors that might affect Rational Demiconductor's value are assumed constant. This is not a necessary assumption, but it simplifies the proof of MM's theory.

[14] The "old" shareholders get all the benefit of the positive NPV project. The "new" shareholders require only a fair rate of return. They are making a zero NPV investment.

= $11 per share. In other words, the price of the old stock falls by the amount of the $1-per-share dividend payment.

Now let us look at the new stock. Clearly, after the issue this must sell at the same price as the rest of the stock. In other words, it must be valued at $11. If the new stockholders get fair value, the company must issue 1,000/$11 or 91 new shares in order to raise the $1,000 that it needs.

Share Repurchase

We have seen that any increased cash dividend payment must be offset by a stock issue if the firm's investment and borrowing policies are held constant. In effect the stockholders finance the extra dividend by selling off part of their ownership of the firm. Consequently, the stock price falls by just enough to offset the extra dividend.

This process can also be run backwards. With investment and borrowing policy given, any *reduction* in dividends must be balanced by a reduction in the number of shares issued or by repurchase of previously outstanding stock. But if the process has no effect on stockholders' wealth when run forward, it must likewise have no effect when run in reverse. We will confirm this by another numerical example.

Suppose that a technical discovery reveals that Rational Demiconductor's new project is not a positive NPV venture, but a sure loser. Management announces that the project is to be discarded, and that the $1,000 earmarked for it will be paid out as an extra dividend of $1 per share. After the dividend payout, the balance sheet is:

Rational Demiconductor's Balance Sheet (market value)			
Cash	$0	$0	Debt
Existing fixed assets	$9,000	$9,000	Equity
New project	$0		
Total asset value	$9,000	$9,000	Total firm value

Since there are 1,000 shares outstanding, the stock price is 10,000/1,000 = $10 before the dividend payment and 9,000/1,000 = $9 *after* the payment.

What if Rational Demiconductor uses the $1,000 to repurchase stock instead? As long as the company pays a fair price for the stock, the $1,000 buys 1,000/10 = 100 shares. That leaves 900 shares worth 900 × 10 = $9,000.

As expected, we find that switching from cash dividends to share repurchase has no effect on shareholders' wealth. They forgo a $1 cash dividend but end up holding shares worth $10 instead of $9.

Note that when shares are repurchased the transfer of value is in favour of those stockholders who do not sell. They forgo any cash dividend but end up owning a larger slice of the firm. In effect they are using their share of Rational Demiconductor's $1,000 distribution to buy out some of their fellow shareholders.

16-4   THE RIGHTISTS

Much of traditional finance literature has advocated high-payout ratios. Here, for example, is a statement of the rightist position made by Graham and Dodd in 1951:

. . . the considered and continuous verdict of the stock market is overwhelmingly in favor of liberal dividends as against niggardly ones. The common stock investor must take this judgment into account in the valuation of stock for purchase. It is now becoming standard practice to evaluate common stock by applying one multiplier to that portion of the earnings paid out in dividends and a much smaller multiplier to the undistributed balance.[15]

Another author has written a book urging the government to enforce full distribution of earnings on the grounds that it "would almost certainly double or treble (within a short period) the market value of equities."[16]

This belief in the importance of dividend policy is common in the business and investment communities. Stockholders and investment advisers continually pressure corporate treasurers for increased dividends. When we had wage–price controls in the United States in 1974 and in Canada in 1975–1978, it was deemed necessary to have dividend controls as well. As far as we know, no labour union objected that "dividend policy is irrelevant." After all, if wages are reduced, the employee is worse off. Dividends are the shareholders' wages, and so if the payout ratio is reduced the shareholder is worse off. Therefore fair play requires that wage controls be matched by dividend controls. Right?

Wrong! You should be able to see through that kind of argument by now. But let us turn to some of the more serious arguments for a high-payout policy.

Do MM Ignore Risk?

One of the most common and immediate objections to MM's argument about the irrelevance of dividends is that dividends are cash in hand while capital gains are at best in the bush. It may be true that the recipient of an extra cash dividend forgoes an equal capital gain, but if the dividend is safe and the capital gain is risky, isn't the stockholder ahead?

It is true that dividends are more predictable than capital gains. Managers can stabilize dividends but they cannot control stock price. From this it seems a small step to conclude that increased dividends make the firm less risky.[17] But the important point is, once again, that as long as investment policy and borrowing are held constant, a firm's *overall* cash flows are the same regardless of payout policy. The risks borne by *all* the firm's stockholders are likewise fixed by its investment and borrowing policies, and unaffected by dividend policy.[18]

A dividend increase creates a transfer of ownership between "old" and "new" stockholders. The old stockholders—those who receive the extra dividend and do

---

[15] These authors later qualified this statement, recognizing the willingness of investors to pay high price-earnings multiples for growth stocks. But otherwise they have stuck to their position. We quoted their 1951 statement because of its historical importance. Compare B. Graham and D.L. Dodd, *Security Analysis: Principles and Techniques*, 3rd ed., McGraw-Hill Book Company, New York, 1951, p. 432, with B. Graham, D.L. Dodd, and S. Cottle, *Security Analysis: Principles and Techniques*, 4th ed., McGraw-Hill Book Company, New York, 1962, p. 480.

[16] See A. Rubner, *The Ensnared Shareholder*, Macmillan International Ltd., London, 1965, p. 139.

[17] By analogy one could presumably argue that interest payments are even more predictable, so that a company's risk would be diminished by increasing the proportion of receipts paid out as interest.

[18] There are a number of variations of the "bird-in-the-hand" argument. Perhaps the most persuasive is found in M.J. Gordon, "Dividends, Earnings and Stock Prices," *Review of Economics and Statistics*, **41**: 99–105 (May 1959). He reasoned that investors run less risk if the firm pays them cash now rather than retaining and reinvesting it in the hope of paying higher future dividends. But careful analysis of Gordon's argument—see M.J. Brennan, "A Note on Dividend Irrelevance and the Gordon Valuation Model," *Journal of Finance*, **26**: 1115–1122 (December 1971), for example—shows that he was really talking about changes in investment policy, not dividend policy.

not buy their part of the stock issue undertaken to finance the dividend—find their stake in the firm reduced. They have indeed traded a safe receipt for an uncertain future gain. But the reason their money is safe is not because it is special "dividend money," but because it is in the bank. If the dividend had not been increased, the stockholders could have achieved an equally safe position just by selling shares and putting the money in the bank.

If we really believed that old stockholders are better off by trading a risky asset for cash, then we would also have to argue that the new stockholders—those who trade cash for the newly issued shares—are worse off. But this doesn't make sense: the new stockholders are bearing risk, but they are getting paid for it. They are willing to buy because the new shares are priced to offer a return adequate to cover the risk.

MM's argument for the irrelevance of dividend policy does not assume a world of certainty: it assumes an efficient capital market. Market efficiency means that the transfers of value created by shifts in dividend policy are carried out on fair terms. And since the *overall* value of (old and new) stockholders' equity is unaffected, nobody gains or loses.

Market Imperfections   We believe—and it is widely believed—that MM's conclusions follow from their assumption of perfect and efficient capital markets. Nobody claims their model is an exact description of the so-called "real-world." Thus the dividend controversy finally boils down to arguments about imperfections, inefficiencies, or whether shareholders are fully rational.[19]

There is a natural clientele for high-payout stocks. For example, some financial institutions are legally restricted from holding stocks lacking established dividend records. Trusts and endowment funds may prefer high-dividend stocks because dividends are regarded as spendable "income," whereas capital gains are "additions to principal," which cannot be spent.

There is also a natural clientele of investors who look to their stock portfolios for a steady source of cash to live on. In principle this cash could be easily generated from stocks paying no dividends at all; the investor could just sell off a small fraction of his or her holdings from time to time. But it is simpler and cheaper for Canadian Pacific to send a quarterly cheque than for its stockholders to sell, say, one share every three months. Canadian Pacific's regular dividends relieve many of its shareholders of transaction costs and considerable inconvenience.

Those advocating generous dividends might go on to argue that a regular cash dividend relieves stockholders of the risk of having to sell shares at "temporarily depressed" prices. Of course, the firm will have to issue shares eventually to finance the dividend, but (the argument goes) the firm can pick the *right time* to sell. If firms really try to do this and if they are successful—two big *ifs*—then stockholders of high payout firms do indeed get something for nothing.

There is another line of argument that you can use to justify high payouts. Think of a market in which investors receive very little reliable information about a firm's earnings. Such markets exist in some European countries where a passion for secrecy and a tendency to construct many-layered corporate organizations

---

[19] Psychologists' experiments show that human beings are not 100% rational decision makers. Shefrin and Statman use some of the psychologists' results to argue that investors may have an irrational preference for cash dividends. See H. Shefrin and M. Statman, "Explaining Investor Preference for Cash Dividends," *Journal of Financial Economics,* **13**: 253–282 (June 1984).

produce asset and earnings figures that are next to meaningless. Some people say that, thanks to creative accounting, the situation is little better in Canada and the United States. How does an investor in such a world separate marginally profitable firms from the real money makers? One clue is dividends. A firm that reports good earnings and pays a generous dividend is putting its money where its mouth is.[20] We can understand why investors would favour firms with established dividend records. We can also see how the information content of dividends would come about. Investors would refuse to believe a firm's reported earnings announcements unless they were backed up by an appropriate dividend policy.

MM regard the informational content of dividends as a temporary thing. A dividend increase signals management's optimism about future earnings, but investors will be able to see *for themselves* whether the optimism is justified. The jump in stock price that accompanies an unexpected dividend increase *would have happened anyway* as information about future earnings comes out through other channels. Therefore, MM expect to find changes in dividends associated with stock price movements, but no permanent relationship between stock price and the firm's long-run target payout ratio. MM believe management should be concerned with dividend *changes*, but not with the average *level* of payout.

16-5   THE TAXATION OF INVESTMENT INCOME

One important market imperfection that can create a preference for or against dividends is taxation. The laws governing the taxation of investment income have changed several times in the last two decades. First we will discuss the 1989 Canadian tax law and see how it makes some investors prefer dividends and other investors prefer capital gains. Then we will discuss how different tax laws have affected the relative merits of dividends and capital gains over time and across countries.

Interest income is taxed as ordinary income when received either by an individual or by a corporation. That is, interest income is taxed at the same rate as wage and salary income for individuals and at the same rate as income from operations for corporations.

Capital gains are taxed only when they are *realized*—that is, when the asset is sold. Only 75% of the capital gain is taxable.[21] This treatment applies to individual as well as corporate investors.

Dividends are not taxed when received by a public corporation, such as one that is traded on a Canadian stock exchange. On the other hand, the **dividend tax credit** (DTC) system applies to the taxation of Canadian dividends received by individual Canadian investors (that is, those who are not corporations). It reduces the burden of the *double taxation* of shareholder income that occurs when cash flows that produce dividends are taxed at the corporate level as well as at the personal level. This principle is called *tax integration* and its rationale is discussed in Appendix 16-1.

---

[20] Of course, firms can cheat in the short run by overstating earnings and scraping up cash to pay a generous dividend. But it is hard to cheat in the long run, for a firm that is not making money will not have the cash flow to pay out. Financing dividends by issuing stock is self-defeating, for it ultimately reduces dividends per share and thereby reveals that the initial dividend was not supported by earnings.

[21] That is, capital gains are normally taxed at 75% of the rate for ordinary income. Generally speaking, private individuals may elect to have this treatment for all their investment gains. However, a stock trader or dealer must take capital gains as ordinary income, so that 100% of the gain is taxable. This 75% "inclusion rate" was introduced in 1990.

Since corporations are not allowed to deduct the dividends they pay from taxable income, corporate cash flows that generate either dividends or retained earnings are taxed in the same manner at the corporate level. The only difference is the personal taxation in the hands of investors. The value of a dividend received by an individual from a Canadian corporation is "grossed-up" by 25% to yield a "taxable dividend" that is taxed as ordinary personal income. This is offset by a dividend tax credit of 13⅓% of the taxable dividend, which is deducted from federal tax payable.[22] Provincial tax is then computed as a proportion of the net federal tax payable. Provincial tax rates in 1989 varied from 43% to 61% except in Québec, which has its own tax system.

Table 16-1 describes the taxation of a $100 dividend or capital gain for the three marginal federal tax rates — 17%, 26%, and 29% — when the province charges tax at 50% of the federal rate. The 26% marginal tax rate corresponds to taxable income between approximately $28,000 and $57,000 in 1990. The overall marginal tax rates for dividend income in those three cases are 6.9%, 23.8%, and 29.4%, respectively. In contrast, if the $100 had been retained in the firm and the investor sold the shares immediately to realize an incremental $100 capital gain that was subject to tax, the marginal personal tax rates on the capital gain would have been 19.1%, 29.3%, and 32.6%, respectively, as in the bottom half of Table 16-1. Thus, from a tax perspective, all investors would prefer dividends to immediately realized taxable capital gains. The tax advantage to dividends is much stronger, however, for the investors in the lower tax brackets — the high-income investor is almost indifferent between dividends and immediately realized capital gains.

Table 16-1
Personal Taxation of Dividends and Capital Gains for a Provincial Tax Rate of 50%

	Marginal Personal Federal Tax Rate		
	17%	26%	29%
Dividend	$100.00	$100.00	$100.00
Taxable or grossed-up dividend	125.00	125.00	125.00
Tax on grossed-up dividend	21.25	32.50	36.25
less DTC (13.33% of taxable dividend)	(16.67)	(16.67)	(16.67)
Net federal personal tax on dividend	4.58	15.83	19.58
Provincial tax (50% of federal tax)	2.29	7.92	9.79
Total personal tax on dividend	$6.87	$23.75	$29.37
After-tax dividend	$93.13	$76.25	$70.63
Capital gain	$100.00	$100.00	$100.00
Taxable capital gain (75% of capital gain)	75.00	75.00	75.00
Federal tax on capital gain	12.75	19.50	21.75
Provincial tax (50% of federal tax)	6.38	9.75	10.88
Total personal tax on capital gain	$19.13	$29.25	$32.63
After-tax capital gain	$80.87	$70.75	$67.37

[22] These gross-up and tax credit rates were introduced in 1988.

On the other hand, starting in 1985, Canadian investors have had a $100,000 lifetime capital gains exemption. Moreover, many investors are in a position to defer some or all of their taxable capital gains because they need not sell their stock. Even those who desire a regular annual income from their investments can defer much of their capital gain on "home-made dividends" because they don't have to sell off all of their investment at once. For example, suppose someone buys $10,000 of non-dividend-paying stock and sells 10% of that stock a year later as a home-made dividend when the stock price has increased by 12% to $11,200. The investor receives $1,120 for shares that cost $1,000, and thus realizes a capital gain of $120 which is only 1.2% of the $10,000 investment. The remaining $1,000 of the home-made dividend is not taxed, and tax on the remaining $1,080 of the gain is deferred. The deferral reduces the present value of any capital gains tax. If the capital gains are deferred far enough into the future, the present value of the capital gains tax is negligible, and the effective tax rate on capital gains approaches zero.

For all these investors who pay little or no tax on capital gains, by virtue of exemption or deferral, it would be more appropriate to compare the net tax on dividends in Table 16-1 to a zero capital gains tax rate. All such investors would prefer capital gains to dividends.

Stock Repurchase and Stock Dividends

Stock repurchases by Canadian corporations generally get one of two tax treatments. If the shares are purchased on the open market, the seller receives a capital gains treatment, since it cannot be determined whether the buyer is a general member of the public or the corporation.[23] If the shares are not repurchased on the open market (for example, the shares are tendered directly to the corporation), the tax situation is more complex. In many cases, for example, when the shareholder is a Canadian dealing at "arm's-length" with the corporation, the sale is also treated as a capital gain. In other cases the share repurchase is treated as a combination of a "deemed dividend," a capital gain, and a return of "paid-up capital" (similar to stated capital), which is not taxed.[24]

Prior to the 1986 tax reform, stock dividends were not taxed on receipt of the dividend, but were treated as an acquisition of shares at a zero cost. In effect, the stock dividend was taxed as a capital gain when the shares were ultimately sold. Since the tax reform eliminated much of the tax on capital gains, it also eliminated the capital gains treatment of stock dividends. Thus, stock dividends are now taxed just like ordinary cash dividends.

Tax-Based Clienteles

So far we have seen that one group of investors, which we will call "clientele D," pays lower taxes on dividends and another group, which we will call "clientele G," pays lower taxes on capital gains. Clientele D includes Canadian investors in low tax brackets as well as investors who buy and sell ("trade") stocks often and cannot avail themselves of any capital gains tax exemption. Clientele G includes investors in high tax brackets, who either do not trade their stocks often or have not used up the $100,000 lifetime capital gains tax exemption. They prefer capital gains to dividends. Since Canadian public corporations pay no tax on dividends they receive from other taxable Canadian corporations, and do not get an exemption from the taxation of capital gains, they are in clientele D.

---

[23] Income Tax Act, subsection 84(6).

[24] In the Income Tax Act, subsection 84(8) provides for the capital gains treatment. Provision for the deemed dividend is in subsection 84(3), and the capital gains associated with it arise in subparagraph 54(h)(x).

How Taxes Affect Values

Corporations can transmute capital gains into dividends by shifting their dividend policies. Such financial alchemy should be welcomed by investors in clientele D. They should be willing to pay more for stocks with high-dividend yields. In other words, they should be willing to accept a lower *pretax* rate of return from securities offering returns in the form of dividends rather than taxable capital gains.

Table 16-2
Effects of a shift in dividend policy when capital gains are taxed more heavily than dividends. The low payout stock (Firm A) must sell at a lower price in order to provide the same after-tax return because capital gains are taxed more heavily than dividends. The net tax rates on dividends and capital gains correspond to the 26% marginal tax bracket and 50% provincial tax rate in Table 16-1.

	Firm A (no dividend)	Firm B (high dividend)
Next year's price	$114.13	$104.13
Dividend	$0.00	$10.00
Total pretax payoff	$114.13	$114.13
Today's stock price	$100.00	$100.68
Capital gain	$14.13	$3.45
Before-tax rate of return	$\frac{14.14}{100} \times 100 = 14.1\%$	$\frac{13.45}{100.68} \times 100 = 13.4\%$
Tax on dividend at 23.75%	$0.00	$0.2375 \times 10 = \$2.38$
Tax on capital gain at 29.25%	$0.2925 \times 14.13 = \$4.13$	$0.2925 \times 3.45 = \$1.01$
Total after-tax income (dividends plus capital gains less taxes)	$(0 + 14.13) - 4.13$ $= \$10.00$	$(10 + 3.45) - (2.38 + 1.01)$ $= \$10.06$
After-tax rate of return	$\frac{10}{100} \times 100 = 10.0\%$	$\frac{10.06}{100.68} \times 100 = 10.0\%$

Table 16-2 illustrates this. The shares of firms A and B are equally risky. Investors expect firm A to be worth $114.13 per share next year. The share price of B is expected to be only $104.13, but a $10 dividend is also forecast, and so the total pretax payoff is the same, $114.13. Yet we find that clientele D investors should be willing to pay more for a share of stock B than of stock A, and hence get a lower pretax rate of return from B. The reason is obvious: clientele D investors are taxed less heavily on dividends and B's return is mainly in the form of dividends. Table 16-2 shows that A and B are exactly equivalent investments to investors who are in the 26% marginal federal tax bracket, pay 50% provincial tax, and pay tax on capital gains annually. Each offers a 10% return after all taxes. The difference between the stock prices of A and B is exactly the present value of the extra taxes such investors face if they buy A.

Exactly the opposite is true for clientele G investors who are taxed more heavily on dividends than capital gains. They would pay more for stocks with low dividend yields. The question is which clientele predominates: will high dividend yield stocks sell for more or less than low dividend yield stocks on the basis of taxes?[25]

---

[25] Michael Brennan has modeled what happens when you introduce taxes into an otherwise perfect market and found that the capital asset pricing model continues to hold, but on an *after-tax* basis. Thus, if A and B have the same beta, they should offer the same after-tax rate of return. The spread between pretax and posttax returns is determined by a weighted average of investors' tax rates on dividends and capital gains. A risky stock must earn a premium for risk as measured by beta, and a premium for its dividend yield. The dividend yield premium is positive if clientele G predominates and negative if clientele D predominates. See M.J. Brennan, "Taxes, Market Valuation and Corporate Financial Policy," *National Tax Journal*, **23**: 417–427 (December 1970).

16-6   CHANGING TAX LAWS: A SWINGING PENDULUM

Since a major tax reform in 1972, Canada has made small changes to the dividend and capital gains taxation system on several occasions. The overall effect has been to gradually shift investors from clientele G to clientele D as well as to reduce the net difference between the taxes on dividends and capital gains.[26]

Prior to 1972, Canada imposed no taxes on capital gains. Dividends were not grossed-up, but there was a 20% dividend tax credit. All but low-income investors were in clientele G. Then Canada introduced a ⅓ dividend gross-up and started to include 50% of realized capital gains in regular income. That shifted some medium-income investors who were frequent traders into clientele D and kept in D low-income investors who already were there. After a one-year transition period, dividend income starting in 1978 was subject to a 50% gross-up and a tax credit of 25% of the taxable dividend. This shifted medium-income investors into clientele D, even if they traded stocks infrequently. In 1985 the capital gains exemption was introduced, moving many frequent traders back into clientele G. After a one-year transition period the gross-up and dividend tax credit were reduced in 1988 to the figures used in Table 16-1, the capital gains inclusion rate was increased to 66⅔%, and the top marginal federal tax rate was reduced from 34% to 29%. The net effect was to shift some investors back into clientele G, especially if they did not frequently trade stocks or did not have high incomes. In 1990, the capital gains inclusion rate was increased to 75%, moving a few frequent stock traders back into clientele D. Thus, the Canadian population has shifted from clientele G to clientele D during the period from 1970 to 1985, with a reversal from clientele D back to clientele G starting in 1985. Also, the net difference between the dividend and capital gains tax rates has become smaller over the years. For example, up to 1986 the dividend tax credit exceeded the tax on the grossed-up dividend for low-income investors who actually faced a negative marginal tax rate on dividends!

American Tax-Based Clienteles

In the United States, dividends received by individuals are taxed as regular income, while 20% of dividends received by corporations are included in regular income. Both individuals and corporations include 100% of their capital gains in income. Thus, corporations are generally in clientele D, but individuals are either in clientele G if they do not trade their stocks often or are on the borderline between clienteles D and G.

Prior to 1986, individuals included all of their dividends in regular income while corporations only included 15% of their dividends in regular income. If an individual derived a capital gain over a period of less than 12 months, all of it was included in regular income and taxed, but if the capital gain was derived over a longer period, it was called a long-term gain and only 40% of the gain was included in income. American corporations had to pay a 30% tax on realized capital gains. Thus, before 1986, American individuals and corporations were in clientele G, except for a few corporations that frequently traded securities.

The Response by Firms to Clientele Effects

We have seen that, depending on the relative numbers of clientele D and clientele G investors, high-dividend-yield stocks can sell at a higher or lower price than low-dividend-yield stocks of the same risk. For example, suppose there is a predominance of clientele D investors who are taxed more heavily on capital

---

[26] For a more detailed discussion, see Jean-Marc Suret and Jean-Marie Gagnon, ''The Canadian Tax Reform and Dividends: A Re-examination,'' *Finance: Revue de l'Association Française de Finance*, **10**: 27–49.

gains than dividends. Then firms could increase their share prices if they increase their dividend payouts because this would make them more attractive to clientele D investors. Under general circumstances,[27] the resulting increase in dividends would satisfy some of the overall demand of investors for high dividend stocks. Thus, they would require less of a pretax return premium per unit of dividend yield to compensate them for the higher tax on *any* low-dividend paying stocks. If enough firms were to convert to a high dividend yield, the premium would vanish and low dividend firms would have the same pretax return (and price) as high dividend firms of the same risk. Exactly the opposite would happen if there is a preponderance of clientele G investors — aggregate dividend yields would fall in response to the higher demand for capital gains as opposed to dividends.

Overall, we would expect to see firms shifting, in aggregate, to an optimal dividend policy at which there is no positive or negative premium required of high dividend stocks. At this point, dividend policy would be irrelevant for each firm, even from a tax viewpoint. However, firms as a *whole* will have an optimal dividend policy.[28]

If this line of reasoning is correct, the following three hypotheses should hold:

1. Canadian firms, on the whole, should have increased their dividend yields throughout the 1970s as capital gains were taxed more heavily and dividends less heavily and investors moved from clientele G to D. After 1985, the overall dividend yields in Canada should fallen, as tax laws changed to move some investors back to clientele D.
2. Canadian firms should generally have higher dividend yields than American firms because the U.S. tax system favours capital gains over dividends more so than the Canadian system. This should be particularly noticeable before 1986 when both countries reformed their tax systems to reduce the differential taxation of dividends and capital gains.
3. When changes in tax laws were announced that shifted investors from clientele G to D, the prices of high-dividend stocks should rise and that of low-dividend stocks should fall, as shown in Table 16-2. That is, firms should have been given the incentive to change their dividend policies.

Let's see whether Canadian firms have responded to the changing tax incentives and have really made Hypotheses 1 and 2 valid. A reasonable measure of the dividends paid out in Canada is the amount of dividends paid out on the Toronto Stock Exchange 300 Composite Index. It can be compared with the Standard and Poor's 500 Composite Index in the United States. Figure 16-3 shows the annual dividend yields on these two indices from 1956 to 1989. From 1956 to 1973, the yields on these two indices were close to each other. Both

---

[27] This actually requires a technical variation on the model developed by Brennan. In his model, the return premium required to compensate for taxes on a unit of dividend yield does not depend on how many firms have high and low dividend yields, nor on the dividend yield of the firm in question: the relationship between the premium and dividend yield is a straight line. Litzenberger and Ramaswamy ("Dividends, Short Selling Restrictions, Tax-Induced Investor Clienteles and Market Equilibrium," *Journal of Finance*, **35**: 469–482 (May 1980)) have incorporated restrictions on short sales of stock in a model like Brennan's and they show that the return premium on a high-dividend yield stock will be largely determined by the marginal tax rates of the clientele attracted to it. In this general setting, a change in dividend policy will change the clientele faced by the firm and, hence, change the tax-based return premium for a unit of dividend yield.

[28] This line of reasoning is analogous to an argument by Merton Miller with regard to taxation and capital structure, which is discussed in Chapter 18.

Figure 16-3   Dividend Yields in Canada and the United States, 1956–1989.

Sources: *The Toronto Stock Exchange 300 Stock Price Indexes Manual,* Toronto, various issues, and *Standard and Poor's Statistical Service Security Price Index Record,* New York, 1990.

dividend yields rose sharply in 1974 (mainly because Canadian and American stock prices fell in 1974). After 1977, however, the TSE yield fell below the S&P yield. The evidence in Figure 16-3 seems to be at odds with both Hypotheses 1 and 2. Canadian dividend yields fell relative to American dividend yields in the 1970s, just when the Canadian tax system swung more heavily in favour of dividends. Also, Canadian dividend yields have never been consistently higher than American dividend yields.

However, we may have overstated the case against Hypothesis 1, because we looked at dividend *yields* rather than dividend *payments*. Figure 16-4 shows the annual rates of change in dividend payments to the TSE 300 and S&P 500 indices. The indices had similar rates of dividend change from 1957 to 1972. But, from 1973 to 1975 and from 1978 to 1980, the TSE rate of dividend increase greatly outpaced the S&P rate of dividend increase. This could very well have been the result of the two major changes in Canada's dividend and capital gains tax laws, which took effect in 1972 and 1978. To reconcile the difference between the evidence in Figure 16-3 and 16-4, note that when the TSE dividend payments were increasing faster than the S&P dividend payments, the value of the TSE 300 Index was increasing at an even greater rate, relative to the value of the S&P 500 Index. As a result, the TSE dividend yield fell below the S&P dividend yield.[29]

---

[29] Khouri and Smith ("Dividend Policy and the Capital Gains Tax in Canada," *Journal of Business Administration,* **8**: 19–38 (Spring 1977)) studied a related pair of hypotheses by comparing the dividend policies of 145 Canadian firms with those of 130 similar American firms for the 1963–73 period. Their conclusions were similar. Note, however, that their time period is shorter and they did not attempt to look at the aggregate effect of all firms' behaviour.

Figure 16-4   Changes in Dividend Payouts in Canada and the United States, 1957–1989.

Sources: *The Toronto Stock Exchange 300 Stock Price Indexes Manual,* Toronto, various issues, and *Standard and Poor's Statistical Service Security Price Index Record,* New York, 1990.

Thus, we have some support for Hypothesis 1. On the other hand, Hypothesis 2 is an open question. Canadian tax law seems to favour dividends over capital gains more than American tax law, but it is not clear that Canadian corporations had relatively higher dividend payouts prior to the mid-1980s in response to this. Perhaps Canadian firms responded to the demand for dividends with preferred share offerings. Since preferred shares are included in neither the TSE 300 nor the S&P 500 indices, these indices may not, in fact, be a good measure of total dividends paid to investors. Further research is needed before we can come to a definitive conclusion on the question.

Ben Amoaku-Adu analyzed Hypothesis 3 by studying the share-price performance of the 30 highest-yielding and 30 lowest-yielding Canadian stocks at the time of the announcements of the 1971 and 1977 tax reforms. After adjusting for overall market effects, he found support for Hypothesis 3. That is, the high-yielding stocks did increase in price, which is consistent with the fact that these tax-law changes generally moved investors from clientele G to D. The low-yielding stocks did decrease in price, but not significantly.[30]

---

[30] See Ben Amoaku-Adu, "Canadian Tax Reform and Its Effect on Stock Prices: A Note," *Journal of Finance,* **38**: 1669–1675 (December 1983).

An obvious way to solve the dividend quandary is to look at the evidence and test whether high-yielding stocks do offer different expected returns. Unfortunately, there are difficulties in measuring these effects.

Suppose that stock A is priced at $100 and is expected to pay a $5 dividend. The *expected* yield is, therefore, $5/100 = 0.05$ or 5%. The company now announces bumper earnings and a $10 dividend. Thus, with the benefit of hindsight, A's *actual* dividend yield is $10/100 = 0.10$ or 10%. If the unexpected increase in earnings causes a rise in A's stock price, we will observe that a high actual yield is accompanied by a high actual return. But that would not tell us anything about whether a high *expected* yield was accompanied by a high *expected* return. In order to measure the effect of dividend policy, we need to estimate the dividends that investors expected.

A second problem is that nobody is quite sure what is meant by a high-dividend yield. For example, utility stocks are generally regarded as offering a high yield. But do they have a high yield all the year or only in months or on days that dividends are paid? Perhaps for most of the year they have zero yield and are perfect holdings for the highly taxed individual.[31] Of course the high taxpayer would not want to hold a utility stock on the days dividends are paid, but he or she could sell the stock temporarily to a security dealer who would "capture" the dividend. The dealer is taxed equally on dividends and capital gains and, therefore, should not demand any different return for holding stocks over the dividend period. If shareholders can pass stocks freely between each other at the time of the dividend payment, we should not observe any tax effects at all.

A third problem is that most empirical studies have looked for a straight-line relationship between yield and return. But if there are any asymmetries in the tax system, the relationship might be more complicated.[32]

Given these difficulties in measuring the relationship between expected yield and return, it is not surprising that different researchers have come up with different results. Table 16-3 summarizes some of the findings in United States and Canadian markets. In all of the American tests, the estimated tax rate is positive. In other words, high-yielding American stocks appear to have lower prices and offer higher returns. But while the dividends-are-bad school can claim that the weight of evidence is on its side, the contest is by no means over. Many respected scholars in the United States, including Merton Miller and Myron Scholes, still believe that dividend policy doesn't matter. They stress the difficulty of measuring dividend yield properly and proving the link between dividend yield and expected return.[33]

The Canadian market studies by Morgan and Rumsey are particularly interesting because they are broken into two periods that are divided by the date (December 1971) when capital gains taxes were introduced in Canada. The implied "tax

---

[31] Suppose there are 250 trading days in a year. Think of a stock paying quarterly dividends. We could say that the stock offers a high dividend yield on four days, but a zero dividend yield on the remaining 246 days.

[32] A restriction on short sales of stock is one such asymmetry, because it prevents tax savings on payments made to cover dividends while an investor is short from being made at the same rate as tax costs on dividends received while an investor is long. See footnote 27.

[33] Miller reviews several of the studies cited in Table 16-2 in "Behavioral Rationality in Finance: The Case of Dividends," *Journal of Business*, **59**: S451–S468 (October 1986).

Table 16-3
Some Tests of the Effect of Yield on Returns

Test	Test Period	Interval	Implied "Tax Rate," %	Standard Error of Tax Rate
American Market				
Brennan	1946–1965	Monthly	34	12
Black & Scholes (1974)	1936–1966	Monthly	22	24
Litzenberger & Ramaswamy (1979)	1936–1977	Monthly	24	3
Litzenberger & Ramaswamy (1982)	1940–1980	Monthly	14–23	2–3
Rosenberg & Marathe (1979)	1931–1966	Monthly	40	21
Bradford & Gordon (1980)	1926–1978	Monthly	18	2
Blume (1980)	1936–1976	Quarterly	52	25
Miller & Scholes (1982)	1940–1978	Monthly	4	3
Stone & Bartter (1979)	1947–1970	Monthly	56	28
Morgan (1982)	1946–1977	Monthly	21	2
Rumsey (1989)	1940–1978	Monthly	9	2–6
Canadian Market				
Morgan (1980)	1968–1971	Monthly	59	17
	1972–1977	Monthly	−10	8
Rumsey (1989)	1968–1971	Monthly	65–67	14–30
	1972–1983	Monthly	19–34	7–13

Sources: M.J. Brennan, "Dividends and Valuation in Imperfect Markets: Some Empirical Tests," unpublished paper, not dated.

F. Black and M. Scholes, "The Effects of Dividend Yield and Dividend Policy on Common Stock Prices and Returns," *Journal of Financial Economics*, **1**: 1–22 (May 1974).

R.H. Litzenberger and K. Ramaswamy, "The Effect of Personal Taxes and Dividends on Capital Asset Prices: Theory and Empirical Evidence," *Journal of Financial Economics*, **7**: 163–195 (June 1979).

R.H. Litzenberger and K. Ramaswamy, "The Effects of Dividends on Common Stock Prices: Tax Effects or Information Effects," *Journal of Finance*, **37**: 429–443 (May 1982).

B. Rosenberg and V. Marathe, "Tests of Capital Asset Pricing Model Hypotheses," in H. Levy (ed.), *Research in Finance I*, Greenwich, Conn.: JAI Press (1979).

D.F. Bradford and R.H. Gordon, "Taxation and the Stock Market Valuation of Capital Gains and Dividends," *Journal of Public Economics*, **14**: 109–136 (1980).

M.E. Blume, "Stock Returns and Dividend Yields: Some More Evidence," *Review of Economics and Statistics*, 567–577 (November 1980).

M.H. Miller and M. Scholes, "Dividends and Taxes: Some Empirical Evidence," *Journal of Political Economy*, **90**: 1118–1141 (1982).

B.K. Stone and B.J. Bartter, "The Effect of Dividend Yield on Stock Returns: Empirical Evidence on the Relevance of Dividends," W.P.E.-76-78, Georgia Institute of Technology, Atlanta, Ga.

I.G. Morgan, "Dividends and Capital Asset Prices," *Journal of Finance*, **37**: 1071–1086 (September 1982).

I.G. Morgan, "Dividends and Stock Price Behaviour in Canada," *Journal of Business Administration*, **12** :91–106 (Fall 1980).

J. Rumsey, "An Efficient Technique for Testing Financial Models with Time Varying Coefficients," Working Paper, York University (May 1989).

rate" in Table 16-3 is more correctly interpreted as (a weighted average across investors of)

$$T = \frac{T_d - T_g}{1 - T_g}$$

where T = "implied tax rate"
T_d = tax rate on dividend income
T_g = tax rate on capital gains income

If $T_g = 0$, then $T = T_d$ is just the tax rate on dividends. Morgan and Rumsey estimated this as 59% to 67% for the period prior to the introduction of the capital gains tax. If the tax rate on capital gains for most investors exceeds that on dividends, the implied tax rate, T, is actually negative. This is consistent with the $T = -10\%$ (which is actually insignificantly different from zero) that Morgan reports for the 1972–1977 period. In other words, Morgan's evidence suggests that the dividends-are-bad school was correct in Canada prior to 1972, but not after 1972. On the other hand, Rumsey's tests do not suggest that dividends are good, but they do suggest that dividends are, at least, not *too* bad, after 1972. In fact, the empirical evidence for 1972–1977 suggests that there was no particular reason to support high or low dividends. The dividend tax credit became more generous after 1977, so it may be that future empirical tests in Canada will favour the dividends-are-good school.

Are We Now Closer to the Middle of the Road?   The empirical tests discussed in the last section were conducted prior to the mid-1980s tax reforms in Canada and United States. These reforms tended to push everyone in Canada and the United States toward the middle of the road. While they may have been a preponderance of clientele D investors in Canada prior to tax reform, the tax savings from moving between high- and low-dividend stocks are not as great as they used to be. Similarly, while there might have been a preponderance of clintele G investors in the United States prior to tax reform, the increased capital gains tax rate has moved many investors out of clientele G and into the middle of the road. With current tax laws, there are still dividend and capital gains clienteles, but their borders are not so clear. It will be interesting to see empirical studies of dividends in the post-tax-reform capital markets.

16-7   SUMMARY

Dividends come in many forms. The most common is the regular cash dividend, but sometimes companies pay an extra or special cash dividend, and sometimes they pay a dividend in the form of stock. A firm is not free to pay whatever dividends it likes. It may have promised its bondholders not to declare large dividends, and it is also prevented by law from paying dividends if it is insolvent or if it has insufficient surplus.

The company's dividend policy does not affect its own tax payments but it can affect the taxes paid by its shareholders. The taxation of dividends is softened by the dividend tax credit system which yields negative taxes on dividends to low income investors. Capital gains are taxed at a reduced rate compared to ordinary personal income and sometimes not taxed at all. From a tax standpoint, capital gains will be strongly preferred to dividends by investors who can defer their capital gains for a long period of time or who have not used up their capital gains tax exemption. Dividends will be strongly preferred to capital gains by low-income investors. High-income investors who realize their capital gains every year will have a slight preference for dividends.

As an alternative to dividend payments, the company can repurchase its own stock. Although this has the same effect of distributing cash to shareholders, the shareholders are generally taxed only on the capital gains that they may realize as a result of the repurchase.

When managers decide on the dividend, their primary concern seems to be to give shareholders a "fair" level of dividends: if that does not leave enough money to finance expansion, the company pays the dividend and makes an issue of shares. Most managers have a conscious or subconscious long-term target payout rate. If firms simply applied the target payout rate to each year's earnings, dividends would fluctuate wildly. Managers, therefore, try to smooth dividend payments by moving only partway toward the target payout in each year. Also they don't just look at past earnings performance: they try to look into the future when they set the payment. Investors are aware of this and they know that a large dividend increase is often a sign of optimism on the part of management.

If we hold the company's investment policy constant, then dividend policy is a trade-off between cash dividends and the issue or repurchase of common stock. Should firms retain whatever earnings are necessary to finance growth and pay out any residual as cash dividends? Or should they increase dividends and then (sooner or later) issue stock to make up the shortfall of equity capital? Or should they reduce dividends below the "residual" level and use the released cash to repurchase stock?

If we lived in an ideally simple and perfect world, there would be no problem, for the choice would have no effect on market value. The controversy centres on the effects of dividend policy in our flawed world. A common—though by no means universal—view in the investment community is that high payout enhances share price. There are natural clienteles for high-payout stocks. But we find it difficult to explain a *general* preference for dividends other than in terms of an irrational prejudice. The case for "liberal dividends" depends largely on a wealth of tradition.

The most obvious and serious market imperfection is the different tax treatment of dividends and capital gains. This creates two investor clienteles: one that prefers low dividends and one that prefers high dividends. This suggest that firms should adjust their dividend policies so that some firms satisfy one clientele and other firms satisfy the other. If this occurs, dividend policy does not matter for an individual firm, but it is important for firms as a whole.

These theories are too incomplete and the evidence is too sensitive to minor changes in specification to warrant any dogmatism. Our sympathies, however, lie with those who stress the tax consequences of dividend policy, and our recommendations to companies would emphasize the following points. First, there is little doubt that sudden shifts in dividend policy can cause abrupt changes in stock price. The principal reason is the information that investors read into the company's actions, although some casual evidence suggests that there may be other less rational explanations.[34] Given such problems, there is a clear case for defining the firm's target payout and making relatively slow adjustments toward it. If it is necessary to make a sharp change in the dividend rate, the company should provide as much forewarning as possible and take considerable care to ensure that the action is not misinterpreted.

Subject to these strictures, we believe that many Canadian firms should, on the whole, have a higher payout rate than American firms because Canadian tax law is more favourable to dividends relative to capital gains than is American law tax. If a firm has many American shareholders, the benefits of dividends for some Canadian shareholders must be weighed against the costs of dividends for the American shareholders, and such firms may find it best to opt for the low dividend clientele. Over the years, Canadian firms and arbitrageurs have sought to give individual shareholders the choice between dividends and capital gains. In the past, firms have offered dual-class shares, in which one class pays cash dividends and the other class pays stock dividends of equivalent value.[35] More recently, investment banking firms have bought blocks of high-dividend bank shares or utility shares and split them into two parts: one that receives the capital gains, and the other that receives the dividends. Such innovation will always be rewarded if there are some investors who have a stong preference to either dividends or capital gains.

FURTHER READING

Lintner's classic analysis of how companies set their dividend payments is provided in:

J. Lintner, "Distribution of Incomes of Corporations among Dividends, Retained Earnings, and Taxes," *American Economic Review*, **46**: 97–113 (May 1956).

There have been a number of tests of how well Lintner's model describes dividend changes. One of the best known is:

E.F. Fama and H. Babiak, "Dividend Policy: An Empirical Analysis," *Journal of the American Statistical Association*, **63**: 1132–1161 (December 1968).

Marsh and Merton have reinterpreted Lintner's findings and used them to explain the aggregate dividends paid by United States corporations:

T.A. Marsh and R.C. Merton, "Dividend Behavior for the Aggregate Stock Market," *Journal of Business*, **60**: 1–40 (January 1987).

The pioneering article on dividend policy in the context of a perfect capital market is:

M.H. Miller and F. Modigliani, "Dividend Policy, Growth and the Valuation of Shares," *Journal of Business*, **34**: 411–433 (October 1961).

---

[34] For example, in an article in *Fortune* Carol Loomis tells the story of General Public Utilities ("A Case for Dropping Dividends," *Fortune*, June 15, 1968, pp. 181 ff.). In 1968 its management decided to reduce its cash dividend to avoid a stock issue. Despite the company's assurances, it encountered considerable opposition. Individual shareholders advised the president to see a psychiatrist, institutional holders threatened to sell their stock, the share price fell nearly 10%, and eventually GPU capitulated.

[35] See, for example, Warren Bailey, "Canada's Dual Class Shares: Further Evidence on the Market Value of Cash Dividends," *Journal of Finance*, **43**: 1143–1160 (December 1988).

There are several interesting models explaining the information content of dividends. Two influential examples are:

S. Bhattacharya, "Imperfect Information, Dividend Policy and the Bird in the Hand Fallacy," *Bell Journal of Economics and Management Science,* **10**: 259–270 (Spring 1979).

M.H. Miller and K. Rock, "Dividend Policy Under Asymmetric Information," *Journal of Finance,* **40**: 1031–1052 (September 1985).

The most powerful advocacy of the "dividends are good" case is Gordon's. Brennan discusses the source of the differences between Gordon and MM.

M.J. Brennan: "A Note on Dividend Irrelevance and the Gordon Valuation Model," *Journal of Finance,* **26**: 1115–1122 (December 1971).

M.J. Gordon, "Dividends, Earnings and Stock Prices," *Review of Economics and Statistics,* **41**: 99–105 (May 1959).

The effect of differential rates of tax on dividends and capital gains is analyzed rigorously in the context of the capital asset pricing model in:

M.J. Brennan, "Taxes, Market Valuation and Corporate Financial Policy," *National Tax Journal,* **23**: 417–427 (December 1970).

The argument that dividend policy is irrelevant even in the presence of taxes is presented in:

F. Black and M.S. Scholes, "The Effects of Dividend Yield and Dividend Policy on Common Stock Prices and Returns," *Journal of Financial Economics,* **1**: 1–22 (May 1974).

M.H. Miller and M.S. Scholes, "Dividends and Taxes," *Journal of Financial Economics,* **6**: 333–364 (December 1978).

A brief review on some of the empirical evidence is contained in:

R.H. Litzenberger and K. Ramaswamy, "The Effects of Dividends on Common Stock Prices: Tax Effects or Information Effects," *Journal of Finance,* **37**: 429–443 (May 1982).

Merton Miller reviews research on the dividend controversy in:

M.H. Miller, "Behavioral Rationality in Finance: The Case of Dividends," *Journal of Business,* **59**: S451–S468 (October 1986).

An empirical analysis of the effect of differential taxation of dividends and capital gains in Canada is in:

I.G. Morgan, "Dividends and Stock Price Behaviour in Canada," *Journal of Business Administration,* **12**: 91–106 (Fall 1980).

An alternative approach to empirically estimating the differential impact of dividend and capital gains taxation involves examining the price drop of shares as they go ex-dividend. With American data, this is done by Elton and Gruber; with Canadian data this is done by Lakonishok and Vermaelen, and by Booth and Johnston:

L.D. Booth and D.J. Johnston, "The Ex-Dividend Day Behavior of Canadian Stock Prices: Tax Changes and Clientele Effects," *Journal of Finance,* **39**: 457–476 (June 1984).

E. Elton and M. Gruber, "Marginal Stockholder Tax Rates and the Clientele Effect," *Review of Economics and Statistics,* **52**: 68–70 (February 1970).

J. Lakonishok and T. Vermaelen, "Tax Reform and Ex-Dividend Day Behavior," *Journal of Finance,* **38**: 1157–1179 (September 1983).

THE DIVIDEND TAX CREDIT AND THE ELIMINATION OF DOUBLE TAXATION

Canadian legislators have made a significant effort to eliminate the double taxation of dividends at the corporate and at the personal level by means of the dividend tax credit (DTC). We will start by discussing the *theory* of the DTC, and conclude by relating it to Canada's tax laws.

The basic idea of the DTC is that the government will pay a tax credit to the shareholder for the corporate tax paid on the pretax cash flow used to generate a dividend, and then tax the shareholder on the total amount received: the dividend *and* the tax credit. In this way, dividends are effectively taxed at the personal level, but not the corporate level.

Let

DIV = dividend paid by a firm
T_c = corporate tax rate
T_p = marginal personal tax rate on ordinary salary and interest income
C = pretax corporate cash flow required to support the dividend

Since dividends are paid out of after-tax cash flows, we have $C(1 - T_c) = $ DIV or $C = $ DIV$/(1 - T_c)$. The cash flow, C, is often called the "grossed-up dividend." The government then permits the shareholder a dividend tax credit equal to the amount of the corporate tax paid. That is,

$$\begin{aligned} \text{DTC} &= T_c C \\ &= \frac{T_c \, \text{DIV}}{1 - T_c} \end{aligned}$$

The system actually used in Canada is complicated by two facts: first, personal tax is assessed at the federal and provincial level, and second, there are two basic corporate tax rates—one for small business and one for ordinary business.

Let

T_{pfed} = marginal personal federal tax rate
T_{prov} = provincial tax as a proportion of federal tax

Then, the overall marginal personal tax rate is $T_p = T_{pfed}(1 + T_{prov})$. (All provinces but Quebec calculate personal taxes in this manner.) Similarly, the dividend tax credit is partly generated by the federal and partly by the provincial governments, so that

$$\text{DTC} = \text{DTC}_{fed}(1 + T_{prov})$$

where DTC_{fed} is the dividend tax credit on the federal tax return.

Starting in 1988, the grossed-up dividend is 125% of the dividend actually paid, so that $T_c = 20\%$ was the corporate tax rate implied by the dividend tax credit system, since $1.25 = 1/(1 - 0.20)$. The federal dividend tax credit is $13\frac{1}{3}\%$ of the grossed-up dividend. From

$$\text{DTC} = \text{DTC}_{fed}(1 + T_{prov}) \text{ and } \text{DTC} = T_c C$$

we have

$$T_c C = 0.1333 \, C \, (1 + T_{prov})$$

so that

$$T_{prov} = 50\%$$

Thus, if the corporate tax rate is 20% and the provincial personal tax is 50% of the federal tax, the dividend tax credit works perfectly to eliminate the double taxation of dividends.[36] In actual fact, in 1989, provincial personal taxes varied from 43% to 61% of federal tax.

Overall, the dividend tax credit system works toward the elimination of double taxation by making the total corporate and personal taxes on corporate equity cash flows equal to what would have resulted from *no corporate taxes,* and personal taxes at the same rates as applied to ordinary personal income. This effect is called the **integration** of the corporate and personal tax systems and was supported by the Carter Royal Commission on Taxation.[37] Full integration has been achieved with wages, salaries, and interest income, because these cash outflows are tax-deductible for the corporation and taxable only in the hands of the recipient. From the calculations above, we can see that full integration is achieved for the dividends of small firms, but not for large firms. A natural question to ask is, "Why should corporations pay any tax at all if the integration concept is appropriate?" The answer is that it prevents the corporate structure from being used to defer taxes (via retention of earnings), thereby reducing their present value. Under full integration, taxes on corporate equity income are merely pre-payments of personal taxes.

QUIZ

1. In 1990, Molson Company paid a regular quarterly dividend of $0.25 a share.
    (a) Match each of the following sets of dates:
(A) Wednesday, May 9	(a) Record date
(B) Monday, May 28	(b) Payment date
(C) Friday, June 1	(c) Ex-dividend date
(D) Friday, May 25	(d) Last with-dividend date
(E) Sunday, July 1	(e) Declaration date
    (b) On one of these dates the stock price is likely to fall by about the value of the dividend. Which date and why?
    (c) The stock price in May was $36. What was the prospective dividend yield?
    (d) The earnings per share for 1990 were forecast at around $4.00. What was the percentage payout rate?
    (e) Suppose that in 1990 the company paid a 10% stock dividend. What would be the expected fall in the stock price?
2. Indicate which of the following statements are false:
    (a) A company may not generally pay a dividend out of paid-up capital.
    (b) A company may not generally pay a dividend if it is insolvent.

[36] This analysis also provides investors with a popular rule of thumb regarding equivalent bond and preferred share yields. The DTC system works in such a way that dividends from preferred shares are equivalent, after personal taxes, to a pretax interest or salary cash flow equal to the grossed-up dividend. Thus, a dividend yield of r is equivalent to a grossed-up bond yield of $1.25r$. For example, an investor should be indifferent between an 8% preferred share and a 10% bond, provided the two securities have the same risk and term to maturity, and the provincial tax is close to 50% of federal tax.

[37] *Report of the Royal Commission on Taxation,* Ottawa, Queen's Printer, 1966.

(c) Realized capital gains are taxed at the marginal rate of income tax.

(d) Corporations are taxed on dividends received.

(e) The stock dividend is taxed as income.

3.   Here are several "facts" about typical corporate dividend policies. Which of the "facts" are true and which false? Write out a corrected version of any false statements.

(a) Most companies set a target dividend payout ratio.

(b) They set each year's dividend equal to the target payout ratio times that year's earnings.

(c) Managers and investors seem more concerned with dividend changes than dividend levels.

(d) Managers often increase dividends temporarily when earnings are unexpectedly high for a year or two.

4.   Between 1964 and 1982 one could explain 80% of the variation in GM's dividend changes by the following equation:

$$\text{DIV}_t - \text{DIV}_{t-1} = 1.66 + 0.77 \,(0.35\ \text{EPS}_t - \text{DIV}_{t-1})$$

What do you think was

(a) GM's target payout ratio?

(b) The rate at which dividends adjusted toward the target?

5.   Suppose the Miller-Modigliani (MM) theory of dividend policy is correct. How would a government-imposed dividend freeze affect

(a) Stock prices?

(b) The volume of capital investment?

6.   Sock price usually rises when there is an unexpected dividend increase, and falls when there is an unexpected dividend cut. Why?

7.   Suppose all investments offered the same expected return *before* tax. Consider two equally risky Canadian shares, Hi and Lo. Hi shares pay a generous dividend and offer low expected capital gains. Lo shares pay low dividends and offer high expected capital gains. Which of the following investors would prefer the Lo shares? Which would prefer the Hi shares? Which wouldn't care? Explain.

(a) An individual in a high tax bracket who rarely trades stocks, and who is

   (i) an American resident

   (ii) a Canadian resident.

(b) An individual in a low tax bracket who is

   (i) an American resident

   (ii) a Canadian resident.

(c) A Canadian pension fund.

(d) A Canadian security dealer that is a public corporation.

8.   Company X pays a dividend of $10 a share. How much would you expect the price to fall on the ex-dividend date in each of the following cases?

(a) The capital market is perfectly competitive and there are no taxes.

(b) Each investor is subject to a 10% tax on dividends.

(c) Each investor is subject to a 10% tax on dividends and 15% on capital gains, which are realized every year.

9.   From 1982 to 1986, Revenue Canada grossed-up dividends by 50% and had a (federal) dividend tax credit of $22\frac{2}{3}\%$ of grossed-up dividends. What corporate and provincial tax rates is this consistent with?

QUESTIONS AND PROBLEMS

1. Look in a recent issue of *The Financial Post* at "Dividends Declared" and "The Markets" and choose a company reporting a regular dividend.
   (a) How frequently does the company pay a regular dividend?
   (b) What is the amount of the dividend?
   (c) By what date must your stock be registered for you to receive the dividend?
   (d) How many weeks later is the dividend paid?
   (e) Look up the stock price and calculate the annual yield on the stock.

2. Respond to the following comment: "It's all very well saying that I can sell shares to cover cash needs, but that may mean selling at the bottom of the market. If the company pays a regular dividend, investors avoid that risk."

3. "Dividends are the shareholder's wages. Therefore, if a government adopts an income policy that restricts increases in wages, it should in all logic restrict increases in dividends." Does this make sense?

4. Refer to the first balance sheet prepared for Rational Demiconductor in Section 16-3. Again it uses cash to pay a $1,000 cash dividend, planning to issue stock to recover the cash required for investment. But this time catastrophe hits before the stock can be issued. A new pollution control regulation increases manufacturing costs to the extent that the value of Rational Demiconductor's existing business is cut in half, to $4,500. The NPV of the new investment opportunity is unaffected, however. Show that dividend policy is still irrelevant.

5. "Risky companies tend to have lower target payout ratios and more gradual adjustment rates." Explain what is meant by this statement. Why do you think it is so?

6. Consider the following two statements: "Dividend policy is irrelevant." "Stock price is the present value of expected future dividends" (see Chapter 4). They *sound* contradictory. This question is designed to show that they are fully consistent.

   The current price of the shares of Charles River Mining Corporation is $50. Next year's earnings and dividends per share are $4 and $2, respectively. Investors expect perpetual growth at 8% per year. The expected rate of return demanded by investors is $r = 12\%$.

   We can use the perpetual-growth model

   $$P_0 = \frac{DIV_1}{r - g} = \frac{2}{0.12 - 0.08} = 50$$

   Suppose that Charles River Mining announces that it will switch to a 100% payout policy, issuing shares as necessary to finance growth. Use the perpetual-growth model to show that current stock price is unchanged.

7. A shareholder receives $100 in dividends from a Canadian corporation after 1982. Suppose her provincial tax is 38.5% of federal tax. What is the net tax on dividends if her marginal federal tax rate is
   (a) 16%?
   (b) 43%?

8. The expected pretax return on three stocks is divided between dividends and capital gains in the following way:

Stock	Expected Dividend	Expected Capital Gain
A	$0	$10
B	5	5
C	10	0

(a) If each stock is priced at $100, what are the expected net returns on each stock to the following investors:

Investor Characteristics	Federal Tax Bracket	Provincial Tax as a Proportion of Federal Tax	Time to Realization of Capital Gain
(i) Pension fund			
(ii) Individual	17%	50%	Indefinite deferral
(iii) Individual	29%	50%	Indefinite deferral
(iv) Individual	29%	50%	One year
(v) American individual	28%		Indefinite deferral
(vi) American individual	28%		One year

(b) Recalculate the expected net returns assuming stock A is priced at $115, B at $100, and C at $90. Other things equal, which stock would be most attractive?

9. An article on stock repurchase in the *Los Angeles Times* noted that "An increasing number of companies are finding that the best investment they can make these days is in themselves." Discuss this view. How is the desirability of repurchase affected by company prospects and the price of its stock?

10. Adherents of the "dividends-are-good" school have sometimes pointed to the fact that stocks with high yields tend to have above-average price-earnings multiples. Is this evidence convincing? Discuss.

11. For each of the following four groups of companies, state whether you would expect them to distribute a relatively high or low proportion of current earnings and whether you would expect them to have a relatively high or low price-earnings ratio.
   (a) High-risk companies
   (b) Companies that have recently experienced an unexpected decline in profits
   (c) Companies that expect to experience a decline in profits
   (d) "Growth" companies with valuable future investment opportunities

12. "Many companies use stock repurchase to increase earnings per share. For example, suppose that a company is in the following position:

Net profit	$10 million
Number of shares before repurchase	1 million
Earnings per share	$10
Price-earnings ratio	20
Share price	$200

The company now repurchases 200,000 shares at $200 a share. The number of shares declines to 800,000 shares and the earnings per share increase to $12.50. Assuming the price-earnings ratio stays at 20, the share price must rise to $250.00." Discuss.

13. (a) The Horner Pie Company pays a quarterly dividend of $1. Suppose that the stock price is expected to fall on the ex-dividend date by 90 cents. Would you prefer to buy on the with-dividend date or the ex-dividend date if you were (1) a tax-free investor, (2) an investor with a marginal tax rate of 40% on income (and 16% on capital gains)?

(b) In a study of ex-dividend behaviour in the United States, Elton and Gruber estimated that the stock price fell on the average by 85% of the dividend. Assuming that the tax rate on capital gains is 40% of the rate on income tax, what does Elton and Gruber's result imply about investors' marginal rate of income tax?

(c) Elton and Gruber also observed that the ex-dividend price fall was different for high-payout stocks and for low-payout stocks. Which group would you expect to show the larger price fall?

(d) Would the fact that investors can trade stocks freely around the ex-dividend date alter your interpretation of Elton and Gruber's study?

14. Booth and Johnston studied ex-dividend behaviour of Canadian stocks from 1970 to 1980.

(a) Their data show that the average price drop in 1972–1976 was 47% of the dividend. In that period, dividends were grossed-up by one-third to get taxable dividends, and the federal dividend tax credit was 20% of the grossed-up dividend. Capital gains were taxed at 50% of the ordinary personal tax rate. Assume that they are realized annually. Suppose the typical investor was in Ontario, where provincial tax was 30.5% of federal tax during 1972–1976. What marginal federal personal tax rate is implied by these data?

(b) Booth's and Johnston's data showed that, in the 1978–1980 period, the average price drop was 62% of the dividend. In that period, dividends were grossed-up by 50% and the federal dividend tax credit was 25% of the grossed-up dividend. Capital gains were still taxed at 50% of the ordinary income rate, but Ontario tax had risen to 44% of federal tax. What marginal federal personal tax rate is implied by these data?

15. Suppose Canadian lawmakers decided to eliminate all of the nominal 36% corporate tax paid on income used to generate dividends for ordinary firms. If provincial personal tax is 50% of federal personal tax, by how much must dividends be grossed-up and what would be the appropriate federal dividend tax credit? You will need to study Appendix 16-1 to answer this.

16. You and your cousins have recently inherited a substantial sum of money and your cousins have come to you for advice regarding how to invest their share. They want to know whether to invest in five-year bonds or high-grade preferred shares. The shares will pay an 8% dividend for each of the next five years, and then will be redeemed for their initial purchase price. You feel that the risks of the two securities are the same, and that the decision should be made on the basis of tax considerations. Your cousins face the following taxes:

	Federal Tax Bracket	Provincial Tax
Bert	26%	52%
Ernie	17%	52%
Hilda	26%	45%
Elsie	17%	45%

Which bond yields are equivalent to the 8% dividend yield, for each of your four cousins?

17. Create a spreadsheet to reproduce Table 16-1. Now adjust the spreadsheet to give a comparison between the taxation of dividends and capital gains for each of the following scenarios:

Period	Gross-up Rate	DTC as Fraction of Taxable Dividend	Capital Gains Inclusion Rate	Provincial Tax as Fraction of Federal Tax	Federal Tax Rate		
					17%	26%	29%
1982–86	50%	22⅔%	50%	50%	16%	26%	34%
1978–81	50%	25%	50%	45%	16%	26%	34%
1972–76	33⅓%	20%	50%	30%	16%	26%	34%
Pre-1972	0%	20%	0%	28%	16%	26%	34%

C · H · A · P · T · E · R

17

DOES DEBT POLICY
MATTER?

A firm's basic resource is the stream of cash flows produced by its assets. When the firm is financed entirely by common stock, all those cash flows belong to the stockholders. When it issues both debt and equity securities, it undertakes to split up the cash flows into two streams, a relatively safe stream that goes to the debt holders and a more risky one that goes to the stockholders.

The firm's mix of different securities is known as its **capital structure**. The choice of capital structure is fundamentally a marketing problem. The firm can issue dozens of distinct securities in countless combinations but it attempts to find the particular combination that maximizes its overall market value.

Are these attempts worthwhile? We must consider the possibility that *no* combination has any greater appeal than any other. Perhaps the really important decisions concern the company's assets, and decisions about capital structure are mere details—matters to be attended to but not worried about.

Modigliani and Miller (MM), who showed that dividend policy doesn't matter in perfect capital markets, also showed that financing decisions don't matter in perfect markets.[1] Their famous "Proposition I" states that a firm cannot change the *total* value of its securities just by splitting its cash flows into different streams: the firm's value is determined by its real assets, not by the securities it issues. Thus capital structure is irrelevant as long as the firm's investment decisions are taken as given.

MM's Proposition I allows complete separation of investment and financing decisions. It implies that any firm could use the capital budgeting procedures

---

[1] MM's paper (F. Modigliani and M.H. Miller, "The Cost of Capital, Corporation Finance and the Theory of Investment," *American Economic Review*, **48**: 261–297 (June 1958)) was published in 1958, but their basic argument was anticipated in 1938 by J.B. Williams and to some extent by David Durand. See J.B. Williams, *The Theory of Investment Value*, Harvard University Press, Cambridge, Mass., 1938, and D. Durand, "Cost of Debt and Equity Funds for Business: Trends and Problems of Measurement," in *Conference on Research in Business Finance*, National Bureau of Economic Research, New York, 1952. For a simple, straightforward presentation of the theory, see F. Modigliani and M.H. Miller, "Reply to Heins and Sprenkle," *American Economic Review*, **59**: 592–595 (September 1969).

presented in Chapters 2 to 12. In those chapters we never worried about where the money for capital expenditures comes from. We assumed all-equity financing without really thinking about it. If Proposition I holds, that is exactly the right approach.

We believe that in practice capital structure *does* matter, but we nevertheless devote all of this chapter to MM's argument. If you don't fully understand the conditions under which MM's theory holds, you won't fully understand why one capital structure is better than another. The financial manager needs to know what kinds of market imperfection to look for.

In Chapter 18 we will undertake a detailed analysis of the imperfections that are most likely to make a difference: taxes, the costs of bankruptcy, and the costs of writing and enforcing complicated debt contracts. We will also argue that it is naive to suppose that investment and financing decisions can be completely separated.

But in this chapter we isolate the decision about capital structure by holding the decision about investment fixed. We also assume that dividend policy is irrelevant.

17-1 THE EFFECT OF LEVERAGE IN A COMPETITIVE TAX-FREE ECONOMY

We have referred to the firm's choice of capital structure as a *marketing problem*. The financial manager's problem is to find the combination of securities that has the greatest overall appeal to investors—the combination that maximizes the market value of the firm. Before tackling this problem, we ought to make sure that a policy that maximizes firm value also maximizes the wealth of the shareholders.

Let D and E denote the market values of the outstanding debt and equity of the Wapshot Mining Company. Wapshot's 1,000 shares sell for $50 apiece. Thus

$$E = 1,000 \times \$50 = \$50,000$$

Wapshot has also borrowed $25,000, and so V, the aggregate market value of all Wapshot's outstanding securities, is

$$V = D + E = \$75,000$$

Wapshot's stock is known as *levered equity*. Its stockholders face the benefits and costs of *financial leverage* or *gearing*. Suppose that Wapshot "levers up" still further by borrowing an additional $10,000 and paying the proceeds out to shareholders as a special dividend of $10 per share. This substitutes debt for equity capital with no impact on Wapshot's assets.

What will Wapshot's equity be worth after the special dividend is paid? We have two unknowns, E and V:

Old debt	$25,000	
New debt	$10,000	$35,000 = D
Equity		? = E
Firm value		? = V

If V is $75,000 as before, then E must be $V - D = \$75,000 - \$35,000 = \$40,000$. Stockholders have suffered a capital loss that exactly offsets the $10,000 special dividend. But if V increases to, say, $80,000 as a result of the change in capital structure, then $E = \$45,000$ and the stockholders are $5,000 ahead. In general, any increase or decrease in V caused by a shift in capital structure accrues to the firm's stockholders. We conclude that a policy that maximizes the market value of the firm is also best for the firm's stockholders.

This conclusion rests on two important assumptions: first, that Wapshot can ignore dividend policy and, second, that after the change in capital structure the old and new debt is *worth* $35,000.

Dividend policy is probably relevant but there is no need to repeat the discussion of Chapter 16. We need only note that shifts in capital structure sometimes force important decisions about dividend policy. Perhaps Wapshot's cash dividend has costs that should be weighed against any benefits achieved by its increased financial leverage.

Our second assumption that old and new debt ends up worth $35,000 seems innocuous. But it could be wrong. Perhaps the new borrowing has increased the risk of the old bonds. If the holders of old bonds cannot demand a higher rate of interest to compensate for the increased risk, the value of their investment is reduced. In this case Wapshot's stockholders gain at the expense of the holders of old bonds even though the overall value of the debt and equity is unchanged.

But this anticipates issues better left to Chapter 18. In this chapter we will assume that any issue of debt has no effect on the market value of existing debt.[2]

Enter Modigliani and Miller

Let us accept the notion that the financial manager would like to find the combination of securities that maximizes the value of the firm. How is this done? MM's answer is that the financial manager should stop worrying: in a perfect market any combination of securities is as good as another. The value of the firm is unaffected by its choice of capital structure.

You can see this by imagining two firms that generate the same stream of operating income and differ only in their capital structure. Firm U is unlevered. Therefore the total value of its equity E_U is the same as the total value of the firm V_U. Firm L, on the other hand, is levered. The value of its stock is, therefore, equal to the value of the firm less the value of the debt: $E_L = V_L - D_L$.

Now think which of these firms you would prefer to invest in. If you don't want to take much risk, you can buy common stock in the unlevered firm U. For example, if you buy 1% of firm U's shares, your investment is $0.01 V_U$ and you are entitled to 1% of the gross profits:

Dollar Investment	Dollar Return
$0.01 V_U$	0.01 Profits

Now compare this with an alternative strategy. This is to purchase the same fraction of both the debt and the equity of firm L. Your investment and return would then be as follows:

	Dollar Investment	Dollar Return
Debt	$0.01 D_L$	0.01 Interest
Equity	$0.01 E_L$	0.01 (Profits − interest)
Total	$0.01 (D_L + E_L)$	0.01 Profits
	$= 0.01 V_L$	

[2] See E.F. Fama, "The Effects of a Firm's Investment and Financing Decisions," *American Economic Review*, **68**: 272–284 (June 1978), for a rigorous analysis of the conditions under which a policy of maximizing the value of the firm is also best for the stockholders.

Both strategies offer the same payoff: 1% of the firm's profits. In well-functioning or perfect markets two investments that offer the same payoff must have the same cost. Therefore $0.01\ V_U$ must equal $0.01\ V_L$: the value of the unlevered firm must equal the value of the levered firm.

Suppose that you are willing to run a little more risk. You decide to buy 1% of the outstanding shares in the *levered* firm. Your investment and return are now as follows:

Dollar Investment	Dollar Return
$0.01\ E_L$ $= 0.01\ (V_L - D_L)$	$0.01\ (\text{Profits} - \text{interest})$

But there is an alternative strategy. This is to borrow $0.01\ D_L$ on your own account and purchase 1% of the stock of the *unlevered* firm. In this case, your borrowing gives you an immediate cash *inflow* of $0.01\ D_L$, but you have to pay interest on your loan equal to 1% of the interest that is paid by firm L. Your total investment and return are, therefore, as follows:

	Dollar Investment	Dollar Return
Borrowing	$-0.01\ D_L$	$-0.01\ \text{Interest}$
Equity	$0.01\ V_U$	$0.01\ \text{Profits}$
Total	$0.01\ (V_U - D_L)$	$0.01\ (\text{Profits} - \text{interest})$

Again both strategies offer the same payoff: 1% of profits, after interest. Therefore, both investments must have the same cost. The quantity $0.01\ (V_U - D_L)$ must equal $0.01\ (V_L - D_L)$ and V_U must equal V_L.

It does not matter whether the world is full of cautious investors, incautious investors, or a mixture of each. All would agree that the value of the unlevered firm U must be equal to the value of the levered firm L. As long as investors can borrow or lend on their own account on the same terms as the firm, they can "undo" the effect of any changes in the firm's capital structure. This is the basis for MM's famous Proposition I: "The market value of any firm is independent of its capital structure."

The Law of the Conservation of Value

MM's argument that debt policy is irrelevant is an application of an astonishingly simple idea. If we have two streams of cash flow, A and B, then the present value of A + B is equal to the present value of A plus the present value of B. We met this principle of *value additivity* in our discussion of capital budgeting, where we saw that in perfect capital markets the present value of two assets combined is equal to the sum of their present values considered separately.

In the present context we are not combining assets, but splitting them up. But value additivity works just as well in reverse. We can slice a cash flow into as many parts as we like; the values of the parts will always sum back to the value of the unsliced stream. (Of course, we have to make sure that none of the stream is lost in the slicing. We cannot say, "The value of a pie is independent of how it is sliced," if the slicer is also a nibbler.)

This is really a *law of conservation of value*. The value of an asset is preserved regardless of the nature of the claims against it. Thus Proposition I: firm value is determined on the *left-hand* side of its balance sheet by real assets—not by the proportions of debt and equity securities issued by the firm.

The simplest ideas often have the widest application. For example, we could apply the law of conservation of value to the choice between issuing preferred stock, common stock, or some combination. The law implies that the choice is irrelevant, assuming perfect capital markets and providing that the choice does not affect the firm's investment, borrowing, and operating policies. If the total value of the equity "pie" (preferred and common combined) is fixed, the firm's owners (its common stockholders) do not care how this pie is sliced.

The law also applies to the *mix* of debt securities issued by the firm. The choices of long-term versus short-term, secured versus unsecured, senior versus subordinated, and convertible versus non-convertible debt all should have no effect on the overall value of the firm.

Combining assets and splitting them up will not affect values as long as they do not affect an investor's choice. When we showed that capital structure does not affect choice, we implicitly assumed that both companies and individuals can borrow and lend at the same risk-free rate of interest. As long as this is so, individuals can "undo" the effect of any changes in the firm's capital structure.

In practice, corporate debt is not risk-free and firms cannot escape with rates of interest appropriate to a government security. Some people's initial reaction is that this alone invalidates MM's proposition. It is a natural mistake, but capital structure can be irrelevant even when debt is risky.

If a company borrows money, it does not *guarantee* repayment: it repays the debt in full only if its assets are worth more than the debt obligation. The shareholders in the company, therefore, have limited liability.

Many individuals would like to borrow with limited liability. They might, therefore, be prepared to pay a small premium for levered shares *if the supply of levered shares was insufficient to meet their needs.*[3] But there are literally thousands of common stocks of companies that borrow. Therefore it is unlikely that an issue of debt would induce them to pay a premium for *your* shares.[4]

An Example of Proposition I

Macbeth Spot Removers is reviewing its capital structure. Table 17-1 shows its current position. The company has no leverage and all the operating income is paid as dividends to the common stockholders (we assume still that there are no taxes). The expected earnings and dividends per share are $1.50, but this figure is by no means certain—it could turn out to be more or less than $1.50. The price of each share is $10. Since the firm expects to produce a level stream of earnings in perpetuity, the expected return on the share is equal to the earnings-price ratio, $1.50/10.00 = 15\%$.[5]

Ms. Macbeth, the firm's president, has come to the conclusion that shareholders would be better off if the company had equal proportions of debt and equity. She therefore proposes to issue $5,000 of debt at an interest rate of 10% and use the proceeds to repurchase 500 shares. To support her proposal, Ms. Macbeth has analyzed the situation under different assumptions about operating income. The results of her calculations are shown in Table 17-2.

---

[3] Of course, individuals could *create* limited liability if they chose. In other words, the lender could agree that borrowers need repay their debt in full only if the assets of company X are worth more than a certain amount. Presumably individuals don't enter into such arrangements because they can obtain limited liability more simply by investing in the stocks of levered companies.

[4] Capital structure is also irrelevant if each investor holds a fully diversified portfolio. In that case he or she owns all the risky securities offered by a company (both debt and equity). But anybody who owns *all* the risky securities doesn't care about how the cash flows are divided between different securities.

[5] See Chapter 4, Section 3.

Table 17-1
Macbeth Spot Removers is entirely equity-financed. Although it *expects* to have an income of $1,500 a year in perpetuity, this income is not certain. This table shows the return to the stockholder under different assumptions about operating incomes. We assume no taxes.

Data

Number of shares	1,000
Price per share	$10
Market value of shares	$10,000

Outcomes

Operating income, dollars	500	1,000	**1,500**	2,000
Earnings per share, dollars	0.50	1.00	**1.50**	2.00
Return on shares, %	5	10	**15**	20
			Expected outcome	

Table 17-2
Macbeth Spot Removers is wondering whether to issue $5,000 of debt at an interest rate of 10% and repurchase 500 shares. This table shows the return to the shareholder under different assumptions about operating income.

Data

Number of shares	500
Price per share	$10
Market value of shares	$5,000
Market value of debt	$5,000
Interest at 10%	$500

Outcomes

Operating income, dollars	500	1,000	**1,500**	2,000
Interest, dollars	500	500	**500**	500
Equity earnings, dollars	0	500	**1,000**	1,500
Earnings per share, dollars	0	1	**2**	3
Return on shares, %	0	10	**20**	30
			Expected outcome	

In order to see more clearly how leverage would affect earnings per share, Ms. Macbeth has also produced Figure 17-1. The solid line shows how earnings per share would vary with operating income under the firm's current all-equity financing. It is, therefore, simply a plot of the data in Table 17-1. The dotted line shows how earnings per share would vary given equal proportions of debt and equity. It is, therefore, a plot of the data in Table 17-2.

Ms. Macbeth reasons as follows: "It is clear that the effect of leverage depends on the company's income. If income is greater than $1,000, the return to the

Earnings per share
(EPS), dollars

Figure 17-1 Borrowing increases Macbeth's EPS (earnings per share) when operating income is greater than $1,000 and reduces EPS when operating income is less than $1,000. Expected EPS rise from $1.50 to $2.

equity holder is *increased* by leverage. If it is less than $1,000, the return is *reduced* by leverage. The return is unaffected when operating income is exactly $1,000. At this point the return on the market value of the assets is 10%, which is exactly equal to the interest rate on the debt. Our capital structure decision, therefore, boils down to what we think about income prospects. Since we expect operating income to be above the $1,000 break-even point, I believe we can best help our shareholders by going ahead with the $5,000 debt issue."

As financial manager of Macbeth Spot Removers, you reply as follows: "I agree that leverage will help the shareholder as long as our income is greater than $1,000. But your argument ignores the fact that Macbeth's shareholders have the alternative of borrowing on their own account. For example, suppose that a person borrows $10 and then invests $20 in two unlevered Macbeth shares. This person has to put up only $10 of his or her own money. The payoff on the investment varies with Macbeth's operating income, as shown in Table 17-3. This is exactly the same set of payoffs as the investor would get by buying one share in the levered company. Therefore a share in the levered company must also sell for $10. If Macbeth goes ahead and borrows, it will not allow investors to do anything that they could not do already, and so it will not increase value."

The argument that you are using is exactly the same as MM used to prove Proposition I.

Table 17-3
Individual investors can replicate Macbeth's leverage.

	Operating Income, Dollars			
	500	1,000	1,500	2,000
Earnings on two shares, dollars	1	2	**3**	4
Less interest at 10%, dollars	1	1	**1**	1
Net earnings on investment, dollars	0	1	**2**	3
Return on $10 investment, %	0	10	**20**	30
			Expected outcome	

17-2 HOW LEVERAGE AFFECTS RETURNS

Implications of Proposition I

Consider now the implications of Proposition I for the expected returns on Macbeth stock:

	Current Structure: All Equity	Proposed Structure: Equal Debt and Equity
Expected earnings per share	$1.50	$2.00
Price per share	$10.00	$10.00
Expected return on share, %	15	20

Leverage increases the expected stream of earnings per share, but *not* the share price. The reason is that the change in the expected earnings stream is exactly offset by a change in the rate at which the earnings are capitalized. The expected return on the share (which for a perpetuity is equal to the earnings-price ratio) increases from 15% to 20%. We now show how this comes about.

The expected return on a firm's assets r_A is equal to the expected operating income divided by the total market value of the firm's securities:

$$\text{Expected return on assets} = r_A = \frac{\text{expected operating income}}{\text{market value of all securities}}$$

We have seen that in perfect capital markets the company's borrowing decision does not affect *either* the firm's operating income *or* the total market value of its securities. Therefore the borrowing decision also does not affect the expected return on the firm's assets r_A.

Suppose that an investor holds all of a company's debt and all its equity. This investor would be entitled to all the firm's operating income; therefore, the expected return on the portfolio would be equal to r_A.

The expected return on a portfolio is equal to a weighted average of the expected returns on the individual holdings. Therefore the expected return on a portfolio consisting of *all* the firm's securities is

$$\begin{pmatrix} \text{Expected return} \\ \text{on assets} \end{pmatrix} = \begin{pmatrix} \text{proportion} \\ \text{in debt} \times \begin{array}{c} \text{expected} \\ \text{return on} \\ \text{debt} \end{array} \end{pmatrix} + \begin{pmatrix} \text{proportion} \\ \text{in equity} \times \begin{array}{c} \text{expected} \\ \text{return on} \\ \text{equity} \end{array} \end{pmatrix}$$

$$r_A = \left(\frac{D}{D+E} \times r_D \right) + \left(\frac{E}{D+E} \times r_E \right)$$

We can rearrange this equation to obtain an expression for r_E, the expected return on the equity of a levered firm:

$$\begin{array}{c}\text{Expected return}\\\text{on equity}\end{array} = \begin{array}{c}\text{expected}\\\text{return on}\\\text{assets}\end{array} + \begin{array}{c}\text{debt-}\\\text{equity}\\\text{ratio}\end{array} \times \left(\begin{array}{c}\text{expected}\\\text{return on}\\\text{assets}\end{array} - \begin{array}{c}\text{expected}\\\text{return on}\\\text{debt}\end{array}\right)$$

$$r_E = r_A + \frac{D}{E}(r_A - r_D)$$

Proposition II This is MM's Proposition II: the expected rate of return on the common stock of a levered firm increases in proportion to the debt-equity ratio (D/E), expressed in market values; the rate of increase depends on the spread between r_A, the expected rate of return on a portfolio of all the firm's securities, and r_D, the expected return on the debt. Note that $r_E = r_A$ if the firm has no debt.

We can check out this formula for Macbeth Spot Removers. Before the decision to borrow

$$r_E = r_A = \frac{\text{expected operating income}}{\text{market value of all securities}}$$

$$= \frac{1{,}500}{10{,}000} = 0.15, \text{ or } 15\%$$

If the firm goes ahead with its plan to borrow, the expected return on assets r_A is still 15%. The expected return on equity is

$$r_E = r_A + \frac{D}{E}(r_A - r_D)$$

$$= 0.15 + \frac{5{,}000}{5{,}000}(0.15 - 0.10)$$

$$= 0.20, \text{ or } 20\%$$

The general implications of MM's Proposition II are shown in Figure 17-2. The figure assumes that the firm's bonds are essentially risk-free at low debt levels. Thus r_D is independent of D/E and r_E increases linearly as D/E increases. As the firm borrows more, the risk of default increases and the firm is required to pay higher rates of interest. Proposition II predicts that when this occurs the rate of increase in r_E slows down. This is also shown in Figure 17-2. The more debt the firm has, the less sensitive r_E is to further borrowing.

Why does the slope of the r_E line in Figure 17-2 taper off as D/E increases? Essentially because holders of risky debt bear some of the firm's business risk. As the firm borrows more, more of that risk is transferred from stockholders to bondholders.

The Risk-Return Trade-off Proposition I says that financial leverage has no effect on shareholders' wealth. Proposition II says that the rate of return they can expect to receive on their shares increases as the firm's debt-equity ratio increases. How can shareholders be indifferent to increased leverage when it increases expected return? Any increase in expected return is exactly offset by an increase in risk and therefore in shareholders' *required* rate of return.

Figure 17-2 MM's Proposition II. The expected return on equity r_E increases linearly with the debt-equity ratio so long as debt is risk-free. But if leverage increases the risk of the debt, debt holders demand a higher return on the debt. This causes the rate of increase in r_E to slow down.

Look at what happens to the risk of Macbeth shares if it moves to equal debt-equity proportions. Table 17-4 shows how a shortfall in operating income affects the payoff to the shareholders.

Table 17-4
Leverage increases the risk of Macbeth shares.

		Operating Income	
		$500	**$1,500**
All equity:	Earnings per share, dollars	0.50	1.50
	Return on shares, %	5	15
50% debt:	Earnings per share, dollars	0	2.00
	Return on shares, %	0	20

You can see that the debt-equity proportion does not affect the *dollar* risk borne by equity holders. Suppose operating income drops from $1,500 to $500. Under all-equity financing, equity earnings drop by $1 per share. There are 1,000 outstanding shares, and so *total* equity earnings fall by $1 × 1,000 = $1,000. With 50% debt, the same drop in operating income reduces earnings per share by $2. But there are only 500 shares outstanding, and so total equity income drops by $2 × 500 = $1,000, just as in the all-equity case.

However, the debt-equity choice does amplify the spread of *percentage* returns. If the firm is all-equity-financed, a decline of $1,000 in the operating income reduces the return on the shares by 10%. If the firm issues risk-free debt with a fixed interest payment of $500 a year, then a decline of $1,000 in the operating income reduces the return on the shares by 20%. In other words, the effect of leverage is to double the amplitude of the swings in Macbeth's shares. Whatever the beta of the firm's shares before the refinancing, it would be twice as high afterwards.

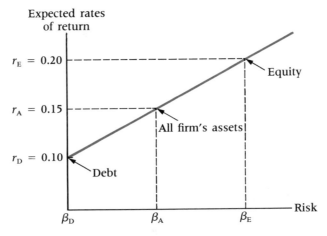

Figure 17-3   If Macbeth is unlevered, the expected return on its equity equals the expected return on its assets. Leverage increases both the expected return on equity (r_E) and the risk of equity (β_E).

Just as the expected return on the firm's assets is a weighted average of the expected return on the individual securities, so likewise is the beta of the firm's assets a weighted average of the betas of the individual securities.[6]

$$\text{Beta of atoms} = \left(\begin{matrix}\text{proportion} \\ \text{of debt}\end{matrix} \times \begin{matrix}\text{beta of} \\ \text{debt}\end{matrix}\right) + \left(\begin{matrix}\text{proportion} \\ \text{of equity}\end{matrix} \times \begin{matrix}\text{beta of} \\ \text{equity}\end{matrix}\right)$$

$$\beta_A = \left(\frac{D}{D+E} \times \beta_D\right) + \left(\frac{E}{D+E} \times \beta_E\right)$$

We can rearrange this equation also to give an expression for β_E, the beta of the equity of a levered firm:

$$\text{Beta of equity} = \begin{matrix}\text{beta of} \\ \text{assets}\end{matrix} + \begin{matrix}\text{debt-equity} \\ \text{ratio}\end{matrix} \times \left(\begin{matrix}\text{beta of} \\ \text{assets}\end{matrix} - \begin{matrix}\text{beta of} \\ \text{debt}\end{matrix}\right)$$

$$\beta_E = \beta_A + \frac{D}{E}(\beta_A - \beta_D)$$

Now you can see why investors require higher returns on levered equity. The required return simply rises to match the increased risk.

In Figure 17-3 we have plotted the expected returns and the risk of Macbeth's securities, assuming that the interest on the debt is risk-free.[7]

17-3   THE TRADITIONAL POSITION

What did financial experts think about debt policy before MM? It is not easy to say because with hindsight we see that they did not think too clearly.[8] However,

---

[6] This equation should look familiar. We used it in Section 9-3 to work out how a change in leverage would affect the beta of stock.

[7] In this case $\beta_D = 0$ and $\beta_E = \beta_A + (D/E)\beta_A$.

[8] Financial economists in the year 2000 may remark on BMSG's blind spots and clumsy reasoning. On the other hand, they may not remember us at all.

a "traditional" position has emerged in response to MM. In order to understand it, we have to discuss the **weighted average cost of capital**.

The expected return on a portfolio of all the company's securities is often referred to as the *weighted average cost of capital*:[9]

$$\text{Weighted average cost of capital} = r_A = \left(\frac{D}{V} \times r_D\right) + \left(\frac{E}{V} \times r_E\right)$$

The weighted average cost of capital is used in capital budgeting decisions to find the net present value of projects that would not change the business risk of the firm.

For example, suppose that a firm has $2 million of outstanding debt and 100,000 outstanding shares selling at $30 per share. Its current borrowing rate is 8% and the financial manager thinks that the stock is priced to offer a 15% return, therefore $r_E = 0.15$. (The hard part is estimating r_E, of course.) This is all we need to calculate the weighted average cost of capital:

$$D = \$2 \text{ million}$$
$$E = 100{,}000 \text{ shares} \times \$30 \text{ per share} = \$3 \text{ million}$$
$$V = D + E = 2 + 3 = \$5 \text{ million}$$

$$\text{Weighted average cost of capital} = \left(\frac{D}{V} \times r_D\right) + \left(\frac{E}{V} \times r_E\right)$$

$$= \left(\frac{2}{5} \times 0.08\right) + \left(\frac{3}{5} \times 0.15\right)$$

$$= 0.122, \text{ or } 12.2\%$$

Note that we are still assuming that Proposition I holds. If it doesn't, we can't use this simple weighted average as the discount rate even for projects that do not change the firm's business "risk class." As we will see in Chapter 19, the weighted average cost of capital is at best a starting point for setting discount rates.

Two Warnings

Sometimes the objective in financing decisions is stated not as "maximize overall market value" but as "minimize the weighted average cost of capital." These are equivalent objectives under the simplifying assumptions we have made so far. If MM's Proposition I does *not* hold, then the capital structure that maximizes the value of the firm also minimizes the weighted average cost of capital, *provided* that operating income is independent of capital structure. Remember that the weighted average cost of capital equals the expected operating income divided by the market value of all securities. Anything that increases the value of the firm reduces the weighted average cost of capital if operating income is constant. But if operating income is varying too, all bets are off.

In Chapter 18 we will show that financial leverage can affect operating income in several ways. Therefore maximizing the value of the firm is *not* always equivalent to minimizing the weighted average cost of capital.

Warning 1   Shareholders want management to increase the firm's value. They are more interested in being rich than in owning a firm with a low weighted average cost of capital.

---

[9] Remember that in this chapter we ignore taxes. In Chapter 19, we shall see that the weighted average cost of capital formula needs to be amended when debt interest can be deducted from taxable profits.

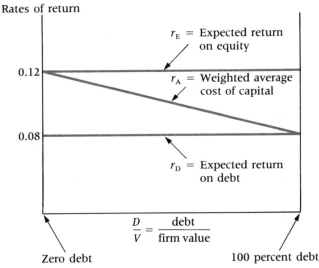

Rates of return

r_E = Expected return on equity

0.12

r_A = Weighted average cost of capital

0.08

r_D = Expected return on debt

$$\frac{D}{V} = \frac{\text{debt}}{\text{firm value}}$$

Zero debt   100 percent debt

Figure 17-4   If the expected rate of return demanded by stockholders r_E is unaffected by financial leverage, then the weighted average cost of capital r_A declines as the firm borrows more. At 100% debt r_A equals the borrowing rate r_D. Of course this is an absurd and totally unrealistic case.

Warning 2   Trying to minimize the weighted average cost of capital seems to encourage logical short circuits like the following. Suppose that someone says: "Shareholders demand—and deserve—higher expected rates of return than bondholders do. Therefore debt is the cheaper capital source. We can reduce the weighted average cost of capital by borrowing more." But this doesn't follow if the extra borrowing leads stockholders to demand a still higher expected rate of return. According to MM's Proposition II, the "cost of equity capital" r_E increases by just enough to keep the weighted average cost of capital constant.

This is not the only logical short circuit you are likely to encounter. We have cited two more in question 5 at the end of this chapter.

Rates of Return on Levered Equity—The Traditional Position   You may ask why we have even mentioned the weighted average cost of capital at this point if it is often wrong or confusing as a financial objective. We had to because the traditionalists accept this objective and argue their case in terms of it.

The logical short circuit we just described rested on the assumption that r_E, the expected rate of return demanded by stockholders, does not rise as the firm borrows more. Suppose, just for the sake of argument, that this is true. Then r_A, the weighted average cost of capital, must decline as the debt-equity ratio rises.

Take Figure 17-4, for example, which is drawn on the assumption that shareholders demand 12% no matter how much debt the firm has, and that bondholders always want 8%. The weighted average cost of capital starts at 12% and ends up at 8%. Suppose that this firm's operating income is a level, perpetual stream of $100,000 a year. Then firm value starts at

$$V = \frac{100,000}{0.12} = \$833,333$$

and ends up at

$$V = \frac{100,000}{0.08} = \$1,250,000$$

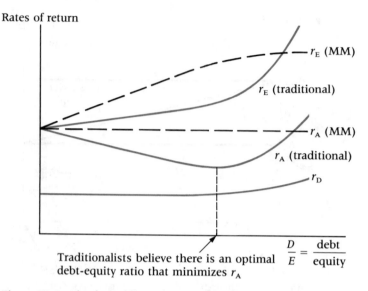

Rates of return

r_E (MM)

r_E (traditional)

r_A (MM)

r_A (traditional)

r_D

Traditionalists believe there is an optimal debt-equity ratio that minimizes r_A

$$\frac{D}{E} = \frac{\text{debt}}{\text{equity}}$$

Figure 17-5   The dashed lines show MM's view of the effect of leverage on the expected return on equity r_E and the weighted-average cost of capital r_A. (See Figure 17-2.) The solid lines show the traditional view. Traditionalists say that borrowing at first increases r_E more slowly than MM predict but that r_E shoots up with excessive borrowing. If so, the weighted-average cost of capital can be minimized if you use just the right amount of debt.

The gain of \$416,667 falls into the stockholders' pockets.[10]

Of course this is absurd: a firm that reaches 100% debt *has to be bankrupt*. If there is *any* chance that the firm could remain solvent, then the equity retains some value, and the firm cannot be 100% debt-financed. (Remember that we are working with the *market* values of debt and equity.)

But if the firm is bankrupt and its original shares are worthless pieces of paper, then its lenders *are* its new shareholders. The firm is back to all-equity financing! We assumed that the original stockholders demanded 12%—why should the new ones demand any less? They have to bear all of the firm's business risk.[11]

The situation described in Figure 17-4 is just impossible.[12] However, it is possible to stake out a position somewhere *between* Figures 17-3 and 17-4. That is exactly what the traditionalists have done. Their hypothesis is shown in Figure 17-5. They hold that a moderate degree of financial leverage may increase the

---

[10] Note that Figure 17-4 relates r_E and r_D to D/V, the ratio of debt to firm value, rather than to the debt-equity ratio D/E. In this figure we wanted to show what happens when the firm is 100% debt-financed. At that point $E = 0$ and D/E is infinite.

[11] We ignore the costs, delays, and other complications of bankruptcy. They are discussed in Chapter 18.

[12] This case is often termed the *net-income* (NI) approach because investors are assumed to capitalize income *after* interest at the same rate regardless of financial leverage. In contrast, MM's approach is a net-operating-income (NOI) approach, because the value of the firm is fundamentally determined by operating income, the total dollar return to *both* bondholders and stockholders. This distinction was emphasized by Durand in his important, pre-MM paper (*op. cit.*).

expected equity return r_E although not to the degree predicted by MM's Proposition II. But irresponsible firms that borrow *excessively* find r_E shooting up faster than MM predict. Consequently, the weighted average cost of capital r_A declines at first, then rises. Its minimum point is the point of optimal capital structure. Remember that minimizing r_A is equivalent to maximizing overall firm value if, as the traditionalists assume, operating income is unaffected by borrowing.

Two arguments might be advanced in support of the traditional position. First, it could be that investors don't notice or appreciate the financial risk created by "moderate" borrowing, although they wake up when debt is "excessive." If so, investors in moderately leveraged firms may accept a lower rate of return than they really should.

That seems naive.[13] The second argument is better. It accepts MM's reasoning as applied to perfect capital markets, but holds that actual markets are imperfect. Imperfections may allow firms that borrow to provide a valuable service for investors. If so, levered shares might trade at premium prices compared to their theoretical values in perfect markets.

Suppose that corporations can borrow more cheaply than individuals. Then it would pay investors who want to borrow to do so indirectly by holding the stock of levered firms. They would be willing to live with expected rates of return that do not fully compensate them for the business and financial risk they bear.

Is corporate borrowing really cheaper? It's hard to say. Interest rates on home mortgages are not too different from rates on high-grade corporate bonds.[14] Rates on margin debt (borrowing from a stockbroker with the investor's shares tendered as security) are not too different from the rates firms pay banks for short-term loans.

There are some individuals who face relatively high interest rates, largely because of the costs lenders incur in making and servicing small loans. There are economies of scale in borrowing. A group of small investors could do better by borrowing via a corporation, in effect pooling their loans and saving transaction costs.[15]

But suppose that this class of investors is large, both in number and in the aggregate wealth it brings to capital markets. Shouldn't the investors' needs be fully satisfied by the thousands of levered firms already existing? Is there really an unsatisfied clientele of small investors standing ready to pay a premium for one more firm that borrows?

Maybe the market for corporate leverage is like the market for automobiles. Canadians need millions of automobiles and are willing to pay thousands of dollars apiece for them. But that doesn't mean that you could strike it rich by going into the automobile business. You're at least 50 years too late.

---

[13] The first argument may reflect a confusion between financial risk and the risk of default. Default is not a serious threat when borrowing is moderate; stockholders worry about it only when the firm goes "too far." But stockholders bear financial risk—in the form of increased volatility of rate of return and higher beta—even when the chance of default is nil. We demonstrated this in Figure 17-3.

[14] One of the authors once obtained a home mortgage at a rate one-half percentage point *less* than the contemporaneous yield on long-term AT&T bonds.

[15] Even here there are alternatives to borrowing on personal account. Investors can draw down their savings accounts or sell a portion of their invesment in bonds. The impact of reductions in lending on the investor's balance sheet and risk position is exactly the same as increases in borrowing.

Where to Look for Violations of MM's Propositions

MM's propositions depend on perfect capital markets. Here we are using the phrase *perfect capital markets* a bit loosely, for scholars have argued about the *degree* of perfection necessary for Proposition I. (We remember an off-the-cuff comment made many years ago by Ezra Solomon: "A perfect capital market should be *defined* as one in which the MM theory holds.")

We believe capital markets are generally well-functioning, but they are not 100% perfect 100% of the time. Therefore, MM must be wrong some times in some places. The financial manager's problem is to figure out when and where.

That is not easy. Just finding market imperfections is insufficient.

Consider the traditionalists' claim that imperfections make borrowing costly and inconvenient for many individuals. That creates a clientele for whom corporate borrowing is better than personal borrowing. That clientele would, in principle, be willing to pay a premium for the shares of a levered firm.

But maybe they don't *have* to pay a premium. Perhaps smart financial managers long ago recognized this clientele and shifted the capital structures of their firms to meet its needs. The shifts would not have been difficult or costly to make. But if the clientele is now satisfied it is no longer willing to pay a premium for levered shares. Only the financial managers who *first* recognized the clientele extracted any advantage from it.

Today's Unsatisfied Clienteles Are Probably Interested in Exotic Securities

So far we have made little progress in identifying cases where firm value might plausibly depend on financing. But our examples illustrate what smart financial managers look for. They look for an *unsatisfied* clientele, investors who want a particular kind of financial instrument but because of market imperfections can't get it or can't get it cheaply.

MM's Proposition I is violated when the firm, by imaginative design of its capital structure, can offer some *financial service* that meets the needs of such a clientele. Either the service must be new and unique, or the firm must find a way to provide some old service more cheaply than other firms or financial intermediaries can.

Now, is there an unsatisfied clientele for garden-variety debt or levered equity? We doubt it. But perhaps you can invent an exotic security and uncover a latent demand for it.

AT&T's Stillborn Savings Bonds

On October 9, 1970, a front-page article appeared in *The Wall Street Journal* with the headline "AT&T Mulls Offering Ma Bell Savings Bonds Similar to Treasury's." The reporter quoted "sources" at AT&T who described the terms of the possible issue. The bonds would be sold directly to investors in $100 denominations through 2,000 AT&T business offices. They would yield at least 6.5%. Investors would not receive cash interest payments. Instead, the value of the bonds would appreciate over time, in the same way that a savings deposit grows when you leave the interest to accumulate. Thus, at a 6.5% yield you might purchase a ten-year bond for $100 and ten years later cash it in for

$$\text{Future value} = \$100(1.065)^{10} = \$187.71$$

This was an almost exact copy of a United States savings bond, except that the interest rate was higher. At the time, United States savings bonds offered only 5%, or 5.5% if held for a full ten years.[16]

---

[16] In this respect, United States savings bonds differ from Canada Savings Bonds, for owners of CSBs can allow their interest to compound as in the United States or can receive regular coupon payments. Bonds that do not pay regular coupons are called **discount bonds**. Some

AT&T's motives were clear. It borrows billions of dollars yearly, and at that time its newly issued bonds were yielding about 8.6%. Borrowing at 6.5% would have been a big improvement.

And there was a natural market for AT&T savings bonds, an unsatisfied clientele of investors who found it difficult to take advantage of the high yields offered in the bond market. Even the most conservative investor could obtain a 7.3% yield in seven-year United States notes: corporate bonds yielded 8% and up.

Yet there were billions of dollars on deposit in bank savings accounts and savings and loan associations. The *maximum* rate offered on these accounts was 6% on deposits committed for a two-year period. Most of the deposits yielded only about 5%.

Why didn't depositors cash in and invest in bonds? Many of them did.[17] But many did not, partly from inertia and unfamiliarity with the bond market, and partly because buying bonds is inconvenient if you only have a few hundred or a few thousand dollars to invest. The minimum denomination for a corporate bond is $1,000. Ten thousand dollars is more common.

AT&T savings bonds would have offered such investors an easy, convenient way to earn 6.5% or more. At the same time it would have saved AT&T a lot of money. It was a great idea.

What created this opportunity? What explained the spread between bond rates and yields on savings accounts? The most important cause was restrictions imposed by the United States government on interest rates offered to small investors.[18] The government was trying to protect savings institutions by limiting competition for their depositors' money. The fear was that depositors would run off in search for higher yields, causing a cash drain that savings institutions would not be able to meet, cutting off the supply of funds from those institutions for new real estate mortgages, and knocking the housing market for a loop. The savings institutions could not compete by offering higher interest rates on deposits — even if the government had allowed them to — because most of their past deposits had been locked up in fixed-rate mortgages issued when interest rates were lower.

These regulations helped the savings institutions, and may have helped the housing market, but they were grossly unjust to small investors, who lost billions in interest income. We have never been able to understand why there was no political pressure to compensate small investors for the cost of these restrictions, or why consumer advocates never took up the small investor's cause.

Anyway, it was no surprise to find both savings institutions and the federal government arrayed against AT&T's plan. AT&T capitulated and its idea died a quiet death.

But if we believe the idea would have worked, then we have found a counterexample to MM's Proposition I. AT&T could have increased its overall market value by issuing savings bonds rather than garden-variety debt and equity.

---

investment dealers in the United States and Canada now buy government bonds, clip off the coupons, and repackage the parts as **strip bonds**, which are mini-bonds that make cash payments at their maturity only. These discount bonds are discussed in Section 23-2.

[17] This is called *disintermediation* (probably the longest word in this book). The investor who withdraws funds from a savings account and invests directly in securities is reducing the role of financial intermediation. The intermediary (the savings institution) is no longer used as a vehicle for investment.

[18] In the United States, this was called Regulation Q. Canada also had ceilings on the interest rates that banks could pay small depositors, but dropped them several years before the erosion of Regulation Q in the United States.

Imperfections and Opportunities

The most serious capital market imperfections often are those created and protected by government. But even these tend to erode. An imperfection which supports a violation of MM's proposition I *also* creates a money-making opportunity. Firms and financial intermediaries will find some way to reach the clientele of investors that the imperfection is frustrating. When they finally get low-cost access to that clientele, MM's proposition is restored.

Thus, in the 1970s "money market funds" were invented. They are mutual funds invested in Treasury bills, commercial paper, and other high-grade, short-term debt instruments. Any saver with a few thousand dollars to invest can gain access to these instruments through a money fund, yet the investor can withdraw funds anytime by writing a cheque against his or her money-fund balance.[19] These money market funds have become enormously popular. By 1990, their assets had increased to about $430 billion in the United States. (Money market funds are not needed in Canada, because banks and other savings institutions can offer money market rates of interest to their depositors.)

The money fund is one of many financial inventions which have extended the menu of opportunities open to investors. Another is the *floating-rate note*, first issued on a large scale, and with terms designed to appeal to individual investors, by Citicorp on July 30, 1974. Floating-rate notes are medium-term debt securities whose interest payments "float" with short-term interest rates. On the Citicorp issue, for example, the coupon rate used to calculate each semiannual interest payment was set at one percentage point above the contemporaneous yield on Treasury bills. The holder of the Citicorp note was therefore hedged against fluctuating interest rates, because Citicorp sent a larger semiannual cheque when interest rates rose (though, of course, a smaller cheque when rates fell).

Citicorp evidently found an untapped clientele of investors, for it was able to raise $650 million in the first offering, and within 5 months an additional $650 million of floating-rate notes was issued by other companies. By the mid-1980s about $43 billion of floating-rate securities was outstanding.[20]

What about the savings institutions? During the 1970s, more and more of their depositors' money left for money funds, floating-rate notes, and other high-yielding investments. The institutions were forced to compete, so they gradually edged up the rates paid to investors willing to salt money away for a few years. They provided extra services in place of higher interest rates. Many offered "free gifts"—toasters, radios, hair dryers—to new depositors. But as they competed, and as money funds and other high-yielding instruments became more easily available, the protection given by government restrictions on savings account rates became less and less helpful. Finally, the restrictions were lifted and savings institutions met their competition head on.[21]

In short, there are many more options open to the small investor now than there were in 1970. AT&T's savings bonds might work today, but there is no longer any special clientele who would buy them on terms attractive to AT&T. If *you* ever find an unsatisfied clientele, do something about it right away or capital markets will evolve and steal it from you.

---

[19] Money funds offer rates slightly lower than on the securities they invest in. This spread covers the funds' operating costs and profits.

[20] A good review of the development of the floating-rate market is Richard S. Wilson, "Domestic Floating-Rate and Adjustable-Rate Debt Securities," in F.J. Fabozzi and I.M. Pollack, eds., *Handbook of Fixed Income Securities,* 2nd ed., Dow Jones-Irwin, Homewood, Ill., 1987.

[21] By 1986, interest rates on regular savings accounts were still limited by government regulation, but banks and savings institutions were free to create other accounts at unrestricted rates. For example, most banks offered "money-market accounts," which closely resembled money-market funds. Thus, the remaining restrictions had little practical effect.

17-4   **SUMMARY**

At the start of this chapter we characterized the firm's financing decision as a marketing problem. Think of the financial manager as taking all of the firm's real assets and selling them to investors as a package of securities. Some financial managers choose the simplest package possible: all-equity financing. Some end up issuing dozens of debt and equity securities. The problem is to find the particular combination that maximizes the market value of the firm.

Modigliani and Miller's (MM's) famous Proposition I states that no combination is better than any other—that the firm's overall market value (the value of all its securities) is independent of capital structure. Firms that borrow do offer investors a more complex menu of securities, but investors yawn in response. The menu is redundant. Any shift in capital structure can be duplicated or "undone" by investors. Why should they pay extra for borrowing indirectly (by holding shares in a levered firm) when they can borrow just as easily and cheaply on their own accounts?

MM agree that borrowing increases the expected rate of return on shareholders' investment. But it also increases the risk of the firm's shares. MM show that the risk increase exactly offsets the increase in expected return, leaving stockholders no better or worse off.

Proposition I is an extremely general result. It applies not just to the debt-equity trade-off but to *any* choice of financing instruments. For example, MM would say that the choice between long-term and short-term debt has no effect on firm value.

The formal proofs of Proposition I all depend on the assumption of perfect capital markets.[22] MM's opponents, the "traditionalists," argue that market imperfections make personal borrowing excessively costly, risky, and inconvenient for some investors. This creates a natural clientele willing to pay a premium for shares of levered firms. The traditionalists say that firms should borrow to realize the premium.

But this argument is incomplete. There may be a clientele for levered equity, but that is not enough; the clientele has to be *unsatisfied*. There are already thousands of levered firms available for investment. Is there still an unsatiated clientele for garden-variety debt and equity? We doubt it.

Proposition I is violated when financial managers find an untapped demand and satisfy it by issuing something new and different. The argument between MM and the traditionalists finally boils down to whether this is difficult or easy. We lean toward MM's view: finding unsatisfied clienteles and designing exotic securities to meet their needs is a game that's fun to play but hard to win.

FURTHER READING

The pioneering work on the theory of capital structure is:

F. Modigliani and M.H. Miller, "The Cost of Capital, Corporation Finance and the Theory of Investment," *American Economic Review*, **48**: 261–297 (June 1958).

However, Durand deserves credit for setting out the issues that MM later solved:

D. Durand, "Cost of Debt and Equity Funds for Business: Trends and Problems in Measurement," in *Conference on Research in Business Finance*, National Bureau of Economic Research, New York, 1952, pp. 215–247.

---

[22] Proposition I can be proved umpteen different ways. The references at the end of this chapter include several more abstract and general proofs. Our formal proofs have been limited to MM's own arguments and (in Appendix 17-1) a proof based on the capital asset pricing model.

A somewhat difficult article that analyzes capital structure in the context of capital asset pricing theory is:

R.S. Hamada, "Portfolio Analysis, Market Equilibrium and Corporation Finance," *Journal of Finance*, **24**: 13–31 (March 1969).

More abstract and general theoretical treatments can be found in:

E.F. Fama, "The Effects of a Firm's Investment and Financing Decisions," *American Economic Review*, **68**: 272–284 (June 1978).
J.E. Stiglitz, "On the Irrelevance of Corporate Financial Policy," *American Economic Review*, **64**: 851–866 (December 1974).

APPENDIX 17-1   MM AND THE CAPITAL ASSET PRICING MODEL

We showed in Section 17-2 that, as the firm increases its leverage, the expected equity return goes up in lockstep with the beta of the equity. Given this, it should be no surprise to find that we can use the capital asset pricing model to derive MM's Proposition I. The following demonstration has been simplified by assuming that the firm can issue risk-free debt.

The firm is initially all-equity financed. Its expected end-of-period value is V_1, which we take to include any operating income for the initial period. We now draw on the certainty-equivalent form of the capital asset pricing model, which we derived in Appendix 9-1. This states that the present value of the firm is

$$V = E = \frac{V_1 - \lambda \text{Cov}(\tilde{V}_1, \tilde{r}_m)}{1 + r_f}$$

where λ is the market price of risk $(r_m - r_f)/(\sigma_m^2)$.

Now suppose that that the firm borrows D at the risk-free rate of interest and distributes the proceeds to stockholders. They get D dollars now but next year they will have to repay the debt with interest. Therefore instead of receiving V_1 at the end of the year, they can expect to receive only $V_1 - (1 + r_f)D$. The present value of their levered equity is, therefore,

$$E = \frac{V_1 - (1 + r_f)D - \lambda \text{Cov}[\tilde{V}_1 - (1 + r_f)D, \tilde{r}_m]}{1 + r_f}$$

But since $(1 + r_f)D$ is known, it has no effect on the covariance. When debt is risk-free, stockholders have to bear *all* the risk associated with $\tilde{V}_1$. Therefore, we substitute Cov $(\tilde{V}_1, \tilde{r}_m)$ for Cov $[\tilde{V}_1 - (1 + r_f)D, \tilde{r}_m]$. This gives us

$$E = \frac{V_1 - (1 + r_f)D - \lambda \text{Cov}(\tilde{V}_1, \tilde{r}_m)}{1 + r_f}$$

$$= \frac{V_1 - \lambda \text{Cov}(\tilde{V}_1, \tilde{r}_m)}{1 + r_f} - D$$

To calculate the value of the *firm* we add the value of the debt D. This gives

$$V = \frac{V_1 - \lambda \text{Cov}(\tilde{V}_1, \tilde{r}_m)}{1 + r_f}$$

The value of the levered firm is identical to the value of the unlevered firm.

QUIZ

1. Assume a perfectly competitive market with no corporate or personal taxes. Companies A and B each earn gross profits of P and differ only in their capital structure—A is wholly equity-financed and B has debt outstanding on which it pays a certain $100 of interest each year. Investor X purchases 10% of the equity of A.
   (a) What profits does X obtain?
   (b) What alternative strategy would provide the same result?
   (c) Suppose investor Y purchases 10% of the equity of B. What profits does Y obtain?
   (d) What alternative strategy would provide the same result?

2. Ms. Kraft owns 50,000 shares of the common stock of Copperhead Corporation with a market value of $2 per share, or $100,000 overall. The company is currently financed as follows:

	Book Value
Common stock (8 million shares)	$2,000,000
Short-term loans	$2,000,000

   Copperhead now announces that it is replacing $1 million of short-term debt with an issue of common stock. What action can Ms. Kraft take to ensure that she is entitled to exactly the same proportion of profits as before? (Ignore taxes.)

3. The common stock and debt of Northern Sludge are valued at $50 million and $30 million, respectively. Investors currently require a 16% return on the common stock and an 8% return on the debt. If Northern Sludge issues an additional $10 million of common stock and uses this money to retire debt, what happens to the expected return on the stock? Assume that the change in capital structure does not affect the risk of the debt and that there are no taxes. If the risk of the debt did change, would your answer underestimate or overestimate the expected return on the stock?

4. Company C is financed entirely by common stock and has a β of 1.0. The stock has a price-earnings multiple of ten and is priced to offer a 10% expected return. The company decides to repurchase half the common stock and substitute an equal value of debt. If the debt yields a risk-free 5%,
   (a) Give:
      (i) The beta of the common stock after the refinancing
      (ii) The beta of the debt
      (iii) The beta of the company (that is, stock and debt combined)
   (b) Give:
      (i) The required return on the common stock before the refinancing
      (ii) The required return on the common stock after the refinancing
      (iii) The required return on the debt
      (iv) The required return on the company (that is, stock and debt combined) after the refinancing
   (c) Assume that the operating profit of firm C is expected to remain constant. Give:
      (i) The percentage increase in earnings per share
      (ii) The new price-earnings multiple

5. Suppose that Macbeth Spot Removers issues $2,500 of debt and uses the proceeds to repurchase 250 shares.
   (a) Rework Table 17-2 to show how earnings per share and share return now vary with operating income.
   (b) If the beta of Macbeth's assets is 0.8 and its debt is risk-free, what would be the beta of the equity after the increased borrowing?
6. True or false? Explain briefly.
   (a) Shareholders always benefit from an increase in company value.
   (b) MM's Proposition I assumes that actions that maximize firm value also maximize shareholder wealth.
   (c) The reason that borrowing increases equity risk is because it increases the probability of bankruptcy.
   (d) If firms did not have limited liability, the risk of their assets would be increased.
   (e) If firms did not have limited liability, the risk of their equity would be increased.
   (f) Borrowing does not affect the return on equity if the return on the firm's assets is equal to the interest rate.
   (g) As long as the firm is certain that the return on assets will be higher than the interest rate, an issue of debt makes the shareholders better off.
   (h) MM's Proposition I implies that an issue of debt increases expected earnings per share and leads to an offsetting fall in the price-earnings ratio.
   (i) MM's Proposition II assumes increased borrowing does not affect the interest rate on the firm's debt.
   (j) Borrowing increases firm value if there is a clientele of investors with a reason to prefer debt.
7. Note the two blank graphs in Figure 17-6. On graph (a), assume MM are right, and plot the relationship between financial leverage and (i) the rates of return on debt and equity and (ii) the weighted average cost of capital. Then fill in graph (b) assuming the traditionalists are right.

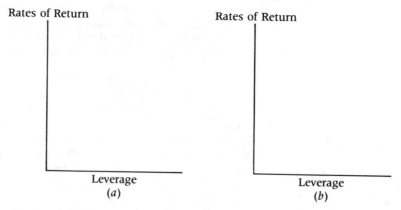

Figure 17-6   See quiz question 7.

QUESTIONS AND PROBLEMS

1. Companies A and B differ only in their capital structure. A is financed by 30% debt and 70% equity; B is financed by 10% debt and 90% equity. The debt of both companies is risk-free.
   (a) Mr. X owns 1% of the common stock of A. What other investment package would produce identical cash flows for Mr. X?
   (b) Mrs. Y owns 2% of the common stock of B. What other investment package would produce identical cash flows for Mrs. Y?
   (c) Show that neither Mr. X nor Mrs. Y would invest in the common stock of B, if the *total* value of company A were less than that of B.

2. Hubbard's Pet Foods is financed 80% by common stock and 20% by bonds. The expected return on the common stock is 12% and the rate of interest on the bonds is 6%. Assuming that the bonds are default-free, draw a graph that shows the expected return of Hubbard's common stock r_E and the expected return on the package of common stock and bonds r_A for different debt-equity ratios.

3. Here is a limerick:

   > There once was a man named Carruthers,
   > Who kept cows with miraculous udders.
   > He said, "Isn't this neat?
   > Th[...]ve cream from one teat,
   > A[...]om each of the others!"

   Wha[...] Carruthers's cows and firms' financing
   deci[...]itably adapted, say about the
   val[...]

4. "M[...]v more, you have to pay higher
   ra[...]this is a valid objection.

5. I[...]rguments:
   ([...]becomes risky, both stock- and
   [...]eturn. Thus, by *reducing* the debt
   [...]bt and the cost of equity, making

   [...]ficantly affect the probability of
   [...]onsequently moderate borrowing
   [...]return demanded by stockholders."
   [...]e or at least misleading. Explain why

6. [...]y offering a 10% DCF rate of return is
   [...]100% debt-financed at an 8% interest

   [...]the higher the interest rate it must pay.
   [...]hy firms should operate at conservative

7. [...]ebt that might be attractive to investors?
   Why do y[...][...]been issued?

8. It has been suggeste[...]isadvantage of common stock financing is that share prices tend to decline in recessions, thereby increasing the cost of

capital and deterring investment. Discuss this view. Is it an argument for greater use of debt financing?

9. People often convey the idea behind MM's proposition I by various supermarket analogies, for example, "The value of a pie should not depend on how it is sliced," or, "The cost of a whole chicken should equal the cost of assembling one by buying two drumsticks, two wings, two breasts, and so on."

Actually, Proposition I doesn't work in the supermarket. You'll pay less for an uncut whole pie than for a pie assembled from pieces purchased separately. Supermarkets charge more for chickens after they are cut up.

Why? What costs or imperfections cause Proposition I to fail in the supermarket? Are these costs or imperfections likely to be important for corporations issuing securities on the world capital market? Explain.

C · H · A · P · T · E · R

18

HOW MUCH SHOULD A FIRM BORROW?

In Chapter 17 we found that debt policy rarely matters in well-functioning capital markets. Few financial managers would accept that conclusion as a practical guideline. If debt policy doesn't matter, then they shouldn't worry about it — financing decisions should be delegated to underlings. Yet financial managers do worry about debt policy. This chapter explains why.

If debt policy were *completely* irrelevant, then actual debt ratios should vary randomly from firm to firm and industry to industry. Yet almost all airlines, utilities, and real estate development companies rely heavily on debt. And so do most firms in capital-intensive industries like steel, aluminum, chemicals, and mining. On the other hand, it is rare to find a drug company or advertising agency that is not predominantly equity-financed. Glamorous "growth" companies like Polaroid, Northern Telecom, Hewlett-Packard, and Apple Computer rarely use much debt despite rapid expansion and often heavy requirements for capital.

The explanation of these patterns lies partly in the things we left out of the last chapter. We ignored taxes. We assumed bankruptcy was cheap, quick, and painless. It isn't, and there are costs associated with financial distress even if legal bankruptcy is ultimately avoided. We ignored potential conflicts of interest between the firm's security holders. For example, we did not consider what happens to the firm's "old" creditors when new debt is issued or when a shift in investment strategy takes the firm into a riskier business. We ignored the possible *interactions* of investment and financing decisions.

Now we will put all these things back in: taxes first, then the costs of bankruptcy and financial distress. This will lead us to conflicts of interest and to possible interactions of financing and investment decisons. In the end we will have to admit that debt policy *does* matter.

However, we will *not* throw away the MM theory we developed so carefully in Chapter 17. We're shooting for a theory combining MM's insights *plus* the effects of taxes, costs of bankruptcy and financial distress, and various other complications. We're not dropping back to the traditional view based on imperfections in the capital market. Instead, we want to see how well-functioning capital markets *respond* to taxes and the other things covered in this chapter.

After finishing with theory, we will have a look at the evidence. We will point out the variables that seem to explain differences in financial leverage from company to company, and the instances in which increases in financial leverage seem to be good news to investors. Finally, we will attempt to draw the theory and evidence together in a checklist for financial managers to use when choosing their firms' debt-equity ratios.

18-1   CORPORATE TAXES

Debt financing has one important advantage under the corporate income tax system in Canada and the United States. The interest that the company pays is a tax-deductible expense. Dividends and retained earnings are not. Thus, the return to bondholders escapes taxation at the corporate level.

Table 18-1 shows simple income statements for firm U, which has no debt, and firm L, which has borrowed $1,000 at 8%. The tax bill of L is $28.80 less than that of U. This is the *tax shield* provided by the debt of L. In effect, the government pays 36% of the interest expense of L. The total income that L can pay out to its bondholders and stockholders increases by that amount.

Table 18-1
The tax-deductibility of interest increases the total income that can be paid out to bondholders and stockholders.

	Income Statement of Firm U	Income Statement of Firm L
Earnings before interest and taxes	$1,000	$1,000,00
Interest paid to bondholders	0	80.00
Pretax income	1,000	920.00
Tax at 36%	360	331.20
Net income to stockholders	$ 640	$ 588.80
Total income to both bondholders and stockholders	$0 + $640 = $640	$80 + $588.80 = $668.80
Interest tax shield (0.36 × interest)	$0	$28.80

Tax shields are valuable assets. Suppose that the debt of L is permanent. (That is, it plans to refinance its present debt obligations when they mature and to keep "rolling over" its debt obligations indefinitely.) It looks forward to a permanent stream of cash flows, $28.80 per year. The risk of these flows is likely to be less than the risk of the operating assets of L. The tax shields depend only on the corporate tax rate[1] and on the ability of L to earn enough to cover interest payments. Now, the corporate tax rate does not vary much over time. And the ability of L to earn its interest payments must be reasonably sure—otherwise it could not have borrowed at 8%.[2] Therefore, we should discount the interest tax shields at a relatively low rate.

---

[1] Always use the marginal corporate tax rate, not the average rate. For large corporations earning taxable income in Canada and the United States, the marginal tax rate is about 36%. Average rates are often much less than this because of the investment tax credit, the small business deduction, and various other adjustments.

[2] If the income of L does not cover interest in some future year, the tax shield is not necessarily lost. L will have a tax loss for the year, which can be used to reduce taxable income in other years. The loss carry-back and carry-forward rules are discussed in Appendix 6-1.

But what rate? The most common assumption is that the risk of the tax shields is the same as that of the interest payments generating them. Thus we discount at 8%, the expected rate of return demanded by investors who are holding the firm's debt:

$$\text{PV tax shield} = \frac{28.80}{0.08} = \$360$$

In effect the government itself assumes 36% of the $1,000 debt obligation of L.

Under these assumptions, the present value of the tax shield is independent of the return on the debt r_D. It equals the corporate tax rate T_c times the amount borrowed D:

$$\text{Interest payment} = \text{return on debt} \times \text{amount borrowed}$$

$$= r_D \times D$$

$$\text{PV tax shield} = \frac{\text{corporate tax rate} \times \text{expected interest payment}}{\text{expected return on debt}}$$

$$= \frac{T_c (r_D D)}{r_D} = T_c D$$

Of course PV tax shield is less if the firm does not plan to borrow permanently, or if it may not be able to use the tax shields in the future.

How Do Interest Tax Shields Contribute to the Value of Stockholders' Equity?

MM's proposition I amounts to saying that "the value of a pie does not depend on how it is sliced." The pie is the firm's assets, and the slices are the debt and equity claims. If we hold the pie constant, then a dollar more of debt means a dollar less of equity value.

But there is really a third slice, the government's. Look at Table 18-2: it shows an *expanded* balance sheet with *pretax* asset value on the left, and the value of the government's tax claim recognized as a liability on the right. MM would still say that the value of the pie—in this case *pretax* asset value—is not changed by slicing. But anything the firm can do to reduce the size of the government's slice obviously makes stockholders better off. One thing it can do is to borrow money, which reduces its tax bill and, as we saw in Table 18-1, increases the cash flows to debt and equity investors. The *after-tax* value of the firm (the sum of its debt and equity values as shown in a normal market value balance sheet) goes up by PV tax shield.

Recasting Canadian Marconi's Capital Structure

Canadian Marconi is a successful firm that uses very little long-term debt. Table 18-3(a) shows simplified book and market value balance sheets for Marconi as of the 1988 year-end, in March 1989.

Suppose that you had been Marconi's financial manager in 1989, with complete responsibility for its capital structure. You decide to borrow an additional 100 million dollars on a permanent basis and use the proceeds to repurchase shares.

Table 18-3(b) shows the new balance sheets. The book version simply has 100 million dollars more long-term debt and $100 million less equity. But we know that Marconi's assets must be worth more, for its tax bill has been reduced by 36% of the interest on the new debt. In other words, Marconi has a new asset, PV tax shield, which is worth $T_c D = 0.36 \times 100 = \$36$ million. If the MM theory

Table 18-2
Normal and expanded market value balance sheets. In a normal balance sheet assets
are valued after-tax. In the expanded balance sheet, assets are valued pretax and the
value of the government's tax claim is recognized on the right-hand side. Interest tax
shields are valuable because they reduce the government's claim.

Normal Balance Sheet (Market Values)

Asset value (present value of after-tax cash flows)	Debt
	Equity
Total assets	Total liabilities

Expanded Balance Sheet (Market Values)

Pretax asset value (present value of *pretax* cash flows)	Debt
	Government's claim (present value of future taxes)
	Equity
Total pretax assets	Total liabilities

Table 18-3(*a*)
Simplified balance sheets for Canadian Marconi, March 31, 1989 (figures in millions).

Book values

Net working capital	$151	$ 6	Long-term debt
Long-term assets	111	8	Deferred taxes
		248	Equity
Total assets	$262	$262	Total liabilities

Market values

Net working capital	$151	$ 6	Long-term debt
Market value of long-term assets	291	8	Deferred taxes
		428	Equity
Total assets	$442	$442	Market value of firm

Notes:
1. The $151 million of net working capital is computed as the reported short-term assets of
   $244 million, net of reported short-term liabilities of $93 million. Thus the total assets and the
   total liabilities shown above are actually $93 million less than those reported in Marconi's
   1988 balance sheet.
2. Market value is assumed to equal book value for net working capital, long-term debt, and
   deferred taxes. Equity is entered at actual market value: number of shares times closing price
   on March 31, 1989. The difference between the market and book values of long-term assets is
   equal to the difference between the market and book values of equity.
3. The market value of long-term assets includes the tax shield on the existing debt. This tax
   shield is assumed to be worth $0.36 \times 6 = \$2$ million.

Table 18-3(*b*)
Balance sheets for Marconi with an additional $100 million of long-term debt substituted for stockholder's equity (figures in millions).

Book values

Net working capital	$151	$106	Long-term debt
Long-term assets	111	8	Deferred taxes
		148	Equity
Total assets	$262	$262	Total liabilities

Market values

Net working capital	$151	$106	Long-term debt
Market value of long-term assets	291	8	Deferred taxes
		364	Equity
Present value of additional tax shields	36		
Total assets	$478	$478	Market value of firm

Notes:
1. The figures in Table 18-3(*b*) for net working capital, long-term assets and deferred taxes are identical to those in Figure 18-3(*a*).
2. Present value of tax shields assumed equal to corporate tax rate (36%) times amount of additional debt obligation.

holds *except* for taxes, firm value must increase by $36 million to $478 million. Marconi's equity ends up worth $364 million.

Now you have repurchased $100 million worth of shares but Marconi's equity value has dropped by only $64 million. Therefore Marconi's stockholders must be $36 million ahead. Not a bad day's work.[3]

MM and Taxes   We have just developed a version of MM's Proposition I as "corrected" by them to reflect corporate income taxes.[4] The new proposition is

Value of firm = value if all-equity-financed + PV tax shield

In the special case of permanent debt,

Value of firm = value if all-equity-financed + T_cD

Our imaginary financial surgery on Canadian Marconi provides the perfect illustration of the problems inherent in this "corrected" theory. That $36 million windfall came too easily; it seems to violate the law that "There is no such thing

---

[3] Notice that as long as the bonds are sold at a fair price, all the benefits from the tax shield go to the shareholders.

[4] MM's original article (F. Modigliani and M.H. Miller, "The Cost of Capital, Corporation Finance and the Theory of Investment," *American Economic Review*, **48**: 261–297 (June 1958)) recognized interest tax shields, but did not value them properly. They put things right in their 1963 article "Corporate Income Taxes and the Cost of Capital: A Correction," *American Economic Review*, **53**: 433–443 (June 1963).

as a money machine." And if Marconi's stockholders would be richer with 106 million dollars of corporate debt, why not $212 or $262 million?[5] Our formula implies that firm value and stockholders' wealth continue to go up as D increases. The implied optimal debt policy is embarrassingly extreme: all firms should be 100% debt-financed.

MM were not that fanatical about it. For one thing, no one would expect the formula to apply at extreme debt ratios. But that does not explain why firms like Marconi thrive with so little debt. Some American firms like Apple, Kodak, and Hewlett-Packard also have no debt. It is hard to believe that the managers of all these firms are simply missing the boat.

Moreover, there are no dramatic differences between corporate debt ratios now and ratios before World War II when the corporate income tax was negligible or nonexistent. How do we explain this if the tax advantages of corporate borrowing are so compelling?

Therefore we have argued ourselves into a corner. There are just two ways out:

1. Perhaps a fuller examination of the system of corporate *and personal* taxation will uncover a tax disadvantage of corporate borrowing, offsetting the present value of the corporate tax shield.
2. Perhaps firms that borrow incur other costs — bankruptcy costs, for example — offsetting the present value of the tax shield.

We will now explore these two escape routes.

18-2   CORPORATE AND PERSONAL TAXES

When personal taxes are introduced, the firm's objective is no longer to minimize the *corporate* tax bill; the firm should try to minimize the present value of *all* taxes paid on corporate income. "All taxes" includes *personal* taxes paid by bondholders and stockholders.

Figure 18-1 illustrates how corporate and personal taxes are affected by leverage. Depending on the firm's capital structure, a dollar of operating income will accrue to investors either as debt interest or equity income (dividends or capital gains). That is, the dollar can go down either branch of Figure 18-1.

Notice that Figure 18-1 distinguishes between T_p, the personal tax rate on interest, and T_{pE}, the effective personal rate on equity income. The quantity T_{pE} is a weighted average of the personal tax rate on dividends and the present value of the personal tax rate on capital gains. The weights depend on the proportions of equity income received as dividends and as capital gains. In general, we always have $T_{pE} \leq T_p$. For many individual investors who do not trade so frequently as to be regarded as security dealers, T_{pE} is much less than T_p.[6] For individual or

---

[5] The last figure would correspond to a 100% *book* debt ratio. But Marconi's *market* value would be $534 million according to our formula for firm value. Marconi's common shares would have an aggregate value of $264 million.

[6] Using the notation of Chapter 16 and its Appendix, we have, for individual investors:

$$T_p = T_{pfcd} \times (1 + T_{prov}) \qquad \text{(tax rate on interest)}$$
$$T_d = 1.25 \times (T_{pfcd} - 0.1333) \times (1 + T_{prov}) \quad \text{(tax rate on dividends)}$$
$$T_g = 0.75 \times T_{pfcd} \times (1 + T_{prov}) \times \text{PV factor} \quad \text{(tax rate on deferred capital gains)}$$

By manipulating these expressions and noting that the highest federal tax rate is $T_{pfcd} = 0.29$, one can see that $T_d < T_p$ and $T_g < T_p$. Of course, T_{pE} is a weighted average of T_d and T_g.

For corporate investors:

$$T_p = T_c$$
$$T_d = 0 \text{ if the investment is in a firm controlled by the corporate investor, and}$$

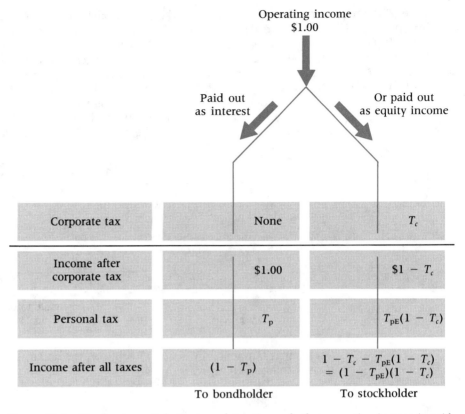

Figure 18-1 The firm's capital structure determines whether operating income is paid out as interest or equity income. Interest is taxed only at the personal level. Equity income is taxed at both the corporate and the personal levels. However, T_{pE}, the personal tax rate on equity income, is less than T_p because of the dividend tax credit and because equity income is received partly as capital gains.

corporate investors such as security dealers or brokers who trade frequently, capital gains are taxed at the full ordinary rate, but still $T_{pE} \leq T_p$ and $T_{pE} < T_p$ if the investor can defer some capital gains tax for more than a year or receive dividends that are taxed at a low rate.[7] For tax-exempt investors and institutions, $T_{pE} = T_p = 0$.

The firm's objective should be to arrange its capital structure so as to maximize after-tax income. You can see from Figure 18-1 that corporate borrowing is better if $(1 - T_p)$ is more than $(1 - T_{pE}) \times (1 - T_c)$; otherwise, it is worse. Corporate debt policy is irrelevant if

$$(1 - T_p) = (1 - T_{pE}) \times (1 - T_c).$$

We seem to have a simple, practical decision rule. Arrange the firm's capital structure to shunt operating income down that branch of Figure 18-1 where the tax is least. We will now try a couple of back-of-the envelope calculations to see what that rule could imply.

$T_g = 0.75 \times T_c \times$ PV factor
If the corporate investor does not control the firm in which it invests, $T_d = T_c$.

[7] To see when capital gains are included in ordinary income without a capital gains exemption, look at Section 2335 of *Canada Income Tax Guide Reports*, CCH Canadian Limited, Don Mills, 1990.

Debt Policy when Interest and Equity Income Are Taxed at the Same Personal Rate

Incorporated investment bankers and dealers trading on their own accounts pay tax on interest and capital gains at the same rate as on ordinary income, although they receive dividends tax-free. We will still use the term "personal taxation" to describe the taxation of such dealers because they are the investors that own the securities and are distinct from the corporation that issues the securities. These dealers are important because they often embark upon transactions to minimize taxes. Consider such a dealer, taxed at a rate of 36%, for whom all equity income is in the form of capital gains that are realized every year. For this dealer, $T_p = T_{pE} = T_g = 36\%$. The income after all taxes is as follows:

	Interest	Equity Income
Income before tax	$1.00	$1.00
Less corporate tax at $T_c = 36\%$	0.00	0.36
Income after corporate tax	1.00	0.64
Less personal tax at $T_p = T_{pE} = 36\%$	0.36	0.23
Income after all taxes	$0.64	$0.41

Advantage to debt
= $0.23

Debt comes out ahead by about 23 cents on the dollar, so there is still a strong tax advantage to borrowing.

Table 18-4
Personal income taxes reduce, but do not eliminate, the annual tax shield generated by corporate borrowing, assuming that equity and interest income are subject to the same personal income tax rate.

	Firm U	Firm L
Total income to both bondholders and stockholders (before personal tax; see Table 18-1)	0 + $640 = $640	$80 + 588.80 = $668.80
Tax shield generated by interest on corporate debt	$ 0.00	$ 28.80
Tax paid by bondholders (36% marginal rate)	$ 0.00	0.36×80 = $ 28.80
Tax paid by stockholders (36% marginal rate)	$0.36 \times \$640$ = $230.40	$0.36 \times \$588.80$ = $211.97
Total personal tax paid	$230.40	$240.77
Total after-tax income to both bondholders and stockholders	$640 − $230.40 = $409.60	$668.80 − $240.77 = $428.03
Tax shield remaining after personal taxes		$428.03 − $409.60 = $ 18.43

In fact, the value of this advantage is exactly as MM calculated it. The existence of personal taxes does not reduce the tax advantages of corporate borrowing *provided that* all kinds of personal income are taxed at the same rate.

Look back at the example in Table 18-1. Firm U is unlevered; firm L has borrowed $1,000 at 8%. The annual corporate tax shield produced by L's borrowing is $0.36 \times 80 = \$28.80$ a year. Therefore, the total income to investors is increased by that $28.80.

In Table 18-4 we have added *personal* taxes to Table 18-1 on the assumption that the income of both bondholders and stockholders is taxed at a rate of 36%. Notice that investors in firm L have to pay personal tax on their extra income of $28.80. Thus, their after-tax income is increased by $28.80 (1 − 0.36) = \$18.43$.

We assumed that the debt of L is permanent. What is the present value of $18.43 per annum in perpetuity? Since this cash flow is computed *after personal taxes*, we have to discount at an opportunity cost of capital *likewise computed after personal taxes*. The stockholders of L can obtain 8% before tax, but after tax only $8 \times (1 − 0.36) = 5.12\%$. Thus,

$$\text{PV tax shield (after personal tax)} = \frac{\$18.43}{0.0512} = \$360.$$

But this is the same answer we got before, when we ignored personal taxes entirely. The cash flow due to the corporate income tax shield is 36% less when personal taxes are recognized, but so is the opportunity cost of capital.[8]

In short, MM's "corrected" theory of debt and taxes does not have to assume away personal taxes. It only requires that debt and equity income be taxed at the same rate.

Debt Policy when Interest Is Taxed at a Higher Rate than Equity Income

Let's now go to the other extreme and suppose that an individual investor in the top tax bracket earns all equity income in the form of capital gains that are deferred virtually forever, so that $T_{pE} = 0$. Then we have:

	Interest	Equity Income
Income before tax	$1.00	$1.00
Less corporate tax at $T_c = 36\%$	0.00	0.36
Income after corporate tax	1.00	0.64
Personal tax $T_p = 43.5\%$ and $T_{pE} = 0\%$	0.435	0
Income after all taxes	$0.565	$0.64

Advantage to equity
= $0.075

---

[8] In general, if investors are willing to lend at a prospective return *before* personal taxes of r_D, then they must also be willing to accept a return *after* personal taxes of $r_D(1 − T_p)$, where T_p is the marginal rate of personal tax. Thus, we can compute the value after personal taxes of the tax shield on permanent debt:

$$\text{PV tax shield} = \frac{T_c \times (r_D D) \times (1 − T_p)}{r_D \times (1 − T_p)} = T_c D$$

This brings us back to our previous formula for firm value:

$$\text{Value of firm} = \text{value if all-equity-financed} + T_c D$$

Now *equity* has a small advantage: it's worth paying the 36% corporate tax to escape the 43.5% tax on interest.

These back-of-the-envelope calculations show some possible outcomes but they don't tell the financial manager what to do, for in real life it isn't clear which investors' tax rates should be used. What's T_{pE}, for example? The shareholder roster of a large corporation may include tax-exempt investors (such as pension funds or university endowments) as well as millionaires. All possible tax brackets will be mixed together. And it's the same with T_p, the personal tax rate on interest. The large corporation's "typical" bondholder might be a tax-exempt pension fund but many taxpaying investors also hold corporate debt. Our simple rule cannot cope with a variety of personal tax rates.

There are two ways of simplifying the analysis: recalling the concept of tax integration in Canada, and employing a model by Merton Miller. We will discuss these in turn.

Tax Integration and Capital Structure

The dividend tax credit system in Canada is intended to "integrate" the personal and corporate tax systems and reduce or eliminate the double taxation of equity income at the personal and corporate level. That is, if the system works perfectly, the "bottom line" income after all taxes should be the same for both branches of Figure 18-1. Let's see what actually happens. First, consider the case of a firm that pays tax at 20% and passes all equity income to shareholders in the form of dividends. In Appendix 16-1, we showed how the dividend tax credit system has the effect of making an owner indifferent between taking ordinary (interest or salary) income out of such a firm and dividend income out of the same firm. That is, if T_d is the personal tax rate on dividend income,

$$1 - T_p = (1 - T_d) \times (1 - 0.20)$$

If the shareholders receive dividend income rather than capital gains, $T_{pE} = T_d$, so that corporate debt policy would be irrelevant.

But the income of large firms faces a higher tax rate of $T_c = 36\%$, so the double taxation of dividend income for their owners is slightly more onerous than the taxation of interest income.[9] Thus, the Canadian tax system is not perfectly integrated and large firms would be *slightly* better off shunting their operating income down the debt branch of Figure 18-1, rather than the equity branch (if they always pay out equity income in the form of dividends).

What if some or all of the equity income is paid out in the form of capital gains? Unfortunately, Canadian legislators have made no attempt to integrate the tax system for equity income that is in the form of capital gains. If the equity income branch of Figure 18-1 is in the form of capital gains, low tax bracket investors would prefer that operating income be passed down the debt branch, and high tax bracket investors would prefer that it be passed down the equity branch.

Certainly the dividend tax credit system has blunted the bald preference for debt implied by the "corrected" MM theory, but there still may be a preference for debt or for equity in Canada, because equity investors receive a mixture of dividends and capital gains, and because all investors face a variety of personal tax rates. Moreover, there is nothing like the dividend tax credit system in the

---

[9] That is, for an individual Canadian investor, and $T_c = 0.36$,

$$1 - T_p = (1 - T_d) \times (1 - 0.20) > (1 - T_d) \times (1 - T_c)$$

United States, yet many American firms have *lower* debt to equity ratios than similar Canadian firms. We will examine another theory that may help resolve these issues.

Merton Miller's "Debt and Taxes"

To discuss these issues, we turn to "Debt and Taxes," Merton Miller's 1976 Presidential Address to the American Finance Association.[10] Miller's model is both insightful and controversial.

Consider a simple world in which all equity income comes as unrealized capital gains. In that case nobody pays any tax on equity income; T_{pE} is zero for all investors. But the rate of tax on bond interest depends on the investor's tax bracket. Tax-exempt institutions do not pay any tax on interest; for them T_p is zero. At the other extreme, millionaires pay tax at a rate of almost 50% on bond interest: for them T_p is 0.50. Most investors fall somewhere between these two extremes.

Suppose that companies are initially financed entirely by equity. If financial managers are on their toes, this cannot represent a stable situation. Think of it in terms of Figure 18-1. If every dollar goes down the equity branch, there are no taxes paid at the personal level (remember, $T_{pE} = 0$). Thus the financial manager need consider only corporate taxes, which we know create a strong incentive for corporate borrowing.

As companies begin to borrow, some investors have to be persuaded to hold corporate debt rather than common stock. There should be no problem in persuading tax-exempt investors to hold debt. They do not pay any personal taxes regardless of whether they hold bonds or stocks. Thus, the initial impact of borrowing is to save corporate taxes and to leave personal taxes unchanged.

But, as companies borrow more, they need to persuade taxpaying investors to migrate from stocks to bonds. Therefore they have to offer a bribe in the form of a higher interest rate on their bonds. Companies can afford to bribe investors to migrate as long as the corporate tax saving *is greater than* the personal tax loss. But there is no way that companies can bribe millionaires to hold their bonds. The corporate tax saving cannot compensate for the extra personal tax that those millionaires would need to pay. Thus, the migrations stop when the corporate tax saving *equals* the personal tax loss. This point occurs when T_p, the personal tax rate of the migrating investor, equals the corporate tax rate T_c.

Let us put some numbers on this. The corporate tax rate T_c is 36%. We continue to assume that T_{pE}, the effective rate of tax on equity income, is zero for all investors. In this case, companies will bribe investors with tax rates below 36% to hold bonds. But there is nothing to be gained (or lost) by persuading investors with tax rates *equal* to 36% to hold bonds. In the case of these investors $1 of operating income will produce income after all taxes of $0.64, regardless of whether the dollar is interest or equity income:

	Income Remaining after All Taxes
Income paid out as interest	$1 - T_p = 1 - 0.36 = \$0.64$
Income paid out as equity income	$(1 - T_{pE})(1 - T_c) = (1 - 0)(1 - 0.36) = \$0.64$

[10] M.H. Miller, "Debt and Taxes," *Journal of Finance*, **32**: 261–276 (May 1977). Some of the issues and ideas in Miller's paper were also discussed in D. Farrar and L.L. Selwyn, "Taxes, Corporate Financial Policy and the Returns to Investors," *National Tax Journal*, **20**: 144–154 (December 1967) and in some unpublished papers by Fischer Black.

In this equilibrium, taxes determine the aggregate amount of corporate debt but not the amount issued by any particular firm. The debt-equity ratio for corporations as a whole depends on the corporate tax rate and the funds available to individual investors in the various tax brackets. If the corporate tax rate is increased, migrations starts again, leading to a higher debt-equity ratio for companies as a whole. If personal tax rates are increased, the migrations reverses, leading to a lower debt-equity ratio. If *both* personal and corporate tax rates are increased by the same amount–10 percentage points, say—there is no migration and no change. That explains why there was no substantial increase in the debt-equity ratio when the corporate income tax rose drastically at the start of World War II. Personal tax rates were simultaneously increased by about the same amount.

The companies in our example that first sold bonds to tax-exempt investors may have gained an advantage. But once the "low" taxpayers have invested in bonds and the migrations have stopped, no single firm can gain an advantage by borrowing more or suffer any penalty by borrowing less. Therefore, there is no such thing as an optimal debt-equity ratio *for any single firm*. The market is interested only in the *total* amount of debt. No single firm can influence that.

One final point about Miller's tax equilibrium: because he assumes equity returns escape personal tax ($T_{pE} = 0$), investors are willing to accept lower rates of return on low-risk common stocks than on debt. Consider a safe (zero-beta) stock. The standard capital asset pricing model would give an expected return of $r = r_f$, the risk-free interest rate. But the investor migrating from equity to debt gives up r and earns $r_f(1 - T_p)$, the *after-tax* interest rate. In equilibrium, the migrating investor is content with either debt or equity, so $r = r_f(1 - T_p)$. Moreover, that investor's T_p equals the corporate rate T_c. Therefore, $r = r_f(1 - T_c)$. If we accept Miller's argument lock, stock, and barrel, the security market line should pass through the after-tax risk-free interest rate.

*Taxes, Debt Policy, and Dividend Policy

Under various choices of dividend and debt policies, the corporation can convert its operating cash flows into any of three types of flows:

1. Dividend equity flows,
2. Capital gain equity flows,
3. Interest flows on debt.

In Canada, the dividend tax credit makes the dividend and interest flows equivalent on a total tax basis if the corporate tax rate is 20%. But if large firms face a tax rate of 36%, interest flows should be preferred to equity flows. Their only important decision should be between capital gains and interest flows.

This is nice in theory, but it flies in the face of actual corporate and investor practice. For example, many large Canadian corporations have preferred shares that provide cash flows mainly in the form of dividends—and they are very popular with individual investors. Also, prior to 1985 many Canadian corporations allowed their shareholders the option of a taxable dividend or capital gains treatment on their dividend flows, and their shareholders often opted for the dividend flow.[11]

---

[11] For more on how the dividend and capital structure incentives have changed over time, see J.-M. Gagnon and J.-M. Suret, "Tax Rules and Corporate Financing: A Canadian Perspective," *Canadian Journal of Administrative Science*, **6**: 36 (March 1988).

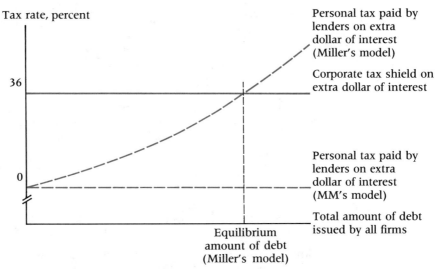

Figure 18-2   It pays companies to borrow as long as the corporate tax saving exceeds the extra personal tax paid by the marginal lender. MM and Miller disagree only about how the extra personal tax varies with total company borrowing.

Dividends are so popular that we must have doubts that the tax situation is as simple as we have stated to this point. Perhaps the *marginal* corporate tax rate is closer to 20% than to 36% for the firms that issue preferred shares. In the next section, we will see how the "risk" of tax losses in the future can drive down the effective marginal tax rate for highly levered corporations.

*A Compromise Theory   The majority of financial managers and economists believe our tax system favours corporate borrowing. Before Miller's paper, they had fallen into the habit of calculating the tax advantage of financial leverage as $T_c D$, the PV of the tax shields generated by a perpetual stream of corporate interest payments. When pressed, they admitted that this is a first approximation only, and they professed a willingness to consider personal taxes too, if only they had a sensible model showing them how to do it.

Enter Miller's model, which recognizes that investors have different personal tax rates, but which says financial managers ought to forget about taxes entirely in choosing between debt and equity. Yet the model is clearly oversimplified: if accepted, it upsets the majority's apple cart without picking up all the apples. How does the majority react? Cautiously. They stick to their old beliefs, but profess them with less vigour than before.

Figure 18-2 summarizes the dilemma. Both MM and Miller agree that there is a corporate tax shield on debt that is equal to 36% of the interest payments. The corporate tax shield is shown by the solid horizontal line in Figure 18-2. It pays companies to issue more debt as long as this corporate tax shield exceeds the personal tax cost to the marginal lender.

This tax cost depends on the difference between that lender's personal tax rate T_p and the effective rate T_{pE} the lender would pay on equity income.

The disagreement between MM and Miller centres on the additional personal taxes paid by debt versus equity investors. MM implicitly assume that personal taxes are the same on debt and equity. In this case the corporate tax shield *always* exceeds the extra taxes paid by the marginal lender, and companies should borrow to the hilt.

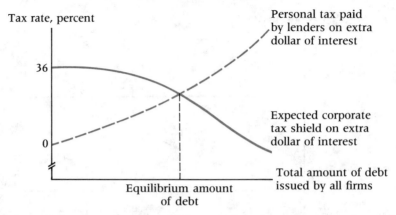

Figure 18-3   If companies cannot be sure of taxable profits in the future, the expected corporate tax saving will be less, and less debt will be issued.

Miller assumes that investors are subject to different tax rates. Therefore, as the total amount of corporate debt increases, investors with higher tax rates must be bribed to hold debt. In this case the tax rate of the marginal lender is shown by the broken *upward-sloping* line in Figure 18-2.[12] The equilibrium amount of debt in Miller's model is reached when the corporate tax benefit to the borrower equals the personal tax cost to the marginal lender. As long as all companies pay the same rate of tax, it is immaterial which firms supply this debt.

Figure 18-2 also provides a clue as to where we might look for a compromise theory. Consider the assumption that the corporate tax shield on debt is a constant 36% regardless of the amount borrowed. In practice few firms can be *sure* they will show a taxable profit in the future. If a firm shows a loss and cannot carry the loss back against past taxes, its interest tax shield must be carried forward with the hope of using it later. The firm loses the time value of money while it waits. If its difficulties are deep enough, the wait may be permanent and the interest tax shield lost forever.

Notice also that borrowing is not the only way to shield income against tax. Firms have accelerated write-offs for plant and equipment. Investment in many intangible assets can be expensed immediately. So can contributions to the firm's pension fund. The more that firms shield income in these other ways, the lower the expected tax shield from borrowing.[13]

If there is a chance that firms will make a loss, the *expected* corporate tax shield is less than 36%. The more a firm borrows, the higher the probability of loss and therefore the lower the expected tax shield.[14] In Figure 18-3 we have redrawn the corporate tax shield line to recognize this. The expected tax shield for the marginal borrower starts close to 36% but it declines as more debt is issued. We continue to represent the personal tax payments on debt interest by an upward-sloping line. The total amount of debt that will be issued is again given by the point at which the tax benefit to the marginal borrower equals the tax payment

---

[12] We have arbitrarily shown this as a smooth curve. In practice, there would be a series of steep sections and plateaus.

[13] For a discussion of the effect of these other tax shields on company borrowing see H. DeAngelo and R. Masulis, "Optimal Capital Structure Under Corporate and Personal Taxation," *Journal of Financial Economics*, **8**: 5–29 (March 1980).

[14] For some evidence on the average marginal tax rate of United States firms see J.J. Cordes and S.M. Sheffrin, "Taxation and the Sectoral Allocation of Capital in the U.S.," *National Tax Journal*, **34**: 419–432 (1981).

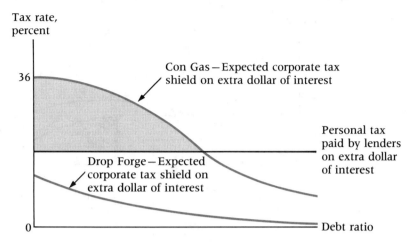

Figure 18-4 Drop Forge is unlikely to earn taxable profits and therefore should not borrow. Con Gas should borrow until the expected corporate tax saved on extra borrowing equals the personal tax paid by the lender. (Note: the personal tax paid by lenders is unaffected by the debt ratio of an individual company.)

by the marginal lender, but this equilibrium differs from Miller's model in three ways.

First, if companies cannot be sure they can take full advantage of the corporate tax shield, the total amount of debt issued will be less than in Miller's model. (The intersection in Figure 18-3 is further left than in Figure 18-2.)

Second, since companies cannot be sure of benefiting from the corporate tax shield, they will not be prepared to pay such a high rate of interest on the debt. (The intersection in Figure 18-3 is lower than in Figure 18-2.)

Third, since companies have different expected tax rates, the corporate tax shields are worth more to some firms than to others. For example, look at Figure 18-4. The lower line depicts the expected corporate tax saving from an additional dollar of interest payments for the Drop Forge and Basic Slag Company. Drop Forge has large accumulated tax loss carry-forwards and uncertain prospects. So there is little chance that it will be able to use any corporate tax shield. Since the expected tax saving is less than the expected personal tax payment by the marginal lender, borrowing has a negative net present value for Drop Forge. By contrast the upper line shows the expected corporate tax saving from an additional dollar of interest payment for Con Gas, a company whose income is relatively high and stable. Since the expected corporate tax saving exceeds the lender's expected personal tax payment, borrowing is a positive-NPV activity for Con Gas. But the more Con Gas borrows, the greater the chance that it will incur future losses. This places a limit on the amount of borrowing the company should undertake.

To maximize value, Con Gas should borrow until the expected tax saving on its last dollar of interest is equal to the expected personal tax payment by the lender. The shaded area in Figure 18-4 shows the total net benefit each year to Con Gas.

We don't pretend that this is the whole story. Our point is that there may be an intermediate position if you are not prepared to go out on a limb for either MM or Miller. Our own view is that there is a moderate tax advantage to corporate borrowing, at least for companies that are reasonably sure they can use the corporate tax shields. For companies that do not expect to be able to use the corporate tax shields we believe there is a moderate tax disadvantage.

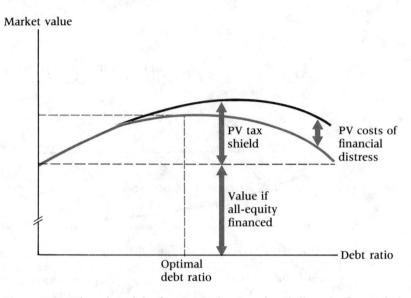

Figure 18-5 The value of the firm is equal to its value if all-equity financed plus PV tax shield minus PV costs of financial distress. The manager should choose the debt ratio that maximizes firm value.

18-3   COSTS OF FINANCIAL DISTRESS

Financial distress occurs when promises to creditors are broken, or honoured with difficulty. Sometimes financial distress leads to bankruptcy. Sometimes it means only that the firm skates on thin ice.

As we will see, financial distress is costly. Investors know that levered firms may fall into financial distress, and they worry about it. That worry is reflected in the current market value of the levered firm's securities. Thus, the value of the firm is:

$$\begin{matrix} \text{Value} \\ \text{of firm} \end{matrix} = \begin{matrix} \text{value if} \\ \text{all-equity-financed} \end{matrix} + \text{PV tax shield} - \begin{matrix} \text{PV costs of} \\ \text{financial distress} \end{matrix}$$

The costs of financial distress depend on the probability of distress and the magnitude of costs encountered if distress occurs.

Figure 18-5 shows how the trade-off between the tax benefits and the costs of distress determines optimal capital structure. PV tax shield initially increases as the firm borrows more. At moderate debt levels the probability of financial distress is trivial, and so PV cost of financial distress is small and tax advantages dominate. But, at some point, the probability of financial distress increases rapidly with additional borrowing; the costs of distress begin to take a substantial bite out of firm value. Also, if the firm can't be sure of profiting from the corporate tax shield, the tax advantage of debt is likely to dwindle and eventually disappear. The theoretical optimum is reached when the present value of tax savings due to additional borrowing is just offset by increases in the present value of costs of distress.

Costs of financial distress covers several specific items. Now we identify these costs and try to understand what causes them and why they cannot be avoided.

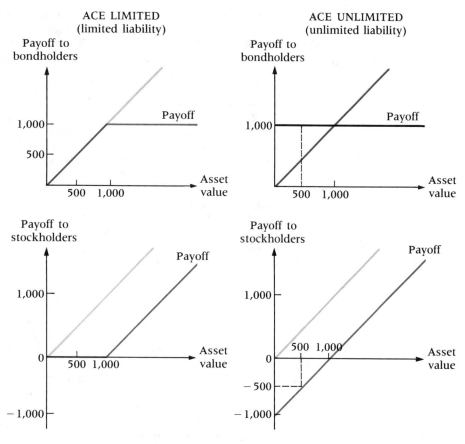

Figure 18-6 Comparison of limited and unlimited liability for two otherwise identical firms. If the two firms' asset values are less than $1,000, Ace Limited stockholders default and its bondholders take over the assets. Ace Unlimited stockholders keep the assets, but they must reach into their own pockets to pay off its bondholders. The total payoff to both stockholders and bondholders is the same for the two firms.

Bankruptcy Costs

You rarely hear anything nice said about corporate bankruptcy. But there is some good in almost everything. Corporate bankruptcies occur when stockholders exercise their *right to default*. That right is valuable; when a firm gets into trouble, limited liability allows stockholders simply to walk away from it, leaving all its troubles to its creditors. The former creditors become the new stockholders, and the old stockholders are left with nothing.

In our legal system all stockholders automatically enjoy limited liability. But suppose that this were not so. Suppose that there were two firms with identical assets and operations. Each firm has debt outstanding and each has promised to repay $1,000 (principal and interest) next year. But only one of the firms, Ace Limited, enjoys limited liability. The other firm, Ace Unlimited, does not; its stockholders are personally liable for its debt.

Figure 18-6 compares next year's possible payoffs to the creditors and stockholders of these two firms. The only differences occur when next year's asset value turns out to be less than $1,000. Suppose that next year the assets of each company are worth only $500. In this case Ace Limited defaults. Its stockholders walk away; their payoff is zero. Bondholders get the assets worth $500. But Ace Unlimited's stockholders can't walk away. They have to cough up $500, the difference between asset value and the bondholders' claim. The debt is paid whatever happens.

Suppose that Ace Limited does go bankrupt. Of course, its stockholders are disappointed that their firm is worth so little, but that is an operating problem having nothing to do with financing. Given poor operating performance, the right to go bankrupt—the right to default—is a valuable privilege. As Figure 18-6 shows, Ace Limited's stockholders are in better shape than Unlimited's are.

The example illuminates a mistake people often make in thinking about the costs of bankruptcy. Bankruptcies are thought of as corporate funerals. The mourners (creditors and especially shareholders) look at their firm's present sad state. They think of how valuable their securities used to be and how little is left. Moreover, they think of the lost value as a cost of bankruptcy. That is the mistake. The decline in the value of assets is what the mourning is really about. That has no necessary connection with financing. The bankruptcy is merely a legal mechanism for allowing creditors to take over when the decline in the value of assets triggers a default. Bankruptcy is not the *cause* of the decline in value. It is the result.

Be careful not to get cause and effect reversed. When a person dies, we do not cite the implementation of his or her will as the cause of death.

We said that bankruptcy is a legal mechanism allowing creditors to take over when a firm defaults. Bankruptcy costs are the costs of using this mechanism. There are no bankruptcy costs at all shown in Figure 18-6. Note that only Ace Limited can default and go bankrupt. But, regardless of what happens to asset value, the *combined* payoff to the bondholders and stockholders of Ace Limited is always the same as the *combined* payoff to the bondholders and stockholders of Ace Unlimited. Thus, the overall market values of the two firms now (this year) must be identical. Of course, Ace Limited's *stock* is worth more than Ace Unlimited's stock because of Ace Limited's right to default. Ace Limited's *debt* is worth correspondingly less.

Our example was not intended to be strictly realistic. Anything involving courts and lawyers cannot be free. Suppose that court and legal fees are $200 if Ace Limited defaults. The fees are paid out of the remaining value of Ace's assets. Thus if asset value turns out to be $500, creditors end up with only $300. Figure 18-7 shows next year's *total* payoff to bondholders and stockholders net of this bankruptcy cost. Ace Limited, by issuing risky debt, has given lawyers and the court system a claim on the firm if it default. The present market value of the firm is reduced by the present value of this claim.

It is easy to see how increased leverage affects the present value of the costs of financial distress. If Ace borrows more, it must promise more to bondholders. This increases the probability of default and the value of the lawyer's claim. It increases PV costs of financial distress and reduces Ace's present market value.

The costs of bankruptcy come out of stockholders' pockets. Creditors foresee the costs and foresee that *they* will pay them if default occurs. For this they demand compensation in advance in the form of higher payoffs when the firm does *not* default. That is, they demand a higher promised interest rate. This reduces the possible payoffs to stockholders and reduces the present market value of their shares.

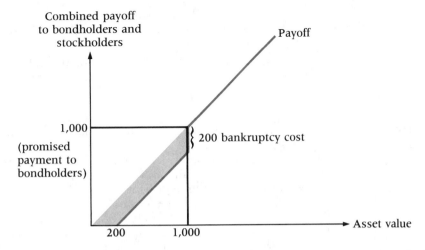

Figure 18-7   Total payoff to Ace Limited security holders. There is a $200 bankruptcy cost in the event of default (shaded area).

Evidence on Bankruptcy Costs

Bankruptcy costs can add up fast. *Aviation Week and Space Technology* reported in 1984 that legal and professional fees of the Braniff International Corporation bankruptcy were $12 million; legal fees in the Continental Airlines bankruptcy were running $2 million per month.[15] Daunting as these numbers may seem, they are not a large fraction of these airlines' *asset* values. For example, in 1984 it cost about $95 million to buy *one* airplane, a Boeing 747.

J.B. Warner has reported legal and administrative costs of 11 railroad bankruptcies.[16] The average cost was about $2 million spread over many years. (On average, it took 13 years before the railroads were reorganized and released from the bankruptcy courts. For one railroad it took 23 years.)

Two million dollars is not small change. But, on average, the costs were only 5.3% of the overall market value of the railroads' debt and equity securities, estimated just before bankruptcy. The costs declined to 1.4% of overall market value estimated five years prior to bankruptcy, when the railroads were in better health. That is a small number. Suppose that you are the financial manager of a railroad facing a 20% chance of bankruptcy in five years.[17] Using Warner's results, you guesstimate the present value of bankruptcy costs as follows:

$$\begin{array}{l}\text{Expected}\\ \text{cost}\end{array} = \begin{array}{l}\text{probability}\\ \text{of bankruptcy}\end{array} \times \begin{array}{l}\text{cost of bankruptcy as proportion}\\ \text{of firm's current market value}\end{array}$$
$$= 0.2 \times 0.014 \text{ (value of firm)} = 0.0028 \text{ (value of firm)}$$

Discount back 5 years at, say, 8%:

---

[15] *Aviation Week and Space Technology*, April 23, 1984, p. 35.

[16] J.B. Warner, "Bankruptcy Costs: Some Evidence," *Journal of Finance,* **26**: 337–348 (May 1977).

[17] Investors weren't able to predict the railroad bankruptcies five years before they happened. We are assuming that railroads like the ones that Warner examined had a 20% chance of going bankrupt in five years. That is one guess, but any other guess will do for present purposes.

$$\text{PV costs of bankruptcy} = \frac{0.0028}{(1.08)^5}(\text{value of firm}) = 0.0019 \ (\text{value of firm})$$

Trivial. Of course, Warner's data apply only to railroads. Legal and administrative costs could be a larger proportion of firm value for, say, a sample of manufacturing firms.[18]

<table><tr><td>**Direct versus Indirect Costs of Bankruptcy**</td><td>So far we have discussed the *direct* (that is, legal and administrative) costs of bankruptcy. There are indirect costs too, which are nearly impossible to measure. But we have circumstantial evidence indicating their importance.</td></tr></table>

The indirect costs reflect the difficulties of running a railroad—or any company—while it is going through bankruptcy. Management's effort to prevent further deterioration in the firm's business are often undermined by the delays and legal tangles that go with bankruptcy as a legal process.

The Penn Central Railroad went under in June 1970. Four years later, with bankruptcy proceedings nowhere near completion, *Business Week* published an article called "Why the Penn Central Is Falling Apart." Here are some excerpts.

As its creditors hound it—some of them want to shut it down to get back their money—the railroad must continue operations at a time when it can barely keep running without pouring in huge sums to rebuild its facilities. Those sums, however, will not be available until the railroad shows that it can be reorganized.

Penn Central could have raised money by selling off some of its assets, but its creditors naturally oppose this:

. . . Scores of other problems arise from a lack of money. Agonizingly for everyone on the Penn Council, there is a tremendous source of capital that cannot be touched. For example, just about every abandoned mine branch in the Allegheny Mountains is chock full of old Penn and Central cars destined for scrap. With today's scrap prices, they are a potential gold mine. But the creditors will not allow this asset to be turned into cash that will be reinvested in the estate since that estate is eroding day by day.

The creditors' interest also got in the way of sensible maintenance:

And the creditors' problems do not stop there. Between Indianapolis and Terre Haute, the former Pennsylvania and New York Central RRs had double-track, high-speed main lines rarely more than three miles apart. After the merger, most traffic was routed over the old New York Central route and the Pennsy line's second track was picked up. There are still 11 mi. of double track on the old Pennsy, though, and the 132-lb. rail is in excellent shape. It is desperately needed on the old New York Central line where double traffic and deferred maintenance have left much of that stretch with 10 mph speed limits.

The obvious thing is to use the good rail on the Penn Central line. Unfortunately,

. . . the rail belongs to a Pennsy subsidiary, itself in reorganization, and the creditors will not permit the asset to be moved to a subsidiary of the New York Central except for "cash on the barrel," which, of course, is unavailable.[19]

We do not know what the sum of direct and indirect costs of bankruptcy amounts to. We suspect it is a significant number, particularly for large firms for which

[18] Bankruptcy costs are likely to be larger for *small* firms; there are economies of scale in going bankrupt, as in many other economic endeavours.

[19] Reprinted from the October 12, 1974, issue of *Business Week* by special permission, © 1974 by McGraw-Hill, Inc., New York, NY 10020. All rights reserved.

proceedings would be lengthy and complex. Perhaps the best evidence is the reluctance of creditors to force bankruptcy. In principle, they would be better off to end the agony and seize the assets as soon as possible. Instead, creditors often overlook defaults in the hope of nursing the firm over a difficult period. They do this in part to avoid costs of bankruptcy.[20] There is an old financial saying, "Borrow $1,000 and you've got a banker. Borrow $10,000,000 and you've got a partner."

Here is one final piece of evidence on the direct plus indirect costs of bankruptcy. On April 10, 1987, Texaco filed for bankruptcy, surprising most investors and financial analysts. Texaco's biggest creditor was Pennzoil, to whom it owed $10.5 billion in damages stemming from Texaco's 1984 takeover of Getty Oil.[21] Texaco had been negotiating with Pennzoil, trying to cut a deal in which Pennzoil would give up its claim—which Texaco was contesting—in exchange for an immediate cash settlement. When these negotiations broke down, Texaco turned to the bankruptcy court.

Table 18-5 reports that Texaco stock fell from $31.875 to $28.50 after the announcement, a fall of $817 million in Texaco's equity value. At the same time Pennzoil's equity value fell by $628 million. We do not know how Texaco's other creditors fared, but the value of their claims cannot have increased. Therefore, bankruptcy reduced the market value of (the claims on) Texaco's assets by at least $817 plus 628 or $1,445 million, roughly $1.5 billion. We can take this loss as the stock market's estimate of the present value of the direct and indirect costs of the Texaco bankruptcy.

But how could bankruptcy cost $1.5 *billion*? Texaco's business operations were healthy and profitable, and thus unlikely to encounter the sort of problems that plagued Penn Central. We are at a loss to explain how a stock market could rationally forecast bankruptcy costs as large as those implied by Table 18-5.[22]

Table 18-5
Texaco's stock price dropped by $3.375 when its bankruptcy filing was announced. Pennzoil was Texaco's largest creditor; its stock price dropped too, by $15.125. The combined market value of the two firms' stock fell $1,445 million.

	Share Price			Number of Shares (Millions)	Change in Value (Millions)
	Friday April 10, 1987	Monday April 13, 1987	Change		
Texaco	$31.875	$28.50	−$ 3.375	242	−$ 817
Pennzoil	92.125	77.00	− 15.125	41.5	− 628
Total					−$1,445

[20] There is another reason. Creditors are not always given absolute priority in bankruptcy. Absolute priority means that creditors must be paid in full before stockholders receive a cent. Sometimes reorganizations are negotiated which provide "something for everyone," even though creditors are *not* paid in full. Thus, creditors can never be sure how they will fare in bankruptcy.

[21] Pennzoil thought it had struck a deal to buy Getty when Texaco arrived with a higher bid. Texaco finally won, but Pennzoil sued, arguing that Texaco had broken up a valid contract between Pennzoil and Getty. The court agreed and ordered Texaco to pay over $11.1 billion. This amount was reduced on appeal, but *with interest* the damages still amounted to $10.5 billion by April 1987.

[22] The Texaco bankruptcy is discussed by L. Summers and D.M. Cutler, "The Costs of Conflict and Financial Distress: Evidence from the Texaco-Pennoil Litigation," *RAND Journal of Economics,* **19**: 157–172 (Summer 1988).

**Financial
Distress
without
Bankruptcy**

Not every firm which gets into trouble goes bankrupt. As long as the firm can scrape up enough cash to pay the interest on its debt, it may be able to postpone bankruptcy for many years. Eventually the firm may recover, pay off its debt, and escape bankruptcy altogether.

When a firm is in trouble, both bondholders and stockholders want it to recover, but in other respects their interests may be in conflict. In times of financial distress the security holders are like many political parties—united on generalities but threatened by squabbling on any specific issue.

Financial distress is costly when these conflicts of interest get in the way of proper operating, investment, and financing decisions. Stockholders are tempted to forsake the usual objective of maximizing the overall market value of the firm and to pursue narrower self-interest instead. They are tempted to play games at the expense of their creditors. We will now illustrate how such games can lead to costs of financial distress.

Here is the Circular File Company's present book balance sheet:

Circular File Company (book values)

Net working capital	$ 20	$ 50	Bonds outstanding
Fixed assets	80	50	Common stock
Total assets	$100	$100	Total liabilities

We will assume there is only one share and one bond outstanding. The stockholder is also the manager. The bondholder is somebody else.

Here is its balance sheet in market values—a clear case of financial distress, since the face value of Circular's debt ($50) exceeds the firm's market value ($30):

Circular File Company (market values)

Net working capital	$20	$25	Bonds outstanding
Fixed assets	10	5	Common stock
Total assets	$30	$30	Total liabilities

If the debt matured today, Circular's owner would default, leaving the firm bankrupt. But suppose that the bond actually matures one year hence, that there is enough cash for Circular to limp along for one year, and that the bondholder cannot "call the question" and force bankruptcy before then.

The one-year grace period explains why the Circular share still has value. Its owner is betting on a stroke of luck that will rescue the firm, allowing it to pay off the debt with something left over. The bet is a long shot—the owner wins only if firm value increases from $30 to more than $50.[23] But the owner has a secret weapon: He controls investment and operating strategy.

**Risk Shifting:
The First Game**

Suppose that Circular has $10 cash. The following investment opportunity comes up:

---

[23] We are not concerned here with how to work out whether $5 is a fair price for stockholders to pay for the debt. We will come to that in Chapter 20 when we discuss the valuation of options.

Now	Possible Payoffs Next Year
	$120 (10% probability)
Invest $10	
	$0 (90% probability)

This is a wild gamble and probably a lousy project. But you can see why the owner would be tempted to take it anyway. Why not go for broke? Circular will probably go under anyway, and so the owner is essentially betting with the bondholder's money. But the owner gets most of the loot if the project pays off.

Suppose that the project's NPV is −$2 but that it is undertaken anyway, thus depressing firm value by $2. Circular's new balance sheet might look like this:

Circular File Company (market values)

Net working capital	$10	$20	Bonds outstanding
Fixed assets	18	8	Common stock
Total assets	$28	$28	Total liabilities

Firm value falls by $2, but the owner is $3 ahead because the bond's value has fallen by $5. The $10 cash that used to stand behind the bond has been replaced by a very risky asset worth only $8.

Thus, a game has been played at the expense of Circular's bondholder. The game illustrates the following general point. Stockholders of levered firms gain when business risk increases. Financial managers who act strictly in their share-holders' interests (and *against* the interests of creditors) will favour risky projects over safe ones. They may even take risky projects with negative NPVs.

This warped strategy for capital budgeting clearly is costly to the firm and to the economy as a whole. Why do we associate the costs with financial distress? Because the temptation to play is strongest when the odds of default are high. Exxon would never invest in our negative-NPV gamble. Its creditors are not vulnerable to this type of game.

Refusing to Contribute Equity Capital: The Second Game

We have seen how stockholders, acting in their immediate, narrow self-interest, may take projects which reduce the overall market value of their firm. These are errors of commission. Conflicts of interest may also lead to errors of omission.

Assume that Circular cannot scrape up any cash, and therefore cannot take that wild gamble. Instead, a *good* opportunity comes up: a relatively safe asset costing $10 with a present value of $15 and NPV = +$5.

This project will not in itself rescue Circular, but it is a step in the right direction. We might therefore expect Circular to issue $10 of new stock and to go ahead with the investment. Suppose that two new shares are issued to the original owner for $10 cash. The project is taken. The new balance sheet might look like this:

Circular File Company (market values)

Net working capital	$20	$33	Bonds outstanding
Fixed assets	25	12	Common stock
Total assets	$45	$45	Total liabilities

The total value of the firm goes up by \$15 (\$10 of new capital and \$5 NPV). Notice that the Circular bond is no longer worth \$25, but \$33. The bondholder receives a capital gain of \$8 because the firm's assets include a new, safe asset worth \$15. The probability of default is less and the payoff to the bondholder if default occurs is larger.

The stockholder loses what the bondholder gains. Equity value goes up not by \$15, but by \$15 − \$8 = \$7. The owner puts in \$10 of fresh equity capital but gains only \$7 in market value. Going ahead is in the firm's interest, but not the owner's.

Again, our example illustrates a general point. If we hold business risk constant, any increase in firm value is shared among bondholders and stockholders. The value of any investment opportunity *to the firm's stockholders* is reduced because project benefits must be shared with bondholders. Thus, it may not be in the stockholders' self-interest to contribute fresh equity capital even if that means forgoing positive-NPV investment opportunities.

This problem theoretically affects all levered firms, but it is most serious when firms land in financial distress. The greater the probability of default, the more bondholders have to gain from investments that increase firm value.

And Three More Games, Briefly

As with other games, the temptation to play is particularly strong in financial distress.

1. *Cash in and Run*: Stockholders may be reluctant to put money into a firm in financial distress, but they are happy to take the money out—in the form of a cash dividend, for example. The market value of the firm's stock goes down by less than the amount of the dividend paid, because the decline in *firm* value is shared with creditors. This game is just "refusing to contribute equity capital" run in reverse.

2. *Playing for Time*: When the firm is in financial distress, creditors would like to salvage what they can by forcing the firm to settle up. Naturally, stockholders want to delay this as long as they can. There are various devious ways of doing this, for example, through accounting changes designed to conceal the true extent of trouble, by encouraging false hopes of spontaneous recovery, or by cutting corners on maintenance, research and development, etc., in order to make this year's operating performance look better.

3. *Bait and Switch*: This game is not always played in financial distress, but it is a quick way to get *into* distress. You start with a conservative policy, issuing a limited amount of relatively safe debt. Then you suddenly switch and issue a lot more. That makes all your debt risky, imposing a capital loss on the "old" bondholders. Their capital loss is the stockholders' gain.

What the Games Cost

Why should anyone object to these games as long as they are played by consenting adults? Because playing them means poor decisions about investment and operations.

The more the firm borrows, the greater the temptation to play the games (assuming the financial manager acts in the stockholders' interest). The increased odds of poor decisions in the future prompt investors to mark down the present market value of the firm. The fall in value comes out of stockholders' pockets. Potential lenders, realizing that games may be played at their expense, protect themselves by demanding better terms.

Therefore, it is ultimately in the stockholders' interest to avoid temptation. The easiest way to do this is to limit borrowing to levels at which the firm's debt is safe or close to it.

But suppose that the tax advantages of debt spur the firm on to a high debt ratio and a significant probability of default or financial distress. Is there any way to convince potential lenders that games will not be played? The obvious answer is to give lenders veto power over potentially dangerous decisions.

There we have the ultimate economic rationale for all that fine print backing up corporate debt. Debt contracts almost always limit dividends or equivalent transfers of wealth to stockholders; the firm may not be allowed to pay out more than it earns, for example. Additional borrowing is almost always limited. For example, many companies are prevented by existing bond indentures from issuing any additional long-term debt unless their ratio of earnings to interest charges exceeds 2.0.

Sometimes firms are restricted from selling assets or making major investment outlays except with the lenders' consent. The risks of "playing for time" are reduced by specifying accounting procedures and by giving lenders access to the firm's books and its financial forecasts.

Of course, fine print cannot be a complete solution for firms that insist on issuing risky debt. The fine print has its own costs; you have to spend money to save money. Obviously, a complex debt contract costs more to negotiate than a simple one. Afterward, it costs the lender more to monitor the firm's performance. Lenders anticipate monitoring costs and demand compensation in the form of higher interest rates; thus, the monitoring costs are ultimately paid by stockholders.

Perhaps the most severe costs of the fine print stem from the constraints it places on operating and investment decisions. For example, an attempt to prevent the "risk shifting" game may also prevent the firm from pursuing *good* investment opportunities. At the minimum there are delays in clearing major investments with lenders. In some cases lenders may veto high-risk investments even if net present value is positive. Lenders can lose from risk shifting even when the firm's overall market value increases. In fact, the lenders may try to play a game of their own, forcing the firm to stay in cash or low-risk assets even if good projects are forgone.

Thus, debt contracts cannot cover every possible manifestation of the games we have just discussed. Any attempt to do so would be hopelessly expensive and doomed to failure in any event. Human imagination is insufficient to conceive of all the possible things that could go wrong. We will always find surprises coming at us on dimensions we never thought to think about.

We hope we have not left the impression that managers and stockholders always succumb to temptation unless restrained. Usually they refrain voluntarily, not only from a sense of fair play, but also on pragmatic grounds: A firm or individual that makes a killing today at the expense of a creditor will be coldly received when the time comes to borrow again. Aggressive game playing is done only by out-and-out crooks and by firms in extreme financial distress. Firms limit borrowing precisely because they don't wish to land in distress and be exposed to the temptation to play.

Costs of Distress Vary with Type of Asset   Suppose your firm's only asset is a large downtown hotel, mortgaged to the hilt. The recession hits, occupancy rates fall, and the mortgage payments cannot be met. The lender takes over and sells the hotel to a new owner and operator. You use your firm's stock certificates for wallpaper.

What is the cost of bankruptcy? In this example, probably very little. The value of the hotel is, of course, much less than you hoped, but that is due to the lack of guests, not to the bankruptcy. The direct bankruptcy costs of Heartbreak Hotel are restricted to items such as legal and court fees, real estate commissions, and the time the lender spends sorting things out.

Suppose we repeat the story of Heartbreak Hotel for Fledgling Electronics. Everything is the same, except for the underlying real assets—not real estate but a high-tech going concern, a growth company whose most valuable assets are technology, investment opportunities, and its employees' human capital.

If Fledgling gets into trouble, the stockholders may be reluctant to put up money to cash in on its growth opportunities. Failure to invest is likely to be much more serious for Fledgling than for a company like Heartbreak Hotel.

If Fledgling finally defaults on its debt, the lender would find it much more difficult to cash in by selling off the assets. Many of them are intangibles which have value only as a part of a going concern.

Could Fledgling be kept as a going concern through default and reorganization? It may not be as hopeless as putting a wedding cake through a car wash, but there are a number of serious difficulties: (1) the odds of defections by key employees are higher than if the firm had never gotten into financial trouble; (2) special guarantees may have to be given to customers who are doubtful whether the firm will be around to service its products; (3) aggressive investment in new products and technology will be difficult; and (4) each class of creditors will have to be convinced that it is in their interest for the firm to invest new money in risky ventures.

Our examples of the hotel and electronics firm illustrate that the values of some assets can pass through bankruptcy and reorganization largely unscathed; the values of other assets are likely to be considerably diminished. The losses are greatest for the intangible assets that are linked to the health of the firm as a going concern—for example, technology, human capital, and brand image. That may be why debt ratios are low in the pharmaceutical industry, where value depends on continued success in research and development, and in many service industries where value depends on human capital. We can also understand why highly profitable growth companies, such as Hewlett-Packard or Apple Computer, use mostly equity finance.[24]

The moral of these examples is: *Do not think only about the probability that borrowing will bring trouble. Think also of the value that may be lost if trouble comes.*

18-4   EXPLAINING FINANCING CHOICES

Financial managers often think of the firm's debt-equity decision as a trade-off between interest tax shields and the costs of financial distress. Of course, there is controversy about how valuable interest tax shields are and what kinds of financial trouble are most threatening, but these disagreements are only variations on a theme. Thus, Figure 18-5 illustrates the debt-equity trade-off.

This *trade-off theory* of capital structure recognizes that target debt ratios may vary from firm to firm. Companies with safe, tangible assets and plenty of taxable

---

[24] Recent empirical research confirms that firms holding largely intangible assets, such as growth opportunities, borrow less. See M. Long and I. Malitz, "The Investment-Financing Nexus: Some Empirical Evidence," *Midland Corporate Finance Journal,* **3**: 53–59 (Fall 1985); and S. Williamson, "The Moral Hazard Theory of Corporate Capital Structure: Empirical Tests," unpublished Ph.D. dissertation, MIT, November 1981.

income to shield ought to have high target ratios. Unprofitable companies with risky, intangible assets ought to rely primarily on equity financing.

If there were no costs of adjusting capital structure, then each firm should always be at its target debt ratio. However, there are costs, and therefore delays, in adjusting to the optimum. Firms cannot immediately offset the random events that bump them away from their capital structure targets, so we should see random differences in actual debt ratios among firms having the same target debt ratio.

All in all, this trade-off theory of capital structure choice tells a comforting story. Unlike the "corrected" MM theory, which seemed to say that firms should take on as much debt as possible, it avoids extreme predictions and rationalizes moderate debt ratios.

But what are the facts? Can the trade-off theory of capital structure explain how companies actually behave?

The answer is "yes and no." On the "yes" side, the trade-off theory successfully explains many industry differences in capital structure. High-tech growth companies, for example, whose assets are risky and mostly intangible, normally use relatively little debt. Airlines can and do borrow heavily because their assets are tangible and relatively safe.[25]

The trade-off theory also helps explain what kinds of companies "go private" in **leveraged buyouts (LBOs)**. LBOs are acquisitions of public companies by private investors who finance a large fraction of the purchase price with debt. The target companies for LBO takeovers are usually mature "cash cow" businesses with established markets for their products, but little in the way of high-NPV growth opportunities. That makes sense by the trade-off theory, because these are exactly the kind of companies that *ought* to have high debt ratios.

The trade-off theory also says that companies saddled with extra heavy debt—too much to pay down with a couple of years' internally generated cash—should issue stock, constrain dividends, or sell off assets to raise cash to rebalance capital structure. Here again, we can find plenty of confirming examples. When Texaco bought Getty Petroleum in January 1984, it borrowed $8 billion from a consortium of banks to help finance the acquisition. (The loan was arranged and paid over to Texaco within 2 weeks!) By the end of 1984, it had raised about $1.8 billion to pay down this debt, mostly by selling assets and forgoing dividend increases. Chrysler, when it emerged from near-bankruptcy in 1983, sold $432 million of new common stock to help regain a conservative capital structure.[26]

On the "no" side, there are other things the trade-off theory cannot explain. It cannot explain why some of the most successful companies thrive with little debt. Think of Canadian Marconi which, as Table 18-3(a) shows, is basically all-equity-financed. Granted, Marconi's most valuable assets are intangible, the fruits of its electronic research and development. We know that intangible assets and conservative capital structures tend to go together. But Marconi also has a large corporate income tax bill ($2 million to $14 million per year in 1985-1989)

---

[25] We are not suggesting that all airline *companies* are safe; many are not. But air*craft* can support debt where air*lines* cannot. If Fly-by-Night Airlines fails, its planes retain their value in another airline's operations. There's a good secondary market in used aircraft, so a loan secured by aircraft can be well-protected even if made to an airline flying on thin ice (and in the dark).

M. Kim and V. Maksimovic, "Debt and Input Misallocation," *Journal of Finance*, **45**: 795–816 (July 1990) found that highly levered airlines do not operate as efficiently as other airlines because the debt distorts their investment incentives—as discussed in the games of Section 18–3.

[26] Note that Chrysler issued stock *after* it emerged from financial distress. It did not *prevent* financial distress by raising equity money when trouble loomed on its horizon. Why not? Refer back to "Refusing to Contribute Equity Capital: The Second Game" in Section 18–3.

and a high credit rating. It could borrow enough to save millions of tax dollars without raising a whisker of concern about possible financial distress.

Marconi illustrates an odd fact about real-life capital structures: The most profitable companies generally borrow the least.[27] Here the trade-off theory fails, for it predicts exactly the reverse: under the trade-off theory, high profits should mean more debt-servicing capacity and more taxable income to shield, and should give a *higher* target debt ratio.[28]

A Pecking Order Theory

There is an alternative story which could explain the inverse relationship between profitability and debt ratios. It goes like this.[29]

1. Firms prefer internal finance.
2. They adapt their target dividend payout ratios to their investment opportunities, while trying to avoid sudden changes in dividends.
3. Sticky dividend policies, plus unpredictable fluctuations in profitability and investment opportunities, mean that internally generated cash flow is sometimes more than capital expenditures and at other times less. If it is more, the firm pays off debt or invests in marketable securities. If it is less, the firm first draws down its cash balance or sells its marketable securities.
4. If external finance is required, firms issue the safest security first. That is, they start with debt, then possibly hybrid securities such as convertible bonds, then perhaps equity as a last resort.

In this story, there is no well-defined target debt-equity mix, because there are two kinds of equity, internal and external, one at the top of the pecking order and one at the bottom. Each firm's observed debt ratio reflects its cumulative requirements for external finance.

The pecking order explains why the most profitable firms generally borrow less—not because they have low target debt ratios, but because they don't need outside money. Less profitable firms issue debt because they do not have internal funds sufficient for their capital investment program, and because debt financing is first on the pecking order of *external* financing.

The pecking order theory rests on (1) sticky dividend policy, (2) a preference for internal funds, and (3) an aversion to issuing equity. We will not revisit dividend policy, which occupied Chapter 16, but items (2) plus (3) deserve a further word.

Some think that financial managers do not strive for optimal financing decisions, but simply finance by the line of least resistance. If so, internal funds would be their first choice. Internal funds relieve financial managers of contact with outside investors and the "disciplining influences of the securities market."

---

[27] For example, Carl Kester, in a study of the financing policies of firms in the United States and in Japan, found that in each country, high book profitability was the most statistically significant variable distinguishing low- from high-debt companies. See "Capital and Ownership Structure: A Comparison of United States and Japanese Manufacturing Corporations," *Financial Management*, **15**: 5–16 (Spring 1986).

[28] Here we mean debt as a fraction of the book or replacement value of the company's assets. Profitable companies might not borrow a greater fraction of their market value. Higher profits imply higher market value as well as stronger incentives to borrow.

[29] The description is paraphrased from S.C. Myers, "The Capital Structure Puzzle," *Journal of Finance*, **39**: 581–582 (July 1984). For the most part, this section follows Myers's arguments.

If these comfortable people have to seek external financing, debt is next on the line of least resistance. Who wants to face "the glare of publicity and public attention generated by a stock issue?"[30]

However, a pecking order might also spring from fully rational economic motives, for example, from differences in *issue costs*. Internal funds of course have no issue costs, but if outside money is needed, issue costs are less for debt than for equity. Thus, it makes sense to use retained earnings, rather than external equity, and to build up *financial slack*, in the form of cash, marketable securities, or unused debt capacity, to reduce the odds that a future stock issue will be necessary.

Financial managers also worry about the adverse *signal* transmitted to investors when equity is issued. Remember from Chapter 15 that stock issues are bad news to investors: the announcement of a stock issue drives down stock price. Issuing debt, on the other hand, seems to be no news at all, or at worst a trifling disappointment.[31] You can appreciate why financial managers, who would rather not see stock price fall, would put debt ahead of equity in the pecking order.[32]

18-5 CHOOSING THE FIRM'S DEBT-EQUITY RATIO

A Checklist
It should be clear that there are no simple answers to the capital structure decision. For example, we can't say that more debt is always better. Debt may be better than equity in some cases, worse in others. We suggest, however, that you use a four-dimensional checklist when thinking about capital structure. These dimensions are taxes, risk, asset type, and the need for financial slack.

1. *Taxes*: If your company is in a taxpaying position, an increase in leverage reduces the income tax paid by the company and increases the tax paid by investors. If the company has large accumulated losses, an increase in leverage cannot reduce corporate taxes but does increase personal taxes.

   Of course, you are not just interested in whether the company is currently paying taxes but whether it will do so throughout the life of the debt. Firms with high and stable income streams are more likely to remain in a taxpaying position, but even they may be unable to take full advantage of the interest tax shields if they borrow too much; hence, our recommendation that there is a tax advantage to borrowing for companies that are reasonably sure that they can use the interest tax shields and a disadvantage for those that are unlikely to use them.

   Remember also that borrowing is not the only way to shield income. For example, accelerated write-offs of plant and equipment can be used to reduce corporate taxes.

2. *Risk*: With or without bankruptcy, financial distress is costly. Other things equal, distress is more likely for firms with high business risk. That is why such firms generally issue less debt.

---

[30] See Chapter 14, Section 14–6.

[31] For example, see B.E. Eckbo, "Valuation Effects of Corporate Debt Offerings," *Journal of Financial Economics,* **15**: 119–151 (January–February 1986).

[32] We have not given a full account of the theoretical underpinnings of the pecking order theory. There is more to it than "managers who would rather not see stock price fall." The theory was developed in S.C. Myers and N.S. Majluf, "Corporate Financing and Investment Decisions When Firms Have Information Investors Do Not Have," *Journal of Financial Economics,* **13**: 187–222 (June 1984).

3. *Asset Type*: The costs of distress are likely to be greater for firms whose value depends on growth opportunities or intangible assets. These firms are more likely to forgo profitable investment opportunities and, if default occurs, their assets may erode rapidly. Hence, firms whose assets are weighted toward intangible assets should borrow significantly less, on average, than firms holding assets you can kick.

4. *Financial Slack*: In the long run, a company's value rests more on its capital investment and operating decisions than on financing. Therefore, you want to make sure your firm has sufficient financial slack, so that financing is quickly accessible when good investment opportunities arise. Financial slack is most valuable to firms that have ample positive-NPV growth opportunities. That is another reason why growth companies usually aspire to conservative capital structures.

Planning Ahead

When you issue debt, you need to persuade the lenders that you will be able to repay their loan. Therefore, companies seeking debt financing usually draw up a set of pro forma income statements and balance sheets. These are simply your best forecasts of the firm's profits, assets, and liabilities.

You may find when you do this that the firm is unlikely to generate sufficient cash internally to repay the loan. That is not in itself a cause for alarm—remember that most growing firms run a financial deficit and are, therefore, repeatedly raising new capital. But such a result should prompt you to ask two questions. First, "Can the maturity of the proposed loan be extended so that the firm *can* repay the loan out of income?" Second, "Is the firm likely to be *able* to raise the additional debt or equity that it will need to repay the proposed loan?"

Most managers are not only interested in the expected outcome; they also want to know what could happen if things go wrong. The techniques that we used in Chapter 10 for examining a single project can also be used to examine the firm as a whole. For example, before their firm issues a large amount of debt, many financial managers conduct a break-even analysis. In other words, they look at how far sales or profits could decline without imperiling the firm's ability to service the loan. Or they look at how well the firm would fare under alternative plausible scenarios. Or they use Monte Carlo simulation to estimate the whole distribution of financial consequences.

The capital structure decision cannot be made in a vacuum. It has to form part of a sensible financial plan that takes into account future investment opportunities, the firm's dividend policy, and so on. That is why the financial manager needs to think about the effects of an issue of debt or equity on future income and balance sheets.

Pro forma income statements and balance sheets will indicate future financing needs. But they won't tell you much about whether you will be able to raise the necessary money. In other words, they won't tell you when you are bankrupt. Remember that bankruptcy occurs when the market value of the firm is less than the payments that have to be made on the debt. When this happens, the shares are worthless and the shareholders have no incentive to put up any further capital. If you want to estimate the risk of bankruptcy, you need to estimate the distribution of future company values. Here again you may find it useful to use simulation to estimate the odds that the market value of the company will be less than the payments that need to be made on the debt.

18-6   **SUMMARY**

Our goal in this chapter was to build a theory of optimal capital structure combining MM's insights with an analysis of taxes and financial distress.

The value of the firm equals

Value if all-equity financed + PV tax shield − PV costs of financial distress

The cost of financial distress can be broken down as follows:

1. Bankruptcy costs
    (a) Direct costs such as court fees
    (b) Indirect costs reflecting the difficulty of managing a company undergoing reorganization
2. Costs of financial distress short of bankruptcy
    (a) Conflicts of interest between bondholders and stockholders or firms in financial distress may lead to poor operating performance and investment decisions. Stockholders acting in their narrow self-interest can gain at the expense of creditors by playing "games" which reduce the overall value of the firm.
    (b) The fine print in debt contracts is designed to prevent these games. But fine print increases the costs of writing, monitoring, and enforcing the debt contract.

The value of the tax shield is more controversial. Let us define the net tax shield as T^* times the interest payment on the debt $r_D D$. To calculate present value, this tax shield is usually discounted at the borrowing rate r_D. In the special case of permanent debt

$$\text{PV tax shield} = \frac{T^*(r_D D)}{r_D} = T^* D$$

The problem is to identify T^*.

Most economists have become accustomed to thinking only of the corporate tax advantages of debt. Because firms do not pay corporate tax on any profits that are paid out as interest, interest payments provide a corporate tax shield. If this is the only tax consequence of debt, then for a taxpaying company the net tax saving, T^*, is simply the marginal corporate tax rate.

The principal difficulty with this view is that many firms seem to thrive with no debt at all despite the strong inducement to borrow. Miller has presented an alternative theory which may explain this. He argued that the net tax saving T^* is really zero when personal taxes as well as corporate taxes are considered. Interest income is not taxed at the corporate level but is taxed at the personal level. Equity income is taxed at the corporate level but may largely escape personal taxes if it comes in the form of capital gains.

In Miller's theory, the supply of corporate debt expands as long as the corporate tax rate exceeds the personal tax rate of the investors absorbing the increased supply. The supply which equates these two tax rates establishes an optimal debt ratio for the aggregate of corporations. But, if the total supply of debt suits investors' needs, any single taxpaying firm must find that debt policy does not matter.

We suggest that borrowing may make sense for some firms but not for others. If a firm can be fairly sure of earning a profit, there is likely to be a net tax saving from borrowing. In these cases T^* is greater than zero but less than 0.36. However, for firms that are unlikely to earn sufficient profits to benefit from the corporate tax shield, there is little, if any, net tax advantage to borrowing. For these firms T^* could even be negative.

There is no neat formula that you can plug in to find the optimal capital structure. But we recommend that you employ a four-dimensional checklist of taxes, risk, asset type, and the need for financial slack. This provides a framework for making sensible borrowing decisions.

We have portrayed the capital structure choice as a trade-off of the tax advantages of borrowing against the costs of financial distress. Corporations are supposed to pick a target capital structure that maximizes firm value. Firms with safe, tangible assets and plenty of taxable income to shield ought to have high targets. Unprofitable companies with risky, intangible assets ought to rely primarily on equity financing.

This "trade-off theory" of capital structure successfully explains many industry differences in capital structure, but it does not explain why the most profitable firms *within* an industry generally have the most conservative capital structures. (Under the trade-off theory, high profitability should mean high debt capacity *and* a strong corporate tax incentive to use that capacity.)

There is an alternative "pecking order" theory, which states that firms use internal finance when available, and choose debt over equity when external finance is needed. This could explain why less profitable firms borrow more—not because they have higher target debt ratios, but because they need more external financing, and because debt is next in the pecking order when internal funds are exhausted. A pecking order in financing could reflect managers' attempts to minimize issue costs and to avoid the adverse signals conveyed to investors when equity issues are announced.

The pecking order theory stresses the value of financial slack. Without financial slack, the company may be caught at the bottom of the pecking order, and may be forced to choose between issuing undervalued shares or passing over a positive-NPV investment opportunity.

FURTHER READING

Modigliani and Miller's analysis of the present value of interest tax shields at the corporate level is in:

F. Modigliani and M.H. Miller, "Corporate Income Taxes and the Cost of Capital: A Correction," *American Economic Review,* **53**: 433–443 (June 1963).

F. Modigliani and M.H. Miller, "Some Estimates of the Cost of Capital to the Electric Utility Industry, 1954–57," *American Economic Review,* **56**: 333–391 (June 1966).

The following articles consider personal as well as corporate taxes:

D. Farrar and L.L. Selwyn, "Taxes, Corporate Financial Policy and the Returns to Investors," *National Tax Journal,* **20**: 144–154 (December 1967).

M.H. Miller, "Debt and Taxes," *Journal of Finance,* **32**: 261–276 (May 1977).

Miller's theory is extended to include depreciation and other tax shields in:

H. DeAngelo and R. Masulis, "Optimal Capital Structure Under Corporate Taxation," *Journal of Financial Economics,* **8**: 5–29 (March 1980).

Estimates of bankruptcy costs are presented in:

J.B. Warner, "Bankruptcy Costs: Some Evidence," *Journal of Finance,* **32**: 337–348 (May 1977).

The following four articles analyze the conflicts of interest between bondholders and stockholders, and their implications for financing policy. (Do not read the first article until you have read Chapter 20).

D. Galai and R.W. Masulis, "The Option Pricing Model and the Risk Factor of Stock," *Journal of Financial Economics,* **3**: 53–82 (January–March 1976).

M.J. Gordon, "Towards a Theory of Financial Distress," *Journal of Finance,* **26**: 347–356 (May 1971).

M.C. Jensen and W.H. Meckling, "Theory of the Firm: Managerial Behavior, Agency Costs and Ownership Structure," *Journal of Financial Economics,* **3**: 305–360 (October 1976).

S.C. Myers, "Determinants of Corporate Borrowing," *Journal of Financial Economics,* **5**: 146–175 (1977).

For an interesting survey of the capital structure controversy, see:

R.H. Gordon and B.G. Malkiel, "Corporate Finance," in H.J. Aaron and J.A. Pechman (eds.), *How Taxes Affect Economic Behavior*, The Brookings Institution, Washington, D.C., 1981.

Donaldson has described how corporations set their borrowing targets. He also suggests how these targets can be set more intelligently.

G. Donaldson, *Corporate Debt Capacity: A Study of Corporate Debt Policy and the Determination of Corporate Debt Capacity*. Division of Research, Graduate School of Business Administration, Harvard University, Boston, 1962.

G. Donaldson, *Strategy for Financial Mobility*, Division of Research, Graduate School of Business Administration, Harvard University, Boston, 1969.

Myers describes the pecking order theory, which is based, in turn, on work by Myers and Majluf:

S.C. Myers, "The Capital Structure Puzzle," *Journal of Finance,* **39**: 575–592 (July 1984).

S.C. Myers and N.S. Majluf, "Corporate Financing and Investment Decisions When Firms Have Information Investors Do Not Have," *Journal of Financial Economics,* **13**: 187–222 (June 1984).

The January–February 1986 issue of the *Journal of Financial Economics* (**15**, No. 1/2) collects a series of empirical studies on the stock price impacts of debt and equity issues and capital structure changes.

QUIZ

1. Compute the present value of interest tax shields generated by these three debt issues. Consider corporate taxes only. The marginal tax rate is $T_c = 0.36$.
   (a) A $1,000, 1-year loan at 8%.
   (b) A 5-year loan of $1,000 at 8%. Assume no principal is repaid until maturity.
   (c) A $1,000 perpetuity at 7%.

2. Here are book and market value balance sheets of the United Frypan Company:

Book				Market			
Net working capital	20	Debt	40	Net working capital	20	Debt	40
Long-term assets	80	Equity	60	Long-term assets	140	Equity	120
	100		100		160		160

Assume that MM's theory holds with taxes. There is no growth and the $40 of debt is expected to be permanent. Assume a 40% corporate tax rate.

   (a) How much of the firm's value is accounted for by the debt-generated tax shield?

   (b) How much better off will UF's shareholders be if the firm borrows $20 more and uses it to repurchase stock?

   (c) Now suppose that a law is passed eliminating the deductibility of interest for tax purposes after a grace period of five years. What will be the new value of the firm, other things equal? (Assume an 8% borrowing rate.)

3.   Suppose that, in an effort to reduce the federal deficit, parliament increases the top personal tax rate on interest to 36%, but most provinces maintain personal tax at 50% of federal tax. The corporate income tax rate stays at 36%. Compute the total corporate plus personal taxes paid on debt versus equity income if (a) all capital gains are realized immediately and (b) capital gains are deferred forever. Capital gains are half of equity income. The dividend tax credit system and the capital gains inclusion rate are unchanged.

4.   Suppose that the rate of corporate income tax is reduced to 24%. What would Miller predict about corporate debt policy?

5.   Compute the total corporate plus personal taxes paid on debt and equity income for each of the following cases. In each case, specify whether the tax advantage lies with debt or equity. Assume the corporate tax rate is T_c = 0.36. Capital gains when realized are taxed at 75% of the rate on debt, which is the ordinary personal tax rate. Taxable dividends are 125% of dividends, but there is a federal dividend tax credit of $13^1/_3\%$ of taxable dividends. Provincial personal tax is 50% of federal tax.

Case	Investor's Federal Tax Bracket	Form of Equity Income
a	0.	All dividends
b	0.17	All dividends
c	0.17	All capital gains, never realized
d	0.26	All capital gains, never realized
e	0.26	All dividends
f	0.29	All dividends
g	0.29	All capital gains, immediately realized

6.   "The firm can't use interest tax shields unless it has (taxable) income to shield." What does this statement imply for the debt policy? Explain briefly.

7.   Let us go back to Circular File's market value balance sheet:

Net working capital	$20	$25	Bonds outstanding
Fixed assets	10	5	Common stock
Total assets	$30	$30	Total liabilities

Who gains and who loses from the following manoeuvres?

(a) Circular scrapes up $5 in cash and pays it as a cash dividend.

(b) Circular halts operations, sells its fixed assets, and converts net working capital into $20 cash. Unfortunately the fixed assets fetch only $6 on the second-hand market. The $26 cash is invested in Treasury bills.

(c) Circular encounters an acceptable investment opportunity, NPV = 0, requiring an investment of $10. The firm borrows to finance the project. The new debt has the same security, seniority, and so on as the old.

(d) Suppose that the new project has NPV = +$2 and is financed by an issue of preferred stock.

(e) The lenders agree to extend the maturity of their loan from one year to two years in order to give Circular a chance to recover.

8. What types of firms would be likely to incur heavy costs in the event of bankruptcy or financial distress? What types would incur relatively light costs? Give a few examples of each type.

9. The conventional theory of optimal capital structure states that firms trade off corporate interest tax shields against the possible costs of financial distress due to borrowing. What does this theory predict about the relationship between book profitability and target book debt ratios? Is the theory's prediction consistent with the facts?

10. What is meant by the "pecking order" theory of capital structure? Could this theory explain the observed relationship between profitability and debt ratios? Explain briefly.

QUESTIONS AND PROBLEMS

1. Montmorency Inc. has assets of $100 million and these are expected to remain unchanged in real terms. Assume that the real interest rate is 5%, the corporate tax rate is 36%, and debt interest is paid at the end of each year. If debt is a constant 30% of the value of the assets, what is PV tax shield
(a) If there is no expected inflation?
(b) If expected inflation is 10% a year?

2. "The trouble with MM's argument is that it ignores the fact that individuals can deduct interest for personal income tax." Show why this is not an objection. What difference would it make if individuals were not allowed to deduct interest for personal tax?

3. Look back at the Marconi example in Section 18–1. Suppose that Marconi moves to a 40% book debt ratio by issuing debt and using the proceeds to repurchase shares. Assume that MM's theory holds except for taxes. Now reconstruct Table 18–3(b) to reflect the new capital structure. Before it changes its capital structure, Marconi has 24 million shares outstanding. What is the stock price before and after the change?

4. Calculate the tax shield for an actual company assuming
(a) debt is permanent.
(b) MM are right.
How would the stock price change if the company announced tomorrow that it intended to replace all its debt with equity?

*5. Explain the implications of Miller's capital structure theory for the debt policy of:
(a) A company that pays corporate income tax.
(b) A company that is not in a taxpaying position.
(c) A company that is paying taxes now, but is unsure that it will have taxable income in the future.

*6. Recalculate Miller's equilibrium assuming that equity returns are taxed at half the rate of personal income tax on interest receipts.

7. Look at some real companies with different types of assets. What operating problems would each encounter in the event of financial distress? How well would the assets keep their value?

8. Imagine the following very simple world. There are three groups of investors with the following tax rates:

Group	Tax Rate, %
A	60
B	40
C	0

They can choose from perpetual American municipal bonds, perpetual corporate bonds, and common stock. Municipals and common stock attract no personal tax. Interest from corporate bonds attracts personal tax but is deductible for corporate tax. The corporate tax rate is 50%. Interest payments on municipals total $20 million. Cash flow (before interest and taxes) from corporations totals $300 million. Each group starts with the same amount of money. Regardless of what changes are made in capital structure, the three groups always invest the same amount as each other, and they require a minimum return of 10% after taxes on any security.

(a) Suppose that companies are financed initially by common stock. Company X now decides to allocate $1 million of its pretax cash flows to interest payments on debt. Which group or groups of investors will buy this debt? What will be the rate of interest? What will be the effect on the value of Company X?

(b) Other companies have followed the example of X and interest payments now total $150 million. At this point Company Y decides to allocate $1 million to interest payments on debt. Which group or groups will buy this debt? What will be the rate of interest? What will be the effect on the value of company Y?

(c) Total interest payments have somehow risen to $250 million. Now company Z substitutes common stock for debt, thereby *reducing* interest payments by $1 million. Which group or groups will sell their debt to Z? At what rate of interest can Z repurchase the debt? What will be the effect on Z's value?

(d) What is the equilibrium capital structure? Which groups will hold which securities? What is the rate of interest? What is the total value of all companies? Show that in equilibrium even an unlevered company has no incentive to issue debt. Similarly show that even a company with above-average leverage has no incentive to reduce its debt.

*9. Here is a difficult problem. What difference does capital cost allowance make to Miller's equilibrium? Try recalculating the equilibrium in problem 8, assuming that companies can deduct CCA of:

(a) $100 million, perpetually.

(b) $50 million, perpetually.

*10. The expected return on (risk-free) equity is 14% and the interest rate is 20%.

    (a) What is the implied personal tax rate of the marginal lender? (Assume that equity income is free of personal tax.)

    (b) Company A has large CCA tax shields and uncertain income. As a result, A's expected marginal rate of corporate tax is 40% if it finances solely with equity. For every 5% increase in A's debt ratio, A's marginal tax rate is expected to decline by 2%. How much should A borrow?

11. A Canadian corporation has a pretax cash flow of $1,000. The cash can either go to create interest for a bondholder or a dividend for a stockholder. The investor has a 26% marginal federal tax rate and lives in a province where provincial tax is 50% of personal federal tax. Dividends are grossed up by 25% for tax purposes and there is a federal dividend tax credit of $13\frac{1}{3}\%$ of grossed-up dividends. How much cash would go to the bondholder or the stockholder, after all taxes, in the following cases:

    (a) The corporate tax rate is 20%.

    (b) The corporate tax rate is 36%.

    Are these answers consistent with what you learned in Section 18–2?

*12. The Salad Oil Storage Company (SOS) has financed a large part of its facilities with long-term debt. There is a significant risk of default, but the company is not on the ropes yet. Explain:

    (a) Why SOS stockholders could lose by investing in a positive-NPV project financed by an equity issue.

    (b) Why SOS stockholders could gain by investing in a negative-NPV project financed by an equity issue.

    (c) Why SOS stockholders could gain from paying out a large cash dividend.

    How might the firm's adherence to a target debt ratio mitigate some or all of the problems noted above?

*13. (a) Who benefits from the "fine print" in bond contracts when the firm gets into financial trouble? Give a one-sentence answer.

    (b) Who benefits from the fine print when the bonds are issued? Suppose the firm is offered the choice of issuing (1) a bond with standard restrictions on dividend payout, additional borrowing, and so on, and (2) a bond with minimal restrictions, but a much higher interest rate? Suppose the interest rates on both (1) and (2) are fair from the viewpoint of lenders. Which bond would you expect the firm to issue? Why?

14. Explain why stock price falls when equity issues are announced but not when debt issues are announced. *Hint*: You'll find part of the answer in Section 15–3.

15. "I was amazed to find that the announcement of a stock issue drives down the value of the issuing firm by *30 percent*, on average, of the proceeds of the issue. That issue cost dwarfs the underwriter's spread and the administrative costs of the issue. It makes common stock issues prohibitively expensive."

    (a) You are contemplating a $100 million stock issue. On past evidence, you anticipate that announcement of this issue will drive down stock price by 3% and that the market value of your firm will fall by 30% of the amount to be raised. On the other hand, additional equity funds are necessary to fund an investment project which you believe has a positive NPV of $40 million. Should you proceed with the issue?

    (b) Is the fall in market value on announcement of a stock issue an *issue cost* in the same sense as an underwriter's spread? Respond to the quote which begins this question.

Use your answer to (a) as a numerical example to explain your response to (b).

16. Ronald Masulis[33] has analyzed the stock price impact of *exchange offers* of debt for equity or vice versa. In an exchange offer, the firm offers to trade freshly issued securities for seasoned securities in the hands of investors. Thus, a firm that wanted to move to a higher debt ratio could offer to trade new debt for outstanding shares. A firm that wanted to move to a more conservative capital structure could offer to trade new shares for outstanding debt securities.

    Masulis found that debt for equity exchanges were good news (stock price increased on announcement) and equity for debt exchanges were bad news.

    (a) Are these results consistent with the "trade-off" theory of capital structure?

    (b) Are the results consistent with the evidence that investors regard announcements of (i) stock issues as bad news, (ii) stock repurchases as good news, and (iii) debt issues as no news, or at most trifling disappointments?

    (c) How could Masulis's results be explained?

17. A recent newspaper column[34] suggests a novel way to help pay down Canada's federal debt. Taxpayers would be offered the chance to reduce their federal tax payable by $1,250 for each $1,000 payment they make to an account that specifically retires the federal debt. While this apparently seems like a loss to the government of $250, proponents of the scheme point out that, at a 13% interest rate on federal debt, the interest on the $1,000 of debt totals $1,000 over a 7.6 year period. Thus, the taxpayers accepting this scheme would actually be paying off the debt not just by $1,000 but by $1,000 + $1,000 or $2,000 over the span of a 7.6 year period. With compound interest and longer time intervals, the saving gets even better.

    (a) Do you think this plan would be an effective policy for the federal government? Explain.

    (b) The anonymous proposer of the plan suggests that the offer should be made only to taxpayers in the top tax bracket because it would transfer wealth from the rich to the poor. Do you think the proposer is in a high or low tax bracket?

---

[33] R.W. Masulis, "The Effects of Capital Structure Change on Security Prices: A Study of Exchange Offers," *Journal of Financial Economics*, **8**: 139–177 (June 1980), and "The Impact of Capital Structure Change on Firm Value," *Journal of Finance*, **38**: 107–126 (March 1983).

[34] "The Insiders" by Diane Francis, *Financial Post*, April 27, 1990.

C·H·A·P·T·E·R

19

INTERACTIONS OF
INVESTMENT AND
FINANCING DECISIONS

We first addressed problems of capital budgeting in Chapter 2. At that point we had said hardly a word about financing decisions; we proceeded under the simplest possible assumption about financing, namely, all-equity financing. We were really assuming an idealized Modigliani-Miller (MM) world in which all financing decisions are irrelevant. In a strict MM world, firms can analyze real investments as if they are to be all-equity-financed; the actual financing plan is a mere detail to be worked out later.

Under MM assumptions, decisions to spend money can be separated from decisions to raise money. In this chapter we reconsider the capital budgeting decision when investment and financing decisions *interact* and cannot be separated.

In the early chapters you learned how to value a capital investment opportunity by a four-step procedure:

1. Forecast the project's incremental after-tax cash flow.
2. Assess the project's risk.
3. Estimate the opportunity cost of capital, that is, the expected rate of return offered to investors by the equivalent-risk investments traded in capital markets.
4. Calculate NPV using the discounted-cash-flow formula.

In effect, we were thinking of each project as a mini-firm, and asking, "How much would that mini-firm be worth if we spun it off as a separate, all-equity-financed enterprise? How much would investors be willing to pay for shares in the project?"

Of course, this procedure rests on the concept of *value additivity*. In well-functioning capital markets the market value of the firm is the sum of the present value of all the assets held by the firm[1] — the whole equals the sum of the parts.

---

[1] *All assets* means intangible as well as tangible assets. For example, a going concern is usually worth more than a haphazard pile of tangible assets. Thus, the aggregate value of a firm's tangible assets often falls short of its market value. The difference is accounted for by going-concern value or by other intangible assets such as accumulated technical expertise, an experienced sales force, or valuable growth opportunities.

If value additivity did *not* hold, then the value of the firm with the project could be more or less than the sum of the separate value of the project and the value of the firm without the project. We could not determine the project's contribution to firm value by evaluating it as a separate mini-firm.

In this chapter we stick with the value-additivity principle, but extend it to include value contributed by financing decisions as well as value contributed by investment decisions. That leads us to a simple and straightforward approach to analyzing the interactions of financing and investment decisions. The idea is to start by estimating the project's "base-case" value as an all-equity-financed mini-firm, and then to adjust this project's base-case NPV to account for the project's impact on the firm's capital structure. Thus,

> Adjusted NPV (ANPV, or just APV for short) = base-case NPV
> + NPV of financing decisions caused by project acceptance

Once you identify and value the side effects of financing a project, calculating its APV (adjusted net present value[2]) is no more than addition or subtraction.

There is another way to capture financing side effects. This alternative procedure is more widely used than APV, and it *looks* simpler: you just change the discount rate for the project's cash flows. We will discuss the pros and cons of the adjusted discount rate after you master APV.

We conclude the chapter by reexamining a basic and apparently simple issue: What should the discount rate be for a risk-free project? Once we recognize the tax deductibility of debt interest, we will find that all risk-free, or *debt-equivalent,* cash flows can be evaluated by discounting at the *after-tax* interest rate.

19-1   THE ADJUSTED-PRESENT-VALUE RULE

The adjusted-present-value rule is easiest to understand in the context of simple numerical examples. We start by analyzing a project under base-case assumptions, and then consider possible financing side effects of accepting the project.

The Base Case   The APV method begins by valuing the project as if it were a mini-firm financed solely by equity. Consider a project to produce solar waterheaters. It requires a $10 million investment and offers a level after-tax cash flow of $1.8 million per year for ten years. The project's opportunity cost of capital is 12%, which reflects the project's business risk. Investors would demand a 12% expected return to invest in the mini-firm's shares.

Thus, the mini-firm's base-case NPV is:

$$NPV = -10 + \sum_{t=1}^{10} \frac{1.8}{(1.12)^t}$$
$$= +\$0.17 \text{ million or } \$170,000$$

Considering the project's size, this figure is not significantly greater than zero. In a pure MM world where no financing decision matters, the financial manager would lean toward taking the project but would not be heartbroken if the project were discarded.

Issue Costs   But suppose that the firm actually has to finance the $10 million investment by issuing stock (it will not have to issue stock if it rejects the project) and that

---

[2] APV is sometimes called *valuation by components.*

issue costs soak up 5% of the gross proceeds of the issue. That means the firm has to issue $10,526,000 in order to obtain $10,000,000 cash. The $526,000 difference goes to underwriters, lawyers, and others involved in the issue process.[3]

The project's APV is calculated by subtracting the issue cost from base-case NPV:

$$APV = \text{base-case NPV} - \text{issue cost} = +170{,}000 - 526{,}000 = -\$356{,}000$$

The firm would reject the project because APV is negative.

Additions to the Firm's Debt Capacity

Consider a different financing scenario. Suppose that the firm has a 50% target debt ratio. Its policy is to limit debt to 50% of the book value of its assets. Thus, if it invests more, it borrows more; in this sense investment adds to the firm's debt capacity.[4]

Is debt capacity worth anything? The most widely accepted answer is "yes" because of the tax shields generated by interest payments on corporate borrowing. (You may wish to look back to our discussion of debt and taxes in Chapter 18.) For example, MM's original theory states that the value of the firm is independent of its capital structure *except* for the present value of interest tax shields:

$$\text{Firm value} = \text{value with all-equity financing} + \text{PV tax shield}$$

This theory tells us to compute the value of the firm in two steps: first compute its base-case value under all-equity financing, and then add the present value of taxes saved due to a departure from all-equity financing. This procedure is like an APV calculation for the firm as a whole.

We can repeat the calculation for a particular project. For example, suppose that the solar heater project increases the firm's assets by $10 million and therefore prompts it to borrow $5 million more. To keep things simple, we assume that this $5 million loan is repaid in equal instalments, so that the amount borrowed declines with the depreciating book value of the solar heater project. We also assume that the loan is *not* subsidized and therefore carries an interest rate of 8%. Table 19-1 shows how the value of the interest tax shields is calculated. This is the value of the additional debt capacity contributed to the firm by the project. We obtain APV by adding this amount to the project's NPV:

$$APV = \text{base-case NPV} + \text{PV tax shield}$$
$$= +170{,}000 + 592{,}000 = \$762{,}000$$

The Value of Interest Tax Shields

In Table 19-1, we boldly assumed that the firm could fully capture interest tax shields of 36 cents on the dollar discounted back to the present. The true value of the tax shield is almost surely less:

1. You can't use tax shields unless you pay taxes, and you don't pay taxes unless you make money. Few firms can be *sure* that future probability will be sufficient to use up the interest tax shields.
2. The government takes two bites out of corporate income: the corporate tax and the tax on bondholders' and stockholders' personal income. The corporate tax favours debt; the personal tax favours equity.

---

[3] Some of these costs may be tax-deductible expenses for the firm. If so, the after-tax transaction costs will be less than $526,000.

[4] *Debt capacity* is potentially misleading because it seems to imply an absolute limit to the amount the firm is *able to* borrow. That is not what we mean. The firm limits borrowing to 50% of assets because it believes that to be the best policy. It could borrow more if it wanted to.

Table 19-1
Calculating the present value of interest tax shields on debt supported by the solar heater project (figures in thousands).

Year	Debt Outstanding at Start of Year	Interest	Interest Tax Shield	Present Value of Tax Shield
1	$5,000	$400	$144	$133
2	4,500	360	130	111
3	4,000	320	115	91
4	3,500	280	101	74
5	3,000	240	86	59
6	2,500	200	72	45
7	2,000	160	58	34
8	1,500	120	43	23
9	1,000	80	29	14
10	500	40	14	7
			Total	$592

Assumptions:

1. Marginal tax rate = 0.36; tax shield = 0.36 × interest.

2. Debt principal repaid at end of year in ten $500,000 instalments.

3. Interest rate on debt is 8%.

4. Present value calculated at the 8% borrowing rate. The assumption here is that the tax shields are just as risky as the interest payments generating them.

In Chapter 18, we argued that the effective tax shield on interest was not 36% (T_c = 0.36), but some lower figure T^*. We were unable to pin down an exact figure for T^* (some respected scholars believe T^* = 0, and it could even be negative[5]).

Suppose, for example, that we believe T^* = 0.30. We can easily recalculate the APV of the solar heater project. Just multiply the present value of the interest tax shields by 30/36. The bottom line of Table 19-1 drops from $592,000 to $592,000 (30/36) or $493,000. APV drops to:

$$APV = \text{base case NPV} + \text{PV tax shield}$$
$$= +170,000 + 493,000 = \$663,000$$

Review of the Adjusted-Present-Value Approach

If the decision to invest in a capital project has important side effects on other financial decisions made by the firm, those side effects should be taken into account when the project is evaluated.

The idea behind APV is "divide and conquer." The approach does not attempt to capture all the side effects in a single calculation. A series of present value calculations is made instead. The first establishes a base-case value for the project: its value as a separate, all-equity-financed mini-firm. Then each side effect is traced out and the present value of its cost or benefit to the firm is calculated. Finally, all the present values are added together to estimate the project's total contribution to the value of the firm. Thus, in general,

---

[5] If your firm faces a tax rate of T_c, but the marginal firm (namely, a firm that is indifferent between debt and equity) faces a tax rate of T_m, then one can calculate T^* as $T^* = T_c - T_m$. In Miller's model, all firms face the same tax rate $T_c = T_m$, so T^* = 0. In the M-M model, $T_m = 0$, so $T^* = T_c$. In reality, the marginal firm is likely taxed at less than the full statutory rate (of about 36%), so a fully-taxed firm with $T_c > T_m$ would have $T^* > 0$, while a firm paying taxes at a low rate $T_c < T_m$ would actually have $T^* < 0$. This is discussed in G.A. Sick, "Tax-Adjusted Discount Rates," *Management Science,* **36**: 1432–1450 (December 1990).

$$\text{Project APV} = \text{base-case NPV} + \begin{array}{l}\text{sum of the present value of the side}\\ \text{effects of accepting the project}\end{array}$$

19-2   ADJUSTED DISCOUNT RATES – AN ALTERNATIVE TO ADJUSTED PRESENT VALUE

Calculating APV is not mathematically difficult, but tracing out and evaluating a project's financial side effects takes financial sophistication. Many firms use a simpler procedure. They adjust the discount rate rather than adjusting present value. This allows them to calculate net present value only once, rather than the two or more times required by APV. They set the discount rate for project acceptance equal to an *adjusted cost of capital* which reflects the opportunity cost of capital *and* the project's financing side effects.

Example: The Geothermal Project

We will explain the adjusted-cost-of-capital approach with an even simpler numerical example. The project calls for tapping geothermal energy to supply heat and air conditioning for a shopping centre. The investment required is one million dollars. Once installed, the project will save $220,000 per year after taxes. To keep the arithmetic simple, we will assume the saving continues indefinitely. The business risk of the venture requires a 20% discount rate – this is r, the opportunity cost of capital. Thus the project's base-case NPV is just positive:

$$\text{Base-case NPV} = -1,000,000 + \frac{220,000}{0.20}$$
$$= +\$100,000$$

We assume that the project has one financing side effect. It expands the firm's borrowing power by $400,000. The project lasts indefinitely, and so we treat it as supporting perpetual debt. In other words, the firm is assumed to borrow $400,000 against the project, and to maintain that borrowing come hell or high water. If the borrowing rate is 14% and the net tax shield per dollar of interest is $T^* = 0.30$, the project supports debt that generates interest tax shields of $0.3 \times 0.14 \times 400,000 = \$16,800$ per year forever. The present value of these tax shields is $\$16,800/0.14 = \$120,000$. Thus, the geothermal project's APV is:

$$\text{APV} = \text{base-case NPV} + \text{PV tax shield}$$
$$= +100,000 + 120,000 = +\$220,000$$

The geothermal project looks even better when its contribution to corporate debt capacity is recognized.

The present value of the interest tax shield is $+\$120,000$. Therefore, the geothermal project would still be acceptable even if base-case NPV were as low as $-\$120,000$. What does that imply for the minimum acceptable *income* from the project? To answer that question, we set base-case NPV at $-\$120,000$ and solve for the project's annual income:

$$\begin{array}{l}\text{Minimum acceptable}\\ \text{base-case NPV}\end{array} = -1,000,000 + \frac{\text{annual income}}{0.20}$$
$$= -120,000$$
$$\text{Annual income} = 0.2(1,000,000 - 120,000) = \$176,000$$

Thus, the minimum acceptable income from the project is \$176,000 a year and the minimum acceptable IRR is $176,000/1,000,000 = 0.176$ or 17.6%.[6] This is the lowest return that the firm would be willing to accept from projects like this one; it is the IRR at which APV is zero.

Suppose that we encounter another perpetuity. Its opportunity cost of capital is also $r = 0.20$, and it also expands the firm's borrowing power by 40% of the investment. We know that if such a project offers an IRR greater than 17.6%, it will have a positive APV. Therefore, we could shorten the analysis by just discounting the project's cash inflows at 17.6%.[7] This discount rate is often called the adjusted cost of capital. It reflects both the project's business risk and its contribution to the firm's debt capacity.

We will denote the adjusted cost of capital by r^*. To calculate r^*, we find the minimum acceptable internal rate of return—the IRR at which APV = 0. The rule is:

Accept projects which have a positive NPV at the adjusted cost of capital r^*.

A General Definition of the Adjusted Cost of Capital

We now have two concepts of the cost of capital:

Concept 1: The Opportunity Cost of Capital (r)   The expected rate of return offered in capital markets by equivalent-risk assets. This depends on the risk of the project's cash flows.

Concept 2: The Adjusted Cost of Capital (r*)   An adjusted opportunity cost or hurdle rate that reflects the financing side effects of an investment project.

Some people just say "cost of capital." Sometimes their meaning is clear in context. At other times, they don't know which concept they are referring to and that can sow widespread confusion.

When financing side effects are important, you should accept projects with positive APVs. But if you know the adjusted discount rate, you don't have to calculate APV; you just calculate NPV at the adjusted rate. If we could find a simple, universally correct method for calculating r^*, we would be all set. Unfortunately, there is no such method. There are some reasonably adequate rules of thumb, however.

MM's Formula   One formula for calculating r^* was suggested by Modigliani and Miller (MM).[8] MM's formula is

$$r^* = r(1 - T^*L)$$

where r is the opportunity cost of capital and L is the project's marginal contribution to the firm's debt capacity as a proportion of the project's present value. The value of L may be higher than the firm's overall debt ratio or lower than the firm's overall debt ratio. Remember, T^* reflects the net tax saving attached to a dollar of future interest payments.

---

[6] Since the project produces a level stream of cash flows in perpetuity, IRR = cash flow divided by investment.

[7] Remember that forecasted project cash flows do *not* reflect the tax shields generated by any debt the project may support.

[8] The formula first appeared in F. Modigliani and M.H. Miller, "Corporate Income Taxes and the Cost of Capital: A Correction," *American Economic Review*, **53**: 433–443 (June 1963). It is explained more fully in M.H. Miller and F. Modigliani, "Some Estimates of the Cost of Capital to the Electric Utility Industry: 1954–1957," *American Economic Review*, **56**: 333–391 (June 1966). In these articles, MM assumed that T^* equals the corporate tax rate T_c.

EXAMPLE   The contribution of the geothermal project to the firm's debt capacity is \$400,000. Therefore, $L = 0.40$. The project's opportunity cost of capital is $r = 0.20$ and we continue to assume that $T^* = 0.30$. We worked out earlier that the project's adjusted cost of capital was $r^* = 0.176$. That is precisely what we get using the MM formula:

$$r^* = r(1 - T^*L)$$
$$= 0.20(1 - 0.3(0.4)) = 0.176 \text{ or } 17.6\%$$

How Reliable is MM's Formula?   The MM formula works for the geothermal project or for any other project that is expected to (1) generate a level, perpetual cash flow and (2) support permanent debt. The formula is exactly right only if these two assumptions are met. Assets offering perpetual cash-flow streams are like abominable snowmen: often referred to but seldom seen. But MM's formula still works reasonably well for projects with limited lives or irregular cash-flow streams. Using the formula to calculate the present value of these projects will typically result in an error of 2% to 6%.[9] This is not too bad when you consider that a biased cash-flow forecast could put project value off the mark by plus or minus 20%.

What Happens when Future Debt Levels Are Uncertain

We wish we could stop at this point and go on to something easier. But conscience won't allow it. Any capital budgeting procedure that assumes debt levels are fixed when a project is undertaken is grossly oversimplified. For example, we assumed that the geothermal project contributed \$400,000 to the firm's debt capacity — not just when the project is undertaken, but "from here to eternity." That amounts to saying that the future value and risk of the project will not change — a strong assumption indeed. Suppose the price of oil shoots up unexpectedly a year after the project is undertaken; since the geothermal project saves oil, its cash flow and value shoot up too. Suppose the project's value doubles. In that case, won't its contribution to debt capacity also double, to \$800,000? It works the other way too: if the oil price falls out of bed, the contribution to debt capacity tumbles.

Suppose the firm's rule is not "Always borrow \$400,000," but "Always borrow 40% of the geothermal project's value." Then, if project value increases, the firm borrows more. If it decreases, it borrows less. Under this policy, you can no longer discount future interest tax shields at the borrowing rate because the shields are no longer certain. Their size depends on the amount actually borrowed and, therefore, on the actual future value of the project.

When the firm adjusts its borrowing to keep a constant debt proportion, it can often be a wearisome task to calculate the project's APV. Fortunately, James Miles and Russell Ezzell have derived an adjusted discount rate formula for this problem:[10]

---

[9] See S.C. Myers, "Interactions of Corporate Financing and Investment Decisions — Implications for Capital Budgeting," *Journal of Finance*, **29**: 1–25 (March 1974).

[10] J. Miles and R. Ezzell, "The Weighted Average Cost of Capital, Perfect Capital Markets, and Project Life: A Clarification," *Journal of Financial and Quantitative Analysis*, **15**: 719–730 (September 1980). The Miles-Ezzel formula is not completely correct when there are different personal tax rates on debt and equity income — the kind of situation that results in the Miller equilibrium and other refinements discussed in Chapter 18. For this more general case, Proposition 5 of Sick, *op cit.*, replaces the Miles-Ezzell formula with

$$r^* = r - Lr_i T^*\left(\frac{1 + r}{1 + r_z}\right)$$

$$r^* = r - Lr_\mathrm{D}T^* \left(\frac{1 + r}{1 + r_\mathrm{D}} \right)$$

where r_D is the borrowing rate. For the geothermal project, we would calculate an adjusted cost of capital of:

$$r^* = 0.20 - 0.4(0.14)(0.3) \left(\frac{1.2}{1.14} \right) = 0.1823 \text{ or } 18.23\%$$

Discounting the project's cash flows at 18.23% gives a net present value of:

$$NPV = -1,000,000 + \frac{220,000}{0.1823}$$
$$= +\$207,000$$

The Miles-Ezzell formula works only for firms that maintain a constant debt proportion, but in these cases, it is exact for any cash-flow pattern or project life.[11] It is also much easier to use than the adjusted-present-value method.

How Useful Are Adjusted-Cost-of-Capital Formulas?

We now have two adjusted-cost-of-capital formulas. The major *conceptual* difference between the two formulas lies in their assumptions about the amount of debt the firm can or will issue against the project. MM assume this amount is fixed. Miles and Ezzell assume it will vary with the project's future value. Miles and Ezzell's assumption is more attractive theoretically but, on the other hand, we have to admit that firms' debt policies are sticky: we don't see firms issuing or retiring debt every time their stock price goes up or down. So the truth may be somewhere in between.

Truth's exact location may not be so important. The geothermal and solar heater projects were attractive, regardless of which method or formula we used. This is one illustration of BMGS's third law: *You can make a lot more money by good investment decisions than by good financing decisions.*

Nevertheless, it's important to understand the assumptions underlying the formulas and their relationship to the more general APV rule. Both formulas assume that financing affects firm value only through interest tax shields. This is a bold simplification. Most financial scholars and practitioners agree that the tax shields have value—although even this is controversial, as we saw in Chapter 18. But practically no one believes that interest tax shields are the *only* thing governing the financing decision. The decision to accept a project may lead to a stock issue and to issue costs. It may force the firm to shift its dividend policy, or it may enable the firm to make use of an advantageous financial lease or government-subsidized financing. The adjusted-cost-of-capital formulas assume that side effects like these do not exist, or, if they do exist, that they do not matter.

Of course firms can, if they wish, derive more complicated formulas for calculating the adjusted cost of capital in cases where these kinds of financing side effects do matter. But such effects are rarely worth the trouble. It is much simpler to

---

where r_f is the rate of return on riskless debt and r_z is the rate of return on riskless equity in the capital asset pricing model. (Recall from Section 18-2 that these two rates of return differ to the extent that they are taxed differently.) Also, Sick shows that this formula should use the return on riskless debt r_f even if the debt is risky and r_D exceeds r_f, because the certainty equivalent of the return on risky debt is the same as that on riskless debt, namely r_f.

[11] Remember that the MM formula was exact, given its assumption about debt policy, only for perpetuities.

calculate the net present value of side effects separately and then work out the adjusted present value.[12]

19-3   THE WEIGHTED-AVERAGE-COST-OF-CAPITAL FORMULA

Formulas are like cheese: too large a helping may cause insomnia. Fortunately, you need learn only one other formula for calculating adjusted present values. This is the *weighted-average cost of capital*. Sometimes we call it the *textbook formula*, since many other textbooks have put heavy emphasis on it. The formula is:[13]

$$r^* = r_D(1 - T_c)\frac{D}{V} + r_E\frac{E}{V}$$

where r^* = the adjusted cost of capital
$\quad r_D$ = the firm's current borrowing rate
$\quad T_c$ = the marginal *corporate* income tax rate — not the effective rate T^* used in Sections 19-1 and 19-2
$\quad r_E$ = the expected rate of return on the firm's stock (a function of the firm's business risk *and* its debt ratio)
$\quad D, E$ = the market values of currently outstanding debt and equity
$\quad V = D + E$ = the total market value of the firm

The first thing to notice about the weighted-average formula is that all variables in it refer to the firm as a whole. As a result the formula gives the right discount rate only for projects that are just like the firm undertaking them. The formula works for the "average" project. It is incorrect for projects that are safer or riskier than the average of the firm's existing assets. It is incorrect for projects whose acceptance would lead to an increase or decrease in the firm's debt ratio.

The idea behind the weighted-average formula is simple and intuitively appealing. If the new project is profitable enough to pay the (after-tax) interest on the debt used to finance it, and also to generate a superior expected rate of return on the equity invested in it, then it must be a good project. What is a "superior" equity return? One that exceeds r_E, the expected rate of return required by investors in the firm's shares. Let us see how this idea leads to the weighted-average formula.

Suppose that the firm invests in a new project that is expected to produce the same yearly income in perpetuity. If the firm maintains the same debt ratio, the amount of debt used to finance the project is

$$\text{Firm's debt ratio} \times \text{investment} = \frac{D}{V} \times \text{investment}$$

Similarly, the equity used to finance the project is

$$\text{Firm's equity ratio} \times \text{investment} = \frac{E}{V} \times \text{investment}$$

---

[12] Of course you can still use the MM formula or the Miles and Ezzell formula to take account of the interest tax shields and then add on the present value of any other financing side effects.

[13] If $T_c = 0$, the weighted-average cost of capital simplifies to

$$r_D\frac{D}{V} + r_E\frac{E}{V}$$

This is exactly the formula that we introduced in Chapter 17, where we assumed that there are no corporate taxes.

If the project is worthwhile, the income must cover after-tax interest charges and provide an acceptable return to equityholders. The after-tax interest costs on the additional debt are equal to

$$\text{After-tax interest rate} \times \text{value of debt} = r_D(1 - T_c) \times \frac{D}{V} \times \text{investment}$$

The minimum acceptable income to equityholders is

$$\text{Expected return on equity} \times \text{value of equity} = r_E \times \frac{E}{V} \times \text{investment}$$

Therefore, for the project to be acceptable, its income *must exceed*:

$$r_D(1 - T_c) \times \frac{D}{V} \times \text{investment} + r_E \times \frac{E}{V} \times \text{investment}$$

This brings us back to the weighted-average formula. Just divide through by the initial investment:

$$\frac{\text{Income}}{\text{Investment}} \ \textit{must exceed} \ r_D(1 - T_c)\frac{D}{V} + r_E\frac{E}{V}$$

Note that the ratio of the project's annual income to investment is just the project's return. Therefore, our formula gives the minimum acceptable rate of return from the project.

We have derived the textbook formula only for firms and projects offering perpetual cash flows. But Miles and Ezzell have shown that the formula works for any cash-flow pattern if the firm adjusts its borrowing to maintain a constant debt ratio D/V regardless of whether things turn out well or poorly. When the firm departs from this policy, the textbook formula is only approximately correct.

Now We Apply the Textbook Formula to the Geothermal Project
Imagine the geothermal project set up as an independent, one-asset firm, which we'll call Geothermal, Inc. Once the project is built, Geothermal's market value will be worth the initial investment of $1,000,000 plus the project's APV.

In Section 19-2, we calculated that if Geothermal maintains a constant debt ratio of 40%, the APV is $207,000. Thus, Geothermal's balance sheet should turn out as follows:

	Geothermal, Inc. (Market Values)		
Assets (initial investment + APV)	1,207,000	482,800	Debt (D) (40% of firm value)
		724,000	Equity (E) (60% of firm value)
	1,207,000	1,207,000	

Each year the equity holders expect to receive the cash flow from the investment, (C) *less* the interest payment on debt ($r_D D$), *plus* the interest tax shield ($T_c r_D D$):

$$
\begin{aligned}
\text{Expected equity income} &= C - r_D D + T_c r_D D \\
&= 220,000 - 0.14(482,800) + 0.36(0.14)(482,800) \\
&= 176,741
\end{aligned}
$$

The expected rate of return on equity is equal to the expected equity income divided by the equity value:

$$\text{Expected equity return} = r_E = \frac{\text{Expected equity income}}{\text{Equity value}}$$

$$= \frac{176,741}{724,200} = 0.244 \text{ or } 24.4\%$$

Now suppose Geothermal unexpectedly encounters another investment opportunity. The second is a clone of the first in all dimensions save profitability: it has the same business risk and the same time pattern of cash flows. Geothermal therefore plans to borrow 40% of the project's value.

If management has forgotten the calculations we did in Section 19-2, it can use the textbook formula to find the appropriate adjusted discount rate.

$$r^* = r_D(1 - T_c)\frac{D}{V} + r_E\frac{E}{V}$$

$$= 0.14(1 - 0.36)(0.4) + 0.244(0.6)$$

$$= 0.1822 \text{ or } 18.22\%$$

That's the same figure that we got earlier using the Miles and Ezzell formula, save for the roundoff error.

Using the Textbook Formula

One of the handy features of the textbook formula is that you can often use stock market data to get an estimate of r_E, the expected rate of return demanded by investors in the company's stock. With that estimate, the textbook r^* is not too hard to calculate, because the borrowing rate r_D and the debt and equity ratios D/V and E/V can be directly observed or estimated without too much trouble.[14]

The textbook r^* is a *company* adjusted cost of capital. Strictly speaking, it works only for projects that are carbon copies of the firm's existing assets, both in business risk and financing. Often it is used as a companywide benchmark discount rate; the benchmark is adjusted upward for unusually risky projects and downward for unusually safe ones.

You can also calculate the textbook r^* for *industries.* Suppose that a pharmaceutical company has a subsidiary which produces specialty chemicals. What discount rate is better for the subsidiary's projects — the company r^* or a weighted-average cost of capital for a portfolio of "pure play" specialty chemical companies? The latter rate is better in principle, and also in practice, if good data are available for firms with operations and markets similar to the subsidiary's.

An Application to the Railroad Industry

In mid-1974 the assets of the Penn Central Railroad were taken over by Conrail, a new, federally sponsored corporation in the United States. Since Penn Central had declared bankruptcy in 1971, the assets taken by Conrail really belonged to the railroad's creditors. Congress set up a special court to determine fair compensation.

Although the Penn Central system was generating hair-curling losses overall, some of its freight lines were potentially profitable. In 1978 one of the authors was asked to estimate a discount rate for valuing the cash flows these lines would

---

[14] Most corporate debt is not actively traded, so its market value cannot be observed directly. But you can usually value a nontraded debt security by looking to securities which *are* traded and which have approximately the same default risk and maturity. See Chapter 23.

have produced, had Conrail not taken them over. He was asked to assume that these freight lines would have had the same business risk and financing as the railroad industry generally. That sounded like a job for the textbook formula. An extensive investigation boiled down to the following calculation:

$$r^*(\text{in mid-}1974) = r_D(1 - T_c)D/V + r_E E/V$$
$$= 0.087(1 - 0.5)(0.45) + 0.16(0.55)$$
$$= 0.1076 \text{ or about } 10^3/_4\%$$

The formula's components were derived as follows:

$r_D = 0.087$, a weighted average of bond yields for ten major railroads in mid-1974

$T_c = 0.50$. The corporate income tax rate in mid-1974 was 48%. Two percentage points were added to cover state income taxes.

$D/V = 0.45$. The estimated average market debt-to-value ratio for ten major railroads. Thus, $E/V = 0.55$.

$r_E = 0.16$. Railroad stocks on average appeared to have about the same risk as the market portfolio. Their betas averaged out close to 1.0. Thus, $r_E = r_M$. The 16% market return equals the sum of the Treasury bill yield in mid-1974 plus the historical risk premium on the market portfolio.

Of course, each of these numbers was to some extent controversial. Other expert witnesses used the same textbook formula to arrive at substantially different answers. Anyone brave enough to estimate a discount rate in public can expect controversy.

Mistakes People Make in Using the Weighted-Average Formula

The real danger with the weighted-average formula is that it tempts people to make logical errors. For example, manager Q, who is campaigning for a pet project, might look at the formula

$$r^* = r_D(1 - T_c)\frac{D}{V} + r_E\frac{E}{V}$$

and think, "Aha! My firm has a good credit rating. It could borrow, say, 90% of the project's cost if it likes. That means $D/V = 0.9$ and $E/V = 0.1$. My firm's borrowing rate r_D is 8% and the required return on equity r_E is 15%. Therefore,

$$r^* = 0.08(1 - 0.36)(0.9) + 0.15(0.1) = 0.061 \text{ or } 6.1\%$$

When I discount at that rate, my project looks great."

Q is wrong on several counts. First, the weighted-average formula only works for projects that are carbon copies of the firm. The firm isn't 90% debt-financed.

Second, the immediate source of funds for a project has no necessary connection with the hurdle rate for the project. What matters is the project's overall contribution to the firm's borrowing power. A dollar invested in Q's pet project will not increase the firm's debt capacity by 90 cents. If it borrows 90% of the project's cost, it is really borrowing in part against its *existing* assets. Any advantage from financing the new project with more debt than normal should be attributed to the old projects, not to the new one.

Third, even if the firm were willing and able to lever up to 90% debt, its cost of capital would not decline to 6.1% (as Q's naive calculation predicts). You cannot increase the debt ratio without creating financial risk for stockholders and thereby increasing r_E, the expected rate of return they demand from the firm's common stock. Going to 90% debt would certainly increase the borrowing rate too.

19-4 DISCOUNTING SAFE, NOMINAL CASH FLOWS

Suppose you're considering purchase of a $100,000 machine. The manufacturer sweetens the deal by offering to finance the purchase by lending you $100,000 for 5 years, with annual interest payments of 5%. You would have to pay 13% to borrow from a bank. Your marginal tax rate is 30% ($T_c = 0.3$).

How much is this loan worth? If you take it, the cash flows are:

Period	0	1	2	3	4	5
Cash flow (in thousands)	$100	−5	−5	−5	−5	−105
Tax shield		+1.5	+1.5	+1.5	+1.5	+1.5
After-tax cash flow	$100	−3.5	−3.5	−3.5	−3.5	−103.5

What is the right discount rate?

Here you are discounting *safe, nominal* cash flows — safe because your company must commit to pay if it takes the loan,[15] and nominal because the payments would be fixed regardless of future inflation. Now, the correct discount rate for safe, nominal cash flows is your company's *after-tax, unsubsidized borrowing rate.*[16] In this case, $r^* = r_D(1 - T_c) = 0.13(1 - 0.3) = 0.091$. Therefore:

$$NPV = +100 - \frac{3.5}{1.091} - \frac{3.5}{(1.091)^2} - \frac{3.5}{(1.091)^3} - \frac{3.5}{(1.091)^4} - \frac{103.5}{(1.091)^5}$$
$$= +21.73, \text{ or } \$21,730$$

The manufacturer has effectively cut the machine's purchase price from $100,000 to ($100,000 − $21,730) = $78,270. You can now go back and recalculate the machine's NPV using this fire-sale price, or you can use the NPV of the subsidized loan as one element of the machine's adjusted present value.

A General Rule   Clearly, we owe an explanation of why $r^* = r_D(1 - T_c)$ for safe, nominal cash flows. It's no surprise that r^* depends on r_D, the unsubsidized borrowing rate, for that is investors' opportunity cost of capital, the rate they would demand from your company's debt. But why should r_D be converted to an *after-tax* figure?

Let's simplify by taking a *1-year* subsidized loan of $100,000 at 5%. The cash flows, in thousands, are:

Period	0	1
Cash flow	$100	−105
Tax shield		+1.5
After-tax cash flow	$100	−103.5

---

[15] In theory, "safe" means literally risk-free, like the cash returns on a Treasury bond. In practice, it means that the risk of not paying or receiving a cash flow is small.

[16] In Section 13-1, we calculated the NPV of subsidized financing using the *pretax* borrowing rate. Now you can see that was a mistake. Using the pretax rate implicitly defines the loan in terms of its pretax cash flows, violating a rule promulgated way back in Section 6-1: *Always* estimate cash flows on an after-tax basis.

Now ask, "What is the maximum amount X that could be borrowed for 1 year through regular channels if \$103,500 is set aside to service the loan?" The cash flows of this *equivalent loan* are:

Period	0	1
Cash flow	X	$-(1+r_\mathrm{D})X = -1.13X$
Tax shield		$+T_c r_\mathrm{D} X = 0.039X$
After-tax cash flow		$-[1+r_\mathrm{D}(1-T_c)]X = -1.091X$

In other words, you will need 109.1% of the amount borrowed to pay back principal plus after-tax interest changes. If $1.091X = 103,500$, $X = 94,867$. Now if you can borrow \$100,000 by a subsidized loan, but only \$94,867 through normal channels, the difference (\$5,133) is money in the bank. Therefore, it must also be the NPV of this one-period subsidized loan.

When you discount a safe, nominal cash flow at an after-tax borrowing rate, you are implicitly calculating the equivalent loan, the amount you could borrow through normal channels using the cash flow at debt service. Note that:

$$\begin{matrix} \text{Equivalent} \\ \text{loan} \end{matrix} = \text{PV}\left(\begin{matrix} \text{cash flow} \\ \text{available for} \\ \text{debt service} \end{matrix}\right) = \frac{103,500}{1.091} = 94,867$$

In some cases, it may be easier to think of taking the lender's side of the equivalent loan rather than the borrower's. For example, you could ask, "How much would my company have to invest today in order to cover next year's debt service on the subsidized loan?" The answer is \$94,867: if you lend that amount at 13%, you will earn 9.1% after tax, and therefore have 94,867(1.091) = 103,500. By this transaction, you can in effect cancel, or "zero out," the future obligation. If you can borrow \$100,000 and then set aside only \$94,867 to cover all the required debt service, you clearly have \$5,133 to spend as you please. That amount is the NPV of the subsidized loan.

Therefore, regardless of whether it's easier to think of borrowing or lending the correct discount rate for safe, nominal cash flows is an after-tax interest rate.[17]

In some ways, this is an obvious result once you think about it. Companies are free to borrow or lend money. If they *lend,* they receive the after-tax interest rate on their investment; if they *borrow* in the capital market, they pay the after-tax interest rate. Thus, the opportunity cost to companies of investing in debt-equivalent cash flows is the after-tax interest rate. This is the adjusted cost of capital for debt-equivalent cash flows.

---

[17] Borrowing and lending rates should not differ by much if the cash flows are truly safe—that is, if the chance of default is small. Usually your decision will not hinge on the rate used. If it does, ask which offsetting transaction—borrowing or lending—seems most natural and reasonable for the problem at hand. Then use the corresponding interest rate.

Some Further Examples

Here are some further examples of debt-equivalent cash flows:

Payout Fixed by Contract Suppose you sign a maintenance contract with a truck leasing firm, which agrees to keep your leased truck in good working order for the next 2 years in exchange for 24 fixed monthly payments. These payments are debt-equivalent flows.[18]

Depreciation Tax Shields Capital projects are normally valued by discounting the total after-tax cash flows they are expected to generate. Depreciation tax shields contribute to project cash flow, but they are not valued separately; they are just folded into project cash flows along with dozens, or hundreds, of other specific inflows and outflows. The project's opportunity cost of capital reflects the average risk of the resulting aggregate.

However, suppose we ask what depreciation tax shields are worth *by themselves*. For a firm that's sure to pay taxes, depreciation tax shields are a safe, nominal flow. Therefore, they should be discounted at the firm's after-tax borrowing rate.[19]

Suppose we buy an asset for $200,000 and sell it 6 years later for $60,000. Assume it is in a class by itself with a CCA rate of 30%. From Section 6-2 we know that the resulting capital cost allowance tax shields are:

Period	1	2	3	4	5	6
UCC	$200.0	140.0	98.0	68.6	48.0	
CCA	$60.0	42.0	29.4	20.6	14.4	
Terminal loss (Recapture)						−12.0
Tax shields at $T_c = 30\%$	$18.0	12.6	8.8	6.2	4.3	−3.6

The after-tax discount rate is $r_D(1 - T_c) = 0.13(1 - 0.3) = 0.091$. (We continue to assume a 13% pretax borrowing rate and a 30% marginal tax rate.) The present value of these shields is:

$$PV = \frac{18}{1.091} + \frac{12.6}{(1.091)^2} + \frac{8.8}{(1.091)^3} + \frac{6.2}{(1.091)^4} + \frac{4.3}{(1.091)^5} - \frac{3.6}{(1.019)^6}$$
$$= +38.9 \text{ or } \$38,900$$

*Adjusted Discount Rates for Debt-Equivalent Cash Flows

You may have wondered whether our procedure for valuing debt-equivalent cash flows is consistent with the adjusted-discount-rate approaches presented earlier in this chapter. Yes, they are consistent, as we will now illustrate.

Remember from Section 18-2 that the value of corporate interest tax shields depends on the personal tax rates paid by debt and equity investors. No one

[18] We assume you are locked into the contract. If it can be cancelled without penalty, you may have a valuable option.

[19] The depreciation tax shields are cash inflows, not outflows as for the contractual payout or the subsidized loan. For safe, nominal inflows, the relevant question is, "How much could the firm borrow today if it uses the inflow for debt service?" You could also ask, "How much would the firm have to lend today to generate the same future inflow?"

knows for sure what the relevant personal rates actually are. The polar views are those of Modigliani and Miller (MM) on the one hand, and Miller on the other. MM assume that investors face the same tax rate on debt and equity income, so that only corporate taxes need be considered; in that case, $T^* = T_c$. But Miller argues that debt investors pay higher effective tax rates than equity investors, so much so that any advantage of the corporate interest tax shield is entirely offset, and $T^* = 0$.

Let's look at a very simple numerical example from each viewpoint. Our problem is to value a $1 million payment to be received from a blue-chip company one year hence. After taxes at 36%, the cash inflow is $660,000. The payment is fixed by contract.

Since the contract generates a debt-equivalent flow, the opportunity cost of capital is the rate investors would demand on a 1-year note issued by the blue-chip company, which happens to be 8%. For simplicity, we'll assume this is your company's borrowing rate too. Our valuation rule for debt-equivalent flows is therefore to discount at $r^* = r_D(1 - T_c) = 0.08(1 - 0.36) = 0.051$.

$$PV = \frac{660,000}{1.051} = \$628,000$$

Valuing Debt-Equivalent Cash Flows under MM Assumptions   Now let's see how MM would address this same problem. The opportunity cost of capital is still $r_D = 0.08$, or 8%. With $T^* = T_c$, the MM adjusted-cost-of-captial formula is $r^* = r_D(1 - T_cL)$.

What is L? In Section 19-2, we defined it as a project's "marginal contribution to the firm's debt capacity," expressed as a fraction of project value, which is normally well below one. But the debt capacity of a safe cash flow is 100% of its value, because the firm could "zero out" the cash flow by taking out an equivalent loan with the same after-tax debt service. Thus, we can think of "debt capacity" as the offsetting equivalent loan. Since the equivalent loan has exactly the same present value as the debt-equivalent flow, $L = 1$.

The MM adjusted-cost-of-capital formula for debt-equivalent cash flows therefore boils down to the same after-tax borrowing rate we used to discount the $660,000 inflow:

$$r^* = r(1 - T_cL) = r_D(1 - T_c) = 0.08(1 - 0.36) = 0.051$$

We get the same result from Miles-Ezzell formula. With $r = r_D$ and $L = 1$:

$$r^* = r - Lr_DT_c\left(\frac{1 + r}{1 + r_D}\right)$$

$$= r_D - 1 \times r_DT_c\left(\frac{1 + r_D}{1 + r_D}\right)$$

$$= r_D - r_DT_c = r_D(1 - T_c)$$

Let's also try an APV calculation under MM assumptions. This a two-part calculation. First, the $660,000 inflow is discounted at the opportunity cost of capital, 8%. Second, we add the present value of interest tax shields on debt supported by the project. Since the firm can borrow 100% of the cash flow's value, the tax shield is r_DT_cAPV, and APV is:

$$APV = \frac{660,000}{1.08} = \frac{0.08(0.36)APV}{1.08}$$

Solving for APV, we get $627,900 which, save for a rounding error, is the same answer we obtained by discounting at the after-tax borrowing rate.

Thus, our valuation rule for debt-equivalent flows is a special case of the APV rule once we adopt MM's assumptions about debt and taxes.

Valuing Debt-Equivalent Cash Flows under Miller's Assumptions   But suppose you share Miller's view that there is no tax advantage to debt, so that $T^* = 0$. That would seem to imply that debt-equivalent cash flows should be discounted at the *pretax* borrowing rate. For example, if we set $T^* = 0$ in the MM adjusted-cost-of-capital formula, $r^* = r(1 - T^*L) = r(1 - 0 \times L) = r$, the opportunity cost of capital, which we would normally set at $r = r_D$ for debt-equivalent flows.

However, the reason that $T^* = 0$ in Miller's theory is that debt investors' personal tax rate equals the corporate rate $(T_p = T_c)$, while the effective tax rate on equity income is zero $(T_{pE} = 0)$. (See Section 18-2.) Thus, debt investors demand a higher pretax rate of return on safe investments than equity investors do. For example, if the after-personal-tax return on debt is $0.8(1 - 0.36) = 0.051$ or 5.1%, then investors will also be content with a 5.1% rate of return on a safe, *untaxed* equity investment.

Therefore, equity investors' opportunity cost of capital for a safe cash flow is the *after-tax* interest rate: $r = r_D(1 - T_p) = r_D(1 - T_c)$.

Thus, although $T^* = 0$ in Miller's world, we nevertheless end up discounting debt-equivalent flows at $r_D(1 - T_c)$, because that is the rate the firm's stockholders demand.

19-5   SUMMARY

Investment decisions always have side effects on financing: every dollar spent has to be raised somehow. Sometimes the side effects are irrelevant or at least unimportant. In an ideal world with no taxes, transaction costs, or other market imperfections, only investment decisions would affect firm value. In such a world firms could analyze all investment opportunities as if they were all-equity-financed. Firms would decide which assets to buy and then worry about getting the money to pay for them. No one would worry about where the money might come from, because debt policy, dividend policy, and all other financing choices would have no impact on stockholder's wealth.

The side effects cannot be ignored in practice. Therefore, in this chapter we showed you how they should be taken into account.

The technique is simple. We first calculate the present value of the project as if there are no important side effects. Then we adjust present value to calculate the project's total impact on firm value. The rule is to accept the project if adjusted net present value (APV) is positive:

$$\text{Accept project if APV} = \text{base-case NPV} + \begin{array}{c} \text{present value of} \\ \text{financing side effects} \end{array} > 0$$

The base-case NPV is the project's NPV computed assuming all-equity financing and perfect capital markets. Think of it as the project's value if it were set up as a separate mini-firm. You would compute the mini-firm's value by forecasting its cash flows and discounting at the opportunity cost of capital for the project. The cash flows should be net of the taxes that an all-equity-financed mini-firm would pay.

Financing side effects are evaluated one by one and their present values added to or subtracted from base-case NPV. We looked at several cases:

1. *Issue costs.* If accepting the project forces the firm to issue securities, then the present value of issue costs should be subtracted from base-case NPV.
2. *Interest tax shields.* Debt interest is a tax-deductible expense. Most people believe that interest tax shields contribute to firm value. Thus a project that prompts the firm to borrow more generates additional value. The project's APV is increased by the present value of interest tax shields on debt the project supports.
3. *Special financing.* Sometimes special financing opportunities are tied to project acceptance. For example, the government might offer subsidized financing for socially desirable projects. You simply compute the present value of the financing opportunity and add it to base-case NPV.

Remember not to confuse *contribution to corporate debt capacity* with the immediate source of funds for investment. For example, a firm might, as a matter of convenience, borrow $1 million for a $1 million research program. But the research would be unlikely to contribute $1 million in debt capacity; a large part of the $1 million new debt would be supported by the firm's other assets.

Also remember that *debt capacity* is not meant to imply an absolute limit on how much the firm *can* borrow. The phrase refers to how much it *chooses* to borrow. Normally the firm's optimal debt level increases as its assets expand; that is why we say that a new project contributes to corporate debt capacity.

Calculating APV may require several steps: one step for base-case NPV, and one for each financing side effect. Many firms try to calculate APV in a single calculation. They do so by the following procedure. After-tax cash flows are forecasted in the usual way — that is, as if the project is all-equity-financed. But the discount rate is adjusted to reflect the financing side effects. If the discount rate is adjusted correctly, the result is APV:

$$\begin{array}{c}\text{NPV at adjusted}\\\text{discount rate}\end{array} = \text{APV} = \begin{array}{c}\text{NPV at opportunity}\\\text{cost of capital}\end{array} + \begin{array}{c}\text{present value of}\\\text{financing side effects}\end{array}$$

Unfortunately, there is no formula for adjusting the discount rate that is simple and generally correct. However, there are two useful rules of thumb. The first is the Modigliani-Miller (MM) formula:

$$r^* = r(1 - T^*L)$$

Here r is the opportunity cost of capital and r^* is adjusted cost of capital. The quantity T^* is the net tax saving per dollar of interest paid, and L is the proportional contribution made by the project to corporate borrowing power.

MM's formula is strictly correct only for projects offering level, perpetual cash-flow streams and supporting permanent debt. But the errors from applying it to other types of projects are not serious.

Miles and Ezzell have developed another formula:

$$r^* = r - Lr_D T^* \left(\frac{1 + r}{1 + r_D}\right)$$

Sick has refined the Miles-Ezzell formula to:

$$r^* = r - Lr_f T^* \left(\frac{1 + r}{1 + r_z}\right)$$

where r_f is the rate of return on riskless debt and r_z is the rate of return on riskless equity in the capital asset pricing model. The Miles-Ezzell and Sick formulas assume the firm will adjust its borrowing to follow every fluctuation in future project value. If this assumption is right, these formulas work for projects of any maturity or cash-flow pattern.

The Miles-Ezzell and Sick formulas typically give adjusted discount rates slightly higher than MM's. The truth is probably somewhere in between. However, all three formulas assume that the present value of additional interest tax shields is the *only* side effect of accepting the project.

To apply the MM, Miles-Ezzell, and Sick formulas, you need to know r, the cost of capital for an all-equity-financed project. If you don't know r, you may be able to calculate the adjusted cost of capital using the weighted-average or textbook formula:

$$r^* = r_D(1 - T_c)\frac{D}{V} + r_E\frac{E}{V}$$

Here, r_D and r_E are the expected rates of return demanded by investors in the firm's bonds and stock, respectively. The quantities D and E are the current *market values* of debt and equity, while the quantity V is the total market value of the firm ($V = D + E$).

Unfortunately, this formula only works for projects that are carbon copies of the existing firm—projects with the same business risk that will be financed to maintain the firm's current, market debt ratio.

Remember that all these formulas are rules of thumb. And remember the assumptions underlying them. When you encounter a project that seriously violates these assumptions, you should go back to APV.

FURTHER READING

For a discussion of adjusted present value, see Myers's article and the subsequent comments:

D. Ashton and D. Atkins, "Interactions of Corporate Financing and Investment Decisions—Implications for Capital Budgeting: A Further Comment," *Journal of Finance*, **33**: 1447–1453 (December 1978).

S. Bar-Yosef, "Interactions of Corporate Financing and Investment Decisions—Implications for Capital Budgeting: Comment," *Journal of Finance*, **32**: 211–217 (March 1977), followed by Myers's "Reply."

S.C. Myers, "Interactions of Corporate Financing and Investment Decisions—Implications for Capital Budgeting," *Journal of Finance*, **29** :1–25 (March 1974).

Formulas for the adjusted discount rate are explained in:

J. Miles and R. Ezzell, "The Weighted Average Cost of Capital, Perfect Capital Markets and Project Life: A Clarification," *Journal of Financial and Quantitative Analysis*, **15**: 719–730 (September 1980).

M.H. Miller and F. Modigliani, "Some Estimates of the Cost of Capital to the Electric Utility Industry: 1954–1957," *American Economic Review*, **56**: 333–391 (June 1966).

F. Modigliani and M.H. Miller, "Corporate Income Taxes and the Cost of Capital: A Correction," *American Economic Review*, **53**: 433–443 (June 1963).

For a discussion of adjusted present value, adjusted discount rates, the determination of the effective tax rate T^* and the weighted-average cost of capital, see:

G.A. Sick, "Tax-Adjusted Discount Rates," *Management Science*, **36**: 1432–1450 (December 1990).

There have been dozens of articles on the weighted-average cost of capital and other issues discussed in this chapter. Here are two representative ones:

M.J. Brennan, "A New Look at the Weighted-Average Cost of Capital," *Journal of Business Finance,* **5**: 24–30 (1973).

D.R. Chambers, R.S. Harris, and J.J. Pringle, "Treatment of Financing Mix in Analyzing Investment Opportunities," *Financial Management,* **11**: 24–41 (Summer 1982).

The valuation rule for safe, nominal cash flows is developed in:

R.S. Ruback, "Calculating the Market Value of Risk-Free Cash Flows," *Journal of Financial Economics,* **15**: 323–339 (March 1986).

QUIZ

1. A project costs $1 million with a base-case NPV of exactly zero (NPV = 0). What is the project's APV in the following cases?
   (a) If the firm invests, it has to raise $500,000 by stock issue. Issue costs are 15% of *net* proceeds.
   (b) The firm has ample cash on hand. But if it invests, it will have access to $500,000 of debt financing at a subsidized interest rate. The present value of the subsidy is $175,000.
   (c) If the firm invests, its debt capacity increases by $500,000. The present value of interest tax shields on this debt is $76,000.
   (d) If the firm invests, it issues equity, as in (a), and borrows, as in (c).
2. Consider the APV of the solar heater project, as calculated in Table 19-1. How would the APV change if the net tax shield per dollar of interest is not $T_c = 0.36$, but $T^* = 0.10$?
3. Consider a project lasting one year only. The initial outlay is $1,000 and the expected inflow is $1,200. The opportunity cost of capital is $r = 0.20$. The borrowing rate is $r_D = 0.10$, the net tax shield per dollar of interest is $T^* = 0.20$, and the firm plans to borrow 30% of project value.
   (a) What is the project's base-case NPV?
   (b) What is its APV?
4. Calculate the adjusted cost of capital for the one-period project discussed in Quiz question 3, just above.
   (a) First, use the MM formula.
   (b) Then use the Miles-Ezzell formula.
   (c) Calculate the project's NPV using the discount rates you calculated in (a) and (b). Which gives the right answer? (Compare your answer to Quiz question 3.)
5. Calculate the weighted-average cost of capital for Federated Junkyards, using the following information.

   • Debt: $75,000,000 outstanding, at book value. The debt is trading at 90% of par. The yield to maturity is 16%.
   • Equity: 2,500,000 shares selling at $42 per share. Assume the expected rate of return on Federated's stock is 25%.
   • Taxes: Federated's marginal tax rate is $T_c = 0.23$.
6. Suppose a project has an opportunity cost of capital of $r = 20\%$ if all-equity financed. It will support debt of 40% of its value. Riskless debt earns 8% and riskless equity earns 6%. The project's risky debt will earn 9%. The firm earns effective interest tax shields at a rate of 25%. Calculate the adjusted cost of capital under each of the formulas of MM, Miles-Ezzell, and Sick.

7. The textbook formula seems to imply that debt is "cheaper" than equity — i.e., that a firm with more debt could use a lower discount rate r^*. Does this make sense? Explain briefly.

8. You are considering a 5-year lease of office space for R&D personnel. Once signed, the lease cannot be cancelled. It would commit your firm to six annual $100,000 payments, with the first payment due immediately. What is the present value of the lease if your company's borrowing rate is 9% and its tax rate is 36%. Note: The lease payments would be tax-deductible.

QUESTIONS AND PROBLEMS

1. Consider another perpetual project like the geothermal project in Section 19-2. Its initial investment is $1,000,000 and the expected cash inflow is $85,000 a year in perpetuity. The opportunity cost of capital with all-equity financing is 10%, and the project allows the firm to borrow an additional $400,000 at 7%. Assume the net tax advantage to borrowing is 30 cents per dollar of interest paid ($T^* = 0.30$). What is the project's APV?

2. Suppose the project described in problem 1 is to be undertaken by a university. Funds for the project will be withdrawn from the university's endowment, which is invested in a widely diversified portfolio of stocks and bonds. However, the university can also borrow at 7%.

   Suppose the university treasurer proposes to finance the project by issuing $400,000 of perpetual bonds at 7%, and by selling $600,000 worth of common stocks from the endowment. The expected return on the common stocks is 10%. He therefore proposes to evaluate the project by discounting at a weighted-average cost of capital, calculated as:

$$r^* = r_D \frac{D}{V} + r_E \frac{E}{V}$$

$$= 0.07 \left(\frac{400,000}{1,000,000} \right) + 0.10 \left(\frac{600,000}{1,000,000} \right)$$

$$= 0.088 \text{ or } 8.8\%$$

   What's right or wrong with the treasurer's approach? Should the university invest? Should it borrow?

3. Digital Organics has the opportunity to invest $1 million now ($t = 0$) and expects after-tax returns of $600,000 in $t = 1$ and $700,000 in $t = 2$. The project will last for two years only. The appropriate cost of capital is 12% with all-equity financing, the borrowing rate is 8%, and DO's target debt ratio for a project of this type is 0.3. Assume debt tax shields have a net benefit of 30 cents per dollar of interest paid. Calculate the project's APV using each of the following methods.
   (a) Use the procedure followed in Table 19-1, where debt ratios were assumed fixed in terms of book values.
   (b) Discount project cash flows at an adjusted rate derived from the Miles-Ezzell formula.
   (c) Use an adjusted rate derived from the MM formula.

4. Refer again to Quiz question 3 for this chapter. Suppose the firm borrows 30% of the project's *value*.
   (a) What is the project's APV?
   (b) What is the minimum acceptable rate of return for projects of this type?

(c) Show that your answer to (b) is consistent with the Miles-Ezzell formula.

5. List the assumptions underlying the MM adjusted-discount-rate formula. Derive the formula algebraically for a perpetual project. Then try to derive it for a one-period project like the one described in Quiz question 3. Keep MM's other assumptions intact. *Hint:* You will end up with the Miles-Ezzell formula. In other words, their formula works for one-period projects; MM's does not.

6. The Bunsen Chemical Company is currently at its target debt ratio of 40%. It is contemplating a $1 million expansion of its existing business. This expansion is expected to produce a cash inflow of $130,000 a year in perpetuity.

   The company is uncertain whether to undertake this expansion and how to finance it. The two options are a $1 million issue of common stock or a $1 million issue of 20-year debt. The flotation costs of a stock issue would be around 5% of the amount raised and the flotation costs of a debt issue would be around 1½%.

   Bunsen's financial manager, Ms. Polly Ethylene, estimates that the required return on the company's equity is 14%, but she argues that the flotation costs increase the cost of new equity to 19%. On this basis, the project does not appear viable.

   On the other hand, she points out that the company can raise new debt on a 7% yield that would make the cost of new debt 8½%. She therefore recommends that Bunsen should go ahead with the project and finance it with an issue of long-term debt.

   Is Ms. Ethylene right? How would you evaluate the project?

7. Can you explain why we use the marginal corporate tax rate (T_c) in the textbook formula, but the *net* tax shield per dollar of interest (T^*) in the MM, Miles-Ezzell, and Sick formulas?

8. Suppose you wanted to figure out the *opportunity* cost of capital (r) for the United States railroad industry in mid-1974. You have an estimate of r^*, the adjusted discount rate: 10¾% as reported in Section 19-3. *Hint*: We presented three formulas linking r and r^*, but one of them can't be used since it also requires knowledge of the riskless rates of return on debt and equity, and these we don't have.

9. Suppose the firm issues not just debt and equity, but preferred stock also. How would this change the weighted-average cost of capital formula? How would it change the MM, Miles-Ezzell, and Sick formulas?

10. Consider a different financing scenario for the solar water heater project discussed in Section 19-1. The project requires $10 million and has a base-case NPV of $170,000. Suppose the firm happens to have $5 million in the bank which could be used for the project.

    The government, eager to encourage solar energy, offers to help finance the project by lending $5 million at a subsidized rate of 5%. The loan calls for the firm to pay the government $647,500 annually for 10 years (this amount includes both principal and interest).

    (a) What is the value of being able to borrow from the government at 5%? Assume the company's normal borrowing rate is 8% and the corporate tax rate is 36%.

    (b) Suppose the company's normal debt policy is to borrow 50% of the book value of its assets. It calculates the present value of interest tax shields by the procedure shown in Table 19-1 and includes this present value in APV. Should it do so here, given the government's offer of cheap financing?

(c) Suppose instead that the firm normally borrows 30% of the *market* value of its assets. Does this change your answer to part (b)? *Hint:* The Miles-Ezzell formula can be used to calculate project APV in this case; that formula does not capture the value of the subsidized loan, however.

11. Suppose a firm's effective tax shield on interest $T^* = 25\%$, the rate of return on riskless equity is $r_z = 6\%$, the rate of return on riskless debt $r_f = 8\%$, and the opportunity cost of capital $r = 12\%$. The firm maintains a target debt ratio $L = 40\%$. Calculate the adjusted cost of capital using the MM, Miles-Ezzell, and Sick formulas under both of the following scenarios:

    (a) $r_D = 8\%$

    (b) $r_D = 10\%$.

P·A·R·T

6

OPTIONS

C · H · A · P · T · E · R

20

CORPORATE LIABILITIES
AND THE VALUATION
OF OPTIONS

The Chicago Board Options Exchange (CBOE) was founded in 1973. It was an almost instant success. Within 5 years investors were trading options to buy or sell more than 10 million shares daily.

Option trading now takes place on a number of exchanges around the world. In addition to options on individual common stocks, there are also options on stock indexes, bonds, commodities, and foreign exchange. A list of the principal traded options is given in Table 20-1.

Option trading is a specialized business and its devotees speak a language of their own. They talk of calls, puts, straddles, butterflies, deep-in-the-money options, and naked options. We will not tell you the meaning of *all* these terms but by the time you have finished this chapter you should know the principal kinds of options and how to value them.

Why should a financial manager of an industrial company be interested in such matters? Because managers routinely use currency, commodity, and interest rate options, and they also come up against a variety of corporate investment and financing problems which have options embedded in them.

Many capital investment proposals include an option to buy additional equipment at some future date. For instance, the company may invest in a patent that allows it to exploit a new technology or it may purchase adjoining land that gives it an opportunity to expand. In each case the company is paying money today for the opportunity to make a further investment. To put it another way, it is acquiring *growth opportunities*. We discussed these options in Chapter 4, and in Chapter 10 we showed how you can use decision trees to analyze Magna Charter's options to expand a project or abandon it. We return to Magna Charter in the next chapter, when we show you how to calculate the value of the abandonment option using option pricing theory.

Here is another disguised option. You are considering the purchase of a tract of desert land that is known to contain gold deposits. Unfortunately, the cost of extraction is higher than the current price of gold. Does that mean the land is almost worthless? Not at all. You are not obliged to mine the gold, but ownership

Table 20-1
Some options and the exchanges on which they are traded

Canadian and U.S. common stocks   AMEX, CBOE, NYSE, PSE, PhilSE, TCO
Canadian and U.S. stock market indexes   AMEX, CBOE, IMM,[f] NASDAQ, NYFE,[f]
                                           NYSE, PSE, PhilSE, TCO

Canadian and U.S. Treasury bonds and notes   CBT,[f] TCO[f]
Eurodollar deposits   IMM,[f] LIFFE[f]

Australian dollars   SFE,[f] IMM[f]
Canadian dollars   IMM,[f] PhilSE, PhilSE*
Deutsche marks   CBOE,* IMM,[f] EOE, LSE, ME, PhilSE
Dutch florin   EOE
ECU (European currency unit)   EOE
French franc   CBOE,* PhilSE
Pound sterling   CBOE,* IMM,[f] EOE, LIFFE, LSE, ME, PhilSE
Swiss franc   CBOE,* IMM,[f] ME, PhilSE
Yen   CBOE,* IMM,[f] PhilSE

Gold   COMEX,[f] EOE, MCE,[f] PhilSE
Silver   CBT,[f] COMEX,[f] EOE
Gold and silver index   PhilSE

Cattle   CME[f]
Corn   CBT[f]
Cotton   NYCE[f]
Crude Oil   NYM[f]
Hogs   CME[f]
Lumber   CME[f]
Soybeans   CBT,[f] MCE[f]
Sugar   CSCE[f]
Wheat   KC,[f] MCE,[f] MPLS[f]

Key:
AMEX   American Stock Exchange
CBOE   Chicago Board Options Exchange
CBT   Chicago Board of Trade
CME   Chicago Mercantile Exchange
COMEX   Commodity Exchange, New York
CSCE   Coffee, Sugar, and Cocoa Exchange, New York
EOE   European Options Exchange
IMM   International Monetary Market (at CME)
KC   Kansas City Board of Trade
LIFFE   London International Financial Futures Exchange
LSE   London Stock Exchange
MCE   MidAmerica Commodity Exchange
MPLS   Minneapolis Grain Exchange
ME   Montreal Exchange
NASDAQ   National Association of Securities Dealers Automated Quotations
NYCE   New York Cotton Exchange
NYFE   New York Futures Exchange
NYM   New York Mercantile Exchange
NYSE   New York Stock Exchange
PSE   Pacific Stock Exchange
PhilSE   Philadelphia Stock Exchange
SFE   Sydney Futures Exchange
TCO   Trans Canada Options (Montreal, Toronto and Vancouver)
TFE   Toronto Futures Exchange
VSE   Vancouver Stock Exchange

[f] denotes option on a future

* European option

Note: futures are orders to buy an asset at a future date. They are described in Chapter 25.

of the land gives you the option to do so. Of course, if you know that the gold price will remain below the extraction cost, then the option is worthless. But if there is uncertainty about future gold prices, you could be lucky and make a killing.[1]

In Chapters 14 and 15 we discussed a variety of options associated with new financing. For example:

1. Warrants and convertible securities give their holders an option to exchange their securities for common stock.
2. A call option on a bond gives the company the right to repurchase the bond before maturity.

In fact, whenever a company borrows it creates an option. The reason is that the borrower is not *compelled* to repay the debt at maturity. If the value of the company's assets is less than the amount of the debt, the company will choose to default on the payment and the bondholders will get to keep the company's assets. Thus, when the firm borrows, the lender effectively acquires the company and the shareholders obtain the option to buy it back by paying off the debt. This is an extremely important insight. It means that anything that we can learn about traded call options applies equally to corporate liabilities.[2]

Our primary goal in this chapter is to tell you how options work and how they are valued. We are asking you to invest to acquire several important ideas. The return to this investment comes primarily in later chapters, where these concepts are applied to a variety of corporate financial problems.

20-1   CALLS, PUTS, AND SHARES

In Chapter 13 we met Louis Bachelier, who in 1900 first suggested that security prices follow a random walk. Bachelier also devised a very convenient shorthand to illustrate the effects of investing in options.[3] Let us use this shorthand to compare three possible investments—buying a call option, buying a put option, and buying the share itself.

A **call option** gives its owner the right to buy stock at a specified **exercise** or **striking** price. In some cases, the option can be exercised only on one particular day, called the **exercise date**, and it is then conventionally known as a **European** call; in other cases, it can be exercised on or before that day and it is then known as an **American** call. We shall initially concentrate on the conceptually simpler European option, but almost all our remarks apply equally well to its American cousin.

The **position diagram** in Figure 20-1(a) shows the possible values just before expiration of a call option that is exercisable at $100. If the share price at that time turns out to be less than this figure, nobody will pay $100 to obtain the share via the call option. Our call option will in that case be valueless and we will throw it away. On the other hand, if the share price turns out to be greater

---

[1] In Chapter 11 we valued King Solomon's gold mine by calculating the value of the gold in the ground and then subtracting the value of the extraction costs. That is strictly correct only if we *know* that the gold will be mined. Otherwise, the value of the mine is increased by the value of the option to leave the gold in the ground if its price is less than the extraction cost.

[2] This relationship was first recognized by Fischer Black and Myron Scholes, in "The Pricing of Options and Corporate Liabilities," *Journal of Political Economy,* **81**: 637–654 (May–June 1973).

[3] L. Bachelier, *Théorie de la Speculation*, Gauthier-Villars, Paris, 1900. Reprinted in English in P.H. Cootner (ed.), *The Random Character of Stock Market Prices*, M.I.T. Press, Cambridge, Mass., 1964.

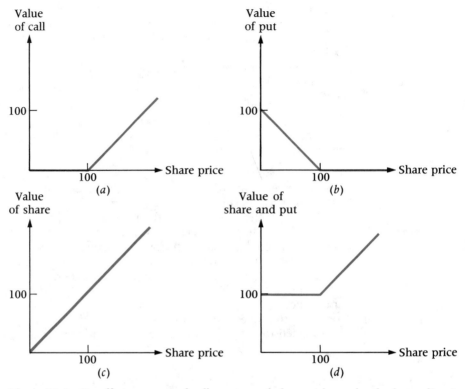

Figure 20-1 Payoffs to owners of calls, puts, and shares (shown by the heavy lines) depend on the share price. (*a*) Result of buying call exercisable at $100. (*b*) Result of buying put exercisable at $100. (*c*) Result of buying share. (*d*) Result of buying share *and* put option exercisable at $100; this is equivalent to owning a call and having $100 in the bank.

than $100, it will pay us to exercise our option to buy the share. In this case the option will be worth the market price of the share minus the $100 that we must pay to acquire it.

Now let us look at a European **put option** with the same exercise price. Whereas the call gives us the right to *buy* a share for $100, the comparable put gives us the right to *sell* it for $100. Therefore, the circumstances in which the put will be valuable are just the opposite of those in which the call will be valuable. We can see this from the position diagram in Figure 20-1(*b*). If the share price immediately before expiration turns out to be *greater* than $100, nobody will want to sell the share at that price. Our put option will be worthless. Conversely, if the share price turns out to be *less* than $100, it will pay to buy the share and then take advantage of the option to sell it for $100. In this case, the value of the put option at expiration is the difference between the $100 proceeds of the sale and the market price of the share. For example, if the share is worth $60, the put is worth $40:

$$\begin{aligned} \text{Value of put option at expiration} &= \text{exercise price} - \text{market price of the share} \\ &= \$100 - \$60 \\ &= \$40 \end{aligned}$$

Our third investment consists of the share itself. Figure 20-1(*c*) betrays few secrets when it shows that the value of this investment is always exactly equal to the market value of the share.

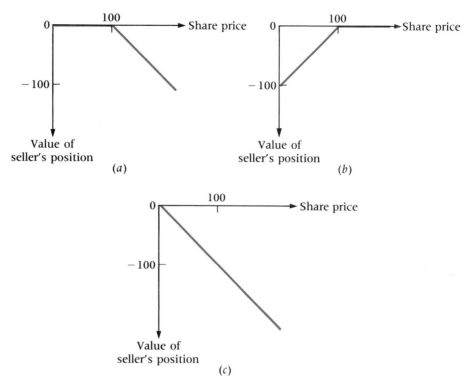

Figure 20-2   Payoffs to sellers of calls, puts, and shares (shown by the heavy lines) depend on the share price. (*a*) Result of selling call exercisable at $100. (*b*) Result of selling put exercisable at $100. (*c*) Result of selling share short.

Selling Calls, Puts, and Shares
Let us now look at the position of an investor who *sells* these investments. The individual who sells, or "writes," a call promises to deliver shares if asked to do so by the call buyer. In other words, the buyer's asset is the seller's liability. If at expiration the share price is below the exercise price, the buyer will not exercise the call and the seller's liability will be zero. If it rises above the exercise price, the buyer will exercise and the seller will give up the shares. The seller loses the difference between the share price and the exercise price received from the buyer.

Suppose that the exercise price is $100 and the stock price turns out to be $150. The call option will be exercised. The seller is forced to sell stock worth $150 for only $100 and therefore loses $50. Of course the buyer gains $50.

In general, the seller's loss is the buyer's gain, and vice versa. Figure 20-2(*a*) shows the payoffs to the seller. Note that Figure 20-2(*a*) is just Figure 20-1(*a*) drawn upside down.

In just the same way we can depict the position of an investor who sells, or "writes," a put by standing Figure 20-1(*b*) on its head. The seller of the put has agreed to pay $100 for the share if the put buyer should request it. Clearly the seller will be safe as long as the share price remains above $100 but will lose money if the share price falls below this figure. The worst thing that can happen is for the stock to be worthless. The seller would then be obliged to pay $100 for a stock worth $0. The "value" of the option position would be −$100.

Finally, Figure 20-2(*c*) shows the position of someone who sells the stock short. Short sellers sell stock which they do not yet own. As they say on Wall Street:

He who sells what isn't his'n
Buys it back or goes to prison.

Eventually, therefore, the short seller will have to buy the stock back. The short seller will make a profit if it has fallen in price and a loss if it has risen.[4] You can see that Figure 20-2(c) is simply an upside-down Figure 20-1(c).

20-2   HOLDING CALLS, PUTS, AND SHARES IN COMBINATION

We now return to the option buyer and see what happens when we add two investments together. Suppose, for example, that our portfolio contains *both* the share and an option to sell (put) it for $100. We can read off the value of each of these holdings from panels (b) and (c) in Figure 20-1. Notice that if the share price rises above $100, the put option will be worthless and the value of our portfolio will be equal to the share price. Conversely, if the share price falls below $100, the decline in the value of the share will be exactly offset by the rise in that of the put. In Figure 20-1(d) we have plotted the total value of these two holdings.

This diagram tells us something about the relationship between a call option and a put option. We can see why if we compare it with Figure 20-1(a). Regardless of the share price, the final value of our combined investment in the share and the put is exactly $100 greater than that of a simple investment in the call. In other words, if you (1) buy the call and (2) put aside enough money to pay the $100 exercise price on the expiration date, you have the same investment as someone who buys the share and also an option to sell it for $100. At the expiration date both strategies give the investor the choice between $100 cash or owning the share. Since the two packages give *identical* payoffs, they should at all times sell for the same price. This gives us a fundamental relationship for European options:

Value of call + present value of exercise price = value of put + share price

To repeat, this relationship holds because the payoff of

[Buy call, invest present value of exercise price in safe asset[5]]

is identical to the payoff of

[Buy put, buy share]

Here is a slightly different example. Suppose that you want to invest in a particular stock but you have no cash on hand. However, you know you will receive $100 3 months hence. Therefore, you borrow the present value of $100 from your bank and invest that amount in the stock. We assume that is enough to buy one share. At the end of 3 months your payoff is the share price less the $100 owed the bank. Now compare this with an alternative strategy to *buy* a 3-month call option with an exercise price of $100 and to *sell* a 3-month put option with an exercise price of $100. The final value of such a package would be equal to the sum of Figure 20-1(a) and (b). Figure 20-3 shows that this sum is always equal to the market price of the share less $100. It is not difficult to see why. If the share price rises, we would exercise our call and pay $100 to obtain the share; if it goes down, the other person would exercise it and sell us a share for $100.

---

[4] Selling short is not as simple as we have described it. For example, a short seller usually has to put up margin, that is, deposit cash or securities with the broker. This assures the broker that the short seller will be able to repurchase the stock when the time comes to do so.

[5] This present value is calculated at the *risk-free rate of interest*. It is the amount you would have to invest today in Treasury bills to realize the exercise price on the option's expiration date.

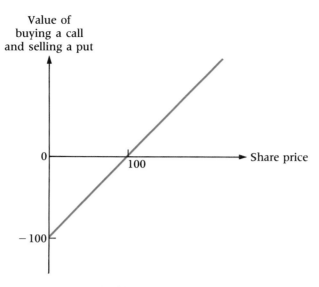

Figure 20-3 Result of buying a call *and* selling a put, each exercisable at $100. Whatever happens to the share price, you end up paying $100 and acquiring the share at the expiration date of the option. You could achieve the same outcome by buying the share and borrowing the present value of $100, to be repaid on the expiration date.

In either case, we would pay $100 and acquire the share. Since our two investment strategies have exactly the same consequences, they should have exactly the same value. In other words, we have the following rearrangement of our earlier equation:

Value of call − value of put = share price − present value of exercise price

which holds because　　　　　　[Buy call, sell put]

is identical to　　　　　　[Buy share, borrow present value of exercise price[6]]

Of course there are many ways to express the basic relationship between share price, call and put values, and the present value of the exercise price. Each expression implies two investment strategies that give identical results.

One more example. Solve the basic relationship for the value of a put:

Value of put = value of call − value of share + present value of exercise price

From this expression you can deduce that　　　[Buy put]

is identical to　　　　[Buy call, sell share, invest present value of exercise price]

In other words, if puts were not available you could create them by buying shares, selling calls, and borrowing.

Maneuvers such as these are called **option conversions**. Calls can be converted into puts, or vice versa, by taking the appropriate position in the share and borrowing or lending. As a result, we do not need calls, puts, shares, *and* borrowing or lending in this world (and we hope not in the next). Given any three of these investment opportunities we can always construct the fourth.

---

[6] Again, present value is computed at the risk-free rate of interest. In other words, the comparison assumes that you are certain to pay off the loan.

In Chapter 18 we discussed the plight of Circular File Company, which borrowed $50 per share. Unfortunately, the firm fell on hard times and the market value of its assets fell to $30. Circular's bond and stock prices fell to $25 and $5, respectively. Circular's *market* value balance sheet is now:

Circular File Company (market values)			
Asset value	$30	$25	Bonds
		5	Stock
	$30	$30	Firm value

If Circular's debt were due and payable now, the firm could not repay the $50 it originally borrowed. It would default, bondholders receiving assets worth $30 and shareholders receiving nothing. The reason Circular stock is worth $5 is that the debt is *not* due now but rather is due a year from now. A stroke of good fortune could increase firm value enough to pay off the bondholders in full, with something left over for the stockholders.

Let us go back to a statement that we made at the start of the chapter. Whenever a firm borrows, the lender effectively acquires the company and the shareholders obtain the option to buy it back by paying off the debt. The stockholders have, in effect, purchased a call option on the assets of the firm. The bondholders have sold them this call option. Thus, the balance sheet of Circular File can be expressed as follows:

Circular File Company (market values)			
Asset value	$30	$25	Bond value = asset value − value of call
		5	Stock value = value of call
	$30	$30	Firm value = asset value

If this still sounds like a strange idea to you, try drawing one of M. Bachelier's position diagrams for Circular File. It should look like Figure 20-4. If the future value of the assets is less than $50, Circular will default and the stock will be worthless. If the value of the assets exceeds $50, the stockholders will receive asset value *less* the $50 paid over to the bondholders. The payoffs in Figure 20-4 are identical to a call option on the firm's assets, with an exercise price of $50.

Now look again at the basic relationship between calls and puts:

Value of call + present value of exercise price = value of put + value of share

To apply this to Circular File, we have to interpret "value of share" as "asset value," because the common stock is a call option on the firm's assets. Also, "present value of exercise price" is the present value of receiving the promised payment of $50 to bondholders *for sure* next year. Thus:

Value of call + present value of promised payment to bondholders
= value of put + asset value

Now we can solve for the value of Circular bonds. This is equal to the firm's asset value less the value of the shareholders' call option on these assets:

Bond value = asset value − value of call
= present value of promised payment to bondholders − value of put

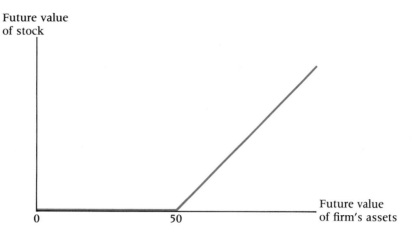

Figure 20-4   The value of Circular's common stock is the same as the value of a call option on the firm's assets with an exercise price of $50.

Circular's bondholders have in effect (1) bought a safe bond, and (2) given the shareholders the option to sell them the firm's assets for the amount of the debt. You can think of the bondholders as receiving the $50 promised payment but they have given the shareholders the option to take the $50 back in exchange for the assets of the company. If firm value turns out to be less than the $50 that is promised to bondholders, the shareholders will exercise their put option.

Circular's risky bond is equal to a safe bond less the value of the shareholders' option to default. To value this risky bond we need to value a safe bond and then subtract the value of the default option. The default option is equal to a put option on the firm's assets.

In the case of Circular File the option to default is extremely valuable because default is likely to occur. At the other extreme, the value of Bell Canada Enterprise's option to default is trivial compared to the value of BCE's assets. Default on BCE bonds is possible but extremely unlikely. Option traders would say that for Circular File the put option is "deep in the money" because today's asset value ($30) is well below the exercise price ($50). For BCE the put option is well "out of the money" because the value of BCE's assets substantially exceeds the value of BCE debt.

We know that Circular's stock is equivalent to a call option on the firm's assets. It is also equal to (1) owning the firm's assets, (2) borrowing the present value of $50 with the obligation to repay regardless of what happens, but also (3) buying a put on the firm's assets with an exercise price of $50.

We can sum up by presenting Circular's balance sheet in terms of asset value, put value, and the present value of a sure $50 payment:

Circular File Company (market values)

Asset value	$30	$25	Bond value = present value of promised payment − value of put
		5	Stock value = asset value − present value of promised payment + value of put
	$30	$30	Firm value = asset value

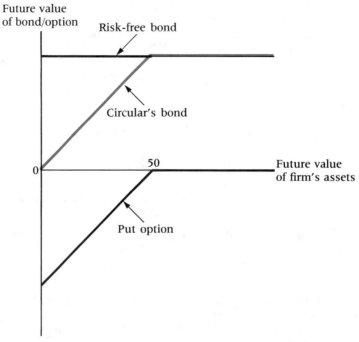

Figure 20-5   You can also think of Circular's bond (the coloured line) as equivalent to a risk-free bond (the upper black line) *less* a put option on the firm's assets with an exercise price of $50 (the lower black line).

Again you can check this with a position diagram. The coloured line in Figure 20-5 shows the payoffs to Circular's bondholders. If the firm's assets are worth more than $50, the bondholders are paid off in full; if the assets are worth less than $50, the firm defaults and the bondholders receive the value of the assets. You could get an identical payoff pattern by buying a safe bond (the upper black line) and selling a put option on the firm's assets (the lower black line).

*Spotting the Option

Options rarely come with a large label attached. Often the trickiest part of the problem is to identify the option. For example, we suspect that until it was pointed out, you did not realize that every risky bond contains a hidden option.

When you are not sure whether you are dealing with a put or a call or a complicated blend of the two, it is a good precaution to draw a position diagram. Here is an example.

The Flatiron and Mangle Corporation has offered its president Ms. Higden the following incentive scheme. If at the end of the year the price of the stock has risen by a minimum of 20% from its present level of $100, Ms. Higden will receive $100,000. Otherwise she will receive nothing.

You can think of Ms. Higden as owning 100,000 tickets each of which pays $1 if the stock price exceeds $120. Figure 20-6 shows the payoffs from just one of these tickets. The payoffs are not the same as those of the simple put and call options that we drew in Figure 20-1, but it is possible to find a combination of options that almost exactly replicates Figure 20-6. Before going on to read the answer, see if you can spot it yourself (if you are someone who enjoys puzzles of the 'make-a-triangle-from-just-two-matchsticks' type, this one should be a walkover).

The answer is in Figure 20-7. The solid black line represents the purchase of a call option with an exercise price of 119.5 and the dotted line the sale of another

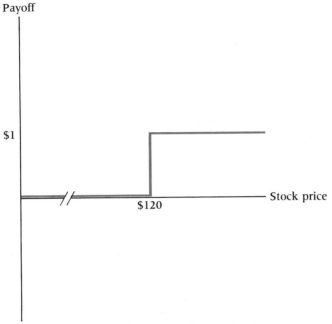

Figure 20-6   The payoff from one of Ms. Hidgen's "tickets" depends on Flatiron's stock price.

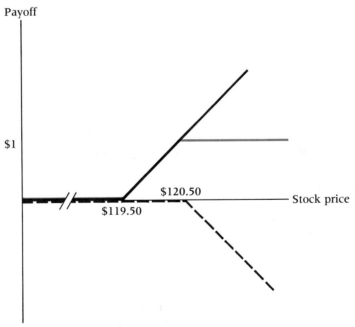

Figure 20-7   The solid black line shows the payoff from buying a call with an exercise price of 119.5. The dotted black line shows the *sale* of a call with an exercise price of 120.5. The combined purchase and sale (shown by the coloured line) closely resembles one of Ms. Higden's "tickets."

call option with an exercise price of 120.5. The coloured line shows the payoff from a combination of the purchase and the sale—almost identical to the payoff from each of Ms. Higden's tickets.

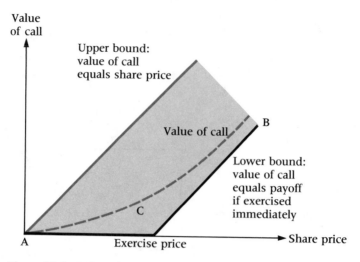

Figure 20-8 Value of a call before its expiration date (dashed line). The value depends on the stock price. It is always worth more than its value if exercised now (heavy line). It is never worth more than the stock price itself.

Thus, if we wish to know how much the incentive scheme is costing the company we need to calculate the difference between the value of 100,000 call options with an exercise price of 119.5 and the value of 100,000 calls with an exercise price of 120.5.[7]

We could have made the incentive scheme depend in a much more complicated way on the stock price. For example, it could pay $100,000 if the stock price is between $120 and $140 and nothing in any other circumstances. (Don't ask why anyone would want to offer such an arrangement—perhaps there's some tax angle.) You could still have represented this scheme as a combination of options. In fact, we can state a general theorem:

> Any set of contingent payoffs—that is, payoffs which depend on the value of some other asset—can be valued as a mixture of simple options on that asset.

For instance, if you needed to value a capital project that would pay off $2 million if the price of copper was less than $1,500 but only $1 million if the price was greater than $1,500, you could use option theory to do so.

20-3   WHAT DETERMINES OPTION VALUES?

So far we have said nothing about how the market value of options is determined. We do know what an option is worth when it matures, however. Consider, for example, our earlier case of an option to buy stock at $100. If the stock price is below $100 at the expiration date, the call will be worthless; if the stock price is above $100, the call will be worth $100 less than the value of the stock. In terms of Bachelier's position diagram, the relationship is depicted by the heavy line in Figure 20-8.

Even before maturity the price of the option can never remain *below* the heavy line in Figure 20-8. For example, if our option were priced at $50 and the stock at $200, it would pay any investor to buy the option, exercise it for an additional

---

[7] The fact that Figure 20-7 is not quite identical to Figure 20-6 means that the value is not exact, but we can make the approximation as close as we choose. For example, for greater accuracy we could calculate the difference between the value of 1 million calls with an exercise price of 119.95 and 1 million calls with an exercise price of 120.05.

$100, and then sell the stock. That would give a money machine with a profit of $50. The demand for options from investors using the money machine would quickly force the option price up at least to the heavy line in the figure. For options that still have some time to run, the heavy line is therefore a *lower* limit on the market price of the option.

The diagonal line in Figure 20-8 is the *upper* limit to the option price. Why? Because the stock gives a higher ultimate payoff, whatever happens. If at the option's expiration the stock price ends up above the exercise price, the option is worth the stock price *less* the exercise price. If the stock price ends up below the exercise price, the option is worthless, but the stock's owner still has a valuable security. Let P be the stock price at the option's expiration date, and assume the option's exercise price is $100. Then the extra dollar returns realized by stockholders are:

	Stock Payoff	Option Payoff	Extra Payoff from Holding Stock Instead of Option
Option exercised (P greater than $100)	P	$P - 100$	$100
Option expires unexercised (P less than or equal to $100)	P	0	P

If the stock and the option have the same price, everyone will rush to sell the option and buy the stock. Therefore, the option price must be somewhere in the shaded region of Figure 20-8. In fact, it will lie on a curved, upward-sloping line like the dashed curve shown in the figure. This line begins its travels where the upper and lower bounds meet (at zero). Then it rises, gradually becoming parallel to the upward-sloping part of the lower bound. This line tells us an important fact about option values: *the value of an option increases as stock price increases*, if the exercise price is held constant.

That should be no surprise. Owners of call options clearly hope for the stock price to rise, and are happy when it does. But let us look more carefully at the shape and location of the dashed line. Three points, *A*, *B*, and *C*, are marked on the dashed line. As we explain each point you will see why the option price has to behave as the dashed line predicts.

Point *A*: *When the stock is worthless, the option is worthless.* A stock price of zero means that there is no possibility the stock will ever have any future value.[8] If so, the option is sure to expire unexercised and worthless, and it is worthless today.

Point *B*: *When the stock price becomes large, the option price approaches the stock price less the present value of the exercise price.* Notice that the dashed line representing the option price in Figure 20-8 eventually becomes parallel to the ascending heavy line representing the lower bound on the option price. The reason is as follows: the higher the stock price, the higher the probability that the option will eventually be exercised. If the stock price is high enough, exercise becomes a virtual certainty; the probability that the stock price will fall below the exercise price before the option expires becomes trivially small.

---

[8] If a stock *can* be worth something in the future, then investors will pay *something* for it today, although possibly a very small amount.

If you own an option which you *know* will be exchanged for a share of stock, you effectively own the stock now. The only difference is that you don't have to pay for the stock (by handing over the exercise price) until later, when formal exercise occurs. In these circumstances, buying the call is equivalent to buying the stock but financing part of the purchase by borrowing. The amount implicitly borrowed is the present value of the exercise price. The value of the call is therefore equal to the stock price less the present value of the exercise price.

This brings us to another important point about options. Investors who acquire stock by way of a call option are buying on installment credit. They pay the purchase price of the option today, but they do not pay the exercise price until they actually take up the option. The delay in payment is particularly valuable if interest rates are high and the option has a long maturity. With an interest rate r_f and the time to maturity t, then we would expect the value of the option to depend on the *product*[9] of r_f and t: *the value of an option increases with both the rate of interest and the time to maturity.*

Point C: *The option price always exceeds its minimum value* (except when stock price is zero). We have seen that the dashed and heavy lines in Figure 20-8 coincide when stock price is zero (point *A*), but elsewhere the lines diverge; that is, the option price must exceed the minimum value given by the heavy line. The reason for this can be understood by examining point *C*.

At point *C*, the stock price exactly equals the exercise price. The option is therefore worthless if exercised today. However, suppose that the option will not expire until 3 months hence. Of course we do not know what the stock price will be at the expiration date. There is roughly a 50% chance that it will be higher than the exercise price, and a 50% chance that it will be lower. The possible payoffs to the option are therefore:

Outcome	Payoff
Stock price rises (50% probability)	Stock price less exercise price (option is exercised)
Stock price falls (50% probability)	Zero (option expires worthless)

If there is a positive probability of a positive payoff, and if the worst payoff is zero, then the option must be valuable. That means the option price at point *C* exceeds its lower bound, which at point *C* is zero. In general, the option prices will exceed their lower-bound values as long as there is time left before expiration.

One of the most important determinants of the *height* of the dashed curve (i.e., of the difference between actual and lower-bound value) is the likelihood of substantial movements in the stock price. An option on a stock whose price is unlikely to change by more than 1 or 2% is not worth much; an option on a stock whose price may halve or double is very valuable.

Panels (*a*) and (*b*) in Figure 20-9 illustrate this point. The panels compare the payoffs at expiration of two options with the same exercise price and the same stock price. The panels assume that stock price equals exercise price (like point *C* in Figure 20-8), although this is not a necessary assumption. The only difference is that the price of stock Y at its option's expiration date (Figure 20-9(*b*)) is much harder to predict than the price of stock X at its option's expiration date. You can see this from the probability distributions superimposed on the figures.

---

[9] Using continuous compounding, the present value of the exercise price is (exercise price $\times e^{-r_f t}$). The discount factor $e^{-r_f t}$ depends on the product of r_f and t.

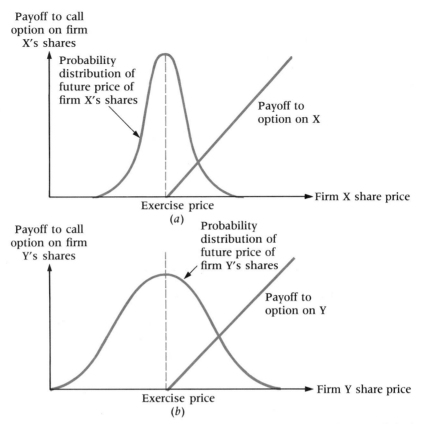

Figure 20-9 Call options are written against the shares of (*a*) firm X and (*b*) firm Y. In each case, the current share price equals the exercise price, so that each option has a 50% chance of ending up worthless (if the share price falls) and a 50% chance of ending up "in the money" (if the share price rises). However, the chance of a *large* payoff is *greater* for the option on firm Y's share, because Y's stock price is more volatile and therefore has more "upside potential."

In both cases there is roughly a 50% chance that the stock price will decline and make the options worthless, but if the prices of stocks X and Y rise, the odds are that Y will rise more than X. Thus, there is a larger chance of a big payoff from the option on Y. Since the chance of a zero payoff is the same, the option on Y is worth more than the option on X. Figure 20-10 illustrates this: the higher curved line belongs to the option on Y.

The probability of large stock price changes during the remaining life of an option depends on two things: (1) the variance (i.e., volatility) of the stock price *per period* and (2) the number of periods until the option expires. If there are t remaining periods, and the variance per period is σ^2, the value of the option should depend on cumulative variability $\sigma^2 t$.[10] Other things equal, you would like to hold an option on a volatile stock (high σ^2). Given volatility, you would like to hold an option with a long life ahead of it (large t). Thus, the value of an option increases *with both the variability of the share and the time to maturity*.

---

[10] Here is an intuitive explanation. If the stock price follows a random walk (see Section 13-2), successive price changes are statistically independent. The cumulative price change before expiration is the sum of t random variables. The variance of a sum of independent random variables is the sum of the variances of those variables. Thus, if σ^2 is the variance of the daily price change, and there are t days until expiration, the variance of the cumulative price change is $\sigma^2 t$.

Figure 20-10 Values of calls on shares of firm X and shares of firm Y. The call on Y's shares is worth more because Y's shares are more volatile (see Figure 20-9). The higher curved line describes the value of a call on Y's shares; the lower curved line describes the value of a call on X's shares.

It's a rare person who can keep all these properties straight at first reading. Therefore, we have summed them up in Table 20-2.

20-4 AN OPTION-VALUATION MODEL

We would now like to replace the qualitative statements of Table 20-2 with an exact option-valuation model—a formula we can plug numbers into and get a definite answer. The search for that formula went on for years before Fischer Black and Myron Scholes finally found it. Before we show you what they found, we should say a few words to explain why the search was so difficult.

Why Discounted Cash Flow Won't Work for Options

Our standard operating procedure of (1) forecasting expected cash flow and (2) discounting at the opportunity cost of capital is not helpful for options. The first step is messy but feasible. Finding *the* opportunity cost of capital is impossible, because the risk of an option changes every time the stock price moves,[11] and we know it *will* move along a random walk through the option's lifetime.

When you buy a call you are *taking a position* in the stock but putting up less of your own money than if you had bought the stock directly. Thus, an option is always riskier than the underlying stock. It has a higher beta and a higher standard deviation of return.

How much riskier the option is depends on the stock price relative to the exercise price. An option that is in the money (stock price greater than exercise price) is safer than one that is out of the money (stock price less than exercise price). Thus, a stock price increase raises the option's price *and* reduces its risk. When the stock price falls, the option's price falls *and* its risk increases. That is why the expected rate of return investors demand from an option changes day by day, or hour by hour, every time the stock price moves.

We repeat the general rule: the higher the stock price relative to the exercise price, the safer the option, although the option is always riskier than the stock. The option's risk changes every time the stock price changes.

---

[11] It also changes over time even with the stock price constant.

Table 20-2
What the price of a call option depends on

1. If the following variables *increase*,	the changes in the call option price are:
Stock price (P)	positive
Exercise price (EX)	negative
Interest rate (r_f)	positive
Time to expiration (t)	positive
Volatility of stock price (σ)	positive

2. Other properties:
   a. Upper bound. The option price is always less than the stock price.
   b. Lower bound. The option price never falls below the payoff to immediate exercise $(P - \text{EX}$ or zero, whichever is larger).
   c. If the stock is worthless, the option is worthless.
   d. As the stock price becomes very large, the option price approaches the stock price less the present value of the exercise price.

Note: The *direct* effects of increases in r_f or σ on option price are positive. There may also be *indirect* effects. For example, an increase in r_f could reduce stock price P. This, in turn, would tend to reduce option price.

Constructing Option Equivalents from Common Stocks and Borrowing

If you've digested what we've said so far, you can appreciate why options are hard to value by standard discounted cash flow formulas, and why a rigorous option-valuation technique eluded economists for many years. The breakthrough came when Black and Scholes exclaimed "Eureka! We have found it!"[12] The trick is to set up an *option equivalent* by combining common stock investment and borrowing. The net cost of buying the option equivalent must equal the value of the option."

We will show you how this works with a simple numerical example. We will work out the value of a 1-year option to buy the stock of Wombat Corporation at an exercise price of $110. To keep matters simple, we will assume that Wombat stock can do only two things over the coming year—either the price will fall to $80 from its current level of $100 or it will rise to $125. We will also assume that the 1-year rate of interest is 10%.

If Wombat's stock price falls to $80, the call option will be worthless, but if the price rises to $125, the option will be worth $125 − 110 = $15. The possible payoffs to the option are therefore:

	Stock Price = 80	Stock Price = 125
1 call option	$0	$15

Now compare these payoffs with what you would get if you bought one share of stock and borrowed $72.73 from the bank:

	Stock Price = 80	Stock Price = 125
1 share of stock	$80	$125
Repayment of loan + interest	− 80	− 80
Total payoff	$ 0	$ 45

---

[12] We do not know whether Black and Scholes, like Archimedes, were sitting in bathtubs at the time.

Notice that the payoffs from the levered investment in the stock are identical to the payoffs from *three* call options. Therefore, both investments must have the same value:

$$\text{Value of 3 calls} = \text{value of share} - \$72.73 \text{ bank loan}$$
$$= 100 - 72.73 = 27.27$$
$$\text{Value of 1 call} = \$9.09$$

Presto! You've valued a call option.

To value the Wombat option we borrowed money and bought stock in such a way that we exactly replicated the payoff from a call option. The number of shares that are needed to replicate one call is often called the **hedge ratio** or **option delta**. In our Wombat example three calls are replicated by a levered position in one share. The option delta is, therefore, 1/3.

How did we know that Wombat's call option is equivalent to a levered position in one third of a share? We used a simple formula that says

$$\text{Option delta} = \frac{\text{Spread of possible option prices}}{\text{Spread of possible share prices}} = \frac{15 - 0}{125 - 80} = \frac{1}{3}$$

You have learned not only to value a simple option. You have also learned that you can replicate an investment in the option by a levered investment in the underlying asset. Thus, if you can't buy or sell an option on an asset, you can create a homemade option by a replicating strategy of buying or selling delta shares and borrowing or lending the balance.

*The Risk-Neutral Method

Notice why the Wombat call option has to sell for $9.09. If the option price is higher than $9.09, you could make a certain profit by buying one share of stock, selling three call options, and borrowing $72.73. Similarly, if the option price is less than $9.09, you could make an equally certain profit by selling the stock, buying three calls, and lending the balance. In either case there would be a money machine.

If there's a money machine, everyone scurries to take advantage of it. So when we say that the option price must be $9.09 or otherwise there would be a money machine, we did not have to know anything about investor attitudes to risk. The price cannot depend on whether investors detest risk or could not care a jot.

This suggests an alternative way to calculate the value of the Wombat option. We can *pretend* that all investors are *indifferent* about risk, work out the expected future value of the option in such a world, and discount it back at the risk-free interest rate to give the current value. Let us check that this method gives the same answer.

If investors are indifferent to risk, the expected return on the stock must be equal to the rate of interest:

$$\text{Expected return on Wombat stock} = 10\% \text{ per annum}$$

We know that Wombat stock can either rise by 25% to $125 or fall by 20% to $80. We can, therefore, calculate the probability of a price rise in our hypothetical risk-neutral world:

$$\text{Expected return} = (\text{probability of rise}) \times 25$$
$$+ (1 - \text{probability of rise}) \times (-20)$$
$$= 10\%$$

Therefore,

$$\text{Probability of rise} = 0.67, \text{ or } 67\%$$

We know that if the stock price rises, the Wombat call option will be worth $15; if it falls, the call will be worth nothing. Therefore, the expected value of the call option is:

$$(\text{Probability of rise} \times 15) + ((1 - \text{probability of rise}) \times 0)$$
$$= (0.67 \times 15) + (0.33 \times 0)$$
$$= \$10$$

And the current value of the call is

$$\frac{\text{Expected future value}}{1 + \text{interest rate}} = \frac{10}{1.10} = \$9.09$$

Exactly the same answer that we got earlier!
We now have two ways to calculate the value of an option:

1. Find the combination of stock and loan that replicates an investment in the option. Since the two strategies give identical payoffs in the future, they must sell for the same price today.
2. Pretend that investors do not care about risk, so that the expected return on the stock is equal to the interest rate. Calculate the expected future value of the option in this risk-neutral world and discount it at the interest rate.

Valuing Options That Last for More than One Period

Our example of the Wombat call option is fanciful in one important respect: there will be more than two possible prices for Wombat's stock at the end of the year. We could make the problem slightly more realistic by assuming that there were two possible changes in the stock price in each 6-month period. That would give a wider range of end-year prices. It would still be possible to construct a series of levered investments in the stock that would give exactly the same prospects as the option.[13]

There is no reason that we should stop at 6-month periods. We could go on to take shorter and shorter intervals, with each interval showing two possible changes in Wombat's stock price. Eventually we would reach a situation in which Wombat's stock price was changing continuously and generating a continuum of possible year-end prices. We could still replicate the call option by a levered investment in the stock, but we would need to adjust the degree of leverage continuously as the year went by.

Calculating the value of this levered investment may sound like a hopelessly tedious business, but Black and Scholes derived a formula that does the trick. It is an unpleasant-looking formula, but its interpretation is the same as in the Wombat example:

Value of option = [delta × share price] − [bank loan]

$$[N(d_1) \times \quad P \quad] - [N(d_2) \times \text{PV(EX)}]$$

where

$N(d)$ = cumulative normal probability density function[14]
EX = exercise price of option; PV(EX) is calculated by discounting at the risk-free interest rate r_f; $\text{PV(EX)} = \text{EX}e^{-r_f t}$

---

[13] We will work through a two-period example in the next chapter.

[14] That is, $N(d)$ is the probability that a normally distributed random variable $\tilde{x}$ will be less than or equal to d. $N(d_1)$ in the Black-Scholes formula is the option delta. Thus the formula tells us that the value of a call is equal to an investment of $N(d_1)$ in the common stock less borrowing of $\text{EX}e^{-r_f t}N(d_2)$.

$$d_1 = \frac{\log{(P/\text{PV(EX)})}}{\sigma \sqrt{t}} + \sigma \sqrt{t}/2$$

$$d_2 = d_1 - \sigma \sqrt{t}$$

t = number of periods to exercise date

P = price of stock now

σ = standard deviation per period of the (continuously compounded) rate of return on the stock

Notice what the value of the option does and does not depend on. The willingness of investors to bear risk does not affect value nor does the expected return on the stock.[15] The value of the option increases with the level of the stock price (P), it decreases with the present value of the exercise price PV(EX), which in turn depends on the interest rate and time to maturity and increases with the time to maturity multiplied by the stock's variability ($\sigma \sqrt{t}$).

Using the Black-Scholes Formula

Does the Black-Scholes option-valuation formula seem a little removed from the real world? It should not. Every day dealers on the options exchanges use this formula to make huge trades. These dealers are not for the most part trained in the formula's mathematical derivation; they just use a specially programmed calculator or a set of tables to find the value of the option.

Appendix Tables 6 and 7 allow you to use the Black-Scholes formula to value a variety of simple options. In order to use the tables, follow these four steps:

Step 1. Multiply the standard deviation of the proportionate changes in the asset's value by the square root of time to the option's expiration. For example, suppose that you wish to value a 4-year option on the stock of Ragwort Corporation and that the standard deviation of the continuously compounded stock price changes is 40% per year.

$$\text{Standard deviation} \times \sqrt{\text{time}} = 0.40 \times \sqrt{4} = 0.80$$

Step 2. Calculate the ratio of the asset value to the present value of the option's exercise price. For example, suppose that Ragwort's stock price is currently $140, that the option's exercise price is $160, and that the interest rate is 12.47%. Then

$$\frac{\text{Asset value}}{\text{PV(exercise price)}} = 140 \div \frac{160}{(1.1247)^4} = 1.4$$

Step 3. Now turn to Table 6 and look up the entry corresponding to the numbers that you calculated in steps 1 and 2. You can see that a 4-year call option on Ragwort stock would be worth 43.1% of the stock price, or $60.34.

If you want to know the value of a put option with the same exercise price, then you can use the simple relationship that we derived in Section 20-2:

$$\text{Value of put} = \text{value of call} + \text{PV(exercise price)} - \text{stock price}$$

$$= 60.34 + \frac{160}{(1.1247)^4} - 140 = \$20.34$$

Step 4. Table 7 tells you the option delta. For example, if you look up the equivalent entry in Table 7, you see that the Ragwort call option has a delta of

---

[15] Although the expected return affects the price of the stock, it does not affect the *relative* value of the stock and option.

0.79. This means that instead of buying a call for $60.34, you could achieve the same result by buying 0.79 shares of stock (at a cost of 0.79 × 140 = $110.60) and borrowing the balance ($110.60 − 60.34 = $50.26).[16]

To find the option delta for the put, you simply subtract 1 from the entry in Table 7. In our example

$$\text{Put option delta} = \text{call option delta} - 1$$
$$= 0.79 - 1 = -0.21$$

In other words, instead of *paying out* $20.34 to buy a Ragwort put option, you could *sell* 0.21 shares of stock (for a cash inflow of 0.21 × 140 = $29.40) and buy a Treasury bill with the available cash (20.34 + 29.40 = $49.74).

20-5   SUMMARY

If you have managed to reach this point, you are probably in need of a rest and a stiff gin and tonic. So we will summarize what we have learned so far and take up the subject of options again in the next chapter when you are rested (or drunk).

There are two basic types of option. An American call is an option to buy an asset at a specified exercise price on or before a specified exercise date. Similarly, an American put is an option to sell the asset at a specified price on or before a specified date. European calls and puts are exactly the same except that they cannot be exercised *before* the specified exercise date. Calls and puts are the basic building blocks that can be combined to give any pattern of payoffs.

What determines the value of a call option? Common sense tells us that it ought to depend on three things:

1. In order to exercise an option you have to pay the exercise price. Other things being equal, the less you are obliged to pay, the better. Therefore, the value of an option increases with the ratio of the asset price to the exercise price.
2. You do not have to pay the exercise price until you decide to exercise the option. Therefore, an option gives you a free loan. The higher the rate of interest and the longer the time to maturity, the more this free loan is worth. Therefore, the value of an option increases with the interest rate multiplied by the time to maturity.
3. If the price of the asset falls short of the exercise price, you won't exercise the option. You will, therefore, lose 100% of your investment in the option no matter how far the asset depreciates below the exercise price. On the other hand, the more the price rises *above* the exercise price, the more profit you will make. Therefore, the option holder does not lose from increased variability if things go wrong, but gains if they go right. The value of an option increases with the variance per period of the stock return multiplied by the number of periods to maturity.

We showed you how to value an option on a stock when there are only two possible changes in the stock price in each subperiod. Black and Scholes have also derived a formula that gives the value of an option when there is a continuum of possible future stock prices. Tables in the Appendix should allow you to apply this formula to a number of simple option problems.

Unfortunately, not all option problems are simple. Therefore, in the next chapter we will look at some of the complications and work through several examples of moderate complexity.

---

[16] Of course, as time passes and the share price changes, the option delta changes. Therefore, you will need to keep adjusting your levered holding in Ragwort stock.

FURTHER READING

The classic articles on option valuation are:

F. Black and M. Scholes: "The Pricing of Options and Corporate Liabilities," *Journal of Political Economy*, **81**: 637–654 (May–June 1973).

R.C. Merton: "Theory of Rational Option Pricing," *Bell Journal of Economics and Management Science*, **4**: 141–183 (Spring 1973).

There are also a number of good texts on option valuation. They include:

J. Cox and M. Rubinstein, *Options Markets*, Prentice-Hall, Inc., Englewood Cliffs, N.J., 1985.

J. Hull, *Options, Futures and other Derivative Securities*, Prentice-Hall, Inc., Englewood Cliffs, N.J. 1989.

R. Jarrow and A. Rudd, *Option Pricing*, Dow Jones-Irwin, Inc., Homewood, Ill., 1983.

QUIZ

1. Complete the following passage: A _____ option gives its owner the opportunity to buy a stock at a specific price which is generally called the _____ price. A _____ option gives its owner the opportunity to sell stock at a specified _____ price.

   Options that can be exercised only at maturity are called _____ options.

   The common stock of firms that borrow is a _____ option. Stockholders effectively sell the firm's _____ to _____ , but retain the option to buy the _____ back. The exercise price is the _____ .

2. Fill in the blanks:
   (a) A firm that issues warrants is selling a _____ option.
   (b) A firm that enters a standby agreement whereby the underwriter to a rights issue guarantees to take up any unwanted stock acquires a _____ option.
   (c) Rights are _____ options on the issuing firm's stock.
   (d) An oil company acquires mining rights to a silver deposit. It is not obligated to mine the silver, however. The company has effectively acquired a _____ option, where the exercise price is the cost of opening the mine.
   (e) Some preferred shareholders have the right to redeem their shares at par value after a specified date. (If they hand over their shares, the firm sends them a cheque equal to the shares' par value.) These shareholders have a _____ option.
   (f) An executive who qualifies for a stock option plan acquires a _____ option.
   (g) An investor who buys stock in a levered firm acquires a _____ option on the firm's assets.
   (h) A firm buys a standard machine with a ready secondhand market. The secondhand market gives the firm a _____ option.

3. Note Figures 20-11(*a*) and 20-11(*b*). Match each figure with one of the following positions:
   (a) Call buyer
   (b) Call seller
   (c) Put buyer
   (d) Put seller

4. Suppose that you hold a share of stock and a put option on that share. What is the payoff when the option expires

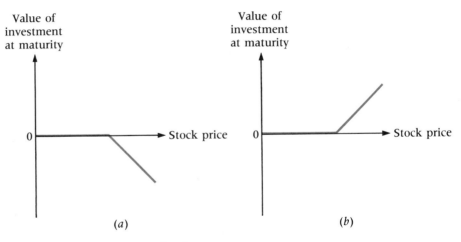

Figure 20-11   See Quiz, question 3.

(a) The stock price is below the exercise price?
(b) The stock price is above the exercise price?

5.   There is another strategy involving calls and borrowing and lending which gives the same payoffs as the strategy described in question 4. What is the alternative strategy?

6.   What is the lower bound to the price of a call option? What is the upper bound?

7.   What is a call option worth if:
(a) The stock price is zero?
(b) The stock price is extremely high relative to the exercise price?

8.   How does the price of a call option respond to the following changes, other things equal? Does the call price go up or down?
(a) Stock price increases.
(b) Exercise price is increased.
(c) Risk-free interest rate increases.
(d) Expiration date of the option is extended.
(e) Volatility of the stock price falls.
(f) Time passes, so the option's expiration date comes closer.

9.   "An option is always riskier than the stock it is written on." True or false? How does the risk of an option change when the stock price changes?

10. Why can't you value options using a standard discounted cash flow formula?

11. Use Appendix Table 6 to value the following options.
(a) A call option written on a stock selling for $60 per share with a $60 exercise price. The stock's standard deviation is 6% per month. The option matures in 3 months. The risk-free interest rate is 1% per month.
(b) A put option written on the same stock at the same time, with the same exercise price and expiration date.
Now for each of these options use Table 7 to calculate the combination of stock and risk-free asset that would replicate the option.

12. Imagine that the range of future prices for Wombat stock widens to $100 to $220 (see Section 20-4). Recalculate the value of the call option using (a) the replicating-portfolio method (b) the risk-neutral method. Explain intuitively why the option value increases.

QUESTIONS AND PROBLEMS

1. Look up the terms of actual call and put options on stocks, currencies, etc. Plot their payoffs at maturity using diagrams like those in Figures 20-1 and 20-2.

2. Explain why the value of a call depends on each of the following:
    (a) The *product* of volatility per period and time to maturity.
    (b) The *product* of the risk-free interest rate and time to maturity.

3. Look at actual trading prices of call options on stocks to check whether they behave as the theory presented in this chapter predicts. For example:
    (a) Follow several options as they approach maturity. How would you expect their prices to behave? Do they actually behave that way?
    (b) Compare two call options written on the same stock with the same maturity but different exercise prices.
    (c) Compare two call options written on the same stock with the same exercise price but different maturities.

*4. How would the value of Circular File common stock (see Section 20-2) change if:
    (a) The value of the firm's assets increases?
    (b) The maturity of its debt is extended?
    (c) The assets become safer (less volatile)?
    (d) The risk-free rate of interest increases (hold the value of the firm's assets constant)?

5. The Rank and File Company is considering a rights issue to raise $50 million. An underwriter offers to "stand by" (i.e., to guarantee the success of the issue by buying any unwanted stock at the issue price). The underwriter's fee is $2 million.
    (a) What kind of option does Rank and File acquire if it accepts the underwriter's offer?
    (b) What determines the value of the option?
    (c) How would you calculate whether the underwriter's offer is a fair deal?

6. Which *one* of the following statements is correct?
    (a) Value of put + present value of exercise price = value of call + share price
    (b) Value of put + share price = value of call + present value of exercise price
    (c) Value of put − share price = present value of exercise price − value of call
    (d) Value of put + value of call = share price − present value of exercise price

    The correct statement equates the value of two investment strategies. Plot the payoffs to each strategy as a function of the stock price. Show that the two strategies give identical payoffs.

7. The price of Backwoods Chemical Company stock on January 20 is $90 per share. Three call options are trading on the stock, one maturing on April 20, one on July 20, and one on October 20. All three options have the same $100 exercise price. The standard deviation of Backwoods stock is 42% per year. The risk-free interest rate is 11% per year. What are the three call options worth?

8. The common stock of Triangular File Company is selling at $90. A 26-week call option written on Triangular File's stock is selling for $8. The call's exercise price is $100. The risk-free interest rate is 10% per year.

    (a) Suppose that puts on Triangular stock are not traded, but you want to buy one. How would you do it?

    (b) Suppose that puts *are* traded. What should a 26-week put with an exercise price of $100 sell for?

9. Test the option conversion formula you used to answer problem 8 by using it to explain the relative prices of traded puts and calls.

*10. Refer again to the Circular File balance sheet given in Section 20-2. Suppose that the federal government suddenly offers to guarantee the $50 principal payment due bondholders next year and also to guarantee the interest payment due next year. (In other words, if firm value falls short of the promised interest and principal payment, the government will make up the difference.) This offer is a complete surprise to everyone. The government asks nothing in return, and so its offer is cheerfully accepted.

    (a) Suppose that the promised interest rate on Circular's debt is 10%. The rate on 1-year federal government bonds is 8%. How will the guarantee affect bond value?

    (b) The guarantee does *not* affect the value of Circular stock. Why? (*Note*: There could be some effect if the guarantee allows Circular to avoid costs of financial distress or bankruptcy. See Section 18-3.)

    (c) How will the value of the firm (debt plus equity) change?

    Now suppose that the government offers the same guarantee for *new* debt issued by *Rectangular* File Company. Rectangular's assets are identical to Circular's, but Rectangular has no existing debt. Rectangular accepts the offer and uses the proceeds of a $50 debt issue to repurchase or retire stock.

    Will Rectangular stockholders gain from the opportunity to issue the guaranteed debt? By how much, approximately? (Ignore taxes.)

11. How would you use Appendix Table 6 to estimate the volatility of a common stock on which call options are written and actively traded?

12. Show how the option delta changes as the stock price rises relative to the exercise price. Explain intuitively why this is the case. (What would happen to the option delta if the exercise price of an option was zero? What would happen if the exercise price became indefinitely large?)

13. Use either the replicating-portfolio method or the risk-neutral method to value a put option on Wombat stock (see Section 20-4) with an exercise price of $160. Use the formula in Section 20-2 to check your answer.

14. Is it more valuable to own an option to buy a portfolio of stocks or a portfolio of options to buy each of the individual stocks? Say briefly why.

15. Discuss briefly the relative risk of the following positions:

    (a) Buy stock and a put option on the stock.

    (b) Buy stock.

    (c) Buy call.

    (d) Buy stock and sell call option on the stock.

    (e) Buy bond.

    (f) Buy stock, buy put, and sell call.

    (g) Sell put.

*16. In Section 20-2 we suggested a more complicated payment scheme for Ms. Higden ($100,000 only if the stock price is between $120 and $140).

    (a) Draw a position diagram showing the payoffs from such a scheme.

    (b) Show that this scheme is a combination of simple options.

    (c) Assume that the current stock price is $100, the standard deviation of the stock price is 30% a year, and the rate of interest is 10%. What is the value of this incentive scheme?

17. A very difficult question: Use our conversion formula (see Section 20-2) and the one-period binomial model to show that the option delta for a put option is equal to the option delta for a call option minus one.

18. Option traders often refer to straddles and butterflies. Here is an example of each:

Straddle   Buy one call with exercise price of $100 and simultaneously buy one put with exercise price of $100.

Butterfly   Simultaneously buy one call with exercise price of $100, sell two calls with exercise price of $110, and buy one call with exercise price of $120.

(a) Draw position diagrams for the straddle and butterfly, showing the payoffs from the investor's net position. Each strategy is a bet on variability. Explain briefly the nature of this bet.

(b) The profitability of a straddle or a butterfly depends on how much the stock price has changed by the time the option matures and not on how it varies *before* maturity. If you believe that volatility *during* the option's life will be higher than expected, how can you construct a hedged position to take advantage of your belief? What if you believe that volatility will be lower than expected?

19. In 1988 the Australian firm Bond Corporation sold a share in some land that it owned near Rome for $110 million and as a result boosted its 1988 earnings by $74 million. In 1989 a television program revealed that the buyer was given a put option to sell its share in the land back to Bond for $110 million and also that Bond had paid $20 million for a call option to repurchase the share in the land for the same price.[17]

(a) What happens if the land is worth more than $110 million when the options expire? What if it is worth less than $110 million?

(b) Use position diagrams to show the net effect of the land sale and the option transactions.

(c) Assume a one-year maturity on the options. Can you deduce the interest rate?

(d) The television program argued that it was misleading to record a profit on the sale of land. What do you think?

20. (a) The Chase Manhattan Bank has offered its more wealthy customers an unusual type of time deposit known as the Guaranteed Market Investment Account. It does not pay a fixed rate of interest but instead the depositor receives a proportion of any rise in the Standard & Poor's index. How should the bank invest the money in order to minimize its risk?

(b) Suppose the interest rate is 10%, the standard deviation of returns on the Standard & Poor's index is 20% per year and the deposit has a maturity of 3 months. What proportion of any appreciation in the index could the bank afford to offer depositors?

(c) You can also make a deposit with Chase which does not pay interest if the market index rises but makes an increasingly large payment as the market index falls. How should the bank protect itself against the risk of offering this deposit?

21. Figure 20-12 shows some complicated position diagrams. Work out the combination of stocks, bonds, and options that produces each of these positions.

---

[17] See *Sydney Morning Herald* March 14, 1989, page 27. The options were subsequently renegotiated.

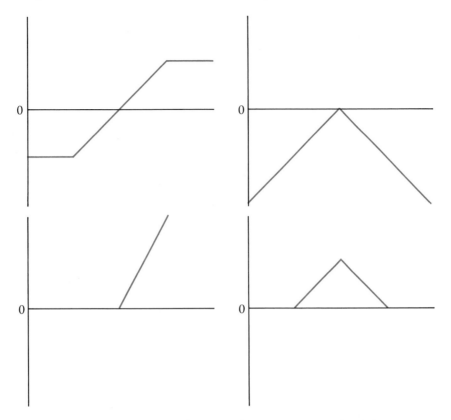

Figure 20-12   Some complicated position diagrams (see Question 21)

22. (a) If you can't sell a share short, you can achieve exactly the same
          final payoff by a combination of bonds and options. What is this
          combination?
     (b) Now work out the mixture of stock and options that gives the same
          final payoff as a bond.
23. A difficult question: Three 6-month call options are traded on Hogswill
     stock:

Exercise price	Call option price
$ 90	$ 5
100	11
110	15

How could you make money by trading in Hogswill options? *Hint:* Draw a
graph with option price on the vertical axis and the ratio of stock price to
exercise price on the horizontal axis. Plot the three Hogswill call options
on your graph. Does this fit with what you know about how option prices
should vary with the ratio of stock price to exercise price? Now look in the
newspaper at options with the same maturity date but different exercise
prices. Can you find any money-making possibilities?

C · H · A · P · T · E · R

21

APPLICATIONS OF OPTION PRICING THEORY

This chapter brings the first reward to your investment in learning about options. We describe three common and important *real options* found in capital investment projects.

- The option to make *follow-on* investments if the immediate investment project succeeds
- The option to abandon a project
- The option to wait (and learn) before investing

Real options such as these allow managers to add value to their firm, by acting to amplify good fortune or to mitigate loss. Managers often do not use option jargon to describe these opportunities; for example, they may refer to "intangibles" rather than to puts or calls. But when they review major investment proposals, these option "intangibles" are often the key to their decisions.

We will also work through some simple numerical examples to show how real options can be valued. These examples ignore many complexities that are encountered in practice, however; think of them as back-of-the-envelope estimates of the value of more realistic but complex real options.

These examples will also provide an opportunity to learn more about the *technique* of option valuation. By the time you have worked through the examples in the chapter, you should know how to use the binomial method to value options on assets that last for more than one period, how to pick sensible figures for the upside and downside price changes and how to value an option on an asset that pays dividends.

Since the only feasible way to solve most practical option problems is with a computer, why do we ask you to work through a number of option problems by hand? The reason is that unless you understand the basics of option valuation, you are likely to make mistakes in setting up an option problem and you won't know how to interpret the computer's answers and explain them to others.

21-1   THE VALUE OF FOLLOW-ON INVESTMENT OPPORTUNITIES

It is 1982. You are assistant to the chief financial officer (CFO) of Blitzen Computers, an established computer manufacturer casting a profit-hungry eye on the rapidly developing personal computer market. You are helping the CFO evaluate the proposed introduction of the Blitzen Mark I Micro.

The Mark I's forecasted cash flows and NPV are shown in Table 21-1. Unfortunately, the Mark I can't meet Blitzen's customary 20% hurdle rate, and has a $46 million negative NPV, contrary to top management's strong gut feeling that Blitzen ought to be in the personal computer market.

Table 21-1
Summary of cash flows and financial analysis of the Mark I microcomputer, (Figures in millions. After-tax operating cash flow is negative in 1982 because of R&D costs.)

Year	1982	1983	1984	1985	1986	1987
After-tax operating cash flow	− 200	+ 110	+ 159	+ 295	+ 185	0
Capital investment	250	0	0	0	0	0
Increase in working capital	0	50	100	100	− 125	− 125
Net cash flow (1) − (2) − (3)	− 450	+ 60	+ 59	+ 195	+ 310	− 125

NPV at 20% = − $46.45, about − $46 million

Table 21-2
Calculating what the option to invest in the Mark II microcomputer could be worth

Assumptions
1. The decision to invest in the Mark II must be made after 3 years, in 1985.
2. The Mark II investment is double the scale of the Mark I (note the expected rapid growth of the industry). Investment required is $900 million (the exercise price), which is taken as fixed.
3. Forecasted cash inflows of the Mark II are also double those of the Mark I, with present value of about $800 million in 1985 and $800/(1.2)^3 = \$463$ million in 1982.
4. The future value of the Mark II cash flows is highly uncertain. This value evolves like a stock price with a standard deviation of 35% per year. (Many high-tech stocks have standard deviations higher than 35%.)

Interpretation
The opportunity to invest in the Mark II is a 3-year call option on an asset worth $463 million with a $900 million exercise price.

Valuation
See Appendix Table 6:

$$\text{Standard deviation} \times \sqrt{\text{time}} = 0.35\sqrt{3} = 0.61$$

$$\frac{\text{Asset value}}{\text{PV (exercise price)}} = \frac{463}{900/(1.1)^3} = 0.68$$

$$\frac{\text{Call value}}{\text{Asset value}} = 0.119 \qquad \text{(closest figure from Appendix Table 6)}$$

$$\text{Call value} = 0.119 \times 463 = 55.1, \text{ or about \$55 million}$$

"The Mark I just can't make it on financial grounds," the CFO says, "but we've got to do it for strategic reasons. I'm recommending we go ahead."

"But you're missing the all-important financial advantage, Chief," you reply.

"Don't call me Chief. What financial advantage?"

"If we don't launch the Mark I, it will probably be too expensive to enter the micro market later, when Apple, IBM, and others are firmly established. If we go ahead, we have the opportunity to make follow-on investments which could be extremely profitable. The Mark I gives not only its own cash flows, but a call option to go on with a Mark II micro. That call option is the real source of strategic value."

"So, it's strategic value by another name. That doesn't tell me what the Mark II investment's worth. The Mark II could be a great investment or a lousy one—we haven't got a clue."

"That's exactly when a call option is worth the most," you point out perceptively. "The call lets us invest in the Mark II if it's great and walk away from it if it's lousy."

"So, what's it worth?"

"Hard to say precisely, but I've done a back-of-the-envelope calculation that suggests the value of the option to invest in the Mark II could more than offset the Mark I's $46 million negative NPV. [The calculations are shown in Table 21-2.] If the option to invest is worth $55 million, the total value of the Mark I is its own NPV, −$46 million, plus the $55 million option attached to it, or +$9 million."

"You're just overestimating the Mark II," the CFO says gruffly. "It's easy to be optimistic when an investment is three years away."

"No, no," you reply patiently. "The Mark II is expected to be no more profitable than the Mark I—just twice as big, and therefore twice as bad in terms of discounted cash flow. I'm forecasting it to have a negative NPV of about $100 million. But there's a chance the Mark II could be extremely valuable. The call option allows Blitzen to cash in on those upside outcomes. The chance to cash in could be worth $55 million."

"Of course, the $55 million is only a trial calculation, but it illustrates how valuable follow-on investment opportunities can be, especially when uncertainty is high and the product market is growing rapidly. Moreover, the Mark II will give us a call on the Mark III, the Mark III on the Mark IV, and so on. My calculations don't take subsequent calls into account."

"I think I'm beginning to understand a little bit of corporate strategy," mumbles the CFO.

Real Options and the Value of Management

Discounted cash flow (DCF) implicitly assumes that firms hold real assets passively. It ignores the options found in real assets—options that sophisticated managers can act to take advantage of. You could say that DCF does not reflect the value of management.

Remember that the DCF valuation method was first developed for bonds and stocks. Investors in these securities are necessarily passive: With rare exceptions, there is nothing investors can do to improve the interest rate they are paid or the dividends they receive. A bond or common stock can be sold, of course, but that merely substitutes one passive investor for another.

Options and securities such as convertible bonds that contain options are fundamentally different. Investors who hold options do not have to be passive. They are given a right to make a decision, which they can exercise to capitalize on good fortune or to mitigate loss. This right clearly has value whenever there is uncertainty. However, calculating that value is not a simple matter of discounting. Option pricing theory tells us what the value is, but the necessary formulas do not look like DCF.

Now consider the firm as an investor in *real* assets. Management can *add value* to those assets by responding to changing circumstances—by taking advantage of good fortune or by mitigating loss.

Management has the opportunity to act because many investment opportunities have real options embedded in them—options that management can exercise when it is in the firm's interest to do so. DCF misses this extra value because it implicitly treats the firm as a passive investor.

21-2   THE OPTION TO ABANDON

In the case of Blitzen Computer we needed to value an option to expand. Sometimes we face the opposite problem and need to value an option to abandon a business. For example, suppose you must choose between two technologies for production of a new product, a Wankel-engined outboard motor.

1. Technology A uses computer-controlled machinery custom-designed to produce the complex shapes required for Wankel engines in high volumes and at low cost. But if the Wankel engine doesn't sell, this equipment will be worthless.
2. Technology B uses standard machine tools. Labour costs are much higher, but the tools can be sold or shifted to another use if the motor doesn't sell.

Technology A looks better in a discounted cash flow (DCF) analysis of the new product because it was designed to have the lowest possible cost at the planned production volume. Yet you can sense the advantage of technology B's flexibility if you doubt whether the new outboard will sink or swim in the marketplace.

In such cases managers may ignore technology A's better DCF value and choose technology B instead for its "intangible" flexibility advantage. But we can make the value of this flexibility more concrete by modeling it as a put option.

For the sake of simplicity, assume that the initial capital outlays for technologies A and B are the same. Technology A, with its low-cost customized machinery, will provide a payoff of $20 million if the outboard is popular with boatowners and $5 million if it is not. Think of these payoffs as the project's cash flow in its first year of production plus the present value of all subsequent cash flows. The corresponding payoffs to Technology B are $18 million and $3 million.

| | Payoffs from producing outboard (millions) | |
	Technology A	Technology B
Buoyant demand	$20	$18
Sluggish demand	5	3

If you are obliged to continue in production regardless of how unprofitable the project turns out to be, then Technology A is clearly the superior choice. But suppose that you can bail out of Technology B for $8 million. If the outboard is not a success in the market, you would do better to sell off the plant and equipment for $8 million rather than continuing with a project with a present value of only $3 million. Thus, once we recognize the option to sell the assets, the payoffs to Technology B change as follows:

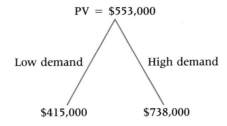

PV = $553,000

Low demand   High demand

$415,000 $738,000

Note:

$$\text{Expected} \atop \text{cash flow} = \left[\begin{array}{c} \text{Probability of} \\ \text{high demand} \end{array} \times 738 \right] + \left[\begin{array}{c} \text{Probability of} \\ \text{low demand} \end{array} \times 415 \right]$$

$$= (0.6 \times 738) + (0.4 \times 415) = 609$$

$$\text{PV} = \frac{609}{1.1} = \$553,000$$

Figure 21-1   The possible payoffs to Magna Charter from investing in a turboprop. (The payoffs assume that the company continues to operate the plane.)

A put option on a stock is an insurance policy that pays off when the stock ends up below the put's exercise price. Technology B provides the same kind of insurance policy: if the outboard's sales are disappointing, you can abandon the machinery and realize its $8 million value. This abandonment option is a put option with an exercise price equal to the sale-value of the machinery. The total value of the project using technology B is its DCF value assuming that the company does not abandon *plus* the value of the abandonment put.[1] When you value this put option you are placing a value on flexibility.

Valuing the Abandonment Put — An Example

In Chapter 10 we introduced you to that airborne pioneer Agnes Magna who was pondering the purchase of a turboprop for her new airline, Magna Charter. Figure 21-1 summarizes the possible payoffs from the turbo. If the airline gets off to a good start and demand is high, Ms. Magna calculates she will have a business worth $738,000 by the end of the first year. If things don't work out, it will be worth only $415,000. Ms. Magna estimates that there is a 60% chance that the business will succeed and therefore calculates the expected value in year 1 as $(0.6 \times 738) + (0.4 \times 415) = 609$ or $609,000. She discounts this at a 10% cost of capital to give a present value of $609/1.1 = \$553,000$.[2]

Note that these calculations do not allow for the possibility of abandonment. If the business does not take off[3] in the first year, Ms. Magna would do better to sell the turboprop for $500,000, rather than retain a business that is worth only $415,000.

---

[1] Imagine a stock which pays off either $3 or $18. If you own both the stock and a put option on the stock with an exercise price of $8, the possible payoffs on your investment are

Stock price $18 → Keep stock → Own stock worth $18
Stock price $3 → Exercise put option → Receive $8 exercise price

Investing in technology B is exactly like owning both the stock and the put option.

[2] If you look back at Chapter 10, you will see that this is not the *total* value of the business to Ms. Magna, since she also expects to earn some income during the first year. This income does not affect the value of the option to abandon at the end of the first year and so we ignore it here.

[3] The pun was (at first) unintentional.

What is the value of this option to bail out? In Chapter 10 we tried to answer that question using standard discounted cash flow (DCF) techniques. We know now that you cannot use standard DCF where there is an option involved because the discount rate changes as the value of the underlying asset changes. To value Ms. Magna's option to abandon, you need to value a 1-year put option on the turboprop with an exercise price of $500,000.

You require the following information to value the put (dollar figures in thousands):

- Present value of business without option to abandon = $553
- Exercise price = $500
- Maturity = 1 year
- Interest rate = 5%
- Future value of business with high demand = $738
- Future value with low demand = $415

Since Ms. Magna can foresee only two outcomes, this problem is tailor-made for the binomial method that we used in Chapter 20 to value the Wombat option. Here is a chance to show that you haven't forgotten it.

We start the risk-neutral method by pretending that Ms. Magna is indifferent about risk. In this case she would be content if the business offered just the 5% risk-free rate of interest. We know that the value of the business will either go from $553,000 to $738,000, a rise of 33%, or it will go to $415,000, a fall of 25%. We can therefore calculate the probability that value will rise in our hypothetical risk-neutral world:

$$\text{Expected return} = \left(\begin{array}{c}\text{probability}\\\text{of rise}\end{array}\right) \times 33 + \left(1 - \begin{array}{c}\text{probability}\\\text{of rise}\end{array}\right) \times (-25)$$

$$= 0.05 \text{ or } 5\%$$

Therefore, *probability of rise* equals 52%.

We know that if the business is successful, the option to abandon will be worthless. If it is unsuccessful, Ms. Magna will sell the turboprop and save herself $500 - 415 = 85$ or $85,000. Therefore, the expected future value of the option to abandon is:

$$\left(\begin{array}{c}\text{Probability}\\\text{of rise}\end{array}\right) \times 0 + \left(1 - \begin{array}{c}\text{probability}\\\text{of rise}\end{array}\right) \times 85$$

$$= (0.52 \times 0) + (0.48 \times 85) = 41 \text{ or } \$41,000$$

And the current value of the option to abandon is:

$$\frac{\text{Expected future value}}{1 + \text{interest rate}} = \frac{41}{1.05} = 39 \text{ or } \$39,000$$

Thus, recognizing the option to abandon increases the value of Ms. Magna's business by $39,000:

$$\begin{array}{c}\text{Value of business}\\\text{with abandonment}\\\text{option}\end{array} = \begin{array}{c}\text{value of business}\\\text{without abandonment}\\\text{option}\end{array} + \begin{array}{c}\text{value}\\\text{of}\\\text{option}\end{array}$$

$$= 553 + 39$$

$$= 592 \text{ or } \$592,000$$

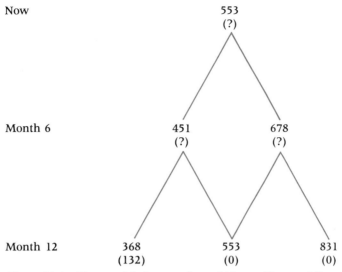

Figure 21-2   The possible future values of Magna Charter airline. Figures in parentheses show the values of an option to sell the airline's assets for $500,000.

*What Happens to Ms. Magna's Option If There Are More than Two Possible Outcomes?

Ms. Magna's option provides a good opportunity to extend our understanding of the binomial model. Notice that Ms. Magna considered only two possible changes to the value of her business—a rise of 33% if demand is high and a fall of 25% if demand is low. As an alternative suppose that in each 6-month period the value of Ms. Magna's firm could either rise by 22.6% or fall by 18.4% (we'll tell you shortly how we picked these figures). Figure 21-2 shows the possible firm values by the year end. You can see that there are now three possible outcomes: firm value could either rise to $831,000, remain unchanged, or decline to $368,000. That might be somewhat more realistic than Ms. Magna's initial "boom or bust" scenario.

We continue to assume that Ms. Magna has the option to sell the plane at the end of the year[4] for $500,000: we show the associated value of this option in brackets underneath the possible year-end values. Thus, if the value of the firm turns out to be $831,000, the abandonment option will be worthless; at the other extreme, if firm value is $368,000, the option will be worth:

$$\text{Exercise price} - \text{firm value} = 500 - 368 = 132 \text{ or } \$132,000$$

Option Values after Six Months

We first use the risk-neutral trick to work out option values at the end of six months. If investors are risk-neutral, the expected return on the firm must be equal to the interest rate, which is 5% a year or 2.5% for 6 months. So:[5]

---

[4] We assume that the plane cannot be sold at the end of six months. In other words, we assume that the abandonment option is European.

[5] The general formula for calculating the probability of a rise is:

$$p = \frac{\text{interest rate} - \text{downside change}}{\text{upside change} - \text{downside change}}$$

Thus, in the case of Magna Charter,

$$p = \frac{2.5 - (-18.4)}{22.6 - (-18.4)} = 0.51$$

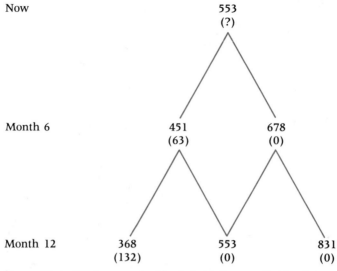

Now   553
                                             (?)

Month 6   451   678
                     (63)   (0)

Month 12   368   553   831
              (132)   (0)   (0)

Figure 21-3 We have worked back from the month-12 values to calculate the value of the Magna Charter abandonment option in month 6.

$$\left(\begin{array}{c}\text{Probability}\\\text{of rise}\end{array}\right) \times 22.6 + \left(1 - \begin{array}{c}\text{probability}\\\text{of rise}\end{array}\right) \times (-18.4) = 2.5$$

Probability of rise = 0.51 or 51%

Suppose that we are in month 6 and firm value is 451. In that case there is a 0.51 chance that at the end of the year the option will be worthless and a 0.49 chance that it will be worth 132. Thus:

$$\text{Expected value of option at end of year} = (0.51 \times 0) + (0.49 \times 132)$$
$$= 65$$

And, with an interest rate of 2.5% every six months,

$$\text{Value at month 6} = \frac{65}{1.025} = 63$$

If firm value at month 6 is 678, the option is certain to be worthless at the year end and, therefore, its value at month 6 is zero.

Option Value Now   We can now get rid of two of the question marks in Figure 21-2. Figure 21-3 shows that if firm value in month 6 is 451, the option value is 63 and, if firm value is 678, option value is zero. It now remains to work back to the value of the option today.

The expected value of the option in month 6 is:

$$\left(\begin{array}{c}\text{Probability}\\\text{of rise}\end{array}\right) \times 0 + \left(1 - \begin{array}{c}\text{probability}\\\text{of rise}\end{array}\right) \times 63 = 0.51 \times 0 + 0.49 \times 63 = 31$$

Therefore, the value today is:

$$\frac{\text{Expected value of option at month 6}}{1 + \text{interest rate}} = \frac{31}{1.025} = 30$$

In the one-step example we assumed that demand could only be high or low and that gave us an option value of $39,000. The two-step calculation allowed us to recognize that demand could take on three possible values and that changed our estimate of the option value to $30,000. It took us longer to value the option in the two-step case, but the principle was exactly the same and it didn't need any math more advanced than multiplication and division.

The General Binomial Method

Moving to two steps when valuing the Magna Charter abandonment option probably added extra realism. But there is no reason to stop there. We could go on to take shorter and shorter intervals in each of which there are only two possible changes in the value of the enterprise. For example, we could divide the year into 12 subintervals of 1 month each. That would give 13 possible year-end values. We could still use the binomial method to work back from the final date to the present. Of course, it would be tedious to do such a calculation by hand but with a computer you can whisk through options with many periods to run.

Since an asset usually can take on an almost limitless number of future values, the binomial method is likely to give a more realistic and accurate measure of the option's value if we work with a large number of subperiods. But that raises an important question: How do we pick sensible figures for the up and down changes in value? For example, why did we pick figures of 22.7% and -18.4% when we revalued the Magna Charter option using two subperiods? Fortunately, there is a neat little formula that relates the up and down changes to the standard deviation of the returns on the asset:

$$1 + \text{upside change} = u = e^{\sigma\sqrt{h}}$$

$$1 + \text{downside change} = d = 1/u$$

Where e = the base for natural logs = 2.718
σ = the standard deviation of (continuously compounded) annual returns on the asset
h = the interval as a fraction of a year

When Ms. Magna said that the value of her business could either rise by 33% or fall by 25% over one year, her figures were consistent with a figure of 28.8% for the standard deviation of the annual returns on her business:

$$1 + \text{upside change (1-year interval)} = u = e^{0.288\sqrt{1}} = 1.33$$

$$1 + \text{downside change} = d = 1/u = 1/1.33 = 0.75$$

To work out the equivalent upside and downside changes when we chop the year into two 6-month intervals, we use the same formula:

$$1 + \text{upside change (6-month interval)} = u = e^{0.288\sqrt{0.5}} = 1.226$$

$$1 + \text{downside change} = d = 1/u = 1/1.226 = 0.816$$

The left-hand columns in Table 21-3 also show the equivalent up and down moves in the value of the firm if we chop the year into monthly or weekly subperiods.

As the number of intervals is increased, the values that you obtain from the binomial method should get closer and closer to the Black-Scholes value. In fact, you can think of the Black-Scholes formula as a shortcut alternative to the binomial method as the number of intervals gets very large. For the Magna

Table 21-3

As the number of intervals is increased, you must adjust the range of possible stock price changes to keep the same standard deviation. But you will get increasingly close to the Black-Scholes measure of the Magna Charter option. (Note that sometimes you may *temporarily* move away from the Black-Scholes value. For example, this happens when the number of intervals is increased from 3 to 4.)

Number of Intervals in a Year (1/h)	Change in interval (%)		Estimated European Put Option Value (thousands)
	Upside	Downside	
1	+33.3	−25	$39.4
2	+22.6	−18.4	30.2
3	+18.2	−15.3	29.8
4	+15.5	−13.4	30.4
12	+ 8.7	− 8.0	29.1
52	+ 4.1	− 3.9	28.3
		Black-Scholes put value =	28.2

Note: The standard deviation is σ = 0.288, exercise price = $500, maturity = 1 year, interest rate = 5%, and value of business without option to abandon = $553.

Figure 21-4 In the left-hand histogram, we assume that only two things can happen to Ms. Magua's venture—high demand or low demand. The histogram shows present values at year 1 assuming no abandonment. The lognormal distribution on the right is more realistic because it recognizes a continuum of possible present values and does not ignore intermediate outcomes. The Black-Scholes model is based on the lognormal distribution.

Charter option the Black-Scholes formula gives a value of $28,200. The right-hand column of Table 21-3 shows that if you divide the year into 52 weekly subperiods, the binomial method gives a good approximation to the Black-Scholes formula. Why do the option values change as we chop time into ever smaller pieces? Figure 21-4 shows the answer. A one-step binomial assumes that only two things can happen—a very good outcome or a very bad one. The Black-Scholes formula is more realistic: it recognizes a continuum of outcomes.

If the Black-Scholes formula is more accurate and quicker to use than the binomial method, why trouble with the binomial method at all? The answer is that there are circumstances in which you cannot use the Black-Scholes formula but where the binomial method will still give you a good measure of the option's value. We will come across one such case in the next section.

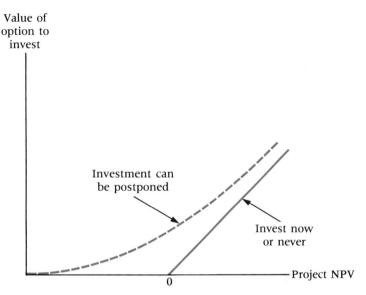

Figure 21-5   The opportunity to invest in the malted herring factory amounts to a call option. If investment is now or never, the call's payoffs are shown by the coloured line. If investment can be postponed, the call option is valuable even if project NPV is zero or negative. Compare Figure 20-8.

21-3   THE TIMING OPTION

Optimal investment timing is easy when there is no uncertainty. You just calculate project NPV at various future investment dates and pick the date that gives the highest current value.[6] Unfortunately, this simple rule breaks down in the face of uncertainty.

Suppose that you have a project which could be a big winner or a big loser. The project's upside outweighs its downside, and it has a positive NPV if undertaken today. However, the project is not "now or never." Should you invest right away or wait? It's hard to say: If the project is truly a winner, waiting means loss or deferral of its early cash flows. But if it turns out a loser, waiting could prevent a bad mistake.

In Chapter 6 we sidestepped this problem of optimal investment timing under uncertainty. Now we have the tools to confront it head on, because the opportunity to invest in a positive-NPV project is equivalent to an in-the-money call option. Optimal investment timing means exercising that call at the best time.

Example of Timing Option   We'll suppose that the project we've been discussing involves construction of a malted herring factory for $180 million. As most of our readers will know, the demand for malted herring fluctuates widely, depending on the price of competing fertilizers.

Assume first that construction of the plant is a now-or-never opportunity. That's the same as having an about-to-expire call option on the factory with an exercise price equal to the $180 million investment required to build it. If the present value of the plant's forecasted cash flows exceeds $180 million, the call option's payoff is the project's NPV. But if project NPV is negative, the call option's payoff is zero, because in that case the firm will not make the investment. We've plotted these payoffs as the solid coloured line in Figure 21-5.

[6] See Section 6-4.

Now suppose that you could choose to delay construction of the plant for up to 2 years. Even though the project may have a zero or negative NPV if undertaken today, your call option has value because 2 years gives room for hope that the volatile malted herring market will take off. We have shown a possible range of option values as the curved line in Figure 21-5.

The decision to launch or defer investment in the malted herring factory amounts to deciding whether to exercise the call option immediately or to wait and possibly exercise later.[7] Naturally, this involves a trade-off. You are reluctant to exercise, because despite today's rosy forecasts, investment in the malted herring plant may still turn out to be a mistake. When you give up your option to wait, you can no longer take advantage of the volatility of the project's future value. Remember, option holders like volatility because it generates upside potential and the option contract limits loss. On the other hand, as long as the project has a positive NPV, you are eager to exercise in order to get your hands on the cash inflows. If the cash flows (and NPV) are high enough, you will gladly exercise your call before its time is up.

The cash flows from an investment project play the same role as dividend payments on a stock. When a stock does not pay dividends, an American call option is always worth more alive than dead, and should never be exercised early. But payment of a dividend before the option matures reduces the ex-dividend price and the possible payoffs to the call option at maturity. Think of the extreme case: if a company pays out all its assets in one bumper dividend, then afterward the stock price must be zero and the call worthless. Therefore, any in-the-money call would be exercised just before this liquidating dividend.

Dividends do not always prompt early exercise, but if they are sufficiently large, call option holders capture them by exercising just before the ex-dividend date. We see managers acting in the same way: when a project's forecasted cash flows are sufficiently large, they "capture" the cash flows by investing right away.[8] But when forecasted cash flows are small, they are inclined to hold on to their call rather than investing, even when project NPV is positive. This explains why managers are sometimes reluctant to commit to positive-NPV projects. This caution is rational as long as the option to wait is open and sufficiently valuable.

*Valuing the Malted Herring Option

We will put some numbers on the malted herring project and then show how to calculate option values when there are cash-flow payouts from the asset. Figure 21-6 shows the possible cash flows and end-of-year values for the malted herring project. You can see that the current value of the project is $200 million. If demand turns out to be low in year 1, the cash flow is only $16 million and the remaining value of the project falls to $160 million. On the other hand, if demand is high in year 1, the cash flow is $25 million and value rises to $250 million. A second year of low demand would cause cash flow to fall to $12.8 million and project value to fall to $128 million, and so on.[9] Although the project lasts

---

[7] We are thinking here of American options. European options cannot be exercised immediately.

[8] In this case the call's value equals its lower-bound value because it is exercised immediately: the two lines in Figure 21-3 touch where project PV is high enough to trigger immediate investment. At this and higher PVs the value of a European call option, which could not be exercised immediately, would lie below the value of a now-or-never investment.

[9] We assume here that in each year there is a 44% probability of a 25% rise in the cash flow and a 56% probability of a 20% fall. The *expected* change in the cash flow is $(0.44 \times 25) + (0.56 \times (-20)) = 0$. Since this cash flow is expected to persist indefinitely, we calculate project value at each point by dividing by a 10% cost of capital. Thus, if the cash flow in year 1 is $16,000, project value at the end of the year is $16/0.10 = 160$ or $160,000.

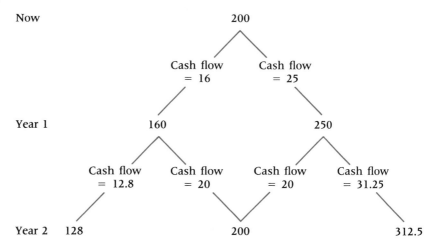

Figure 21-6   The possible cash flows and end-of-period values for the first two years of the malted herring project.

indefinitely, we assume that investment cannot be postponed beyond the end of the second year and, therefore, we show only the cash flows for the first two years and the possible values at the end of the two years. Notice that if you undertake the investment right away, you capture the first year's cash flow ($16 million or $25 million); if you delay, you miss out on this cash flow but you now have more information on how the project is likely to work out.

If demand is high in the first year, the malted herring plant has a cash flow of $25 million and a year-end value of $250 million. The total return is ($25 + 250)/ 200 − 1 = 0.375 or 37.5%. If demand is low, the plant has a cash flow of 16 million dollars and a year-end value of $160 million. Total return is (16 + 160)/ 200 − 1 = −0.12 or −12%. In a *risk-neutral* world the expected return would be equal to the interest rate, which we assume is 5%:

$$\begin{pmatrix} \text{Expected} \\ \text{return} \end{pmatrix} = \begin{pmatrix} \text{Probability of} \\ \text{high demand} \end{pmatrix} \times 37.5 + \left(1 - \begin{pmatrix} \text{probability of} \\ \text{low demand} \end{pmatrix}\right) \times (-12)$$

$$= 0.05 \text{ or } 5\%$$

Therefore, probability of high demand is 34.3%.

We want to value a call option on the malted herring project with an exercise price of $180 million. We begin as usual at the end and work backwards. The bottom row of Figure 21-7 shows the possible values of this option at the end of year 2. If project value is $128 million, the option to invest is worthless. At the other extreme, if project value is $312.5 million, option value is 312.5 − 180 = $132.5 million.

To calculate option values at year 1 we work out the expected payoffs in a risk-neutral world and discount at the interest rate of 5%. Thus, if project value in year 1 is $160 million, option value is:

$$\frac{(0.343 \times 20) + (0.657 \times 0)}{1.05} = \$6.5 \text{ million}$$

If project value in year 1 is $250 million, option value is:

$$\frac{(0.343 \times 132.5) + (0.657 \times 20)}{1.05} = \$55.8 \text{ million}$$

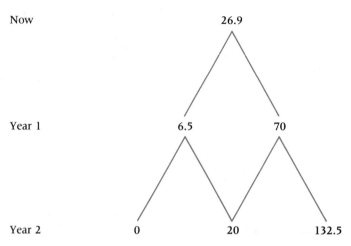

Now   26.9

Year 1   6.5   70

Year 2   0   20   132.5

Figure 21-7 The values of the option to build a malted herring factory. The option to build the factory in the future is worth more than the NPV of the factory if built today.

But here is where we need to recognize the opportunity to exercise the option early. The option is worth $55.8 million if we keep it open, but it is worth 250 − 180 = $70 million if exercised. Thus, if demand is high in year 1, there will be no point in delaying investment further. We will exercise our option to invest in the malted herring plant.

We know now that if demand is low in year 1, the option at the end of the year is worth $6.5 million and, if demand is high, the option is worth $70 million. We now work back to the value today by calculating the expected payoff on the option and discounting at the interest rate.

$$\text{Option value today} = \frac{(0.343 \times 70) + (0.657 \times 6.5)}{1.05} = \$26.9 \text{ million}$$

The value of the malted herring option is 200 − 180 = $20 million if exercised immediately. But the option is worth $26.9 million if we keep it open for at least a year. Thus, the fact that the malted herring project had a positive NPV was not sufficient reason for investing. There was a still better strategy—"Wait and See."

Notice how we worked this out. We worked back from the final period in the usual way but at each step we checked whether the option was worth more dead than alive and we used the higher of the two values as we worked back through the binomial tree. You can use the same technique whenever you need to value an American option on a dividend-paying stock.

Option Valuation and Decision Trees   Calculating option values by the binomial method is basically a process of solving decision trees. You start at some future date and work back through the tree to the present, checking at each decision point to determine the best future action. Eventually, the possible cash flows generated by future events and actions are folded back to a present value.

Is the binomial method merely another application of decision trees, a tool of analysis that you learned about in Chapter 10? The answer is no, for at least two reasons. First, option theory gives us a simple, powerful framework for describing complex decision trees. The complete decision tree for our malted herring factory would overflow the largest classroom blackboard. Now that you know about options, we can refer to the opportunity to invest in malted herring production as just "an American call on a perpetuity with a constant dividend yield." Of course not all real problems have such easy options analogues, but we can often approximate complex decision trees by some simple package of assets and options. A custom decision tree may get closer to "reality" but the time and expense may not be worth it. Most men buy their suits off the rack even though a custom-tailored suit from Saville Row would fit better and look nicer.

Second, and more important, option pricing theory is absolutely essential for discounting within decision trees. Standard discounted cash flow doesn't work within decision trees for the same reason that it doesn't work for puts and calls. As we pointed out in Section 20-4, there is no single, constant discount rate for options because the risk of the option changes as time and the price of the underlying asset change. There is no single discount rate inside a decision tree, because if the tree contains meaningful future decisions, it also contains options. The market value of the future cash flows described by the decision tree has to be calculated by option pricing methods.

21-4   A CHECKLIST

When we introduced option valuation in the last chapter, we focused on the valuation of European calls. In the course of this chapter we have encountered European and American options, calls and puts, options on assets that pay dividends and on those that don't. You may find it useful to have the following checklist of how different combinations of features affect option value.

American calls—no dividends   We know that in the absence of dividends the value of a call option increases with time to maturity. So, if you exercised an American call option early, you would needlessly reduce its value. Since an American call should not be exercised before maturity, its value is the same as that of a European call, and the Black-Scholes formula applies to both options.

European puts—no dividends   If we wish to value a European put, we can use a formula that we developed in Chapter 20:

$$\text{Value of put} = \text{value of call} - \text{value of stock} + \text{PV(exercise price)}$$

American puts—no dividends   It can sometimes pay to exercise an American put before maturity in order to reinvest the exercise price. For example, suppose that immediately after buying an American put the stock price falls to zero. In this case there is no advantage to holding on to the option since it *cannot* become more valuable. It is better to exercise the put and invest the exercise money. Thus, an American put is always more valuable than a European put. In our extreme example, the difference is equal to the present value of the interest that you could earn on the exercise price. In all other cases, the difference is less.

Because the Black-Scholes formula does not allow for early exercise, it cannot be used to value an American put exactly. But you can use the step-by-step binomial method as long as you check at each point whether the option is worth more dead than alive and then use the higher of these two values.

European calls on dividend-paying stocks   Part of the share value is composed of the present value of dividends to which the option holder is not entitled.

Therefore, when using the Black-Scholes model to value a European call on a dividend-paying stock, you should reduce the price of the stock by the present value of dividends paid before the option's maturity.[10]

EXAMPLE   Dividends don't always come with a label attached; so look out for instances where the asset holder gets a benefit and the option does not. For example, when you buy foreign currency, you can invest it to earn interest, but if you own an option to buy foreign currency, you miss out on this income.

Suppose that in spring 1991 you are offered a 1-year option to buy sterling at the current exchange rate of $1.75; i.e., C$1.75 = £1. You have the following information:

- Maturity of option $t = 1$
- Exercise price $E = \$1.75$
- Current price of sterling $P = \$1.75$
- Standard deviation of exchange rate changes $\sigma = 0.10$
- Dollar interest rate $r_\$ = 0.10$
- Sterling interest rate $r_£ = 0.12$

If you buy sterling, you can invest it to earn interest at 12%. By buying the option rather than sterling itself you miss out on this "dividend." Therefore, to value the call option you must first reduce the current price of sterling by the amount of the lost interest:[11]

$$\text{Adjusted price of sterling} = P^* = \frac{\text{current price}}{1 + r_£} = \frac{1.75}{1.12} = \$1.56$$

Now you can apply the Black-Scholes formula:

$$\text{Standard deviation} \times \sqrt{\text{time}} = 0.10\sqrt{1} = 0.10$$

$$\frac{\text{Price}}{\text{PV(exercise price)}} = \frac{P^*}{E/(1 + r_s)} = \frac{1.56}{1.75/1.10} = 0.98$$

Using the call option tables in Appendix Table 6 gives

$$\text{Value of call} = 0.031 \times P^* = 0.031 \times 1.56 = 0.048$$

That is, 4.8 cents per pound. An option to purchase £1 million on these terms would be worth $48,000.

American Calls on Dividend-Paying Stocks

We have seen that when the stock does not pay dividends, an American call option is *always* worth more alive than dead. That way you both keep your option open *and* earn interest on the exercise money. Even when there are dividends, you should never exercise early if the dividend you gain is less than the interest that you lose by having to pay the exercise price early. However, if the dividend is sufficiently large, you might want to capture it by exercising the option just before the ex-dividend date.

---

[10] For real options the "dividends" are cash flows generated by some real asset. The present value of these cash flows would be excluded from the asset's present value when you value an option on the asset. For example, our valuation of the abandonment option for Magna Charter's turboprop ignored the income that the plane would generate in year 1, before the option to sell the plane could be exercised.

[11] Note that current price − PV(interest) = $P - \dfrac{r_£ P}{1 + r_£} = \dfrac{P}{1 + r_£}$

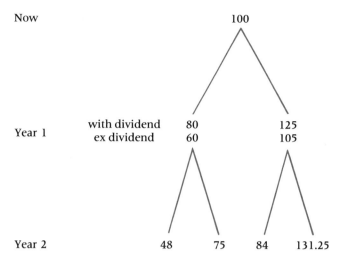

Figure 21-8   Possible values of Consolidated Pork Bellies stock.

The only general method for valuing an American call on a dividend-paying stock is to use the step-by-step binomial method. In this case you must check at each stage whether the option is more valuable if exercised just before the ex-dividend date or if you should hold it for at least one more period.

EXAMPLE   Here is a last chance to practice your option valuation skills by valuing an American call on a dividend-paying stock. Figure 21-8 summarizes the possible price movements in Consolidated Pork Bellies stock. The stock price is currently $100 but over the next year it could either fall by 20% to $80 or rise by 25% to $125. In either case the company will then pay its regular dividend of $20. Immediately after payment of this dividend the stock price will fall to $80 − $20 = $60, or 125 − 20 = $105. Over the second year the price will again either fall by 20% from the ex-dividend price or rise by 25%.[12]

Suppose that you wish to value a 2-year American call option on Consolidated stock. Figure 21-9 shows the possible option values at each point assuming an exercise price of $70 and an interest rate of 12%. We won't go through all the calculations behind these figures but we will just focus on the option values at the end of Year 1.

Suppose that the stock price has fallen in the first year. What is the option worth if you hold on to it for a further period? You should be used to this problem by now. First pretend that investors are risk-neutral and calculate the probability that the stock will rise in price. This probability turns out to be 71%.[13] Now calculate the expected payoff on the option and discount at 12%.

$$\begin{matrix} \text{Option value if} \\ \text{not exercised} \\ \text{in Year 1} \end{matrix} = \frac{(0.71 \times 5) + (0.29 \times 0)}{1.12} = 3.18$$

---

[12] Notice that the payment of a fixed dividend in Year 1 results in four possible stock prices at the end of Year 2. In other words, 60 × 1.25 does not equal 105 × 0.8. Don't let that put you off. You still start from the end and work back one step at a time to find the possible option values at each date.

[13] Using the formula in footnote 5 gives:

$$p = \frac{r - d}{u - d} = \frac{12 - (-20)}{25 - (-20)} = 0.71$$

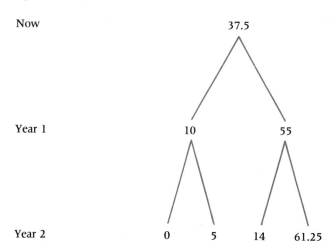

Figure 21-9 Values of a two-year call option on Consolidated Pork Bellies stock. Exercise price is $70. Although we show option values for year 2, the option will not be alive then. It will be exercised in year 1.

Thus, if you hold on to the option, it is worth $3.18. However, if you exercise the option just before the ex-dividend date, you pay an exercise price of $70 for a stock worth $80. This $10 value from exercising is greater than the $3.18 from holding on to the option. Therefore, in Figure 21-9 we put in an option value of $10 if the stock price falls in Year 1.

Similarly, you want to exercise if the stock price *rises* in Year 1. The option is worth only $42.45 if you hold on to it but $55 if you exercise. Therefore, in Figure 21-9 we put in a value of $55 if the stock price rises.

The rest of the calculation is routine. Calculate the expected option payoff in Year 1 and discount by 12% to give the option value today:

$$\text{Option value today} = \frac{(0.71 \times 55) + (0.29 \times 10)}{1.12} = \$37.5$$

21-5 SUMMARY

In Chapter 20 you learned the basics of option valuation. In this chapter we described three important real options.

1. *The option to make follow-on investments.* Companies often cite "strategic" value when taking on negative-NPV projects. A close look at the projects' payoffs reveals a call option on follow-on projects in addition to the immediate projects' cash flows. Today's investments can generate tomorrow's opportunities.
2. *The option to abandon.* The option to abandon a project provides partial insurance against failure. This is a put option; the put's exercise price is the value of the project's assets if sold or shifted to a more valuable use.
3. *The option to wait* (and learn) before investing is equivalent to owning a call option on the investment project. The call is exercised when the firm commits to the project. But often it's better to defer a positive-NPV project in order to keep the call alive. Deferral is most attractive when uncertainty is great and immediate project cash flows, which are lost or postponed by waiting, are small.

We should offer here a health warning. The real options encountered in practice are usually considerably more complex than the simple examples that we examined in this chapter. For instance, you may be able to bail out from a project at any time rather than the single occasion that we assumed for Magna Charter. The price at which you can bail out is likely to change over time and will rarely be known in advance. Also, once you have abandoned you may be able to reinstate the project if business improves. Handling such complexities typically requires a number-crunching computer.

Modeling the problem also requires informed judgement. For example, when we discussed the option to postpone investment, we assumed that postponement causes you to miss out on the first year's cash flow although you learn what this flow would have been if you had undertaken the project. But that may not always be the case. Sometimes you may learn nothing by waiting, so that at the end of the year you are at exactly the same position as when you started. Obviously, how much you learn by waiting makes a considerable difference to your estimate of option value.

These examples of real options provided an opportunity to review and extend the option-valuation methods introduced in Chapter 20.

The binomial method assumes that the time to the option's maturity can be divided into a number of subintervals in each of which there are only two possible price changes. In the last chapter we valued an option with only one period to expiration. Here we showed you how to value an option with many periods to expiration. The advantage of chopping the life of the option into many subperiods is that it allows you to recognize that the asset may take on many future values. You can think of the Black-Scholes formula as a shortcut solution when there is an indefinite number of these subperiods and therefore an indefinite number of possible future asset prices.

Regardless of the number of subperiods, the basic idea behind the binomial method is the same. You start at the option's maturity and work back one step at a time to find the option's initial value. But that raises a question: How do we pick sensible numbers for the up and down moves in the asset values? We introduced you to a formula that allows you to derive the up and down moves that are consistent with a given standard deviation of asset returns.

One of the advantages of holding the asset is that you may receive dividends; the option holder generally doesn't get these dividends. If there are no dividends, you would never want to exercise a call option before maturity. (Even if you *knew* that you were going to exercise it, you would prefer to pay the exercise money later rather than sooner.) But when the asset does pay a dividend, it may pay to exercise a call option early in order to capture the dividend. You can still use the binomial method to value the option but at each point you need to check whether the option is worth more dead than alive.

FURTHER READING

Sick discusses real options and also shows how to build a large spreadsheet to analyze binomial option models:

G.A. Sick, *Capital Budgeting with Real Options*, Monograph 1989–3, Salomon Brothers Center for the Study of Financial Institutions, Stern School of Business, New York University (1989).

The spring 1987 issue of the *Midland Corporate Finance Journal* contains several articles on real options and capital investment decisions. See also Kester for a discussion of options and corporate strategy:

W.C. Kester, "Today's Options for Tomorrow's Growth," *Harvard Business Review*, **62**: 153–160 (March–April 1984).

Mason and Merton review a range of option applications to corporate finance:

S.P. Mason and R.C. Merton, "The Role of Contingent Claims Analysis in Corporate Finance," in E.I. Altman and M.G. Subrahmanyam (eds.), *Recent Advances in Corporate Finance*, Richard D. Irwin, Inc., Homewood, Ill., 1985.

Brennan and Schwartz have worked out an interesting application to natural resource investments:

M.J. Brennan and E.s. Schwartz, "Evaluating Natural Resource Investments," *Journal of Business*, **58**: 135–157 (April 1985).

The texts given under Further Reading in Chapter 20 can be referred to for further discussion of the binomial method and the practical complications of applying option pricing theory.

QUIZ

1. Describe the real option in each of the following cases.
   (a) Backwoods Chemical postpones a major plant expansion. The expansion has positive NPV on a discounted cash flow basis, but top management wants to get a better fix on product demand before proceeding.
   (b) Western Telecom commits to production of digital switching equipment specially designed for the European market. The project has a negative discounted cash flow NPV, but is justified by the need for a strong market position in the rapidly growing, and potentially very profitable, market.
   (c) Western Telecom vetos a fully integrated, automated production line for the new digital switches. It relies on standard, less expensive equipment. The automated line is more efficient overall, according to a discounted cash flow analysis.

2. Backwoods Chemical's stock price changes only once a month: Either it goes up by 20% or it falls by 10%. Its price now is 40. The interest rate is 12.7% per year, or about 1% per month.
   (a) What is the value of a 1-month call option with an exercise price of 40?
   (b) What is the option delta?
   (c) Show how the payoffs of this call option can be replicated by buying Backwoods stock and borrowing.
   (d) What is the value of a 2-month call option with an exercise price of 40?
   (e) What is the option delta of the 2-month call over the first 1-month period?

3. "The Black-Scholes formula gives the same answer as the binomial method when _____." Fill in the blank and briefly explain.

4. For which of these options *might* it be rational to exercise before maturity? Say briefly why or why not.
   (a) American put on a nondividend-paying stock.
   (b) American call—the dividend payment is $5 per annum, the exercise price is $100, and the interest rate is 10%.

(c) American call — the interest rate is 10% and the dividend payment is 5% of future stock price. *Hint:* Stock price may rise or fall.

(d) American call on deutsche marks.

5. Suppose a stock price can go up by 15% or down by 13% over the next period. You own a one-period put on the stock. The interest rate is 10%, and the current stock price is 60.

(a) What exercise price leaves you indifferent between holding the put or exercising it now?

(b) How does this "break-even" exercise price change if the interest rate is increased?

6. Dr. Livingstone I. Presume holds £600,000 in East African gold stocks. Bullish as he is on gold mining, he requires absolute assurance that at least £500,000 will be available in 6 months to fund an expedition. Describe two ways for Dr. Presume to achieve this goal. There is an active market for puts and calls on East African gold stocks, and the sterling rate of interest is 12.4% per year.

QUESTIONS AND PROBLEMS

1. Describe each of the following situations in the language of options.

(a) Drilling rights to undeveloped heavy crude oil in Saskatchewan. Development and production of the oil now is a negative-NPV endeavour. (The break-even oil price is $32 per barrel, versus a spot price of $20.) However, the decision to develop can be put off for up to 5 years. Development costs are expected to increase by 5% per year.

(b) A restaurant producing net cash flows, after all out-of-pocket expenses, of $700,000 per year. There is no upward or downward trend in the cash flows, but they fluctuate, with an annual standard deviation of 15%. The real estate occupied by the restaurant is owned, not leased, and could be sold for $5 million. The interest rate is 10%. Ignore taxes.

(c) A variation on part (b): Assume the restaurant faces known fixed costs of $300,000 per year incurred so long as the restaurant is operating. Thus:

$$\text{Net cash flow} = \begin{array}{c} \text{revenue} \\ \text{less variable} \\ \text{costs} \end{array} - \text{fixed costs}$$
$$\$700,000 = 1,000,000 - 300,000$$

The annual standard deviation of the forecast error of revenue less variable costs is 10.5%. The interest rate is 10%. Ignore taxes.

(d) The British-French treaty giving a concession to build a railroad link under the English Channel also requires the concessionaire to propose by the year 2000 to build a "drive-through link" if "technical and economic conditions permit . . . and the increase in traffic shall justify it without undermining the expected return on the first [rail] link." Other companies will not be permitted to build a link before the year 2020.

2. Perform a sensitivity analysis on Table 21-2. The CFO would like to know how the present value of the option on the Mark II depends on

(a) The degree of uncertainty (standard deviation)

(b) The forecasted NPV of the Mark II

(c) The rate of growth of the micro market (which determines the possible *scale* of the Mark II project)

3. You own a 1-year call option on 1 acre of Toronto real estate. The exercise price is $2 million, and the current, appraised market value of the land is $1.7 million. The land is currently used as a parking lot, generating just enough money to cover real estate taxes. Over the last 5 years, similar properties have appreciated by 20% per year. The annual standard deviation is 15% and the interest rate 12%. How much is your call worth? Use the Black-Scholes formula and Appendix Table 6.

4. A variation on question 3: Suppose the land is occupied by a warehouse, generating rents of $150,000 after real estate taxes and all other out-of-pocket costs. The value of the land plus warehouse is again $1.7 million. Other facts are as in question 3. You have a *European* call option. What is it worth?

5. The price of Wigeon Corp. stock is 100. During each of the next two 6-month periods the price may either rise by 25% or fall by 20% (equivalent to a standard deviation of 31.5% a year). At month 6 the company will pay a dividend of $20. The interest rate is 10% per 6-month period. What is the value of a one-year American call option with an exercise price of 80? Now recalculate option value assuming that the dividend is equal to 20% of the with-dividend stock price.

6. Buffelhead stock price is $220 and could halve or double in each six month period (equivalent to an annual standard deviation of 98%). A one-year call option on Buffelhead has an exercise price of $165. The interest rate is 21% a year.
    (a) What is the value of the Buffelhead call?
    (b) Now calculate the option delta for the second 6 months if (i) the stock price rises to $440; (ii) the stock price falls to $110.
    (c) How does the call option delta vary with the level of the stock price? Explain, intuitively, why.
    (d) Suppose that in month 6 the Buffelhead stock price is $110. How at that point could you replicate an investment in the stock by a combination of call options and risk-free lending? Show that your strategy does indeed produce the same returns as an investment in the stock.

7. Recalculate the value of the Buffelhead option (see question 6) assuming that the option is American and that at the end of the first 6 months the company pays a dividend of $25. (Thus, the price at the end of the year is either double or half the *ex*-dividend price in month 6.) How would your answer change if the option were European?

8. Suppose that you have an option which allows you to sell Buffelhead stock in month 6 for $165 *or* to buy it in month 12 for $165 (see question 6). What is the value of this unusual option?

9. The current price of Northern Airlines stock is $100. During each 6-month period it will either rise by 11.1% or fall by 10% (equivalent to an annual standard deviation of 14.9%). The interest rate is 5% per 6-month period.
    (a) Calculate the value of a 1-year European put option on Northern stock with an exercise price of 102.
    (b) Recalculate the value of the Northern put option, assuming that it is an American option.

10. The current price of United Carbon (UC) stock is $200. The standard deviation is 22.3% a year and the interest rate is 21% a year. A 1-year call option on UC has an exercise price of $180.
    (a) Use the Black-Scholes model to value the call option on UC.
    (b) Use the formula given in Section 21-3 to calculate the up and down

' moves that you would use if you valued the UC option with the one-period binomial method. Now value the option using the one-period binomial method.

(c) Now recalculate the up and down moves and revalue the option using the two-period binomial method.

(d) Use your answer to part (c) to calculate the option delta (i) today, (ii) next period if the stock price rises, and (iii) next period if the stock price falls. Show at each point how you would replicate a call option with a levered investment in the company's stock.

11. Options have many uses. They allow you (a) to take a levered position in the asset, (b) to sell the asset short, (c) to insure against a fall in the value of the asset, (d) to hedge against any changes in the asset value and (e) to bet on the asset's variability. Explain *how* you can use options in these ways. Are there other means to achieve the same ends?

12. Suppose you construct an option hedge by buying a levered position in delta shares of stock and selling one call option. As the share price changes the option delta changes and you will need to adjust your hedge. You can minimize the cost of adjustments if changes in the stock price have only a small effect on the option delta. Construct an example to show whether the option delta is likely to vary more if you hedge with an in-the-money option, an at-the-money option, or an out-of-the-money option.

13. Suppose you expect to need a new plant ready to produce turbo-encabulators in 36 months. If design A is chosen, construction must begin immediately. Design B is more expensive, but you can wait 12 months before breaking ground. Figure 21-10 shows the cumulative present value of construction costs for the two designs up to the 36-month deadline. Assume

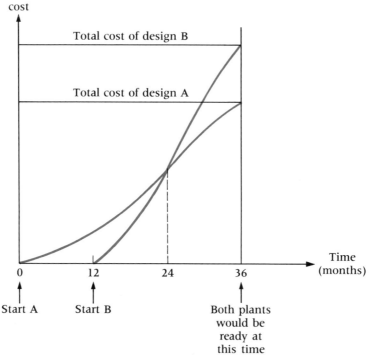

Figure 21-10 Cumulative construction cost of the two plant designs. Plant A takes 36 months to build, plant B only 24. But plant B costs more.

that the designs, once built, are equally efficient and have equal production capacity.

A standard discounted cash flow analysis ranks design A ahead of design B. But suppose the demand for turbo-encabulators falls and the new factory is not needed; then, as Figure 21-10 shows, the firm is better off with design B provided the project is abandoned before month 24.

Describe this situation as the choice between two (complex) call options. Then describe the same situation in terms of (complex) abandonment put options. The two descriptions should imply identical payoffs to each design, given optimal exercise strategies.

14. In August 1986 Salomon Brothers issued 4-year Standard & Poor's 500 Index Subordinated Notes (SPINS). These pay no interest but at maturity the investor receives the face value plus a possible bonus. This bonus is equal to $1,000 times the proportionate appreciation in the market index.
   (a) What would be the value of SPINS if issued today?
   (b) If Salomon Brothers wished to hedge itself against a rise in the market index, how should it do so?

15. Other things equal, which of these American options are you most likely to want to exercise early:
   (a) A put option on a stock with a large dividend or a call on the same stock
   (b) A put option on a stock that is selling well below exercise price or a call on the same stock
   (c) A put option when the interest rate is high or the same put option when the interest rate is low?

Illustrate your answer with examples using the two-step binomial method.

16. Is it better to exercise a call option on the with-dividend date or on the ex-dividend date? How about a put option? Explain.

C · H · A · P · T · E · R

22

WARRANTS AND
CONVERTIBLES

Many debt issues are either packages of bonds and warrants or convertible bonds. The warrant gives its owner the right to buy other securities issued by the company. A convertible bond gives its owner the right to exchange the bond for other securities.

There is also convertible preferred stock — it is often used to finance mergers, for example. Convertible preferred gives its owner the right to exchange the preferred share for other securities.

What are these strange hybrids, and how should you value them? Why are they issued? We will answer each of these questions in its turn.

22-1 WHAT IS A WARRANT?

A significant proportion of private placement bonds and a smaller proportion of public issues are sold with warrants. In addition, warrants are sometimes attached to issues of common stock or preferred stock or are given to underwriters as compensation for their services.[1]

Here is an example of an issue of warrants. In April of 1990 BCE Inc. — the parent company of Bell Canada, Northern Telecom, Montreal Trust, and others — raised $417.5 million by issuing 10 million packages of preferred shares and warrants. Each package contained one variable rate preferred share[2] and one

---

[1] The term warrant usually refers to a long-term option issued by a company on its own stock or bonds, but in recent years investment banks and other financial institutions have issued ''warrants'' to buy the stock of another firm. For example, in August 1989 Bankers Trust in the United States sold 125,000 covered warrants, each of which entitled the holder to buy one share of J.C. Penny, two shares of Toys-R-Us, and one share of Wal-Mart Stores. The term ''covered warrant'' indicates that Bankers Trust had covered its risk by holding a package of these stocks.

[2] The preferreds were cumulative, a feature that we discussed in Chapter 14. The fact that they were redeemable means Bell has an option to buy them back at a pre-specified price. The retraction feature allows investors the option to sell the shares back to Bell at a pre-specified price. We discuss redemption and retraction in Chapter 24. The fact that they were variable rate means that the dividend payments are adjusted periodically. We'll take another look at floating rate preferreds in Chapter 32.

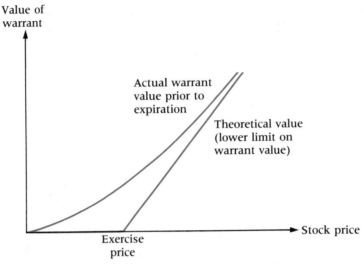

Figure 22-1   Relationship between warrant value and stock price. The heavy line is the lower limit for warrant value. Warrant value falls to the lower limit just before the option expires. Before expiration, warrant value lies on a curve like the one shown here.

warrant. Each warrant gave the right to buy one share of common stock for $45.75 at any time before April 28, 1995. Since the price of the common stock at the time of issue was $38.38, the exercise price was 10% above the initial share price. The package or "unit" was issued at $41.75.

Occasionally, bonds and warrants can be traded only as a package but the BCE warrants were detachable. This means that they can be traded separately.

The BCE issue had a special features. Instead of paying out $45.75 in cash to exercise the warrant, the holder can choose to hand over one of the preferred shares plus $4.00. If the preferred share is worth less than $41.75, it pays to hand over the share; if it is worth more than $41.75, it is better to use cash.

The warrant holder is not entitled to vote or to receive dividends but the exercise price of the warrant is adjusted for any stock dividends or splits. For example, if BCE has a 2 for 1 stock split, the exercise price is automatically cut in half to $22.88.

Most warrant issues resemble that of BCE Inc., but occasionally they are more exotic. In 1984, for example, Lac Minerals Ltd. issued $50 million of 8% $1,000 debentures with each debenture having attached four gold purchase warrants. This type of warrant is unusual because it is not written on the company's common stock. Rather, this warrant provides its holder with the right to buy a physical commodity, specifically 0.5 troy ounces of gold at a purchase price of $230 (U.S.).[3]

But even stock purchase warrants are not without complication. In 1968 Loew's Theaters in the United States acquired Lorillard Corporation. For each share, Loew's offered a subordinated debenture with a face value of $62, plus one warrant. The warrant entitled its owner to buy one share of Loew's common stock at any time between 1968 and 1980. The exercise price was set at $35.00 for the first four years, $37.50 for the next four years, and $40.00 for the final four years.

---

[3] In 1981 Echo-Bay Mines introduced an even more complex gold purchase warrant. The warrant was only exercisable if Echo-Bay met certain production levels prior to the exercise date. These warrants are analyzed in "Pricing Complex Options: Echo-Bay Ltd. Gold Purchase Warrants," *Canadian Journal of Administrative Studies*, **2**: 294–306 (1985).

Valuing Warrants

As a trained option spotter (having read Chapter 20), you have probably already classified the BCE Inc. warrant as a five-year American call option exercisable at $45.75. You can depict the relationship between the value of the warrant and the value of the common stock with our standard option shorthand, as in Figure 22-1. The lower limit on the value of the warrant is the heavy line in the figure. If the price of BCE stock is less than $45.75, the lower limit on the warrant price is zero: if the price of the stock is greater than $45.75, the lower limit is equal to the stock price minus $45.75.[4] Investors in warrants sometimes refer to this lower limit as the *theoretical* value of the warrant. It is a misleading term because both theory and practice tell us that before the final exercise date the value of the warrant should lie *above* the lower limit, on a curve like the one in Figure 22-1.

The height of this curve depends on two things. As we explained in Section 20-4, it depends on the variance of the stock returns per period (σ^2) times the number of periods before the warrant expires ($\sigma^2 t$). It also depends on the rate of interest times the length of the option period ($r_f t$). If the warrant has no unusual features and the stock pays no dividends, then the value of the option can be estimated from the Black-Scholes formula described in Section 20-4.

Of course, as time runs out on a warrant, its price snuggles closer and closer to the lower bound. On the final day of its life, its price hits the lower bound.

Two Complications: Dividends and Dilution

Thus far our discussion of warrants has just repeated what was said about call options in Chapter 20, but special problems are often encountered in applying these principles to warrants. For example, we have seen that the exercise price may change over time. Another problem occurs when warrants are issued against dividend-paying stocks. The warrant holder is not entitled to dividends. In fact, the warrant holder loses every time a cash dividend is paid, because paying the dividend reduces stock price and thus reduces the value of the warrant. It may pay to exercise the warrant before maturity in order to capture the extra income.[5]

Remember that the Black-Scholes option-valuation formula assumes that the stock pays no dividends. Thus, it will not give the theoretically correct value for a warrant issued by a dividend-paying firm. However, we showed in Chapter 21 how you can use the one step at a time binomial method to value options on dividend paying stocks.

Another complication is that exercising the warrants increases the number of shares. Therefore, exercise means that the firm's assets and profits are spread over a larger number of shares. For example, BCE's earnings in 1990 were $3.50 per share on an "undiluted" basis (that is, ignoring warrants). If the warrants had been exercised in 1990 and if *total* earnings had been unaffected by the influx of cash from exercise, earnings *per share* would have been only $3.39. In other words, *diluted earnings* per share were $3.39.[6] Firms with significant amounts of

---

[4] Do you remember why this is a lower limit? What would happen if, by some accident, the warrant price was *less* than the stock price minus $45.75? (See Section 20-3.)

[5] This may make sense if the dividend payment is larger than the interest that could be earned on the exercise price. By *not* exercising, the warrant holder keeps the exercise price and can put this money to work.

[6] BCE Inc.'s undiluted earnings per share (EPS) for 1990 equal actual 1990 net income ($1,062 million) divided by the average number of shares outstanding in 1990 (303 million):

$$EPS = \frac{\$1,032}{303} = \$3.50$$

There were 10 million new warrants issued. If they had been converted in 1990 the number of outstanding shares would have increased to 313 million. EPS would have declined to $3.39:

$$EPS \text{ (diluted)} = \frac{\$1,032}{313} = \$3.39$$

warrants or convertible issues outstanding are now required to report earnings on a fully diluted basis.

The problem of dilution never arises with call options. If you buy or sell an option on the Toronto Stock Exchange, you have no effect on the assets of the company or the number of shares outstanding.

Example: Valuing United Glue's Warrants

United Glue has just issued a $2 million package of debt and warrants. Here are some basic data that we can use to value the warrants:

- Number of shares outstanding $= N = 1$ million
- Current stock price $= P = \$12$
- Number of warrants issued per share outstanding $= q = 0.10$
- Total number of warrants issued $= Nq = 100,000$
- Exercise price of warrants $= EX = \$10$
- Time to expiration of warrants $= t = 4$ years
- Annual standard deviation of stock price changes $= \sigma = 0.40$
- Rate of interest $= r = 10\%$

Suppose that without the warrants the debt is worth $1.5 million. Then investors must be paying $0.5 million for the warrants:

$$\begin{array}{ccc} \text{Cost of} & = \text{total amount} & - \text{value of loan} \\ \text{warrants} & \text{of financing} & \text{without warrants} \end{array}$$

$$500,000 = 2,000,000 \quad - 1,500,000$$

$$\text{Each warrant costs investors } \frac{500,000}{100,000} = \$5$$

The following table shows the market value of United's assets and liabilities both before and after the issue:

Before the issue:

Market Value Balance Sheet (in millions)

Existing assets	$16	$ 4	Existing loans
			Common stock
			(1 million shares
		12	at $12 a share)
Total	$16	$16	Total

After the issue:

Market Value Balance Sheet (in millions)

Existing assets	$16	$ 4	Existing loans
New assets financed			New loan without
by debt and warrants	2	1.5	warrants
		5.5	Total debt
		0.5	Warrants
		12	Common stock
		12.5	Total equity
Total	$18	$18	Total

Now let us take a stab at checking whether the warrants are really worth the $500,000 that investors are paying for them. Remember that the warrant is a call option to buy United stock. The stock does not pay a dividend. Therefore, we can use the call option tables in Appendix Table 6 to value the warrants. First we need two items of data:

$$\begin{array}{c}\text{Standard} \\ \text{deviation}\end{array} \times \begin{array}{c}\text{square root} \\ \text{of time}\end{array} = \sigma\sqrt{t} = 0.40\sqrt{4} = 0.80$$

$$\begin{array}{c}\text{Share price divided by} \\ \text{PV (exercise money)}\end{array} = \frac{P}{\text{PV(EX)}} = \frac{12}{10/(1.1)^4} = 1.75$$

From Appendix Table 6, we find

$$\frac{\text{Call option value}}{\text{Share price}} = \frac{C}{P} = 0.511$$

Therefore, $\begin{array}{c}\text{Call option} \\ \text{value}\end{array} = 0.511 \times \begin{array}{c}\text{share} \\ \text{price}\end{array} = 0.511 \times 12 = \$6.13$

Thus, the warrant issue looks to be a good deal for investors and a bad deal for United. Investors are paying $5 a share for warrants that are worth $6.13.

*How the Value of United Warrants Is Affected by Dilution

Unfortunately, our calculations for United warrants do not tell the whole story. Remember that when investors exercise a traded call or put option, there is no change in either the company's assets or the number of shares outstanding. But, if United's warrants are exercised, the number of shares outstanding will increase by $Nq = 100,000$. Also the assets will increase by the amount of the exercise money ($Nq \times EX = 100,000 \times \$10 = \$1$ million). In other words, there will be dilution. We need to allow for this dilution when we value the warrants.

Let us call the value of United's equity V:

$$\begin{array}{c}\text{Value of} \\ \text{equity}\end{array} = V = \begin{array}{c}\text{value of United's} \\ \text{total assets}\end{array} - \begin{array}{c}\text{value of} \\ \text{debt}\end{array}$$

If the warrants are exercised, equity value will increase by the amount of the exercise money to $V + NqEX$. At the same time the number of shares will increase to $N + Nq$. So the share price after the warrants are exercised will be

$$\text{Share price after exercise} = \frac{V + NqEX}{N + Nq}$$

At maturity the warrant holder can choose to let the warrants lapse or to exercise them and receive the share price less the exercise price. Thus, the value of the warrants will be the share price minus the exercise price or zero, whichever is higher. Another way to write this is:

$$\begin{array}{c}\text{Warrant value} \\ \text{at maturity}\end{array} = \text{maximum}\left(\begin{array}{c}\text{share} \\ \text{price}\end{array} - \begin{array}{c}\text{exercise} \\ \text{price,}\end{array} 0\right)$$

$$= \text{maximum}\left(\frac{V + NqEX}{N + Nq} - EX, 0\right)$$

$$= \text{maximum}\left(\frac{V/N - EX}{1 + q}, 0\right)$$

$$= \frac{1}{1 + q}\,\text{maximum}\left(\frac{V}{N} - EX, 0\right)$$

This tells us the effect of dilution on the value of United's warrants. The warrant value is the value of $1/(1 + q)$ call options written on the stock of an alternative firm with the same total equity value V, *but with no outstanding warrants.* The alternative firm's stock price would be equal to V/N—that is, the total value of United's equity (V) divided by the number of shares outstanding (N).[7] The stock price of this alternative firm is more variable than United's stock price. So when we value the call option on the alternative firm, we must remember to use the standard deviation of the changes in V/N.

Now we can recalculate the value of United's warrants allowing for dilution. First, we find the value of one call option on the stock of an alternative firm with a stock price of V/N:

$$\begin{array}{c}\text{Current equity value} \\ \text{of alternative firm}\end{array} = V = \begin{array}{c}\text{value of United's} \\ \text{total assets}\end{array} - \begin{array}{c}\text{value of} \\ \text{loans}\end{array}$$

$$= 18 - 5.5 = \$12.5 \text{ million}$$

$$\begin{array}{c}\text{Current share price of} \\ \text{alternative firm}\end{array} = \frac{V}{N} = \frac{12.5 \text{ million}}{1 \text{ million}} = \$12.50$$

To use the option table we calculate:

$$\begin{array}{c}\text{Share price divided by} \\ \text{PV (exercise price)}\end{array} = 12.50 \div \frac{10}{(1.1)^4} = 1.83$$

Also, suppose the standard deviation of the share price changes of the alternative firm is $\sigma^* = 0.41$.[8] Then:

$$\begin{array}{c}\text{Standard} \\ \text{deviation}\end{array} \times \begin{array}{c}\text{square root} \\ \text{of time}\end{array} = \sigma^* \times \sqrt{t} = 0.41 \times \sqrt{4} = 0.82$$

---

[7] The modifications to allow for dilution when valuing warrants were originally proposed in F. Black and M. Scholes, "The Pricing of Options and Corporate Liabilities," *Journal of Political Economy,* **81**: 637–654 (May–June 1973), pp. 648, 649. Our exposition follows a discussion in D. Galai and M.I. Schneller, "Pricing of Warrants and the Valuation of the Firm," *Journal of Finance,* **33**: 1333–1342 (December 1978).

[8] How in practice could we compute σ^*? It would be easy if we could wait until the warrants had been trading for some time. In that case, σ^* could be computed from the returns on a package of *all* the company's shares and warrants. In the present case we need to value the warrants *before* they start trading. We argue as follows. The standard deviation of the *assets* before the issue is equal to the standard deviation of a package of the common stock and the existing loans. For example, suppose that the company's debt is risk-free and that the standard deviation of stock returns *before* the bond-warrant issue is 38% (slightly lower than the standard deviation of the common stock after the issue). Then we calculate the standard deviation of the initial assets as follows:

$$\begin{array}{c}\text{Standard deviation} \\ \text{of initial assets}\end{array} = \begin{array}{c}\text{proportion in} \\ \text{common stock}\end{array} \times \begin{array}{c}\text{standard deviation} \\ \text{of common stock}\end{array}$$

$$= \frac{12}{16} \times 38 = 28.5\%$$

Now suppose that the assets after the issue are equally risky. Then:

$$\begin{array}{c}\text{Standard deviation of} \\ \text{assets after issue}\end{array} = \begin{array}{c}\text{proportion of equity} \\ \text{after issue}\end{array} \times \begin{array}{c}\text{standard deviation} \\ \text{of equity } (\sigma^*)\end{array}$$

$$28.5 = \frac{12.5}{18} \times \begin{array}{c}\text{standard deviation} \\ \text{of equity } (\sigma^*)\end{array}$$

$$\text{Standard deviation of equity } (\sigma^*) = 41\%$$

Using a little interpolation in Appendix Table 6, we find:

$$\frac{\text{Call option value}}{\text{share price}} = \frac{C}{P} = 0.53 \text{ (approximately)}$$

Therefore,

$$\frac{\text{Value of call on}}{\text{alternative firm}} = \frac{C}{P} \times \frac{V}{N} = 0.53 \times 12.50 = \$6.63$$

The value of United warrants is equal to:

$$\frac{1}{1 + q} \times \frac{\text{value of call on}}{\text{alternative firm}} = \frac{1}{1.1} \times 6.63 = \$6.02$$

This is a somewhat lower value than we computed when we ignored dilution, but still a bad deal for United.

It may sound from all this as if you need to know the value of United warrants to compute their value. This is not so. The formula does not call for warrant value but for V, the value of United's equity (that is, the shares *plus* warrants). Given equity value, the formula calculates how the overall value of equity should be split up between stock and warrants. Thus, suppose that United's underwriter advises that \$500,000 extra can be raised by issuing a package of bonds and warrants rather than the bonds alone. Is this a fair price? You can check using the Black-Scholes formula with the adjustment for dilution.

Finally, notice that these modifications are necessary to apply the Black-Scholes formula to value a warrant. They are not needed by the warrant holder, who must decide whether to exercise at maturity. If at maturity the price of the stock exceeds the exercise price of the warrant, the warrant holder will, of course, exercise.

Warrants on Bonds

Most warrants are changeable into common stock, but some companies and governments have issued warrants on bonds.[9] For example, the province of British Columbia sold warrants that gave the option to buy 10.6%, 30-year bonds. The warrants expired Sept. 5, 1990.

The Black-Scholes option model assumes that the price of the underlying asset is free to wander randomly, so that the further you look out into the future, the wider is the range of possible prices. But the price of a bond is not free to wander in this happy-go-lucky fashion; as maturity approaches, the bond price gets pulled back to its face value. Because bonds have a date with destiny, the Black-Scholes model gives only a rough estimate of the value of a long-term warrant on a bond. In these cases you need to use an option valuation model that recognizes the way that bond prices vary over time.[10]

---

[9] Now and then you encounter "option warrants" that give you a choice between buying equity or debt.

[10] The following authors have developed more elaborate versions of the Black-Scholes model that can be used for pricing warrants on bonds: G. Courtadon "The Pricing of Options on Default-Free Bonds," *Journal of Financial and Quantitative Analysis*, **17**: 75–100 (March 1982); M.J. Brennan and E.S. Schwartz, "Alternative Methods for Valuing Debt Options," *Finance*, **4**: 119–137 (October 1983).

22-2   WHAT IS A CONVERTIBLE BOND?

The convertible bond is a close relative to the bond-warrant package. Also, many companies choose to issue convertible preferred as an alternative to issuing packages of preferred stock and warrants. We will concentrate on convertible bonds, but almost all our comments also apply to convertible preferred issues.

Here is an example of a convertible bond.

In 1986 PWA Corp. issued \$250 million of 7⅞% convertible subordinated debentures due in 1996.[11] Each bond with a face value of \$1,000 could be converted into 41.66 shares of common stock at any time prior to maturity. In other words, the owner had a 10-year option to return the bond to PWA and receive 41.66 shares of PWA stock in exchange. The number of shares for each bond is called the bonds *conversion ratio*. The conversion ratio of the PWA bond is 41.66.

The conversion ratio for the PWA debenture was computed on the basis of the face value of the bond and the *conversion price* for the shares. Both of these terms are stated in the bond indenture. In order to receive the shares of PWA stock you have to surrender debentures with a face value of \$1,000. This \$1,000 could be applied to the purchase of common shares at a conversion price of \$24.00 per share. Therefore, the conversion ratio of this PWA issue is \$1,000/\$24 or approximately 41.66.

At the time the bond was issued, the price of PWA stock was about \$19. Therefore, the conversion price was about 26% greater than the stock price.

Convertibles are usually protected against stock splits or stock dividends. If PWA were to split its stock 2 for 1 the conversion ratio would increase from 41.66 to 83.33. Thus, the conversion price would drop to \$1,000/83.33 = \$12.00.

The PWA convertible is a fairly typical issue, but you can come across more complicated cases. Often the conversion price is stepped up over time. Litton Industries in the United States, on the other hand, once issued a convertible in which the conversion price was stepped down.[12] Occasionally, the owner must surrender the bond and pay a cash conversion fee in order to receive the common stock. Also, in the last few years it has been increasingly common for firms to issue convertibles that can be exchanged for other bonds. So-called "flip-flop" bonds give the investor the option to flip back and forth several times.

Valuing Convertible Bonds

The owner of a convertible bond owns a bond and a call option on the firm's stock. So does the owner of a bond-warrant package. There are differences, of course, the most important being the requirement that a convertible owner give up the bond in order to exercise the call option. The owner of a bond-warrant package can exercise the warrant for cash and keep the bond. Nevertheless, understanding convertibles is easier if you analyze them first as bonds and then as call options.

---

[11] The PWA issue was a convertible subordinated debenture. The term *subordinated* indicates that the bond is a junior debt—its holders will be at the bottom of the heap of creditors in the event of default. A *debenture* is simply an unsecured bond. Therefore, there are no specific assets that have been reserved to pay off the holders in the event of default. There is more about these terms in Chapter 24.

[12] Convertibles are usually issued at their face value, that is, 100% of par. Since they consist of a bond plus an option, the underlying bond at issue is worth less than 100. Thus, the value of the bond can be expected to increase between issue and maturity. This means that for most convertibles the value of the bond that must be surrendered (i.e., the exercise price of the option) increases over time. For very low coupon convertibles these changes in exercise price can be dramatic.

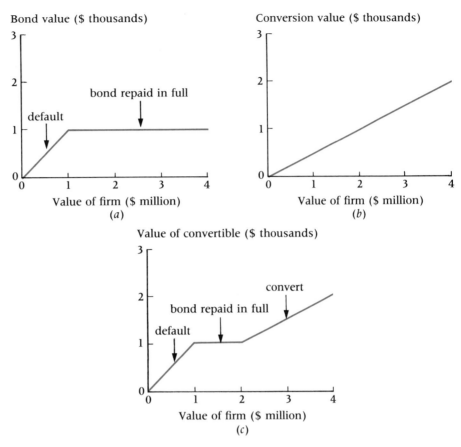

Figure 22-2   (*a*) The bond value when Eastman Kojak's convertible bond matures. If firm value is at least $1 million, the bond is paid off in full; if it is less than $1 million, the bondholders receive the value of the firm's assets. (*b*) The conversion value at maturity. If converted, the value of the convertible bond rises in proportion to firm value. (*c*) At maturity the convertible bondholder can choose to receive the principal repayment on the bond or convert into common stock. The value of the convertible bond is therefore the higher of its bond value and its conversion value.

Imagine that Eastman Kojak has issued convertible bonds with a total face value of $1 million and that these can be converted at any stage into 1 million shares of common stock. The price of Kojak's convertible bond depends on its **bond value** and its **conversion value**. The bond value is what each bond would sell for if it could *not* be converted. The conversion value is what the bond would sell for if it had to be converted immediately.

The Value at Maturity   Figure 22-2(*a*) shows the possible *bond values* when the Kojak convertible matures. As long as the value of the firm's assets does not fall below $1 million, the bond will pay off in full. But, if firm value is *less* than $1 million, there will not be enough to pay off the bondholders. In the extreme case that the assets are worthless, the bondholders will receive nothing. Thus, the horizontal line in Figure 22-2(*a*) shows the payoff if the bond is repaid in full and the sloping line shows the payoffs if the firm defaults.[13]

---

[13] You may recognize this as the position diagram for a default-free bond *minus* a put option on the assets with an exercise price equal to the face value of the bonds. See Section 20–1.

You can think of the bond value as a lower bound, or "floor", to the price of the convertible. But, remember, if the firm falls on hard times, the bonds may not be worth very much. So the "floor" has a nasty slope.

Figure 22-2(*b*) shows the possible **conversion values** at maturity. We assume that Kojak already has 1 million shares of common stock outstanding, so that the convertible holders will be entitled to half the value of the firm. For example, if the firm is worth $2 million,[14] the 1 million shares obtained by conversion would be worth $1 each. Each convertible bond can be exchanged for 1,000 shares of stock and therefore would have a conversion value of 1,000 × 1 = $1,000.

Kojak's convertible also cannot sell for less than its conversion value. If it did, smart investors would buy the convertible, exchange it rapidly for stock, and sell the stock. Their profit would be equal to the difference between the conversion value and the price of the convertible.

Therefore, there are *two* lower bounds to the price of the convertible; its bond value and its conversion value. Investors will not convert if bond value exceeds conversion value; they will do so if conversion value exceeds bond value. In other words, the price of the convertible at maturity is represented by the higher of the two lines in Figures 22-2(*a*) and 22-2(*b*). This is shown in Figure 22-2(*c*).

Value before Maturity   We can also draw a similar picture to Figure 22-2 when the convertible is *not* about to mature. Because even healthy companies may subsequently fall sick and default on their bonds, other things equal bond value will be lower when the bond has some time to run. Thus, bond value before maturity is represented by the curved line in Figure 22-3(*a*).[15]

Figure 22-3(*c*) shows that the lower bound to the price of a convertible before maturity is again the lower of the bond value and conversion value. However, before maturity the convertible bondholders *do not have to make a now-or-never choice for or against conversion*. They can wait and then, with the benefit of hindsight, take whatever course turns out to give them the highest payoff. Thus, before maturity a convertible is always worth more than its lower-bound value. Its actual selling price will behave as shown in Figure 22-3(*d*). The difference between the value of convertible and the lower bound is the value of a call option on the firm. Remember, however, that this option can only be exercised by giving up the bond. In other words, the option to convert is a call option with an exercise price equal to the bond value.

Dilution and Dividends Revisited   If you want to value a convertible, it is easiest to break the problem down into two parts. First estimate bond value, then add the value of the conversion option.

When you value the conversion option, you need to look out for the same things that make warrants more tricky to value than traded options. For example, dilution may be important. If the bonds are converted, the company saves on its interest payments and is relieved of having to eventually repay the loan; on the other hand, net profits have to be divided among a larger number of shares.[16]

---

[14] Firm value is equal to the value of Kojak's common stock *plus* the value of its convertible bonds.

[15] Remember, the value of a risky bond is the value of a safe bond *less* the value of a put option on the firm's assets. The value of this option increases with maturity.

[16] In practice, investors often ignore dilution and calculate conversion value as the share price times the number of shares into which the bonds can be converted. A convertible bond actually gives an option to acquire a fraction of the "new equity"—the equity *after* conversion. When we calculated the conversion value of Kojak's convertible, we recognized this by multiplying the proportion of common stock that the convertible bondholders would receive by the total value of the firm's assets (i.e., the value of the common stock plus the value of the convertible).

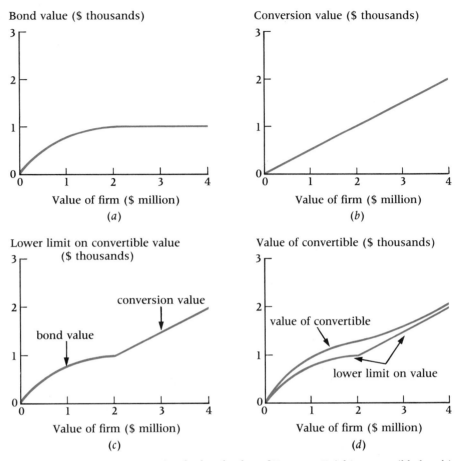

Figure 22-3   (*a*) Beore maturity the bond value of Eastman Kojak's convertible bond is close to that of a similar default-free bond when firm value is high; but it falls sharply if firm value falls to a very low level. (*b*) The conversion value at maturity. If converted, the value of the convertible bond rises in proportion to firm value. (*c*) If investors were obliged to make an immediate decision for or against conversion, the value of the convertible would be equal to the higher of bond value or conversion value. (*d*) Since convertible bondholders do not have to make a decision until maturity, (*c*) represents a lower limit. The value of the convertible bond is worth *more* than either bond value or conversion value.

Companies are obliged to show in their financial statements how earnings would be affected by conversion.[17]

Also you must remember that the convertible owner is missing out on the dividends on the common stock. If these dividends are higher than the interest on the bonds, it may pay to convert before the final exercise date in order to pick up the extra cash income.

Forcing Conversion   Companies usually retain an option to buy back or call the convertible bond at a preset price. If the company calls the bond, the owner has a brief period, usually about 30 days, within which to either convert the bond or surrender it. If the bond is surrendered, the investor receives the call price in cash.

---

[17] These "diluted" earnings take into account the extra shares but not the savings in interest payments.

Calling the bond obviously does not affect the total size of the company pie, but it can affect the size of the individual slices. In other words, conversion has no effect on the total value of the firm's assets, but it does affect how asset value is *distributed* among the different classes of security holders. Therefore, if you want to maximize your shareholders' slice of the pie, you must minimize the convertible bondholders'. That means you must not call the bonds if they are worth *less* than the call price, for that would be giving the bondholders an unnecessary present. Similarly, you must not allow the bonds to remain uncalled if their value is *above* the call price, for that would not be minimizing the value of the bonds. Therefore, the rule for calling a convertible debenture is exactly the same as the rule for calling any other bond: *call the bond when, and only when, its value reaches the call price.*

Managers are fickle creatures. No sooner do they issue convertibles, than they seem to want to get rid of them. They often complain of "overhanging" convertibles — that is, ones that are not being converted. They feel that overhanging convertibles limit their freedom of action. In view of these complaints, you might expect that managers would be only too eager to call their convertibles. But Ingersoll has found that in practice it is just the reverse. Firms seldom call their convertibles until they are worth much *more* than the call price. For example, Ingersoll looked at 124 firms that called their convertible debentures between 1968 and 1975. All but six delayed the call too long, and the typical company waited until conversion value was 44% above the call price.[18]

Table 22-1 shows several convertible issues outstanding in the United States during January 1991. Each of the issues has current conversion value well above the current call price. Therefore, these companies could have called the bonds and forced conversion. Finance theory implies they should have done so. The reason for firms' reluctance to call convertibles is not known.[19]

Of course Table 22-1 is not a random sample of convertible issues. We chose extreme cases to illustrate a point. We could have presented another table of convertible issues with conversion values well below call prices.

22-3 THE DIFFERENCE BETWEEN WARRANTS AND CONVERTIBLES

We have dwelt on the basic similarity between warrants and convertibles. Now let us look at some of the differences.

1. *Warrants are usually issued privately.* Packages of bonds with warrants or preferred stock with warrants tend to be more common in private placements. By contrast, most convertible bonds or preferreds are issued publicly.

---

[18] J.E. Ingersoll, "An Examination of Corporate Call Policies on Convertible Securities," *Journal of Finance*, **32**: 463–478 (May 1977). Also, see A. Kraus, "An Analysis of Call Provisions and the Corporate Refunding Decision," *Midland Corporate Finance Journal*, **1**: 46-60 (1983).

[19] Here is one ingenious explanation. Imagine two firms, each with a convertible bond that is selling above its call price. The manager of the first firm believes his stock is undervalued. He will therefore be confident that the bond will be converted eventually and will conclude that there is little to be lost by not forcing conversion now. The manager of the second firm believes her stock is *over*valued. So she can help her shareholders by forcing conversion before the stock price falls. Of course, investors will realize that managers of overvalued stocks have the greater incentive to force conversion and will mark down the price of the stock when the bond is called. The managers of the undervalued firms will prefer not to be tarred with the same brush and, therefore, will not force conversion even though they would otherwise do so. See M. Harris and A. Raviv, "A Sequential Signalling Model of Convertible Debt Call Policy." *Journal of Finance*, **40**: 1263–1282 (December 1985).

Table 22-1
Convertible bonds outstanding in January 1991 with high conversion values relative to call price.

Issuing Firm	Coupon	Maturity	Call Price	Conversion Value
Crane Co.	5.00	1993	100	540.50
Baxter Travenol	4.75	2001	100.55	237.75
Ford	4.5	1996	100.00	191.63
McGraw Hill	3.875	1992	100.00	168.38
J.P. Morgan	4.75	1998	100.72	221.88
Pfizer Inc.	4.00	1997	100.50	339.88
Ralston Purina	5.75	2000	100.44	668.5
Rockwell Int'l.	4.25	1991	100.00	482.5
Skil Corp.	5.00	1992	100.00	253.38
McDonnel Douglas	4.75	1991	100.00	126.88

Notes:
1. Data is from Moody's *Bond Record*.
2. All issues except J.P. Morgan are subordinated debentures. J.P. Morgan is not subordinated.
3. Coupons, call prices, and conversion values are given as percentages of par value.

2. *Warrants can be detached.* When you buy a convertible, the bond and the option are bundled up together. You cannot sell them separately. This may be inconvenient. If your tax position or attitude to risk inclines you to bonds, you may not want to hold options as well. Sometimes warrants are also "nondetachable." But usually you can keep the bond or preferred and sell off the warrant.

3. *Warrants may be issued on their own.* Warrants do not have to be issued in conjunction with other securities. Often they are used to compensate investment bankers for underwriting services. Many companies also give their executives long-term options to buy stock. These executive stock options are not usually called warrants but that is exactly what they are. Companies rarely sell warrants directly to investors for cash (except as part of a package), but there is no reason that they shouldn't.

4. *Warrants are exercised for cash.* When you exercise warrants, you generally put up extra cash, though occasionally you have to surrender the bond (or can choose to do so). When you convert a debenture, you simply exchange your bond for common stock. Therefore, bond-warrant packages and convertible bonds have different effects on the company's cash flow and on its capital structure.

5. *Receipts from warrants may be taxable.* There is an important tax difference between warrants and convertibles. When a company issues a package of bonds and warrants, the value of each of the two instruments is written into the prospectus. If the warrants subsequently expire without being exercised, Revenue Canada will generally insist that the company treat the money that is received for the warrants as capital gain.[20] Therefore, if a company issues warrants, it may later have to pay tax on one-half of their value. This is an odd rule, completely inconsistent with the tax treatment of other securities. If your firm issues a convertible bond, but the conversion option subsequently proves worthless, is the firm taxed on the amount investors originally paid for the conversion option? No. If it issues *any* other kind of security, which later declines in value, is the investor's capital loss treated as taxable income to the firm? No.

---

[20] The Internal Revenue Service in the United States deems the money received from unexercised warrants to be ordinary income at the time the warrant expires.

6. *You cannot call warrants.* Suppose that a company issues a bond-warrant package and then several years later decides that it would like to tidy up its financial structure by getting rid of the warrants. It may be able to call the *bonds* but it cannot usually call the warrants.[21] It can raise the dividend on the stock and try to force exercise that way. Or it can tempt the warrant holders by a temporary reduction in the exercise price. The company that issues a convertible debenture has a much simpler way to extinguish the conversion option. It just calls the bond.

22-4   WHY DO COMPANIES ISSUE WARRANTS AND CONVERTIBLES?

You hear many arguments for issuing warrants and convertibles but most of them have a "Heads I win, tails you lose" flavour. For example, here is one such argument:[22]

> A company that wishes to sell common stock must usually offer the new stock at 10 percent to 20 percent below the market price for the flotation to be a success.[23] However, if warrants are sold for cash, exercisable at 20 percent to 50 percent above the market price of the common, the result will be equivalent to selling common stock at a premium rather than a discount; and if the warrants are never exercised, the proceeds from their sale will become a clear profit to the company.

There is something that you should find immediately suspicious about an argument like this. If the shareholder inevitably wins, the warrant holder must inevitably lose. But that doesn't make sense. Surely there must be some price at which it pays to buy warrants.

Suppose that your company's stock is priced at $100 and that you are considering an issue of warrants exercisable at $120. You believe that you can sell these warrants at $10. If the stock price subsequently fails to reach $120, the warrants will not be exercised. You will have sold warrants for $10 each, which with the benefit of hindsight proved to be worthless to the buyer. If the stock price reaches $130, say, the warrants will be exercised. Your firm will have received the initial payment of $10 *plus* the exercise price of $120. On the other hand, it will have issued to the warrant holders stock worth $130 per share. The net result is a standoff. You have received a payment of $130 in exchange for a liability worth $130.

Think now what happens if the stock price rises above $130. Perhaps it goes to $200. In this case the warrant issue will end up producing a loss of $70. This is not a cash outflow but an opportunity loss. The firm receives $130, but in this case it could have sold stock for $200. On the other hand, the warrant holders gain $70: They invest $130 in cash to acquire stock that they can sell, if they like, for $200.

Our example is oversimplified—for instance, we have kept quiet about the time value of money and risk—but we hope it has made the basic point. When you sell warrants, you are selling options and getting cash in exchange. Options are valuable securities. If they are properly priced this is a fair trade—in other words, it is a zero NPV transaction.

---

[21] A small fraction of warrant issues is callable.

[22] See S. T. Kassouf: *Evaluation of Convertible Securities*, Analytical Investors, New York, 1966, p. 6. We hasten to add that Kassouf's lapse is *not* characteristic of him. He is a respected scholar who has made important contributions to finance.

[23] This is an overestimate of the discount associated with seasoned issues. See Section 15–2.

You can see why the quotation is misleading. When it refers to "selling stock at a premium," the implicit comparison is with the market value of the stock today. The relevant comparison is with what it may be worth tomorrow.

Managers often use similar arguments to justify the sale of convertibles. For example, several surveys have revealed two main motives for their use. A large number of managers look on convertibles as "cheap debt." A somewhat higher proportion regard them as a deferred sale of stock at an attractive price.[24]

We have seen that a convertible is like a package of a straight bond and an option. The difference between the market value of the convertible and that of the straight bond is therefore the price investors place on the call option. The convertible is "cheap" only if this price overvalues the option.

What then of the other managers—those who regard the issue as a deferred sale of common stock? A convertible bond gives you the right to buy stock by giving up a bond.[25] Bondholders may decide to do this, but then again they may not. Thus issues of a convertible bond *may* amount to a deferred stock issue. But if the firm *needs* equity capital, a convertible issue is an unreliable way of getting it.

Taken at their face value the motives of management are irrational. Convertibles are not just cheap debt nor are they a deferred sale of stock. But we suspect that these simple phrases encapsulate some more complex and rational motives.

Notice that convertibles tend to be issued by the smaller and more speculative firms. They are almost invariably unsecured and generally subordinated. Now put yourself in the position of a potential investor. You are approached by a small firm with an untried product line that wants to issue some junior unsecured debt. You know that if things go well, you will get your money back but, if they do not, you could easily be left with nothing. Since the firm is in a new line of business, it is difficult to assess the chances of trouble. Therefore, you don't know what the fair rate of interest is. Also you may be worried that once you have made the loan, management will be tempted to run extra risks. It may borrow additional senior debt or it may decide to expand its operations and go for broke on your money. In fact, if you charge a very high rate of interest, you could be encouraging this to happen.

What can management do to protect you against an incorrect estimate of the risk and to assure you that its intentions are honourable? In crude terms, it can give you a piece of the action. You don't mind the company running unanticipated risks, as long as you share in the gains as well as the losses.[26]

Convertible securities and warrants make sense whenever it is unusually costly to assess the risk of debt or whenever investors are worried that management may not act in the bondholders' interest.

The relatively low coupon rate on convertible bonds may also be a convenience for rapidly growing firms facing heavy capital expenditures. They may be willing to give up the conversion option to reduce immediate cash requirements for debt

---

[24] See, for example, E.F. Brigham: "An Analysis of Convertible Debentures: Theory and Some Empirical Evidence," *Journal of Finance*, **21**: 35–54 (March 1966).

[25] That is much the same as already having the stock together with the right to sell it for the convertible's bond value. In other words, instead of thinking of a convertible as a bond plus a call option, you could think of it as the stock plus a put option. Now you see why it is wrong to think of a convertible as equivalent to the sale of stock; it is equivalent to the sale of both stock *and* a put option. If there is any possibility that investors will want to hold onto their bond, the put option will have some value.

[26] See M. J. Brennan and E. S. Schwartz, "The Case for Convertibles," *Chase Financial Quarterly*, **1**: 27–46 (Spring 1982).

service. Without the conversion option, lenders might demand extremely high (promised) interest rates to compensate for the probability of default. This would not only force the firm to raise still more capital to pay for debt service, it would increase the risk of financial distress. Paradoxically, lenders' attempts to protect themselves against default may actually increase the probability of financial distress by increasing the burden of debt service on the firm.[27]

22-5 SUMMARY

Instead of issuing straight bonds, companies may sell either packages of bonds and warrants or convertible bonds.

A warrant is just a long-term call option issued by the company. You already know a good deal about valuing call options. You know from Chapter 20 that call options must be worth at least as much as the stock price less the exercise price. You know that their value is greatest when they have a long time to expiration, when the underlying stock is risky, and when the interest rate is high.

Warrants are somewhat trickier to evaluate than the call options that are traded on the options exchanges. First, because they are long-term options, it is important to take into account the fact that the warrant holder does not receive any dividends. Second, dilution must be allowed for.

A convertible bond gives its holder the right to swap the bond for common stock. The rate of exchange is usually measured by the *conversion ratio* — that is, the number of shares that the investor gets for each bond. Sometimes the rate of exchange is expressed in terms of the *conversion price* — that is, the face value of the bond that must be given up in order to receive one share.

Convertibles are like a package of a bond and a call option. When you evaluate the conversion option you must again remember that the convertible holder does not receive dividends and that conversion results in dilution of the common stock. There are two other things to watch out for. One is the problem of default risk. If the company runs into trouble, you may not only have a worthless conversion option, you may also have a worthless bond. Second, the company may be able to force conversion by calling the bond. It should do this as soon as the market price of the convertible reaches the call price. Many companies do not call their bonds until well after this point. Nobody knows why.

You hear a variety of arguments for issuing warrants or convertibles. Convertible bonds and bonds with warrants are almost always junior bonds and are frequently issued by risky companies. We think this says something about the reasons for their issue. Suppose that you are lending subordinated debt to a untried company. You are worried that the company may turn out to be riskier than you thought or that it may issue additional senior bonds. You can try to protect yourself against such eventualities by imposing very restrictive conditions on the debt, but it is often simpler to say that you don't mind the company taking some extra risk as long as you get a piece of the action. The convertible and bond-warrant package give you a chance to participate in the firm's successes as well as its failures. They diminish the possible conflicts of interest between bondholder and stockholder.

---

[27] This fact led to an extensive body of literature on "credit rationing." A lender rations credit if it is irrational to lend more to a firm regardless of the interest rate the firm is willing to *promise* to pay. Whether this can happen in efficient, competitive capital markets is controversial. We give an example of credit rationing in Chapter 32. For a review of this literature see E. Baltensperger, "Credit Rationing: Issues and Questions," *Journal of Money, Credit and Banking*, **10**: 170–183 (May 1978).

FURTHER READING

The items listed in Chapter 20 under "Further Reading" are also relevant to this chapter, in particular, Black and Scholes's discussion of warrant valuation.
Ingersoll's work represents the "state of the art" in valuing convertibles:

J.E. Ingersoll, "A Contingent Claims Valuation of Convertible Securities." *Journal of Financial Economics*, **4**: 289–322 (May 1977).

Ingersoll also examines corporate call policies on convertible bonds in:

J.E. Ingersoll, "An Examination of Corporate Call Policies on Convertible Securities," *Journal of Finance*, **32**: 463–478 (May 1977).

Brennan and Schwartz's paper was written at about the same time as Ingersoll's and reaches essentially the same conclusions. They also present a general procedure for valuing convertibles.

M.J. Brennan and E.S. Schwartz, "Convertible Bonds: Valuation and Optimal Strategies for Call and Conversion," *Journal of Finance*, **32**: 1699–1715 (December 1977).

Two useful articles on warrants are:

D. Galai and M.A. Schneller, "Pricing of Warrants and the Value of the Firm," *Journal of Finance*, **33**: 1333–1342 (December 1978).

E.S. Schwartz, "The Valuation of Warrants: Implementing a New Approach," *Journal of Financial Economics*, **4**: 79–93 (January 1977).

For a nontechnical discussion of the pricing of convertibles and the reasons for their use, see:

M.J. Brennan and E.S. Schwartz, "The Case for Convertibles," *Chase Financial Quarterly*, **1**: 27–46 (Spring 1982).

QUIZ

1. Associated Elk warrants entitle the owner to buy one share at $40.
   (a) What is the theoretical value of the warrant if the stock price is
       (i) $20?
       (ii) $30?
       (iii) $40?
       (iv) $50?
       (v) $60?
   (b) Plot the theoretical value of the warrant against the stock price.
   (c) Suppose the stock price is $60 and the warrant price is five dollars. What would you do?
2. In 1984 BC Sugar Refinery issued one-half million warrants attached to a 1 million share common stock issue. Each warrant could have been exercised before 1988 at a price of $25 per share. Suppose the current share price is $23.00.
   (a) Does the warrant holder have a vote?
   (b) Does the warrant holder receive dividends?
   (c) If the stock were to split 5-for-1, how would the exercise price be adjusted?
   (d) Suppose that, instead of reducing the exercise price after the 5-for-1 split, the company gave each warrant holder the right to buy *five* shares at $25 apiece. Would this have the same effect?
   (e) Is there any benefit to exercising the warrant today?
   (f) If there is no benefit to exercising the warrant today, does that mean the current warrant price should be equal to zero?

(g) *Other things being equal,* would the warrant be more or less valuable if:
  (i) The company increased its dividend payout rate?
  (ii) The interest rate declined?
  (iii) The stock became riskier?
  (iv) The company extended the exercise period?
  (v) The company reduced the exercise price?
(h) A few companies issued perpetual warrants (that is, warrants with no final exercise date). Suppose that the BC Sugar warrants are perpetual. In what circumstances might it make sense for investors to exercise their warrants?

3. Amalgamated Sludge has outstanding 10 million warrants, each of which may be converted into one share of common stock. Assume
Net income = $40 million
Number of shares outstanding = 20 million
(a) Calculate earnings per share.
(b) Calculate earnings per share on a fully diluted basis.

4. Suppose that Maple Aircraft has issued a 4¾% convertible subordinated debenture due 1998. The conversion price is $47.00 and the debenture is callable at 102.75. The market price of the convertible is 91% of face value and the price of the common is $41.50. Assume the value of the bond in the absence of a conversion feature is about 65% of face value.
(a) What is the conversion ratio of the debenture?
(b) If the conversion ratio were 50, what would be the conversion price?
(c) What is the conversion value?
(d) At what stock price is the conversion value equal to the bond value?
(e) Can the market price be less than the conversion value?
(f) How much is the convertible holder paying for the option to buy one share of common stock?
(g) By how much does the common have to rise by 1998 to justify conversion?
(h) When should Maple call the debenture?

QUESTIONS AND PROBLEMS

1. Refer again to the BCE Inc. warrant discussed in Section 22-1. BCE had approximately 303 million shares and 10 million warrants outstanding. The warrant's exercise price was $45.75.
(a) Suppose that BCE's stock price had been $50 per share just before expiration. What would the warrants have sold for? Is this the warrants' theoretical value?
(b) Suppose that stock price had been $50 per share a year *prior* to expiration. Would the warrants have sold for more or less than your answer to (a)? Would they have sold for their theoretical value? Explain.
(c) Suppose that BCE's undiluted earnings had been $4 per share in 1990. Calculate its diluted earnings per share.
*2. Describe how you would use the Black-Scholes formula to compute the value of the BCE's warrant a year before its expiration, assuming a stock price of $50 and a warrant price of $20. What ratio of exercise price to stock price would you use in the formula? Is this significantly different from 45.75/50 = 0.92?

3. Occasionally firms extend the life of warrants that would otherwise expire unexercised. What is the cost of doing this? Could such an extension be rational despite the cost? (*Hint*: See point 5, Section 22-3.)

*4. Here's a question on dilution: The Electric Bassoon Company has outstanding 2,000 shares with a total market value of $20,000 *plus* 1,000 warrants with a total market value of $5,000. Each warrant gives its holders the option to buy one share at $20.
   (a) To value the warrants you first need to value a call option on an alternative share. What is the current price on this alternative share? How might you calculate its standard deviation?
   (b) Suppose that the value of a call option on this alternative share were $6. Calculate whether the Electric Bassoon warrants were undervalued or overvalued.

5. The Surplus Value Company had $10 million (face value) of convertible bonds outstanding in 1980. Each bond has the following features:

Conversion price	$25
Current call price	105 (percent of face value)
Current trading price	130 (percent of face value)
Maturity	1990
Current stock price	$30 (per share)
Interest rate	10 (coupon as percent of face value)

   (a) What is the bond's conversion value?
   (b) Can you explain why the bond is selling above conversion value?

6. Growth-Tech has issued $10 million of a 10% subordinated convertible debenture. Assume:

   Net income = $50 million
   Number of shares outstanding = 2.5 million
   Conversion ratio = 50
   Tax rate = 50%

   (a) Calculate earnings per share.
   (b) Calculate earnings per share on a fully diluted basis.

7. Associated Elk warrants have an exercise price of $40. The share price is $50. The dividend on the stock is $3 and the interest rate is 10%.
   (a) Would you exercise your warrants now or later? State why.
   (b) If the dividend increased to $5, it could pay to exercise now if the stock price had low variability and it could be better to exercise later if the stock price had high variability. Explain why.

8. "The company's decision to issue warrants should depend on the management's forecast of likely returns on the stock." Do you agree?

9. In each case, state which of the two securities is likely to provide the higher return:
   (a) When the stock price rises (stock *or* convertible bond?).
   (b) When interest rates fall (straight bond *or* convertible bond?).
   (c) When the specific risk of the stock decreases (straight bond *or* convertible bond?).
   (d) When the dividend on the stock increases (stock *or* convertible bond?).

10. Towncorp has issued three-year warrants to buy 12% perpetual debentures at a price of 120%. The current interest rate is 12% and the standard deviation of returns on the bond is 20%. Use the Black-Scholes model to obtain a rough estimate of the value of Towncorp warrants.

11. Moose Stores has outstanding 1 million shares of common stock with a total market value of $40 million. It now announces an issue of 1 million warrants at $5 each. Each warrant entitles the owner to buy one Moose share for a price of $30 at any time within the next five years. Moose Stores has stated that it will not pay a dividend within this period.

  The standard deviation of the returns on Moose's equity is 20% a year, and the interest rate is 8%.

  (a) What is the market value of each warrant?

  (b) What is the market value of each share after the warrant issue? (*Hint*: The value of the shares is equal to the total value of the equity less the value of the warrants.)

12. Look again at question 11. Suppose that Moose now forecasts the following dividend payments:

End Year	Dividend
1	$2.00
2	3.00
3	4.00
4	5.00
5	6.00

Reestimate the market values of the warrant and stock.

13. Occasionally it is said that issuing convertible bonds is better than issuing stock when the firm's shares are undervalued. Suppose that the financial manager of the Butternut Furniture Company does in fact have inside information indicating that the Butternut stock price is too low. Butternut's future earnings will in fact be higher than investors expect. Suppose further that the inside information cannot be released without giving away a valuable competitive secret. Clearly, selling shares at the present low price would harm Butternut's existing shareholders. Will they also lose if convertible bonds are issued? If they do lose in this case, is the loss more or less than if common stock is issued?

  Now suppose that investors forecast earnings accurately, but still undervalue the stock because they overestimate Butternut's actual business risk. Does this change your answers to the questions posed in the preceding paragraph? Explain.

14. Banks or insurance companies sometimes negotiate "equity kickers" when lending money. The firm pays interest and also gives warrants to the lender. Thus the lender has an equity interest in the firm (via the warrants) and shares in the rewards if the firm is successful. Of course, in negotiating the loan, the lender always has the alternative of forgoing the warrants and demanding a higher interest rate instead. What are the advantages of the "equity kicker" arrangement compared to this alternative? In what circumstances would use of the equity kicker be more sensible?

15. In April 1984 Lac Minerals attached gold purchase warrants to a debenture issue. The warrant provides the right to buy 0.5 ounces of gold at an exercise price of $230 at any time up to and including April 1989. If the riskless rate of interest was 10% at that time, the standard deviation of the rate of return on gold 30% and the market price of gold $300 per ounce (that is, $150 per 0.5 ounces), what was the approximate value of the gold purchase warrant?

(*Hint*: An investment in gold is like an investment in a non-dividend-paying stock, so an American call option on gold may be priced using the European call option formula.)

16. Rupert Thorndike, the autocratic CEO of Thorndike Oil, was found dead this morning in a pool of blood on his office floor. He had been shot through the head. Yesterday Thorndike had flatly rejected an offer by T. Spoone Dickens to buy all of Thorndike Oil's assets for $1 billion cash, effective January 1, 1992. With Thorndike out of the way, Dickens's offer will be immediately accepted.

The immediate suspects were Thorndike's two nieces, Doris and Patsy, and his nephew John.

Thorndike Oil's capital structure is as follows:

- *Debt:* $250 million face value, issued in 1965 at a coupon rate of 5%, with market value of 60% of face value. This debt will be paid off at par if Dickens's offer goes through.
- *Stock:* 30 million shares closing yesterday at $10 per share.
- *Warrants:* Warrants to buy an additional 20 million shares at $10 per share, expiring December 31, 1991. The last trade of the warrants was at $1 per warrant.

Here are Doris, John, and Patsy's stakes in Thorndike Oil:

	Debt (Market Value)	Stock (Number of Shares)	Warrants (Number)
Doris	$6 million	1 million	0
John	0	0.5 million	2 million
Patsy	0	1.5 million	1 million

Which niece or nephew stood to gain most (in portfolio value) by eliminating old Thorndike and allowing Dickens's offer to succeed? Explain. Make additional assumptions if you find them necessary.

P·A·R·T

7

DEBT FINANCING

C·H·A·P·T·E·R

23

VALUING RISKY DEBT

How do you estimate the present value of a company's bonds? The answer is simple. You take the cash flows and discount them at the opportunity cost of capital. Therefore if a bond is expected to produce cash flows of C dollars per year for N years and then to repay its face value ($1,000), the present value is

$$PV = \frac{C}{1 + r_1} + \frac{C}{(1 + r_2)^2} + \cdots + \frac{C}{(1 + r_N)^N} + \frac{\$1,000}{(1 + r_N)^N}$$

where $r_1, r_2, \ldots, r_N$ are the appropriate discount rates for the cash flows to be received by the bond's owner in years 1, 2, ..., N.

That is correct as far as it goes but it does not tell us anything about what *determines* the discount rate. For example:

1. In 1948 Canadian Treasury bills offered an average return of 0.4%: in April 1991 they offered a return of 9.4%. Why does the same security offer radically different yields at different points in time?
2. In April 1991 the Government of Canada could borrow for one to three years at an average interest rate of about 9.4%, but it had to pay an average rate of nearly 10% for loans of ten years and longer. Why do bonds maturing at different dates offer different rates of interest? In other words, why is there a *term structure* of interest rates?
3. In April 1991 the Canadian government could issue bonds with more than ten years to maturity at a rate of nearly 10%. You could not have borrowed at that rate. Why not? What explains the premium you have to pay?

These questions lead to deep issues that will keep economists simmering for years. But we can give general answers and at the same time present some fundamental ideas.

Why should the financial manager care about these ideas? Who needs to know how bonds are priced as long as the bond market is active and efficient? Efficient markets protect the ignorant trader. If it is necessary to check whether the price is right for a proposed bond issue, you can check the prices of similar bonds. There is no need to worry about the historical behaviour of interest rates, about the term structure, or about the other issues discussed in this chapter.

We do not believe that ignorance is desirable even when it is harmless. At least you ought to be able to read *The Financial Post* or *The Globe and Mail* and talk to underwriters and securities dealers. More important, you will encounter many problems of bond pricing where there are no similar instruments already traded. How do you evaluate a private placement with a custom-tailored repayment schedule? How about financial leases? In Chapter 26 we will see that they are essentially debt contracts, but often extremely complicated ones, for which traded bonds are not close substitutes. You will find that the terms, concepts, and facts presented in this chapter are essential to the analysis of these and other practical problems in financing covered in later chapters.

We begin, therefore, with our first question: "Why does the general level of interest rates change over time?"

23-1 THE CLASSICAL THEORY OF INTEREST

Real Interest Rates

Suppose that everyone knows that there is not going to be any inflation. If so, all interest rates are *real* rates—they include no premium for anticipated inflation. What are the essential determinants of the rate of interest in such a world? The classical economist's answer to this question is summed up in the title of Irving Fisher's great book: *The Theory of Interest: As Determined by Impatience to Spend Income and Opportunity to Invest It.*[1] The real interest rate, according to Fisher, is the price that equates the supply and demand for capital. The supply depends on people's willingness to save—that is, to postpone consumption.[2] The demand depends on the opportunities for productive investment.

For example, suppose that investment opportunities generally improve. Firms have more good projects, and so are willing to invest more at any interest rate. Therefore, the rate has to rise to induce individuals to save the additional amount that firms want to invest.[3] Conversely, if investment opportunities deteriorate, there will be a fall in the real interest rate.

Fisher's theory emphasizes that the real rate of interest depends on real phenomena. A high aggregate willingness to save may be associated with such factors as high aggregate wealth (because wealthy people usually save more), an uneven distribution of wealth (an even distribution would mean few rich people, who do most of the saving), and a high proportion of middle-aged people (the young don't need to save and the old don't want to—"You can't take it with you"). Correspondingly, a high propensity to invest may be associated with a high level of industrial activity or major technological advances.

Inflation and Interest Rates

Now let us see what Irving Fisher had to say about the effect of inflation on interest rates. Suppose that consumers are equally happy with 100 apples today or 105 apples in a year's time. Then the real or "apple" rate of interest is 5%. Suppose also that I know the price of apples will increase over the year by 10%. Then I will part with $100 today if I am repaid $115 at the end of the year. That $115 is needed to buy me 5% more apples than I can get for my $100 today. In

---

[1] Augustus M. Kelley, Publishers, New York, 1965; originally published 1930.

[2] Some of this saving is done indirectly. For example, if you hold 100 shares of CP stock, and CP retains earnings of $1 per share, CP is saving $100 on your behalf.

[3] We assume that investors save more as interest rates rise. It doesn't have to be that way; here is an example of how higher interest rates can mean less savings. Suppose that you need $10,000 20 years hence for your children's university expenses. How much will you have to set aside today to cover this obligation? The answer is the present value of $10,000 after 20 years, or $10,000/(1 + r)^{20}$. The higher r, the lower the present value and the less you have to set aside.

other words, the nominal or "money" rate of interest must equal the real or "apple" rate plus the prospective rate of inflation. A change of one percentage point in the expected inflation rate produces a change of one percentage point in the nominal interest rate.[4] That is Fisher's theory: a change in the expected rate of inflation will cause the same change in the nominal interest rate.

In principle, there is no upper limit to the real rate of interest. But is there any lower limit? For example, is it possible for the money rate of interest to be 5% and the expected rate of inflation to be 10%, thus giving a negative real interest rate? If this happens, you may be able to make money in the following way. You borrow $100 at an interest rate of 5% and you use the money to buy apples. You store the apples and sell them at the end of the year for $110, which leaves you enough to pay off your loan plus $5 for yourself.

Since easy ways to make money are rare, we can conclude that, if it doesn't cost anything to store goods, the money rate of interest is unlikely to be less than the expected rise in prices. But many goods are even more expensive to store than apples, and others cannot be stored at all (you can't store haircuts, for example). For these goods, the money interest rate can be less than the expected price rise.

Comment   If you look back to our discussion of inflation and discount rates in Section 6-1, you will see that our apple example is a bit oversimplified. If apples cost $1.00 apiece today and $1.10 next year, you need $1.10 \times 105 = \$115.50$ next year to buy 105 apples. The money interest rate is 15.5%, not 15.

The exact formula relating real and money rates is

$$1 + r_{money} = (1 + r_{real})(1 + i)$$

where i is the expected inflation rate. Thus:

$$r_{money} = r_{real} + i + i(r_{real})$$

In our example, the money rate should be

$$r_{money} = 0.05 + 0.10 + 0.10(0.05) = 0.155$$

When we said the money rate should be 15%, we ignored the "cross-product" term $i(r_{real})$. This is a common rule of thumb, because the cross-product is usually small. But there are countries where i is large (sometimes 100% per year or more). In such cases it pays to use the full formula.

Back to Fisher's Theory   Not all economists would agree with Fisher that the real rate of interest is not changed by the inflation rate. For example, if changes in prices are associated with changes in the level of industrial activity, then in inflationary conditions I might want more or less than 105 apples in a year's time to compensate me for the loss of 100 today.

We wish we could show you the past behaviour of interest rates and *expected* inflation. Instead, we have done the next best thing and plotted in Figure 23-1 the return on Canadian Treasury bills against *actual* inflation. Notice, first, that since 1949 the return on Treasury bills often has been below the inflation rate. Hence, our earlier argument that the *real* interest rate has averaged about 1%. Throughout the 1980s and into 1990 the return on bills has been significantly higher than inflation. If you knew for sure that these positive real rates were to persist, you could make yourself a bundle and retire to the Caribbean.

---

[4] The apple example was taken from R. Roll, "Interest Rates on Monetary Assets and Commodity Price Index Changes," *Journal of Finance*, **27**: 251–278 (May 1972).

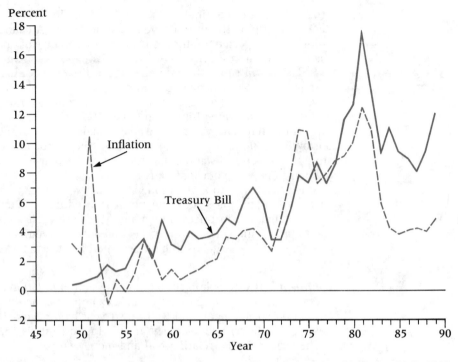

Figure 23-1 The yield on Canadian Treasury bills and the rate of inflation 1949–1989.
Source: International Monetary Fund, International Financial Statistics.

Fisher's theory states that changes in anticipated inflation produce correspond-ing changes in the rate of interest. But there is very little evidence of this in the early years shown in Figure 23-1. During this period, the return on Treasury bills scarcely changed even though inflation fluctuated sharply. Either these changes in inflation were unanticipated or Fisher's theory was wrong. Since 1954, there appears to have been a closer relationship between interest rates and inflation in Canada.[5] Therefore, it is worth looking more carefully at how well Fisher's theory has worked in these recent years.

Eugene Fama has suggested that one way to test Fisher's theory is to twist it around and measure whether the inflation rate can be forecasted by subtracting a constant real rate from the observed nominal interest rate. That is, if Fisher is right,

$$\text{Nominal interest rate} = \text{real interest rate} + \text{inflation rate forecasted by investors}$$

or

$$\text{Inflation rate forecasted by investors} = \text{nominal interest rate} - \text{real interest rate}$$

Of course, investors cannot predict the actual inflation rate perfectly—there will be a random forecast error. But in an efficient market, we expect them to be right on the average. Thus, the forecast error should be zero on the average.

---

[5] Until 1954, Treasury bills were not an important source of financing for the Government of Canada. Trading in Treasury bills was largely confined to chartered banks and the Bank of Canada. In an attempt to develop an organized money market, the Canadian government introduced a weekly Treasury bill auction market in early 1953 and then later in the same year allowed and encouraged money market dealers to trade Treasury bills. With the more active and liquid market came a more competitive interest rate.

Suppose that we observe the nominal returns on Treasury bills and the *actual* rates of inflation. We fit the following equation to these data:

$$\frac{\text{Actual}}{\text{inflation rate}} = a + b(\text{nominal interest rate}) + \text{random forecasting error}$$

If Fisher is correct, the coefficient b should be close to 1.0 and the constant term a should be equal to minus the real interest rate.

We estimated b on Canadian data for the period 1953 to 1989 as 0.71 and on U.S. data for same period as 0.81. Both of these estimates are a bit less than we should expect if Fisher is right *and* the real interest rate is constant.[6]

Before leaving this topic, we must add two qualifications. First, the real interest rate is really an *expected* rate. When you buy a Treasury bill and hold it to maturity, you know what the dollar payoff will be, but the *real* payoff is uncertain because future inflation is not wholly predictable. Thus, to be perfectly precise, we should define the real interest rate as follows:

$$\begin{aligned}\text{Real interest rate} &= \textit{expected} \text{ real rate of return from investment in Treasury bills} \\ &= \text{nominal rate of return on Treasury bills} \\ &\quad - \textit{expected} \text{ rate of inflation}\end{aligned}$$

Second, Nelson and Schwert, and Hess and Bicksler have pointed out that the (expected) real interest rate *does* vary over time. Indeed, we have seen that the real rate appears to have been unusually high throughout the 1980s. If that is so, Fama's test may be inappropriate.[7]

Until these problems have been resolved, we recommend that you look on Fisher's theory simply as a useful rule of thumb. Thus, if the expected inflation rate changes, your best bet is that there will be a corresponding change in the interest rate.

23-2 TERM STRUCTURE AND YIELDS TO MATURITY

We turn now to the relationship between short-term and long-term rates of interest. Suppose that we have a simple loan which pays \$1 at time 1. The present value of this loan is

$$PV = \frac{1}{1 + r_1}$$

Thus, we discount the cash flow at r_1, the rate appropriate for a one-period loan. This rate is fixed today; it is often called today's one-period **spot rate**.

If we have a loan that pays \$1 at both times 1 and 2, its present value is:

$$PV = \frac{1}{1 + r_1} + \frac{1}{(1 + r_2)^2}$$

---

[6] Fama fitted his equation to quarterly U.S. data for the period 1953 to 1971. His estimate of b was 0.98, which is almost identical to the figure that Fisher would predict. See E.F. Fama, "Short-Term Interest Rates as Predictors of Inflation," *American Economic Review,* **65**: 269–282 (June 1975).

[7] C.R. Nelson and G. Schwert, "Short-Term Interest Rates as Predictors of Inflation: On Testing the Hypothesis that the Real Rate of Interest is Constant," *American Economic Review,* **67**: 478–486 (June 1977); P. Hess and J. Bicksler, "Capital Asset Prices versus Time Series Models as Predictors of Inflation," *Journal of Financial Economics,* **2**: 341–360 (December 1975).

Thus, the first period's cash flow is discounted at today's one-period spot rate and the second period's flow is discounted at today's two-period spot rate. The series of spot rates r_1, r_2, and so on is one way of expressing the **term structure of interest rates.**

Yield to Maturity

Rather than discounting each of the payments at a different rate of interest, we could find a single rate of discount that would produce the same present value. Such a rate is known as the **yield to maturity**, though it is in fact no more than our old acquaintance, the internal rate of return (IRR), masquerading under another name. If we call the yield to maturity y, we can write the present value as:

$$PV = \frac{1}{1 + y} + \frac{1}{(1 + y)^2}$$

All you need to calculate y is the price of a bond, its annual payment, and its maturity. You can then rapidly work out the yield with the aid of a preprogrammed calculator or you can find it in a set of bond tables.

Look at Table 23-1, which contains eight pages from a mini-book of bond tables. Each page shows yields for bonds with a particular coupon. For example, suppose that you have an 8% bond maturing in ten years and priced at 85. (Bond prices are quoted as percentages of the bonds' face value.) Look at the fourth page of our mini bond tables. This shows yields for bonds with an 8% coupon, then run your eye down the column for ten years. A bond priced at 87.54 yields 10% and a bond priced at 82.07 yields 11%. Obviously the yield on your bond lies somewhere in between, about 10.5%.

Real books of bond tables contain several hundred pages, each crammed with bond prices for different combinations of coupon, yield and maturity, but in all other respects, they are the same as our mini-book of Table 23-1.

AN EXAMPLE   The yield to maturity is unambiguous and easy to calculate. It is the stock in trade of any bond dealer. By now, however, you should have learned to treat any internal rate of return with suspicion.[8] The more closely we examine the yield to maturity, the less informative it is seen to be. Here is an example.

It is 1993. You are contemplating an investment in Government of Canada bonds. You come across the following quotations for two bonds:

Bond	Price	Yield to Maturity, % (IRR)
5s of '98	85.21	8.78
10s of '98	105.43	8.62

The phrase "5s of '98" means a bond maturing in 1998 paying annual interest amounting to 5% of the bond's face value. The interest payment is called a *coupon* payment. Bond investors would say that these bonds have a 5% coupon. Face

---

[8] See Section 5-5.

Table 23-1
Each page of this mini-book of bond tables shows bond prices for a different coupon level.

Coupon = 5% Page 1

Yield	6	8	10	12	14
6.00%	95.02	93.72	92.56	91.53	90.62
7.00	90.34	87.91	85.79	83.94	82.33
8.00	85.92	82.52	79.61	77.13	75.01
9.00	81.76	77.53	73.98	71.01	68.51
10.00	77.84	72.91	68.84	65.50	62.75
11.00	74.14	68.61	64.15	60.54	57.64
12.00	70.66	64.63	59.86	56.07	53.08
13.00	67.37	60.93	55.93	52.04	49.01
14.00	64.26	57.49	52.33	48.39	45.38

Coupon = 6% Page 2

Yield	6	8	10	12	14
6.00%	100.00	100.00	100.00	100.00	100.00
7.00	95.17	93.95	92.89	91.97	91.17
8.00	90.61	88.35	86.41	84.75	83.34
9.00	86.32	83.15	80.49	78.26	76.39
10.00	82.27	78.32	75.08	72.40	70.20
11.00	78.45	73.84	70.12	67.12	64.70
12.00	74.85	69.68	65.59	62.35	59.78
13.00	71.44	65.81	61.44	58.03	55.39
14.00	68.23	62.21	57.62	54.12	51.45

Coupon = 7% Page 3

Yield	6	8	10	12	14
6.00%	104.98	106.28	107.44	108.47	109.38
7.00	100.00	100.00	100.00	100.00	100.00
8.00	95.31	94.17	93.20	92.38	91.67
9.00	90.88	88.77	86.99	85.50	84.26
10.00	86.71	83.74	81.31	79.30	77.65
11.00	82.76	79.08	76.10	73.70	71.76
12.00	79.04	74.74	71.33	68.62	66.48
13.00	75.52	70.70	66.94	64.03	61.76
14.00	72.20	66.94	62.92	59.86	57.52

Coupon = 8% Page 4

Yield	6	8	10	12	14
6.00%	109.95	112.56	114.88	116.94	118.76
7.00	104.83	106.05	107.11	108.03	108.83
8.00	100.00	100.00	100.00	100.00	100.00
9.00	95.44	94.38	93.50	92.75	92.13
10.00	91.14	89.16	87.54	86.20	85.10
11.00	87.07	84.31	82.07	80.27	78.82
12.00	83.23	79.79	77.06	74.90	73.19
13.00	79.60	75.58	72.45	70.02	68.13
14.00	76.17	71.66	68.22	65.59	63.59

Table 23-1
(Continued)

Coupon = 9%						Page 5

| | Years | | | | |
Yield	6	8	10	12	14
6.00%	114.93	118.84	122.32	125.40	128.15
7.00	109.66	112.09	114.21	116.06	117.67
8.00	104.69	105.83	106.80	107.62	108.33
9.00	100.00	100.00	100.00	100.00	100.00
10.00	95.57	94.58	93.77	93.10	92.55
11.00	91.38	89.54	88.05	86.85	85.88
12.00	87.42	84.84	82.80	81.17	79.89
13.00	83.68	80.46	77.96	76.02	74.51
14.00	80.14	76.38	73.51	71.33	69.66

Coupon = 10%						Page 6

| | Years | | | | |
Yield	6	8	10	12	14
6.00%	119.91	125.12	129.75	133.87	137.53
7.00	114.50	118.14	121.32	124.09	126.50
8.00	109.39	111.65	113.59	115.25	116.66
9.00	104.56	105.62	106.50	107.25	107.87
10.00	100.00	100.00	100.00	100.00	100.00
11.00	95.69	94.77	94.02	93.42	92.94
12.00	91.62	89.89	88.53	87.45	86.59
13.00	87.76	85.35	83.47	82.01	80.88
14.00	84.11	81.11	78.81	77.06	75.73

Coupon = 11%						Page 7

| | Years | | | | |
Yield	6	8	10	12	14
6.00%	124.89	131.40	137.19	142.34	146.91
7.00	119.33	124.19	128.42	132.12	135.33
8.00	114.08	117.48	120.39	122.87	124.99
9.00	109.12	111.23	113.01	114.50	115.74
10.00	104.43	105.42	106.23	106.90	107.45
11.00	100.00	100.00	100.00	100.00	100.00
12.00	95.81	94.95	94.27	93.72	93.30
13.00	91.84	90.23	88.98	88.01	87.25
14.00	88.09	85.83	84.11	82.80	81.79

Coupon = 12%						Page 8

| | Years | | | | |
Yield	6	8	10	12	14
6.00%	129.86	137.68	144.63	150.81	156.29
7.00	124.16	130.24	135.53	140.15	144.17
8.00	118.77	123.30	127.18	130.49	133.33
9.00	113.68	116.85	119.51	121.74	123.61
10.00	108.86	110.84	112.46	113.80	114.90
11.00	104.31	105.23	105.98	106.58	107.06
12.00	100.00	100.00	100.00	100.00	100.00
13.00	95.92	95.12	94.49	94.00	93.63
14.00	92.06	90.55	89.41	88.53	87.86

value plus interest are paid back at maturity, 1998. The price of each bond is quoted as a percent of face value. Therefore, if face value is $1,000, you would have to pay $852.10 to buy the bond and your yield would be 8.78%. Letting 1993 be $t = 0$, 1994 be $t = 1$, and so on, we have the following discounted cash-flow calculation.[9]

			Cash Flows				Yield
Bond	C_0	C_1	C_2	C_3	C_4	C_5	%
5s of '98	− 852.10	+ 50	+ 50	+ 50	+ 50	+ 1,050	8.78
10s of '98	− 1,054.30	+ 100	+ 100	+ 100	+ 100	+ 1,100	8.62

Although the two bonds mature at the same date, they presumably were issued at different times, the 5s when interest rates were low, and the 10s when interest rates were high.

Are the 5s of '98 a better buy? Is the market making a mistake by pricing these two issues at different yields? The only way you will know for sure is to calculate the bond's present values using spot rates of interest, r_1 for 1994, r_2 for 1995, and so on. This is done in Table 23-2.

Table 23-2
Calculating present value of two bonds when long-term interest rates are higher than short-term rates.

		Present Value Calculations			
		5s of '98		10s of '98	
Period	Interest Rate	C_1	PV at r_t	C_t	PV at r_t
$t = 1$	$r_1 = 0.05$	$ 50	$ 47.62	$ 100	$ 95.24
$t = 2$	$r_2 = 0.06$	50	44.50	100	89.00
$t = 3$	$r_3 = 0.07$	50	40.81	100	81.63
$t = 4$	$r_4 = 0.08$	50	36.75	100	73.50
$t = 5$	$r_5 = 0.09$	1,050	682.43	1,100	714.92
	Totals	$1,250	$852.11	$1,500	$1,054.29

The important assumption in Table 23-2 is that long-term interest rates are higher than short-term interest rates. We have assumed that the one-year interest rate is $r_1 = 0.05$, the two-year rate is $r_2 = 0.06$, and so on. When each year's cash flow is discounted at the rate appropriate to that year, we see that each bond's present value is exactly equal to the quoted price. Thus, each bond is *fairly priced*.

Why do the 5s have a higher yield? Because, for each dollar that you invest in the 5s you receive relatively little cash inflow in the first four years and a relatively high cash inflow in the final year. Therefore, although the two bonds have identical maturity dates, the 5s provide a greater proportion of their cash flows in 1998. In this sense the 5s are a longer-term investment than the 10s. Their higher yield to maturity just reflects the fact that long-term interest rates are higher than short-term rates.

---

[9] Coupon payments are actually made semiannually—the owners of the 5s of '98 would receive $25 every six months. Thus, our calculations are a little bit off what you would get from using bond tables like Table 23-1.

Problems with Yield to Maturity

With this example in mind, we can sum up the problems with the yield to maturity.

First, when a bond's yield to maturity is calculated, the *same* rate is used to discount *all* payments to the bondholder. The bondholder may actually demand different rates of return ($r_1, r_2,$ and so on) for different periods. Unless two bonds offer exactly the same pattern of cash flow over time, they are likely to have different yields to maturity. Therefore, the yield to maturity on one bond can offer only a rough guide to the appropriate yield on another.

Second, yields to maturity do not determine bond prices. It is the other way around. The demand by companies for capital and the supply of savings by individuals combine to determine the spot rates $r_1, r_2,$ and so on. These rates then determine the value of any package of future cash flows. Finally, *given* the value, we can compute the yield to maturity. We cannot, however, derive the appropriate yield to maturity *without* first knowing the value. We cannot, for example, assume that the yield should be the same for two bonds with the same maturity unless they also happen to have the same coupon.

The yield to maturity is a complicated average of spot rates of interest. Suppose that r_2 is greater than r_1. Then the yield on a two-year coupon bond must lie between r_1 and r_2. In this case, the yield on the two-year bond provides an underestimate of the two-year spot rate. Of course, if r_2 is less than r_1, it would be the other way around—the yield on the two-year bond would overestimate the two-year spot rate. Sometimes these differences can be dramatic. For example, in Britain in 1977 the 20-year spot rate of interest r_{20} was nearly 20%. But the *yield* on high-coupon bonds maturing in 20 years was only about 13%. The reason was that short-term spot rates of interest were much lower than 20%. The yield on 20-year bonds was an average of short-term and long-term rates.[10]

In Chapter 5 we asserted that one problem with internal rates of return is that they don't add up. In other words, even if you know the return on A and the return on B, you cannot generally work out the return on A + B. Let us illustrate. Suppose your portfolio is evenly divided between two bonds both priced at 100. Bond A is a 1-year bond with a 10% coupon and therefore yields 10%. Bond B is a 2-year bond with an 8% coupon and therefore yields 8%. You might think that the yield on your portfolio would be halfway between: at 9%. You would be wrong. The yield is 8.68%. In other words:

$$200 = \frac{110 + 8}{1.0868} + \frac{108}{1.0868^2}$$

Thus it is dangerous to rely on the yield to maturity—like most averages, it hides much of the interesting information.

*Measuring the Term Structure

If you just want a quick, summary measure of the return offered on a bond, look at the yield to maturity. But if you want to understand why different bonds sell at different prices, you are going to have to dig deeper to estimate spot rates of interest. That is not something that most bond analysts do at the moment. Here's your chance to be ahead of the game.

Look back at Table 23-2, which shows how investors value the 5% bonds of '98. Five years before maturity, each bond is like a package of five mini-bonds.

---

[10] For a good analysis of the relationship between the yield to maturity and spot interest rates, see S.M. Schaefer, "The Problem of Redemption Yields," *Financial Analysts Journal,* **33**: 59–67 (July–August 1977).

The package contains one mini-bond paying $50 at $t = 1$, another paying $50 at $t = 2$, and so on up to the fifth mini-bond, which pays $1,050 at $t = 5$.

To calculate the spot rates of interest, we must first work out the price of each mini-bond. For example, in 1993, you could buy the following packages:

1. Invest $1,704.22 to buy *two* 5s of '95.
2. Invest $1,054.30 to buy *one* 10 of '95.

Each package provides a $100 cash flow for four years. But in year 5, when the bonds mature, the first package gives $2 \times \$1,050 = \$2,100$, and the second package gives $1 \times \$1,100 = \$1,100$. Thus, the only cash-flow advantage of package 1 occurs in year 5. It costs $649.93 more to buy package 1 ($1,704.22 − $1,054.29 = $649.93), but you gain $1,000 in year 5 ($2,100 − $1,100 = $1,000).

Investors must be indifferent between the two packages—if they were not, they would dump one bond and buy the other, and the bond prices would change. Thus, an extra $1,000 received in year 5 must be worth $649.93 now:

$$PV(\$1,000 \text{ in year } 5) = \$649.93$$

But this present value depends on the five-year spot rate r_5:

$$PV = \frac{1,000}{(1 + r_5)^5} = 649.93$$

Solving for r_5, we find that it equals 0.09 or 9%.

In this example, we had two bonds with the same five-year maturity, but different coupons. This allowed us to work out the price of a mini-bond that made a payment only in year 5 and this in turn gave us the five-year spot rate. In order to work out the exact prices of mini-bonds and spot rates for all other periods, we would need a complete series of matching bonds. In practice, we are never so fortunate, but as long as we have a fair spread of coupons and maturities, we can get quite satisfactory estimates of the spot rates.[11] For example, the solid line in Figure 23-2 shows some estimates by Barra Rosenberg of spot interest rates in July 1989.

In Canada the more common name for mini-bonds is **strip bonds**. The name arose because a typical government bond issue consists of two parts. The first is a certificate bearing a face value ranging from $1,000 to $1 million and is redeemable 20 to 30 years from the issue date, and the second is a detachable "strippable" sheet of 40 to 60 interest coupons, which are redeemable on specified dates during the bond's life. The term *strip bond* then refers to the first part of the bond, that is, the bond stripped of its coupons.

Recently, a number of financial institutions in Canada and the United States have purchased long-term government bond issues and have reissued them as strip bonds, each of which makes only one payment at maturity.[12] These strip bonds are popular with individual investors who want to provide themselves with

---

[11] You may also have to adjust for the fact that low-coupon bonds, because they sell at a discount, get a tax break relative to high-coupon bonds. Part of the low-coupon bonds' expected return comes as capital gains, because the discount diminishes over time. Also, bonds may have differing call provisions (see Section 24-3).

[12] These strip bonds have a variety of exotic names. In Canada, for example, Guaranty Trust issues are known as *Cougar Residuals* and North West Trust issues as *The Nugget*. In the United States, Merrill Lynch labeled their mini-bond issues TIGRs (Treasury Investment Growth Receipts) and at Salomon Brothers they were known as CATS (Certificates of Accrual on Treasury Securities).

Figure 23-2   Estimated spot rates on U.S. Treasury securities, July 1989. The coloured line gives estimates made by BARRA. The black line shows rates on U.S. Treasury "strips."

a future nest-egg to combine with their retirement savings plans. The price of a $100,000, 20-year strip bond with a promised yield of 12% annually is as little as 10% of the face value.

The strip bond or mini-bond yields provide another way to measure spot interest rates. Simply look at the interest rates on each of these bonds. For example, the broken line in Figure 23-2 shows the rates of interest on U.S. Treasury "stripped" bonds. Notice that these rates are almost indistinguishable from Barra's estimates of the interest rates on packages of Treasury coupon bonds.

*Pricing Bonds of Different Maturity   Do you remember how we valued options? The profit or loss on an option depends only on what happens to the underlying stock. You can, therefore, create a mixture of a risk-free loan and the stock which gives exactly the same payoffs as the option. If both packages give the same payoff, they must sell for the same price.

We can use a similar idea to check that bonds of different maturity are consistently priced. For example, suppose that the price of each bond depends only on what happens to the short-term rate of interest. Then you could exactly duplicate the payoffs on any bond by holding a mixture of two other bonds. If both investments give the same payoff, you know that they should sell for the same price. If they don't, you unload the expensive investment and buy the cheap one. Investors are now starting to use these ideas to price different bonds.

23-3   EXPLAINING THE TERM STRUCTURE

The term structure in Figure 23-2 is upward-sloping. In other words, long rates of interest are higher than short rates. This is the more common pattern but sometimes it is the other way around, with short rates higher than long rates. Why do we get these shifts in term structure?

Table 23-3
Two investment strategies for Ms. Long, who wants to invest $1,000 for two years.

Strategy	Now	Year 1	Year 2 (Final Payoff)
L1 invest in 2 one-year bonds	$1,000 $\xrightarrow[\substack{\text{Invest in} \\ \text{first bond} \\ \text{yielding } r_1}]{}$	$1,000(1 + r_1)\xrightarrow[\substack{\text{Invest in} \\ \text{second bond} \\ \text{yielding } r_2}]{}$	$1,000(1 + r_1)(1 + {}_1r_2)$
L2 invest in 1 two-year bond	$1,000 \xrightarrow[\substack{\text{Invest in bond} \\ \text{yielding } r_2}]{}$		$1,000(1 + r_2)^2$
Strategy L2 can be expressed as	$1,000 \xrightarrow[\substack{\text{Invest for} \\ \text{one year at } r_1}]{}$	$1,000(1 + r_1)\xrightarrow[\substack{\text{Invest for} \\ \text{second year} \\ \text{at implicit} \\ \text{forward rate} \\ f_2}]{}$	$1,000(1 + r_1)(1 + f_2)$

Ms. Long's Problem

Let us look at a simple example. Ms. Long wants to invest $1,000 for two years. Two strategies open to her are described in Table 23-3. Strategy L1 is to put the money in a one-year bond at an interest rate of r_1. At the end of the year she must then take her money and find another one-year bond. Let us call the rate of interest on this second bond ${}_1r_2$—that is, the spot rate of interest at time 1 on a loan maturing at time 2.[13] As Table 23-3 shows, the final payoff to this strategy is $1,000(1 + r_1)(1 + {}_1r_2)$.

Of course Ms. Long cannot know for sure what the one-period spot rate of interest ${}_1r_2$ will be next year. Suppose that she *expects* it to be 11%. That is, $E({}_1r_2) = 0.11$. The current one-period spot rate is 10%. The expected final payoff is:

$$1,000(1 + r_1)[1 + E({}_1r_2)] = 1,000(1.10)(1.11) = \$1,221$$

Instead of making two separate investments of one year each, Ms. Long could invest her money today in a bond that pays off in year 2 (strategy L2 in Table 23-3). That is, she would invest at the *two-year* spot rate r_2, and receive a final payoff of $1,000 (1 + r_2)^2$. If $r_2 = 0.105$, the payoff is $1,000(1.105)^2 = \$1,221$.

Now, look below the dashed line in Table 23-3. The table shows that strategy L2 can be reinterpreted as investing for one year at the spot rate r_1 and for the second year at a **forward rate** f_2. The forward rate is *implicit* in the two-year spot rate r_2. It is also *guaranteed*: by buying the two-year bond, Ms. Long can "lock in" an interest rate of f_2 for the second year she invests.

Suppose that the two-year spot rate is 10.5% as before. Then the forward rate f_2 must be 11%. By definition, the forward rate for $t = 2$ is the implicit interest rate in the second year of the two-year loan:

$$(1 + r_2)^2 = (1 + r_1)(1 + f_2)$$
$$(1.105)^2 = (1.10)(1 + f_2)$$
$$f_2 = \frac{(1.105)^2}{1.10} - 1 = 0.11$$

or 11%.[14] The two-year spot rate of 10.5% is an average of the 10% one-year spot rate and the 11% forward rate.

---

[13] Be careful to distinguish ${}_1r_2$ from r_2, the spot interest rate on a *two-year* bond held from time 0 to time 2. The quantity ${}_1r_2$ is a *one-year* spot rate established at time 1.

[14] Actually, 11.002%. We rounded.

What should Ms. Long do? One possible answer is that she should follow the strategy that gives the highest *expected* payoff. That is, she should compare:

Expected Payoff to Strategy L1	To	(Certain) Payoff to Strategy L2
$1,000(1 + r_1)[1 + E(_1r_2)]$	to	$1,000(1 + r_2)^2$
	or to	$1,000(1 + r_1)(1 + f_2)$

Strategy L1 gives the higher expected return if $E(_1r_2)$, the expected future spot rate, exceeds the forward rate f_2 implicit in the two-year spot rate r_2. In our numerical example, with $r_1 = 0.10$, $r_2 = 0.105$, and $E(_1r_2) = 0.11$, the two strategies give the same expected return:

	Payoff
Strategy L1	$1,000(1.10)(1.11) = \$1,221$ (expected)
Strategy L2	$1,000(1.105)^2 = \$1,221$ (certain)

Mr. Short's Problem

Now let us look at the decision faced by Mr. Short. He also has $1,000 to invest, but he wants it back in one year. An obvious strategy is to invest in a one-year bond. In this case, his payoff is $1,000(1 + r_1)$—see strategy S1 in Table 23-4. A second strategy (S2 in the table) is to buy a two-year bond and sell it after one year. The sale price will be the bond's present value in year 1. At that time, the bond will have one year to maturity. Its present value will be equal to its year-2 payoff $1,000(1 + r_2)^2$ discounted at $_1r_2$, the one-period spot rate prevailing in year 1:

$$\text{PV of two-year bond at year 1} = \frac{1,000(1 + r_2)^2}{1 + \,_1r_2}$$

Table 23-4
Two investment strategies for Mr. Short, who wants to invest $1,000 for one year.

Strategy	Now		Year 1 (Final Payoff)
S1 invest in one-year bond	$1,000	Invest in r_1	$1,000(1 + r_1)$
S2 invest in two-year bond, but sell in year 1	$1,000	Invest, sell for PV at year 1	$\dfrac{1,000(1 + r_2)^2}{1 + \,_1r_2}$

We know from Ms. Long's problem that the two-period rate r_2 can be expressed in terms of the one-period spot rate r_1 and the forward rate f_2. Thus:

$$\text{PV of two-year bond at year 1} = \frac{1,000(1 + r_1)(1 + f_2)}{1 + \,_1r_2}$$

Of course, Mr. Short cannot predict the future spot rate, and, therefore, he cannot predict the price at year 1 of the two-year bond. But if $r_2 = 0.105$, and he expects the spot rate to be $_1r_2 = 0.11$, then the expected price is:

$$\frac{1,000(1.105)^2}{1.11} = \frac{1,221}{1.11} = \$1,100$$

What should Mr. Short do? Suppose that he prefers the strategy that gives the highest expected payoff. Then he should compare:[15]

(Certain) Payoff to Strategy S1	To	Expected Payoff to Strategy S2
$1,000(1 + r_1)$	to	$\dfrac{1,000(1 + r_2)^2}{1 + E(_1r_2)}$
	or to	$\dfrac{1,000(1 + r_1)(1 + f_2)}{1 + E(_1r_2)}$

Strategy S2 is better if the forward rate f_2 exceeds the expected future spot rate $E(_1r_2)$. If Mr. Short faces the same interest rates as Ms. Long [$r_1 = 0.10$, $r_2 = 0.105$, $E(_1r_2) = 0.11$, $f_2 = 0.11$], the two strategies give the same expected return:

	Payoff
Strategy S1	$1,000(1.10) = \$1,100$ (certain)
Strategy S2	$\dfrac{1,000(1.105)^2}{1.11} = \dfrac{1,000(1.10)(1.11)}{1.11} = \$1,100$ (expected)

The Expectations Hypothesis

You can see that if the world is made up of people like Ms. Long and Mr. Short, all trying to maximize their expected return, then the one-year and two-year bonds can exist side by side only if

$$f_2 = E(_1r_2)$$

This condition was satisfied in our numerical example—both f_2 and $E(_1r_2)$ equalled 11%. But what happens if the forward rate exceeds the expected future

---

[15] Here we are making an approximation because the expected payoff of S2 in $t = 1$ is not exactly equal to $[1,000(1 + r_2)^2]/[1 + E(_1r_2)]$. We should calculate the expected price of the two-year bond at $t = 1$. Call this $\tilde{P}$. By definition:

$$\tilde{P} = \frac{1,000(1 + r_2)^2}{1 + {}_1r_2}$$

and

$$E(\tilde{P}) = E\left[\frac{1,000(1 + r_2)^2}{1 + {}_1r_2}\right]$$

But

$$E\left[\frac{1,000(1 + r_2)^2}{1 + {}_1r_2}\right] \text{ is only approximately equal to } \frac{1,000(1 + r_2)^2}{1 + E(_1r_2)}$$

In general, for any positive random variable $\tilde{x}$, $E(1/\tilde{x})$ is greater than $1/E(\tilde{x})$. This is an example of *Jensen's inequality*. Ignoring Jensen's inequality can be dangerous if the variance of $\tilde{x}$ is large.

spot rate? Then both Long and Short prefer investing in two-year bonds. If the world were entirely made up of expected-return maximizers, and f_2 exceeds $E(_1r_2)$, no one would be willing to hold one-year bonds. On the other hand, if the forward rate were less than the expected future spot rate, no one would be willing to hold two-year bonds. Since investors *do* hold both one-year and two-year bonds, it follows that forward rates of interest must equal expected future spot rates (providing that investors are only interested in expected return).

This is the **expectations hypothesis** of the term structure.[16] It says that the *only* reason for an upward-sloping term structure is that investors expect future spot rates to be higher than current spot rates; the *only* reason for a declining term structure is that investors expect spot rates to fall below current levels. The expectations hypothesis also implies that investing in short-term bonds (as in strategies L1 and S1) gives exactly the same expected return as investing in long-term bonds (as in strategies L2 and S2).

The Liquidity-Preference Theory

One problem with the expectations theory is that it says nothing about risk. Look back for a moment at our two simple cases. Ms. Long wants to invest for two years. If she buys a two-year bond, she can nail down her final payoff today. If she buys a one-year bond, she knows her return for the first year but she does not know at what rate she will be able to reinvest her money. If she does not like this uncertainty, she will tend to prefer the two-year bond, and she will hold one-year bonds only if

$$E(_1r_2) \text{ is greater than } f_2$$

What about Mr. Short? He wants to invest for one year. If he invests in a one-year bond, he can nail down his payoff today. If he buys the two-year bond, he will have to sell it next year at an unknown price. If he does not like this uncertainty, he will prefer the one-year investment, and he will hold two-year bonds only if

$$E(_1r_2) \text{ is less than } f_2$$

Here we have the basis for the **liquidity-preference** theory of term structure.[17] Other things being equal, Ms. Long will prefer to invest in two-year bonds and Mr. Short in one-year bonds. If more companies want to issue two-year bonds than there are Ms. Longs to hold them, they will need to offer a bonus to tempt some of the Mr. Shorts to hold them. Conversely, if more companies want to issue one-year bonds than there are Mr. Shorts to hold them, they will need to offer a bonus to tempt some of the Ms. Longs to hold them.

Any bonus shows up as a difference between forward rates and expected future spot rates. This difference is usually called the **liquidity premium**.

Suppose that there is a shortage of people like Ms. Long. Then the liquidity premium will be positive—that is, the forward rate will exceed the expected spot rate. Advocates of the liquidity-preference theory believe that for the most part, investors want to lend short and companies want to borrow long, so that liquidity premiums are positive.

---

[16] The expectations hypothesis is usually attributed to Lutz and Lutz. See F.A. Lutz and V.C. Lutz, *The Theory of Investment in the Firm*, Princeton University Press, Princeton, N.J., 1951.

[17] The liquidity-preference hypothesis is usually attributed to Hicks. See J.R. Hicks, *Value and Capital: An Inquiry into Some Fundamental Principles of Economic Theory*, 2nd ed., Oxford University Press, Oxford, 1946. For a theoretical development, see R. Roll, *The Behavior of Interest Rates: An Application of the Efficient Market Model to U.S. Treasury Bills*, Basic Books, Inc., Publishers, New York, 1970.

If the liquidity-preference theory is right, the term structure should be upward-sloping more often than not. A positive liquidity premium rewards investors for lending long. This reward shows up in higher long-term rates of interest. Of course, if future spot rates are expected to fall, the term structure could be downward-sloping and *still* reward investors for lending long. But the liquidity-preference hypothesis would predict a less dramatic downward slope than the expectations hypothesis would.

Introducing Inflation

We argued above that Ms. Long could nail down her return by investing in two-year bonds. What do we mean by that? If the bonds are issued by the Canadian government, she can be virtually certain that she will be paid the promised number of dollars. But she cannot be certain what that money will buy. The expectations theory and the liquidity-preference theory of term structure implicitly assume that future inflation rates are known. Let us consider the opposite case in which the *only* uncertainty about interest rates stems from uncertainty about inflation.[18]

Suppose that Irving Fisher is right and short rates of interest always incorporate fully the market's latest views about inflation. Suppose also that the market learns more as time passes about the likely inflation rate in a particular year. Perhaps today it has only a very hazy idea about inflation in year 2, but in a year's time it expects to be able to make a much better prediction.

Because future inflation rates are never known with certainty, neither Ms. Long nor Mr. Short can make a completely risk-free investment. But since they expect to learn a good deal about the inflation rate in year 2 from experience in year 1, next year they will be in a much better position to judge the appropriate interest rate in year 2. It is therefore more risky for either of them to make a forward commitment to lend in year 2. Even Ms. Long, who wants to invest for two years, would be incurring unnecessary risk by buying a two-year bond. Her least risky strategy is to invest in successive one-year bonds. She does not know what her reinvestment rate will be, but at least she knows that it will incorporate the latest information about inflation in year 2.

Of course, this means that borrowers must offer some incentive if they want investors to lend long. Therefore, the forward rate of interest f_2 must be greater than the expected spot rate $_1r_2$ by an amount that compensates investors for the extra inflation risk.

EXAMPLE Suppose that the real interest rate is always 2%. Nominal interest rates therefore equal 2% plus the expected rate of inflation. Suppose that the *expected* inflation rate is 8% for both year 1 and year 2. However, inflation may accelerate to 10% in year 1, or it may decrease to 6%. To keep things simple, assume that the actual inflation rate for year 1 continues for year 2:

	Actual Inflation in Year 1	Actual Inflation in Year 2
Expected inflation rate = 0.08	0.10	0.10
	0.08	0.08
	0.06	0.06

Each outcome has a probability of one-third.

---

[18] The following is based on R.A. Brealey and S. Schaefer, "Term Structure and Uncertain Inflation," *Journal of Finance,* **32**: 277–290 (May 1977).

Now reconsider Ms. Long's problem. Suppose that she can lend for either one or two years at 10% (the 2% real rate plus the 8% expected inflation rate). If she invests in a one-year bond, she will get $1,000(1.1) = \$1,100$ in year 1. This amount is reinvested, but at what rate? The answer is that the future spot rate $_1r_2$ will be 2% plus the inflation rate experienced in year 1 and projected for year 2:

Actual Inflation Rate	Spot Interest Rate in Year 1
0.10	0.12
0.08	0.10
0.06	0.08

Thus, the final payoffs to lending short are:

	Year 1	Reinvest at	Final Payoff in Year 2
Invest for first year at $r_1 = 0.10$	$1,100	$_1r_2 = 0.12$	$1,232
	1,100	$_1r_2 = 0.10$	1,210
	1,100	$_1r_2 = 0.08$	1,188

Note that this strategy gives high payoffs when inflation turns out high.

Now, Ms. Long could lock in a $1,210 payoff in year 2 by purchasing a two-year bond at 10% $[1,000(1 + r_2)^2 = 1,000(1.1)^2 = \$1,210]$. But this would not lock in her *real* return. In fact, lending short is the *safer* strategy when the final payoffs are converted back to current dollars:

Strategy	Final Payoffs	Inflation Rate	Inflation-Adjusted Payoffs[19]
Buy two-year bond	$1,210	0.10	$1,000.00
	1,210	0.08	1,037.38
	1,210	0.06	1,076.90
Buy one-year bond and reinvest at year 1	1,232	0.10	1,018.18
	1,210	0.08	1,037.38
	1,188	0.06	1,057.32

A Comparison of Theories of Term Structure

We have described three views about why long- and short-term interest rates differ. The first view, the expectations theory, is somewhat extreme, and not fully supported by the facts. For example, if we look back to Table 7-1 we find that the average annual return on investment in long-term government bonds for the period 1926 to 1988 was 5.2% in Canada and 4.2% in the United States, while the average annual return on an investment in short-term Treasury bills was 4.4% and 3.6% respectively. Perhaps the short-term interest rates did not go up as much as investors expected, but it seems more likely that investors wanted a

---

[19] The inflation-adjusted payoffs are calculated by dividing by $(1 + i)^2$. In this case i is the *actual* inflation rate.

higher expected return for holding long bonds, and that, on the average, they got it. If so, the expectations theory is wrong.

The expectations theory states that if the forward rate of interest is 1% above the spot rate of interest, then your best estimate is that the spot rate of interest will rise by 1%. In a study of the U.S. Treasury bill market between 1959 and 1982, Eugene Fama found that a forward premium *does* on average precede a rise in the spot rate but the rise is less than the expectations theory would predict.[20]

The expectations theory has few strict adherents, but Fama's study confirms that long-term interest rates reflect, in part, investors' expectations about future short-term rates.

Our other two theories suggest that long-term bonds ought to offer some additional return to compensate for additional risk. The liquidity-preference theory supposes that risk comes solely from the uncertainty about the underlying real rates. This may be a fair approximation in periods of price stability such as the 1960s. The inflation-premium theory supposes that the risk comes solely from uncertainty about the inflation rate, which may be a fair approximation in periods of fluctuating inflation such as the 1970s.

If short-term rates of interest are significantly lower than long-term rates, it is often tempting to borrow short-term rather than long-term. Our discussion of term structure theories should serve to warn against such naive strategies. One reason for higher long rates could be that short rates are expected to rise in the future. Also, investors who buy long bonds may be accepting liquidity or inflation risks for which they correctly want compensation. You should borrow short when the term structure is upward sloping only if you feel that investors are *overestimating* future increases in interest rates or *overestimating* the risks of lending long.

If the risk of bond investment comes primarily from uncertainty about the real rate, then the safest strategy for investors is to hold bonds that match their liabilities. For example, the firm's pension fund generally has long-term liabilities. The liquidity-preference theory, therefore, implies that the pension fund should favour long-term bonds. If the risk comes from uncertainty about the inflation rate, then the safest strategy is to hold short bonds. For example, most pension funds have real liabilities that depend on the level of wage inflation. The inflation-premium theory implies that, if a pension fund wants to minimize risk, it should favour short-term bonds.

*Some New Theories of the Term Structure

These term structure theories are static theories—they tell us how bond prices may be determined at one point in time. More recently, financial economists have proposed some important theories of how price *movements* of different bonds are related.

The basic idea underlying these new theories is that the returns on bonds with different maturities tend to move together. For example, if short-term interest rates are high, there is a good bet that long-term rates will be high also. If short-term rates fall, long-term rates usually keep them company.

These linkages between interest rate movements can tell us something about consistent relationships between bond prices. Let us illustrate.[21]

[20] See E.F. Fama, "The Information in the Term Structure," *Journal of Financial Economics,* **13**: 509–528 (Dec. 1984).

[21] We are grateful to John Cox from whom we have borrowed and adapted the following example.

Period   Interest rate, percent

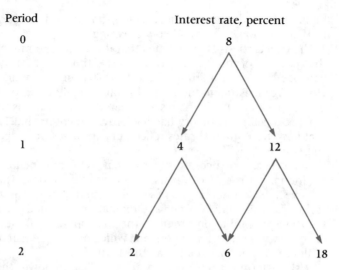

Figure 23-3 The current one-period interest rate is 8%. We assume that in each future period the rate will either halve or increase 1.5 times.

Each branch in Figure 23-3 shows what could happen to the short-term rate of interest. The rate is currently 8% but next period we assume that it could either be halved to 4% or rise to 12%. Then, in period 2 it could again either be halved or rise 1.5 times giving possible interest rates of 2, 6, or 18%.

Now look at the prices of the three zero coupon bonds shown in Figure 23-4. Each branch in the diagram shows how the price of the bond and its yield to maturity will vary, depending on what happens to the short-term interest rate:

1. SHORT is a one-period bond that pays off 100 in period 1. It offers the one-period interest rate of 8% and is therefore priced at $100/1.08 = 92.59$.
2. MEDIUM is a two-period bond. We know that next period the one-period interest rate will be either 4% or 12%. So, in period 1, MEDIUM will be priced at either $10/1.04 = 96.15$ or $100/1.12 = 89.29$. We *assume* (you'll see why shortly) that today MEDIUM has a yield to maturity of 8.73% and, therefore, its price is $100/1.0873^2 = 84.58$.
3. LONG is a three-period bond. We know that in period 2 it must offer a yield of 2, 6, or 18% and we *assume* that in period 1 it will yield either 4.38% or 13.05% and that today it is priced to yield 9.48%.

Now consider the following two strategies:

	Cash flow today	Cash flow period 1	
		Interest rate = 4%	Interest rate = 12%
Strategy 1:			
Buy 1 MEDIUM bond	−84.58	+96.15	+89.29
Strategy 2:			
Buy 0.4965 SHORT bonds	−45.97	+49.65	+49.65
Buy 0.507 LONG bonds	−38.61	+46.50	+39.64
Total	−84.58	+96.15	+89.29

			Bond			
Period		Short	Medium		Long	
0	Yield	8.0	8.73		9.48	
	Price	92.59	84.58		76.20	
1	Yield		4.0	12.0	4.38	13.05
	Price	100	96.15	89.29	91.78	78.24
2	Yield				2.0	6.0	18.0
	Price		100	100	98.04	94.34	84.75
3	Price				100	100	100

Figure 23-4 We show below how the yield to maturity and the price of three bonds might vary with the short-term rate of interest (shown in Figure 23-3). These prices are consistent prices—that is, they offer no arbitrage opportunities.

Notice that, regardless of whether interest rates rise or fall, one MEDIUM bond provides exactly the same payoff as a mixture of a SHORT and a LONG bond. Since the two investments provide exactly the same payoffs, they must cost the same today—that is, they must cost 84.58. If they didn't, there would be arbitrage opportunities. For example, if the yield to maturity of MEDIUM was greater than 8.73% and all other yields were unchanged, you could make money by simultaneously buying one MEDIUM bond and selling the package of SHORT and LONG bonds.[22]

We saw in Figure 23-3 that in each period interest rates could either be halved or rise 1.5 times. Suppose that these two outcomes are equally likely. In this case the expected payoff from holding the long bond for one period is $(0.5 \times 91.78) + (0.5 \times 78.24) = 85.01$ and the expected return over this period is $(85.01 - 76.20)/76.20 = 0.1156$ or 11.56%. So the long bond is relatively risky[23] but it also offers the higher expected return. Thus our set of consistent prices assumes that investors require a particular premium for taking on interest rate risk. But that is not the only set of consistent bond prices. For example, there is another set of consistent prices that would offer a higher or lower premium for risk.

Our simple example should give you a flavour for these modern theories of term structure but you can probably think of a number of improvements that would make the example more realistic. First, short-term interest rates have more built-in stability than we implied. If they rise this year, they are more likely to fall back to a "normal" level next year. If they fall next year, they are more likely

---

[22] If you have read Chapter 20, you will recognize that the approach to finding consistent bond prices is almost identical to the binomial method that we used to value an option.

[23] The return on LONG in period 1 could be *either* $(78.24 - 76.20)/76.20 = 2.7\%$ or $(91.78 - 76.20)/76.20 = 20.5\%$.

than not to bounce back later. Second, short-term interest rates fluctuate more than long-term rates. Third, short-term interest rates and long-term rates do not move in perfect lockstep as our example implied. Sometimes, for example, short-term rates rise but the spread between short- and long-term rates falls. In this case, it might be more realistic to assume that the return on each bond depends on both the change in the short-term interest rate and the change in the spread between the long and short rate. Making the model more realistic also makes it more complex; but, if we know how interest rates can change and how the returns on different bonds are linked, we can still say something about consistent patterns of bond prices.

23-4   ALLOWING FOR THE RISK OF DEFAULT

You should by now be familiar with some of the basic ideas about why interest rates change and why short rates may differ from long rates. It only remains to consider our third question: "Why do some borrowers have to pay a higher rate of interest than others?"

The answer is obvious: bond prices go down, and interest rates go up, when the probability of default increases. But when we say "interest rates go up," we mean *promised* interest rates. If the borrower defaults, the *actual* interest rate paid to the lender is less than the promised rate. The *expected* interest rate may go up with increasing probability of default, but this is not a logical necessity.

These points can be illustrated by a simple numerical example. Suppose that the interest rate on one-year *risk-free* bonds is 9%. Backwoods Chemical Company has issued 9% notes with face values of $1,000, maturing in one year. What will the Backwoods notes sell for?

The answer is easy—if the notes are risk-free: just discount principal ($1,000) and interest ($90) at 9%:

$$\text{PV of notes} = \frac{\$(1,000 + 90)}{1.09} = \$1,000$$

Suppose instead that there is a 20% chance that Backwoods will default. If default does occur, holders of its notes receive nothing. In this case, the possible payoffs to the note holder are:

	Payoff	Probability
Full payment	$1,090	0.8
No payment	0	0.2

The expected payment is 0.8($1,090) + 0.2($0) = $872.

We can value the Backwoods notes like any other risky asset, by discounting their expected payoff ($872) at the appropriate opportunity cost of capital. We might discount at the risk-free interest rate (9%) if Backwoods's possible default is totally unrelated to other events in the economy. In this case the default risk is wholly diversifiable, and the beta of the notes is zero. The notes would sell for:

$$\text{PV of notes} = \frac{\$872}{1.09} = \$800$$

An investor who purchased these notes for $800 would receive a *promised* yield of about 36%:

$$\text{Promised yield} = \frac{\$1,090}{\$800} - 1 = 0.363$$

That is, an investor who purchased the notes for $800 would earn a 36.3% rate of return *if* Backwoods does not default. Bond traders therefore might say that the Backwoods notes "yield 36%." But the smart investor would realize that the bond's *expected* yield is only 9%, the same as on risk-free bonds.

This, of course, assumes that risk of default with these notes is wholly diversifiable, so that they have no market risk. In general, risky bonds do have market risk (that is, positive betas) because default is more likely to occur in recessions when all businesses are doing poorly. Suppose that investors demand a 2% risk premium and an 11% expected rate of return. Then, the Backwoods notes will sell for 872/1.11 = $785.59 and offer a promised yield of (1,090/785.59) − 1 = 0.388, or about 39%.

You rarely see traded bonds offering 39% yields, although we shall encounter shortly an example of one company's bonds that had a promised yield of 50%.

Bond Ratings The relative quality of most bonds traded in Canada can be judged to some extent from bond ratings given by Canadian Bond Rating Service (CBRS) and Dominion Bond Rating Service. Some Canadian bond issues are also rated by United States financial service companies, Moody's and Standard and Poor's. These issues are usually ones sold in the United States as well as in Canada.

Table 23-5 provides the categories in which CBRS classifies bonds.[24] Bonds rated B + + or above are generally considered to be *investment grade* bonds. Commercial banks and many pension funds and other financial institutions are not allowed to invest in bonds unless they are investment grade.

Bond ratings are judgements about firms' financial and business prospects. If there is insufficient information to permit a judgement, the bond will not be rated. There is no fixed formula by which ratings are calculated. Nevertheless, underwriters, bond portfolio managers, and others who follow the bond market closely can get a fairly good idea of how a bond will be rated by looking at a few key numbers, such as the firm's debt-equity ratio, the ratio of earnings to interest and the return on assets.[25]

Examples of corporate bond issues in the various CBRS categories are provided in Table 23-6. It is interesting to note that the bond ratings reflect the perceived riskiness of the industry within which the company operates. AEC Power Ltd. is in the relatively stable utilities industry and has an A + + rating on its first mortgage bonds. Its parent, Alberta Energy Company is an oil and gas producer that faces more risk, so its debentures have a rating of A (Low). Doman is in the more volatile paper and forest products industries and has a B rating on its sinking fund debentures.[26] The "Low" and "High" remarks beside some of the ratings reflect the companys' relative strength within the rating category.

Since bond ratings reflect the probability of default, it is not surprising that there is also a close correspondence between a bond's rating and its promised yield. For example, at the end of March 1991, long-term Canadian government bonds promised a yield of 9.79%, while long-term A + + corporate bonds prom-

---

[24] About 10% of rated bonds are classified A + +, 15% A +, 25% A, 25% B + +, and 20% B +. The remainder are predominantly B or C.

[25] See, for example, R.S. Kaplan and G. Urwitz, "Statistical Models of Bond Ratings: A Methodological Inquiry," *Journal of Business*, **52**: 231–261 (April 1979).

[26] The different kinds of debt are discussed in Chapter 24. For example secured debt provides an extra guarantee and is safer than general unsecured debt. Thus, the security of Provigo's Series E and F collateralized debentures generate an A + (High) rating, while Provigo's unsecured Series 1987 and 1991 Debentures are only rated A (Low).

ised a 10.27% yield and B+ bonds offered an 11.85% yield. Thus, the risk-premium or spread on A+ bonds was about 0.5% while the spread of B+ bonds over long Canada bonds was about 2%.

Once a bond rating service such as CBRS or Moody's rates a bond, the rating is not changed unless there is a significant shift in the company's financing or prospects. If a company's conditions change for the worse, the rating agencies put the company on a "Credit Watch," until it becomes clear whether the rating should be changed.

Table 23-5
Key to CBRS bond ratings

A+ +   Highest Quality

This category encompasses bonds of outstanding quality. They possess the highest degree of protection of principal and interest. Companies rated A+ + are generally large national and/or multi-national corporations whose products or services are essential to the Canadian economy.

These companies are the acknowledged leaders in their respective industries and have clearly demonstrated their ability to best withstand adverse economic or trade conditions either national or international in scope. Characteristically these companies have had a long and creditable history of superior debt protection, in which the quality of their assets and earnings has been constantly maintained or improved, with strong evidence that this will continue.

A+   Very Good Quality

Bonds rated A+ are very similar in characteristics to those rated A+ + and can also be considered superior in quality. These companies have demonstrated a long and satisfactory history of growth with above-average protection of principal and interest on their debt securities.

These bonds are generally rated lower in quality because the margin of assets or earnings protection may not be as large or as stable as those rated A+ +. In both these categories the nature or quality of the asset and earning coverages are more important than the numerical values of the ratios.

A   Good Quality

Bonds rated A are considered to be good quality securities and to have favourable long-term investment characteristics. The main feature that distinguishes them from the higher rated securities is that these companies are more susceptible to adverse trade or economic conditions and the protection is consequently lower than for the categories A+ + and A+.

In all cases the A rated companies have maintained a history of adequate assets and earnings protection. There may be certain elements that may impair this protection sometime in the future. Confidence that the current overall financial position will be maintained or improved is slightly lower than for the above rated securities.

B+ +   Medium Grade

Issues rated B+ + are classified as medium or average grade credits and are considered to be investment grade. These companies are generally more susceptible than any of the higher rated companies to swings in economic or trade conditions that would cause a deterioration in protection should the company enter a period of poor operating conditions.

There may be factors present either from within or from without the company that may adversely affect the long-term level of protection of the debt. These companies bear closer scrutiny but in all cases both interest and principal are adequately protected at the present time.

Table 23-5
(*Continued*)

B+   Lower Medium Grade

Bonds which are rated B+ are considered to be lower medium grade securities and have limited long-term protective investment characteristics. Assets and earnings coverage may be modest or unstable.

A significant deterioration in interest and principal protection may occur during periods of adverse economic or trade conditions. During periods of normal or improving economic conditions, assets and earnings protection are adequate; however, the company's ability to continually improve its financial position and the level of debt protection is at present limited.

B   Poor Quality

Securities rated B lack most qualities necessary for long-term fixed income investment. Companies in this category have a general history of volatile operating conditions, and the assurance has been in doubt that principal and interest protection will be maintained at an adequate level. Current coverages may be below industry standards and there is little assurance that debt protection will significantly improve.

C   Speculative

Securities in this category are clearly speculative. The companies are generally junior in many respects and there is little assurance that the adequate coverage of principal and interest can be maintained uninterruptedly over a period of time.

D   Default

Bonds in this category are in default of some provisions in their trust deed and the companies may or may not be in the process of liquidation.

Rating Suspended

A company that has its rating suspended is experiencing severe financial or operating problems of which the outcome is uncertain. The company may or may not be in default but at present there is uncertainty as to the company's ability to pay off its debt.

Source: *An Introduction to Bond and Commercial Paper Ratings*, Canadian Bond Rating Service, 1985.

Table 23-6
CBRS bond ratings for selected Canadian corporate bond issues

Company	Bonds Rated	Rating
AEC Power Ltd.	First Mortgage Bonds	A++
Alberta Energy Company	Debentures	A (Low)
Bombardier	Debentures	A (High)
Canadian Tire	Sinking Fund Debentures	A+
Doman Industries	Sinking Fund Debentures	B
Hudson's Bay Acceptance	Secured Debentures	B++ (High)
Provigo	Series E & F Collateralized Debentures	A+ (High)
Provigo	Series 1987 & 1991 Debentures	A (Low)
Stelco	Subordinated Debentures	B+
Teleglobe Canada	Unsecured Debentures	A

Source: *Master Index*, Canadian Bond Rating Service, April, 1991.

In July 1965 the issue of an additional $175 million of New York City bonds led Moody's to downrate the city's debt from A to Baa.[27] In subsequent testimony to the congressional Subcommittee on Economic Progress, a city official claimed that the rating services were "causing leading cities to be shortchanged out of hundreds of millions of dollars in unwarranted interest charges." Suggested remedies included the idea that a federal agency be established that could rate municipal bonds "more objectively." We leave it to the reader to judge whether Moody's is likely to have *caused* the increased interest charges, as New York City suggested, or whether the rating change just reflected a widespread disillusionment with the city's debt. Ten years later, after New York had nearly defaulted, Moody's was again the subject of criticism—this time for overoptimistic ratings. "Moody's," complained Senator Eagleton, "continued to signal 'All is well,'" even while the city "was floundering on the financial rocks and was being abandoned by its crew of bankers and money men." A bond rater's lot is not always a happy one.

Junk Bonds

Bonds rated below B + + by CBRS or Baa by Moody's are often known as **junk bonds.** Until recently most junk bonds were "fallen angels"—that is, they were bonds of companies that had fallen on hard times. But during the 1980s new issues of junk bonds multiplied tenfold as more and more companies issued large quantities of low-grade debt to finance takeovers or to defend themselves against being taken over.

The development of this market for low-grade corporate bonds was largely the brainchild of the investment banking firm, Drexel Burnham Lambert. The result was that for the first time corporate midgets were able to take control of corporate giants and they could finance this activity by issues of debt. However, issuers of junk bonds often had debt ratios of 90 or 95%. Many worried that these high levels of leverage resulted in undue risk and pressed for legislation to ban junk bonds.

Between 1986 and 1988 Campeau Corporation amassed a huge retailing empire by acquiring major department store chains such as Federated Department Stores and Allied Stores. Unfortunately, it also amassed $10.9 billion in debt, which was supported by just $0.9 billion of book equity. So, in September 1989 when Campeau announced that it was having difficulties meeting the interest payments on its debt, the junk bond market took a nose dive and worries about the riskiness of junk bonds intensified. Campeau's own bonds fell to the point at which they offered a promised yield of nearly 50%. Investors with large holdings of junk bonds took large losses. Among them was the originator of junks, Drexel Burnham Lambert, which was driven into bankruptcy.

Most junk bonds have not defaulted but that doesn't mean much since most junk bonds have not been around for very long. However, a study by Asquith, Mullins and Wolff,[28] found that of the junk bonds issued between 1977 and 1982 almost a third had defaulted by the end of 1988. A further third of the bonds had been called, thus depriving their holders of the prospect of a continuing

---

[27] In descending order of probability of default, the Moody's bond ratings are Aaa, Aa, A, Baa, Ba, B, Caa, Ca and C. Like CBRS, the first four of these categories are considered to be investment quality.

[28] See P. Asquith, D.W. Mullins, and E.D. Wolff, "Original Issue High Yield Bonds: Aging Analyses of Defaults , Exchanges, and Calls," *Journal of Finance,* **44**: 923–952 (September 1989). Edward Altman reached essentially the same conclusions in E. Altman, "Measuring Corporate Bond Mortality and Performance," *Journal of Finance,* **44**: 909–922 (September 1989).

stream of high coupon payments. In 1989 companies defaulted on $8.1 billion of debt and in the first half of 1990 the figure was $4.8 billion. Not surprisingly, the market for *new* low grade bonds largely dried up.

*Option Pricing and Risky Debt

In Section 20-2 we showed that holding a corporate bond is equivalent to lending money with no chance of default *but* at the same time giving stockholders a put option on the firm's assets. When a firm defaults, its stockholders are in effect exercising their put. The put's value is the value of limited liability—of stockholders' right to walk away from their firm's debts in exchange for handing over the firm's assets to its creditors. To summarize:

Bond value = bond value assuming no chance of default − value of put

Thus, valuing bonds should be a two-step process. The first step is easy: calculate the bond's value assuming no default risk. (Discount promised interest and principal payments at the yield on comparable Government of Canada issues.) Second, calculate the value of a put written on the firm's assets, where the maturity of the put equals the maturity of the bond, and the exercise price of the put equals the interest and principal payments promised to bondholders.

Owning a corporate bond is *also* equivalent to owning the firm's assets *but* giving a call option on these assets to the firm's stockholders.[29]

Bond value = asset value − value of call on assets

Thus, you also can calculate a bond's value, given the value of the firm's assets, by valuing a call on these assets, and subtracting the call value from the asset value. (The call value is just the value of the firm's common stock.)

Therefore, if you can value puts and calls on a firm's assets, you can value its debt.[30]

In practice, this is a bit more difficult than it sounds. The put or call you have to value is usually not the simple option described in Chapter 20, but a much more complex one. Suppose, for example, that Backwoods Chemical issues a ten-year bond that pays interest annually and is retired by ten sinking fund payments starting a year after issue. We can still think of Backwoods stock as a call option that can be exercised by making interest and sinking fund payments. But there is not one such payment but ten of them. To value Backwoods stock we would have to value ten sequential one-year call options. The first option can be exercised by making the first interest and sinking fund payment when it comes due. By exercise stockholders obtain a second call option, which can be exercised by making the second interest and sinking fund payment. The reward of exercising is a third call option, and so on. When the tenth option is finally exercised, the debt is fully repaid and stockholders regain unencumbered ownership of Backwoods's assets.

Of course, if the firm does not make interest and sinking fund payments when due, bondholders take over and stockholders are left with nothing. In other words, by not exercising one call option, stockholders give up all subsequent call options.

[29] Again, see Section 20-2.

[30] However, option valuation procedures cannot value the *assets* of the firm. Puts and calls must be valued as a proportion of asset value. For example, note that the Black-Scholes formula (Section 20-5) requires stock price in order to compute the value of a call option.

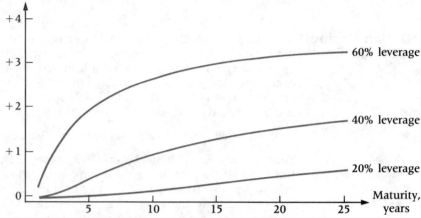

Differences between
interest rate on bond
and risk-free interest rate

Figure 23-5   How the interest rate on risky corporate debt changes with leverage and maturity. These curves are calculated using option pricing theory under the following simplifying assumptions: (1) The risk-free interest rate is constant for all maturities. (2) The standard deviation of the return on the company's assets is 25% per annum. (3) No dividends are paid. (4) Debt is in the form of discount bonds (that is, only one payment is made, at maturity). (5) Leverage is the ratio of the *market* value of the debt to the *market* value of the debt plus equity.

Valuing Backwoods stock when the ten-year bond is issued is equivalent to valuing the first of the ten call options. But you cannot value the first option without prospectively valuing the nine following ones.[31] Even this example under-states the practical difficulties, because large firms may have dozens of outstand-ing debt issues with different interest rates, sinking fund schedules, seniority, and maturities, and also convertible issues, preferred shares, and so on. But do not lose heart. Computers can solve these problems, more or less by brute force, even in the absence of simple, exact evaluation formulas.

Figure 23-5 shows a simple application. The figure is designed to give you some feel for the effect of default risk on (promised) bond yields. It takes a company with average operating risk and shows how the interest rate should increase with the amount of bonds that are issued and their maturity. You can see, for example, that, if the company raises 20% of its capital in the form of 20-year bonds, it should pay about one-half of a percentage point above the government borrowing rate to compensate for the default risk. Companies with more leverage or with longer-maturity bonds ought to pay higher premia.[32]

In practice, interest rate differentials tend to be greater than those shown in Figure 23-5. High-grade corporate bonds typically offer promised yields about one percentage point greater than Government of Canada bonds. Does this mean that these companies are paying too much for their debt?

Probably not; there are a number of other possible explanations. For example, notice that Figure 23-5 makes several artificial assumptions. One assumption is that the company does not pay dividends. If it does regularly pay out part of its

---

[31] The other approach to valuing Backwoods's (subtracting put value from risk-free bond value) is no easier. The analyst would be confronted by not one simple put, but by a package of ten sequential puts.

[32] But beyond a certain point (not shown in Figure 23-5), the yield premia begin to decline with increasing maturity.

assets to stockholders, there may be substantially fewer assets to protect the bondholder in the event of trouble. In this case, the market may be quite justified in requiring a higher yield on the company's bonds. Also, most publicly issued corporate bonds are less marketable than federal government bonds, which trade every day in large quantities. Lawrence Fisher has conducted an important study of the corporate bond market in which he concluded that differences in market-ability were a principal reason for differences in interest rates.[33]

*Valuing Government Loan Guarantees

In the summer of 1971 Lockheed Corporation was in trouble. It was nearly out of cash after absorbing heavy cost overruns on military contracts and, at the same time, committing more than $800 million[34] to the development of the L1011 TriStar airliner. Introduction of the TriStar had been delayed by unexpected problems with its Rolls-Royce engines, and it would be many years before the company could recoup its investment in the plane. Lockheed was on the brink of bankruptcy. (Rolls-Royce was itself driven to the brink by the costs of fixing the engine problems. It was taken over by the British government.)

After months of suspense and controversy, the United States government rescued Lockheed by agreeing to guarantee up to $250 million of new bank loans. If Lockheed had defaulted on these loans, the banks could have gotten their money back directly from the government.

From the banks' point of view, these loans were as safe as Treasury notes. Thus, Lockheed was assured of being able to borrow up to $250 million at a favourable rate.[35] This assurance in turn gave Lockheed's banks the confidence to advance the rest of the money the firm needed.

The loan guarantee was a helping hand—a subsidy—to bring Lockheed through a difficult period. What was it worth? What did it cost the government?

This loan guarantee did not turn out to cost the government anything, because Lockheed survived, recovered, and paid off the loans the government guaranteed. Does that mean that the value of the guarantee to Lockheed was also zero? Does it mean the government absorbed no risks when it gave the guarantee in 1971, when Lockheed's survival was still uncertain? Of course not. The government absorbed the risk of default. Obviously, the banks' loans to Lockheed were worth more with the guarantee than they would have been without it.

The present value of a loan guarantee is the amount lenders would be willing to pay to relieve themselves of all risk of default on an otherwise equivalent unguaranteed loan. It is the difference between the present value of the loan with the guarantee and its present value without the guarantee. A guarantee can clearly have substantial value on a large loan when the chance of default by the firm is high.

It turns out that a loan guarantee can be valued as a put on the firm's assets, where the put's maturity equals the loan's maturity, and its exercise price equals the interest and principal payments promised to lenders. We can easily show this equivalence by starting with the definition of the value of the guarantee.

Value of guarantee = value of guaranteed loan − loan value without guarantee

---

[33] L. Fisher, "Determinants of Risk Premiums on Corporate Bonds," *Journal of Political Economy,* **67**: 212–237 (June 1959).

[34] See U. Reinhardt, "Break-Even Analysis for Lockheed's TriStar: An Application of Financial Theory," *Journal of Finance,* **28**: 821–838 (September 1973).

[35] Lockheed paid the current Treasury bill rate plus a fee of roughly 2% to the government.

Without a guarantee, the loan becomes an ordinary debt obligation of the firm. We know from Section 20-2 that

Value of ordinary loan = value assuming no chance of default − value of put

The loan's value, assuming no chance of default, is exactly its guaranteed value. Thus, the put value equals the difference between the values of a guaranteed and an ordinary loan. This is exactly the value of the loan guarantee.

Thus, option pricing theory should lead to a way of calculating the actual cost of the government's many loan guarantee programs. This will be a healthy thing. The government's possible liability under existing guarantee programs is enormous: for example, the Canadian Deposit Insurance Corporation (CDIC) insures certain bank and trust company customer deposits up to a maximum of $60,000. Should a particular financial institution fail, each of its customers is guaranteed to receive the amount of his or her deposit or $60,000, whichever is less. Recently, option pricing theory has been used to estimate the value of deposit insurance provided by CDIC. In some cases, the estimated value was several times larger than the amount paid by the banks for the insurance.[36]

23-5 SUMMARY

Efficient debt management presupposes that you understand how bonds are valued. That means you need to consider three problems:

1. What determines the general level of interest rates?
2. What determines the difference between long-term and short-term rates?
3. What determines the difference between the interest rates on company and government debt?

Here are some things to remember.

The rate of interest depends on the demand for savings and the supply. The *demand* comes from firms who wish to invest in new plant and equipment. The *supply* of savings comes from individuals who are willing to consume tomorrow rather than today. The equilibrium interest rate is the rate that produces a *balance* between the demand and supply.

The best-known theory about the effect of inflation on interest rates is that suggested by Irving Fisher. He argued that the nominal, or money rate of interest, is equal to the expected real rate plus the expected inflation rate. If the expected inflation rate increases by 1%, so too will the money rate of interest. During the past 30 years Fisher's simple theory has done a good job of explaining changes in short-term interest rates in the United States and Canada.

The value of any bond is equal to the cash payments discounted at the spot rates of interest. For example, the value of a ten-year bond with a 5% coupon equals:

$$PV \text{ (percent of face value)} = \frac{5}{1 + r_1} + \frac{5}{(1 + r_2)^2} + \cdots + \frac{105}{(1 + r_{10})^{10}}$$

Bond dealers generally look at the yield to maturity on a bond. This is simply the internal rate of return, y, the discount rate at which:

---

[36] See R. Giammarino, E. Schwartz, and J. Zechner, "Market Valuation of Bank Assets and Deposit Insurance in Canada," *Canadian Journal of Economics*, **22**: 109–127 (1989).

$$\text{Bond price} = \frac{5}{1 + y} + \frac{5}{(1 + y)^2} + \cdots + \frac{105}{(1 + y)^{10}}$$

The yield to maturity y is a complex average of the spot interest rates r_1, r_2, and so on. Like most averages it can be a useful summary measure but it can also hide a lot of interesting information. We would like you to use some of the new techniques that produce estimates of the spot rates of interest.

The one-period spot rate r_1 may be very different from the two-period spot rate r_2. In other words, investors often want a different annual rate of interest for lending for one year than for two years. Why is this? The *expectations theory* says that bonds are priced so that the expected rate of return from investing in bonds over any period is independent of the maturity of the bonds held by the investor. The expectations theory predicts that r_2 will exceed r_1 only if *next* year's one-period interest rate is expected to rise.

The *liquidity-preference* theory points out that you are not exposed to risks of changing interest rates and changing bond prices if you buy a bond that matures exactly when you need the money. However, if you buy a bond that matures *before* you need the money, you face the risk that you may have to reinvest your savings at a low rate of interest. And, if you buy a bond that matures *after* you need the money, you face the risk that the price will be low when you come to sell it. Investors don't like risk and they need some compensation for taking it. Therefore, when we find that r_2 is generally higher than r_1, it may mean that investors have relatively short horizons and have to be offered an inducement to hold long bonds.

No bonds are risk-free in real terms. If inflation rates are uncertain, the safest strategy for an investor is to keep investing in short bonds and to trust that the rate of interest on these bonds will vary as inflation varies. Therefore, another reason r_2 may be higher than r_1 is that investors have to be offered an inducement to accept additional inflation risk.

In addition to looking at how spot rates at a point in time are determined, we have also considered how changes in spot rates over time affect bond prices. The main idea here is that returns on bonds with different maturities tend to move together. The common element in the returns changes have implications for consistent bond prices.

Finally, we come to our third question: "What determines the difference between interest rates on company and government debt?" Company debt sells at a lower price than government debt. This discount represents the value of the company's option to default. We showed you how the value of this option varies with the degree of leverage and time to maturity. In Canada, Canadian Bond Rating Service and Dominion Bond Rating Service and, in the United States, Moody's and Standard and Poor's rate company bonds according to their default risk, and the price of bonds is closely related to these ratings.

FURTHER READING

The classic work on interest rates is:

Irving Fisher, *The Theory of Interest: As Determined by Impatience to Spend Income and Opportunity to Invest It*, Augustus M. Kelley, Publishers, New York, 1965. Originally published in 1930.

Fisher's work also anticipated Lutz and Lutz's expectations hypothesis of the term structure of interest rates.

F.A. Lutz and V.C. Lutz, *The Theory of Investment of the Firm*, Princeton University Press, Princeton, N.J., 1951.

The liquidity-premium hypothesis is due to Hicks, and our description of the effect of inflation on term structure is taken from Brealey and Schaefer.

R.A. Brealey and S. Schaefer, "Term Structure and Uncertain Inflation," *Journal of Finance*, **32**: 277–290 (May 1977).

J.R. Hicks, *Value and Capital: An Inquiry into Some Fundamental Principles of Economic Theory*, 2nd ed., Oxford University Press, Oxford, 1946.

Good reviews of the term structure literature may be found in Nelson and Roll. Roll applies modern finance theory to the term structure problem.

C.R. Nelson, "The Term Structure of Interest Rates: Theories and Evidence," in J.L. Bicksler, ed., *Handbook of Financial Economics*, North-Holland Publishing Company, Amsterdam, 1980.

R. Roll, *The Behavior of Interest Rates: An Application of the Efficient Market Model to U.S. Treasury Bills*, Basic Books, Inc., Publishers, New York, 1970.

Dobson, Sutch, and Vanderford review empirical tests of term structure theories. Two more recent tests of term structure theories are provided by Fama.

S. Dobson, R. Sutch, and D. Vanderford, "An Evaluation of Alternative Empirical Models of the Term Structure of Interest Rates," *Journal of Finance*, **31**: 1035–1066 (September 1976).

E.F. Fama, "The Information in the Term Structure." *Journal of Financial Economics*, **13**: 509–528 (December 1984).

E.F. Fama, "Term Premiums in Bond Returns," *Journal of Financial Economics*, **13**: 529–546 (December 1984).

Here are three papers that discuss measurement of the term structure:

W. Carleton and I. Cooper, "Estimation and Uses of the Term Structure of Interest Rates," *Journal of Finance*, **31**: 1067–1084 (September 1976).

J. McCulloch, "Measuring the Term Structure of Interest Rates," *Journal of Business*, **44**: 19–31 (January 1971).

S.M. Schaefer, "Measuring a Tax Specific Term Structure of Interest Rates in the Market for British Government Securities," *Economic Journal*, **91**: 415–438 (June 1981).

The Cox, Ingersoll, and Ross paper uses no-arbitrage conditions to derive a rigorous model of the term structure. The Brennan and Schwartz paper is a readable description of a model that links each bond's return to both the short-term and long-term interest rate and then derives consistent bond prices.

M.J. Brennan and E.S. Schwartz, "Bond Pricing and Market Efficiency," *Financial Analysts Journal*, **38**:49–56 (September–October 1982).

J.C. Cox, J.E. Ingersoll, and S.A. Ross, "A Theory of the Term Structure of Interest Rates," *Econometrica*, **53**: 385–407 (May 1985).

Fama's tests indicate that the expected real rate of interest was essentially constant between 1953 and 1971. However, if you read Fama's paper, you should also read the replies by Hess and Bicksler and by Nelson and Schwert.

E.F. Fama, "Short-Term Interest Rates as Predictors of Inflation," *American Economic Review*, **65**: 269–282 (June 1975).

P. Hess and J. Bicksler, "Capital Asset Prices versus Time Series Models as Predictors of Inflation," *Journal of Financial Economics*, **2**: 341–360 (December 1975).

C.R. Nelson and G. Schwert, "Short-Term Interest Rates as Predictors of Inflation: On Testing the Hypothesis That the Real Rate of Interest is Constant," *American Economic Review*, **67**: 478–486 (June 1977).

Evidence on long-run average interest rates in Canada and the United States, respectively, may be found in:

P.P. Boyle, H.H. Panjer, and K.P. Sharp, "Report on Canadian Economic Statistics 1924–1988," Canadian Institute of Actuaries, Waterloo, (1989).

Ibbotson Associates, *Stocks, Bonds, Bills, and Inflation: 1989 Yearbook,* Ibbotson Associates, Chicago, 1989.

The classic empirical study on valuing risky debt is by Lawrence Fisher. Robert Merton has shown how option pricing theory can be applied to risky debt.

L. Fisher, "Determinants of Risk Premiums on Corporate Bonds," *Journal of Political Economy,* **67**: 212–237 (June 1959).

R. Merton, "On the Pricing of Corporate Debt: The Risk Structure of Interest Rates," *Journal of Finance,* **29**: 449–470 (May 1974).

QUIZ

1. The real interest rate is determined by the demand and supply for capital. Draw a diagram to show how the demand by companies for capital and the supply of capital by investors vary with the interest rate. Use this diagram to show:
    (a) What will happen to the amount of investment and saving if firms' investment prospects improve? How will the equilibrium interest rate change?
    (b) What will happen to the amount of investment and saving if individuals' willingness to save increases at each possible interest rate? How will the equilibrium interest rate change? Assume firms' investment opportunities do not change.

2. (a) What is the formula for the value of a two-year, 5% bond in terms of spot rates?
    (b) What is the formula for its value in terms of yield to maturity?
    (c) If the two-year spot rate is higher than the one-year rate, is the yield to maturity greater or less than the two-year spot rate?
    (d) In each of the following sentences choose the correct term from within the parentheses:
        "The (yield-to-maturity/spot-rate) formula discounts all cash flows from one bond at the same rate even though they occur at different points in time." "The (yield-to-maturity/spot-rate) formula discounts all cash flows received at the same point in time at the same rate even though the cash flows may come from different bonds."

3. Use Table 23-1 to check your answers to the following:
    (a) If interest rates rise, do bond prices rise or fall?
    (b) If the bond yield is greater than the coupon, is the price of the bond greater or less than 100?
    (c) If the price of a bond exceeds 100, is the yield greater or less than the coupon?
    (d) Do high coupon bonds sell at higher or lower prices than low coupon bonds?

4. Use Table 23-1 to answer the following questions:
    (a) What is the yield to maturity on a 7%, eight-year bond selling at 74¾?
    (b) What is the approximate price of a 5%, nine-year bond yielding 10%?
    (c) A 9%, 12-year bond yields 14%. If the yield remains unchanged, what will be its price six months hence? Calculate the investor's total return over the six months.

5. (a) Suppose that the one-year spot rate of interest at time 0 is 1% and the two-year spot rate is 3%. What is the forward rate of interest for year 2?

(b) What does the expectations theory of term structure say about the relationship between this forward rate and the one-year spot rate at time 1?

(c) Over a very long period of time, the term structure in Canada has been, on average, upward-sloping. Is this evidence for or against the expectations theory?

(d) What does the liquidity-preference theory say about the relationship between the forward rate and the one-year rate at time 1?

(e) If the liquidity-preference theory is a good approximation and you have to meet long-term liabilities (university tuition for your children, for example), is it safer to invest in long-term or short-term bonds? Assume inflation is predictable.

(f) If the inflation-premium theory is a good approximation and you have to meet long-term real liabilities, is it safer to invest in long-term or short-term bonds?

(g) What does the inflation-premium theory say about the relationship between the forward rate and the one-year spot rate at time 1?

6. (a) State the four CBRS ratings that are generally known as "investment grade" ratings.

(b) Other things equal, would you expect the yield to maturity on a corporate bond to increase or decrease with:
   (i) The company's business risk?
   (ii) The expected rate of inflation?
   (iii) The risk-free rate of interest?
   (iv) The degree of leverage?

7. (a) How in principle would you calculate the value of a government loan guarantee?

(b) The difference between the price of a government bond and a simple corporate bond is equal to the value of an option. What is this option and what is its exercise price?

QUESTIONS AND PROBLEMS

1. Why might Fisher's theory about inflation and interest rates *not* be true?
2. You have estimated spot interest rates as follows:

Year	Spot Rate, %
1	$r_1 = 5.00$
2	$r_2 = 5.40$
3	$r_3 = 5.70$
4	$r_4 = 5.90$
5	$r_5 = 6.00$

(a) What are the discount factors for each date (that is, the present value of $1 paid in year t)?

(b) What are the forward rates for each period?

(c) Calculate the PV of each of the following:

      (i) 5%, two-year bond
      (ii) 5%, five-year bond
      (iii) 10%, five-year bond
    (d) Explain intuitively why the yield to maturity on the 10% bond is less than on the 5% bond.

3. Look at the spot interest rates shown in problem 2. Suppose that someone told you that the six-year spot interest rate was 4.80%. Why would you not believe him or her? How could you make money if he or she was right? What is the minimum sensible value for the six-year spot rate?

4. Look just one more time at the spot interest rates shown in problem 2. What can you deduce about the one-year spot interest rate in four years if:
    (a) The expectations theory of term structure is right?
    (b) The liquidity-preference theory of term structure is right?
    (c) The term structure contains an inflation uncertainty premium?

5. Assume the term structure of interest rates is upward-sloping, as in Figure 23-2. How would you respond to the following comment? "The present term structure of interest rates makes short-term debt more attractive to corporate treasurers. Firms should avoid new long-term debt issues."

6. Here is a harder one: It has been suggested that the Fisher theory is a tautology. If the real rate of interest is defined as the difference between the nominal rate and the expected inflation rate, then the nominal rate *must* equal the real rate plus the expected inflation rate. In what sense is Fisher's theory *not* a tautology?

7. Look up the prices of ten Government of Canada bonds with different coupons and different maturities. Use bond tables to calculate how their prices would change if the yield to maturity increased by one percentage point. Are long-term bonds or short-term bonds most affected by the change in yields? Are high-coupon bonds or low-coupon bonds most affected?

8. Look up prices of ten corporate bonds with different coupons and maturities. Be sure to include some low-rated bonds on your list. Now estimate what these bonds would sell for if the Canadian government had guaranteed them. Calculate the value of the guarantee for each bond. Can you explain the differences between the ten guaranteed values?

9. Look in a recent issue of *The Financial Post* at the Corporate Bonds price quotations.
    (a) Bid and ask prices are reported for each of the corporate bonds listed in *The Financial Post*. The bid price is the price at which the bond dealer is standing ready to buy the bond from you, and the ask price is the price at which the bond dealer is standing ready to sell the bond to you. Thus, the difference between the bid and ask prices (that is, the spread) is the mark-up the dealer demands as compensation for market making services. If you buy the Bell Canada 9.40s of 2002, what is your promised yield to maturity? (Assume annual interest payments.)
    (b) How much higher is the yield on this Bell Canada issue than on a Government of Canada issue with similar maturity?
    (c) Glance quickly through the list of corporate bonds and find one with a very high yield to maturity. Why do you think the yield on this bond is so high?
    (d) Would the expected return be more or less than the yield to maturity?

10. Under what conditions can the expected real interest rate be negative?

11. Bond rating services usually charge corporations for rating their bonds.
   (a) Why do they do this, rather than charge those investors who use the information?
   (b) Why will a company pay to have its bonds rated even when it knows that the service is likely to assign a below-average rating?
   (c) A few companies are not willing to pay for their bonds to be rated. What can investors deduce about the quality of these bonds?

12. A 6%, six-year bond yields 12% and a 10%, six-year bond yields 8%. Calculate the six-year spot rate. (Assume semiannual coupon payments.)

13. In 1985, North West Trust "Nuggets" were priced as follows:

Maturity	Price
1990	54.345
1992	43.713
1994	35.161
1995	31.346
2000	18.951
2004	12.372
2006	9.996

   (a) Estimate the spot rates of interest.
   (b) If the expectations theory is correct, what is the expected one-year rate of interest (that is, the one-year forward rate) in 1994?
   (c) Again, if the expectations theory is correct, what is the expected two-year interest rate in 2004?

14. Are high-coupon bonds more likely to yield more than low-coupon bonds when the term structure is upward-sloping or when it is downward-sloping?

*15. Look back to the first Backwoods Chemical example at the start of Section 23-4. Suppose that the firm's book balance sheet is:

Backwoods Chemical Company (Book Values)			
Net working capital	$ 400	$1,000	Debt
Net fixed assets	1,600	1,000	Equity (net worth)
Total assets	$2,000	$2,000	Total liabilities and net worth

   The debt has a one-year maturity and a promised interest rate of 9%. Thus, the promised payment to Backwoods's creditors is $1,090. The market value of the assets is $1,200 and the standard deviation of asset value is 45% per year. Use Appendix Table 6 to value the Backwoods debt and equity.

*16. Assume that Figure 23-4 correctly describes the path of short-term interest rates. The prices and yields of the three bonds that we described in Section 23-3 have changed. The yield to maturity of MEDIUM is 8.18%. The yield to maturity on LONG is currently 7.80%. Next period it will fall to 3.98% if the short-term interest rate falls and rise to 11.84% if the short-term rate rises.
   (a) Are these yields consistent or are there arbitrage profits to be made?
   (b) How would your answer change if the yield of MEDIUM was currently 7.93% and all other yields were unchanged?
   (c) Suppose that short-term rates are equally likely to rise or fall. What can you deduce about the expected return on the three bonds and investors attitude to risk?

C · H · A · P · T · E · R

24

MANY DIFFERENT KINDS
OF DEBT

In Chapter 14 we introduced you to some of the different kinds of debt. For example, we saw that debt may be short term or long term, it may consist of straight bonds or it may be convertible into common stock, it may be issued domestically or sold overseas, and so on.

As financial manager, you need to choose the type of debt that makes sense for your company. We begin our analysis of this problem by looking in this chapter at the different kinds of straight bonds. After describing the form of the debt contract, we will examine the differences between senior and junior bonds and between secured and unsecured bonds. Then we will describe how bonds are repaid by means of a sinking fund and how the borrower or the lender may have an option for early repayment. Finally, we will look at some of the restrictive provisions that seek to prevent the company from doing anything that would reduce the value of the bonds.

We will not only describe the different features of corporate debt, but also try to say *why* sinking funds, repayment options, and the like exist. They are not simply matters of custom; there are generally good economic reasons for their use.

Debt may be sold to the public by means of a general cash offer or may be placed privately with a limited number of financial institutions. One important kind of private debt is the bank term loan. This may run from 1 to 8 years, shorter than most bonds. We will cover these term loans in more detail in Chapter 32 when we describe short-term bank lending.

Another form of private debt is project finance. This is the glamorous part of the debt market. The words "project finance" conjure up images of multi-million-dollar loans to finance mining ventures in exotic parts of the world. You'll find there's something to the popular image, but it's not the whole story.

Finally, there is a large market for standard long-term private placement bonds. These private placements are closely related to the publicly issued bonds that we look at in this chapter. Whether you decide to make a private placement or a public issue will depend partly on the relative issue costs, for a public issue involves higher fixed costs but a lower rate of interest.[1] But your choice should

---

[1] See Section 15-5.

not depend solely on these costs. There are three other ways in which the private placement bond may differ from its public counterpart.

First, if you place an issue privately with one or two financial institutions, it may be necessary to sign only a simple promissory note. This is simply an IOU which lays down certain conditions that the borrower must observe. However, when you make a public issue of debt, you must worry about who is to represent the bondholders in any subsequent negotiations and what procedures are needed for paying interest and principal. Therefore, the contractual arrangement has to be that much more complicated.

The second characteristic of publicly issued bonds is that they are highly standardized products. They *have* to be—investors are constantly buying and selling them without checking the fine print in the agreement. This is not so necessary in private placements. They are not regularly traded; they are bought and held by large institutions that are well-equipped to evaluate any unusual features. Furthermore, because private placements involve lower fixed issue costs, they tend to be issued by smaller companies. These are the very companies that most need custom-tailored debt.

All bond agreements seek to protect the lender by imposing a number of conditions on the borrower. In the case of private placements these restrictions may be severe. For example, if the borrower wishes to issue any more bonds, the firm may need the permission of the existing bondholders. Because there are only one or two lenders involved, this permission is usually easily obtained. That would not be possible with publicly issued debt. Therefore, the limitations tend to be less stringent in the case of public issues.

We are not going to discuss private placement bonds separately in this chapter because the greater part of what we have to say about public issues is also true of private placements. Just bear the following in mind:

1. The private placement contract is simpler than the public issue contract.
2. The private placement contract is more likely to have nonstandard features.
3. The private placement contract often imposes more stringent conditions on the borrower, but it is more easily renegotiated.

24-1   DOMESTIC BONDS, FOREIGN BONDS, AND EUROBONDS

A borrower can either issue in the domestic market or raise money overseas, for example by a **foreign bond** issue. In this case, it issues bonds on a foreign capital market just like any local firm. The bond must, of course, be denominated in the local currency and the terms must conform to local custom. For North American borrowers the most important markets for foreign bonds have been Switzerland and Japan.

Foreign bonds are issued nationally and are subject to local regulations. There is also an international market for long-term debt known as the **eurobond** market. A eurobond is a bond that is sold simultaneously in a number of foreign countries by an international syndicate of underwriters. Although eurobonds may be sold throughout the world, eurobond underwriters and dealers are mainly located in London. They include the London branches of American, European, Japanese, and Canadian commercial and investment banks.

Eurobond issues are generally made in currencies that are actively traded, fully convertible, and relatively stable. The U.S. dollar has been the most popular choice, followed by the Japanese yen, the British pound Sterling, and the deutsche mark. The Canadian dollar is also popular. There is also a growing market in ECU bonds. An ECU, or European Currency Unit, is simply a basket of currencies that is used as the benchmark for the European Monetary System.[2] Occasionally, when a eurobond has been denominated in a weak currency the holder has been given an option to ask for payment to be made in another currency. There are also dual currency bonds that pay interest in one currency and principal in another.

The eurobond market grew up during the 1960s because the American government imposed an interest-equalization tax on the purchase of foreign securities and because it discouraged American corporations from exporting capital. Therefore, both European and American multinationals were forced to tap an international market for capital. The interest-equalization tax was removed in 1974 and there are no longer any controls on capital exports.[3] Since firms in the United States can now choose whether to borrow in New York or London, the interest rates in the two markets are usually similar. However, the eurobond market is not directly subject to regulation by the American authorities and, therefore, the financial manager needs to be alert to small differences in the costs of borrowing in one market rather than another. For the same reasons, markets for eurobonds denominated in other currencies, such as Canadian dollars, exist.

24-2
Indenture or
Trust Deed

THE BOND CONTRACT

The contract for a private issue of debt is typically just a promissory note or IOU. The contract in any public issue of bonds usually takes the form of an **indenture** or **trust deed** between the borrower and a trust company. The trust company represents the bondholders. It must see that the terms of indenture are observed, administer any sinking fund, and look after the bondholders' interests in the event of default.

A copy of the bond indenture is filed with the securities commission. It is a turgid legal document,[4] and its main provisions are summarized in the prospectus to the issue. To give you some feel for these provisions, the Appendix to this chapter contains details of a debenture issue by Interprovincial Pipe Line (NW) Ltd.

We will use the prospectus to illustrate some features of the bond contract. As we do so, you might consider whether even these summary documents are not unduly obscure. In particular, like most legal documents, they review only the conditions and safeguards that exist and do nothing to draw your attention to any omissions or unusual features.

---

[2] When an ECU bond matures, lenders don't receive a mixture of currencies. They take payment in the currency of their choice at the current exchange rate for ECUs.

[3] Also, until 1984 the United States imposed a withholding tax on interest payments to foreign investors. Investors could avoid this tax by buying a eurobond issued in London rather than a similar bond issued in New York.

[4] For example, Section 1.03 of the indenture for a bond issue by J.C. Penney, a large general merchandise retailer in the United States, says: "In any case where several matters are required to be certified by, or covered by an opinion of, any specified Person, it is not necessary that all such matters be certified by, or covered by the opinion of, only one such Person, or that they be so certified or covered by only one document, but one such Person may certify or give an opinion with respect to some matters and one or more other such Persons as to other matters, and any such Person may certify or give an opinion as to such matters in one or several documents." Try saying that three times very fast.

The Bond Terms

The first page of the prospectus contains a table showing the price and cost of the issue. Notice two things about the price. First, although the bonds have a face value of $1,000, their prices are always shown as a percentage of face value. Second, bond prices in Canada and the United States are usually quoted *net of accrued interest*. That means the bond buyer must pay out not only the quoted price, but also the amount of any interest that may have accrued. Interprovincial planned to issue the bonds on November 15, exactly the interest date, and so in this case the accrued interest is 0%. But suppose the bonds have been issued on December 15. In that case, one month of interest would have accumulated. One month of interest at 12.7% a year is $1/12 \times 12.7 = 1.06\%$. Therefore, the buyer would have had to pay a price of 100% plus 1.06% accrued interest.[5]

The bonds were offered to the public at a price of 100% but Interprovincial sold the issue to the underwriters at 98.85%. The difference represented the underwriters' fee. The total amount of the issue was $75 million of which $900,000 went to the underwriters.

Turn now to the second page of the prospectus, entitled "Prospectus Summary." This section provides a summary of the salient features of the bond issue. Notice that interest is to be paid semiannually at a fixed rate of 12.7% a year. Thus, every 6 months, investors receive interest of $12.7/2 = 6.35\%$. A comparable eurobond would generally pay interest annually.[6]

Sometimes bonds are sold at a discount on their face value, so that investors receive a significant part of their return in the form of capital appreciation.[7] The ultimate is the zero coupon bond, which pays no interest at all; in this case all the return consists of price appreciation.[8]

The Interprovincial interest payment is fixed for the life of the bond, but in some issues the payment varies with the general level of interest rates. For example, the payment may be tied to the Treasury bill rate or to the London interbank offered rate (LIBOR), which is the rate at which banks lend eurodollars to one another. These floating-rate (FRNs) are particularly common in the eurobond market.

Until 1974 floating-rate notes were relatively rare. In that year Citicorp issued $850 million of FRNs. These notes had a special attraction for Citicorp. Since they were a long-term debt of the bank holding company, the terms of the offer were not subject to the United States Regulation Q, which placed a ceiling on the rate that banks could pay for time deposits. Eventually, Regulation Q was repealed, but by that time banks and industrial firms had found other attractions in floating-rate notes.[9]

---

[5] The exact method of calculating accrued interest depend on the market. In some bond markets calculations are based on the assumption that a year is composed of twelve 30-day months; in other markets calculations recognize the actual number of days in each calendar month.

[6] In Table 23-1 we showed you an extract from a book of yields to maturity. These yields were semiannually compounded; in other words, they are equal to twice the 6-month yield. Because eurobonds pay interest annually, it is conventional to quote yields to maturity on eurobonds on an *annually* compounded basis. Remember this when comparing yields.

[7] A zero coupon is often called a "pure discount bond." Any bond that is issued at a discount is known as an *original issue discount* (OID) bond.

[8] The ultimate of ultimates was an issue on behalf of a charity of a perpetual zero coupon bond.

[9] In 1985 a change in government regulation again led Citicorp to make an issue of floating-rate notes. The SEC required that investments made by money-market funds must have an average maturity of no more than 120 days, where maturity was defined as "the period until the next readjustment of the interest rate." Citicorp therefore reset the interest rate on the notes each *week*. SEC regulations also required that money-market funds should only buy debt due within 1 year. The Citicorp notes had a maturity of 364 days, but each quarter the notes were automatically extended unless the investor requested otherwise. Therefore, the notes could be held by money-market funds even though the final repayment could be extended indefinitely.

Often floating-rate notes specify a minimum (or "floor") interest rate or, less frequently, they specify a maximum (or "cap") on the rate.[10] You may also come across "collars," which stipulate both a maximum and a minimum payment or "drop-locks," which provide that, if the rate falls to a specified trigger point, the payment is then fixed for the remainder of the bond's life.

The regular interest payment is like a hurdle the company must keep jumping.[11] If the company ever fails to pay the interest on its debt, the lender can demand his or her money back immediately instead of waiting until matters have deteriorated further. Thus, interest payments provide protection for the lenders.[12]

Registered and Bearer Bonds

Now look at the "Details of the Offering" on the eighth page of Interprovincial's prospectus. The principal and semiannual interest payments will be payable at any branch of the Canadian bank designated in the debentures. These bonds are said to be in **bearer** form. The bond certificate constitutes evidence of ownership, so the bondholder must detach each coupon and claim his or her interest as well as final principal at the designated bank.

Sometimes bonds are issued in **registered** form. This means that the company's registrar will record the ownership of each bond. If the bond is **fully registered**, the company will pay both the interest and the principal directly to each owner. Occasionally a bond issue is **registered as to principal**. This means that the bondholder will receive his or her final principal directly from the company and must claim the interest payments by redeeming the detachable coupons on the bond certificate.

24-3 SECURITY AND SENIORITY

The Interprovincial Pipe Line (NW) issue is a **debenture**. This means that it is an unsecured (or occasionally secured) obligation of the company.[13] The word also usually indicates that the debt has a maturity of 15 years or more—shorter unsecured loans are usually termed **notes**. Both debentures and notes may be senior claims (like the Interprovincial issue, where the Series B Debenture ranks *pari passu* with the firm's other senior debentures), or they may be subordinated to the senior bonds or to *all* other creditors. Occasionally, they may be guaranteed by another company (like the Interprovincial issue) or jointly guaranteed by several companies. Private placements are sometimes guaranteed by the company's management. It does not necessarily matter that the manager is not personally wealthy—the threat of personal ruin always concentrates the mind wonderfully.

---

[10] Instead of issuing a straight (uncapped) FRN, a company will sometimes issue a capped FRN and at the same time sell the cap to another investor. The first investor receives a coupon payment up to the specified maximum and the second investor receives any interest in excess of this maximum.

[11] There is one type of bond where the borrower is obliged to pay interest only if it is covered by the year's earnings. These so-called *income bonds* have largely been issued as part of railroad reorganizations. For a discussion of the attractions of income bonds, see J.J. McConnell and G.G. Schlarbaum: "Returns, Risks, and Pricing of Income Bonds, 1956–1976 (Does Money Have an Odor?)," *Journal of Business*, **54**: 33–64 (January 1981).

[12] See F. Black and J.C. Cox: "Valuing Corporate Securities: Some Effects of Bond Indenture Provisions," *Journal of Finance*, **31**: 351–367 (May 1976). Black and Cox point out that the interest payment would be a trivial hurdle if the company could sell assets to make the payment. Such sales are, therefore, restricted.

[13] There are international differences in terminology. In Great Britain, *debenture* usually signifies bonds that have a *prior* claim on the firm's assets.

Other bonds are secured by a pledge of specific assets of the company. When a company defaults on a secured obligation, the trustee or debtor may take possession of the relevant assets. If these are insufficient to satisfy the claim, the remaining debt will have a general claim alongside any unsecured debt against the other assets of the firm.

The vast majority of secured debt consists of **mortgage bonds**. Some of these mortgages are *closed*, so that no more bonds may be issued against the mortgage. However, usually there is no specific limit to the amount of bonds that may be secured (in which case the mortgage is said to be *open* or there is a specific limit that has not been reached (in which case the mortgage is said to be *limited open end*). Mortgage bonds sometimes provide a claim against a specific building but they are more often secured on substantially all of the company's property.[14] The issuer undertakes to insure this property and to keep it in good repair. Frequently, the indenture will provide for a fixed annual contribution for such maintenance with any unspent balance being used to redeem bonds. Of course, the value of any mortgage depends not only on how well the property is maintained but on whether it has value in alternative uses. A custom-built machine for producing buggy whips will not be worth much if the market for buggy whips dries up.

Collateral trust bonds closely resemble mortgage bonds except that in this case the claim is against securities held by the corporation. Generally, these bonds are issued by railroad or industrial holding companies — that is, firms whose main assets consist of common stock in a number of subsidiaries. This stock can be pledged as collateral for borrowing by the parent company. The problem for the lender is that the stock is junior to *all* other claims on the assets of the subsidiaries, and so the collateral trust issue will usually include detailed restrictions on the freedom of the subsidiaries to issue debt or preferred stock.

The third principal form of secured debt is the **equipment trust certificate**. This is most frequently used to finance new railroad rolling stock. Under this arrangement a trustee obtains formal ownership of the equipment. The railroad makes a down payment of 10% to 25% of the cost and the balance is provided by a package of trust certificates with different maturities that might typically run from 1 to 15 years. Only when all these debts have finally been paid off does the railroad become the formal owner of the equipment. Because the trustee holds the title to the pledged equipment and can immediately repossess it in the event of default, equipment trust certificates offer good security to their holders. Bond rating agencies such as CBRS and Moody's, therefore, usually rate equipment trust certificates one grade higher than the railroad's regular debt. In the case of Canadian Pacific Ltd., CBRS rates the equipment trust certificates as A + +, while the collateral trust certificates are rated as A +.

Bonds may be senior claims or they may be subordinated to the senior bonds or to *all* other creditors.[15] if the firm defaults, the senior bonds come first in the pecking order. For example, a company may issue first and second mortgage bonds. The first mortgage bonds have the first claim against the assets, then come the second mortgage bonds.

---

[14] Many mortgage bonds are secured not only by existing property but also by "after-acquired" property. However, if the company buys only property that is already mortgaged, the bondholder would have only a junior claim on the new property. Therefore, mortgage bonds with after-acquired property clauses also restrict the extent to which the company can purchase additional mortgaged property.

[15] If a bond does not specifically state that it is junior, you can assume that it is senior.

24-4   REPAYMENT PROVISIONS

Sinking Funds

Information on the repayment of the Interprovincial's debt issue is provided on the ninth page of the prospectus. Although the issue does not mature for 20 years, part of the issue is repaid earlier by means of a *sinking fund*. From the end of third year, the company is obliged to pay $3 million to the trustee annually — that is, 4% of the total amount of the issue. This payment can be in the form of either cash or bonds that the company has bought back. If it is cash, then the trustee will use the money to repurchase bonds in the marketplace or it will select bonds by lottery and redeem them at par.[16] This mandatory payment is sufficient to redeem 68% of the issue before maturity and to reduce the average life of the bond from 20 to 13.9 years.[17]

Interprovincial, like most borrowers, can *choose* between repurchasing the bonds in the market or calling them at par.[18] If the price of the bond is low, the firm will satisfy the sinking fund requirement by buying bonds in the market; if the price is high, it will call the bonds by lottery. This option tends to reduce the value of sinking fund bonds.

Generally, there is a mandatory fund that *must* be satisfied and an optional fund which can be satisfied if the borrower chooses. Utility first mortgage bonds often have a wholly optional fund. A number of private placements (particularly those in extractive industries) require a payment only when net income exceeds some specified level.[19]

Most "sinkers" begin to operate after about ten years. For lower-quality issues the payments are usually sufficient to redeem the entire issue in equal instalments over the life of the bond. In contrast, high-quality bonds often have light sinking fund requirements with large "balloon" payments at maturity. Generally, bonds may be redeemed for the sinking fund at par but some issues provide for a gently declining schedule of repayment prices.[20]

We saw earlier that interest payments provide a regular test of the company's solvency. Sinking funds are an additional check that the firm must keep jumping. If it cannot pay the cash into the sinking fund, the lenders can demand their money back. That is why long-dated, low-quality issues usually involve larger sinking funds.

Unfortunately, a sinking fund is a weak test of solvency *if the firm is allowed to repurchase bonds in the market*. Since the *market* value of the debt must always be

---

[16] Every investor dreams of buying up the entire supply of a sinking fund bond that is selling way below face value and then forcing the company to buy the bonds back at face value. "Cornering the market" in this way is fun to dream about but difficult to do. For a discussion, see K.B. Dunn and C.S. Spatt, "A Strategic Analysis of Sinking Fund Bonds," *Journal of Financial Economics*, **13**: 399–424 (September 1984).

[17] 4% of (3 + 4 + ... + 19) plus 32% of 20 = 13.9 years. This is the conventional method of calculating average life, although it might be useful if each period were weighted by the *present value* of the amount retired (that is, if we measured the bond's *duration*: see Section 23-2).

[18] If the bonds are privately placed, the company cannot repurchase the bonds in the marketplace — it must call them at par. Similarly, equipment trust certificates consist of a package of bonds that mature in successive years. Such bonds are usually called *serial bonds*. A package of serial bonds is rather like a sinking fund bond. Both provide regular repayments of the debt. But the serial bond does not give the borrower the option to buy the bonds in the marketplace — the borrower *must* redeem the bonds at par.

[19] Repayment provisions for privately placed debt are simpler than for public issues. For example, private placements cannot be repurchased in the bond market and there is no need for a formal sinking fund.

[20] Some bonds have a *purchase fund*. In this case the company agrees to put aside money which is to be used to repurchase bonds in the market only if the price is below par.

less than the value of the firm, the troubles of the firm reduce the cost of repurchasing debt in the market. So, the sinking fund is like a hurdle that gets progressively lower as the hurdler gets weaker.

Call or Redemption Provisions

Interprovincial also has an option to buy back or **call** or **redeem** the entire bond issue. If it does so, it is required to pay a premium that is equal in the first year to the annual coupon and that declines progressively to zero. Interprovincial is subject to a particular limitation on the use of the call option. During the first 15 years after issue, it is prohibited from calling the bond in order to replace it with another issue yielding less than the 12.7% offering yield on the original bond.

The repayment provisions of the Interprovincial bond are typical of Canadian industrial debentures. The majority of such issues mature in 20 years, are callable at a premium that is virtually equal to the coupon, and are "nonrefundable" (NR) for ten years or more "below interest cost."

Other kinds of bonds tend to provide more limited call options. For example, notes or medium-maturity mortgage bonds typically have a maturity of seven to ten years and are noncallable for all except the last two years of this time. Short-maturity issues and equipment trust certificates cannot be called at any time.

The option to call a bond is obviously attractive to the issuer. If interest rates decline and bond prices rise, the issuer has the opportunity to repurchase the bonds below their potential value. For example, suppose that by the year 2000, yields on investment-quality bonds have fallen to 6%. A 12.7% bond with four years to maturity would then be worth 123.2% or $1,232. The call provision allows Interprovincial to repurchase the bonds that are worth $1,232 for only $1,021. Or the company can, if it chooses, hold on and hope to do better by calling the bonds in the year 2001.

How can Interprovincial know when to call its bonds? The answer is simple. Other things being equal, if it wishes to maximize the value of its stock, it must minimize the value of its bond. Therefore, it should never call the bond if its market value is less than the call price, for that would just be giving a present to the bondholders. Equally, it *should* call the bond if it is worth *more* than the call price.

Of course, investors take the call option into account when they buy or sell the bond. They know that the company will call the bond as soon as it is worth more than the call price. Therefore no investor will be willing to pay more than the call price for the bond. The market price of the bond may, therefore, reach the call price but it will not rise above it. This gives the company the following rule for calling its bonds:[21] *Call the bond when, and only when, the market price reaches the call price.*

If we know how bond prices behave over time, we can modify our basic option-valuation model of Chapter 20 to give us the value of the callable bond, *given* that investors know the company will call the issue if ever the market price reaches the call price. For example, look at Figure 24-1. It illustrates the relationship

---

[21] See M.J. Brennan and E.S. Schwartz, "Savings Bonds, Retractable Bonds, and Callable Bonds," *Journal of Financial Economics,* **5**: 67–88 (1977). Of course this assumes that the bond is correctly priced, that investors are acting rationally, and that investors expect the *firm* to act rationally. Also, we ignore some complications. First, you may not wish to call a bond if you are prevented by a nonrefunding clause from issuing new debt. Second, the call premium is a tax-deductible expense for the company but is taxed as a capital gain to the bondholder. Third, there are other possible tax consequences to both the company and the investor from replacing a low-coupon bond with a higher-coupon bond. Fourth, there are costs to calling and reissuing debt.

Figure 24-1   Relationship between the value of a callable bond and that of a straight (noncallable) bond. Assumptions: (1) Both bonds have an 8% coupon and a 5-year maturity. (2) The callable bond may be called at any time before maturity. (3) The short-term interest rate follows a random walk, and the expected returns on bonds of all maturities are equal.

Source: M.J. Brennan and E.S. Schwartz, "Savings Bonds, Retractable Bonds, and Callable Bonds," *Journal of Financial Economics* **5**: 67–88 (1977).

between the value of a straight 8% 5-year bond and the value of an 8% 5-year callable bond. Suppose that the value of the straight bond is very low. In this case, there is little likelihood that the company will ever wish to call its bonds. (Remember that it will only call the bonds if they are worth more than the call price.) Therefore, the value of the callable bond will be almost identical to the value of the straight bond. Now suppose that the straight bond is worth exactly 100. In this case there is a good chance that the company will wish at some time to call its bonds. Therefore, the value of our callable bond will be slightly less than that of the straight bond. If interest rates decline further, the price of the straight bond will move above 100. But nobody will ever pay *more* than 100 for the callable bond.

The Extendible/ Retractable Provision

From time to time the Government of Canada and some Canadian corporations issue **extendible** or **retractable bonds**. Both of these types of bonds are like callables, in the sense that they provide an option to redeem the bond at a time other than the stated maturity. The difference between callable bonds and extendible/retractables is that the bondholder, not the issuer, owns the option.

An *extendible bond* allows its holder to extend the maturity of the bond for an additional specified period. For example, Inland Natural Gas Co. currently has outstanding a 10.55% extendible bond with a maturity date of June 1999. At any time prior to May 1999, this bond may be exchanged at par value for another bond with the same coupon interest rate but with a maturity date of June 2009.

In other words, this bond provides its owner with the right to buy (or with a call option on) a longer-term bond where the exercise price is equal to the par value of the existing bond. Such a bond provides investors with protection from decreases in the interest rate.

A *retractable bond* is just the reverse of an extendible bond. The bondholder holds an option to sell back or "put" the long-term bond to the issuer at a specified time before maturity. The exercise price of the option is again the par value of the original issue. Stelco Inc. has outstanding a 10.4% retractable debenture maturing in November 2009. This issue provides the bondholder with the right to redeem the bond at par on November 30, 1999. Should the bondholder choose not exercise the option at that point in time, the bond will revert to a straight debenture maturing in 2009. Retractable bonds protect the investor from increases in interest rates after the bond is issued.

*Valuing the Extendible/ Retractable Provision

Extendible bonds and retractable bonds are essentially the same creature. Each is equivalent to a short-term bond plus a call option or to a long-term bond with a put option. For this reason we will focus on the retractable provision. The reader is left to develop a comparable analysis for the extendible provision.

The option to shorten the maturity of a bond protects the bondholder from increases in the interest rate. If interest rates rise and bond prices fall, the bondholder has the opportunity to put the bonds to the issuer at the par value, which may be well above the current market value. Suppose, for example, that the interest rate on nonretractable issues comparable to the Stelco retractable issue rises to 13% on November 30, 1999. A 10.4% bond with 10 years to maturity would then be worth about $856.76. The retractability feature allows the holder of an a Stelco bond to redeem the bond for $1,000 when the current market value is $143.24 less.

Like callable bonds, investors take the value of the option into account when they buy or sell the bond. With retractables, however, it is the bondholder who receives the privilege, so prospective buyers are willing to pay more for a retractable bond than an otherwise comparable bond with no retractability feature.

24-5 RESTRICTIVE COVENANTS

The difference between a corporate bond and a comparable government bond is that the company has an option to default — the government supposedly doesn't. That is a valuable option.[22] If you don't believe us, think whether, other things being equal, you would prefer to be a shareholder in a company with limited liability or in a company with unlimited liability. Of course you would prefer to have the option to walk away from your debts. Unfortunately, every silver lining has its cloud, and the drawback to having a default option is that corporate bondholders expect to be compensated for giving it to you. That is why corporate bonds sell at lower prices and therefore higher yields than government bonds.

Investors know that there is a risk of default when they buy a corporate bond. But they still want to make sure that the company plays fair. They don't want it

---

[22] In Chapters 20 and 23 we showed that this option to default is equivalent to a put option on the assets of the firm.

to gamble with their money or to take unreasonable risks.[23] Therefore, the bond agreement may include a number of restrictive covenants to prevent the company from purposely increasing the value of its default option.

Suppose Nocturnal Aviation Ltd. has a market value of $100 million and total senior debt of $10 million. The debt-to-value ratio is 10%. That means that the value of Nocturnal could fall by about 90% before the company would want to default. To put it another way, the point at which the company would want to exercise its option is about 10% of the value of the assets.

Now suppose that Nocturnal announces a further $10 million bond issue. The company now has a market value of $110 million and senior debt of $20 million. The debt-to-value ratio has increased to 18%. It would now be willing to default if the value of the assets falls by only 82%. The original debenture holders are slightly worse off. If they had known about the new issue, they would not have been willing to pay quite such a high price for their bonds.

The new issue hurts the original debenture holders by increasing the *ratio* of senior debt to company value. They would not object to the bond issue if the company kept the ratio the same by simultaneously issuing common stock. Therefore, the bond agreement often states that the company may issue more senior debt only if the ratio of senior debt to the net asset value is below a specified limit.

Why don't senior lenders demand limits on *subordinated* debt? The answer is that the subordinated lender does not get *any* money until the senior bondholders are paid in full. The senior bondholders, therefore, view subordinated debentures in almost the same way that they view equity: they would be happy to see an issue of either.[24] Of course, the converse is not true. A holder of subordinated debentures does care both about the total amount of debt and the proportion that is senior to their claim. As a result, the indenture for an issue of subordinated debt generally includes a restriction on both total debt and senior debt.

All bondholders worry that the company may issue more secured debt. An issue of mortgage bonds usually imposes a limit on the amount of secured debt. This is not necessary when you are issuing debentures. As long as the debenture holders are given equal protection, they do not care how much you mortgage your assets. Therefore, the bond agreement for a debenture issue usually includes a so-called **negative pledge clause**, in which the debenture holders simply say, "Me too."[25]

During the 1950s and 1960s many companies found that they could circumvent some of these restrictions if, instead of borrowing money to buy an asset, they entered into a long-term agreement to rent or lease it. For the debtholder this arrangement was very similar to secured borrowing. Therefore, indentures began to include limitations on leasing.

---

[23] We described in Section 18-3 some of the games that managers could play at the expense of the bondholders.

[24] In practice the courts do not always observe the strict rules of precedence. Therefore, the subordinated debtholder may receive *some* payment even when the senior debtholder is not fully paid off.

[25] "Me too" is not acceptable legal jargon. Instead, the bond agreement usually says something like, "The company will not issue, or guarantee any debt secured by a lien upon any principal property without providing that the (existing) securities shall be secured equally and ratably." If the firm *does* subsequently issue secured debt, this negative pledge clause allows the debenture holder to demand repayment. But it does not invalidate the security given to the other debtholders.

Leases are an example of a hidden debt. After their fingers had been burned, bondholders began to impose restrictions on leases. But you want to impose restrictions *before* your fingers are burned. Perhaps, therefore, lenders should be placing restrictions on other kinds of hidden debt such as those that we describe in Section 24-7, "Project Finance," or such as unfunded pension liabilities, which we describe in Chapter 35.

We have talked about how an unscrupulous company can try to increase the value of the default option by issuing more debt. But that is not the only way in which it can exploit its existing bondholders. For example, we know that the value of an option is affected by dividend payments. If the company pays out large dividends to its shareholders and doesn't replace the cash with an issue of stock, there are less assets available to cover the debt. Therefore, most bond issues restrict the amount of dividends that the company may pay. Usually these restrictions prohibit the company from paying dividends if their cumulative amount would exceed the sum of (1) cumulative consolidated net income, (2) the proceeds from the sale of stock or conversion of debt, and (3) a dollar amount equal to about one year's dividend.

Changes in Covenant Protection

Before 1980 most bonds had covenants limiting further issues of debt and payments of dividends. But then large institutions relaxed their requirements for large public companies and accepted bonds with no such restrictions. This was the case with RJR Nabisco, the food and tobacco giant, which had in 1988 $5 billion of A-rated debt outstanding. In that year the company was taken over and $19 billion of additional debt was substituted for equity. Immediately, the value of the existing debt fell by about 12% and it was downrated to BB. For one of the bondholders, Metropolitan Life Insurance, this meant a $40 million loss. Metropolitan sued the company, arguing that the bonds contained an *implied* covenant preventing major financial changes that would undercut existing bondholders.[26] However, Metropolitan lost: the courts held that only the written covenants count.

Restrictions on debt issues and dividend payments quietly returned to fashion. Bond analysts and lawyers began to look more closely at "event risks" like the debt-financed takeovers that socked Metropolitan. Some companies offered **poison put** clauses that oblige the borrower to repay the bonds if a large quantity of stock is bought by a single investor and the firm's bonds are downrated.

Would covenants have protected Metropolitan Life and the other bondholders against loss? A study by Paul Asquith and Thierry Wizman suggests that they would.[27] On average, the announcement of a leveraged buyout led to a fall of 5.2% in the value of the bond if there were no restrictions on further debt issues, dividend payments, or mergers. However, where the bond was protected by strong covenants, announcement of a leveraged buyout led to a *rise* in the bond price of 2.6%.[28]

---

[26] Metropolitan Life Insurance Company (plaintiff) v. RJR Nabisco, Inc. and F. Ross Johnson (defendants), Supreme Court of the State of New York, County of New York, Complaint, November 16, 1988.

[27] P. Asquith and T.A. Wizman, "Event Risk, Bond Covenants, and the Return to Existing Bondholders in Corporate Buyouts," Unpublished Paper, Sloan School of Management, MIT, June 1990.

[28] One reason for the price rise is that bonds with strong covenant protection were often called or repurchased following the buyout.

Positive Covenants   The restrictions on new debt issues or dividend payments prevent the company from doing things that would benefit the shareholders at the expense of the bondholders, but they don't make the bonds safe. Therefore, lenders also seek to protect themselves by arrangements that give them the chance to demand repayment at the first sign of trouble. For example, bank loans sometimes specify that the bank can demand repayment if there is a "material adverse change" which impairs the borrower's ability to repay the loan.[29]

We have already seen that lenders impose a number of hurdles which the company must keep jumping. The most obvious of these hurdles are the regular interest payments and sinking fund contributions. If these obligations are not met, the loan becomes repayable immediately. That is why the company will always try to make the payment if it possibly can. Another, rather different hurdle is the repayment of other outstanding debt. Many issues contain a **cross-default** clause. This says that the company is in default if it fails to meet its obligations on any of its debt issues. Thus, a cross-default clause may enable the lender to get out from under before the firm has missed a payment on that particular loan.

Most indentures also include so-called **positive covenants**, which impose certain duties on the borrower. In the case of public bond issues, many of these affirmative covenants are innocuous. For example, the company may be obliged to furnish bondholders with a copy of its annual accounts. If it doesn't do so, it is in default on the bonds.

Many privately placed issues impose much more onerous affirmative covenants. The most common of these are covenants to maintain at all times some minimum level of working capital or of net worth. If the amount of working capital or net worth is a good guide to the value of the company, the lenders are putting a ceiling on the amount they can lose.

We do not want to give the impression that the lenders are constantly seeking an opportunity to cry "default" and then demand their money back. If the company does default, the lenders have the *right* to claim repayment but they will not generally do so. The more usual result is that the lenders or the trustee will seek a detailed explanation from the company and discuss possible changes in its operating policy. It is only as a last resort that lenders demand early repayment and force the company into bankruptcy.

24-6   INNOVATION IN THE BOND MARKET

Domestic bonds, foreign bonds, and eurobonds; fixed-rate and floating-rate bonds; coupon bonds and zeros; callable, extendable, and retractable bonds; secured and unsecured bonds; senior and junior bonds—you might think that all this would give you as much choice as you need. Yet almost every day some new type of bond seems to be issued. Here are some examples of exotic bonds.

Pay-in-kind bonds (PIKs) make regular interest payments but, in the early years of the bonds' life, the issuer can choose to pay interest in the form of either

---

[29] "Material adverse change" is usually not specifically defined—the clause protects the lender in scenarios where the borrower falls into default without triggering specific covenants.
Of course, this clause might be a dangerous weapon in the hands of a short-sighted and unscrupulous lender, who could pretend to see an adverse change and try to extort a higher interest rate by threatening to demand immediate repayment. Fortunately, few if any financial institutions play this game. They would be sued for trying it, and their reputation for *not* taking unfair advantage of their customers is a valuable business asset.

cash or more bonds with the equivalent face value.[30] That can be a valuable option. If the company falls on hard times and bond prices fall, it can hand over low-priced bonds instead of hard cash. Many of the companies that have issued PIKs have been taken over in a leveraged buyout. These firms are often very short of cash in the initial years and therefore find the option to pay interest in the form of bonds particularly attractive. For example, when Kohlberg, Kravis, and Roberts took over RJR Nabisco, the shareholders were partly paid off in PIKs.[31]

A liquid yield option note (LYON) is a callable and retractable, convertible, zero coupon bond (and you can't get anything much more complicated than that). In August 1990 Chemical Waste Management issued a LYON at a price of 30.7%. It was a 20-year zero coupon bond that was convertible at any time into a fixed number of shares, though the company could instead pay out the cash equivalent of these shares. In addition, the bondholder had an annual option to sell the bond back to the company for cash and Chemical Waste Management had the option to *call* the bond for cash. The exercise price of these two options increased each year.[32]

Some of the most exotic bonds are eurobonds.[33] Here is an example of a complicated euroyen bond. In 1989 the Norwegian Christiania Bank issued a three-year bond that came in two tranches. Tranche A pays interest equal to the long-term prime rate but subject to a maximum (or "cap") of 12.8%. Tranche B pays interest of 12.8% *less* the long-term prime rate. Thus, if the general level of interest rates rises, the interest payment on tranche B falls.[34] However, it is not allowed to fall below zero. You may like to check for yourself that, if you invested an equal amount in each tranche, the average interest rate on your two holdings would be 6.4%. This was well above the going interest rate for Japanese bonds.

That is not the end of the complications of tranche B, since the principal repayment was not fixed at 100%. Instead, it declines if the Japanese stock market index falls. If the index falls by about 50%, the bondholder does not receive any principal repayment at all. You can think of the investor in tranche

---

[30] For a discussion of PIKs see L.S. Goodman and A.H. Cohen, "Pay-in Kind Debentures: An Innovation," *Journal of Portfolio Management*, **15**: 9–16 (Winter 1989).

[31] The use of PIKs to finance highly leveraged buyouts earned them a bad reputation. Ross Johnson, the President of RJR Nabisco, was reported to have marveled at the potential for PIKs. " 'I mean,' Johnson went on, 'we have found something better than the U.S. printing press. And they've got it all down here on Wall Street. And nobody knows it's going on. I wonder if the World Bank knows about it. You could solve the third world debt crisis with this stuff. It's a brand new currency . . .' " B. Burrough and J. Helyar, *Barbarians at the Gate: The Fall of RJR Nabisco*, Harper & Row, New York, 1990, p. 489.

[32] To complicate matters, the company could exercise its call option immediately but investors could not exercise their put option until 1993. Thereafter, both options had the same exercise price. However, in the first 2 years the company could not call the bond if the price of the common stock was below a specified minimum. If the bond is called, investors have a final chance to decide whether to convert into common stock. For an interesting discussion of an earlier LYON issue by Chemical Waste Management's parent company see J. McConnell and E.S. Schwartz, "Taming LYONS," *Journal of Finance*, **41**: 561–576 (July 1986).

[33] Perhaps the winner in the competition for the most exotic bond is a eurobond issued in 1990 by the Swedish company Electrolux. The principal repayment on this bond depends on whether an earthquake occurs in Japan.

[34] Bonds whose interest payments move in the opposite direction to the general level are called *reverse floaters* or *yield-curve notes*. Our favourite example of a reverse floater is an issue in 1986 by Hong Kong Mass Transit Railway which offered a 5-year United States dollar floater with warrants. The warrants had a maturity of 1 year and gave the holder the right to buy a 5-year, Hong Kong dollar, reverse floater paying 15.15% *less* the short-term Hong Kong interest rate (HIBOR).

B as buying an unusual variable rate note and also selling a put option on the Japanese stock market. The high yield on the bonds is offset, therefore, by the possible capital loss.

In recent years about 60% of public euroyen issues have involved some option such as this. Why? One reason is that life insurance companies in Japan cannot distribute capital gains to policyholders and, therefore, have a powerful appetite for high-yielding bonds even if it means taking on the risk of a capital loss. Christiania Bank pays a high interest rate on the package but it gets a put option in exchange. If it does not want to hold on to this put option, it can easily sell it to foreign investors who are worried that the Japanese equity market may be overpriced and would like to protect themselves against a fall in the Japanese equity market.

The Causes of Innovation

It is often difficult to foresee which new securities will become popular and which will never get off the ground. However, Merton Miller believes that government often has a crucial role to play. He compares government regulation and tax with the grain of sand which irritates the oyster and produces the pearl.[35] This would suggest that the wave of innovation that has swept capital markets in recent years may be prompted by the increasing strains of a tax and regulatory system that dates back to the 1930s and 1940s.

We have seen how one unusual bond, the option-linked euroyen bond, is a consequence of Japanese insurance regulation. Let us also look at how a quirk in the tax rules brought about a new type of bond in the United States.

EXAMPLE   In June 1981 General Motors Acceptance Corporation issued $750 million of 10-year zero coupon notes. The issue price was $252.50 for each note. Thus, the investor faced a prospective fourfold increase in value over 10 years, which is equivalent to a compound return of about 14.8% a year.

Table 24-1 shows the expected yearly change in the value of the GMAC notes. In year 1, the prospective appreciation is $0.148 \times 252.5 = \$37.3$. At the start of year 2, the expected value of the notes is $252.5 + 37.3 = \$289.8$. Thus, the appreciation in year 2 is $0.148 \times 289.8 = \$42.8$, and so on. Of course, the total appreciation over the 10 years is $1,000 - 252.5 = \$747.5$.

The attraction to GMAC of zero coupon debt arose from an IRS mistake. The IRS correctly recognized that even if debt does not pay interest, it is still costly to the issuer. Therefore, it allowed the company to deduct a portion of the original issue discount from taxable income. But, in calculating this deduction, the IRS employed simple, rather than compound, interest. Thus, GMAC was permitted to deduct the same amount in each year, $747.5/10 = \$74.75$.

If you compare columns 2 and 3 of Table 24-1, you will see that in the early years of the loan's life, GMAC could deduct more than the cost of the loan from its taxable income. For example, in year 1, each note *cost* GMAC $37.3 or 14.8% of the amount of the loan. However, when calculating taxable profits, GMAC could deduct $74.75 or 29.6% of the amount of the loan. From year 7 onward, the deduction is less than the cost of the loan but, other things equal, GMAC benefitted from having the extra tax shield in the early years.

Of course, this is not the whole story. Just as the IRS pretended that GMAC paid interest of $74.75 a year, so it pretended that the noteholders received

---

[35] See M.H. Miller, "Financial Innovation: The Last Twenty Years and the Next," *Journal of Financial and Quantitative Analysis*, **21**: 459–471 (December 1986).

Table 24-1
GMAC's original issue discount bonds were expected to appreciate by an increasing percentage amount each year, but the IRS allowed GMAC to deduct the same *dollar* amount each year from taxable income.

Year	(1) PV at Start of Year	(2) Change in PV During Year	(3) Allowable Tax Write-off
1	$252.5	$ 37.3	$ 74.75
2	289.8	42.8	74.75
3	332.5	49.1	74.75
4	381.6	56.3	74.75
5	437.9	64.6	74.75
6	502.5	74.1	74.75
7	576.6	85.1	74.75
8	661.7	97.6	74.75
9	759.4	112.0	74.75
10	871.4	128.6	74.75
		$747.5	$747.50

interest of $74.75 a year. But as long as GMAC notes were bought by tax-exempt investors, this was no disadvantage.[36]

The tax advantage to zero coupon bonds led to a flurry of issues in 1981. By 1982, the IRS had become sufficiently concerned about the loss of revenue that it began to use compound interest to calculate the tax deduction. From the point on, the tax incentive to issue zero coupon debt disappeared. Yet zeros survived. Companies continued to issue them, though at a much slower rate than before.[37]

The Gains from Innovation

Initially, the benefits of zero coupon debt went to those investment banks that were smart enough to devise and market the idea, and to issuers such as GMAC. But, remember, there was an advantage to zero coupon debt only if the marginal investor had a lower tax rate than the borrower. This takes us back to the capital structure controversy of Chapter 18. As long as only a few companies issued zero coupons, there were enough tax-exempt investors who were happy to hold them. But, as more such debt was issued, those companies who came late on the scene faced higher rates of interest. Thus, as soon as everyone had cottoned on to the idea, all the benefits went to the tax-exempt investors in the form of this higher interest rate.[38]

The lesson is a simple one. Investment banks and companies can be sure of benefiting from an innovation only if they are early in the field. Once the market is in equilibrium, all the benefits go to the players that are in short supply (in our example, the tax-exempt investors).

Lasting Innovations

You can think of the IRS as subsidizing the development of zero coupon bonds. But the important and worthwhile innovations are those like zero coupon bonds

---

[36] Zero coupon bonds were popular with the Japanese, since the Japanese tax authorities treated the price appreciation as a capital gain. This ruling was changed in 1985.

[37] For a further analysis of the tax incentives of OID debt, see D. Pyle, "Is Deep Discount Debt Financing a Bargain?," *Chase Financial Quarterly*, **1**: 39–61 (1981).

[38] We may oversimplify: If tax-exempt investors foresee that further issues are going to force up the interest rate on zero coupon bonds, they may be reluctant to buy the early issues at the lower interest rate.

that survive once such subsidies have been removed. Some endure because they reduce costs. Often an idea starts as a one-off deal between a bank and its customer. As demand grows, the tailer-made product is replaced by tradeable securities that perform a similar function.

There are economics of scale in the securities markets just as there are in other businesses, and this creates a continuing pressure for standardization. In the next chapter we shall see how the increased volatility of interest rates and exchange rates brought about a demand for low-cost ways to hedge these risks. The huge volume of potential business made it possible to offer standardized futures contracts at very low cost.[39]

Innovations also survive because they widen investor choice. When economists smile in their sleep, they are probably dreaming of a complete capital market in which there are many different securities as there are possible future states of the world. Such a market would give investors the wides possible choice and allow them to select portfolios that would protect them against any combination of hazards.

Of course complete markets are just make-believe, but we do observe a constant demand for new securities to protect against new dangers. For example, in countries such as Israel or Brazil that suffer from persistent inflation, investors don't want bonds that offer a fixed money return; they want ones that give a fixed *real* return. Therefore, in these countries payments on most debt are indexed to the rate of inflation.

Indexed bonds were almost unknown in the United States until 1988 when Franklin Savings Association made history by issuing a twenty-year bond whose interest (but not principal) was tied to the rate of inflation. Since then several other companies have followed suit.[40]

Instead of being tied to the general rate of inflation, payments are sometimes indexed to the price of a particular commodity. French Rail, for example, has issued a bond which is linked to the price of rail travel and which therefore resembles a long-term transferable season ticket. A few companies in the United States have also sought to limit shareholders' risk by tying bond payments to the price of a particular commodity. For instance, in June 1986 Standard Oil issued a zero coupon note maturing in 1992. At maturity the lenders are repaid at least the $1,000 face value. In addition, they are entitled to a bonus equal to 200 times the amount by which the oil price exceeds $25 a barrel.[41] The Standard Oil bond gives the firm protection against the vagaries of oil prices. If the price of oil is low in 1992, so is the company's income. However, this is partly mitigated by the fact that the cost of its debt is also low.

24-7   PROJECT FINANCE

Privately placed loans are usually direct obligations of the parent or one of its principal subsidiaries. In recent years there has been considerable interest in a new type of private loan that is tied as far as possible to the fortunes of a particular

[39] For a general discussion of the way that market innovations have stemmed from a drive for more efficient ways to provide a financial service, see 1. A. Cooper, "Innovations: New Market Instruments," *Oxford Review of Economic Policy*, **2**: 1–17 (1986).

[40] Franklin Savings was not quite the first United States company to issue an indexed bond. In 1925 the Rand Kardex company issued a bond that was linked to the wholesale price index, but the experiment was short-lived and the bond was converted shortly after issue.

[41] However, the bonus could not be greater than 200 × $15 = $3,000 per bond. In the same month Standard Oil also issued a 4½-year note. The bonus on this note was equal to 170 times the amount by which the oil price exceeded $25 a barrel.

Figure 24-2 Financing for the Forties Field project. The banks made a loan to Norex, which then made an advance payment to BP Development for future deliveries of oil. This oil was resold to BP Trading at an agreed-on price. These payments by BP Trading allowed Norex to repay the banks. The heavy arrows show how the banks provided financing: the lighter arrows show how BP repaid the banks.

project and that minimizes the exposure of the parent. Such a loan is usually referred to as **project finance** and is a specialty of large international banks.[42]

An Example from the Oil Industry

Let us look at how British Petroleum (BP) used project financing in 1972 to pay for development of its huge Forties Field in the North Sea. Since BP needed to finance very large capital expenditures elsewhere in the world, management wanted to segregate the financing of the Forties Field project as far as possible from BP's other fund-raising activities. Ideally, it would have liked to isolate its other business completely from the fate of the North Sea but no bank could be expected to take the risk of lending solely on the security of a field that was not yet producing.

BP's solution is illustrated in Figure 24-2. A syndicate of 66 major banks agreed in 1972 to lend a total of $945 million—the largest industrial bank loan in history. But instead of lending the money directly to BP, they lent it to a company called Norex, which was controlled by the banks. Norex, in turn, paid the money to BP Development, the subsidiary of BP that was responsible for developing the Forties Field. But Norex's payment to BP Development was not in the form of a loan; it was an advance payment for future deliveries of oil. In other words, in return for the money BP Development promised to deliver to Norex an agreed quantity of oil. Of course, the last thing that the banks wanted was a load of oil on their doorsteps. Therefore, they also arranged for another BP subsidiary, BP Trading, to repurchase the oil from Norex at a prescribed price.

Payments to Norex had to be completed within ten years. But, because a number of unpredictable factors affected the development of the Forties Field, the speed with which Norex was paid off was tied to the production rate of the field.

The banks consented to bear the ultimate risk that the oil reserves were insufficient to service their loan. However, they were protected against three other hazards. The first was the possible failure of BP Development to construct the necessary facilities. The agreement, therefore, specified in considerable detail the manner in which the field should be developed and BP guaranteed that its subsidiary would carry out this plan.

---

[42] Project financing is not exclusively made through private loans. The publicly issued International Pipe Line (NW) debentures discussed in this chapter were used to finance the costs of the construction of a pipeline from Norman Wells in the Northwest Territories to Zama, Alberta.

The second danger was that the field might be depleted more rapidly than was envisaged. To protect the banks against this possibility BP guaranteed that the difference between the market value of the oil produced and the amount needed to service the loan should be paid into a "reclaim account," which could be drawn upon by Norex if the oil flow was subsequently reduced.

The third risk was that of force majeure. If it proved impossible to produce any oil before the end of six years and if the assessed reserves would have been adequate to service the loan, then Norex could claim repayment from a restitution account that was guaranteed by BP.

One effect of this complicated financing arrangement was that the banks accepted some of the risk associated with the Forties Field. For example, if the oil reserves were inadequate to service the banks' loan to Norex, the banks had no claim against BP's other assets. A second difference between the Forties project financing and a straight bank loan was that the project financing did not show up in BP's balance sheet as a debt. Instead, BP Trading's promise to repurchase the oil from Norex was recorded as a deferred liability against future oil delivery.

Who Uses Project Finance? The basic requirement of any project financing is that the project can be physically isolated from the parent and that it offers the lender tangible security. The additional research and legal costs also mean that project financing makes sense only when the sums involved are large.

Traditionally, project finance has been widely used for major mineral extraction and processing developments often involving joint ventures with overseas firms. More recently in the United States the most common use of project finance has been for electric power plants.[43] For example, electric utility companies often get together with industrial companies to construct cogeneration plants that provide electricity to the utility and waste heat to a nearby industrial plant.

Project finance for production of electric power was stimulated by the Public Utility Regulatory Power Act of 1978 (PURPA), which requires utilities to buy from independent producers under long-term contracts. These contracts may lock in a fixed price, or may contain a *fuel adjustment clause*, that requires the utility to absorb fluctuations in the cost of the oil, gas, or coal required to run the plant.

Such a contract is excellent security for a loan. The utility stands behind the cogeneration project and guarantees its revenue stream. Once the plant is completed, and competent operating management is installed, cash flow for debt service is insulated from most of the risks facing normal businesses. Thus, some power projects have been more than 90% debt-financed.[44]

---

[43] Kensinger and Martin estimate that between January 1987 and August 1988 almost 50% of the funds raised in the United States by project finance were used for power generation—about $5.7 billion. See J.W. Kensinger and J.D. Martin, "Project Finance: Raising Money the Old-Fashioned Way," *Journal of Applied Corporate Finance*, **1**: 69–81 (Fall 1988).

[44] Such extremely high-debt ratios must rest on the utility's credit worthiness. In a sense, the utility has borrowed money "off balance sheet," since the contract to purchase power is a fixed, debt-like, long-term commitment. Other things equal, including the amount of on-balance-sheet debt, this fixed commitment should act like financial leverage and increase the volatility of utility earnings and shareholder returns.

There are some interesting regulatory implications, however. When a utility builds a power plant, it is entitled to a fair return on its investment: regulators are supposed to set customer charges to allow the utility to earn its cost of capital. Unfortunately, the cost of capital is not easily measured and is a natural focus for argument in regulatory hearings. But when a utility contracts for power, the cost of capital is rolled into the contract price and treated as an operating cost. In this case, the pass-through to consumers may be less controversial.

Project Finance — Some Common Features

Project finance is often provided in the form of a straight loan. However, the BP Forties financing is an example of an alternative arrangement known as a *production payment*. In this case the banks do not lend to either the parent or the operating company. Instead, they lend to an intermediate company (such as Norex) which is controlled by them. This company then uses the money to make an advance payment to the project's owner against future delivery of the product. When the product is delivered, the intermediate company can sell it and use the proceeds to repay the banks.

We can classify project financings according to the contractual obligations of the project's owners. The purest, but least common, method of financing offers the lender **no recourse** against the owners at any stage. This notion of "no recourse" is somewhat imprecise, for the banks may well require a general assurance from the parent that it will do its best to ensure the success of the project. Although these "comfort letters" are usually too general to be sued upon, they do represent a potentially embarrassing commitment on the part of the parent.

One of the most common threats to a successful project loan is a serious delay in completion. Occasionally, the project may even turn out to be technically infeasible. Our second class of loans, therefore, consists of those that are supported by a *completion guarantee*. Such a guarantee may be provided by the parent company or by an insurance company in the form of *completion bonding*.

Most project loans provide lenders with more recourse against the parent. For instance, we saw that BP promised to repurchase oil for Nortex at a prescribed price. Here are three other examples of how the parent companies may provide some limited guarantees:

1. *The throughput agreement.* Many oil pipeline loans involve a throughput agreement. This states that if other companies do not make sufficient use of the pipeline, the owners will themselves will ship enough oil through it to provide the pipeline company with the cash that it needs to service the loan.
2. *The cost company arrangement.* Under a cost company arrangement the project's owners receive all of the project's output free of charge. In exchange, they agree to pay all operating costs including loan service. Thus, the project has no net income, and each parent firm simply deducts from its own profits its share of the project's expenses.
3. *The cash deficiency arrangement.* Under this arrangement, the project's owners agree to provide the operating company with enough funds to maintain a certain level of net working capital.

In any project financing the payments on the loan should correspond as closely as possible to the ability of the project to generate cash. For example, if the project's completion date is uncertain, the first payment date may simply be set as a specified number of months after completion. If the loan involves a large final payment, it is common to include an *earnings recapture* clause under which a proportion of any surplus earnings is applied to the final payment. A lender who bears the risk of inadequate reserves will wish to ensure that the reserves are not depleted too rapidly. In these cases, therefore, it is common to assign a *proportion* of revenues to loan repayments rather than a fixed sum.

The Benefits of Project Finance

Various motives have been suggested for the use of project finance rather than direct borrowing by the parent company. It is tempting to believe that the value of a project to the parents is enhanced if it can be made to stand alone as a self-financing entity, so that the parents from its success and is isolated from its failure. Such a result is improbable. When we look at actual project loans, we find that not only is the parent rarely isolated from the vicissitudes of the project but the rate of interest on the project loan is directly related to the degree of support that the parent provides. However, project finance does allow the parent to transfer specific risks to the lenders. For example, if BP had borrowed on its general credit, it would have remained exposed to the risk of inadequate North Sea reserves, whereas the Forties financing effectively provided insurance against this contingency. Correspondingly, with many loans for projects in politically unstable countries the lenders are taking on the risk of adverse government action. Many companies believe that expropriate by a foreign government is *less likely* when they raise money by a project financing.

Project financing may not be shown as debt in the company's balance sheet. For example, we have already seen how BP's financing of the Forties Field showed up as a deferred liability against future oil deliveries. In some cases the owner's guarantees may not be shown in the balance sheet at all. In this case, the financing is said to be "off balance sheet." This attracts some financial managers—but lenders or shareholders usually recognize these hidden liabilities.

Project finance can often be costly to arrange, but sometimes the arrangement is simpler than a direct loan. Projects are often jointly owned, and it may by easier to negotiate one project loan than separate financing to each of several parents. Also, security for project lenders commonly derives as much from contractual arrangements as from tangible assets. For example, a bank's security for a pipeline load depends on throughput agreements and its security for a tanker loan depends on charter agreements. In such instances, it may be simplest to tie the loan directly to these contracts.

24-8   SUMMARY

Now that you have read this chapter, you should have a fair idea of what you are letting yourself in for when you make a public issue of bonds. You can make an issue of bonds in the domestic market or you can do so in a foreign bond market or in the eurobond market. Eurobonds are bonds that are marketed simultaneously in a number of foreign countries, usually by the London branches of international banks and security dealers.

The detailed bond agreement is set out in the indenture between your company and a trustee, but the main provisions are summarized in the prospectus to the issue.

The indenture states whether the bonds are senior or subordinated and whether they are secured or unsecured. Most bonds are unsecured debentures or notes. This means that they are general claims on the corporation. The principal exceptions are utility first mortgage bonds, collateral trust bonds, and equipment trust certificates. In the event of a default the trustee to these issues can repossess the company's assets in order to pay off the debt.

Most long-term bond issues have a *sinking fund*. This means that the company must set aside enough money each year to retire a specified number of bonds. A sinking fund reduces the average life of the bond and (as long as the company is not allowed to repurchase bonds in the marketplace) it provides a yearly test of the company's ability to service its debt. It, therefore, protects the bondholders against the risk of default.

Most long-dated bonds may be called at a premium which is initially equal to the coupon and which declines progressively to zero. There is one common limitation to this right—companies are generally prohibited from calling the bond in the first few years if they intend to replace it with another bond at a lower rate of interest. The option to call the bond may be very valuable: if interest rates decline and bond values rise, you may be able to call a bond that would be worth substantially more than the call price. Of course, if investors know that you may call the bond, the call price will act as a ceiling on the market price. Your best strategy, therefore, is to call the bond as soon as the market price hits the call price. You are unlikely to do better than that.

The bond indenture also lays down certain conditions. Here are some examples of things the company must *not* do:

1. Issues of senior bonds often prohibit the company from issuing further senior or junior debt if the ratio of senior debt to net tangible assets would exceed a specified maximum.
2. Issues of subordinated bonds may also prohibit the company from issuing further senior or junior debt if the ratio of *all* debt to net tangible assets would exceed a specified maximum.
3. Unsecured bonds incorporate a *negative pledge* clause, which prohibits the company from securing additional debt without giving equal treatment to the existing unsecured bonds.
4. Many bonds place a limit on the company's dividend payments.

Conditions that require the company to take positive steps to protect the bondholders are known as *positive covenants*. In public bond issues these conditions are generally innocuous. The really important positive covenants are those that give the bondholder the chance to claim a default and get money out while the company still has a substantial value. For example, some bond issues require the company to maintain a minimum level of working capital or net worth. Since a deficiency in either is a good indication of financial weakness, this condition is tantamount to giving the bondholders the right to demand their money back as soon as life appears hazardous.

Private placements are less standardized than public issues and they impose more stringent covenants. Otherwise, they are close counterparts of publicly issued bonds.

There is an enormous variety of bond issues, and new forms of bonds are spawned almost daily. By a principle of natural selection some of these new instruments become popular and may even replace existing species. Others are ephemeral curiosities. We don't know all the reasons for the success of some innovations but we suggest that many new securities owe their origin to tax rules and government regulation. The lasting innovations are those that reduce costs or widen investor choice.

Project finance is used for large projects to limit the risk borne by the project developer and pass on some of the risk to the lenders. In the extreme case, a *non-recourse* loan provides the project's assets and cash flows as the only security for the loan—the lenders have no recourse to the developer if the loan is in default.

APPENDIX 24-1: EXCERPTS FROM A PROSPECTUS FOR A DEBENTURE ISSUE

Additional Issue   *Project Financing*

$75,000,000

Interprovincial Pipe Line (NW) Ltd.
(a wholly-owned subsidiary of Interprovincial Pipe Line Limited)

12.70% Debentures, Series B

To be dated November 15, 1984   To mature November 15, 2004

   The 12.70% Debentures, Series B (the "Series B Debentures") will be secured by an assignment by the Company of the Norman Wells Pipeline Agreement among Imperial Oil Limited, Interprovincial Pipe Line (NW) Ltd. (the "Company") and Interprovincial Pipe Line Limited. The Series B Debentures will not be redeemable before November 15, 1999, for other than sinking fund purposes, from the proceeds of funds borrowed at a lower interest cost. Particulars of sinking fund, redemption and other material attributes are set forth under "Details of the Offering".

Financial support provided by

Imperial Oil Limited

Under the terms of the Norman Wells Pipeline Agreement, Imperial Oil Limited is required to pay to the Company amounts which will enable the Company to service the Series B Debentures. Reference is made to "The Norman Wells Pipeline Agreement".

   In the opinion of counsel, the Series B Debentures will be eligible for investment under the Canadian and British Insurance Companies Act and other statutes as set forth under "Eligibility for Investment".

Price: 100 and accrued interest, if any

   We, as principals, conditionally offer these Series B Debentures, subject to prior sale, if, as and when issued by the Company and accepted by us in accordance with the conditions contained in the underwriting agreement referred to under "Plan of Distribution" and the approval of certain legal matters on behalf of the Company by Osler, Hoskin & Harcourt, Toronto and on our behalf by Blake, Cassels & Graydon, Toronto.

	Price to the public (1)	Underwriters' fee	Net proceeds to the Company (2)
Per Debenture	100.00%	1.15%	98.85%
Total	$75,000,000	$862,500	$74,137,500

(1) Plus accrued interest, if any, to the date of delivery.
(2) Before deducting expenses of issue estimated at $175,000 which will be paid out of the general funds of the Company.

   Subscriptions will be received subject to rejection or allotment in whole or in part and the right is reserved to close the subscription books at any time without notice. It is expected that the Series B Debentures will be available for delivery on or about November 15, 1984.
October 24, 1984

Source: International Pipe Line (NW) Ltd., 12.70% Debentures.

TABLE OF CONTENTS

ELIGIBILITY FOR INVESTMENT

In the opinion of Osler, Hoskin & Harcourt, counsel to the Company, and in the opinion of Blake, Cassels & Graydon, counsel to the underwriters, the Series B Debentures offered by this prospectus, on the date of issue, will be eligible investments, without resort to the so-called "basket" provisions, but subject to general investment provisions for:

(i) insurance companies registered or licensed under the Canadian and British Insurance Companies Act (Canada), the Foreign Insurance Companies Act (Canada) and the Insurance Act (Alberta) and insurance companies incorporated or organized under the Insurance Act (Ontario);

(ii) loan companies regulated under the Loan Companies Act (Canada) and loan corporations registered under the Loan and Trust Corporations Act (Ontario);

(iii) trust companies regulated or registered under the Trust Companies Act (Canada), the Loan and Trust Corporations Act (Ontario) and the Loan and Investment Societies Act (Quebec); and

(iv) pension funds regulated or registered under the Pension Benefits Standards Act (Canada), the Pension Benefits Act (Ontario), the Pension Benefits Act (Alberta) and An Act respecting supplemental pension plans (Quebec).

In the opinion of such counsel, the Series B Debentures will also be eligible investments for registered retirement savings plans and for registered home ownership savings plans under the Income Tax Act (Canada), and the provisions of An Act respecting Insurance (Quebec) would not preclude the investment by an insurance company in the Series B Debentures, subject to the general investment provisions of that act.

Metric Conversion Table

To Convert from	To	Multiply by
Cubic metres (m³)	Barrels	6.3
Kilometres (km)	Miles	0.6
Metres (m)	Feet	3.3
Millimetres (mm)	Inches	0.04

Note: In this prospectus "cubic metres per day" has been abbreviated to "m³/d".

2

INTERPROVINCIAL PIPE LINE (NW) LTD.

PROSPECTUS SUMMARY

Issue:	$75,000,000 12.70% Debentures, Series B.
Price:	100% and accrued interest, if any.
Interest Payment Dates:	Payable semi-annually on May 15 and November 15, commencing May 15, 1985.
Sinking Fund:	An annual sinking fund commencing on November 15, 1987 to produce an average life of approximately 13.9 years.
Redemption:	Not redeemable for financial advantage prior to November 15, 1999. Otherwise redeemable at par plus a premium of 12.70% in the first year, declining to par after November 15, 2002, together with accrued interest.
Financial Support:	The Series B Debentures will be direct obligations of Interprovincial Pipe Line (NW) Ltd. and will be secured by an assignment of the benefits of the Norman Wells Pipeline Agreement including the right to receive moneys payable by Imperial Oil Limited.
Use of Proceeds:	The net proceeds of this issue will be applied toward the costs of construction of the Norman Wells Pipeline System. The Company is financing the Pipeline System on the basis of a debt to equity ratio by 75% to 25%.
Norman Wells Pipeline System:	The Company is engaged in the construction of an oil pipeline extending 866 km from the Norman Wells oil field being developed by a subsidiary of Imperial Oil Limited in the Northwest Territories to connect with the pipeline of Rainbow Pipe Line Company, Ltd. at Zama in northern Alberta. The initial design capacity of the Pipeline System is approximately $4\,800$ m^3/d of crude oil and other liquid hydrocarbons. The construction and operation of the Pipeline System are regulated by the National Energy Board.

3

THE COMPANY

Interprovincial Pipe Line (NW) Ltd. was incorporated on March 3, 1980 under the Canada Business Corporations Act. All of the Company's outstanding shares are owned by Interprovincial Pipe Line Limited ("Interprovincial"). The registered office of the Company is at 1202 Interprovincial Pipe Line Tower, 10201 Jasper Avenue, Edmonton, Alberta.

The Company is constructing a 324 mm diameter pipeline extending 866 km (the "Pipeline System") from the Norman Wells oil field being developed by Esso Resources Canada Limited, a wholly-owned subsidiary of Imperial Oil Limited ("Imperial"), in the Northwest Territories to connect with the pipeline of Rainbow Pipe Line Company, Ltd. (the "Rainbow Pipeline") at Zama in northern Alberta. Crude oil and other liquid hydrocarbons will be transported through the facilities of the Company and the Rainbow Pipeline to Edmonton, Alberta, for delivery to refineries in the Edmonton area, or to the pipelines of Interprovincial or other carriers for transportation to Canadian or U.S. refineries.

The Pipeline System is expected to be completed at a capital cost of $400 million, including a capitalized allowance for debt and equity funds used during construction of $62 million. Construction progress has exceeded targets and installation of two-thirds of the pipe for the total project has been completed. The Company expects to complete the Pipeline System in the spring of 1985 and it is anticipated that full operations will commence shortly thereafter. The initial design capacity of the Pipeline System is approximately 4 800 m^3/d of crude oil and other liquid hydrocarbons.

The portion of the Rainbow Pipeline to be used for shipment of oil to Edmonton has a capacity of approximately 39 200 m^3/d. The average throughput of the Rainbow Pipeline during 1983 was approximately 22 800 m^3/d. The Company is confident that there will be sufficient capacity in the Rainbow Pipeline to accommodate the throughput of the Pipeline System. Imperial is a one-third shareholder of Rainbow Pipe Line Company, Ltd.

All services required by the Company for the construction, operation, maintenance and management of the Pipeline System are provided by Interprovincial pursuant to a management agreement.

Imperial, the Company and Interprovincial are parties to the Norman Wells Pipeline Agreement dated as of January 1, 1980 as amended by an agreement made as of April 1, 1982 and clarified by a letter agreement dated August 29, 1983 (collectively the "Pipeline Agreement"). The Pipeline Agreement specifies the terms and conditions governing the financing, construction and operation of the Pipeline System.

The Company and Interprovincial are parties to an agreement with two Canadian chartered banks (the "Bank Loan Agreement") to provide financing for the Pipeline System, including a facility to finance cost overruns. A total of $275 million remains available to the Company under the Bank Loan Agreement.

The principal properties of the Company comprise rights of way, the partly constructed Pipeline System, materials and work in progress for the completion of construction and a portfolio of short term securities being maintained pending requirement of funds for construction.

NORMAN WELLS OIL FIELD

The Norman Wells oil field is located at Norman Wells, which is situated on the Mackenzie River in the Northwest Territories. The Norman Wells oil field was discovered by Imperial in 1920. Following reservoir studies and evaluation well drilling, Imperial has concluded that there are significant volumes of oil in place in the reservoir beneath the Mackenzie River. Esso Resources Canada Limited is undertaking a field-wide water flood of the Norman Wells oil field and Imperial expects that this will increase total field production of crude oil and natural gas liquids from 500 m^3/d to 4 600 m^3/d. The Government of Canada has a one-third carried interest in the Norman Wells oil field.

Imperial estimates probable reserves to be some 43 million m^3 of oil and natural gas liquids recoverable by primary recovery techniques and by a field-wide water flood project. Based on information supplied by Imperial, the Company estimates that pipeline throughput in 1985 will be 4 100 m^3/d. This level is expected to increase to 4 600 m^3/d by 1990 at which time throughput will begin to decline, reaching 1 000 m^3/d over 20 years.

4

The Pipeline System has the potential for transporting crude oil and other liquid hydrocarbons provided by other shippers. Several companies are engaged in exploration for oil in the vicinity of the route of the Pipeline System. In August 1984 the southernmost 29 km of the Pipeline System was placed in service to transport approximately 400 m³/d for another shipper.

IMPERIAL OIL LIMITED

Imperial is an integrated oil company and is active in all phases of the petroleum industry in Canada, including the exploration for and production of crude oil and natural gas. In Canada, it is a major producer of crude oil, a large refiner and marketer of petroleum products and a significant supplier of natural gas. Imperial is a major participant in Syncrude, a joint venture for the production of upgraded crude oil. It is also engaged in mineral exploration, development and production and in the manufacture and sale of chemicals, fertilizers and building materials. Exxon Corporation owns 69.6% of the outstanding shares of Imperial, with the remaining shares being publicly held.

Imperial's financial performance for the periods indicated is summarized below.

	Year ended December 31				
	1983	1982	1981	1980	1979
	(millions of dollars)				
Total revenues	$9,027	$8,618	$8,185	$6,349	$4,906
Net income	290	267	465	682	493
Internal funds from operations	708	830	839	893	702
Long term debt and other obligations	1,180	1,028	946	618	611
Shareholders' equity	4,231	4,103	4,042	3,789	2,440
Total assets	8,049	7,486	7,096	6,244	4,668

Source: Imperial

INTERPROVINCIAL PIPE LINE LIMITED

Interprovincial, directly and through its wholly-owned United States subsidiary, Lakehead Pipe Line Company, Inc. ("Lakehead"), owns and operates an oil pipeline system for the transportation of crude oil and other liquid hydrocarbons. The pipeline system constitutes the only crude oil pipeline connecting the oil fields of Alberta across the Canadian prairies through the Great Lakes region of the United States to Toronto, Ontario and Montreal, Quebec, with lateral lines to Nanticoke, Ontario and Buffalo, New York, and includes a line between Superior, Wisconsin and Sarnia, Ontario, via Chicago, Illinois. Deliveries are made en route in the Canadian prairies and the midwestern United States.

Interprovincial and Lakehead are primarily engaged in the business of transporting, at established tariffs, crude oil and other liquid hydrocarbons through their common carrier pipeline system. During 1983, 41 shippers tendered 49 types of products for shipment through the system. The five principal shippers were Gulf Canada Limited, Imperial, Petro-Canada, Shell Canada Limited and Texaco Canada Limited. Products shipped averaged 198 900 m³/d during 1983 and can be grouped into the following classifications:

(i)   light, medium and heavy crude oil from conventional sources;

(ii) crude oils extracted from Alberta oil sands deposits;

(iii) natural gas liquids which include propane, butane and condensate; and

(iv) refined petroleum products such as gasoline, diesel fuel and heating fuel.

In Canada, interprovincial pipeline operations are regulated by the National Energy Board (the "NEB" or the "Board"). In the United States, the Federal Energy Regulatory Commission (the "FERC") has regulatory authority over the rates, regulations and accounting practices of Lakehead. In 1982, an industry-wide decision by the FERC concerning ratemaking for oil pipelines prescribed that companies will be allowed to set tariffs to recover operating and interest costs and to provide a return on equity. The return is applied to a rate base which incorporates a weighted average of the reproduction cost and the original cost of the pipeline facility. This decision is currently under review by the FERC.

5

THE NORMAN WELLS PIPELINE AGREEMENT

The Company, Interprovincial and Imperial entered into the Pipeline Agreement to provide for the financing, construction and operation of the Pipeline System for the transportation of crude oil and other liquid hydrocarbons from the Norman Wells oil field to Zama, Alberta. The Pipeline Agreement has a term of 25 years from the date when "leave to open" the Pipeline System is granted by the NEB but will end earlier if and when the debt for financing the construction of the Pipeline System is retired.

The Pipeline Agreement provides that the Company will construct, maintain and operate the Pipeline System and that Interprovincial will enter into a management agreement with the Company to provide the services required for the construction, operation, maintenance and management of the Pipeline System. The Pipeline Agreement also contemplates that Imperial will tender for transportation in the Pipeline System all petroleum production from the Norman Wells oil field (except that needed for local requirements), and will pay transportation tolls based on the full cost of service with the requirement to pay a Minimum Bill in the circumstances described below. Both Imperial and the Company have a right to withdraw from the arrangements contemplated by the Pipeline Agreement in accordance with the terms of abandonment described below. Interprovincial has agreed to cause the Company to perform its obligations under the Pipeline Agreement and Imperial has agreed to cause its subsidiary, Esso Resources Canada Limited, to proceed with diligence to increase the production capacity of the Norman Wells oil field.

The Company is required to finance the Pipeline System on the basis of a debt to equity ratio of 75% to 25%. Pursuant to the Pipeline Agreement, Imperial has agreed to the Bank Loan Agreement and to the issue of the Series A and Series B Debentures; future consents of Imperial will be obtained as required for the debt financing of the Pipeline System.

Shippers which tender petroleum for transportation through the Pipeline System will pay the full cost of service for transportation based upon a tariff which includes an agreed rate of return of 16% on equity. The full cost of service tariff includes the following items:

(i)   operating expenses including maintenance, transportation and general expenses;

(ii) depreciation and amortization expense;

(iii) normalized income taxes;

(iv) interest expense; and

(v)   the return on equity mentioned above.

The Pipeline Agreement also provides for a Minimum Bill, which is payable by Imperial to the Company to the extent amounts collected by the Company from all shippers, including Imperial, in any operating month during the term of the Pipeline Agreement do not aggregate an amount equal to one-twelfth of the estimated annual Minimum Bill. The Minimum Bill includes the following items:

(i)   operating expenses including maintenance, transportation and general expenses;

(ii) income taxes currently payable;

(iii) interest expense; and

(iv) depreciation, defined for purposes of the Minimum Bill as the amount required to retire the Company's debt in accordance with its terms.

The Pipeline Agreement provides that either the Company or Imperial may abandon the Pipeline System at any time for any reason. In the event that either party initiates the abandonment, the other party has the right to elect to continue the Pipeline System under certain conditions.

6

In the event of abandonment of the Pipeline System prior to commencement of operations:

(i)   if notice is given by Imperial that it does not wish to proceed with the arrangement and the Company then elects to abandon. Imperial will assume the Company's debt obligations relating to the Pipeline System, pay to the Company that portion of the cost of the Pipeline System not included in the debt obligations so assumed, and pay those costs reasonably incurred to abandon the Pipeline System;

(ii) if notice of abandonment is given by the Company and Imperial does not then elect to continue the Pipeline System, Imperial will assume the Company's debt obligations relating to the Pipeline System; and

(iii) if notice of abandonment is given by the Company and Imperial elects to continue the Pipeline System, the Company will sell the Pipeline System to Imperial and Imperial will assume the Company's debt relating to the Pipeline System and pay to the Company that portion of the cost of the Pipeline System not included in the debt obligations so assumed.

In the event of abandonment of the Pipeline System after the commencement of operations and prior to the expiration of the Pipeline Agreement:

(i)   if Imperial gives, or is deemed to have given, notice that it is unwilling or unable to tender petroleum for the remainder of the term, and the Company then elects to abandon, Imperial will pay to the Company the Minimum Bill for the remaining term of the Pipeline Agreement;

(ii) if the Company elects to abandon, or is deemed to have done so, and Imperial then elects not to continue the Pipeline System, Imperial will pay to the Company the Minimum Bill until the Pipeline Agreement expires; and

(iii) if the Company elects to abandon and Imperial elects to continue the Pipeline System, the Company will sell the Pipeline System to Imperial and Imperial will assume the Company's debt obligations relating to the Pipeline System.

If Imperial gives notice of abandonment either prior to or after commencement of operations, the Company may elect to continue the Pipeline System in which event the Pipeline Agreement terminates. However, the trust indenture securing the Series A and Series B Debentures provides that the Company cannot so elect unless it has provided the Trustee with a guarantee or letter of credit with respect to the payment of principal and interest on the Debentures from one or more of the existing five largest Schedule A chartered banks.

THE MANAGEMENT AGREEMENT

The Company and Interprovincial have entered into a management agreement dated as of January 1, 1982 (the "Management Agreement") under which the Company appointed Interprovincial to provide the services required for the construction, operation, maintenance and management of the Pipeline System. Interprovincial is being reimbursed by the Company for services provided and related overheads pursuant to this agreement. Amounts charged for services under the Management Agreement were as follows: in 1982, $733,542, in 1983, $1,158,518 and $1,300,833 to August 31, 1984.

THE BANK LOAN AGREEMENT

The Company, Interprovincial and two chartered banks entered into the Bank Loan Agreement to provide initial financing for the Pipeline System. The Bank Loan Agreement now provides that up to $275 million may be advanced prior to the completion of the Pipeline System or December 31, 1987, whichever is earlier. Funds available under the Bank Loan Agreement will be reduced by the amount of this issue and any further long-term fixed rate indebtedness incurred to finance the construction of the Pipeline System. Funds may be drawn in Canadian or U.S. dollars at floating rates of interest or at fixed rates of interest by way of LIBOR loans or bankers' acceptances. The Bank Loan Agreement also provides a backup line of credit for commercial paper issued by the Company.

The loans outstanding at the time "leave to open" the Pipeline System is obtained are repayable over a ten year term commencing on that date, and with minor exceptions may be prepaid at any time without penalty. Mandatory quarterly repayments of principal are required to be the greater of 1% of the loans outstanding at the time of "leave to open" or an amount equal to a portion of the depreciation expense of the Pipeline System determined by rateably allocating the depreciation expense over all debt relating to the Pipeline System.

Advances pursuant to the Bank Loan Agreement are secured by the Bank Debentures. See "Details of the Offering".

7

GOVERNMENT REGULATION

Under the National Energy Board Act (the "NEB Act"), the NEB has regulatory power over the construction, operation and maintenance of pipelines within federal jurisdiction. The NEB Act provides that a company subject to the Board's jurisdiction shall not make any unjust discrimination in tolls, service or facilities against any person or locality. The Board has power to disallow any tariff or toll and to require a company to substitute a tariff satisfactory to the Board for a tariff originally determined by that company. A company's accounting records must be kept according to standards established by the Oil Pipeline Uniform Accounting Regulations and are subject to audit by the Board.

In its reasons for the decision which resulted in the granting of the Certificate of Public Convenience and Necessity No. OC-35 which authorizes construction of the Pipeline System, the Board set forth a number of conditions to be met by the Company. These included filing a variety of studies and other material data for Board approval prior to construction. These approvals have been obtained.

The NEB approved the form and content of the Company's "full cost of service" tariff, including the 16% return on equity, and the Rules and Regulations which will apply to the transportation of petroleum through the Pipeline System, all as contained in the Pipeline Agreement.

The Board in its order respecting tariffs declared that if additional shippers intend to use the Pipeline System the Board may review the structure of the full cost of service tariff. The order requires the Company to submit for review and approval its estimate of the full cost of service prior to the beginning of each operating year, and requires that any operating expenses in excess of the approved estimate not be included in the actual full cost of service until such amounts are approved by the Board. The Board is currently reviewing the allocation among shippers of the full cost of service tariff.

Following completion of the Pipeline system, a "leave to open" order is required from the Board before the Pipeline System may be operated. "Leave to open" the southernmost 29 km of the Pipeline System has been obtained.

CAPITALIZATION

	Authorized	Outstanding June 30, 1984	Outstanding August 31, 1984	Outstanding August 31, 1984 after giving effect to this issue
		(Unaudited)	(Unaudited)	(Unaudited)
Debt				
Debentures				
13.40% Series A due April 1, 2004	$100,000,000	$100,000,000	$100,000,000	$100,000,000
12.70% Series B due November 15, 2004	$200,000,000	–	–	75,000,000
Project financing (1)		46,600,000	60,200,000	–
		$146,600,000	$160,200,000	$175,000,000
Shareholder's Equity				
Common Shares	unlimited	$ 81,025,000	$ 81,025,000	$ 81,025,000
		(81,026 shs)	(81,026 shs)	(81,026 shs)
Retained Earnings		11,432,000	11,432,000(2)	11,432,000(2)
		$ 92,457,000	$ 92,457,000	$ 92,457,000

Notes:

1. All amounts owed by the Company under the Bank Loan Agreement are collaterally secured by the pledge of Bank Debentures which rank pari passu with the Series A and Series B Debentures (see "Details of the Offering"). The Bank Debentures are deemed to be outstanding at any time only to the extent of all amounts then owing by the Company under the Bank Loan Agreement. A total of $275 million remains available to the Company under the Bank Loan Agreement.
2. Amounts shown for retained earnings in the August 31, 1984 columns are as of June 30, 1984.

USE OF PROCEEDS

The net proceeds from this sale of the Series B Debentures will amount to approximately $73,962,500, and will be applied as required toward the costs of construction of the Pipeline System. These proceeds will initially be used to reduce borrowings under the Bank Loan Agreement and, on an interim basis, the balance will be invested in short term securities.

The total debt requirement of the Pipeline System is expected to be $300 million. The Company proposes to fund the remaining requirements by incurring further indebtedness pursuant to the Bank Loan Agreement and through the issue of additional debt securities. The Company's current intention is to replace bank borrowing on a timely basis as financial market conditions and other factors dictate. The equity requirement for the project, anticipated to be $100 million, will be satisfied by Interprovincial through its share investment in the Company and the accumulated retained earnings from the project.

PLAN OF DISTRIBUTION

Under an agreement dated October 24, 1984, between the Company and Wood Gundy Inc. and McLeod Young Weir Limited as underwriters, the Company has agreed to sell and the underwriters have agreed to purchase, on November 15, 1984, or such other date as the Company and the underwriters may agree upon but in any event not later than November 29, 1984, subject to the terms and conditions stated therein, all but not part of the $75,000,000 principal amount of Series B Debentures at an aggregate price of $75,000,000 plus accrued interest, if any, from November 15, 1984 to the date of delivery, payable to the Company against delivery of such Series B Debentures. This agreement provides for the Company to pay the underwriters out of its general funds a fee of $862,500 on account of the services rendered by the underwriters. The obligation of the underwriters to take up the Series B Debentures under such agreement may be terminated at their discretion on the basis of their assessment of the state of the financial markets and may also be terminated upon the occurrence of certain stated events. In connection with the offering, the underwriters may overallot or effect transactions which stabilize or maintain the market price of the Series B Debentures at a level above that which might otherwise prevail in the open market; such transactions, if commenced, may be discontinued at any time.

DETAILS OF THE OFFERING

The following is a summary of the material attributes and characteristics of the Series B Debentures which does not purport to be complete. For full particulars reference should be made to the Trust Indenture referred to below.

Trust Indenture

The Series B Debentures will be issued pursuant to the provisions of a trust indenture dated as of March 1, 1984, between the Company and Montreal Trust Company of Canada, as trustee (the "Trustee") providing for the creation and issue of debentures (the "Debentures") and a supplemental indenture to be made as of November 15, 1984, (together the "Trust Indenture"). The aggregate principal amount of the Debentures which may be issued by the Company is not limited by the Trust Indenture, but Debentures may only be issued to finance construction of the Pipeline System.

The Series B Debentures will be direct obligations of the Company and will rank pari passu with the Series A Debentures, the Bank Debentures and all other Debentures (except as to sinking funds pertaining exclusively to any particular series).

The Company issues Bank Debentures under the Trust Indenture, which are pledged to two chartered banks as security for loans from those banks to the Company under the Bank Loan Agreement. Notwithstanding the stated principal amount of Bank Debentures at any time issued, they are deemed to be outstanding only to the extent of all amounts owing by the Company to the said banks under the Bank Loan Agreement from time to time and are repayable only in accordance with the terms of the Bank Loan Agreement.

Interest

The Series B Debentures will bear interest at the rate of 12.70% per annum from November 15, 1984. The principal of and half-yearly interest on the Series B Debentures will be payable in lawful money of Canada on May 15 and November 15 in each year commencing May 15, 1985 at any branch in Canada of the bank designated in the Series B Debentures.

Denominations

Series B Debentures will be issued in coupon form registrable as to principal only in the denominations of $1,000, $25,000 and $100,000 and in fully registered form in denominations of $1,000 and integral multiples thereof.

Security

All outstanding Debentures are secured pursuant to the Trust Indenture by an assignment to the Trustee by the Company of substantially all its rights under any Shipping Agreement and under the Pipeline Agreement, including a right to receive all moneys due thereunder and a right to give a notice of abandonment under the Pipeline Agreement following the occurrence of an Event of Default under the Trust Indenture.

9

The Trust Indenture also provides for a first and specific mortgage (subject to Permitted Encumbrances) upon the real estate, rights of way and other immovable properties that form part of the Pipeline System and are described in the Schedule to the Trust Indenture and fixed plant and fixed equipment situate thereon, together with cash balances and evidences of indebtedness deposited from time to time with the Trustee. The Trust Indenture contains provisions for the release of property from the said mortgage when the disposal of such property would not interfere with the operation of the Pipeline System. In some circumstances, certain of the Bank Debentures, for a limited period, may not have the benefit of the said mortgage.

Sinking Fund

The Company will covenant in the Trust Indenture to make payments to the Trustee, as and by way of a sinking fund, sufficient to retire 4% of the total of original issues of Series B Debentures on November 15 in each of the years 1987 to 2003 inclusive, so as to retire 68% of the issue prior to maturity. The sinking fund will produce an average life for the Series B Debentures of approximately 13.9 years.

Series B Debentures redeemed (other than for sinking fund purposes) or purchased will establish a sinking fund credit equal to the principal amount thereof which may be applied to the satisfaction in whole or in part of any subsequent sinking fund payment. Series B Debentures will be redeemable out of sinking fund moneys at the principal amount thereof plus accrued interest.

Redemption and Purchase

The Series B Debentures will not be redeemable prior to November 15, 1999, other than for sinking fund purposes, unless the Company shall have filed with the Trustee a certified copy of a resolution of its directors declaring that such Series B Debentures are being redeemed otherwise than as part of a refunding or anticipated refunding operation involving the application, directly or indirectly, of funds borrowed in connection with or in anticipation of such refunding operation having an interest rate or cost of less than 12.70% per annum. Subject to the foregoing, the Series B Debentures will be redeemable prior to maturity, other than for sinking fund purposes, in whole at any time or in part from time to time, at the option of the Company on not less than 30 days' notice, at prices equal to the following percentages of the principal amount thereof, together in every case with accrued and unpaid interest to the date fixed for redemption:

If redeemed in the 12 months ending November 15	Percentage	If redeemed in the 12 months ending November 15	Percentage
1985	112.70	1995	105.60
1986	111.95	1996	104.90
1987	111.20	1997	104.20
1988	110.50	1998	103.50
1989	109.80	1999	102.80
1990	109.10	2000	102.10
1991	108.40	2001	101.40
1992	107.70	2002	100.70
1993	107.00	2003	100.00
1994	106.30	2004	100.00

The Company will reserve the right to purchase Series B Debentures in the market or by tender to all Series B Debenture holders, at any price, or by private contract at prices not exceeding the foregoing percentages of the principal amount thereof plus accrued and unpaid interest and the costs of purchase.

10

Covenants

The following is a summary of certain covenants which will be applicable under the Trust Indenture so long as any Series B Debentures remain outstanding.

Additional Debentures
The Company will not issue additional Debentures except in accordance with the Pipeline Agreement.

Completion of Pipeline System
The Company will use its best endeavours to construct and complete the Pipeline System on or before December 31, 1987 subject to the terms of the Pipeline Agreement.

Maintenance of Agreements
The Company will use its best efforts (i) to keep the Pipeline Agreement in full force and effect and to collect all amounts from time to time payable to the Company under that agreement, (ii) to keep the Management Agreement in full force and effect and (iii) to collect all amounts from time to time payable to the Company under any Shipping Agreement. The Company will not assign or consent to the assignment of any rights or obligations under the Pipeline Agreement or the Management Agreement or terminate, amend or modify the terms thereof in any respect which, in the opinion of the Trustee, is adverse to the interests of the Debenture holders. The Company will not assign or consent to the assignment of any Shipping Agreement. Notwithstanding these covenants, the Company may assign or encumber the Pipeline Agreement or any Shipping Agreement to secure equally with the Debentures any issue of additional debt securities the proceeds of which are used exclusively to finance the Pipeline System. The Company shall not give a notice of its intention to continue the Pipeline System in response to a notice of abandonment given by Imperial (if to do so would cause the termination of the Pipeline Agreement), unless it has provided the Trustee with a guarantee or letter of credit with respect to the payment of principal and interest on the Debentures from one or more of the existing five largest Schedule A chartered banks.

Creation of Security
The Company will not:

(i) create or assume any encumbrance on property comprising the Pipeline System, other than Permitted Encumbrances and encumbrances to secure Debentures; or

(ii) create or assume any encumbrance on property not comprising part of the Pipeline System, other than Permitted Encumbrances, if the indebtedness of the Company to which the encumbrance relates has been created or assumed upon terms which, in the opinion of the Trustee, permit the lender to have any recourse to or interfere, in any way which is materially adverse to the interests of the Debenture holders, with the operation of the Pipeline System.

Modification

The rights of a Debenture holder under the Trust Indenture may be modified. For that purpose, among others, the Trust Indenture contains provisions for making binding upon all Debenture holders resolutions passed by the affirmative vote of holders of not less than $66^2/_3\%$ of the principal amount of the Debentures voting at a meeting of Debenture holders or by instruments in writing signed by the holders of not less than $66^2/_3\%$ of the principal amount of the outstanding Debentures, subject to the provisions of the Trust Indenture.

11

FURTHER READING

Ananthanarayanan and Schwartz and Brennan and Schwartz focus on valuing the options implicit in callable, extendible, and retractable bonds. Kraus provides a general discussion of call provisions.

A.L. Ananthanarayanan and E.S. Schwartz, "Retractable and Extendible Bonds: The Canadian Experience," *Journal of Finance*, **35**: 31–47 (May 1980).

M.J. Brennan and E.S. Schwartz, "Savings Bonds, Retractable Bonds and Callable Bonds," *Journal of Financial Economics*, **5**: 67–88 (1977).

A. Kraus, "An Analysis of Call Provisions and the Corporate Refunding Decision," *Midland Corporate Finance Journal*, **1**: 46–60 (Spring 1983).

Smith and Warner provide an extensive survey and analysis of covenants:

C.W. Smith and J.B. Warner, "On Financial Contracting: An Analysis of Bond Covenants," *Journal of Financial Economics*, **7**: 117–161 (June 1979).

A useful general work on debt securities is:

F.J. Fabozzi and I.M. Pollack, eds., *Handbook of Fixed Income Securities*, 2nd ed., Dow Jones-Irwin, Inc., Homewood, IL, 1987.

For recent developments in project finance, see:

J.W. Kensinger and J.D. Martin, "Project Finance: Raising Money the Old-Fashioned Way," *Journal of Applied Corporate Finance*, **1**: 69–81 (Fall 1988).

QUIZ

1. Select the most appropriate term from within the parentheses:
   (a) (High-grade utility bonds/Low-grade industrial bonds) generally have only light sinking fund requirements.
   (b) (Short-dated notes/Long-dated debentures) are often noncallable.
   (c) Collateral trust bonds are often issued by (utilities/industrial holding companies).
   (d) (Utility bonds/Industrial bonds) are usually unsecured.
   (e) Equipment trust certificates are usually issued by (railroads/financial companies).
2. (a) If interest rates rise, will callable or noncallable bonds fall more in price?
   (b) The Belgian government has issued bonds that may be repaid after a specified date at the option of *either* the government or the bondholder. If each side acts rationally, what will happen on that date?
3. Which of the following sinking funds increase the value of a bond at the time of issue?
   (a) An optional sinking fund operating by drawings at par
   (b) A mandatory sinking fund operating by drawings at par *or* by purchases in the market
   (c) A mandatory sinking fund operating by drawings at par
4. (a) As a senior debtholder would you like the company to issue more junior debt, would you prefer it not to do so, or would you not care?
   (b) You hold debt secured on the company's existing property. Would you like the company to issue more unsecured debt, would you prefer it not to do so, or would you not care?
5. Use the Interprovincial prospectus (but not the text) to answer the following questions:

(a) Who are the underwriters of the issue?

(b) Who is the trustee for the issue?

(c) How many dollars does the company receive for each debenture after the deduction of *all* expenses?

(d) Is the debenture "bearer" or "registered"?

(e) What proportion of the issue is retired each year by the mandatory sinking fund?

(f) At what price is the issue callable in 1995?

(g) Can the company call the bond in 1995 and replace it with a debenture yielding 7%?

6. Look at the Interprovincial prospectus:

(a) How much would you have to pay to buy one bond on January 15,1985? Don't forget accrued interest.

(b) When is the first interest payment on the bond and what is the amount of that payment?

(c) On what date do the bonds finally mature and what is the principal amount of the bonds that is due to be repaid that date?

(d) Suppose that the market price of the bonds rises to 102 and thereafter does not change. When should the company call the issue?

QUESTIONS AND PROBLEMS

1. After a sharp change in interest rates, newly issued bonds generally sell at yields different from outstanding bonds of the same quality. One suggested explanation is that there is a difference in the value of the call provision. Explain how this could arise.

2. Obtain a prospectus for a recent issue of debentures and compare the terms and conditions with the Interprovincial issue.

3. What restrictions are imposed on a company's freedom to issue further debt? Be as precise as possible. Explain carefully the reasons for such restrictions.

4. Explain carefully why senior and subordinated bond indentures place different restrictions on a company's freedom to issue additional debt.

5. An extendible bond is a bond whose maturity may be extended at the investor's option. Describe the relationship between the value of a straight bond and an extendible bond.

6. What determines the value of an indexed bond? Should the rate of interest on an indexed bond be higher or lower than the expected real rate on a nominal bond?

7. Explain carefully why bond indentures place limitations on the following actions:

(a) Sale of the company's assets

(b) Payment of dividends to shareholders

(c) Issue of additional senior debt

8. Look up the terms of a commodity-linked bond (for example, the Standard Oil bond *or* the International Refining gold bond). Find out what has happened to the payments on these bonds as the commodity price has changed. Have these bonds increased shareholders' risk or reduced it?

9. Suppose that instead of issuing the original issue discount bonds, GMAC had raised the same amount of money by an issue of 14.80% ten-year notes at a price of $100.

(a) What face amount of notes would GMAC have needed to issue?

(b) Value the gain to GMAC from the issue of OID debt rather than the 14.80% notes. (You may assume either the MM or Miller theory of debt and taxes.)

(c) Show that the gain to GMAC disappears if the annual tax deduction is calculated using compound interest rather than simple interest.

10. Does the issue of additional junior debt harm senior bondholders? Would your answer be the same if the junior debt matured *before* the senior debt? Explain.

11. Estimate the value of the Standard Oil "oil bond" (see Section 24-6).

12. State as precisely as you can the circumstances in which each of the options on Chemical Waste Management's LYONs will be exercised. What does this imply about the upper and lower limits on the price of the bond in each year?

13. In Section 24-6 we referred to Christiana Bank's exotic bond. Explain how you would value tranche B. Assume that the principal repayment is fixed at 100% of par. (*Hint:* Find a package of other securities that would produce identical cash flows.) What does this tell you about the riskiness of Hong Kong Mass Transit Railway's warrants (see footnote 34).

14. Dorlcote Milling has outstanding a $1 million 3% mortgage bond maturing in 10 years. The coupon on any new debt issued by the company is 10%. The finance director, Mr. Tulliver, cannot decide whether there is a tax benefit to repurchasing the existing bonds in the marketplace and replacing them with new 10% bonds. What do you think? Start by assuming that all bondholders are tax-exempt. Then introduce Miller's idea that higher-rate taxpayers will gravitate to tax-efficient securities and force up their prices.

15. Look up a recent issue of an unusual bond in, say, a recent issue of the periodical *Euromoney*. Why do you think this bond was issued? What investors do you think it would appeal to? How would you value the unusual features?

16. In a number of countries such as France it is not uncommon for firms to band together to make a debt issue. A portion of the receipts is put aside in a safe government bond and the remainder is parcelled out among the different issuers. Each firm is responsible for its portion of the total debt, but in the event of default by any one firm the lenders can draw on the money invested in the government bond. Do you think this is a good idea? How would you value this debt?

17. Some eurobonds involve payments in more than once currency. For example, in 1985 Anheuser-Busch issued a 10-year yen bond at a price of 101. The coupon payment is made in yen but the final repayment of principal is in dollars at an exchange are of 208 yen to the dollar. How would you value such a bond?

C · H · A · P · T · E · R

25

HEDGING FINANCIAL RISK

Most of the time we take risk as God-given. An asset or business has its beta, and that's that. Its cash flow is exposed to unpredictable changes in selling price, labour cost, tax rates, technology, and a long list of other variables. There's nothing the manager can do about it.

That's not wholly true. To some extent a manager can *select* the risks of an asset or business. Some risks can be *hedged* (i.e., offset) by trading in options, **futures**, or other financial instruments.[1]

Suppose your company harvests trees and manufactures building products. Here are some of its principal sources of risk:

- Selling prices of standardized products, such as:
  Lumber
- Exchange rates including:
  U.S. versus Canadian dollars, because some of your major competitors are American
  U.S. dollars versus Japanese yen, because Japan is a major market for lumber and building products
- New housing starts in Canada and the United States, which (among other things) depend on:
  Interest rates
- Changes in the energy cost of running your factories, which largely reflect:
  Crude oil prices

All the risks shown in italics can be hedged. For example, you can cancel out the unpredictable fluctuations in the selling price of your lumber by trading in futures contracts. As Tables 25-1 and 25-2 show, there is a futures market for each of the variables in italics, and for many other commodities and financial instruments. You may also be able to use options and other securities to hedge risks.

This chapter will explain *how* firms can hedge out unpredictable fluctuations in many business and financial variables. But first we should give some of the reasons *why* they do it.

---

[1] Risks can also be *amplified* by trading, but operating managers do not usually speculate in this way. They leave speculation to professional traders.

Table 25-1
Commodity futures and the exchanges on which they are traded

Future	Exchange
Barley	BFE, WPG
Corn	CBT, MCE
Oats	CPT, WPG
Rye	WPG
Wheat	BFE, CBT, KC, MCE, MPLS, WPG
Flaxseed	WPG
Rapeseed	WPG
Soybeans	CBT, MCE
Soybean meal	BFE, CBT, MCE
Soybean oil	CBT
Cattle	CME, MCE
Hogs	BFE, CME, MCE
Pork bellies	CME
Cocoa	CSCE, FOX
Coffee	CSCE, FOX
Cotton	CTN
Lumber	CME
Orange juice	CTN
Sugar	CSCE, FOX, PCE
Aluminum	COMEX, LME
Copper	COMEX, LME
Gold	CBT, COMEX
Lead	LME
Nickel	LME
Palladium	NYMEX
Platinum	NYMEX
Silver	CBT, COMEX, MCE
Tin	LME
Zinc	LME
Crude oil	IPE, NYMEX
Fuel oil	IPE
Gas oil	IPE
Heating oil	NYMEX
Unleaded gas	NYMEX
Freight rates	BFE

Key to abbreviations:

BFE	Baltic Futures Exchange
CBT	Chicago Board of Trade
CME	Chicago Mercantile Exchange
COMEX	Commodity Exchange, New York
CSCE	Coffee, Sugar and Cocoa Exchange, New York
CTN	New York Cotton Exchange
FOX	London Futures and Options Exchange
IPE	International Petroleum Exchange of London
KC	Kansas City Board of Trade
LME	London Metal Exchange
MCE	MidAmerica Commodity Exchange
MPLS	Minneapolis Grain Exchange
NYMEX	New York Mercantile Exchange
PCE	Paris Commodity Exchange
WPG	Winnipeg Commodity Exchange

Table 25-2
Some financial futures contracts

Future	Exchange
U.S. Treasury bills	IMM, MCE
U.S. Treasury notes	CBT, FINEX
U.S. Treasury bonds	CBT, LIFFE, MCE
Canadian Government bonds	ME
Eurodollar deposits	IMM, LIFFE
Canadian Bankers Acceptances	ME
Mortgage-backed bonds	CBT
U.S. corporate bond index	CBT, COMEX
U.S. municipal bond index	CBT
Standard & Poor's Index	IMM
Toronto Stock Exchange 35	TFE
Australian dollar	IMM, PhilSE
Canadian dollar	IMM, MCE, PhilSE
Deutschemark	IMM, LIFFE, MCE, PhilSE
European Currency Unit	FINEX, PhilSE
French franc	IMM, PhilSE
Sterling	IMM, LIFFE, MCE, PhilSE
Swiss franc	IMM, LIFFE, MCE, PhilSE
Yen	IMM, LIFFE, MCE, PhilSE

Key to abbreviations:

CBT	Chicago Board of Trade
COMEX	Commodity Exchange, New York
FINEX	Financial Instrument Exchange (at the New York Cotton Exchange)
IMM	International Monetary Market (at the CME)
LIFFE	London International Financial Futures Exchange
MCE	MidAmerica Commodity Exchange
ME	Montreal Exchange
PhilSE	Philadelphia Stock Exchange
TFE	Toronto Futures Exchange

Like insurance, hedging is seldom free. Most businesses hedge to reduce risk, not to make money.[2]

Why then bother to hedge? For one thing, it makes financial planning easier and reduces the odds of an embarrassing cash shortfall. A shortfall might only mean an unexpected trip to the bank, but in extreme cases it could trigger financial distress or even bankruptcy. Why not reduce the odds of these awkward outcomes with a hedge?

In some cases hedging also makes it easier to decide whether an operating manager deserves a stern lecture or a pat on the back. Suppose your lumber export division shows a 60% profit increase in a period when the yen unexpectedly jumps by 12% against the dollar. How much of the increase is due to the exchange rate shift, and how much to good management? If the exchange rate was hedged, it's probably good management. If it was not, things have to be sorted out with

---

[2] Hedging transactions are zero-NPV when trading is costless and markets are completely efficient. In practice the firm has to pay small trading costs. Sometimes also it may be less well informed than professional traders on the other side of the market.

hindsight, probably by asking, "What would profits have been *if* the yen had been hedged?"[3]

Finally, hedging extraneous events can help focus the operating manager's attention. We know we shouldn't worry about events outside our control, but most of us do anyway. It's naive to expect the sawmill manager not to worry about lumber prices if her bottom line and bonus depend on them. That worrying time would be better spent if the prices were hedged.[4]

In this chapter we explain how to set up a hedge and introduce you to some of the basic tools of hedging, including forward and futures contracts and swaps.

25-1   THE TECHNIQUE OF HEDGING

In Chapter 7 we saw how risk can be reduced by diversifying across a number of securities that are not closely correlated. The idea behind hedging is somewhat different. Ideally you want to find two investments that are *perfectly* correlated. You then buy one and sell the other so that the net position is absolutely safe. In practice, the correlation is often not perfect and, therefore, some residual risk remains despite the hedge.

Whether the correlation is perfect or not, the techniques for setting up a hedge are the same. Suppose that you already have a liability A. You now wish to hedge this liability by an offsetting purchase of asset B. The object is to minimize the uncertainty of your net position.

The size of your investment in B depends on how the values of A and B are related. Suppose, for example, you estimate that percentage changes in the value of A are related in the following way to percentage changes in the value of B

$$\begin{pmatrix} \text{Expected change in} \\ \text{value of A} \end{pmatrix} = a + \delta \begin{pmatrix} \text{change in value} \\ \text{of B} \end{pmatrix}$$

Delta (δ) measures the sensitivity of A to changes in the value of B. It is also equal to the hedge ratio—that is, the number of units of B which should be purchased to hedge the liability of A. You minimize risk if you offset your liability by the purchase of delta units of B.[5]

Let us illustrate. Imagine that an investment dealer has sold short $10 million of Molson Companies A stock. If the market rises, it is likely that the price of Molson will rise also and the dealer will lose money on her sale of Molson. She can reduce this risk by making an offsetting purchase of the market portfolio. (In practice, rather than attempting to buy the market portfolio, she would buy an index future. More about that later.) To judge how much she should invest in the market, the dealer must first estimate the sensitivity of Molson's stock price to changes in the market index. On past evidence this relationship is as follows:

---

[3] Many large firms hedge away operating divisions' risk exposures by setting up internal, make-believe markets between the divisions and the treasurer's office. Trades in the internal markets are at real (external) market prices. The object is to relieve the operating manager of risks outside his or her control. The treasurer makes a separate decision on whether to hedge the *firm's* exposure.

[4] A Texas oilman who lost hundreds of millions in various ill-fated deals protested, "Why should I worry? Worry is for strong minds and weak characters." If there are any financial managers with weak minds and strong characters, we especially advise them to hedge whenever they can.

[5] Notice that A, the item that you wish to hedge, is the dependent variable. Delta is the sensitivity of A to changes in B.

$$\begin{pmatrix}\text{Expected monthly change}\\ \text{in value of Molson}\end{pmatrix} = a + \delta \begin{pmatrix}\text{monthly change}\\ \text{in market index}\end{pmatrix}$$

$$= 0.81 + 0.92 \times (\text{change in market index})$$

In this case the sensitivity of Molson's stock price is identical to our old friend, beta. To minimize risk the investment dealer should combine her short position in Molson with an offsetting investment of $0.92 \times 10 = \$9.2$ million in the market portfolio.

Note that we said "minimize" risk, not "eliminate." Market movements explained only 36% of the variance of price changes in Molson stock.[6] Hedging with the market index cannot offset the remaining 64%, the unique, or diversifiable, risk of Molson stock. The correlation between the returns on the market index and the returns on a diversified portfolio of stocks is much higher than for Molson alone. If the market index is used to hedge a short position in a diversified portfolio, the proportionate reduction in risk is much greater.

Notice that our investment dealer hedges a $10 million short position by making a $9.2 million investment in the market portfolio. Although she is hedged against *changes* in the value of Molson stock, the value of her short position in Molson is not equal to the value of her investment in the market portfolio. To create a *zero-value hedge* the investment dealer would also need to set aside $0.8 million in a bank deposit:

Assets (Millions)		Liability (Millions)	
PV (market investment)	$ 9.2	PV (Molson stock)	$10
PV (bank deposit)	0.8		
	$10.0		$10

As time passes, the investment dealer is likely to find that the value of her assets is no longer equal to that of her liability. For example, suppose the market index falls 5% and the price of Molson stock rises 10%. (Remember the hedge is not perfect. Molson stock will not always move by 0.92 times the market change.) Now the value of the market investment is $8.74/11.0 = 79\%$ of the short position in Molson and the risk of her position is no longer minimized. She must invest $11 \times 0.92 - 8.74 = \$1.38$ more in the market to regain the 0.92 hedge ratio.

Thus, the investment dealer needs to follow a dynamic hedging strategy in which she periodically buys or sells the market portfolio to maintain the desired hedge ratio. Later in the chapter we will come across cases where the hedge ratio itself changes over time. Here, too, you will need to follow a dynamic hedging strategy.

*How Hedging Instruments Allow You to Separate Your Bets

When our investment dealer sold Molson stock, she was placing at least two bets. She was betting on what would happen to the market as a whole and she was betting on how Molson would perform *relative* to the market. By simultaneously investing in the market index, she changed this double bet into a single bet—on Molson's relative performance.

Suppose that you are pessimistic about the outlook for Molson but optimistic about the prospects for the market as a whole. You could place a bet on the

[6] That is, $R^2 = 0.36$. See Section 9-1.

Table 25-3
The first four columns show that the final cash flow accounts for only 70.1% of the present value of the 9¼s of 1996. The final column shows how to calculate a weighted average of the time to each cash flow. This average is the bond's duration.

Year	C_t	PV(C_t) at 9.35%	Proportion of Total Value PV(C_t)/V	Proportion of Total Value × Time
1	$ 92.50	84.59	0.085	0.085
2	92.50	77.36	0.078	0.155
3	92.50	70.74	0.071	0.213
4	92.50	64.69	0.065	0.260
5	1,029.50	698.76	0.701	3.507
	V =	996.15	1.000	Duration = 4.220 years

relative performance of Molson by investing in the market index and selling Molson.

Many financial decisions involve a package of bets. For example, when Jaguar decides to launch a new model aimed at the North American market—a 10- or 15-year commitment—it is betting amongst other things on the exchange rate between dollars and pounds (since Jaguar's costs are in pounds and the revenues are in dollars). It is also betting on the exchange rate between dollars and deutschemarks (since this affects the competitive position of Mercedes and Porsche). Perhaps Jaguar is optimistic about everything except the short-run dollar-pound exchange rate—it fears that the pound will appreciate making British cars expensive in North America. Should that pessimism stop Jaguar from going ahead with the new model? It might if there were no way to hedge out the exchange rate bet. But Jaguar can use the currency forward markets to place a separate bet on the exchange rate.[7] Therefore, management should ask two questions:

1. Should we go ahead with the new model assuming that the company hedges the currency risk?
2. What bets, if any, should be placed on the currency?

There is a general message here. Since investment decisions involve a package of bets, it is important to work out what factors you are betting on and why a particular investment looks good. It could be that there are more efficient ways to bet on these factors. For example, suppose that a cable manufacturer's production plans are based on the assumption that copper prices are going to take off. Producing cables is not the only way to place a bet on copper prices; the manufacturer would do better to base his production plans on a "normal" copper price and use copper futures to bet on the forecast price increase.

One final point. If Jaguar's worries about the exchange rate are confirmed, is the company in a stronger competitive position if it has hedged against a change in the exchange rate? It is certainly true that it makes more money if it has hedged. But there is a general maxim that you should not let the profits in one part of your business (currency hedging) cross-subsidize losses in another part (making cars). If, for example, the pound should appreciate to the point where Jaguar would do better to stop exporting to North America, it should do just that. It should *not* go on selling cars at a loss just because it is making large profits on its currency position.

---

[7] We explain later how currency forward markets work.

25-2 DURATION AND VOLATILITY

Let us return now to the problem of finding the hedge ratio. When we estimated the hedge ratio for our investment dealer, we relied on past history to tell us the sensitivity of Molson's stock price to changes in the value of the market. We will now see how a little theory can sometimes help to estimate the hedge ratio.

In April 1991 Canada 9¼s of 1996 had a price of 99.62 and yielded 9.35%. Table 25-3 shows where this present value comes from. Notice that the cash flow in year 5 accounts for only 70.1% of value. About one-third of the value comes from earlier cash flows. Therefore, it is somewhat misleading to describe the bond as a 5-year bond; the average time to each cash flow is less than 5 years.

Bond analysts often use the term *duration* to describe the average time to each payment. If we call the total value of the bond V, then duration is calculated as follows:[8]

$$\text{Duration} = \left[\frac{(\text{PV}(C_1)}{V} \times 1\right] + \left[\frac{\text{PV}(C_2)}{V} \times 2\right] + \left[\frac{\text{PV}(C_3)}{V} \times 3\right] + \cdots$$

For the 9¼s of 1996,

$$\begin{aligned}\text{Duration} &= (0.085 \times 1) + (0.078 \times 2) + (0.071 \times 3) + \cdots \\ &= 4.220 \text{ years}\end{aligned}$$

Suppose there is another Government of Canada bond also maturing in 1996, with a coupon of 13%. The first 4 years' coupon payments of the 13s account for a larger fraction of the bond's value than they do for the 9¼s. In this sense the 13s are a shorter bond than the 9¼s. The duration of the 13s is 4.043 years.

Consider now what happens to the prices of our two bonds as interest rates change:

	9¼s of 1996		13s of 1996	
	New Price	Change	New Price	Change
Yield falls 0.5%	101.56	1.95%	116.21	1.87%
Yield rises 0.5%	97.72	−1.91%	111.99	−1.83%
Difference	3.85	3.86%	4.22	3.70%

Thus, a 1% variation in yield causes the price of the 9¼s to change by 3.86%. We can say that the 9¼s have a *volatility* of 3.86%.

Notice that the 13% bonds have a lower volatility and they also have a shorter duration. In fact, a bond's volatility is directly related to its duration:

$$\frac{\text{Volatility}}{(\%)} = \frac{\text{duration}}{1 + \text{yield}}$$

In the case of the 13s,

$$\frac{\text{Volatility}}{(\%)} = \frac{4.043}{1.0935} = 3.70$$

Volatility is a useful summary measure of the likely effect of a change in interest rates on a debt portfolio.

---

[8] We assume annual coupon payments. Actual payments are semiannual.

Potterton Leasing has just purchased some equipment and arranged to rent it out for $2 million a year over 8 years. At an interest rate of 12%, Potterton's rental income has a present value of $9.94 million:[9]

$$PV = \frac{2}{1.12} + \frac{2}{(1.12)^2} + \cdots + \frac{2}{(1.12)^8} = \$9.94 \text{ million}$$

The duration of the rental income is 3.9 years; that is,

$$\text{Duration} = \frac{1}{9.94}\left[\left(\frac{2}{1.12} \times 1\right) + \left(\frac{2}{1.12^2} \times 2\right) + \cdots + \left(\frac{2}{1.12^8} \times 8\right)\right]$$
$$= 3.9 \text{ years}$$

Potterton proposes to finance the deal by issuing a package of $1.91 million of 1-year debt and $8.03 million of 6-year debt, each with a 12% coupon. Think of its new asset (the stream of rental income) and the new liability (the issue of debt) as a package. Does Potterton stand to gain or lose on this package if interest rates change?

We can answer this question by calculating the duration of Potterton's new liability. The duration of the 1-year debt is 1 year and the duration of the 6-year debt is 4.6 years. The duration of the package of 1- and 6-year debt is a weighted average of the durations of the individual issues:

$$\begin{array}{l}\text{Durability of} \\ \text{liability}\end{array} = \left(\frac{1.91}{9.94} \times \begin{array}{l}\text{duration of} \\ \text{1-year debt}\end{array}\right) + \left(\frac{8.03}{9.94} \times \begin{array}{l}\text{duration of} \\ \text{6-year debt}\end{array}\right)$$
$$= (0.192 \times 1) + (0.808 \times 4.6) = 3.9 \text{ years}$$

Thus, both the asset (the lease) and the liability (the debt package) have a duration of 3.9 years. Therefore, both are affected equally by a change in interest rates. If rates rise, the present value of Potterton's rental income will decline, but the value of its debt obligation will also decline by the same amount. Rental income will decline, but the value of its debt obligation will also decline by the same amount. By equalizing the duration of the asset and the liability, Potterton has *immunized* itself against any change in interest rates. It looks as if Potterton's financial manager knows a thing or two about hedging.

Notice several things about this example. First, the hedge ratio is measured by the ratio of the durations of the liability and the asset. Since both the lease and the debt package have the same duration, the hedge ratio is 1.0: Potterton minimizes uncertainty by ensuring that the amount of debt issued is equal to the present value of the rental payments ($9.94 million). Could Potterton have hedged itself simply by issuing 6-year debt? Certainly. The duration of the lease is 85% of the duration of the 6-year debt:

$$\frac{\text{Duration of lease}}{\text{Duration of 6-year debt}} = \frac{3.9}{4.6} = 0.85$$

Therefore, Potterton could have hedged itself against changes in interest rates simply by using 0.85 × PV (lease) = $8.45 million of 6-year debt. If interest rates change, the change in the value of the lease will be equal to the change in the value of the debt issue. However, in this case the amount of the debt issue will not be equal to the value of the lease. To create a zero-value hedge, Potterton

---

[9] We ignore tax in this example.

Table 25-4
Potterton can hedge by issuing this sinking fund bond that pays out $2 million per year

Year	Cash Flows, in Millions							
	1	2	3	4	5	6	7	8
Balance at start of year	$9.94	9.13	8.23	7.22	6.08	4.81	3.39	1.79
Interest at 12%	1.19	1.10	0.99	0.87	0.73	0.58	0.40	0.21
Sinking fund payment	0.81	0.90	1.01	1.13	1.27	1.42	1.60	1.79
Interest plus sinking fund payment	$2.00	2.00	2.00	2.00	2.00	2.00	2.00	2.00

would also need to issue a further 9.94 − 8.45 = $1.49 million of very short-term debt with a duration of zero.

Second, notice that Potterton's debt package protects the firm only against an across-the-board change in interest rates. For example, if short-term and long-term interest rates do not move exactly together, Potterton would have to consider two volatility measures. It would need to ensure that its assets and liabilities were equally affected by changes in the short-term rate and also that they were equally affected by changes in the long rate.[10]

Third, as interest rates change and time passes, the duration of Potterton's asset may no longer be the same as that of its liability. Thus, to remain hedged against interest rate changes, Potterton must be prepared to keep adjusting the duration of its debt.

If Potterton is not disposed to follow this dynamic hedging strategy, it has an alternative. It can devise a debt issue whose cash flows exactly match the rental income from the lease. For example, suppose that it issues an 8-year sinking fund bond; the amount of the sinking fund is $810,000 in year 1 and the payment increases by 12% annually. Table 25-4 shows that the bond payments (interest plus sinking fund) are $2 million in each year.

Since the cash flows on the asset exactly match those on the liability, Potterton's financial manager can now relax. Each year the manager simply collects the $2 million rental income and hands it to the bondholders. Whatever happens to interest rates, the firm is always perfectly hedged.

Why would not Potterton's financial manager *always* prefer to construct matching assets and liabilities? One reason is that it may be relatively costly to devise a bond with a specially tailored pattern of cash flows. Another may be that Potterton is continually entering into new lease agreements and issuing new debt. In this case the manager can never relax; it may be simpler to keep the duration of the assets and liabilities equal than to maintain an exact match between the cash flows.

In our Molson example the dealer hedged by buying a diversified portfolio of shares. In the case of Potterton Leasing the company hedged by selling bonds. We now need to introduce you to a number of instruments that are specially designed for hedging. These are **futures**, **forwards**, **swaps**, and (your old friend) options. They are all referred to as **derivative instruments** because their value

---

[10] In practice short-term and long-term interest rates do not move in exact lockstep. In addition short rates vary *more* than long rates. Despite this, hedging policies based on a simple duration measure are hard to beat. (See J. Nelson and S. M. Schaefer, "The Dynamics of the Term Structure and Alternative Portfolio Immunization Strategies" in G. O. Bierwag, G. G. Kaufman, and A. Toevs, eds., *Innovations in Bond Portfolio Management: Duration Analysis and Immunization*, Greenwich, Conn.: JAI Press, 1983.) As so often in finance, simple rules are hard to beat.

depends on the value of another asset. You can think of them as side-bets on the value of the underlying asset.[11]

We start with the oldest actively traded derivative instruments, futures contracts. Futures were originally developed for agricultural and similar commodities.

25-3   HEDGING WITH FUTURES

Before the harvest, a wheat farmer cannot be sure of the price at which he will be able to sell his crop. If he does not like this uncertainty, he can reduce it by selling wheat **futures**. In this case he agrees to deliver so many bushels of wheat in the future at a price that is set today. Do not confuse this futures contract with an option where the holder has a choice whether or not to make delivery; the farmer's futures contract is a firm promise to deliver wheat.

A miller is in the opposite position. She needs to *buy* wheat after the harvest. If she would like to fix the price of this wheat ahead of time, she can do so by *buying* wheat futures. In other words, she agrees to take delivery of wheat in the future at a price that is fixed today. The miller also does not have an option; if she holds the contract to maturity, she is obliged to take delivery.

Both the farmer and the miller have less risk than before.[12] The farmer has hedged risk by *selling* wheat futures; this is termed a *short hedge*. The miller has hedged risk by *buying* wheat futures; this is known as a *long hedge*.

Hedgers are not the only buyers and sellers of futures. The market also needs speculators who are prepared to take on risk. For example, if there is an excess of short hedgers like our farmer, the price of futures will be forced down until a sufficient number of speculators are prepared to buy in hope of a profit. If there is an excess of long hedgers like our miller, the futures price will rise until a sufficient number of speculators are prepared to sell wheat futures.

The price of wheat for immediate delivery is known as the **spot price**. When the farmer sells wheat futures, the price that he agrees to take for his wheat may be very different from the spot price. But as the date for delivery approaches, a futures contract becomes more and more like a spot contract and the price of the future gets closer and closer to the spot price.

The farmer may decide to wait until his futures contract matures and then deliver wheat to the buyer. In practice such delivery is very rare, for it is more convenient for the farmer to buy back the wheat futures just before maturity.[13] If he is properly hedged, any loss of his wheat crop will be exactly offset by the profit on his sale and subsequent repurchase of wheat futures.

Commodity and Financial Futures

Futures contracts are bought and sold on organized futures exchanges. Table 25-1 lists the principal commodity futures contracts and the exchanges on which they are traded. Notice that our farmer and miller are not the only businesses that

---

[11] "Side-bets" conjures up an image of wicked speculators. Derivative instruments attract their share of speculators, some of whom may be wicked, but they are also used by sober and prudent business people who simply want to reduce risk.

[12] We are oversimplifying. The miller won't reduce risk if bread prices vary in proportion to the post-harvest wheat price. In this case the miller is in the hazardous position of having fixed her cost but not her selling price. This point is discussed in A. C. Shapiro and S. Titman, "An Integrated Approach to Corporate Risk Management," *Midland Corporate Finance Journal*, **3**: 41–56 (Summer 1985).

[13] In the case of some of the financial futures described below, you *cannot* deliver the asset. At maturity the buyer simply receives (or pays) the difference between the spot price and the price at which he or she agreed to purchase the asset.

can hedge risk with commodity futures. The lumber company and the builder can hedge against changes in timber prices, the copper producer and cable manufacturer against changes in copper prices, the oil producer and the trucker against changes in gasoline prices, and so on.[14]

For many firms the wide fluctuations in interest rates and exchange rates have become at least as important a source of risk as changes in commodity prices. The financial futures listed in Table 25-2 allow firms also to hedge against these risks. Financial futures are similar to commodity futures but, instead of placing an order to buy or sell a commodity at a future date, you place an order to buy or sell a financial asset at a future date.

Financial futures have been a remarkably successful innovation. They were invented in 1972; within a few years, trading in financial futures significantly exceeded trading in commodity futures.

The Mechanics of Futures Trading

When you buy or sell a futures contract, the price is fixed today but payment is not made until later. You will, however, be asked to put up margin in the form of either cash or Treasury bills to demonstrate that you have the money to honour your side of the bargain. As long as you earn interest on the margined securities, there is no cost to you.

In addition, futures contracts are *marked to market*. This means that each day any profits or losses on the contract are calculated; you pay the Exchange any losses and receive any profits. For example, suppose that our farmer agreed to deliver 100,000 bushels of wheat at $2.50 a bushel. The next day the price of wheat futures declines to $2.45 a bushel. The farmer now has a profit on his sale of $100,000 \times \$0.05 = \$5,000$. The Exchange's clearinghouse therefore pays this $5,000 to the farmer. You can think of the farmer as closing out his position every day and then opening up a new position. Thus, after the first day the farmer has realized a profit of $5,000 on his trade and now has an obligation to deliver wheat for $2.45 a bushel.

Of course, our miller is in the opposite position. The fall in the futures price leaves her with a *loss* of 5 cents a bushel. She must, therefore, pay over this loss to the Exchange's clearinghouse. In effect, the miller closes out her initial purchase at a 5-cent loss and opens a new contract to take delivery at $2.45 a bushel.

Spot and Futures Prices — Financial Futures

If you want to buy a security, you have a choice. You can buy it for immediate delivery at the spot price. Alternatively, you can place an order for later delivery; in this case you buy at the futures price. When you buy a financial future, you end up with exactly the same security that you would have if you bought in the spot market. However, there are two differences. First, you don't pay for the security "up front," and so you can earn interest on its purchase price. Second, you miss out on any dividends or interest that are paid in the interim. This tells us something about the relationship between the spot and futures prices.[15]

---

[14] By the time you read this, the list of futures contracts will almost certainly be out of date. Unsuccessful contracts are regularly dropped and at any time the Exchanges are seeking approval for literally dozens of new contracts.

[15] This relationship is strictly true only if the contract is not marked to market. Otherwise, the value of the future depends on the path of interest rates up to the delivery date. In practice, this qualification is usually unimportant. See J. C. Cox, J. E. Ingersoll, and S. A. Ross, "The Relationship between Forward and Futures Prices," *Journal of Financial Economics*, **9**: 321–346 (1981).

$$\frac{\text{Futures price}}{(1 + r_f)^t} = \frac{\text{spot}}{\text{price}} - \text{PV} \begin{pmatrix} \text{dividends or} \\ \text{interest payments} \\ \text{forgone} \end{pmatrix}$$

Here r_f is the t-period risk-free interest rate.

Two examples will show how and why this formula works.

EXAMPLE: STOCK INDEX FUTURES   Suppose 6-month stock index futures trade at 320.28 when the index is 314. The 6-month interest rate is 8.2% and the average dividend yield of stocks in the index is 4% per year. Are these numbers consistent?

Suppose you buy the futures contract and set aside the money to exercise it. At an 8.2% annual rate, you'll earn about 4% interest over the next 6 months. Thus you invest:

$$\frac{\text{Futures price}}{(1 + r_f)^t} = \frac{320.28}{1.04} = 307.96$$

What do you get in return? Everything you would have gotten by buying the index now at the spot price, except for the dividends paid over the next 6 months. If we assume for simplicity that a half-year's dividends are paid on month 6 (rather than evenly over 6 months), your payoff is:

$$\frac{\text{Spot}}{\text{price}} - \text{PV (dividends)} = 314 - \frac{314(.02)}{1.04}$$
$$= 307.96$$

You get what you pay for.

EXAMPLE: FOREIGN EXCHANGE FUTURES   Suppose that you decide to buy 1-year Swiss franc futures rather than buying spot francs. Since you don't take delivery of the francs for a year, you earn an extra year's interest on your dollars. On the other hand, you also miss the opportunity to earn a year's interest on the francs. That lost interest plays the same role as the lost dividends on the stock index contract. Thus, if $r_\$$ is the dollar interest rate,

$$\frac{\begin{array}{c}\text{Futures price}\\\text{of Swiss francs}\end{array}}{1 + r_\$} = \frac{\text{spot}}{\text{price}} - \text{PV} \begin{pmatrix} \text{forgone} \\ \text{interest on} \\ \text{Swiss francs} \end{pmatrix}$$

Now the interest forgone is at the Swiss franc rate r_{sf}, and

$$\text{PV} \begin{pmatrix} \text{forgone} \\ \text{interest} \end{pmatrix} = \frac{r_{sf} \times \text{spot price}}{1 + r_{sf}}$$

A bit of algebra gives:

$$\begin{array}{c}\text{Futures}\\\text{price of}\\\text{Swiss francs}\end{array} = \text{spot price} \times \left(\frac{1 + r_\$}{1 + r_{sf}} \right)$$

This relationship between the futures and spot prices of currency is an important one which we will come back to in Chapter 34, International Financial Management.

Spot and
Futures
Prices —
Commodities

The difference between buying *commodities* today and commodity futures is more complicated. First, because payment is again delayed, the buyer of the future earns interest on her money. Second, she does not need to store the commodities and, therefore, savings warehouse costs, wastage, and so on. On the other hand, the futures contract gives no *convenience yield*, which is the value of being able to get your hands on the real thing. The manager of a supermarket can't burn heating oil futures if there's a sudden cold snap and he can't stock the shelves with orange juice futures if he runs out of inventory at 1 P.M. on a Saturday. All this means that for commodities,

$$\frac{\text{Futures price}}{(1 + r_f)^t} = \frac{\text{spot}}{\text{price}} + \text{PV}\left(\frac{\text{storage}}{\text{costs}}\right) - \text{PV}\left(\frac{\text{convenience}}{\text{yield}}\right)$$

No one would be willing to hold the futures contract at a higher futures price or to hold the commodity at a lower futures price.[16]

You can't observe PV (storage costs) or PV (convenience yield) separately, but you can infer the difference between them by comparing the spot price to the discounted futures price. Table 25-5 does this for a half-dozen commodities in March 1990. For copper, orange juice, and soybean oil the convenience yield outweighed the storage costs. For coffee it was the other way around. For cocoa and corn, storage cost and convenience yield more or less balanced out.

Though interesting, these figures are not necessarily typical. Spreads between commodity spot and futures prices can bounce around. For example, convenience yields on oil and gasoline can rise to very high levels when troubles in the Middle East revive fears of an interruption of supply.

Table 25-5
Spreads between spot and discounted futures prices reveal the difference between storage costs and convenience yield. These figures are based on 1-year futures contracts in mid-March 1990.

Commodity	Futures Price	Futures Price Discounted[a]	Spot Price[b]	PV (Storage Costs) Less PV (Convenience Yield)[c]
Cocoa, per ton	$113.8	109.25	$109.5	−0.25 (−0.2%)
Coffee, per pound	1.1	1.056	1.0188	0.037 (3.7%)
Copper, per pound	1.020	0.979	1.198	−0.219 (−18.3%)
Corn, per bushel	2.5675	2.4649	2.43	0.0349 (1.4%)
Frozen orange juice, per pound	1.7255	1.6565	1.9125	−0.256 (−13.4%)
Soybean oil, per pound	0.21	0.2016	0.2212	−0.0196 (−8.9%)

[a] Interest rate of 8% assumed.

[b] Spot prices assumed equal to prices of futures maturing in March 1990.

[c] Figures in parentheses are percentages of spot prices.

---

[16] The futures price could be less than given by our formula if no one is willing to hold the commodity, that is, if inventories fall to zero or some absolute minimum.

Setting Up a
Futures Hedge

Setting up a hedge with futures is no different from setting up any other hedge. Suppose that you are a farmer with 100,000 bushels of wheat to sell next September. You are worried that the price of wheat may decline in the interim and therefore decide to hedge by selling 100,000 bushels of September wheat futures. This effectively fixes the price at which you will sell your wheat.

Think about your position. You have an asset (wheat) and an offsetting liability (the sale of wheat futures). As long as the asset you own and the asset that you have promised to deliver are identical, you don't need complicated calculations to tell you that the two are likely to change equally in price. In other words, the hedge delta is 1.0:

$$\text{Expected change in value of wheat you own} = 1.0 \times \text{change in value of wheat you promise to deliver}$$

That is why you hedge your 100,000 bushels of wheat by selling 100,000 bushels of wheat futures.

In practice, the wheat that you expect to own and the wheat that you have sold in the futures markets are *unlikely* to be identical. For example, if you sell wheat futures on the Kansas City exchange, you agree to deliver hard red winter wheat in Kansas City in September. But perhaps you are growing northern spring wheat in Canada many miles from Kansas City. If the prices of the two wheats do not move exactly together, you will not be able to hedge away all your risk. Futures traders describe this remaining risk as *basis risk*.

25-4 FORWARD CONTRACTS

Each day billions of dollars of futures contracts are bought and sold. This liquidity is possible only because futures contracts are standardized and mature on a limited number of dates each year.

Fortunately there is usually more than one way to skin a financial cat. If the terms of futures contracts do not suit your particular needs, you may be able to buy or sell a **forward contract**. Forward contracts are simply tailor-made futures contracts. For example, suppose that you know that at the end of 6 months you are going to need a 3-month loan. You can lock in the interest rate on that loan by buying a **forward rate agreement** (FRA) from a bank.[17] For example, the bank might offer to sell you a 6-month forward rate agreement on 3-month LIBOR at 7%. If at the end of 6 months the 3-month LIBOR rate is greater than 7%, the bank will pay you the difference: If the 3-month LIBOR is less than 7%, you pay the bank the difference.[18]

Turnover in FRAs has now reached $500 billion a year, but this is very small beer compared with the huge volume of business in forward currency. Banks regularly buy and sell forward currency for dates up to 1 year ahead, and in the case of the major currencies they are increasingly prepared to enter into contracts for 5 years or more.

All this may make forwards sound more attractive than futures. However, banks charge a higher rate if you want to buy forward currency for odd amounts

---

[17] Notice that the party that profits from a rise in rates is described as the "buyer." In our example she is usually said to buy "6 against 9 months" money, meaning that the forward agreement is for a 3-month loan in 6 months' time.

[18] Unlike futures contracts, forwards are not marked to market. Thus, all profits or losses are settled when the contract matures.

or for odd periods. And, if you change your mind and decide that you want to sell your forward contract, you must renegotiate with the bank.

Homemade Forward Contracts

Suppose that you borrow $90.91 for 1 year at 10% and lend $90.91 for 2 years at 12%. These interest rates are for loans made today; therefore, they are spot interest rates.

The cash flows on your transactions are as follows:

	Year		
	0	1	2
Borrow for 1 year at 10%	+90.91	−100	
Lend for 2 years at 12%	−90.91		+114.04
Net cash flow	0	−100	+114.04

Notice that you do not have any net cash outflow today but you have contracted to pay out money in year 1. The interest rate on this forward commitment is 14.04%. To calculate this forward interest rate we simply worked out the extra return for lending for 2 years rather than 1:

$$\text{Forward interest rate} = \frac{(1 + 2\text{-year spot rate})^2}{1 + 1\text{-year spot rate}} - 1$$
$$= \frac{1.12^2}{1.10} - 1 = 0.1404, \text{ or } 14.04\%$$

In our example you manufactured a forward loan by borrowing short-term and lending long. But you can also run the process in reverse. If you wish to fix today the rate at which you borrow next year, you borrow long and lend short.

You can also construct a do-it-yourself forward contract to buy or sell foreign exchange. For example, suppose that you want to place an order today to buy Swiss frances in 1 year. The current (or spot) exchange rate is 1 france = $0.50, the 1-year dollar interest rate is 6%, and the 1-year franc interest rate is 4%. You now borrow $50 for 1 year, exchange these dollars into francs, and lend your francs for a year. Your cash flows are as follows:

	Now		After 1 Year	
	Dollars	Francs	Dollars	Francs
Borrow dollars at 6%	+50		−53	
Change dollars into francs	−50	+100		
Lend francs at 4%		−100		+104
Net cash flow	0	0	−53	+104

Your net cash flow today is zero but you have committed to pay out $53 at the end of the year and receive 104 francs. Thus, you have constructed a homemade forward contract to buy Swiss francs at an exchange rate of 1 franc = 53/104 = $0.51.

We stated in Section 25-3 that the 1-year futures price for Swiss francs is

$$\text{Spot price of francs} \times \frac{1 + \text{dollar interest rate}}{1 + \text{franc interest rate}}$$

That better turn out to equal $0.51, the cost of our homemade forward contract. It does:

$$\text{Futures price of francs} = 0.50 \times \frac{1.06}{1.04} = \$0.51$$

What would happen if the price of futures were higher than this figure? Everyone would rush to sell futures, borrow dollars, and lend francs. If the futures price were lower, they would do the reverse. Sharp-eyed arbitrageurs with families to support are constantly on the lookout for such discrepancies.

If you can make your own forward contracts for interest rates or currencies, why does anyone bother to trade on the financial futures exchanges? The answer is, "Convenience and cost." Some of the most popular futures contracts are the interest rate and currency futures contracts that are closest to maturity. In principle, these are the easiest to replicate but the huge volume of business in financial futures makes them a very low-cost tool for hedging (or speculation).

25-5   SWAPS

Suppose that the Possum Company wishes to borrow deutschemarks to help finance its European operations. Since Possum is better known in Canada, the financial manager believes that the company can obtain more attractive terms on a dollar loan than on a deutschemark loan. Therefore, the company issues $10 million of 5-year 12% notes in Canada. At the same time Possum arranges with a bank to **swap** its future dollar liability for deutschemarks. Under this arrangement the bank agrees to pay Possum sufficient dollars to service its dollar loan; in exchange Possum agrees to make a series of annual payments in deutschemarks to the bank.

Here are Possum's cash flows (in millions):

	Year 0		Years 1–4		Year 5	
	$	**DM**	**$**	**DM**	**$**	**DM**
1. Issue dollar loan	+10		−1.2		−11.2	
2. Swap dollars for deutschemarks (DM)	−10	+20	+1.2	−1.6	+11.2	−21.6
3. Net cash flow	0	+20	0	−1.6	0	−21.6

The combined effect of Possum's two steps (line 3) is to convert a 12% dollar loan into an 8% deutschemark loan. The device that makes this possible is the currency swap. You can think of the cash flows for the swap (line 2) as a series of forward currency contracts. In each of years 1 through 4 Possum agrees to purchase $1.2 million at a cost of 1.6 million deutschemarks; in year 5 it agrees to buy $11.2 million at a cost of 21.6 million deutschemarks.[19]

---

[19] Usually in a currency swap the two parties make an initial payment to each other (i.e., Possum pays the bank $10 million and receives 20 million deutschemarks). However, this is not necessary, and in the case of interest rate swaps that are in the *same* currency no initial payments occur and there are no final principal repayments. Interest rate swaps are explained below.

The bank's cash flows from the swap are the reverse of Possum's. It has undertaken to pay out dollars in the future and receive deutschemarks. Since the bank is now exposed to the risk that the deutschemark will weaken unexpectedly against the dollar, it will try to hedge this risk by a series of futures or forward contracts or by swapping deutschemarks for dollars with another counterparty. As long as Possum and the other counterparty honour their promises, the bank is fully protected against risk. The recurring nightmare for swap managers is that one party will default, leaving the bank with a large unmatched position.

Swaps are not new. For many years the British government limited purchases of foreign currency to invest abroad. These restrictions led many British firms to arrange so-called back-to-back loans. The firm would lend sterling to a company in the United States and simultaneously borrow dollars which could then be used for foreign investment. In taking out the back-to-back loan the British firm agreed to make a series of future dollar payments in exchange for receiving a flow of sterling income.

In 1979 these limits on overseas investment were removed and British firms no longer needed to take out back-to-back loans. However, during the 1980s the banks did a "respray" job on the back-to-back loan and relaunched it as a swap. Swaps turned out to be very popular with corporate customers; in recent years, about 70% of dollar eurobond issues have been accompanied by a swap.[20]

Swaps are not limited to future exchanges of currency. For example, firms often swap fixed-interest-rate loans for floating-rate loans. In this case one party promises to make a series of fixed annual payments in return for receiving a series of payments that are linked to the level of short-term interest rates. Sometimes, also, swaps are used to convert between floating-rate loans that are tied to different base rates. For example, a firm might wish to swap a series of payments that are linked to the prime rate for a series of payments that are linked to the Treasury bill rate. It is even possible to swap commodities. In this case you don't need to deliver the commodities, you just settle up any differences in their value.[21]

For example, an oil producer could lock in its selling price of oil by agreeing to pay an amount that goes up and down with an index of oil prices, while the other party pays the oil company a fixed stream of payments. In contrast, an airline could lock in the price at which it *buys* oil by paying a fixed cash amount while the other party pays an amount that is linked to oil prices.

25-6 HEDGING WITH OPTIONS

In Chapter 20 we came across options. These give you the right, but not the obligation, to buy or sell an asset. Options are another example of a derivative instrument—that is, their value depends only on what happens to the price of the underlying asset.

The *option delta* summarizes the link between the option and the asset. For example, if you own an option to buy a share of Molson stock, the change in the value of your investment will be the same as if you held delta shares of Molson.

Since the option price is tied to the asset price, options can be used for hedging.

---

[20] See *Euromoney Corporate Finance*, May 1987, p. 70.

[21] You also encounter forwards on swaps, options on swaps (or "swaptions"), callable swaps, and puttable swaps.

Thus, if you own the option to buy a share of Molson and at the same time you sell delta shares of Molson, any change in the value of your position in the stock will be exactly offset by a change in the value of your option position. In other words, you will be perfectly hedged.

EXAMPLE   Here is another example. Imagine that you have won the contract for a large construction project in France. Payment will be in francs but many of your costs will be in U.S. dollars.[22] Therefore, if the value of the franc declines, you could have a large loss on your hands.

There are several ways to hedge yourself against this currency risk:

• sell franc futures, or
• sell the franc forward, or
• acquire an option to sell the franc at today's price.

If you use options to hedge the currency risk, there are two things to look out for. First, as we showed in Chapter 20, the option delta depends on the volatility of the asset: if you misestimate volatility, you will not buy the correct number of options and you will not be properly hedged. Second, as time passes and the exchange rate changes, the option delta will also change. So you need to continually adjust your holdings in order to remain hedged.

This may make options seem a less natural tool for risk management, but there are occasions when it is simpler to use options than futures or forwards. Consider the following problem. Imagine that you have only just bid for the construction project and that it will be several months before you know whether your bid is successful. In the meantime the value of the franc may have declined and the contract may no longer be profitable.

In this situation there is no straightforward way to avoid *all* currency risk because you can't hedge against whether you are awarded the contract. For example, if you sell futures and you don't get the contract, then you will lose money if the franc *appreciates*.

In these cases companies often use options to insure against extreme outcomes. In our example you would do this by taking out an option to sell francs. If you get the contract and the franc depreciates, the profit on the option should offset the reduction in the value of the contract. If you *don't* get the contract, you have got an option which could turn out to be very valuable if the franc depreciates.

Of course, insurance doesn't come free; the price you pay for the option is the insurance premium. If the franc appreciates, you have with hindsight bought unnecessary insurance.

25-7   SUMMARY

As a manager, you are paid to take risks, but you are not paid to take *any* risks. Some are simply bad bets and others could jeopardize the success of the firm. In these cases you should look for ways to hedge.

---

[22] If your costs will be in Canadian dollars, you may have to first hedge francs against U.S. dollars and then U.S. dollars against Canadian dollars. There are many more financial contracts denominated in U.S. dollars than Canadian dollars. You may even be comfortable absorbing the risk that the Canadian dollar will move against the U.S. dollar by hedging into U.S. dollars only.

The idea behind hedging is straightforward. You find two closely related assets. You then buy one and sell the other in proportions that minimize the risk of your net position. If the assets are *perfectly* correlated, you can make the net position risk-free.

The trick is to find the hedge ratio, or delta—that is, the number of units of one asset that is needed to offset changes in the value of the other asset. Sometimes the best solution is to look at how the prices of the two assets have moved together in the past. For example, suppose that a 1% change in the value of B has been accompanied on average by a 2% change in the value of A. Then delta equals 2.0; to hedge each dollar invested in A you need to sell $2 of B.

On other occasions a little theory can help to find delta. For example, we showed how the average life of a fixed income stream can be measured by its "duration." If you buy a bond to hedge a fixed money liability, delta depends on the relative durations of the liability and the bond.

If the value of the asset *equals* the value of the liability, the net investment in the hedge is zero. We described this as a "zero-value" hedge. You can always convert any hedge into a zero-value hedge. If the value of the asset is *less* than the value of the liability, you put the difference into a bank deposit. If the value of the asset *exceeds* the liability, you can convert to a zero-value hedge by borrowing from the bank.

Some hedging strategies are static. Once you have set up the hedge, you can take a long vacation, confident that the firm is well-protected. Most hedging strategies are dynamic. As time passes and prices change, you may need to rebalance your position to maintain the hedge.

Firms use a number of tools to hedge:

1. Futures contracts are advance orders to buy or sell an asset. The price is fixed today but payment does not occur until the delivery date. The futures markets allow firms to place advance orders for dozens of different commodities, securities, and currencies.
2. Futures contracts are highly standardized and are traded in huge volume on the futures exchanges. Instead of buying or selling a standardized futures contract, you may be able to arrange a tailor-made contract with a bank. These tailor-made futures contracts are usually called "forward" contracts. Firms regularly protect themselves against exchange rate changes by buying or selling forward currency contracts.
3. It is also sometimes possible to construct homemade forward contracts. For example, as an alternative to buying forward currency, you could borrow dollars, exchange them for foreign currency, and then lend the foreign currency until it is needed. This would have exactly the same cash-flow consequences as a purchase of forward currency.
4. In recent years firms have entered into a variety of swap arrangements. For example, you may arrange for the bank to make all the future payments on your dollar loan in exchange for paying the bank the cost of servicing a deutschemark loan. Swaps are like packages of forward contracts.
5. If you own an option, you have the right to buy or sell the asset but you are not obliged to do so. The value of an option is linked to the value of the underlying asset by the option delta. So you can hedge against risk by taking offsetting positions in the option and in delta units of the underlying asset. Instead of trying to eliminate all risk, managers may also use options to insure themselves against extreme outcomes.

FURTHER READING

The following are general articles on corporate risk management:

R. W. Anderson and J. P. Danthine, "Cross Hedging," *Journal of Political Economy*, **89**: 1182–1196 (1981).

A. C. Shapiro and S. Titman, "An Integrated Approach to Corporate Risk Management," *Midland Corporate Finance Journal*, **3**: 41–56 (Summer 1985).

C. W. Smith and R. M. Stultz, "The Determinants of Firms' Hedging Policies," *Journal of Financial and Quantitative Analysis*, **20**: 391–405 (December 1985).

The following book is a general study of market innovation but it includes very useful material on swaps, forward rate agreements, and so forth:

Bank for International Settlements, *Recent Innovations in International Banking*, Basel, April 1986.

Hodges and Schaefer's article provides an example of how to hedge interest rate risk with exactly matching portfolios. Schaefer's paper is a useful review of how duration measures are used to immunize fixed liabilities:

S. D. Hodges and S. M. Schaefer, "A Model for Bond Portfolio Improvement," *Journal of Financial and Quantitative Analysis*, **12**: 243–260 (1977).

S. M. Schaefer, "Immunisation and Duration: A Review of Theory, Performance and Applications," *Midland Corporate Finance Journal*, **3**: 41–58 (Autumn 1984).

For material on futures and swaps see:

D. Duffie, *Futures Markets*, Prentice Hall, Englewood Cliffs N.J., 1988.

S. Figlewski, K. John, and J. Merrick, *Hedging with Financial Futures for Institutional Investors: From Theory to Practice*, Ballinger Publishing Company, Cambridge, Mass., 1986.

S. K. Henderson and J. A. M. Price, *Currency and Interest Rate Swaps*, Butterworths & Co., London, 1984.

D. R. Siegel and D. F. Siegel, *Futures Markets*, Dryden Press, Hinsdale IL, 1990.

C. W. Smith, C. W. Smithson, and L. M. Wakeman, "The Evolving Market for Swaps," *Midland Corporate Finance Journal*, **3**: 20–32 (Winter 1986).

QUIZ

1. True or false?
   (a) A perfect hedge of asset A requires an asset B that's perfectly correlated with A.
   (b) Hedging transactions in an active futures market have zero or slightly negative NPVs.
   (c) Longer maturity bonds necessarily have longer durations.
   (d) The longer a bond's duration, the lower is its volatility.
   (e) When you buy a futures contract, you pay now for delivery at a future date.
   (f) The holder of a futures contract receives the convenience yield on the underlying commodity.
   (g) The holder of a financial futures contract misses out on any dividend or interest payments made on the underlying security.
2. You own a $1 million portfolio of aerospace stocks with a beta of 1.2. You are enthusiastic about aerospace but uncertain about the prospects for the overall stock market. Explain how you could "hedge out" your market exposure by selling the market short. How much would you sell? How in practice would you go about "selling the market"?
3. Calculate the durations and volatilities of securities A, B, and C. Their cash flows are shown below. The interest rate is 8%.

	Period		
	1	2	3
A	40	40	40
B	20	20	120
C	10	10	110

4. Suppose you have promised to pay out $100 in period 3. Explain how you could hedge the present value of this liability by investing in Security A from Quiz question 3. Could you also hedge by buying B or C?

5. Calculate the value of a 6-month futures contract on a Treasury bond. You have the following information:

   • 6-month interest rate = 10% per year, or 4.9% for 6 months.
   • Spot price of bond = 95.
   • Coupon payments on the bond over the next 6 months have a present value of 4.

6. Calculate PV (convenience yield) for magnoosium scrap from the following information:

   • Spot price = $2,550 per ton.
   • Futures price = $2,408 for a 1-year contract.
   • Interest rate = 12%.
   • PV (storage costs) = $100 per year.

7. What is the currency swap? An interest-rate swap? Give one example of how each might be used.

QUESTIONS AND PROBLEMS

1. Legs Diamond owns shares in Vanguard Index 500 mutual fund worth $1 million on July 15. (This is an index fund that tracks the Standard & Poor's 500.) He wants to cash in now but his accountant advises him to wait 6 months so as to defer a large capital gains tax. Explain to Legs how he can use stock index futures to hedge out his exposure to market movements over the next 6 months. Could Legs "cash in" without actually selling his shares? Explain.

2. Refer back to question 1. Suppose that the nearest index futures contract matures in 7 months rather than 6. Show how Legs Diamond can still use index futures to hedge his position. How would the maturity date affect the hedge ratio?

3. Price changes on two gold-mining stocks have shown strong positive correlation. Their historical relationship is

$$\text{Average percentage change in A} = 0.001 + 0.75 \left(\text{percentage change in B} \right)$$

Changes in B explain 60% of the variation of the changes in A ($R^2 = 0.6$).
(a) Suppose you own $100,000 of A. How much of B should you sell to minimize the risk of your net position?
(b) What is the hedge ratio?

(c) How would you construct a zero-value hedge?

(d) Here is the historical relationship between A and gold prices:

$$\text{Average percentage change in A} = -0.002 + 1.2 \begin{pmatrix} \text{percentage} \\ \text{change in} \\ \text{gold price} \end{pmatrix}$$

If $R^2 = 0.5$, can you lower the risk of your net position by hedging with gold (or gold futures) rather than with stock B? Explain.

4. In Section 25-2, we stated that the duration of the 13s of 1996 was 4.043 years. Construct a table like Table 25-2 to show that this is so.

5. In Section 25-2, we stated that the duration of Potterton's lease equals the duration of its debt.

(a) Show that this is so.

(b) Now suppose that the interest rate falls to 3%. Show how the value of the lease and the debt package are now affected by a 0.5% rise or fall in the interest rate. What would Potterton need to do to reestablish the interest-rate hedge?

6. Line 1 of the following table shows cash outflows that your company has just promised to make. Below that are the cash flows on a blue-chip corporate note. The interest rate is 10%. Your company can borrow at this rate if it wishes.

	Year			
	1	2	3	4
Liability in millions	0	0	−$20	−$20
Note's cash payments as percent of face value	12	12	12	12

(a) Calculate the durations of the liability and the note.

(b) How much must you invest in the note to hedge the liability?

(c) How would you construct a zero-value hedge?

(d) Would this hedge continue to protect your company
   (i) If interest rates dropped by 3%?
   (ii) If short-term interest rates fluctuate while longer-terms remain basically constant?
   (iii) If interest rates remain the same but 2 years pass?

(e) Can you set up a hedge portfolio that relieves the financial manager of all the worries mentioned in (d)? Describe that portfolio.

7. Explain the chief differences between futures and forward contracts, e.g., for foreign exchange.

8. In March 1990, 6-month futures on the New York Stock Exchange Composite Index traded at 189.75. Spot was 185.77. Assume an interest rate of 8.5%. What was the PV of the average dividend yield on the stocks in this index?

9. Table 25-6 contains spot and 6-month futures prices for several commodities and financial instruments. There may be some money-making opportunities. See if you can find them, and explain how you would trade to take advantage of them. The interest rate is 14.5% or 7% over the 6-month life of the contracts.

CHAPTER 25 Hedging Financial Risk   **685**

Table 25-6
Spot and 6-month futures prices for selected commodities and securities

Commodity	Spot Price	Futures Price	Comments
Magnoosium, per ton	$ 2,550	$ 2,728.50	PV (storage costs) = PV (convenience yield)
Frozen Quiche, per pound	0.50	0.514	PV (storage costs) = 0.10 per pound; PV (convenience yield) = 0.05 per pound
PEI Hydro 8s of 2002	77	78.39	4% semiannual coupon payment due just before futures contract expires
Costaguanan Pulgas (currency), in Pulgas per dollar	9,300	6,900	Costaguanan interest rate is 95% per year
Establishment Industries common stock	95	97.54	Establishment pays dividends of $2 per quarter. Next dividend is paid 2 months from now
Cheap white wine, per 10,000 gallon tank	$12,500	$14,200	PV (convenience yield) = $250 per tank. Your company unexpectedly has surplus storage and can store 50,000 gallons at no cost

10. The following table shows gold futures prices for varying contract lengths. Gold is predominantly an investment good, not an industrial commodity. Investors hold gold because it diversifies their portfolios and because they hope its price will rise. They do not hold it for its convenience yield.

   Calculate the interest rate faced by traders in gold futures for each of the contract lengths shown below. The spot price is $456.90 per ounce.

	Contract Length (Months)				
	1	3	9	15	21
Futures price	$458.90	464.50	483.30	503.90	425.70

11. The Commodities and Futures Trading Commission in the U.S. needs to be assured that new futures contracts serve the public interest. One of the tests that it applies is that the contract should provide price discovery — that is, the futures price should provide the public with new information on investors' forecasts of changes in spot prices. In justifying their proposals to trade index futures the exchanges have argued that index futures provide information about investor views on future prices. Evaluate this claim.

12. Firms A and B face the following borrowing rates for making a 5-year fixed-rate debt issue in dollars or Swiss francs:

	Dollars	Swiss Francs
Firm A	10%	7%
Firm B	8	6

Suppose that A wishes to borrow dollars and B wishes to borrow Swiss francs. Show how a swap could be used to reduce the borrowing costs of each company. Assume a spot exchange rate of 2 Swiss francs per dollar.

13. "Last year we had a substantial income in sterling, which we hedged by selling sterling forward. In the event sterling rose and our decision to sell forward cost us a lot of money. I think that in future we should either stop hedging our currency exposure or just hedge when we think sterling is overvalued." As financial manager, how would you respond to this chief executive's comment?

14. "Speculators want futures contracts to be incorrectly priced; hedgers want them to be correctly priced." Why?

15. Hoopoe Corp. wants to borrow 100 million dollars at a fixed rate with a maturity of 5 years. It calculates that it can make a eurobond issue with the following terms:

- Interest: $10\frac{5}{8}\%$ payable annually
- Maturity: 5 years
- Commissions: $1\frac{1}{8}\%$
- Agency fees: 0.15% on coupon; 0.075% on principal
- Issue expenses: 0.2%

A bank has presented Hoopoe with a proposal for a Swiss franc issue combined with a currency swap in dollars. The proposed terms for the Swiss franc issue are:

- Amount: 200 million Swiss francs
- Interest: $5\frac{3}{8}\%$ annually
- Maturity: 5 years
- Commissions: 2.8%
- Agency fees: 0.75% on coupon; 0.30% on principal
- Issue expenses: 0.2%

The counterparty of the swap would raise fixed dollars on the following terms:

- Amount: 100 million dollars (equivalent to 200 million Swiss francs)
- Interest: $10\frac{5}{8}\%$ annually
- Maturity: 5 years
- Commissions: 1.8%
- Agency expenses: 0.15% on coupon; 0.075% on principal
- Issue expenses: 0.2%

The counterparty would be happy with an all-in cost in Swiss francs of 6.4%.

(a) Which alternative should Hoopoe undertake? (Ignore credit risk in your analysis.)

(b) Suppose that you are the corporate finance manager of Hoopoe. Discuss the credit risk issues involved in the alternatives.

16. If you buy a 9-month Treasury bill future, you undertake to buy a 3-month bill in 9 months time. Suppose that Treasury bills currently offer the following yields:

Months to maturity	Annual Yield (%)
3	6
6	6.5
9	7
12	8

What is the value of a 9-month bill future?

17. In 1985 a German corporation bought $250 million forward to cover a future purchase of goods from the United States. However, the dollar subsequently depreciated and the company found that, if it had waited and then bought spot dollars, it would have paid DM 225 million less. One financial manager pointed out that the company could have waited to buy the dollars and meanwhile covered its exposure using options. In that case it would have saved itself DM 225 million and would have lost only the cost of the option—around DM 20 million.[23] Evaluate the company's decision and the financial manager's criticism.

[23] Example cited in *Managing Risks and Costs through Financial Innovation*, Business International Corporation, New York, 1987.

C · H · A · P · T · E · R

26

LEASING

Most of us occasionally rent a car, bicycle, or boat. Usually such personal rentals are short-lived—we may rent a car for a day or week. But, in corporate finance, longer-term rentals are common. A rental agreement that extends for a year or more and involves a series of fixed payments is called a **lease**.

Firms lease as an alternative to buying capital equipment. Computers are often leased; so are trucks, railroad cars, aircraft, and ships. Just about every kind of asset including electric power plants, nuclear fuel, handball courts, and zoo animals,[1] has been leased sometime by somebody.

Every lease involves two parties. The *user* of the asset is called the **lessee**. The lessee makes periodic payments to the *owner* of the asset, who is called the **lessor**. For example, if you sign an agreement to rent an apartment for a year, you are the lessee and the owner is the lessor.

You often see references to the *leasing industry*. This refers to lessors. (Almost all firms are lessees to at least a minor extent.) Who are the lessors?

Some of the largest lessors are equipment manufacturers. For example, GATX is the largest lessor of railcars (it leased about 55,000 cars at the end of 1989); IBM is the largest lessor of computers, and Xerox is the largest lessor of copiers.

The other two major groups of lessors are banks and independent leasing companies. The latter offer a variety of services. Some act as lease brokers (arranging lease deals) as well as lessors. Others specialize in leasing automobiles, trucks, and standardized industrial equipment; they succeed because they can buy equipment in quantity, service it efficiently, and if necessary resell it at a good price. Independent computer leasing companies got started because some people believed that IBM's leasing charges were too high. Computer leasing companies buy equipment, mainly from IBM, and lease it to computer users at rates below IBM's.

---

[1] In 1988 computers accounted for just over 20% of new leasing business and aircraft for 15%. We don't have a figure for zoo animals. (See American Association of Equipment Lessors, *1988 Survey of Industry Activity*.)

26-1   WHAT IS A LEASE?

Leases come in many forms, but in all cases the lessee (user) promises to make a series of payments to the lessor (owner). The lease contract specifies the monthly or semi-annual payments, with the first payment usually due as soon as the contract is signed. The payments are usually level, but their time pattern can be tailored to the user's needs. For example, suppose that a manufacturer leases a machine to produce a complex new product. There will a year's "shake-down" period before volume production starts. In this case, it might be possible to arrange for lower payments during the first year of the lease.

When a lease is terminated, the leased equipment reverts to the lessor. However, the lease agreement often gives the user the option to purchase the equipment or take out a new lease.

Some leases are short-term and cancellable during the contract period at the option of the lessee: these are generally known as **operating leases**. Others extend over most of the estimated economic life of the asset and cannot be cancelled or can be cancelled only if the lessor is reimbursed for any losses: these are called **capital, financial**, or **full-payout leases**.[2]

Financial leases are a *source of financing*. Signing a financial lease contract is like borrowing money. There is an immediate cash inflow because the lessee is relieved of having to pay for the asset. But the lessee also assumes a binding obligation to make the payments specified in the lease contract. The user could have borrowed the full purchase price of the asset by accepting a binding obligation to make interest and principal payments to the lender. Thus, the cash flow consequences of leasing and borrowing are similar. In either case, the firm raises cash now and pays it back later. A large part of this chapter will be devoted to comparing leasing and borrowing as financing alternatives.

Leases also differ in the services provided by the lessor. Under a **full-service** or **rental** lease, the lessor promises to maintain and insure the equipment and to pay any property taxes due on it. In a **net** lease, the lessee agrees to maintain the asset, insure it, and pay any property taxes. Most financial leases are net leases.

Most financial leases are arranged for brand new assets. The lessee identifies the equipment, arranges for the leasing company to buy it from the manufacturer, and signs a contract with the leasing company. This is called a **direct** lease. In other cases, the firm sells an asset it already owns and leases it back from the buyer. These **sale and lease-back** arrangements are common in real estate. For example, firm X may wish to raise cash by selling a factory, but still retain use of the factory. It could do this by selling the factory for cash to a leasing company and simultaneously signing a long-term lease contract for the factory. Legal ownership of the factory passes to the leasing company but the right to use it stays with firm X.

You may also encounter **leveraged** leases. These are financial leases in which the lessor borrows part of the purchase price of the leased asset, using the lease contract as security for the loan. Leveraged lease deals are complicated, and so we defer discussion of them to the end of this chapter.

26-2   WHY LEASE?

You hear many suggestions about why companies should lease equipment rather than buy it. Let us look at some sensible reasons and then at four that are more dubious.

---

[2] In the shipping industry, a financial lease is often termed a *bareboat charter* or *demise hire*.

Sensible Reasons for Leasing

Short-Term Leases are Convenient   Suppose you want the use of a car for a week. You could buy one and sell it seven days later, but that would be silly. Quite apart from the fact that registered ownership is a nuisance, you would spend some time selecting a car, negotiating purchase, and arranging insurance. Then, at the end of the week, you must negotiate resale, and cancel registration and insurance. When you need a car for only a short time, it clearly makes sense to rent it. You save the trouble of registering ownership and you know the effective cost. In the same way, it pays a company to lease equipment that it needs for only a short time. Of course, this kind of lease is always an operating lease.

Sometimes the cost of short-term rentals may seem prohibitively high, for you may find it difficult to rent at any price. This can happen for equipment that is easily damaged by careless use. The owner knows that short-term users are unlikely to take the same care they would give to their own equipment. When the danger of abuse becomes too high, short-term rental markets do not survive. Thus, it is easy enough to buy a Maserati Bora, provided your pockets are deep enough, but nearly impossible to rent one.

Cancellation Options are Valuable   Computers are frequently leased on a short-term cancellable basis. It is difficult to estimate how rapidly such equipment will become obsolete, because the technology of computers is advancing rapidly and somewhat unpredictably. Leasing with an option to cancel passes the risk of premature obsolescence from the user to the lessor. Usually the lessor is a computer manufacturer or a computer leasing specialist and, therefore, knows more about the risk of obsolescence than the user. Thus, the lessor is better equipped than the user to bear these risks. It makes sense for the user to pay the lessor for the option to cancel. The payment comes in the form of higher lease payments. Some leases that *appear* expensive really are fairly priced once the option to cancel is recognized.

Maintenance is Provided   Under a full-service lease, the user receives maintenance and other services. Many lessors are well equipped to provide efficient maintenance. However, bear in mind that these benefits are likely to be reflected in higher lease payments.

Standardization Leads to Low Administrative and Transaction Costs   Suppose that you operate a leasing company that specializes in financial leases for trucks. You are effectively lending money to a large number of firms (the lessees), which may differ considerably in size and risk. But, because the underlying asset is in each case the same saleable item (a truck), you can safely "lend" the money (lease the truck) without conducting a detailed analysis of each firm's business. You can also use a simple, standard lease contract. This standardization makes it possible to "lend" small sums of money without incurring large investigative, administrative, or legal costs. Therefore, leasing is often a relatively cheap source of cash for the small company. It offers long-term financing on a flexible, piece-meal basis, with lower transaction costs than in a private placement or a public bond or stock issue.

Tax Shields Can be Used   The lessor owns the leased asset and deducts its depreciation (CCA) from taxable income. If the lessor can make better use of the CCA than an asset's user, it may make sense for the leasing company to own the equipment and pass on some of the tax benefits to the lessee in the form of low lease payments. We will see exactly how this works in the next section.

Some Dubious Reasons for Leasing

Leasing Avoids Capital Expenditure Controls   In many companies lease proposals are scrutinized as carefully as capital expenditure proposals, but in others leasing may enable an operating manager to avoid the elaborate approval procedures needed to buy an asset. Although this is a dubious reason for leasing, it may be influential, particularly in the public sector. For example, city hospitals have sometimes found it politically more convenient to lease their medical equipment than to ask the city government to provide funds for purchase.

Leasing Preserves Capital   Leasing companies provide "100% financing"; they advance the full cost of the leased asset. Consequently, they often claim that leasing preserves capital, allowing the firm to save its cash for other things.

But the firm can also "preserve capital" by borrowing money. If Greymare Bus Lines leases a $100,000 bus rather than buying it, it does conserve $100,000 cash. It could also (1) buy the bus for cash and (2) borrow $100,000 using the bus as security. Its bank balance ends up the same whether it leases or buys and borrows. It has the bus in either case, and it incurs a $100,000 liability in either case. What's so special about leasing?

Leases May Be Off-Balance-Sheet Financing   Until the end of 1976 financial leases were **off-balance-sheet-financing**. That is, a firm could buy an asset, finance it through a financial lease, and show neither the asset nor the lease contract on its balance sheet. The firm was required only to add a brief footnote to its accounts describing its lease obligation. Accounting standards now require that all *capital* (financial) leases be **capitalized**.[3] That is, the present value of the lease payments must be calculated and shown alongside debt on the right-hand side of the balance sheet. The same amount must be shown as an asset on the left-hand side of the balance sheet.[4]

In order to implement this new requirement, accountants had to come up with objective rules for distinguishing between operating and capital (financial) leases. They defined capital leases as leases that meet *any one* of the following requirements:

1. The lease agreement transfers ownership to the lessee before the lease expires.
2. The lessee can purchase the asset for a bargain price when the lease expires.
3. The lease lasts for at least 75% of the asset's estimated economic life.
4. The present value of the lease payments is at least 90% of the asset's value (less any investment tax credit taken by the lessor).

All other leases are operating leases as far as the accountants are concerned.

Some financial managers have tried to take advantage of this arbitrary boundary between operating and financial leases. Suppose that you wanted to finance a computer-controlled machine tool costing $1 million. The machine tool is expected to last for 12 years. You could sign a lease contract for 8 years, 11 months (just missing requirement 3) with lease payments having a present value of $899,000 (just missing requirement 4). You also make sure the lease contract avoids requirements 1 and 2. Result? You have off-balance-sheet financing. This

---

[3] See "Accounting for Leases," *Statement of Financial Accounting Standards No. 13*, Financial Accounting Standards Board, Stamford, Conn., 1976; and "Leases," Section 3065, *CICA Handbook, Accounting Recommendations*, Canadian Institute of Chartered Accountants, Toronto, 1978.

[4] This "asset" is then amortized over the life of the lease. The amortization is deducted from book income, just as depreciation is deducted for a purchased asset.

lease would not have to be capitalized, although it is clearly a long-term, fixed obligation.

Now we come to the $64 question: "Why should anyone *care* whether financing is off balance sheet or on balance sheet?" Shouldn't the financial manager worry about substance rather than appearance?

When a firm obtains off-balance-sheet financing, the conventional measures of financial leverage, such as the debt-equity ratio, understate the true degree of financial leverage. Some believe that financial analysts do not always notice off-balance-sheet lease obligations (which are still referred to in footnotes) or the greater volatility of earnings that results from the fixed lease payments. They may be right, but we would not expect such an imperfection to be widespread.

When a company borrows money, it must usually consent to certain restrictions on future borrowing. Early bond indentures did not include any restrictions on the extent to which the company could lease. Therefore, leasing was seen as a way to circumvent restrictive covenants. Loopholes such as these are easily stopped and most bond indentures now include limits on leasing.

Long-term lease obligations ought to be regarded as debt whether or not they appear on the balance sheet. Financial analysts may overlook minor debts. But major lease obligations are generally recognized and taken into account.

In May 1979, *Business Week* described the financial problems facing San Diego Gas and Electric Company (SDG&E). A "cash squeeze" on the company led to the following sale and lease-back deal:

> In March [the company] sold a new generating unit for $132 million to a group of banks headed by Bank of America and then took a lease on the plant . . Its near-term profit picture has not been affected. But ultimately, the desperate measure will remove a huge asset from the utility's rate [i.e., asset] base, thus lowering potential profits and further weakening SDG&E's bond rating. "The rating agencies look at the $132 million obligation as if it were long-term debt," explains [Robert E. Morris, the company's president].[5]

Leasing Affects Book Income   Leasing can make the firm's balance sheet and income statement *look* better by increasing book income or decreasing book asset value, or both.

A lease that qualifies as off-balance-sheet financing affects book income in only one way: the lease payments are an expense. If the firm buys the asset instead, and borrows to finance it, both depreciation and interest expense are deducted. Leases are usually set up so that payments in the early years are less than depreciation plus interest under the buy-and-borrow alternative. Consequently, leasing increases book income in the early years of an asset's life. The book rate of return can increase even more dramatically, because the book value of assets (the denominator in the book-rate-of-return calculation) is understated if the leased asset never appears on the firm's balance sheet.

Leasing's impact on book income should in itself have no effect on firm value. In efficient capital markets investors will look through the firm's accounting results to the true value of the asset and the liability incurred to finance it.

26-3   VALUING FINANCIAL LEASES

Leasing does offer special advantages to some firms in some circumstances. However, there is no point in further discussion of these advantages until you know how to value financial lease contracts.

---

[5] Reprinted from the May 28, 1979, issue of *Business Week* by special permission; © 1979 by McGraw-Hill Inc., New York, N.Y. 10020. All rights reserved, p. 110.

Table 26-1

Direct cash-flow consequences of the lease contract offered to Greymare Bus Lines (figures in thousands). The tax rate is 36% and the CCA rate is 30%. Under the half-year rule, CCA is taken at 15% for the first year and at 30% thereafter.

	Year							
	0	1	2	3	4	5	6	7
1. Cost of new bus/ salvage	100.00							
2. Lost CCA tax shield and terminal loss benefit	−5.40	−9.18	−6.43	−4.50	−3.15	−2.20	−1.54	−3.60
3. Lease payment	−18.50	−18.50	−18.50	−18.50	−18.50	−18.50	−18.50	
4. Tax shield of lease payment	6.66	6.66	6.66	6.66	6.66	6.66	6.66	
Cash flow of lease	82.76	−21.02	−18.27	−16.34	−14.99	−14.04	−13.38	−3.60

Example of a Financial Lease

Imagine yourself in the position of Thomas Pierce, III, president of Greymare Bus Lines. Your firm was established by your grandfather, who was quick to capitalize on the growing demand for transportation between Greymare and nearby townships. The company has owned all of its vehicles from the time it was formed; you are now reconsidering that policy. Your operating manager wants to buy a new bus costing $100,000. Greymare will own the bus for seven years and then scrap it for $0.

You are convinced that the investment in additional equipment is worthwhile. However, the representative of the bus manufacturer has pointed out that her firm would also be willing to lease the bus to you for seven years for an annual payment of $18,500. Greymare would remain responsible for all maintenance, insurance, and operating expenses.

Table 26-1 shows the direct cash-flow consequences of signing the lease contract. (An important indirect effect is considered later.) The consequences are:

1. Greymare does not have to pay for the bus. This is equivalent to a cash inflow of $100,000.
2. Greymare no longer owns the bus, so it cannot claim capital cost allowance (CCA) on it. Therefore, it gives up a valuable CCA tax shield in years 0 to 6. In Table 26-1, we have assumed the bus would be in Asset Class 10, with a 30% CCA rate. Moreover, Greymare loses the tax effects of scrapping the bus in year 7. We have assumed that the bus would have been the only asset in its class, so Greymare also gives up a terminal loss tax benefit.[6]
3. Greymare must pay $18,500 per year for 7 years to the lessor. The first payment is due immediately.
4. However, these lease payments are fully tax-deductible. At a 36% marginal tax rate, the lease payments generate tax shields of $6,600 per year. You could say that the after-tax cost of the lease payment is $18,500 − $6,660 = $11,840.

Analyzing leases usually requires a sharp pencil because the value of the benefits is often very close to that of the costs. We have taken care to incorporate

---

[6] As discussed in Chapter 6, the bus would often be grouped with the other assets in Class 10 but, in this case, we'll suppose that the bus is to be used on a new route, which Revenue Canada deems to be a separate business for tax purposes. If the bus is grouped with other Class 10 assets, and the UCC of the class exceeds the salvage value, Greymare would be left with a perpetual CCA tax shield instead of a terminal loss.

the exact tax effects of the half-year rule, as discussed in Appendix 6-1. Thus, CCA is taken at half the normal rate in year 0, and at the full 30% rate for years 1 to 6. The undepreciated capital cost (UCC) at the end of year 6 is

$$100 \times (1 - 0.15) \times (1 - 0.30)^6 = 10.00 \text{ or } \$10,000$$

If Greymare had owned the bus, it could have claimed a terminal loss in year 7 and achieved a tax saving of $(10,000 - 0) \times 0.36 = \$3,600$.

We must emphasize that Table 26-1 assumes that Greymare will pay taxes at the full 36% marginal rate. If the firm were sure to lose money, and therefore pay no taxes, lines 2 and 4 would be left blank.

Table 26-1 also assumes the bus will be worthless when it goes to the scrapyard at year 7. Otherwise, there would be an entry for salvage value lost.

Who *Really* Owns the Leased Asset?

To a lawyer or a tax accountant, this would be a silly question: the lessor is clearly the *legal* owner of the leased asset. That is why the lessor is allowed to deduct depreciation from taxable income, and to claim the investment tax credit.

From an *economic* point of view, you might say that the *user* is the real owner, because in a *financial* lease the user faces the risks and receives the rewards of ownership. If the new bus turns out to be hopelessly costly and unsuited for Greymare's routes, that is Greymare's problem, not the lessor's. If it turns out to be a great success, the profit goes to Greymare, not the lessor. The success or failure of the firm's business operations does not depend on whether the buses are financed by leasing or some other financial instrument.

In many respects, a financial lease is equivalent to the secured loan. The lessee must make a series of fixed payments and, if the lessee fails to do so, the lessor can repossess the asset. Thus, we can think of a balance sheet like this:

Greymare Bus Lines (figures in thousands of dollars)			
Bus	100	100	Loan secured by bus
All other assets	1,000	450	Other loans
		550	Net worth
Total assets	1,100	1,100	Total liabilities and net worth

as being economically equivalent to a balance sheet like this:

Greymare Bus Lines (figures in thousands of dollars)			
Bus	100	100	Financial lease
All other assets	1,000	450	Other loans
		550	Net worth
Total assets	1,100	1,100	Total liabilities and net worth

Having said this, we must immediately add two qualifications. First, legal ownership makes a big difference when a financial lease expires, because the lessor gets the salvage value of the asset. Once a secured loan is paid off the user owns the asset free and clear.

Second, legal ownership also makes a difference in bankruptcy or reorganization. When a lessee fails to make a lease payment, the lessor can of course recover the asset. But suppose that the asset is worth much less than the future payments the lessee had promised to make. Obviously the lessor loses. The lessor can try to recoup this loss from the firm, but the lessor is an unsecured creditor.

Contrast what happens when a firm defaults on payments to a secured lender. The lender has a prior claim on the asset that secured the loan, and if this asset's value is less than the loan principal plus unpaid interest, the lender can enter a claim for the *full* amount of the difference.

Of course, neither the lessor nor the secured lender can be sure its claim will be paid. Each has to get in line with other creditors. Our point is that lessees and secured creditors have different rights when the asset user gets into trouble.

Leasing and Revenue Canada

We have already noted that the lessor, as legal owner, usually enjoys the CCA tax shields and any investment tax credit generated by the leased asset. Lease payments are then treated as rents which are taxable income for the lessor and a tax-deductible expense for the lessee.

However, the tax authorities are suspicious by nature, and they will require a different tax treatment unless they are satisfied that the arrangement is a genuine lease rather than a disguised instalment purchase. Here are examples of "lease-option" contracts that may be treated as a sale. In these cases, the lessee gets CCA, and is deemed to have received a loan where the lease payment is regarded as a combination of interest and principal repayment. The lessor is deemed to have made a sale and taken back a loan.

1. The lessee receives an option to acquire the asset for, say, $1 when the lease expires. Such a provision would effectively give the asset's salvage value to the lessee.
2. The lessee guarantees an "option" purchase price that will be paid to the lessor at the expiration of the lease.

Revenue Canada is also suspicious of "sale-leaseback" agreements where someone sells an asset but continues to use it under a lease. These are treated as secured loans if, for example, the asset is sold for less than market value and the lease contract has one of the features described above.

Lessors also face another type of tax problem: they cannot use tax losses generated by the capital cost allowances on their leasing assets to "shelter" or reduce their other taxable income.[7] This is a potential problem since the transfer of CCA tax shields from the lessee to the lessor is often the main reason why a lease can be negotiated. However, the CCA tax shields can be pooled within the leasing business and applied against taxable income generated by leasing. CCA tax shields are largest in the early years of the life of an asset, while lease payments are usually constant over time. This means that any given lease will often generate a tax loss early in its life and taxable income later. Thus, the lessor would we well-advised to have a whole portfolio of leases of different ages, in order to avoid having to carry forward the tax losses.

Finally, in 1990, the federal government introduced Regulations that further limit the availability of CCA tax shields to the lessor.[8] Essentially, the new Regulations limit the lessor's CCA by an amount of depreciation measured as the amortization of the principal of a loan that has blended principal and interest payments equal to the lease payment and an interest rate equal to a prescribed

---

[7] See Sections 1100 (11) to (16) of the Canadian Income Tax Regulations.

[8] See Income Tax Regulations 1100 (1.01) to (1.12). The original reason for these Regulations was to prevent the sale and leaseback of assets from a tax-exempt entity (such as a university) to a taxable entity, but the Regulations have a broader impact and affect many other transactions.

rate of 1% more than the long-Canada-bond rate. If the CCA rate is high, the allowable CCA is then limited to this alternative depreciation measure. Note that this alternative depreciation measure has higher deductions in later years than in the earlier years, unlike ordinary declining balance CCA, so the limit is more likely to be binding in the early years of a lease than the later years. This rule does *not* apply to several common types of leasing property, such as: computer systems software and hardware, office furniture and equipment, automobiles, trucks, buildings, and railway cars.

Finally, note that some leases are designed *not* to qualify as a lease for tax purposes. Suppose a firm finds it convenient to lease a new computer but wants to keep the CCA tax shields. This is easily accomplished by giving the firm the option to purchase the computer for $1 at the end of the lease. Then, Revenue Canada treats the lease as an instalment sale and the firm can deduct CCA and the interest component of the lease payment for tax purposes. But the lease is still a lease for all other purposes.

A First Pass at Valuing a Lease Contract

When we left Thomas Pierce, III, president of Greymare Bus Lines, he had just set down in Table 26-1 the *direct* cash-flow consequences of the financial lease contract proposed by the bus manufacturer.

The direct cash flows are typically assumed to be *safe* flows that investors would discount at approximately the same rate as the interest and principal payments on a secured bond issued by the lessee. This assumption is reasonable for the lease payments because the lessor is effectively making a loan to the lessee. But the various tax shields might carry enough risk to deserve a higher rate. For example, Greymare might be confident it could make the lease payments, but not confident that it could earn enough taxable income to use these tax shields. In that case the cash flows generated by the tax shields would probably deserve a higher discount rate than the borrowing rate used for the lease payments.

A lessee might, in principle, end up using a separate discount rate for each line of Table 26-1, each rate chosen to fit the risk of that line's cash flow. But established, profitable firms usually find it reasonable to simplify by discounting the types of flows shown in Table 26-1 at a single rate based on the rate of interest the firm would pay if it borrowed rather than leased. We will assume Greymare's borrowing rate is 10%.

At this point we must go back to our discussion in Chapter 19 of debt-equivalent flows. When a company lends money, it pays tax on the interest it receives. Its net return is the after-tax interest rate. When a company borrows money, it can *deduct* interest payments from its taxable income. The net cost of borrowing is the after-tax interest rate. Thus, the after-tax interest rate is the effective rate at which a company can transfer debt-equivalent flows from one time period to another. Therefore, to value the incremental cash flows stemming from the lease we need to discount them at the after-tax interest rate.

Since Greymare can borrow at 10%, we should discount the lease cash flows at $r^* = 0.10 (1 - 0.36) = 0.064$ or 6.4%. This gives:

$$\begin{aligned} \text{NPV} \atop \text{lease} &= +82.76 - \frac{21.02}{1.064} - \frac{18.27}{(1.064)^2} - \frac{16.34}{(1.064)^3} - \frac{14.99}{(1.064)^4} - \frac{14.04}{(1.064)^5} \\ &\quad - \frac{13.38}{(1.064)^6} - \frac{3.60}{(1.064)^7} \\ &= -0.24 \text{ or } -\$240 \end{aligned}$$

Since the lease has a negative NPV, Greymare is better off buying the bus.

Why Leasing Would Make Greymare's Shareholders Worse Off

A positive or negative NPV is not an abstract concept; in this case Greymare's shareholders really are $240 poorer if the company leases. Let us now check how this comes about.

Look once more at Table 26-1. The lease cash flows are:

	Year						
	0	1	2	3	4	5	6	7

Lease cash flows $\left(\begin{array}{c}\text{thousands}\\\text{of dollars}\end{array}\right)$ 82.76 −21.02 −18.27 −16.34 −14.99 −14.04 −13.38 −3.60

The lease payments are contractual obligations like the principal and interest payments on secured debt. Thus, you can think of the incremental lease cash flows in years 1 through 7 as the "debt service" of the lease. Table 26-2 shows a loan with *exactly* the same debt service as the lease. The initial amount of the loan is 83.00 thousand dollars. If Greymare borrowed this sum, it would need to pay interest in the first year of $0.10 \times 83.00 = 8.30$ and would *receive* a tax shield on this interest of $0.36 \times 8.30 = 2.99$. Greymare could then repay 15.71 of the loan, leaving a net cash outflow of 21.02 (exactly the same as for the lease) in year 1, and an outstanding debt at the start of year 2 of 67.30.

As you walk through the calculations in Table 26-2, you see that it costs exactly the same to service a loan that brings an immediate inflow of 83.00 as it does to service the lease, which brings in only 82.76. That is why we say that the lease has a net present value of $82.76 - 83.00 = -0.24$ or $-\$240$. If Greymare leases the bus rather than raising an equivalent loan,[9] there will be $240 less in Greymare's bank account.

Our example illustrates two general points about leases and equivalent loans. First, if you can devise a borrowing plan that gives the same cash flow as the lease in every future period but a higher immediate cash flow, then you should not lease. If, however, the equivalent loan provides the same future cash outflows as the lease but a lower immediate inflow, then leasing is the better choice.

Second, our example suggests two ways to value a lease:

1. *Hard way:* Construct a table like Table 26-2 showing the equivalent loan.
2. *Easy way:* Discount the lease cash flows at the *after-tax* interest rate that the firm would pay on an equivalent loan. Both methods give the same answer—in our case an NPV of $-\$240$.

The Story So Far

We concluded that the lease contract offered to Greymare Bus Lines was *not* attractive because the lease provided $240 less financing than the equivalent loan. The underlying principle is as follows: a financial lease is superior to buying and borrowing if the financing provided by the lease exceeds the present value of the liability created by the lease.

The principle implies this formula:

$$\begin{array}{c}\text{Net value}\\\text{of lease}\end{array} = \begin{array}{c}\text{initial financing}\\\text{provided}\end{array} - \sum_{t=1}^{N} \frac{\text{LCF}_t}{[1 + r(1 - T_c)]^t}$$

[9] When we compare the lease to its equivalent loan, we do not mean to imply that the bus alone could support all of that loan. Some part of the loan would be supported by Greymare's other assets. Some part of the lease would likewise be supported by the other assets.

Table 26-2
Details of the equivalent loan for the lease offered to Greymare Bus Lines (figures in thousands, cash outflows shown with a negative sign)

	Year						
	0	**1**	**2**	**3**	**4**	**5**	**6**	**7**
Amount borrowed at year-end	83.00	67.30	53.34	40.41	28.01	15.76	3.38	0
Interest paid at 10%		−8.30	−6.73	−5.33	−4.04	−2.80	−1.58	−0.34
Interest tax shield at 36%		2.99	2.42	1.92	1.45	1.01	0.57	0.12
Interest paid after tax		−5.31	−4.31	−3.41	−2.59	−1.79	−1.01	−0.22
Principal repaid		−15.71	−13.96	−12.92	−12.40	−12.25	−12.37	−3.38
Net cash flow of equivalent loan	83.00	−21.02	−18.27	−16.34	−14.99	−14.04	−13.38	−3.60

where LCF_t is the cash outflow attributable to the lease in period t and N is the term of the lease. Initial financing provided equals the cost of the leased asset minus any immediate lease payment or other cash outflow attributable to the lease.

Notice that the value of the lease is its incremental value relative to borrowing via an equivalent loan. A positive lease value means that *if* you acquire the asset, lease financing is advantageous. It does not prove you should acquire the asset.

However, sometimes favourable lease terms rescue a capital investment project. Suppose that Greymare had decided *against* buying a new bus because the NPV of the $100,000 investment was −$5,000 assuming normal financing. The bus manufacturer could rescue the deal by offering a lease with a value of, say, +$8,000. By offering such a lease, the manufacturer would in effect cut the price of the bus to $92,000, giving the bus-lease package a positive value to Greymare. We could express this more formally by treating the lease's NPV as a favourable financing side effect which adds to project adjusted present value (APV):[10]

$$APV = \text{NPV of project} + \text{NPV of lease}$$
$$= -5,000 + 8,000 = +\$3,000$$

Notice also that our formula applies to net financial leases. Any insurance, maintenance, and other operating costs picked up by the lessor have to be evaluated separately and added to the value of the lease. If the asset has salvage value at the end of the lease, that value should be taken into account also.

Suppose, for example, that the bus manufacturer offers to provide routine maintenance that would otherwise cost $3,000 per year after tax. However, Mr. Pierce reconsiders and decides that the bus will probably be worth $10,000 after 7 years. (Previously he assumed the bus would be worthless at the end of the lease.) Then the value of the lease increases by the present value of the maintenance savings and decreases by the present value of the lost salvage value.

Maintenance and salvage value are harder to predict than the cash flows shown in Table 26-1, and so they normally deserve a higher discount rate. Suppose that Mr. Pierce uses $r^* = 12\%$. We'll assume the maintenance savings occur in years 0 to 6. They are worth:

$$\sum_{t=0}^{6} \frac{3,000}{(1.12)^t} = \$15,330$$

[10] See Section 19-1.

Determining the change in the value of the lease that results from the increase in the risk of the salvage value requires more care, since the salvage value *and* the terminal loss are affected. Denote the undepreciated capital cost of the bus just prior to salvage by UCC. We previously calculated it to be $10,000, but we'll just call it UCC, partly to remind us that it is riskless, unlike the salvage value. Let the expected salvage value be S. The expected salvage value plus terminal loss benefit is then:

$$S + 0.36 \,(UCC - S) = 0.64 \, S + 0.36 \, UCC$$

Of this cash flow, 0.64 S is risky and 0.36 UCC is riskless. When we previously calculated the value of the lease as $-\$240$, we assumed $S = \$0$, but did include the amount 0.36 $\times$ UCC as a terminal loss benefit. Thus, we can account for the change in NPV resulting from the new estimate of salvage value $S = \$10,000$ by simply discounting the amount $0.64 \times 10,000 = 6,400$ at 12%.

The revised value of the lease is, therefore,

$$-\$240 + 15,330 - \frac{6,400}{(1.12)^7} = \$12,190$$

Now the lease looks like a good deal.

*A General Formula

Monthly payments Leases usually involve monthly payments. Let's denote the monthly lease payment by $\$L$. To discount these payments, we need the equivalent monthly interest rate, as discussed in Section 3-3. This monthly rate must compound over 12 months to the annual rate $r(1 - T_c)$. If we let r_m denote the after-tax monthly interest rate, then

$$r_m = (1 + r(1 - T_c))^{1/12} - 1$$

This will usually give an interest rate that doesn't appear in the Appendix tables to this book, so we need to use a financial calculator or a computer. Alternatively, we can use the formula for the present value of an annuity given in Section 3-2. Remember that lease payments are in advance (at the beginning of each period), while Section 3-2 gives the present value of an annuity in arrears (with payments at the end of each period). We can adjust for this by subtracting 1 period from the life of the annuity, and adding 1 to the total, as the present value of the first payment. If the lease has n years to maturity, it has $12n$ months, so the present value of the lease payments is:

$$\begin{matrix} \text{PV of} \\ \text{after-tax monthly} \\ \text{lease payments} \end{matrix} = -L \times (1 - T_c) \times \begin{matrix} \text{PV of} \\ \text{annuity in advance} \\ \text{for } 12n \text{ months} \end{matrix}$$

$$= -L(1 - T_c)\left(1 + \frac{1}{r_m}\left(1 - \frac{1}{(1 + r_m)^{12n-1}}\right)\right)$$

Capital cost The lease saves the lessor the initial capital cost of the asset, $\$C$.

Present Value of CCA We can deal with the CCA tax shields on an annual basis. Since leasing is a "sharp-pencil business," we'll use the refined formulas of Appendix 6-1. Let's assume the asset is in a CCA class by itself. The undepreciated capital cost of the asset at year $n - 1$, just prior to salvage, is

$$UCC_{n-1} = C \,(1 - d)^{n-1}\left(1 - \frac{d}{2}\right)$$

where d is the CCA rate. The present value of the CCA tax shields lost, using the half-year rule, is then:

$$\text{PV of CCA tax shields} = -\frac{CdT_c}{r(1-T_c)+d}\left(1+\frac{r(1-T_c)}{2}\right)+\frac{1}{(1+r(1-T_c))^{n-1}}\left(\frac{\text{UCC}_{n-1}dT_c}{r(1-T_c)+d}\right)$$

Note that we lose the perpetual stream of CCA tax shields starting in year n, but the formula $\dfrac{\text{UCC}_{n-1}dT_c}{r(1-T_c)+d}$ for the PV of the perpetual CCA tax shield discounts back to one year prior to the first tax shield, so we need only discount it back from year $n-1$.

Salvage, Recapture and Terminal Loss   Assume the lessor has the capital asset in a CCA class by itself. We have seen that the expected salvage value plus terminal loss benefit or tax on recaptured depreciation is $S + T_c(\text{UCC}_{n-1} - S)$ $= (1 - T_c)S + T_c\,\text{UCC}_{n-1}$. Since the salvage value is risky, we discount the first term at the rate r^*, but the second term is discounted at the after-tax debt rate $r(1 - T_c)$. Thus,[11]

$$\text{PV of lost salvage net of terminal loss or recapture} = -\frac{(1-T_c)S}{(1+r^*)^n} - \frac{T_c\,\text{UCC}_{n-1}}{(1+r(1-T_c))^n}$$

Annual Maintenance Saving   Finally, let the annual pretax maintenance cost saved be M, and assume this occurs as an annuity in advance. Discount this at r^*:

$$\text{PV of annual maintenance cost saved} = M(1-T_c)\left(1+\frac{1}{r^*}\left(1-\frac{1}{(1+r^*)^{n-1}}\right)\right)$$

EXAMPLE   To illustrate this approach, let us assume the Greymare lease involves monthly payments of $18.50/12 = 1.542$ or $1,542. All other data are as described earlier.

---

[11] These formulas are slightly different than those given in Appendix 6-1, but they give the same result. Here, we are not taking the CCA for the salvage year n, so recapture is based on the UCC left after taking CCA for years 0 through $n-1$. The formula $\dfrac{\text{UCC}_{n-1}dT_c}{r(1-T_c)+d}$ discounts the impact of the lost CCA stream back to one year before salvage, or year $n-1$, so to it we apply the present value factor $\dfrac{1}{(1+r(1-T_c))^{n-1}}$.

In Appendix 6-1 we took the CCA for the salvage year n, which is $T_c d\,\text{UCC}_{n-1}$. Therefore, the recapture/terminal loss and lost perpetual CCA tax shields were based on UCC_n, which is the UCC left after taking CCA for years 0 through n. However, there is no extra tax saving because we also increase our tax payable in year n through the recapture/terminal loss calculation. With this calculation, the first lost tax shield occurs in year $n+1$, so we discounted $\dfrac{\text{UCC}_n dT_c}{r(1-T_c)+d}$ by n periods, rather than $n-1$.

In mathematical terms, we have just shown that

$$\frac{T_c\,\text{UCC}_{n-1}}{(1+r(1-T_c))^n} - \frac{1}{(1+r(1-T_c))^{n-1}}\left(\frac{\text{UCC}_{n-1}dT_c}{r(1-T_c)+d}\right)$$

$$= \frac{1}{(1+r(1-T_c))^n}\left(T_c\,\text{UCC}_n - \frac{\text{UCC}_n dT_c}{r(1-T_c)+d}\right)$$

The capital cost saved is $C = \$100,000$.

We earlier calculated the UCC of the bus just prior to salvage as $UCC_{n-1} = \$10,000$, so the present value of lost CCA tax shields is:

$$\begin{array}{l}\text{PV of lost} \\ \text{CCA tax shields}\end{array} = -\frac{100 \times 0.30 \times 0.36}{0.064 + 0.30}(1.032) + \frac{1}{(1.064)^7}\left(\frac{10 \times 0.30 \times 0.36}{0.064 + 0.30}\right)$$

$$= -30.62 + 2.04 = -28.58 \text{ or } -\$28,580$$

The after-tax monthly interest rate is:

$$r_m = (1 + 0.10 \times (1 - 0.36))^{1/12} - 1 = 0.00518 \text{ or } 0.518\%$$

The seven-year lease has 84 monthly payments in advance, so the PV of the annuity in advance is:

$$-L\,(1 - T_c)\left(1 + \frac{1}{r_m}\left(1 - \frac{1}{(1 + r_m)^{12n-1}}\right)\right)$$

$$= -1.542 \times (1 - 0.36) \times \left(1 + \frac{1}{0.00518}\left(1 - \frac{1}{(1.00518)^{83}}\right)\right)$$

$$= -1.542 \times (1 - 0.36) \times 68.32 = 67.42 \text{ or } \$67,420$$

The after-tax PV of the lost salvage opportunity is:

$$\begin{array}{l}\text{PV of lost salvage} \\ \text{net of terminal loss} \\ \text{or recapture}\end{array} = -\frac{0.64 \times 10}{(1.12)^7} - \frac{0.36 \times 10}{(1.064)^7}$$

$$= -2.90 - 2.33 = -5.23 \text{ or } \$5,230$$

The annual maintenance saving after tax is $M(1 - T_c) = \$3,000$, so

$$\begin{array}{l}\text{PV of} \\ \text{annual maintenance} \\ \text{cost saved}\end{array} = 3 \times \left(1 + \frac{1}{0.12}\left(1 - \frac{1}{(1.12)^6}\right)\right)$$

$$= 3 \times 5.111 = 15.33 \text{ or } \$15,330$$

Thus, the NPV of the lease with monthly payments is:

$$100 - 28.58 - 67.42 - 5.23 + 15.33 = 14.1 \text{ or } \$14,100$$

Pooling of Assets in Capital Cost Allowance Classes   If the lessor pools the asset with other assets in the same CCA class and the class always has a large UCC, then the incremental effect of salvage is different from the salvage recapture and terminal loss treatment described above. As in Appendix 6-1, when the asset is scrapped, the sale price S is deducted from the balance of the asset class. As of year n when the asset is sold, this results in a loss of CCA tax shields of

$$\frac{SdT_c}{r(1 - T_c) + d}\left(1 + \frac{r(1 - T_c)}{2}\right)$$

But this value is risky because the salvage value S is risky. Therefore, we discount it back to the present at the rate r^*. Overall, we have:

$$\begin{array}{l} \text{PV of CCA} \\ \text{tax shields} \end{array} = -\frac{CdT_c}{r(1-T_c)+d}\left(1+\frac{r(1-T_c)}{2}\right)$$
$$+\frac{1}{(1+r^*)^n}\left(\frac{SdT_c}{r(1-T_c)+d}\right)\left(1+\frac{r(1-T_c)}{2}\right)$$

In the example above, we would have:

$$\begin{array}{l} \text{PV of lost} \\ \text{CCA} \\ \text{tax shields} \end{array} = \frac{100\times0.30\times0.36}{0.064+0.30}(1.032)+\frac{1}{(1.12)^7}\left(\frac{10\times0.30\times0.36}{0.064+0.30}\right)(1.032)$$
$$= -30.62+1.39 = -29.23 \text{ or } -\$29,230$$

Since there is no terminal loss or recapture:

$$\text{PV of lost salvage} = -\frac{(1-T_c)S}{(1+r^*)^n}$$

In our example, this is -2.90 or $-\$2,900$.

Overall, the NPV of the lease becomes:

$$100 - 29.23 - 67.42 - 2.90 + 15.33 = 15.78 \text{ or } \$15,780$$

26-4   WHEN DOES LEASING PAY?

We have examined the value of a lease from the viewpoint of the lessee. However, the lessor's criterion is simply the reverse. As long as the lessor and lessee are in the same tax bracket, every cash outflow to the lessee is an inflow to the lessor, and vice versa. In our numerical example, the bus manufacturer would project cash flows in a table like Table 26-1, but with the signs reversed. The value of the lease to the bus manufacturer would be:

$$\begin{array}{l} \text{Value of lease} \\ \text{to lessor} \end{array} = -82.76 + \frac{21.02}{1.064} + \frac{18.27}{(1.064)^2} + \frac{16.34}{(1.064)^3} + \frac{14.99}{(1.064)^4} + \frac{14.04}{(1.064)^5}$$
$$+ \frac{13.38}{(1.064)^6} + \frac{3.60}{(1.064)^7}$$
$$= +0.24 \text{ or } \$240$$

In this case, the values to lessee and lessor exactly offset ($-240 + 240 = 0$). The lessor can win only at the lessee's expense.

But both lessee and lessor can win if their tax rates differ. Suppose that Greymare paid no tax ($T_c = 0$). Then, the only cash flows of the bus lease would be:

	\multicolumn{8}{c}{Year}
	0	1	2	3	4	5	6	7
Cost of new bus	100							
Lease payment		−18.50	−18.50	−18.50	−18.50	−18.50	−18.50	−18.50	0.00

These flows should be discounted at 10%, because $r_D(1 - T_c) = r_D$ when $T_c = 0$.

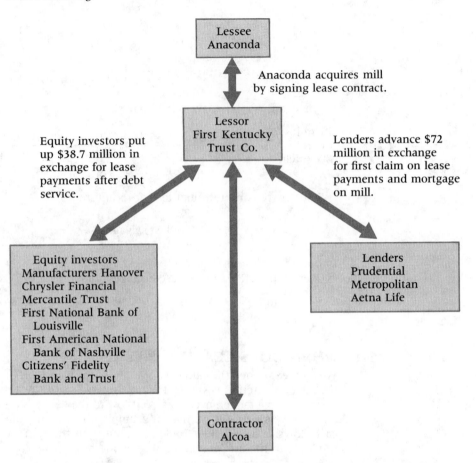

Figure 26-1 How Anaconda arranged a lease on its aluminum reduction mill. This is a leveraged lease because part of the cost of the plant was raised by borrowing.

The value of the lease is:

$$\text{Value of lease} = 100 - \sum_{t=0}^{6} \frac{18.50}{(1.10)^t}$$
$$= +0.93 \text{ or } \$930$$

In this case there is a net gain of $240 to the lessor (who has the 36% tax rate) and a net gain of $930 to the lessee (who pays zero tax). This mutual gain is at the expense of the government. On the one hand, the government gains from the lease contract because it can tax the lease payments. On the other hand, the contract allows the lessor to take advantage of depreciation and interest tax shields, which are of no use to the lessee. However, because the depreciation is accelerated, and the interest rate is positive, the government suffers a net loss in the present value of its tax receipts as a result of the lease.

Now you should begin to understand the circumstances in which the government makes a loss on the lease and the other two parties gain. Other things being equal, there are potential gains to lessor and lessee when:

1. The lessor's tax rate is higher than the lessee's.
2. The CCA rate is high so that the depreciation tax shield is received early in the lease period.

3. The lease period is long and the lease payments are concentrated toward the end of the period.
4. The interest rate r_D is high—if it were zero there would be no advantage, in present value terms, to postponing tax.

It is not hard to find situations where these four requirements are not met and, hence, a lease is not worthwhile. For example, if the bus had only a 20% CCA rate rather than a 30% rate, a lease offers tax advantages to the lessee and the lessor only if the lessor's tax rate is *lower* than the lessee's. Alternatively, if you shorten the life of the asset (and tenure of the lease), it is very difficult to find a lease rate that is acceptable to both the lessee and lessor. It is foolish to rely on rules of thumb when analyzing leases. You have to sharpen your pencil and calculate the present values of the after-tax flows to know whether it is possible to strike a worthwhile lease deal.

26-5   EVALUATING A LARGE, LEVERAGED LEASE

Now let us try using our new-found knowledge to evaluate a large leasing deal. In 1971 Anaconda began to build a $138 million aluminum-reduction mill at Sebree, Kentucky. The company's original intention was to finance the project largely by a private placement of debt but, before it could do so, two things happened. First, the Allende government expropriated Anaconda's Chilean copper mines and so provided the company with a $356 million tax-deductible loss. Second, the United States Congress reinstated the investment tax credit (then 7%).

Anaconda clearly was unlikely to pay taxes for a number of years. If it went ahead and bought the mill, it could not make immediate use of the investment tax credit or the depreciation tax shields. By leasing the mill, however, Anaconda could pass on these benefits to someone who could use them.[12] It therefore decided to purchase only the real estate at Sebree and to pay $1.1 million to a leasing broker, U.S. Leasing International, to put together a leveraged lease for the $110.7 million of plant and equipment. Figure 26-1 shows how this was arranged. First Kentucky Trust Company issued $39 million of equity to a group of banks and leasing companies and $72 million of debt to a group of insurance companies. It then used this money to purchase the mill and lease it to Anaconda. Anaconda agreed to make 40 lease payments, prepaid semiannually, over a 20-year period. The first 21 payments were set at $3.99 million each and the last 19 at $5.46 million each.

The $72 million loan was secured by a first claim on Anaconda's lease payments and by a mortgage on the plant. It was *not* secured by First Kentucky or the equity investors. It was a *nonrecourse* loan: if Anaconda had defaulted on the lease payments, the insurance companies' only protection would have been the value of the mill, and a general claim against Anaconda.

This is called a *leveraged* lease because part of the cost of the plant was raised by a loan secured by the asset and the lease payments. The lessor, First Kentucky Trust, really acted as an intermediary, receiving the lease payments from Anaconda, paying the debt service, and distributing what was left over to the equity

---

[12] The Anaconda lease was described in P. Vanderwicken, "Powerful Logic of the Leasing Boom," *Fortune*, **87**: 132–161 (November 1973). Our analysis of its present value is taken from S. C. Myers, D. A. Dill, and A. J. Bautista, "Valuation of Financial Lease Contracts," *Journal of Finance*, **31**: 799–819 (June 1976), and J. R. Franks and S. D. Hodges, "Valuation of Financial Lease Contracts: A Note," *Journal of Finance*, **33**: 647–669 (May 1978).

investors. First Kentucky, in effect, financed the lease contract by selling off debt and equity claims against it.

But let's look at the lease contract itself from the lessor's viewpoint. The initial outlay was $110.7 million less the investment tax credit of $7.75 million and the initial prepaid lease payment. The major subsequent cash inflows were the 39 semiannual lease payments, the depreciation tax shields, and the salvage value in 1993.

As frequently happens in financial analysis, the hardest problem is to choose the right discount rate. Here is one way to look at it. The interest rate on the insurance companies' loan was 9.125%. Because this debt is also protected by the lessor's equity, the lease payments must be *riskier* than the debt. On the other hand, the depreciation tax shield must be *safer* than the lease payments for, once the contract is signed, the size of the shields is independent of Anaconda's fortunes. Since our formula calls for a single rate of discount for both the after-tax lease payments and the depreciation tax shield, we will compromise on a discount rate of 9.125%. The adjusted discount rate is 4.5625%, assuming a marginal tax rate of 50%.

The present value calculations are set out in Table 26-3 along with a list of the other assumptions we have made. You can see that for the lessor the lease was moderately profitable: its net value was roughly 3% of the plant's cost.[13]

It is not so easy to evaluate the lease from Anaconda's side because we do not know when Anaconda expected to resume paying taxes. But we can work out how much the lease was worth to Anaconda under varying assumptions about its future tax position. The results are presented in Figure 26-2. Notice that if Anaconda paid taxes immediately, it would lose exactly the $3.0 million that the lessor gained. The break-even point comes after only three years and, thereafter, the value of the lease arrangement to Anaconda rises rapidly to the maximum of about $35 million. It appears that the deal was a good one for Anaconda.

26-6   SUMMARY

A lease is just an extended rental agreement. The owner of the equipment (the *lessor*) allows the user (the *lessee*) to operate the equipment in exchange for regular lease payments.

There is a wide variety of possible arrangements. Short-term, cancellable leases are known as *operating leases*: in these cases the lessor bears the risk of obsolescence. Long-term, noncancellable leases are called *full payout*, *financial*, or *capital leases*: in these cases the lessee bears the risk of obsolescence. Operating leases make sense when you want to use the equipment for only a short time or where the lessor has some control over the obsolescence rate. Financial leases are *sources*

---

[13] The NPV calculation in Table 26-3 takes no notice of the $72 million partial financing of the lessor's purchase of Anaconda's mill. The calculation doesn't look to the sources of the up-front money required of the lessors. It looks at alternative uses of this money: it compares the lease to an *equivalent loan to Anaconda*.

For lessors the equivalent loan method compares leasing and lending. Suppose we add up all the after-tax cash flows of the proposed lease, including lease payments, depreciation tax shields, investment tax credit, and salvage value. How much debt would these cash flows support? Table 26-3 tells us the answer; about $3 million more than the $110.7 million cost of the mill. That is why we say the lease has an NPV of $3 million to the lessors.

Does the availability of the $72 million loan add anything to this NPV? Not unless the loan is at an especially favourable rate. (Note that the loan has NPV = 0 if its cash flows are discounted at 9.125%.) If the loan does add value in some way, we would just add that value to the $3 million NPV given in Table 26-3.

Table 26-3
Value of Anaconda lease to lessor (figures in millions of dollars)

Item	Present Value
1. Price	−110.7
2. Investment tax credit	+7.7
3. Depreciation tax shield	+44.3
4. After-tax lease payments	+60.8
5. Salvage value	+0.9
Total value to *lessor*	+3.0

Notes:

1. Assumed tax rate is $T_c = 0.5$.
2. The adjusted discount rate for items 3 and 4 is 4.5625%. (The present values were actually calculated assuming semiannual cash flows and an equivalent semiannual rate.)
3. The discount rate for item 5 is 15%, our guesstimate of the average cost of capital for Anaconda's assets.
4. The depreciation schedule was based on an 11-year depreciable life and a 5% book salvage value. The double-declining-balance method was used for the first two years and then a switch was made to sum-of-the-years' digits. This appears to be the fastest write-off available under 1973 regulations.
5. The lessor's estimate of the plant's after-tax salvage value appears to be $10.9 million. This is not from the horse's mouth; it is inferred from other information.
6. In principle, ownership of the salvage value also creates debt capacity. We have not included an estimate of the NPV of this capacity to the lessors. It is in any event a small number.

Source: S. C. Myers, D. A. Dill, and A. J. Bautista, "Valuation of Financial Lease Contracts," *Journal of Finance*, **31**: 799–819 (June 1976), table 1, p. 809.

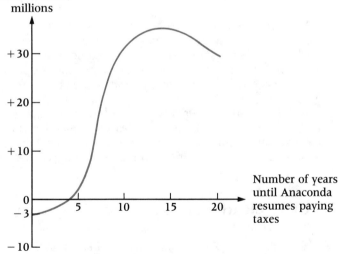

Figure 26-2 The value of the aluminum reduction mill to Anaconda increases rapidly as its "tax holiday" is extended. If the holiday extends for 15 years, the lease is worth about $36 million.

Source: J.R. Franks and S.D. Hodges, "Value of Financial Lease Contracts: A Note," *Journal of Finance*, **33**: 667 (May 1978), Table 3.

of financing for assets the firm wishes to acquire and use for an extended period.

Many vehicle or office equipment leases include insurance and maintenance. They are *full-service* leases. If the lessee is responsible for insurance and maintenance, the lease is a *net* lease.

Frequently, the lessor acquires the asset directly from the manufacturer. This is a *direct* lease. Sometimes the lessor acquires the asset from the user and then leases it back to the user. This is a *sale and lease-back*.

Most leases involved only the lessee and the lessor. But, if the asset is very costly, it may be convenient to arrange a *leveraged lease*, in which the cost of the leased asset is financed by issuing debt and equity claims against the asset and the future lease payments.

There are a number of reasons that companies sometimes prefer to lease equipment rather than buying it. For example, there may be good tax reasons. If the operator cannot use the capital cost allowance tax shield, it makes sense to sell the equipment to someone who can. Also, the lessor may be better able to bear the risk of obsolescence, or be in a better position to resell second-hand assets. The lessor may be able to offer a very good deal on maintenance. Finally, it may be much less costly in time and effort to arrange a simple lease contract on a standard item of equipment than to arrange a normal loan.

A financial lease is like a secured bond. If a firm invests in bonds, it earns the after-tax interest rate on its investment; if it issues bonds, it pays the after-tax rate of interest on its debt. Therefore, the opportunity cost of lease financing is the after-tax rate of interest on the firm's bonds. To value the lease, we need to discount the incremental cash flows from leasing by the after-tax interest rate.

An equivalent loan to a lease is one that commits the firm to exactly the same future cash flows. When we calculate the net present value of the lease we are measuring the difference between the amount of financing provided by the lease and the financing provided by the equivalent loan:

$$\frac{\text{Value}}{\text{of lease}} = \frac{\text{financing provided}}{\text{by lease}} - \frac{\text{value of}}{\text{equivalent loan}}$$

We can also analyze leases from the lessor's side of the transaction using the same approaches we developed for the lessee. If lessee and lessor are in the same tax bracket, they will receive exactly the same cash flows, but with signs reversed. Thus, the lessee can gain only at the lessor's expense, or vice versa. However, if the lessee's tax rate is lower than the lessor's, then both can gain at the government's expense.

Although this chapter was mostly devoted to financial leases, we included a few hints on analyzing operating leases. Remember that many operating leases have valuable options attached to them — for example, the right to renew the lease at a prespecified rate or to purchase the asset at a prespecified price.

FURTHER READING

The approach to lease valuation presented in this chapter is based on:

J. R. Franks and S. D. Hodges, "Valuation of Financial Lease Contracts: A Note," *Journal of Finance*, **33**: 647–669 (May 1978).

S. C. Myers, D. A. Dill, and A. J. Bautista, "Valuation of Financial Lease Contracts," *Journal of Finance*, **31**: 799–819 (June 1976).

Other useful works include Nevitt and Fabozzi's book and the theoretical discussions of Miller and Upton, and Lewellen, Long, and McConnell:

W. G. Lewellen, M. S. Long, and J. J. McConnell, "Asset Leasing in Competitive Capital Markets," *Journal of Finance*, **31**: 787–798 (June 1976).

M. H. Miller and C. W. Upton, "Leasing, Buying and the Cost of Capital Services," *Journal of Finance*, **31**: 761–786 (June 1976).

P. K. Nevitt and F. J. Fabozzi, *Equipment Leasing*, 3rd ed., Dow Jones–Irwin, Inc., Homewood, Ill., 1988.

The options embedded in some lease contracts are discussed in:

T. E. Copeland and J. F. Weston, "A Note on the Evaluation of Cancellable Operating Leases," *Financial Management*, **11**: 68–72 (Summer 1982).

J. J. McConnell and J. S. Schallheim, "Valuation of Asset Leasing Contracts," *Journal of Financial Economics*, **12**: 237–261 (August 1983).

QUIZ

1. The following terms are often used to describe leases:
   (A) Direct
   (B) Full-service
   (C) Operating
   (D) Financial
   (E) Rental
   (F) Net
   (G) Leveraged
   (H) Sale and lease-back
   (I) Full-payout
   Match each of these terms with one of the following statements:
   (A) The initial lease period is shorter than the economic life of the asset.
   (B) The initial lease period is long enough for the lessor to recover the cost of the asset.
   (C) The lessor provides maintenance and insurance.
   (D) The lessee provides maintenance and insurance.
   (E) The lessor buys the equipment from the manufacturer.
   (F) The lessor buys the equipment from the prospective lessee.
   (G) The lessor finances the lease contract by issuing debt and equity claims against it.

2. Some of the following reasons for leasing are rational. Others are irrational, or assume imperfect or inefficient capital markets. Which of the following reasons are the rational ones?
   (a) The lessee's need for the leased asset is only temporary.
   (b) Specialized lessors are better able to bear the risk of obsolescence.
   (c) Leasing provides 100% financing and thus preserves capital.
   (d) Leasing allows firms with low marginal tax rates to "sell" CCA tax shields.
   (e) Leasing increases earnings per share.
   (f) Leasing reduces the transaction cost of obtaining external financing.
   (g) Leasing avoids restrictions on capital expenditures.

3. True or false?
   (a) Leasing payments are usually made at the start of each period. Thus, the first payment is usually made as soon as the lease contract is signed.
   (b) Financial leases can still provide off-balance-sheet financing.
   (c) The cost of capital for a financial lease is the interest rate the company would pay on a bank loan.
   (d) An equivalent loan's principal plus after-tax interest payments exactly match the after-tax cash flows of the lease.
   (e) A financial lease should not be undertaken unless it provides more financing than the equivalent loan.

(f) It makes sense for firms that pay no taxes to lease from firms that do.

(g) Other things equal, the net tax advantage to leasing increases as normal interest rates increase.

4. Suppose that National Waferonics has before it a four-year lease proposal for a machine it may invest in. The firm constructs a table like Table 26-1. The bottom line of its table shows the lease cash flows:

	Year			
	0	1	2	3
Lease cash flow	+ 62,000	− 26,800	− 22,200	− 17,600

These flows reflect the cost of the machine, lost investment tax credits, CCA tax shields and the after-tax payments. Ignore salvage value. Assume the firm could borrow at 10% and faces a 36% marginal tax rate.

(a) What is the value of the equivalent loan?

(b) What is the value of the lease?

(c) Suppose the machine's NPV under normal financing is − $5,000. Should National Waferonics invest? Should it sign the lease?

QUESTIONS AND PROBLEMS

1. Look again at the bus lease as discussed in Section 26-3 and Table 26-1.

(a) What is the value of the lease if Greymare's marginal tax rate is $T_c = 0.20$?

(b) What would the lease value be if Greymare had to use straight-line depreciation as CCA, for tax purposes? Assume the bus is to be depreciated to a value of $10,000 over seven years, and that the half-year rule does not apply.

2. In Section 26-4 we showed that the lease offered to Greymare Bus Lines had a positive NPV of $930 if Greymare paid no tax, and *also* a + $240 NPV to a lessor paying 36% tax. What is the minimum lease payment the lessor could accept under these assumptions? What is the maximum amount that Greymare could pay?

3. Recalculate the value of the lease to Greymare Bus Lines if the company pays no taxes until year 3. Calculate the lease cash flows by modifying Table 26-1. Remember that the after-tax borrowing rate for periods 1 and 2 differs from the rate for periods 3 through 7.

4. In Section 26-4, we asserted that, if the bus to be leased by Greymare has a 20% CCA rate rather than a 30% rate, then there are tax advantages to the lessee and the lessor only if the lessor's tax rate is lower than the lessee's. Check this by supposing the lessor has a 0% tax rate and the lessee has a 36% tax rate. Make all other assumptions as in Table 26-1. Find the minimum acceptable lease payment for the lessor and the maximum acceptable lease payment for the lessee, and see whether there is room in between to strike a deal.

5. NNW Airlines proposes to lease a $10 million aircraft. The terms require six annual lease payments of $1.65 million prepaid. NNW pays tax at 36%. If it purchases the aircraft, it would put the aircraft cost in a 25% CCA class, separate from its other Class 9 assets. The half-year rule applies, and the

aircraft will be worthless after six years. The interest rate is 10%. Draw up a schedule like Table 26-1 showing the incremental cash flows from leasing. What is the equivalent loan? How does it change over the life of the lease?

Suppose the plane is expected to have a $4 million salvage value after 7 years, and that investors in airplanes require a 15% expected return. Should NNW accept the lease as offered?

6. Nodhead College needs a new computer. It can either buy it for $250,000 or lease it from Compulease. The lease terms require Nodhead to make six annual payments (prepaid) of $50,000. Nodhead pays no tax. Compulease pays tax at 36%. Compulease would place the computer in Class 10 (30%) with all its other computers. It runs a multimillion dollar leasing business and always has a substantial UCC in Class 10. The half-year rule for CCA applies. The computer will have no residual value at the end of year 5. The interest rate is 8%.
   (a) What is the NPV of the lease for Nodhead College?
   (b) What is the NPV for Compulease?
   (c) What is the overall gain to the two parties if the lease is undertaken?

7. Many companies calculate the internal rate of return of the incremental after-tax cash flows from leasing. What problems do you think this may give rise to? To what rate should the IRR be compared?

8. The overall gain to leasing is the sum of the lease's value to the lessee and its value to the lessor. Construct simple numerical examples showing how this gain is affected by:
   (a) The rate of interest
   (b) The choice of CCA rate
   (c) The difference between the tax rates of the lessor and lessee
   (d) The length of the lease.

9. Discuss the following two opposite statements. What do you think makes the most sense?
   (a) "Leasing is tax avoidance and should be legislated against."
   (b) "Leasing ensures that the government's investment incentives work. It does so by allowing companies in non-taxpaying positions to take advantage of CCA."

10. The Safety Razor Company has a large tax loss carry-forward and does not expect to pay taxes for another 15 years. The company is therefore proposing to lease $100,000 of new machinery. The lease terms consist of eight equal lease payments prepaid annually. The lessor would group the machinery with its other Class 8 (20%) assets, and this class always has a large UCC. There is no salvage value at the end of the lease. The tax rate is 36% and the interest rate is 10%. Wilbur Occam, the president of Safety Razor, wants to know the maximum lease payment that his company should be willing to make and the minimum payment that the lessor is likely to accept. Can they negotiate a deal? How would your answer differ if the lessor is allowed a 50% CCA rate on the machinery?

*11. Here is a very hard question: Merton Miller argues that companies that pay corporate income tax should be indifferent between issuing debt and equity (see Section 18-2). Suppose that he is right. Then companies that do not pay income tax should prefer to issue equity rather than debt. They should also prefer to lease rather than issue debt. Does this mean that they should be indifferent between leasing and issuing equity?

12. In Section 26-4 we stated that if the interest rate is zero there would be no advantage in postponing tax and therefore no advantage to leasing. Value

the Greymare Bus Lines lease with an interest rate of zero. (Assume that Greymare does not pay tax.) Can you devise any lease terms that would make both a lessee and lessor happy? (If you can, we would like to hear from you.)

*13.   A lease with a varying rental schedule is known as a "structured lease." Try structuring the Greymare Bus Lines lease to increase value to the lessee while preserving the value to the lessor. (Assume that Greymare does not pay tax.) Note: In practice, the tax authorities will allow some structuring of rental payments but might be unhappy with some of the schemes you devise.

14.   In Section 26-4 we listed four circumstances in which there are potential gains from leasing. Check them out by conducting a sensitivity analysis on the Greymare Bus Lines lease assuming that Greymare does not pay tax. Try in turn: (a) A lessor tax rate of 50% (rather than 36%), (b) Immediate 100% depreciation in Year 0 (rather than 30% CCA), (c) A lease with four annual rentals (rather than a six-year lease), and (d) An interest rate of 20% (rather than 10%). In each case, find the minimum rental that would satisfy the lessor and look at the NPV to the lessee.

P · A · R · T

8

FINANCIAL PLANNING

C · H · A · P · T · E · R

27

ANALYZING FINANCIAL PERFORMANCE

"Divide and conquer" is the only practical strategy for presenting an extensive, complex field like financial management. We have broken the financial manager's job down into a series of clearly but narrowly defined topics, including capital budgeting, dividend policy, stock issue procedures, debt policy, and leasing. But in the end the financial manager has to consider the combined effects of these decisions on the firm as a whole.

In this chapter we look at how you can use financial data to analyze a firm's overall performance and assess its current financial standing. For example, you may need to check whether your own firm's financial performance is in the ballpark of standard practice. Or you may wish to understand the policies of a competitor or to check on the financial health of a customer.

Understanding the past is a necessary prelude to contemplating the future. Therefore, the other chapters in Part 8 are devoted to financial planning. Chapter 28 shows how managers use long-term financial plans to establish concrete goals and to anticipate surprises. Chapter 29 then discusses short-term planning, where the focus is on ensuring that the firm has enough cash to pay its bills and puts any spare cash to good use. Chapter 29 also serves as an introduction to Part 9, which covers the management of the firm's short-term assets and liabilities.

But all that comes later. The business at hand is to analyze financial performance. We start with the time-honoured method of financial ratio analysis. We discuss how ratios are used, and we note the limitations of the accounting data, which most of the ratios are based on.

27-1 FINANCIAL RATIOS

We have all heard stories of financial whizzes who in minutes can take a company's accounts apart and find its innermost secrets in financial ratios. The truth, however, is that financial ratios are no substitute for a crystal ball. They are just a convenient way to summarize large quantities of financial data and to compare firms' performance. Ratios help you to ask the right questions: they seldom answer them.

We will describe and calculate four types of financial ratios:

- Leverage ratios show how heavily the company is in debt,
- Liquidity ratios measure how easily it can lay its hands on cash,
- Profitability ratios are used to judge how efficiently the firm is using its assets, and
- Market value ratios show how highly it is valued by investors.

Table 27-1 contains the basic information that you need to calculate these financial ratios for Dofasco Inc. The income statement shows the amount that the company earned during 1989. After deducting the costs of goods sold and other expenses, Dofasco had total earnings before interest and taxes (EBIT) of $466 million. Of this sum, $132 million was used to pay debt interest (remember interest is paid out of pretax income) and $117 million was set aside for taxes. Preferred stock dividends took up $27 million of the aftertax profit, and the balance belonged to the common stockholders. However, Dofasco did not pay out all its earnings to the stockholders; $108 million was plowed back into the business.[1]

The balance sheet in Table 27-1 shows a snapshot of Dofasco's assets and liabilities at the end of 1989. Both the assets and the liabilities are listed in declining order of liquidity. For example, you can see that the accountant first lists the assets that are most likely to be turned into cash in the near future. They include cash itself, short-term securities, receivables (that is, unpaid bills by the firm's customers), and inventories of raw materials, work-in-process, and finished goods. These assets are all known as *current assets*. The second main group of assets consists of long-term assets such as steel mills and office buildings. Note that the balance sheet does not show the *current* value of each asset. Instead, the accountant records the amount that the asset originally cost and then, in the case of plant and equipment, deducts an annual amount to represent the anticipated depreciation.

Dofasco's liabilities are also classified into current and long term. Current liabilities are bills that the company expects to pay in the near future. They include debts that are due to be repaid within the next year and payables (that is, amounts owed by the company to its suppliers). In addition to these short-term obligations, Dofasco has issued bonds and leases that will not be repaid for many years. These are shown as long-term liabilities. After all these liabilities and the preferred stock have been paid off, the remaining assets belong to the common stockholders. The common shareholders' equity is simply the total value of the assets less the current and long-term liabilities and the preferred stock. It is also equal to common stock plus retained earnings—that is, the net amount that the firm has received from stockholders or reinvested on their behalf.

Table 27-1 also provides some other financial information about Dofasco. For example, it shows the market value of the common stock. It is often helpful to compare the *book value* of the equity (shown in the company's accounts) with the *market value* established in the capital markets.

Leverage Ratios

When a firm borrows money, it promises to make a series of fixed payments. Because the shareholders get only what is left over after the debtholders have been paid, debt is said to create *financial leverage*. Our first set of ratios measures this leverage.

---

[1] This is in addition to $242 million of cash flow earmarked as depreciation.

Table 27-1
Summary of financial statements of Dofasco Inc. (figures are in millions of dollars[a])

	1989	1988
Income statement:		
Sales	3,908	2,982
Other income	54	25
Cost of goods sold	3,201	2,375
Other expenses	295	224
Depreciation	242	187
Earnings before interest and tax (EBIT)	466	409
Interest	132	76
Tax	117	111
Net income	218	222
Preferred stock dividend	27	27
Earnings applicable to common stock	191	195
Balance Sheet:		
Cash and short-term securities	141	92
Receivables	447	521
Inventories	1,151	1,077
Total current assets	1,739	1,689
Plant and equipment	3,213	3,143
Other long-term assets	138	40
Total assets	5,091	4,872
Debt due	172	52
Payables	632	546
Total current liabilities	804	598
Long-term debt	1,337	1,426
Other long-term liabilities	692	728
Preferred stock	341	341
Common stock	1,918	1,779
Total liabilities	5,091	4,872
Other financial information:		
Market value of common equity[b]	$1,601	$1,689
Average number of shares[c] (in millions)	65	58
Earnings per share	$2.95	$3.37
Dividends per share	$1.28	$1.06
Share price (December close)	$24.5	$26.25

[a] Columns may not add due to rounding
[b] Based on year end values
[c] Based on average number of shares outstanding during the year

Debt Ratio   Financial leverage is usually measured by the ratio of long-term debt to total long-term capital. Since long-term lease arrangements also commit the firm to a series of payments, it makes sense to include the value of lease obligations with the long-term debt.[2]

---

[2] Preferred dividends also involve a series of fixed payments and are sometimes included with debt in the numerator of the debt ratio. In the context of the leverage ratios considered here, however, preferred shares are regarded as equity and are combined with common shares to compute total shareholders' equity.

Thus, for Dofasco:

$$\text{Debt ratio} = \frac{\text{long-term debt} + \text{value of leases}}{\text{long-term debt} + \text{value of leases} + \text{shareholders' equity}}$$

$$= \frac{1,337}{1,337 + 341 + 1,918} = 0.37$$

Another way to measure this is in terms of the company's debt-equity ratio:

$$\text{Debt-equity ratio} = \frac{\text{long-term debt} + \text{value of leases}}{\text{equity}} = \frac{1,337}{341 + 1,918} = 0.59$$

Notice that both these measures make use of book (that is, accounting) values rather than market values.[3] The market value of the company finally determines whether debtholders get their money back, so you would expect analysts to look at the face amount of the debt as a proportion of the total market value of debt and equity. The main reason that they don't do this is that market values are often not readily available. Does it matter much? Perhaps not; after all, the market value includes the value of intangible assets generated by research and development, advertising, staff training, and so on. These assets are not readily saleable and, if the company falls on hard times, the value of these assets may disappear altogether. For some purposes, it may be just as well to follow the accountant and to ignore these intangible assets entirely.

Also, notice that this measure of leverage takes account only of long-term debt obligations. Managers sometimes also define debt to include all liabilities other than equity:

$$\frac{\text{Total liabilities} - \text{equity}}{\text{Total liabilities}} = \frac{5,091 - 2,259}{5,091} = 0.56$$

Times Interest Earned   Another measure of financial leverage is the extent to which interest is covered by earnings before interest and taxes (EBIT) plus depreciation. In the case of Dofasco:[4]

$$\text{Times interest earned} = \frac{\text{EBIT} + \text{depreciation}}{\text{interest}} = \frac{466 + 242}{132} = 5.4$$

The regular interest payment is a hurdle that companies must keep jumping if they are to avoid default. The "times interest earned" ratio measures how much clear air there is between hurdle and hurdler. Always bear in mind that such summary measures tell only a part of the story. For example, it would make sense

---

[3] In the case of leased assets the accountant tries to estimate the present value of the lease commitments. In the case of long-term debt he or she simply shows face value. This can sometimes be very different from present value. For example, the present value of low-coupon debt may be only a fraction of its face value.

[4] The numerator of "times interest earned" can be defined in several ways. Sometimes depreciation is excluded. Sometimes it is just net earnings plus interest—that is, earnings before interest but after tax. This last definition seems nutty to us, because the point of "times interest earned" is to assess the risk that the firm won't have enough money to pay interest. If EBIT falls below interest obligations, the firm won't have to worry about taxes. Interest is paid before the firm pays income taxes.

to include other fixed charges such as regular repayments of existing debt or long-term lease payments.[5]

Liquidity Ratios   If you are extending credit or lending to a company for a short period, you are not just interested in the total asset coverage of the debt. You want to know whether the company will be able to lay its hands on the cash to repay you. That is why credit analysts and bankers look at several measures of liquidity.

Another reason that managers focus on liquid assets is that the figures are more reliable. The book value of a catalytic cracker may be a fairly poor guide to its true value, but at least you know what cash in the bank is worth.

Liquidity ratios also have some *less* desirable characteristics. Because short-term assets and liabilities are easily changed, measures of liquidity can rapidly become out of date. You might not know what that catalytic cracker is worth but you can be fairly sure that it won't disappear overnight. Also, companies generally choose a slack period for the end of their financial year. For example, retailers may end their financial year in January after the Christmas boom. At these times the companies are likely to have more cash and less short-term debt than during busier seasons.

Net Working Capital to Total Assets   Current assets are those assets that the company expects to turn into cash in the near future; current liabilities are liabilities that it expects to meet in the near future. The difference between the current assets and the current liabilities is known as *net working capital*. It roughly measures the company's potential reservoir of cash. Managers often express net working capital as a proportion of total assets:

$$\frac{\text{Net working capital}}{\text{Total assets}} = \frac{1{,}739 - 804}{5{,}091} = 0.18$$

Current Ratio   Another measure that serves a similar purpose is the current ratio:

$$\text{Current ratio} = \frac{\text{current assets}}{\text{current liabilities}} = \frac{1{,}739}{804} = 2.2$$

Changes in the current ratio can mislead. For example, suppose that a company borrows a large sum from the bank and invests it in marketable securities. If nothing else alters, net working capital is unaffected, but the current ratio changes. For this reason it might be preferable to net out the short-term investments and the short-term debt when calculating the current ratio.

Quick (or Acid-Test) Ratio   Some assets are closer to cash than others. If trouble comes, inventories may not sell at anything above fire-sale prices. (Trouble typically comes *because* the firm can't sell its finished product inventory for more than production cost.) Thus, managers often focus only on cash, marketable securities, and bills that customers have not yet paid.

$$\text{Quick ratio} = \frac{\text{cash + marketable securities + receivables}}{\text{current liabilities}} = \frac{141 + 447}{804} = 0.73$$

---

[5] In 1989 Dofasco used $87 million to reduce long-term debt. So,

$$\frac{\text{EBIT + depreciation}}{\text{interest + repayments of long-term debt}} = \frac{466 + 242}{132 + 87} = 3.2$$

Cash Ratio   A company's most liquid assets are its holdings of cash and marketable securities. That is why financial analysts also look at the cash ratio:

$$\text{Cash ratio} = \frac{\text{cash + marketable securities}}{\text{current liabilities}} = \frac{141}{804} = 0.18$$

Of course, lack of cash may not matter if the firm can borrow on short notice. Who cares whether a firm has actually borrowed from the bank or whether it has a guaranteed line of credit that enables it to borrow if it chooses? None of the standard liquidity measures takes the firm's "reserve borrowing power" into account.

Interval Measure   Instead of looking at a firm's liquid assets relative to its current liabilities, it may be useful to measure whether they are large relative to the firm's regular cash outgoings. One suggestion is the so-called interval measure:

$$\text{Interval measure} = \frac{\text{cash + marketable securities + receivables}}{\text{average daily expenditures from operations}}$$

$$= \frac{141 + 447}{3,496 \div 365} = 61 \text{ days}$$

Thus, Dofasco has sufficient liquid assets to finance operations for 61 days, even if it receives no further cash.

Profitability or Efficiency Ratios   Financial analysts employ another set of ratios to judge how efficiently companies are using their assets. As we will see, there is a much greater degree of ambiguity in these ratios. For example, we can be fairly sure that it is safer to lend to a company that has relatively little leverage and a predominance of liquid assets. But how should the lender interpret the fact that a firm has a high profit margin? Perhaps it is in a low-volume, high-markup business. (Jewellers operate on higher profit margins than food wholesalers but they are not necessarily safer.) Or perhaps it is more vertically integrated than its rivals. Again, that is not necessarily safer. Perhaps it charges higher prices, which is a bad sign. Or perhaps it has lower costs, which is a good sign. We think that you should use these profitability ratios to help you *ask* the important questions and *perhaps* to help answer them.

Sales to Total Assets   The sales-to-assets ratio shows how hard the firm's assets are being put to use.

$$\frac{\text{Sales}}{\text{Average total assets}} = \frac{3,908}{(5,091 + 4,872)/2} = 0.78$$

A high ratio could indicate that the firm is working close to capacity. It may prove difficult to generate further business without an increase in invested capital.

Notice that, since the assets are likely to change over the year, we have the *average* of the assets at the beginning of the year and the end of the year. Averages are usually used when a flow figure (in this case, *sales*) is compared with a snapshot figure (*total assets*).

Sales to Net Working Capital   Net working capital can be measured more accurately than other assets. Also the level of net working capital can be adjusted more rapidly to reflect temporary fluctuations in sales. Thus managers sometimes focus on how hard working capital has been put to use.

$$\frac{\text{Sales}}{\text{Average net working capital}} = \frac{3,908}{(935 + 1,091) \div 2} = 3.9$$

Net Profit Margin   If you want to know what proportion of sales finds its way into profits, you look at the profit margin. Thus:

$$\text{Net profit margin} = \frac{\text{EBIT} - \text{tax}}{\text{sales}} = \frac{466 - 117}{3,908} = 0.089 \text{ or } 8.9\%$$

Inventory Turnover   Managers sometimes look at the rate at which companies turn over their inventories. In Dofasco's case,

$$\text{Inventory turnover} = \frac{\text{cost of goods sold}}{\text{average inventory}} = \frac{3,201}{(1,151 + 1,077) \div 2} = 2.9$$

A high inventory turnover is often regarded as a sign of efficiency. But don't jump to conclusions — it may simply indicate that the firm is living from hand to mouth.

Average Collection Period   The average collection period measures the speed with which customers pay their bills:

$$\text{Average collection period} = \frac{\text{average receivables}}{\text{average daily sales}}$$
$$= \frac{(447 + 521) \div 2}{3,908 \div 365} = 45 \text{ days}$$

A low ratio is again believed to indicate an efficient collection department, but it sometimes results from an unduly restrictive credit policy.[6]

Return on Total Assets   Managers often measure the performance of a firm by the ratio of income to total assets. Income is usually defined as earnings before interest but after taxes.[7]

$$\text{Return on total assets} = \frac{\text{EBIT} - \text{taxes}}{\text{average total assets}}$$
$$= \frac{466 - 117}{(5,091 + 4,872) \div 2} = 0.070 \text{ or } 7.0\%$$

---

[6] If possible, it would make sense to divide average receivables by average daily *credit* sales. Otherwise, a low ratio might simply indicate that only a small portion of sales were made on credit.

[7] This measure is sometimes misleading if it is used to compare firms with different capital structures. The reason is that firms that pay more interest pay less taxes. Thus, this ratio reflects differences in financial leverage as well as in operating performance. If you want a measure of operating performance alone, we suggest adjusting taxes by adding back interest tax shields (interest payments × marginal tax rate). This gives the taxes the firm would pay if all-equity financed. Thus:

$$\text{Return on total assets} = \frac{\text{EBIT} - (\text{taxes} + \text{interest tax shields})}{\text{average total assets}}$$
$$= \frac{466 - (117 + 0.25(132))}{(5,091 + 4,872) \div 2} = 6.3\%$$

We could use this measure to compare the operating performance of two firms even if they had radically different debt ratios.

Sometimes net income after interest and taxes is used in the numerator. This is an odd measure: equity income ought to be compared with equity investment, not with total assets.

Another measure focuses on the return on the firm's equity:

$$\text{Return on equity} = \frac{\text{earnings available for common}}{\text{average common equity}}$$

$$= \frac{191}{(1{,}918 + 1{,}779) \div 2} = 0.103 \text{ or } 10.3\%$$

Some profitability or efficiency ratios can be linked together in useful ways. For example, the return on assets depends on the firm's sales-to-assets ratio and profit margin:

$$\frac{\text{Income}}{\text{Assets}} = \frac{\text{sales}}{\text{assets}} \times \frac{\text{income}}{\text{sales}}$$

All firms would like to earn a higher return on assets, but their ability to do so is limited by competition. If the expected return on assets is fixed by competition, firms face a trade-off between the sales-to-assets ratio and the profit margin. Thus, we find that fast-food chains, which turn over their capital frequently, also tend to operate on low profit margins. Hotels have relatively low sales-to-assets ratios but tend to compensate for this with higher margins.

Firms often seek to increase their profit margin by becoming more vertically integrated—for example, they may acquire a supplier or one of their sales outlets. Unfortunately, unless they have some special skill in running these new businesses, they are likely to find that any gain in profit margin is offset by a decline in the sales-to-assets ratio.

Payout Ratio The payout ratio measures the proportion of earnings that is paid out as dividends. For Dofasco:

$$\text{Payout ratio} = \frac{\text{dividend}}{\text{earnings per share}} = \frac{1.28}{2.95} = 0.43$$

We saw in Section 16-2 that managers don't like cutting dividends because of a temporary shortfall in earnings. Therefore, if a company's earnings are particularly variable, management is likely to play safe by setting a low average payout ratio.

When earnings fall unexpectedly, the payout ratio is likely to rise temporarily. Likewise, if earnings are expected to rise next year, management may feel that it can pay slightly more generous dividends than it would otherwise have done.

Earnings not paid out as dividends are plowed back into the business.

$$\text{Proportion of earnings plowed back} = 1 - \text{payout ratio}$$

$$= \frac{\text{earnings} - \text{dividend}}{\text{earnings}}$$

If you multiply this figure by the return on equity, you can see how rapidly the shareholders' investment is growing as a result of plowback. We used this growth measure in the constant-growth DCF model of Section 4-3. Thus, for Dofasco:

$$\text{Growth in equity from plowback} = \frac{\text{earnings} - \text{dividend}}{\text{earnings}} \times \frac{\text{earnings}}{\text{equity}}$$

$$= 0.57 \times 0.103 = 0.059 \text{ or } 5.9\%$$

If Dofasco can continue to earn 10.3% on its book equity, both earnings and equity will grow at 5.9% a year. Analysts sometimes refer to this figure as the *sustainable rate of growth*.

Is this a reasonable prospect? On past evidence, probably not. Dofasco's return on equity has fluctuated between 9% and 17% since 1983. So you would not want to bet too heavily that the 1989 return on equity will persist.

Market Value Ratio

There is no law that prohibits the financial manager from introducing data that are not in the company accounts. For example, if you were analyzing a steel company, you might want to look at the cost per tonne of steel produced or the sales per employee. Frequently managers find it helpful to look at ratios that combine accounting and stock market data. Here are four of these market-based ratios.

Price-Earnings Ratio   The price-earnings, or *P/E*, ratio is a common measure of the esteem in which the company is held by investors. In the case of Dofasco:[8]

$$P/E \text{ ratio} = \frac{\text{stock price}}{\text{earnings per share}} = \frac{24.5}{2.95} = 8.3$$

What does it mean when a company's stock sells on a high or low *P/E*? To answer this question you may find it helpful to look back to a formula that we introduced in Chapter 4. If a company's dividends are expected to grow at a steady rate, then the current stock price is:

$$P_0 = \frac{DIV_1}{r - g}$$

In this formula DIV_1 measures the expected dividend next year, r is the return that investors require from similar investments, and g is the expected rate of dividend growth. In order to find the *P/E* ratio, simply divide through by expected earnings per share:

$$\frac{P_0}{EPS_1} = \frac{DIV_1}{EPS_1} \times \frac{1}{r - g}$$

Thus, a high *P/E* ratio may indicate that (1) investors expect high dividend growth (g); or (2) that the stock has low risk and, therefore, that investors are content with a low prospective return (r); or (3) the company is expected to achieve average growth while paying out a high proportion of earnings (DIV_1/EPS_1).

Dividend Yield   The stock's dividend yield is simply the expected dividend as a proportion of the stock price. Thus, for Dofasco:

$$\text{Dividend yield} = \frac{\text{dividend per share}}{\text{stock price}} = \frac{1.28}{24.50} = 0.052 \text{ or } 5.2\%$$

Again, it is helpful to consider a company with a steady expected growth in dividends. In this case:

$$\text{Dividend yield} = \frac{DIV_1}{P_0} = r - g$$

---

[8] We use 1989 earnings per share and the price per share at the end of 1989. Since stockholders always look forward, not back, it would be better to use earnings that were forecasted for 1990. See Section 4-4.

Thus, a high yield may indicate that investors expect low dividend growth or that the stock's risk merits a high expected return.

Market-to-Book Ratio The market-to-book ratio is the ratio of stock price to book value per share. For Dofasco:

$$\text{Market-to-book ratio} = \frac{\text{stock price}}{\text{book value per share}} = \frac{24.5}{1,918 \div 65} = 0.83$$

Book value per share is just stockholders' book equity (net worth) divided by the number of shares outstanding. Book equity equals common stock plus retained earnings—the net amount that the firm has received from stockholders or reinvested on their behalf. Thus, Dofasco's market-to-book ratio of 0.83 means that the firm is worth 17% less than past and present stockholders have put into it.

Tobin's q The ratio of the market value of a company's debt and equity to the replacement cost of its assets is often referred to as Tobin's q, after the economist James Tobin.[9]

$$q = \frac{\text{market value of assets}}{\text{estimated replacement cost}}$$

This ratio is like the market-to-book ratio, but there are several important differences. The numerator q includes all the firm's debt and equity securities, not just its common stock. The denominator includes all assets, not just the firm's net worth. Moreover, these assets are not entered at original cost, as shown in the company's books, but at what it would cost to replace them. Inflation has driven many assets' replacement cost well above original cost. In Canada, companies of a certain minimum inventory and asset size are required to report the estimated replacement cost as a supplement to their regular financial statements.[10]

Tobin argued that firms have an incentive to invest when q is greater than one (that is when capital equipment is worth more than it costs to replace), and that they will stop investing only when q falls to one. Conversely, there may be occasions when q is less than one (that is, when equipment is worth less than it would cost to replace), and at these times firms have no incentive to invest.

Of course, it is possible to think of cases when the existing assets are worth much more than they cost but there is no scope for further profitable investment. Nevertheless, a high market value is usually a sign that investors believe there are good opportunities in your business.

The reverse is also true. Just because an asset is worth *less* than it would cost to buy today, it does not necessarily mean that it can be better employed elsewhere. But companies whose assets are valued below replacement cost ought to

---

[9] J. Tobin, "A General Equilibrium Approach to Monetary Theory," *Journal of Money, Credit, and Banking*, **1**: 15–29 (February 1969).

For estimates of q see R. H. Gordon and D. F. Bradford, "Taxation and the Stock Market Valuation of Capital Gains and Dividends: Theory and Empirical Results," *Journal of Public Economics*, **14** (October 1980); G. Von Furstenberg, "Corporate Investment: Does Market Valuation Really Matter?" *Brookings Papers on Economic Activity*, **2**: 347–397 (1977); and E. B. Lindberg and S. A. Ross, "Tobin's q Ratio and Industrial Organization," *Journal of Business*, **54**: 1–33 (January 1981).

[10] The conditions under which a publicly traded firm must report replacement cost information are given in the *CICA Handbook*, Section 4510.

Table 27.2
Average values of Tobin's q, 1960–1977

	High q's		Low q's
Avon Products	8.53	Cone Mills	0.45
Polaroid	6.42	Holly Sugar	0.50
Xerox	5.52	Federal Paper Bond	0.52
Searle	5.27	National Steel	0.53
MMM	4.87	Graniteville	0.55
Schering-Plough	4.30	Publicker Industries	0.59
IBM	4.21	Medusa Corp.	0.60
Coca-Cola	4.21	Lowenstein	0.61
Smithkline	4.19	U.S. Steel	0.62
Eli Lilly	4.02	Dan River	0.67

Source: E. B. Lindberg and S. A. Ross, "Tobin's q Ratio and Industrial Organization," *Journal of Business*, **54**: 1–33 (January 1981).

look over their shoulder to see whether predators are threatening to take them over and redeploy the assets.

We should also expect that q would be higher for firms with a strong competitive advantage. Table 27-2 seems to bear this out. The companies with the highest values of q tend to be those that have had very strong brand images or patent protection. Those with the lowest values have generally been in highly competitive and shrinking industries.

Accounting Definitions

Many years ago a British bank chairman observed that not only did the bank's accounts show its true position but the actual situation was a little better still.[11] Since that time accounting standards have been much more carefully defined but companies still have considerable discretion in calculating profits and deciding what to show on the balance sheet. Thus, when you calculate financial ratios, you need to look below the surface and understand some of the decisions taken by the firm's accountants.

Here are some examples of things you might want to think about when interpreting Dofasco's financial ratios:

1. Dofasco reports interest income plus other income as one item on the income statement and then has a separate entry for interest expense. There is nothing wrong with doing this but you have to be careful when comparing this with gross and net interest figures shown by other firms.

2. The income shown in Dofasco's financial statements is smaller than the income that is reported to the tax authorities. The main reason is that in the income statement provided to shareholders Dofasco uses primarily a straight line depreciation method whereas Revenue Canada allows the firm to use a declining balance CCA. This means that there will be differences in income reported to shareholders relative to income reported to Revenue Canada. In 1989 these differences meant that the company actually paid $28.7 million more in taxes than the amount shown on the income statement. Thus, net income was actually lower than reported.[12]

---

[11] Speech by the Chairman of the London and County Bank at the Annual Meeting, February 1901. Reported in *The Economist* 1901, p. 204, and cited in C. A. E. Goodhart. *The Business of Banking 1891–1914*, Weidenfeld (George) and Nicholson, Ltd., London, 1972, p. 15.

[12] Of course, in other years the company pays less tax than is shown on its income statement. This amount is set aside in the balance sheet as an "income tax allocation relating to future years," which is also commonly referred to as deferred tax.

3. Dofasco's assets include equity in Algoma Steel which, at year end 1989, was valued at $687 million dollars. However, Dofasco indicated in its statements that it planned to write off its investment in Algoma completely. This is an obvious case where the reported asset value should be treated with caution. A less obvious example is a company's investment in goodwill which is usually entered as an asset when a company acquires another company for a price that exceeds book value. We don't want to get into a discussion as to whether goodwill is really an asset, but we should warn you about the dangers of comparing ratios of firms whose balance sheets include a substantial goodwill element with those that do not.

4. Not all assets and liabilities show up on the balance sheet. For example, the pension that firms promise to employees is like a debt. To pay future pension, companies make contributions to a pension fund. Although the obligation and the pension fund are significant assets and liabilities they are not directly reported on the balance sheet. Instead, the difference between the asset and liability is authorized and reported as an accrual.

For instance, in 1989 Dofasco's pension fund portfolio was valued at $1.73 billion while its pension liability was considered to be $156 million more than that. This deficit is then amortized over the average expected service life of the employee group. The amortization is then reflected in the company's accrual for net pension benefits.

Choosing a Benchmark

We have shown you how to calculate the principal financial ratios for Dofasco. But you still need some way of judging whether a ratio is high or low.

A good starting point is to compare the 1989 ratios with equivalent figures for Dofasco in earlier years. For example, you can see from the first two columns of Table 27-3 that Dofasco appears to be a weaker company in 1989 than it had been during the previous five years. It was less profitable, although it was more highly levered, and it was more illiquid. Investors also seemed to be more pessimistic about Dofasco's products, for they placed a lower value on its earnings and assets than in earlier years.[13] But you should now dig behind these figures. For example, check that Dofasco has not increased its research and development expenditures, for that would lower current earnings to the benefit of future earnings. Find out what was happening to inventories. In 1989, inventories increased by 6%. This also can't recur indefinitely. Also, examine the 44% increase in the debt ratio and the 40% decrease in the current ratio. Are they a source of concern? In sum, don't just measure whether Dofasco's financial ratios have changed: try to understand *why* they have changed.

It is also helpful to compare Dofasco's financial position with that of other firms. However, you would not expect companies in different industries to have similar financial ratios. For example, a steel producer is unlikely to have the same profit margin as a jeweller or the same leverage as a finance company. It makes sense, therefore, to limit the comparison to other firms in the same industry. The third column of Table 27-3 sets out the average financial ratios for other steel producers. Although Dofasco's 1989 performance was weaker than in previous years, it still appears to be more profitable and financially stronger than the other steel companies. But once again you should not stop there. For example, notice

[13] Averages of ratios are somewhat odd animals. For example, you wouldn't want to take an average of *P/E* ratios if one company had negligible earnings. In Table 27-3 we have scaled all the industry data by dividing by the year's total assets. Then we have calculated the ratio of the average of one item to the average of the other item.

Table 27-3
Financial ratios for Dofasco, Inc. and other steel companies

	1989	1984–1988	Other Companies in the Steel Industry, 1989*
Leverage ratios:			
Debt ratio	0.372	0.259	0.388
Total liabilities − equity / Total liabilities	0.556	0.458	0.581
Times interest earned	5.376	9.367	4.274
Liquidity ratios:			
Net working capital to total assets	0.184	0.293	0.257
Current ratio	2.164	3.482	2.495
Quick ratio	0.732	1.654	0.971
Cash ratio	0.175	0.840	0.293
Interval measure (in days)	61.404	112.604	64.412
Profitability (or efficiency) ratios:			
Sales to average total assets	0.785	0.779	1.028
Sales to average working capital	3.857	2.665	4.091
Net profit margin (%)	0.089	0.101	0.059
Inventory turnover	2.873	2.921	3.318
Average collection period (days)	45.201	44.697	46.668
Return on total assets	0.070	0.079	0.060
Return on equity	0.103	0.120	0.063
Market value ratios:			
Price-earnings ratio	8.305	9.337	14.853
Dividend yield	0.052	0.039	0.042
Market-too-book ratio	0.835	1.037	0.840

* Stelco, IPSCO, and Ivaco.

that Dofasco's leverage and liquidity ratios are now in line with industry averages. Note also that the difference in the return on assets stems largely from the difference in profit margins. Was this due to greater efficiency or to a difference in the type of business? You can obtain some clues by comparing segment counts, which break profitability down according to product and area of operation. Are there any indications that the difference in margins may be temporary? A closer examination of the cost of goods sold may help you decide.

Financial ratios for industries are published by Dun and Bradstreet Canada, Statistics Canada, and others. Table 27-4 gives selected leverage, liquidity, and profitability ratios for major industry groups. This should give you a feel for some differences between industries.

Which Financial Ratios? Be selective in your choice of financial ratios, because many ratios tell you similar things. For illustration, Table 27-5 shows the correlation between the nine financial ratios.[14] Notice that the correlation between the times interest earned and the return on equity ratio is 0.7. This suggests that you may not need to calculate both these ratios. Conversely, there is almost no relationship between

[14] The correlations are Spearman rank correlations. In other words, they measure whether a company's ranking in terms of one ratio corresponds to its ranking in terms of the second ratio.

Table 27-4
Selected financial ratios for major industry groups, 1989

Industry[a]	Debt-Equity Ratio	Current Ratio	Net Profit Margin	Collection Period[b]	Return on Equity[c]
All manufacturers	1.25	1.6	0.035	38	0.104
Food (wholesale)	2.41	1.3	0.001	22	0.144
Tobacco	0.51	2.5	0.131	36	0.113
Paper products	0.94	1.9	0.033	43	0.095
Publishing and printing	1.43	1.2	0.070	49	0.190
Iron and steel mills	1.39	2.2	0.037	46	0.076
Electrical equipment, industrial	0.90	1.9	0.037	68	0.099
Retail trade	2.21	1.3	0.032	10	0.278

[a] The industry classifications and ratios are from *Key Business Ratios, 1989 Edition*, Dun and Bradstreet Canada.

[b] Collection period is average daily sales divided by end-of-year receivables.

[c] Return on equity includes preferred dividends in numerator and the value of the preferred shares in the denominator.

Table 27-5
Correlations and co-movements between representative financial ratios of different categories

	(1)	(2)	(3)	(4)	(5)	(6)	(7)	(8)
(1)	1.000							
(2)	0.423	1.000						
(3)	0.206	−0.016	1.000					
(4)	−0.337	−0.446	−0.132	1.000				
(5)	0.256	0.339	0.241	−0.591	1.000			
(6)	0.257	0.110	0.186	−0.154	0.700	1.000		
(7)	0.013	0.209	−0.450	−0.219	0.369	0.239	1.000	
(8)	0.111	0.281	0.162	−0.226	0.432	0.201	0.221	1.000

(1) = (Cash + mkt securities) / Total assets
(2) = Current ratio
(3) = Cash flow from operations / Sales
(4) = Debt − equity ratio
(5) = Times interest earned
(6) = Return on equity
(7) = Sales to total assets
(8) = Price / Earnings ratio

Source: G. Foster, *Financial Statement Analysis*, Prentice-Hall, Inc., Englewood Cliffs, N.J., 1986.

a firm's sales to total assets and cash and marketable securities to total assets. You can get additional information by looking at both figures.

27-2   THE EARNINGS RECORD

Figure 27-1 summarizes Dofasco's earnings record over the past five years. To interpret this record you need to take into account what was happening to other companies. The reason for this is that Dofasco is affected by the state of the economy as a whole and by the prosperity of its particular industry. The impor-

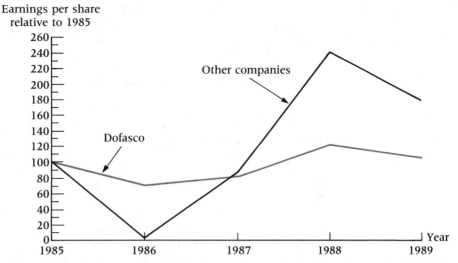

Figure 27-1   Earnings per share of Dofasco and a sample of other steel companies, 1985–89, expressed as a percent of 1985 earnings per share.

Table 27-6
Industry breakdown of industry and economy influences on first differenced net income series, 1964–1983

Industry Title	Economy Influence	Industry Influence
Crude petroleum and natural gas	0.14	0.23
Paper and allied products	0.49	0.60
Drugs	0.14	0.26
Petroleum refining	0.37	0.54
Steel and blast furnaces	0.35	0.53
General industrial machinery and equipment	0.23	0.29
Radio and TV transmitting equipment	0.14	0.17
Electronic components	0.32	0.37
Trucking	0.21	0.42
Air transportation	0.12	0.15
Electric services	0.08	0.39
Natural gas distribution	0.13	0.11
Electric and other service combinations	0.06	0.45
Retail, grocery stores	0.09	0.17
State banks, federal reserve system	0.05	0.25
Total	0.17	0.36

Source: G. Foster, *Financial Statement Analysis*, Prentice-Hall, Inc., Englewood Cliffs, N.J., 1986.

tance of these external influences on a company's income is shown in Table 27-6 for American companies. On average an estimated 17% of the yearly variation in income is due to changes in the aggregate income of all corporations. A further 36% is explained by changes in the industry's income.

Figure 27-1 shows the average earnings performance of other Canadian companies doing business in the steel industry. We can now start to ask sensible questions about Dofasco's record. For example, why were the earnings of the other steel companies so weak in 1986? Was it because of a slowdown in business conditions in other countries that prompted an influx of imports from competitors trying to increase their capacity utilization? If so, we know two danger signals to look out for in the future. Why did Dofasco buck the industry trend to some extent in 1986? Is it related to its role as the dominant supplier of flat-rolled steel in Canada?

Although Dofasco avoided the 1986 set-back experienced by others, it also seems to have missed the growth in earnings that others have experienced since. Does this mean that the industry has entered into a period of continued growth that Dofasco will miss out on?

Not necessarily. Statisticians who have studied the time path of reported earnings conclude that earnings behave much like stock prices — that is, they seem to follow a random walk.[15] There is almost no relationship between a company's earnings growth in one period and that in the next. Therefore, do not extrapolate growth mechanically. A firm with above-average earnings growth may sustain it, but it is equally likely to be followed by below-average growth.

Since earnings changes are unrelated from one year to the next, your best measure of past growth is the simple average of past annual percentage growth rates. There is little point in fitting a trend line to past earnings, and such a trend line tells you little about likely future earnings.

Of course there are many other sources of information that may help you forecast earnings. For example, when a firm enjoys a high *P/E* ratio despite disappointing earnings, it suggest investors expect an earnings rebound. Or suppose a firm announces a significant technological jump ahead of its competitors: you don't need a Ph.D. to figure out the likely impact on earnings.

*The Meaning of Accounting Earnings

Economists often define earnings as cash flow plus the change in value of the company's assets. But we know from looking at the behaviour of stock prices that changes in asset values are fundamentally unpredictable. So it looks as if the company's published earnings follow a much smoother path than economic earnings.

Accountants don't really try to track year-to-year economic income. They seem more interested in showing the long-run average profitability of the firm's assets.[16] However, they often don't achieve that objective either.

We described the biases in accounting profitability measures in Chapter 12. A few more words are needed here because accountants provide most of the input for financial ratios.

How Accounting Earnings Are Calculated   We emphasized in Chapter 6 that accounting earnings differ from cash flow. Accountants start with cash flow, but they allocate cash outflows to two categories — current and capital expenditures. Current expenditures are deducted from earnings right away.[17] Capital expenditures are capitalized and then depreciated over the following years.

Which outflows should be capitalized? When a company builds a new factory, there is an outflow of cash but shareholders also acquire an asset that is likely to bring higher cash flows in the future. Therefore, accountants are prepared to

---

[15] See, for example, R. Ball and R. Watts, "Some Time Series Properties of Accounting Income," *Journal of Finance*, **27**: 663–682 (June 1972).

[16] Fischer Black has made this point in an extreme but very interesting way. See F. Black, "The Magic in Earnings: Economic Earnings versus Accounting Earnings," *Financial Analysts Journal*, **36**: 3–8 (November–December 1980).

[17] This is obviously an oversimplification. Accountants also try to record income and expenditure in the year in which it accrues rather than when the bills are paid.

treat such expenditures as capital investments. But what about the cost of research and development, or staff training, or a new advertising campaign? These expenditures are also investments in the future but accountants are reluctant to recognize investments in intangible assets. Therefore, they deduct such expenditures from current earnings.[18]

If a high-tech company makes a large investment in research and development (R&D), financial statements are likely to understate true earnings. But investors recognize that some of the expenses are really an investment in the future. Therefore, the stock sells at a high price relative to published earnings. Subsequently, when the investment in R&D begins to pay off, published earnings are likely to rise rapidly. But investors are aware that the company is now running down its capital; so the stock price will not keep pace with earnings.[19]

A company's income statement shows the actual operating cash flows but it does not show the actual change in asset value. Instead, accountants set up a depreciation schedule ahead of time and, except in abnormal circumstances, they stick to it. Thus, the company's income statement reflects partly what actually happened (the operating cash flow) and partly what was forecast to happen (the depreciation in asset value).

When accountants set up the depreciation schedule in advance, they do not make detailed forecasts of how the value of each asset is likely to vary over time. Instead, they rely on a few standard rules of thumb such as straight-line depreciation. If an investment takes several years to reach full profitability, then in the early years straight-line depreciation will overstate the likely fall in the investment's value and in the later years it will understate it. For example, suppose that a paper manufacturer opens a new mill. Large paper mills take a notoriously long time to reach maximum efficiency. Therefore, if the company depreciates its assets straight-line, the financial statements will initially understate true earnings and the stock will sell at a high price relative to the published figure.

Of course, decisions on which items to capitalize and how to depreciate them are not the only potential sources of distortion in earnings. Our message, however, is a general one. If you wish to use a company's earnings as a guide to its value, you need to "normalize" those earnings for temporary distortions that stem from particular accounting techniques.

*How Inflation Affects Book Returns

We will steer clear of "inflation accounting" because the subject is so complex when one gets down to practical proposals. We will just remind you how inflation bears on standard book earnings.

First, inflation increases the nominal value of work-in-process and finished inventory. Suppose you are a clothing manufacturer. In January you make up 1,000 men's suits worth $300 apiece, but you do not sell the suits until June. During this time your competitors have raised their prices by 6% and you have quite literally followed suit. Thus, the goods are finally sold for $300 \times 1.06 = $318.

Part of your profit on this batch of suits can be attributed to inflation while the suits sat in inventory. You receive an inventory profit of $18 per suit.

---

[18] Accountants prefer assets you can kick. Since you can't see or touch intangible assets, how can you be *sure* they are there?

[19] When the stock price does not respond to the increased earnings, managers sometimes feel that investors are irrational or ungrateful. They forget that the *real* increase in earnings occurred several years earlier.

Inventory profits are profits. You are better off with them than without. They are properly included in nominal income. However, they are not a part of real income, except to the extent that inventories appreciate faster than the general price level.

There is a second problem. As inflation progresses, the net book value of fixed assets gets more and more out of date—that is, book value understates current value or replacement cost. Thus, book depreciation is too low.

Inflation has a third effect on book profits of firms that borrow. Lenders are paid back in inflated future dollars, so they demand a higher interest rate to compensate for the declining real value of their loan. The part of the interest rate that compensates for expected inflation is called the *inflation premium*.

The full interest payment, including the inflation premium, is deducted from the firm's net book income. But book income does not recognize the compensating gain that the stockholders make at the expense of lenders. Remember, lenders gain from the inflation premium but lose as inflation drives down the real value of their asset. Stockholders lose by paying the inflation premium but gain because inflation drives down the real value of their obligation. Book income recognizes stockholders' loss but not the offsetting gain.[20]

27-3   APPLICATIONS OF FINANCIAL ANALYSIS

We have discussed how to calculate and interpret summary measures of a company's financial position. We conclude this chapter with a brief glimpse at some of the ways that these measures can help the financial manager.

Using Financial Ratios in Credit Analysis

Suppose that you are a credit analyst or bank lending officer with the job of deciding whether a particular company is likely to repay its debts. What can you learn from the company's financial statements?

To answer this question William Beaver compared the financial ratios of 79 firms that subsequently failed with the ratios of 79 that remained solvent.[21] Beaver's sample of failed firms behaved much as you would expect. They had more debt than the surviving firms and they had a lower return on sales and assets. They had less cash but more receivables. As a result they had somewhat lower current ratios and dramatically lower cash ratios. Contrary to popular belief, the failed firms had less, rather than more, inventory.

Figure 27-2 provides some idea of the predictive power of these financial ratios. You can see that five years before failure the group of failed firms appeared to be consistently less healthy. As we move progressively closer to the date of collapse, the difference between the two groups becomes even more marked.

Instead of looking at a number of separate clues, it may be more useful to combine the different bits of information into a single measure of the likelihood of bankruptcy. We will describe in Chapter 30 how companies construct such a measure.

---

[20] For a good, provocative discussion of inflationary biases in book income see F. Modigliani and R. A. Cohn, "Inflation, Rational Valuation and the Market," *Financial Analysts Journal*, **35**: 24–44 (March–April 1979).

[21] See W. H. Beaver, "Financial Ratios and Predictors of Failure," *Empirical Research in Accounting: Selected Studies. Supplement to Journal of Accounting Research*, 1966, 77–111.

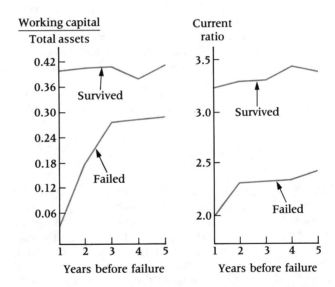

Figure 27-2 Beaver's study showed that the financial ratios of firms that subsequently fail are different from those of firms that survive. Note that the horizontal axis measures the number of years *before* failure: thus moving from right to left brings the failed firms *closer* to failure.

Source: W.H. Beaver, "Financial Ratios and Predictors of Failure," *Empirical Research in Accounting: Selected Studies. Supplement to Journal of Accounting Research*, 1966, pp. 77–111, fig. 1, p. 82.

Using Financial Ratios to Estimate Market Risk

Chapter 9 described how the return that investors require from a company's stock depends on its market risk or beta. If you have a sufficient history of stock price data, you can estimate beta by looking at the extent to which the price was affected by fluctuations in the market.

Because such stock price data are not always available, financial economists have examined whether accounting data can be used to estimate beta. The

Table 27-7
Correlations between stock market betas and financial ratios

	1947–1956	1957–1965
Accounting beta	0.44	0.23
Leverage	0.23	0.22
Average payout ratio	−0.49	−0.29
Asset size	−0.06	−0.16
Asset growth	0.27	0.01
Liquidity	−0.13	0.05

Source: W. H. Beaver, P. Kettler, and M. Scholes, "The Association Between Market-Determined and Accounting-Determined Measures of Risk Measures," *The Accounting Review,* **45**: 654–682 (October 1970).

pioneering study is by Beaver, Kettler, and Scholes.[22] In addition to calculating the usual financial ratios, Beaver, Kettler, and Scholes calculated an "accounting beta." In other words, they estimated the sensitivity of each company's earnings changes to changes in the aggregate earnings of all companies. An accounting beta of less than 1.0 means that on average the company's earnings changed by less than 1% for each 1% change in aggregate earnings. Conversely an accounting beta of more than 1.0 implies that the firm's earnings changed by more than 1% for each 1% change in aggregate earnings.

Table 27-7 summarizes the findings of this study. Not only the accounting beta but also the firm's leverage and payout ratio appear to provide useful clues to market risk.

Instead of looking at financial ratios one by one, Rosenberg and Marathe looked at a combination of ratios and obtained a single estimate of beta that was about as accurate as you could get from stock price data.[23] They suggested that you can get even better estimates of risk by taking both accounting measures and stock price data into account.

Using Financial Ratios to Predict Bond Ratings

DBRS's and Moody's bond ratings are widely used as a yardstick of bond quality. Therefore, they are a pointer as to which investors are likely to buy your company's bonds and what interest rate they will require. Financial managers pay considerable attention to their company's bond ratings and would like to know in advance how a new issue of bonds would be rated and how a change in circumstances would affect the ratings on existing debt.

Kaplan and Urwitz found that issuers of the more highly rated bonds generally had lower debt ratios, a higher ratio of earnings to interest, and a higher return on assets. The bonds were also more likely to be senior issues and the companies tended to be larger with lower market and unique risk.

Kaplan and Urwitz also combined these variables into a single measure of bond quality and looked at how well it could forecast Moody's ratings for a sample of newly issued bonds. Table 27-8 shows that their forecast was spot on two-thirds of the time and that it was never out by more than one category.

---

[22] W. H. Beaver, P. Kettler, and M. Scholes, "The Association Between Market-Determined and Accounting-Determined Risk Measures," *The Accounting Review,* **45**: 654–682 (October 1970).

[23] See B. Rosenberg and V. Marathe, "The Prediction of Systematic and Residual Risk," *Proceedings of the Seminar on the Analysis of Security Prices.* Center for Research in Security Prices, Graduate School of Business, University of Chicago, November 1975.

Table 27-8
Moody's bond ratings for a sample of new issues were similar to the predicted ratings (for example, a total of 46 bonds were predicted to have A ratings and, of these, 33 actually received an A rating)

Actual Ratings	Predicted Ratings						
	Aaa	Aa	A	Baa	Ba	B	Total
Aaa	2						2
Aa	2	2	5				9
A		1	33	2			36
Baa			8	7			15
Ba				1			1
B					1		1
Total	4	3	46	10	1		64

Source: R. S. Kaplan and G. Urwitz, "Statistical Models of Bond Ratings: A Methodological Inquiry," *Journal of Business*, **52**: 231–261 (April 1979).

27-4   SUMMARY

If you are analyzing a company's financial statement, there is a danger of being overwhelmed by the sheer volume of data. That is why managers use a few salient ratios to summarize the firm's leverage, liquidity, profitability, and market valuation. We have described some of the more popular financial ratios.

We offer the following general advice to users of financial ratios.

1. Financial ratios seldom provide answers but they do help you ask the right questions.
2. There is no international standard for financial ratios. A little thought and common sense is worth far more than blind application of formulas.
3. Be selective in your choice of ratios. Different ratios often tell you similar things.
4. You need a benchmark for assessing a company's financial position. It is usual to compare financial ratios with the company's ratios in earlier years and with the ratios of other firms in the same business.

You can learn something about why a company's earnings change by comparing its earnings record with that of other firms. But be careful not to extrapolate past rates of earnings growth—earnings follow approximately a random walk.

Accounting earnings don't incorporate the year-by-year fluctuations in the value of the company's assets. Instead, accountants try to provide a picture of long-run sustainable earnings. Therefore, you can often get some idea of a company's value by multiplying its earnings by a standard price-earnings multiple. Sometimes the procedures used by accountants may temporarily depress earnings. For example, accountants generally deduct expenditure on intangible assets from current earnings. Also, if an investment takes a while to reach maximum profitability, straight-line depreciation will lead to an understatement of earnings in the early years. In these cases the earnings should be capitalized at a higher multiple.

Financial statement analysis helps you understand what makes the firm tick. We looked briefly at three particular applications. First, healthy firms have different financial ratios than firms that are heading for insolvency. Second, financial ratios provide valuable clues about a firm's market risk. Finally, we saw that a company's financial ratios can be used to predict the rating on a new issue of bonds.

FURTHER READING

There are some good general texts on financial statement analysis. See, for example:

G. Foster, *Financial Statement Analysis*, Prentice-Hall, Inc., Englewood Cliffs, N.J., 1986.

B. Lev, *Financial Statement Analysis: A New Approach*, Prentice-Hall, Inc., Englewood Cliffs, N.J., 1978.

Fischer Black's provocative paper argues that the object of accounting rules is to produce an earnings figure that moves as nearly as possible in line with company values:

F. Black, "The Magic in Earnings: Economic Earnings versus Accounting Earnings," *Financial Analysts Journal*, **36**: 3–8 (November–December 1980).

Three classic articles on the application of financial ratios to specific problems are:

W. H. Beaver, "Financial Ratios and Predictors of Failure," *Empirical Research in Accounting: Selected Studies. Supplement to Journal of Accounting Research*, 1966, 77–111.

W. H. Beaver, P. Kettler, and M. Scholes, "The Association Between Market-Determined and Accounting-Determined Risk Measures," *The Accounting Review*, **45**: 654–682 (October 1970).

J. O. Horrigan, "The Determination of Long Term Credit Standing with Financial Ratios," *Empirical Research in Accounting: Selected Studies. Supplement to Journal of Accounting Research*, 1966, 44–62.

QUIZ

1. Table 27-9 gives abbreviated balance sheets and income statements for Tuktoyaktuk Manufacturing Inc. Calculate the following financial ratios:
   (a) Debt ratio
   (b) Current ratio
   (c) Quick ratio
   (d) Net profit margin
   (e) Inventory turnover
   (f) Return on net worth
   (g) Payout ratio

2. There are no universally accepted definitions of financial ratios, but five of the following ratios make no sense at all. Substitute the correct definitions.

   (a) Debt-equity ratio $= \dfrac{\text{long-term debt} + \text{value of leases}}{\text{long-term debt} + \text{value of leases} + \text{equity}}$

   (b) Return on equity $= \dfrac{\text{EBIT} - \text{tax}}{\text{average equity}}$

   (c) Payout ratio $= \dfrac{\text{dividend}}{\text{stock price}}$

   (d) Profit margin $= \dfrac{\text{EBIT} - \text{tax}}{\text{sales}}$

   (e) Inventory turnover $= \dfrac{\text{sales}}{\text{average inventory}}$

   (f) Current ratio $= \dfrac{\text{current liabilities}}{\text{current assets}}$

   (g) Sales to net working capital $= \dfrac{\text{average sales}}{\text{net working capital}}$

   (h) Interval measure $= \dfrac{\text{current assets} - \text{inventories}}{\text{average daily expenditure from operations}}$

   (i) Average collection period $= \dfrac{\text{sales}}{\text{average receivables} \div 365}$

Table 27-9
**Income statement and balance sheets for Tuktoyaktuk Manufacturing, Inc.
for fiscal year ending December 31, 1990**

Income statement

Sales	$2,979
Cost of goods sold	2,053
Selling, general and administrative expenses	598
Operating income	328
Interest expense	64
Income before taxes	264
Taxes	128
Net earnings	136
Dividends	31

	Start of Year	End of Year
Balance sheet		
Assets:		
Cash and marketable securities	$ 43	$ 74
Inventory	437	502
Accounts receivable	74	84
Other current assets	16	19
Total current assets	570	679
Net property, plant, and equipment	726	740
Other assets	181	200
Total assets	$1,477	$1,619
Liabilities:		
Accounts payable	317	330
Other current liabilities	133	157
Total current liabilities	450	487
Long-term debt, including capitalized leases	232	221
Other long-term liabilities	98	110
Stockholders' equity	697	801
Total liabilities and stockholder's equity	$1,477	$1,619

(j) Quick ratio $= \dfrac{\text{current assets } - \text{ inventories}}{\text{current liabilities}}$

(k) Tobin's $q = \dfrac{\text{market value of assets}}{\text{replacement cost of assets}}$

3. True or false?
    (a) A company's debt-equity ratio is always less than one.
    (b) The quick ratio is always less than the current ratio.
    (c) The return on equity is always less than the return on assets.
    (d) Successive earnings levels are unrelated to each other.
    (e) Successive earnings changes are unrelated to each other.
    (f) Earnings follow roughly a random walk. This means that if earnings
        turn out to be higher than expected, you should revise upward your
        forecast of future earnings by a similar proportion.
    (g) Accounting earnings follow a less smooth path than economic earnings.
    (h) If a project is slow to reach full profitability, straight-line depreciation
        is likely to produce an overstatement of profits in the early years.

      (i) A substantial new advertising campaign by a cosmetics company will tend to depress earnings and cause the stock to sell at a low price-earnings multiple.

4. In each of the following cases, explain briefly which of the two companies is likely to be characterized by the higher ratio:

    (a) Debt-equity ratio: a shipping company or a computer software company

    (b) Payout ratio: United Foods Inc. or Computer Graphics Inc.

    (c) Ratio of sales to assets: an integrated pulp and paper manufacturer or a paper mill

    (d) Average collection period: A supermarket chain or a mail order company

    (e) Price-earnings multiple: Basic Sludge Company or Fledgling Electronics

    (f) Tobin's q: an iron foundry or a pharmaceutical company with strong patent protection

QUESTIONS AND PROBLEMS

1. Discuss alternative measures of financial leverage. Should the market value of equity be used or the book value? Is it better to use the market value of debt, the book value, or the book value discounted at the risk-free interest rate? How should you treat off-balance-sheet obligations such as pension liabilities? How would you treat preferred stock, deferred tax reserves, and minority interest?

2. As you can see, someone has spilt ink over some of the entries in the balance sheet and income statement of Transylvania Railroad (Table 27-10). Can you use the following information to work out the missing entries?

- Debt ratio   = 0.4
- Current ratio   = 1.4
- Quick ratio   = 1.0
- Cash ratio   = 0.2
- Return on total assets   = 0.18
- Return on equity   = 0.41
- Inventory turnover   = 5.0
- Receivables' collection period = 71.2 days

3. Use financial ratio analysis to compare two companies chosen from the same industry.

4. Read and discuss Fischer Black's paper "The Magic in Earnings."

5. Describe some of the ways that the choice of accounting technique can temporarily depress or inflate earnings.

6. Suppose that at year end 1989 Dofasco had unused lines of credit which would have allowed it to borrow a further $300 million. Suppose that it used this line of credit to raise short-term loans of $300 million and invested the proceeds in marketable securities. Would the company have appeared to be (a) more or less liquid or (b) more or less highly levered? Calculate the appropriate ratios.

7. Recalculate Dofasco's financial ratios at the end of 1990. What problems arise in ensuring comparable figures with 1989?

8. Here are some data for five companies in the saucepan industry:

Company	A	B	C	D	E
Net income (millions of $)	10	0.5	6.67	−1	6.67
Total book assets (millions of $)	300	30	120	50	120
Shares outstanding (millions)	3	4	2	5	10
Share price ($)	100	5	50	8	10

Table 27-10
Balance sheet and income statement of Transylvania Railroad

	Millions of Dollars	
	December 1991	December 1990
Balance sheet		
Fixed assets, net	■ ■ ■	25
Cash	■ ■ ■	20
Accounts receivable	■ ■ ■	34
Inventory	■ ■ ■	26
Total current assets	■ ■ ■	80
Total	■ ■ ■	105
Equity	■ ■ ■	30
Long-term debt	■ ■ ■	20
Notes payable	30	35
Accounts payable	25	20
Total current liabilities	■ ■ ■	55
Total	115	105
Income statement		
Sales	■ ■ ■	
Cost of goods sold	■ ■ ■	
Selling, general and administrative expenses	10	
Depreciation	20	
EBIT	■ ■ ■	
Interest	■ ■ ■	
Earnings before tax	■ ■ ■	
Tax	■ ■ ■	
Available for common shareholders	■ ■ ■	

You have been asked to calculate some measure of the industry price-earnings ratio. Discuss the possible ways that you might calculate such a measure. Does changing the method of calculation make a significant difference in the end result?

9. "When calculating 'times interest earned,' we average earnings over the past 5 years. This gives a better measure of the company's typical earnings."

"For simplicity we just divide current earnings by interest payments."

"We fit a trend line to earnings and then measure 'times interest earned' using the current trend value."

"We also fit a trend line to earnings and then use that trend to forecast earnings. We then measure 'times interest earned' using forecasted earnings. After all, it is the future not the past that any credit analyst is concerned with."

What assumptions is each of these speakers making? If you wished to measure the creditworthiness of a business, what would be the best way to compute "times interest earned" (perhaps there are alternatives that none of the speakers has considered)?

10. Look at the segment accounts of Dofasco. Calculate three profitability measures: sales to assets, profit margin, and return on assets for the different segments. Which appear to be the most profitable parts of the business? Do segments with a high sales-to-assets ratio tend to have a high or low profit margin? Why?

C · H · A · P · T · E · R

28

APPROACHES TO
FINANCIAL PLANNING

A camel looks like an animal designed by a committee. If the firm made all its financial decisions piecemeal, it would end up with a financial camel. Therefore, smart financial managers consider the overall effect of financing and investment decisions. This process is called *financial planning*, and the end result is a *financial plan*.

Financial planning is necessary because investment and financing decisions interact and should not be made independently. In other words, the whole may be more or less than the sum of the parts.

It is also necessary to help financial managers avoid surprises and think ahead about how they should react to unavoidable surprises. In Chapter 10 we stressed that financial managers are unwilling to treat capital investment proposals as "black boxes." They insist on understanding what makes projects work and what could go wrong with them. They attempt to trace out the possible impact of today's decisions on tomorrow's opportunities. The same approach is, or should be, taken when financing and investment decisions are considered in the aggregate. Without financial planning, the firm itself becomes a black box.

Finally, financial planning helps establish concrete goals to motivate managers and provide standards for measuring performance.

Planning should never be the exclusive preserve of the planners. Unless management is widely involved in the process, it will lack faith in the output. Also, financial plans should be tied in closely to the firm's business plans. A series of financial forecasts has little operational value unless management has thought about the production and marketing decisions that are needed to make those forecasts come about.

Financial planning is not easy to write about — it is the sort of topic that attracts empty generalities or ponderous detail. A full, formal treatment is beyond the scope of this book and probably beyond the capability of its authors. But there are a few specific, helpful points we can make. We will first summarize what financial planning is and what it is not. Second, we will describe the contents of a typical completed financial plan, and we will describe what the firm has to be able to do in order to plan successfully. Finally, we will discuss the use of *financial models* in the planning process.

28-1   WHAT IS FINANCIAL PLANNING?

Financial planning is a *process* of:

1. Analyzing the interactions of the financing and investment choices open to the firm
2. Projecting the future consequences of present decisions, in order to avoid surprises and understand the links between present and future decisions
3. Deciding which alternatives to undertake (these decisions are embodied in the final financial plan)
4. Measuring subsequent performance against the goals set in the financial plan

Of course, there are different kinds of planning. Short-term financial planning is discussed in the next chapter. In short-term planning the *planning horizon* is rarely longer than the next 12 months. The firm wants to make sure it has enough cash to pay its bills and that short-term borrowing and lending are arranged to the firm's advantage.

Here we are more concerned with long-term planning, where a typical horizon is five years, although some firms look out ten years or more. For example, it can take ten years or more for an electric utility to design, obtain approval for, build, and test a major generating plant.

Financial Planning Focuses on the Big Picture   Financial planners try to look at the big picture, and to avoid getting bogged down in detail. Thus, the long-term planning process usually looks only at the *total* capital investment outlays of divisions or business units. A large number of small investment proposals are aggregated and, in effect, treated as a single project.

For example, at the beginning of the planning process the corporate staff might ask each division to submit three alternative business plans covering the next five years:

1. An *aggressive growth* plan calling for heavy capital investment and new products, increased share of existing markets, or entry of new markets
2. A *normal growth* plan in which the division grows with its markets but not significantly at the expense of its competitors
3. A plan of *retrenchment* and specialization designed to minimize required capital outlays — this may amount to gradual liquidation of the division

The planners might add a fourth option:

4. *Divestiture* — Sale or liquidation of the division

Each alternative has a stream of forecasted cash flows associated with it. Therefore, the alternatives can be analyzed as four mutually exclusive capital projects.

Financial planners normally abstain from capital budgeting analysis on a project-by-project basis. Planners address capital investment on a grander scale. Of course, some projects are large enough to have significant individual impact. When in 1978 Boeing committed $3 *billion* to two new planes (the 757 and 767 models), you can safely bet that these two capital projects were explicitly analyzed in the context of Boeing's long-range financial plan.

Financial Planning Is Not Just Forecasting   Forecasting concentrates on the most likely future outcome. Financial planners are not concerned solely with forecasting, for they need to take into account unlikely events as well as likely ones. If you think ahead about what could go wrong, then you are less likely to ignore the danger signals and you can react faster to trouble.

Also, financial planning does not attempt to *minimize* risk. Instead, it is a process of deciding which risks to take and which are unnecessary or not worth taking.

Companies have developed a number of ways of looking at these "what if" questions. Some work through the consequences of the plan under the most likely set of circumstances and then vary the assumptions one at a time. For example, they might look at how badly the company would be hit if a policy of aggressive growth coincided with a recession. Other companies might look at the consequences of each business plan under a couple of plausible scenarios.[1] For example, one scenario might envisage high interest rates leading to a slowdown in world economic growth and lower commodity prices. The second scenario might involve a buoyant domestic economy, high inflation, and a weak currency.

28-2 CONTENTS OF A COMPLETED FINANCIAL PLAN

A completed financial plan for a large corporation is a substantial document. A smaller corporation's plan would have the same elements but less detail and documentation. For the smallest, youngest businesses, the financial plan may be entirely in the financial manager's head. The basic elements of the plans will be similar, however, for firms of any size.

The plan will present *pro forma* (that is, forecasted) balance sheets, income statements, and statements describing sources and uses of cash. Because these statements embody the firm's financial goals, they may not be strictly unbiased forecasts. The earnings target in the plan may be somewhere between an honest forecast and the earnings management *hopes* to achieve.

The plan will also describe planned capital expenditure, usually broken down by category (investment for replacement, for expansion, for new products, for mandated expenditures like pollution control equipment, and so on) and by division or line of business. There will be a narrative description of why these amounts are needed for investment, and also of the business strategies to be used to reach the financial goals. The descriptions might cover areas such as research and development efforts, steps to improve productivity, design and marketing of new products, pricing strategy, and so on.

These written descriptions, record the end result of discussions and negotiation between operating managers, corporate staff, and top management. They ensure that everyone involved in implementing the plan understands what is to be done.[2]

Planned Financing
Most plans contain a summary of planned financing together with narrative backup as necessary. This part of the plan should logically include a discussion of dividend policy, because the more the firm pays out, the more capital it will have to find from sources other than retained earnings.

The complexity and importance of financing plans varies tremendously from firm to firm. A firm with limited investment opportunities, ample operating cash flow, and a moderate dividend payout accumulates considerable "financial slack" in the form of liquid assets and unused borrowing power. Life is relatively easy

---

[1] For a description of the use of different planning scenarios in the Royal Dutch/Shell group see P. Wack, "Scenarios: Uncharted Waters Ahead," *Harvard Business Review,* **63** (September–October 1985) and "Scenarios: Shooting the Rapids," *Harvard Business Review,* **63** (November–December 1985).

[2] Also, managers come up with better strategies when they are forced to present them formally and expose them to criticism. Haven't you often found that you didn't *really* understand an issue until you were forced to explain it to someone else?

for the managers of such firms, and their financing plans are routine. Whether that easy life is in the interest of their stockholders is another matter.

Other firms have to raise capital in large amounts by selling securities. Naturally, they give careful attention to planning what kinds of securities are to be sold, and when. Such firms may also find their financing plans complicated by covenants on their existing debt. For example, electric utility bonds usually prohibit the firm from issuing more bonds if interest coverage drops below a certain level. Typically, the minimum level is two times earnings.

Utilities have enormous appetites for capital and relatively generous dividend payouts. In normal times they may issue a new series of bonds every year, almost like clockwork. But when earnings are depressed, as they were in the mid-1970s, alternative financing plans have to be developed. A common response was much heavier reliance on short-term loans from banks, coupled with more frequent stock issues than the utilities liked. But whatever the response, considerable midnight oil was burned by utility financial managers during this period.

| **Three Requirements for Effective Planning** | The requirements for effective planning follow from the purposes of planning and the desired end result. Three points deserve emphasis. |

Forecasting   First is the ability to forecast accurately and consistently. Perfect or even good accuracy may not be obtainable—if it were, the need for planning would be much less. Still the firm must do the best it can.

Forecasting cannot be reduced to a mechanical exercise. Naive extrapolation or fitting trends to past data is of limited value. It is because the future is not likely to resemble the past that planning is needed.

To supplement their judgement, forecasters rely on a variety of data sources and forecasting methods. For example, forecasts of the economic and industry environment may involve use of econometric models that take account of interactions between economic variables. In other cases the forecaster may employ statistical techniques for analyzing and projecting time series. Forecasts of demand will partly reflect these projections of the economic environment, but they may also be based on formal models that marketing specialists have developed for predicting buyer behaviour or on recent consumer surveys to which the firm has access.[3]

Because information and expertise may be inconveniently scattered throughout the firm, effective planning requires administrative procedures to ensure that this information is not passed by. Also, many planners reach outside the firm. Many organizations such as Data Resources, Inc. (DRI) and the Conference Board of Canada specialize in preparing macroeconomic and industry forecasts for use by corporations.

It is tempting to conduct planning in a vacuum and to ignore the fact that the firm's competitors are concurrently developing their own plans. Your ability to implement an aggressive growth plan and increase market share depends on what the competition is likely to do. In fact, we can generalize by paraphrasing a recommendation that we made in Chapter 11. *When you are presented with a set of corporate forecasts, do not accept them at face value. Probe behind the forecasts and try to identify the economic model on which they are based.*

Inconsistency of forecasts is a potential problem because planners draw on information from many sources. Forecasted sales may be the sum of separate

---

[3] For an interesting example of how forecasting is organized in one company see R.N. Dino, R.E. Riley, and P.G. Yatrakis, "The Role of Forecasting in Corporate Strategy: the Xerox Experience," *Journal of Forecasting*, **1**: 335–348 (October–December 1982).

forecasts made by managers of several business units. Left to their own devices, these managers may make different assumptions about inflation, growth of the national economy, availability of raw materials, and so on. Achieving consistency is particularly hard for vertically integrated firms, where the raw material for one business unit is the output of another. For example, an oil company's refining division might plan to produce more gasoline than the marketing division plans to sell. The oil company's planners would be expected to uncover this inconsistency and align the plans of the two divisions.

Corporations often find that working out a consistent aggregate forecast of sales, cash flow, income, and so on, is complex and time-consuming. However, many of the calculations can be automated by using a corporate model. We will comment on corporate models in a moment.

Finding the Optimal Financial Plan   In the end the financial manager has to be able to judge which plan is best. We would like to present a model or theory that tells the manager exactly how to make that judgement, but we cannot. There is no model or procedure that comprehends all the complexity and intangibles encountered in financial planning.

As a matter of fact, there never will be one. This bold statement is based on BMSG's third law.[4]

- *Axiom*. The supply of unsolved problems is infinite.
- *Axiom*. The number of unsolved problems that humans can hold in their minds is at any time limited to ten.
- *The law*. Therefore, in any field there will always be ten problems that can be addressed but that have no formal solution.

You will note that the last chapter of this book discusses ten unsolved problems in finance.

Financial planners have to face the unsolved issues, and cope as best they can by judgement. Take dividend policy, for example. At the end of Chapter 16 we were unable to say for sure whether a generous dividend policy was a good or bad thing. Nevertheless, financial planners have to *decide* on the dividend policy.

You sometimes hear managers stating corporate goals in terms of accounting numbers. They might say "Our objective is to achieve an annual sales growth of 20%," or "We want a 25% return on book equity and a profit margin of 10%."

On the surface such objectives don't make sense. Shareholders want to be richer, not to have the satisfaction of a 10% profit margin. Also, a goal that is stated in terms of accounting ratios is nonoperational unless it is translated back into what that means for business decisions. For example, what does a 10% profit margin imply—higher prices, lower costs, a move into new, high-margin products, or increased vertical integration?

So why do managers define objectives in this way? In part, such goals may be a mutual exhortation to try harder, like singing the company song before work. But we suspect that managers are often using a code to communicate real concerns. For example, the goal to increase sales rapidly may reflect managers' belief that increased market share is needed to achieve scale economies, or a target profit margin may be a way of saying that the firm has been pursuing sales growth at the expense of margins.

The danger is that everyone may forget the code and the accounting targets may be seen as goals in themselves.

---

[4] The second law is presented in Section 12-2.

Watching the Financial Plan Unfold   Long-term plans have an annoying habit of falling out of date almost as soon as they are made. They are then left to gather dust. Of course, you can always restart the planning process from scratch but it may help if you can think ahead of time how to revise your forecasts in the light of unexpected events. For example, suppose that profits in the first 6 months turn out to be 10% below forecast. Profits follow roughly a random walk, so they have no tendency to bounce back after a fall. Unless you have special information to the contrary, you should revise your profit forecasts for later years downward by 10%.

We have mentioned that long-term plans are also used as a benchmark to judge subsequent performance. But performance appraisals have little value unless you also take into account the business background against which they were achieved. If you know how a downturn in the economy is likely to throw you off plan, then you have a standard to judge your performance during such a downturn.

Financial Planning as Managing a Portfolio of Options

Another problem that is often crucial in financial planning is the dependency of future investment opportunities on today's capital investment decisions. You often find firms investing to enter a market for "strategic" reasons: that is, not because the *immediate* investment has positive net present value by itself, but because it establishes the firm in the market and creates *options* for possibly valuable follow-up investments.

In other words, there is a two-stage decision. At the second stage (the follow-up project) the financial manager faces a standard capital budgeting problem. But, at the first stage, projects may be valuable primarily for the options they bring with them. We saw how a financial manager could value a first-stage project's "strategic value" using option pricing theory.[5]

Sometimes there are three or more stages. Think of the progress of a technological innovation from its inception in basic research, to product development, to pilot production and market testing, and finally to full-scale commercial production. The decision to produce at commercial scale is a standard capital budgeting problem. The decision to proceed with pilot production and test marketing is like purchasing an option to produce at commercial scale. The commitment of funds to development is like purchasing an option for pilot production and test marketing: the firm acquires an option to purchase an option. The investment in research at the very first stage is like acquiring an option to purchase an option to purchase an option.

Here we will stick our necks out by predicting the increasing use of option pricing theory for formal analysis of sequential investment decisions like the ones just discussed. Financial planning eventually will be thought of not as a search for a single investment plan, but rather as the management of the portfolio of options held by the firm. This portfolio consists not of traded puts and calls, but of *real options* (options to purchase real assets on possibly favourable terms) or options to purchase other real options.[6]

---

[5] See the Blitzer Computers example in Section 21-1.

[6] The concept of real options was introduced in S.C. Myers, "Determinants of Corporate Borrowing," *Journal of Financial Economics,* **5**: 147–175 (November 1977). The importance of real options to strategic decision making is emphasized in S.C. Myers, "Finance Theory and Financial Strategies," *Interfaces,* **14**: 126–137 (January–February 1984). For a general discussion of some of the more technical aspects of real options, see G.A. Sick, *Capital Budgeting with Real Options,* Monograph 1989–3, Salomon Brothers Center for the Study of Financial Institutions, Stern School of Business, New York University (1989).

You can think of financial planning as, in part, a process of:

- Acquiring real options
- Maintaining these options — unlike financial options, real options based on technology, product design, or other competitive edges usually erode if put on the shelf and forgotten
- Exercising valuable real options at the right time
- Disposing of options that are too far "out of the money" and too expensive to maintain

28-3   FINANCIAL PLANNING MODELS

Most corporate financial models are simulation models designed to project the financial consequences of alternative financial strategies under specified assumptions about the future. The models range from general-purpose ones, not much more complicated than the illustration presented later in this section, to models containing literally hundreds of equations and interacting variables.

Most large firms have a financial model, or have access to one. Sometimes they may use more than one, perhaps a detailed model integrating capital budgeting and operational planning, a simpler model focusing on the aggregate impacts of financing strategy, and a special model for evaluating mergers.

The reason for the popularity of such models is a simple and practical one. They support the financial planning process by making it easier and cheaper to construct pro forma financial statements. The models automate an important part of planning that used to be boring, time-consuming, and labour-intensive.

Programming these financial planning models used to consume large amounts of high-priced programming talent and computer time. These days standard spreadsheet programs such as LOTUS 1-2-3 or Excel are regularly used to solve quite complex financial planning problems.

Executive Fruit's Financial Model

Table 28-1 shows current (year-end 1989) financial statements for Executive Fruit Company. Judging by these figures, the company is ordinary in almost all respects. Its earnings before interest and taxes were 10% of sales revenue. Net earnings were $90,000 after paying of taxes and 9% interest on $400,000 outstanding debt. The company paid out 60% of its earnings as dividends.

Executive Fruit's operating cash flow was not sufficient to pay the dividend and also to provide the cash needed for investment and to expand net working capital. Therefore, $64,000 of common stock was issued. The firm ended the year with debt equal to 40% of total capitalization.

Now suppose that you are asked to prepare pro forma statements for Executive Fruit Company for 1990. You are told to assume business as usual *except* that (1) sales and operating costs are expected to be up 30% over 1989, and (2) common stock is not to be issued again. You interpret "business as usual" to mean that (3) interest rates will remain at 9%, (4) the firm will stick to its traditional 60% dividend payout, and (5) net working capital and fixed assets will increase by 30% to support the larger sales volume.

These assumptions lead to the pro forma statements shown in Table 28-2. Note that projected net income is up by 23%, to $111,000, which is heartening. But a glance at the "sources and uses of funds" statement shows that $404,000 has to be raised for additional working capital and for replacement and expansion of

Table 28-1
1989 Financial Statements for Executive Fruit Company (all figures in thousands of dollars)

Income Statement

Revenue (REV)	2,160
Cost of goods sold (CGS)	1,944
Earnings before interest and taxes	216
Interest (INT)[a]	36
Earnings before taxes	180
Tax at 50% (TAX)	90
Net income (NET)	90

Sources and Uses of Funds

Sources	
Net income (NET)	90
Depreciation (DEP)[b]	80
Operating cash flow	170
Borrowing (ΔD)	0
Stock issues (SI)	64
Total sources	234
Uses	
Increase in net working capital (ΔNWC)	40
Investment (INV)	140
Dividends (DIV)	54
Total uses	234

Balance Sheets

	1989	1988	Change
Assets			
Net working capital (NWC)[c]	200	160	+40
Fixed assets (FA)	800	740	+60[d]
Total assets	1,000	900	+100
Liabilities			
Debt (D)	400	400	0
Book equity (E)	600	500	+100[e]
Total liabilities	1,000	900	+100

[a] Interest is 9% of the $400 in outstanding debt.

[b] Depreciation or capital cost allowance is a non-cash expense. Therefore, we add it back to net income to find operating cash flow.

[c] Net working capital is defined as current assets less current liabilities.

[d] The increase in the book value of fixed assets equals investment less depreciation. Change in FA is ΔFA = INV − DEP = 140 − 80 = 60.

[e] Book equity increases by retained earnings less dividends plus stock issues. Change in E is ΔE = NET − DIV + SI = 90 − 54 + 64 = 100.

Table 28-2
1990 Pro Forma Financial Statements for Executive Fruit Company (all figures in thousands of dollars)

Income Statement

Revenue (REV)	2,808 ⎱	(+30%)
Cost of goods sold (CGS)	2,527 ⎰	
Earnings before interest and taxes	281	
Interest (INT)	59	
Earnings before taxes	222	
Tax (TAX)	111	
Net income (NET)	111	(+23%)

Sources and Uses of Funds

Sources	
Net income (NET)	111
Depreciation (DEP)	104
Operating cash flow	215
Borrowing (ΔD)	255.6
Stock issues (SI)	0
Total sources	470.6

Uses		
Increase in net working capital (ΔNWC)	60	(+30%)
Investment (INV)	344	
Dividends (DIV)	66.6	
Total uses	470.6	

Balance Sheets

	1990	1989	Change
Assets			
Net working capital (NWC)	260	200	+ 60
Fixed assets (FA)	1,040	800	+240
Total assets	1,300	1,000	+300
Liabilities			
Debt (D)	655.6	400	+255.6
Book equity (E)	644.4	600	+ 44.4
Total liabilities	1,300.0	1,000	+300.0

Assumptions:

CGS	Assumed to remain at 90% of REV.
INT	Nine percent of debt (D). This assumes all new debt is taken out early in 1990 so that a full year's interest must be paid.
TAX	Tax rate remains at 50%.
DEP	Capital cost allowance or depreciation remains at 10% of fixed assets. This assumes that a full year's depreciation is taken on all new investment made in 1990.
ΔD	Balancing item. Executive Fruit must borrow $255.6 to cover planned expenditures.
SI	Executive Fruit's management has decided not to issue stock in 1990, therefore SI = 0.
ΔNWC, NWC	Net working capital expands in proportion to the increase in REV.
INV, FA	Required fixed assets FA are assumed to expand in proportion to the growth in sales. Investment must therefore cover depreciation plus the increase in FA.
DIV	Payout stays at 60% of NET.
E	The increase in equity equals retained earnings (NET − DIV) plus stock issues (SI). NET − DIV + SI = 111 − 66.6 + 0 = 44.4

fixed capital.[7] Executive Fruit's generous dividend payout and its decision against another stock issue mean that $255,600 has to be raised by additional borrowing. The result is an increase in the book debt ratio to more than 50% and a reduction in pretax interest coverage ratio to 4.8. (Earnings before interest and taxes divided by interest is 231/59 = 4.8.)

We have spared you the trouble of actually calculating the figures necessary for Table 28-2. The calculations do not take more than a few minutes for this simple example, *provided* you set up the calculations correctly and make no arithmetic mistakes.

If that time requirement seems trivial, remember that in reality you probably would be asked for four similar sets of statements covering each year from 1991 to 1994. Probably you would be asked for alternative projections under different assumptions (for example, a 25% instead of 30% growth rate of revenue) or, different financial strategies (for example, freezing dividends at their 1989 level of $54,000). This would be lots of work. Building a model and letting the computer toil in your place has obvious attractions.

Table 28-3 shows a 15-equation model for Executive Fruit. There is one equation for each variable needed to construct pro forma statements like Tables 28-1 and 28-2. Of the equations, six are accounting identities ensuring that the income statement adds up, the balance sheet balances, and sources of funds match uses. The functions of the equations are as follows: (1) and (8) set revenues and stock

Table 28-3
Financial Model for Executive Fruit Company

Income Statement Equations

(1) REV = forecast by model user	
(2) CGS = a_1REV	
(3) INT = a_2D	(a_2 = interest rate)
(4) TAX = a_3(REV − CGS − INT)	(a_3 = tax rate)
(5) NET = REV − CGS − INT − TAX	(accounting identity)

Sources and Uses Statement Equations

(6) DEP = a_4FA	
(7) ΔD = ΔNWC + INV + DIV − NET − DEP − SI	(accounting identity)
(8) SI = value specified by model user	
(9) ΔNWC = NWC − NWC(−1)	(accounting identity)
(10) INV = DEP + FA − FA(−1)	(accounting identity)
(11) DIV = a_5NET	(a_5 = dividend payout ratio)

Balance Sheet Equations

(12) NWC = a_6REV	
(13) FA = a_7REV	
(14) D = ΔD + D(−1)	(accounting identity)
(15) E = E(−1) + NET − DIV + SI	(accounting identity)

Note: (−1) means a number taken from the previous year's balance sheet. These numbers are constants, not variables.

---

[7] Executive Fruit's existing fixed capital is assumed to depreciate by $104,000 in 1989. Thus, it has to invest $104,000 simply to maintain the net book value of its fixed assets. Total investment is $104,000 plus the growth in net fixed assets required by the increased sales volume. Incidentally, we realize that requiring the net book value of fixed assets to grow in lockstep with sales volume is an arbitrary and probably unrealistic assumption. We adopt it only to keep things simple.

issues equal to values specified by the model user. Equations (2), (12), and (13) specify cost of goods sold, net working capital, and fixed assets as constant proportions of sales. The remaining equations relate interest to debt outstanding (3), taxes to income (4), depreciation to fixed assets (6), and dividends to net income (11).

The *input* for our model comprises nine items: a sales forecast (REV), a decision on the amount of stock to be issued (SI), and seven coefficients, a_1 through a_7, tying cost of goods sold to revenue, interest payments to borrowing, and so on. Take the coefficient a_5, for example. In developing Table 28-2 we assumed dividends to be 60% of net income. In the model this would be expressed as $a_5 = 0.6$.

Table 28-4 shows that our model works. In the table we insert the value for REV, SI, and a_1 through a_7 that correspond to the assumptions underlying Table 28-2. And we get the right answers, confirming that the model can be used to forecast Executive Fruit's financial results. All we would have to do is to give the computer the 9 input items, tell it to solve the 15 simultaneous equations, and instruct it to print out the results in the format of Table 28-2.

Table 28-4
Model Forecast for Table 28-2

Income Statement

(1) REV = forecast = 2,808
(2) CGS = 0.9 REV $(a_1 = 0.9)$
       = 0.9 (2,808) = 2,527
(3) INT = 0.09D $(a_2 = 0.09)$
       = 0.09(655.6) = 59
(4) TAX = 0.5 (REV − CGS − INT) $(a_3 = 0.5)$
       = 0.5(2,808 − 2,527 − 59) = 111
(5) NET = REV − CGS − INT − TAX
       = 2,808 − 2,527 − 59 − 111 = 111

Sources and Uses of Funds Statement

(6) DEP = 0.1 FA $(a_4 = 0.1)$
       = 0.1 (1,040) = 104
(7) ΔD = ΔNWC + INV + DIV − NET − DEP − SI
       = 60 + 344 + 66.6 − 111 − 104 − 0 = 255.6
(8) SI = specified as 0
(9) ΔNWC = NWC − NWC(−1)
       = 260 − 200 = 60
(10) INV = DEP + FA − FA(−1)
       = 104 + 1,040 − 800 = 344
(11) DIV = 0.6 NET $(a_5 = 0.6)$
       = 0.6(111) = 66.6

Balance Sheet

(12) NWC = 0.093 REV $(a_6 = 0.093)$
       = 0.093(2,808) = 260
(13) FA = 0.37 REV $(a_7 = 0.37)$
       = 0.37(2,808) = 1,040
(14) D = ΔD + D(−1)
       = 255.6 + 400 = 655.6
(15) E = E(−1) + NET − DIV + SI
       = 600 + 111 − 66.6 + 0 = 644.4

Pitfalls in Model Design

The Executive Fruit model is too simple for practical application. You probably have already thought of several ways to improve it—by keeping track of the number of outstanding shares, for example, and printing out earnings and dividends per share. Or you might want to distinguish short-term lending and borrowing opportunities, now buried in net working capital.

But beware: there is always the temptation to make a model bigger and more detailed. You may end up with an exhaustive model that is too cumbersome for routine use.

Exhaustive detail gets in the way of the intended use of corporate planning models, namely, to project the financial consequences of a variety of strategies and assumptions. The fascination of detail, if you give in to it, distracts attention from crucial decisions like stock issues and dividend policy, debt policy, and allocation of capital by business area. Sometimes decisions like these end up being made not by the financial manager, but by rules of thumb "wired into" the model, just as the Executive Fruit model arbitrarily sets dividends equal to a constant proportion of net income.

There is No Finance in Corporate Financial Models

Why do we say that there is no finance in corporate financial models? The first reason is that most such models incorporate an accountant's view of the world. They are designed to forecast accounting statements, and their equations naturally embody the accounting conventions employed by the firm. Consequently, the models do not emphasize the tools of financial analysis: incremental cash flow, present value, market risk, and so on.

Second, corporate financial models produce no signposts pointing toward optimal financial decisions. They do not even tell which alternatives are worth examining. All this is left up to their users.

BMSG's third law implies that no model can find the best of all financial strategies. However, it is possible to build linear programming models that help search for the best financial strategy subject to specified assumptions and constraints. These "intelligent" financial planning models should prove more flexible tools for sensitivity analysis and more effective in screening alternative financial strategies. Ideally, they will suggest strategies that would never occur to the unaided financial manager.

The appendix to this chapter sketches a linear programming model based on the modern finance theory presented in this book.

28-4   SUMMARY

Most firms take financial planning seriously and devote considerable resources to it. What do they get for this effort?

The tangible product of the planning process is a financial plan describing the firm's financial strategy and projecting its future consequences by means of pro forma balance sheets, income statements, and statements of sources and uses of funds. The plan establishes financial goals and is a benchmark for evaluating subsequent performance. Usually it also describes why that strategy was chosen and how the plan's financial goals are to be achieved.

The plan is the end result. The process that produces the plan is valuable in its own right. First, planning forces the financial manager to consider the combined effects of all the firm's investment and financing decisions. This is important because these decisions interact and should not be made independently.

Second, planning, if it is done right, forces the financial manager to think about events that could upset the firm's financial progress and to devise strategies to be held in reserve for counterattack when unhappy surprises occur. Planning is more than forecasting, because forecasting deals with the most likely future. Planners also have to think about events that may occur even though they are unlikely.

To repeat: financial planning is a *process* of:

1. Analyzing the interactions of the financing and investment choices open to the firm
2. Projecting the future consequences of present decisions, in order to avoid surprises and understand the links between present and future decisions
3. Deciding which alternatives to undertake (these decisions are embodied in the final financial plan)
4. Measuring subsequent performance against the goals set in the financial plan.

In this chapter we discussed "long-range" or "strategic" planning, in which the *planning horizon* is usually five years or more in the future. This kind of planning deals with aggregate decisions: for example, the planner would worry about whether the broadaxe division should invest in heavy capital investment and rapid growth but not whether the division should choose machine tool A versus tool B. In fact, planners must be constantly on guard against the fascination of detail, because giving in to it means slighting crucial issues like investment strategy, debt policy, and the choice of a target dividend payout ratio.

There is no theory or model that leads straight to *the* optimal financial strategy. Consequently, financial planning proceeds by trial and error. Many different strategies may be projected under a range of assumptions about the future before one strategy is finally chosen.

The dozens of separate projections that may be made during this trial and error process generate a heavy load of arithmetic and paperwork. Firms have responded by developing corporate planning models to forecast the financial consequences of specified strategies and assumptions about the future. These models are efficient and widely used. But remember that there is not much finance in them. Their primary purpose is to produce accounting statements. It is often difficult to calculate a strategy's present value from model output. The models do not search for the best financial strategy, but only trace out the consequences of a strategy specified by the model user.

One of the most difficult aspects of deciding what strategies to examine closely is that the best strategy may not be an obvious one. In the appendix to this chapter we describe a linear programming model that is based on the concepts of finance rather than accounting, and that does help the financial manager search for the best financial plan.

FURTHER READING

Corporate planning has an extensive literature of its own. Good books and articles include:

G. Donaldson, "Financial Goals and Strategic Consequences," *Harvard Business Review,* **63**: 57–66 (May–June 1985).

G. Donaldson, *Strategy for Financial Mobility*, Harvard Business School Press, Boston, 1986.

A.C. Hax and N.S. Majluf, *Strategic Management: An Integrative Perspective*, Prentice-Hall, Inc., Englewood Cliffs, N.J., 1984.

P. Lorange, and R.F. Vancil, *Strategic Planning Systems*, Prentice Hall, Inc., Englewood Cliffs, N.J., 1977.

Our description of what planning is and is not was influenced by:

P. Drucker, "Long-Range Planning: Challenge to Management Science," *Management Science*, **5**: 238–249 (April 1959).

Here are three references on corporate models:

W.T. Carleton, C.L. Dick, Jr., and D.H. Downes, "Financial Policy Models: Theory and Practice," *Journal of Financial and Quantitative Analysis*, **8**: 691–709 (December 1973).

W.T. Carlton and J.M. McInnes, "Theory, Models and Implementation in Financial Management," *Management Science*, **28**: 957–978 (September 1982).

T.H. Taylor and H. Schauland, "A Survey of Users of Corporate Planning Models," *Management Science*, **28**: 957–978 (September 1982).

LONGER is presented in:

S.C. Myers and G.A. Pogue, "A Programming Approach to Corporate Financial Management," *Journal of Finance*, **29**: 579–599 (May 1974).

APPENDIX 28-1

LONGER

This appendix is a brief introduction to LONGER, a linear programming model devised by Myers and Pogue to support financial planners.[8] Other applications of linear programming to financial planning are described in "Further Reading" for this chapter.

LONGER differs from the typical corporate financial model described in this chapter in two important respects. First, it *optimizes*: it calculates the *best* financial plan, given specified assumptions, and constraints. The typical planning model merely *projects* the consequences of a financial strategy chosen by the model user. Second, the model is based on finance theory rather than accounting. It assumes well-functioning capital markets. Consequently, its objective is to maximize the firm's net present value. It relies on value additivity and the Modigliani-Miller theory that the chief advantage of debt is the tax shields created by debt interest payments.

LONGER will be introduced by a simple numerical example. Then extensions of the model are briefly described. The final part of this appendix shows how the shadow prices generated as part of LONGER's solution are interpreted. The shadow prices are an easy way to understand *adjusted present value* or APV, which measures the value of capital projects which have important financing side effects. APV and its practical implications were covered more fully in Chapter 19. This appendix should give a deeper appreciation of the APV method and the assumptions underlying it.

EXAMPLE[9]   Consider a firm that has to decide how much to invest or borrow in the coming year. Let:

x = New investment, in millions of dollars. (We assume for simplicity that the firm has only one project.)

y = New borrowing, in millions of dollars.

Also, assume that:

---

[8] S.C. Myers and G.A. Pogue, "A Programming Approach to Corporate Financial Management," *Journal of Finance*, **29**: 579–599 (May 1974).

[9] This example is based on one presented by Myers and Pogue, *op. cit.*

1. Available investment opportunities can absorb $1 million at most. The investments generate a perpetual stream of after-tax cash flows. Let the expected average value of these flows be C. In this case $C = 0.09x$; thus, the project offers a 9% internal rate of return.
2. Assume that the market will capitalize the returns at the rate $r = 0.10$. Thus, if all-equity financing is used, these assets generate a net present value of $-\$0.10$ per dollar invested $(-x + 0.09x/0.10 = -0.1x)$.
3. The firm's policy is to limit new debt to 40% of new investment.
4. The firm has $800,000 in cash available.
5. Any excess cash is paid out in dividends.
6. The additions to debt and equity are expected to be permanent.

For simplicity we begin with the Modigliani-Miller valuation formula for the firm.[10] If the firm does nothing $(x$ and $y = 0)$ then V will be given by:

$$V = V_0 + T_c D$$

where V_0 = market value of firm's *existing* assets if they were all-equity financed

$\quad\quad T_c$ = marginal corporate income tax rate (0.5 in this example)

$\quad\quad D$ = amount of debt *already* outstanding, excluding any borrowing for new project

The amount $T_c D$ is the present value of the tax shields generated by the outstanding debt, assuming the debt is permanent.

For our example,

$$V = V_0 + 0.5D - 0.1x + 0.5y$$

Now V_0 and D are fixed and, therefore, not relevant to the choice of x and y. Consequently, we can just maximize the quantity $-0.1x + 0.5y$, subject to constraints on the amount invested $(x \leq 1)$, the amount of debt issued $(y \leq 0.4x)$, and the balance of sources and uses of funds $(x \leq y + 0.8)$.

The Solution   This is the linear programming problem depicted in Figure 28-1. First look at the shaded area representing the set of feasible solutions. The feasible region is below the line $x = 1$ because the firm's investment opportunity will absorb $1 million at most. It is below the line $x = 0.8 + y$ because the amount invested is limited to cash on hand ($0.8 million) plus additional borrowing. It is above and to the left of the line $y = 0.4x$ because new debt is limited to 40% of new investment.

The firm does not want to invest (because NPV $= -\$0.10$ per dollar invested) but it does want to borrow and, in order to borrow, it has to invest. Thus, firm value is maximized when $x = 1, y = 0.4$. The firm invests and borrows as much as it can.

However, note that the constraint $x \leq 0.8 + y$ is not binding at the optimal solution. The firm borrows $200,000 more than it needs for investment. Thus, it has $200,000 available for dividends.

Why does the optimal solution call for investing in a project with a negative net present value? The reason is that the project allows the firm to issue more debt, and the value of tax savings generated by the debt more than offsets the investment's inadequate return. (In fact, the optimal solution remains $x = 1.0$, $y = 0.4$ so long as the investment generates more than $-\$0.20$ per dollar invested.

---

[10] See Section 18-1.

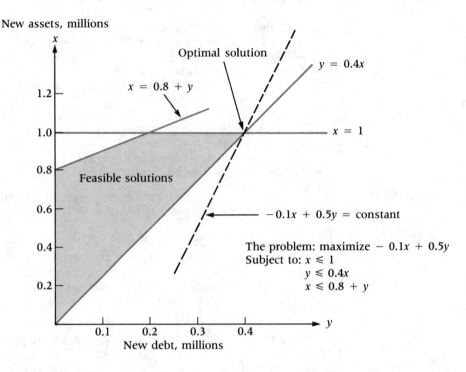

New assets, millions

Figure 28-1 In this example, the firm can invest at most $1 million and borrow 40% of new investment. Funds for the new investment must come from existing cash ($0.8 million) or new borrowing. The investment is not attractive in its own right (NPV = −$0.1x), but the firm is willing to invest in order to borrow because the tax shields created by borrowing outweigh the net loss in value attributable to the new investment.

If it generates less than that, −$0.30, for example, the solution becomes $x = y = 0$.) The debt capacity constraint thus makes financing and investment decisions interdependent.

Effects of Dividend Policy   The sources-uses constraint is not binding in the example, and therefore does not create an interaction of financing and investment decisions. However, what if it is binding? What if the firm has, say, only $500,000 cash on hand?

At first glance the effect is to change the sources-uses constraint to $x \leq 0.5 + y$, which changes the optimal solution to $x = \frac{5}{6}$, $y = \frac{1}{3}$. However, if we consider dividend policy, then we should also allow new issues of equity. The constraint should really be:

$$x + \text{DIV} \leq 0.5 + y + \text{SI}$$

where DIV and SI are dividends paid and equity issued in millions. If dividend policy is irrelevant, then DIV and SI have no effect in the objective function, and the constraint itself is irrelevant. Thus, the optimal solution remains at $x = 1$, $y = 0.4$. The firm must make a $100,000 stock issue, but this is a mere detail once the investment and borrowing decisions are made.

However, in practice there would be transaction costs associated with the stock issue. These costs would have to be subtracted from the objective function, and the sources-uses constraint would become relevant and binding. The solution values for x and y will clearly be affected, if the transaction cost is large enough.

Thus, the sources-uses constraint becomes important only if there are transaction costs to security issues or dividend policy matters for other reasons.

Extending the Model

The example we have just examined was limited to two variables by our goal of presenting it graphically on the two dimensions of the printed page. But the computer does not need a picture like Figure 28-1 to solve a linear program. We can extend LONGER to a practical level of detail by adding variables and constraints.

We have already referred to one extension. Suppose that the firm can pay dividends or issue common stock, but that cash available is cut to $0.5 million. The linear program becomes

$$\text{Maximize: } -0.1x + 0.5y + a\text{DIV} + b\text{SI}$$

$$\text{Subject to: } x \le 1$$
$$y \le 0.4x$$
$$x + \text{DIV} \le 0.5 + y + \text{SI}$$

If dividend policy is irrelevant, then both a and b are set at zero. But in practice b would have to be negative to reflect the transaction costs of a stock issue, and a might be positive, negative, or zero depending on your position on the dividend controversy (see Chapter 16).

Now suppose that there is a second investment opportunity to invest up to $2 million in a project offering $0.12 of NPV per dollar invested. However, the performance of project 2 is less predictable than project 1's performance, and so the firm is willing to borrow only 20% of the amount invested in project 2. Our model now becomes:

$$\text{Maximize: } -0.1x_1 + 0.12x_2 + 0.5y + a\text{DIV} + b\text{SI}$$

$$\text{Subject to: } x_1 \le 1$$
$$x_2 \le 2$$
$$y \le 0.4x_1 + 0.2x_2$$
$$x_1 + x_2 + \text{DIV} \le 0.5 + y + \text{SI}$$

Because present values add, we can include as many projects as we like without upsetting the linear form of the objective. Moreover, there is no need for included projects to have the same risk or time pattern of cash flows. There is nothing wrong with setting an office building alongside a wildcat oil well, so long as you can come up with a net present value for each.

If we introduce projects with irregular patterns of cash flow over time, we would naturally want to allow borrowing to vary period by period. Suppose that the firm has a five-year planning horizon. Then we could replace the debt variable y with five new variables $y_1, y_2, \ldots, y_5$, where y_t is planned total borrowing for year t. This naturally suggests that dividends and stock issues should be allowed to vary over time also. Our objective function becomes:

$$\begin{aligned}\text{Maximize: } & -0.1x_1 + 0.12x_2 \\ & + c_1y_1 + c_2y_2 + \cdots + c_5y_5 \\ & + a_1\text{DIV}_1 + a_2\text{DIV}_2 + \cdots a_5\text{DIV}_5 \\ & + b_1\text{SI}_1 + b_2\text{SI}_2 + \cdots + b_5\text{SI}_5\end{aligned}$$

Also, we will now need 12 constraints: two limiting the amount that can be invested in each project, five limiting the amount that can be borrowed in each of the five years covered by the financial plan, and five constraints ensuring that planned uses of funds do not exceed planned sources in any year.

Still more constraints might be added. The financial manager might wish to try to avoid any planned cut in dividends, for example. This would call for five more constraints:

$$\text{DIV} \geq \text{dividends in period 0}$$
$$\text{DIV}_2 \geq \text{DIV}_1$$
$$\text{DIV}_3 \geq \text{DIV}_2$$
$$\text{DIV}_4 \geq \text{DIV}_3$$
$$\text{DIV}_5 \geq \text{DIV}_4$$

Some firms might require that their financial plan generate a steady growth in reported (book) earnings. Suppose that the target growth rate is g. Then we would need five more constraints of the form $Z_t \geq (1 + g)Z_{t-1}$, where Z_t represents forecasted earnings in year t. The variable Z_t would be determined by the other decision variables in the programming model.

But we must immediately add a caveat: any constraint on acceptable *book* earnings, as opposed to economic earnings, raises difficult issues. Should the firm be willing to sacrifice present value just to achieve regular growth in reported earnings? If capital markets are efficient, investors ought to be able to look through any fluctuations of short-run earnings to the true, underlying value of the firm. If so, any constraint on earnings is superfluous at best.

Constraints on the growth of book earnings might perhaps be useful for keeping track of how pursuit of present value affects reported earnings. It may be that the financial plan can be changed to generate a pretty earnings pattern. If there is a real conflict between value and book earnings, comparing solutions with and without this constraint will at least awaken financial managers to the cost of that pretty pattern.[11]

There are several other items of optional equipment that most might wish to add to LONGER, but we will stop at this point. You may wish to refer to Myers and Pogue's paper and the other suggested readings for the full story.

Comparison of LONGER with the Typical Corporate Planning Model

A full-scale linear programming model for financial planning would become formidably complex, but no more so than a typical simulation model.[12] The two models applied to the same firm would have approximately the same number of variables, and the number of constraints included in LONGER would about match the number of equations in the simulation model. But the input requirements for LONGER would be greater because an objective function must be specified. In return, LONGER allows the planner to screen all feasible financial strategies, to reject the inferior ones automatically, and to identify the best strategy consistent with the assumptions and constraints embodied in the model.

However, linear programming models do not automate the *decisions* required by the financial plan. No model can capture all the issues that the financial manager must face. Nor would access to an optimization model change the trial and error process of developing a financial plan; it only promises to make that process somewhat more efficient. The optimum plan generated by any run of

[11] Eugene Lerner and Arnold Rappaport demonstrate the conflicts between pursuit of value and short-run earnings in "Limit DCF in Capital Budgeting," *Harvard Business Review,* **46**: 133–139 (September–October 1968).

[12] Note our warning on the temptation to excessive detail. See Section 28-3.

LONGER does no more than reflect the assumptions and constraints specified by the model user, who will naturally explore a variety of assumptions and constraints before reaching a final decision.[13]

Shadow Prices or Marginal Costs   The solution to any linear program includes a shadow price or marginal cost for each constraint. There are three constraints in the simple numerical example introduced at the start of this appendix and, therefore, three shadow prices:

Constraint	Shadow Price	Explanation
Limit on investment ($x \leq 1$)	0.1	Project NPV is $-0.1x$. But investment supports $0.4x$ in debt worth $0.50 per dollar borrowed. $-0.1x + 0.4(0.5x) = +0.1x$
Limit on debt ($y \leq 0.4x$)	0.5	$1 of additional debt generates tax shields worth $0.50.
Limit on available cash ($x \leq 0.8 + y$)	0	Firm has surplus cash at optimal solution. Additional cash has NPV of zero.

A shadow price is defined as the change in the objective per unit change in the constraint.[14] In our example the objective is to increase net present value. Therefore, the shadow price of 0.1 on the investment limit means that, if the firm were allowed to invest $1,000,001 instead of $1 million, net present value would increase by 10 cents. The shadow price of 0.5 on the debt limit means that if the firm were allowed to borrow $400,001 instead of $400,000, holding investment fixed at $1 million, value would increase by 50 cents.

The limit on available cash is not binding at the optimal solution. The firm borrows $200,000 more than it needs, and so the shadow price on that constraint is zero. That is, extra cash would have a *net* present value of zero.

Consider a slightly more complex example. Cash on hand is reduced to $500,000. Equity issues and dividend payments are allowed, but transactions cost absorb 10% of the net proceeds of any issue. The linear programming problem changes to:

$$\text{Maximize: } -0.1x + 0.5y + (0)\text{DIV} - 0.1\text{SI}$$

$$\text{Subject to: } x \leq 1$$
$$y \leq 0.4x$$
$$x + \text{DIV} \leq 0.5 + y + \text{SI}$$

The solution is $x = 1$, $y = 0.4$, DIV $= 0$, and SI $= 0.1$. The firm invests and borrows as before, but has to issue $100,000 of equity to raise the necessary cash for investment.

The shadow prices for this problem are as follows:

---

[13] Williard T. Carleton, Charles L. Dick, Jr., and David H. Downes give a comprehensive and insightful discussion of the differences in design and use of the two model types, and argue that optimization models are potentially more useful, in "Financial Policy Models: Theory and Practice," *Journal of Financial and Quantitative Analysis,* **8**: 691–709 (December 1973).

[14] Shadow prices are valued only for marginal shifts in the constraints. The range over which shifts qualify as marginal varies from problem to problem.

Constraint	Shadow Price	Explanation
Limit on investment ($x \leq 1$)	0.04	(See below.)
Limit on debt ($y \leq 0.4x$)	0.6	$1 of additional debt generates tax shields worth $0.50 *and* reduces equity issued by $1, saving $0.01 in issue costs.
Limit on available cash ($x + \text{DIV} \leq 0.5 + y + \text{SI}$)	0.1	Extra cash reduces equity issued and saves $0.10 per $1.

The shadow price on project investment goes down by 0.06, from $0.10 to $0.04 per dollar invested. This occurs because additional investment can be only 40% debt-financed. The remainder must come from issuing new equity. Therefore, the value of the opportunity to invest an additional dollar decreases by $0.6 \times 0.1 = 0.06$.

The shadow prices on the investment limits are particularly interesting because they show the project's net marginal contribution to firm value, when all of the project's financing side effects are accounted for. In this example the project's marginal contribution is 4 cents per dollar invested. Remember that the project has negative NPV separately considered. But it has one favourable side effect (investment allows the firm to borrow) and one unfavourable side effect (investment requires equity issues and generates issue costs).

The shadow price for the project can be calculated by starting with its base-case NPV of −0.1, adding the value of its marginal contribution to corporate borrowing, and subtracting the marginal cost of the equity issue needed to finance it:

$$
\begin{array}{c}
\text{Net contribution} \\
\text{to firm value}
\end{array}
=
\begin{array}{c}
\text{base-case} \\
\text{NPV}
\end{array}
+
\begin{array}{c}
\text{value of project's} \\
\text{marginal contribution} \\
\text{to borrowing power}
\end{array}
-
\begin{array}{c}
\text{marginal cost} \\
\text{of equity issue} \\
\text{needed to finance} \\
\text{project}
\end{array}
$$

Investing $1 more effectively loosens the debt constraint by $0.40 and tightens the cash constraint by $1. Therefore, we can "price out" the project's financing side effects by noting the shadow prices on these two constraints. Extra borrowing power is worth 60 cents per dollar and cash used up costs 10 cents per dollar. Therefore:

Net contribution to firm value $= -0.1 + 0.4(0.6) - (1.00)(0.1) = 0.04$

"Net contribution to firm value" is no more or less than *adjusted present value*, or APV. APV is calculated automatically as a by-product of LONGER. But, as you saw in Chapter 19, for simple problems you can calculate APV by hand. You need APV because it is the only generally reliable approach to capital budgeting when investment decisions have important financing side effects.

QUIZ

1. True or false?
   - (a) Financial planning should attempt to minimize risk.
   - (b) The primary aim of financial planning is to obtain better forecasts of future cash flows and earnings.
   - (c) Financial planning is necessary because financing and investment decisions interact and should not be made independently.
   - (d) Firms' planning horizons rarely exceed three years.
   - (e) Individual capital investment projects are not considered in a financial plan unless they are very large.
   - (f) Financial planning requires accurate and consistent forecasting.
   - (g) Financial planning models should include as much detail as possible.
2. List the major elements of a completed financial plan.
3. "There is no finance in financial planning models." Explain.

QUESTIONS AND PROBLEMS

1. What are the dangers and disadvantages of using a financial model? Discuss.
2. Should a financial plan be considered an unbiased forecast of future cash flows, earnings, and other financial variables? Why or why not?
3. How would Executive Fruit's financial model change is dividends were cut to zero in 1990? Use the revised model to generate a new financial plan for 1990. Show how the financial statements given in Table 28-2 would change. Do you think the new plan is an improvement on the old one? Discuss.
4. The balancing item in the Executive Fruit model is borrowing. What is meant by *balancing item*? How would the model change if dividends were made the balancing item instead? In that case how would you suggest that planned borrowing be determined?
5. Construct a new model for Executive Fruit based on your answer to question 4. Does your model generate a feasible financial plan for 1990? (*Hint:* If it doesn't you may have to allow the firm to issue stock.)
6. Executive Fruit's financial manager believes that revenues in 1990 could rise by as much as 50% or by as little as 10%. Recalculate the pro forma financial statements under these two assumptions. How does the rate of growth in revenues affect the firm's borrowing requirement?
7. (a) Use the Executive Fruit model (Table 28-3) to produce pro forma income statements, balance sheets, and sources and uses of funds statements for 1991 and 1992. Assume "business as usual" except that sales and costs expand by 30% per year as do fixed assets and net working capital. The interest rate is forecasted to remain at 9%, and stock issues are ruled out. Executive Fruit also plans to stick to its 60% dividend payout ratio. (*Hint:* Interest expense depends on additional borrowing, which in turn depends on profit after interest and taxes. You may find it helpful to rearrange the equations so that you can calculate interest first.)
   - (b) What are the firm's debt ratio and interest coverage under this plan?
   - (c) Can the company continue to finance expansion by borrowing?
8. Discuss the relative merits of descriptive financial models, such as the Executive Fruit model, and optimizing models such as LONGER. Descriptive models are much more commonly used in practice. Why do you think this is so?

Table 28-5
Financial statements for Executive Cheese Company (figures in thousands of dollars)

Income Statement for 1990

Revenue	$1,785
Fixed costs	53
Variable costs (80% of revenue)	1,428
Depreciation	80
Interest (at 10%)	24
Taxes (at 40%)	80
Net income	$ 120

Sources and Uses of Funds for 1990

Sources	
Operating cash flow	$ 200
Borrowing	36
Stock issues	104
Total sources	$ 340
Uses	
Increase in net working capital	60
Investment	200
Dividends	80
Total uses	$ 340

Balance Sheet, Year-End

	1990	1989
Assets		
Net working capital	$ 400	$ 340
Fixed assets	800	680
Total assets	$1,200	$1,020
	1990	1989
Liabilities		
Debt	$ 240	$ 204
Book equity	960	816
Total liabilities	$1,200	$1,020

9. Table 28-5 shows the 1990 financial statements for the Executive Cheese Company. Annual depreciation is 10% of fixed assets at the beginning of this year, plus 10% of new investment. The company plans to invest a further $200 per year in fixed assets for the next five years (over and above the capital needed to replace depreciated assets), and forecasts that the ratio of revenues to total assets at the start of each year will remain at 1.75. Fixed costs are expected to remain at $53 and variable costs at 80% of revenue. Net working capital is one-third of total assets. The company's policy is to pay out two-thirds of net income as dividends and to maintain a book debt ratio of 20%.

    (a) Construct a model like the one in Table 28-3 for Executive Cheese.

    (b) Use your model to produce a set of financial statements for 1991.

10. Our model for Executive Fruit is an example of a "top down" planning model. Some firms use a "bottom up" financial planning model, which incorporates forecasts of revenues and costs for particular products, advertising plans, major investment projects, and so on. What are the advantages and disadvantages of the two model types? What sort of firms would you expect to use each type and what would they use them for?

11. Corporate financial plans are often used as a basis for judging subsequent performance. What do you think can be learned from such comparisons? What problems are likely to arise and how might you cope with these problems?

12. What problems are likely to be encountered in keeping the corporate financial plan up to date?

C·H·A·P·T·E·R

29

SHORT-TERM FINANCIAL PLANNING

Most of this book is devoted to long-term financial decisions such as capital budgeting and the choice of capital structure. Such decisions are called *long-term* for two reasons. First, they usually involve long-lived assets or liabilities. Second, they are not easily reversed, and therefore may commit the firm to a particular course of action for several years.

Short-term financial decisions generally involve short-lived assets and liabilities, and usually they *are* easily reversed. Compare, for example, a 60-day bank loan for $50 million with a $50 million issue of 20-year bonds. The bank loan is clearly a short-term decision. The firm can repay it two months later and be right back where it started. A firm might conceivably issue a 20-year bond in January and retire it in March, but it would be extremely inconvenient and expensive to do so. In practice, such a bond issue is a long-term decision, not only because of the bond's 20-year maturity, but because the decision to issue it cannot be reversed on short notice.

A financial manager responsible for short-term financial decisions does not have to look far into the future. The decision to take the 60-day bank loan could properly be based on cash-flow forecasts for the next few months only. The bond issue decision will normally reflect forecasted cash requirements five, ten, or more years into the future.

Managers concerned with short-term financial decisions can avoid many of the difficult conceptual issues encountered elsewhere in this book. In a sense, short-term decisions are easier than long-term decisions — but they are not less important. A firm can identify extremely valuable capital investment opportunities, find the precise optimal debt ratio, follow the perfect dividend policy, and yet founder because no one bothers to raise the cash to pay this year's bills. Hence, the need for short-term planning.

In this chapter, we will review the major classes of short-term assets and liabilities, show how long-term financing decisions affect the firm's short-term financial planning problem, and describe how financial managers trace changes in cash and working capital. We will also describe how managers forecast month-by-month cash requirements or surpluses and how they develop short-term investment and financing strategies.

Part 9 of the book takes a more detailed look at working capital management. Chapter 30 examines the decision to extend credit to the firm's customers. Chapter 31 describes the decisions to hold cash (instead of investing cash to earn interest) and the relationship between firms and commercial banks. Chapter 32 describes the many channels firms can use to invest or raise funds for short periods.

29-1   THE COMPONENTS OF WORKING CAPITAL

Short-term or *current* assets and liabilities are collectively known as **working capital**. Table 29-1 gives a breakdown of current assets and current liabilities for all Canadian manufacturing firms with more than $10 million in assets in the third quarter of 1990. Note that total current assets were 86.9 billion and current liabilities were $60.3 billion. **Net working capital** (current assets less current liabilities) was $26.6 billion.

Table 29-1
Current assets and liabilities for manufacturing corporations in Canada, third quarter, 1990 (figures in millions of dollars)

Current Assets[a]		Current Liabilities[a]	
Cash	2,659	Short-term loans	22,373
Short-term loans to affiliates	2,955	Accounts payable	32,275
Marketable securities	6,118	Corporate income taxes payable	1,422
Accounts receivable	36,464	Portion of long-term debt payable within one year	1,841
Inventories	35,793		
Other current assets	2,929	Other current liabilities	2,408
Total	86,918	Total	60,319

[a] Net working capital (current assets − current liabilities) is $86,918 − $60,319 = $26,599.

Source: Statistics Canada, *Industrial Corporations*, Financial Statistics, Catalogue 61-003, Third Quarter, 1990, pp. 22–25. Reproduced by permission of the Minister of Supply and Services Canada.

One important current asset is *accounts receivable*. When one company sells goods to another company or a government agency, it does not usually expect to be paid immediately. These unpaid bills or *trade credit* make up the bulk of accounts receivable. Companies also sell some goods on credit to the final consumer. This *consumer credit* makes up the remainder of accounts receivable.[1] We will discuss the management of receivables in Chapter 30. You will learn how companies decide which customers are good or bad credit risks and when it makes sense to offer credit.

Another important current asset is *inventory*. Inventories may consist of raw materials, work in process, or finished goods awaiting sale and shipment.

---

[1] Sales of all manufacturing corporations were $61,507 million in the third quarter of 1990. Table 29-1 shows that accounts receivable were $36,464 million, about 59% of the quarter's sales. Since the accounts receivable are measured at the quarter's end, they must represent the last 59% of the quarter's sales. This amounts to $0.59 \times 13 = 7.7$ weeks. If this ratio of accounts receivable to annual sales is maintained, accounts receivable will always reflect the 7.7 weeks' sales.

Firms *invest* in inventory. The cost of holding inventory includes not only storage cost and the risk of spoilage or obsolescence, but also the opportunity cost of capital—that is, the rate of return offered by other, equivalent-risk investment opportunities.[2] The benefits to holding inventory are often indirect. For example, a large inventory of finished goods (large relative to expected sales) reduces the chance of a "stockout" if demand is unexpectedly high. A producer holding a small finished goods inventory is more likely to be caught short, unable to fill orders promptly. Similarly, large raw materials inventories reduce the chance that an unexpected shortage would force the firm to shut down production or use a more costly substitute material.

Bulk orders for raw materials, although they lead to large average inventories, may be worthwhile if the firm can obtain lower prices from suppliers. (That is, bulk orders may yield quantity discounts.) Firms will often hold large inventories of finished goods, for similar reasons. A large inventory of finished goods allows longer, more economical production runs. In effect, the production manager gives the firm a quantity discount.

The task of inventory management is to assess these benefits and costs and to strike a sensible balance. In manufacturing companies the production manager is best placed to make this judgement. Since the financial manager is not usually directly involved in inventory management, we will not discuss the inventory problem in detail.

The remaining current assets are cash and marketable securities. The cash consists of currency, demand deposits (funds in chequing accounts), and time deposits (funds in savings accounts). The principal marketable security is commercial paper (short-term unsecured notes sold by other firms) and bankers' acceptances (short-term promissory notes sold by other firms and backed by chartered banks). Other securities include Treasury bills and sales finance paper (secured or unsecured notes sold by finance companies or firms with finance subsidiaries).

In choosing between cash and marketable securities, the financial manager faces a task like that of the production manager. There are always advantages to holding large "inventories" of cash—they reduce the risk of running out of cash and having to raise more on short notice. On the other hand, there is a cost to holding idle cash balances rather than putting the money to work in marketable securities. In Chapter 31 we will tell you how the financial manager collects and pays out cash and decides on an optimal cash balance.

We have seen that a company's principal current asset consists of unpaid bills from other companies. One firm's credit must be another's debit. Therefore it is not surprising that a company's principal current liability consists of *accounts payable*—that is, outstanding payments to other companies.

To finance its investment in current assets, a company may rely on a variety of short-term loans. Commercial banks are by far the largest source of such loans, but an industrial firm may also borrow from other sources. Other ways of borrowing include issuing bankers' acceptances and selling commercial paper.

Many short-term loans are unsecured, but sometimes the company may offer its inventory or receivables as security. For example, a firm may decide to borrow

---

[2] How risky are inventories? It is hard to generalize. Many firms just assume inventories have the same risk as typical capital investments and therefore calculate the cost of holding inventories using the firm's average opportunity cost of capital. You can think of many exceptions to this rule of thumb, however. For example, some electronics components are made with gold connections. Should an electronics firm apply its average cost of capital to its inventory of gold? (See Section 11-3.)

short-term money secured by its accounts receivable. When its customers have paid their bills, it can use the cash to repay the loan. An alternative procedure is to *sell* the receivables to a financial institution and let it collect the money. In other words, some companies solve their financing problem by borrowing on the strength of their current assets; others solve it by selling their current assets. In Chapter 32 we will look at the varied and ingenious methods of financing current assets.

29-2 LINKS BETWEEN LONG-TERM AND SHORT-TERM FINANCING DECISIONS

All businesses require capital—that is, money invested in plant, machinery, inventories, accounts receivable, and all the other assets it takes to run a business efficiently. Typically, these assets are not purchased all at once but obtained gradually over time. Let us call the total cost of these assets the firm's *cumulative capital requirement.*

Most firms' cumulative capital requirement grows irregularly, like the wavy line in Figure 29-1. This line shows a clear upward trend, as the firm's business grows. But there is also seasonal variation around the trend: in the figure the capital-requirements line peaks late in each year. Finally, there would be unpredictable week-to-week and month-to-month fluctuations, but we have not attempted to show these in Figure 29-1.

The cumulative capital requirement can be met from either long-term or short-term financing. When long-term financing does not cover the cumulative capital requirement, the firm must raise short-term capital to make up the difference. When long-term financing *more* than covers the cumulative capital requirement, the firm has surplus cash available for short-term investment. Thus, the amount of long-term financing raised, given the cumulative capital requirement, determines whether the firm is a short-term borrower or lender.

Lines *A*, *B*, and *C* in Figure 29-1 illustrate this. Each depicts a different long-term financing strategy. Strategy *A* always implies a short-term cash surplus. Strategy *C* implies a permanent need for short-term borrowing. Under *B*, which is probably the most common strategy, the firm is a short-term lender during part of the year and a borrower during the rest.

What is the *best* level of long-term financing relative to the cumulative capital requirement? It is hard to say. There is no convincing theoretical analysis of this question. We can make several practical observations, however.

Matching Maturities

Most financial managers attempt to "match maturities" of assets and liabilities. That is, they finance long-lived assets like plant and machinery with long-term borrowing and equity.

Permanent Working-Capital Requirements

Most firms make a permanent investment in net working capital (current assets less current liabilities). They finance this investment from long-term sources.[3]

---

[3] In a sense this statement is true by definition. If net working capital (current assets less current liabilities) is positive, it must be financed by long-term debt or equity. Our point is that firms *plan* it that way.

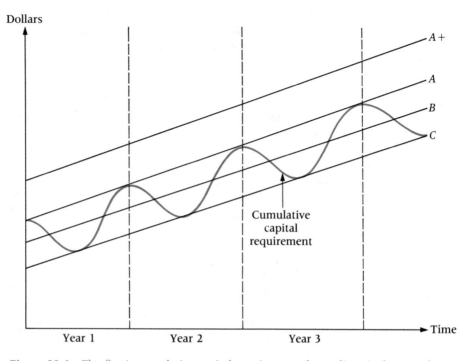

Figure 29-1   The firm's cumulative capital requirement (heavy line) is the cumulative investment in plant, equipment, inventory and all other assets needed for the business. In this case the requirement grows year by year, but there is seasonal fluctuation within each year. The requirement for short-term financing is the difference between long-term financing (lines $A+$, A, B, and C) and the cumulative capital requirement. If long-term financing follows line C, the firm *always* needs short-term financing. At line B, the need is seasonal. At lines A and $A+$, the firm never needs short-term financing. There is always extra cash to invest.

The Comforts of Surplus Cash

Many financial managers would feel more comfortable under strategy A than strategy C. Strategy $A+$ (the highest line) would be still more relaxing. A firm with a surplus of long-term financing never has to worry about borrowing to pay next month's bills. But is the financial manager paid to be comfortable? Firms usually put surplus cash to work in Treasury bills or other marketable securities. This is at best a zero-NPV investment for a tax-paying firm.[4] Thus, we think that firms with a *permanent* cash surplus ought to go on a diet, retiring long-term securities to reduce long-term financing to a level at or below the firm's cumulative capital requirement. That is, if the firm is on line $A+$, it ought to move down to line A, or perhaps even lower.

---

[4] But what is the NPV of an investment in Treasury bills? The answer depends on your position on the "debt and taxes" controversy discussed in Section 18-2. If there is a tax advantage to borrowing, as most people believe, there must be a corresponding tax *dis*advantage to lending, and investment in Treasury bills has a negative NPV.

Table 29-2
**Year-end balance sheets for 1989 and 1990 for Cimarron Mattress Company
(figures in millions of dollars)**

	1989	1990
Current assets		
Cash	4	5
Marketable securities	0	5
Inventory	26	25
Accounts receivable	25	30
Total current assets	55	65
Fixed assets		
Gross investment	56	70
Less depreciation	−16	−20
Net fixed assets	40	50
Total assets	95	115
Current liabilities		
Bank loans	5	0
Accounts payable	20	27
Total current liabilities	25	27
Long-term debt	5	12
Net worth (equity and retained earnings)	65	76
Total liabilities and net worth	95	115

29-3 TRACING CHANGES IN CASH AND WORKING CAPITAL

Table 29-2 compares 1989 and 1990 year-end balance sheets for Cimarron Mattress Company. Table 29-3 shows the firm's income statement for 1990. Note that Cimarron's cash balance increased by $1 million during 1990. What caused this increase? Did the extra cash come from Cimarron Mattress Company's additional long-term borrowing, from reinvested earnings, from cash released by reducing inventory, or from extra credit extended by Cimarron's suppliers? (Note the increase in accounts payable.)

The correct answer is "all the above," as well as many other activities and actions taken by the firm during the year. All we can say is that *sources* of cash exceeded *uses* by $1 million.

Financial analysts often summarize sources and uses of cash in a statement like the one shown in Table 29-4. The statement shows that Cimarron *generated* cash from the following sources:

1. It issued $7 million of long-term debt.
2. It reduced inventory, releasing $1 million.
3. It increased its accounts payable, in effect borrowing an additional $7 million from its suppliers.
4. By far the largest source of cash was Cimarron's operations, which generated $16 million. See Table 29-3, and note: income ($12 million) understates cash flow because depreciation is deducted in calculating income. Depreciation is *not* a cash outlay. Thus, it must be added back in order to obtain operating cash flow.

Cimarron *used* cash for the following purposes:

Table 29-3
Income statement for 1990 for Cimarron Mattress Company (figures in millions of dollars)

Sales	350
Operating costs	−321
	29
Depreciation	−4
	25
Interest	−1
Pretax income	24
Tax at 50%	−12
Net income	12

Note:

Dividend   = $1 million
Retained earnings = $11 million

Table 29-4
Sources and uses of cash for 1990 for Cimarron Mattress Company (figures in millions of dollars)

Sources	
Issued long-term debt	7
Reduced inventories	1
Increased accounts payable	7
Cash from operations:	
Net income	12
Depreciation	4
Total sources	31
Uses	
Repaid short-term bank loan	5
Invested in fixed assets	14
Purchased marketable securities	5
Increased accounts receivable	5
Dividend	1
	30
Increase in cash balance	1

1. It paid a $1 million dividend. (*Note*: The $11 million increase in Cimarron's equity is due to retained earnings: $12 million of equity income, less the $1 million dividend.)
2. It repaid a $5 million short-term bank loan.[5]
3. It invested $14 million. This shows up as the increase in gross fixed assets in Table 29-2.
4. It purchased $5 million of marketable securities.
5. It allowed accounts receivable to expand by $5 million. In effect, it lent this additional amount to its customers.

---

[5] This is principal repayment, not interest. Sometimes interest payments are explicitly recognized as a use of funds. If so, operating cash flow would be defined *before* interest, that is, as net income plus interest plus depreciation.

Table 29-5

Condensed year-end balance sheets for 1989 and 1990 for Cimarron Mattress Company (figures in millions of dollars)

	1989	1990
Net working capital	30	38
Fixed assets		
Gross investment	56	70
Less depreciation	−16	−20
Net fixed assets	40	50
Total assets	70	88
Long-term debt	5	12
Net worth	65	76
Long-term liabilities and net worth[a]	70	88

[a] When only *net* working capital appears on a firm's balance sheet, this figure (the sum of long-term liabilities and net worth) is often referred to as *total capitalization.*

Tracing Changes in Net Working Capital

Financial analysts often find it useful to collapse all current assets and liabilities into a single figure for net working capital. Cimarron's net working capital balances were (in millions):

	Current Assets	Less	Current Liabilities	Equals	Net Working Capital
Year-end 1989	$55	−	$25	=	$30
Year-end 1990	$65	−	$27	=	$38

Table 29-5 gives balance sheets that report only net working capital, not individual current asset or liability items.

"Sources and uses" statements can likewise be simplified by defining "sources" as actions or activities that contribute to net working capital, and "uses" as actions or activities that use up working capital. In this context, working capital is usually referred to as *funds,* and a *"sources and uses of funds" statement* is presented.

In 1990 Cimarron contributed to net working capital by:

1. Issuing $7 million of long-term debt
2. Generating $16 million from operations

It used up net working capital by:

1. Investing $14 million
2. Paying a $1 million dividend

The year's changes in net working capital are thus summarized by Cimarron Mattress Company's "sources and uses of funds" statement, given in Table 29-6.

Profits and Cash Flow

Now look back to Table 29-4, which shows sources and uses of *cash.* We want to register two warnings about the entry called *cash from operations.* It may not actually represent real dollars — dollars you can buy beer with.

First, depreciation may not be the only noncash expense deducted in calculating income. For example, most firms use different accounting procedures in their tax books than in their reports to shareholders. The point of special tax accounts is to minimize current taxable income. The effect is that the shareholder books

Table 29-6
Sources and uses of funds (net working capital) for 1990 for Cimarron Mattress Company (figures in millions of dollars)

Sources	
Issued long-term debt	7
Cash from operations	
Net income	12
Depreciation	4
	23
Uses	
Invested in fixed assets	14
Dividend	1
	15
Increase in net working capital	8

overstate the firm's current asset tax liability,[6] and after-tax cash flow from operations is therefore understated.

Second, income statements record sales when made, not when the customer's payment is received. Think of what happens when Cimarron sells goods on credit. The company records a profit at the time of sale but there is no cash inflow until the bills are paid. Since there is no cash inflow, there is no change in the company's cash balance, although there is an increase in working capital in the form of an increase in accounts receivable. No net addition to cash would be shown in a "sources and uses" statement like Table 29-4. The increase in cash from operations would be offset by an increase in accounts receivable.

Later, when the bills are paid, there is an increase in the cash balance. However, there is no further profit at this point and no increase in working capital. The increase in the cash balance is exactly matched by a decrease in accounts receivable.

That brings up interesting characteristics of working capital. Imagine a company that conducts a very simple business. It buys raw materials for cash, processes them into finished goods, and then sells these goods on credit. The whole cycle of operations looks like this:

---

[6] The difference between taxes reported and paid to Revenue Canada shows up on the balance sheet as an increased deferred tax liability. The reason a liability is recognized is that accelerated depreciation and other devices used to reduce current taxable income do not eliminate taxes, they only delay them. Of course this reduces the present value of the firm's tax liability, but still the ultimate liability has to be recognized. In the "sources and uses" statements an increase in deferred taxes would be treated as a source of funds. In the Cimarron Mattress example we ignore deferred taxes.

If you draw up a balance sheet at the beginning of the process, you see cash. If you delay a little, you find the cash replaced by inventories of raw materials and, still later, by inventories of finished goods. When the goods are sold, the inventories give way to accounts receivable and finally, when the customers pay their bills, the firm draws out its profit and replenishes the cash balance.

There is only one constant in this process—namely, working capital. The components of working capital are constantly changing. That is one reason that (net) working capital is a useful summary measure of current assets or liabilities.

The strength of the working capital measure is that it is unaffected by seasonal or other temporary movements between different current assets or liabilities. But the strength is also its weakness, for the working capital figure hides a lot of interesting information. In our example cash was transformed into inventory, then into receivables, and back into cash again. But these assets have different degrees of risk and liquidity. You can't pay bills with inventory or with receivables—you must pay with cash.

29-4   CASH BUDGETING

The past is interesting only for what one can learn from it. The financial manager's problem is to forecast *future* sources and uses of cash. These forecasts serve two purposes. First, they alert the financial manager to future cash needs. Second, the cash-flow forecasts provide a standard, or budget, against which subsequent performance can be judged.

Preparing the Cash Budget: Inflow

There are at least as many ways to produce a quarterly cash budget as there are to skin a cat. Many large firms have developed elaborate "corporate models;" others use a spread-sheet program to plan their cash needs. The procedures of smaller firms may be less formal. But there are common issues that all firms must face when they forecast. We will illustrate these issues by continuing the example of Cimarron Mattress.

Most of Cimarron's cash inflow comes from the sale of mattresses. We therefore start with a sales forecast by quarter[7] for 1991:

	Quarter			
	First	Second	Third	Fourth
Sales (millions of dollars)	87.5	78.5	116	131

But sales become accounts receivable before they become cash. Cash flow comes from *collections* on accounts receivable.

Most firms keep track of the average time it takes customers to pay their bills. From this they can forecast what proportion of a quarter's sales are likely to be converted into cash in that quarter, and what proportion is likely to be carried over to the next quarter as accounts receivable. Suppose that 80% of sales are "cashed in" in the immediate quarter and 20% in the next. Table 29-7 shows forecasted collections under this assumption.

---

[7] Most firms would forecast by month instead of by quarter. Sometimes weekly or even daily forecasts are made. But presenting a monthly forecast would triple the number of entries in Table 29-7 and subsequent tables. We wanted to keep the examples as simple as possible.

Table 29-7
To forecast Cimarron Mattress's collections on accounts receivables you have to forecast
sales and collection rates (figures in millions of dollars)

	First Quarter	Second Quarter	Third Quarter	Fourth Quarter
1. Receivables at start of period	30	32.5	30.7	38.2
2. Sales	87.5	78.5	116	131
3. Collections				
Sales in current period (80%)	70	62.8	92.8	104.8
Sales in last period (20%)	15[a]	17.5	15.7	23.2
Total collections	85	80.3	108.5	128.0
4. Receivables at end of period	32.5	30.7	38.2	41.2
4 = 1 + 2 − 3				

[a] Sales in the fourth quarter of the previous year were $75 million.

In the first quarter, for example, collections from current sales are 80% of $87.5,
or $70 million. But the firm also collects 20% of the previous quarter's sales, or
0.2(75) = $15 million. Therefore, total collections are $70 + $15 = $85 million.

Cimarron started the first quarter with $30 million of accounts receivable. The
quarter's sales of $87.5 million were *added* to accounts receivable, but $85 million
of collections were *subtracted*. Therefore, as Table 29-7 shows, Cimarron ended
the quarter with accounts receivable of $30 + 87.5 − 85 = $32.5 million. The
general formula is:

$$\text{Ending accounts receivable} = \text{beginning accounts receivable} + \text{sales} - \text{collections}$$

The top section of Table 29-8 shows forecasted sources of cash for Cimarron
Mattress. Collection of receivables is the main source but it is not the only one.
Perhaps the firm plans to dispose of some land, or expects a tax refund or payment
of an insurance claim. All such items are included as "other" sources. It is also
possible that you may raise additional capital by borrowing or selling stock, but
we don't want to prejudge that question. Therefore, for the moment, we just
assume that Cimarron will not raise further long-term finance.

**Preparing the
Cash Budget:
Outflow**

So much for the incoming cash. Now for the outgoing cash. There always seems
to be many more uses for cash than there are sources. For simplicity, we have
condensed the uses into four categories in Table 29-8:

1. *Payments on accounts payable.* You have to pay your bills for raw materials, parts,
   electricity, and so on. The cash-flow forecast assumes all these bills are paid
   on time, although Cimarron could probably delay payment to some extent.
   Delayed payment is sometimes called *stretching your payables*. Stretching is one
   source of short-term financing, but for most firms it is an expensive source,
   because by stretching they lose discounts given to firms that pay promptly.
   This is discussed in more detail in Section 30-1.
2. *Labour, administrative, and other expenses.* This category includes all other regular
   business expenses.
3. *Capital expenditures.* Note that Cimarron Mattress plans a major capital outlay
   in the first quarter.
4. *Taxes, interest, and dividend payments.* This includes interest on presently outstanding long-term debt, but does not include interest on any additional

Table 29-8
Cimarron Mattress's cash budget for 1991 (figures in millions of dollars)

	First Quarter	Second Quarter	Third Quarter	Fourth Quarter
Sources of cash				
Collections on accounts receivable	85	80.3	108.5	128
Other	0	0	12.5	0
Total sources	85	80.3	121	128
Uses of cash				
Payments on accounts payable	65	60	55	50
Labour, administrative, and other expenses	30	30	30	30
Capital expenditures	32.5	1.3	5.5	8
Taxes, interest, and dividends	4	4	4.5	5
Total uses	131.5	95.3	95	93
Sources minus uses	−46.5	−15.0	+26	+35
Calculation of short-term financing requirement				
1. Cash at start of period	5	−41.5	−56.5	−30.5
2. Change in cash balance (sources less uses)	−46.5	−15.0	+26	+35
3. Cash at end of period[a] 1 + 2 = 3	−41.5	−56.5	−30.5	+4.5
4. Minimum operating cash balance	5	5	5	5
5. Cumulative short-term financing required[b] 5 = 4 − 3	46.5	61.5	35.5	0.5

[a] Of course, firms cannot literally hold a negative amount of cash. This is the amount the firm will have to raise to pay its bills.

[b] A negative sign would indicate a cash *surplus*. But in this example the firm must raise cash for all quarters.

borrowing to meet cash requirements in 1991. At this stage in the analysis, Cimarron does not know how much it will have to borrow, or whether it will have to borrow at all.

The forecasted net inflow of cash (sources minus uses) is shown in the box in Table 29-8. Note the large negative figure for the first quarter: a $46.5 million forecasted *outflow*. There is a smaller forecasted outlay in the second quarter, and then substantial cash inflows in the second half of the year.

The bottom part of Table 29-8 (below the box) calculates how much financing Cimarron will have to raise if its cash-flow forecasts are right. It starts the year with $5 million in cash. There is a $46.5 million cash outflow in the first quarter, and so Cimarron will have to obtain at least $46.5 − $5 = $41.5 million of additional financing. This would leave the firm with a forecasted cash balance of exactly zero at the start of the second quarter.

Most financial managers regard a planned cash balance of zero as driving too close to the edge of the cliff. They establish a *minimum operating cash balance* to absorb unexpected cash inflows and outflows. Also, banks usually require firms to maintain a minimum average cash balance as partial compensation for services the bank provides to the firm—this is described in more detail in Chapter 31. We will assume that Cimarron's minimum operating cash balance is $5 million. That means it will have to raise the full $46.5 million cash outflow in the first quarter, and $15 million more in the second quarter. Thus, its cumulative financing requirement is $61.5 million in the second quarter. This is the peak, fortunately: the cumulative requirement declines in the third quarter by $26 million to $35.5 million. In the final quarter, Cimarron is almost out of the woods: its cash balance is $4.5 million, just $0.5 million shy of its minimum operating balance.

The next step is to develop a *short-term financing plan* that covers the forecasted requirements in the most economical way possible. We will move on to that topic after two general observations.

1. The large cash outflows in the first two quarters do not necessarily spell trouble for Cimarron Mattress. In part, they reflect the capital investment made in the first quarter: Cimarron is spending $32.5 million, but it should be acquiring an asset worth that much or more. In part, the cash outflows reflect low sales in the first half of the year; sales recover in the second half.[8] If this is a predictable seasonal pattern, the firm should have no trouble borrowing to tide it over the slow months.

2. Table 29-8 is only a best guess about future cash flows. It is a good idea to think about the *uncertainty* in your estimates. For example, you could undertake a sensitivity analysis, in which you inspect how Cimarron's cash requirements would be affected by a shortfall in sales or by a delay in collections. The trouble with such sensitivity analyses is that you are only changing one item at a time, whereas in practice a downturn in the economy might affect, say, sales levels *and* collection rates. An alternative but more complicated solution is to build a model of the cash budget, and then to simulate to determine the probability of cash requirements significantly above or below the forecasts shown in Table 29-8.[9] If cash requirements are difficult to predict, you may wish to hold additional cash or marketable securities to cover a possible unexpected cash outflow.

29-5   THE SHORT-TERM FINANCING PLAN

Cimarron's cash budget defines its problem: its financial manager must find short-term financing to cover the firm's forecasted cash requirements. There are dozens of sources of short-term financing, but for simplicity we start by assuming that there are just two options.

Options for Short-Term Financing

1. Unsecured Bank Borrowing   Cimarron has an existing arrangement with its bank allowing it to borrow up to $41 million at an interest cost of 11.5% per year or 2.875% per quarter. The firm can borrow and repay whenever it wants so long as it does not exceed the credit limit. Cimarron does not have to pledge any specific assets as security for the loan. This kind of arrangement is called a **line of credit**.[10]

---

[8] Maybe people buy more mattresses late in the year when the nights are longer.

[9] In other words, you could use Monte Carlo simulation. See Section 10-2.

[10] Lines of credit are discussed in more detail in Chapter 32.

When a company borrows on an unsecured line of credit, it is generally obliged to maintain a **compensating balance** on deposit at the bank. In our example, Cimarron has to maintain a balance of 20% of the amount of the loan. In other words, if the firm wants to raise $100, it must actually borrow $125, because $25 (20% of $125) must be left on deposit in the bank.

2. Stretching Payables   Cimarron can also raise capital by putting off paying its bills. The financial manager believes that Cimarron can defer the following amounts in each quarter:

Quarter	1	2	3	4
Amount deferrable (millions of dollars)	52	48	44	40

That is, $52 million can be saved in the first quarter by *not* paying bills in that quarter. (Table 29-8 assumes these bills *are* paid in the first quarter.) If deferred, these payments *must* be made in the second quarter. Similarly, $48 million of quarter 2's bills can be deferred to quarter 3 and so on.

Stretching payables is often costly, however, even if no ill will is incurred. The reason is that suppliers often offer discounts for prompt payment. Cimarron loses this discount if it pays late. In this example we assume the lost discount is 5% of the amount deferred. In other words, if a $100 payment is delayed, the firm must pay $105 in the next quarter.

The First Financing Plan   With these two options, the short-term financing strategy is obvious: use the line of credit first, if necessary up to the $41 million credit limit. If cash requirements exceed the credit limit, stretch payables.

Table 29-9 shows the resulting financing plan. In the first quarter the plan calls for borrowing the full amount available under the line of credit ($41 million) and stretching $3.6 million of payables (see lines 1 and 2 in the table). In addition, the firm sells the $5 million of marketable securities it held at the end of 1990 (line 8). Thus, under this plan it raises $49.6 million in the first quarter (line 10).

Why raise $49.6 million when Table 29-8 shows a cash requirement of only $46.5 million? The major reason is that the $41 million borrowed under the line of credit requires a compensating balance of 20% of $41 million, or $8.2 million. Cimarron can cover part of this with its $5 million minimum balance, but $3.2 million still has to be raised (line 15).

In the second quarter, the plan calls for Cimarron to maintain line of credit borrowing at the upper limit and stretch $20 million in payables. This raises $16.4 million after the $3.6 million of payables stretched in the first quarter are paid.

Again, the amount of cash raised exceeds the amount required for operations ($16.4 versus $15 million). In this case, the difference is the interest cost of the first quarter's borrowing: $1.2 million for the line of credit and $0.2 million for the stretched payables (lines 11 and 12).[11]

In the third and fourth quarters the plan calls for Cimarron to pay off its debt. In turn, this releases cash tied up by the compensating balance requirement of the line of credit.

---

[11] The interest rate on the line of credit is 11.5% per year or 11.5/4 = 2.875% per quarter. Thus, the interest due is 0.02875(41) = 1.2, or $1.2 million. The "interest" cost of the stretched payables is actually the 5% discount lost by delaying payment. Five percent of $3.6 million is $180,000 or about $0.2 million.

Table 29-9
Cimarron Mattress's first financing plan (figures in millions of dollars)

	First Quarter	Second Quarter	Third Quarter	Fourth Quarter
New borrowing				
1. Line of credit	41	0	0	0
2. Stretching payables	3.6	20	0	0
3. Total	44.6	20	0	0
Repayments				
4. Line of credit	0	0	4.8	36.2
5. Stretched payables	0	3.6	20	0
6. Total	0	3.6	24.8	36.2
7. Net new borrowing	44.6	16.4	−24.8	−36.2
8. Plus securities sold	5[a]	0	0	0
9. Less securities bought	0	0	0	0
10. Total cash raised	49.6	16.4	−24.8	−36.2
Interest payments				
11. Line of credit	0	1.2	1.2	1.0
12. Stretching	0	0.2	1.0	0
13. Less interest on marketable securities	−0.1[a]	0	0	0
14. Net interest paid	−0.1	1.4	2.2	1.0
15. Additional funds for compensating balance[b]	3.2	0	−1.0	−2.2
16. Cash required for operations[c]	46.5	15	−26	−35
17. Total cash required	49.6	16.4	−24.8	−36.2

[a] Cimarron held $5 million in marketable securities at the end of 1990. The yield is assumed to be 2.4% per quarter.

[b] Twenty percent of the amount borrowed on the line of credit in excess of $25 million. Cimarron's $5 million minimum operating cash balance serves as compensating balance for loans up to $25 million.

[c] From Table 29-8.

Evaluating the First Plan   Does the plan shown in Table 29-9 solve Cimarron's short-term financing problem? No: the plan is feasible, but Cimarron can probably do better. The most glaring weakness of this first plan is its reliance on stretching payables, an extremely expensive financing device. Remember that it costs Cimarron 5% *per quarter* to delay paying bills — 20% per year at simple interest. The first plan would merely stimulate the financial manager to search for cheaper sources of short-term borrowing. Perhaps the $41 million limit on the line of credit could be increased, for example.

The financial manager would ask several other questions as well. For example:

1. Does Cimarron need a larger reserve of cash or marketable securities to guard against, say, its customers stretching their payables (thus slowing down collections on accounts receivable?)

2. Does the plan yield satisfactory current and quick ratios?[12] Its bankers may be worried if these ratios deteriorate.[13]
3. Are there intangible costs of stretching payables? Will suppliers begin to doubt Cimarron's creditworthiness?
4. Does the plan for 1991 leave Cimarron in good financial shape for 1992? (Here the answer is yes, since Cimarron will have paid off all short-term borrowing by the end of the year.)
5. Should Cimarron try to arrange long-term financing for the major capital expenditure in the first quarter? This seems sensible, following the rule of thumb that long-term assets deserve long-term financing. It would also reduce the need for short-term borrowing dramatically. A counter argument is that Cimarron is financing the capital investment *only temporarily* by short-term borrowing. By year-end, the investment is paid for by cash from operations. Thus, Cimarron's initial decision not to seek immediate long-term financing may reflect a preference for ultimately financing the investment with retained earnings.
6. Perhaps the firm's operating and investment plans can be adjusted to make the short-term financing problem easier. Is there any easy way of deferring the first quarter's large cash outflow? For example, suppose that the large capital investment in the first quarter is for new mattress-stuffing machines to be delivered and installed in the first half of the year. The new machines are not scheduled to be ready for full-scale use until August. Perhaps the machine manufacturer could be persuaded to accept 60% of the purchase price on delivery and 40% when the machines are installed and operating satisfactorily.

Short-term financing plans are developed by trial and error. You lay out one plan, think about it, then try again with different assumptions on financing and investment alternatives. You continue until you can think of no further improvements.

Trial and error is important because it helps you understand the real nature of the problem the firm faces. Here we can draw a useful analogy between the *process* of planning and Chapter 10, "A Project is Not a Black Box." In Chapter 10 we described sensitivity analysis and other tools used by firms to find out what makes capital investment projects tick and what can go wrong with them. Cimarron's financial manager faces the same kind of task: not just to choose a plan, but to understand what can go wrong with it, and what will be done if conditions change unexpectedly.[14]

We cannot trace through each trial and error in Cimarron Mattress's search for the best short-term financing plan. The reader may be buried in numbers already. Instead we will wrap up this chapter by looking at Cimarron's second try.

The Second Financing Plan   The second financing plan, shown in Table 29-10, reflects two significant new assumptions.

---

[12] These ratios are discussed in Chapter 27.

[13] We have not worked out these ratios explicitly, but you can infer from Table 29-9 that they would be fine at the end of the year but relatively low in midyear, when Cimarron's borrowing is high.

[14] This point is even more important in *long-term* financial planning. See Chapter 28.

Table 29-10
Cimarron Mattress's second financing plan (figures in millions of dollars)

	First Quarter	Second Quarter	Third Quarter	Fourth Quarter
New borrowing				
1. Line of credit	41	0	0	0
2. Secured borrowing (receivables pledged)	6.1	16.4	0	0
3. Total	47.1	16.4	0	0
Repayments				
4. Line of credit	0	0	2.0	36.7
5. Secured borrowing	0	0	22.4	0
6. Total	0	0	24.4	36.7
7. Net new borrowing	47.1	16.4	−24.4	−36.7
8. Plus securities sold	2.5	0	0	0
9. Less securities bought	0	0	0	0
10. Total cash raised	49.6	16.4	−24.4	−36.7
Interest payments				
11. Line of credit	0	1.2	1.2	1.1
12. Secured borrowing	0	0.2	0.8	0
13. Less interest on marketable securities	−0.1[a]	−0.1	−0.1	−0.1
14. Net interest paid	−0.1	1.3	2.0	1.0
15. Additional funds for compensating balance[b]	3.2	0	−0.4	−2.8
16. Cash required for operations[c]	46.5	15	−26	−35
17. Total cash required	49.6	16.4	−24.4	−36.7

[a] Cimarron held $5 million in marketable securities at the end of 1990.
[b] Twenty percent of the amount borrowed on the line of credit in excess of $25 million. Cimarron's $5 million minimum operating cash balance serves as compensating balance for loans up to $25 million.
[c] From Table 29-8.
Note: There are minor inconsistencies in this table because of rounding.

1. A commercial financial company[15] has offered to lend Cimarron up to 80% of its accounts receivable at an interest rate of 15% per year or 3.75% per quarter. In return, Cimarron is to pledge accounts receivable as security for the loan. This is clearly cheaper than stretching payables. It appears much more expensive than the bank line of credit — but remember that the line of credit requires a 20% compensating balance, whereas every dollar borrowed against receivables can be spent.
2. The financial manager is uncomfortable with the first plan, which includes no cushion of marketable securities. The second plan calls for a $2.5 million marketable securities portfolio held throughout the year.

A comparison of Table 29-9 and Table 29-10 shows that the second plan is broadly similar to the first, except that borrowing against receivables replaces stretching payables, and the firm holds $2.5 million of marketable securities. The

---

[15] Commercial finance companies are nonbank financial institutions that specialize in lending to businesses.

second plan is also cheaper than the first. This can be seen by comparing net interest paid (line 14) under the two plans.

	Quarter				Total
	1	2	3	4	
First plan	−0.1	1.4	2.2	1.0	4.5
Second plan	−0.1	1.3	2.0	1.0	4.2

Over the year the second plan saves $4.5 − $4.2 = $0.3 million, or about $300,000 of interest.[16]

A Note on Short-Term Financial Planning Models

Working out a consistent short-term plan requires burdensome calculations.[17] Fortunately, much of the arithmetic can be delegated to a computer. Many large firms have built *short-term financial planning models* to do this. Smaller companies like Cimarron do not face so much detail and complexity and find it easier to work with a spread-sheet program on a personal computer. In either case the financial manager specifies forecasted cash requirements or surpluses, interest rates, credit limits, and so on, and the model grinds out a plan like those shown in Tables 29-9 and 29-10. The computer also produces balance sheets, income statements, and whatever special reports the financial manager may require.

Smaller firms that do not want custom-built models can rent general-purpose models offered by banks, accounting firms, management consultants, or specialized computer "software" firms.

Most of these models are *simulation* programs.[18] They simply work out the consequences of the assumptions and policies specified by the financial manager. *Optimization* models for short-term financial planning are also available. These models are usually linear programming models. They search for the *best* plan from a range of alternative policies identified by the financial manager.

As a matter of fact, we used a linear programming model developed by Pogue and Bussard[19] to generate Cimarron Mattress's financial plans. Of course in that simple example we hardly needed a linear programming model to identify the best strategy: it was obvious that Cimarron should always use the line of credit first, turning to the second-best alternative (stretching payables or borrowing against receivables) only when the limit on the line of credit was reached. The Pogue-Bussard model nevertheless did the arithmetic quickly and easily.

Optimization helps when the firm faces complex problems with many interdependent alternatives and restrictions for which trial and error might never identify the *best* combination of alternatives.

---

[16] These are pretax figures. We simplified this example by forgetting that each dollar of interest paid is a tax-deductible expense.

[17] If you doubt that, look again at Table 29-9 or 29-10. Notice that the cash requirements in each quarter depend on borrowing in the previous quarter, because borrowing creates an obligation to pay interest. Also, borrowing under a line of credit may require additional cash to meet compensating balance requirements; if so that means still more borrowing and still higher interest charges in the next quarter. Moreover, the problem's complexity would have been tripled had we not simplified by forecasting per quarter rather than by month.

[18] Like the simulation models described in Section 10-2, except that the short-term planning models rarely include uncertainty explicitly. The models referred to here are built and used in the same way as the long-term financial planning models described in Section 28-3.

[19] G.A. Pogue and R.N. Bussard, "A Linear Programming Model for Short-Term Financial Planning under Uncertainty," *Sloan Management Review*, **13**: 69–99 (Spring 1972).

Of course, the best plan for one set of assumptions may prove disastrous if the assumptions are wrong. Thus, the financial manager has to explore the implications of alternative assumptions about future cash flows, interest rates, and so on. Linear programming can help identify good strategies, but even with an optimization model the financial plan is still sought by trial and error.

29-6 SUMMARY

Short-term financial planning is concerned with the management of the firm's short-term, or *current* assets and liabilities. The most important current assets are cash, marketable securities, inventory, and accounts receivable. The most important current liabilities are bank loans and accounts payable. The difference between current assets and current liabilities is called *(net) working capital*.

Current assets and liabilities are turned over much more rapidly than the other items on the balance sheet. Short-term financing and investment decisions are more quickly and easily reversed than long-term decisions. Consequently, the financial manager does not need to look so far into the future when making them.

The nature of the firm's short-term financial planning problem is determined by the amount of long-term capital it raises. A firm that issues large amounts of long-term debt or common stock, or which retains a large part of its earnings, may find that it has permanent excess cash. In such cases there is never any problem paying bills, and short-term financial planning consists of managing the firm's portfolio of marketable securities. We think that firms with permanent cash surpluses ought to return the excess cash to their stockholders.

Other firms raise relatively little long-term capital and end up as permanent short-term debtors. Most firms attempt to find a golden mean by financing all fixed assets and part of current assets with equity and long-term debt. Such firms may invest cash surpluses during part of the year and borrow during the rest of the year.

The starting point for short-term financial planning is an understanding of sources and uses of cash.[20] Firms forecast their net cash requirements by forecasting collections on accounts receivable, adding other cash inflows, and subtracting all forecasted cash outlays.

If the forecasted cash balance is insufficient to cover day-to-day operations and to provide a buffer against contingencies, you will need to find additional finance. It may make sense to raise long-term finance if the deficiency is permanent and large. Otherwise, you may choose from a variety of sources of short-term finance. For example, you may be able to borrow from a bank on an unsecured line of credit, you may borrow offering receivables or inventory as security, or you may be able to finance the deficit by not paying your bills for a while. In addition to the explicit interest costs of short-term financing, there are often implicit costs. For example, the firm may be required to maintain a compensating balance at the bank, or it may lose its reputation as a prompt payer if it raises cash by delaying payment on its bills. The financial manager must choose the financing package that has lowest total cost (explicit and implicit

---

[20] We pointed out in Section 29-3 that sources and uses of *funds* are often analyzed rather than sources and uses of cash: anything that contributes to working capital is called *source of funds*; anything that diminishes working capital is called a *use of funds*. "Sources and uses of funds" statements are relatively simple because many sources and uses of cash are buried in changes in working capital. However, in forecasting, the emphasis is on cash flow: you pay bills with cash, not working capital.

costs combined) and yet leaves the firm with sufficient flexibility to cover contingencies.

The search for the best short-term financial plan inevitably proceeds by trial and error. The financial manager must explore the consequences of different assumptions about cash requirements, interest rates, limits on financing from particular sources, and so on. Firms are increasingly using computerized financial models to help in this process. The models range from simple spread-sheet programs that merely help with the arithmetic to linear programming models that help find the best financial plan.

FURTHER READING

Here are some general textbooks on working capital management:

G.W. Gallinger and P.B. Healey, *Liquidity Analysis and Management*, Addison-Wesley Publishing Company, Inc., Reading, Mass., 1987.

K.V. Smith, *Readings on the Management of Working Capital*, 2nd ed., West Publishing Company, New York, 1980.

J.H. Vander Weide and S.F. Maier, *Managing Corporate Liquidity: An Introduction to Working Capital Management*, John Wiley & Sons, Inc., New York, 1985.

J.D. Wilson and J.F. Duston, *Financial Information Systems Manual*, Warren, Gorham and Lamont, Inc., Boston, 1986.

Pogue and Bussard present a linear programming model for short-term financial planning:

G.A. Pogue and R.N. Bussard, "A Linear Programming Model for Short-Term Financial Planning under Uncertainty," *Sloan Management Review,* **13**: 69–99 (Spring 1972).

QUIZ

1. Listed below are six different transactions that Cimarron Mattress might make. Indicate how each transaction would affect each of the following:
    (a) Cash
    (b) Working capital
    The transactions are:
    1. Pay out $2 million cash dividend
    2. A customer pays a $2,500 bill resulting from a previous sale
    3. Cimarron pays $5,000 previously owed to one of its suppliers
    4. Borrow $1 million long-term and invest the proceeds in inventory
    5. Borrow $1 million short-term and invest the proceeds in inventory
    6. Sell $5 million of marketable securities for cash

2. Here is a forecast of sales by National Bromide for the first four months of 1992 (figures in thousands of dollars):

Month	1	2	3	4
Cash sales	15	24	18	14
Sales on credit	100	120	90	70

On the average 50% of credit sales are paid for in the current month, 30% in the next month, and the remainder in the month after that. What is the expected cash inflow from operations in months 3 and 4?

3. Fill in the blanks in the following statements:
    (a) A firm has a cash surplus when its _____ capital exceeds its _____. The surplus is normally invested in _____.

(b) In developing the short-term financial plan, the financial manager starts with a _____ budget for the next year. This budget shows the _____ generated or absorbed by the firm's operations, and also the minimum _____ needed to support these operations. The financial manager may also wish to invest in _____ as a reserve for unexpected cash requirements.

(c) Short-term financing plans are developed by _____ and _____, often aided by computerized _____.

4. State how each of the following events would affect the firm's balance sheet. State whether each change is a source or use of cash and whether it is a source or use of funds.

(a) An automobile manufacturer increases production in response to a forecasted increase in demand. Unfortunately, the demand does not increase.

(b) Competition forces the firm to give customers more time to pay for their purchases.

(c) Inflation increases the value of raw material inventories by 20%.

(d) The firm sells a parcel of land for $100,000. The land was purchased five years earlier for $200,000.

(e) The firm repurchases its own common stock.

(f) The firm doubles its quarterly dividend.

(g) The firm issues $1 million of long-term debt and uses the proceeds to repay a short-term bank loan.

QUESTIONS AND PROBLEMS

1. Table 29-11 shows Cimarron Mattress's year-end 1988 balance sheet, and Table 29-12 shows its income statement for 1989. Work out statements of sources and uses of cash and sources and uses of funds for 1989.

2. Work out a short-term financing plan for Cimarron Mattress Company assuming the limit on the line of credit is raised from $41 to $50 million. Otherwise adhere to the assumptions used in developing Table 29-10.

3. Look again at Cimarron Mattress's second plan in Table 29-10. Note that the line of credit is cheaper than borrowing against accounts receivable. Would you expect this to be true in practice? Why or why not?

Table 29-11
Year-end balance sheet for 1988 (figures in millions of dollars)

Current assets		Current liabilities	
Cash	4	Bank loans	4
Marketable securities	2	Accounts payable	15
Inventory	20	Total current liabilities	19
Accounts receivable	22		
Total current assets	48	Long-term debt	5
		Net worth (equity and	
Fixed assets		retained earnings)	60
Gross investment	50	Total liabilities	
Less depreciation	−14	and net worth	84
Net fixed assets	36		
Total assets	84		

Table 29-12
Income statement for 1989 (figures in millions of dollars)

Sales	300
Operating costs	−285
	15
Depreciation	−2
	13
Interest	−1
Pretax income	12
Tax at 50%	−6
Net income	6

Note:
Dividend   = $1 million
Retained earnings = $5 million

4. Suppose that Cimarron's bank offers to forget about the compensating balance requirement if the firm pays interest at a rate of 3.375% per quarter. Should the firm accept this offer? Why or why not? (Except for this change, follow the assumptions underlying Table 29-10.) Would your answer change if Cimarron's cash requirements in quarters 1 and 2 were much smaller— say, only $20 million and $10 million, respectively?

5. In some countries the market for long-term corporate debt is limited, and firms turn to short-term bank loans to finance long-term investments in plant and machinery. When a short-term loan comes due, it is replaced by another one, so that the firm is always a short-term debtor. What are the disadvantages of such an arrangement? Does it have any advantages? (*Hint:* See Section 23-3, especially "Introducing Inflation.")

6. Suppose a firm has surplus cash, but is *not* paying taxes. Would you advise it to invest in Treasury bills or other safe, marketable securities? How about investment in the preferred or common stock of other companies? (*Hint:* Your answer will reflect your stand on the "debt and taxes" controversy. See Section 18-2).

P·A·R·T

9

SHORT-TERM FINANCIAL DECISIONS

C·H·A·P·T·E·R

30

CREDIT MANAGEMENT

Chapter 29 provided an overall idea of what is involved in short-term financial management. It is time to get down to detail.

When companies sell their products, they sometimes demand cash on or before delivery, but in most cases they allow some delay in payment. If you turn back to the balance sheet in Table 29-1, you can see that these accounts receivable constitute on the average about one-third of a firm's current assets. These receivables include both trade credit and consumer credit. The former is by far the larger and will, therefore, be the main focus of this chapter.

Credit management involves five main steps:

1. First, you must determine the terms on which you propose to sell your goods. How long are you going to give customers to pay their bills? Are you prepared to offer a cash discount for prompt payment?
2. Second, you must decide what evidence you need of indebtedness. Do you just ask the buyer to sign a receipt, or do you insist on some more formal IOU?
3. Third, you must consider which customers are likely to pay their bills. Do you judge this from the customers' past records or past financial statements? Or do you rely on bank references?
4. Fourth, you must decide how much credit you are prepared to extend to each customer. Do you play safe by turning down any doubtful prospects? Or do you accept the risk of a few bad debts as part of the cost of building up a large regular clientele?
5. Finally, after you have granted credit, you have the problem of collecting the money when it becomes due. How do you keep track of payments? What do you do about reluctant payers?

We will discuss each step in turn.

30-1 TERMS OF SALE

Not all business transactions involve credit. For example, if you are producing goods to the customer's specification or incurring substantial delivery costs, then it may be sensible to ask for cash before delivery (CBD). If you are supplying goods to a wide variety of irregular customers, you may require cash on delivery (COD).

If your product is expensive and custom-designed, a formal sales contract will be signed. Often such contracts provide for **progress payments** as work is carried out. For example, a large, extended consulting contract might call for 30% payment after completion of field research, 30% more on submission of a draft report, and the remaining 40% when the project is finally completed.

When we look at transactions that do involve credit, we encounter a wide variety of arrangements and considerable jargon. In fact, each industry seems to have its own particular usage with regard to payment terms. These norms have a rough logic. The seller will naturally demand earlier payment if its customers are in a high-risk business, if their accounts are small, or if the goods are perishable or quickly resold.

In order to induce customers to pay before the final date, it is common to offer a cash discount for prompt settlement.[1] For example, a manufacturer may require payment within 30 days but offer a 5% discount to customers who pay within 10 days. These terms are referred to as *5/10, net 30*. If a firm sells goods on terms of 2/30, net 60, customers receive a 2% discount for payment within 30 days and must pay in full within 60 days.

Cash discounts are often very large. For example, a customer who buys on terms of 5/10, net 30 may decide to forgo the cash discount and pay on the 30th day. This means that the customer obtains an extra 20 days' credit but pays about 5% more for the goods. This is equivalent to borrowing money at a rate of 155% per annum.[2] Of course, any firm that delays payment beyond the due date gains a cheaper loan but damages its reputation for creditworthiness.

You can think of the terms of sale as fixing both the price for the cash buyer and the rate of interest charged for credit. For example, suppose that a firm reduces the cash discount from 5% to 4%. That would represent an *increase* in the price for the cash buyer of 1% but a *reduction* in the implicit rate of interest charged the credit buyer from just over 5% per 20 days to just over 4% per 20 days.

For many items that are bought on a recurrent basis, it is inconvenient to require separate payment for each delivery. A common solution is to pretend that all sales during the month, in fact, occur at the end of the month. Thus goods may be sold on terms of 8/10, EOM, net 60. This allows the customer a cash discount of 8% if the bill is paid within ten days of the end of month (EOM); otherwise the full payment is due within 60 days of the invoice date.[3] When purchases are subject to seasonal fluctuations, manufacturers often encourage customers to take early delivery by allowing them to delay payment until the usual order season. This practice is known as "season dating."

30-2 COMMERCIAL CREDIT INSTRUMENTS

The terms of sale define the amount of any credit but not the nature of the contract. Repetitive sales to domestic customers are almost always made on **open**

---

[1] In addition, many companies allow an "anticipation rate"—that is, a discount calculated to give a normal rate of interest to those customers who miss the cash discount but pay before the final date. Some firms also add a service charge for late payment.

[2] The cash discount allows you to pay $95 rather than $100. If you do not take the discount, you get a 20-day loan but you pay $\frac{5}{95}$ = 5.26% more for your goods. There are $\frac{365}{20}$ = 18.25 20-day periods in a year. A dollar invested for 18.25 periods at 5.26% per period grows to $(1.0526)^{18.25}$ = $2.55, a 155% return on the original investment.

[3] Terms of 8/10, prox., net 60 would entitle the customer to a discount if the bill was paid within ten days of the end of the following (or "proximo") month.

account and involve only an implicit contract. There is simply a record in the seller's books and a receipt signed by the buyer.

If an order is very large and there is no complicating cash discount, the customer may be asked to sign a **promissory note**. This is just a straightforward IOU, worded along the following lines:

> Antigonish, N.S.
> April 1, 1991
>
> Sixty days after date I promise to pay to the order of the XYZ Company one thousand dollars ($1,000.00) for value received.
>
> Signature

Such an arrangement is not common, but it has two advantages. First, as long as it is payable to "order" or to "bearer," the holder may sell this note or use it as security for a loan. Second, the note eliminates the possibility of any subsequent disputes about the existence of the debt; the customer knows that he or she may be sued immediately for failure to pay on the due date.

If you want a clear commitment from the buyer, it is more useful to have it *before* you deliver the goods. In this case the simplest procedure is to arrange a **commercial draft**.[4] It works as follows. The seller draws a draft ordering payment by the customer and sends this draft to the customer's bank together with the shipping documents. If immediate payment is required, the draft is termed a **sight draft**; otherwise, it is known as a **time draft**. Depending on whether it is a sight or a time draft, the customer either pays up or acknowledges the debt by adding the word *accepted* and his or her signature. The bank then hands the shipping documents to the customer and forwards the money or the **trade acceptance** to the seller.[5] The latter may hold the trade acceptance to maturity or may use it as security for a loan.

If the customer's credit is for any reason suspect, the seller may ask the customer to arrange for his or her bank to accept the time draft. In this case, the bank guarantees the customer's debt. These **bank acceptances** are often used in overseas trade; they have a higher standing and greater negotiability than a trade acceptance.

The exporter who requires greater certainty of payment can ask the customer to arrange for an **irrevocable letter of credit**. In this case the customer's bank sends the exporter a letter stating that it has established a credit in his or her favour at a bank in Canada. The exporter then draws a draft on the customer's bank and presents it to the bank in Canada together with the letter of credit and the shipping documents. The bank in Canada arranges for this draft to be accepted or paid and forwards the documents to the customer's bank.

If you sell goods to a customer who proves unable to pay, you cannot get your goods back. You simply become a general unsecured creditor of the company, in common with other unfortunates. You can avoid this situation by making a **conditional sale**, so that title to the goods remains with the seller until full payment is made. It is used for goods that are bought on an instalment basis. In this case, if the customer defaults on the payments, the goods can be immediately repossessed by the seller.

---

[4] Commercial drafts are sometimes known by the more general term *bills of exchange*.

[5] You often see the terms of sale defined as SD–BL. This means that the bank will hand over the bill of lading in return for payment on a sight draft.

30-3 CREDIT ANALYSIS

Firms are not allowed to discriminate between customers by charging them different prices. Neither may they discriminate by offering the same prices but different credit terms.[6] You *can* offer different terms of sale to different *classes* of buyer. You can offer volume discounts, for example, or discounts to customers willing to accept long-term purchase contracts. But as a rule, if you have a customer of doubtful standing, you keep to your regular terms of sale for that customer class. You protect yourself by restricting the volume of goods that the customer may buy on credit.

There are a number of ways in which you can find out whether customers are likely to pay their debts. The most obvious indication is whether they have paid promptly in the past. Prompt payment is generally a good omen; but beware of the customer who establishes a high credit limit on the basis of a series of small payments and then disappears, leaving you with a large unpaid bill.

If you are dealing with a new customer, you will probably check with a credit agency. Dun and Bradstreet is by far the largest of these agencies: its regular *Reference Book* provides credit ratings on nearly 3 million domestic and foreign firms. Figure 30-1 tells you how to interpret these ratings. In addition to its rating service, Dun and Bradstreet provides on request a full credit report on a potential customer.

Credit agencies usually report the experience that other firms have had with your customer. You can also get this information by contacting the firms directly or through a credit bureau or through a better business bureau.

Your bank can also make a credit check. It will contact the customer's bank and ask for information on the customer's average bank balance, access to bank credit, and general reputation.

In addition to checking with your customer's bank, it might make sense to check what everybody else in the financial community thinks about your customer's credit standing. Does that sound expensive? Not if your customer is a public company. You just look at the Canadian Bond Rating Service rating for the customer's outstanding bonds.[7] You can also compare prices of these bonds to prices of other firms' bonds. (Of course, the comparisons should be between bonds of similar maturity, coupon, and so on.) Finally, you can look at how the customer's stock price has been behaving recently. A sharp fall in price doesn't mean that the company is in trouble, but it does suggest that prospects are less bright than formerly.

Financial Ratio Analysis   We have suggested a number of ways to check whether your customer is a good risk. You can ask your collection manager, a specialized credit agency, a credit bureau, a banker, or the financial community at large. But, if you don't like relying on the judgement of others, you can do your own homework. Ideally, this would involve a detailed analysis of the company's business prospects and financing, but this is usually too expensive. Therefore, credit analysts concentrate on the company's financial statements, using rough rules of thumb to judge

---

[6] Price discrimination, and by implication credit discrimination, is prohibited by law. However, it is possible to offer buyers a menu of choices amongst combinations of price and credit terms that will cause customers to "self-select" or discriminate amongst themselves. See M.J. Brennan, V. Maksimovic, and J. Zechner, "Vendor Financing," *Journal of Finance,* **43**: 1127–1141 (1988).

[7] See Section 23-4.

Key to Ratings

ESTIMATED FINANCIAL STRENGTH			HIGH	GOOD	FAIR	LIMITED
			COMPOSITE CREDIT APPRAISAL			
5A	$50,000,000	and over	1	2	3	4
4A	$10,000,000 to	49,999,999	1	2	3	4
3A	1,000,000 to	9,999,999	1	2	3	4
2A	750,000 to	999,999	1	2	3	4
1A	500,000 to	749,999	1	2	3	4
BA	300,000 to	499,999	1	2	3	4
BB	200,000 to	299,999	1	2	3	4
CB	125,000 to	199,999	1	2	3	4
CC	75,000 to	124,999	1	2	3	4
DC	50,000 to	74,999	1	2	3	4
DD	35,000 to	49,999	1	2	3	4
EE	20,000 to	34,999	1	2	3	4
FF	10,000 to	19,999	1	2	3	4
GG	5,000 to	9,999	1	2	3	4
HH	Up to	4,999	1	2	3	4

GENERAL CLASSIFICATION

ESTIMATED FINANCIAL STRENGTH			GOOD	FAIR	LIMITED
			COMPOSITE CREDIT APPRAISAL		
1R	$125,000	and over	2	3	4
2R	$50,000 to	$124,999	2	3	4

EXPLANATION

When the designation "**1R**" or "**2R**" appears, followed by a 2, 3 or 4, it is an indication that the Estimated Financial Strength, while not definitely classified, is presumed to be in the range of the ($) figures in the corresponding bracket, and while the Composite Credit Appraisal cannot be judged precisely, it is believed to fall in the general category indicated.

"**INV**," shown in place of a rating indicates that the report was under investigation at the time of going to press. It has no other significance.

"**FB**" (Foreign Branch). Indicates that the headquarters of this company is located in a foreign country (including Canada). The written report contains the location of the headquarters.

ABSENCE OF RATING, expressed by two hyphens (--), is not to be construed as unfavorable but signifies the circumstances difficult to classify within condensed rating symbols. It suggests the advisability of obtaining a report for additional information.

EMPLOYEE RANGE DESIGNATIONS IN REPORTS ON NAMES NOT LISTED IN THE REFERENCE BOOK

		KEY TO EMPLOYEE RANGE DESIGNATIONS	
Certain businesses do not lend themselves to a	ER 1	1000 or more	Employees
Dun & Bradstreet rating and are not listed in the	ER 2	500–999	Employees
Reference Book. Information on these names,	ER 3	100–499	Employees
however, continues to be stored and updated in	ER 4	50– 99	Employees
the D&B Business Information File. Reports are	ER 5	20– 49	Employees
available on such businesses and instead of a rat-	ER 6	10– 19	Employees
ing they carry an Employee Range Designation	ER 7	5– 9	Employees
(ER) which is indicative of size in terms of number	ER 8	1– 4	Employees
of employees. No other significance should be	ER N		Not Available
attached.			

Figure 30–1 Key to Dun and Bradstreet ratings.

Source: Used by permission of Dun and Bradstreet Canada Limited.

whether the firm is a good credit risk. The rules of thumb are based on *financial ratios*. Chapter 27 described how these ratios are calculated and interpreted.

Numerical Credit Scoring

Analyzing credit risks is like police detective work. You have a lot of clues — some important, some minor, some fitting into a neat pattern, others contradictory. You must weigh these clues to come up with an overall judgement.

In a small village the local police officer can generally rely on experience and knowledge of the locality. Personal judgement is everything. In a large city the police force cannot operate like this. It needs a systematic way to gather and sort all the information that comes into police headquarters. Likewise, when the firm has a small, regular clientele, the credit manager can easily handle the investigation process informally. But when the company is dealing directly with consumers or with a large number of small trade accounts, some streamlining is essential. In these cases it may make sense to use a mechanical scoring system to prescreen credit applications.

If you apply for a credit card or bank loan, you will be asked various questions about your job, home, and financial position. One medium-sized bank required each loan applicant to answer a standard questionnaire, of which a condensed version is shown in Table 30-1.[8] It found that only 1.2% of these loans subsequently defaulted. Some categories of borrower, however, proved to be much worse credit risks than others. We have added the actual default rates for each category in the right-hand margin of Table 30-1. For example, you can see that 7.0% of the borrowers who had no telephone subsequently defaulted. Similarly, borrowers who lived in rented rooms, had no bank account, needed the loan to pay medical bills, and so on, were much worse credit risks than the average.

Given this experience, it might make sense for the bank to calculate an overall risk index for each applicant.[9] For example, it could construct a rough-and-ready index simply by adding up all the probabilities in Table 30-1. The wretch who gave the most unfavourable response to each question would have a risk index of

$$7.0 + 7.3 + 2.6 + \cdots + 2.6 = 51.8$$

As if he (or she) didn't have enough troubles!

The questionnaire in Table 30-1 is, of course, dated — not many loan applicants have a monthly income below $200! We wish we could give a real, current example, but they are all Top Secret: a bank with a superior method for identifying good and bad borrowers has a significant edge on its competition.

Constructing Better Risk Indexes

Many lenders that use credit scoring systems employ ad hoc formulas. You should be able to do better than this.

Just adding up the separate probabilities, as in our bank example, isn't the answer, for it ignores the interactions between the different factors. It may be much more alarming when single applicants have a family of eight than when married ones do. On the other hand, you may not be so concerned when single applicants live in a rented room (unless, of course, they also have a family of eight).

Suppose that you take just two factors — time spent in last residence and time spent in last job. You then plot a scatter diagram like Figure 30-2. The x's represent customers that subsequently paid their debts: the o's represent customers that defaulted. Now try to draw a straight dividing line between the two groups. You

---

[8] See P.F. Smith, "Measuring Risk on Consumer Installment Credit," *Management Science,* **11**: 327–340 (November 1964).

[9] There are some measures you *cannot* use in calculating this risk index or in any other credit evaluation: the applicant's sex or race, for example.

Table 30-1
A condensed version of a questionnaire used by a bank for personal loan applicants.
We have added in parentheses the percentage of borrowers in each category who
subsequently defaulted.

1.	Do you have:	
	1 or more telephones?	(0.7)
	No telephone?	(7.0)
2.	Do you:	
	Own your home?	(0.7)
	Rent a house?	(2.2)
	Rent an apartment	(3.3)
	Rent a room?	(7.3)
3.	Do you:	
	Have one or more bank accounts?	(0.8)
	No bank account?	(2.6)
4.	Is the purpose of the loan:	
	To buy an automobile?	(0.8)
	To buy household goods?	(0.6)
	To pay medical expenses?	(2.5)
	Other?	(1.3)
5.	How long did you spend in your last residence?	
	6 months or less?	(3.1)
	7 to 60 months?	(1.4)
	More than 60 months?	(0.8)
6.	How long did you spend in your last job?	
	6 months?	(3.2)
	7 to 60 months?	(1.5)
	More than 60 months?	(0.9)
7.	What is your marital status:	
	Single?	(1.6)
	Married?	(1.0)
	Divorced?	(2.9)
8.	What is your postal zone?	(0.1 to 11.4)
9.	For how long do you require the loan:	
	12 months or less?	(1.6)
	More than 12 months?	(1.0)
10.	What is your occupation?	(0.4 to 3.5)
11.	What is your monthly income:	
	$200 or less?	(2.3)
	$200 to $1,000?	(1.1)
	More than $1,000	(0.7)
12.	What is your age:	
	25 or under?	(1.5)
	26 to 30?	(1.8)
	More than 30?	(1.0)
13.	How many are there in your family:	
	One?	(1.6)
	Two to seven?	(1.1)
	Eight or more?	(2.6)

Source: Reprinted by permission from P.F. Smith, "Measuring Risk on Consumer Installment
Credit," *Management Science,* **11**: 327–340 (November 1964), Copyright 1964 The Institute of
Management Science.

can't wholly separate them but the line in our diagram keeps the two groups as
far apart as possible. (Note that there are only three x's below the line and three
o's above it.) This line tells us that, if we wish to *discriminate* between the good

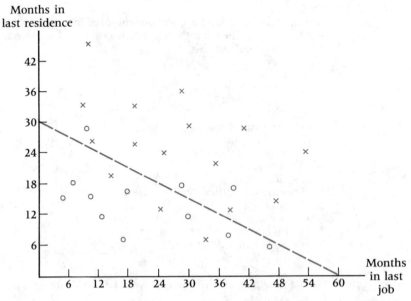

Figure 30-2   The x's represent a hypothetical group of bank borrowers that subsequently repaid their loans; the o's represent those that defaulted. The sloping line discriminates between the two groups on the basis of time spent in last home and time spent in last job. The line represents the equation $Z = 2$ (months in last residence) $+ 1$ (months in last job) $= 60$. Borrowers who plot above the line have "Z-scores" greater than 60.

and bad risks, we should give only half as much weight to job stability as we give to home stability. The index of creditworthiness is:

$$\text{Index of creditworthiness} = Z = 2 \text{ (months in last residence)} \\ + 1 \text{ (months in last job)}$$

You minimize the degree of misclassification if you predict that applicants with Z scores over 60 will pay their bills and that those with Z scores below 60 will not pay.[10]

In practice, we do not need to confine our attention to just two variables nor do we need to estimate the equation by eye. Multiple discriminant analysis (MDA) is a straightforward statistical technique for calculating how much weight to put on each variable in order to separate the sheep from the goats.[11]

Edward Altman has used MDA to predict bad business risks. Altman's object was to see how well financial ratios could be used to distinguish which firms would go bankrupt during the period 1946–1965. MDA gave him the following index of creditworthiness:[12]

---

[10] The quantity 60 is an arbitrary constant. We could just as well have used 6. In that case the Z score is $Z = 0.2$ (months in last residence) $+ 0.1$ (months in last job).

[11] MDA is not the only statistical technique that you can use for this purpose. Probit and logit are two other potentially useful techniques. These estimate the probability of some event—e.g., default—as a function of observable attributes.

[12] EBIT is earnings before interest and taxes. E.I. Altman, "Financial Ratios, Discriminant Analysis and the Prediction of Corporate Bankruptcy," *Journal of Finance,* **23**: 589–609 (September 1968).

$$Z = 3.3 \frac{\text{EBIT}}{\text{total assets}} + 1.0 \frac{\text{sales}}{\text{total assets}} + 0.6 \frac{\text{market value equity}}{\text{book value of debt}}$$

$$+ 1.4 \frac{\text{retained earnings}}{\text{total assets}} + 1.2 \frac{\text{working capital}}{\text{total assets}}$$

This equation did a good job at distinguishing the bankrupt and nonbankrupt firms. Of the former, 94% has Z scores of *less* than 2.7 the year before they went bankrupt. In contrast, 97% of the nonbankrupt firms had Z scores *above* this level.[13]

Credit scoring systems should carry a health warning. When you construct a risk index, it is tempting to experiment with many different combinations of variables until you find the equation that would have worked best in the past. Unfortunately, if you "mine" the data in this way, you are likely to find that the system works less well in the future than it did previously. If you are misled by these past successes into placing too much faith in your model, you may refuse credit to a number of potentially good customers. The profits that you lose by turning away customers could more than offset the gains that you make from avoiding a few bad eggs. As a result you could be worse off than if you had pretended that you could not tell one customer from another and extended credit to all of them.

Does this mean that you should not use credit scoring systems? Not a bit. It simply implies that it is not sufficient to have a good credit scoring system; you also need to know how much to rely on it. That is the topic of the next section.

30-4   THE CREDIT DECISION

Let us suppose that you have taken the first three steps toward an effective credit operation. In other words, you have fixed your terms of sale; you have decided whether to sell on open account or to ask your customers to sign an IOU; and you have established a procedure for estimating the probability that each customer will pay up. Your next step is to work out which of those customers should be offered credit.

If there is no possibility of repeat orders, the decision is relatively simple. Figure 30-3 summarizes your choice. On the one hand, you can refuse credit. In this case you make neither a profit nor a loss. The alternative is to offer credit. Suppose that the probability that the customer will pay up is p. If the customer does pay, you receive additional revenues (REV) and you incur additional costs; your net gain is the present value of REV − COST. Unfortunately, you can't be certain that the customer will pay; there is a probability $(1 - p)$ of default. Default means you receive nothing and incur the additional costs. The *expected* profit from the two courses of action is therefore as follows:

	Expected Profit
Refuse credit	0
Grant credit	$p\text{PV}(\text{REV} - \text{COST}) - (1 - p)\, \text{PV}(\text{COST})$

You should grant credit if the expected profit from doing so is greater than the expected profit from refusing.

---

[13] This equation was fitted with hindsight. The equation did slightly less well when used to predict bankruptcies after 1965.

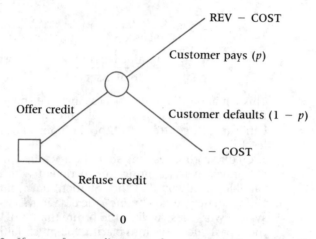

Figure 30-3   If you refuse credit, you make neither profit nor loss. If you offer credit, there is a probability p that the customer will pay and you will make REV − COST; there is a probability $(1 - p)$ that the customer will default and you will lose COST.

Consider for example the case of the Cast Iron Company. On each nondelinquent sale Cast Iron receives revenues with a present value of $1,200 and incurs costs with a value of $1,000. Therefore, the company's expected profit if it offers credit is:

$$p\,PV(REV - COST) - (1 - p)\,PV(COST) = p \times 200 - (1 - p) \times 1,000$$

If the probability of collection is ⅚, Cast Iron can expect to break even:

$$\text{Expected profit} = \frac{5}{6} \times 200 - \left(1 - \frac{5}{6}\right) \times 1,000 = 0$$

Therefore, Cast Iron's policy should be to grant credit whenever the chances of collection are better than five out of six.

*When to Stop Looking for Clues   We told you earlier where to *start* looking for clues about a customer's creditworthiness, but we never said anything about when to *stop*. Now we can work out how your profits would be affected by more detailed credit analysis.

Suppose that Cast Iron Company's credit department undertakes a study to determine which customers are most likely to default. It appears that 95% of its customers have been prompt payers and 5% have been slow payers. On the other hand, customers with a record of slow payment are much more likely to default on the next order than those with a record of prompt payment. On the average 20% of the slow payers subsequently default but only 2% of the prompt payers do so.

In other words, consider a sample of 1,000 customers, none of which has defaulted yet. Of these 950 have a record of prompt payment and 50 have a record of slow payment. On the basis of past experience Cast Iron should expect 19 of the prompt payers to default in the future and 10 of the slow payers to do so:

Category	Number of Customers	Probability of Default	Expected Number of Defaults
Prompt payers	950	0.02	19
Slow payers	50	0.20	10
All customers	1,000	0.029	29

Now the credit manager faces the following decision: Should the company refuse to give any more credit to customers that have been slow payers in the past?

If you are aware that a customer has been a slow payer, the answer is clearly "yes." Every sale to slow payers has only an 80% chance of payment ($p = 0.8$). Selling to a *slow* payer, therefore, gives an expected *loss* of $40:

$$\text{Expected profit} = p\text{PV}(\text{REV} - \text{COST}) - (1 - p)\text{PV}(\text{COST})$$
$$= 0.8(200) - 0.2(1,000) = -\$40$$

But suppose that it costs $10 to search through Cast Iron's records to determine whether a customer has been a prompt or slow payer. Is it worth doing so? The expected payoff to such a check is:

$$\text{Expected payoff to credit check} = \text{probability of identifying a slow payer}$$
$$\times \text{ gain from not extending credit}$$
$$- \text{ cost of credit check}$$
$$= (0.05 \times 40) - 10 = -\$8$$

In this case checking isn't worth it. You are paying $10 to avoid a $40 loss 5% of the time. But suppose that a customer orders ten units at once. Then checking is worthwhile because you are paying $10 to avoid a *$400* loss 5% of the time:

$$\text{Expected payoff to credit check} = (0.05 \times 400) - 10 = \$10$$

The credit manager therefore decides to check customers' past payment records only on orders of more than five units. You can verify that a credit check on a five-unit order just pays for itself.

Our illustration is simplistic, but you have probably grasped the message. You don't want to subject each order to the same credit analysis. You want to concentrate your efforts on the large and doubtful orders.

Credit Decisions with Repeat Orders

So far we have ignored the possibility of repeat orders. But one of the reasons for offering credit today is that you may get yourself a good, regular customer.

Figure 30-4 illustrates the problem.[14] Cast Iron has been asked to extend credit to a new customer. You can find little information on the firm and you believe that the probability of payment is no better than 0.8. If you grant credit, the expected profit on this order is:

---

[14] Our example is adapted from H. Bierman, Jr. and W.H. Hausman, "The Credit Granting Decision," *Management Science,* **16**: B519–B532 (April 1970).

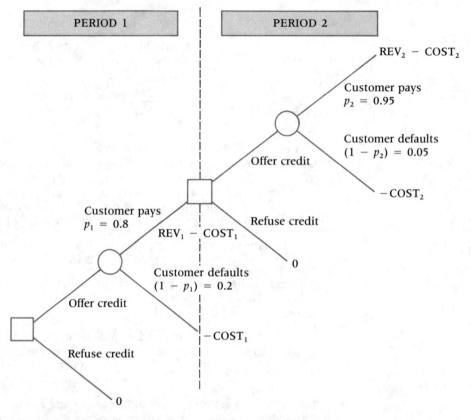

Figure 30-4   In this example there is only a 0.8 probability that your customer will pay in period 1; but if payment is made, there will be another order in period 2. The probability that the customer will pay for the second order is 0.95. The possibility of this good repeat order more than compensates for the expected loss in period 1.

$$\text{Expected profit on initial order} = p_1 \times PV(REV - COST)$$
$$- (1 - p_1) \times PV(COST)$$
$$= (0.8 \times 200) - (0.2 \times 1,000) = -\$40$$

You decide to refuse credit.

This is the correct decision if there is no chance of a repeat order. But look again at the example shown in the decision tree, Figure 30-4. If the customer does pay up, there will be a reorder next year. Because the customer has paid once, you can be 95% sure that he or she will pay again. For this reason any repeat order is very profitable:

$$\text{Next year's expected profit on repeat order} = p_2 PV(REV_2 - COST_2)$$
$$- (1 - p_2) PV(COST_2)$$
$$= (0.95 \times 200) - (0.05 \times 1,000)$$
$$= \$140$$

Now you can re-examine today's credit decision. If you grant credit today, you receive the expected profit on the initial order *plus* the possible opportunity to extend credit next year:

$$\text{Total expected profit} = \text{expected profit on initial order}$$
$$+ \text{probability of payment and repeat order}$$
$$\times PV \text{ (next year's expected profit on repeat order)}$$
$$= -40 + 0.80 \times PV(140)$$

At any reasonable discount rate you ought to extend credit. For example, if the discount rate is 20%,

$$\text{Total expected profit (present value)} = -40 + \frac{0.8(140)}{1.2} = \$53.33$$

In this example you should grant credit even though you expect to make a loss on the order. The expected loss is more than outweighed by the possibility that you will secure a reliable and regular customer.

Some General Principles Sometimes the credit manager faces clear-cut choices. In these circumstances it may be possible to estimate fairly precisely the consequences of a more liberal or a more stringent credit policy. But real-life situations are generally far more complex than our simple examples. Customers are not all good or bad. Many of them pay consistently late: you get your money, but it costs more to collect and you lose a few months' interest. Then there is the question of risk. You may be able to measure the revenues and costs, but at what rate do you discount them?

Like almost all financial decisions, credit allocation involves a strong dose of judgement. Our examples are intended as reminders of the issues involved rather than as cookbook formulas. Here are the basic things to remember.

1. Maximize Profit   As credit manager your job is not to minimize the number of bad accounts; it is to maximize expected profit. You must, therefore, recognize that you are concerned with a trade-off. The best that can happen is that the customer pays promptly; the worst is default. In the one case the firm receives the full additional revenues from the sale less the additional costs; in the other it receives nothing and loses the costs. You must weigh the chances of these alternative outcomes. If the margin of profit is high, you are justified in a liberal credit policy; if it is low, you cannot afford many bad debts.

2. Concentrate on the Dangerous Accounts   You should not expend the same effort or analyzing all credit applications. If an application is small or clear-cut, your decision should be largely routine; if it is large or doubtful, you may do better to move straight to a detailed credit appraisal. Most credit managers don't make credit decisions on an order-by-order basis. Instead they set a credit limit for each customer. The sales representative is required to refer the order for approval only if the customer exceeds this limit.

3. Look Beyond the Immediate Order   The credit decision is a dynamic problem. You cannot look only at the immediate future. Sometimes it may be worth accepting a relatively poor risk as long as there is a likelihood that the customer will grow into a regular and reliable buyer. New businesses must, therefore, be prepared to incur more bad debts than established businesses. This is part of the cost of building up a good customer list.

30-5 COLLECTION POLICY

It would be nice if all customers paid their bills by the due date. But they don't, and, since you may also occasionally "stretch" your payables, you can't altogether blame them.

The credit manager keeps a record of payment experiences with each customer. The manager knows that company A always takes the discount and that company Z is generally slow 90 days. In addition the manager monitors overdue payments

Table 30-2
An aging schedule of receivables (figures in dollars)

Customer's Name	Amount Not Yet Due	1 Month Overdue	2 Months Overdue	More Than 2 Months Overdue	Total Owed
A	10,000	—	—	—	10,000
.	.	.	.	.	.
.	.	.	.	.	.
.	.	.	.	.	.
Z	5,000	4,000	6,000	15,000	30,000
Total	200,000	40,000	15,000	43,000	265,000

by drawing up a schedule of the aging of receivables. This may look roughly like Table 30-2.

When a customer is in arrears, the usual procedure is to send a statement of account and to follow this at intervals with increasingly insistent letters, telephone calls, or telex or fax messages. If none of these has any effect, most companies turn the debt over to a collection agency or an attorney. The fee for such services is usually between 15% and 40% of the amount collected. An insolvent customer may become bankrupt. In Appendix 30-1 we describe what happens when an individual or firm files for bankruptcy.

There is always a potential conflict of interest between the collection department and the sales department. Sales representatives commonly complain that they no sooner win new customers than the collection department frightens them off with threatening letters. The collection manager, on the other hand, bemoans the fact that the sales force is concerned only with winning orders and does not care whether the goods are subsequently paid for.

There are also many instances of cooperation between sales managers and the financial managers who worry about collections. For example, the specialty chemicals division of a major pharmaceutical company actually made a business loan to an important customer which had been suddenly cut off by its bank. The pharmaceutical company bet that it knew its customer better than the customer's bank did—and it was right. The customer arranged alternative bank financing, paid back the pharmaceutical company, and became an even more loyal customer. It was a nice example of financial management supporting sales.

Factoring and Credit Insurance

The large firm has some advantages in managing its accounts receivable. First, it may be possible for divisions to pool information on the creditworthiness of their customers. Second, there are potential economies of scale in record keeping, billing, and so on, especially if the process can be computerized. Third, debt collection is a specialized business that calls for experience and judgement. The small firm may not be able to hire or train a specialized credit manager. However, it may be able to obtain some of these economies by farming part of the job out to a **factor**.

Factoring works as follows. The factor and the client agree on credit limits for each customer and on the average collection period. The client then notifies each customer that the factor has purchased the debt. Thereafter, for any sale the client sends a copy of the invoice to the factor, the customer makes payment directly to the factor, and the factor pays the client on the basis of the agreed average collection period regardless of whether the customer has paid. There are, of course, costs to such an operation, and the factor typically charges a fee of 1% to 2% of the value of the invoice.[15]

This factoring arrangement provides assistance with collection and insurance against bad debts. It is known as *maturity factoring*. In addition to these services, the factor is generally also willing to advance 70% to 80% of the value of the accounts at an interest cost of 2% or 3% above the prime rate. Factoring that provides collection, insurance, and finance is generally termed *old-line factoring*.[16]

If you don't want help with collection but do want protection against bad debts, you can obtain credit insurance. The credit insurance company obviously wants to be certain that you do not throw caution to the winds by extending boundless credit to the most speculative accounts. It, therefore, generally imposes a maximum amount that it will cover for accounts with a particular credit rating. Thus it may agree to insure up to a total of $100,000 of sales to customers with the highest Dun and Bradstreet rating, up to $50,000 to those with the next highest rating, and so on. You may claim not only if the customer actually becomes insolvent but also if an account is overdue. Such a delinquent account is then turned over to the insurance company, which makes vigorous efforts to collect.

The Export Development Corporation (EDC), a federal Crown corporation, has several credit-related programs for Canadian exporters. It provides insurance for up to 90% of a short-term credit transaction. Banks are more willing to lend against such insured receivables. The EDC itself also provides financing, particularly for large transactions, for which bank financing may be hard to obtain.

30-6   SUMMARY

Credit management involves five steps. The first task is to establish normal terms of sale. This means that you must decide the length of the payment period and the size of any cash discounts. In most industries these conditions are standardized.

Your second step is to decide the form of the contract with your customer. Most domestic sales are made on open account. In this case the only evidence that the customer owes you money is the entry in your ledger and a receipt signed by the customer. Particularly if the customer is foreign, you may require a more formal contract. We looked at three such devices — the promissory note, the trade acceptance, and the letter of credit.

The third task is to assess each customer's creditworthiness. There is a variety of sources of information — your own experience with the customer, the experience of other creditors, the assessment of a credit agency, a check with the customer's bank, the market value of the customer's securities, and an analysis of the customer's financial statements. Firms that handle a large volume of credit information often use a formal system for combining the various sources into an overall credit score. These numerical scoring systems help to separate the borderline cases from the obvious sheep or goats. We showed how you can use statistical techniques such as multiple discriminant analysis to give an efficient measure of default risk.

---

[15] Many factors are subsidiaries of banks. Their typical client is a relatively small manufacturing company selling on a repetitive basis to a large number of industrial or retail customers. Factoring is particularly common in the clothing industry.

[16] Under an arrangement known as *with-recourse factoring*, the company is liable for any delinquent accounts. In this case the factor provides collection, but not insurance.

When you have made an assessment of the customer's credit standing, you can establish sensible credit limits. The job of the credit manager is not to minimize the number of bad debts; it is to maximize profits. This means that you should increase the customer's credit limit as long as the probability of payment times the expected profit is greater than the probability of default times the cost of the goods. Remember not to be too shortsighted in reckoning the expected profit. It is often worth accepting the marginal applicant if there is a chance the applicant may grow into a regular and reliable customer.

Finally, you must *collect*. This requires tact and judgement. You want to be firm with the truly delinquent customer, but you don't want to offend the good one by writing demanding letters just because a cheque has been delayed in the mail. You will find it easier to spot troublesome accounts if you keep a careful record of the aging of receivables.

These five steps are interrelated. For example, you can afford more liberal terms of sale if you are very careful about to whom you grant credit. You can accept higher-risk customers if you are very active in pursuing any late payers. A good credit policy is one that adds up to a sensible whole.

FURTHER READING

Two of the standard texts on the practice and institutional background of credit management are:

T.N. Beckman and R.S. Foster, *Credits and Collections: Management and Theory*, 8th ed., McGraw-Hill Book Company, New York, 1969.

R.H. Cole, *Consumer and Commercial Credit Management*, 8th ed., Richard D. Irwin, Inc., Homewood, Ill., 1987.

Much more analytical discussions of the credit granting decision are contained in:

H. Bierman, Jr., and W.H. Hausman, "The Credit Granting Decision," *Management Science*, **16**: B519–B532 (April 1970).

D.R. Mehta, *Working Capital Management*, Prentice-Hall, Inc., Englewood Cliffs, N.J., 1974.

Altman's paper is the classic on numerical credit scoring:

E.I. Altman, "Financial Ratios, Discriminant Analysis and the Prediction of Corporate Bankruptcy," *Journal of Finance*, **23**: 589–609 (September 1968).

Altman's book provides a general survey of the bankruptcy decision. The studies listed below are principally concerned with an analysis of the conflicting interests of different security holders and the costs and consequences of reorganization:

E.I. Altman, *Corporate Bankruptcy in America*, Heath, Lexington Books, Lexington, Mass., 1971.

J.I. Bulow and J.B. Shoven, "The Bankruptcy Decision," *Bell Journal of Economics and Management Science*, **9**: 437–457 (Autumn 1978).

J.R. Franks and W.N. Torous, "An Empirical Investigation of U.S. Firms in Reorganization," *Journal of Finance*, **44**: 747–770 (July 1989).

R.M. Giammarino, "The Resolution of Financial Distress," *The Review of Financial Studies*, **2**: 25–47 (1989).

J.B. Warner, "Bankruptcy, Absolute Priority, and the Pricing of Risky Debt Claims," *Journal of Financial Economics*, **4**: 239–276 (May 1977).

M. White, "The Corporate Bankruptcy Decision," *Journal of Economic Perspectives*, **3**: 129–152 (Spring 1989).

<table>
<tr><td>APPENDIX
30-1</td><td># BANKRUPTCY PROCEDURES</td></tr>
</table>

APPENDIX 30-1   BANKRUPTCY PROCEDURES

In 1990 about 43,000 individuals and 12,000 businesses were declared bankrupt in Canada. We are sure that nobody who reads this book is likely to go bankrupt. But you may still have occasion to deal with individuals or companies that are bankrupt or insolvent. In this appendix, we outline the procedures involved in bankruptcy. We will first discuss things that are common to personal and business bankruptcy, and then discuss some issues that are important only for personal (consumer) bankruptcy. Business bankruptcies in Canada account for about 21% of all bankruptcies, but they account for over 59% of the dollar value of liabilities in bankruptcies.

Bankruptcy law in Canada is largely a federal matter, and the main body of law regarding bankruptcy is the *Bankruptcy Act* of 1950, although the *Winding-up Act* and the *Companies Creditors' Arrangement Act* also deal with insolvency. Several replacement acts have been drafted since then, but none have been passed into law. It is reasonable to expect a new act regarding bankruptcy and insolvency in the near future.

Security and the Priority of Creditors

Creditors can be secured by instruments such as the trust indenture of a bond, a charge on specific assets (as in a mortgage), a conditional sale, or a floating charge on inventories or accounts receivable.

The secured creditors do not need to force the debtor into bankruptcy to "realize their security" (that is, to be paid). They seize the secured assets by means of a **receivership**. In this case, a **receiver** (typically someone who is also a licensed **trustee** in bankruptcy), seizes, forecloses, or repossesses the secured assets for disposition and often operates the debtor's business. Any value realized by the sale over and above the amount of secured debt reverts to the **estate** of the debtor. If the liquidation of the assets providing the security does not extinguish the debt, federal law allows the creditor an unsecured claim on the remaining amount of unpaid debt in any bankruptcy proceeding involving the debtor. However, provincial law may prevent the secured creditor from realizing any value beyond the sale of the underlying asset. A notorious example of this occurred in Alberta during the recession of the early 1980s. Many householders, finding the value of their house to be less than the amount of their mortgage, defaulted on their mortgages. The lenders found they had no recourse to the borrower beyond the foreclosure and sale of the house. Some bold householders even engaged in a "dollar-deal": they sold their houses to third parties for $1, yet were able to continue living in the houses for several months as the lengthy foreclosure proceedings went on. Neither party would make mortgage payments during that period, because they had little, if any, incentive to do so.

The claims of unsecured creditors are satisfied under the *Bankruptcy Act* according to the following priority scheme:

1. Funeral expenses of a deceased bankrupt.
2. Administrative costs, in the following order (a) expenses and fees of a bankruptcy trustee[17]; (b) legal costs of bankruptcy.
3. A levy paid to the federal government to defray the costs of supervising the bankruptcy.[18]

---

[17] The trustee's fee structure is voted upon by the creditors and typically depends on the amount of money distributed to the creditors.

[18] This levy is usually paid out of the total disbursement made to the unsecured creditors. It is 5% of the first $1,000,000, plus 1¼% of the next $1,000,000 and ¼% of any larger amounts. See L.W. Houlden and C.H. Morawetz, *The Annotated Bankruptcy Act 1990* for more detail.

4. Wages, salaries, and commissions earned within the three months prior to the bankruptcy (up to $500), by employees of the bankrupt.
5. Municipal taxes owed within 2 years of bankruptcy.
6. Up to three months arrears of rent for any property in which the bankrupt is a tenant.
7. The legal costs of the creditor who petitions the debtor into bankruptcy.
8. Debts owed to the government under a Workers' Compensation Act, the *Unemployment Insurance Act* and the *Income Tax Act*.
9. Liabilities to employees for injuries sustained that are not covered by Workers' Compensation, but only to the extent of any monies received by the bankrupt debtor from a third party insurer.
10. Any other debts owed to federal or provincial governments.
11. All other unsecured creditors.

The creditors listed in the first ten categories above are called **preferred creditors**. Creditors who are in the same category rank equally in their claim on the debtor's estate (assets), and prior to creditors in subsequent categories. That is, the creditors in one category must be fully paid before those in the next category receive anything.

Who Is Involved in a Bankruptcy?

Besides the creditors and debtor, bankruptcy law entails appointment of a trustee who acts on behalf of the unsecured creditors to liquidate the debtor's estate and distribute the funds to the creditors. The creditors also appoint one to five **inspectors**, who essentially act as corporate directors overseeing the work of the trustee.

The **official receiver** is an officer of the court in bankruptcy who ensures that the trustee follows the law. If the creditors are concerned that assets of the debtor will be lost to them between the time of the filing of a petition for bankruptcy with the courts and the time of granting a receiving order allowing the trustee to liquidate and distribute the assets, the creditors can apply for the appointment of an **interim receiver**. This person is usually also the trustee and can take possession of the debtor's property and conserve the value of assets (this may include selling perishable property), but otherwise is not supposed to interfere with the debtor's business.[19]

How a Bankruptcy Occurs

A debtor is **insolvent** if it has liabilities exceeding $1,000, and is unable to meet its debt obligations as they come due. An insolvent debtor or business may voluntarily go into bankruptcy by making an **assignment** of its property for the benefit of its creditors. Alternatively, the creditors may **petition** the courts for a **receiving order**, which will involuntarily force the insolvent debtor into bankruptcy. In either event, the debtor loses most of its assets, which the trustee distributes to the creditors in the form of **dividends**. The advantage of an assignment is timeliness: the insolvent may be able to extinguish its debt obligations before the value of the assets in the estate drops substantially, and perhaps may be even able to work its way out of bankruptcy.

Within 3 to 12 months of the date of the assignment or receiving order, the estate has been liquidated and the trustee applies to the court to obtain a **dis-**

---

[19] The person (typically a bankruptcy trustee) appointed to seize and dispose of the assets providing security for a debt is also called a receiver. We pointed out earlier that the seizure of secured assets does not involve bankruptcy law, so there is no relation between the official receiver in bankruptcy and the receiver who seizes a secured asset. The former is an officer of the court, while the latter is typically a licensed bankruptcy trustee.

charge for the debtor from its debts. The court may refuse the discharge if the bankrupt person has displayed reprehensible conduct, but more likely it will give an absolute, conditional, or suspended discharge.

An Alternative to Bankruptcy: The Proposal

An insolvent debtor may propose an alternative to bankruptcy called a **proposal** or a **proposal for arrangement**. This can provide an extension of time for the repayment of some or all of the debt. This procedure (like many legal procedures) does not recognize the time value of money, so the economic value of the repayment is less than the true economic value of the liability. Alternatively, the proposal may provide for a **composition**, in which case the creditors agree to forgive some of the debt.

Creditors will often accept a proposal, if they believe the debtor can generate a higher present value of payments as a "going concern" that stays in business than would be realized by an immediate liquidation of the debtor's assets in a bankruptcy. As soon as the debtor files a proposal, all creditor actions are **stayed**, or suspended, until the proposal (or a modification of it) is accepted. Thus, both the proposal and the filing of the proposal "buy time" for the debtor. The debtor will often offer a proposal to avoid impairment of its credit rating and to keep alive the call option on the firm's future cash flows (where the exercise price is the proposed scheme of repayments).

Clearly, a proposal is more workable if the debtor is not too insolvent. Indeed, the proposal can be struck down by the courts if it does not provide reasonable security for the payment of "50 cents on the dollar" for the debts owing to the unsecured creditors. The total assets of all insolvent debtors that filed proposals in 1981 was 65% of the total liabilities, whereas the total assets of all debtors that went bankrupt in 1981 was only 34% of the total liabilities. Proposals are used in fewer than 5% of insolvencies. The payment scheme set out in the proposal must be consistent with the priority scheme we discussed earlier for the creditors in a bankruptcy.

The creditors must meet and vote on a **special resolution** to decide whether to accept the proposal. Acceptance requires the approval of creditors representing 75% of the value of the claims against the debtor, as well as 50% of the number of creditors. (These percentages are taken as a proportion of the creditors present or represented by proxy at the meeting.) If the creditors reject the proposal, the debtor becomes bankrupt.

Attacking Fraudulent Conveyances and Fraudulent Preferences

If a debtor knows it is likely to become bankrupt in the near future, it may be tempted to voluntarily convey or give property to friends, relatives, or associated corporations, or to pay off debts to certain creditors without regard to the preference rules or priority rules set for payment to unsecured creditors in a bankruptcy. These transfers are called **fraudulent conveyance** and **fraudulent preference**, respectively. These can be **attacked** by the trustee, who asks the courts to **set aside** or **void** such transfers. To be attacked, they must have occurred within 3 months of the bankruptcy, or if the transfer was to a related person or corporation, within 12 months of the bankruptcy. A fraudulent conveyance can be an indictable or criminal offence.

Special Issues for Personal Bankruptcies

The bankrupt person is exempted from losing certain basic items, such as some furniture, clothing, personal effects, and some tools of a trade. Provincial laws may enhance this exemption. Part of the person's salary (typically 50% of the salary in excess of the poverty line) may be **garnisheed** or paid over to the trustee in bankruptcy for the benefit of the creditors, but this ceases once the bankrupt receives a discharge from the bankruptcy. So-called **after-acquired property**—that is, property acquired between the date of bankruptcy (when the receiving order or assignment was made) and the date of discharge (the date the court relieves the bankrupt of further obligations)—goes to the benefit of the creditors. This makes little difference to a bankrupt corporation, since it generally acquires property only in exchange for assets that would have gone to the estate for the benefit of the creditors anyway. However, it does mean that a consumer bankrupt who receives a large bequest on the death of a relative between the date of bankruptcy and the date of discharge will lose that bequest to the creditors.

Bankruptcy does not relieve the bankrupt of certain liabilities, such as matrimonial debts (alimony and maintenance), liabilities arising out of fraud or embezzlement, and debts owing to suppliers of "necessaries of life." The rationale for not relieving a bankrupt person from liabilities associated with obtaining the necessaries of life is to avoid inducing the suppliers to withhold such items from people in financial distress.

The administrative costs of a proposal are too high for it to be a viable alternative to bankruptcy for many consumer debtors. As a result, Part X of the *Bankruptcy Act* was added to allow a **consolidation order** to provide for the orderly payment of consumer debt as an alternative to bankruptcy. Like a proposal, it only provides for the deferral of the repayment of debt, rather than a reduction in its amount. If the amount of the debt exceeds $1,000 or if it is an arrears of wages that would normally come under a mechanics' lien act, the consolidation order can only proceed with the consent of the creditor. Moreover, only six provinces allow consolidation orders. In particular, Ontario and Québec do not allow consolidation orders.

The Choice between Liquidation and Reorganization

Here is a simple view of the bankruptcy decision. Whenever a payment is due to creditors, management checks the value of the equity. If the value is positive, the firm pays the creditors (if necessary raising the cash by an issue of shares). If the equity is valueless, the firm defaults on its debt and petitions for bankruptcy. If the assets of the bankrupt firm can be put to better use elsewhere, the firm is liquidated and the proceeds are used to pay off the creditors. Otherwise, the creditors simply become the new owners and the firm continues to operate.[20]

In practice, matters are rarely so simple. For example, we observe that firms often petition for bankruptcy even when the equity has a positive value. And firms are often reorganized even when the assets could be used more efficiently elsewhere. Here are some reasons.[21]

---

[20] If there are several classes of creditor, the junior creditors initially become the owners of the company and are responsible for paying off the senior debt. They now face exactly the same decision as the original owners. If their equity is valueless, they will also default and turn over ownership of the company to the next class of creditors.

[21] Giammarino examines the incentives that lead debtors and creditors to engage in costly 'game playing' during financial distress. See R.M. Giammarino, "The Resolution of Financial Distress," *The Review of Financial Studies*, **2**: 25–47 (1989).

1. Although the reorganized firm is legally a new entity, it is entitled to any tax-loss carry-forwards belonging to the old firm. If the firm is liquidated rather than reorganized, any tax-loss carry-forwards disappear.[22] Thus, there is an incentive to continue in operation.

2. If the firm's assets are sold off, it is easy to determine what is available to pay the creditors. However, when the company is reorganized, it needs to conserve cash as far as possible. Therefore, claimants are generally paid in a mixture of cash and securities. This makes it less easy to judge whether they receive their entitlement. For example, each bondholder may be offered $300 in cash and $700 in a new bond that pays no interest for the first two years and a low rate of interest thereafter. A bond of this kind in a company that is struggling to survive may not be worth much, but the bankruptcy court usually looks at the face value of the new bonds and may therefore regard the bondholders as paid off in full.

   Senior creditors who know they are likely to get a raw deal in a reorganization are likely to press for a liquidation. Shareholders and junior creditors prefer a reorganization. They hope that the court will not interpret the pecking order too strictly and that they will receive some crumbs.[23]

3. Although shareholders and junior creditors are at the bottom of the pecking order, they have a secret weapon — they can play for time. Bankruptcies often take several years before a plan is presented to the court and agreed to by each class of creditor. (The bankruptcy proceedings of the Missouri Pacific Railroad took a total of 22 years.) When they use delaying tactics, the junior claimants are betting on a stroke of luck that will rescue their investment. On the other hand, the senior claimants know that time is working against them, so they may be prepared to accept a smaller payoff as part of the price for getting a plan accepted.

4. While a reorganization plan is being drawn up, the company is likely to need additional working capital. It is therefore allowed to buy goods on credit and borrow money.[24] Postpetition creditors have priority over the old creditors and their debt may even be secured by assets that are already mortgaged to existing debtholders. This also gives the prepetition creditors an incentive to settle quickly, before their claim on assets is diluted by the new debt.

5. Sometimes profitable companies have filed for Chapter 11 bankruptcy in the United States to protect themselves against "burdensome" suits.[25] For example, Continental Airlines, which was bedeviled by a costly labour contract, filed for Chapter 11 in 1982 and immediately cut pay by up to 50%. In 1983 Manville Corp. was threatened by 16,000 damage suits alleging injury from asbestos. Manville filed for bankruptcy under Chapter 11, and the bankruptcy judge agreed to stay the damage suits. Needless to say, lawyers and legislators worry that these actions were contrary to the original intent of the bankruptcy acts.

---

[22] However, the dollar amount of debt that is forgiven in a consolidation proposal is applied to reduce the dollar amount of the tax-loss carry-forward.

[23] Franks and Torous found that stockholders in U.S. bankruptcies received some payoff — usually securities — in two-thirds of reorganizations conducted under Chapter 11 of the U.S. bankruptcy law.

[24] Of course, the debtor must inform any new creditors that it is a bankrupt.

[25] See, for example, A. Cifelli, "Management by Bankruptcy," *Fortune*, October 1983, pp. 69–73.

QUIZ

1. Company X sells on a 1/30, net 60, basis. Customer Y buys goods with an invoice of $1,000.
   (a) How much can Y deduct from the bill if he or she pays on day 30?
   (b) What is the effective annual rate of interest if Y pays on the due date rather than day 30?
   (c) Indicate if you would expect X to require shorter or longer payment if each of the following were true:
       (i)   The goods are perishable.
       (ii) The goods are not rapidly resold.
       (iii) The goods are sold to high-risk firms.

2. The lag between purchase date and the date at which payment is due is known as the "terms lag." The lag between the due date and the initial payment date is termed the "due lag," and the lag between the purchase and payment dates is the "pay lag." Thus,

$$\text{pay lag} = \text{terms lag} + \text{due lag}$$

   State how you would expect the following events to affect each type of lag.
   (a) The company imposes a service charge on late payers.
   (b) A recession causes customers to be short of cash.
   (c) The company changes its terms from net 10 to net 20.

3. Complete the following passage by selecting the appropriate terms from the following list (some terms may be used more than once): *acceptance, open, commercial, trade, Canada, his or her own, note, draft, account, promissory, bank, the customer's, letter of credit, shipping documents, irrevocable, Canadian.*

   Most goods are sold on _____ _____. In this case the only evidence of the debt is a record in the seller's books and a signed receipt. When the order is very large, the customer may be asked to sign a _____ _____, which is just a simple IOU. An alternative is for the seller to arrange a _____ _____ ordering payment by the customer. In order to obtain the _____ _____, the customer must acknowledge this order and sign the document. This signed acknowledgement is known as a _____ _____. Sometimes the seller may also ask _____ bank to sign the document. In this case it is known as a _____. The fourth form of contract is used principally in overseas trade. The customer's bank sends the exporter a _____ stating that it has established a credit in his or her favour at a bank in Canada. The exporter then draws a draft on _____ bank and presents it to _____ bank together with the _____ and _____. The bank then arranges for this draft to be accepted and forwards the _____ to the customer's bank.

4. The Branding Iron Company sells its irons for $50 a piece wholesale. Production cost is $40 per iron. There is a 25% chance that wholesaler Q will go bankrupt within the next year. Q orders 1,000 irons and asks for six months' credit. Should you accept the order? Assume a 10% per year discount rate, no chance of a repeat order, and that Q will pay either in full or not at all.

*5. Look back at Section 30-4. Cast Iron's costs have increased from $1,000 to $1,050. Assuming there is no possibility of repeat orders, answer the following:
   (a) When should Cast Iron grant or refuse credit?
   (b) If it costs $12 to determine whether a customer has been a prompt or slow payer in the past, when should Cast Iron undertake such a check?

*6. Look back at the discussion in Section 30-4 of credit decisions with repeat orders. If $p_1 = 0.8$, what is the minimum level of p_2 at which Cast Iron is justified in extending credit?

7. True or false?
    (a) Exporters who require greater certainty of payment arrange for the customers to sign a bill of lading in exchange for a sight draft.
    (b) Multiple discriminant analysis is often used to construct an index of creditworthiness. This index is generally called a "Z score."
    (c) It makes sense to monitor the credit manager's performance by looking at the proportion of bad debts.
    (d) If a customer refuses to pay despite repeated reminders, the company will usually turn the debt over to a factor or an attorney.
    (e) The Export Development Corporation insures export credits.

8. (This question refers to Appendix 30-1.) True or false?
    (a) Individuals may file for bankruptcy or opt for an arrangement. In the latter case, a repayment plan is drawn up and approved by the creditors.
    (b) When a company becomes bankrupt, it is usually in the interests of the equityholders to seek a liquidation rather than a reorganization.
    (c) The Department of National Revenue has first claim on the company's assets in the event of bankruptcy.
    (d) In a reorganization, creditors may be paid off with a mixture of cash and securities.
    (e) When a company is liquidated, one of the most valuable assets to be sold is often the tax-loss carry-forward.

QUESTIONS AND PROBLEMS

1. Here are some common terms of sale. Can you explain what they mean?
    (a) 2/30, net 60
    (b) net 10
    (c) 2/5, net 30, EOM
    (d) 2/10 prox, net 60

2. Some of the items in question 1 involve a cash discount. Calculate the rates of interest paid by customers who pay on the due date instead of taking the cash discount.

3. As treasurer of the Universal Bed Corporation, Aristotle Procrustes is worried about his bad-debt ratio, which is currently running at 6%. He believes that imposing a more stringent credit policy might reduce sales by 5% and reduce the bad-debt ratio to 4%. If the cost of goods sold is 80% of the selling price, should Mr. Procrustes adopt the more stringent policy?

4. Jim Khana, the credit manager of Velcro Saddles, is reappraising the company's credit policy. Velcro sells on terms of net 30. Cost of goods sold is 85% of sales and fixed costs are a further 5% of sales. Velcro classifies customers on a scale of 1 to 4. During the past five years, the collection experience was as follows:

Classification	Defaults as % of Sales	Average Collection Period in Days for Nondefaulting Accounts
1	0.0	45
2	2.0	42
3	10.0	50
4	20.0	80

The average interest rate was 15%.

What conclusions (if any) can you draw about Velcro's credit policy? What other factors should be taken into account before changing this policy?

5. Look again at question 4. Suppose (a) that it costs $95 to classify each new credit applicant and (b) that an almost equal proportion of new applicants fall into each of the four categories. In what circumstances should Mr. Khana not bother to undertake a credit check?

6. Until recently, Augean Cleaning Products sold its products on terms of net 60, with an average collection period of 75 days. In an attempt to induce customers to pay more promptly, it has changed its terms to 2/10, EOM, net 60. The initial effect of the changed terms is as follows:

Percent of Sales With Cash Discount	Average Collection Periods (days)	
	Cash Discount	Net
60	30[a]	80

[a] Some customers deduct the cash discount even though they pay after the specified date.

Calculate the effect of the changed terms assuming that the change does not affect sales volume. Assume:
(a) The interest rate is 12%.
(b) There are no defaults.
(c) Cost of goods sold is 80% of sales.

7. Look back at question 6. Assume that the change in credit terms results in a 2% increase in sales. Recalculate the effect of the changed credit terms.

8. Financial ratios were described in Chapter 27. If you were the credit manager, to which financial ratios would you pay most attention? Which do you think would be the least informative?

9. Discuss in which ways real-life decisions are more complex than the decision illustrated in Figure 30-4. How do you think these differences ought to affect the credit decision?

10. Discuss the problems with developing a numerical credit scoring system for evaluating personal loans.

11. If a company experiences a sudden decrease in sales, the aging schedule in Figure 30-2 will suggest that an abnormally high proportion of payments is overdue. Show why this happens. Can you suggest an alternative form of presentation that would make it easier to recognize a change in customer payment patterns?

12. Why do firms grant "free" credit? Would it be more efficient if all sales were for cash and late payers were charged interest?

13. Sometimes a firm sells its receivables at a discount to a wholly owned "captive finance company." This captive finance company is financed partly by the parent, but it also issues substantial amounts of debt. What are the possible advantages to such an arrangement?

14. Explain why equity can sometimes have a positive value even when companies petition for bankruptcy.

15. Reliant Umbrellas has been approached by Plumpton Variety Stores of Manitoba. Plumpton has expressed interest in an initial purchase of 5,000 umbrellas at $10 each on Reliant's standard terms of 2/30, net 60. Plumpton estimates that if the umbrellas prove popular with customers, its purchases could be in the region of 30,000 umbrellas a year. After deducting variable costs, this would provide an addition of $47,000 to Reliant's profits.

Reliant has been anxious for some time to break into the lucrative Manitoba market, but its credit manager has some doubts about Plumpton. In the past five years, Plumpton had embarked on an aggressive program of store openings. In 1983, however, it went into reverse. The recession combined with aggressive price competition caused a cash shortage. Plumpton laid off employees, closed one store, and deferred store openings. The company's Dun and Bradstreet rating is only fair and a check with Plumpton's other suppliers reveals that, although Plumpton has traditionally taken cash discounts, it has recently been paying 30 days slow. A check through Reliant's bank indicates that Plumpton has unused credit lines of $350,000 but has entered into discussions with the banks for a renewal of a $1,500,000 term loan due at the end of the year.

Table 30-3 summarizes Plumpton's latest financial statements.

As credit manager of Reliant, what is your attitude to extending credit to Plumpton?

Table 30-3
Plumpton Variety Stores: Summary Financial Statements (figures in millions)

	1991	1990		1991	1990
Cash	$ 1.0	$ 1.2	Payables	$ 2.3	$ 2.5
Receivables	1.5	1.6	Short-term loans	3.9	1.9
Inventory	10.9	11.6	Long-term debt	1.8	2.6
Fixed assets	5.1	4.3	Equity	10.5	11.7
Total assets	$18.5	$18.7	Total liabilities	$18.5	$18.7

	1991	1990
Sales	$55.0	$59.0
Cost of goods, sold	32.6	35.9
Selling, general and administrative expenses	20.8	20.2
Interest	0.5	0.3
Tax	0.5	1.3
Net income	$ 0.6	$ 1.3

16. Galenic, Inc. is a wholesaler for a range of pharmaceutical products. Before deducting any losses from bad debts, Galenic operates on a profit margin of 5%. The firm has for a long time employed a numerical credit scoring system based on a small number of key ratios. This has resulted in a bad debt ratio of 1%.

Galenic has recently commissioned a detailed statistical study of the payment record of its customers over the past eight years and, after considerable experimentation, has identified five variables that would form the basis of a new credit scoring system. On the evidence of the past eight years, Galenic calculates that for every 10,000 accounts it would have experienced the following default rates:

Credit score under proposed system	Number of accounts		
	Defaulting	Paying	Total
Less than 80	60	9,100	9,160
Greater than 80	40	800	840
Total	100	9,900	10,000

By refusing credit to firms with a low credit score (less than 80) Galenic calculates that it would reduce its bad debt ratio to 60/9,160 or just under 0.7%. While this may not seem a big deal, Galenic's credit manager reasons that this is equivalent to a fall of a third in the bad debt ratio and would result in a significant improvement in the profit margin.

(a) What is Galenic's current profit margin, allowing for bad debts?

(b) Assuming that the firm's estimates of default rates are right, how would the new credit scoring system affect profits?

(c) Why might you suspect that Galenic's estimates of default rates will not be realized in practice? What are the likely consequences of overestimating the accuracy of such a credit scoring scheme?

(d) Suppose that one of the variables in the proposed new scoring system is whether the customer has an existing account with Galenic (new customers are more likely to default). How would this affect your assessment of the proposal?

C · H · A · P · T · E · R

31

CASH MANAGEMENT

At the end of 1990, citizens and corporations in Canada held approximately $41 billion in cash. This included $20 billion of currency and $21 billion of demand deposits with banks. Cash pays no interest. Why, then, do sensible people hold it? Why, for example, don't you take all your cash and invest it in interest-bearing securities? The answer, of course, is that cash gives you more *liquidity* than securities. You can use it to buy things. It is hard enough getting cab drivers to give you change for a $10 bill, but try asking them to split a Treasury bill!

In equilibrium all assets in the same risk class are priced to give the same expected marginal benefit. The benefit from holding Treasury bills is the interest that you receive; the benefit from holding cash is that it gives you a convenient store of liquidity. In equilibrium the marginal value of this liquidity is equal to the marginal value of the interest on an equivalent investment in Treasury bills. This is just another way of saying that Treasury bills are investments with zero net present value — they are fair value relative to cash.

Does this mean that it does not matter how much cash you hold? Of course not. The marginal value of liquidity declines as you hold increasing amounts of cash. When you have only a small proportion of your assets in cash, a little extra can be extremely useful; when you have a substantial holding, any additional liquidity is not worth much. Therefore, as financial manager you want to hold cash balances up to the point where the marginal value of the liquidity is equal to the value of the interest forgone.

If that seems more easily said than done, you may be comforted to know that production managers must make a similar trade-off. Ask yourself why they carry inventories of raw materials. They are not obliged to do so; they could simply buy materials day by day, as needed. But then they would pay higher prices for ordering in small lots, and they would risk production delays if the materials were not delivered on time. That is why they order more than the firm's immediate needs.[1]

---

[1] Not much more, though, in many manufacturing operations. "Just-in-time" assembly systems provide for a continuous stream of parts deliveries, with no more than two or three hours of parts inventory on hand. Financial managers likewise strive for just-in-time cash management systems, in which no cash lies idle anywhere in the company's business. This ideal is never quite reached because of the costs and delays discussed in this chapter. Large corporations get close, however.

But there is a cost to holding inventories. Interest is lost on the money that is tied up in inventories, storage must be paid for, and often there is spoilage and deterioration. Therefore, production managers try to strike a sensible balance between the costs of holding too little inventory and those of holding too much.

That is all we are saying you need to do with cash. Cash is just another raw material that you require to carry on production. If you keep too small a proportion of your funds in the bank, you will need to make repeated small sales of securities every time you want to pay your bills. On the other hand, if you keep excessive cash in the bank, you are losing interest. The trick is to hit a sensible balance.

The trade-off between the benefits and costs of liquidity is one essential part of cash management. The other part is making sure that the collection and disbursement of cash is as efficient as possible. To understand this we will have to look closely at the relationships between firms and their banks. Most of the latter part of this chapter is devoted to the mechanics of cash collection and disbursement and the services offered by banks to assist firms in cash management.

31-1   INVENTORIES AND CASH BALANCES

Let us take a look at what economists have had to say about managing inventories and then see whether some of these ideas may help us to manage cash balances. Here is a simple inventory problem.

Everyman's Bookstore experiences a steady demand for *Principles of Corporate Finance* from customers who find that it makes a serviceable bookend. Suppose that the bookstore sells 100 copies of the book a year and that it orders Q books at a time from the publishers. Then it will need to place $100/Q$ orders per year:

$$\text{Number of orders per year} = \frac{\text{sales}}{Q} = \frac{100}{Q}$$

Just before each delivery, the bookstore has effectively no inventory of *Principles of Corporate Finance*. Just *after* each delivery it has an inventory of Q books. Therefore, its *average* inventory is midway between 0 books and Q books:

$$\text{Average inventory} = \frac{Q}{2} \text{ books}$$

For example, if the store increases its regular order by one book, the average inventory increases by ½ book.

There are two costs to holding this inventory. First, there is the carrying cost. This includes the cost of the capital that is tied up in inventory, the cost of shelf space, and so on. Let us suppose that these costs work out to a dollar per book per year. The effect of adding one more book to each order is therefore to increase the average inventory by ½ book and the carrying cost by ½ × $1.00 = $0.50. Thus, the marginal carrying cost is a constant $0.50:

$$\text{Marginal carrying cost} = \frac{\text{carrying cost per book}}{2} = \$0.50$$

The second type of cost is the order cost. Imagine that each order placed with the publisher involves a fixed clerical and handling expense of $2. Table 31-1 illustrates what happens to order costs as you increase the size of each order. You can see that the bookstore gets a large reduction in costs when it orders two books at a time rather than one, but thereafter the savings from increases in order size steadily diminish. In fact, the *marginal* reduction in order cost depends on the *square* of the order size:[2]

$$\text{Marginal reduction in order cost} = \frac{\text{sales} \times \text{cost per order}}{Q^2} = \frac{\$200}{Q^2}$$

Table 31-1
How order cost varies with order size

Order Size, Number of Books	Number of Orders Per Year	Total Order Costs, Dollars
1	100	200
2	50	100
3	33	66
4	25	50
10	10	20
100	1	2

Here, then, is the kernel of the inventory problem. As the bookstore increases its order size, the number of orders falls but the average inventory rises. Costs that are related to the number of orders decline; those that are related to inventory size increase. It is worth increasing order size as long as the decline in order cost outweighs the increase in carrying cost. The optimal size is the point at which these two effects exactly offset each other. In our example this occurs when $Q = 20$:

$$\text{Marginal reduction in order cost} = \frac{\text{sales} \times \text{cost per order}}{Q^2} = \frac{\$200}{20^2} = \$0.50$$

$$\text{Marginal carrying cost} = \frac{\text{carrying cost per book}}{2} = \$0.50$$

The optimal order size is 20 books. Five times a year the bookstore should place an order for 20 books, and it should work off this inventory over the following ten weeks. Its inventory of *Principles of Corporate Finance* will therefore follow the sawtoothed pattern in Figure 31-1.

The general formula for optimum order size is found by setting marginal reduction in order cost equal to the marginal carrying cost and solving for Q:

Marginal reduction in order cost = marginal carrying cost

$$\frac{\text{Sales} \times \text{cost per order}}{Q^2} = \frac{\text{carrying cost}}{2}$$

$$Q^2 = \frac{2 \times \text{sales} \times \text{cost per order}}{\text{carrying cost}}$$

$$Q = \sqrt{\frac{2 \times \text{sales} \times \text{cost per order}}{\text{carrying cost}}}$$

---

[2] Let T = total order cost, S = sales per year, and C = cost per order. Then

$$T = \frac{SC}{Q}$$

Differentiate with respect to Q:

$$\frac{dT}{dQ} = -\frac{SC}{Q^2}$$

Thus, an *increase* of dQ reduces T by SC/Q^2.

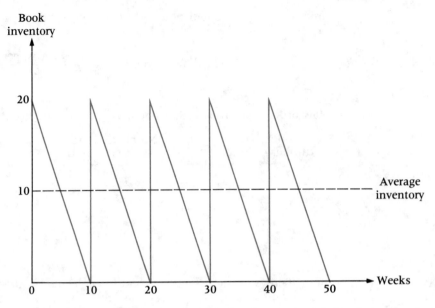

Figure 31-1   Everyman's bookstore minimizes inventory costs by placing 5 orders per year for 20 books per order. That is, it places orders at about ten week intervals.

In our example,

$$Q = \sqrt{\frac{2 \times 100 \times 2}{1}} = \sqrt{400} = 20$$

The Extension to Cash Balances

William Baumol was the first to notice that this simple inventory model can tell us something about the management of cash balances.[3] Suppose that you keep a reservoir of cash that is steadily drawn down to pay bills. When it runs out you replenish the cash balance by selling Treasury bills. The main carrying cost of holding this cash is the interest that you are losing. The order cost is the fixed administrative expense of each sale of Treasury bills. In these circumstances your inventory of cash also follows a sawtoothed pattern like Figure 31-1.

In other words, your cash management problem is exactly analogous to the problem of optimum order size faced by Everyman's Bookstore. You just have to redefine variables. Instead of books per order, Q becomes the amount of Treasury bills sold each time the cash balance is replenished. Cost per order becomes cost per sale of Treasury bills. Carrying cost is just the interest rate. Total cash disbursements take the place of books sold. The optimum Q is:

$$Q = \sqrt{\frac{2 \times \text{annual cash disbursements} \times \text{cost per sale of Treasury bills}}{\text{interest rate}}}$$

Suppose that the interest rate on Treasury bills is 8%, but every sale of bills costs you $20. Your firm pays out cash at a rate of $105,000 per month or $1,260,000 per year. Therefore, the optimum Q is:

---

[3] W.J. Baumol, "The Transactions Demand for Cash: An Inventory Theoretic Approach," *Quarterly Journal of Economics*, **66**: 545–556 (November 1952).

Cash balance

Figure 31-2   In Miller and Orr's model the cash balance is allowed to meander until it hits an upper or lower limit. At this point the firm buys or sells securities to restore the balance to the return point, which is the lower limit plus one-third of the spread between the upper and lower limits.

$$Q = \sqrt{\frac{2 \times 1,260,000 \times 20}{0.08}}$$

$$= \$25,100 \text{ or about } \$25,000$$

Thus, your firm would sell approximately $25,000 of Treasury bills four times a month—about once a week. Its average cash balance will be $25,000/2 or $12,500.

In Baumol's model a higher interest rate implies a lower Q.[4] In general, when interest rates are high, you want to hold small average cash balances. On the other hand, if you use up cash at a high rate or if there are high costs to selling securities, you want to hold large average cash balances. Think about that for a moment. *You can hold too little cash.* Many financial managers point with pride to the tight control that they exercise over cash and to the extra interest that they have earned. These benefits are highly visible. The costs are less visible but they can be very large. When you allow for the time that the manager spends in monitoring her cash balance, it may make sense to forgo some of that extra interest.

The Miller-Orr Model   Baumol's model works well as long as the firm is steadily using up its cash inventory. But that is not what usually happens. In some weeks the firm may collect some large unpaid bills and therefore receive a net *inflow* of cash. In other weeks it may pay its suppliers and so incur a net *outflow* of cash.

Economists and management scientists have developed a variety of more elaborate and realistic models that allow for the possibility of both cash inflows and outflows. Let us look briefly at a model developed by Miller and Orr.[5] It represents a nice compromise between simplicity and realism.

Miller and Orr consider how the firm should manage its cash balance if it cannot predict day-to-day cash inflows and outflows. Their answer is shown in Figure 31-2. You can see that the cash balance meanders unpredictably until it

---

[4] Note that the interest rate is in the denominator of the expression for optimal Q. Thus, increasing the interest rate reduces the optimal Q.

[5] M.H. Miller and D. Orr, "A Model of the Demand for Money by Firms," *Quarterly Journal of Economics,* **80**: 413–435 (August 1966).

reaches an upper limit. At this point the firm buys enough securities to return the cash balance to a more normal level. Once again the cash balance is allowed to meander until this time it hits a lower limit. When it does, the firm *sells* enough securities to restore the balance to its normal level. Thus, the rule is to allow the cash holding to wander freely until it hits an upper or lower limit. When this happens, the firm buys or sells securities to regain the desired balance.

How far should the firm allow its cash balance to wander? Miller and Orr show that the answer depends on three factors. If the day-to-day variability in cash flows is large or if the fixed cost of buying and selling securities is high, then the firm should set the control limits far apart. Conversely, if the rate of interest is high, it should set the limits close together. The formula for the distance between barriers is[6]

$$\begin{matrix} \text{Spread between} \\ \text{upper and lower} \\ \text{cash balance limits} \end{matrix} = 3\left(\frac{3}{4} \times \frac{\text{transaction cost} \times \text{variance of cash flows}}{\text{interest rate}}\right)^{1/3}$$

Have you noticed one odd feature about Figure 31-2? The firm does not return to a point halfway between the lower and upper limits. The firm always returns to a point one-third of the distance from the lower to the upper limit. In other words, the return point is

$$\text{Return point} = \text{lower limit} + \frac{\text{spread}}{3}$$

Always starting at this return point means the firm hits the lower limit more often than the upper limit. This does not minimize the number of transactions — that would require always starting exactly in the middle of the spread. However, always starting in the middle would mean a larger average cash balance and larger interest costs. The Miller-Orr return point minimizes the sum of transaction costs and interest costs.

Using the Miller-Orr Model

The Miller-Orr model is easy to use. The first step is to set the lower limit for the cash balance. This may be zero, some minimum safety margin above zero, or a balance necessary to keep the bank happy—more on bank requirements later in the chapter. The second step is to estimate the variance of cash flows. For example, you might record net cash inflows or outflows for each of the last 100 days and compute the variance of those 100 sample observations. More sophisticated measurement techniques could be applied if there were, say, seasonal fluctuations in the volatility of cash flows. The third step is to observe the interest rate and the transaction cost of each purchase or sale of securities. The final step is to compute the upper limit and the return point and to give this information to a clerk with instructions to follow the "control limit" strategy built into the Miller-Orr model. Table 31-2 gives a numerical example.

This model's practical usefulness is limited by the assumptions it rests on. For example, few managers would agree that cash inflows and outflows are entirely unpredictable, as Miller and Orr assume. The manager of a toy store knows that there will be substantial cash inflows around Christmas time. Financial managers

---

[6] This formula assumes the expected daily change in the cash balance is zero. Thus, it assumes that there are no systematic upward or downward trends in the cash balance. If the Miller-Orr model is applicable you need only know the variance of the daily cash flows, that is the variance of the daily *changes* in the cash balance.

know when dividends will be paid and when income taxes will be due. In Chapter 29 we described how firms forecast cash inflows and outflows and how they arrange short-term investment and financing decisions to supply cash when needed and put cash to work earning interest when it is not needed.

Table 31-2
Numerical example of the Miller-Orr model

A.   Assumptions:
    1. Minimum cash balance = $10,000
    2. Variance of daily cash flows = 6,250,000 (equivalent to a standard deviation of $2,500 per day.)
    3. Interest rate = 0.025% per day
    4. Transaction cost for each sale or purchase of securities = $20

B.   Calculation of spread between upper and lower cash balance limits:

$$\text{Spread} = 3\left(\frac{^3/_4 \times \text{transaction cost} \times \text{variance of cash flows}}{\text{interest rate}}\right)^{1/3}$$

$$= 3\left(\frac{^3/_4 \times 20 \times 6,250,000}{0.00025}\right)^{1/3}$$

$$= 21,634 \text{ or about } \$21,600$$

C.   Calculate upper limit and return point:
    Upper limit = lower limit + 21,600 = $31,600

$$\text{Return point} = \text{lower limit} + \frac{\text{spread}}{3} = 10,000 + \frac{21,600}{3} = \$17,200$$

D.   Decision rule:
    If cash balance rises to $31,600, invest $31,600 − 17,200 = $14,400 in marketable securities; if cash balance falls to $10,000, sell $7,200 of marketable securities and replenish cash.

This kind of short-term financial plan is usually designed to produce a cash balance that is stable at some lower limit. But there are always fluctuations that financial managers cannot plan for, certainly not on a day-to-day basis. You can think of the Miller-Orr policies as responding to the cash inflows and outflows that cannot be predicted, or that are not *worth* predicting. Trying to predict *all* cash flows would chew up enormous amounts of management time.

The Miller-Orr model has been tested on daily cash-flow data for several firms. It performed as well as or better than the intuitive policies followed by these firms' cash managers. However, the model was not an unqualified success; in particular, simple rules of thumb seem to perform just as well.[7] The Miller-Orr model may improve our *understanding* of the problem of cash management, but it probably will not yield substantial savings compared with policies based on a manager's judgement, providing of course that the manager understands the trade-offs we have discussed.

Raising Cash by Borrowing   So far we have assumed that surplus cash is invested in securities such as Treasury bills and that cash is replenished when necessary by selling these securities. The alternative may be to replenish cash by borrowing—for example, by drawing on a bank line of credit.

---

[7] For a review of tests of the Miller-Orr model, see D. Mullins and R. Homonoff, "Applications of Inventory Cash Management Models," in S.C. Myers, ed., *Modern Developments in Financial Management*, Frederick A. Praeger, Inc., New York, 1976.

Borrowing raises another problem. The interest rate that you pay to the bank is likely to be higher than the rate that you receive on securities. As financial manager, you therefore face a trade-off. To earn the maximum interest on your funds, you want to hold low cash balances, but this means that you are more likely to have to borrow to cover an unexpected cash outflow. For example, suppose you can either hold cash that pays no interest or you can invest in securities that pay interest at 10%. The cost of keeping cash balances is the interest forgone by not investing the money in securities.

$$\text{Cost of cash balances} = 10\%$$

If you need more cash at short notice, it may be difficult or costly to sell securities, but you can borrow from the bank at 12%. In this case, there is a simple rule for maximizing expected return. You should adjust the cash balances until the probability that you will need to borrow from the bank equals:[8]

$$\frac{\text{Cost of cash balances}}{\text{Cost of borrowing}} = \frac{10}{12} = 0.83$$

When we look at the problem this way, the best cash balance depends on the cost of borrowing and the extent of uncertainty about future cash flow. If the cost of borrowing is high relative to the interest rate on securities, you should make sure that there is only a low probability that you will be obliged to borrow. If you are very uncertain about the future cash flow, you may need to keep a large cash balance in order to be confident that you will not have to borrow. If you are fairly sure about cash flow, you can keep a lower cash balance.

Cash Management in the Largest Corporations

For very large firms, the transaction costs of buying and selling securities become trivial compared with the opportunity cost of holding idle cash balances. Suppose that the interest rate is 8% per year or roughly $^8\!/_{365} = 0.022\%$ per day. Then, the daily interest earned by $1 million is $0.00022 \times 1,000,000 = \$220$. Even at a cost of $50 per transaction, which is generous, it pays to buy Treasury bills today and sell them tomorrow rather than to leave $1 million idle overnight.

A corporation with $1 billion of annual sales has an average daily cash flow of $1,000,000,000/365, about $2.7 million. Firms of this size end up buying or selling securities once a day, every day, unless by chance they have only a small positive cash balance at the end of the day.

---

[8] See, for example, J.H.W. Gosling, "One-Period Optimal Cash Balances," unpublished paper presented to the European Finance Association, Scheviningen, Holland, 1981. Instead of keeping the money in cash you may be able to keep it in very liquid securities that are therefore easily sold, but pay only a low rate of interest. The model works in this case also. For example, suppose that the interest rate on these liquid balances is 4%. Then the cost of investing in liquid balances is the interest that you forgo by not investing in the less marketable securities:

$$\text{Cost of liquid balances} = 10 - 4 = 6\%$$

The cost of borrowing is the difference between the interest that you pay on the borrowing and the rate that you earn on liquid balances:

$$\text{Cost of borrowing} = 12 - 4 = 8\%$$

Our rule states that you should adjust the liquid balances until the probability that you will need to borrow equals

$$\frac{\text{Cost of liquid balances}}{\text{Cost of borrowing}} = \frac{6}{8} = 0.75$$

Why do such firms hold any significant amounts of cash? There are basically two reasons. First, cash may be left in non-interest-bearing accounts to compensate banks for the services they provide. Second, large corporations may have literally hundreds of accounts with many different banks and bank branches. It is often better to leave idle cash in some of these accounts than to monitor each account daily and make daily transfers between them.

One major reason for the proliferation of bank accounts is decentralized management. You cannot give a subsidiary operating autonomy without giving its managers the right to spend and receive cash.

Good cash management nevertheless implies some degree of centralization. You cannot maintain your desired inventory of cash if all the subsidiaries in the group are responsible for their own private pools of cash. And you certainly want to avoid situations in which one subsidiary is investing its spare cash at 7% while another is borrowing at 8%. It is not surprising, therefore, that even in highly decentralized companies there is generally central control over cash balances and bank relations.

31-2   CASH COLLECTION AND DISBURSEMENT SYSTEMS

We have talked loosely about a firm's cash balance; it is now time to be more precise about how cash enters and exits the corporation and how the available cash balance is computed. The first necessary step is understanding the *float*.

Suppose that the United Carbon Company has $1 million on demand deposit with its bank. It now pays one of its suppliers by writing a cheque for $200,000. The company's ledgers are immediately adjusted to show a cash balance of $800,000. But the company's bank won't learn anything about this cheque until it has been deposited at the supplier's bank and presented to United Carbon's bank for payment.[9] During this time, United Carbon's bank continues to show in its ledger that the company has a balance of $1 million. The company obtains the benefit of an extra $200,000 in the bank while the cheque is clearing. This sum is often called *payment float*.

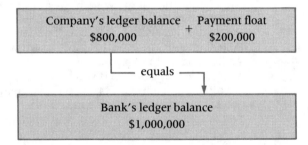

This "float" sounds like a marvellous invention, but unfortunately it can also work in reverse. Suppose that in addition to paying its supplier, United Carbon *receives* a cheque for $100,000 from a customer. It deposits the cheque, and both the company and the bank increase the ledger balance by $100,000:

---

[9] Cheques deposited with a bank are cleared internally if the cheque is drawn on the same bank in which it is deposited, and otherwise through the Canadian Payments Association clearing system. These systems are fast and only take one or two days. However, the time taken in the mail system and the time taken by the supplier to process the cheque can be substantial. Bills are generally regarded as being paid on the date stamped on the payment envelope.

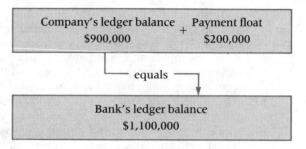

But this money isn't available to the company until the bank has presented the cheque and received the funds from the customer's bank. In the meantime, the bank will show that United Carbon has an *available balance* of $1 million and an *availability float* of $100,000:

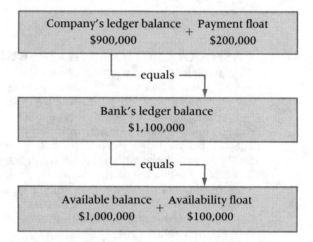

Notice that the company gains as a result of the payment float and loses as a result of the availability float. The difference is often termed the *net float*. In our example, the net float is $100,000. The company's available balance is therefore $100,000 greater than the balance shown in its ledger.

As financial manager your concern is with the available balance, not with the company's ledger balance. If you know that it is going to be a week or two before some of your cheques are presented for payment, you may be able to get by on a smaller cash balance. This game is often called *playing the float*.

You can increase your available cash balance by increasing your net float. This means that you want to ensure that cheques paid in by customers are cleared rapidly and those paid to suppliers are cleared slowly. Perhaps this may sound like rather small beer, but think what it can mean to a company like Ford. Ford's daily sales average over $250 million. Therefore, if it can speed up the collection process by one day, it frees more than $250 million, which is available for investment or payment to Ford's stockholders.

Some financial managers have become overenthusiastic at managing the float. In 1985 E.F. Hutton in the United States pleaded guilty to 2,000 separate counts of mail and wire fraud. Hutton admitted that it had created nearly $1 billion of float by shuffling funds between its branches, and through various accounts at different banks. These activities cost the company a $2 million fine and its agreement to repay the banks any losses they may have incurred.

Managing Float   Float is the child of delay. Actually, there are several kinds of delay, so people in the cash management business refer to several kinds of float. Figure 31-3 summarizes:

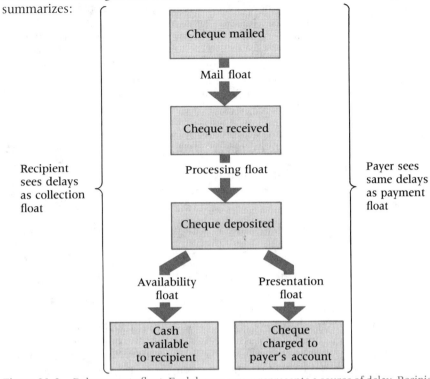

Figure 31-3   Delays create float. Each heavy arrow represents a source of delay. Recipients try to reduce delay to get available cash sooner. Payers prefer delay so they can use their cash longer. *Note:* The delays causing availability float and presentation float are equal on average, but can differ from case to case.

Of course, the delays that help the payer hurt the recipient. Recipients try to speed up collections. Payers try to slow down disbursements.

Speeding Up   One way to speed up collections is by a method known as **concentration**
Collections   **banking**. In this case, customers in a particular area make payment to a local branch office rather than to company headquarters. The local branch office then deposits the cheques into a local branch bank account. Surplus funds are periodically transferred to the company's principal branch, which is known as the *concentration branch*. Sometimes the company's branch office does not even have its own bank account, and instead makes a deposit at a local bank branch directly into the head office account. Sometimes the company's branch office deals with a different bank from the head office, in which case the funds are transferred to the bank of the head office by a *depository transfer cheque*. The main advantage of concentration banking is the reduction in mailing time that arises because the branch office is nearer to the customer.[10]

---

[10] If the company is in the United States, another advantage to concentration banking arises because banks are not allowed to branch across state lines. Thus, it is often faster to clear the customer's cheque in the same locality as the bank on which it is written. The company's head office and branch will usually have to deal with different banks, so the branch office will transfer the funds to the head office with a wire transfer or a depository transfer cheque.

Often concentration banking is combined with a **lock-box system**. It works as follows: The company rents a locked post office box in each principal region. All customers within a region are instructed to send their payments to the post office box. The local bank branch, as agent for the company, empties the box at regular intervals and deposits the cheques in the company's account.

How many collection points do you need if you use a lock-box system or concentration banking? The answer depends on where your customers are and on the speed of Canada Post. For example, suppose that you are thinking of opening a lock box. The bank shows you a map of mail delivery times. From that and knowledge of your customers' locations, you come up with the following data:

- Average number of daily payments to lock box   = 150
- Average size of payment   = $1,200
- Rate of interest *per day*   = 0.02%
- Saving in mailing time   = 1.2 days
- Saving in clearing time   = 0.8 days

On this basis, the lock box would increase your collected balance by:

150 items per day × $1,200 per item × (1.2 + 0.8) days saved = $360,000

Invested at 0.02% per day, that gives a daily return of:

$$0.0002 \times \$360,000 = \$72.00$$

The bank's charge for operating the lock-box system depends on the number of cheques processed. Suppose that the bank charges $0.26 per cheque. That works out at 150 × 0.26 = $39.00 per day. You are ahead by $72.00 − 39.00 = $33.00 per day, plus whatever your firm saves from not having to process the cheques itself.

Our example assumes that the company has only two choices. It can do nothing or it can operate the lock box. But maybe there is some other lock-box location, or some mixture of locations, that would be still more effective. Of course, you can always find this out by working through all possible combinations, but it may be simpler to solve the problem by linear programming. Many banks offer linear programming models to solve the problem of locating lock-boxes.[11]

Canadian firms can also arrange for lock boxes to receive payments from American customers. For example, the 1984 takeover of the Harris Bank of Chicago by the Bank of Montreal gave the latter bank access to a lock-box network of six banks in key American cities. Other Canadian banks provide lock boxes in U.S. cities near the border and transfer the material by courier to a nearby Canadian city for processing.

Controlling Disbursements

Speeding up collections is not the only way to increase the net float. You can also do so by slowing down disbursements. One tempting strategy is to increase mail time. For example, suppose that United Carbon pays one of its Toronto suppliers with a cheque mailed from Toronto. The cheque might spend one or two days in the mail, one day being processed by the supplier, and one day in the cheque clearing system before the funds are drawn from its bank account. But if United Carbon mails the cheque from Vancouver or Halifax, it will spend more time in the mail, thereby increasing its float.

[11] See, for example, A. Kraus, C. Janssen, and A. McAdams, "The Lock-Box Location Problem," *Journal of Bank Research,* **1**: 50–58 (Autumn 1970).

In the United States, this scheme is often extended to take advantage of the slow United States cheque clearing system by also making the cheque payable from a bank in a remote location.[12] The United States Federal Reserve guarantees a maximum clearing time of two days on all cheques cleared through its system, so the supplier can use the funds within two days of presenting the cheque at its bank. However, because United States banks cannot branch across state lines, because the United States Federal Reserve is itself an amalgamation of distinct Federal Reserve Districts, and because the Federal Reserve System does not even have a monopoly on the clearing business, the actual clearing time is typically longer than this. The resulting float that is created is at the expense of the United States Federal Reserve system and is called "Fed float." The Federal Reserve does object and has been trying to prevent remote disbursement.

The Canadian Payments Association clearing system is much more efficient, because it is unified. All banks in Canada must join the system and near-banks (such as trust companies, credit unions, and caisses populaires) are allowed to join the system. The system has ten clearing centres located in major Canadian cities to facilitate the exchange of cheques and magnetic tapes. Items presented before 15:00 Eastern Time are settled on the same day. With same-day settlement, there is very little float created by the clearing system.

31-3   BANK RELATIONS

Much of the work of cash management—processing cheques, transferring funds, running lock boxes, helping to keep track of the company's accounts—is done by banks. And banks provide many other services not so directly linked to cash management; for example, handling payments and receipts in foreign currency, executing the purchase or sale of Treasury securities, or acting as a custodian for securities. Of course, banks also lend money, or give firms the *option* to borrow under a *line of credit*.[13]

All these services have to be paid for. Banks demand fees for processing cheques, operating lock boxes, or standing by ready to lend. These fees can be paid directly—a monthly charge based on services provided—or indirectly by letting money sit in noninterest-bearing accounts. Banks like demand deposits. After setting aside a portion of the deposit in a reserve account with the Bank of Canada, they can relend these deposits and earn interest on them. Banks would, therefore, be prepared to pay interest to attract demand deposits, but the government prohibits them from doing so.

One thing that governments never learn is that it is very difficult to legislate prices. Although they stop banks from offering money in payment for demand deposits, they do not stop them from offering services to attract deposits. Therefore, if a firm keeps a sufficiently large balance with the bank, the bank will process the firm's cheques without charge, it will operate a lock-box system—it will provide all kinds of advice and services.[14]

---

[12] Remote disbursement accounts are described in I. Ross, "The Race is to the Slow Payer," *Fortune*, 75–80, (April 1983).

[13] See Section 32-3.

[14] Often the bank will allow your balance to do double duty—that is, it can both pay for cheque handling and similar services, and also serve as compensating balance for a loan. This means that it is worth borrowing from those banks that provide you with tangible services. See G.A. Pogue, R.B. Faucett, and R.N. Bussard, "Cash Management: A Systems Approach," *Industrial Management Review*, **11**: 55–76 (Winter 1970).

Thus, firms can pay for bank services by maintaining interest-free demand deposits. These deposits generate 'earnings credits' which are used to pay for bank services. These earnings credits are interest by another name.[15]

Demand deposits earmarked to pay for bank services are termed *compensating balances*. There has been a steady trend toward direct fees for bank services and away from compensating balances. But some banks still request them; for example, in exchange for a line of credit. In some cases *you* may request them. Suppose you had other reasons to keep a working balance in a certain bank, perhaps to support local operations. This money may also serve as compensating balances. In other words, it may be more efficient to let the money sit in the bank and generate earnings credits than to pay the costs of frequent transfers into or out of interest-bearing securities.

What Happens if Money Pays Interest?

The prohibition on paying interest on demand deposits is breaking down gradually. Individuals have access to savings accounts with cheque-writing privileges. Of course, banks are less likely to offer "free" services, such as cheque processing, on interest-bearing accounts.

Even if interest-bearing chequing accounts become the norm, firms and individuals will still face a trade-off between liquidity and forgone interest, because chequing accounts will normally offer lower interest rates than direct investment in securities. (Otherwise banks will lose money; and in the long run they cannot offer a money-losing service.) Thus, the less money kept in the chequing account, the more interest earned. Yet low balances in chequing accounts means frequent sales or purchases of securities, and thus frequent transaction costs. This is the same problem we started the chapter with.

31-4 SUMMARY

Cash provides liquidity, but it doesn't pay interest. Securities pay interest, but you can't use them to buy things. As financial manager you want to hold cash up to the point where the marginal value of liquidity is equal to the interest that you could earn on securities.

Cash is just one of the raw materials that you need to do business. It is expensive keeping your capital tied up in large inventories of raw materials when it could be earning interest. Why do you hold inventories at all? Why not order materials as and when you need them? The answer is that it is also expensive to keep placing many small orders. You need to strike a balance between holding too large an inventory of cash (and losing interest on the money) and making too many small adjustments to your inventory (and incurring additional administrative costs). If interest rates are high, you want to hold relatively small inventories of cash. If your cash needs are variable and your administrative costs are high, you want to hold relatively large inventories.

If the securities are not easily sold, you have the alternative of borrowing to cover a cash deficiency. Again, you face a trade-off. Since banks charge a high interest rate on borrowing, you want to keep sufficiently large liquid funds that you don't need to keep borrowing. On the other hand, by having large liquid balances, you are also not earning the maximum return on your cash.

---

[15] Under this system of indirect rewards, the bank will insist that you maintain a specified average level of balances over the month. Therefore, you don't want your cash inventory to run down to zero before replenishing it.

The cash shown in the company ledger is not the same as the net collected balance in your bank account. The difference is the net float. When you have written a large number of cheques awaiting clearance, the net collected balance will be larger than the ledger balance. When you have just deposited a large number of cheques that have not yet been collected by the bank, the net collected balance will be smaller. If you can predict how long it will take cheques to clear, you may be able to "play the float" and get by on a smaller cash balance.

You can also *manage* the float by speeding up collections and slowing down payments. One way to speed collections is by *concentration banking*. Customers make payment to a regional office that then pays the cheques into a local bank branch account. Surplus funds are transferred from the local account to a concentration bank. An alternative technique is *lock-box banking*. In this case customers send their payments to a local post office box. A local bank branch empties the box at regular intervals and clears the cheques. Concentration banking and lock-box banking reduce mailing time and the time required to clear cheques.

Banks provide many services. They handle cheques, manage lock boxes, provide advice, obtain references, and so on. Sometimes firms pay cash for these services, but more often they pay for them by maintaining sufficient cash balances with the bank.

In many cases you will want to keep larger balances than are needed to pay for the tangible services. One reason is that the bank may be a valuable source of ideas and business connections. Another reason is that you may use the bank as a source of short-term funds. Leaving idle cash at your bank may be implicit compensation for the willingness of the bank to stand ready to advance credit when needed. A large cash balance may, therefore, be good insurance against a rainy day.

FURTHER READING

Baumol and Miller and Orr were the pioneers in applying inventory models to cash management.

W.J. Baumol, "The Transactions Demand for Cash: An Inventory Theoretic Approach," *Quarterly Journal of Economics,* **66**: 545–556 (November 1952).

M.H. Miller and D. Orr, "A Model of the Demand for Money by Firms," *Quarterly Journal of Economics,* **80**: 413–435 (August 1966).

Mullins and Homonoff review tests of inventory models for cash management.

D. Mullins and R. Homonoff, "Applications of Inventory Cash Management Models," in S.C. Myers, ed., *Modern Developments in Financial Management*, Frederick A. Praeger, Inc., 1976.

The next two articles analyze the design of lock-box and concentration banking systems. The third article by Bernell Stone gives an overview of banking and cash management.

A. Kraus, C. Janssen, and A. McAdams, "The Lock-Box Location Problem," *Journal of Bank Research,* **1**: 50–58 (Autumn 1970).

S.F. Maier and J.H. Vander Weide, "What Lock-Box and Disbursement Models Really Do," *Journal of Finance,* **37**: 361–371 (May 1983).

B.K. Stone, "The Design of a Company's Banking System," *Journal of Finance,* **37**: 373–385 (May 1983).

The Journal of Cash Management, published by the National Corporate Cash Management Association, is a good reference for recent developments. Useful specialized texts include:

N.C. Hill and W.L. Sartoris, *Short-Term Financial Management*, New York, Macmillan Publishing Company, 1988.

J.G. Kallberg, K.L. Parkinson, and J.R. Ochs, eds., *Essentials of Cash Management*, National Corporate Cash Management Association, 1989.

J. Vander Weide and S.F. Maier, *Managing Corporate Liquidity: An Introduction to Working Capital Management*, New York, John Wiley & Sons Inc., 1985.

QUIZ

1. Everyman's Bookstore has experienced an increase in demand for *Principles of Corporate Finance*. It now expects to sell 200 books a year. Unfortunately inventory carrying costs have increased to $2 per book per year whereas order costs have remained steady at $2 per order.
   (a) What is the marginal carrying cost (for a unit increase in order size)?
   (b) At what point does the marginal carrying cost equal the marginal reduction in order cost?
   (c) How many orders should the store place per year?
   (d) What is its average inventory?
2. Now assume that Everyman's Bookstore uses up cash at a steady rate of $20,000 a year. The interest rate is 2% and each sale of securities costs $2.
   (a) What is the marginal carrying cost of the cash (for a $1 increase in order size)?
   (b) At what point does the marginal carrying cost equal the marginal reduction in order costs?
   (c) How many times a year should the store sell securities?
   (d) What is its average cash balance?
3. In the Miller and Orr cash balance model the firm should allow the cash balance to move within limits.
   (a) What three factors determine how far apart these limits are?
   (b) How far should the firm adjust its cash balance when it reaches the upper or lower limit?
   (c) Why does it not restore the cash balance to the halfway point?
4. Suppose that you can hold cash that pays no interest or invest in securities paying interest of 8%. The securities are not easily sold on short notice and, therefore, you must make up any cash deficiency by drawing on a bank line of credit, that charges interest at 10%. Should you invest more or less in securities if
   (a) You are unusually uncertain about future cash flows?
   (b) The interest rate on bank loans rises to 11%?
   (c) The interest rate on securities and on bank loans both rise by the same proportion?
   (d) You revise downward your forecast of future cash needs?
5. A company has the following cash balances:

   Company's ledger balance = $600,000
   Bank's gross ledger balance = $625,000
   Net collected balance = $550,000

   (a) Calculate the payment float and collection float.
   (b) Why does the company gain from the payment float?
   (c) Suppose the company adopts a policy of writing cheques on a remote

bank branch. How is this likely to affect the three measures of cash balance?

6. Anne Teak, the financial manager of a furniture manufacturer, is considering operating a lock-box system. She forecasts that 300 payments a day will be made to lock boxes with an average payment size of $1,500. The bank's charge for operating the lock boxes is *either* $0.40 a cheque *or* compensating balances of $800,000.

(a) If the interest rate is 9%, which method of payment is cheaper?

(b) What reduction in the time to collect and process each cheque is needed to justify use of the lock-box system?

7. Complete the following passage by choosing the appropriate term from the following list: *lock-box banking, payment float, concentration banking, collection float, net float*.

The firm's net collected balance is equal to its ledger balance plus the _____ and minus the _____. The difference between the collected balance and the ledger balance is often called the _____. Firms can increase their cash resources by speeding up collections. One way to do this is to arrange for payments to be made to regional offices, which pay the cheques into local bank branches. This is known as _____. Surplus funds are then transferred from the local branch to one of the company's main bank branches. Another technique is to arrange for a local bank branch to collect the cheques directly from a post office box. This is known as _____.

QUESTIONS AND PROBLEMS

1. Indicate how you would expect a firm's cash balance to respond to the following changes:
(a) Interest rates increase.
(b) The volatility of daily cash flow decreases.
(c) The transaction cost of buying or selling marketable securities goes up.

2. A firm maintains a separate account for cash disbursements. Total disbursements are $100,000 per month spread evenly over the month. Administrative and transaction costs of transferring cash to the disbursement account are $10 per transfer. Marketable securities yield 1% per month. Determine the size and number of transfers that will minimize the cost of maintaining the special account.

3. Refer again to Table 31-2. Calculate the optimal strategy for each of the following variations on the basic assumptions:
(a) Minimum cash balance = $20,000.
(b) Standard deviation of daily cash flows = $5,000.
(c) Interest rate = 0.03% per day.
(d) Transaction cost of each purchase or sale of securities = $25.

4. Suppose that the rate of inflation accelerates from 5% to 10% per year. Would firms' cash balances go up or down relative to sales? Explain.

5. A Canadian company with subsidiaries in the United States settles the collection fund balances of its subsidiaries once a week. (That is, each week it transfers any balances in their accounts to a central account.) The cost of a wire transfer is $2. A depository transfer cheque costs $0.20. Cash transferred by wire is available the same day, but the parent must wait three days for depository transfer cheques to clear. Cash can be invested at 12% per year. How much money must be in a collection account before it pays to use a wire transfer?

6. The financial manager of JAC Cosmetics is considering opening a lock box in Calgary. Cheques cleared through the lock box will amount to $300,000 per month. The lock box will make cash available to the company three days earlier.

   (a) Suppose that the bank offers to run the lock box for a $20,000 compensating balance. Is the lock box worthwhile?

   (b) Suppose that the bank offers to run the lock box for a fee of $0.10 per cheque cleared instead of a compensating balance. What must the average cheque size be for the fee alternative to be less costly? Assume an interest rate of 6% per year.

   (c) Why did you need to know the interest rate to answer (b) but not to answer (a)?

7. On January 25, Coot Company has $250,000 deposited with a bank. On January 27, the company writes and mails cheques of $20,000 and $60,000 to suppliers. At the end of the month, Coot's financial manager deposits a $45,000 cheque received from a customer in the morning mail and picks up the end-of-month account summary from the bank. The manager notes that only the $20,000 payment of the 27th has cleared the bank. What are the company's ledger balance and payment float? What is the company's net float?

8. Knob, Inc., is a nationwide distributor of furniture hardware. The company now uses a central billing system for credit sales of $180 million annually. First Commercial, Knob's principal bank, offers to establish a new concentration banking system for a flat fee of $100,000 per year. The bank estimates that mailing and collection time can be reduced by three days. By how much will Knob's collection float be reduced under the new system? How much extra interest income will the new system generate if the extra funds are used to reduce borrowing under Knob's line of credit with First Commercial? Assume the borrowing rate is 12%. Finally, should Knob accept First Commercial's offer if collection costs under the old system are $40,000 per year?

9. A few years ago, the U.S. brokerage firm of Merrill Lynch increased its float by mailing cheques drawn on west coast banks to customers in the east and cheques drawn on east coast banks to customers in the west. A subsequent class action suit against Merrill Lynch revealed that, in 28 months from September 1976, Merrill Lynch disbursed $1.25 billion in 365,000 cheques to New York State customers alone. The plaintiff's lawyer calculated that by using a remote bank branch Merrill Lynch had increased its average float by 1½ days.[16]

   (a) How much did Merrill Lynch disburse per day to New York State customers?

   (b) What was the total gain to Merrill Lynch over the 28 months, assuming an interest rate of 8%?

   (c) What was the present value of the increase in float if the benefits were expected to be permanent?

   (d) Suppose that the use of remote bank branches had involved Merrill Lynch in extra expenses. What was the maximum extra cost per cheque that Merrill Lynch would have been prepared to pay?

---

[16] See, for example, I. Ross, "The Race is to the Slow Payer," *op. cit.*

C · H · A · P · T · E · R

32

SHORT-TERM LENDING
AND BORROWING

If a company has a temporary cash surplus, it can invest in short-term securities. If it has a temporary deficiency, it can replenish cash by selling securities or by borrowing on a short-term basis. In Chapter 31 you learned something about when to make such changes. But you need to know more than that. There is an elaborate menu of short-term securities; you should be familiar with the most popular entrées. Similarly, there are many kinds of short-term debts and you should know their distinguishing characteristics. That is why we have included the present chapter on short-term lending and borrowing. You will encounter little in the way of new theory, but there is a good deal of interesting institutional material.

32-1 SHORT-TERM LENDING

The market for short-term investments is generally known as the **money market**. The money market has no physical marketplace. It consists of a loose agglomeration of banks and dealers linked together by telex, telephones, and computers. But a huge volume of securities is regularly traded on the money market, and competition is vigorous.

Most large corporations manage their own money-market investments, buying and selling securities denominated in multiples of $50,000 or $100,000 through banks or dealers. Small companies sometimes find it more convenient to put their cash into a money-market fund. This is a mutual fund that invests only in short-term securities. In return for a fee, money market funds provide professional management and a diversified portfolio of high-quality, short-term securities. We discussed money-market mutual funds in Section 17-4.

In Chapter 24 we pointed out that there are two main markets for long-term dollar bonds. There is a domestic market in Canada and there is an international market for eurobonds. Similarly, in this chapter we shall see that in addition to the Canadian money market, there is also an international market for short-term eurodollar investments.

A eurodollar is not some strange bank note—it is simply a dollar deposit in a bank outside of Canada. For example, suppose that a Canadian oil company buys crude oil from an Arab sheik and pays for it with a $1 million cheque drawn on the Bank of Montreal. The sheik then deposits the cheque with his account at Barclays Bank of London. As a result, Barclays has an asset in the form of a $1 million credit in its account with the Bank of Montreal. It also has an offsetting liability in the form of a Canadian dollar deposit. The dollar deposit is placed outside of Canada: it is, therefore, a eurodollar deposit.

We will describe in this chapter the principal domestic and eurodollar investment, but bear in mind that there is also a market for investments in other eurocurrencies. For instance, if a Canadian company wishes to make a short-term investment in deutsche marks, it can do so either in the Frankfurt money market or in the international eurocurrency market.

If we lived in a world without regulation and taxes, the interest rate on a eurodollar loan would have to be the same as on an equivalent domestic dollar loan, the rate on a eurosterling loan would have to be the same as on a domestic sterling loan, and so on. However, the eurocurrency markets exist only because individual governments attempt to regulate domestic bank lending. For example, between 1963 and 1974 the U.S. government controlled the export of funds for corporate investment. Therefore, companies that wished to expand abroad were forced to turn to the eurodollar market. This additional demand for eurodollar loans tended to push the eurodollar interest rate above the domestic rate. At the same time the government limited the rate of interest that banks in the United States could pay on domestic deposits; this also tended to keep the eurodollar rate of interest above the domestic rate. By early 1974 the restrictions on the export of funds had been removed and for large deposits the interest rate ceiling had also been abolished. In consequence, the differential between the interest rate on eurodollars and the rate on domestic deposits narrowed. But banks are not subject to reserve requirements on eurodollar deposits and are not obliged to insure these deposits. On the other hand, depositors are exposed to the unlikely chance that a foreign government could prohibit banks from repaying eurodollar deposits. For these reasons eurodollar investments continue to offer slightly higher rates of interest than domestic dollar deposits.

The term *eurodollar* indicates that most of the business is conducted in Europe and principally in London. In addition there is a growing market for Asian dollar deposits. The government of Canada has become increasingly concerned that one consequence of regulation has been to drive banking business overseas to foreign banks and the overseas branches of Canadian banks. In an attempt to attract some of this business back to Canada, the government has designated Vancouver and Montreal as International Financial Centres (IFC's). An IFC is the financial equivalent of a free-trade zone; it is physically situated in Canada, but as long as it conducts business with only non-Canadian customers, it is not required to maintain reserves and is exempt from certain taxes.

Valuing Money-Market Investments   When we value long-term debt, it is important to take default risk into account. Almost anything may happen in 20 years; even today's most respectable company may get into trouble eventually. This is the basic reason corporate bonds offer higher yields than Treasury bonds.

Short-term debt is not risk-free either. When Penn Central failed in the United States, it had $82 million of short-term commercial paper outstanding. After that shock, investors became much more discriminating in their purchases of commercial paper and the spread between interest rates on high- and low-quality paper widened dramatically.

Such examples of failure are exceptions that prove the rule; in general the danger of default is less for money-market securities issued by corporations than for corporate bonds. There are two reasons for this. First, the range of possible outcomes is less for short-term investments. Even though the distant future may be clouded, you can usually be confident that a particular company will survive for at least the next month. Second, only well-established companies can borrow in the money market. If you are only going to lend money for one day, you can't afford to spend too much time or resources in evaluating the loan. Thus, you will consider only blue-chip borrowers.

Despite the high quality of money-market investments, there are often significant differences in yield between corporate and Canadian government securities. For example, in April 1991, the rate of interest on three-month commercial paper was almost one-quarter of a percentage point higher than on Treasury bills. Why is this? One answer is the risk of default on commercial paper. Another is that the investments have different degrees of liquidity or "moneyness." Investors prefer Treasury bills because they are a little easier to turn into cash on short notice. Securities that can be converted quickly and cheaply into cash offer relatively low yields.

Calculating the Yield on Money-Market Investments

Many money-market investments are pure discount securities. This means that they don't pay interest: the return consists of the difference between the amount you pay and the amount you receive at maturity. Unfortunately, it is no good trying to persuade Revenue Canada that this difference represents a capital gain. It is wise to that one and will tax your return as ordinary income.

Yields in Canada are quoted in two different ways: the **true yield basis** and the **commercial discount basis**. Treasury bills in Canada are quoted on a true yield basis. For example, on Thursday April 25, 1991 the Government of Canada issued 91-day treasury bills at a price of 97.75% of face value. For each $97.75 that you invested on April 25, the government agreed to pay $100 to you 91 days later. That means that an investment in 91-day T-bills will provide a 91-day return of

$$\frac{100 - 97.75}{97.75} = 0.023 \text{ or } 2.3\%$$

The T-bill rate quoted for the issue (on a true yield basis) was 9.24% which is approximately equal to $2.3 \times (365/91)$. This rate is compounded quarterly, since the investor can reinvest the interest 365/91 or 4 times per year.[1]

At the same time, 90-day paper commercial paper (which we will discuss below) was quoted on a commercial discount basis at 9.58%. This is a way of saying that the price of the paper was $100 - 9.58 \times (90/365) = \$97.64$. For each $97.64 that you invested, the borrower would pay $100 to you 90 days later. The yield over 90 days was $(\$100 - 97.64)/97.64 = 2.4\%$, equivalent over a 365-day year to 9.6% interest compounded quarterly and 10.1% interest compounded annually.[2]

---

[1] The annually compounded rate of return on the T-bills is $(1.023)^{\frac{365}{91}} - 1 = 0.0955$ or 9.55%. See Section 3-3.

[2] By way of comparison, we should note that U.S. money market securities are quoted on a *360-day discount basis*. That is, in the United States, the paper is said to be discounted at

$$\frac{(100 - 97.66)}{100} \times \frac{360}{90} = 0.0937 \text{ or } 9.37\%$$

Notice that the quoted American discount is less than both the equivalent Canadian true yield and the equivalent Canadian commercial discount.

Government of Canada Treasury Bills

Table 32-1 summarizes the characteristics of the principal money-market investments. The first item on our list is Government of Canada Treasury bills. These mature in 91 days, 182 days, or 1 year.[3] The 91- and 182-day bills are issued every week, and the 1-year bills are usually issued every two weeks, in multiples of $1,000. Sales are by auction on Thursdays. You enter a bid through a bank or an investment dealer and take your chance of receiving an allotment at your bid price.[4] You don't have to submit a bid in the auction in order to invest in Treasury bills. There is an excellent secondary market in which millions of dollars of bills are bought and sold every day.

Part of the "depth" of this market arises because banks can use T-bills as part of their secondary reserves,[5] and they buy and sell T-bills to adjust their overall liquidity. Another source of depth is that T-bills can be used by **jobbers** as security for a loan from the Bank of Canada. Jobbers are investment dealers who maintain an inventory in and make a market in Government of Canada securities. In return for this service, they (like the banks) are given the privilege of using the Bank of Canada as a lender of last resort. (They use the privilege much more frequently than the banks.) They borrow from the Bank of Canada by means of a **purchase and resale agreement** (PRA). To accomplish this, they sell Government of Canada securities, like Treasury bills, to the Bank of Canada and repurchase them at a later pre-specified date and price. The security acts as a form of collateral for the loan.

Treasury bills are quoted on a true yield basis.

Provincial and Municipal Securities

The provinces, municipalities, and their Crown corporations and agencies issue various short-term securities, such as treasury bills and short-term **paper**. Sometimes they also issue **tax-anticipation notes**, which are short-term notes that will be paid off by the receipt of tax payments. The provinces and municipalities have reduced their reliance on bank loans by going directly into the money market for short-term financing in recent years. There is a good secondary market for their securities. While each situation must be dealt with on an individual basis, these securities are regarded as secure and generally pay only a small interest premium over federal T-bills.

Bank Time Deposits and Certificates of Deposit[6]

If a firm puts its money in a **demand deposit**, it can withdraw it whenever it chooses. On the other hand, the bank does not pay interest on the deposit. An alternative is to place the money in a **time** or **notice deposit**, but there may be a wait before the money can be withdrawn.

---

[3] They are often cited more simply as being 90-, 180-, or 360-day bills, respectively.

[4] In the United States Treasury bill auction, such bids are called *competitive* bids. Individuals are also allowed to place *noncompetitive* bids, which are filled at the average price of the successful competitive bids. The advantage of these bids is that you can be sure of getting your bills with a noncompetitive bid.

[5] Banks are required to maintain primary reserves in the form of cash and non-interest-bearing deposits with the Bank of Canada. They also must maintain secondary reserves in the form of certain securities like T-bills.

[6] There are "near-banks" that accept interest-bearing deposits, including trust companies, credit unions, caisses populaires, and provincial treasury branches. They cater mainly to individuals rather than corporations, and they offer deposit instruments that are similar to those offered by banks. For simplicity, we will refer to banks in the following material, even though it would be more accurate to continually use the phrase "banks, trust companies and many other near-banks."

Table 32-1
Money-Market Instruments

Investment	Borrower	Maturities When Issued	Marketability	Basis for Calculating Interest	Notes
Treasury bills	Government of Canada	91, 182 days and 1 year	Excellent secondary market	Discounted	91- and 182-day bills auctioned weekly, 1-year bills auctioned bi-weekly
Treasury bills and paper	Provinces, municipalities, and their agencies	Various maturities	Good secondary market	Discounted	Tax-anticipation notes also issued
Bank savings deposits and certificates of deposit (CDs)	Banks and trust companies	Overnight to 7 years	No secondary market	Yield basis, interest at maturity	Deposits in Canadian or United States dollars; CDs sometimes can be cashed early
Negotiable certificates of deposit (CDs)	Banks and trust companies	30 days to 1 year	Good secondary market	Discounted	Cannot be cashed before maturity
Swapped deposits	Banks	30 days to 1 year	No secondary market	All-in yield, interest at maturity	Deposit in United States dollars or pounds sterling is hedged against exchange risk
Eurodollar deposits	Foreign (branches of) banks	Overnight to 1 year; also on demand basis	No secondary market	Yield basis, interest at maturity	Dollar time deposits at overseas banks
Negotiable London dollar certificates of deposit	London branches of American, Canadian, Japanese, and British banks	30 days to 1 year	Good secondary market	Yield basis, interest at maturity	Receipts for dollar time deposits at overseas banks
Finance company paper	Sales and finance companies	Typically 30 to 365 days	Good secondary market in prime paper	Usually discounted	Placed directly with investors, or through dealers
Corporate paper	Leading industrial firms	Typically 30 to 90 days	Modest secondary market; see buy-backs	Can be discounted or interest bearing	Placed through dealers; sometimes can be cashed early
Bankers' acceptances	Corporations	A few days to 1 year; typically 30 to 90 days	Good secondary market	Discounted	Repayment guaranteed by borrower and bank
Buy-back agreements and call loans	Dealers in Government of Canada securities	Overnight to about 3 months	No secondary market	Yield basis, interest at maturity	Collateral provided by money-market securities; terms set to suit lender (perhaps including daily call privilege)

The risk of default on a bank time deposit is small. Until the 1985 failures of the Canadian Commercial Bank and the Northlands Bank, Canada had gone for over half a century without a bank failure. Moreover, bank and trust company deposits that mature within five years are insured for up to $60,000 with the Canada Deposit Insurance Corporation (CDIC), a federal Crown corporation. Therefore, you can be sure of getting at least that much of your money back. The government may also choose to bail out uninsured depositors when a bank fails. Since this is a political decision, it is not something a corporate treasurer can count on.

There are several kinds of time deposits. One of the most popular is the regular **savings account**. You may invest almost any sum you choose in a savings account. The bank can insist that you give 15 days' notice before withdrawing funds, but in practice it is always prepared to pay out on demand. Savings accounts are, therefore, very liquid; and, although they offer fairly low rates of interest, they are widely used by individuals and small companies.

Investment in a savings account is for an undefined period. In other words, you can withdraw funds as you need them. An alternative form of time deposit is the **fixed-term deposit**, sometimes just called a **term deposit**. In this case you lend your money for a fixed period. If you find that you need the money before maturity, the bank will often allow you to withdraw, but you suffer a penalty in the form of a reduced rate of interest.

Term deposits are rather like short-term bonds. The company "lends" the bank so many dollars; in return, the bank promises to repay the money with interest at the end of the period agreed on. As evidence of the debt, the borrower may give the company a **certificate of deposit** (CD), **term note**, or **term deposit receipt**. (The terminology varies amongst the banks and trust companies.) The certificate is just the bank's promise to repay the loan. These term deposits are typically for a period of 30 days to 5 years, however, they have been issued for terms as short as 1 day and as long as 7 years. They are not transferable or negotiable: the only way the company can get cash is to sell the certificate back to the bank, usually facing a penalty in the form of a lower interest rate.

However, there are bank deposits of $100,000 or more that are negotiable securities. They are called **bearer notes** or **negotiable certificates of deposit**. Therefore, if you decide that you need the money before maturity, you don't have to ask the bank: you just sell your bearer note to another investor. When the loan matures, the new owner of the note presents it to the bank and receives payment. There is an active market in these notes, so they are quite "liquid." They are typically sold at a discount.

Unlike domestic banking, eurocurrency banking is a wholesale rather than a retail business. The customers are corporations and governments—not individuals. They don't want chequing accounts; they want to earn interest on their money. Therefore, all eurodollar bank deposits are either for a fixed term that may vary from one day to several years or they are for an undefined term but may be called at one day's notice. These fixed term deposits are a more important source of funds for eurobanks than for domestic Canadian banks. However, the London branches of the major banks also issue eurodollar CDs, which are often for longer maturities than are available in Canada.

Swapped Deposits

Another type of time deposit that you can get in Canada is the **swapped deposit**. It is an American dollar deposit combined with a spot exchange of Canadian dollars to American dollars and a forward exchange of American dollars to Canadian dollars at the maturity date of the deposit. (The forward transaction guarantees the rate of exchange that will apply at the termination of the deposit, and we will discuss this more in Chapter 34.)

At first, this seems like an overly complicated combination of three different transactions for a short-term investment, but fortunately the banks are in the business of providing each of the three types of transaction separately. With a swap deposit, they put the whole package together and quote you a single "all-in yield" or Canadian-dollar interest rate. You are "hedged" and not exposed to foreign-exchange risk. The all-in yield can be compared directly with the interest rates quoted on interest-bearing Canadian dollar deposits. They are not negotiable or transferable, and it is difficult, if not impossible, to withdraw the funds early.[7]

Swap deposits are also available with exchange into other currencies, such as the pound sterling, but most use the American dollar.

The main difference between a swapped deposit and a eurodollar deposit is the currency the lender uses. A swapped deposit uses the lender's currency, but a eurodollar deposit uses the borrower's (or some third) currency. Thus, the eurodollar deposit exposes the lender to foreign exchange risk. Both are "offshore" sources of funds in the sense that the loan is made in a country that is foreign to the borrower.

In addition to eurodollar CDs you can hold eurodollar commercial paper and bankers' acceptances (described below).

Commercial Paper

A bank is an intermediary that borrows short-term funds from one group of firms or individuals[8] and relends the money to another group. It makes its profit by charging the borrower a higher rate of interest than it offers the lender.

Sometimes it is very convenient to have a bank in the middle. It saves lenders the trouble of looking for borrowers and assessing their creditworthiness, and it saves borrowers the trouble of looking for lenders. Depositors do not care whom the bank lends to: they only need to satisfy themselves that the bank as a whole is safe.

There are also occasions on which it is *not* worth paying an intermediary to perform these functions. Large, safe, and well-known companies can bypass the banking system by issuing their own short-term notes. These notes are known as **commercial paper**. If the company is a finance company, the paper is sometimes called **acceptance paper** or **finance paper**; otherwise, it is often called **corporate paper**.[9] While many finance companies, such as General Motors Acceptance Corporation, provide financing for consumer and industrial goods, many also engage in other types of lending, including term loans and mortgages.

Often these firms set up their own marketing department and sell their issues directly to investors. Others issue their paper through dealers (who maintain an inventory in these securities) or agents, who find a suitable investor and are paid a commission for their services.

---

[7] To allow you to withdraw your money, the bank has to negotiate the early withdrawal of the U.S. dollar deposit, engage in a spot exchange of U.S. dollars to Canadian dollars, and close out the forward contract for the exchange of U.S. dollars to Canadian dollars. The terms of these transactions cannot be determined in advance.

[8] Remember that any bank deposit can be thought of as a loan from the depositor to the bank.

[9] Commercial paper is also issued by U.S. bank holding companies. A bank holding company is a firm that owns a bank and some other subsidiaries, such as a leasing subsidiary. The holding company is often used to get around some of the U.S. restrictions on widespread branch banking by selling commercial paper outside the state in which the bank is located.

Maturities of commercial paper may range from a few days to a year[10] or more, but corporate paper typically matures in 30 to 90 days. There is a good secondary market for "prime" paper, and some paper can be repaid early, at the option of the lender. Sometimes commercial paper is interest-bearing, and sometimes it is issued at a discount. In the latter case, the yield is generally quoted on a commercial discount basis.

Only nationally known companies can find a market for their commercial paper, and even then dealers are reluctant to handle a company's paper if there is any uncertainty about its financial position.[11] Companies generally back their issue of commercial paper by arranging a special backup line of credit with a bank. This guarantees that they can find the money to repay the paper.

Sometimes, commercial paper is secured. The security can consist of a pledge of accounts receivable or a floating charge on all assets of the company. If the paper is issued by a "captive" finance company—one that provides financing to purchasers of goods produced by its parent—it is usually guaranteed by the parent. The risk of default is small for commercial paper. The most notable default in Canada arose from the 1965 failure of Atlantic Acceptance, a finance company.

By cutting out the intermediary, major companies are able to borrow at rates that may be 1% to 1½% below the prime rate charged by banks. Even after allowing for a dealer's commission and the cost of compensating balances on any backup line of credit, there is still a substantial saving. Banks have felt the competition from commercial paper and have been prepared to reduce their rates to blue-chip customers. Banks also have had to make their prime rates more sensitive to the changing money market conditions that affect the yields on commercial paper and other money market instruments. Otherwise, if interest rates rise, for example, and banks are slow to increase their prime rates, corporate borrowers will switch from commercial paper to bank loans just at a time when the cost of borrowing to the bank rises. Previously, banks tried to "administer" their prime rates with gradual adjustments. In recent years two new markets in commercial paper have developed. One is the growing eurocommercial paper market.[12] The other is the market for tax exempt commercial paper issued by municipalities in the United States.

| Bankers' Acceptances | A banker's acceptance begins life as a **draft** (which is effectively a post-dated cheque) for the bank to pay a given sum at a future date. The bank then guarantees this draft by writing "accepted" on it, although there is a clear agreement that the writer of the draft (the borrower) will deposit enough funds with the bank in time to cover the future payment. Once accepted, the draft becomes the bank's *and* the borrower's IOU. It is a negotiable security. |

This security can then be bought or sold at a discount and is quoted on a true yield basis. The yield is slightly greater than that on Treasury bills of the same maturity. However, the borrower must compensate the bank for taking on some risk, by paying a **stamping fee** and there may be requirements associated with maintaining a line of credit with the bank.

---

[10] To avoid having to file a prospectus, the borrower often has the issue mature within one year and sells the debt in multiples of $50,000 or more.

[11] Bond rating firms such as Canadian Bond Rating Service and Moody's publish quality ratings for commercial paper. Investors rely on these ratings, along with other information, when they compare the quality of different firms' paper.

[12] For a general discussion of commercial paper, see R. Felix (ed.), *Commercial Paper*, Euromoney Publications, London, 1987, and Bank of England, "Commercial Paper Market: An International Survey," *Bank of England Quarterly Bulletin*, **27**: 46–53 (1987).

A banker's acceptance may arise in one of two ways. We saw in Chapter 30 that an acceptance may be arranged when a company is buying goods on credit. In this case the draft is originally made payable to the supplier of the goods. Another important way of creating a banker's acceptance in Canada arose in 1962. A corporate borrower can make a draft payable to itself, get it accepted by a bank, and then endorse it, without making it payable to any particular party. In this way, it becomes payable to the bearer and is very marketable. Money market dealers[13] and banks maintain inventories and make markets in these securities, and there is an active secondary market.

Buy-backs   We have seen that the money market dealers can borrow from the Bank of Canada against the collateral of Government of Canada securities by means of a purchase and resale agreement. They also borrow from corporations and institutional investors under similar terms by means of a **repurchase agreement** or **buy-back**,[14] in which case the lenders are known colloquially as **country banks** or **offstreet** lenders.[15] The country bank is protected by the collateral of the security involved as well as the backing of the investment dealer doing the borrowing. Other types of collateral used in country banking include corporate, provincial, and municipal securities.

The terms of a buy-back are usually customized to the needs of the lender. Thus, if a lender is accumulating cash in preparation for a dividend, interest, or other known payment at a specific date, the buy-back is arranged to be liquidated on that date. On other occasions, buy-backs are set to mature on a daily basis, or are for an indefinite period, but with a daily call or renegotiation privilege accorded to both the borrower and the lender. Such loans are called **call loans**.

32-2   FLOATING-RATE PREFERRED STOCK — AN ALTERNATIVE TO MONEY-MARKET SECURITIES

There is no law preventing firms from making short-term investments in long-term securities. If your firm has $1 million set aside for an income tax payment, it could buy a long-term bond on April 1 and sell in on April 30, when the tax instalment is due. However, the danger in this strategy is obvious: what happens if bond prices fall by 10% in April? There you are, with a $1 million liability to the Receiver General of Canada and bonds worth only $900,000. Of course bond prices could also go up, but why take the chance? Corporate treasurers entrusted with excess funds for short-term investment are naturally averse to the price volatility of long-term bonds.

You might think that common and preferred stocks would be equally unattractive short-term investments for excess cash, but that is not quite right, because these securities have an important tax advantage for corporations and individuals. Canadian corporations do not have to pay any tax on dividend income received

---

[13] From 1962 to 1981, investment dealers could use a banker's acceptance in a purchase and resale agreement (PRA) with the Bank of Canada, when using the central bank as a lender of last resort. The intent was to improve the marketability of bankers' acceptances. Parliament decided that the bankers' acceptance market was sufficiently well-established, so it stopped this with the 1980 revision of the *Bank of Canada Act*. See Daryl Merrett, "The Evolution of Bankers' Acceptances in Canada," *Bank of Canada Review*, 3–12, October 1981.

[14] In the United States, such agreements are also called "RPs" or "repos."

[15] Buy-backs can use a broad range of collateral, including commercial paper and bankers' acceptances. Banks provide day loans, call loans, and special call loans to investment dealers, and these are similar to buy-backs.

from other Canadian corporations, and individuals can take advantage of the dividend tax credit. We discussed this in Chapter 16.

If you invest the firm's surplus cash in a short- or long-term debt, the firm must pay tax on the interest it receives. Thus, for $1 of interest, a firm in a 46% marginal tax bracket ends up with only $0.54. However, if you invest the surplus cash in stock and receive $1 of dividends, you get to keep it all. The tax rate on dividends received is zero.

Suppose you consider putting that $1 million in some other corporation's preferred shares.[16] The zero tax rate is very tempting. On the other hand, since preferred dividends are fixed, the prices of preferred shares change when long-term interest rates change. A $1 million investment in preferred shares could be worth only $900,000 on April 30, when the tax instalment is due. Wouldn't it be nice if someone invented a preferred share that was insulated from fluctuating interest rates?

Well, there are such securities—the so-called floating-rate preferreds, which pay dividends that go up and down with the general level of interest rates.[17] The prices of these securities are less volatile than fixed-dividend preferreds, and they are a safer haven for firms' excess cash. Indeed, some of these preferreds have their dividend adjusted *exactly* when their market price moves away from the initial issue price.

Why would any firm want to *issue* floating-rate preferreds? Dividends must be paid out of *after-tax* income, interest from before-tax income. Thus, if a taxpaying firm wants to issue a floating-rate security, it would normally prefer to issue debt rather than equity in order to generate interest tax shields.

But there are plenty of firms that either are not paying taxes or are facing a low marginal tax rate because they have other ways of shielding taxable income. These firms cannot make full use of an interest tax shield. Moreover, they have been able to issue floating-rate preferreds at yields *lower* than the yields they would have to pay on a floating-rate debt issue. The corporations and individuals buying the preferreds are happy with this lower yield because they either pay no tax on the dividends or receive a dividend tax credit.

Floating-rate preferreds were invented in Canada in the mid-1970s, and they were bought mainly by banks, often in a private placement. However, Parliament noticed that heavy use of these non-taxable investments allowed many banks to pay little or no tax, so it changed the law to make banks pay tax on so-called **term preferred** dividends—that is, dividends on preferred shares that could be redeemed within ten years of their initial issue. This cooled off the market for awhile.

Then they were reinvented in the United States in May 1982, when Chemical New York Corporation, the holding company for Chemical Bank, raised $200 million. The securities proved so popular that over $4 billion of floating-rate preferreds were issued by spring 1983, including $1.5 billion in one four-day period in February 1983. Then the novelty wore off and the frequency of new issues slowed down.

Meanwhile, the Canadian banks decided to try another angle with floating-rate preferreds. In addition to *buying* floating-rate preferreds, they decided to *sell*

---

[16] Preferred shares are usually better short-term investments for a corporation than common shares. The preferred shares' expected return is virtually all dividends; most common shares are expected to generate capital gains, too. The corporate tax on capital gains is usually $0.75 \times 36 = 27\%$, as discussed in Chapter 16. Corporations therefore have a strong incentive to like dividends and dislike capital gains.

[17] Often there are limits on the maximum and minimum dividends that can be paid. Thus, if interest rates leap to 100%, the preferred dividend rate would hit a ceiling of, say, 15%. If interest rates fall to 1%, the preferred dividend rate would hit a floor at, say, 5%.

them. Many industrial corporations have done the same. There is another item in the menu of investment opportunities open to corporate money managers.

When investment bankers latch onto a good idea, they can't stop tinkering with it. In 1984 American Express invented auction-rate preferred. In this case the dividend is reset every 49 days by means of a Dutch auction which is open to all investors. An existing shareholder can enter the auction by stating the minimum dividend he is prepared to accept; if this turns out to be higher than the rate that is needed to sell the issue, the shareholder sells the stock on to the new investors at par. Alternatively, the shareholder can simply enter a noncompetitive bid, in which case he keeps his shares and receives whatever dividend is set by the other bidders. Since auction-rate preferred can be resold for par every 49 days, it has proved popular with corporate treasurers as a temporary home for cash.[18]

32-3   SHORT-TERM BORROWING

You now know where to invest your surplus cash. But suppose that you have the opposite problem and face a temporary cash deficit. Where can you find the short-term funds?

We have in part already answered that question. Remember that all those money-market investments that we discussed above must be *issued* by someone. So your firm may be able to raise short-term money by issuing commercial paper or discounting a banker's acceptance or (in the case of a bank) issuing CDs. But there are also other possible sources of cash that we have not yet discussed. In particular, you may take out a loan from a bank or finance company.

Obviously, if you approach a bank for a loan, the bank's lending officer is likely to ask searching questions about your firm's financial position and its plans for the future. Also the bank will want to monitor the firm's subsequent progress. There is a good side to this. Other investors know that banks are hard to convince and, therefore, when a company announces that it has arranged a large bank facility, the share price tends to rise.[19]

Credit Rationing   Before we discuss the different types of bank loan, we should notice an interesting general point. The more that you borrow from the bank, the higher the rate of interest that you will be required to pay. However, there may come a stage at which the bank will refuse to lend you more, no matter how high an interest rate you are prepared to pay.

This takes us back to our discussion in Chapter 18 of the games that borrowers can play with lenders. Suppose that Henrietta Ketchup is a budding entrepreneur with two possible investment projects offering the following payoffs:

	Investment	Payoff	Probability of Payoff
Project 1	− 12	+ 15	1.0
Project 2	− 12	$\begin{cases} +24 \\ 0 \end{cases}$	0.5 0.5

---

[18] The dividend rate on straight floating-rate preferred stock is typically linked to the long-term interest rate and reset every 13 weeks. As a result the price of this stock is likely to vary more than that of auction-rate preferred. See M.J. Alderson, K.C. Brown and S.L. Lummer, "Dutch Auction Rate Preferred Stock," *Financial Management,* **16**: 68–73 (Summer 1987).

[19] See C. James, "Some Evidence on the Uniqueness of Bank Loans," *Journal of Financial Economics,* **19**: 217–235 (1987).

Project 1 is sure-fire and very profitable; project 2 is risky and a rotten project. Ms. Ketchup now approaches her bank and asks to borrow the present value of $10 (the remaining money she will find out of her own purse). The bank calculates that the payoff will be split as follows:

	Expected Payoff to Bank	Expected Payoff to Ms. Ketchup
Project 1	+10	+5
Project 2	$(0.5 \times 10) + (0.5 \times 0) = +5$	$0.5 \times (24 - 10) = +7$

If Ms. Ketchup accepts project 1, the bank's debt is certain to be paid in full; if she accepts project 2, there is only a 50% chance of payment and the expected payoff to the bank is only $5. Unfortunately, Ms. Ketchup will prefer to take project 2, for if things go well she gets most of the profit and if they go badly, the bank bears most of the loss. Unless the bank can specify in the fine print which project must be undertaken, it will not lend to Ms. Ketchup the present value of $10. Suppose, however, that the bank agrees to lend the present value of $5. Then the payoffs would be

	Expected Payoff to Bank	Expected Payoff to Ms. Ketchup
Project 1	+5	+10
Project 2	$(0.5 \times 5) + (0.5 \times 0) = +2.5$	$0.5 \times (24 - 5) = +9.5$

By rationing Ms. Ketchup to a smaller loan the bank has now made sure that she will not be tempted to speculate with its money.[20]

Unsecured Loans

We have so far referred to bank loans as if they were a standard product, but in practice they come in a variety of flavours. The simplest and most common solution is to arrange an unsecured loan from your bank. For example, many companies rely on unsecured bank loans to finance a temporary increase in inventories. Such loans are described as *self-liquidating*—in other words, the sale of the goods provides the cash to repay the loan. Another popular use of bank loans is for construction or "bridging" finance. In this case the loan serves as interim financing until a project is completed and long-term financing is arranged.

Companies that frequently require short-term bank loans often ask their bank for a line of credit. This allows them to borrow at any time up to an established limit.[21] A line of credit usually extends for a year and is then subject to review

---

[20] You might think that if the bank suspects Ms. Ketchup will undertake project 2, it should raise the interest rate on its loan. In this case, Ms. Ketchup will not want to take on project 2 (they can't *both* be happy with a lousy project). But Ms. Ketchup also would not want to pay a high rate of interest if she is going to take on project 1 (she would do better to borrow less money at the risk-free rate). So, simply raising the interest rate is not the answer. If you find this surprising, imagine that you offered to lend someone a large sum at 100%. Would you be happier if he accepted or declined?

[21] Most lines of credit are not formal commitments. The bank reserves the right to refuse additional credit if there is a significant deterioration in the borrower's financial position. If the borrower requires an unconditional guarantee that money will be available, the bank commonly charges an additional standby fee.

by the bank's loan committee. Banks are often anxious that companies not use a line of credit to cover their need for long-term finance. Thus, they often require the company to "clean up" its short-term bank loans for at least one month during the year.

The interest rate on a line of credit is usually tied to the bank's prime rate of interest or at the CD rate—that is, the rate at which the bank can raise additional funds. In addition to the interest charge, banks usually insist that in return for a line of credit the firm must maintain an interest-free demand deposit at the bank. A typical requirement is that the firm maintain a minimum average compensating balance equal to 10% of funds potentially available under the line of credit plus 10% of the amount actually borrowed. If, as a result, the firm maintains a higher cash balance than it otherwise would, the interest forgone on the additional deposit represents an extra cost to the loan.

Earlier in the chapter we noted that large companies sometimes bypass the banking system and issue their own short-term unsecured debt, that is, commercial paper. Even after allowing for the issue expenses and the cost of backup lines of credit, commercial paper is generally substantially cheaper than a bank loan. Remember, however, that when times are hard and money is tight, the bank will give priority to its regular customers. Thus few firms bypass the banking system entirely, even in good times when commercial paper is cheap and easy to sell.

Loans Secured by Receivables

Banks often ask firms to provide security for loans. Since the bank is lending on a short-term basis, the security generally consists of liquid assets such as receivables, inventories, or securities. Sometimes the bank will accept a "floating lien" or "floating charge" against receivables and inventory. This gives it a general claim against these assets, but it does not specify them in detail, and it sets few restrictions on what the company can do with the assets. More commonly, banks will require specific collateral.

If the bank is satisfied with the credit standing of your customers and the soundness of your product, it may be willing to lend you as much as 80% of the value of accounts receivable. In return, you pledge your receivables or "assign your book debts" as collateral for the loan. If you fail to pay your debt, the bank can collect the receivables and apply the proceeds to repaying the debt. If the proceeds are insufficient, you are liable for any deficiency. The loan is therefore said to be *with recourse*.

When you pledge receivables, you must keep the bank up to date on credit sales and collections. When you deliver goods to your customers, you send the bank a copy of the invoice, together with a form of assignment, which gives the bank the right to the money your customers owe you. Then the firm can borrow up to the agreed proportion of this collateral.[22]

Each day, as you make new sales, your collateral increases and you can borrow more money. Each day customers pay their bills. This money is placed in a special collateral account under the bank's control and is periodically used to reduce the size of the loan. Therefore, as the firm's business fluctuates, so does the amount of collateral and the size of the loan.

---

[22] Thus, there are three main pieces of documentation: (1) the collateral agreement (or security agreement), which defines the terms under which the collateral is given; (2) the form of assignment, under which specific assets are pledged; and (3) a promissory note against which money is borrowed.

A few receivables loans are on a notification basis. In this case the bank informs your customer of the lending arrangement and asks for the money to be paid directly to the bank. Firms generally do not like their customers to know they are in debt, and therefore such loans are made more frequently without notification.

Receivables loans can be obtained not only from banks but also from finance companies that specialize in lending to businesses.

Loans against receivables are flexible, and they provide a continuous source of funds. Also, banks are willing to lend the firm more with collateral than without it. However, it can be costly for borrower and lender alike to supervise and record changes in the collateral. Therefore, the rate of interest on receivables financing is usually high, and there may be an additional service charge on the loan.

We discussed factoring in Chapter 30. Don't confuse factoring with lending against receivables. Factors *buy* your receivables and, if you wish, advance a proportion of the money. They are, therefore, responsible for collecting the debt and suffer any losses if the customers don't pay up. When you pledge your receivables as collateral for a loan, *you* remain responsible for collecting the debt and *you* suffer if a customer is delinquent.

If it moves, an investment banker will try to turn it into a security. In recent years receivables have sometimes been repackaged into securities. For instance, in 1986 First Boston Corporation set up a special-purpose subsidiary, which bought 367,000 vehicle loans from General Motors Acceptance Corporation (GMAC). It then bundled these loans into three packages, each with a different maturity, and resold the packages to investors in the form of notes with the huge total value of $4 billion. GMAC provided a limited guarantee on these notes, but if a large number of car buyers defaulted on their payments, the noteholders would suffer a loss.

The GMAC notes are known as CARs (Certificates for Automobile Receivables). Other companies have bundled together a large number of credit card loans and sold these packages to investors. As you might guess, these packages are called CARDs (Certificates for Amortizing Revolving Debts).

The biggest development in this area in Canada has been mortgage-backed securities (MBS). MBS's are securities backed by pools of residential mortgages guaranteed by Canada Mortgage and Housing Corporation.

Loans Secured by Inventory

Banks and finance companies also lend on the security of inventory, but they are choosy about the collateral they will accept. They want to make sure that they can identify and sell the inventory if you default. Automobiles and other standardized, nonperishable commodities are good collateral for a loan; work in process and ripe Camemberts are poor collateral.

The procedure for lending against inventories depends on where the goods are stored. If you place goods in a public warehouse,[23] the warehouse company gives you a **warehouse receipt** and will then release the goods only on the instructions of the holder of the receipt.[24] Because the holder of the receipt controls the inventory, the receipt can be used as collateral for a loan.[25] Notice, however, that

---

[23] Also called a *terminal warehouse*.

[24] Most warehouse receipts are nonnegotiable. In this case the warehouse company merely requires written instructions from the holder. If they are negotiable, the company will release goods only on presentation of the receipt itself.

[25] A similar procedure may be followed when goods are in transit. In this case the bank exercises control over the goods by holding the bill of lading.

the warehouse receipt only identifies the goods and where they are stored. It doesn't guarantee the grade of the goods, nor does it guarantee your claim to the goods, nor does it provide insurance against fire, theft, and other hazards. Therefore, the lender will also need to be satisfied on all these matters.

Lenders want to make sure that goods are not released without their permission. Therefore, the law states that a warehouse receipt can be issued only by a bona fide warehouse company independent of the company that owns the goods. That is fine if you want to store your goods in a large public warehouse—but what do you do if you want to keep them on your own premises? The answer is that you establish a **field warehouse**. In other words, you arrange for a warehouse company to lease your warehouse or storage area. The warehouse company puts up signs stating that a field warehouse is being operated. It then remains responsible for storing your pledged goods and releases them only on the instructions of the holder of the warehouse receipt.

The important feature of warehouse loans is that goods are physically segregated and under the control of an independent warehouse company. Suppose, however, that you are an automobile dealer who needs to finance an inventory of new cars. You can't put the cars in a warehouse; you need to keep them in the showroom under your control. The common solution is to enter into a **floor planning** arrangement. Under this arrangement the finance company buys the cars from the manufacturer and you hold them in trust for the finance company. As evidence of this, you sign a *trust receipt* that identifies the cars involved. You are free to sell the cars, but when you do so, the proceeds are used to redeem the trust receipt. To make sure that the collateral is properly maintained, the finance company will make periodic inspections of the inventory.

The fact that liquid assets are easily saleable does not always make them good collateral. It also means the lender has to make sure that the borrower doesn't suddenly sell the assets and run off with the money. If you want to make your hair stand on end, read the story of the great salad oil swindle.[26] Fifty-one banks and companies made loans of nearly $200 million to the Allied Crude Vegetable Oil Refining Corporation. Warehouse receipts issued by a field warehousing company were taken as security. Unfortunately, the cursory inspections by the employees of the field warehousing company failed to uncover the fact that, instead of containing salad oil, Allied's storage tanks were mainly filled with soap stock, seawater, and unidentifiable sludge. When the fraud was discovered, the president of Allied went to jail, the field warehousing company went into bankruptcy, and the 51 lenders were left out in the cold, looking for their $200 million. Lenders have been more careful since then, but no doubt they'll be caught by some new scam sooner or later.

32-4   TERM LOANS

The principal form of medium-term debt financing is the **term loan**. Most such loans are made by banks and have maturities of one to eight years. Insurance companies often make longer-maturity term loans, and a number of term loans are split between banks and insurance companies.

Term loans are usually repaid in level amounts over the period of the loan, although sometimes there may be no payment for the first couple of years, or there may be a large final "balloon" or just a single "bullet" payment at maturity.

---

[26] For an excellent account see N. Miller, *The Great Salad Oil Swindle*, Victor Gollancz, Ltd. London, 1966.

Banks can accommodate repayment patterns to the anticipated cash flows of the borrowing firm. For example, the first principal repayment might be delayed for a year pending completion of a new factory. Often term loans are renegotiated in midstream—that is, before maturity. Banks are usually willing to do this if the borrowing firm is an established customer, remains creditworthy, and has a sound business reason for making the change.

The rate of interest on the term loan is sometimes fixed for the life of the loan. But usually it is linked to the prime rate. Thus, if the rate is set at "1% over prime," the borrower may pay 5% in the first year when prime is 4%, 5½% in the second year when prime is 4½%, and so on. Occasionally these variable-rate term loans include a "collar," which sets upper and lower limits on the interest that can be charged, or a "cap" which sets an upper limit only.

In addition to the interest cost the borrower is usually obliged to maintain a minimum interest-free demand deposit with the bank. This compensating balance is commonly set at 10% to 20% of the amount of the loan, so that the true interest rate, calculated on the money the firm can actually use, may be significantly higher than the quoted interest rate.

Term loans are for the most part unsecured debt. The conditions of a term loan are like those of the most unsecured bonds. They generally do not include the very restrictive negative conditions of private placement bonds, but they do stipulate minimum levels of net worth and working capital. Because many term loans are made to small companies, they often impose conditions on senior management. For example, the bank may require the company to insure the lives of senior managers, may place limits on management's remuneration, and may require personal guarantees for the loan.

A variant on the straight loan is the *revolving line of credit*. This is a legally assured line of credit that is reviewed annually. The company pays interest on any borrowings plus an "insurance premium" of about ½% on the unused amount, as well as maintains a compensating balance with the bank.

Revolving credit agreements are relatively expensive compared to straight lines of credit or short-term bank loans. But, in exchange for the extra cost, the firm receives a valuable option: it has guaranteed access to the bank's money at a fixed spread above the prime rate. This amounts to a put option, because the firm can sell its debt to the bank on fixed terms even if its own creditworthiness deteriorates.[27]

Eurodollar Lending

The major international banks also make unsecured eurodollar loans with short- or medium-term maturities. The interest rate on such loans is usually tied to the London interbank offered rate (LIBOR), which is the rate at which the banks lend eurodollars to one another. When the sums involved are very large, these eurodollar loans have traditionally been made by a syndicate of banks where each bank has a separate loan agreement with the borrower.[28]

---

[27] Gregory Hawkins has analyzed revolving credit agreements using option pricing theory. See "An Analysis of Revolving Credit Agreements," *Journal of Financial Economics*, **10**: 59–81 (March 1982).

[28] Occasionally, banks would like to sell their share in a syndicated loan. They could do this by arranging for another bank to "participate" in their portion. Therefore, loan agreements sometimes make it possible for each bank to transfer its portion of the loan. Transferable syndicated loans are a response by the banks to the trend away from bank lending and toward marketable securities.

Other firms have preferred to borrow by means of **note issuance facilities** (NIFs).[29] NIFs have been one of the great growth products of the 1980s. A NIF is a line of credit that allows the borrower to issue a series of short-term euronotes, typically over a period of 5 to 7 years. These euronotes are marketed on behalf of the firm by one or more banks or investment banks. In order to make sure that the firm gets its money, a (possibly different) group of banks underwrites the issue by promising to take up any unsold notes. In exchange for this facility the firm usually pays an initial fee and an annual underwriting fee.[30]

Most of the euronotes issued under a note issuance facility have a 3- to 6-month maturity, but sometimes the firm will have a wide choice as to the maturity and currency of any debt that it issues. Many firms do not take up their option to issue euronotes but instead use the NIF either as an emergency source of funds or as a backup line of credit for their commercial paper programs.

Instead of arranging syndicated eurodollar loans, many firms during the 1980s moved toward more marketable types of debt. This process is generally known as "securitization."

Securitization in the eurodollar market has taken two principal forms. Some firms, who would previously have borrowed by means of a syndicated bank loan, have chosen instead to issue floating-rate notes in the eurobond market. (We described these notes in Section 24-2.)

32-5 SUMMARY

If you have more cash than you currently need, you can invest the surplus in the money market. The principal money-market investments are:

- Treasury bills
- Certificates of deposit
- Swapped deposits
- London dollar certificates of deposit
- Commercial paper
- Bankers' acceptances
- Buy-back agreements

If none of these catches your fancy, you can make a short-term eurocurrency investment, such as a eurodollar time deposit.

No two of these securities are exactly the same. If you want to make effective use of your cash, you need to be aware of the differences in their liquidity, risk, and yield. Table 32-1 summarizes the main features of money-market instruments. Figure 32-1 shows money-market rates as reported in *The Globe and Mail* for April 30, 1991.

Most corporations making short-term investments of excess cash buy one or more of the instruments described in Table 32-1. But there are many alternatives, including floating-rate preferreds. These securities are attractive for two reasons. First, corporations pay no tax on the dividends received. Second, the dividend

---

[29] Other similar facilities are termed revolving underwriting facilities (RUFs) or note purchase facilities. Eurocommercial paper programs are sometimes referred to as nonunderwritten NIFs. The bank will agree to market the firm's short-term debt but will not promise to take up any unsold paper.

[30] See *Recent Innovations in International Banking*, Bank for International Settlements, Basel, April 1986.

MONEY MARKETS

ADMINISTERED RATES	
Bank of Canada	9.49%
Canadian prime	10–10.25%

MONEY MARKET RATES	
(for transactions of $1-million or more)	
3-month treasury bills	9.22%
6-month treasury bills	9.12%
1-year treasury bills	9.22%
2001 Canada bonds	9.53%
2014 Canada bonds	9.83%
30-day comm. paper	9.45%
60-day comm. paper	9.43%
90-day comm. paper	9.40%
30-day banker's accept.	9.33%
6-day banker's accept.	9.30%
90-day banker's accept.	9.25%
1-month dollar swaps	9.24%
2-month dollar swaps	9.16%
3-month dollar swaps	9.19%
6-month dollar swaps	9.28%
1-year dollar swaps	9.34%
Call money	9.375%

UNITED STATES

NEW YORK (AP) — Money rates for Monday as reported by Telerate Systems Inc:

Telerate interest rate index: 5.980
Prime Rate: 9.00
Discount Rate: 6.00
Broker call loan rate: 7.50–8.50
Federal funds market rate:
High 5.9375, low 5.875, last 5.875
Dealers commercial paper:
30–180 days: 6.00–6.00
Commercial paper by finance company: 30–270 days: 5.90–5.91
Bankers acceptances dealer indications: 30 days, 5.95; 60 days, 5.92; 90 days, 5.92; 120 days, 5.93; 150 days, 5.95; 180 days, 5.95
Certificates of Deposit Primary: 30 days, 5.62; 90 days, 5.65; 180 days, 5.75

Certificates of Deposit by dealer: 30 days, 6.02; 60 days, 6.05; 90 days, 6.10; 120 days, 6.15; 150 days, 6.18; 180 days, 6.20
Eurodollar rates: Overnight, 5.875–6.00; 1 month, 5.9375–6.0625; 3 months, 6.0625–6.1875; 6 months, 6.1875–6.3125; 1 year 6.625–6.75
London Interbank Offered Rate: 3 months, 6.1875; 6 months, 6.3125
Treasury Bill auction results: average discount rate: 3-month as of Apr. 29: 5.60; 6-month as of Apr. 29: 5.68
Treasury Bill, annualized rate on weekly average basis, yield adjusted for constant maturity, 1-year, as of Apr. 29: 6.25
Treasury Bill marked rate, 1-year: 5.83–5.81
Treasury Bond market rate, 30-year: 8.22

Figure 32–1   Short-term interest rates in April 1991.
Source: The Globe and Mail, Report on Business.

paid moves up and down with changes in interest rates, so the preferred shares' prices are more or less stabilized. For many companies surplus cash is not a worry: their problem is to finance a temporary cash deficiency. One of the main sources of short-term funds is the unsecured bank loan. This is often taken out under a bank line of credit, which entitles the firm to borrow up to an agreed limit. The interest rate that banks charge on unsecured loans must be sufficient to cover not only the opportunity cost of capital for the loans but also the costs of running a loan department. As a result large, regular borrowers have found it cheaper to bypass the banking system and issue their own short-term unsecured debt. This debt is known as *commercial paper*.

Bank loans with maturities exceeding one year are called *term loans*. The firm agrees to pay interest based on the bank's prime rate and to repay principal in regular instalments. Special patterns of principal payments over time can often be negotiated to meet the firm's special needs, however. Usually compensating balances are required.

Another form of medium-term bank finance is revolving credit, which guarantees the firm access to a line of credit. Revolving credit can often be converted into regular term loans.

The international banks also make unsecured loans of eurodollars. The rate on these loans is usually tied to the London interbank offered rate (LIBOR). Sometimes a group of banks will arrange a line of credit that allows the borrower to issue euronotes up to some agreed limit. Such lines of credit are generally called *Note Issuance Facilities* (NIFs).

If you ask to borrow more and more, you will eventually be asked to provide security for the loan. Sometimes this security consists of a floating lien on receivables and inventories, but more frequently you will be asked to pledge specific assets. The bank or finance company will take precautions to make sure that the collateral is properly identified and within its control. For example, when you borrow against receivables the bank must be informed of all sales of goods and the resulting accounts receivable must be pledged to the bank. As customers pay their bills, the money is paid into a special collateral account under the bank's control. Similarly, when you borrow against stocks of raw materials, the bank will insist that the goods are held by an independent warehouse company. As long as the bank holds the warehouse receipt for these goods, they cannot be released without the bank's permission. Loans secured on finished goods are usually made under a floor planning arrangement. In this case you will be required to sign a trust receipt that you are merely holding the specified goods in trust for the lender, and the lender will make periodic inspections to see that you are keeping your promise.

You may also find that there comes a point at which the bank will not increase its lending no matter how high a rate of interest you are prepared to pay. Banks know that the more they lend, the more they are encouraging you to gamble with their money. Your aims and the bank's are more likely to coincide if your borrowing is kept to a responsible level.

FURTHER READING

For a detailed description of the money market and short-term lending opportunities in Canada and the United States, respectively, see:

S. Sarpkaya, *The Money Market in Canada*, 4th ed., CCH Canadian Ltd., Don Mills, Ont., 1989.

M. Stigum, *The Money Market: Myth, Reality and Practice*, 2nd ed., Richard D. Irwin, Inc., Homewood, Illinois, 1983.

A good book discussing the borrowing and lending practices of Canadian banks is:

J.A. Galbraith, *Canadian Banking*, Ryerson Press, Toronto, 1970.

QUIZ

1. Choose the investment that best fits the accompanying description.
   (a) Maturity often overnight: repurchase agreements or bankers' acceptances?
   (b) No secondary market: bankers' acceptances or swapped deposits?
   (c) Issued by banks: Treasury bills or certificates of deposit?
   (d) Can be deposited with the Bank of Canada by a money-market jobber: bankers' acceptances or Treasury bills?
   (e) Used in country banking: savings deposits or Treasury bills?
   (f) Discounted: bankers' acceptances or swapped deposits?
   (g) Sold by auction: bearer notes or Treasury bills?
2. On April 19, 1991, 91-day Treasury bills were quoted at a yield of 9.41%.
   (a) What was the price of a 91-day T-bill?
   (b) What was the equivalent annually compounded yield?
   (c) If these T-bills were offered for sale in the United States, at what discount would they be quoted?
3. Complete the following passage by selecting the most appropriate terms from the following list: *floating lien, field warehouse, clean-up provision, commercial paper, floor planning, line of credit, prime rate, public warehouse, compensating balance, trust receipt, warehouse receipt, collateral, with resource.*

   Companies with fluctuating capital needs often arrange a _____ with their bank. To make sure that this facility is not used to provide permanent funds, the bank sometimes incorporates a _____. The interest on any borrowing is tied to the bank's _____. In addition the bank generally requires that the company keep a _____ on deposit at the bank. Some large companies bypass the banking system and issue their own short-term unsecured debt. This is called _____.

Secured short-term loans are sometimes covered by a _____ on all receivables and inventory. Generally, however, the borrower pledges specific assets as _____. If these assets are insufficient to repay the debt, the borrower is liable for the deficiency. Therefore, such loans are said to be _____. Warehouse loans are examples of secured short-term loans. The goods may be stored in a _____ or in a _____ that is established by the warehouse company on the borrower's premises. The warehouse company issues a _____ to the lender and releases the goods only on his or her instructions. Loans to automobile dealers are usually made on a different basis. The dealer holds the inventory on behalf of the lender and issues a _____. This arrangement is known as _____.

4. Consider three securities:
   (a) A floating-rate bond
   (b) A preferred share paying a fixed dividend
   (c) A floating-rate preferred
   A financial manager responsible for short-term investment of excess cash would probably choose the floating-rate preferred over *either* of the other two securities. Why? Explain briefly.

5. Here are six questions about term loans:
   (a) Who makes term loans?
   (b) Are compensating balances usually required?
   (c) Are term loans usually secured loans? That is, are they usually backed up by specific collateral?
   (d) How is the interest rate usually determined?
   (e) What is a balloon payment?
   (f) What is a revolving line of credit?

QUESTIONS AND PROBLEMS

1. Look up current interest rates offered by short-term investment alternatives. Suppose that your firm has $1 million excess cash to invest for the next two months. How would you invest this excess cash? How would your answer change if the excess cash is $5,000, $20,000, $100,000, or $100 million?

2. On April 21, 1991, Government of Canada 90-day Treasury bills were quoted at 9.4%, 90-day bankers' acceptances were quoted at 9.47%, commercial paper was quoted at 9.60%, and United States 90-day Treasury bills were quoted at 5.69%.
   (a) What was the effective yield of each of these investments, compounded annually?
   (b) Why were bankers' acceptances quoted at the same rate as commercial paper, even though bankers' acceptances are guaranteed by the borrower *and* a bank?
   (c) Would you infer that Canadian or American T-bills were a better investment? Why?

3. Interest rates on bank loans exceed rates on commercial paper. Why don't all firms issue commercial paper rather than borrowing from banks?

4. Do you think you could make money by setting up a firm that would (a) issue commercial paper and (b) relend money to businesses at a rate slightly higher than the commercial paper rate, but still less than the rate charged by banks?

5. Roy's Toys needs an extra $1 million in October to build up inventory for the Christmas season. First Commercial has offered to lend at 9% subject to a 20% compensating balance. The Bank of Anyprovince will lend at 11% with no strings attached. Which bank is offering the better deal? Why? Would your answer change if Roy's Toys already had a $100,000 normal working balance at First Commercial? (Assume in this case that the working balance can be used to cover part of the compensating balance.)

6. Axle Chemical Corporation's treasurer has forecast a $1 million cash deficit for the next quarter. However, there is only a 50% chance this deficit will actually occur. The treasurer estimates that there is a 20% probability the company will have no deficit at all, and a 30% probability that it will actually need $2 million in short-term financing. The company can either take out a 90-day unsecured loan at 1% per month or establish a line of credit costing 1% per month on the amount borrowed plus a commitment fee of $20,000. Both alternatives also require a 20% compensating balance for outstanding loans. If excess cash can be reinvested at 9%, which source of financing gives the lower expected cost?

7. Suppose that you are a banker responsible for approving corporate loans. Nine firms are seeking secured loans. They offer the following assets as collateral:
   (a) Firm A, a heating oil distributor, offers a tanker load of fuel oil in transit from the Middle East.
   (b) Firm B, a wine wholesaler, offers 1,000 cases of Beaujolais Nouveau, located in a field warehouse.
   (c) Firm C, a stationer, offers an account receivable for office supplies sold to the city of Regina.
   (d) Firm D, a bookstore, offers its entire inventory of 15,000 used books.
   (e) Firm E, a wholesale grocer, offers a boxcar full of bananas.
   (f) Firm F, an appliance dealer, offers his inventory of electric typewriters.
   (g) Firm G offers 100 ounces of gold.
   (h) Firm H, a government securities dealer, offers its portfolio of Treasury bills.
   (i) Firm I, a boat builder, offers a half-completed luxury yacht. The yacht will take four months more to complete.
   Which of these assets are most likely to be good collateral? Which are likely to be poor collateral? Explain.

8. Any one of the assets mentioned in the preceding question *could* be acceptable collateral under certain circumstances if appropriate safeguards were taken. What circumstances? What safeguards? Explain.

9. The first floating-rate preferreds were successfully issued at initial dividend yields *below* yields on Treasury bills. How was this possible? The preferreds were clearly riskier than the bonds. What would you predict for the *long-run* relationship between yields on bills and floating-rate preferreds? (We say "long-run" to give time for all firms who will want to issue floating-rate preferreds to get around to doing so.)

10. Most floating-rate preferreds have both a "floor" and a "ceiling" on their dividend rate. (See Section 32-2, fn. 17.) How do these limits affect the behaviour of the *prices* of these securities as interest rates change? Why do you think the issuing companies included the limits in the first place?

11. Term loans usually require firms to pay a fluctuating interest rate. For example, the interest rate may be set at "1% above prime." The prime rate sometimes varies by several percentage points within a single year.

   Suppose that your firm has decided to borrow $40 million for five years. It has three alternatives:

   (a) Borrow from a bank at the prime rate, currently 10%. The proposed loan agreement requires no principal repayments until the loan matures in five years.

   (b) Issue 26-week commercial paper, currently having a true yield of 9%. Since funds are required for five years, the commercial paper will have to be "rolled over" semiannually. That is, financing the $40 million requirement for five years will require ten successive commercial paper sales.

   (c) Borrow from an insurance company at a fixed rate of 11%. As in the bank loan, no principal has to be repaid until the end of the five-year period.

   What factors would you consider in analyzing these alternatives? Under what circumstances would you choose (a)? Under what circumstances would you choose (b) or (c)? (*Hint:* Don't forget Chapter 23.)

P·A·R·T

10

MERGERS, INTERNATIONAL FINANCE, AND PENSIONS

C · H · A · P · T · E · R

33

MERGERS

The scale and scope of merger activity in Canada is remarkable. For example, Table 33-1 lists just a few of the more important mergers that occurred during the years 1978 through 1990. You can see that they involve big money. During periods of intense merger activity financial managers spend significant amounts of time either searching for firms to acquire or worrying whether some other firm will acquire them.

Table 33-1
Some important mergers, 1978–1990

Acquiring Company	Selling Company	Payment (millions of dollars)
Campeau Corp.	Federated Stores (U.S.)	4,300
Campeau Corp.	Allied Stores (U.S.)	8,800
Amoco Canada	Dome Petroleum	5,500
Gulf Canada	Hiram Walker Resources	3,000
Olympia and York	Gulf Canada	2,850
JMB Realty Corp. (U.S.)	Cadillac Fairview	2,590
Imasco Limited	Genstar	2,500

Sources: R.S. Khemani, D.M. Shapiro, and W.T. Stanbury, *Mergers, Corporate Concentration and Power in Canada*, The Institute for Research on Public Policy, 1988. The Financial Post.

When you buy another company, you are making an investment, and the basic principles of capital investment decisions apply. You should go ahead with the purchase if it makes a net contribution to shareholders' wealth. But mergers are often awkward things to evaluate. First, you have to be careful to define benefits and costs properly. Second, buying a company is more complicated than buying a new machine; in particular, special tax, legal, and accounting issues must often be addressed. Third, you must be aware of the offensive and defensive tactics used in hostile takeovers, just in case a friendly deal cannot be consummated. Finally, you need to have a general understanding of why mergers occur and who typically gains or loses as a result of them.

We will start by defining the benefits and costs of a merger. We will also comment on the legal, tax, and accounting problems encountered in putting two firms together.

Many mergers are arranged amicably, but in other cases one firm will make a hostile take-over bid for the other. We will describe the principal techniques of modern merger warfare, and since the threat of hostile take-overs has stimulated corporate restructurings and **leverage buyouts (LBOs)**, we will describe them too, and also attempt to explain why these deals are generating such enormous rewards for investors.

We close with a look at the public policy issues raised by the recent boom in leveraged buyouts and the aggressive use of debt in corporate restructurings.

33-1 ESTIMATING THE ECONOMIC GAINS AND COSTS FROM MERGERS[1]

Suppose that you are the financial manager of firm A and that you wish to analyze the possible purchase of firm B. The first thing to think about is whether there is an *economic gain* from the merger. There is an economic gain *only if the two firms are worth more together than apart*. For example, if you think that the combined firm would be worth PV_{AB}, and that the separate firms are worth $PV_A + PV_B$, then

$$GAIN = PV_{AB} - (PV_A + PV_B)$$

If this gain is positive, there is an economic justification for merger. But you also have to think about the *cost* of acquiring firm B. Take the easy case in which payment is made in the form of cash. Then the cost of acquiring B is equal to the cash payment minus B's value as a separate entity. Thus:

$$COST = CASH - PV_B$$

The net present value to A of a merger with B is measured by the difference between the gain and the cost. Therefore, you should go ahead with the merger if its net present value, defined as

$$NPV = GAIN - COST = PV_{AB} - (PV_A + PV_B) - (CASH - PV_B)$$

is positive.

We like to write the merger criterion in this way because it focuses attention on two distinct questions. When you estimate the benefit, you concentrate on whether there are any gains to be had from the merger. When you estimate cost, you are concerned with the division of these gains between the two companies.

An example may help make this clear. Firm A has a value of $100 million, B a value of $50 million. Merging the two would allow cost savings with a present value of $25 million. This is the gain to be had from the merger. Thus:

$$PV_A = \$100$$
$$PV_B = \$50$$
$$GAIN = +\$25$$
$$PV_{AB} = \$175$$

Suppose that B is bought for cash, say for $65 million. The cost of the merger is

$$COST = CASH - PV_B$$
$$= \$65 - \$50 = \$15 \text{ million}$$

---

[1] This chapter's definitions and interpretations of the gains and costs of merger generally follow those set out in S.C. Myers, "A Framework for Evaluating Mergers," in S.C. Myers, ed., *Modern Developments in Financial Management*, Frederick A. Praeger, Inc., New York, 1976.

Note that the stockholders of firm B — the people on the other side of the transaction — are ahead by $15 million. *Their* gain is *your* cost.[2] They have captured $15 million of the $25 million merger gain. Thus, when we write down the NPV of the merger from A's viewpoint, we are really calculating that part of the gain that A's stockholders get to keep, less the part of the gain captured by B's stockholders.

$$NPV = \$25 - \$15 = + \$10 \text{ million}$$

Just as a check, let's confirm that A's stockholders really come out $10 million ahead. They start with a firm worth $PV_A = \$100$ million. They pay out $65 million cash to B's stockholders and end up with a firm worth $175 million. Thus, their net gain is

$$
\begin{aligned}
NPV &= \text{wealth with merger} - \text{wealth without merger} \\
&= (PV_{AB} - \text{CASH}) - PV_A \\
&= (\$175 - \$65) - \$100 \\
&= + \$10 \text{ million}
\end{aligned}
$$

Suppose investors do not anticipate the merger between A and B. The announcement will cause the value of B's stock to rise from $50 to $65 million, a 30% increase. If investors share management's assessment of the merger gains, the market value of A's stock will increase by $10 million, or only a 5% increase.

It makes sense to keep an eye on what investors think the gains from merging are. If A's stock price falls when the deal is announced, then investors are sending a message that the merger benefits are doubtful or that A is paying too much for them.

Right and Wrong Ways to Estimate the Benefits of Mergers

Some companies begin their merger analyses with a forecast of the target firm's future cash flows. Any revenue increases or cost reductions attributable to the merger are included in the forecasts, which are then discounted back to the present and compared with the purchase price:

$$
\begin{matrix}
\text{Estimated} \\
\text{net gain}
\end{matrix}
=
\begin{matrix}
\text{DCF valuation} \\
\text{of target, including} \\
\text{merger benefits}
\end{matrix}
-
\begin{matrix}
\text{Cash required} \\
\text{for acquisition}
\end{matrix}
$$

This is a dangerous procedure. Even the brightest and best-trained analyst can make large errors in valuing a business. The estimated net gain may come up positive not because the merger makes sense, but simply because the analyst's cash flow forecasts are overoptimistic. On the other hand, a good merger may not be pursued if the analyst fails to recognize the target's potential as a stand-alone business.

Our procedure *starts* with the target's stand-alone market value (PV_B) and concentrates on the *changes* in cash flow that would result from the merger. *Ask yourself why the two firms should be worth more together than apart.*

The same advice holds when you are contemplating the *sale* of part of your business. There is no point saying to yourself, "This is an unprofitable business and should be sold." Unless the buyer can run the business better than you can, the price you receive will reflect the poor prospects.

---

[2] In practice, B's gain may be less than A's cost because money leaks out in fees for underwriters, lawyers, and accountants. For example, the leveraged buyout of RJR Nabisco (discussed below in Section 33-7) provides a recent and dramatic example. Total fees for banks, investment banks, lawyers, and accountants were roughly U.S. $1.1 billion out of a $25 billion purchase price.

Sometimes you may come across managers who believe that there are simple rules for identifying good acquisitions. For example, they may say that they always seek to buy into growth industries or that they have a policy of acquiring companies that are selling below book value. But our comments in Chapter 11 about the characteristics of a good investment decision also hold true when you are buying a whole company. *You add value only if you can generate additional economic rents*—some competitive edge that other firms can't match and the target firm's managers can't achieve on their own.

One final piece of horse sense. Often two companies bid against one another to acquire the same target firm. In effect, the target firm puts itself up for auction. In these cases ask yourself whether the target is worth more to you than to the other bidder. If the answer is no, you should be cautious about getting into a bidding contest. Winning such a contest may be more expensive than losing it. If you lose, you have simply wasted your time; if you win, you may have paid too much.

33-2   SENSIBLE MOTIVES FOR MERGERS

Mergers are often categorized as *horizontal, vertical,* or *conglomerate.* A horizontal merger is one that takes place between two firms in the same line of business; most of the mergers around the turn of the century were of this type. Recent examples include oil industry mergers, such as Gulf Canada's take-over of Hiram Walker Resources in 1986.

During the 1920s vertical mergers were predominant. A vertical merger is one in which the buyer expands backward toward the source of raw materials or forward in the direction of the ultimate consumer.

A conglomerate merger involves companies in unrelated lines of business. Conglomerate mergers became common in the 1960s and 1970s. However, the fraction of conglomerate mergers declined in the 1980s. In fact, much of the action in the 1980s came from breaking up the conglomerates that had been formed 10 to 20 years earlier.

With these distinctions in mind, we will go on to consider motives for mergers—that is, reasons why two firms may be worth more together than apart. But first, a caveat. It would be nice if we could say that certain types of mergers are generally successful and other types fail. Unfortunately, we know of no such simple generalizations. Many mergers which seem to make economic sense fail because they are badly implemented. Others fail because the buyer misestimates the value of assets or fails to notice hidden liabilities. For example, the buyer may underestimate the value of stale inventory or the costs of renovating elderly plant and equipment, or may overlook the warranties on a defective product. Buyers must be particularly careful about environmental liabilities. If there is pollution from the seller's operations, or toxic waste on its property, the costs of cleaning up will probably fall on the buyer.

Economies of Scale   Just as most of us believe that we would be happier if only we were a little richer, so every manager seems to believe that his or her firm would be more competitive if only it were just a little bigger.[3]

---

[3] Economies of scale are enjoyed when the average unit cost of production goes down as production increases. One way of achieving economies of scale is by spreading fixed costs over a larger volume of production.

These economies of scale are the natural goal of horizontal mergers. But such economies have been claimed in conglomerate mergers too. The architects of these mergers have pointed to the economies that come from sharing central services such as office management and accounting, financial control, executive development, and top-level management.

There are innumerable examples of possible economies of scale. But merging isn't always the best way of achieving them. It is always easier to buy another business than it is to integrate it with yours afterwards. Even economies in central services may be elusive. The complicated structure of conglomerate companies may actually increase the administrative staff. And top-level managers of conglomerates often find that their general skills are not easily applied to the specialized problems of individual subsidiaries.

Economies of Vertical Integration

Vertical mergers seek economies in vertical integration. Large industrial companies commonly like to gain as much control as possible over the production process by expanding back toward the output of the raw material and forward to the ultimate consumer. One way to achieve this is to merge with a supplier or a customer.

One reason for vertical integration is that it makes coordination and administration easier. We can illustrate by a somewhat extreme example. Think of an airline that does not own any planes. If it schedules a flight from Toronto to Vancouver, it sells tickets and then rents a plane for that flight from a separate company. This strategy might work on a small scale, but it would be an administrative nightmare for a major carrier which would have to coordinate hundreds of rental agreements daily. In view of these difficulties, it is not surprising that all major airlines have integrated backwards, away from the consumer, by buying and flying airplanes rather than patronizing "rent-a-plane" companies.

Do not assume that more vertical integration is better than less. Carried to extremes it is absurdly inefficient, as in the case of LOT, the Polish state airline, which in the late 1980s found itself raising pigs to make sure that its employees had fresh meat on their tables. (Of course, in a centrally managed economy it may be necessary to grow your own meat since you can't be sure you'll be able to buy it.)

Combining Complementary Resources

Many small firms are acquired by large ones which can provide missing ingredients necessary for the firm's success. The small firm may have a unique product but lack the engineering and sales organizations necessary to produce and market it on a large scale. The firm could develop engineering and sales talent from scratch, but it may be quicker and cheaper to merge with a firm that already has ample talent. The two firms have *complementary resources*—each has what the other needs—and so it can make sense for them to merge. The two firms are worth more together than apart because each acquires something it does not have and gets it cheaper than it would acting on its own. Also, the merger may open up opportunities that neither firm would pursue otherwise.

Unused Tax Shields

Sometimes a firm may have potential tax shields but not have the profits to take advantage of them. For example, after the expropriation of its Cuban sugar plantations, Bangor Punta had substantial tax-loss carry-overs, which it could not use. It therefore combined with other firms that were generating taxable profits so that the tax-loss carry-over could be used.[4]

---

[4] Mergers undertaken *just* to use tax-loss carry-forwards may be challenged by Revenue Canada, and the use of the carry-forwards may be denied. Suppose that you own a profitable firm.

Mergers as a Use for Surplus Funds

Here's another argument for mergers. Suppose that your firm is in a mature industry. It is generating a substantial amount of cash, but it has few profitable investment opportunities. Ideally, such a firm should distribute the surplus cash to shareholders by increasing its dividend payment or by a stock repurchase. Unfortunately, energetic managers are often reluctant to adopt a policy of shrinking their firm in this way.

If the firm is not willing to purchase its own shares, it can instead purchase someone else's. Thus, firms with a surplus of cash and a shortage of good investment opportunities often turn to mergers *financed by cash* as a way of redeploying their capital.

Some firms have excess cash and do not pay it out to stockholders or redeploy it by acquisition. Such firms often find themselves targets for take-over by other firms who propose to redeploy the cash for them.[5] During the oil price slump of the early 1980s many cash-rich oil companies found themselves threatened by take-over. This was not because their cash was a unique asset. The acquirers wanted to capture the companies' cash flow to make sure it was not frittered away on negative-NPV oil exploration projects. We will return to this *free cash flow* motive for take-overs later in this chapter.

Eliminating Inefficiencies

Cash is not the only asset that can be wasted by poor management. There are always firms with unexploited opportunities to cut costs and increase sales and earnings. Such firms are natural candidates for acquisition by other firms with better management. In some cases "better management" may simply mean the determination to force painful cuts or realignments of the company's operations.

If this motive is important, one would expect that firms that perform *poorly* would tend to be targets for acquisition. This seems to be the case. Palepu, for example, found that investors in firms that were subsequently acquired earned relatively low rates of return over several years before the merger.[6] Apparently, many of these firms fell on bad times and were rescued, or reformed, by merger.

Of course, a merger is not the only way to improve management. But sometimes it is the only simple and practical way. Managers are naturally reluctant to fire or demote themselves, and stockholders of large public firms do not usually have much *direct* influence on how their firm is run or who runs it.[7]

Of course, it is easy to critize another firm's management and less easy to do better. Some of the self-appointed scourges of poor management turn out to be

---

You find another company on the ropes, with large cumulative losses. If you bought up that company and then liquidated its assets, Revenue Canada would probably regard the tax-loss carry-forwards as liquidated also and not allow them to use them to reduce your taxable income. But the tax rules are funny: if the company on the rocks bought *you*, then gradually and discreetly closed down its own business and continued with yours, Revenue Canada may accept the deal and let it use the tax-loss carry-forwards.

[5] Take-overs in this case often take the form of leveraged buyouts. In 1988 $77 billion was distributed to selling stockholders in 214 LBOs. This was 71% of the $108 billion of corporate dividends paid in that year. See M.C. Jensen, "The Eclipse of the Public Corporation," *Harvard Business Review* **67**: 61–74 (September–October 1989).

[6] K. Palepu, "Predicting Takeover Targets: A Methodological and Empirical Analysis," *Journal of Accounting and Economics*, **8**: 3–36 (March 1986).

[7] It is difficult to assemble a large enough block of stockholders to effectively challenge management and the incumbent board of directors. Stockholders can have enormous indirect influence, however. Their displeasure shows up in the firm's stock price. A low stock price may encourage a take-over bid by another firm.

less competent than those they replace. Here is how Warren Buffet, the Chairman of Berkshire Hathaway, summarizes the matter.[8]

> Many managers were apparently over-exposed in impressionable childhood years to the story in which the imprisoned, handsome prince is released from the toad's body by a kiss from the beautiful princess. Consequently, they are certain that the managerial kiss will do wonders for the profitability of the target company. Such optimism is essential. Absent that rosy view, why else should the shareholders of company A want to own an interest in B at a take-over cost that is two times the market price they'd pay if they made direct purchases on their own? In other words, investors can always buy toads at the going price for toads. If investors instead bankroll princesses who wish to pay double for the right to kiss the toad, those kisses better pack some real dynamite. We've observed many kisses, but very few miracles. Nevertheless, many managerial princesses remain serenely confident about the future potency of their kisses, even after their corporate backyards are knee-deep in unresponsive toads.

33-3   SOME DUBIOUS REASONS FOR MERGERS

The benefits that we have described so far all make economic sense. Other arguments that are sometimes given for mergers are more dubious. Here are a few of these.

Diversification   We have suggested that the managers of a cash-rich company may prefer to see that cash used for acquisitions rather than distribute it as extra dividends. That is why we often see cash-rich firms in stagnant industries merging their way into fresh woods and pastures new.

But what about diversification as an end in itself? It is obvious that diversification reduces risk. Isn't that a gain from merging?

The trouble with that argument is that diversification is easier and cheaper for the stockholder than for the corporation. No one has shown that investors pay premiums for diversified firms—in fact, discounts are common. For example, Kaiser Industries was dissolved as a United States holding company in 1977 because its diversification apparently *subtracted* from its value. Kaiser Industries' main assets were shares of Kaiser Steel, Kaiser Aluminium, and Kaiser Cement. These were independent companies, and the stock of each was publicly traded. Thus, you could value Kaiser Industries by looking at the stock prices of Kaiser Steel, Kaiser Aluminium, and Kaiser Cement. But Kaiser Industries' stock was selling at a price reflecting a significant *discount* from the value of its investment in these companies. The discount vanished with Kaiser Industries revealed its plan to sell its holdings and distribute the proceeds to its stockholders.

Why the discount existed in the first place is a puzzle. But the example at least shows that diversification does not increase value. The appendix to this chapter provides a simple proof that corporate diversification does not affect value in perfect capital markets as long as investors' diversification opportunities are unrestricted.

There are exceptional cases in which personal diversification may be more expensive than corporate diversification. Suppose you are the president and majority owner of a closely held corporation. You may be wealthy, but you have

---

[8] Berkshire Hathaway 1981 Annual Report, cited in G. Foster, "Comments on M&A Analysis and the Role of Investment Bankers," *Midland Corporate Finance Journal*, **1**: 36–38 (Winter 1983).

Table 33-2
Impact of merger on market value and earnings per share of World Enterprises

	World Enterprises (before merger)	Muck and Slurry	World Enterprises (after acquiring Muck and Slurry)
1. Earnings per share	$2.00	$2.00	$2.67
2. Price per share	$40.00	$20.00	$40.00
3. Price-earnings ratio	20	10	15
4. Number of shares	100,000	100,000	150,000
5. Total earnings	$200,000	$200,000	$400,000
6. Total market value	$4,000,000	$2,000,000	$6,000,000
7. Current earnings per dollar invested in stock (line 1 divided by line 2)	$0.05	$0.10	$0.067

Note: When World Enterprises purchases Muck and Slurry, there are no gains. Therefore, total earnings and total market value should be unaffected by the merger. But earnings *per share* increase. World Enterprises only issues 50,000 of its shares (priced at $40) to acquire the 100,000 Muck and Slurry shares (priced at $20).

all your eggs in that one corporate basket. You could sell off a substantial part of your shares to diversify but this could result in a large liability for capital gains tax. It may be better to merge with a firm in another line of business, and hold on to the shares of that firm. If the deal is properly structured you can defer the capital gains tax and you will have your eggs in two baskets rather than one.

The Bootstrap Game: Mergers and Earnings per Share[9]

During the 1960s some conglomerate companies made acquisitions that offered no evident economic gains. Nevertheless, the conglomerates' aggressive acquisition strategy produced several years of rising earnings per share and stock prices. To see how this can happen, let us look at the acquisition of Muck and Slurry by the well-known conglomerate World Enterprises.

The position before the merger is set out in the first two columns of Table 33-2. Notice that because Muck and Slurry has relatively poor growth prospects, its stock sells at a lower price-earnings ratio than World Enterprises (line 3). The merger, we assume, produces no economic benefits, and so the firms should be worth exactly the same together as apart. The market value of World Enterprises after the merger should be equal to the sum of the separate values of the two firms (line 6).

Since World Enterprises stock is selling for double the price of Muck and Slurry stock (line 2), World Enterprises can acquire the 100,000 Muck and Slurry shares for 50,000 of its own shares. Thus World will have 150,000 shares outstanding after the merger.

Total earnings double as a result of the merger (line 5), but the number of shares increases by only 50%. Earnings *per share* rise from $2.00 to $2.67. We call this a *bootstrap effect* because there is no real gain created by the merger and no increase in the two firms' combined value. Since stock price is unchanged, the price-earnings ratio falls (line 3).

Figure 33-1 illustrates what is going on here. Before the merger $1 invested in World Enterprises bought 5 cents of current earnings and rapid growth prospects.

---

[9] The discussion of the bootstrap game follows S.C. Myers, "A Framework for Evaluating Mergers," *op. cit.*

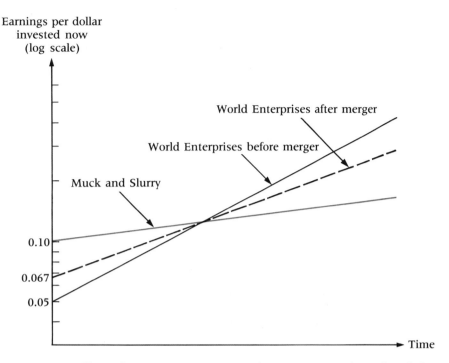

Figure 33-1 Effects of merger on earnings growth. By merging with Muck and Slurry, World Enterprises increases current earnings but accepts a slower rate of future growth. Its stockholders should be no better or worse off unless investors are fooled by the bootstrap effect.

Source: S.C. Myers, "A Framework for Evaluating Mergers," in S.C. Myers (ed.), *Modern Developments in Financial Management*, Frederick A. Praeger, Inc., New York, 1976, fig. 1, p. 639.

On the other hand, $1 invested in Muck and Slurry bought 10 cents of current earnings but slower growth prospects. If the *total* market value is not altered by the merger, then $1 invested in the merged firm gives 6.7 cents of immediate earnings. Thus, World Enterprises' shareholders see a jump in immediate earnings but slower growth, and the Muck and Slurry shareholders get lower immediate earnings but faster growth. Neither side gains or loses provided everybody understands the deal.

Financial manipulators sometimes try to ensure that the market does *not* understand the deal. Suppose that investors are fooled by the exuberant confidence of the president of World Enterprises and by plans to introduce modern management techniques into the Earth Sciences Division (formerly known as Muck and Slurry). They could easily mistake the 33% post-merger increase in earnings per share for real growth. If they do, the price of World Enterprises' stock rises and the shareholders of both companies receive something for nothing.

You should now see how to play the bootstrap, or "chain letter," game. Suppose that you manage a company enjoying a high price-earnings ratio. The reason it is high is that investors anticipate rapid growth in future earnings. You achieve this growth not by capital investment, product improvement, or increased operating efficiency, but by purchasing slow-growing firms with low price-earnings ratios. The long-run result will be slower growth and a depressed price-earnings ratio, but in the short run earnings per share can increase dramatically. If this fools investors, you may be able to achieve the higher earnings per share without suffering a decline in your price-earnings ratio. But in order to *keep* fooling investors, you must continue to expand by merger *at the same compound rate*. Obviously, you cannot do this forever; one day expansion must slow down or stop. Then earnings growth will cease, and your house of cards will fall.

This kind of game is not played much now, after investors' bitter experience with it in the 1960s. But there is still a widespread belief that you should not acquire companies with higher price-earnings ratios (*P/E*s) than your own. Of course, you know better than to believe that low-*P/E* stocks are cheap and high-*P/E* stocks are dear. If life were as simple as that, we should all be wealthy by now. Beware of false prophets who suggest that you can appraise mergers on the basis of their immediate impact on earnings per share.

Lower Financing Costs

You often hear it said that merged firms are able to borrow more cheaply than the separate units. In part this is true. We have already seen (in Section 15-4) that there are significant economies of scale in making new issues. Therefore, if firms can make fewer, larger security issues by merging, there is a genuine saving.

But when people say that borrowing costs are lower for the merged firm, they usually mean something more than lower issue costs. They mean that when two firms merge, they can borrow at lower interest rates than they could separately. This, of course, is exactly what we should expect in a well-functioning bond market. While the two firms are separate, they do not guarantee each other's debt; if one fails, the bondholder in that company cannot ask the other for money. But after the merger each enterprise effectively does guarantee the other's debt — if one part of the business fails, the bondholders can still take their money out of the other part. Because these mutual guarantees make the debt less risky, lenders demand a lower interest rate.

Does the lower interest rate mean a net gain to the merger? Not necessarily. Compare the following two situations:

1. *Separate issues*: Firm A and firm B each make a $50 million bond issue.
2. *Single issue:* Firm A and B merge and the new firm AB makes a single $100 million issue.

Of course, AB would pay a lower interest rate, other things being equal. But it does not make sense for A and B to merge just to get that lower rate. The firm's shareholders do gain from the lower rate but they lose by having to guarantee each other's debt. In other words, they get the lower interest rate only by giving bondholders better protection. There is no *net* gain.

In Sections 20-2 and 23-4 we showed that

$$\text{Bond value} = \text{bond value (assuming no chance of default)} \\ - \text{value of shareholders' (put) option to default}$$

Merger increases bond value (or reduces the interest payments necessary to support a *given* bond value) only by reducing the value of stockholders' options to default. In other words, the value of the default option for AB's $100 million issue is less than the combined values of the two default options on A and B's separate $50 million issues.

Now suppose that A and B each borrow $50 million and *then* merge. If the merger is a surprise, it will be a happy surprise for the bondholders. The bonds they thought were guaranteed by one of the two firms end up guaranteed by both. The stockholders lose, other things being equal, because they have given bondholders better protection but have received nothing for it.

There is one situation in which mergers can create value by making debt safer. In Section 18-3 we described the choice of an optimal debt ratio as a trade-off of the value of tax shields on interest payments made by the firm against the present value of possible costs of financial distress due to borrowing too much. Merging decreases the probability of financial distress, other things being equal. If it allows increased borrowing, and increased value from the interest tax shields, there will be a net gain to the merger.[10]

33-4 ESTIMATING THE COST OF A MERGER

To recapitulate: You should go ahead with a merger if the gain exceeds the cost. The gain is the difference between the value of the merged firm and the value of the separate entities.

$$\text{Gain} = PV_{AB} - (PV_A + PV_B)$$

We have looked at where these gains may come from and how to estimate them. It is now time to focus on the costs.

Estimating Cost When the Merger Is Financed by Cash

The cost of a merger is the premium that the buyer pays for the selling firm over its value as a separate entity. It is a straightforward problem to estimate cost as long as the merger is financed by cash. However, it is important to bear in mind that if investors *expect* A to acquire B, the market value of B may be a poor measure of its value as a separate entity. Thus, it may help to rewrite our formula for cost as

$$\begin{aligned} COST &= (CASH - MV_B) + (MV_B - PV_B) \\ &= \text{premium paid over market value of B} \\ &\quad + \text{difference between market value of B} \\ &\quad\quad \text{and its value as a separate entity} \end{aligned}$$

This is one of the few places in this book where we have drawn an important distinction between market value (MV) and the true or "intrinsic" value (PV) of the firm as a separate entity. The problem here is not that the market value of B is wrong, but that it may not be the value of firm B as a separate entity. Potential investors in B's stock will see two possible outcomes and two possible values:

Outcome	Value of B's Stock
1. No merger	PV_B: Value of B as a separate firm
2. Merger occurs	PV_B: *plus* some part of the benefits of the merger

If the second outcome is possible, MV_B, the stock price we observe for B, will overstate PV_B. This is exactly what *should* happen in a competitive capital market. Unfortunately, it complicates the task of a financial manager evaluating a merger.

---

[10] This merger rationale was first suggested by W.G. Lewellen, "A Pure Financial Rationale for the Conglomerate Merger," *Journal of Finance*, **26**: 521–537 (May 1971). If you want to see some of the controversy and discussion this idea led to, look at R.C. Higgins and L.D. Schall, "Corporate Bankruptcy and Conglomerate Merger," *Journal of Finance*, **30**: 93–114 (March 1975), and D. Galai and R.W. Masulis, "The Option Pricing Model and the Risk Factor of Stock," *Journal of Financial Economics*, **3**: 53–81, esp. pp. 66–69 (January–March 1976).

Here is an example. Suppose that just before the merger announcement we observe the following:

	Firm A	Firm B
Market price per share	$75	$15
Number of shares	1,000,000	600,000
Market value of firm	$75 million	$9 million

Firm A intends to pay $12 million cash for B. If B's market price reflects only its value as a separate entity, then

$$COST = (CASH - MV_B) + (MV_B - PV_B)$$
$$= (12 - 9) + (9 - 9) \text{ or } \$3 \text{ million}$$

However, suppose that B's share price has already risen $2 because of rumours of a favourable merger offer. That means MV_B overstates PV_B by $2 \times 600,000 = 1,200,000$ or $1.2 million. The true value of PV_B is only $7.8 million. Then,

$$COST = (CASH - MV_B) + (MV_B - PV_B)$$
$$= (12 - 9) + (9 - 7.8) \text{ or } \$4.2 \text{ million}$$

Notice that if the market made a mistake and the market value of B were *less* than its true value as a separate entity, the cost would be negative. In other words, B would be a *bargain* and the merger would be worthwhile from A's point of view, even if the two firms are worth no more together than apart. Of course, A's stockholders' gain would be B's stockholders' loss, because B is being sold for less than its true value.

Firms have made acquisitions just because their managers believed they had spotted a company whose intrinsic value was not fully appreciated by the stock market. However, we know from the evidence on market efficiency that, as often as not, "cheap" stocks turn out to be expensive. It is not easy for outsiders, whether investors or managers, to find firms that are truly undervalued by the market.

Of course, if the shares are bargain-priced, A doesn't need a merger to profit by its special knowledge. It can just buy up B's shares on the open market and hold them passively, waiting for other investors to wake up to B's true value.[11]

If firm A is wise, it will not go ahead with a merger if the cost exceeds the gain. Conversely, firm B will not consent to a merger if it thinks the cost is negative, for a negative cost to A means a negative gain to B. This gives us a range of possible cash payments that would allow the merger to take place. Whether the payment is at the top or the bottom of this range depends on the relative bargaining power of the two participants. For example, if A makes an acquisition solely in order to use a tax-loss carry-over, then it could equally well merge with B, C, D, or X; firm B has nothing special to offer, and its management is in no position to demand a large fraction of the gains. In this case, the cost of the merger to A is likely to be relatively low.

---

[11] However, it's hard to buy a substantial number of shares without tipping your hand. Rules governing take-over bids are determined provincially but share the common theme of providing equitable treatment to all shareholders. In Ontario, for instance, all shareholders must be sent details of take-over bids.

Estimating cost is more complicated when a merger is financed by an exchange of shares. Suppose that firm A offers 160,000 shares instead of $12 million in cash. Since A's share price before the announcement is $75 and B's market value is $9 million,[12] the cost *appears* to be

$$\text{Apparent cost} = 160{,}000 \times \$75 - \$9{,}000{,}000 = \$3{,}000{,}000$$

However, the apparent cost may not equal the true cost. Are A's shares really worth $75 each?

These shares may be worth $75 before the merger is announced but not afterwards. Suppose the merger is expected to generate cost savings worth $4.75 million:

$$\begin{aligned}\text{Gain} &= PV_{AB} - (PV_A + PV_B) \\ &= 88.75 - (75 + 9) = \$4.75 \text{ million}\end{aligned}$$

Given the gain and the terms of the deal, we can calculate share prices and market values *after* the merger is negotiated and announced. Note that the new firm will have 1,160,000 shares outstanding. Therefore:

$$\text{New Share Price} = P_{AB} = \frac{88{,}750{,}000}{1{,}160{,}000} = \$76.50$$

The true cost is:

$$\text{Cost} = (160{,}000 \times \$76.50) - \$9{,}000{,}000 = \$3{,}240{,}000$$

The true cost can also be calculated by figuring out the gain to B's shareholders. They end up with 160,000 shares or 13.8% of the new firm AB. Their gain is:

$$0.138(88{,}750{,}000) - \$9{,}000{,}000 = \$3{,}240{,}000$$

In general, if B's shareholders are given the fraction x of the combined firms,

$$\text{Cost} = xPV_{AB} - PV_B$$

We can now understand the first key distinction between cash and stock as financing instruments. If cash is offered, the cost of the merger is unaffected by the merger gains. If stock is offered, cost depends on the gains because the gains show up in the post-merger share price.

Stock financing also mitigates the effect of overvaluation or undervaluation of either firm. Suppose, for example, that A overestimates B's value as a separate entity, perhaps because it has overlooked some hidden liability. Thus, A makes too generous an offer. Other things being equal, A's stockholders are better off if it is a stock offer rather than a cash offer. With a stock offer, the inevitable bad news about B's value will fall partly on the shoulders of B's stockholders.

There is a second key difference between cash and stock financing for mergers. A's managers will usually have access to information about A's prospects that is not available to outsiders. Economists call this asymmetric information.

Suppose A's managers are more optimistic than outside investors. They may think that A's shares will really be worth $80 after the merger, rather than the

---

[12] In this case we will assume that B's market value reflects only its value as a separate firm.

$76.50 market price we just calculated. If they are right, the true cost of a stock-financed merger with B is:

$$\text{Cost} = 160,000 \times \$80 - \$9,000,000 = \$3,800,000$$

B's shareholders would get a "free gift" of $3.50 for every A share they receive—an extra gain of $3.50 × 160,000, or $560,000 in all.

Of course, if A's managers were really this optimistic, they would strongly prefer to finance the merger with cash. Financing with stock would be favoured by *pessimistic* managers who think their company's shares are *over*valued.

Does this sound like "win-win" for A—just issue shares when overvalued, cash otherwise? No, it's not that easy, because B's shareholders, and outside investors generally, understand what's going on. Suppose you are negotiating on behalf of B. You find that A's managers keep suggesting stock rather than cash financing. You quickly infer A's managers' pessimism, mark down your own opinion of what the shares are worth, and drive a harder bargain. Investors who would pay $76.50 for A shares after a cash deal might value the shares at, say, only $74 if A insists on stock financing. A would have to hand over more than 160,000 shares to get the deal done.

This asymmetric information story might explain why buying firms' share prices often fall when stock-financed mergers are announced. Asquith, Bruner, and Mullins found an average market-adjusted fall of 2.5% on the announcement of stock-financed mergers between 1973 and 1983. There was a small *gain* (0.8%) for a sample of cash-financed deals.[13]

However, this is not the case in Canada. In a study of take-overs announced between 1964 and 1982 Eckbo, Giammarino, and Heinkel found that buying firms' shares actually increased in both all-cash and all-stock offers and, in fact, all-stock offers had a *greater* average gain than all-cash offers: the announcement of cash financed take-overs resulted in an average 1.43% market-adjusted share price increase while all stock take-overs led to a 2.7% gain. However, unlike the United States, many Canadian take-overs involve offers of a mixture of cash and stock. The gain to buying firms that used 'mixed' offers was a surprisingly large 5.7%.[14]

33-5 THE MECHANICS OF A MERGER

Buying a company is a much more complicated affair than buying a piece of machinery. Thus, we should look at some of the problems encountered in arranging mergers. In practice these problems are often *extremely* complex, and specialists must be consulted. We are not trying to replace those specialists; we simply want to alert you to the kinds of legal, tax, and accounting issues they deal with.

Anti-Combines Law One subject on which you may need early advice is federal anti-combines law. From 1911 to 1986, mergers were governed by the *Combines Investigation Act* which treated combinations that were detrimental to the public interest as criminal offences. Because of the high standard of proof required for a criminal conviction, and the difficulty of introducing and interpreting economic evidence in a criminal case, the Act was ineffective. In the 75-year history of the Combines Investigation

[13] P. Asquith, R.F. Bruner, and D.W. Mullins, "Merger Returns and the Form of Financing," Working Paper, MIT Sloan School of Management, August 1990, Table 4.

[14] B.E. Eckbo, R. Giammarino, and R. Heinkel, "Asymmetric Information and the Medium of Exchange: Theory and Test," *The Review of Financial Studies 3*, (1990): 651–675.

Act only eight charges were laid, resulting in seven acquittals and one guilty plea.

On June 19, 1986 the new *Competition Act* was passed into law, replacing the *Combines Investigation Act*.[15] One of the biggest changes in the law was that anti-combines law moved from criminal to non-criminal status. With this change came a more appropriate standard against which the impact of a merger could be judged. Moreover, enforcement of the law focuses on the abuse of market power and not necessarily on size. In fact, the law explicitly includes an 'efficiency defence' which " . . . recognizes that the restructuring of an industry can, in certain circumstances, result in net benefits for the economy, even though such a merger may result in higher levels of concentration."[16] Finally, instead of presenting cases in a criminal court, the new reviewing body is a tribunal that can be made up of judges, business people, and economists.

The net result of all this seems to be a much more active system of merger regulation. Companies planning a merger must report to the Bureau of Competition Policy which reviews the case. Often, alterations to the merger are made during the review process. In cases where agreement cannot be reached between the competition watch dog and the merging parties, the potential merger might be dropped or the case might be referred to the tribunal. The greater regulatory power contained in the new law is reflected in the fact that potential buyers now often talk to the Bureau of Competition Policy before they talk to the firm they wish to acquire. Moreover, in contrast to the one conviction in the 75-year history of the *Combines Investigation Act*, in the first nine months of operation under the new Act 2 cases were heard by the Tribunal, 5 proposed transactions were dropped, and 21 proceeded following negotiation between the Bureau and the firms involved.[17]

The Form of Acquisition

Let us suppose that you have been advised that the purchase of company B would not be challenged by the Bureau of Competition Policy. The next thing you will want to consider is the best way to effect the acquisition. You have the following choices.

Statutory Amalgamation or Merger   We have been using the term *merger* to indicate *any* combination of two companies, but this convention is too broad in the legal sense. In Canada, a merger or, more precisely, a *statutory amalgamation* refers to the case where all of the assets and all of the liabilities of the selling company are transferred to, and absorbed by, the buying corporation, and where the selling company disappears as a separate entity. It also applies to the case where an entirely new corporation is formed and both selling entities disappear.[18]

In a merger the buyer automatically assumes *all* the assets and *all* the liabilities of the seller, and so the mechanics of a merger are comparatively simple. This is an advantage. For example, it is not necessary to transfer separate title to each individual asset.

---

[15] For an excellent discussion of the structure of the new Act see C.S. Goldman "Corporate Concentration and Canada's New Competition Act," in R.S. Khemani, D.M. Shapiro, and W.T. Stanbury, eds., *Mergers Corporate Concentration and Power in Canada*, The Institute for Research on Public Policy, Halifax: 489–503, 1988.

[16] Goldman, *op. cit.*

[17] Goldman, *op. cit.*

[18] In the United States, the term *merger* refers to the case where one of the firms continues to exist and the term *amalgamation* or consolidation is reserved for the case where an entirely new entity is formed.

However, there are drawbacks to merger. The automatic assumption of liabilities places a greater onus on the buyer to ensure that no liabilities have been overlooked; after the two firms have merged, there is no one to whom the buyer can complain if a mistake has been made. The complete absorption of the seller also requires broad agreement among shareholders. Under the various federal and provincial business corporations acts, a merger must have the approval of a required majority (usually two-thirds or three-quarters) of the stockholders. Even with majority approval, however, the acts also provide dissenting shareholders with the right to challenge the merger agreement in court if they feel the price per share is below "fair value."

Acquisition of Stock   The essential feature of a merger is that the buyer acquires all the seller's assets and all its liabilities. An alternative procedure is for the buyer to purchase the seller's stock in exchange for cash, shares, or other securities issued by the buyer.[19] Generally speaking, the mechanics of such an exchange are simple. However, since the buyer's post-purchase holdings of the selling company's shares are expected to exceed 20% of the voting shares, the purchase is labelled a "take-over bid" and must comply with provincial securities act rules that are designed to ensure equitable treatment of the selling firm's shareholders.[20] In Ontario, for example, the take-over bid rules require, among other things, that the buying company send the details of the take-over bid to all shareholders of the selling company.

There is one major disadvantage in acquiring a firm by buying up its stock. As long as Aunt Agatha holds out and refuses to sell her ten shares, the two businesses cannot be completely integrated. Complete integration requires a further step—a formal amalgamation.

Acquisition of Assets   A third approach is to buy the seller's assets. Payment is made to the selling *firm* (not directly to its stockholders). The payment can be in the form of cash, the buyer's shares, or other securities issued by the buyer. The selling company can then, if it chooses, dissolve itself. If it does so, the receipts from the sale of its assets are paid out to its stockholders.

In this approach the buyer acquires individual, specific assets. (The buyer may also assume specific liabilities.) Thus, the buyer can acquire only part of the seller's business, and can be more confident of *not* acquiring a hidden liability. Also, since the buyer is acquiring property rather than a share interest in property, the buyer does not have to worry about having minority shareholders. Although federal and provincial business corporation acts go some way in protecting shareholders who are unhappy about the sale of assets, they do not require the same degree of acquiescence by shareholders as they do in mergers. For example, there is usually no need for specific approval from the buyer's shareholders, and typically it is necessary to obtain only a 50% vote of the seller's shareholders. Neither group of shareholders can force an independent valuation of the acquired assets.

But the acquisition of assets also has disadvantages. First, the courts may hold that a particular exchange is effectively a merger and, therefore, require additional attention to the rights of the selling shareholders. A second problem is that

[19] S. Martin, "Business Combinations in Canada: 1960–1968," in D. Morin and W. Chippindale, eds., *Acquisitions and Mergers in Canada*, Methuen, Toronto, 1970 reported that 80% of acquisitions in Canada were through acquisition of shares.

[20] All of the rules regarding take-over bids in Ontario are presented in sections 88 through 100 of the Securities Act, 1978 in *Ontario Securities Legislation*, CCH Clearinghouse Limited, 1980.

Table 33-3
**Purchasing versus pooling in the merger of A Corporation and B Corporation
(figures in millions of dollars)**

Initial Balance Sheets								
A Corporation				B Corporation				
NWC	2.0	3.0	D	NWC	0.1	0	D
FA	8.0	7.0	E	FA	0.9	1.0	E
	10.0	10.0			1.0	1.0	

Balance Sheets of AB Corporation				
	AB Corporation			
Under pooling of interests:	NWC	2.1	3.0	D
	FA	8.9	8.0	E
		11.0	11.0	
	AB Corporation			
Under purchase accounting, assuming that	NWC	2.1	3.0	D
A Corporation pays $1.8 million for	FA	8.9	8.8	E
B Corporation:	Goodwill	0.8		
		11.8	11.8	

Key:
NWC = Net working capital
FA   = Net book value of fixed assets
D   = Debt
E   = Book value of equity

transferring assets individually is likely to create additional legal and administrative costs.

A Note on Merger Accounting

Mergers sometimes raise complex accounting issues. One such issue is whether a merger should be treated as a *purchase of assets* or as a *pooling of interests*.[21] In efficient capital markets, the choice between these two methods should make no difference whatsoever, but the *CICA Handbook*, Section 1580.18, recommends that the " . . . purchase method should be used to account for all business combinations, except for those rare transactions where an acquirer cannot be identified."

The essential differences between the two methods are illustrated in Table 33-3. The table shows what happens when A Corporation buys B Corporation, leading to a new AB Corporation. The two firms' initial (book) balance sheets are shown at the top of the table. The next balance sheet shown is AB Corporation's under *pooling of interest*. Note that this is nothing more than the two firms' separate balance sheets added together.

The final balance sheet shows what happens when purchase accounting is used. We assume that B Corporation has been purchased for $1.8 million, 180% of book value.

---

[21] When two or more companies join through an exchange of voting shares in which none of the companies can be identified as the acquirer, a *new entity* has been created. Under the new entity method, the assets and liabilities are combined in the new entity's financial statements at fair value. See Section 1580.10 of the *CICA Handbook*.

Why did A Corporation pay an $800,000 premium over book value? There are two possible reasons. First, the true values of A's *tangible assets*—its working capital, plant, and equipment—may be greater than $1 million. We will assume this is *not* the reason; that is, we assume the assets listed on its balance sheet are valued there correctly.[22] Second, A Corporation may be paying for *intangible* assets that are not listed on B Corporation's balance sheet. The intangible asset may be a promising product or technology developed by B Corporation, for example. Or it may be no more than B Corporation's share of the economic gains of the merger.

Under the purchase method of accounting, A Corporation is viewed as buying an asset worth $1.8 million—as indeed it is. The problem is how to show that asset on the left-hand side of AB Corporation's balance sheet. B Corporation's tangible assets are worth only $1 million. This leaves $0.8 million. The accountant takes care of this by creating a new asset category called *goodwill* and assigning $0.8 million to it.

All this is somewhat arbitrary, but reasonable enough. Intangible assets do have value, and so there's no reason such assets shouldn't be shown on the balance sheet when a firm buys them.

Nevertheless, most managers prefer to pool when they can. The reason is that goodwill has to be amortized over a period not exceeding 40 years, and the periodic amortization charges have to be deducted from reported income. Thus, AB Corporation's reported income will be reduced by at least $800,000/40 = $20,000 each year. Under pooling, goodwill never appears, and so reported income is at least $20,000 higher.

Now all this has absolutely no cash consequences. The amortization charges are *not* cash outflows and they are not tax-deductible expenses. Thus, the choice between purchase and pooling should have no effect on the value of the merged firms.

Hong, Mandelker, and Kaplan tested this proposition by looking at a sample of 159 acquisitions made between 1954 and 1964, a period in which there were fewer restrictions on pooling than there are now.[23] They found no evidence that acquiring firms did better under pooling than under purchase accounting.

Some Tax Considerations

An acquisition may be either taxable or tax-free. In a taxable acquisition, the selling stockholders are treated, for tax purposes, as having *sold* their shares, and they must report any capital gains or losses on their income tax forms. In a tax-free acquisition, the selling shareholders are viewed as *exchanging* their old shares for essentially similar new ones; no capital gains or losses are recognized.

The tax status of the acquisition also affects the taxes paid by the firm afterwards. After a tax-free acquisition, the firm is taxed as if the two firms had always been together. In a taxable acquisition, the assets of the selling firm are revalued and the depreciation deductible for tax purposes is recalculated.

---

[22] If the assets were worth more than their previous book values, they would be reappraised and their current values entered on AB Corporation's balance sheet. Goodwill (see below) would be decreased by an amount equal to the write-up of tangible assets.

[23] H. Hong, G. Mandelker, and R.S. Kaplan, "Pooling vs. Purchase: The Effects of Accounting for Mergers on Stock Prices," *Accounting Review*, **53**: 31–47 (January 1978). The requirements for pooling were tightened in 1970 by the Accounting Principles Board of the American Institute of Certified Public Accountants. The requirements are set out in Opinions No. 16 and No. 17 of the board (New York, 1970). The opinions state, among other requirements for pooling, that the seller's stockholders must remain stockholders of the merged firm, and that the buyer must finance the merger by exchanging its common stock for at least 90% of the seller's shares.

A very simple example will illustrate these distinctions. In 1992 Captain B forms Seacorp, which purchases a fishing boat for $300,000. The boat is depreciated for tax purposes over 20 years on a straight-line basis (no salvage value). Thus, annual depreciation is $300,000/20 = $15,000, and in 2002 the boat has a net book value of $150,000.

But in 2002 Captain B finds that, owing to inflation, careful maintenance, and good times in the fishing industry, the boat is really worth $280,000. In addition, Seacorp holds $50,000 of marketable securities.

Now suppose that Captain B sells the firm to Baycorp for $330,000. The possible tax consequences of the acquisition are as shown in the accompanying table.

	Taxable	Tax-Free
1. Impact on Captain B	Captain B must recognize a $30,000 capital gain	Capital gain can be deferred until Captain B sells the Baycorp shares
2. Impact on Baycorp	Boat is revalued at $280,000; annual depreciation increases to $280,000/10 = $28,000 (assuming ten years of remaining life)	Boat's value remains at $150,000, and depreciation at $15,000 per year

Captain B is better off with a tax-free deal, because capital gains taxes can be deferred. Baycorp, on the other hand, should prefer a taxable deal because depreciation tax shields are higher.

It should be clear from these remarks that tax-free status is not an unmitigated blessing and that there can often be a divergence of interests between the buying corporation and the selling stockholders. The latter will generally prefer a tax-free arrangement if they are showing a profit on their original investment; they will prefer a taxable arrangement if they are showing a loss. Correspondingly, the buying corporation will prefer a taxable arrangement if the current values of depreciable assets are substantially larger than their depreciable values in the hands of the seller.

Requirements for Tax-Free Status

We have not yet told you what determines whether an acquisition is tax-free. The basic requirement is that the selling stockholders receive common or preferred shares in the surviving corporation. The detailed rules for each form of acquisition are somewhat more complex, but they are sketched below:[24]

- **Amalgamation or merger** To establish tax-free status for a merger, all of the property of the selling corporation must become the property of the buying corporation; all of the liabilities of the selling corporation must become the liabilities of the buying corporation; and, all of the shareholders of the selling corporation must become shareholders in the buying corporation.
- **Acquisition of stock** When the shares of the selling firm are acquired, it will be treated as tax-free only if payment is *entirely* in the form of the buying corporation's shares and only if, immediately after the acquisition, the buyer has 10% of the voting shares of the selling corporation. Also, prior to the

---

[24] For a readable discussion of the roll-over tax treatment of amalgamations and share-for-share exchanges, see Chapter 15 of I.G. Riehl and G.W. Riehl, *Incorporation and Income Tax in Canada*, CCH Canadian Limited, 1984.

exchange, the buying and selling companies must be dealing with each other "at arm's length," and the selling company must not control or own more than 50% of the shares of the buying company.

- **Acquisition of assets**   A tax-free exchange of assets for shares is a trickier proposition, but, under certain conditions,[25] it may be possible. Again, the payment must be entirely in the form of the buying corporation's shares.

The discussion above is the last point in this chapter where we will need to distinguish the three ways of arranging a combination of two firms. Henceforth, we will relapse into using the word *merger* in its everyday sense to refer to any combination of two firms into one.

33-6   MERGER TACTICS

Many mergers are agreed upon by both parties, but in other cases the acquirer will go over the heads of the target firm's management and appeal directly to its stockholders. There are two ways of doing this. First, it can seek the support of the target firm's stockholders at its next annual meeting. This is called a *proxy fight* because the right to vote someone else's share is called a *proxy*.[26]

Proxy fights are expensive and difficult to win. The alternative is for the would-be acquirer to make a *tender offer* directly to the shareholders. The management of the target firm may advise its shareholders to accept the tender or it may attempt to fight the bid.

Tender battles resemble a complex game of poker. The rules are set mostly by provincial securities regulations, federal competition policy, and the Courts. We will return to the game and its rules after looking at one classic contest.

Merger Negotiations and Battles   Consider the acquisition of Cities Service in 1982.[27] Cities is a leading U.S. oil producer that holds a 13.2% interest in the Syncrude Oil Sands project in Northern Alberta.

The Fight for Cities Service   The battle for Cities began in May when Boone Pickens, the chairman of Mesa Petroleum, began buying Cities shares as preparation for a take-over bid. Foreseeing the bid, Cities made an issue of equity that diluted Mesa's holding and followed this up with a retaliatory offer for Mesa.[28] Over the following month Mesa's bid was revised once and Cities' bid was revised twice before both companies agreed to drop their bids for one another. Cities repurchased Mesa's holdings — at a $80 million profit to Mesa — and in exchange Mesa agreed not to attempt a hostile take-over of Cities for 5 years.

The principal reason for the cessation of hostilities between Mesa and Cities was the announcement that Cities had found a more congenial partner in Gulf Oil. Also, Gulf was prepared to pay substantially more than Mesa for Cities' stock.

---

[25] The technical rules for such exchanges are provided in subsection 85(1) of the *Income Tax Act*.

[26] Peter Dodd and Jerrold Warner have written a detailed description and analysis of proxy fights. See "On Corporate Governance: A Study of Proxy Contexts," *Journal of Financial Economics*, **11**: 401–438 (April 1985).

[27] The Cities Service take-over is described in R.S. Ruback, "The Cities Service Takeover: A Case Study," *Journal of Finance*, **38**: 319–330 (May 1983).

[28] This practice of defending yourself against a merger by making a counterbid for the predator's stock is sometimes known as the "Pacman defence."

Unfortunately, this proposal fell afoul of the Federal Trade Commission (FTC), which issued a temporary restraining order. Shortly thereafter, Gulf withdrew its offer.

In response, Cities charged Gulf with not attempting to resolve the FTC's objections and it filed a $3 billion lawsuit against Gulf. At the same time it began to look for another *white knight* who would take it over. The only interested suitor was Occidental Petroleum. Occidental's initial offer for Cities was revised twice and finally accepted. The battle for Cities Service had lasted 3 months and involved a total of nine bids from four separate companies.

Many of these bids consisted of a *two-tier offer*. For example, Occidental's final offer for Cities consisted of a tender offer of $55 a share for 45% of the stock, followed by a package of fixed-income securities worth about $40 a share for the remaining stock. In effect, Occidental was saying, "Last one through the door does the washing up," since there was a big advantage in selling for cash rather than waiting for the securities. The plan worked, for almost all Cities' stockholders rushed to take advantage of the cash offer, and Occidental gained control.

In several instances the bidders employed both carrot and stick; for example. Occidental followed up its initial friendly offer for Cities with a hostile tender offer before finally reaching a friendly agreement.

The generous Gulf offer would have provided Cities' shareholders with a cumulative profit of almost 80%, but the collapse of that offer and the shortage of other suitors caused Cities' stock price to lose all its earlier gains. From then on Cities was in a relatively weak bargaining position and the Occidental offer resulted in a profit of only 12% for Cities' stockholders. The merger scarcely affected Occidental's stock price, which suggests that investors believed the merger to be a zero-NPV investment. Gulf's stockholders fared the worst. Its high-priced offer led to a 14% fall in the price of Gulf stock. Even though this offer was subsequently withdrawn, the prospect of a costly lawsuit left Gulf's stock price depressed.

As with many real-life stories, there is an epilogue. One year after losing its battle for Cities, Gulf itself became a take-over target, when Mesa Petroleum proposed to buy Gulf stock in order to break the company up and sell it in pieces. At this point Chevron came to the rescue and acquired Gulf for $13.2 billion, more than double its value of 6 months earlier. Chevron's bid gave Mesa a profit of $760 million on the Gulf shares that it had bought. Asked for his views, Pickens commented, "Shucks, I guess we lost another one."

Is It Better to Sell Than Buy?

Though Cities' stockholders gained "only" 12%, they still did better than Occidental's or Gulf's stockholders. In mergers, is it better for stockholders to sell than to buy?

In general, yes although how much better off shareholders are seems to depend on whether or not the take-over occurs in Canada or the United States.

Eckbo looked at the abnormal returns to almost 1,700 buying firms and over 400 selling firms in take-overs that occurred between 1964 and 1983.[29] Figure 33-2 summarizes the results of the study which shows that the selling firms did better than the buying firms during the 24-month period around the announcement of the take-over, although both buyers and sellers experienced significant increases in wealth. (Note also how much of this gain occurs before press day.

---

[29] B.E. Eckbo, "Mergers and the Market For Corporate Control: the Canadian Evidence," *Canadian Journal of Economics,* **19**: 236–260 (May 1986).

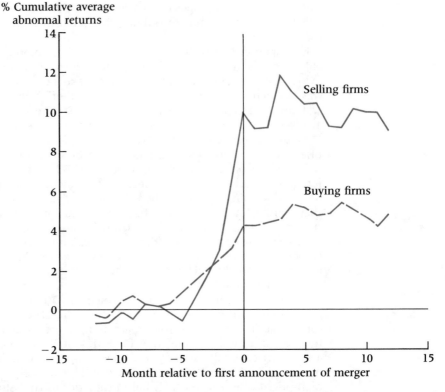

Figure 33-2   Eckbo's study shows that both selling firms and buying firms in Canada experience gains from takeovers, although the gains to selling firms are larger.

Source: B.E. Eckbo, "Mergers and the Market For Corporate Control: the Canadian Evidence," *Canadian Journal of Economics,* **19**: 236–260 (May 1986).

Investors anticipate the announcement of the acquisition and the good news it brings.)

Eckbo's study is notable both because it provides a comprehensive examination of Canadian merger activity and because it provides evidence that both buying and selling firms seem to gain from take-overs. This is quite different from the evidence that had been obtained by studying takeovers in the United States.

For instance, Figure 33-3 summarizes the results of a study by Asquith of about 200 mergers during the period 1962 to 1976. The study tracked abnormal returns to shareholders over 120-day periods centred on the press dates when the acquisitions were first announced. You can see that selling stockholders received a healthy gain. On the other hand the acquiring companies' stockholders gained much less. On average, it appears that investors expect acquiring companies to just about break even.[30]

Asquith's study is one of dozens on the gains to acquiring firms and targets in contests for corporate control. Jensen and Ruback reviewed these studies,[31] find-

---

[30] The small initial gain to the shareholders of acquiring firms is not statistically significant, although most researchers observe a similar small positive return.

[31] See M.C. Jensen and R.S. Ruback, "The Market for Corporate Control: The Scientific Evidence," *Journal of Financial Economics,* **11**: 5–50 (April 1983).

Average cumulative excess returns on stock

Figure 33-3   Asquith's study confirms that selling firms receive substantial premiums. Stockholders of buying firms roughly break even. *Note:* The cumulative returns are adjusted to remove price fluctuations attributable to movements of the overall stock market.

Source: P. Asquith, "Merger Bids, Uncertainty, and Stockholder Returns," *Journal of Financial Economics*, **11**: 51–83 (April 1983), figures 1 and 2, pp. 62–63.

ing positive abnormal returns to acquiring firms' shareholders of only about 4% in tender offers and no gains at all in mergers. Selling stockholders, on the other hand, gained 30% in tender offers and 20% in mergers. (Of course, these are averages; sometimes returns are much higher. When DuPont acquired Conoco in 1981, it paid a premium of 81%, of $3 billion, for Conoco stock.[32])

How do we explain the conflicting evidence? There are two possible explanations. First, buyers in the United States are typically much larger than sellers whereas in Eckbo's study of Canada they were about the same size. In mergers where the buyer is bigger it might be that they are so much larger that even substantial net benefits would not show up clearly in the buyers' share price. Suppose, for example, that company A buys another company B which is only one-tenth A's size. Suppose the dollar value of the net gain to the merger is split equally between A and B.[33] Each company's shareholders receive the same *dollar* profit, but B's receive ten times A's *percentage* return.

A second reason is that competition among potential bidders may actually be keeping the gains to buyers down. Once the first bidder puts the target company "in play," one or more additional suitors often jump in, sometimes as *white knights* at the invitation of the target firm's management. Every time one suitor tops

---

[32] Presumably Du Pont foresaw gains worth more than $3 billion, but it is not easy to spot where they were likely to come from. The two companies were in different industries, and Du Pont did not plan to change Conoco's management or to merge any part of its operations. The merger led to a fall of $800 million in the value of Du Pont stock, so presumably investors thought that the merger created more than $2 billion of additional value. For an interesting account of the Du Pont-Conoco merger, see R.S. Ruback, "The Conoco Takeover and Stockholder Returns," *Sloan Management Review*, **23**: 13–33 (Winter 1982).

[33] In other words, the *cost* of the merger to A is one-half the gain ΔV_{AB}.

another's bid, more of the merger gain slides toward the target. At the same time the target firm's management may mount various legal and financial counterattacks, insuring that capitulation, if and when it comes, is at the highest attainable price. Hence, it may be that competition among bidders in the United States is more significant.

Of course, bidders and targets are not the only possible winners. Unsuccessful bidders often win too by selling off their holdings in target companies at substantial profits. Such shares may be sold on the open market or sold back to the target company in a *greenmail* transaction. Sometimes they are sold to the successful suitor. We saw how Mesa Petroleum earned $80 million by selling its Cities Service shares back to Cities Service, and $760 million by selling its Gulf stock to Chevron, the winning bidder.

Other winners include investment bankers, lawyers and accountants, and in some cases arbitrageurs, or "arbs," who speculate on the likely success of take-over bids.[34]

"Speculate" has a negative ring, but it can be a useful social service. A tender offer may present shareholders with a difficult decision. Should they accept, should they wait to see if someone else produces a better offer, or should they sell their stock in the market? This dilemma presents an opportunity for the arbs. In other words, they buy from the target's shareholders and take on the risk that the deal will not go through.

Of course, as Ivan Boesky demonstrated, arbs can make even more money if they learn about the offer *before* it is publicly announced. Because arbitrageurs may accumulate large amounts of stock, they can have an important effect on whether a deal goes through, and the bidding company or its investment bankers may be tempted to take the arbitrageurs into their confidence. This is the point at which a legitimate and useful activity shades into an illegal and harmful one.

Take-over Defences

The Cities Service case illustrates several tactics managers use to fight take-over bids. Frequently, they don't wait for a bid before taking defensive action. Instead, they deter potential bidders by devising *poison pills* that make their companies unappetizing, or they persuade shareholders to agree to *shark repellent* changes to the company charter. Table 33-4 summarizes the principal first and second levels of defence.

Why do managers contest take-over bids? One reason is to extract a higher price from the bidder. Another possible reason is that managers believe their jobs may be at risk in the merged company. These managers are not trying to obtain a better price; they want to stop the bid altogether.

Some companies reduce these conflicts of interest by offering their managers *golden parachutes* — that is, generous payoffs if they lose their jobs as the results of a take-over. Sometimes these payoffs can be very large; for example, in 1989 Canadian Pacific put golden parachutes in place for their managers estimated to be worth $30 million.[35] It may seem odd to reward managers for being taken

---

[34] Strictly speaking, an arbitrageur refers to an investor who takes a fully hedged, that is, riskless position. Arbitrageurs in merger battles often take very large risks indeed. Their activities are sometimes known as "risk arbitrage."

[35] See Deirdre McMurdy, "Canadian Executives Savour Poison Pills," *Globe and Mail Report on Business*, Saturday April 7, 1990.

Table 33-4
A summary of take-over defences

Type of Defence	Description
Preoffer defences	
Shark repellent charter amendments:	
Staggered board	Board is classified into three equal groups. Only one group is elected each year. Therefore, bidder cannot obtain control of the target immediately after obtaining majority.
Supermajority Fair price	High percentage of shares needed to approve a merger usually 80%. Restricts mergers with shareholders owning more than specified percentage of outstanding shares unless fair price (determined by formula or appraisal) is paid.
Other:	
Poison pills	Existing shareholders are issued rights which, if there is a significant purchase of shares by a bidder, can be used to purchase the company's common stock at a bargain price, usually half the market price. In the case of a merger, the rights can be used to buy shares of the acquiring firm.
Dual class recapitalization	Distributes a new class of equity with superior voting rights. Allows target's managers to obtain a majority vote without owning a majority of shares.
Postoffer defences	
Pacman defence	Make counterbid for stock of bidder.
Litigation	File suit against bidder for violating antitrust or securities laws.
Asset restructuring	Buy assets that bidder does not want or that will create antitrust problem. Sell the "crown jewels," i.e., assets that bidder wants.
Liability restructuring	Issue shares to a friendly third party or increase number of shareholders. Repurchase shares from existing shareholders at a premium.

Source: This table is loosely adapted from R.S. Ruback, "An Overview of Takeover Defenses," Working Paper No. 1836–86. Sloan School of Management, MIT, September 1986, tables 1 and 2. See also L. Herzel and R.W. Shepro, *Bidders and Targets: Mergers and Acquisitions in the U.S.*, Basil Blackwell, Inc., Cambridge, MA, Chapter 8, 1990.

over. However, if it overcomes their opposition to take-over bids, even $30 million may be a small price to pay.[36]

Defensive tactics such as poison pills have been more common in the United States than they have been in Canada. In fact the first poison pill in Canada was one introduced by Inco in 1989. During the following year, however, 20 companies introduced plans to implement a poison pill but these plans were not enthusiastically welcomed by shareholders. In fact, pressure from institutional investors caused Canadian Pacific, Dofasco, and Moore Corp. to water down their poison pills.

Any management that tries to develop improved weapons of defence must expect challenges from shareholders, both informally and in the courts. In the

---

[36] Of course, excessively lavish parachutes may have the opposite effect and cause managers to throw themselves into the arms of almost any suitor.

early 1980s the courts tended to give managers the benefit of the doubt and respect their business judgement about whether a take-over should be resisted. But the courts' attitudes to take-over battles are changing. For example, they have ruled against some poison pills on the grounds that they discriminate against major shareholders. Also, they have forced directors of the target company to "determine, seek, and obtain maximum value for its shareholders."[37] As a result, managers have become much more careful in opposing bids and do not throw themselves blindly into the arms of just any white knight.

At the same time governments, especially in the United States, have provided some new defensive weapons. In 1987 the U.S. Supreme Court upheld a state law that allows companies to deprive an investor of voting rights as soon as the investor's share in the company exceeds a certain level. Since then, state antitake-over laws have proliferated. Many allow boards of directors to block mergers with hostile bidders for several years, and to consider the interests of employees, customers, suppliers, and their communities in deciding whether to try to block a hostile bid.

New laws, legal challenges, and antitake-over devices will keep cropping up. All we can say is, "Stay tuned." However, there is one further take-over defence that we haven't yet mentioned. Here is the story of how Phillips Petroleum restructured its balance sheet to keep its independence.

Phillips Restructures to Stave Off Take-over

The main protagonist is once again—you guessed it—Boone Pickens of Mesa Petroleum. In 1982 Mesa had been involved in a battle for General American Oil Co. (GAO) but had dropped its bid when GAO agreed to sell out to Phillips Petroleum. Two years later Mesa bought 6% of Phillips stock at an average price of $38 a share and then bid for a further 15% at $60 a share.

Phillips responded in three ways.[38] First, it agreed to buy back Mesa's holding, giving Mesa a profit on the deal of $89 million.[39] Second, it raised its dividend by 25%, reduced capital spending, and announced a program to sell $2 billion of assets. Third, it agreed to repurchase about 50% of its stock and to issue instead $4.5 billion of debt. Table 33-5 shows how this leveraged repurchase changed Phillips's balance sheet. The new debt ratio was about 80%, and book equity shrunk by $5 billion to $1.6 billion.

This massive debt burden put Phillips on a strict cash diet. It was forced to sell assets and pinch pennies wherever possible. Capital expenditures were cut back from $1,065 million in 1985 to $646 million in 1986. In the same years, the number of employees fell from 25,300 to 21,800.

---

[37] In *Edelman v. Fruehauf Corporation*, 1986. No. 86 CV 71332 DT, unpublished transcript at 22 (E.D. Mich. July 24, 1986). In 1985 a shiver ran through many boardrooms when the directors of Trans Union Corporation were held personally liable for being too hasty in accepting a take-over bid. Changes in judicial attitudes to take-over defences are reviewed in L. Herzel and R.W. Shepro, *Bidders and Targets: Mergers and Acquisitions in the U.S.*, Basil Blackwell, Inc., Cambridge, MA, 1990.

[38] Phillips also devised a poison pill that would make it a less appetizing morsel for future predators. This poison pill gave shareholders the right to exchange their stock for notes worth $62 a share if anyone bought 30% or more of Phillips's stock. (The purchaser who triggered this provision would not be entitled to any of the notes.)

[39] Phillips's move to deter Mesa by buying out its holding at a premium is another example of greenmail. But giving in to greenmail can be dangerous, as Phillips soon discovered. Just six weeks later a group led by another corporate raider, Carl Icahn, acquired nearly 5% of Phillips's stock and made an offer to buy the remainder. Phillips responded with a second greenmail payment: it bought out Icahn and his pals, giving them a profit of about $35 million.

Table 33-5
Phillips's balance sheet was dramatically changed by its leveraged repurchase (figures in billions)

	1985	1984		1985	1984
Current assets	$ 3.1	$ 4.6	Current liabilities	$ 3.1	$ 5.3
Fixed assets	10.3	11.2	Long-term debt	6.5	2.8
Other	0.6	1.2	Other long-term liabilities	2.8	2.3
			Equity	1.6	6.6
Total assets	$14.0	$17.0	Total liabilities	$14.0	$17.0

Austerity continued through the late 1980s. By the end of the decade long-term debt was reduced to $3.9 billion, and Phillips had regained an investment-grade debt rating. Employment was steady and capital expenditures gradually increasing, although not to the levels of the early 1980s. Phillips emerged from the decade leaner, but healthy and still independent.

Why did this restructuring shield Phillips from take-over? Certainly not by making purchase of the company more expensive — on the contrary, restructuring drastically reduced the total market value of Phillips's outstanding stock and, therefore, reduced the likely cost of buying out its remaining shareholders.

But restructuring removed the chief *motive* for take-over, which was to force Phillips to generate and pay out more cash to investors. Before the restructuring, investors sensed that Phillips was not running a tight ship, and worried that it would plow back its ample operating cash flow into mediocre capital investments or ill-advised expansion. They wanted Phillips to pay out its free cash flow rather than let it be soaked up by a too-comfortable organization or plowed into negative-NPV investments. Consequently, Phillips's share price did not reflect the potential value of its assets and operations. *That* created the opportunity for a take-over. One can almost hear the potential raider thinking:

> So what if I have to pay a 30 or 40% premium to take over Phillips? I can borrow most of the purchase price, and then pay off the loan by selling surplus assets, cutting out all but the best capital investments, and wringing out slack in the organization. It'll be a rough few years, but if surgery's necessary, I might as well be the doctor and get paid for doing it.

Phillips management did not agree that the company was slack or prone to overinvestment. Nevertheless, they bowed to pressure from the stock market and undertook the surgery themselves. They paid out billions to repurchase stock and to service the $6.5 billion in long-term debt. They sold assets, cut back capital investment, and put their organization on the diet investors were calling for.

When the merger motive is to eliminate inefficiency or distribute excess cash, the target's best defence is to do what the bidder would do, and thus avoid the cost, confusion, and random casualties of a take-over battle.

Divestitures and Spin-offs

Firms not only acquire businesses; they also sell them. In recent years the number of divestitures has been about a third of the number of mergers. Many of them are a consequence of merger; others result from the threat of merger.

Instead of selling a business to another firm, companies may spin off a subsidiary by distributing its stock to the shareholders of the parent company. Some spin-offs have tax or regulatory advantages. Others may widen investor choice by allowing them to invest directly in just one part of the business. However, probably the most frequent motive for spin-offs is that they improve efficiency. Companies sometimes refer to a business as being a "poor fit." By spinning it off, the management of the parent company can concentrate on its main activity. If each business must stand on its own feet, there is no risk that funds will be siphoned off from one in order to support unprofitable investments in the other. Moreover, if the two parts of the business are independent, it is easy to see the value of each and to reward managers accordingly.

It seems that corporate spin-offs have been well received in Canada. Burnie, Gunay, and Kleiman looked at the stock market reaction to 97 spin-off announcements in Canada between 1981 and 1986. They found that shareholders experienced on abnormal return of 1.6% over the two days ending with the announcement day.[40]

33-7 LBOs

LBOs, or leveraged buyouts, differ from ordinary acquisitions in two ways. First, a large fraction of the purchase price is debt-financed. Some, perhaps all, of this debt is junk, that is, below investment grade. Second, the shares of the LBO no longer trade on the open market.[41] The remaining equity in the LBO is privately held by a small group of (usually institutional) investors. When this group is led by the company's management, the acquisition is called a *MBO*, or *management buyout*.

In the 1970s and 1980s many management buyouts were arranged for unwanted divisions of large, diversified companies. Smaller divisions outside the companies' main lines of business often lacked top management's interest and commitment, and divisional management chafed under corporate bureaucracy. Many such divisions flowered when spun off as MBOs. Their managers, encouraged by a substantial personal stake in the business, found ways to cut costs and compete more effectively.

In the 1980s MBO/LBO activity shifted to buyouts of entire businesses, including large, mature public corporations. We will start with the largest, most dramatic, and best documented LBO of them all: the $25 billion U.S. take-over of RJR Nabisco in 1988 by Kohlberg, Kravis, and Roberts (KKR). The players, tactics, and controversies of LBOs are writ large in this case.

RJR Nabisco On October 28th, 1988, the Board of Directors of RJR Nabisco revealed that Ross Johnson, the company's Chief Executive Officer, had formed a group of investors prepared to buy all of RJR's stock for $75 per share in cash and take the company private. Johnson's group was backed up and advised by Shearson Lehman Hutton, the investment bank subsidiary of American Express.

RJR's share price immediately moved to about $75, handing shareholders a one-day 36% gain over the previous day's price of $56. At the same time RJR's bonds fell, as it was clear that existing bondholders would soon have a lot more company.[42]

[40] D.A. Burnie, E. Gunay, and R.J. Kleiman, "The Wealth Effects of Voluntary Corporate Divestitures," *Proceedings of the Administrative Sciences Association of Canada, Finance Division*, 1989.

[41] Sometimes a small "stub" of shares is left over and continues to trade.

[42] N. Mohan and C.R. Chen track the abnormal returns of RJR securities in "A Review of the RJR-Nabisco Buyout," *Journal of Applied Corporate Finance*, **3**: 102–108 (Summer 1990).

Johnson's offer lifted RJR onto the auction block. Once the company was in play, its Board of Directors was obliged to consider other offers—which were not long coming. Four days later Kohlberg, Kravis, and Roberts (KKR) bid $90 per share, $79 in cash plus PIK preferred valued at $11. ("PIK" means "pay in kind." The preferred dividends would be paid not in cash, but in more preferred shares.[43])

The resulting bidding contest had as many turns and surprises as a Dickens novel. RJR's board set up a Committee of Independent Directors, advised by the investment bank Lazard Freres, to set rules for the bidding. Financial projections for RJR were made available to KKR and another bidding group put together by First Boston.

The bidding finally closed on November 30, 32 days after the initial offer was revealed. In the end, it was Johnson's group against KKR. KKR offered $109 per share, after adding $1 per share (roughly $230 million) in the last hour.[44] The KKR bid was $81 in cash, convertible subordinated debentures valued at about $10, and PIK preferred shares valued at about $18. Johnson's group bid $112 in cash and securities.

But the RJR board chose KKR. True, Johnson's group had offered $3 per share more, but its security valuations were viewed as "softer" and perhaps overstated. Also, KKR's planned asset sales were less drastic; perhaps their plans for managing the business inspired more confidence. Finally, the Johnson group's proposal contained a management compensation package that seemed extremely generous and had generated an avalanche of bad press.

But where did the merger benefits come from? What could justify offering $109 per share, about $25 billion in all, for a company that only 33 days previously was selling for $56 per share?

KKR and the other bidders were betting on two things. First, they expected to generate billions of additional cash from interest tax shields, reduced capital expenditures, and sales of assets not strictly necessary to RJR's core businesses. Asset sales alone were projected to generate $5 billion. Second, they expected to make those core businesses significantly more profitable, mainly by cutting back on expenses and bureaucracy. Apparently, there was plenty to cut, including the RJR "Air Force," which at one point included ten corporate jets.

In the year after KKR took over, new management was installed which sold assets and cut back operating expenses and capital spending. There were also layoffs. As expected, high interest charges meant a net loss of $976 million for 1989, but pre-tax operating income actually increased despite extensive asset sales, including the sale of RJR's European food operations.

Inside the firm, things were going well. But outside there was confusion and rapidly declining prices in the junk bond market, implying much higher future interest charges for RJR and stricter terms on any refinancing. In mid-1990 KKR made an additional equity investment and, in December 1990, announced an offer of cash and new shares in exchange for $753 million of junk bonds. RJR's chief financial officer described the exchange offer as "one further step in the deleveraging of the company."[45] For RJR, the world's largest LBO, it seemed that high debt was a temporary, not permanent virtue.

---

[43] See Section 24-6.

[44] The whole story is reconstructed by B. Burrough and J. Helyar in *Barbarians at the Gate: The Fall of RJR Nabisco*, New York, Harper & Row, 1990. See especially Chapter 18.

[45] G. Andress, "RJR Swallows Hard, Offers $5-a-share Stock," *Wall Street Journal*: C1–C2, December 18, 1990.

Barbarians at the Gate?

The RJR LBO crystalized views on LBOs, the junk bond market, and the M&A business. For many, it exemplified all that was wrong with finance in the 1980s, especially the willingness of "raiders" to carve up established companies and leave them with enormous debt burdens—basically, to get rich quick.

There was plenty of confusion, stupidity, and greed in the LBO business. Not all of the people involved were nice. On the other hand, LBOs generated enormous increases in market value, and most of the gains went to selling stockholders, not to the raiders. For example, the biggest winners in the RJR-Nabisco LBO were that company's stockholders.

We should, therefore, consider briefly where these gains may have come from before we try to pass judgement on LBOs. There are several possibilities.

The Junk Bond Markets   LBOs and debt-financed take-overs may have been driven by artificially cheap funding from the junk bond markets. With hindsight it seems that investors in junk bonds underestimated the risks of default in junk bonds. Default rates climbed painfully in 1989 and 1990; for example, Edward Altman reported $4.8 billion in defaults in the first six months of 1990.[46] At the same time the junk bond market became much less liquid after the demise of Drexel Burnham, the chief market maker. Yields climbed dramatically, and new issues dried up. Suddenly junk-financed LBOs became as scarce as great blind dates.

If junk bond investors in 1985 had appreciated the risk of what actually happened in 1990, junk finance would have been dearer. That would have slowed down LBOs and other highly leveraged transactions.

Leverage and Taxes   Borrowing money saves taxes, as we explained in Chapter 18. But taxes were not the main driving force behind LBOs. The value of interest tax shields was just not big enough to explain the observed gains in market value.[47] For example, Richard Ruback has estimated the present value of additional interest tax shields generated by the RJR LBO at $1.8 billion.[48] But the gain in market value to RJR stockholders was about $8 billion.

Of course, if interest tax shields were the main motive for LBOs' high debt, then LBO managers would not be so concerned to pay debt off. We saw that this was one of the first tasks facing RJR Nabisco's new management, and also the management of Phillips Petroleum after its leveraged recapitalization.

Other Stakeholders   We should look at the total gain to *all* investors in an LBO, not just the selling stockholders. It's possible that their gain is just someone else's loss, and that no value is generated overall.

Bondholders are the obvious losers. The debt they thought was well-secured may turn into junk when the borrower goes through an LBO. We noted how market prices of RJR Nabisco debt fell sharply when Ross Johnson's first LBO offer was announced. But again, the value losses suffered by bondholders in LBOs are not nearly large enough to explain stockholder gains. For example, Mohan and Chen's estimate of losses to RJR bondholders was at most $575 million[49]—painful to the bondholders, but far below stockholders' gain.

---

[46] E.I. Altman, "Setting the Record Straight on Junk Bonds: A Review of Research on Default Rates and Returns," *Journal of Applied Corporate Finance*, **3**: 82–95 (Summer 1990). See also Section 23-4.

[47] Moreover, there are some tax costs to LBOs. For example, selling shareholders realize capital gains and pay taxes that otherwise could be deferred.

[48] R.S. Ruback, "RJR Nabisco," Case Study, Harvard Business School, 1989.

[49] Mohan and Chen, *op. cit.*

Leverage and Incentives   Managers and employees of LBOs work harder and often smarter. They have to generate cash for debt service. Moreover, managers' personal fortunes are riding on the LBO's success. They become owners rather than organization men.

It's hard to measure the payoff from better incentives, but there is some preliminary evidence of improved operating efficiency in LBOs. Kaplan, who studied 48 MBOs between 1980 and 1986, found average increases in operating income of 24% three years after the MBO. Ratios of operating income and net cash flow to assets and sales increased dramatically. He observed cutbacks in capital expenditures but not in employment. Kaplan suggests that these "operating changes are due to improved incentives rather than layoffs or managerial exploitation of shareholders through inside information."[50]

Free Cash Flow   The free cash flow theory of take-overs is basically that mature firms with a surplus of cash will tend to waste it. This contrasts with standard finance theory, which says that firms with more cash than positive-NPV investment opportunities should give the cash back to investors through higher dividends, share repurchases, or other devices. But we see firms like RJR Nabisco spending on corporate luxuries and questionable capital investments. One benefit of LBOs is to put such companies on a diet and force them to pay out cash to service debt.

The free cash flow theory predicts that mature, "cash cow" companies will be the most likely targets of LBOs. We can find many examples that fit the theory, including RJR Nabisco. The theory says that the gains in market value generated by LBOs are just the present value of the future cash flows that would otherwise have been frittered away.[51]

We do not endorse the free cash flow theory as an exclusive explanation for LBOs. We have mentioned several other plausible reasons, and suspect that most LBOs are driven by a mixture of motives. Nor do we say that all LBOs are positive. On the contrary, there are many mistakes, and even soundly motivated LBOs are dangerous, as the bankruptcies of Campeau, Revco, National Gypsum, and many other highly leveraged companies prove. However, we do quarrel with those who portray LBOs *simply* as Wall Street barbarians breaking up the traditional strengths of corporate North America. LBOs have in many cases generated true gains.

In the next section we attempt to sum up the longer run impact of mergers, including LBOs, in the economy. We warn you, however, that there are no neat answers. Our assessment has to be mixed and tentative.

33-8   MERGERS AND THE ECONOMY

Merger Waves   Mergers come in waves. The first episode of intense merger activity occurred at the turn of the century and the second in the 1920s. There was a further boom from 1967 to 1969 and then again in the 1980s. Each episode coincided with a period of buoyant stock prices, though in each case there were substantial differences in the types of companies that merged and the ways they went about it.

We don't really understand why merger activity is so volatile. If mergers are prompted by economic motives, at least one of these motives must be "here today

---

[50] S. Kaplan, "The Effects of Management Buyouts on Operating Performance and Value, *Journal of Financial Economics*, **24**: 217–254 (October 1989).

[51] The free cash flow theory's chief proponent is Michael Jensen. See "The Eclipse of the Public Corporation," *op. cit.*, and "The Agency Costs of Free Cash Flow, Corporate Finance and Takeovers," *American Economic Review*, **76**: 323–329 (May 1986).

and gone tomorrow," and it must somehow be associated with high stock prices. But none of the economic motives that we review in this chapter has anything to do with the general level of the stock market. None burst on the scene in 1967, departed in 1970, and reappeared for most of the 1980s.

Some mergers may result from mistakes in valuation on the part of the stock market. In other words, the buyer may believe that investors have underestimated the value of the seller or may hope that they *will* overestimate the value of the combined firm. But we see (with hindsight) that mistakes are made in bear markets as well as bull markets. Why don't we see just as many firms hunting for bargain acquisitions when the stock market is low? It is possible that "suckers are born every minute," but it is difficult to believe that they can be harvested only in bull markets.

Companies are not the only active buyers and sellers in a bull market. Investors also trade much more heavily after a rise in share prices. Again, nobody has a good explanation of why this should be the case. Perhaps the answer has nothing to do with economics. Perhaps merger booms and stock market trading are behavioural phenomena—human beings, like some animals, are more active when the weather is sunny.

Although we can't explain the timing of merger waves, we can do a bit better interpreting recent history. We have seen that in the 1980s corporations in mature industries such as oil, tobacco, and forest products found themselves with large operating cash flows and limited investment opportunities within their existing businesses. Many of these companies used their cash surpluses to buy into new areas. But they were also themselves the target for take-overs that obliged them to distribute cash.

During the 1980s "merger boom" no company, except a handful of the very largest, was immune from attack from a rival management team. For example, in 1985 Pantry Pride, a small supermarket chain recently emerged from bankruptcy, made a bid for the cosmetics company, Revlon. Revlon's assets were more than five times Pantry Pride's. What made the bid possible (and eventually successful) was the ability of Pantry Pride to finance the take-over by borrowing $2.1 billion. The growth of leveraged buyouts during the 1980s depended on the development of a junk bond market that allowed bidders to place low-grade bonds rapidly and in high volume.[52]

By the end of the decade the merger environment had changed. Many of the obvious targets had disappeared, and the battle for RJR Nabisco highlighted the increasing cost of victory. Institutions were reluctant to increase their holdings of junk bonds. Moreover, the market for these bonds had depended to a remarkable extent on one individual, Michael Milken of the investment bank, Drexel Burnham. By the late 1980s Milken and his employer were in trouble. Milken was indicted by a federal grand jury on 98 counts, and was subsequently sentenced to jail for 10 years and ordered to pay $600 million. Drexel likewise pleaded guilty to six felony counts and paid $650 million in penalties. In early 1990 Drexel filed for bankruptcy, but by that time the junk bond market was moribund and the finance for highly leveraged buyouts had largely dried up.[53]

---

[52] Because speed is important in take-overs, most junk bond issues in leveraged buyouts were private placements. Pantry Pride's public junk bond issue was unusual.

[53] For a readable history of the role of Milken in the development of the junk bond market see C. Bruck, The Predators' Ball: *The Junk Bond Raiders and the Man Who Staked Them*, Simon and Schuster, New York, 1988.

Do Mergers Generate Net Benefits?

There are undoubtedly good acquisitions and bad acquisitions, but economists find it hard to agree as to whether acquisitions are *on balance* beneficial. We do know that mergers generate substantial gains to acquired firms' stockholders.[54]

Since buyers seem at least to break even and sellers make substantial gains, it seems that there are positive overall benefits to merger.[55] But not everybody is convinced. Some believe that investors analyzing mergers pay too much attention to short-term earnings gains and don't notice that these gains are at the expense of long-term prospects.[56]

Since we can't observe how companies would have fared in the absence of a merger, it is difficult to measure the effects on profitability. Ravenscroft and Scherer, who looked at mergers during the 1960s and early 1970's, argued that productivity declined in the years following merger.[57] But the studies of more recent merger activity suggest that mergers *do* seem to improve real productivity. For example, Paul Healy, Krishna Palepu, and Richard Ruback examined 50 large mergers between 1979 and 1983 and found an average increase in the companies' pretax returns of 2.4 percentage points.[58] They argue that this gain came from generating a higher level of sales from the same assets. There was no evidence that the companies were mortgaging their long-term future by cutting back on long-term investments; expenditures on capital equipment and research and development tracked the industry average.[59]

---

[54] See Eckbo, *op. cit.*, and Jensen and Ruback, *op. cit.*, and the discussion in Section 33-6. See also J.R. Franks and R.S. Harris, "Shareholder Wealth Effects of Corporate Takeovers: The UK Experience 1955–1985," *Journal of Financial Economics,* **23**: 225–250 (1989).

[55] Jensen and Ruback, *op. cit.*, after an extensive review of empirical work, conclude that "corporate takeovers generate positive gains" (p. 47). Richard Roll reviews the same evidence and argues that "takeover gains may have been overestimated if they exist at all." See "The Hubris Hypothesis of Corporate Takeovers," *Journal of Business,* **59**: 198–216 (April 1986).

[56] There have been a number of attempts to test whether investors are myopic. For example, McConnell and Muscarella examined the reaction of stock prices to announcements of capital expenditure plans. If investors were interested in short-term earnings, which are generally depressed by major capital expenditure programs, then these announcements should depress stock price. But they found that increases in capital spending were associated with *increases* in stock prices and reductions were associated with *falls.* Similarly, Jarrell, Lehn, and Marr found that announcements of expanded R&D spending prompted a *rise* in the stock price. See H. McConnell and C. Muscarella, "Corporate Capital Expenditure Decisions and the Market Value of the Firm, *Journal of Financial Economics,* **14**: 399–422 (July 1985) and G. Jarrell, K. Lehn, and W. Marr, "Institutional Ownership, Tender Offers, and Long-Term Investments," The Office of the Chief Economist, Securities and Exchange Commission (April 1985).

[57] See D.J. Ravenscroft and F.M. Scherer, "Mergers and Managerial Performance, in J.C. Coffee, Jr., L. Lowenstein, and S. Rose-Ackerman, eds., *Knights, Raiders, and Targets: The Impact of the Hostile Takeover,* Oxford University Press, 1988.

[58] See P. Healy, K. Palepu, and R. Ruback, "Does Corporate Performance Improve After Mergers?," NBER Working Paper No. 3348, 1990. The study examined the pretax returns of the merged companies relative to industry averages. A study by Lichtenberg and Siegel comes to similar conclusions. Before merger acquired companies had lower levels of productivity than other firms in their industries, but by seven years after the control change two-thirds of the productivity gap had been eliminated. See F. Lichtenberg and D. Siegel, "The Effect of Control Changes on the Productivity of U.S. Manufacturing Plants," *Journal of Applied Corporate Finance,* **2**: 60–67 (Summer 1989).

[59] Maintained levels of capital spending and R&D are also observed by Lichtenberg and Siegel, *op. cit.*, and B.H. Hall, "The Effect of Takeover Activity on Corporate Research and Development," in A.J. Auerbach, ed., *Corporate Takeover: Causes and Consequences,* University of Chicago Press, 1988.

If you are concerned with public policy toward mergers, you do not want to look only at their impact on the shareholders of the companies concerned. For instance, we have already seen that in the case of RJR Nabisco some part of the shareholders' gain was at the expense of the bondholders and the Internal Revenue Service (through the enlarged interest tax shield). The acquirer's shareholders may also gain at the expense of the target firm's employees who, in some cases, are laid off or are forced to take pay cuts after take-overs. Andrei Schleifer and Lawrence Summers argue that such activities may involve a loss of trust between employer and employee which can spread through the economic system.[60]

Many people worry that the merger wave of the 1980s has led to excessive debt levels and left many companies ill-equipped to survive a recession. Also, many banks and some large insurance firms invested heavily in junk bonds. Defaults on these bonds threatened and, in some cases, extinguished their solvency.

Perhaps the most important effect of acquisitions is on the managers of companies that are *not* taken over. For example, one effect of LBOs was that managers of even the largest corporations could not feel safe from challenge. Perhaps the threat of take-over spurs the whole of corporate America to try harder. Unfortunately, we don't know whether on balance the threat of merger makes more for active days or sleepless nights.

But merger activity is also very costly. For example, in the RJR Nabisco buyout the total fees paid to the investment banks, lawyers, and accountants amounted to over $1 billion. Phillips Petroleum spent an estimated $150 million defending itself. And that does not include the amount of time Phillips's management spent on the defences rather than running their business.

Even if the gains to the community exceed the costs, it is worth considering whether the same benefits could not be achieved more cheaply than by acquisition. For example, are leveraged buyouts necessary to make managers work harder? Perhaps the problem lies in the way many corporations reward and penalize their managers. Michael Jensen and Kevin Murphy calculate that in the 250 largest corporations a $1,000 change in corporate value corresponds to a change of just 6.7 cents in the chief executives' salary and bonus over two years.[61] Perhaps many of the gains from take-over could be captured by linking management compensation more directly to performance.

33-9 SUMMARY

A merger generates an economic gain if the two firms are worth more together than apart. Suppose that firms A and B merge to form a new entity AB. Then the gain from the merger is

$$\text{GAIN} = \text{PV}_{AB} - (\text{PV}_A + \text{PV}_B)$$

Gains from mergers may reflect economies of scale, economies of vertical integration, improved efficiency, fuller use of tax shields, the combination of complementary resources, or redeployment of surplus funds. We don't know how common these benefits are, but they do make economic sense. Sometimes mergers are

---

[60] See A. Schleifer and L.H. Summers, "Breach of Trust in Corporate Takeovers," in A.J. Auerbach, ed., *Corporate Takeovers: Causes and Consequences*, University of Chicago Press, 1988. However, Lichtenberg and Siegel, *op. cit.*, found no evidence that on average ownership changes lead to layoffs or wage cuts.

[61] See M.C. Jensen and K.J. Murphy, "CEO Incentives—It's Not How Much You Pay, But How," *Harvard Business Review* (May/June 1990).

undertaken to reduce the costs of borrowing, diversify risks, or play the bootstrap game. These motives are dubious.

You should go ahead with the merger if the gain exceeds the cost. Cost is the premium that the buyer pays for the selling firm over its values as a separate entity. It is easy to estimate when the merger is financed by cash. In that case,

$$\text{COST} = \text{CASH} - \text{PV}_B$$

When payment is in the form of shares, the cost depends on the value of the combined firm. For example, if B's shareholders end up owning the fraction x of the combined firm

$$\text{COST} = x\text{PV}_{AB} - \text{PV}_B$$

The mechanics of buying a firm are much more complex than those of buying a machine. First, you have to make sure that the purchase is unlikely to fall foul of the new *Competition Act*. This requires that you report the proposed deal to the Bureau of Competition Policy before making a public announcement. Second, you have a choice of procedures. In a merger[62] all the assets and liabilities of the buyer are absorbed into those of the seller. In an acquisition of stock the buyer acquires the stock of the seller rather than the company itself. In an acquisition of assets the buyer purchases the individual assets of the seller. Third, you have to worry about the tax status of the merger. In a tax-free merger the tax position of the corporation and the stockholders is not changed. In a taxable merger the buyer can depreciate the full cost of the tangible assets acquired, but the stockholders in the selling corporation may be taxed on any capital gains. Finally, remember that most mergers are amicably negotiated between the directors of the two companies; but if the seller is reluctant, the would-be buyer can decide to make a tender offer or engage in a proxy fight.

We sketched some of the offensive and defensive tactics used in take-over battles. We also observed that when the target firm loses, its shareholders typically win: selling shareholders earn abnormal returns averaging about 20% in mergers and 30% in tender offers. The bidding firm's shareholders also gain in Canadian take-overs but seem to break even in the U.S. The typical merger generates positive net benefits to investors, but competition among bidders, plus active defence by target managements, pushes most of the gains toward selling shareholders.

LBOs and other debt-financed take-overs are driven by a mixture of motives, including the value of interest tax shields; transfers of value from lenders, who sometimes see the market values of their securities fall as the borrowing firm piles up more debt; and the opportunity to create better incentives for managers and employees, who have a greater personal financial stake in the company but must work harder to service debt. In addition, many such take-overs were designed to force firms with cash surpluses to distribute cash rather than plowing it back. Investors feared such companies would channel free cash flow into negative-NPV investments.

Mergers seem to generate net economic gains, but they are also costly. Investment banks, lawyers, arbitrageurs, and greenmailers thrived during the 1980s merger and LBO boom. Many companies were left with heavy debt burdens and will have to sell assets or improve performance to stay solvent. By the end of 1990, the new issue junk bond market had dried up and the corporate jousting field was strangely quiet. The merger wave of the 1980s was over, and investors and managers began to think about the size, shape, and timing of the next one.

---

[62] In this sentence the word *merger* is used in its technical, legal sense.

FURTHER READING

The approach to analyzing mergers presented in this chapter is based on:

S.C. Myers, "A Framework for Evaluating Mergers," in S.C. Myers, ed., *Modern Developments in Financial Management*, Frederick A. Praeger, Inc., New York, 1976.

The first chapters of Reid's book provide a useful history of merger "waves." Morin and Chippindale and the Royal Commission Report provide some general background of mergers and their effects in Canada, and Steiner provides a general treatment of mergers and their impact on the economy of the United States. Khemani, Shapiro, and Stanbury provide an excellent review of public policy issues surrounding mergers in Canada.

R.S. Khemani, D.M. Shapiro, and W.T. Stanbury, *Mergers Corporate Concentration and Power in Canada*, The Institute for Research on Public Policy, Halifax, 1988.

D. Morin and W. Chippindale, eds., *Acquisitions and Mergers in Canada*, Methuen, Toronto, 1970.

S.R. Reid, *Mergers, Managers and the Economy*, McGraw-Hill Book Company, New York, 1968.

Report of the Royal Commission on Corporate Concentration, Minister of Supply and Services Canada, 1978.

P.O. Steiner, *Mergers: Motives, Effects, Policies*, The University of Michigan Press, Ann Arbor, 1975.

Eckbo examined take-overs in Canada while Jensen and Ruback have recently reviewed the extensive empirical work on mergers in the United States. The same issue of the *Journal of Financial Economics* also contains a collection of some of the more important empirical studies.

B.E. Eckbo, "Mergers and the Market for Corporate Control: The Canadian Evidence," *Canadian Journal of Economics,* **19**: 236–260 (May 1986).

M.C. Jensen and R.S. Ruback, "The Market for Corporate Control: The Scientific Evidence," *Journal of Financial Economics,* **11**: 5–50 (April 1983).

Here are two useful recent books on take-overs.

L. Herzel and R. Shepro, *Bidders and Targets: Mergers and Acquisitions in the U.S.*, Basil Blackwell, Inc., Cambridge, MA, 1990.

J.F. Weston, K.S. Chung, and S.E. Hoag, *Mergers, Restructuring, and Corporate Control*, Prentice-Hall, Inc., Englewood Cliffs, New Jersey, 1990.

Kaplan provides evidence on the performance of a sample of LBOs undertaken in the 1980s. Jensen, the chief proponent of the free cash flow theory of take-overs, provides a spirited and controversial defence of LBOs.

M.C. Jensen, "The Eclipse of the Public Corporation," *Harvard Business Review,* **67**: 61–74 (September–October 1989).

S. Kaplan, "The Effects of Management Buyouts on Operating Performance and Value," *Journal of Financial Economics,* **24**: 217–254 (October 1989).

Finally, here are some informative case studies.

B. Burrough and J. Helyar, *Barbarians at the Gate: The Fall of RJR Nabisco*, Harper & Row, New York, 1990.

R.S. Ruback, "The Conoco Takeover and Shareholder Returns," *Sloan Management Review,* **23**: 13–33 (Winter 1982).

R.S. Ruback, "The Cities Service Takeover: A Case Study," *Journal of Finance,* **38**: 319–330 (May 1983).

APPENDIX 33-1   CONGLOMERATE MERGERS AND VALUE ADDITIVITY

A pure conglomerate merger is one that has no effect on the operations or profitability of either firm. If corporate diversification is in stockholders' interests, a conglomerate merger would give a clear demonstration of its benefits. But, if present values add up, the conglomerate merger would not make stockholders better or worse off.

In this appendix we examine more carefully our assertion that present values add. It turns out that values *do* add as long as capital markets are perfect and investors' diversification opportunities are unrestricted.

Call the merging firms A and B. Value additivity implies

$$PV_{AB} = PV_A + PV_B$$

where

PV_{AB} = the market value of the combined firms just after the merger

and

PV_A, PV_B = the separate market values of A and B just before the merger

For example, we might have

PV_A = $100 million ($200 per share times 500,000 shares outstanding)

and

PV_B = $200 million ($200 per share times 1,000,000 shares outstanding)

Suppose A and B are merged into a new firm AB, with one share in AB exchanged for each share of A or B. Thus, there are 1,500,000 AB shares issued. *If* value additivity holds, then PV_{AB} must equal the sum of the separate values of A and B just before the merger: that is, $300 million. That would imply a price of $200 per share of AB stock.

But note that the AB shares represent a portfolio of the assets of A and B. Before the merger investors could have bought one share of A and two of B for $600. Afterwards they can obtain a claim on *exactly* the same real assets by buying three shares of AB.

Suppose that the opening price of AB shares just after the merger is $200, so that $PV_{AB} = PV_A + PV_B$. Our problem is to determine if this is an equilibrium price; that is, whether we can rule out excess demand or supply at this price.

In order for there to be excess demand, there must be some investors who are willing to increase their holdings of A and B as a consequence of the merger. Who could they be? The only thing new created by the merger is diversification, but those investors who want to hold assets of A *and* B will have purchased A's and B's stock before the merger. The diversification is redundant and consequently won't attract new investment demand.

Is there a possibility of excess supply? The answer is yes. For example, there will be some shareholders in A who did not invest in B. After the merger they cannot invest solely in A, but only in a fixed combination of A and B. Their AB shares will be less attractive to them than the pure A shares, so they will sell part or all their AB stock. In fact, the only AB shareholders who will *not* wish to sell are those who happened to hold A and B in exactly a 1:2 ratio in their premerger portfolios!

Since there is no possibility of excess demand, but a definite possibility of excess supply, we seem to have

$$PV_{AB} \leq PV_A + PV_B$$

That is, corporate diversification can't help, but it may hurt investors by restricting the types of portfolios they can hold. This is not the whole story, however, since investment demand for AB shares might be attracted from other sources if PV_{AB} drops below $PV_A + PV_B$. To illustrate, suppose there are two other firms, A* and B*, which are judged by investors to have the same risk characteristics as A and B, respectively. Then, before the merger,

$$r_A = r_{A^*} \text{ and } r_B = r_{B^*}$$

where r is the rate of return expected by investors. We'll assume $r_A = r_{A^*} = 0.08$ and $r_B = r_{B^*} = 0.20$.

Consider a portfolio one-third invested in A* and two-thirds in B*. This portfolio offers an expected return of 16%.

$$r = x_{A^*}r_{A^*} + x_{B^*}r_{B^*}$$
$$= \tfrac{1}{3}(0.08) + \tfrac{2}{3}(0.20) = 0.16$$

A comparable portfolio of A and B before their merger also offered a 16% return.

As we have noted a new firm AB is really a portfolio of firms A and B, with portfolio weights of ⅓ and ⅔. Thus, it is equivalent in risk to the portfolio of A* and B*. Thus, the price of AB shares must adjust so that it likewise offers a 16% return.

What if AB shares dropped below $200, so that PV_{AB} is less than $PV_A + PV_B$? Since the assets and earnings of firms A and B are the same, the price drop means that the expected rate of return on AB shares has risen above the return offered by the A*B* portfolio. That is, if r_{AB} exceeds $\tfrac{1}{3}r_A + \tfrac{2}{3}r_B$, then r_{AB} must also exceed $\tfrac{1}{3}r_{A^*} + \tfrac{2}{3}r_{B^*}$. But this is untenable: investors A* and B* could sell part of their holdings (in a 1:2 ratio), buy AB, and obtain a higher expected rate of return with no increase in risk.

On the other hand, if PV_{AB} rises above $PV_A + PV_B$, the AB shares will offer an expected return less than that offered by the A*B* portfolio. Investors will unload the AB shares, forcing their price down.

The only stable result is for AB shares to stick at $200. Thus, value additivity will hold exactly in a perfect-market equilibrium if there are ample substitutes for the assets A and B. If A and B have unique risk characteristics, however, then PV_{AB} can fall below $PV_A + PV_B$. The reason is that the merger curtails investors' opportunity to custom-tailor their portfolios to their own needs and preferences. This makes investors worse off, reducing the attractiveness of holding the shares of firm AB.

In general, the condition for value additivity is that investors' opportunity set—that is, the range of risk characteristics attainable by investors through their portfolio choices—is independent of the particular portfolio of real assets held by the firm. Diversification per se can never expand the opportunity set given perfect security markets. Corporate diversification may reduce the investors' opportunity set, but only if the real assets the corporations hold lack substitutes among traded securities or portfolios.

In a few cases the firm may be able to expand the opportunity set. It can do so if it finds an investment opportunity that is unique—a real asset with risk characteristics shared by few or no other financial assets. In this lucky event the firm should not diversify, however. It should set up the unique asset as a separate firm so as to expand investors' opportunity set to the maximum extent. If Gallo by chance discovered that a small piece of its vineyards produced wine comparable to Chateau Margaux, it would not throw that wine into the Hearty Burgundy vat.

QUIZ

1. Indicate which of the following hypothetical mergers is horizontal, vertical, or conglomerate:
   (a) IBM acquires Control Data.
   (b) Control Data acquires Safeway.
   (c) Safeway acquires General Foods.
   (d) General Foods acquires IBM.

2. Velcro Saddles is contemplating the acquisition of Pogo Ski Sticks, Inc. The values of the two companies as separate entities are $20 million and $10 million respectively. Velcro Saddles estimates that by combining the two companies, it will reduce marketing and administrative costs by $500,000 per year in perpetuity. Velcro Saddles can either pay $14 million cash for Pogo or offer Pogo a 50% holding in Velcro Saddles. If the opportunity cost of capital is 10%,
   (a) What is the gain from merger?
   (b) What is the cost of the cash offer?
   (c) What is the cost of the stock alternative?
   (d) What is the NPV of the acquisition under the cash offer?
   (e) What is its NPV under the stock offer?

3. Indicate which of the following mergers are *not* likely to be classed as tax-free:
   (a) A merger undertaken solely for the purpose of taking advantage of tax-loss carry-forwards.
   (b) An acquisition of assets, which are immediately resold.
   (c) Payment is entirely in the form of voting stock.
   (d) Firm A acquires firm B for cash.

4. Indicate whether each of the following is true or false:
   (a) Sellers almost always gain in mergers.
   (b) Buyers almost always gain in mergers.
   (c) Firms that do unusually well tend to be acquisition targets.
   (d) Merger activity in Canada varies dramatically from year to year.
   (e) On the average, mergers produce substantial economic gains.
   (f) Tender offers require the approval of the selling firm's management.
   (g) If a merger can be treated as a pooling of interest rather than a purchase, reported earnings are usually increased.
   (h) The cost of a merger is always independent of the economic gain produced by the merger.
   (i) The cost of a merger to the buyer equals the gain realized by the seller.

5. Indicate which of the following motives for mergers make economic sense:
   (a) Merging to achieve economies of scale
   (b) Merging to reduce risk by diversification
   (c) Merging to redeploy cash generated by a firm with ample profits but limited growth opportunities
   (d) Merging to make fuller use of tax-loss carry-forwards
   (e) Merging just to increase earnings per share

6. Connect each term to its correct definition or description.

   - LBO
   - Poison pill
   - Tender offer
   - Greenmail
   - Golden parachute

   - Payment to target firm's managers who leave after a take-over
   - Attempt to gain control of a firm by winning the votes of its stockholders
   - Offer to buy shares directly from stockholders

- Proxy fight
  - Target company buys out shareholders threatening take-over; repurchase price exceeds market price
  - Shareholders issued rights which must be repurchased by acquiring firm or which can be used to acquire shares of acquiring firm
  - Company or business bought out by private investors, largely debt-financed

QUESTIONS AND PROBLEMS

1. Examine several recent mergers and suggest the principal motives for merging in each case.

2. Examine a recent merger in which at least part of the payment made to the seller was in the form of stock. Use stock market prices to obtain an estimate of the gain from the merger and the cost of the merger.

3. The Muck and Slurry merger has fallen through (see Section 33-3). But World Enterprises is determined to report earnings per share of $2.67. It therefore acquires the Wheelrim and Axle Company. You are given the following facts:

	World Enterprises	Wheelrim and Axle	Merged Firm
Earnings per share	$2.00	$2.50	$2.67
Price per share	$40.00	$25.00	?
Price-earnings ratio	20	10	?
Number of shares	100,000	200,000	?
Total earnings	$200,000.00	$500,000.00	?
Total market value	$4,000,000.00	$5,000,000.00	?

Once again there are no gains from merging. In exchange for Wheelrim and Axle shares, World Enterprises issues just enough of its own shares to ensure its $2.67 earnings per share objective.

(a) Complete the above table for the merged firm.

(b) How many shares of World Enterprises are exchanged for each share of Wheelrim and Axle?

(c) What is the cost of the merger to World Enterprises?

(d) What is the change in the total market value of those World Enterprises shares that were outstanding before the merger?

4. Explain the distinction between a tax-free and a taxable merger. State the circumstances in which you would expect buyer and seller to agree to a taxable merger.

5. As treasurer of Leisure Products, Inc., you are investigating the possible acquisition of Plastitoys. You have the following basic data:

	Leisure Products	Plastitoys
Earnings per share	$5.00	$1.50
Dividend per share	$3.00	$0.80
Number of shares	1,000,000	600,000
Stock price	$90.00	$20.00

You estimate that investors currently expect a steady growth of about 6% in Plastitoys' earnings and dividends. Under new management this growth rate would be increased to 8% per year, without any additional capital investment required.

(a) What is the gain from the acquisition?

(b) What is the cost of the acquisition of Leisure Products pays $25 in cash for each share of Plastitoys?

(c) What is the cost of the acquisition if Leisure Products offers one share of Leisure Products for every three shares of Plastitoys?

(d) How would the cost of the cash offer and the share offer alter if the expected growth rate of Plastitoys were not changed by the merger?

6. Look again at Table 33-3. Suppose that B Corporation's fixed assets are re-examined and found to be worth $1.2 million instead of $0.9 million. How would this affect the AB Corporation's balance sheet under purchase accounting? How would the value of AB Corporation change? Would your answer depend on whether the merger is taxable?

7. Do *you* have any rational explanation for the great fluctuations in aggregate merger activity and the apparent relationship between merger activity and stock prices?

8. "Legislation is needed to ensure that shareholders of target companies are fairly treated."

"Acquiring companies need some inducement to act. Legislation to protect the target shareholders is likely to remove this inducement."

What do you think? For example, do you think that there should be a ban on two-tier bids, such as the Occidental bid for Cities Service?

9. What was the common theme in the Phillips Petroleum restructuring and the RJR Nabisco LBO? Why was financial leverage a necessary part of both deals?

10. Explain why the fall in value of RJR Nabisco bonds caused by its LBO represented a gain to the *equity* investors in the LBO. (*Hint*: See Section 18-3.)

11. Read *Barbarians at the Gate* (see Further Reading). Does this story support Michael Jensen's free cash flow theory of take-overs?

12. What costs, dangers, and inequities did the boom of the 1980s in LBOs and debt financed take-overs create? Would you support new legislation designed to restrict such transactions in the 1990s? Can you think of other ways companies could realize the benefits of these transactions without financing at very high-debt ratios?

C·H·A·P·T·E·R

34

INTERNATIONAL
FINANCIAL MANAGEMENT

So far we have talked principally about doing business at home. But many companies have substantial interests in other countries. Of course, your objectives in international financial management are still the same. You want to buy assets that are worth *more* than they cost, and you want to pay for them by issuing liabilities that are worth *less* than the money raised. It is when you come to apply these criteria to your international business that you come up against some additional problems.

The unique feature of international financial management is that you need to deal with more than one currency. We will, therefore, look at how foreign exchange markets operate, why exchange rates change, and what you can do to protect yourself against exchange risks.

The financial manager must also remember that interest rates differ from country to country. For example, in spring 1990 the rate of interest was about 11% in Canada, 15% in Britain, 8% in the United States, and 40,000% in Brazil. We are going to discuss the reasons for these differences in interest rates, along with some of the implications for financing overseas operations. Should the parent company provide the money? Should it try to finance the operation locally? Or should it treat the world as its oyster and borrow wherever interest rates are lowest?

We will also discuss how international companies decide on capital investments. How do they choose the discount rate? And how does the financing method affect the choice of project? You'll find that the basic principles of capital budgeting are the same but there are a few pitfalls to look out for.

34-1 THE FOREIGN EXCHANGE MARKET

A Canadian company that imports goods from Japan buys yen in order to pay for the purchase. A Canadian company exporting to Japan receives yen, which it sells in exchange for dollars. Both firms make use of the foreign exchange market.[1]

---

[1] Alternatively, trade may take place in dollars. In this case, the Canadian importer pays for goods in dollars and the Japanese exporter sells those dollars to buy yen. Similarly, the Canadian exporter may demand payment in dollars; in this case, the Japanese importer must sell yen to buy those dollars.

FOREIGN EXCHANGE

Mid-market rates in Toronto at noon, May 16, 1991. Prepared by the Bank of Montreal Treasury Group.

	$1 U.S. in Cdn.$ =	$1 Cdn. in U.S.$ =
U.S./Canada spot	1.1488	0.8705
1 month forward	1.1520	0.8681
2 months forward	1.1546	0.8661
3 months forward	1.1575	0.8639
6 months forward	1.1652	0.8582
12 months forward	1.1784	0.8486
3 years forward	1.2223	0.8181
5 years forward	1.2526	0.7983
7 years forward	1.2813	0.7805
10 years forward	1.3388	0.7468
Canadian dollar High	1.1460	0.8726
in 1991: Low	1.1665	0.8573
Average	1.1546	0.8661

Country	Currency	Cdn.$ per unit	U.S.$ per unit
Britain	Pound	2.0052	1.7455
1 month forward		2.0009	1.7369
2 months forward		1.9965	1.7292
3 months forward		1.9938	1.7225
6 months forward		1.9856	1.7041
12 months forward		1.9754	1.6764
Germany	Mark	0.6772	0.5895
1 month forward		0.6773	0.5880
3 months forward		0.6771	0.5850
6 months forward		0.6769	0.5809
12 months forward		0.6776	0.5750
Japan	Yen	0.008352	0.007270
1 month forward		0.008361	0.007258
3 months forward		0.008379	0.007239
6 months forward		0.008411	0.007218
12 months forward		0.008499	0.007213
Algeria	Dinar	0.0661	0.0576
Antigua, Grenada and St. Lucia	E.C. Dollar	0.4263	0.3711
Argentina	Austral	0.00012	0.00010
Australia	Dollar	0.9003	0.7837
Austria	Schilling	0.09661	0.08410
Bahamas	Dollar	1.1488	1.0000
Barbados	Dollar	0.5750	0.5005
Belgium	Franc	0.03303	0.02875
Bermuda	Dollar	1.1488	1.0000
Brazil	Cruzeiro	0.00391	0.00340
Bulgaria	Lev	0.0499	0.0434
Chile	Peso	0.0034	0.0029
China	Renminbi	0.2165	0.1884
Cyprus	Pound	2.4469	2.1299
Czechoslovakia	Koruna	0.0397	0.0345
Denmark	Krone	0.1777	0.1547

Country	Currency	Cdn.$ per unit	U.S.$ per unit
Egypt	Pound	0.3576	0.3113
Fiji	Dollar	0.7783	0.6775
Finland	Markka	0.2871	0.2499
France	Franc	0.1996	0.1737
Greece	Drachma	0.00621	0.00540
Hong Kong	Dollar	0.1475	0.1284
Hungary	Forint	0.01529	0.01331
Iceland	Krona	0.01919	0.01671
India	Rupee	0.05662	0.04929
Indonesia	Rupiah	0.00059	0.00051
Ireland	Punt	1.8182	1.5827
Israel	N. Shekel	0.48688	0.42382
Italy	Lira	0.000909	0.000791
Jamaica	Dollar	0.14113	0.12285
Jordan	Dinar	1.7380	1.5129
Lebanon	Pound	0.00125	0.00109
Luxembourg	Franc	0.03303	0.02875
Malaysia	Ringgit	0.4174	0.3633
Mexico	Peso	0.00038	0.00033
Netherlands	Guilder	0.6004	0.5226
New Zealand	Dollar	0.6792	0.5912
Norway	Krone	0.1742	0.1516
Pakistan	Rupee	0.04882	0.04250
Philippines	Peso	0.04124	0.03590
Poland	Zloty	0.00012	0.00011
Portugal	Escudo	0.00776	0.00675
Romania	Leu	0.0191	0.0167
Saudi Arabia	Riyal	0.3063	0.2666
Singapore	Dollar	0.6514	0.5671
South Africa	Rand	0.4129	0.3595
South Korea	Won	0.001581	0.001376
Spain	Peseta	0.01095	0.00953
Sudan	Pound	0.1010	0.0879
Sweden	Krona	0.1886	0.1642
Switzerland	Franc	0.7975	0.6942
Taiwan	Dollar	0.0424	0.0369
Thailand	Baht	0.0449	0.0391
Trinidad, Tobago	Dollar	0.2706	0.356
USSR	Ruble	1.9330	1.6827
Venezuela	Bolivar	0.02082	0.01812
Yugoslavia	Dinar	0.051081	0.044464
Zambia	Kwacha	0.0201	0.0175
European Currency Unit		1.3954	1.2147
Special Drawing Right		1.5509	1.3500

The U.S. dollar closed at $1.1498 in terms of Canadian funds, up $0.0007 from Wednesday. The pound sterling closed at $2.0127, down $0.0028.

In New York, the Canadian dollar closed down $0.0005 at $0.8697 in terms of U.S. funds. The pound sterling was down $0.0035 to $1.7505.

Figure 34–1   An example of the foreign currency table in *The Globe and Mail*, Friday May 17, 1991, page B8.

Except in a few European centres, the foreign exchange market has no central marketplace. All business is conducted by telephone or telex. The principal dealers are the larger commercial banks and the central banks. Any corporation that wants to buy or sell currency usually does so through a commercial bank.

Turnover in the foreign exchange markets is huge. In London nearly $200 billion of currency changes hands each day. Volume in both New York and Tokyo is well over $100 billion a day.

Exchange rates in Canada are quoted in terms of the number of dollars needed to buy one unit of foreign currency. Therefore, a rate of $0.008352/¥ means that each yen costs you $0.008352. Or, to put it another way, you get 1/0.008352 = 119.73 ¥ for your dollar.

Figure 34-1 reproduces a table of exchange rates from *The Globe and Mail*. Except where otherwise stated, the table gives the price of the currency for immediate delivery. This is known as the **spot exchange rate**. You can see that the spot rate for the yen is $0.008352/¥.

The term *immediate delivery* is a relative one, for spot currency is usually purchased for two-day delivery. For example, suppose that you need 10 million yen to pay for imports from Japan. On Monday you telephone your bank in Toronto and agree to purchase 10,000,000 ¥ at $0.008352/¥. The bank does not hand you a wad of banknotes over the counter. Instead it instructs its Japanese correspondent bank to transfer 10,000,000 ¥ to the account of the Japanese supplier on Wednesday. The bank debits your account by $83,520 on Monday, or, if you are a good customer, on Wednesday.

In addition to the spot exchange market, there is also a **forward market**. In the forward market you buy and sell currency for future delivery—usually 1, 3, 6, or 12 months' time although, in the major currencies, banks are prepared to buy or sell up to 10 years forward. If you know that you are going to pay out or receive foreign currency at some future date, you can insure yourself against loss by buying or selling forward. Thus, if you need 10 million yen three months hence, you can enter into a three-month **forward contract**. The **forward rate** on this contract is the price you agree to pay in three months when the 10 million yen are delivered.

If you look again at Figure 34-1, you see that the three-month forward rate for the yen is quoted at $0.008379/¥. If you buy yen for three months' delivery, you pay more dollars than if you buy the spot. In this case, the yen is said to trade at a forward **premium** relative to the dollar, because forward yen are more expensive than spot ones. Expressed as an annual rate, the forward premium is:

$$4 \times \frac{0.008379 - 0.008352}{0.008352} \times 100 = 1.293$$

You could say that the *dollar* was selling at a 1.29% **forward discount**.

A forward purchase or sale is a made-to-measure transaction between you and the bank. It can be for any currency, any amount, and any delivery day. There is also an organized market for currency for future delivery known as the currency *futures* market. Futures contracts are highly standardized—they exist only for the main currencies, they are for specified amounts, and for a limited choice of delivery dates. The advantage of this standardization is that there is a liquid market in currency futures. Huge numbers of contracts are bought and sold daily on the futures exchanges.[2]

When you buy a forward or a futures contract, you are committed to taking delivery of the currency. As an alternative, you can take out an *option* to buy or sell currency in the future at a price that is fixed today. Made-to-measure currency options can be bought from the major banks, and standardized options are traded on the options exchanges.[3]

Finally, you can agree with the bank that you will buy foreign currency in the future at whatever is the prevailing spot rate *but subject to a maximum and minimum*

---

[2] See Chapter 25 for further discussion of the difference between forward and futures contracts and Table 25-2 for a list of currency futures. Chapter 25 also discusses swaps, which are (effectively) packages of forward contracts.

[3] A list of the traded currency options is given in Table 20-1. Some investment banks have also made one-off issues of currency warrants (i.e., long-term options to buy currency).

service. Without the conversion option, lenders might demand extremely high (promised) interest rates to compensate for the probability of default. This would not only force the firm to raise still more capital to pay for debt service, it would increase the risk of financial distress. Paradoxically, lenders' attempts to protect themselves against default may actually increase the probability of financial distress by increasing the burden of debt service on the firm.[27]

22-5 SUMMARY

Instead of issuing straight bonds, companies may sell either packages of bonds and warrants or convertible bonds.

A warrant is just a long-term call option issued by the company. You already know a good deal about valuing call options. You know from Chapter 20 that call options must be worth at least as much as the stock price less the exercise price. You know that their value is greatest when they have a long time to expiration, when the underlying stock is risky, and when the interest rate is high.

Warrants are somewhat trickier to evaluate than the call options that are traded on the options exchanges. First, because they are long-term options, it is important to take into account the fact that the warrant holder does not receive any dividends. Second, dilution must be allowed for.

A convertible bond gives its holder the right to swap the bond for common stock. The rate of exchange is usually measured by the *conversion ratio*—that is, the number of shares that the investor gets for each bond. Sometimes the rate of exchange is expressed in terms of the *conversion price*—that is, the face value of the bond that must be given up in order to receive one share.

Convertibles are like a package of a bond and a call option. When you evaluate the conversion option you must again remember that the convertible holder does not receive dividends and that conversion results in dilution of the common stock. There are two other things to watch out for. One is the problem of default risk. If the company runs into trouble, you may not only have a worthless conversion option, you may also have a worthless bond. Second, the company may be able to force conversion by calling the bond. It should do this as soon as the market price of the convertible reaches the call price. Many companies do not call their bonds until well after this point. Nobody knows why.

You hear a variety of arguments for issuing warrants or convertibles. Convertible bonds and bonds with warrants are almost always junior bonds and are frequently issued by risky companies. We think this says something about the reasons for their issue. Suppose that you are lending subordinated debt to a untried company. You are worried that the company may turn out to be riskier than you thought or that it may issue additional senior bonds. You can try to protect yourself against such eventualities by imposing very restrictive conditions on the debt, but it is often simpler to say that you don't mind the company taking some extra risk as long as you get a piece of the action. The convertible and bond-warrant package give you a chance to participate in the firm's successes as well as its failures. They diminish the possible conflicts of interest between bondholder and stockholder.

[27] This fact led to an extensive body of literature on "credit rationing." A lender rations credit if it is irrational to lend more to a firm regardless of the interest rate the firm is willing to *promise* to pay. Whether this can happen in efficient, competitive capital markets is controversial. We give an example of credit rationing in Chapter 32. For a review of this literature see E. Baltensperger, "Credit Rationing: Issues and Questions," *Journal of Money, Credit and Banking,* **10**: 170–183 (May 1978).

FURTHER READING

The items listed in Chapter 20 under "Further Reading" are also relevant to this chapter, in particular, Black and Scholes's discussion of warrant valuation.

Ingersoll's work represents the "state of the art" in valuing convertibles:

J.E. Ingersoll, "A Contingent Claims Valuation of Convertible Securities." *Journal of Financial Economics*, **4**: 289–322 (May 1977).

Ingersoll also examines corporate call policies on convertible bonds in:

J.E. Ingersoll, "An Examination of Corporate Call Policies on Convertible Securities," *Journal of Finance*, **32**: 463–478 (May 1977).

Brennan and Schwartz's paper was written at about the same time as Ingersoll's and reaches essentially the same conclusions. They also present a general procedure for valuing convertibles.

M.J. Brennan and E.S. Schwartz, "Convertible Bonds: Valuation and Optimal Strategies for Call and Conversion," *Journal of Finance*, **32**: 1699–1715 (December 1977).

Two useful articles on warrants are:

D. Galai and M.A. Schneller, "Pricing of Warrants and the Value of the Firm," *Journal of Finance*, **33**: 1333–1342 (December 1978).

E.S. Schwartz, "The Valuation of Warrants: Implementing a New Approach," *Journal of Financial Economics*, **4**: 79–93 (January 1977).

For a nontechnical discussion of the pricing of convertibles and the reasons for their use, see:

M.J. Brennan and E.S. Schwartz, "The Case for Convertibles," *Chase Financial Quarterly*, **1**: 27–46 (Spring 1982).

QUIZ

1. Associated Elk warrants entitle the owner to buy one share at $40.
    (a) What is the theoretical value of the warrant if the stock price is
        (i) $20?
        (ii) $30?
        (iii) $40?
        (iv) $50?
        (v) $60?
    (b) Plot the theoretical value of the warrant against the stock price.
    (c) Suppose the stock price is $60 and the warrant price is five dollars. What would you do?
2. In 1984 BC Sugar Refinery issued one-half million warrants attached to a 1 million share common stock issue. Each warrant could have been exercised before 1988 at a price of $25 per share. Suppose the current share price is $23.00.
    (a) Does the warrant holder have a vote?
    (b) Does the warrant holder receive dividends?
    (c) If the stock were to split 5-for-1, how would the exercise price be adjusted?
    (d) Suppose that, instead of reducing the exercise price after the 5-for-1 split, the company gave each warrant holder the right to buy *five* shares at $25 apiece. Would this have the same effect?
    (e) Is there any benefit to exercising the warrant today?
    (f) If there is no benefit to exercising the warrant today, does that mean the current warrant price should be equal to zero?

In deriving the expectations theory we assumed that traders don't care about risk. If they do care, the forward rate can be either higher or lower than the expected spot rate. For example, suppose that you have contracted to receive ItL 100 million in three months. You can wait until you receive the money before you change it into dollars, but this leaves you open to the risk that the price of lira may fall over the next three months. Your alternative is to *sell* the lira forward. In this case, you are fixing today the price at which you will *sell* the lira. Since you avoid risk by selling lira forward, you may be willing to do so even if the forward price of lira is a little *lower* than the expected spot price.

Thus, some companies find it safer to *sell* lira forward, while others find it safer to *buy* lira forward. If the first group predominates, the forward price of lira is likely to be less than the expected spot price. If the second group predominates, the forward price is likely to be greater than the expected spot price.

Changes in the Exchange Rate and Inflation Rates

Now we come to the third side of our quadrilateral—the relationship between changes in the spot exchange rate and inflation rates. Suppose that you notice that silver can be bought in Toronto for $8.50 a troy ounce and sold in Milan for ItL 9,800. You think you may be on to a good thing. You decide to buy silver for $8.50 and put it on the first plane to Milan where you sell it for ItL 9,800. Then you exchange your ItL 9,800 into 9,800 × 0.000909 = $8.91. You have a gross profit of $0.41 an ounce. Of course, you have to pay transportation and insurance costs out of this, but there should still be something left over for you.

Money machines don't exist—not for long. As others notice the disparity between the price of silver in Milan and the price in Toronto, the price will be forced down in London and up in Milan until the profit opportunity disappears. Arbitrage ensures that the dollar price of silver is about the same in the two countries.

Of course, silver is a standard and easily transportable commodity, but to some degree you might expect that the same forces would be acting to equalize the domestic and foreign prices of other goods. Those goods that can be bought more cheaply abroad will be imported, and that will force down the price of the domestic product. Similarly, those goods that can be bought more cheaply in Canada will be exported, and that will force down the price of the foreign product.

This is often called the **law of one price**.[5] Just as the price of goods in Eaton's must be roughly the same as the price of goods in Sears, so the price of goods in Italy when converted into dollars must be roughly the same as the price in Canada.

The law of one price implies that any differences in the rate of inflation will be offset by a change in the exchange rate. For example, if inflation is 5% in Canada and 8.8% in Italy, then in order to equalize the dollar price of goods in the two countries, the price of Italian lire must fall by (1.05/1.088) − 1, or about −3.5%. Therefore, the law of one price suggests that in order to estimate changes in the spot rate of exchange, you need to estimate differences in inflation rates:[6]

---

[5] Economists tend to use the phrase *law of one price* when they are talking about the price of a single good. The notion that the price level of goods in general must be the same in two countries is called **purchasing power parity**.

[6] We are suggesting here that the *expected* difference in the inflation rate equals the *expected* change in the exchange rate. Notice, however, that the law of one price also implies that the *actual* difference in the inflation rate always equals the *actual* change in the exchange rate.

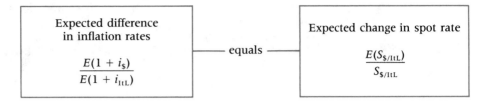

$$\boxed{\begin{array}{c}\text{Expected difference}\\ \text{in inflation rates}\\[4pt] \dfrac{E(1 + i_\$)}{E(1 + i_{ItL})}\end{array}} \;\;\text{---- equals ----}\;\; \boxed{\begin{array}{c}\text{Expected change in spot rate}\\[4pt] \dfrac{E(S_{\$/ItL})}{S_{\$/ItL}}\end{array}}$$

In our example,

$$\begin{array}{ccc}\begin{array}{c}\text{Current spot}\\ \text{rate}\end{array} & \times & \begin{array}{c}\text{Expected difference}\\ \text{in inflation rates}\end{array} & = & \begin{array}{c}\text{Expected spot}\\ \text{rate}\end{array}\\[6pt] 0.000909 & \times & \dfrac{1.05}{1.088} & = & 0.00877\end{array}$$

Interest Rates and Inflation Rates

Now for the fourth leg! Just as water flows downhill, so capital always flows where the returns are greatest. In equilibrium the expected *real* return on capital is the same in different countries.

But bonds don't promise you a fixed *real* return: they promise a fixed *money* payment. Therefore, we have to think about how the money rate of interest in each country is related to the real rate of interest. One answer to this has been provided by Irving Fisher, who argued that the money rate of interest will reflect the amount of expected inflation.[7] In this case Canada and Italy will both offer the same expected *real* rate of interest and the difference in money rates will be equal to the expected difference in inflation rates:

$$\boxed{\begin{array}{c}\text{Difference in}\\ \text{interest rates}\\[4pt] \dfrac{1 + r_\$}{1 + r_{ItL}}\end{array}} \;\;\text{---- equals ----}\;\; \boxed{\begin{array}{c}\text{Expected difference}\\ \text{in inflation rates}\\[4pt] \dfrac{E(1 + i_\$)}{E(1 + i_{ItL})}\end{array}}$$

In other words, capital market equilibrium requires that *real* interest rates be the same in any two countries. In Italy, the real interest rate is about 3%:

$$r_{ItL}\,(\text{real}) = \frac{1 + r_{ItL}}{E\,(1 + i_{ItL})} - 1 = \frac{1.12}{1.088} - 1 = 0.029$$

and the same for Canada:

$$\begin{aligned}r_\$\,(\text{real}) &= \frac{1 + r_\$}{E\,(1 + i_\$)} - 1\\[4pt] &= \frac{1.08}{1.05} - 1\\[4pt] &= 0.029\end{aligned}$$

Is Life Really That Simple?

We have described above four simple theories that link interest rates, forward rates, spot exchange rates, and inflation rates. Notice that the four theories are mutually consistent. This means that if any three are correct, the fourth must also be correct. Conversely, if any one is wrong, at least one other must be wrong.

---

[7] We discussed the Fisher effect in Sections 6-1 and 23-1.

11. Moose Stores has outstanding 1 million shares of common stock with a total market value of $40 million. It now announces an issue of 1 million warrants at $5 each. Each warrant entitles the owner to buy one Moose share for a price of $30 at any time within the next five years. Moose Stores has stated that it will not pay a dividend within this period.

The standard deviation of the returns on Moose's equity is 20% a year, and the interest rate is 8%.

(a) What is the market value of each warrant?

(b) What is the market value of each share after the warrant issue? (*Hint*: The value of the shares is equal to the total value of the equity less the value of the warrants.)

12. Look again at question 11. Suppose that Moose now forecasts the following dividend payments:

End Year	Dividend
1	$2.00
2	3.00
3	4.00
4	5.00
5	6.00

Reestimate the market values of the warrant and stock.

13. Occasionally it is said that issuing convertible bonds is better than issuing stock when the firm's shares are undervalued. Suppose that the financial manager of the Butternut Furniture Company does in fact have inside information indicating that the Butternut stock price is too low. Butternut's future earnings will in fact be higher than investors expect. Suppose further that the inside information cannot be released without giving away a valuable competitive secret. Clearly, selling shares at the present low price would harm Butternut's existing shareholders. Will they also lose if convertible bonds are issued? If they do lose in this case, is the loss more or less than if common stock is issued?

Now suppose that investors forecast earnings accurately, but still undervalue the stock because they overestimate Butternut's actual business risk. Does this change your answers to the questions posed in the preceding paragraph? Explain.

14. Banks or insurance companies sometimes negotiate "equity kickers" when lending money. The firm pays interest and also gives warrants to the lender. Thus the lender has an equity interest in the firm (via the warrants) and shares in the rewards if the firm is successful. Of course, in negotiating the loan, the lender always has the alternative of forgoing the warrants and demanding a higher interest rate instead. What are the advantages of the "equity kicker" arrangement compared to this alternative? In what circumstances would use of the equity kicker be more sensible?

15. In April 1984 Lac Minerals attached gold purchase warrants to a debenture issue. The warrant provides the right to buy 0.5 ounces of gold at an exercise price of $230 at any time up to and including April 1989. If the riskless rate of interest was 10% at that time, the standard deviation of the rate of return on gold 30% and the market price of gold $300 per ounce (that is, $150 per 0.5 ounces), what was the approximate value of the gold purchase warrant?

(*Hint*: An investment in gold is like an investment in a non-dividend-paying stock, so an American call option on gold may be priced using the European call option formula.)

16. Rupert Thorndike, the autocratic CEO of Thorndike Oil, was found dead this morning in a pool of blood on his office floor. He had been shot through the head. Yesterday Thorndike had flatly rejected an offer by T. Spoone Dickens to buy all of Thorndike Oil's assets for $1 billion cash, effective January 1, 1992. With Thorndike out of the way, Dickens's offer will be immediately accepted.

The immediate suspects were Thorndike's two nieces, Doris and Patsy, and his nephew John.

Thorndike Oil's capital structure is as follows:

- *Debt:* $250 million face value, issued in 1965 at a coupon rate of 5%, with market value of 60% of face value. This debt will be paid off at par if Dickens's offer goes through.
- *Stock:* 30 million shares closing yesterday at $10 per share.
- *Warrants:* Warrants to buy an additional 20 million shares at $10 per share, expiring December 31, 1991. The last trade of the warrants was at $1 per warrant.

Here are Doris, John, and Patsy's stakes in Thorndike Oil:

	Debt (Market Value)	Stock (Number of Shares)	Warrants (Number)
Doris	$6 million	1 million	0
John	0	0.5 million	2 million
Patsy	0	1.5 million	1 million

Which niece or nephew stood to gain most (in portfolio value) by eliminating old Thorndike and allowing Dickens's offer to succeed? Explain. Make additional assumptions if you find them necessary.

Figure 34-2 A decline in a currency's purchasing power and a decline in the exchange rate usually go hand in hand. In this diagram, each point represents the experience of a different country between 1983 and 1988. The vertical axis shows the change in the value of a foreign currency relative to the average. The horizontal axis shows the change in the currency's purchasing power relative to the average.

On the other hand, there is clearly some relationship between inflation and changes in exchange rates. For example, by 1988 prices in Bolivia were about 8,800 times their level in 1983. Or, to put it another way, you could say that the purchasing power of the Boliviano declined by about 99.99% relative to other countries. If exchange rates had not adjusted, Bolivian exporters would have found it impossible to sell their goods. But, of course, exchange rates did adjust. In fact, on average, one Boliviano bought 99.99% fewer units of foreign currency than before. Thus, a 99.99% relative decline in purchasing power was offset by a 99.99% decline in the value of the Bolivian currency.

Bolivia is an extreme case, but in Figure 34-2 we have plotted the relative change in purchasing power for a sample of countries against the change in the exchange rate. Bolivia is tucked in the bottom left-hand corner. You can see that although the relationship is far from exact, large differences in inflation rates are generally accompanied by an offsetting change in the exchange rate.

Strictly speaking, the law of one price implies that the differential inflation rate is always identical to the change in the exchange rate. But we don't need to go as far as that. We should be content if the *expected* difference in the inflation rate equals the *expected* change in the spot rate. That's all we wrote on the third side of our quadrilateral. In order to test this, Richard Roll looked at exchange rates of 23 countries between 1957 and 1976.[15] He found that, on average, today's exchange rate provided the best estimate of the inflation-adjusted exchange rate. In other words, your estimate of the inflation differential is also your best estimate of the change in the exchange rate.

---

[15] R. Roll, "Violations of the 'Law of One Price' and Their Implications for Differentially Denominated Assets," in M. Sarnat and G. Szego, eds., *International Finance and Trade*. Ballinger Press, Cambridge, Mass., 1979.

(Dec. 1982–1987)

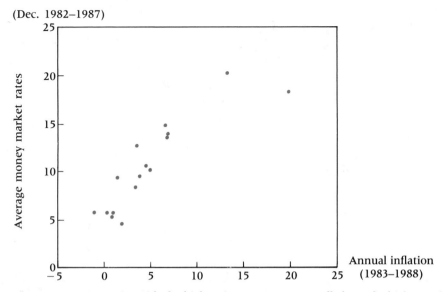

Figure 34-3   Countries with the highest interest rates generally have the highest subsequent inflation rates. In this diagram, each point represents the experience of a different country between 1983 and 1988.

Source: Morgan Guaranty Bank, *World Financial Markets.*

4. Capital market equilibrium   Finally we come to the relationship between interest rates in different countries. Do we have a single world capital market with the same *real* rate of interest in all countries? Can we even extend the notion and think of a single world market for risk capital, so that the real opportunity cost of capital for risky investments is the same in all countries? It is an attractive idea. Unfortunately, the evidence is scanty.

Since governments cannot directly control interest rates in the international eurocurrency markets, we might expect that in these markets, differences between the expected real rates of interest would be small. Governments have more control over their domestic rates of interest, at least in the short run. Therefore, it's possible for a country to have a real rate of interest in the domestic market that is below the real rate in other countries. But it is not easy to maintain this position indefinitely. Individuals and companies are capable of great ingenuity in transferring their cash from countries with low real rates of interest to those with high real rates of interest.

We cannot show the relationship between interest rates and *expected* inflation, but in Figure 34-3 we have plotted the average interest rate in each of 16 countries against the inflation that subsequently occurred. You can see that, in general, the countries with the highest interest rates also had the highest inflation rates. There were much smaller differences between the real rates of interest than between the nominal (or money) rates.

34-3   INSURING AGAINST CURRENCY RISKS

To hedge or not to hedge? Laker Airlines went bankrupt because it didn't. It had borrowed dollars aggressively, when much of its revenue was in sterling. When the dollar "took off" in the early 1980s. Laker could not meet debt service.

With misfortunes like this in mind, most companies hedge or at least limit their foreign exposures. For example, in 1989 another British company, Enterprise Oil, bought some oil properties from Texas Eastern for $440 million. Since the

C · H · A · P · T · E · R

23

VALUING RISKY DEBT

How do you estimate the present value of a company's bonds? The answer is simple. You take the cash flows and discount them at the opportunity cost of capital. Therefore if a bond is expected to produce cash flows of C dollars per year for N years and then to repay its face value ($1,000), the present value is

$$ PV = \frac{C}{1 + r_1} + \frac{C}{(1 + r_2)^2} + \cdots + \frac{C}{(1 + r_N)^N} + \frac{\$1,000}{(1 + r_N)^N} $$

where $r_1, r_2, \ldots, r_N$ are the appropriate discount rates for the cash flows to be received by the bond's owner in years $1, 2, \ldots, N$.

That is correct as far as it goes but it does not tell us anything about what *determines* the discount rate. For example:

1. In 1948 Canadian Treasury bills offered an average return of 0.4%: in April 1991 they offered a return of 9.4%. Why does the same security offer radically different yields at different points in time?
2. In April 1991 the Government of Canada could borrow for one to three years at an average interest rate of about 9.4%, but it had to pay an average rate of nearly 10% for loans of ten years and longer. Why do bonds maturing at different dates offer different rates of interest? In other words, why is there a *term structure* of interest rates?
3. In April 1991 the Canadian government could issue bonds with more than ten years to maturity at a rate of nearly 10%. You could not have borrowed at that rate. Why not? What explains the premium you have to pay?

These questions lead to deep issues that will keep economists simmering for years. But we can give general answers and at the same time present some fundamental ideas.

Why should the financial manager care about these ideas? Who needs to know how bonds are priced as long as the bond market is active and efficient? Efficient markets protect the ignorant trader. If it is necessary to check whether the price is right for a proposed bond issue, you can check the prices of similar bonds. There is no need to worry about the historical behaviour of interest rates, about the term structure, or about the other issues discussed in this chapter.

34-4   INTERNATIONAL INVESTMENT DECISIONS

Outland Steel's export business has risen to the point at which it is worth establishing a subsidiary in the Netherlands to hold inventories of steel. Outland's decision to invest overseas should be based on the same criteria as the decision to invest in Canada—that is, the company must identify the incremental cash flows, discount them at a rate that reflects the opportunity cost of capital, and accept all projects with a positive NPV.

Here are two ways that Outland could calculate the net present value of its Dutch venture:

- *Method 1:* Outland could follow the practice of many multinational companies and do all its capital budgeting calculations in dollars. In this case it must first estimate the guilder cash flows from its Dutch operation and convert these into dollars at the projected exchange rate. These dollar cash flows can then be discounted at the dollar cost of capital to give the investment's net present value in dollars.
- *Method 2:* In order to avoid making forecasts of the exchange rate, Outland could simply calculate the project's net present value entirely in terms of guilders. Outland could then convert this figure into dollars at the current exchange rate.

Each method has three steps, but the orders of steps 2 and 3 are different:

	Method 1	Method 2
Step 1	Estimate future cash flow in guilders	Estimate future cash flow in guilders
Step 2	Convert to dollars (at forecasted exchange rates)	Calculate present value (use guilder discount rate)
Step 3	Calculate present value (use dollar discount rate)	Convert to dollars (use spot rate)

Suppose Outland uses method 1. Where do the exchange rate forecasts come from? It would be foolish for Outland to accept a poor project just because management is particularly optimistic about the guilder—if Outland wishes to speculate in this way, it can simply buy guilders forward. Equally, it would be foolish for Outland to reject a good project just because it is pessimistic about the prospects for the guilder. The company would do much better to go ahead with the project and sell guilders forward. In that way, it would get the best of both worlds.

Thus, as long as company can alter its exchange exposure, its international capital expenditure decisions should *not* depend on whether the manager feels that a currency is wrongly valued. Instead of using its own exchange rate forecasts, Outland should base its capital investment decision on the foreign exchange market's consensus forecasts. To measure this consensus forecast, Outland can make use of the simple relationships described earlier in the chapter. If investors are on their financial toes, the expected movement in the exchange rate is equal to the difference between the interest rates in the two countries.

If Outland uses either of our two methods, its investment decision is also going to be heavily influenced by its assumption about the Dutch inflation rate. Although Outland's financial manager may well have her own views about Dutch inflation, it would again be foolish to let these views influence the investment decision. After all, there are more efficient ways to speculate on the inflation rate than by building (or not building) a steel distribution depot.[22] So the financial manager of Outland would do much better to assume that in efficient capital markets, the difference between the Dutch and Canadian interest rates reflects the likely difference in the inflation rates.[23]

Does it matter which of our two methods Outland uses to appraise its investment? It does if Outland employs its own forecasts of the exchange rate and inflation rate. However, as long as Outland assumes our simple parity relationships between interest rates, exchange rates, and inflation, the two methods will give the same answer.

EXAMPLE   We will illustrate with a simple example. Suppose Outland's Dutch facility is expected to generate the following cash flows in guilders:

	YEAR				
	1	2	3	4	5
Cash flow in thousands of guilders	400	450	510	575	650

How much is this cash flow worth today if Outland wants a 16% *dollar* return from its Dutch investment?

Outland's financial manager looks in the newspaper and finds that the risk-free interest rate is 8% in Canada ($r_\$ = 0.08$) and 9% in the Netherlands ($r_\text{fl} = 0.09$). She sees right away that if real interest rates are expected to be the same in the two countries, then the consensus forecast of the Dutch inflation rate (i_fl) must be approximately one percentage point higher than the inflation rate in Canada ($i_\$$). For example, if the expected rate of inflation in Canada is 5%, then the real rate of interest and the expected Dutch inflation rate are calculated as follows:

	(1 + Nominal Interest Rate)	=	(1 + Real Interest Rate)	×	(1 + Expected Inflation Rate)
In dollars	1.08	=	1.029	×	1.05
In guilders	1.09	=	1.029	×	1.06

The financial manager therefore checks that the guilder cash flow forecasts are consistent with this inflation rate.

Suppose the current spot rate is $0.50 to the guilder. Since the expected inflation rate in the Netherlands is higher than in Canada, the guilder is likely to depreciate against the dollar:

$$\begin{matrix} \text{Expected spot rate} \\ \text{at end of year} \end{matrix} = \begin{matrix} \text{spot rate at} \\ \text{start of year} \end{matrix} \times \begin{matrix} \text{inflation rate} \\ \text{differential} \end{matrix}$$

$$E(S_{\$/\text{fl}}) = S_{\$/\text{fl}} \times \frac{E(1 + i_\$)}{E(1 + i_\text{fl})}$$

---

[22] For example, if the manager believes that investors have underestimated the Dutch inflation rate, she should issue long-term guilder bonds and invest in short-term guilder bills or notes.

[23] There is a general point here that is not confined to international investment. Whenever you face an investment that appears to have a positive NPV, decide what it is that you are betting on and then think whether there is a more direct way to place the bet. For example, if a copper mine looks profitable only because you are unusually optimistic about the price of copper, then maybe you would do better to buy copper futures rather than open a copper mine.

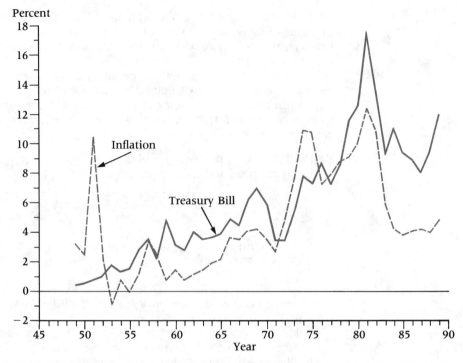

Figure 23-1   The yield on Canadian Treasury bills and the rate of inflation 1949–1989.
Source: International Monetary Fund, International Financial Statistics.

Fisher's theory states that changes in anticipated inflation produce corresponding changes in the rate of interest. But there is very little evidence of this in the early years shown in Figure 23-1. During this period, the return on Treasury bills scarcely changed even though inflation fluctuated sharply. Either these changes in inflation were unanticipated or Fisher's theory was wrong. Since 1954, there appears to have been a closer relationship between interest rates and inflation in Canada.[5] Therefore, it is worth looking more carefully at how well Fisher's theory has worked in these recent years.

Eugene Fama has suggested that one way to test Fisher's theory is to twist it around and measure whether the inflation rate can be forecasted by subtracting a constant real rate from the observed nominal interest rate. That is, if Fisher is right,

$$\text{Nominal interest rate} = \text{real interest rate} + \text{inflation rate forecasted by investors}$$

or

$$\text{Inflation rate forecasted by investors} = \text{nominal interest rate} - \text{real interest rate}$$

Of course, investors cannot predict the actual inflation rate perfectly—there will be a random forecast error. But in an efficient market, we expect them to be right on the average. Thus, the forecast error should be zero on the average.

---

[5] Until 1954, Treasury bills were not an important source of financing for the Government of Canada. Trading in Treasury bills was largely confined to chartered banks and the Bank of Canada. In an attempt to develop an organized money market, the Canadian government introduced a weekly Treasury bill auction market in early 1953 and then later in the same year allowed and encouraged money market dealers to trade Treasury bills. With the more active and liquid market came a more competitive interest rate.

Suppose that we observe the nominal returns on Treasury bills and the *actual* rates of inflation. We fit the following equation to these data:

$$\frac{\text{Actual}}{\text{inflation rate}} = a + b(\text{nominal interest rate}) + \text{random forecasting error}$$

If Fisher is correct, the coefficient b should be close to 1.0 and the constant term a should be equal to minus the real interest rate.

We estimated b on Canadian data for the period 1953 to 1989 as 0.71 and on U.S. data for same period as 0.81. Both of these estimates are a bit less than we should expect if Fisher is right *and* the real interest rate is constant.[6]

Before leaving this topic, we must add two qualifications. First, the real interest rate is really an *expected* rate. When you buy a Treasury bill and hold it to maturity, you know what the dollar payoff will be, but the *real* payoff is uncertain because future inflation is not wholly predictable. Thus, to be perfectly precise, we should define the real interest rate as follows:

Real interest rate = *expected* real rate of return from investment in Treasury bills
    = nominal rate of return on Treasury bills
    − *expected* rate of inflation

Second, Nelson and Schwert, and Hess and Bicksler have pointed out that the (expected) real interest rate *does* vary over time. Indeed, we have seen that the real rate appears to have been unusually high throughout the 1980s. If that is so, Fama's test may be inappropriate.[7]

Until these problems have been resolved, we recommend that you look on Fisher's theory simply as a useful rule of thumb. Thus, if the expected inflation rate changes, your best bet is that there will be a corresponding change in the interest rate.

23-2   TERM STRUCTURE AND YIELDS TO MATURITY

We turn now to the relationship between short-term and long-term rates of interest. Suppose that we have a simple loan which pays $1 at time 1. The present value of this loan is

$$PV = \frac{1}{1 + r_1}$$

Thus, we discount the cash flow at r_1, the rate appropriate for a one-period loan. This rate is fixed today; it is often called today's one-period **spot rate**.

If we have a loan that pays $1 at both times 1 and 2, its present value is:

$$PV = \frac{1}{1 + r_1} + \frac{1}{(1 + r_2)^2}$$

---

[6] Fama fitted his equation to quarterly U.S. data for the period 1953 to 1971. His estimate of b was 0.98, which is almost identical to the figure that Fisher would predict. See E.F. Fama, "Short-Term Interest Rates as Predictors of Inflation," *American Economic Review*, **65**: 269–282 (June 1975).

[7] C.R. Nelson and G. Schwert, "Short-Term Interest Rates as Predictors of Inflation: On Testing the Hypothesis that the Real Rate of Interest is Constant," *American Economic Review*, **67**: 478–486 (June 1977); P. Hess and J. Bicksler, "Capital Asset Prices versus Time Series Models as Predictors of Inflation," *Journal of Financial Economics*, **2**: 341–360 (December 1975).

markets like Chile, India, Thailand, or Hungary. Also, recall from Section 8-3 that Chrisman and Suret found little diversification benefit to Canadian investors by adding the opportunity to invest in foreign securities. Perhaps Canadians already invest in foreign markets through their domestic investments because Canadian firms already do much of their business in foreign markets.

Cooper and Kaplanis have tried to estimate the costs of foreign investment by asking how large the costs would need to be for the American holdings in foreign shares to make sense. They calculated that in the United States, investors behave *as if* the extra cost of investing in foreign shares is about 0.3% a year.[25]

Cooper and Kaplanis's estimates suggest a standard for American corporations that are investing abroad. If Americans are willing to pay a shade more for investing in overseas shares, they should be happy to see American corporations invest abroad even if they expect to earn a shade less than local companies.

Does Japan Enjoy a Lower Cost of Capital?

If there are costs in investing across national borders, then the cost of capital may not be identical in all countries. For example, you often hear people say that Japanese companies enjoy a lower cost of capital than their North American rivals. This difference, it is argued, shows up in the higher price-earnings ratio of Japanese stocks.[26]

This argument is two parts possible confusion and one part probable truth. What has the earnings-price ratio got to do with the cost of capital? Think back to Section 4-4 where we showed that this ratio, EPS_1/P_0, depends on the cost of equity capital, r, and the present value of growth opportunities, PVGO:

$$\frac{EPS_1}{P_0} = r\left(1 - \frac{PVGO}{P_0}\right)$$

When we observe a lower earnings-price ratio for Japanese stocks, it could mean three things:[27]

1. Japanese accountants measure earnings more conservatively than their North American cousins.[28] Since investors look through book earnings to true economic income, stock price is unaffected. Thus, the ratio of reported income to price is lower in Japan.
2. PVGO is higher—that is, Japanese firms have more growth opportunities.
3. r is lower—that is, investors are satisfied with a lower expected return from Japanese companies.

---

[25] I. Cooper and E. Kaplanis, "What Explains the Home Bias in Portfolio Investment?," Working Paper, London Business School (September 1990).

[26] At year-end 1989 the earnings-price ratio for the Japanese stock market was about 1.9 compared with 6.7 for the United States. The argument that differences in earnings-price ratios indicate a lower cost of capital in Japan is put forward in R.N. McCauley and S.A. Zimmer, "Explaining International Differences in the Cost of Capital," *Federal Reserve Bank of New York Quarterly Review,* **14**: 7–28 (Summer 1989). Note: McCauley and Zimmer adjust the ratios for differences in accounting practices.

[27] For a discussion of these possible explanations see K.R. French and J.M. Poterba, "Were Japanese Stock Prices Too High?," forthcoming *Journal of Financial Economics* (1991).

[28] For example, Japanese companies use accelerated tax depreciation for their reports to shareholders. This practice reduces their reported EPS compared to Canadian and U.S. firms, most of which use straight-line depreciation.

Of course, choice of depreciation method doesn't affect reported EPS in a no-growth steady rate—although it does affect the book rate of return, as we explained in Section 12-4. However, most firms grow. Many Japanese firms have grown rapidly.

Simply looking at earnings-price ratios won't tell us whether Japan has the lower cost of capital. But explanation 3, that r really is lower, is nevertheless plausible. Think again about the costs of overseas investment. Japan has substantial excess savings that cannot be absorbed by Japanese industry and therefore must be invested overseas. Japanese investors are not *compelled* to invest overseas: they need to be tempted to do so. If there are costs to buying foreign stocks, then the relative price of Japanese stocks must rise and the expected return must fall until Japanese investors are happy to hold foreign investments.

There is a general message here. If investors have large surpluses that must be invested overseas, of if they incur unusually large costs to get their money out, then the domestic cost of capital is likely to be forced down.

Avoiding Fudge Factors in International Investment Decisions

We certainly don't pretend that we can put a precise figure on the cost of capital for foreign investment. But you can see that we disagree with the frequent practice of automatically marking *up* the domestic cost of capital when foreign investment is considered. We suspect that managers mark up the required return for foreign investment to cover the risk of expropriation, foreign exchange restrictions, or unfavourable tax changes. A fudge factor is added to the discount factor to cover these costs.

We think managers should leave the discount rate alone and reduce expected cash flows instead. For example, suppose that Outland is expected to earn 450,000 guilders in the first year *if no penalties are placed on the operations of foreign firms.* Suppose also that there is a 10% chance that Outland's operation may be expropriated without compensation.[29] The *expected* cash flow is not 450,000 guilders but $0.9 \times 450 = 405,000$ guilders.

The end result may be the same when you add a fudge factor to the discount rate. Nevertheless, adjusting cash flows brings management's assumptions about "political risks" out in the open for scrutiny and sensitivity analysis.

34-6   FINANCING FOREIGN OPERATIONS

Outland can pay for its Dutch venture in three ways. It can export capital from Canada, it can borrow Dutch guilders, or it can borrow wherever interest rates are lowest.

Notice that if the guilder is devalued, other things equal, the Dutch assets will be worth fewer dollars than before. In this case, Outland could protect itself against exchange risk by borrowing guilders. It would then have both a Dutch asset and an offsetting Dutch liability. If the guilder is devalued, the dollar value of the asset falls, but that is offset by the fact that Outland now needs fewer dollars to service its guilder debt.

Unfortunately, other things are rarely equal, for the devaluation may be accompanied by changes in the guilder value of Outland's assets. Remember that the law of one price states that any change in the guilder exchange rate will be exactly offset by a change in the relative price of Dutch goods. Of course, you know better than to take that theory literally, but it may not be too bad an approximation in the case of readily exportable goods such as steel inventory. In other words, even if the guilder is devalued, Outland's steel inventory may largely hold its value in terms of dollars. Therefore, rather than finance the entire venture by guilder debt, it may be safer to finance it with a mixture of guilders and dollars.

---

[29] Our example is fanciful. Most measures of political risk place the Netherlands as one of the most stable environments for investment.

Table 23-1
(Continued)

Coupon = 9%   Page 5

Yield	\multicolumn{5}{c}{Years}

Yield	6	8	10	12	14
6.00%	114.93	118.84	122.32	125.40	128.15
7.00	109.66	112.09	114.21	116.06	117.67
8.00	104.69	105.83	106.80	107.62	108.33
9.00	100.00	100.00	100.00	100.00	100.00
10.00	95.57	94.58	93.77	93.10	92.55
11.00	91.38	89.54	88.05	86.85	85.88
12.00	87.42	84.84	82.80	81.17	79.89
13.00	83.68	80.46	77.96	76.02	74.51
14.00	80.14	76.38	73.51	71.33	69.66

Coupon = 10%   Page 6

Yield	6	8	10	12	14
6.00%	119.91	125.12	129.75	133.87	137.53
7.00	114.50	118.14	121.32	124.09	126.50
8.00	109.39	111.65	113.59	115.25	116.66
9.00	104.56	105.62	106.50	107.25	107.87
10.00	100.00	100.00	100.00	100.00	100.00
11.00	95.69	94.77	94.02	93.42	92.94
12.00	91.62	89.89	88.53	87.45	86.59
13.00	87.76	85.35	83.47	82.01	80.88
14.00	84.11	81.11	78.81	77.06	75.73

Coupon = 11%   Page 7

Yield	6	8	10	12	14
6.00%	124.89	131.40	137.19	142.34	146.91
7.00	119.33	124.19	128.42	132.12	135.33
8.00	114.08	117.48	120.39	122.87	124.99
9.00	109.12	111.23	113.01	114.50	115.74
10.00	104.43	105.42	106.23	106.90	107.45
11.00	100.00	100.00	100.00	100.00	100.00
12.00	95.81	94.95	94.27	93.72	93.30
13.00	91.84	90.23	88.98	88.01	87.25
14.00	88.09	85.83	84.11	82.80	81.79

Coupon = 12%   Page 8

Yield	6	8	10	12	14
6.00%	129.86	137.68	144.63	150.81	156.29
7.00	124.16	130.24	135.53	140.15	144.17
8.00	118.77	123.30	127.18	130.49	133.33
9.00	113.68	116.85	119.51	121.74	123.61
10.00	108.86	110.84	112.46	113.80	114.90
11.00	104.31	105.23	105.98	106.58	107.06
12.00	100.00	100.00	100.00	100.00	100.00
13.00	95.92	95.12	94.49	94.00	93.63
14.00	92.06	90.55	89.41	88.53	87.86

value plus interest are paid back at maturity, 1998. The price of each bond is quoted as a percent of face value. Therefore, if face value is $1,000, you would have to pay $852.10 to buy the bond and your yield would be 8.78%. Letting 1993 be $t = 0$, 1994 be $t = 1$, and so on, we have the following discounted cash-flow calculation.[9]

Bond	C_0	C_1	C_2	C_3	C_4	C_5	Yield %
			Cash Flows				
5s of '98	−852.10	+50	+50	+50	+50	+1,050	8.78
10s of '98	−1,054.30	+100	+100	+100	+100	+1,100	8.62

Although the two bonds mature at the same date, they presumably were issued at different times, the 5s when interest rates were low, and the 10s when interest rates were high.

Are the 5s of '98 a better buy? Is the market making a mistake by pricing these two issues at different yields? The only way you will know for sure is to calculate the bond's present values using spot rates of interest, r_1 for 1994, r_2 for 1995, and so on. This is done in Table 23-2.

Table 23-2
Calculating present value of two bonds when long-term interest rates are higher than short-term rates.

Period	Interest Rate	5s of '98		10s of '98	
		C_1	PV at r_t	C_t	PV at r_t
			Present Value Calculations		
$t = 1$	$r_1 = 0.05$	$ 50	$ 47.62	$ 100	$ 95.24
$t = 2$	$r_2 = 0.06$	50	44.50	100	89.00
$t = 3$	$r_3 = 0.07$	50	40.81	100	81.63
$t = 4$	$r_4 = 0.08$	50	36.75	100	73.50
$t = 5$	$r_5 = 0.09$	1,050	682.43	1,100	714.92
	Totals	$1,250	$852.11	$1,500	$1,054.29

The important assumption in Table 23-2 is that long-term interest rates are higher than short-term interest rates. We have assumed that the one-year interest rate is $r_1 = 0.05$, the two-year rate is $r_2 = 0.06$, and so on. When each year's cash flow is discounted at the rate appropriate to that year, we see that each bond's present value is exactly equal to the quoted price. Thus, each bond is *fairly priced*.

Why do the 5s have a higher yield? Because, for each dollar that you invest in the 5s you receive relatively little cash inflow in the first four years and a relatively high cash inflow in the final year. Therefore, although the two bonds have identical maturity dates, the 5s provide a greater proportion of their cash flows in 1998. In this sense the 5s are a longer-term investment than the 10s. Their higher yield to maturity just reflects the fact that long-term interest rates are higher than short-term rates.

---

[9] Coupon payments are actually made semiannually—the owners of the 5s of '98 would receive $25 every six months. Thus, our calculations are a little bit off what you would get from using bond tables like Table 23-1.

Table 34-2
How to calculate Canadian tax on income earned in a foreign country (figures in dollars)

(a) *Outland Steel's Dutch subsidiary*
Note that the Netherlands and Canada have a tax treaty, so the dividend is out of exempt surplus.

	Dutch Corporate Tax at 40%	Dutch Corporate Tax at 20%
Profits before tax	1,000	1,000
Dutch corporate income tax	400	200
Net profits in the Netherlands, paid as dividend	600	800
Withholding tax	15% of 60 = 90	15% of 80 = 120
Received in Canada	510	680
Canadian tax payable	0	0
Available for dividend in Canada	510	680

(b) *Outland Steel's Algerian subsidiary*
Note that Canada has no tax treaty with Algeria, so that the dividend is out of taxable surplus.

	Algerian Corporate Tax at 40%		Algerian Corporate Tax at 20%	
Profits before tax		1,000		1,000
Algerian corporate income tax		400		200
Net profits in Algeria, paid as dividend		600		800
Withholding tax	15% of 60 =	90	15% of 80 =	120
Received in Canada		510		680
Taxable dividend revenue in Canada	600		800	
Deductions for foreign tax:				
For foreign income tax	− 1.63158 × 400 =	(653)	−1.63158 × 200 =	(326)
For withholding tax	− 2.63158 × 90 =	(237)	−2.63158 × 120 =	(316)
Net		(290)		158
Taxable income*		0		158
Canadian corporate income tax at 36%		0		57
Available for dividend in Canada		510		623

* Canadian taxable income is maximum ($0, dividend − deductions for foreign tax).

Now, consider the case of Outland's Algerian subsidiary. Algeria does not have a tax treaty with Canada, so dividend income may be exposed to double taxation when it is repatriated to Canada. The system is similar to a foreign tax credit scheme in which a credit is allowed for foreign income tax and withholding tax that is paid. The idea is that the total Canadian and Algerian tax paid should equal the tax that would be paid if the income is taxed at the *higher* of the Canadian and Algerian rates. Thus, if the total Algerian tax (income and withholding tax) exceeds the Canadian income tax that would be paid on the same pretax income, then no further Canadian tax is owed. If the total Algerian tax is less than the Canadian income tax that would be paid, then Canada charges a tax just large enough to raise the total tax bill to what would be owed if the subsidiary were located in Canada.

Of course, we are talking about tax law and by now you are suspicious of any explanation of tax law that takes only two brief paragraphs. Indeed, the tax calculations for Outland's Algerian subsidiary are slightly more complex than we just described. They are shown in Table 34-2(b). Instead of a tax credit scheme, Outland actually gets a deduction from earnings calculated on a "relevant tax factor" that is based on the assumption that the Canadian corporate tax rate is 38%. Overall, you can see that, if the Algerian subsidiary has a higher tax rate than Outland has in Canada, then no Canadian tax is paid on the dividend income. However, if the Algerian subsidiary has a low tax rate, then a small amount of Canadian tax is owed.[34,35]

Overall, if the subsidiary is operating in a high-tax country, dividend payments are not subject to additional taxes in Canada. On the other hand, you may do better to arrange a loan from the parent to the subsidiary. The parent company must pay Canadian tax on the interest, but the foreign subsidiary can deduct the interest before paying local tax. Another way to transfer income from high-tax areas to low-tax areas is to levy royalties or management fees on the subsidiary. Or it may be possible to change the transfer prices on sales of goods within the group. Needless to say, the tax and customs authorities are well aware of these incentives to minimize taxes and they will insist that all such intergroup payments be reasonable.

34-7   POLITICAL RISK

Think about what the political risk of a foreign investment really is. It is the threat that a foreign government will change the rules of the game—that is, break a promise or understanding—*after* the investment is made. Some managers think of political risks as an act of God, like a hurricane or earthquake. But the most successful multinational companies structure their business to reduce political risks.

Foreign governments are not likely to expropriate a local business if it cannot operate without the support of its parent. For example, the foreign subsidiaries of computer manufacturers or pharmaceutical companies would have relatively little value if they were cut off from the know-how of their parents. Such operations are much less likely to be expropriated than, say, a mining operation which can be operated as a stand-alone venture.

We are not recommending that you turn your silver mine into a pharmaceutical company, but you may be able to plan overseas manufacturing operations to improve your bargaining position with foreign governments. For example, Ford has integrated its overseas operations so that the manufacture of components,

---

[34] A similar tax credit scheme is the dividend tax credit allowed to individuals, as discussed in Section 16-5 and Appendix 16-1.

[35] The dividend for the Algerian subsidiary comes out of *taxable surplus*. The deductions for foreign tax are in paragraphs 113(1)(*b*) and (*c*) of the *Income Tax Act*. The "relevant tax factor" 2.63158 = 1/0.38. See K.J. Dancey, *et al.*, pp. 48–49 for a discussion of the similarity between a tax credit scheme and the actual taxation of a dividend out of taxable surplus. (However, note that the tax law was changed in 1988 so that their relevant tax factor is outdated.)

If the Algerian subsidiary is wholly owned by Outland, the foreign subsidiary may pay part of its income as a dividend and Outland can receive a further "tax credit" for the tax on retained income. This credit cannot be so large as to exceed the Canadian income tax on the dividend. Thus, if the foreign income tax rate is much higher than the Canadian tax rate, the Canadian owner need not wait until the dividends are repatriated to get the benefit of the "credit"—to a limited extent a credit is allowed against taxes paid on earnings that are retained by the foreign subsidiary.

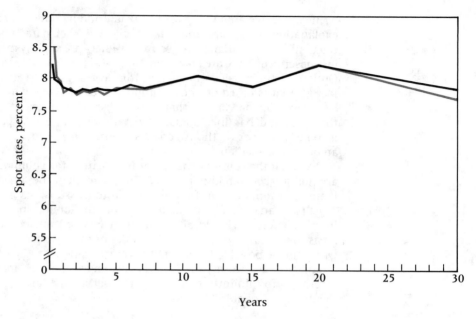

Figure 23-2 Estimated spot rates on U.S. Treasury securities, July 1989. The coloured line gives estimates made by BARRA. The black line shows rates on U.S. Treasury "strips."

a future nest-egg to combine with their retirement savings plans. The price of a $100,000, 20-year strip bond with a promised yield of 12% annually is as little as 10% of the face value.

The strip bond or mini-bond yields provide another way to measure spot interest rates. Simply look at the interest rates on each of these bonds. For example, the broken line in Figure 23-2 shows the rates of interest on U.S. Treasury "stripped" bonds. Notice that these rates are almost indistinguishable from Barra's estimates of the interest rates on packages of Treasury coupon bonds.

*Pricing Bonds of Different Maturity

Do you remember how we valued options? The profit or loss on an option depends only on what happens to the underlying stock. You can, therefore, create a mixture of a risk-free loan and the stock which gives exactly the same payoffs as the option. If both packages give the same payoff, they must sell for the same price.

We can use a similar idea to check that bonds of different maturity are consistently priced. For example, suppose that the price of each bond depends only on what happens to the short-term rate of interest. Then you could exactly duplicate the payoffs on any bond by holding a mixture of two other bonds. If both investments give the same payoff, you know that they should sell for the same price. If they don't, you unload the expensive investment and buy the cheap one. Investors are now starting to use these ideas to price different bonds.

23-3 EXPLAINING THE TERM STRUCTURE

The term structure in Figure 23-2 is upward-sloping. In other words, long rates of interest are higher than short rates. This is the more common pattern but sometimes it is the other way around, with short rates higher than long rates. Why do we get these shifts in term structure?

Table 23-3
Two investment strategies for Ms. Long, who wants to invest $1,000 for two years.

Strategy	Now	Year 1	Year 2 (Final Payoff)
L1 invest in 2 one-year bonds	$1,000 → (Invest in first bond yielding r_1)	$1,000(1 + r_1)$ → (Invest in second bond yielding r_2)	$1,000(1 + r_1)(1 + {}_1r_2)$
L2 invest in 1 two-year bond	$1,000 ⟶ (Invest in bond yielding r_2)		$1,000(1 + r_2)^2$
Strategy L2 can be expressed as	$1,000 → (Invest for one year at r_1)	$1,000(1 + r_1)$ → (Invest for second year at implicit forward rate f_2)	$1,000(1 + r_1)(1 + f_2)$

Ms. Long's Problem

Let us look at a simple example. Ms. Long wants to invest $1,000 for two years. Two strategies open to her are described in Table 23-3. Strategy L1 is to put the money in a one-year bond at an interest rate of r_1. At the end of the year she must then take her money and find another one-year bond. Let us call the rate of interest on this second bond ${}_1r_2$—that is, the spot rate of interest at time 1 on a loan maturing at time 2.[13] As Table 23-3 shows, the final payoff to this strategy is $1,000(1 + r_1)(1 + {}_1r_2)$.

Of course Ms. Long cannot know for sure what the one-period spot rate of interest ${}_1r_2$ will be next year. Suppose that she *expects* it to be 11%. That is, $E({}_1r_2) = 0.11$. The current one-period spot rate is 10%. The expected final payoff is:

$$1,000(1 + r_1)[1 + E({}_1r_2)] = 1,000(1.10)(1.11) = \$1,221$$

Instead of making two separate investments of one year each, Ms. Long could invest her money today in a bond that pays off in year 2 (strategy L2 in Table 23-3). That is, she would invest at the *two-year* spot rate r_2, and receive a final payoff of $1,000 (1 + r_2)^2$. If $r_2 = 0.105$, the payoff is $1,000(1.105)^2 = \$1,221$.

Now, look below the dashed line in Table 23-3. The table shows that strategy L2 can be reinterpreted as investing for one year at the spot rate r_1 and for the second year at a **forward rate** f_2. The forward rate is *implicit* in the two-year spot rate r_2. It is also *guaranteed*: by buying the two-year bond, Ms. Long can "lock in" an interest rate of f_2 for the second year she invests.

Suppose that the two-year spot rate is 10.5% as before. Then the forward rate f_2 must be 11%. By definition, the forward rate for $t = 2$ is the implicit interest rate in the second year of the two-year loan:

$$(1 + r_2)^2 = (1 + r_1)(1 + f_2)$$
$$(1.105)^2 = (1.10)(1 + f_2)$$
$$f_2 = \frac{(1.105)^2}{1.10} - 1 = 0.11$$

or 11%.[14] The two-year spot rate of 10.5% is an average of the 10% one-year spot rate and the 11% forward rate.

---

[13] Be careful to distinguish ${}_1r_2$ from r_2, the spot interest rate on a *two-year* bond held from time 0 to time 2. The quantity ${}_1r_2$ is a *one-year* spot rate established at time 1.

[14] Actually, 11.002%. We rounded.

34-9 SUMMARY

The international financial manager has to cope with different currencies, interest rates, and inflation rates and must be familiar with a variety of different capital markets and tax systems. The most we can hope to do in these pages is to whet your appetite.

To produce order out of chaos, the international financial manager needs some model of the relationship between exchange rates, interest rates, and inflation rates. We described four very simple but useful theories.

Interest rate parity theory states that the interest differential between two countries must be equal to the difference between the forward and spot exchange rates. In the international markets, arbitrage ensures that parity almost always holds. There are two ways to hedge against exchange risk—one is to take out forward cover, the other is to borrow or lend abroad. Interest rate parity tells us that the cost of the two methods should be the same.

The expectations theory of exchange rates tells us that the forward rate equals the expected spot rate. If you believe the expectations theory, you will generally insure against exchange risks.

In its strict form, the law of one price states that $1 must have the same purchasing power in every country. That doesn't square very well with the facts, for differences in inflation rates are not perfectly related to changes in exchange rates. This means that there may be some genuine exchange risks in doing business overseas. On the other hand, the difference in the inflation rates is just as likely to be above as below the change in the exchange rate.

Finally, we saw that in an integrated world capital market real rates of interest would have to be the same. In practice, government regulation and taxes can cause differences in real interest rates. But do not simply borrow where interest rates are lowest. Those countries are also likely to have the lowest inflation rates and the strongest currencies.

With these precepts in mind we looked at three common problems in international finance. First, we showed how you can use the forward markets or the loan markets to price and insure long-term export contracts.

Second, we considered the problem of international capital budgeting. We warned against making stupid investment decisions simply because you have a strong view about future exchange rates. And we showed that it makes no difference which currency you use for your calculations as long as you assume that prices, interest rates, and exchange rates are linked by the simple theories that we described above. The main difficulty is to select the right discount rate. If there is a free market for capital, the discount rate for your project is the return that your shareholders expect from investing in foreign securities. This rate is difficult to measure, but we argued against just adding a premium for the "extra risks" of overseas investment.

Finally, we looked at the problem of financing overseas subsidiaries. There are at least three issues that you should think about. Other things equal, you would like to protect yourself against exchange risk: you may be able to do this by borrowing part of the money in the local currency. Second, you need to think about tax: for example, you can reduce tax by borrowing in high-tax countries and lending in low-tax countries. Third, you should consider whether you can structure the financing to reduce the risk that governments will change the rules of the game.

The cash flow that the parent company receives from its overseas operations depends on the way that they are financed. Therefore, an adjusted present value approach is needed to analyze international investment proposals.

FURTHER READING

There are a number of useful textbooks in international finance. Here is a small selection:

R.Z. Aliber, ed., *Handbook of International Financial Management*, Dow Jones-Irwin, Homewood, IL, 1989.

K.K. Eiteman and A.I. Stonehill, *Multinational Business Finance*, 5th ed., Addison-Wesley Publishing Company, Inc., Reading, Mass., 1989.

M.D. Levi, *International Finance: The Markets and Financial Management of Multinational Business*, 2nd ed., McGraw-Hill, New York, 1990.

R. Rodriquez and E. Carter, *International Financial Management*, 3rd ed., Prentice-Hall, Inc., Englewood Cliffs, New Jersey, 1984.

A.C. Shapiro, *Multinational Financial Management*, 3rd ed., Allyn and Bacon, Inc., Boston, 1989.

Also, it's worth leafing through *Euromoney* and *Euromoney Corporate Finance* for current events and developments in international finance.

Here are some general discussions of international investment decisions and associated exchange risks:

B. Cornell and A.C. Shapiro, "Managing Foreign Exchange Risks," *Midland Corporate Finance Journal*, **1**: 16–31 (Fall 1983).

E. Flood and D. Lessard, "On the Measurement of Operating Exposure to Exchange Rates: A Conceptual Approach," *Financial Management*, **15**: 25–36 (Spring 1986).

A.C. Shapiro, "International Capital Budgeting," *Midland Corporate Finance Journal*, **1**: 26–45 (Spring 1983).

And here is a sample of the articles on some of the relationships between interest rates, exchange rates, and inflation rates:

Forward Rates and Spot Rates

B. Cornell, "Spot Rates, Forward Rates and Exchange Market Efficiency," *Journal of Financial Economics*, **5**: 55–65 (1977).

E.F. Fama, "Forward and Spot Exchange Rates," *Journal of Monetary Economics*. **14**: 319–338 (1984).

R.M. Levich, "Tests of Forecasting Models and Market Efficiency in the International Money Market," in J.A. Frenkel and H.G. Johnson, eds., *The Economics of Exchange Rates: Selected Studies*, Addison-Wesley Publishing Company, Inc., Reading, Mass., 1978.

C.P. Wolff, "Forward Foreign Exchange Rates, Expected Spot Rates and Premia: A Signal Extraction Approach," *Journal of Finance*, **42**: 395–406 (June 1987).

Interest Rate Parity

K. Clinton, "Transaction Costs and Covered Interest Advantage: Theory and Evidence," *Journal of Political Economy*, **96**: 358–370 (April 1988).

J.A. Frenkel and R.M. Levich, "Covered Interest Arbitrage: Unexploited Profits?" *Journal of Political Economy*, **83**: 325–338 (April 1975).

Law of One Price

N. Abuaf and P. Jorian, "Purchasing Power Parity in the Long Run," *Journal of Finance*, **45**: 157–174 (March 1990).

M. Adler and B. Lehmann, "Deviations from Purchasing Power Parity in the Long Run," *Journal of Finance*, **38**: 1471–1487 (December 1983).

L.H. Officer, "The Purchasing Power Theory of Exchange Rates: A Review Article," *IMF Staff Papers*, March 1976.

R. Roll, "Violations of the 'Law of One Price' and Their Implications for Differentially Denominated Assets," in M. Sarnat and G. Szego, eds., *International Finance and Trade*, Ballinger Press, Cambridge, Mass., 1979.

spot rate? Then both Long and Short prefer investing in two-year bonds. If the world were entirely made up of expected-return maximizers, and f_2 exceeds $E(_1r_2)$, no one would be willing to hold one-year bonds. On the other hand, if the forward rate were less than the expected future spot rate, no one would be willing to hold two-year bonds. Since investors *do* hold both one-year and two-year bonds, it follows that forward rates of interest must equal expected future spot rates (providing that investors are only interested in expected return).

This is the **expectations hypothesis** of the term structure.[16] It says that the *only* reason for an upward-sloping term structure is that investors expect future spot rates to be higher than current spot rates; the *only* reason for a declining term structure is that investors expect spot rates to fall below current levels. The expectations hypothesis also implies that investing in short-term bonds (as in strategies L1 and S1) gives exactly the same expected return as investing in long-term bonds (as in strategies L2 and S2).

The Liquidity-Preference Theory

One problem with the expectations theory is that it says nothing about risk. Look back for a moment at our two simple cases. Ms. Long wants to invest for two years. If she buys a two-year bond, she can nail down her final payoff today. If she buys a one-year bond, she knows her return for the first year but she does not know at what rate she will be able to reinvest her money. If she does not like this uncertainty, she will tend to prefer the two-year bond, and she will hold one-year bonds only if

$$E(_1r_2) \text{ is greater than } f_2$$

What about Mr. Short? He wants to invest for one year. If he invests in a one-year bond, he can nail down his payoff today. If he buys the two-year bond, he will have to sell it next year at an unknown price. If he does not like this uncertainty, he will prefer the one-year investment, and he will hold two-year bonds only if

$$E(_1r_2) \text{ is less than } f_2$$

Here we have the basis for the **liquidity-preference** theory of term structure.[17] Other things being equal, Ms. Long will prefer to invest in two-year bonds and Mr. Short in one-year bonds. If more companies want to issue two-year bonds than there are Ms. Longs to hold them, they will need to offer a bonus to tempt some of the Mr. Shorts to hold them. Conversely, if more companies want to issue one-year bonds than there are Mr. Shorts to hold them, they will need to offer a bonus to tempt some of the Ms. Longs to hold them.

Any bonus shows up as a difference between forward rates and expected future spot rates. This difference is usually called the **liquidity premium**.

Suppose that there is a shortage of people like Ms. Long. Then the liquidity premium will be positive—that is, the forward rate will exceed the expected spot rate. Advocates of the liquidity-preference theory believe that for the most part, investors want to lend short and companies want to borrow long, so that liquidity premiums are positive.

---

[16] The expectations hypothesis is usually attributed to Lutz and Lutz. See F.A. Lutz and V.C. Lutz, *The Theory of Investment in the Firm*, Princeton University Press, Princeton, N.J., 1951.

[17] The liquidity-preference hypothesis is usually attributed to Hicks. See J.R. Hicks, *Value and Capital: An Inquiry into Some Fundamental Principles of Economic Theory*, 2nd ed., Oxford University Press, Oxford, 1946. For a theoretical development, see R. Roll, *The Behavior of Interest Rates: An Application of the Efficient Market Model to U.S. Treasury Bills*, Basic Books, Inc., Publishers, New York, 1970.

If the liquidity-preference theory is right, the term structure should be upward-sloping more often than not. A positive liquidity premium rewards investors for lending long. This reward shows up in higher long-term rates of interest. Of course, if future spot rates are expected to fall, the term structure could be downward-sloping and *still* reward investors for lending long. But the liquidity-preference hypothesis would predict a less dramatic downward slope than the expectations hypothesis would.

Introducing Inflation

We argued above that Ms. Long could nail down her return by investing in two-year bonds. What do we mean by that? If the bonds are issued by the Canadian government, she can be virtually certain that she will be paid the promised number of dollars. But she cannot be certain what that money will buy. The expectations theory and the liquidity-preference theory of term structure implicitly assume that future inflation rates are known. Let us consider the opposite case in which the *only* uncertainty about interest rates stems from uncertainty about inflation.[18]

Suppose that Irving Fisher is right and short rates of interest always incorporate fully the market's latest views about inflation. Suppose also that the market learns more as time passes about the likely inflation rate in a particular year. Perhaps today it has only a very hazy idea about inflation in year 2, but in a year's time it expects to be able to make a much better prediction.

Because future inflation rates are never known with certainty, neither Ms. Long nor Mr. Short can make a completely risk-free investment. But since they expect to learn a good deal about the inflation rate in year 2 from experience in year 1, next year they will be in a much better position to judge the appropriate interest rate in year 2. It is therefore more risky for either of them to make a forward commitment to lend in year 2. Even Ms. Long, who wants to invest for two years, would be incurring unnecessary risk by buying a two-year bond. Her least risky strategy is to invest in successive one-year bonds. She does not know what her reinvestment rate will be, but at least she knows that it will incorporate the latest information about inflation in year 2.

Of course, this means that borrowers must offer some incentive if they want investors to lend long. Therefore, the forward rate of interest f_2 must be greater than the expected spot rate $_1r_2$ by an amount that compensates investors for the extra inflation risk.

EXAMPLE   Suppose that the real interest rate is always 2%. Nominal interest rates therefore equal 2% plus the expected rate of inflation. Suppose that the *expected* inflation rate is 8% for both year 1 and year 2. However, inflation may accelerate to 10% in year 1, or it may decrease to 6%. To keep things simple, assume that the actual inflation rate for year 1 continues for year 2:

	Actual Inflation in Year 1	Actual Inflation in Year 2
Expected inflation rate = 0.08	0.10	0.10
	0.08	0.08
	0.06	0.06

Each outcome has a probability of one-third.

[18] The following is based on R.A. Brealey and S. Schaefer, "Term Structure and Uncertain Inflation," *Journal of Finance*, **32**: 277–290 (May 1977).

4. Look in *The Globe and Mail*. How many French francs can you buy for $1? How many German marks can you buy? What rate do you think a German bank would quote for buying or selling French francs? Explain what would happen if it quoted a rate that was substantially above your figure.

5. What do our four basic relationships imply about the relationship between two countries' interest rates and the expected change in the exchange rate? Explain why you would or would not expect them to be related.

6. Ms. Rosetta Stone, the treasurer of International Reprints, Inc., has noticed that the interest rate in Switzerland is below the rates in most other countries. She is, therefore, suggesting that the company should make an issue of Swiss franc bonds. What considerations ought she first to take into account?

7. What considerations should a Canadian company take into account when deciding how to finance its overseas subsidiaries?

8. A Canadian firm is evaluating an investment in Switzerland. The project costs 20 million Swiss francs and it is expected to produce an income of 3 million francs a year in real terms for each of the next 10 years. The expected inflation rate in Switzerland is 1% a year and the firm estimates that an appropriate discount rate for the project would be about 8% above the risk-free rate of interest. Calculate the net present value of the project in dollar using each of the two methods described in this chapter. Exchange rates are given in Figure 34-1. The interest rate was about 4% in Switzerland and 10% in Canada.

9. 'The decline in the value of the dollar has made chemical producers in Canada attractive targets for takeover by European companies." Discuss.

10. Suppose you are the treasurer of Lufthansa. How is the company value likely to be affected by exchange rate changes? What policies would you adopt to reduce exchange rate risk?

11. Suppose that you do use your own views about inflation and exchange rates when valuing an overseas investment proposal. Specifically, suppose that you believe that inflation will be 2% in the Netherlands and 5% in Canada but that the exchange rate will remain unchanged. Recalculate the NPV of the Outland project using both of our methods. Each NPV implies a different financing strategy. What are they?

12. Companies may be affected by changes in the nominal exchange rate or in the real exchange rate. Explain how this can occur. Which risks are easiest to hedge against?

13. We suggested that a Ford dealer in Canada may be exposed to devaluation in the yen if this leads to a cut in the price of Japanese cars. Suppose that the dealer estimates that a 1% decline in the value of the yen would result in a permanent decline of 5% in the dealer's profits. How should she hedge against this risk and how should she calculate the size of the hedge position?

14. You have bid for a possible export order which would provide a cash inflow of 1 million DM in 6 months. The spot exchange rate is $0.55/DM and the 6-month forward rate is $0.58/DM. There are two sources of uncertainty—(1) the deutsche mark could appreciate or depreciate, and (2) you may or may not receive the export order. Illustrate in each case the profits or losses that you would make if
   (a) You sell 1 million DM forward
   (b) You buy a 6-month put option on deutsche marks with an exercise price of $0.58/DM.

C·H·A·P·T·E·R

35

PENSION PLANS

At the end of 1988, current and past employees of Bethlehem Steel in the United States had earned the right to pensions valued at $4.0 billion. To help cover this liability, the company had put aside $2.8 billion in its pension fund, leaving a deficiency of $1.2 billion.[1]

This pension liability is a debt that one day the company will be obliged to honour. In fact, it is Bethlehem's largest debt, five times the total amount of long-term loans shown on Bethlehem's balance sheet. The pension fund is also one of Bethlehem's largest assets, amounting to 40% of the book value of all its plant and equipment.

The company's pension plan is a major responsibility for you as financial manager. You can always call on the advice of specialists such as the actuary, pension consultant, and investment manager, but the buck (or lack of bucks) stops on your desk. Therefore, you must understand the arguments behind the advice you receive and grasp its implications for company policy. That is the reason we have included a chapter on pensions.

First, we consider briefly the pension benefits companies offer. Second, we look at how the actuary calculates the cost of these benefits by drawing up a pension plan balance sheet. This balance sheet affects the amount of money that the company must put aside each year in its pension fund. Finally, we see how the financial manager helps to set the objectives of the pension fund and to monitor its performance.

35-1 TYPES OF PENSION PLANS

When they retire, most employees draw three pensions. One is the Old Age Security (OAS) benefit that is provided by the federal government. Every Canadian citizen is allowed to draw this benefit once he or she has reached the age of 65. The second is a Canada Pension Plan (CPP) benefit, which is paid from the Canada Pension Plan premiums the employee has contributed during his or her

---

[1] We singled out Bethlehem Steel because it had an unusually large unfunded liability. Most large companies in 1988 had pension plans that were in surplus, i.e., the assets in the pension fund more than covered the accumulated liability. However, for many companies this reversed by 1990 with companies like Imperial Oil and Imasco finding they had deficits instead of the surpluses from the previous year.

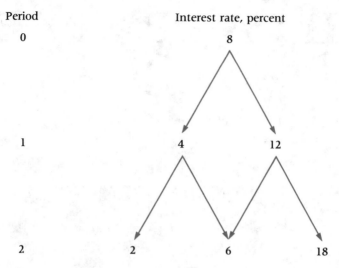

Period | Interest rate, percent

0 — 8

1 — 4, 12

2 — 2, 6, 18

Figure 23-3   The current one-period interest rate is 8%. We assume that in each future period the rate will either halve or increase 1.5 times.

Each branch in Figure 23-3 shows what could happen to the short-term rate of interest. The rate is currently 8% but next period we assume that it could either be halved to 4% or rise to 12%. Then, in period 2 it could again either be halved or rise 1.5 times giving possible interest rates of 2, 6, or 18%.

Now look at the prices of the three zero coupon bonds shown in Figure 23-4. Each branch in the diagram shows how the price of the bond and its yield to maturity will vary, depending on what happens to the short-term interest rate:

1. SHORT is a one-period bond that pays off 100 in period 1. It offers the one-period interest rate of 8% and is therefore priced at 100/1.08 = 92.59.
2. MEDIUM is a two-period bond. We know that next period the one-period interest rate will be either 4% or 12%. So, in period 1, MEDIUM will be priced at either 10/1.04 = 96.15 or 100/1.12 = 89.29. We *assume* (you'll see why shortly) that today MEDIUM has a yield to maturity of 8.73% and, therefore, its price is $100/1.0873^2 = 84.58$.
3. LONG is a three-period bond. We know that in period 2 it must offer a yield of 2, 6, or 18% and we *assume* that in period 1 it will yield either 4.38% or 13.05% and that today it is priced to yield 9.48%.

Now consider the following two strategies:

	Cash flow today	Cash flow period 1	
		Interest rate = 4%	Interest rate = 12%
Strategy 1:			
Buy 1 MEDIUM bond	−84.58	+96.15	+89.29
Strategy 2:			
Buy 0.4965 SHORT bonds	−45.97	+49.65	+49.65
Buy 0.507 LONG bonds	−38.61	+46.50	+39.64
Total	−84.58	+96.15	+89.29

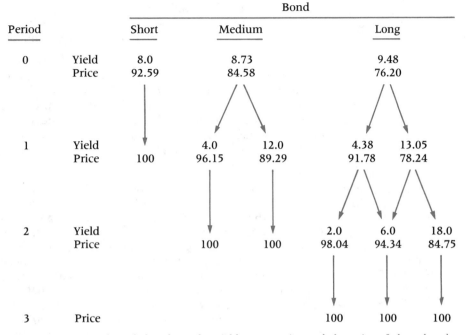

			Bond			
Period		Short	Medium		Long	
0	Yield	8.0	8.73		9.48	
	Price	92.59	84.58		76.20	
1	Yield		4.0	12.0	4.38	13.05
	Price	100	96.15	89.29	91.78	78.24
2	Yield				2.0	6.0	18.0
	Price		100	100	98.04	94.34	84.75
3	Price				100	100	100

Figure 23-4 We show below how the yield to maturity and the price of three bonds might vary with the short-term rate of interest (shown in Figure 23-3). These prices are consistent prices—that is, they offer no arbitrage opportunities.

Notice that, regardless of whether interest rates rise or fall, one MEDIUM bond provides exactly the same payoff as a mixture of a SHORT and a LONG bond. Since the two investments provide exactly the same payoffs, they must cost the same today—that is, they must cost 84.58. If they didn't, there would be arbitrage opportunities. For example, if the yield to maturity of MEDIUM was greater than 8.73% and all other yields were unchanged, you could make money by simultaneously buying one MEDIUM bond and selling the package of SHORT and LONG bonds.[22]

We saw in Figure 23-3 that in each period interest rates could either be halved or rise 1.5 times. Suppose that these two outcomes are equally likely. In this case the expected payoff from holding the long bond for one period is $(0.5 \times 91.78) + (0.5 \times 78.24) = 85.01$ and the expected return over this period is $(85.01 - 76.20)/76.20 = 0.1156$ or 11.56%. So the long bond is relatively risky[23] but it also offers the higher expected return. Thus our set of consistent prices assumes that investors require a particular premium for taking on interest rate risk. But that is not the only set of consistent bond prices. For example, there is another set of consistent prices that would offer a higher or lower premium for risk.

Our simple example should give you a flavour for these modern theories of term structure but you can probably think of a number of improvements that would make the example more realistic. First, short-term interest rates have more built-in stability than we implied. If they rise this year, they are more likely to fall back to a "normal" level next year. If they fall next year, they are more likely

---

[22] If you have read Chapter 20, you will recognize that the approach to finding consistent bond prices is almost identical to the binomial method that we used to value an option.

[23] The return on LONG in period 1 could be *either* $(78.24 - 76.20)/76.20 = 2.7\%$ or $(91.78 - 76.20)/76.20 = 20.5\%$.

$$\text{Unfunded liability} = \text{Accrued liability for past service} -$$
$$\text{pension fund assets}$$
$$= 120 - 110 \text{ or } \$10 \text{ million}$$

The second asset in the pension plan is the stream of contributions that the company has undertaken to pay into the pension fund to cover future service. Does it seem odd to you that contributions which will be made some time in the future are an asset? If so, you may find it helpful to think of these future contributions as a debt that the company has undertaken to pay. The pension plan's entitlement to future contributions is as much an asset to the pension plan as an investment in the company's bonds.

Determining the Pension Contribution

The pension plan balance sheet provides the actuary with the basis for calculating how much the company needs to pay into the pension fund.

Suppose that the assets in Eastinghouse's pension fund were sufficient to cover the accrued liability for past service. In this case, there would be no unfunded liability and the company would simply need to pay into the pension fund each year the value of any extra pensions that have been earned during the year. These regular contributions are generally referred to as *normal costs*.

Actuaries use several methods to estimate normal cost. One approach is to estimate how much would need to be invested now to provide for any benefits that have been earned during the year.[2] When the employees are young, there is more time for these investments to earn interest and, therefore, the amount that you would need to put aside is relatively small. However, as employees approach retirement, you would need to make increasingly large annual contributions.

Instead of providing an *increasing* annual contribution as employees approach retirement, a majority of actuaries use a method that seeks to even out contributions. Under the *level cost method* the company provides an equal dollar amount per employee per year or an equal proportion of its annual wage bill.

As accrued liabilities grow, so the company makes a matching contribution to the pension fund. Thus, if all goes well, the value of the investments in the pension fund should keep pace with the accrued liabilities. But things do not always go without a hitch and the value of the pension fund may fall short of the accrued liabilities. In this case the plan is said to be "underfunded." In the case of Eastinghouse, the plan was underfunded to the tune of $10 million.

Here are some of the things that can lead to underfunding:

• There may be a decline in the value of securities in the pension fund.
• The actuary may revise upward his assumption about the rate of salary inflation.
• The union may negotiate increased pensions.[3]

Of course, you can also get pleasant surprises. For example, if the investments perform better than expected, the value of the pension assets may be *greater* than the accrued liability. Such a pension plan is said to be "overfunded."

The unexpected surpluses or shortfalls are referred to as "experience gains" and are amortized over the average service life of the pension plan member.[4]

---

[2] This method is known as the **accrued benefit cost method**.

[3] These three types of misfortune are often known respectively as "experience losses," "assumption change losses," and "supplemental liabilities."

[4] See CICA *Accounting Recommendations*, April 1986, Section 3460.

A Comment on Actuarial Assumptions

When you look at a pension plan's assets and liabilities, remember that the figures involve a strong injection of judgement. Two of the actuary's most difficult problems are to pick a figure for the likely rate of wage inflation and to choose the rate at which to discount the projected pension payments. Some plans assume a discount rate which is *less* than the projected rate of salary increase and others assume a discount rate that can be 5% *higher* than the rate of salary increase. These choices can make a considerable difference to the estimated value of the plan liabilities.

Many companies have found that a change in actuarial assumptions can do wonders to improve the earnings picture. For example, increasing the discount rate reduces the present value of the liabilities, reduces the annual contribution to the fund, and increases reported earnings.

Actuarial discount rates are usually "sticky"—they don't increase right away even when market interest rates rise dramatically. But many pension plans have loosened up their actuaries by earmarking the portion of the fund that is needed to pay their fixed pensions, and then investing this money in a "dedicated" bond portfolio which generates future cash flows that exactly cover the fixed obligations.[5] In 1984 Bethlehem Steel dedicated 45% of its portfolio by investing $1.3 billion in bonds yielding 14.25%. As a result, the liabilities covered by this bond portfolio were discounted at 14.25% rather than the 8% rate used for other liabilities.

Fund Contributions and Pension Insurance

You can easily envisage a system in which pension plans are not funded. The company does not put anything aside. It just waits until the pensions become due and then pays them out of current income. That system is all very well as long as the company continues to grow and prosper; but if it runs into difficulties, there may be no money to pay the pensioners. In Canada, provincial laws try to prevent such problems by requiring the company to make regular contributions to the pension fund. In the United States, regulation is carried one step further and also provides a guarantee that the pensions will be paid.

Since the various provincial laws are not uniform with respect to fund contributions[6] and since no province has initiated comprehensive pension benefit guarantee program, our discussion will focus on the more complete federal pension regulation in the United States—the 1974 Employee Retirement Security Act (ERISA) and its attendent Pension Benefit Guarantee Corporation (PBGC).

Before the introduction of ERISA in 1974, U.S. companies were obliged to fund only normal costs (and the interest on supplemental liabilities). Some companies offered substantial increases in pension benefits but did not make any contributions to cover the supplemental liabilities. As a result the value of their pension funds fell far short of its accrued liabilities. ERISA imposes more stringent funding rules. Basically, companies are now obliged to cover normal costs and to amortize any supplemental liabilities or other deficiency.

In 1964 Studebaker closed its plant at South Bend, Indiana, and terminated the pension plan. Employees at South Bend became entitled to all accrued benefits. But there was not enough money in the pension fund to cover these benefits

---

[5] The investment manager tries to find the least expensive package of bonds that exactly hedges these pension obligations (see Chapter 25). This problem can be solved using a linear program. See S.D. Hodges and S.M. Schaefer, "A Model for Bond Portfolio Improvement," *Journal of Financial and Quantitative Analysis,* **12**: 243–260 (June 1977).

[6] There is considerable public interest in providing uniform pension policy across Canada. Unfortunately, such reform is still in its planning stage.

and most employees were left without a pension. To guard against such misfortunes, ERISA set up a new agency, the Pension Benefit Guarantee Corporation (PBGC).[7] If any plan is terminated and there is not enough money in the fund to pay pensions, the PBGC will make up most of the deficiency. But Congress did not want companies to be able to walk away from their pension promises. Therefore, it also legislated that the PBGC could recover this money from the company itself. Its claim ranks alongside the tax collector's claim and ahead of all unsecured creditors.

Notice the importance of this change. Before ERISA, pension plans were essentially paper promises. A company could terminate a plan whenever it chose. If the fund was insufficient to cover benefits, the employees suffered. Since ERISA, the employee's pension is effectively guaranteed. On the other hand, any unfunded liabilities are now a very senior debt of the corporation. When the bank is deciding whether to lend a company money or when a bond analyst is rating the company's bonds, it should be looking not just at the debt shown on the balance sheet but at the potentially very large debt to the PBGC.[8]

Plan Terminations

We have seen that the actuary calculates the present value of the pension liability by discounting the projected pension payments. A high interest rate reduces this present value; a low rate increases it. Of course the level of interest rates also affects the value of the bonds and stocks held in the pension fund, but to a lesser extent. Using the terminology of Chapter 25, we would say that pension fund assets have a lower duration than the liabilities. Thus, when interest rates rise, pension plans move into surplus; when they fall, deficits are more common.

The high interest rates and booming equity prices during the first half of the 1980s caused most pension plans to move into surplus. Many companies tried to lay their hands on this surplus and use it for their stockholders. For example, in 1986 Hollinger Inc. withdrew a $38 million surplus from the pension plan of one of its subsidiaries, Dominion Stores. The union representing the store employees fought the move. The Ontario Supreme Court ordered that the funds be repaid.

Companies also worry that other firms may be tempted to take them over in order to terminate the pension plan and get their hands on the surplus. Their response is either to repossess the surplus for themselves[9] or to enter into an agreement with the pension plan that in the event of a take-over the employees get to keep the surplus.

Accounting for Pension Plans

The Canadian Institute of Chartered Accountants (CICA) sets out rules on how pension plan activity should be reported.[10]

When plans are initiated or amended the actuarial value of the pension liability is compared with the value of the assets held by the pension fund. The difference

---

[7] The PBGC is financed by a levy on companies with qualified pension plans. In 1982, this levy was $2.60 per employee per year.

[8] For an account of how Moody's bond ratings reflect the company's pension liabilities, see "ERISA—A Bond Rater's View," *Moody's Bond Survey*, February 1978. Of course, lenders are not the only ones affected by large unfunded pension liabilities. Feldstein and Seligman have produced evidence that share prices also fully reflect such liabilities: see M. Feldstein and S. Seligman, "Pension Funding, Share Prices and National Savings," *Journal of Finance*, **36**: 801–824 (September 1981).

[9] The firm's announcement that it intends to recover the pension surplus generally leads to an abnormal rise in the share price. See, for example, M.J. Alderson and K.C. Chen, "The Stockholder Consequences of Terminating the Pension Fund," *Midland Corporate Finance Journal*, **4**: 55–61 (Winter 1987).

[10] CICA *Accounting Recommendations*, April 1986, Section 3460.

between these figures, if one exists, is amortized over a period of time that corresponds to the average number of years that the employees are expected to continue working for the company. The amortized amount becomes part of the year's pension expense.

Once set up, a defined contribution plan involves an annual pension expense (in addition to the amortized initiation or amendment charges) that is equal to the employees' contribution to the plan. The assets of the fund will equal the liabilities since the liability is the promise to pay each employee their share of the market value of the assets.

Because the nature of the liability is so different, accounting for a defined-benefit plan is more complex. In addition to the employee pension contributions, pension expenses include the amortization of:

1. adjustments arising from changes in assumptions being used in the actuarial estimates of the pension liability (for example, a change in the expected return on the assets of the fund),
2. "experience" gains or losses that are changes that are not due to changes in assumptions.

The expenses are totalled up and compared to the contributions made to the fund in that year. Differences between contributions and expenses are reflected in the balance sheet as a deferred charge or an accrual for pension costs.

35-3   MANAGING THE PENSION FUND

There are two methods of funding a pension plan. The employer can enter into a contract with an insurance company by which the employer agrees to pay the pension contributions over to the insurance company, which guarantees to provide a certain level of retirement benefits. The more common procedure (accounting for about 70% of contributions) is to pay the contributions into a trust fund.

Some companies appoint their own investment manager to run the trust fund but, in the majority of cases, management of the fund is given to one or more banks or investment management companies. The financial manager still retains responsibility for setting fund objectives and monitoring the performance of the investment manager. We will discuss these responsibilities in turn.

Risk and Pension Fund Policy

Some managers believe that they can reduce the cost of a pension scheme by investing in securities with greater risk and greater expected return. But if the securities are properly priced, you cannot increase the present value of the pension fund by changing its composition.

Although the fund's composition cannot alter the size of the total pie, there are circumstances in which it can affect the size of the individual slices. Because pensions in Canada are not guaranteed, if the fund performed badly, employees could lose their pensions. On the other hand, if the fund performed better than expected, employees are not entitled to any of the extra return and the company could reap the reward in the form of reduced contributions. Thus, employees bear part of the risk of the pension fund's investments but receive none of the extra rewards that risk-bearing may bring.[11]

---

[11] The opportunistic company gains the value of the company's option to default on its promise. By increasing the riskiness of the fund, management increases the value of this default option. As we explained in Chapter 20, the option to default is like a put option. The pension put was first discussed in W. Bagehot (pseud.), "Risk and Reward in Corporate Pension Funds," *Financial Analysts Journal*, **28**: 80–84 (January–February 1982). See also J.L. Treynor, W. Priest, and P. Reagan, *The Financial Reality of Pension Funding Under ERISA*, Dow Jones-Irwin, Inc., Homewood, Ill., 1976.

In contrast, because of the Pension Benefit Guarantee Corporation, employees in the United States are now protected against the consequences of a risky investment policy, and so to some extent is the PBGC itself. Therefore, the present value of the pension promise and the present value of the company's shares are largely unaffected by the composition of the pension fund. This means that the shareholders ultimately bear all the risk of the pension fund's investments, so that any change in the value of these investments comes straight out of the shareholders' pockets.

Taxes and Pension Fund Policy

We have seen that since the company can default on its pension promise, both the size of the pension fund and its investment policy may be important to shareholders and employees. But suppose that pension benefit guarantees were introduced which made it impossible for the company to default. Does it then matter whether it makes more than the minimum contribution to the pension fund or whether the fund is invested in stocks or bonds? Fisher Black and Irwin Tepper have suggested an interesting reason that these decisions may matter very much.[12]

Imagine that a firm needs to pay pensions of P a year in perpetuity and that it does not set up a pension fund—it just makes each pension payment as it comes due. Since the pension payment is a tax-deductible expense, the net annual cost to the firm is $(1 - T_c)P$.

Table 35-2 outlines an alternative strategy. Rather than waiting until the pension becomes due, the firm can borrow P/r and put it in the pension fund. Since this pension fund contribution is tax-deductible, the firm receives an immediate tax saving of T_cP/r. If the pension fund invests in corporate bonds, it earns an annual income of $r \times (P/r) = P$, which is just sufficient to pay the future pensions. In addition, the firm has to pay interest on its borrowing, which after tax is equal to

$$(1 - T_c)r \times \frac{P}{r} = (1 - T_c)P$$

Both strategies involve future cash payments of $(1 - T_c)P$, but the second strategy provides an immediate cash benefit of T_cP/r. So it is best to borrow and give the proceeds to the pension fund to invest in bonds.

It is tempting to think that this benefit comes from the decision to fund the pension scheme, but this is not so. Funding the pension scheme offers no advantage in itself. The benefit arises only when the pension fund is invested in corporate bonds. In this case, the firm can borrow at the after-tax rate of interest and earn the pretax rate of interest on corporate bonds held in the pension fund.[13] Of course, the more you put in the pension fund now, the more you can make from this tax arbitrage.

---

[12] See F. Black, "The Tax Consequences of Long-Run Pension Policy," *Financial Analysts Journal*, 1–28 (July–August 1980), and I. Tepper, "Taxation and Corporate Pension Policy," *Journal of Finance*, **36**: 1–14 (March 1981).

[13] Suppose the earnings of the pension fund were taxed at the corporate rate T_c. Then under strategy 2 the firm would have to contribute $P/r(1 - T_c)$ to the pension fund. The after-tax cost would be $(1 - T_c)[P/r(1 - T_c)] = P/r$, which exactly offsets the amount borrowed. Thus, strategy 2 would have no current cash-flow advantage over strategy 1. Try reworking Table 35-3 under this assumption.

Table 35-2
Two strategies for paying pension of $P a year in perpetuity

	Current Cash Flows	Future Cash Flows
Strategy 1:		
Pay pensions when due	—	$-(1 - T_c)P$
Strategy 2:		
1. Borrow P/r	$+ P/r$	$-(1 - T_c)r \times (P/r) =$
		$-(1 - T_c)P$
2. Place P/r in pension fund	$-(1 - T_c)P/r$	—
3. Invest fund in corporate bonds	—	$r \times (P/r) = +P$
4. Pay pensions from pension fund income	—	$-P$
Total cash flows, strategy 2:	$+T_cP/r$	$-(1 - T_c)P$
Cash-flow advantage of strategy 2 over strategy 1	$+T_cP/r$	—

AN EXAMPLE   We will put some numbers on this. Suppose that your company plans to set aside $10 million a year in perpetuity for the payment of pensions. Since this is a tax-deductible expense, the after-tax cash outlay is $(1 - 0.36)10 = \$6.4$ million per year. This is set out in the first line of Table 35-3.

Table 35-3
Two strategies for paying pensions of $10 a year in perpetuity (figures in millions)

	Current Cash Flows	Future Cash Flows
Strategy 1:		
Pay pensions when due	—	$-(1 - 0.36)10 = -\$6.4$
Strategy 2:		
1. Borrow $10/0.10 = \$100$	$+100$	$-(1 - 0.36)10 = -\$6.4$
2. Place $100 in pension fund	$-(1 - 0.36)100 = -64$	—
3. Invest fund in corporate bonds	—	$(+0.10 \times 100) = +10$
4. Pay pensions from pension fund income	—	-10
Total cash flows, strategy 2:	$+\$36$	$-\$6.4$
Cash-flow advantage of strategy 2 over strategy 1	$+\$36$	—

The second section of Table 35-3 shows what happens if you follow Black and Tepper's advice. You arrange for your firm to borrow $100 million at 10%. The annual tax-rate interest payment on this debt is $(1 - 0.36)10 = \$6.4$ million— exactly the same as the after-tax pension expense. The $100 million is placed in the pension fund and invested in bonds earning 10%. Thus, each year the fund generates income of $0.10 \times 100 = \$10$ million, which is just enough to pay the annual pensions. You have now substituted one fixed expense of $6.4 million a year (interest on the debt) for another (the cost of the pension). So all future cash flows are unchanged. But by contributing $100 million to the pension fund today, you also earn an immediate tax shield of $0.36 \times 100 = \$36$ million. Thus, Black and Tepper's strategy has made your shareholders $36 million better off.

Notice that your firm issues an additional $100 million of bonds but, through the pension fund, it also *owns* an additional $100 million of bonds. So the firm's *aggregate* leverage is unchanged.[14]

In view of these gains, we would expect to see pension funds of tax-paying companies almost entirely invested in bonds — but only about 1 in 10 are, and we don't know whether their managers are Black-Tepper fans. Other funds hold more than $500 billion in stocks, plus large investments in real estate and a miscellany of other assets such as venture capital partnership interests.

If pension funds hold $500 billion of common stock, it seems that Black and Tepper's idea is potentially worth 0.36 × $500 or $180 billion. Some find this difficult to believe. Others agree that it works but believe that the gain comes from the issue of debt to fund the pension plan and that it doesn't matter whether the fund invests in debt or equity. A third group believes that it doesn't matter whether contributions are financed by borrowing as long as the pension fund invests in bonds.[15]

Setting Objectives

We might expect funding and investment policy to be pulled towards one of two extremes. Because of the option to default, firms in financial distress are tempted to underfund the pension plan and invest in riskier assets. For profitable, tax-paying firms we are more likely to see them borrowing in order to overfund and invest in bonds. And firms do, in fact, seem to behave in roughly this way.[16]

It is not sensible to play these games too hard. The government imposes a tax penalty on firms that fail to keep within the maximum and minimum funding levels. Firms that stick close to these limits may find that they have to make sharp adjustments to their funding if they wish to avoid these penalties. Also, most firms are concerned with how the pension liability shows up in the balance sheet and how it affects the current earnings per share. A policy that makes sense on other counts doesn't necessarily do wonders for reported earnings.

No manager likes to be caught by surprise, so investment companies and consultants have developed a range of tools that help the manager explore the consequences of any investment policy. For example, in Chapter 10 we saw how firms use Monte Carlo simulation to probe more deeply into their capital budgeting decisions.[17] In just the same way, financial managers sometimes use simulation to analyze their pension plans. It doesn't tell them the optimal investment or funding policy, but it does illustrate the possible consequences of any policy.

---

[14] What if the pension fund invests in equities rather than bonds? In this case, the aggregate leverage would increase. Therefore, if your firm was at its optimal debt-equity ratio before the bond issue, it would no longer be so afterward.

[15] Where you believe the gain comes from depends on your view on the debt and taxes controversy. See Section 18-2. If Miller's theory of debt and taxes is right, the pretax return on debt is higher than on (risk-free) equity and it is necessary to invest the pension fund in bonds in order to capture the tax advantage. If MM are right, the fund would earn the same pretax return regardless whether it invested in debt or equity. However, the company would need to finance the pension fund contribution by an issue of debt in order to capture the interest tax shield.

[16] See Z. Bodie, J.O. Light, R. Morck, and R.A. Taggart, Jr., "Corporate Pension Policy: An Empirical Investigation," *Financial Analysts Journal*, **41**: 10–16. (September–October 1985).

[17] See Section 10-2. Irwin Tepper discusses pension plan simulation in "Risk vs. Return in Pension Fund Investment," *Harvard Business Review*, **55**: 100–107 (March–April 1977).

35-4   MEASURING FUND PERFORMANCE

Since you are likely to pay an investment company a substantial fee for managing your pension fund, it makes sense to monitor how well it is doing its job. The need to measure pension fund performance has spawned an industry of consultants and analysts.

The first step in performance measurement is to calculate the fund's rate of return. Your concern is with *total* return. Therefore, you must include in your calculations both dividends and capital appreciation. You are also interested only in market values. Therefore, you must look at market prices and ignore the prices at which securities may be recorded in the fund's books.

One way to calculate the fund's rate of return is to list all cash flows in and out of the fund together with the final value of the fund; then you find the rate of discount that equates these benefits to the initial fund value:

$$\text{Initial fund value} = \frac{\text{year 1 cash flow}}{1+y} + \frac{\text{year 2 cash flow}}{(1+y)^2} + \cdots$$
$$+ \frac{\text{year } N \text{ fund value}}{(1+y)^N}$$

The quantity y in this formula is our old friend the internal rate of return.

Unfortunately, the internal rate of return is inappropriate for measurement of performance, because it is affected by the timing of cash flows that may be beyond the manager's control. For example, suppose that you have two managers, each of whom follows a strategy of investing an entire fund in the market index. Each manager starts with $10 million. Over the first year the index falls by 50% leaving each manager with an investment of $5 million. At that point company A puts $1 million more *into* its pension fund and company B takes $1 million *out* of its fund. Therefore, A has $6 million invested in the market and B has $4 million. Over the second year the market recovers to its initial level giving A a fund worth $12 million and B a fund worth $8 million. To find the internal rate of return we set out the cash flows and final value and solve for the return y:

$$\text{Fund A:} \quad 10 = \frac{-1}{1+y} + \frac{12}{(1+y)^2} \quad y = 4.7\%$$

$$\text{Fund B:} \quad 10 = \frac{+1}{1+y} + \frac{8}{(1+y)^2} \quad y = -5.4\%$$

Notice that the manager of fund A was fortunate to receive a cash *inflow* at the bottom of the market and so has a positive rate of return. The manager of fund B was unfortunate to have a cash *outflow* at the bottom of the market and so has a negative rate of return. But you wouldn't want to conclude from this that the manager of A was more skilled at picking stocks than the manager of B.

The internal rate of return is sometimes called the **dollar-weighted rate of return** — it gives equal weight to each dollar invested. In performance measurement you need a measure of the return that gives equal weight to each unit of time. A familiar example of a **time-weighted rate of return** is the return on a share in a mutual fund. The value of *your* investment in a mutual fund is not directly affected by whether other people are putting money into the fund or taking it out.

When you measure the performance of a pension fund, you need to pretend that it is a mutual fund and then look at the performance of one share in the fund. In our example that is easy. Regardless of whether you bought a share in fund A or fund B, the value of your investment would have halved in the first year and doubled in the second year. Therefore, by the end of the two years you would have been back where you started. The time-weighted return is the same for both fund A and fund B.

To calculate the time-weighted rate of return you need to identify how much of the gain in the value of the fund was attributable to new cash. You can do that precisely only if you know the date of each cash flow *and* the market value of the fund at that date. Mutual funds value their portfolios every day, but some pension funds leave as much as a year between valuations. The Bank Administration Institute in the United States in cooperation with the University of Chicago sponsored a study of performance measurement which, among other things, devised two possible ways to *estimate* time-weighted rates of return when you don't have frequent fund valuations. It was an extremely careful study, and its recommendations have become a standard for performance measures throughout the world.

Choosing the Performance Yardstick

Suppose that you now have an estimate of the time-weighted returns on your pension fund. That in itself won't tell you whether the investment manager has done a good job. Maybe the average return was high because interest rates were high or because the stock market rose or because the manager held particularly volatile stocks.

The object of performance measurement is to work out how far the fund's return was due to general market movements and how much was due to the skill of the manager.

Step 1   If a fund invests in Treasury bills, it can be sure of earning the risk-free rate of interest. If it invests in risky securities, the return may turn out to be higher or lower than the risk-free rate of interest. The premium that the fund receives for taking on risk is equal to the difference between the return on the fund and the risk-free rate of interest:[18]

$$\text{Fund risk premium} = \text{average fund return} - \text{average rate of interest}$$
$$= r - r_f$$

Step 2   The fund may obtain a positive risk premium because markets in general have been buoyant or because the manager has been successful at picking stocks. It may obtain a negative risk premium because markets have been depressed or because the manager has picked the wrong stocks. You can break down the premium into two further components — the premium *anyone* could have achieved and the additional premium that your manager achieved.

Suppose that the manager has invested in a portfolio with a beta (β) of 0.8. Anyone could have constructed a portfolio with a beta of 0.8 just by putting 80% of the portfolio in the market index and the remainder in Treasury bills. The risk premium on this benchmark portfolio would have been:

$$\text{Benchmark portfolio's risk premium} = 0.8 \times \text{risk premium on market}$$
$$= \beta(r_m - r_f)$$

The quantity $\beta(r_m - r_f)$ measures the risk premium on an unmanaged portfolio with the same market risk as your fund. This is the premium anyone could have

---

[18] Notice that in judging performance you are concerned with the *arithmetic* average of the returns.

achieved. The difference between the risk premium on the actual fund and the risk premium on the benchmark portfolio must be due to the manager's success in picking stocks. This gain from picking stocks is often called alpha (α).[19]

$$\alpha = \text{gain from picking stocks}$$
$$= \text{fund risk premium} - \text{benchmark portfolio's risk premium}$$
$$= (r - r_f) - \beta(r_m - r_f)$$

Step 3   Unfortunately, a manager who tries to pick stocks cannot simultaneously hold the entire market. In other words, to some extent all the manager's eggs must be put into a limited number of baskets. Some of the gains from picking stocks are, therefore, needed just to compensate for this unnecessary unique risk that has been taken on.

In step 2 we measured the gains from picking stocks by comparing the reward on the actual fund with the reward on an unmanaged benchmark portfolio. The actual fund had the same market risk as the benchmark portfolio but it also had unique risk. Therefore, it had more *total* risk.

You can imagine a second benchmark portfolio that is constructed to have the same *total* risk as the fund. If we call the total risk of the fund σ and the total risk of the market σ_m, then this second benchmark portfolio would consist of the fraction σ/σ_m invested in the market index and the remainder invested in Treasury bills. The risk premium on the portfolio would be:

$$\frac{\sigma}{\sigma_m}(r_m - r_f)$$

You can now measure the net gain from your manager's stock selection:

Net gain from picking stocks = fund risk premium
$$\qquad\qquad - \text{risk premium on second benchmark portfolio}$$
$$= (r - r_f) - \frac{\sigma}{\sigma_m}(r_m - r_f)$$

The difference between the gain and the *net* gain from picking stocks is the extra return that the manager needed just in order to compensate for the avoidable unique risk.[20]

Measuring Performance— An Example   Here is a free gift for you. You can use these techniques to measure the performance of your own common stock portfolio. Let us work through an example.

Table 35-4 sets out all the necessary data. It shows the risk-free interest rate and the yearly returns on your portfolio and the market index. At the bottom of

---

[19] Step 2 is equivalent to measuring the difference between the actual return and the return predicted by the capital asset pricing model. Thus, the case for step 2 is strongest if we are sure that the capital asset pricing model is right and that we have measured the true market portfolio. Since we cannot be sure, we do not know that the benchmark portfolio is the *best possible* naive strategy. Nevertheless, the benchmark is plausible and provides a useful way to adjust for market fluctuations.

[20] Our measures for gain from picking stocks and net gain from picking stocks were originally suggested by M.C. Jensen in "The Performance of Mutual Funds in the Period 1945–64," *Journal of Finance,* **23**: 389–416 (May 1968), and in a slightly different form by W.F. Sharpe in "Mutual Fund Performance," *Journal of Business,* **39**: 119–138 (January 1966). Our description of these measures follows E.F. Fama, "Components of Investment Performance," *Journal of Finance,* **27**: 551–568 (June 1972).

Table 35-4
To measure the performance of your portfolio, you need the following data

Year	Return on Your Portfolio	Return on TSE 300 Total Return Composite Index
1976	10.75	11.02
1977	10.09	10.71
1978	26.05	29.72
1979	38.38	44.77
1980	27.68	30.13
1981	4.61	−10.25
1982	7.26	5.54
1983	30.89	35.49
1984	5.40	−2.39
1985	22.11	25.07
1986	19.22	8.95
1987	6.40	5.88
1988	11.18	11.08
1989	19.83	21.37
1990	9.67	−14.80
Average return, %	$r = 16.6$	$r_m = 14.2$
Beta	$\beta = 0.79$	$\beta_m = 1.00$
Standard deviation, %	$\sigma = 10.2$	$\sigma_m = 16.8$

Note: The average Treasury bill rate from 1976 to 1990 was 10.8%.

the table we have calculated three numbers — the average return, the market risk (β), and the total risk (σ).

Now we can start to analyze the average return on your portfolio.

Step 1   By investing in Treasury bills, you could have gotten an average return of $r_f = 10.8\%$. Instead of investing in Treasury bills, you took a risk in your portfolio: you got an average return of $r = 16.6\%$. Taking risk has resulted in a premium of 5.8%:

$$r - r_f = 16.6 - 10.8 = 5.8\%$$

Step 2   Your portfolio had a beta of 0.79. Anyone could have constructed a portfolio with a beta of 0.79, just by putting 79% of his or her money in the market portfolio and the remainder in Treasury bills. The risk premium on this easy-to-pick portfolio would have been

$$\beta(r_m - r_f) = 0.79 \times (14.2 - 10.8) = 2.7$$

You got an average risk premium of 5.8%. Therefore, your gain from picking stocks was:

$$(r - r_f) - \beta(r_m - r_f) = 5.8 - 2.7 = 3.1$$

Step 3   If you tried to pick stocks, you must have been less than fully diversified. Therefore, you took on some unique risk. Your total risk was $\sigma = 10.2\%$. Anyone could have constructed a portfolio with a total risk of 10.2% just by putting $\sigma/\sigma_m = 10.2/16.8 = 0.61$ or 61% of the money in the market portfolio and the remainder in Treasury bills. The risk premium on this second easy-to-pick portfolio would have been:

$$\frac{\sigma}{\sigma_m}(r_m - r_f) = 0.61(14.2 - 10.8) = 2.1\%$$

The *net* gain from your efforts was, therefore,

$$(r - r_f) - \frac{\sigma}{\sigma_m}(r_m - r_f) = 5.8 - 2.1 = 3.7\%$$

It appears that you have outperformed most professional managers.

Some Cautions about Performance Measurement

We should issue three warnings about performance measurement. First, investment management is a highly competitive business, so that it is extremely rare to find managers that consistently outperform naive strategies by any dramatic amount. Occasionally, you find portfolios that are very inferior to the unmanaged benchmark portfolio, so the principal value of performance measurement may well lie in spotlighting gross incompetence. But also remember that there are many aspects of the manager's job that are not being measured, such as choosing an appropriate level of risk and undertaking various administrative functions.

Second, since you are looking for relatively minor differences in performance, it is all the more important to be careful in your comparisons.

Third, unusual performance in any one year will more often than not be due to chance rather than skill. To sort skill from chance, you need to examine performance over a very long period. While you are waiting, don't attach statistical confidence to modest differences in performance.

35-5 SUMMARY

By tradition, corporate finance texts ignore the company's pension plan. But the financial manager is spending more and more time worrying about it. The obligation not covered by the pension fund is often substantially greater than the long-term debt shown in the balance sheet. That is why we have included this brief discussion of how the financial manager assesses the cost of the plan and oversees the management of the fund.

Most private pension plans are of two kinds. Some are regularly negotiated with the labour union: they typically offer their employees a flat benefit related solely to years of service. Others are provided for nonunion or salaried employees: they generally offer a pension that is related to both years of service and final salary. Pension schemes differ in the benefit they give to employees who quit *before* retirement age. But the recent federal and provincial pension laws now lay down certain minimum standards for vesting.

The plan's actuary draws up a regular balance sheet of the plan. The liabilities consist of the value of all the benefits that the company expects to pay to current participants. They include those that have already accrued to them as a result of past service and those that are expected to accrue as a result of future service. To meet these liabilities the pension plan has two principal assets. One is the value of the pension fund; the other is the present value of the planned contributions. If these assets fall short of the liabilities, there is a deficiency and the company must generally make additional contributions to eliminate this deficiency.

Even with provincial regulation governing fund contributions, however, employees can be sure that they will get their pensions only if there are sufficient assets in the pension fund. In the United States the Pension Benefit Guarantee Corporation (PBGC) insures employees' pensions. And the PBGC can recover from the company whatever is needed to pay the pensions. That makes the pension promise a very important and senior debt.

Company contributions may be paid to an insurance company, which will in exchange contract to provide future benefits. More commonly, the contributions are paid into a trust fund, which is run by a bank or investment management company. The financial executive generally has the responsibility for coordination with the manager of the fund and thus has at least two things to worry about — first, deciding on the appropriate objectives for the fund, and, second, monitoring the performance of the fund manager.

It is pointless looking for *the* optimal risk strategy for a pension fund. In an efficient market all securities are zero-NPV investments. Therefore, you are unlikely to find a balance between bonds and stocks that makes *everyone* better off. If the pension obligation is really risk-free, your choice of investments may not even make one group better off at the expense of another. Nevertheless, it makes sense to know what you are letting yourself in for.

Because the income of the pension fund is not taxed, money held in the pension fund earns the pretax rate of return. That provides an incentive for the company to borrow, then fund the pension plan to the hilt and invest in bonds.

Thus, the risk-shifting incentive tempts companies to underfund their pension plan and invest in risky stocks, while the tax effect tempts them to overfund and invest in safe bonds. The government has established minimum and maximum funding rules that prevent firms from playing these games to the limit. If you try to do so, you may find that you need to make rapid changes to your annual pension contribution if you are to avoid a tax penalty.

To measure the performance of the pension fund you first need to calculate its rate of return. It is useless to look at the internal rate of return, because that depends on when the company decides to put more money into the fund. You need to pretend that the fund is a mutual fund and that the contributions are used to buy additional shares in the mutual fund. Then, calculate the average return per share. In the pension business this is called the time-weighted rate of return.

Of course you need some benchmark against which to compare the fund's performance. The trick here is to compare the fund return with the return on a benchmark portfolio which has the same risk as the fund, but which anyone could have picked.

FURTHER READING

Some interesting views on the status of pension funds in Canada are provided in

D.D. Ezra and K.P. Ambachtsheer, *The Struggle for Pension Fund Wealth*, Pagurian Press, Toronto, 1983.

The Bodie, Shoven, and Wise books are useful collections of recent research studies on pensions:

Z. Bodie, J.B. Shoven, and D.A. Wise, eds., *Pensions in the U.S. Economy*, University of Chicago Press, Chicago, 1988.

Z. Bodie, J.B. Shoven, and D.A. Wise, eds., *Issues in Pension Economics*, University of Chicago Press, Chicago, 1987.

A useful general review of pension funding policy and the impact of ERISA is given in

J. Bulow, "Analysis of Pension Funding Under ERISA," National Bureau of Economic Research, Working Paper No. 402, November 1979.

Bagehot's article (which was written before ERISA) shows that the company's pension obligation resembles a risky debt. The value of this debt is reduced if the pension plan is unfunded or if the pension fund invests in risky securities. The studies by Sharpe and Treynor, Priest, and Regan discuss how funding policy is affected by ERISA.

W. Bagehot (pseud.), "Risk and Reward in Corporate Pension Funds," *Financial Analysts Journal,* **28**: 80–84 (January–February 1972).
W.F. Sharpe, "Corporate Pension Funding Policy," *Journal of Financial Economics,* **3**: 183–193 (June 1976).
J.L. Treynor, W. Priest, and P. Regan, *The Financial Reality of Pension Funding Under ERISA,* Dow Jones-Irwin, Inc., Homewood, Ill., 1976.

Irwin Tepper provides a very useful discussion of pension plan simulation in:

I. Tepper, "Risk vs. Return in Pension Fund Investment," *Harvard Business Review,* **55**: 100–107 (March–April 1977).

The following articles discuss the implications of the pension fund's tax-free status for funding and investment policy:

F. Black, "The Tax Consequences of Long-Run Pension Policy," *Financial Analysts Journal,* 1–28 (July–August 1980).
A.F. Ehrbar, "How to Slash Your Company's Tax Bill," *Fortune,* 122–124 (February 23, 1981).
I. Tepper, "Taxation and Corporate Pension Policy," *Journal of Finance,* **36**: 1–14 (March 1981).

The Bank Administration Institute provides a standard reference on the measurement of pension fund performance. The articles by Jensen, Sharpe, and Fama are concerned with the problem of adjusting for risk in performance measurement. Roll's article offers a contrary view and criticizes the modern theory of performance measurement.

Measuring the Investment Performance of Pension Funds, Bank Administration Institute, Park Ridge, Ill., 1968.
E.F. Fama, "Components of Investment Performance," *Journal of Finance,* **27**: 551–568 (June 1972).
M.C. Jensen, "The Performance of Mutual Funds in the Period 1945–64," *Journal of Finance,* **23**: 389–416 (May 1968).
R. Roll, "Ambiguity When Performance is Measured by the Securities Market Line," *Journal of Finance,* **33**: 1051–1069 (September 1978).
W.F. Sharpe, "Mutual Fund Performance," *Journal of Business,* **39**: 119–138 (January 1966).

QUIZ

1. Which of the following statements are true?
    (a) The time-weighted return is unaffected by the timing of cash flows into or out of the fund.
    (b) Vested benefits are those that are invested on behalf of the employee or pensioner.
    (c) If a pension plan defaults on its promise, the Pension Benefit Guarantee Corporation will make up the major part of any deficiency.
    (d) The PBGC's claim on the company's assets is limited to 30% of net worth.
    (e) Most pensions are linked to the employee's final salary.
    (f) Black and Tepper recommend that companies should increase their own borrowing and invest the money in the pension fund in bonds.

2. By the end of the year 1981, Ford's balance sheet was as follows (figures in millions):

Current assets	$10,177	Current liabilities	$ 9,940
Plant, equipment,		Debt and other liabilities	5,719
and other assets	12,844	Equity	7,362
Total assets	$23,021	Total liabilities	$23,021

The company's pension plan for its U.S. employees had vested accrued liabilities of $6,830 million, and the pension fund had total assets of $6,170 million.

(a) Construct an augmented balance sheet for Ford that includes both the pension plan's assets and liabilities.

(b) Show how the published balance sheet and the augmented balance sheet would change if Ford contributed $1,000 million cash to the pension fund.

(c) Show how both balance sheets would change if the value of the securities in the pension fund fell by $2,000 million.

Table 35-5
See Quiz, question 3

Assets	Liabilities
PV pension fund	PV expected benefits for past service
PV future normal costs	PV expected future service costs
Deficit (surplus)	
Total assets	PV expected benefits

3. Table 35-5 shows a pension plan balance sheet. Indicate where in the balance sheet you would enter the value of each of the following items:

(a) 5,000 shares of IBM, which are held in trust for members of the pension scheme

(b) A pension of $10,000 a year, which is currently being paid to Ms. Smith

(c) A pension worth $20,000 a year, which you expect to have to pay to Mr. Brown (age 25), who has just joined the firm

(d) An amount equal to 5% of Mr. Brown's salary, which the company plans to put aside each month in order to pay his pension

(e) The total amount of $600 million that the company needs to earmark for pensions

(f) Additional benefits worth $50 million that have just been negotiated by the union

Table 35-6
See Quiz, question 4

Assets (millions of dollars)		Liabilities (millions of dollars)	
Pension fund	720	Vested accrued benefits	540
Future normal costs	600	Unvested accrued benefits	220
Unamortized experience losses	90	Expected future service costs	900
Unamortized supplemental liabilities	100	Expected benefits	1,660
Losses from changes in actuarial assumptions	150		
Total assets	1,660		

4. Table 35-6 is the balance sheet for the pension plan of Mealy and Briars, Inc.
    (a) Explain the meaning of each of the terms in the table.
    (b) Calculate the unfunded liability.
    (c) Assuming that normal costs are not altered, show how the balance sheet would change if:
        (i) The value of securities in the pension fund falls by $50 million
        (ii) The union negotiates increased pensions worth $80 million

5. If a pension fund is obliged to make a large cash disbursement near the bottom of the market, will the time-weighted rate of return be (a) the same as (b) greater than, or (c) less than the internal rate of return?

6. The financial manager of Olde's Rope Company has observed that the average return was 10% on common stocks, 5% on Treasury bills, and 11% on the firm's pension fund. The market return had an annual standard deviation of 20% and the fund return had an annual standard deviation of 16% and a beta of 0.6.
    (a) What was the risk premium on the pension fund?
    (b) What was the total gain from picking stocks?
    (c) After allowing for the unique risk — what was the *net* gain from picking stocks?

7. A pension fund starts the year with $50 million. By midyear it has appreciated to $60 million, at which point it pays out pensions of $20 million. In the second half of the year, the fund appreciates by a further 50%.
    (a) What is the annually compounded time-weighted rate of return?
    (b) Is the annually compounded dollar-weighted rate of return
        (i) 21.7%
        (ii) 72.5%
        (iii) 8%
    (c) Suppose that the fund had a midyear cash inflow of $20 million rather than an outflow. Would this increase or reduce the time-weighted rate of return?
    (d) Would it increase or reduce the dollar-weighted rate of return?

QUESTIONS AND PROBLEMS

1. Look at the annual report and accounts of any Canadian company and calculate an augmented balance sheet that includes the assets and liabilities of the pension plan.

2. You have been asked to evaluate the performance of your firm's pension fund over the last five years. You fit the following equation to 60 *monthly* returns:

$$r = \alpha + \beta(r_m - r_f)$$

where r = portfolio return
r_m = market return
r_f = risk-free interest rate

You estimate that $\alpha = 5.8\%$ per month and $\beta = 0.63$.

Other facts:

1. The average of the r's was 0.23%
2. The average of the r_m's was 0.14%
3. The average of the r_f's was 0.38%

4. The ratio of the standard deviation of the r's to the standard deviation of the r_m's was 0.90.

What can you infer from these statistics?

Can you say whether the fund management did a good job?

3. (a) Show how an increase in the inflation rate is likely to affect the pension plan's surplus or deficit when most members of the plan:

    (i) Are still employed

    (ii) Are retired

  (b) It is sometimes said that, as long as the actuary makes a good forecast of the *difference* between the rate of return and the inflation rate, the precise levels don't matter. Is this true?

*4. Suppose that a company must pay pensions of $10 million a year in perpetuity. The rate of interest is 10% and the corporate tax rate is 36%.

  (a) If the company does not fund the pension liability, what is the net annual cost to the company of these pensions?

  (b) If it does fund the pension liability, it eliminates this fixed future outflow. It can, therefore, increase its borrowings. How much more can the company afford to borrow if it funds the pension?

  (c) How much must the pension fund invest today in bonds to ensure that it can pay each year's pensions?

  (d) What is the net cost to the company of placing this money in the pension fund?

  (e) If the company borrows and funds the pension scheme in this way, what is the increase in stockholder wealth?

*5. To illustrate Black and Tepper's strategy, we analyzed a company that has a fixed pension obligation in perpetuity. But their strategy does not assume perpetuities. Can you rework Table 35-2 for a company that must pay pensions of $P in year t only?

*6. In Section 35-2, we illustrated the Black and Tepper strategy with an example of a company paying pensions of $10 million a year. Assume that this company has assets of $200 million and no outstanding debt. Construct balance sheets for the company both before and after it follows the Black and Tepper strategy. Then construct the augmented balance sheets that include the assets and liabilities of the pension plan.

*7. Does Black and Tepper's strategy increase the risk for (a) the bondholders, (b) the shareholders, or (c) the PBGC? Would the risk be any different if the company made an issue of new equity, which was then placed in the pension fund and invested in common stocks?

*8. "Black and Tepper's strategy assumed that there is a tax shield to debt. If Miller's 'Debt and Taxes' article is right, the strategy no longer works." Is this true?

9. "Funded pension plans impose an excessive cost on the economy. We will be forced to change to a 'pay-as-you-go' system." What does the speaker mean? Is the statement right?

10. During the past decade, two pension funds had exactly the same cash inflows and outflows and provided the same internal rate of return over the period. However, they provided different time-weighted rates of return. How is this possible?

11. Here is a hard one: Should the pension fund's *current* investment policy be affected by the company's plans for future recruiting?

12. Here is another hard one: "If the pension fund performs badly, the company will have to make extra contributions. If the fund performs well, the company may be able to reduce its level of contributions. Since contributions to the fund are a charge before tax, the pension fund should behave *as if* its returns are taxed at the corporate income tax rate." Does the speaker have a point?

13. Why do we have company pension schemes? Would it be better to let individuals make their own savings arrangements for their old age?

P·A·R·T

11

CONCLUSIONS

C·H·A·P·T·E·R

36

CONCLUSION: WHAT WE DO AND DO NOT KNOW ABOUT FINANCE

We have had our say and it is time to sign off. Let us finish by thinking about some of the things that we do and do not know about finance.

36-1 WHAT WE DO KNOW: THE SEVEN MOST IMPORTANT IDEAS IN FINANCE

What would you say if you were asked to name the seven most important ideas in finance? Here is our list.

1 Net Present Value

When you wish to know the value of a used car, you look at prices in the secondhand car market. Similarly, when you wish to know the value of a future cash flow, you look at prices quoted in the capital markets, where claims to future cash flows are traded (remember, those highly paid investment bankers are just secondhand cash-flow dealers). So when you wish to know the value of a future cash flow, you can look at the prices quoted in the capital market. If you can buy cash flows for your shareholders at a cheaper price than they would have to pay in the capital market, you have increased the value of their investment.

This is the simple idea behind *net present value* (NPV). When we calculate a project's NPV, we are asking whether the project is worth more than it costs. We are estimating its value by calculating what its cash flows would be worth if a claim on them were offered separately to investors and traded in the capital markets.

That is why we calculate NPV by discounting future cash flows at the opportunity cost of capital—that is, at the expected rate of return offered by securities having the same degree of risk as the project. In well-functioning capital markets, all equivalent-risk assets are priced to offer the same expected return. By discounting at the opportunity cost of capital, we calculate the price at which investors in the project could expect to earn that rate of return.

Like most good ideas, the net present value rule is "obvious when you think about it." But notice what an important idea it is. The NPV rule allows thousands of shareholders, who may have vastly different levels of wealth and attitudes toward risk, to participate in the same enterprise and to delegate its operation to a professional manager. They give the manager one simple instruction: "Maximize present value."

2 The Capital Asset Pricing Model

Some people say that modern finance is all about the capital asset pricing model. That's nonsense. If the capital asset pricing model had never been invented, our advice to financial managers would be essentially the same. The attraction of the model is that it gives us a manageable way of thinking about the required return on a risky investment.

Again, it is an attractively simple idea. There are two kinds of risk—those that you can diversify away and those that you can't. You can measure the *nondiversifiable*, or *market*, risk of an investment by the extent to which the value of the investment is affected by a change in the *aggregate* value of all the assets in the economy. This is called the *beta* of the investment. The only risks that people care about are the ones that they can't get rid of—the nondiversifiable ones. This is why the required return on an asset increases in line with its beta.

Many people are worried by some of the rather strong assumptions behind the capital asset pricing model, or they are concerned about the difficulties of estimating a project's beta. They are right to be worried about these things. In 10 or 20 years' time we will probably have much better theories than we do now. But we will be extremely surprised if those future theories do not still insist on the crucial distinction between diversifiable and nondiversifiable risk—and that, after all, is the main idea underlying the capital asset pricing model.

3 Efficient Capital Markets

The third fundamental idea is that security prices accurately reflect available information and respond rapidly to new information as soon as it becomes available. This *efficient-market theory* comes in three flavours, corresponding to different definitions of "available information." The weak form (or random-walk theory) says that prices reflect all the information in past prices. The semistrong form says that prices reflect all publicly available information, and the strong form holds that prices reflect all acquirable information.

Don't misunderstand the efficient-market idea. It doesn't say that there are no taxes or costs; it doesn't say that there aren't some clever people and some stupid ones. It merely implies that competition in capital markets is very tough—there are no money machines, and security prices reflect the true underlying values of assets.

4 Value Additivity and the Law of the Conservation of Value

The principle of *value additivity* states that the value of the whole is equal to the sum of the values of the parts. It is sometimes called the *law of the conservation of value.*

When we appraise a project that produces a succession of cash flows, we always assume that values are additive. In other words, we assume

$$PV(\text{project}) = PV(C_1) + PV(C_2) + \cdots + PV(C_t)$$
$$= \frac{C_1}{1 + r} + \frac{C_2}{(1 + r)^2} + \cdots + \frac{C_t}{(1 + r)^t}$$

We similarly assume that the sum of the present values of projects A and B equals the present value of a composite project AB.[1] But value additivity also means that you can't increase value by putting two whole companies together unless you thereby increase the total cash flow. In other words, there are no benefits to mergers solely for diversification. And if the rule works for addition, it also works for subtraction. Therefore, financing decisions that simply subdivide the same cash flows in a different way just change the packaging: they don't increase overall firm value. This is the basic idea behind Modigliani and Miller's famous article. Other things being equal, changes in capital structure do not affect value. As long as the *total* cash flow generated by the firm's assets and operations is unchanged by capital structure, total value is independent of capital structure. The value of the whole pie does not depend on how it is sliced.[2]

5 Option Theory

In everyday conversation we often use the word *option* as synonymous with *choice* or *alternative*; thus, we speak of someone as *having a number of options*. In finance an option refers specifically to the opportunity to trade in the future on terms that are fixed today. Smart managers know that it is often worth paying today for the option to buy or sell an asset tomorrow.

If options are so important, the financial manager needs to know how to value them. Finance experts have known for some time the relevant variables — the exercise price and the exercise date of the option, the risk of the underlying asset, and the rate of interest. But it was Black and Scholes who first showed how these can be put together in a usable formula.

The Black-Scholes formula was developed for simple call options. It does not directly apply to the more complicated options often encountered in corporate finance. That is why one of the hottest areas of research is extending the basic principles of option valuation to cover the more complicated cases.

6 Absence of Arbitrage Opportunities

We have used "no-arbitrage" arguments (or, "arbitrage arguments" for short) to develop several other fundamental ideas about finance, so the idea merits its own spotlight.

The value-additivity principle rests on the absence of arbitrage. If the total value of the parts is less than the value of the whole, you can earn unlimited riskless profits by simply assembling the parts into the whole. If the total value of the parts is more than the value of the whole, you can earn unlimited riskless profits by simply tearing the whole up into its constituent parts. Since such money machines don't exist, we must have value additivity.

Option pricing theory is based on arbitrage arguments. The option is priced every period by replicating its payoff with a portfolio of the underlying stock and the bond. If the option price does not equal the portfolio price, an arbitrage profit can be earned.

Arbitrage arguments are regularly used to price bonds, foreign exchange, and a variety of new financial instruments.

---

[1] That is, if

$$PV(A) = PV[C_1(A)] + PV[C_2(A)] + \cdots + PV[C_t(A)] + \cdots$$
$$PV(B) = PV[C_1(B)] + PV[C_2(B)] + \cdots + PV[C_t(B)] + \cdots$$

and if for each period t, $C_t(AB) = C_t(A) + C_t(B)$, then

$$PV(AB) = PV(A) + PV(B)$$

[2] If you *start* with the cash flow $C_t(AB)$ and split it into two pieces, $C_t(A)$ and $C_t(B)$, then total value is unchanged. That is, $PV[C_t(A)] + PV[C_t(B)] = PV[C_t(AB)]$. See footnote 1.

Arbitrage arguments can also be subtle. For example, we may be studying the relative merits of the capital asset pricing model, the consumption capital asset pricing model, and arbitrage pricing theory for many years to come. Maybe a new theory will come along. But, an arbitrage argument, combined with a little high-powered math, has been used to show that we will always be able to find some systematic market factor such that the risk premium on any asset will equal a market price of risk times the covariance of that asset's returns with the systematic factor.[3] It's comforting to know that, even though the details will change, the basic principles won't.

7 Management Incentives, Monitoring, and Information

A modern corporation is a complex team effort involving a large number of players. Some of these players are the obvious ones: the current management, employees, shareholders, and bondholders. Other players are less obvious but no less important. They include potential owners who might mount a take-over of the firm, investment bankers whose reputation depends on how well a firm they helped finance ends up performing, investors who are considering buying the firm's securities but are not now security holders, and the public who may or may not be affected by whether or not the company has been a 'good' corporate citizen.

For a long time economists argued that a competitive market place would induce all players to act for the common good. In the last twenty years they have had a lot more to say about the possible conflicts of interest and how companies try to overcome such conflicts. The areas of economics that have been used to shed light on these issues are known as **agency theory** and **game theory**.

We devoted at least one chapter of this book to each of the other important ideas in finance. We didn't allocate a chapter to agency theory and game theory but these theories have helped us think about such questions as:

• How can an entrepreneur persuade venture capital investors to join in his or her enterprise?
• What are the reasons for all the fine print in bond agreements?
• Why might a bank sometimes be unwilling to lend a firm more money at any price?
• Are LBOs simply attempts to "rip off" the other players, or do they change management's incentives to maximize company value?

Are these seven ideas exciting theories or plain common sense? Call them what you will, they are basic to the financial manager's job. If by reading this book you really understand these ideas and know how to apply them, you have learned a great deal.

36-2 WHAT WE DO NOT KNOW: 10 UNSOLVED PROBLEMS IN FINANCE

Since the unknown is never exhausted, the list of what we do not know about finance could go on forever. But, following Brealey, Myers, Sick, and Giammarino's third law (see Section 28-2), we will list and briefly discuss 10 unsolved problems that seem ripe for productive research.

---

[3] This so-called martingale pricing theory was first discussed by J.M. Harrison and D.M. Kreps in "Martingales and Arbitrage in Multiperiod Securities Markets," *Journal of Economic Theory,* **20**: 381–408 (1979).

1 How Are Major Financial Decisions Made?

Arnold Sametz commented in 1964 that "we know very little about how the great nonroutine financial decisions are made."[4] That is no less true today. We know quite a bit about asset values, but we do not know very much about the decisions that give rise to these values. What is the process that causes one company to make a major investment and another to reject it? Why does one company decide to issue debt and another to issue equity? If we knew why companies make particular decisions, we would be better able to help improve those decisions.

Our ignorance is largest when it comes to major *strategic* decisions. In Section 12-1 we described strategic planning as "capital budgeting on a grand scale." Strategic planning attempts to identify the lines of business where the firm has the greatest long-run opportunities and to develop a plan for achieving success in those businesses. But it is hard to calculate the NPV of major strategic decisions. Think, for example, of a firm which makes a major commitment to the design and manufacture of computer memories. It is really embarking on a long-term effort which will require capital outlays over many years. It cannot identify all those future projects, much less evaluate their NPVs. Instead, it decides to go ahead because the computer memory business is growing rapidly, because firms already in that business are doing well, and because it has intangible assets—special technology, perhaps—which it thinks will give it a leg up on the competition.

Strategic planning is a "top-down" approach to capital budgeting: you choose the businesses you want to be in and make the capital outlays necessary for success. It's perfectly sensible and natural for firms to look at capital investments that way *in addition to* looking at them "bottom-up." The trouble is that we understand the bottom-up part of the capital budgeting process better than the top-down part.

Top-down and bottom-up should not be competing approaches to capital budgeting. They should be two aspects of a single integrated procedure. Not all firms integrate the two approaches successfully. No doubt some firms do so, but we don't really know how.

In Section 28-2 we suggested that option pricing theory might help unravel some of the mysteries of strategic planning. We will have to wait and see whether it does.

2 What Determines Project Risk and Present Value?

A good capital investment is one that has a positive NPV. We have talked at some length about how to calculate NPV, but we have given you very little guidance about how to find positive-NPV projects, except to say in Section 11-4 that projects have positive NPVs when the firm can earn economic rents. But why do some companies earn economic rents while others in the same industry do not? Are the rents merely windfall gains, or can they be anticipated and planned for? What is their source, and how long do they persist before competition destroys them? Very little is known about any of these important questions.

Here is a related question: Why are some real assets risky and others relatively safe? In Section 9-5 we suggested a few reasons for the differences in project betas—differences in operating leverage, for example, or in the extent to which a project's cash flows respond to the performance of the national economy. These are useful clues, but we have as yet no general procedure for estimating project betas. Assessing project risk is therefore still largely a seat-of-the-pants matter.

---

[4] A.W. Sametz, "Trends in the Volume and Composition of Equity Finance," *Journal of Finance,* **19**: 450–469 (September 1964). See p. 469.

3 Risk and Return—Have We Missed Something?

In 1848 John Stuart Mill wrote, "Happily there is nothing in the laws of value which remains for the present or any future writer to clear up; the theory is complete." Economists today are not so sure about that. For example, the capital asset pricing model is an enormous step toward understanding the effect of risk on the value of an asset, but there are many puzzles left, some statistical and some theoretical.

The statistical problems arise because the capital asset pricing model is hard to prove or disprove conclusively. It appears that average returns from low-beta stocks are too high (that is, higher than the capital asset pricing model predicts), and those from high-beta stocks are too low; but this could be a problem with the way the tests are conducted and not with the model itself.[5] In addition, some tests indicate that average return has been related to diversifiable risk as well as to beta.[6] This is, of course, inconsistent with the capital asset pricing model, which states that diversifiable risk does not bother investors and, therefore, does not affect expected or average return. Of course, these statistical results could be spurious—an accidental result of inadequate testing procedures. But if they are true, they pose a puzzle: if investors are concerned with diversifiable risk, then corporations ought to be able to increase value just by diversifying. Yet there is evidence that investors do *not* pay extra for firms that diversify. It is hard to see why they would pay extra, because investors can usually diversify more cheaply and effectively than firms can. Maybe diversifiable risk only *appears* to matter because it happens to be correlated with some other variable x that, along with beta, truly determines the expected rates of return demanded by investors. That would resolve the puzzle; but we cannot yet identify variable x and prove that it matters.

Meanwhile, work is proceeding on the theoretical front to relax the simple assumptions underlying the capital asset pricing model. We discussed this work in Section 8-5 but, just for fun, here is another example: Suppose that you love fine wine. It may make sense for you to buy shares in a grand cru chateau, even if that soaks up a large fraction of your personal wealth and leaves you with a relatively undiversified portfolio. However, you are *hedged* against a rise in the price of fine wine: your hobby will cost you more in a bull market for wine, but your stake in the chateau will make you correspondingly richer. Thus, you are holding a relatively undiversified portfolio for a good reason. We would not expect you to demand a premium for bearing that portfolio's undiversifiable risk.

In general, if two people have different tastes, it may make sense for them to hold different portfolios. You may hedge your consumption needs with an investment in wine making, whereas somebody else may do better to invest in Baskin and Robbins. The capital asset pricing model isn't rich enough to deal with such a world. It assumes that all investors have similar tastes: the "hedging motive" does not enter, and therefore they hold the same portfolio of risky assets.

Merton has extended the capital asset pricing model to accommodate the hedging motive.[7] If enough investors are attempting to hedge against the same thing, their model implies a more complicated risk-return relationship. However,

[5] See R. Roll, "A Critique of the Asset Pricing Theory's Tests; Part 1: On Past and Potential Testability of the Theory," *Journal of Financial Economics,* **4**: 129–176 (March 1977); and for a critique of the critique, D. Mayers and E.M. Rice, "Measuring Portfolio Performance and the Empirical Content of Asset Pricing Models," *Journal of Financial Economics,* **7**: 3–28 (March 1979).

[6] For example, see I. Friend, R. Westerfeld, and M. Granito, "New Evidence on the Capital Asset Pricing Model," *Journal of Finance,* **33**: 903–916 (June 1978).

[7] See R. Merton, "An Intertemporal Capital Asset Pricing Model," *Econometrica,* **41**: 867–887 (1973).

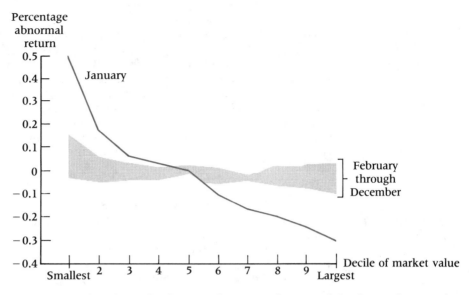

Figure 36-1   The relationship between firm size and average daily abnormal returns for each month, 1963–1979.

Source: D.B. Keim; "Size-Related Anomalies and Stock Return Seasonality: Further Empirical Evidence," *Journal of Financial Economics,* **12**: 21 (June 1983), figure 2.

it is not yet clear who is hedging against what, and so the model remains difficult to test.

4 Are There Important Exceptions to the Efficient-Market Theory?

The efficient-market theory is strong, but no theory is perfect—there must be exceptions. What are the exceptions and how well does the evidence stand up?

We noted some apparent exceptions in Section 13-2. For example, we saw that the stocks of small companies appear to have yielded higher average returns than those of large companies with comparable betas. Thus, whatever your target portfolio beta, you can apparently generate superior average returns by investing in small companies.

Now this could mean one of several things:

1. The stock market is inefficient and consistently underprices stocks of small firms.
2. The difference between the stock market performance of small and large firms is just a coincidence. (The more researchers study stock performance, the more strange coincidences they are likely to find.)
3. Firm size happens to be correlated with variable x, that mysterious second risk variable that investors may rationally take into account in pricing shares.

In searching for an explanation of the small-firm phenomenon, researchers have uncovered other puzzles. For example, look at Figure 36-1, which shows the abnormal return on small- and large-company stocks for each month of the year. You can see that almost all the extra return on small-company stocks occurred in January. So the mystery deepens. Does the turn-of-the-year effect provide a clue to the explanation of the small-company effect or is it just a false trail? Sorting out what is really going on in these cases will take considerable work and thought.

If stocks were fairly priced, there would be no easy ways to make superior profits. That is why most tests of market efficiency have analyzed whether there are simple rules that produce superior investment performance. Unfortunately, the converse does *not* hold: stock prices could deviate substantially from fair value and yet it could be difficult to make superior profits.

For example, suppose that the price of IBM stock is always one half of its fair value. As long as IBM is *consistently* underpriced, the percentage capital gain is the same as it would be if the stock always sold at a fair price. Of course, if IBM stock is underpriced, you get correspondingly more future dividends for your money, but for low-yield stocks that does not make much difference to your total return. So, while the bulk of the evidence shows that it is difficult to earn high returns, we should be cautious about assuming that stocks are *necessarily* fairly priced.

5 Is Management an Off-Balance-Sheet Liability?

Closed-end funds are firms whose only asset is a portfolio of common stocks. One might think that if you knew the value of these common stocks, you would also know the value of the firm. However, this is not the case. The stock of the closed-end fund often sells for substantially less than the value of the fund's portfolio.[8]

All this might not matter much except that it could be just the tip of the iceberg. For example, bank stocks appear to sell for less than the market value of the firms' net assets; so do real estate stocks. In the late 1970s and early 1980s the market value of many large oil companies was less than the market value of their oil reserves. Analysts joked that you could buy oil cheaper on Wall Street and Bay Street than in West Texas or Alberta.

All these are special cases in which it was possible to compare the market value of the whole firm with the values of its separate assets. But perhaps if we could observe the value of other firms' separate parts, we might find that the value of the whole was often less than the sum of the values of the parts.

We don't understand why closed-end investment companies or any of the other firms sell at a discount from the market value of their assets. One explanation is that the value added by the firm's management is less than the cost of the management. That is why we suggest that management may be an off-balance-sheet liability. For example, one rationalization of the discount of oil company shares from oil-in-the-ground value is that investors expected the profits from oil production to be frittered away in negative-NPV investments and bureaucratic excess. The present value of growth opportunities (PVGO) was negative!

Whenever firms calculate the net present value of a project, they implicitly assume that the value of the whole project is simply the sum of the values of each year's cash flow. We referred to this earlier as the law of the conservation of value. If we cannot rely on that law, the tip of the iceberg could turn out to be a very hot potato.

6 How Can We Explain the Success of New Securities and New Markets?

In the last 20 years companies and the securities exchanges have created an enormous number of new securities — options, futures, options on futures; zero coupon bonds, floating-rate bonds; bonds with collars, caps, and droplocks; dual currency bonds; bonds with currency options. . . . The list is endless. In some cases it is easy to explain the success of new markets or securities — perhaps they

---

[8] There are relatively few closed-end funds. Most mutual funds are *open-end*. This means that they stand ready to buy or sell additional shares at a price equal to the fund's net asset value per share. Therefore, the share price of an open-end fund always equals net asset value.

allow investors to insure themselves against new risks or they result from a change in tax or in regulation. Sometimes a market develops because of a change in the costs of issuing or trading different securities. But there are many successful innovations that cannot be explained so easily. Are we really better off by being able to trade options on stocks as well as the stocks themselves? Why do investment bankers continue to invent, and successfully sell, complex new securities that outstrip our ability to value them? The truth is we don't understand why some innovations in markets succeed and others never get off the ground.

7 How Can We Explain Capital Structure?

Modigliani and Miller's article about capital structure emphasized that the value of a firm depends on real variables — the goods it produces, the prices it charges, and the costs it incurs. Financing decisions merely affect the way the cash flows are packaged for distribution to investors. What goes into the package is more important than the package itself.

Does it really not matter how much your firm borrows? We have come across several reasons that it *may* matter. Tax is one possibility. Debt provides a corporate tax shield and this tax shield may more than compensate for any extra personal tax that the investor has to pay on debt interest. Perhaps managers are concerned with potential bankruptcy costs. Perhaps managers use capital structure to signal information to their shareholders.[9] Perhaps differences in capital structure reflect differences in the relative importance of growth opportunities. So far, none of these possibilities has been either proved relevant or definitely excluded.

The upshot of the matter is that we still don't have an accepted, coherent theory of capital structure. It is not for want of argument on the subject.

8 How Can We Resolve the Dividend Controversy?

We spent all of Chapter 16 on dividend policy without being able to resolve the dividend controversy. Many people believe dividends are good, others believe they are bad, and still others believe they are irrelevant. If pressed, we stand somewhere in the middle, but we can't be dogmatic about it.

We don't mean to disparage existing research; rather, we say that more is in order. Whether future research will change anybody's mind is another matter. In 1979 Joel Stern wrote an article for the editorial page of *The Wall Street Journal* arguing for low dividends and citing statistical tests in support of his position.[10] The article attracted several strongly worded responses, including one manager who wrote, "While Mr. Stern is gamboling from pinnacle to pinnacle in the upper realms of the theoretical, those of us in financial management are down below slogging through the foothills of reality."[11]

9 What Is the Value of Liquidity?

Unlike Treasury bills, cash pays no interest. On the other hand, cash provides more liquidity than Treasury bills. People who hold cash must believe that this additional liquidity offsets the loss of interest. In equilibrium, the marginal value of the additional liquidity must equal the interest rate on bills.

---

[9] See S. Ross, "The Determination of Financial Structure: The Incentive-Signaling Approach," *Bell Journal of Economics,* **8**: 23–40 (Spring 1977).

[10] Joel Stern, "The Dividend Question," *Wall Street Journal,* July 16, 1973, p. 13.

[11] *Wall Street Journal,* August 20, 1979, p. 16. The letter was from A.J. Sandblute, senior vice-president of Minnesota Light and Power Company.

Now what can we say about corporate holdings of cash? It is wrong to ignore the liquidity gain and to say that the cost of holding cash is the lost interest. This would imply that cash always has a *negative* NPV. It is equally foolish to say that, because the marginal value of liquidity is equal to the loss of interest, it doesn't matter how much cash the firm holds. This would imply that cash always has a *zero* NPV.

We know that the marginal value of cash to a holder declines with the size of the cash holding, but we don't really understand how to value the liquidity service of cash. In our chapters on working-capital management we largely finesse the problem by presenting models that are really too simple,[12] or by speaking vaguely of the need to ensure an "adequate" liquidity reserve. We cannot successfully tackle the problem of working-capital management until we have a theory of liquidity.

The problem is that liquidity is a matter of degree. A Treasury bill is less liquid than cash, but it is still a highly liquid security because it can be sold and turned into cash easily and almost instantaneously.[13] Corporate bonds are less liquid than Treasury bills; trucks are less liquid than corporate bonds; specialized machinery is less liquid than trucks; and so on.[14] But even specialized machinery can be turned into cash if you are willing to accept some delay and cost of sale. The broad question is therefore not "How much cash should the firm hold?" but "How should it divide its total investment between relatively liquid and relatively illiquid assets?" — holding other things constant of course. That question is hard to answer. Obviously, every firm must be able to raise cash on short notice, but we have no good theory of how much cash is enough or how readily the firm should be able to raise it. To complicate matters further, we note that cash can be raised on short notice by borrowing, or selling other securities, as well as by selling assets. The financial manager with a $1 million unused line of credit may sleep just as soundly as one whose firm holds $1 million in marketable securities.

10   How Can We Explain Merger Waves?

In 1968, at the first peak of the postwar merger movement, Joel Segall noted: "There is no single hypothesis which is both plausible and general and which shows promise of explaining the current merger movement. If so, it is correct to say that there is nothing known about mergers; there are no useful generalizations."[15] Of course, there are many plausible reasons why two firms might wish to merge. If you single out a *particular* merger, it is usually possible to think up a reason why that merger could make sense. But that leaves us with a special hypothesis for each merger. What we need is a *general* hypothesis to explain merger waves. For example, everybody seemed to be merging in 1968 and nobody 5 years later. Why?

---

[12] For example, models based only on the transaction costs of switching between cash and interest-bearing assets. See Section 29-1.

[13] That is, you can realize the asset's true economic value in a quick sale. Liquidity means that you don't have to accept a discount from true value if you want to see the asset quickly.

[14] It also happens that investments are very liquid except when you want to sell them. In the heyday of the junk bond market, institutions were able to trade these bonds in volume with little impact on prices. But then Michael Milken, the founder of the junk bond market, was indicted for securities fraud, his employer Drexel Burnham Lambert filed for bankruptcy, and a number of junk bond issuers defaulted on their debt. The result: many investors (including Drexel) found themselves stuck with junk bonds that were unmarketable at almost any price.

[15] J. Segall, "Merging for Fun and Profit," *Industrial Management Review,* **9**: 17–30 (Winter 1968).

We can think of other instances of financial fashions. For example, from time to time there are hot new issue periods when there seems to be an insatiable supply of speculative new issues and an equally insatiable demand for them. In recent years economists have been developing new theories of speculative bubbles. Perhaps such theories will help to explain these mystifying financial fashions.

36-3   A FINAL WORD

That concludes our list of unsolved problems. We have given you the 10 uppermost in our minds. If there are others that you find more interesting and challenging, by all means construct your own list and start thinking about it.

It will take years for our 10 problems to be finally solved and replaced with a fresh list. In the meantime, we invite you to go on to further study of what we *already* know about finance. We also invite you to apply what you have learned from reading this book.

Now that the book is done, we sympathize with Huckleberry Finn. At the end of his book he says:

> So there ain't nothing more to write, and I am rotten glad of it, because if I'd a'knowed what a trouble it was to make a book I wouldn't a' tackled it, and I ain't a'going to no more.

APPENDIX: FINANCIAL TABLES

Appendix Table 1 Discount factors: Present value of \$1 to be received after t years $= \dfrac{1}{(1 + r)^t}$

t	\multicolumn{15}{c}{Interest rate r}
	1%	2%	3%	4%	5%	6%	7%	8%	9%	10%	11%	12%	13%	14%	15%
1	.990	.980	.971	.962	.952	.943	.935	.926	.917	.909	.901	.893	.885	.877	.870
2	.980	.961	.943	.925	.907	.890	.873	.857	.842	.826	.812	.797	.783	.769	.756
3	.971	.942	.915	.889	.864	.840	.816	.794	.772	.751	.731	.712	.693	.675	.658
4	.961	.924	.888	.855	.823	.792	.763	.735	.708	.683	.659	.636	.613	.592	.572
5	.951	.906	.863	.822	.784	.747	.713	.681	.650	.621	.593	.567	.543	.519	.497
6	.942	.888	.837	.790	.746	.705	.666	.630	.596	.564	.535	.507	.480	.456	.432
7	.933	.871	.813	.760	.711	.665	.623	.583	.547	.513	.482	.452	.425	.400	.376
8	.923	.853	.789	.731	.677	.627	.582	.540	.502	.467	.434	.404	.376	.351	.327
9	.914	.837	.766	.703	.645	.592	.544	.500	.460	.424	.391	.361	.333	.308	.284
10	.905	.820	.744	.676	.614	.558	.508	.463	.422	.386	.352	.322	.295	.270	.247
11	.896	.804	.722	.650	.585	.527	.475	.429	.388	.350	.317	.287	.261	.237	.215
12	.887	.788	.701	.625	.557	.497	.444	.397	.356	.319	.286	.257	.231	.208	.187
13	.879	.773	.681	.601	.530	.469	.415	.368	.326	.290	.258	.229	.204	.182	.163
14	.870	.758	.661	.577	.505	.442	.388	.340	.299	.263	.232	.205	.181	.160	.141
15	.861	.743	.642	.555	.481	.417	.362	.315	.275	.239	.209	.183	.160	.140	.123
16	.853	.728	.623	.534	.458	.394	.339	.292	.252	.218	.188	.163	.141	.123	.107
17	.844	.714	.605	.513	.436	.371	.317	.270	.231	.198	.170	.146	.125	.108	.093
18	.836	.700	.587	.494	.416	.350	.296	.250	.212	.180	.153	.130	.111	.095	.081
19	.828	.686	.570	.475	.396	.331	.277	.232	.194	.164	.138	.116	.098	.083	.070
20	.820	.673	.554	.456	.377	.312	.258	.215	.178	.149	.124	.104	.087	.073	.061
21	.811	.660	.538	.439	.359	.294	.242	.199	.164	.135	.112	.093	.077	.064	.053
22	.803	.647	.522	.422	.342	.278	.226	.184	.150	.123	.101	.083	.068	.056	.046
23	.795	.634	.507	.406	.326	.262	.211	.170	.138	.112	.091	.074	.060	.049	.040
24	.788	.622	.492	.390	.310	.247	.197	.158	.126	.102	.082	.066	.053	.043	.035
25	.780	.610	.478	.375	.295	.233	.184	.146	.116	.092	.074	.059	.047	.038	.030
26	.772	.598	.464	.361	.281	.220	.172	.135	.106	.084	.066	.053	.042	.033	.026
27	.764	.586	.450	.347	.268	.207	.161	.125	.098	.076	.060	.047	.037	.029	.023
28	.757	.574	.437	.333	.255	.196	.150	.116	.090	.069	.054	.042	.033	.026	.020
29	.749	.563	.424	.321	.243	.185	.141	.107	.082	.063	.048	.037	.029	.022	.017
30	.742	.552	.412	.308	.231	.174	.131	.099	.075	.057	.044	.033	.026	.020	.015

E.g.: If the interest rate is 10% per year, the present value of \$1 to be received at the end of year 5 is \$0.621.

						Interest rate r									
16%	17%	18%	19%	20%	21%	22%	23%	24%	25%	26%	27%	28%	29%	30%	t
.862	.855	.847	.840	.833	.826	.820	.813	.806	.800	.794	.787	.781	.775	.769	1
.743	.731	.718	.706	.694	.683	.672	.661	.650	.640	.630	.620	.610	.601	.592	2
.641	.624	.609	.593	.579	.564	.551	.537	.524	.512	.500	.488	.477	.466	.455	3
.552	.534	.516	.499	.482	.467	.451	.437	.423	.410	.397	.384	.373	.361	.350	4
.476	.456	.437	.419	.402	.386	.370	.355	.341	.328	.315	.303	.291	.280	.269	5
.410	.390	.370	.352	.335	.319	.303	.289	.275	.262	.250	.238	.227	.217	.207	6
.354	.333	.314	.296	.279	.263	.249	.235	.222	.210	.198	.188	.178	.168	.159	7
.305	.285	.266	.249	.233	.218	.204	.191	.179	.168	.157	.148	.139	.130	.123	8
.263	.243	.225	.209	.194	.180	.167	.155	.144	.134	.125	.116	.108	.101	.094	9
.227	.208	.191	.176	.162	.149	.137	.126	.116	.107	.099	.092	.085	.078	.073	10
.195	.178	.162	.148	.135	.123	.112	.103	.094	.086	.079	.072	.066	.061	.056	11
.168	.152	.137	.124	.112	.102	.092	.083	.076	.069	.062	.057	.052	.047	.043	12
.145	.130	.116	.104	.093	.084	.075	.068	.061	.055	.050	.045	.040	.037	.033	13
.125	.111	.099	.088	.078	.069	.062	.055	.049	.044	.039	.035	.032	.028	.025	14
.108	.095	.084	.074	.065	.057	.051	.045	.040	.035	.031	.028	.025	.022	.020	15
.093	.081	.071	.062	.054	.047	.042	.036	.032	.028	.025	.022	.019	.017	.015	16
.080	.069	.060	.052	.045	.039	.034	.030	.026	.023	.020	.017	.015	.013	.012	17
.069	.059	.051	.044	.038	.032	.028	.024	.021	.018	.016	.014	.012	.010	.009	18
.060	.051	.043	.037	.031	.027	.023	.020	.017	.014	.012	.011	.009	.008	.007	19
.051	.043	.037	.031	.026	.022	.019	.016	.014	.012	.010	.008	.007	.006	.005	20
.044	.037	.031	.026	.022	.018	.015	.013	.011	.009	.008	.007	.006	.005	.004	21
.038	.032	.026	.022	.018	.015	.013	.011	.009	.007	.006	.005	.004	.004	.003	22
.033	.027	.022	.018	.015	.012	.010	.009	.007	.006	.005	.004	.003	.003	.002	23
.028	.023	.019	.015	.013	.010	.008	.007	.006	.005	.004	.003	.003	.002	.002	24
.024	.020	.016	.013	.010	.009	.007	.006	.005	.004	.003	.003	.002	.002	.001	25
.021	.017	.014	.011	.009	.007	.006	.005	.004	.003	.002	.002	.002	.001	.001	26
.018	.014	.011	.009	.007	.006	.005	.004	.003	.002	.002	.002	.001	.001	.001	27
.016	.012	.010	.008	.006	.005	.004	.003	.002	.002	.002	.001	.001	.001	.001	28
.014	.011	.008	.006	.005	.004	.003	.002	.002	.002	.001	.001	.001	.001	.000	29
.012	.009	.007	.005	.004	.003	.003	.002	.002	.001	.001	.001	.001	.000	.000	30

Appendix Table 2 Accumulation factors: Future value of $1 by the end of t years $= (1 + r)^t$

								Interest rate r							
t	1%	2%	3%	4%	5%	6%	7%	8%	9%	10%	11%	12%	13%	14%	15%
1	1.010	1.020	1.030	1.040	1.050	1.060	1.070	1.080	1.090	1.100	1.110	1.120	1.130	1.140	1.150
2	1.020	1.040	1.061	1.082	1.102	1.124	1.145	1.166	1.188	1.210	1.232	1.254	1.277	1.300	1.322
3	1.030	1.061	1.093	1.125	1.158	1.191	1.225	1.260	1.295	1.331	1.368	1.405	1.443	1.482	1.521
4	1.041	1.082	1.126	1.170	1.216	1.262	1.311	1.360	1.412	1.464	1.518	1.574	1.630	1.689	1.749
5	1.051	1.104	1.159	1.217	1.276	1.338	1.403	1.469	1.539	1.611	1.685	1.762	1.842	1.925	2.011
6	1.062	1.126	1.194	1.265	1.340	1.419	1.501	1.587	1.677	1.772	1.870	1.974	2.082	2.195	2.313
7	1.072	1.149	1.230	1.316	1.407	1.504	1.606	1.714	1.828	1.949	2.076	2.211	2.353	2.502	2.660
8	1.083	1.172	1.267	1.369	1.477	1.594	1.718	1.851	1.993	2.144	2.305	2.476	2.658	2.853	3.059
9	1.094	1.195	1.305	1.423	1.551	1.689	1.838	1.999	2.172	2.358	2.558	2.773	3.004	3.252	3.518
10	1.105	1.219	1.344	1.480	1.629	1.791	1.967	2.159	2.367	2.594	2.839	3.106	3.395	3.707	4.046
11	1.116	1.243	1.384	1.539	1.710	1.898	2.105	2.332	2.580	2.853	3.152	3.479	3.836	4.226	4.652
12	1.127	1.268	1.426	1.601	1.796	2.012	2.252	2.518	2.813	3.138	3.498	3.896	4.335	4.818	5.350
13	1.138	1.294	1.469	1.665	1.886	2.133	2.410	2.720	3.066	3.452	3.883	4.363	4.898	5.492	6.153
14	1.149	1.319	1.513	1.732	1.980	2.261	2.579	2.937	3.342	3.797	4.310	4.887	5.535	6.261	7.076
15	1.161	1.346	1.558	1.801	2.079	2.397	2.759	3.172	3.642	4.177	4.785	5.474	6.254	7.138	8.137
16	1.173	1.373	1.605	1.873	2.183	2.540	2.952	3.426	3.970	4.595	5.311	6.130	7.067	8.137	9.358
17	1.184	1.400	1.653	1.948	2.292	2.693	3.159	3.700	4.328	5.054	5.895	6.866	7.986	9.276	10.76
18	1.196	1.428	1.702	2.026	2.407	2.854	3.380	3.996	4.717	5.560	6.544	7.690	9.024	10.58	12.38
19	1.208	1.457	1.754	2.107	2.527	3.026	3.617	4.316	5.142	6.116	7.263	8.613	10.20	12.06	14.23
20	1.220	1.486	1.806	2.191	2.653	3.207	3.870	4.661	5.604	6.727	8.062	9.646	11.52	13.74	16.37
21	1.232	1.516	1.860	2.279	2.786	3.400	4.141	5.034	6.109	7.400	8.949	10.80	13.02	15.67	18.82
22	1.245	1.546	1.916	2.370	2.925	3.604	4.430	5.437	6.659	8.140	9.934	12.10	14.71	17.86	21.64
23	1.257	1.577	1.974	2.465	3.072	3.820	4.741	5.871	7.258	8.954	11.03	13.55	16.63	20.36	24.89
24	1.270	1.608	2.033	2.563	3.225	4.049	5.072	6.341	7.911	9.850	12.24	15.18	18.79	23.21	28.63
25	1.282	1.641	2.094	2.666	3.386	4.292	5.427	6.848	8.623	10.83	13.59	17.00	21.23	26.46	32.92
26	1.295	1.673	2.157	2.772	3.556	4.549	5.807	7.396	9.399	11.92	15.08	19.04	23.99	30.17	37.86
27	1.308	1.707	2.221	2.883	3.733	4.822	6.214	7.988	10.25	13.11	16.74	21.32	27.11	34.39	43.54
28	1.321	1.741	2.288	2.999	3.920	5.112	6.649	8.627	11.17	14.42	18.58	23.88	30.63	39.20	50.07
29	1.335	1.776	2.357	3.119	4.116	5.418	7.114	9.317	12.17	15.86	20.62	26.75	34.62	44.69	57.58
30	1.348	1.811	2.427	3.243	4.322	5.743	7.612	10.06	13.27	17.45	22.89	29.96	39.12	50.95	66.21

E.g.: If the interest rate is 10% per year, an investment of $1 today will be worth $1.611 at the end of year 5.

						Interest rate r									
16%	17%	18%	19%	20%	21%	22%	23%	24%	25%	26%	27%	28%	29%	30%	t
1.160	1.170	1.180	1.190	1.200	1.210	1.220	1.230	1.240	1.250	1.260	1.270	1.280	1.290	1.300	1
1.346	1.369	1.392	1.416	1.440	1.464	1.488	1.513	1.538	1.562	1.588	1.613	1.638	1.664	1.690	2
1.561	1.602	1.643	1.685	1.728	1.772	1.816	1.861	1.907	1.953	2.000	2.048	2.097	2.147	2.197	3
1.811	1.874	1.939	2.005	2.074	2.144	2.215	2.289	2.364	2.441	2.520	2.601	2.684	2.769	2.856	4
2.100	2.192	2.288	2.386	2.488	2.594	2.703	2.815	2.932	3.052	3.176	3.304	3.436	3.572	3.713	5
2.436	2.565	2.700	2.840	2.986	3.138	3.297	3.463	3.635	3.815	4.002	4.196	4.398	4.608	4.827	6
2.826	3.001	3.185	3.379	3.583	3.797	4.023	4.259	4.508	4.768	5.042	5.329	5.629	5.945	6.275	7
3.278	3.511	3.759	4.021	4.300	4.595	4.908	5.239	5.590	5.960	6.353	6.768	7.206	7.669	8.157	8
3.803	4.108	4.435	4.785	5.160	5.560	5.987	6.444	6.931	7.451	8.005	8.595	9.223	9.893	10.60	9
4.411	4.807	5.234	5.695	6.192	6.727	7.305	7.926	8.594	9.313	10.09	10.92	11.81	12.76	13.79	10
5.117	5.624	6.176	6.777	7.430	8.140	8.912	9.749	10.66	11.64	12.71	13.86	15.11	16.46	17.92	11
5.936	6.580	7.288	8.064	8.916	9.850	10.87	11.99	13.21	14.55	16.01	17.61	19.34	21.24	23.30	12
6.886	7.699	8.599	9.596	10.70	11.92	13.26	14.75	16.39	18.19	20.18	22.36	24.76	27.39	30.29	13
7.988	9.007	10.15	11.42	12.84	14.42	16.18	18.14	20.32	22.74	25.42	28.40	31.69	35.34	39.37	14
9.266	10.54	11.97	13.59	15.41	17.45	19.74	22.31	25.20	28.42	32.03	36.06	40.56	45.59	51.19	15
10.75	12.33	14.13	16.17	18.49	21.11	24.09	27.45	31.24	35.53	40.36	45.80	51.92	58.81	66.54	16
12.47	14.43	16.67	19.24	22.19	25.55	29.38	33.76	38.74	44.41	50.85	58.17	66.46	75.86	86.50	17
14.46	16.88	19.67	22.90	26.62	30.91	35.85	41.52	48.04	55.51	64.07	73.87	85.07	97.86	112.5	18
16.78	19.75	23.21	27.25	31.95	37.40	43.74	51.07	59.57	69.39	80.73	93.81	108.9	126.2	146.2	19
19.46	23.11	27.39	32.43	38.34	45.26	53.36	62.82	73.86	86.74	101.7	119.1	139.4	162.9	190.0	20
22.57	27.03	32.32	38.59	46.01	54.76	65.10	77.27	91.59	108.4	128.2	151.3	178.4	210.1	247.1	21
26.19	31.63	38.14	45.92	55.21	66.26	79.42	95.04	113.6	135.5	161.5	192.2	228.4	271.0	321.2	22
30.38	37.01	45.01	54.65	66.25	80.18	96.89	116.9	140.8	169.4	203.5	244.1	292.3	349.6	417.5	23
35.24	43.30	53.11	65.03	79.50	97.02	118.2	143.8	174.6	211.8	256.4	309.9	374.1	451.0	542.8	24
40.87	50.66	62.67	77.39	95.40	117.4	144.2	176.9	216.5	264.7	323.0	393.6	478.9	581.8	705.6	25
47.41	59.27	73.95	92.09	114.5	142.0	175.9	217.5	268.5	330.9	407.0	499.9	613.0	750.5	917.3	26
55.00	69.35	87.26	109.6	137.4	171.9	214.6	267.6	333.0	413.6	512.9	634.9	784.6	968.1	1193	27
63.80	81.13	103.0	130.4	164.8	208.0	261.9	329.1	412.9	517.0	646.2	806.3	1004	1249	1550	28
74.01	94.93	121.5	155.2	197.8	251.6	319.5	404.8	512.0	646.2	814.2	1024	1286	1611	2015	29
85.85	111.1	143.4	184.7	237.4	304.5	389.8	497.9	634.8	807.8	1026	1301	1646	2078	2620	30

Appendix Table 3 Annuity table: Present value of $1 *per year* for each of t years $= \dfrac{1}{r} = \dfrac{1}{r(1+r)^t}$

t	Interest rate r														
	1%	2%	3%	4%	5%	6%	7%	8%	9%	10%	11%	12%	13%	14%	15%
1	.990	.980	.971	.962	.952	.943	.935	.926	.917	.909	.901	.893	.885	.877	.870
2	1.970	1.942	1.913	1.886	1.859	1.833	1.808	1.783	1.759	1.736	1.713	1.690	1.668	1.647	1.626
3	2.941	2.884	2.829	2.775	2.723	2.673	2.624	2.577	2.531	2.487	2.444	2.402	2.361	2.322	2.283
4	3.902	3.808	3.717	3.630	3.546	3.465	3.387	3.312	3.240	3.170	3.102	3.037	2.974	2.914	2.855
5	4.853	4.713	4.580	4.452	4.329	4.212	4.100	3.993	3.890	3.791	3.696	3.605	3.517	3.433	3.352
6	5.795	5.601	5.417	5.242	5.076	4.917	4.767	4.623	4.486	4.355	4.231	4.111	3.998	3.889	3.784
7	6.728	6.472	6.230	6.002	5.786	5.582	5.389	5.206	5.033	4.868	4.712	4.564	4.423	4.288	4.160
8	7.652	7.325	7.020	6.733	6.463	6.210	5.971	5.747	5.535	5.335	5.146	4.968	4.799	4.639	4.487
9	8.566	8.162	7.786	7.435	7.108	6.802	6.515	6.247	5.995	5.759	5.537	5.328	5.132	4.946	4.772
10	9.471	8.983	8.530	8.111	7.722	7.360	7.024	6.710	6.418	6.145	5.889	5.650	5.426	5.216	5.019
11	10.37	9.787	9.253	8.760	8.306	7.887	7.499	7.139	6.805	6.495	6.207	5.938	5.687	5.453	5.234
12	11.26	10.58	9.954	9.385	8.863	8.384	7.943	7.536	7.161	6.814	6.492	6.194	5.918	5.660	5.421
13	12.13	11.35	10.63	9.986	9.394	8.853	8.358	7.904	7.487	7.103	6.750	6.424	6.122	5.842	5.583
14	13.00	12.11	11.30	10.56	9.899	9.295	8.745	8.244	7.786	7.367	6.982	6.628	6.302	6.002	5.724
15	13.87	12.85	11.94	11.12	10.38	9.712	9.108	8.559	8.061	7.606	7.191	6.811	6.462	6.142	5.847
16	14.72	13.58	12.56	11.65	10.84	10.11	9.447	8.851	8.313	7.824	7.379	6.974	6.604	6.265	5.954
17	15.56	14.29	13.17	12.17	11.27	10.48	9.763	9.122	8.544	8.022	7.549	7.120	6.729	6.373	6.047
18	16.40	14.99	13.75	12.66	11.69	10.83	10.06	9.372	8.756	8.201	7.702	7.250	6.840	6.467	6.128
19	17.23	15.68	14.32	13.13	12.09	11.16	10.34	9.604	8.950	8.365	7.839	7.366	6.938	6.550	6.198
20	18.05	16.35	14.88	13.59	12.46	11.47	10.59	9.818	9.129	8.514	7.963	7.469	7.025	6.623	6.259
21	18.86	17.01	15.42	14.03	12.82	11.76	10.84	10.02	9.292	8.649	8.075	7.562	7.102	6.687	6.312
22	19.66	17.66	15.94	14.45	13.16	12.04	11.06	10.20	9.442	8.772	8.176	7.645	7.170	6.743	6.359
23	20.46	18.29	16.44	14.86	13.49	12.30	11.27	10.37	9.580	8.883	8.266	7.718	7.230	6.792	6.399
24	21.24	18.91	16.94	15.25	13.80	12.55	11.47	10.53	9.707	8.985	8.348	7.784	7.283	6.835	6.434
25	22.02	19.52	17.41	15.62	14.09	12.78	11.65	10.67	9.823	9.077	8.422	7.843	7.330	6.873	6.464
26	22.80	20.12	17.88	15.98	14.38	13.00	11.83	10.81	9.929	9.161	8.488	7.896	7.372	6.906	6.491
27	23.56	20.71	18.33	16.33	14.64	13.21	11.99	10.94	10.03	9.237	8.548	7.943	7.409	6.935	6.514
28	24.32	21.28	18.76	16.66	14.90	13.41	12.14	11.05	10.12	9.307	8.602	7.984	7.441	6.961	6.534
29	25.07	21.84	19.19	16.98	15.14	13.59	12.28	11.16	10.20	9.370	8.650	8.022	7.470	6.983	6.551
30	25.81	22.40	19.60	17.29	15.37	13.76	12.41	11.26	10.27	9.427	8.694	8.055	7.496	7.003	6.566

E.g.: If the interest rate is 10% per year, the present value of $1 to be received at the end of each of the next 5 years is $3.791.

						Interest rate r									
16%	17%	18%	19%	20%	21%	22%	23%	24%	25%	26%	27%	28%	29%	30%	t
.862	.855	.847	.840	.833	.826	.820	.813	.806	.800	.794	.787	.781	.775	.769	1
1.605	1.585	1.566	1.547	1.528	1.509	1.492	1.474	1.457	1.440	1.424	1.407	1.392	1.376	1.361	2
2.246	2.210	2.174	2.140	2.106	2.074	2.042	2.011	1.981	1.952	1.923	1.896	1.868	1.842	1.816	3
2.798	2.743	2.690	2.639	2.589	2.540	2.494	2.448	2.404	2.362	2.320	2.280	2.241	2.203	2.166	4
3.274	3.199	3.127	3.058	2.991	2.926	2.864	2.803	2.745	2.689	2.635	2.583	2.532	2.483	2.436	5
3.685	3.589	3.498	3.410	3.326	3.245	3.167	3.092	3.020	2.951	2.885	2.821	2.759	2.700	2.643	6
4.039	3.922	3.812	3.706	3.605	3.508	3.416	3.327	3.242	3.161	3.083	3.009	2.937	2.868	2.802	7
4.344	4.207	4.078	3.954	3.837	3.726	3.619	3.518	3.421	3.329	3.241	3.156	3.076	2.999	2.925	8
4.607	4.451	4.303	4.163	4.031	3.905	3.786	3.673	3.566	3.463	3.366	3.273	3.184	3.100	3.019	9
4.833	4.659	4.494	4.339	4.192	4.054	3.923	3.799	3.682	3.571	3.465	3.364	3.269	3.178	3.092	10
5.029	4.836	4.656	4.486	4.327	4.177	4.035	3.902	3.776	3.656	3.543	3.437	3.335	3.239	3.147	11
5.197	4.988	4.793	4.611	4.439	4.278	4.127	3.985	3.851	3.725	3.606	3.493	3.387	3.286	3.190	12
5.342	5.118	4.910	4.715	4.533	4.362	4.203	4.053	3.912	3.780	3.656	3.538	3.427	3.322	3.223	13
5.468	5.229	5.008	4.802	4.611	4.432	4.265	4.108	3.962	3.824	3.695	3.573	3.459	3.351	3.249	14
5.575	5.324	5.092	4.876	4.675	4.489	4.315	4.153	4.001	3.859	3.726	3.601	3.483	3.373	3.268	15
5.668	5.405	5.162	4.938	4.730	4.536	4.357	4.189	4.033	3.887	3.751	3.623	3.503	3.390	3.283	16
5.749	5.475	5.222	4.990	4.775	4.576	4.391	4.219	4.059	3.910	3.771	3.640	3.518	3.403	3.295	17
5.818	5.534	5.273	5.033	4.812	4.608	4.419	4.243	4.080	3.928	3.786	3.654	3.529	3.413	3.304	18
5.877	5.584	5.316	5.070	4.843	4.635	4.442	4.263	4.097	3.942	3.799	3.664	3.539	3.421	3.311	19
5.929	5.628	5.353	5.101	4.870	4.657	4.460	4.279	4.110	3.954	3.808	3.673	3.546	3.427	3.316	20
5.973	5.665	5.384	5.127	4.891	4.675	4.476	4.292	4.121	3.963	3.816	3.679	3.551	3.432	3.320	21
6.011	5.696	5.410	5.149	4.909	4.690	4.488	4.302	4.130	3.970	3.822	3.684	3.556	3.436	3.323	22
6.044	5.723	5.432	5.167	4.925	4.703	4.499	4.311	4.137	3.976	3.827	3.689	3.559	3.438	3.325	23
6.073	5.746	5.451	5.182	4.937	4.713	4.507	4.318	4.143	3.981	3.831	3.692	3.562	3.441	3.327	24
6.097	5.766	5.467	5.195	4.948	4.721	4.514	4.323	4.147	3.985	3.834	3.694	3.564	3.442	3.329	25
6.118	5.783	5.480	5.206	4.956	4.728	4.520	4.328	4.151	3.988	3.837	3.696	3.566	3.444	3.330	26
6.136	5.798	5.492	5.215	4.964	4.734	4.524	4.332	4.154	3.990	3.839	3.698	3.567	3.445	3.331	27
6.152	5.810	5.502	5.223	4.970	4.739	4.528	4.335	4.157	3.992	3.840	3.699	3.568	3.446	3.331	28
6.166	5.820	5.510	5.229	4.975	4.743	4.531	4.337	4.159	3.994	3.841	3.700	3.569	3.446	3.332	29
6.177	5.829	5.517	5.235	4.979	4.746	4.534	4.339	4.160	3.995	3.842	3.701	3.569	3.447	3.332	30

Appendix Table 4 Values of e^{rt}: Future value of $1 invested at a *continuously compounded* rate r for t years

rt	.00	.01	.02	.03	.04	.05	.06	.07	.08	.09
.00	1.000	1.010	1.020	1.030	1.041	1.051	1.062	1.073	1.083	1.094
.10	1.105	1.116	1.127	1.139	1.150	1.162	1.174	1.185	1.197	1.209
.20	1.221	1.234	1.246	1.259	1.271	1.284	1.297	1.310	1.323	1.336
.30	1.350	1.363	1.377	1.391	1.405	1.419	1.433	1.448	1.462	1.477
.40	1.492	1.507	1.522	1.537	1.553	1.568	1.584	1.600	1.616	1.632
.50	1.649	1.665	1.682	1.699	1.716	1.733	1.751	1.768	1.786	1.804
.60	1.822	1.840	1.859	1.878	1.896	1.916	1.935	1.954	1.974	1.994
.70	2.014	2.034	2.054	2.075	2.096	2.117	2.138	2.160	2.181	2.203
.80	2.226	2.248	2.270	2.293	2.316	2.340	2.363	2.387	2.411	2.435
.90	2.460	2.484	2.509	2.535	2.560	2.586	2.612	2.638	2.664	2.691
1.00	2.718	2.746	2.773	2.801	2.829	2.858	2.886	2.915	2.945	2.974
1.10	3.004	3.034	3.065	3.096	3.127	3.158	3.190	3.222	3.254	3.287
1.20	3.320	3.353	3.387	3.421	3.456	3.490	3.525	3.561	3.597	3.633
1.30	3.669	3.706	3.743	3.781	3.819	3.857	3.896	3.935	3.975	4.015
1.40	4.055	4.096	4.137	4.179	4.221	4.263	4.306	4.349	4.393	4.437
1.50	4.482	4.527	4.572	4.618	4.665	4.711	4.759	4.807	4.855	4.904
1.60	4.953	5.003	5.053	5.104	5.155	5.207	5.259	5.312	5.366	5.419
1.70	5.474	5.529	5.585	5.641	5.697	5.755	5.812	5.871	5.930	5.989
1.80	6.050	6.110	6.172	6.234	6.297	6.360	6.424	6.488	6.554	6.619
1.90	6.686	6.753	6.821	6.890	6.959	7.029	7.099	7.171	7.243	7.316
2.00	7.389	7.463	7.538	7.614	7.691	7.768	7.846	7.925	8.004	8.085
2.10	8.166	8.248	8.331	8.415	8.499	8.585	8.671	8.758	8.846	8.935
2.20	9.025	9.116	9.207	9.300	9.393	9.488	9.583	9.679	9.777	9.875
2.30	9.974	10.07	10.18	10.28	10.38	10.49	10.59	10.70	10.80	10.91
2.40	11.02	11.13	11.25	11.36	11.47	11.59	11.70	11.82	11.94	12.06
2.50	12.18	12.30	12.43	12.55	12.68	12.81	12.94	13.07	13.20	13.33
2.60	13.46	13.60	13.74	13.87	14.01	14.15	14.30	14.44	14.59	14.73
2.70	14.88	15.03	15.18	15.33	15.49	15.64	15.80	15.96	16.12	16.28
2.80	16.44	16.61	16.78	16.95	17.12	17.29	17.46	17.64	17.81	17.99
2.90	18.17	18.36	18.54	18.73	18.92	19.11	19.30	19.49	19.69	19.89

E.g.: If the continuously compounded interest rate is 10% per year, an investment of $1 today will be worth $1.105 by the end of year 1, $1.162 by the end of year 1.5, and $1.221 by the end of year 2.

r t	.00	.01	.02	.03	.04	.05	.06	.07	.08	.09
3.00	20.09	20.29	20.49	20.70	20.91	21.12	21.33	21.54	21.76	21.98
3.10	22.20	22.42	22.65	22.87	23.10	23.34	23.57	23.81	24.05	24.29
3.20	24.53	24.78	25.03	25.28	25.53	25.79	26.05	26.31	26.58	26.84
3.30	27.11	27.39	27.66	27.94	28.22	28.50	28.79	29.08	29.37	29.67
3.40	29.96	30.27	30.57	30.88	31.19	31.50	31.82	32.14	32.46	32.79
3.50	33.12	33.45	33.78	34.12	34.47	34.81	35.16	35.52	35.87	36.23
3.60	36.60	36.97	37.34	37.71	38.09	38.47	38.86	39.25	39.65	40.04
3.70	40.45	40.85	41.26	41.68	42.10	42.52	42.95	43.38	43.82	44.26
3.80	44.70	45.15	45.60	46.06	46.53	46.99	47.47	47.94	48.42	48.91
3.90	49.40	49.90	50.40	50.91	51.42	51.94	52.46	52.98	53.52	54.05
4.00	54.60	55.15	55.70	56.26	56.83	57.40	57.97	58.56	59.15	59.74
4.10	60.34	60.95	61.56	62.18	62.80	63.43	64.07	64.72	65.37	66.02
4.20	66.69	67.36	68.03	68.72	69.41	70.11	70.81	71.52	72.24	72.97
4.30	73.70	74.44	75.19	75.94	76.71	77.48	78.26	79.04	79.84	80.64
4.40	81.45	82.27	83.10	83.93	84.77	85.63	86.49	87.36	88.23	89.12
4.50	90.02	90.92	91.84	92.76	93.69	94.63	95.58	96.54	97.51	98.49
4.60	99.48	100.5	101.5	102.5	103.5	104.6	105.6	106.7	107.8	108.9
4.70	109.9	111.1	112.2	113.3	114.4	115.6	116.7	117.9	119.1	120.3
4.80	121.5	122.7	124.0	125.2	126.5	127.7	129.0	130.3	131.6	133.0
4.90	134.3	135.6	137.0	138.4	139.8	141.2	142.6	144.0	145.5	146.9
5.00	148.4	149.9	151.4	152.9	154.5	156.0	157.6	159.2	160.8	162.4
5.10	164.0	165.7	167.3	169.0	170.7	172.4	174.2	175.9	177.7	179.5
5.20	181.3	183.1	184.9	186.8	188.7	190.6	192.5	194.4	196.4	198.3
5.30	200.3	202.4	204.4	206.4	208.5	210.6	212.7	214.9	217.0	219.2
5.40	221.4	223.6	225.9	228.1	230.4	232.8	235.1	237.5	239.8	242.3
5.50	244.7	247.2	249.6	252.1	254.7	257.2	259.8	262.4	265.1	267.7
5.60	270.4	273.1	275.9	278.7	281.5	284.3	287.1	290.0	292.9	295.9
5.70	298.9	301.9	304.9	308.0	311.1	314.2	317.3	320.5	323.8	327.0
5.80	330.3	333.6	337.0	340.4	343.8	347.2	350.7	354.2	357.8	361.4
5.90	365.0	368.7	372.4	376.2	379.9	383.8	387.6	391.5	395.4	399.4

Appendix Table 5 Continuous annuity table: Present value of $1 per year received in a continuous stream for each of t years discounted at an *annually compounded* rate r is $\dfrac{1}{\ln(1 + r)}\left(1 + \dfrac{1}{(1 + r)^t}\right)$

t	Interest rate r														
	1%	2%	3%	4%	5%	6%	7%	8%	9%	10%	11%	12%	13%	14%	15%
1	.995	.990	.985	.981	.976	.971	.967	.962	.958	.954	.950	.945	.941	.937	.933
2	1.980	1.961	1.942	1.924	1.906	1.888	1.871	1.854	1.837	1.821	1.805	1.790	1.774	1.759	1.745
3	2.956	2.913	2.871	2.830	2.791	2.752	2.715	2.679	2.644	2.609	2.576	2.543	2.512	2.481	2.450
4	3.921	3.846	3.773	3.702	3.634	3.568	3.504	3.443	3.383	3.326	3.270	3.216	3.164	3.113	3.064
5	4.878	4.760	4.648	4.540	4.437	4.338	4.242	4.150	4.062	3.977	3.896	3.817	3.741	3.668	3.598
6	5.824	5.657	5.498	5.346	5.202	5.063	4.931	4.805	4.685	4.570	4.459	4.353	4.252	4.155	4.062
7	6.762	6.536	6.323	6.121	5.930	5.748	5.576	5.412	5.256	5.108	4.967	4.832	4.704	4.582	4.465
8	7.690	7.398	7.124	6.867	6.623	6.394	6.178	5.974	5.780	5.597	5.424	5.260	5.104	4.956	4.816
9	8.609	8.244	7.902	7.583	7.284	7.004	6.741	6.494	6.261	6.042	5.836	5.642	5.458	5.285	5.121
10	9.519	9.072	8.658	8.272	7.913	7.579	7.267	6.975	6.702	6.447	6.208	5.983	5.772	5.573	5.386
11	10.42	9.884	9.391	8.935	8.512	8.121	7.758	7.421	7.107	6.815	6.542	6.287	6.049	5.826	5.617
12	11.31	10.68	10.10	9.572	9.083	8.633	8.218	7.834	7.478	7.149	6.843	6.559	6.294	6.048	5.818
13	12.19	11.46	10.79	10.18	9.627	9.116	8.647	8.216	7.819	7.453	7.115	6.802	6.512	6.242	5.992
14	13.07	12.23	11.46	10.77	10.14	9.571	9.048	8.570	8.131	7.729	7.359	7.018	6.704	6.413	6.144
15	13.93	12.98	12.12	11.34	10.64	10.00	9.423	8.897	8.418	7.980	7.579	7.212	6.874	6.563	6.276
16	14.79	13.71	12.75	11.88	11.11	10.41	9.774	9.201	8.681	8.209	7.778	7.385	7.024	6.694	6.390
17	15.64	14.43	13.36	12.41	11.55	10.79	10.10	9.482	8.923	8.416	7.957	7.539	7.158	6.809	6.490
18	16.48	15.14	13.96	12.91	11.98	11.15	10.41	9.742	9.144	8.605	8.118	7.676	7.275	6.910	6.577
19	17.31	15.83	14.54	13.39	12.38	11.49	10.69	9.983	9.347	8.777	8.263	7.799	7.380	6.999	6.652
20	18.14	16.51	15.10	13.86	12.77	11.81	10.96	10.21	9.533	8.932	8.394	7.909	7.472	7.077	6.718
21	18.95	17.18	15.65	14.31	13.14	12.11	11.21	10.41	9.704	9.074	8.511	8.007	7.554	7.145	6.775
22	19.76	17.83	16.17	14.74	13.49	12.40	11.44	10.60	9.861	9.203	8.618	8.095	7.626	7.205	6.824
23	20.56	18.47	16.69	15.15	13.82	12.67	11.66	10.78	10.01	9.320	8.713	8.173	7.690	7.257	6.868
24	21.35	19.10	17.19	15.55	14.14	12.92	11.87	10.94	10.14	9.427	8.799	8.243	7.747	7.303	6.905
25	22.13	19.72	17.67	15.93	14.44	13.16	12.06	11.10	10.26	9.524	8.877	8.305	7.797	7.344	6.938
26	22.91	20.32	18.14	16.30	14.73	13.39	12.24	11.24	10.37	9.612	8.947	8.360	7.841	7.379	6.966
27	23.68	20.91	18.60	16.65	15.01	13.60	12.40	11.37	10.47	9.692	9.010	8.410	7.880	7.410	6.991
28	24.44	21.49	19.04	16.99	15.27	13.80	12.56	11.49	10.56	9.765	9.066	8.454	7.915	7.437	7.012
29	25.19	22.06	19.47	17.32	15.52	13.99	12.70	11.60	10.65	9.831	9.118	8.494	7.946	7.461	7.031
30	25.94	22.62	19.89	17.64	15.75	14.17	12.84	11.70	10.73	9.891	9.164	8.529	7.973	7.482	7.047

E.g.: If the interest rate is 10% per year, a continuous cash flow of $1 per year for each of 5 years is worth $3.977. A continuous flow of $1 in year 5 only is worth 3.977 − 3.326 = $0.651.

					Interest rate r										
16%	17%	18%	19%	20%	21%	22%	23%	24%	25%	26%	27%	28%	29%	30%	t
.929	.925	.922	.918	.914	.910	.907	.903	.900	.896	.893	.889	.886	.883	.880	1
1.730	1.716	1.703	1.689	1.676	1.663	1.650	1.638	1.625	1.613	1.601	1.590	1.578	1.567	1.556	2
2.421	2.392	2.365	2.337	2.311	2.285	2.259	2.235	2.211	2.187	2.164	2.141	2.119	2.098	2.077	3
3.016	2.970	2.925	2.882	2.840	2.799	2.759	2.720	2.682	2.646	2.610	2.576	2.542	2.509	2.477	4
3.530	3.464	3.401	3.340	3.281	3.223	3.168	3.115	3.063	3.013	2.964	2.917	2.872	2.828	2.785	5
3.972	3.886	3.804	3.724	3.648	3.574	3.504	3.436	3.370	3.307	3.246	3.187	3.130	3.075	3.022	6
4.354	4.247	4.145	4.048	3.954	3.865	3.779	3.696	3.617	3.542	3.469	3.399	3.331	3.266	3.204	7
4.682	4.555	4.434	4.319	4.209	4.104	4.004	3.909	3.817	3.730	3.646	3.566	3.489	3.415	3.344	8
4.966	4.819	4.680	4.547	4.422	4.302	4.189	4.081	3.978	3.880	3.786	3.697	3.612	3.530	3.452	9
5.210	5.044	4.887	4.739	4.599	4.466	4.340	4.221	4.108	4.000	3.898	3.801	3.708	3.619	3.535	10
5.421	5.237	5.063	4.900	4.747	4.602	4.465	4.335	4.213	4.096	3.986	3.882	3.783	3.689	3.599	11
5.603	5.401	5.213	5.036	4.870	4.713	4.566	4.428	4.297	4.173	4.057	3.946	3.841	3.742	3.648	12
5.759	5.542	5.339	5.150	4.972	4.806	4.650	4.503	4.365	4.235	4.112	3.997	3.887	3.784	3.686	13
5.894	5.662	5.446	5.245	5.058	4.882	4.718	4.564	4.420	4.284	4.157	4.036	3.923	3.816	3.715	14
6.010	5.765	5.537	5.326	5.129	4.945	4.774	4.614	4.464	4.324	4.192	4.068	3.951	3.841	3.737	15
6.111	5.853	5.614	5.393	5.188	4.998	4.820	4.655	4.500	4.355	4.220	4.092	3.973	3.860	3.754	16
6.197	5.928	5.679	5.450	5.238	5.041	4.858	4.687	4.529	4.381	4.242	4.112	3.990	3.875	3.767	17
6.272	5.992	5.735	5.498	5.279	5.076	4.889	4.714	4.552	4.401	4.259	4.127	4.003	3.887	3.778	18
6.336	6.047	5.782	5.538	5.313	5.106	4.914	4.736	4.571	4.417	4.273	4.139	4.014	3.896	3.785	19
6.391	6.094	5.821	5.571	5.342	5.130	4.935	4.754	4.586	4.430	4.284	4.149	4.022	3.903	3.791	20
6.439	6.134	5.855	5.600	5.366	5.150	4.952	4.768	4.598	4.440	4.293	4.156	4.028	3.908	3.796	21
6.480	6.168	5.883	5.623	5.385	5.167	4.966	4.780	4.608	4.448	4.300	4.162	4.033	3.913	3.800	22
6.516	6.197	5.908	5.643	5.402	5.181	4.977	4.789	4.616	4.455	4.306	4.167	4.037	3.916	3.802	23
6.546	6.222	5.928	5.660	5.416	5.192	4.986	4.797	4.622	4.460	4.310	4.170	4.040	3.918	3.804	24
6.573	6.244	5.945	5.674	5.427	5.201	4.994	4.803	4.627	4.464	4.314	4.173	4.042	3.920	3.806	25
6.596	6.262	5.960	5.686	5.437	5.209	5.000	4.808	4.631	4.468	4.316	4.175	4.044	3.922	3.807	26
6.615	6.277	5.973	5.696	5.445	5.216	5.005	4.813	4.635	4.471	4.318	4.177	4.046	3.923	3.808	27
6.632	6.291	5.983	5.705	5.452	5.221	5.010	4.816	4.637	4.473	4.320	4.179	4.047	3.924	3.809	28
6.647	6.302	5.992	5.712	5.457	5.225	5.013	4.819	4.640	4.474	4.322	4.180	4.048	3.925	3.810	29
6.659	6.312	6.000	5.718	5.462	5.229	5.016	4.821	4.641	4.476	4.323	4.181	4.048	3.925	3.810	30

Appendix Table 6 Call option prices (Black-Scholes model): Call option value as a *percent* of share price when the time to expiration of the option is t and the stock returns have a variance of σ^2 per period.

	Share price divided by PV of exercise price																		
$\sigma\sqrt{t}$	.40	.45	.50	.55	.60	.65	.70	.75	.80	.82	.84	.86	.88	.90	.92	.94	.96	.98	1.00
.05	.0	.0	.0	.0	.0	.0	.0	.0	.0	.0	.0	.0	.0	.0	.1	.3	.6	1.2	2.0
.10	.0	.0	.0	.0	.0	.0	.0	.0	.0	.1	.2	.3	.5	.8	1.2	1.7	2.3	3.1	4.0
.15	.0	.0	.0	.0	.0	.0	.1	.2	.5	.7	1.0	1.3	1.7	2.2	2.8	3.5	4.2	5.1	6.0
.20	.0	.0	.0	.0	.0	.1	.4	.8	1.5	1.9	2.3	2.8	3.4	4.0	4.7	5.4	6.2	7.1	8.0
.25	.0	.0	.0	.1	.2	.5	1.0	1.8	2.8	3.3	3.9	4.5	5.2	5.9	6.6	7.4	8.2	9.1	9.9
.30	.0	.1	.1	.3	.7	1.2	2.0	3.1	4.4	5.0	5.7	6.3	7.0	7.8	8.6	9.4	10.2	11.1	11.9
.35	.1	.2	.4	.8	1.4	2.3	3.3	4.6	6.2	6.8	7.5	8.2	9.0	9.8	10.6	11.4	12.2	13.0	13.9
.40	.2	.5	.9	1.6	2.4	3.5	4.8	6.3	8.0	8.7	9.4	10.2	11.0	11.7	12.5	13.4	14.2	15.0	15.9
.45	.5	1.0	1.7	2.6	3.7	5.0	6.5	8.1	9.9	10.6	11.4	12.2	12.9	13.7	14.5	15.3	16.2	17.0	17.8
.50	1.0	1.7	2.6	3.7	5.1	6.6	8.2	10.0	11.8	12.6	13.4	14.2	14.9	15.7	16.5	17.3	18.1	18.9	19.7
.55	1.7	2.6	3.8	5.1	6.6	8.3	10.0	11.9	13.8	14.6	15.4	16.1	16.9	17.7	18.5	19.3	20.1	20.9	21.7
.60	2.5	3.7	5.1	6.6	8.3	10.1	11.9	13.8	15.8	16.6	17.4	18.1	18.9	19.7	20.5	21.3	22.0	22.8	23.6
.65	3.6	4.9	6.5	8.2	10.0	11.9	13.8	15.8	17.8	18.6	19.3	20.1	20.9	21.7	22.5	23.2	24.0	24.7	25.5
.70	4.7	6.3	8.1	9.9	11.9	13.8	15.8	17.8	19.8	20.6	21.3	22.1	22.9	23.6	24.4	25.2	25.9	26.6	27.4
.75	6.1	7.9	9.8	11.7	13.7	15.8	17.8	19.8	21.8	22.5	23.3	24.1	24.8	25.6	26.3	27.1	27.8	28.5	29.2
.80	7.5	9.5	11.5	13.6	15.7	17.7	19.8	21.8	23.7	24.5	25.3	26.0	26.8	27.5	28.3	29.0	29.7	30.4	31.1
.85	9.1	11.2	13.3	15.5	17.6	19.7	21.8	23.8	25.7	26.5	27.2	28.0	28.7	29.4	30.2	30.9	31.6	32.2	32.9
.90	10.7	13.0	15.2	17.4	19.6	21.7	23.8	25.8	27.7	28.4	29.2	29.9	30.6	31.3	32.0	32.7	33.4	34.1	34.7
.95	12.5	14.8	17.1	19.4	21.6	23.7	25.7	27.7	29.6	30.4	31.1	31.8	32.5	33.2	33.9	34.6	35.2	35.9	36.5
1.00	14.3	16.7	19.1	21.4	23.6	25.7	27.7	29.7	31.6	32.3	33.0	33.7	34.4	35.1	35.7	36.4	37.0	37.7	38.3
1.05	16.1	18.6	21.0	23.3	25.6	27.7	29.7	31.6	33.5	34.2	34.9	35.6	36.2	36.9	37.6	38.2	38.8	39.4	40.0
1.10	18.0	20.6	23.0	25.3	27.5	29.6	31.6	33.5	35.4	36.1	36.7	37.4	38.1	38.7	39.3	40.0	40.6	41.2	41.8
1.15	20.0	22.5	25.0	27.3	29.5	31.6	33.6	35.4	37.2	37.9	38.6	39.2	39.9	40.5	41.1	41.7	42.3	42.9	43.5
1.20	21.9	24.5	27.0	29.3	31.5	33.6	35.5	37.3	39.1	39.7	40.4	41.0	41.7	42.3	42.9	43.5	44.0	44.6	45.1
1.25	23.9	26.5	29.0	31.3	33.5	35.5	37.4	39.2	40.9	41.5	42.2	42.8	43.4	44.0	44.6	45.2	45.7	46.3	46.8
1.30	25.9	28.5	31.0	33.3	35.4	37.4	39.3	41.0	42.7	43.3	43.9	44.5	45.1	45.7	46.3	46.8	47.4	47.9	48.4
1.35	27.9	30.5	33.0	35.2	37.3	39.3	41.1	42.8	44.4	45.1	45.7	46.3	46.8	47.4	47.9	48.5	49.0	49.5	50.0
1.40	29.9	32.5	34.9	37.1	39.2	41.1	42.9	44.6	46.2	46.8	47.4	47.9	48.5	49.0	49.6	50.1	50.6	51.1	51.6
1.45	31.9	34.5	36.9	39.1	41.1	43.0	44.7	46.4	47.9	48.5	49.0	49.6	50.1	50.7	51.2	51.7	52.2	52.7	53.2
1.50	33.8	36.4	38.8	40.9	42.9	44.8	46.5	48.1	49.6	50.1	50.7	51.2	51.8	52.3	52.8	53.3	53.7	54.2	54.7
1.55	35.8	38.4	40.7	42.8	44.8	46.6	48.2	49.8	51.2	51.8	52.3	52.8	53.3	53.8	54.3	54.8	55.3	55.7	56.2
1.60	37.8	40.3	42.6	44.6	46.5	48.3	49.9	51.4	52.8	53.4	53.9	54.4	54.9	55.4	55.9	56.3	56.8	57.2	57.6
1.65	39.7	42.2	44.4	46.4	48.3	50.0	51.6	53.1	54.4	54.9	55.4	55.9	56.4	56.9	57.3	57.8	58.2	58.6	59.1
1.70	41.6	44.0	46.2	48.2	50.0	51.7	53.2	54.7	56.0	56.5	57.0	57.5	57.9	58.4	58.8	59.2	59.7	60.1	60.5
1.75	43.5	45.9	48.0	50.0	51.7	53.4	54.8	56.2	57.5	58.0	58.5	58.9	59.4	59.8	60.2	60.7	61.1	61.5	61.8
2.00	52.5	54.6	56.5	58.2	59.7	61.1	62.4	63.6	64.6	65.0	65.4	65.8	66.2	66.6	66.9	67.3	67.6	67.9	68.3
2.25	60.7	62.5	64.1	65.6	66.8	68.0	69.1	70.0	70.9	71.3	71.6	71.9	72.2	72.5	72.8	73.1	73.4	73.7	73.9
2.50	67.9	69.4	70.8	72.0	73.1	74.0	74.9	75.7	76.4	76.7	77.0	77.2	77.5	77.7	78.0	78.2	78.4	78.7	78.9
2.75	74.2	75.4	76.6	77.5	78.4	79.2	79.9	80.5	81.1	81.4	81.6	81.8	82.0	82.2	82.4	82.6	82.7	82.9	83.1
3.00	79.5	80.5	81.4	82.2	82.9	83.5	84.1	84.6	85.1	85.3	85.4	85.6	85.8	85.9	86.1	86.2	86.4	86.5	86.6
3.50	87.6	88.3	88.8	89.3	89.7	90.1	90.5	90.8	91.1	91.2	91.3	91.4	91.5	91.6	91.6	91.7	91.8	91.9	92.0
4.00	92.9	93.3	93.6	93.9	94.2	94.4	94.6	94.8	94.9	95.0	95.0	95.1	95.2	95.2	95.3	95.3	95.4	95.4	95.4
4.50	96.2	96.4	96.6	96.7	96.9	97.0	97.1	97.2	97.3	97.3	97.3	97.4	97.4	97.4	97.5	97.5	97.5	97.5	97.6
5.00	98.1	98.2	98.3	98.3	98.4	98.5	98.5	98.6	98.6	98.6	98.6	98.7	98.7	98.7	98.7	98.7	98.7	98.7	98.8

E.g.: If the share price is $0.90, the present value of the exercise price is $1.00, the variance of stock returns is $(0.5)^2$ per year, and the time to expiration of the option is one year, the call option value is 15.7% of the share price or $0.157 \times 0.90 = \$0.1413$.

To obtain corresponding European put values, add the present value of the exercise price and subtract the share price. The put option in the above example is $0.1413 + 1 - 0.90 = \$0.1513$.

1.02	1.04	1.06	1.08	1.10	1.12	1.14	1.16	1.18	1.20	1.25	1.30	1.35	1.40	1.45	1.50	1.75	2.00	2.50	$\sigma\sqrt{t}$
3.1	4.5	6.0	7.5	9.1	10.7	12.3	13.8	15.3	16.7	20.0	23.1	25.9	28.6	31.0	33.3	42.9	50.0	60.0	.05
5.0	6.1	7.3	8.6	10.0	11.3	12.7	14.1	15.4	16.8	20.0	23.1	25.9	28.6	31.0	33.3	42.9	50.0	60.0	.10
7.0	8.0	9.1	10.2	11.4	12.6	13.8	15.0	16.2	17.4	20.4	23.3	26.0	28.6	31.1	33.3	42.9	50.0	60.0	.15
8.9	9.9	10.9	11.9	13.0	14.1	15.2	16.3	17.4	18.5	21.2	23.9	26.4	28.9	31.2	33.5	42.9	50.0	60.0	.20
10.9	11.8	12.8	13.7	14.7	15.7	16.7	17.7	18.7	19.8	22.3	24.7	27.1	29.4	31.7	33.8	42.9	50.0	60.0	.25
12.8	13.7	14.6	15.6	16.5	17.4	18.4	19.3	20.3	21.2	23.5	25.8	28.1	30.2	32.3	34.3	43.1	50.1	60.0	.30
14.8	15.6	16.5	17.4	18.3	19.2	20.1	21.0	21.9	22.7	24.9	27.1	29.2	31.2	33.2	35.1	43.5	50.2	60.0	.35
16.7	17.5	18.4	19.2	20.1	20.9	21.8	22.6	23.5	24.3	26.4	28.4	30.4	32.3	34.2	36.0	44.0	50.5	60.1	.40
18.6	19.4	20.3	21.1	21.9	22.7	23.5	24.3	25.1	25.9	27.9	29.8	31.7	33.5	35.3	37.0	44.6	50.8	60.2	.45
20.5	21.3	22.1	22.9	23.7	24.5	25.3	26.1	26.8	27.6	29.5	31.3	33.1	34.8	36.4	38.1	45.3	51.3	60.4	.50
22.4	23.2	24.0	24.8	25.5	26.3	27.0	27.8	28.5	29.2	31.0	32.8	34.5	36.1	37.7	39.2	46.1	51.9	60.7	.55
24.3	25.1	25.8	26.6	27.3	28.1	28.8	29.5	30.2	30.9	32.6	34.3	35.9	37.5	39.0	40.4	47.0	52.5	61.0	.60
26.2	27.0	27.7	28.4	29.1	29.8	30.5	31.2	31.9	32.6	34.2	35.8	37.4	38.9	40.3	41.7	48.0	53.3	61.4	.65
28.1	28.8	29.5	30.2	30.9	31.6	32.3	32.9	33.6	34.2	35.8	37.3	38.8	40.3	41.6	43.0	49.0	54.0	61.9	.70
29.9	30.6	31.3	32.0	32.7	33.3	34.0	34.6	35.3	35.9	37.4	38.9	40.3	41.7	43.0	44.3	50.0	54.9	62.4	.75
31.8	32.4	33.1	33.8	34.4	35.1	35.7	36.3	36.9	37.5	39.0	40.4	41.8	43.1	44.4	45.6	51.1	55.8	63.0	.80
33.6	34.2	34.9	35.5	36.2	36.8	37.4	38.0	38.6	39.2	40.6	41.9	43.3	44.5	45.8	46.9	52.2	56.7	63.6	.85
35.4	36.0	36.6	37.3	37.9	38.5	39.1	39.6	40.2	40.8	42.1	43.5	44.7	46.0	47.1	48.3	53.3	57.6	64.3	.90
37.2	37.8	38.4	39.0	39.6	40.1	40.7	41.3	41.8	42.4	43.7	45.0	46.2	47.4	48.5	49.6	54.5	58.6	65.0	.95
38.9	39.5	40.1	40.7	41.2	41.8	42.4	42.9	43.4	44.0	45.2	46.5	47.6	48.8	49.9	50.9	55.6	59.5	65.7	1.00
40.6	41.2	41.8	42.4	42.9	43.5	44.0	44.5	45.0	45.5	46.8	48.0	49.1	50.2	51.2	52.2	56.7	60.5	66.5	1.05
42.3	42.9	43.5	44.0	44.5	45.1	45.6	46.1	46.6	47.1	48.3	49.4	50.5	51.6	52.6	53.5	57.9	61.5	67.2	1.10
44.0	44.6	45.1	45.6	46.2	46.7	47.2	47.7	48.2	48.6	49.8	50.9	51.9	52.9	53.9	54.9	59.0	62.5	68.0	1.15
45.7	46.2	46.7	47.3	47.8	48.3	48.7	49.2	49.7	50.1	51.3	52.3	53.3	54.3	55.2	56.1	60.2	63.5	68.8	1.20
47.3	47.8	48.4	48.8	49.3	49.8	50.3	50.7	51.2	51.6	52.7	53.7	54.7	55.7	56.6	57.4	61.3	64.5	69.6	1.25
48.9	49.4	49.9	50.4	50.9	51.3	51.8	52.2	52.7	53.1	54.1	55.1	56.1	57.0	57.9	58.7	62.4	65.5	70.4	1.30
50.5	51.0	51.5	52.0	52.4	52.9	53.3	53.7	54.1	54.6	55.6	56.5	57.4	58.3	59.1	59.9	63.5	66.5	71.1	1.35
52.1	52.6	53.0	53.5	53.9	54.3	54.8	55.2	55.6	56.0	56.9	57.9	58.7	59.6	60.4	61.2	64.6	67.5	71.9	1.40
53.6	54.1	54.5	55.0	55.4	55.8	56.2	56.6	57.0	57.4	58.3	59.2	60.0	60.9	61.6	62.4	65.7	68.4	72.7	1.45
55.1	55.6	56.0	56.4	56.8	57.2	57.6	58.0	58.4	58.8	59.7	60.5	61.3	62.1	62.9	63.6	66.8	69.4	73.5	1.50
56.6	57.0	57.4	57.8	58.2	58.6	59.0	59.4	59.7	60.1	61.0	61.8	62.6	63.3	64.1	64.7	67.8	70.3	74.3	1.55
58.0	58.5	58.9	59.2	59.6	60.0	60.4	60.7	61.1	61.4	62.3	63.1	63.8	64.5	65.2	65.9	68.8	71.3	75.1	1.60
59.5	59.9	60.2	60.6	61.0	61.4	61.7	62.1	62.4	62.7	63.5	64.3	65.0	65.7	66.4	67.0	69.9	72.2	75.9	1.65
60.9	61.2	61.6	62.0	62.3	62.7	63.0	63.4	63.7	64.0	64.8	65.5	66.2	66.9	67.5	68.2	70.9	73.1	76.6	1.70
62.2	62.6	62.9	63.3	63.6	64.0	64.3	64.6	64.9	65.3	66.0	66.7	67.4	68.0	68.7	69.2	71.9	74.0	77.4	1.75
68.6	68.9	69.2	69.5	69.8	70.0	70.3	70.6	70.8	71.1	71.7	72.3	72.9	73.4	73.9	74.4	76.5	78.3	81.0	2.00
74.2	74.4	74.7	74.9	75.2	75.4	75.6	75.8	76.0	76.3	76.8	77.2	77.7	78.1	78.5	78.9	80.6	82.1	84.3	2.25
79.1	79.3	79.5	79.7	79.9	80.0	80.2	80.4	80.6	80.7	81.1	81.5	81.9	82.2	82.6	82.9	84.3	85.4	87.2	2.50
83.3	83.4	83.6	83.7	83.9	84.0	84.2	84.3	84.4	84.6	84.9	85.2	85.5	85.8	86.0	86.3	87.4	88.3	89.7	2.75
86.8	86.9	87.0	87.1	87.3	87.4	87.5	87.6	87.7	87.8	88.1	88.3	88.5	88.8	89.0	89.2	90.0	90.7	91.8	3.00
92.1	92.1	92.2	92.3	92.4	92.4	92.5	92.6	92.6	92.7	92.8	93.0	93.1	93.3	93.4	93.5	94.0	94.4	95.1	3.50
95.5	95.5	95.6	95.6	95.7	95.7	95.7	95.8	95.8	95.9	96.0	96.1	96.2	96.2	96.3	96.6	96.8	97.2	4.00
97.6	97.6	97.6	97.6	97.7	97.7	97.7	97.7	97.8	97.8	97.8	97.9	97.9	97.9	98.0	98.0	98.2	98.3	98.5	4.50
98.8	98.8	98.8	98.8	98.8	98.8	98.8	98.8	98.9	98.9	98.9	98.9	98.9	99.0	99.0	99.0	99.1	99.1	99.2	5.00

Appendix Table 7 Hedge ratios (Black-Scholes model): Hedge ratios as a *percent* of a share when the time to expiration of the option is t and the stock returns have a variance of σ^2 per period.

$\sigma\sqrt{t}$	.40	.45	.50	.55	.60	.65	.70	.75	.80	.82	.84	.86	.88	.90	.92	.94	.96	.98	1.00
.05	.0	.0	.0	.0	.0	.0	.0	.0	.0	.0	.0	.1	.6	1.9	5.0	11.3	21.4	35.2	51.0
.10	.0	.0	.0	.0	.0	.0	.0	.2	1.5	2.7	4.5	7.2	11.0	15.8	21.7	28.5	36.0	44.0	52.0
.15	.0	.0	.0	.0	.0	.3	1.1	3.3	7.9	10.6	13.8	17.6	21.9	26.5	31.5	36.8	42.2	47.6	53.0
.20	.0	.0	.0	.2	.7	2.0	4.6	9.0	15.5	18.6	22.0	25.7	29.5	33.5	37.6	41.7	45.9	50.0	54.0
.25	.0	.1	.4	1.2	2.8	5.5	9.7	15.3	22.1	25.2	28.4	31.6	35.0	38.3	41.7	45.1	48.5	51.8	55.0
.30	.2	.6	1.5	3.3	6.0	9.9	14.9	20.9	27.6	30.4	33.3	36.2	39.1	42.0	44.9	47.8	50.6	53.3	56.0
.35	.7	1.8	3.6	6.3	9.9	14.6	19.9	25.9	32.2	34.8	37.3	39.9	42.5	45.0	47.5	49.9	52.3	54.7	56.9
.40	1.8	3.6	6.3	9.8	14.1	19.0	24.5	30.2	36.0	38.4	40.7	43.0	45.2	47.5	49.7	51.8	53.9	55.9	57.9
.45	3.5	6.1	9.4	13.5	18.1	23.2	28.5	33.9	39.3	41.4	43.5	45.6	47.6	49.6	51.6	53.5	55.3	57.1	58.9
.50	5.7	8.9	12.8	17.2	22.0	27.0	32.2	37.2	42.2	44.2	46.1	47.9	49.8	51.6	53.3	55.0	56.7	58.3	59.9
.55	8.2	12.0	16.2	20.8	25.7	30.6	35.4	40.2	44.8	46.6	48.3	50.0	51.7	53.3	54.9	56.5	58.0	59.4	60.8
.60	11.0	15.1	19.6	24.3	29.1	33.8	38.4	42.9	47.1	48.8	50.4	51.9	53.5	55.0	56.4	57.8	59.2	60.5	61.8
.65	13.9	18.3	22.9	27.6	32.2	36.8	41.1	45.3	49.3	50.8	52.3	53.7	55.1	56.5	57.8	59.1	60.3	61.6	62.7
.70	16.9	21.5	26.1	30.7	35.2	39.5	43.7	47.6	51.2	52.7	54.0	55.4	56.6	57.9	59.1	60.3	61.5	62.6	63.7
.75	19.9	24.5	29.1	33.6	38.0	42.1	46.0	49.7	53.1	54.4	55.7	56.9	58.1	59.3	60.4	61.5	62.6	63.6	64.6
.80	22.8	27.5	32.0	36.4	40.6	44.5	48.2	51.6	54.8	56.0	57.2	58.4	59.5	60.6	61.6	62.7	63.6	64.6	65.5
.85	25.7	30.3	34.8	39.0	43.0	46.7	50.2	53.4	56.5	57.6	58.7	59.8	60.8	61.8	62.8	63.8	64.7	65.6	66.5
.90	28.5	33.1	37.4	41.5	45.3	48.9	52.1	55.2	58.0	59.1	60.1	61.1	62.1	63.0	64.0	64.8	65.7	66.6	67.4
.95	31.2	35.7	40.0	43.9	47.5	50.9	54.0	56.8	59.5	60.5	61.5	62.4	63.3	64.2	65.1	65.9	66.7	67.5	68.3
1.00	33.9	38.3	42.3	46.1	49.6	52.8	55.7	58.4	60.9	61.9	62.8	63.7	64.5	65.3	66.2	66.9	67.7	68.4	69.1
1.05	36.4	40.7	44.6	48.2	51.5	54.6	57.4	59.9	62.3	63.2	64.0	64.9	65.7	66.4	67.2	67.9	68.7	69.3	70.0
1.10	38.9	43.0	46.8	50.3	53.4	56.3	58.9	61.4	63.6	64.4	65.2	66.0	66.8	67.5	68.2	68.9	69.6	70.3	70.9
1.15	41.2	45.2	48.9	52.2	55.2	57.9	60.4	62.7	64.8	65.6	66.4	67.1	67.9	68.6	69.2	69.9	70.5	71.1	71.7
1.20	43.5	47.4	50.9	54.1	56.9	59.5	61.9	64.1	66.1	66.8	67.5	68.2	68.9	69.6	70.2	70.8	71.4	72.0	72.6
1.25	45.7	49.4	52.8	55.8	58.6	61.0	63.3	65.4	67.2	67.9	68.6	69.3	69.9	70.6	71.2	71.8	72.3	72.9	73.4
1.30	47.8	51.4	54.6	57.5	60.1	62.5	64.6	66.6	68.4	69.1	69.7	70.3	70.9	71.5	72.1	72.7	73.2	73.7	74.2
1.35	49.9	53.3	56.4	59.2	61.7	63.9	65.9	67.8	69.5	70.1	70.7	71.3	71.9	72.5	73.0	73.5	74.0	74.5	75.0
1.40	51.8	55.2	58.1	60.8	63.1	65.3	67.2	69.0	70.6	71.2	71.8	72.3	72.9	73.4	73.9	74.4	74.9	75.4	75.8
1.45	53.7	56.9	59.8	62.3	64.5	66.6	68.4	70.1	71.6	72.2	72.7	73.3	73.8	74.3	74.8	75.2	75.7	76.1	76.6
1.50	55.5	58.6	61.3	63.7	65.9	67.8	69.6	71.2	72.6	73.2	73.7	74.2	74.7	75.2	75.6	76.1	76.5	76.9	77.3
1.55	57.3	60.3	62.8	65.1	67.2	69.0	70.7	72.2	73.6	74.1	74.6	75.1	75.6	76.0	76.5	76.9	77.3	77.7	78.1
1.60	59.0	61.8	64.3	66.5	68.5	70.2	71.8	73.2	74.6	75.0	75.5	76.0	76.4	76.9	77.3	77.7	78.1	78.4	78.8
1.65	60.6	63.3	65.7	67.8	69.7	71.4	72.9	74.2	75.5	76.0	76.4	76.8	77.3	77.7	78.1	78.5	78.8	79.2	79.5
1.70	62.2	64.8	67.1	69.1	70.9	72.5	73.9	75.2	76.4	76.8	77.3	77.7	78.1	78.5	78.8	79.2	79.6	79.9	80.2
1.75	63.7	66.2	68.4	70.3	72.0	73.5	74.9	76.1	77.3	77.7	78.1	78.5	78.9	79.2	79.6	79.9	80.3	80.6	80.9
2.00	70.6	72.6	74.3	75.8	77.2	78.4	79.4	80.4	81.3	81.6	81.9	82.2	82.5	82.8	83.1	83.4	83.6	83.9	84.1
2.25	76.4	77.9	79.3	80.5	81.5	82.5	83.3	84.1	84.8	85.0	85.3	85.5	85.7	86.0	86.2	86.4	86.6	86.8	87.0
2.50	81.2	82.4	83.5	84.4	85.2	85.9	86.6	87.2	87.7	87.9	88.1	88.3	88.5	88.6	88.8	89.0	89.1	89.3	89.4
2.75	85.1	86.1	86.9	87.6	88.3	88.8	89.3	89.8	90.2	90.4	90.5	90.7	90.8	90.9	91.1	91.2	91.3	91.4	91.5
3.00	88.4	89.1	89.8	90.3	90.8	91.3	91.6	92.0	92.3	92.4	92.5	92.6	92.7	92.9	93.0	93.0	93.1	93.2	93.3
3.50	93.2	93.6	94.0	94.3	94.6	94.8	95.0	95.2	95.4	95.5	95.5	95.6	95.7	95.7	95.8	95.8	95.9	95.9	96.0
4.00	96.2	96.4	96.6	96.8	96.9	97.1	97.2	97.3	97.4	97.4	97.5	97.5	97.5	97.6	97.6	97.6	97.7	97.7	97.7
4.50	98.0	98.1	98.2	98.3	98.4	98.4	98.5	98.6	98.6	98.6	98.6	98.7	98.7	98.7	98.7	98.7	98.7	98.8	98.8
5.00	99.0	99.0	99.1	99.1	99.2	99.2	99.2	99.3	99.3	99.3	99.3	99.3	99.3	99.3	99.3	99.4	99.4	99.4	99.4

E.g.: If the share price is $0.90, the present value of the exercise price is $1.00, the variance of stock returns is $(0.5)^2$ per year, and the time to expiration of the option is one year, the call option value hedges the risk of 0.516 shares.

    Subtract 1.0 to obtain the corresponding hedge ratios for European puts. In the above example, a put option hedges the risk of $0.516 - 1.0 = -0.484$ shares. That is, the put option hedges a short position in 0.484 shares.

Share price divided by PV of exercise price																			
1.02	1.04	1.06	1.08	1.10	1.12	1.14	1.16	1.18	1.20	1.25	1.30	1.35	1.40	1.45	1.50	1.75	2.00	2.50	$\sigma\sqrt{t}$
66.3	79.1	88.3	94.1	97.3	98.9	99.6	99.9	100.	100.	100.	100.	100.	100.	100.	100.	100.	100.	100.	.05
59.8	67.1	73.7	79.4	84.2	88.2	91.3	93.8	95.6	96.9	98.9	99.6	99.9	100.	100.	100.	100.	100.	100.	.10
58.2	63.2	67.8	72.2	76.1	79.7	82.9	85.6	88.1	90.2	94.1	96.6	98.1	99.0	99.5	99.7	100.	100.	100.	.15
57.9	61.6	65.2	68.6	71.8	74.8	77.5	80.0	82.3	84.4	88.8	92.1	94.5	96.3	97.5	98.3	99.8	100.	100.	.20
58.1	61.1	64.0	66.7	69.4	71.8	74.2	76.4	78.4	80.4	84.6	88.0	90.7	92.9	94.6	96.0	99.1	99.8	100.	.25
58.6	61.1	63.5	65.8	68.0	70.1	72.1	74.0	75.9	77.6	81.4	84.7	87.5	89.8	91.8	93.3	97.8	99.3	99.9	.30
59.2	61.3	63.4	65.4	67.3	69.1	70.9	72.5	74.1	75.7	79.2	82.2	84.9	87.2	89.2	90.9	96.2	98.4	99.7	.35
59.9	61.7	63.5	65.3	66.9	68.6	70.1	71.6	73.0	74.4	77.6	80.4	82.9	85.1	87.1	88.8	94.5	97.3	99.4	.40
60.6	62.3	63.9	65.4	66.9	68.3	69.7	71.0	72.3	73.6	76.5	79.0	81.4	83.5	85.3	87.0	92.9	96.1	98.8	.45
61.4	62.9	64.3	65.7	67.0	68.3	69.6	70.8	71.9	73.1	75.7	78.1	80.2	82.2	84.0	85.6	91.5	94.9	98.1	.50
62.2	63.5	64.8	66.1	67.3	68.5	69.6	70.7	71.8	72.8	75.2	77.4	79.4	81.2	82.9	84.4	90.2	93.8	97.4	.55
63.0	64.3	65.4	66.6	67.7	68.8	69.8	70.8	71.8	72.7	74.9	77.0	78.8	80.5	82.1	83.5	89.1	92.7	96.6	.60
63.9	65.0	66.1	67.1	68.1	69.1	70.1	71.0	71.9	72.8	74.8	76.7	78.4	80.0	81.5	82.9	88.2	91.8	95.9	.65
64.7	65.8	66.8	67.7	68.7	69.6	70.4	71.3	72.1	72.9	74.8	76.6	78.2	79.7	81.1	82.4	87.5	91.0	95.1	.70
65.6	66.5	67.5	68.4	69.2	70.1	70.9	71.7	72.4	73.2	74.9	76.6	78.1	79.5	80.8	82.0	86.9	90.3	94.5	.75
66.4	67.3	68.2	69.0	69.8	70.6	71.4	72.1	72.8	73.5	75.1	76.7	78.1	79.4	80.6	81.8	86.4	89.7	93.9	.80
67.3	68.1	68.9	69.7	70.4	71.2	71.9	72.6	73.2	73.9	75.4	76.8	78.2	79.4	80.6	81.6	86.1	89.3	93.4	.85
68.2	68.9	69.7	70.4	71.1	71.8	72.4	73.1	73.7	74.3	75.7	77.1	78.3	79.5	80.6	81.6	85.8	88.9	92.9	.90
69.0	69.7	70.4	71.1	71.7	72.4	73.0	73.6	74.2	74.8	76.1	77.4	78.5	79.6	80.7	81.6	85.6	88.6	92.5	.95
69.8	70.5	71.2	71.8	72.4	73.0	73.6	74.2	74.7	75.2	76.5	77.7	78.8	79.9	80.8	81.7	85.5	88.4	92.2	1.00
70.7	71.3	71.9	72.5	73.1	73.7	74.2	74.7	75.3	75.8	77.0	78.1	79.1	80.1	81.0	81.9	85.5	88.2	91.9	1.05
71.5	72.1	72.7	73.2	73.8	74.3	74.8	75.3	75.8	76.3	77.4	78.5	79.5	80.4	81.3	82.1	85.5	88.1	91.7	1.10
72.3	72.9	73.4	74.0	74.5	75.0	75.5	75.9	76.4	76.8	77.9	78.9	79.8	80.7	81.5	82.3	85.6	88.1	91.5	1.15
73.1	73.7	74.2	74.7	75.2	75.6	76.1	76.5	77.0	77.4	78.4	79.4	80.2	81.1	81.8	82.6	85.7	88.1	91.4	1.20
73.9	74.4	74.9	75.4	75.8	76.3	76.7	77.1	77.6	78.0	78.9	79.8	80.7	81.4	82.2	82.9	85.8	88.1	91.3	1.25
74.7	75.2	75.6	76.1	76.5	76.9	77.4	77.8	78.2	78.5	79.4	80.3	81.1	81.8	82.5	83.2	86.0	88.2	91.2	1.30
75.5	75.9	76.4	76.8	77.2	77.6	78.0	78.4	78.7	79.1	80.0	80.8	81.5	82.2	82.9	83.5	86.2	88.3	91.2	1.35
76.2	76.7	77.1	77.5	77.9	78.3	78.6	79.0	79.3	79.7	80.5	81.3	82.0	82.6	83.3	83.9	86.4	88.4	91.2	1.40
77.0	77.4	77.8	78.2	78.5	78.9	79.3	79.6	79.9	80.3	81.0	81.8	82.4	83.1	83.7	84.2	86.7	88.6	91.3	1.45
77.7	78.1	78.5	78.9	79.2	79.5	79.9	80.2	80.5	80.8	81.6	82.2	82.9	83.5	84.1	84.6	86.9	88.7	91.3	1.50
78.5	78.8	79.2	79.5	79.9	80.2	80.5	80.8	81.1	81.4	82.1	82.7	83.4	83.9	84.5	85.0	87.2	88.9	91.4	1.55
79.2	79.5	79.9	80.2	80.5	80.8	81.1	81.4	81.7	82.0	82.6	83.2	83.8	84.4	84.9	85.4	87.5	89.1	91.5	1.60
79.9	80.2	80.5	80.8	81.1	81.4	81.7	82.0	82.3	82.5	83.2	83.7	84.3	84.8	85.3	85.8	87.8	89.3	91.6	1.65
80.6	80.9	81.2	81.5	81.8	82.0	82.3	82.6	82.8	83.1	83.7	84.2	84.8	85.3	85.7	86.2	88.1	89.6	91.8	1.70
81.2	81.5	81.8	82.1	82.4	82.6	82.9	83.1	83.4	83.6	84.2	84.7	85.2	85.7	86.2	86.6	88.4	89.8	91.9	1.75
84.4	84.6	84.8	85.0	85.3	85.5	85.7	85.9	86.1	86.2	86.7	87.1	87.5	87.9	88.2	88.5	90.0	91.1	92.8	2.00
87.2	87.3	87.5	87.7	87.8	88.0	88.2	88.3	88.5	88.6	89.0	89.3	89.6	89.9	90.1	90.4	91.5	92.4	93.7	2.25
89.6	89.7	89.9	90.0	90.1	90.2	90.4	90.5	90.6	90.7	91.0	91.2	91.5	91.7	91.9	92.1	93.0	93.7	94.7	2.50
91.7	91.8	91.9	92.0	92.1	92.2	92.3	92.3	92.4	92.5	92.7	92.9	93.1	93.3	93.4	93.6	94.3	94.8	95.6	2.75
93.4	93.5	93.6	93.6	93.7	93.8	93.9	93.9	94.0	94.1	94.2	94.4	94.5	94.7	94.8	94.9	95.4	95.8	96.4	3.00
96.0	96.1	96.1	96.2	96.2	96.3	96.3	96.3	96.4	96.4	96.5	96.6	96.7	96.8	96.8	96.9	97.2	97.4	97.8	3.50
97.8	97.8	97.8	97.8	97.9	97.9	97.9	97.9	97.9	98.0	98.0	98.1	98.1	98.1	98.2	98.2	98.4	98.5	98.7	4.00
98.8	98.8	98.8	98.8	98.8	98.9	98.9	98.9	98.9	98.9	98.9	99.0	99.0	99.0	99.0	99.0	99.1	99.2	99.3	4.50
99.4	99.4	99.4	99.4	99.4	99.4	99.4	99.4	99.4	99.4	99.5	99.5	99.5	99.5	99.5	99.5	99.5	99.6	99.6	5.00

Appendix Table 8
Cumulative normal probability: *N(d)* = the probability that a unit
normally distributed random variable will be less than *d*.

d	-.00	-.01	-.02	-.03	-.04	-.05	-.06	-.07	-.08	-.09
-3.40	.0003	.0003	.0003	.0003	.0003	.0003	.0003	.0003	.0003	.0002
-3.30	.0005	.0005	.0005	.0004	.0004	.0004	.0004	.0004	.0004	.0003
-3.20	.0007	.0007	.0006	.0006	.0006	.0006	.0006	.0005	.0005	.0005
-3.10	.0010	.0009	.0009	.0009	.0008	.0008	.0008	.0008	.0007	.0007
-3.00	.0013	.0013	.0013	.0012	.0012	.0011	.0011	.0011	.0010	.0010
-2.90	.0019	.0018	.0018	.0017	.0016	.0016	.0015	.0015	.0014	.0014
-2.80	.0026	.0025	.0024	.0023	.0023	.0022	.0021	.0021	.0020	.0019
-2.70	.0035	.0034	.0033	.0032	.0031	.0030	.0029	.0028	.0027	.0026
-2.60	.0047	.0045	.0044	.0043	.0041	.0040	.0039	.0038	.0037	.0036
-2.50	.0062	.0060	.0059	.0057	.0055	.0054	.0052	.0051	.0049	.0048
-2.40	.0082	.0080	.0078	.0075	.0073	.0071	.0069	.0068	.0066	.0064
-2.30	.0107	.0104	.0102	.0099	.0096	.0094	.0091	.0089	.0087	.0084
-2.20	.0139	.0136	.0132	.0129	.0125	.0122	.0119	.0116	.0113	.0110
-2.10	.0179	.0174	.0170	.0166	.0162	.0158	.0154	.0150	.0146	.0143
-2.00	.0228	.0222	.0217	.0212	.0207	.0202	.0197	.0192	.0188	.0183
-1.90	.0287	.0281	.0274	.0268	.0262	.0256	.0250	.0244	.0239	.0233
-1.80	.0359	.0351	.0344	.0336	.0329	.0322	.0314	.0307	.0301	.0294
-1.70	.0446	.0436	.0427	.0418	.0409	.0401	.0392	.0384	.0375	.0367
-1.60	.0548	.0537	.0526	.0516	.0505	.0495	.0485	.0475	.0465	.0455
-1.50	.0668	.0655	.0643	.0630	.0618	.0606	.0594	.0582	.0571	.0559
-1.40	.0808	.0793	.0778	.0764	.0749	.0735	.0721	.0708	.0694	.0681
-1.30	.0968	.0951	.0934	.0918	.0901	.0885	.0869	.0853	.0838	.0823
-1.20	.1151	.1131	.1112	.1093	.1075	.1056	.1038	.1020	.1003	.0985
-1.10	.1357	.1335	.1314	.1292	.1271	.1251	.1230	.1210	.1190	.1170
-1.00	.1587	.1562	.1539	.1515	.1492	.1469	.1446	.1423	.1401	.1379
-0.90	.1841	.1814	.1788	.1762	.1736	.1711	.1685	.1660	.1635	.1611
-0.80	.2119	.2090	.2061	.2033	.2005	.1977	.1949	.1922	.1894	.1867
-0.70	.2420	.2389	.2358	.2327	.2296	.2266	.2236	.2206	.2177	.2148
-0.60	.2743	.2709	.2676	.2643	.2611	.2578	.2546	.2514	.2483	.2451
-0.50	.3085	.3050	.3015	.2981	.2946	.2912	.2877	.2843	.2810	.2776
-0.40	.3446	.3409	.3372	.3336	.3300	.3264	.3228	.3192	.3156	.3121
-0.30	.3821	.3783	.3745	.3707	.3669	.3632	.3594	.3557	.3520	.3483
-0.20	.4207	.4168	.4129	.4090	.4052	.4013	.3974	.3936	.3897	.3859
-0.10	.4602	.4562	.4522	.4483	.4443	.4404	.4364	.4325	.4286	.4247
0.00	.5000	.4960	.4920	.4880	.4840	.4801	.4761	.4721	.4681	.4641

E.g.: The probability that a unit normally distributed random variable will
be less than −1.96 is 0.025, and the probability that a unit normally
distributed random variable will be less than 2.00 is 0.9772.

d	.00	.01	.02	.03	.04	.05	.06	.07	.08	.09
0.00	.5000	.5040	.5080	.5120	.5160	.5199	.5239	.5279	.5319	.5359
0.10	.5398	.5438	.5478	.5517	.5557	.5596	.5636	.5675	.5714	.5753
0.20	.5793	.5832	.5871	.5910	.5948	.5987	.6026	.6064	.6103	.6141
0.30	.6179	.6217	.6255	.6293	.6331	.6368	.6406	.6443	.6480	.6517
0.40	.6554	.6591	.6628	.6664	.6700	.6736	.6772	.6808	.6844	.6879
0.50	.6915	.6950	.6985	.7019	.7054	.7088	.7123	.7157	.7190	.7224
0.60	.7257	.7291	.7324	.7357	.7389	.7422	.7454	.7486	.7517	.7549
0.70	.7580	.7611	.7642	.7673	.7704	.7734	.7764	.7794	.7823	.7852
0.80	.7881	.7910	.7939	.7967	.7995	.8023	.8051	.8078	.8106	.8133
0.90	.8159	.8186	.8212	.8238	.8264	.8289	.8315	.8340	.8365	.8389
1.00	.8413	.8438	.8461	.8485	.8508	.8531	.8554	.8577	.8599	.8621
1.10	.8643	.8665	.8686	.8708	.8729	.8749	.8770	.8790	.8810	.8830
1.20	.8849	.8869	.8888	.8907	.8925	.8944	.8962	.8980	.8997	.9015
1.30	.9032	.9049	.9066	.9082	.9099	.9115	.9131	.9147	.9162	.9177
1.40	.9192	.9207	.9222	.9236	.9251	.9265	.9279	.9292	.9306	.9319
1.50	.9332	.9345	.9357	.9370	.9382	.9394	.9406	.9418	.9429	.9441
1.60	.9452	.9463	.9474	.9484	.9495	.9505	.9515	.9525	.9535	.9545
1.70	.9554	.9564	.9573	.9582	.9591	.9599	.9608	.9616	.9625	.9633
1.80	.9641	.9649	.9656	.9664	.9671	.9678	.9686	.9693	.9699	.9706
1.90	.9713	.9719	.9726	.9732	.9738	.9744	.9750	.9756	.9761	.9767
2.00	.9772	.9778	.9783	.9788	.9793	.9798	.9803	.9808	.9812	.9817
2.10	.9821	.9826	.9830	.9834	.9838	.9842	.9846	.9850	.9854	.9857
2.20	.9861	.9864	.9868	.9871	.9875	.9878	.9881	.9884	.9887	.9890
2.30	.9893	.9896	.9898	.9901	.9904	.9906	.9909	.9911	.9913	.9916
2.40	.9918	.9920	.9922	.9925	.9927	.9929	.9931	.9932	.9934	.9936
2.50	.9938	.9940	.9941	.9943	.9945	.9946	.9948	.9949	.9951	.9952
2.60	.9953	.9955	.9956	.9957	.9959	.9960	.9961	.9962	.9963	.9964
2.70	.9965	.9966	.9967	.9968	.9969	.9970	.9971	.9972	.9973	.9974
2.80	.9974	.9975	.9976	.9977	.9977	.9978	.9979	.9979	.9980	.9981
2.90	.9981	.9982	.9982	.9983	.9984	.9984	.9985	.9985	.9986	.9986
3.00	.9987	.9987	.9987	.9988	.9988	.9989	.9989	.9989	.9990	.9990
3.10	.9990	.9991	.9991	.9991	.9992	.9992	.9992	.9992	.9993	.9993
3.20	.9993	.9993	.9994	.9994	.9994	.9994	.9994	.9995	.9995	.9995
3.30	.9995	.9995	.9995	.9996	.9996	.9996	.9996	.9996	.9996	.9997
3.40	.9997	.9997	.9997	.9997	.9997	.9997	.9997	.9997	.9997	.9998

GLOSSARY

Accelerated cost recovery system (ACRS) Schedule of depreciation rates allowed for tax purposes.

Accelerated depreciation Any depreciation method that produces larger deductions for depreciation in the early years of a project's life; e.g., *double-declining-balance depreciation, sum-of-the-years' digits depreciation.*[1]

Acceptance paper/finance paper Short-term promissory notes issued by a finance company. After issue, these instruments are traded on the money market.

Accounts payable (payables, trade debt) Money owed to suppliers.

Accounts receivable (receivables, trade credit) Money owed by customers.

Accrued-benefit cost method Method for estimating the *normal costs* of a pension plan. Its principle is that the company should contribute each year the present value of any benefits that have accrued (cf. *level cost method*).

Accrued interest Interest that has been earned but not yet paid.

Acid-test ratio *Quick ratio.*

ACRS *Accelerated cost recovery system.*

AcSC Accounting Standards Committee of the Canadian Institute of Chartered Accountants.

Adjusted present value *Net present value* of an asset if financed solely by equity plus the present value of financing side effects.

Adverse selection A situation in which a pricing policy causes only the least desirable customers to do business, e.g., a rise in insurance prices that leads only the worst risks to buy insurance.

Agency theory Theory concerning the relationship between a principal, e.g., a shareholder, and an agent of the principal, e.g., the company's manager.

Aging schedule Record of the length of time that *accounts receivable* have been outstanding.

AIBD Association of International Bond Dealers.

Allowance A reduction in taxable income.

All-or-none underwriting Underwriting whereby the issue is cancelled if the *underwriter* is unable to resell the entire issue.

American depositary receipt (ADR) A security issued in the United States to represent shares of a foreign company.

American option Option that can be exercised any time before the final exercise date (cf. *European option*).

AMEX American Stock Exchange.

Amortization Repayment of a loan by instalments.

Annuity Investment that produces a level stream of cash flows for a limited number of periods.

Anticipation Plan whereby customers who pay before the final due date may be entitled to deduct a normal rate of interest.

Appropriation request Formal request for funds for a capital investment project.

APT Arbitrage pricing theory.

---

[1] Italicized words are defined elsewhere in the glossary.

APV *Adjusted present value.*

Arbitrage Purchase of one security and simultaneous sale of another to give a risk-free profit.

"Arbitrage" or "risk arbitrage" Often used loosely to describe the taking of offsetting positions in related securities, e.g., at the time of a takeover bid.

ASE Alberta Stock Exchange.

Asset beta The beta of all the cash flows generated by a specific asset.

Asset classes Each depreciable asset is assigned to an asset class for tax purposes. The definition as well as the maximum allowable depreciation rate for each category is set by Revenue Canada.

ATS accounts Automatic transfer from savings to demand deposit accounts.

Auction-rate preferred A variant of *floating-rate preferred stock* where the dividend is reset every 49 days by auction.

Authorized share capital Maximum number of shares that a company can issue, as specified in the firm's articles of incorporation.

Availability float Cheques deposited by a company that have not yet been cleared.

Aval Bank guarantee for debt purchased by *forfaiter.*

BA *Banker's acceptance.*

Balloon payment Large final payment (e.g., when a loan is repaid in instalments).

Bank acceptance (cf. *banker's acceptance*)

Banker's acceptance (BA) Written demand that has been accepted by a bank to pay a given sum at a future date (cf. *trade acceptance*).

Basis point 0.01%.

Basis risk Residual risk that results when the two sides of a hedge do not move exactly together.

Bear market Widespread decline in security prices (cf. *bull market*).

Bearer note A negotiable note issued by a bank that is payable to the bearer of the note at maturity.

Bearer security Security for which primary evidence of ownership is possession of the certificate (cf. *registered security*).

Benefit-cost ratio *Profitability index.*

Best-efforts underwriting *Underwriters* do not commit themselves to selling a security issue but promise only to use best efforts.

Beta Measure of *market risk.*

Bill of exchange General term for a document demanding payment.

Bill of lading Document establishing ownership of goods in transit.

Blue-chip company Large and creditworthy company.

Blue-sky laws State laws covering the issue and trading of securities.

Boilerplate Standard terms and conditions, e.g, in a debt contract.

Bond Long-term debt.

BONUS (borrowers' options for notes and underwritten standby) A borrowing facility that allows the firm to issue either euronotes or U.S. domestic debt. Also called *global note facility.*

Book rate of return The average forecasted profits after depreciation and taxes divided by the average book value of the investment.

Book runner The managing *under-writer* for a new issue. The book runner maintains the book of securities sold.

Bracket A term signifying the extent of an *underwriter's* commitment in a new issue, e.g., major bracket, minor bracket.

Break-even analysis Analysis of the level of sales at which a project would just break even.

Bridging loan Short-term loan to provide temporary financing until more permanent financing is arranged.

Bull FRN *Reverse FRN.*

Bull market Widespread rise in security prices (cf. *bear market*).

Bull-bear bonds *Bonds* whose principal repayment is linked to the price of another security. The bonds are issued in two tranches: In the first the repayment increases with the price of the other security; in the second the repayment decreases with the price of the other security.

Bulldog bond *Foreign bond* issue made in London.

Bullet payment Single final payment, e.g., of a loan (in contrast to payment in instalments).

Bunny bonds *Multiplier bonds.*

Buy-back *Repurchase agreement; purchase and resale agreement.*

Call To exercise a contractual right to purchase an asset at a contractually specified price.

Call loan A buy-back that is for an indefinite period of time but can be called or renegotiated daily at the option of the borrower and the lender.

Call option Option to buy an asset at a specified *exercise price* on or before a specified exercise date (cf. *put option*).

Call premium (1) Difference between the price at which a company can call its *bonds* and their *face value*; (2) price of an option.

Cap An upper limit on the interest rate on a *floating-rate note*.

Capital budget List of planned investment projects, usually prepared annually.

Capital gain The size of the gain that is realized when an asset is sold for more than it cost to purchase.

Capital lease *Financial lease.*

Capital market Financial market (particularly the market for long-term securities).

Capital rationing Shortage of funds that forces a company to choose between projects.

Capital structure Mix of different securities issued by a firm.

Capitalization Long-term debt, *preferred stock*, plus *net worth*.

CAPM Capital asset pricing model.

CARs (Certificates of Automobile Receivables) *Pass-through* securities backed by automobile *receivables*.

CARDs (Certificates for Amortizing Revolving Debt) *Pass-through* securities backed by credit card *receivables*.

Career-average plan Pension plan offering a pension that depends on the employee's average compensation during his or her years of membership (cf. *final average plan*).

Carry-back When a tax credit or deduction from one tax year is applied to income earned in a previous year.

Carry-forward When a tax credit or deduction in one year is applied to income earned in a future period.

Cash and carry Purchase of a security and the simultaneous sale of a *future*, with the balance being financed with a loan or *repo*.

Cash budget Forecast of sources and uses of cash.

Cash-deficiency arrangement Arrangement whereby a project's shareholders agree to provide the operating company with sufficient *net working capital*.

CAT A U.S. Treasury *bond* reissued by Salomon Brothers as a series of *zero coupon bonds*.

CBOE Chicago Board Options Exchange.

CBRS Canadian Bond Rating Service.

CCA Capital cost allowance: the tax depreciation system in Canada.

CD *Certificate of Deposit*.

CDIC Canadian Deposit Insurance Corporation.

CEDEL A centralized clearing system for *eurobonds*. Also *Euroclear*.

Certainty-equivalent cash flow Certain cash flow that would have the same value as a particular risky cash flow.

Certificate of deposit (CD) Certificate issued by a bank as evidence of a time deposit.

Characteristic line Line representing the relationship between *expected returns* on an asset and returns on the market.

CICA The Canadian Institute of Chartered Accountants.

Clean-up provision Requirement by banks that companies "clean up" their short-term bank loans for at least one month during the year.

Closed-end mortgage Mortgage against which no more debt may be issued (cf. *open-end mortgage*).

Collar Upper and lower limits on the interest rate charged on a *floating rate bond*.

Collateral Assets that are given as security for a loan.

Collateral trust bonds *Bonds* secured by common stocks that are owned by the borrower.

Collection float Cheques deposited by a company that have not yet been cleared (cf. *payment float*).

Commerical discount basis The basis on which certain money market instruments are quoted. For example, commercial paper is quoted on a commercial discount basis.

Commercial draft (Bill of exchange) Demand for payment.

Commercial paper/corporate paper Short-term promissory notes issued by large, well-known companies. After issue, these instruments are traded on the money market.

Commodity-linked bond Bond with an opportunity to share in the potential price appreciation of a physical commodity—e.g., the price of silver.

Compensating balance Non-interest-bearing demand deposit to compensate banks for bank loans or services.

Competitive bidding Means by which public utility *holding companies* are required to choose their *underwriter* (cf. *negotiated underwriting*).

Completion bonding Insurance that a construction contract will be successfully completed.

Compound interest Reinvestment of each interest payment on money invested, to earn more interest (cf. *simple interest*).

Concentration banking System whereby customers make payments to a regional collection centre. The collection centre pays the funds into a regional bank account and surplus money is transferred to the company's principal bank.

Conditional sales Sales in which ownership does not pass to the buyer until payment is completed.

Conglomerate merger *Merger* between two companies in unrelated businesses (cf. *horizontal merger, vertical merger*).

Consol Name of a perpetual *bond* issued by the British government. Sometimes used as a general term for *perpetuity*.

Contingent project Project that cannot be undertaken unless another project is also undertaken.

Continuous compounding Interest compounded continuously rather than at fixed intervals.

Continuously compounded rate A rate of return that is used in continuous compounding.

Controller Officer responsible for budgeting, accounting, and auditing in a firm (cf. *treasurer*).

Conversion price *Par value* of a *convertible security* divided by the number of shares into which it may be exchanged.

Conversion ratio Number of shares for which a *convertible security* may be exchanged.

Convertible security *Bond* or *preferred stock* that may be converted into another security at the holder's option.

Correlation coefficient Measure of the closeness of the relationship between two variables.

Cost company arrangement Arrangement whereby the shareholders of a project receive output free of charge but agree to pay all operating and financing charges of the project.

Cost of capital *Opportunity cost of capital*.

Coupon (1) Specifically, a coupon attached to the certificate of a *bearer bond* that must be surrendered to collect interest payment. (2) More generally, interest payment on debt.

Covariance Measure of the comovement between two variables.

Covenant Clause in a loan agreement.

CPP Canada Pension Plan.

Country banks/offstreet lenders Corporations or institutional investors who lend money to money market dealers through a repurchase agreement.

Credit scoring A procedure for assigning scores to companies on the basis of the risk of default.

Cross-default clause Clause in a loan agreement stating that the company is in default if it fails to meet its obligation on any other debt issue.

Cum dividend *With dividend*.

Cum rights *With rights*.

Cumulative preferred stock Stock which takes priority over common stock in regard to dividend payments. Dividends may not be paid on the common stock until all past *dividends* on the *preferred stock* have been paid.

Cumulative voting A stockholder may cast all his or her votes for one candidate for the board of directors (cf. *majority voting*).

Current asset Asset that will normally be turned into cash within a year.

Current liability Liability that will normally be repaid within a year.

Current ratio *Current assets* divided by *current liabilities*—a measure of liquidity.

DBRS Dominion Bond Rating Service.

DCF Discounted cash flow.

Debenture Unsecured *bond*, usually with maturity of 15 years or more.

Decision tree Method of representing alternative sequential decisions and the possible outcomes from those decisions.

Dedicated portfolio *Bond* portfolio that provides the cash flows to meet a series of fixed pension obligations at minimum cost.

Defeasance Borrower sets aside cash or *bonds* sufficient to service the borrower's debt. Both the borrower's debt and the offsetting cash or bonds are removed from the balance sheet.

Delta *Hedge ratio.*

Demand deposit A bank account that allows the depositor to withdraw funds upon demand.

Depository transfer cheque Cheque made out directly by a local bank to a particular company.

Depreciation (1) Reduction in the book or market value of an asset. (2) Portion of an investment that can be deducted from taxable income.

Depreciation tax shield The tax savings associated with the capital cost allowance.

Derivative instrument A security whose value depends on the value of another asset.

Dilution Diminution in the proportion of income to which each share is entitled.

Direct lease *Lease* in which the *lessor* purchases new equipment from the manufacturer and leases it to the *lessee* (cf. *sale and lease-back*).

Discount bond Debt sold for less than its *principal* value. If a discount bond pays no interest, it is called a "pure" discount bond.

Discount factor *Present value* of $1 received at stated future date.

Discount rate Rate used to calculate the *present value* of future cash flows.

Discounted cash flow Future cash flows multiplied by *discount factors* to obtain *present value*.

Discounted payback rule A capital budgeting rule under which projects are accepted if the number of years required for the cumulative discounted cash flows to equal the initial investment is less than or equal to a cutoff number.

Disintermediation Withdrawal of funds from a financial institution in order to invest them directly (cf. *intermediation*).

Dividend Payment by a company to its stockholders.

Dividend tax credit Personal tax credit that reduces double taxation of dividends from Canadian firms.

Dividend yield Annual *dividend* divided by share price.

Dollar-weighted rate of return *Internal rate of return* (cf. *time-weighted rate of return*).

Double-declining-balance depreciation Method of *accelerated depreciation*.

Double-tax agreement Agreement between two countries that taxes paid abroad can be offset against domestic taxes levied on foreign *dividends*.

Drop lock An arrangement whereby the interest rate on a *floating-rate note* or *preferred* becomes fixed if it falls to a specified level.

Dual-currency bond *Bond* with interest paid in one currency and *principal* paid in another.

Duration The average time to an asset's *discounted cash flows*.

EBIT Earnings before interest and taxes.

Economic depreciation Any reduction in the present value of an asset.

Economic income Cash flow plus change in *present value*.

Economic rents Profits in excess of the competitive level.

ECU *European currency unit*.

EDC Export Development Corporation.

Efficient capital market A capital market in which the purchase or sale of an asset at prevailing prices is never a positive NPV transaction.

Efficient market Market in which security prices reflect information instantaneously.

Efficient portfolio Portfolio that offers the lowest risk (*standard deviation*) for its *expected return* and the highest expected return for its level of risk.

Employee stock ownership plan (*ESOP*) Companies contribute to a trust fund that buys stock on behalf of employees.

EPS Earnings per share.

Equipment trust certificate Form of *secured debt* generally used to finance railroad equipment. The trustee retains ownership of the equipment until the debt is repaid.

Equity (1) Common stock and *preferred stock*. Often used to refer to common stock only. (2) *Net worth*.

Equivalent annual cash flow *Annuity* with the same *net present value* as the company's proposed investment.

ERISA Employee Retirement Income Security Act.

ESOP *Employee stock ownership plan*.

Eurobond *Bond* that is marketed internationally.

Euroclear A centralized clearing system for *eurobonds*. Also *CEDEL*.

Eurodollar deposit Dollar deposit with a bank outside Canada.

Eurodollar loan A short-term debt instrument issued in a foreign country.

European currency unit (*ECU*) A basket of different European currencies.

European option Option that can be exercised only on final exercise date (cf. *American option*).

Evergreen credit *Revolving credit* without maturity.

Ex dividend Purchase of shares in which the buyer is not entitled to the *dividend* (cf. *with dividend, cum dividend*).

Ex rights Purchase of shares in which the buyer is not entitled to the rights to buy shares in the company's *rights issue* (cf. *with rights, cum rights, rights on*).

Exchange of assets Acquisition of another company by purchase of its assets in exchange for cash or shares.

Exchange of stock Acquisition of another company by the purchase of its stock in exchange for cash or shares.

Exercise price (Striking price) Price at which a *call option* or *put option* may be exercised.

Expectations hypothesis The hypothesis that the term structure of interest rates is determined only by investors' expectations regarding future spot rates.

Expected return Average of possible returns weighted by their probability.

Experience losses In a pension plan, losses resulting from any difference between expectations and experience (e.g., a decline in the value of the pension fund's securities).

Extendible bond A bond whose maturity can be extended at the option of the holder.

External finance Finance that is not generated by the firm: new borrowing or an issue of stock (cf. *internal finance*).

Extra dividend *Dividend* that may or may not be repeated.

Face value *Par value.*

Factor A firm that provides factoring services.

Factoring Arrangement under which a financial institution buys a company's *accounts receivable* and collects the debt.

FASB Financial Accounting Standards Board in the United States.

FCIA Foreign Credit Insurance Association in the United States.

FDIC Federal Deposit Insurance Corporation in the United States.

Federal funds Non-interest-bearing deposits by banks at the Federal Reserve. Excess reserves are lent by banks to each other.

Field warehouse Warehouse rented by a warehouse company on another firm's premises (cf. *public warehouse*).

Final-average plan Pension plan offering a pension that depends on the employee's average compensation in his or her final years of service (cf. *career-average plan*).

Financial assets Pieces of paper that represent claims on *real assets*.

Financial engineering Combining, or dividing, existing instruments to create new financial products.

Financial lease (*capital lease, full-payout lease*) Long-term, noncancelable *lease* (cf. *operating lease*).

Financial leverage (*gearing*) Use of debt to increase the *expected return* on *equity*. Financial leverage is measured by the ratio of debt to debt plus equity (cf. *operating leverage*).

Financing decision Deciding how to raise the cash required for investment.

Fiscal agency agreement An alternative to a bond *trust deed*. Unlike the trustee, the fiscal agent acts as an agent of the borrower.

Fixed term or term deposit A deposit in which a promised interest is earned only if the funds are deposited for an agreed-upon period of time. Early withdrawal may be allowed but will involve an interest reduction penalty.

Flip-flop note *Note* which allows investors to switch backward and forward between two different types of debt.

Float See *collection float, payment float.*

Floating lien General *lien* against a company's assets or against a particular class of assets.

Floating-rate bond *Bond* whose interest payment varies with the short-term interest rate.

Floating-rate note (*FRN*) *Note* whose interest payment varies with the short-term interest rate.

Floating-rate preferred *Preferred stock* paying dividends which vary with short-term interest rates.

Floor planning Arrangement used to finance inventory. A finance company buys the inventory, which is then held in trust by the user.

Foreign bond A bond issued on the domestic *capital market* of another country.

Forex Foreign exchange.

Forfaiting Purchase of promises to pay (e.g., *bills of exchange* or *promissory notes*) issued by importers.

Forward cover Purchase or sale of forward foreign currency in order to offset a known future cash flow.

Forward exchange rate Exchange rate fixed today for exchanging currency at some future date (cf. *spot exchange rate*).

Forward interest rate Interest rate fixed today on a loan to be made at some future date (cf. *spot interest rate*).

Forward market A market where contracts for foreign exchange, delivered at a future point in time, are traded.

FRA *Forward rate agreement.*

Forward rate agreement (*FRA*) A loan agreement in which the interest rate is locked in in advance of the loan date.

Forward rate of interest One-year interest rates for future years implicitly contained in a multi-year bond.

Forwards or forward contract A contract to buy a commodity or security on a future date at a given price that is fixed today. Unlike future contracts, these are not generally traded on organized exchanges and are not marked to market.

Free cash flow Cash not required for operations or reinvestment.

FRN *Floating-rate notes.*

Full-payout lease *Financial lease.*

Full-service lease (*rental lease*) Lease in which the *lessor* promises to maintain and insure the equipment (cf. *net lease*).

Funded debt Debt maturing after more than 1 year (cf. *unfunded debt*).

Future A contract to buy a commodity or security on a future date at a price that is fixed today. Unlike forward contracts futures are generally traded on organized exchanges and are *marked-to-market* daily.

Future service costs Value of the pensions that are expected to accrue from employees' future service.

Garnishment A procedure allowing debt to be paid off by deductions from the debtor's wages.

Gearing *Financial leverage.*

General cash offer Issue of securities offered to all investors (cf. *rights issue*).

Global Note Facility *BONUS.*

Golden parachute A large termination payment due to a company's management if they lose their jobs as a result of a merger.

Gray market Purchases and sales of *eurobonds* that occur before the issue price is finally set.

Greenmail A large block of stock is held by an unfriendly company, which forces the target company to repurchase the stock at a substantial premium to prevent a take-over.

Growth stocks Stocks of companies that have an opportunity to invest money to earn more than the *opportunity cost of capital* (cf. *income stocks*).

Harmless warrant *Warrant* that allows the user to purchase a *bond* only by surrendering an existing bond with similar terms.

Heaven-and-hell bonds *Dual-currency bonds* whose principal repayment is in a currency different from the interest payments. The size of the principal repayment is partially increased if the value of the currency falls, and vice versa.

Hedge ratio (*delta, option delta*) The number of shares to buy for each option sold in order to create a safe position. More generally, the number of units of an asset that should be bought to hedge one unit of a liability.

Hedging Buying one security and selling another in order to reduce risk. A perfect hedge produces a riskless portfolio.

Hell-or-high-water clause Clause in a *lease* agreement that obliges the *lessee* to make payments regardless of what happens to the *lessor* or the equipment.

Holding company Company whose sole function is to hold stock in other companies or subsidiaries.

Horizontal merger *Merger* between two companies that manufacture similar products (cf. *vertical merger, conglomerate merger*).

Horizontal spread The simultaneous purchase and sale of two options that differ only in their exercise date (cf. *vertical spread*).

Hurdle rate Minimum acceptable rate of return on a project.

IBF *International Banking Facility.*

ICON *Indexed currency option note.*

IMM (International Monetary Market) The financial futures market within the Chicago Mercantile Exchange.

Immunization Construction of a portfolio of investments whose value is unaffected by interest rate changes.

Income bonds *Bonds* on which interest is payable only if earned.

Income stocks Stocks of companies that earn only the *opportunity cost of capital* on their new investments (cf. *growth stocks*).

Indenture Formal agreement, e.g., establishing the terms of a *bond* issue.

Indexed bonds *Bonds* whose payments are linked to an index, e.g., a consumer price index.

Indexed currency option note (*ICON*) A *eurobond* providing a principal repayment that is linked to the value of the bond's currency (e.g., a dollar bond whose principal repayment declines if the dollar appreciates against the yen).

Individual Retirement Account (*IRA*) An *IRS*-approved pension plan for individuals.

Industrial revenue bond (*IRB*) Issued by local government agencies on behalf of corporations.

Initial public offering (*IPO*) A company's first public issue of common stock.

Intangible assets Nonmaterial assets such as technical expertise, trademarks, and patents (cf. *tangible assets*).

Integer programming Variant of *linear programming* where the solution values must be integers.

Interest cover *Times interest earned.*

Interest equalization tax Tax on foreign investment by residents of the United States (abolished 1974).

Interest-rate parity Theory that the differential between the *forward exchange rate* and the *spot exchange rate* is equal to the differential between the foreign and domestic interest rates.

Intermediation Investment through

a financial institution (cf. *disinter-mediation*).

Internal finance Finance generated within a firm by retained earnings and *depreciation* (cf. *external finance*).

Internal rate of return (*dollar-weighted rate of return, IRR*) Discount rate at which investment has zero *net present value*.

International Banking Facility (*IBF*) A branch that an American bank establishes in the United States to do eurocurrency business.

Interval measure The number of days that a firm can finance operations without additional cash income.

In-the-money option An option that would be worth exercising if it expired immediately (cf. *out-of-the-money option*).

Investment banker *Underwriter*.

Investment decision Deciding how much the firm should invest in real assets and determining the specific assets that should be acquired.

Investment-grade bonds *Bonds* rated Baa or above.

Investment tax credit Proportion of new capital investment that can be used to reduce a company's tax bill (abolished 1986).

IPO *Initial public offering.*

IRA *Individual Retirement Account.*

IRB *Industrial revenue bond.*

IRR *Internal rate of return.*

Irrevocable letter of credit A letter sent by a customer's bank to a vendor stating that a credit has been established in favour of the vendor at the bank.

IRS Internal Revenue Service in the United States.

Junior debt *Subordinated debt.*

Junk bond Debt that is rated below investment grade.

Keogh plan An *IRS*-approved pension plan for the self-employed and owners of unincorporated businesses.

Lease Long-term rental agreement.

Legal capital Value at which a company's shares are recorded in its books.

Lessee User of a leased asset (cf. *lessor*).

Lessor Owner of a leased asset (cf. *lessee*).

Letter of credit Letter from a bank stating that it has established a credit in a company's favour.

Letter stock Privately placed common stock, so called because the securities commissions require a letter from the purchaser that the stock is not intended for resale.

Level cost method (projected-benefit cost method) Method for estimating the *normal costs* of a pension plan. Its principle is that the company should contribute each year an equal amount per employee or an equal proportion of its wage bill (cf. *accrued-benefit cost method*).

Leverage See *financial leverage, operating leverage*.

Leveraged buyouts (LBO's) Acquisitions of public companies by private individuals who finance a large fraction of their purchase with debt.

Leveraged lease *Lease* in which the *lessor* finances part of the cost of the asset by an issue of debt secured by the asset.

Liabilities, total liabilities Total value of financial claims on a firm's assets. Equals (1) total assets *or* (2) total assets minus *net worth*.

LIBOR (London interbank offered rate)   The interest rate at which major international banks in London lend to each other. (LIBID is London Interbank Bid Rate; LIMEAN is mean of bid and offered rate.)

Lien   Lender's claims on specified assets.

Limited liability   Limitation of a shareholder's losses to the amount invested.

Line of credit   Agreement by a bank that a company may borrow at any time up to an established limit.

Linear programming (*LP*)   Technique for finding the maximum value of some equation subject to stated linear constraints.

Liquid assets   Assets that are easily and cheaply turned into cash — notably cash itself and short-term securities.

Liquidating dividend   *Dividend* that represents a return of capital.

Liquidity preference   The hypothesis that, in addition to expectations, the term structure of interest rates is determined by investor preference for short-term debt.

Liquidity premium   The difference between forward rates and expected future spot rates.

Load-to-load   Arrangement whereby the customer pays for the last delivery when the next one is received.

Lock-box system   Form of *concentration banking*. Customers send payments to a post office box. A local bank collects and processes the cheques and transfers surplus funds to the company's principal bank.

Lookback option   A *call (put) option* whose *exercise price* is fixed in retrospect as the lowest (hightest) price of the asset during the life of the option.

LP   *Linear programming*.

Maintenance margin   Minimum margin that must be maintained on a *futures* contract.

Majority voting   Voting system under which each director is voted upon separately (cf. *cumulative voting*).

Management or standby fee   An amount paid to underwriters in exchange for standing ready to purchase any unsubscribed shares sold through a rights issue.

Margin   Cash or securities set aside by an investor as evidence that he or she can honour a commitment.

Marked-to-market   An arrangement whereby the profits or losses on a *futures* contract are settled up each day.

Market capitalization rate   *Expected return* on a security.

Market risk (*systematic risk*)   Risk that cannot be diversified away.

Maturity factoring   *Factoring* arrangement that provides collection and insurance of *accounts receivable*.

MDA   *Multiple discriminant analysis*.

ME   Montreal Exchange.

Medium-term note   Debt with a typical maturity of 1 to 10 years that is offered regularly by a company using the same procedure as *commercial paper*.

Merger   Acquisition in which all assets and liabilities are absorbed by the buyer (cf. *exchange of assets, exchange of stock*). More generally, any combination of two companies.

Minimax bond   *Floating-rate note* whose interest payments are subject to a narrow *collar*.

Mismatch bond   *Floating-rate note* whose interest rate is reset at more frequent intervals than the roll-over period (e.g., a note whose payments are set quarterly on the basis of the 1-year interest rate).

MMDA (money-market deposit account) In return for maintaining a minimum balance, the depositor receives both interest on the account and limited chequing privileges.

Money market The market for short-term investments. The usual security traded in this market is a debt with a maturity of less than three years.

Money-market fund *Mutual fund* which invests solely in short-term safe securities.

Money market jobbers Investment dealers who maintain an inventory in and make a market for money market securities.

Monte Carlo simulation Method for calculating the probability distribution of possible outcomes, e.g., from a project.

Moral hazard The risk that the existence of a contract will change the behaviour of one or both parties to the contract; e.g., an insured firm may take fewer fire precautions.

Mortgage bond *Bond* secured against plant and equipment.

MTN *Medium-term note.*

Multiple-discriminant analysis (*MDA*) Statistical technique for distinguishing between two groups on the basis of their observed characteristics.

Multiplier bonds *Bonds* that provide the option of taking the interest payment in the form of additional multiplier bonds. Also called *bunny bonds.*

Mutual fund Managed investment fund whose shares are sold to investors.

Mutually exclusive projects Two projects that cannot both be undertaken.

Naked option Option held on its own, i.e., not used to hedge a holding in the asset or other options.

NASD National Association of Security Dealers in the United States.

Negative pledge clause Clause under which the borrower agrees not to permit an exclusive *lien* on any of its assets.

Negotiable certificate of deposit A certificate of deposit that is payable to the bearer at maturity.

Negotiated underwriting Method of choosing underwriters. Most firms may choose their *underwriter* by negotiation (cf. *competitive bidding*).

Net lease *Lease* in which the *lessee* promises to maintain and insure the equipment (cf. *full-service lease*).

Net present value A project's net contribution to wealth—*present value* minus initial investment.

Net working capital *Current assets* minus *current liabilities.*

Net worth Book value of a company's common stock, surplus, and retained earnings.

NIF *Note issuance facility.*

Nominal interest rate Interest rate expressed in money terms (cf. *real interest rate*).

Nonrefundable debt Debt that may not be called in order to replace it with another issue at a lower interest cost.

Normal costs Stream of contributions to a pension plan that is required to cover future employee service.

Normal distribution Symmetric bell-shaped distribution that can be completely defined by its mean and *standard deviation.*

Note Unsecured debt, usually with maturity of less than 15 years.

Note issuance facility (*NIF*) A line of credit that allows a borrower to issue short-term euronotes over a period of 5-7 years. The issues are underwritten by a group of banks.

NOW account "Negotiable order of withdrawal" account; a savings account that offers checking privileges.

NYSE New York Stock Exchange.

Off-balance-sheet financing Financing that is not shown as a liability in a company's balance sheet.

OID debt *Original issue discount* debt.

Old-line factoring *Factoring* arrangement that provides collection, insurance, and finance for *accounts receivable*.

On the run The most recently issued (and, therefore, typically the most liquid) Treasury *bond* in a particular maturity range.

Open account Arrangement whereby sales are made with no formal debt contract. The buyer signs a receipt, and the seller records the sale in the sales ledger.

Open-end mortgage Mortgage against which additional debt may be issued (cf. *closed-end mortgage*).

Operating lease Short-term, cancelable *lease* (cf. *financial lease*).

Operating leverage Fixed operating costs, so called because they accentuate variations in profits (cf. *financial leverage*).

Opportunity cost of capital (*hurdle rate, cost of capital*) *Expected return* that is foregone by investing in a project rather than in comparable financial securities.

Option See *call option, put option*.

Option delta *Hedge ratio*.

Original issue discount debt (*OID debt*) Debt that is initially offered at a price below *face value*.

OSC Ontario Securities Commission.

Out-of-the-money option A call option whose exercise price is above the current underlying stock price, or a put option whose exercise price is below the current stock price.

Paper A short-term promissory note traded on the money market.

Par value (*face value*) Value of security shown on certificate.

Pass-through securities *Notes* or *bonds* backed by a package of assets (e.g., mortgage pass-throughs, *CARs*, *CARDs*).

Payables *Accounts payable*.

Payback period The number of years required before the cumulative cash flows from the project equals the initial investment.

Payment float Cheques written by a company that have not yet cleared (cf. *collection float*).

Payout ratio *Dividend* as a proportion of earnings per share.

PBGC Pension Benefit Guarantee Corporation.

P/E ratio Share price divided by earnings per share.

Perpetuity Investment offering a level stream of cash flows in perpetuity (cf. *consol*).

PN *Project note*.

Poison pill An issue of securities that is convertible in the event of a merger into the shares of the acquiring firm or must be repurchased by acquiring firm.

Poison put A *covenant* allowing the *bond*holder to demand repayment in the event of a hostile merger.

Pooling of interest Method of accounting for *mergers*. The consolidated balance sheet of the merged firm is obtained by combining the balance sheets of the separate firms.

Postaudit Evaluation of an investment project after it has been undertaken.

Preemptive right Common stockholder's right to anything of value distributed by the company.

Preferred stock Stock that takes priority over common stock in regard to *dividends*. Dividends may not be paid on common stock unless the dividend is paid on all preferred stock (cf. *cumulative preferred stock*). The dividend rate on preferred is usually fixed at time of issue.

Preliminary prospectus A prospectus submitted to a Securities commission for approval prior to the public issue of securities. (Also called a red herring.)

Present value Discounted value of future cash flows.

Present value of growth opportunities (PVGO) That part of the value of the firm that represents future earnings growth. That is, the value of the firm is made up of the present value of constant or no growth earnings plus the present value of the future increases in earnings above this no-growth level.

Price-earnings ratio The stock market price divided by the firm's earnings per share.

Primary issue Issue of new securities by a firm (cf. *secondary issue*).

Primary offering When new securities of a firm are sold.

Prime rate Rate at which banks lend to their most favoured customers.

Principal Amount of debt that must be repaid.

Privileged subscription issue *Rights issue.*

Pro forma Projected.

Production payment Loan in the form of advance payment for future delivery of a product.

Profitability index (*benefit-cost ratio*) Ratio of a project's *present value* to the initial investment.

Project finance Debt that is largely a claim against the cash flows from a particular project rather than against the firm as a whole.

Project note (*PN*) *Note* issued by public housing agencies or urban renewal agencies.

Projected-benefit cost method *Level cost method.*

Promissory note Promise to pay.

Prospectus Summary of the *registration* statement providing information on an issue of securities.

Proxy vote Vote cast by one person on behalf of another.

Public warehouse (Terminal warehouse) Warehouse operated by an independent warehouse company on its own premises (cf. *field warehouse*).

Purchase and resale agreement (PRA) *Repurchase agreement.*

Put option Option to sell an asset at a specified exercise price on or before a specified exercise date (cf. *call option*).

q The ratio of the market value of an asset to its replacement cost.

Quadratic programming Variant of *linear programming* where the equations are quadratic rather than linear.

Quick ratio (acid-test ratio) Measure of liquidity: (Current assets − inventory) divided by current liabilities.

Rate of return   The rate at which a dollar invested at one point in time increases with time. The rate of return is the reciprocal of the discount factor minus one.

Real assets   *Tangible assets* and *intangible assets* used to carry on business (cf. *financial assets*).

Real interest rate   Interest rate expressed in terms of real goods; i.e., *nominal interest rate* adjusted for inflation.

Recaptured depreciation   When the sale of an asset would result in an asset class with a negative balance, the amount of the negative balance is referred to as recaptured depreciation and is included in taxable income.

Receivables   *Accounts receivable*.

Record date   Date set by directors when making dividend payment. *Dividends* are sent to stockholders who are registered on the record date.

Recourse   Term describing a type of loan. If a loan is with recourse, the lender has a general claim against the parent company if the *collateral* is insufficient to repay the debt.

Red herring   Preliminary *prospectus*.

Redeem   To repurchase and retire a company's securities.

Refunding   Replacement of existing debt with a new issue of debt.

Registered security   Security whose ownership is recorded by the company's *registrar* (cf. *bearer security*).

Registrar   Financial institution appointed to record issue and ownership of company securities.

Registration   The process of obtaining United States *SEC* approval for a public issue of securities.

Regression analysis   In statistics, a technique for finding the line of best fit.

Regular cash dividend   *Dividend* that the company expects to maintain in the future.

Regulation A issue   Security issues of under $400,000. Regulation A issues are partially exempt from United States SEC *registration* requirements.

Regulation Q   Limit on the rate of interest that United States banks may pay on (small) deposits.

Rental lease   *Full-service lease*.

Repo   *Repurchase agreement*.

Repurchase agreement/buyback (*RP*)   A loan to a security dealer from a corporation or institutional investor where a Government of Canada security is used as collateral.

Residual risk   *Unique risk*.

Retained earnings   Earnings not paid out as *dividends*.

Retractable bond   A bond that, at the option of the holder, can be sold or "put" back to the company at a pre-specified price.

Return on equity   Usually, equity earnings as a proportion of the book value of equity.

Revenue Canada   Reviews and assesses tax returns.

Reverse FRN (*bull FRN, yield-curve note*)   *Floating-rate note* whose payments rise as the general level of interest rates falls, and vice versa.

Revolving credit   Legally assured *line of credit* with a bank.

Revolving underwriting facility (*RUF*)   Issuance facility for short-term euronotes.

Rights issue (*privileged subscription issue*)   Issue of securities that is offered to current stockholders (cf. *general cash offer*).

Rights on   *With rights.*

Risk premium   Expected additional return for making a risky investment rather than a safe one.

ROI   Return on investment. Generally, book income as a proportion of net book value.

Roll-over CD   A package of successive *certificates of deposit.*

RP   *Repurchase agreement.*

R squared   Square of the *correlation coefficient* — the proportion of the variability in one series that can be explained by the variability of one or more other series.

RUF   *Revolving underwriting facility.*

Sale and lease-back   Sale of an existing asset to a financial institution that then *leases* it back to the user (cf. *direct lease*).

Salvage value   Scrap value of plant and equipment.

Samurai bond   A yen *bond* issued in Tokyo by a non-Japanese borrower (cf. *bulldog bond, Yankee bond*).

Savings account   A particular type of time deposit that allows almost any sum to be deposited. The bank can insist on 15-days notice prior to withdrawal.

SBIC   Small Business Investment Company.

Season datings   Extended credit for customers who order goods out of the peak season.

Seasoned issue   Issue of a security for which there is an existing market (cf. *unseasoned issue*).

SEC   Securities and Exchange Commission in the United States.

Secondary issue   Procedure for selling blocks of *seasoned issues* of stock. More generally, sale of already issued stock.

Secondary market   Market in which one can buy or sell *seasoned issues* of securities.

Secondary offering   When securities previously sold by a firm (through a primary offering) are resold.

Secured debt   Debt which, in the event of default, has first claim on specified assets.

Securitization   Substituting tradable securities for privately negotiated instruments.

Security market line   Line representing the relationship between *expected return* and *market risk*.

Self-liquidating loan   Loan to finance *current assets*. The sale of the current assets provides the cash to repay the loan.

Self-selection   Consequence of a contract that induces only one group (e.g., the low-risk individuals) to participate.

Semistrong-form efficient market   Market in which security prices reflect all publicly available information (cf. *weak-form efficient market* and *strong-form efficient market*).

Senior debt   Debt which, in the event of bankruptcy, must be repaid before *subordinated debt* receives any payment.

Sensitivity analysis   Analysis of the effect on project profitability of possible changes in sales, costs, and so on.

Serial bonds   Package of *bonds* that mature in successive years.

Series bond   *Bond* which may be issued in several series under the same *indenture*.

Shark repellants Amendments to company charters intended to protect them against take-over.

Shelf registration A procedure that allows firms to file one *registration* statement covering several issues of the same security.

Shogun bond Dollar *bond* issued in Japan by a non-resident.

Short sale Sale of a security that the investor does not own.

Sight draft Demand for immediate payment (cf. *time draft*).

Signal Action that demonstrates an individual's unobservable characteristics (because it would be unduly costly for someone without those characteristics to take the action).

Simple interest Interest calculated only on the initial investment (cf. *compound interest*).

Simulation *Monte Carlo simulation.*

Sinker *Sinking fund.*

Sinking fund (*sinker*) Fund that is established by a company to retire debt before maturity.

Skewed distribution Probability distribution in which an unequal number of observations lie below and above the mean.

Special dividend (*extra dividend*) *Dividend* that is unlikely to be repeated.

Specific risk *Unique risk.*

Spot exchange rate Exchange rate on currency for immediate delivery (cf. *forward exchange rate*).

Spot interest rate Interest rate fixed today on a loan that is made today (cf. *forward interest rate*).

Spot price The price of an asset or commodity that will be delivered immediately.

Spread (underwriter's spread) Difference between the price at which an *underwriter* buys an issue from a firm and the price at which the underwriter sells it to the public.

Standard deviation Square root of the *variance*—a measure of variability.

Standard error In statistics, a measure of the possible error in an estimate.

Standby agreement In a *rights issue*, agreement that the *underwriter* will purchase any stock that is not purchased by investors.

Statutory amalgamation Merger where all of the assets and all of the liabilities of the selling company are absorbed by the buying company and where the selling company disappears.

Step-up bond *Bond* whose *coupon* is stepped up over time. (Also step-down bonds.)

Stock dividend *Dividend* in the form of stock rather than cash.

Stock split "Free" issue of shares to existing shareholders.

Straddle The combination of a *put option* and a *call option* with the same exercise price.

Striking price *Exercise price* of an *option*.

Strip bond A *bond* that can be subdivided into a series of *zero coupon bonds*.

Strong-form efficient market Market in which security prices reflect instantaneously *all* information available to investors (cf. *weak-form efficient market* and *semistrong-form efficient market*).

Subordinated debt A debt claim that, in the event of default, is paid only after all senior creditors are satisfied.

Sum-of-the-years' digits depreciation Method of *accelerated depreciation*.

Sunk costs Costs which have been incurred and cannot be reversed.

Supermajority A provision in a company's charter requiring a majority of, say, 80% of shareholders to approve certain changes, such as a merger.

Super-NOW account Chequing account with a specified minimum balance and on which interest is paid.

Supplemental liability Additional liability to a pension plan that results from an increase in promised benefits.

Sushi bond A eurobond issued by a Japanese corporation.

Swap An arrangement whereby two companies lend to each other on different terms, e.g., in different currencies, or one at a fixed rate and the other at a floating rate.

Swapped deposit An American dollar deposit combined with a spot exchange of Canadian dollars to American dollars and a forward exchange of American dollars to Canadian dollars.

Swingline facility Bank borrowing facility to provide finance while the firm replaces U.S. *commercial paper* with eurocommercial paper.

Systematic risk *Market risk.*

Take-up fee Fee paid to *underwriters* of a *rights issue* on any stock that they are obliged to purchase.

Tangible assets Physical assets such as plant, machinery, factories, and offices (cf. *intangible assets*).

Tax anticipation notes Short-term notes issued by the provinces that will be paid off by the receipt of tax payments.

Tax credit A reduction in taxes owing.

Tax-free merger Generally, merger that does not change the tax position of the corporation or its stockholders.

Tax integration A tax system which leaves equity cash flow to shareholders as they would be if all corporate income was taxed only as personal income of the shareholder.

Tender offer General offer made directly to a firm's shareholders to buy their stock.

Tender panel Panel of underwriting banks established to bid for *notes* issued under a *note issuance facility.*

Term deposit receipt A receipt providing evidence of a bank time deposit.

Term loans Medium-term privately placed loans, usually made by banks.

Term note A note providing evidence of a bank time deposit.

Term preferred dividends Dividends on preferred shares that can be redeemed within 10 years of their initial issue.

Term structure of interest rates Relationship between interest rates on loans of different maturities.

Term to maturity The length of time between the current date and the date at which the balance of a loan must be repaid.

Terminal loss The amount remaining in an asset class after the last asset in the class is sold, provided that the asset class balance is positive.

Terminal warehouse *Public warehouse.*

Throughput arrangement Arrangement by which shareholders of a pipeline company agree to make sufficient use of the pipeline to enable the pipeline company to service its debt.

Time draft Demand for payment at a stated future date (cf. *sight draft*).

Time/notice deposit A bank account that may require that notice be given several days before a withdrawal is made.

Times interest earned (interest cover) Earnings before interest and tax, divided by interest payments.

Time-weighted rate of return Rate of return that gives equal weight to each time period; used in investment performance measurement (cf. *dollar-weighted rate of return*).

Tombstone Advertisement listing the *underwriters* to a security issue.

Trade acceptance Written demand that has been accepted by an industrial company to pay a given sum at a future date (cf. *bank acceptance*).

Trade credit *Accounts receivable.*

Trade debt *Accounts payable.*

Transfer agent Individual or institution appointed by a company to look after the transfer of newly issued securities.

Treasurer Principal financial manager (cf. *controller*).

Treasury bill Short-term discount debt maturing in less than one year, issued regularly by the federal government.

Treasury stock Common stock that has been repurchased by the company and held in the company's treasury.

True yield basis The basis on which certain money market instruments are quoted. For example, treasury bills are quoted on a true yield basis.

Trust deed Agreement between trustee and borrower setting out terms of *bond*.

Trust receipt Receipt for goods that are to be held in trust for the lender.

TSE Toronto Stock Exchange.

TSE 300 Index Value-weighted stock index comprised of 300 TSE stocks.

Undeprecitated capital cost (UCC) The amount of an asset class that has not been depreciated for tax purposes.

Underpricing Issue of securities below their market value.

Underwriter (investment banker) Firm which buys an issue of securities from a company and resells it to investors.

Unfunded debt Debt maturing within one year (cf. *funded debt*).

Unique risk (residual risk, specific risk, unsystematic risk) Risk that can be reduced by diversification.

Unpaid balance The amount that is owed on a loan.

Unseasoned issue Issue of a security for which there is no existing market (cf. *seasoned issue*).

Unsystematic risk *Unique risk.*

Valuation horizon The value of an investment is usually computed as the discounted value of the investment's cash flows from the current period to a future point in time. This future point is known as the valuation horizon.

Value additivity Rule that the value of the whole must equal the sum of the values of the parts.

Variance Mean squared deviation from the expected value—a measure of variability.

Variation margin The daily gains or losses on a *futures* contract that are credited to the investor's margin account.

Venture capital Capital to finance a new firm.

Vertical merger *Merger* between a

supplier and its customer (cf. *horizontal merger, conglomerate merger*).

Vertical spread The simultaneous purchase and sale of two options that differ only in their exercise price (cf. *horizontal spread*).

Vesting Employee's entitlement to a part of his or her pension if he or she leaves before retirement.

VSE Vancouver Stock Exchange.

Warehouse receipt Evidence that a firm owns goods stored in a warehouse.

Warrant Long-term *call option* issued by a company.

Weak-form efficient market Market in which security prices instantaneously reflect the information contained in the past history of security prices. In such a market security prices follow a random walk (cf. *semistrong-form efficient market* and *strong-form efficient market*).

Weighted-average cost of capital *Expected return* on a portfolio of all the firm's securities.

White knight A friendly potential acquirer sought out by a target company threatened by a less welcome suitor.

With dividend (*cum dividend*) Term describing a purchase of shares by which the buyer is entitled to the forthcoming *dividend* (cf. *ex dividend*).

With rights (*cum rights, rights on*) Purchase of shares in which the buyer is entitled to the rights to buy shares in the company's *rights issue* (cf. *ex rights*).

Withholding tax Tax levied on *dividends* paid abroad.

Working capital *Current assets* and *current liabilities*. The term is commonly used as synonymous with *net working capital*.

Writer *Option* seller.

Yankee bond A dollar *bond* issued in the United States by a non-U.S. borrower (cf. *bulldog bond, Samurai bond*).

Yield curve *Term structure of interest rates*.

Yield-curve note *Reverse FRN.*

Yield to maturity *Internal rate of return* on a *bond*.

Zero coupon bond *Discount bond* making no *coupon* payments.

ANSWERS TO QUIZ QUESTIONS

CHAPTER 1

1. (a) Real
   (b) Executive airplanes
   (c) Brand names
   (d) Financial
   (e) Bonds
   (f) Investment
   (g) Capital budgeting
   (h) Financing

2. a, c, and d

3. c, d,e, and g are real assets. Others are financial.

CHAPTER 2

1. (a) Negative
   (b) $\text{NPV} = \dfrac{C_1}{1 + r}$
   (c) $\text{NPV} = C_0 + \dfrac{C_1}{1 + r}$
   (d) It is the return foregone by investing in the project rather than the capital market.
   (e) The return offered by default-free government bonds.

2. $\text{DF}_1 = 0.867$; discount rate $= 0.154$, or 15.4%.

3. (a) 0.090
   (b) 0.833
   (c) 0.769

4. (a) $\text{Return} = \dfrac{\text{profit}}{\text{investment}}$
   $= \dfrac{132 - 100}{100}$
   $= 0.32$, or 32%.
   (b) Negative (if the rate of interest r *equals* 32%, NPV = 0).
   (c) $\text{PV} = \dfrac{132}{1.10} = 120$, or $120,000
   (d) $\text{NPV} = -100 + 120 = 20$, or $20,000

5. Net present value rule: Invest if NPV is positive. Rate-of-return rule: Invest if the rate of return exceeds the opportunity cost of capital. They give the same answer.

6. (a) $1 + r = 5/4$. Therefore $r = 0.25$, or 25%
   (b) $2.6 - 1.6 = \$1$ million
   (c) $3 million
   (d) $\text{Return} = (3 - 1)/1 = 2.0$, or 200%
   (e) Marginal return = rate of interest = 25%
   (f) $\text{PV} = 4 - 1.6 = \$2.4$ million
   (g) $\text{NPV} = -1.0 + 2.4 = \$1.4$ million
   (h) $4 million ($2.6 million cash + NPV)
   (i) $1 million
   (j) $3.75 million

7. They will vote for (a) only. The other tasks can be carried out just as efficiently by stockholders.

CHAPTER 3

1. $1.00

2. $125/139 = 0.899$

3. $596 \times 0.285 = 170$

4. $\dfrac{374}{(1.09)^9} = 172$

5. $\text{PV} = \dfrac{432}{1.15} + \dfrac{137}{(1.15)^2} + \dfrac{797}{(1.15)^3}$
   $= 375.84 + 103.57 + 524.42$
   $= 1{,}003.83$

6. $100 \times (1.15)^8 = 305.90$

7. $232 \times (1 + r)^2 = 312.18$ implies $r = 0.16$, or 16%.

8. $\text{NPV} = -1{,}548 + \dfrac{138}{0.09} = -14.67$

9. Find g so that NPV = 0.
   $\text{NPV} = -2{,}590 + \dfrac{220}{0.12 - g} = 0$
   implies $g = 0.035$, or 3.5%.

10. $PV = \dfrac{4}{0.14 - 0.04} = \$40$

11. PV of \$502 at $t = 1, 2, \ldots, 9$ at 13% $= 502 \times 5.132 = 2{,}576.26$. Future value $= 2{,}576 \times (1.13)^9 = 7{,}739.19$.

12. (a) Let S_t = salary in year t

$$PV = \sum_{t=1}^{30} \frac{S_t}{(1.08)^t}$$

$$= \sum_{t=1}^{30} \frac{20{,}000\,(1.05)^{t-1}}{(1.08)^t}$$

$$= \sum_{t=1}^{30} \frac{20{,}000/1.05}{(1.08/1.05)^t}$$

$$= \sum_{t=1}^{30} \frac{19{,}048}{(1.029)^t}$$

$$= 19{,}048 \left[\frac{1}{0.029} - \frac{1}{0.029\,(1.029)^{30}} \right]$$

$$= 378{,}222$$

(b) PV (salary $\times$ 0.05) $= 18{,}911$. Future value $= 18{,}911 \times (1.08)^{30} = 190{,}295$.

(c) Annual payment = initial value $\div$ annuity factor; 20-year annuity factor at 8% $= 9.818$; annual payment $= 190{,}295/9.818 = 19{,}382$.

13.

Period	Discount Factor	Cash Flow	Present Value
0	1.0	$-400{,}000$	$-400{,}000$
1	0.893	$+100{,}000$	$+89{,}300$
2	0.797	$+200{,}000$	$+159{,}400$
3	0.712	$+300{,}000$	$+213{,}600$
		Total = NPV =	62,300

14. (a) $PV = 1/0.10 = \$10$

(b) $PV = \dfrac{1}{0.10\,(1.10)^7} = \dfrac{10}{2}$
$= \$5$ (approx.)

(c) $PV = 10 - 5 = \$5$ (approx.)

(d) $PV = \dfrac{C}{r - g} = \dfrac{10{,}000}{0.10 - 0.05}$
$= \$200{,}000$

15. Annuity factor for 30 periods at 2% per period $= 22.40$. Payments $= 50{,}000/22.40 = \$2{,}232.14$ per month. After 2 years, 6 months remain in the mortgage, and the annuity factor is 5.601. Remaining balance $= 2{,}232.14 \times 5.601 = \$12{,}502.23$.

16. (a) $r_m = (1 + 0.11/2)^{1/6} - 1 = 0.008963$ or 0.8963% per month

(b) Annuity factor $= \dfrac{1}{0.008963}$
$\left[1 - \dfrac{1}{1.008963^{360}} \right] = 107.0735$
Payment $= 75{,}000/107.0735$
$= \$700.45$

(c) Annuity factor $= \dfrac{1}{0.008963}$
$\left[1 - \dfrac{1}{1.008963^{300}} \right] = 103.8930$
Remaining balance $= 700.45 \times 103.8930 = \$72{,}771.82$

17. (a) From Appendix Table 1, $1/(1.05)^5 = 0.784$. You therefore need to set aside $10{,}000 \times 0.784 = \$7{,}840$.

(b) From Appendix Table 3, the present value of \$1 a year for six years at 8% is \$4.623. Therefore you need to set aside $1{,}200 \times 4.623 = \$5{,}548$.

(c) From Appendix Table 2, $1.08^6 = 1.587$. Therefore, at the end of six years you would have $1.587 \times (6{,}048 - 5{,}548) = 794$.

(d) From Appendix Table 2, \$1 grows to \$1.762 by year 5 at an annually compounded rate of 12%. From Appendix Table 4, \$1 grows to \$1.762 by year 5 at a continuously compounded rate of about 11.4%.

CHAPTER 4

1. $PV_A = \dfrac{1,060}{1.08} = 981.48$

   $PV_B = \dfrac{60}{1.08} + \dfrac{1,060}{1.08^2} = 964.33$

   $PV_C = \sum\limits_{t=1}^{3} \dfrac{60}{1.08^t} + \dfrac{1,060}{1.08^4} = 933.76$

   $PV_D = \dfrac{100}{1.08} + \dfrac{1,100}{1.08^2} = 1,035.67$

   $PV_E = \sum\limits_{t=1}^{3} \dfrac{100}{1.08^t} + \dfrac{1,100}{1.08^4}$
   $\qquad = 1,066.24$

2. The increased return has larger impact on the longer-term bonds.

   $PV_A = \dfrac{1,060}{1.10} = 963.64$

   $PV_B = \dfrac{60}{1.10} + \dfrac{1,060}{1.10^2} = 930.58$

   $PV_C = \sum\limits_{t=1}^{3} \dfrac{60}{1.10^t} + \dfrac{1,060}{1.10^4} = 873.21$

   $PV_D = \dfrac{100}{1.10} + \dfrac{1,100}{1.10^2} = 1,000$

   $PV_E = \sum\limits_{t=1}^{3} \dfrac{100}{1.10} + \dfrac{1,100}{1.10^4} = 1,000$

3. $P_0 = \dfrac{10 + 110}{1.10} = \$109.09$

4. $r = \dfrac{5}{40} = 0.125$

5. $P_0 = \dfrac{10}{0.08 - 0.05} = \$333.33$

6. $\dfrac{15}{0.08} + PVGO = 333.33$; therefore

   $PVGO = \$145.83$

7. (b) and (c); (a) ignores the cost of the investments needed to produce the earnings.

8. If present value of growth opportunities (PVGO) is zero.

CHAPTER 5

1. The opportunity cost of capital is the expected rate of return investors could earn at any given level of risk.

2. (a) A = three years, B = two years, C = three years
   (b) B
   (c) A, B, and C
   (d) B and C ($NPV_B = \$3.378$; $NPV_C = \$2,405$)
   (e) False
   (f) True

3. (a) $\dfrac{1,000}{4,000} = 0.25$, or 25%

4. (a) True
   (b) False

5. (a) \$15,750; \$4,250; \$0
   (b) 100%

6. (a) (i) Both (IRR is greater than the cost of capital). (ii) The *incremental* cash flows on B are: $-2,000, +1,100, +1,210$. The IRR on these incremental flows is 10%. Since this is greater than the cost of capital, the incremental investment in A is worthwhile.
   (b) NPV of incremental investment = $690 - 657 = \$33$

7. (a) A = 2,000/1,600 = 1.25; B = 2,400/2,100 = 1.14
   (b) (i) Both. (ii) The incremental flows on B are $-500, +240, +288$. The profitability index on the incremental investment is 400/500 = 0.8. Therefore, accept A.

8. C (if both projects have NPV = 0 at the same discount rate, the project with the later cash flows must have the higher NPV if we use a lower discount rate).

9. No (you are effectively "borrowing" at a higher rate of interest).

CHAPTER 6

1. a, b, d, g, h.

2. Real cash flow = 100,000/1.1
= 90,909; real discount rate
= (1.15/1.1) − 1 = 0.0455

$$PV = \frac{90,909}{1.0455} = 86,953, \text{ four}$$

francs short because of rounding error.

3. (a) NPV_A = \$100,000;
NPV_B = \$180,000
(b) Equivalent cash flow of A
= 100,000/1.736 = \$57,604;
equivalent cash flow of B
= 180,000/2.487 = \$72,376
(c) Machine B.

4. Replace at end of five years
(\$80,000 > 72,376).

5. 1, 2, 4, and 6.

6. Soft rationing means provisional capital constraints imposed by management as an aid to financial control. This doesn't rule out raising more money if necessary. Firms facing hard rationing can't raise money from capital markets.

7. Purchase cost and PV of after-tax net revenue stream = − 150,000 + 89,418 = − 60,582. PV of perpetual CCA tax shield on

$$\$150,000 = \frac{150,000 \times 0.2 \times 0.4}{0.12 + 0.2}$$

= 37,500

7. (a) (i) $NPV = -60,582 + 37,500 + \dfrac{20,000}{(1.12)^9} - \dfrac{20,000 \times 0.2 \times 0.4}{0.12 + 0.2}$

$\times \dfrac{1}{(1.12)^9} = -17,673$

(ii)
$NPV = -60,582 + 37,500 + \left(200,000 - 0.4 \times \dfrac{(200,000 - 150,000)}{2}\right)$

$\times \dfrac{1}{(1.12)^9} - \dfrac{150,000 \times 0.2 \times 0.4}{0.12 + 0.2} \times \dfrac{1}{(1.12)^9} = 31,911$

(b) UCC in year 9 = $150,000 \times (1 - 0.2)^9 = 20,133$
(i) $NPV = -60,582 + 37,500 + (20,000 + 0.4 \times (20,133 - 20,000))$

$\times \dfrac{1}{(1.12)^9} - \dfrac{20,133 \times 0.2 \times 0.4}{0.12 + 0.2} \times \dfrac{1}{(1.12)^9} = -17,666$

(ii) $NPV = -60,582 + 37,500 + (30,000 + 0.4 \times (20,133 - 30,000))$

$\times \dfrac{1}{(1.12)^9} - \dfrac{20,133 \times 0.2 \times 0.4}{0.12 + 0.2} \times \dfrac{1}{(1.12)^9} = -15,502$

(iii) $NPV = -60,582 + 37,500 + (200,000 + 0.4 \times (20,133 - 150,000))$

$\times \dfrac{1}{(1.12)^9} - 0.4 \times \dfrac{1}{2} \times (200,000 - 150,000) \times \dfrac{1}{(1.12)^9}$

$- \dfrac{20,133 \times 0.2 \times 0.4}{0.12 + 0.2} \times \dfrac{1}{(1.12)^9} = 24,866$

(c) UCC in year 0 = $150,000 - 100,000 = 50,000$
UCC in year 9 = $50,000 \times (1 - 0.2)^9 = 6,711$

$NPV = -60,582 + 0.4 \times 100,000 + \dfrac{50,000 \times 0.2 \times 0.4}{0.12 + 0.2}$

$+ (20,000 + 0.4 \times (6,711 - 20,000)) \times \dfrac{1}{(1.12)^9}$

$- \dfrac{6,711 \times 0.2 \times 0.4}{0.12 + 0.2} \times \dfrac{1}{(1.12)^9} = -3,392$

8. The only reason you may want to take CCA at a reduced rate would be that you are going to have a higher tax rate in the future so that a CCA tax shield is more valuable then, but suppose this is not the case here. Recaptured depreciation merely forces you to take into income "excess" CCA that you took earlier and received a tax shield for. That is, at recapture time, you merely pay for the same dollar benefit you already received earlier. Under the time value of money, facing a recapture like this is the best thing to do, so you should claim CCA at the maximum rate.

9. The real discount rate is 3% and the nominal discount rate is $1.03 \times 1.05 - 1 = 0.0815$ or approximately 8%. Everything but the CCA tax shield is nominal. By Appendix Table 2, the nominal salvage value is $1,500 \times 1.05^6 = 1,500 \times 1.340 = \$2,010$.

9. (a) NPV = $-C$ + PV of perpetual nominal CCA + PV of 5 years of real after-tax operating flows + PV of nominal salvage $-$ PV of lost nominal CCA on salvage = $-10,000 + \dfrac{10,000 \times 0.20 \times 0.36}{0.08 + 0.20} + (1 - 0.36)$

$\times$ 3,000 $\times$ (5-year annuity factor at 3%) + $\dfrac{2,010}{1.08^6} - \dfrac{1}{1.08^6}$

$\times \dfrac{2,010 \times 0.20 \times 0.36}{0.08 + 0.20} = -10,000 + 2,571 + 8,794 + 1,266 - 326$

= 2,305.

(b) UCC in year 6 = $10,000 \times (1 - 0.20)^6$
$\qquad\qquad\qquad = \$2,621.$

Nominal terminal loss in year 6 is $2,621 - 2,010$
= \$611.

NPV is as in (a) except that the last term is replaced by

$-\dfrac{1}{1.08^6} \times \dfrac{2.621 \times 0.20 \times 0.36}{0.08 + 0.20} + \dfrac{0.36 \times 611}{1.08^6}$

Thus, NPV = $-10,000 + 2,571 + 8,794 + 1,266 - 425 + 139$
= 2,345.

CHAPTER 7

1. (a) About 12%
   (b) 7-8%
   (c) About 1%
   (d) About 20%
   (e) Less (diversification reduces risk)

2. Standard deviation of returns, correlated, less, unique, market.

3. (a) False
   (b) True
   (c) True
   (d) True
   (e) False

4. A: 1.0; B: 2.0; C: 1.5; D: 0; E: -1.0

5. (a) 26%
   (b) zero
   (c) 0.75
   (d) Less than 1.0 (the portfolio's risk is the same as the market, but some of this risk is unique risk).

6. 1.3 (Diversification does not affect market risk.)

7. $\sigma^2 = 330$; $\sigma = 18.2\%$

8. (d)

9.

$x_1^2\sigma_1^2$	$x_1x_2\sigma_{12}$	$x_1x_3\sigma_{13}$
$x_1x_2\sigma_{12}$	$x_2^2\sigma_2^2$	$x_2x_3\sigma_{23}$
$x_1x_3\sigma_{13}$	$x_2x_3\sigma_{23}$	$x_3^2\sigma_3^2$

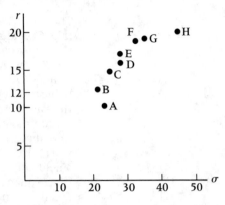

Figure 2   Chapter 8, Quiz question 4 (a).

CHAPTER 8

1. (a) Figure 8-14: Diversification reduces risk (e.g., a mixture of portfolios A and B would have less risk than the average of A and B).
   (b) Those along line *AB* in Figure 8-13.
   (c) See Figure 1, below.

2. (a) Portfolio A (higher expected return, same risk)
   (b) Cannot say (depends on investor's attitude toward risk)
   (c) Portfolio F (lower risk, same expected return)

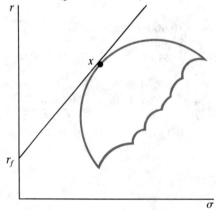

Figure 1   Chapter 8, Quiz question 1 (c).

3. a, b

4. (a) See Figure 2, next column.
   (b) A, D, G
   (c) F
   (d) 15% in C
   (e) Put 25/32 of your money in F and lend 7/32 at 12%:
       Expected return = 7/32 × 12 + 25/32 × 18 = 16.7%
       Standard deviation = 7/32 × 0 + 25/32 × 32 = 25%

If you could borrow without limit, you would achieve as high an expected return as you'd like, with correspondingly high risk of course.

5. (a) True
   (b) False (it offers twice the market *risk premium*)
   (c) False

6. (a) 9.3%
   (b) 12.0% (Denison Mines)
   (c) 6.3% (Bell Canada Ent.)
   (d) lower (11.3 vs. 11.9%)
   (e) higher (7.5 vs. 6.3%)

7. b

CHAPTER 9

1. It will tend to overinvest in risky projects, and pass valuable safe projects by.

2. Suppose $r_f = 7\%$.
   $r = r_f + \beta(r_m - r_f)$
   $= 7 + 2.0\ (8) = 23\%$

   $NPV = -100,000 + \dfrac{150,000}{1.23}$

   $= +21,950$

3. Beta = market risk measure. Average risk would imply beta = 1.0.
   Std. error = measure of extent of possible error in beta estimate.
   Alpha = average price change on stock when market return was zero.

Std. error = measure of extent of possible error in alpha estimate.

R^2 = ratio of market risk to total risk — that is, proportion of variance of stock attributable to market risk.

Resid. Std. dev. = stock's unique risk measured as a standard deviation.

Number of obs. = number of monthly returns used to estimate beta and alpha.

4. $\beta_{ASSETS} = 0 \times 0.40 + 0.5 \times 0.60$
   $= 0.30$
   $r = 10 + 0.30 (20 - 10) = 13\%$

5. (a) $r_f + \beta (r_m - r_f) = 8 + 1.5 \times 10 = 23\%$

   (b) β_{ASSETS}
   $= \beta_{DEBT}\left(\dfrac{debt}{debt + equity}\right) +$
   $\beta_{EQUITY}\left(\dfrac{equity}{debt + equity}\right)$
   $= 0 \times \dfrac{4}{4 + 6} + 1.5 \times \dfrac{6}{4 + 6}$
   $= 0.9$

   (c) $r_f + \beta_{ASSETS} (r_m - r_f)$
   $= 8 + 0.9 \times 10$
   $= 17\%$

   (d) $r = 17\%$

   (e) $r_f + \beta(r_m - r_f)$
   $= 8 + 1.2 \times 10 = 20\%$

6. Expected cash flow is an average of the cash flow from a dry hole and the cash flow from a producing well. The possibility of a dry hole should affect the discount rate only if the project's market risk is increased.

7. (a) A (higher fixed cost).
   (b) C (more cyclical revenues).

8. $CEQ_t/[(1 + r_f)^t]$; less than; $r_f + \beta(r_m - r_f)$; declines at a constant rate

9. (a) $PV = \dfrac{110}{1 + r_f + \beta(r_m - r_f)} +$

$\dfrac{121}{[1 + r_f + \beta(r_m - r_f)]^2}$
$= \dfrac{110}{1.10} + \dfrac{121}{1.10^2} = \$200$

   (b) $\dfrac{CEQ_1}{1.05} = \dfrac{110}{1.10}$, $CEQ_1 = \$105$
   $\dfrac{CEQ_2}{1.05^2} = \dfrac{121}{1.10^2}$,
   $CEQ_2 = \$110.25$

   (c) $Ratio_1 = \dfrac{105}{110} = 0.95$
   $Ratio_2 = \dfrac{110.25}{121} = 0.91$

CHAPTER 10

1. (a) Detailed analysis of capital investment projects, to identify what cash flows depend on, what can go wrong, whether the project could be abandoned if performance is disappointing, and so on.

   (b) Analysis of how project profitability and NPV changes if different assumptions are made about sales, cost, and other key variables.

   (c) Determines the level of future sales at which project profitability or NPV equals zero.

   (d) An extension of sensitivity analysis which explores all possible outcomes and weighs each by its probability.

   (e) A graphical technique for displaying possible future events and decisions taken in response to those events.

   (f) The additional present value created by the option to bail out of a project, and recover part of the initial investment, if the project performs poorly.

   (g) The additional present value created by the option to invest more and expand output, if a project performs well.

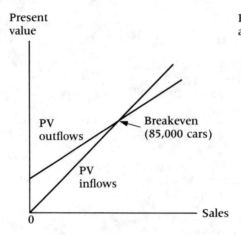

Figure 3 Chapter 10, Quiz question 3 (c).

2. −$30 million.

3. (a) NPV = old NPV

    − additional investment

    + reduction in net variable costs

    + increase in depreciation tax shield

$$= 34.3 - 150$$
$$+ \sum_{t=1}^{10} \frac{(0.5 \times 40)}{(1.10)^t}$$
$$+ \sum_{t=1}^{10} \frac{(0.5 \times 15)}{(1.10)^t}$$
$$= \$53 \text{ million}$$

(b) Variable costs = $260 million on 100,000 cars.

(c) The left-hand chart in Figure 3 shows that expected sales have to be at least 85,000 for the project to have a positive NPV. The right-hand graph shows that the firm can report an *accounting* profit if sales exceed 52,000.

4. (a) "Optimistic" and "pessimistic" rarely show the full probability distribution of outcomes.

(b) Sensitivity analysis changes variables one at a time; in practice, all variables change, and the changes are often interrelated. Sensitivity analysis using scenarios can help in this regard.

5. (a) False
  (b) True
  (c) True
  (d) True
  (e) True
  (f) False
  (g) True
  (h) True

6. (a) Describe how project cash flow depends on the underlying variables.

(b) Specify probability distributions for forecast errors for these cash flows.

(c) Draw from the probability distributions to simulate the cash flows.

7. NPV (pretest) = 34.3 − 0.1
$$= \$34.2 \text{ million}$$
NPV (don't pretest) = 0.9 × 34.3
$$+ 0.1$$
$$\times (-27.1)$$
$$= \$28.2$$
$$\text{million}$$

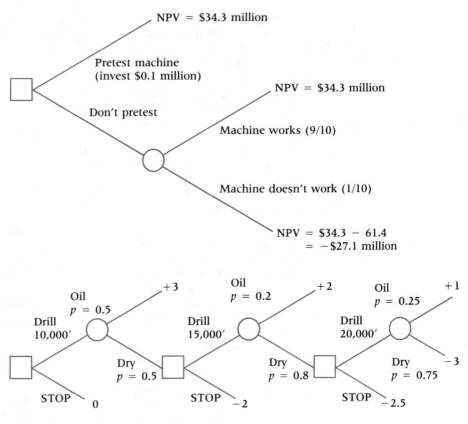

Table 1   See Quiz question 8, Chapter 10.

8. See Table 1. The decision tree shows the probability of finding oil earlier. At 15,000 feet, the expected payoff to further drilling is $(0.25 \times 1) + (0.75 \times -3) = -\$2$ million. This is greater than the payoff to stopping. Therefore Big should drill to 20,000 feet. At 10,000 feet the expected payoff to drilling to 15,000 feet is $0.8 \times [(0.25 \times 1) + (0.75 \times -3)] + (0.2 \times 2) = -\$1.2$ million. This is greater than the payoff to stopping. Therefore Big should drill to 15,000 feet. The expected payoff to drilling to 10,000 feet is $(0.5 \times 3) + (0.5 \times -1.2) = \$0.9$ million. As long as the certainty equivalent value of this payoff is positive, Big should drill

to 10,000 feet initially, but be prepared to go all the way to 20,000 feet.

CHAPTER 11

1. Your best estimate is $2,000 per hectare, the actual market value. Why do a discounted-cash-flow analysis to estimate market value when you can observe it directly?

2. (a) False
   (b) True
   (c) True
   (d) False

3. $15

4. DC-8s should have been valued at market prices for used airplanes. The *low book* depreciation charge

was irrelevant. Alitalia should have compared the total costs of operating 747s and DC-8s, in which the DC-8s' cost includes the opportunity cost of capital on, and depreciation of, their actual secondhand value. *Note:* If 747s and DC-8s were perfect substitutes in terms of range, passenger comfort, and so on, we would expect the DC-8s' secondhand value to adjust until their total operating costs per seat mile were the same as the 747s'.

5. It depends first on competition among capital equipment producers. If other producers can quickly match the new machine, its advantages are passed on to its buyers. But then the buyers will compete to pass on the machine's advantages to their customers. In the end, producers will realize positive NPVs from buying the machine only if they are in a position to make better use of it than their competitors.

CHAPTER 12

1. (a) False
   (b) False — top management usually makes the final decision on major projects.
   (c) True
   (d) True
   (e) False
   (f) True

2. Cash flow, economic, less, greater.

3.

	Year 1	Year 2	Year 3
Cash flow	0	78.55	78.55
PV at start of year	100.00	120.00	65.46
PV at end of year	120.00	65.46	0
Change in value during year	+ 20.00	− 54.54	− 65.46
Expected economic income	+ 20.00	+ 24.00	+ 13.09

4. (a) False
   (b) False — firms have a considerable range of choice.
   (c) True
   (d) True

CHAPTER 13

1. c

2. Weak, semistrong, strong, fundamental, strong, technical, weak

3. c and f

4. (a) Decline to $200
   (b) Remain at 2%
   (c) Less
   (d) A slight abnormal fall (the split is likely to have led investors to expect an above-average rise in dividends)

5. (a) False
   (b) True
   (c) False
   (d) True
   (e) False
   (f) True (a small change in price *in the absence of new information* causes a large increase in demand)

CHAPTER 14

1. | Common stock | $ 60,000 |
   |---|---|
   | Additional paid-in capital | 10,000 |
   | Retained earnings | 30,000 |
   | Common equity | $100,000 |

2. (a) 80 votes
   (b) 10 × 80 = 800 votes

3. (a) Long-term
   (b) Eurobond
   (c) Subordinated
   (d) Debentures
   (e) Sinking fund
   (f) Call
   (g) Prime rate
   (h) Floating rate
   (i) Lease
   (j) Convertible
   (k) Warrant, exercise price

4. Internally generated cash, 64; Financial deficit, 34; New share issues, 10; Long-term debt issues, 31; Short-term debt issue, 1.

5. (a) False
   (b) True
   (c) True
   (d) True
   (e) False
   (f) True
   (g) True

CHAPTER 15

1. (a) Issue of seasoned stock
   (b) Bond issue by utility holding company
   (c) Bond issue by industrial company
   (d) Bond issue by large industrial company

2. A (d); B (f); C (c); D (a); E (b); F(e)

3. (a) A large issue
   (b) A bond issue
   (c) A large competitive bond issue
   (d) A small private placement of bonds

4. (a) 50,000 shares
   (b) Primary: 500,000 shares
       Secondary: 400,000 shares
   (c) $15 or 19%, which is the same as observed by Ibbotson, Sindelar, and Ritter.

(d)

	Millions
Underwriting cost	$ 4.5
Administrative cost	0.82
Underpricing	13.5
Total	$18.82

5. (a) Net proceeds of public issue
   $$= 10,000,000 - 150,000$$
   $$- 80,000 = \$9,770,000$$
   Net proceeds of private placement = $9,970,000
   (b) PV of extra interest on private placement
   $$= \sum_{t=1}^{10} \frac{0.005 \times 10,000,000}{1.085^t}$$
   = $328,000, i.e., extra cost of higher interest on private placement more than outweighs saving in issue costs. N.B. We ignore taxes.
   (c) Private placement debt can be custom-tailored and the terms more easily renegotiated.

6. (a) Number of rights needed to purchase one share: 2
   (b) Number of new shares: 50,000
   (c) Amount of new investment: $500,000
   (d) Total value of company after issue: $4,500,000
   (e) Total number of shares after issue: 150,000
   (f) Rights-on price: $40
   (g) Ex-rights price: $30
   (h) Price of a right: $10

CHAPTER 16

1. (a) A, e; B, d; C, c; D, a; E, b
   (b) June 1 = ex-dividend date
   (c) (4 × 0.25)/36 = 0.028 or 2.8%
   (d) 1/4 = 0.25 or 25%
   (e) $3.60 or 10%

2. c, d, and e are false

3. (a) True
   (b) False (Managers prefer a smooth progression of dividends and move only partway to the dividend target.)
   (c) True
   (d) False (If earnings are expected to decline again, managers are less likely to increase dividends.)

4. (a) 0.35 or 35%
   (b) 0.77 or 77%

5. (a) Under MM's theory, the freeze should make no difference. Firms will have higher retained earnings and will either reduce the volume of new stock issues, repurchase more stock, or simply invest any extra cash in marketable securities. In any case, what investors lose in cash dividends is made up in capital gains.
   (b) If firms keep their investment decisions separate from their dividend and financing decisions, then the freeze will have no effect on real investment. If the freeze restricts dividends, the firm can repurchase shares or "park" excess cash in marketable securities, possibly the shares of other firms.

   Some economists believe that firms do not separate investment from dividend and financing decisions, but look less critically at investments which can be financed from internal funds. In this case a dividend freeze could lead to increased real investment. (Of course if this investment is in negative-NPV projects, share prices will fall, but that would not disprove the MM argument. Prices would not fall because

of forgone dividend increases, but because of the negative-NPV investments.)

6. A dividend increase signals management's optimism about future earnings (the company is putting its money where its mouth is).

7. (a) (i) Lo, (ii) Lo
   (b) (i) Lo, (ii) Hi
   (c) Indifferent
   (d) Hi (dividends are untaxed, but capital gains are taxed as regular income)

8. (a) $10
   (b) $9
   (c) $9/0.85 = $10.59. (An investor who buys with-dividend and sells immediately ex-dividend receives the ex-price + $9 after-tax income + a tax loss worth 0.15 × (with-dividend price − ex-dividend price). Therefore, in equilibrium, the with-dividend price = ex-dividend price + $9 + 0.15 × (with-dividend price − ex-dividend price).

9. The implicit corporate tax rate T_c solves $\dfrac{1}{1 - T_c} = 1 + 1/3$ so that $T_c = 25\%$. The provincial tax rate T_{prov} solves $T_c = (0.2)(1 + T_{prov})$ so that $T_{prov} = 25\%$.

CHAPTER 17

1. (a) 0.10P
   (b) Buy 10% of B's debt + 10% of B's equity
   (c) $0.10(P - 100)$
   (d) Borrow an amount equal to 10% of B's debt and buy 10% of A's equity.

2. Note the market value of Copperhead is far in excess of its book value:

	Market Value
Common stock (8 million shares at $2)	$16,000,000
Short-term loans	$2,000,000

Ms. Kraft owns 0.625% of the firm, which proposes to increase common stock to $17 million and cut short-term debt. Ms. Kraft can offset this by (a) borrowing $0.00625 \times 1,000,000 = \$6250$, and (b) buying that much more Copperhead stock.

3. Expected return on assets is
$$r_A = 0.08 \times 30/80 + 0.16 \times 50/80 = 0.13$$
The new return on equity will be
$$r_E = 0.13 + 20/60\,(0.13 - 0.08) = 0.147$$
If stockholders pass on more of the firm risk to debtholders, expected return on equity will be *less* than 14.7%.

4. (a) (i) $\beta_A = \left(\dfrac{D}{D + E} \times \beta_D\right)$
$$+ \left(\dfrac{E}{D + E} \times \beta_E\right)$$
$$1.0 = (0.5 \times 0)$$
$$+ (0.5 \times \beta_E)$$
$$\therefore \beta_E = 2.0$$
   (ii) $\beta_D = 0$
   (iii) $\beta_A = 1.0$

(b) (i) 0.10
   (ii) $r_A = \left(\dfrac{D}{D + E} \times r_D\right)$
$$+ \left(\dfrac{E}{D + E} \times r_E\right)$$
$$0.10 = (0.5 \times 0.05)$$
$$+ (0.5 \times r_E)$$
$$r_E = 0.15$$
   (iii) $r_D = 0.05$
   (iv) $r_A = 0.10$

(c) (i) 50%
   (ii) 6.7 (i.e., the P/E ratio falls to offset the increase in EPS).

5. (a)

Operating income, dollars	500	1,000	1,500	2,000
Interest, dollars	250	250	250	250
Equity earnings, dollars	250	750	1,250	1,750
Earnings per share	0.33	1.00	1.67	2.33
Return on shares, %	3.3	10	16.7	23.3

(b) $\beta_A = \left(\dfrac{D}{D + E} \times \beta_D\right)$
$$+ \left(\dfrac{E}{D + E} \times \beta_E\right)$$
$$0.8 = (0.25 \times 0)$$
$$+ (0.75 \times \beta_E)$$
$$\beta_E = 1.07$$

6. (a) True, so long as the market value of "old" debt does not change.
(b) False. MM's Proposition I says only that overall firm value ($V = D + E$) does not depend on capital structure.
(c) False. Borrowing increases equity risk even if debt is default-risk free.

(d) False. Limited liability affects the relative values of debt and equity, not their sum.
(e) True. Limited liability protects shareholders if the firm defaults.
(f) True—but the required rate of return on equity and the firm's assets are the same only if the firm holds risk-free assets. In this case, r_A, r_D, and r_E all equal the risk-free rate of interest.
(g) False. The shareholders could make the same debt issue on their own account.
(h) True. To put it more precisely, it assumes that the expected

rate of return to equity goes up, but stockholders' required rate of return goes up proportionately. Therefore, stock price is unchanged.

(i) False. The formula $r_E = r_A + D/E(r_A - r_D)$ does not require r_D = a constant.

(j) False. The clientele has to be willing to pay extra for the debt, which they will not do if plenty of corporate debt issues are already available.

CHAPTER 18

1. (a) PV tax shield
$$= \frac{T_C(r_D D)}{1 + r_D}$$
$$- \frac{0.36(0.08 \times 1,000)}{1.08}$$
$$= \$26.67$$

(b) PV tax shield
$$= \sum_{t=1}^{5} \frac{T_C(r_D D)}{(1 + r_D)^t}$$
$$= \sum_{t=1}^{5} \frac{0.36(0.08 \times 1,000)}{(1.08)^t}$$
$$= \$114.99$$

(c) PV tax shield $= T_C D = \$360$

2. (a) PV tax shield $= T_C D = \$16$

(b) $T_C \times 20 = \$8$

(c) New PV tax shield
$$= \sum_{t=1}^{5} \frac{0.40(0.08 \times 60)}{(1.08)^t}$$
$$= \$7.67$$

Therefore, company value $= 168 - 24 + 7.67 = \$151.67$

3. (a)

	Equity	Debt
corporate tax	0.36	0
personal income tax	0	$0.36 \times 1.5 = 0.54$
dividend tax	$0.5(1.25)(1.5)\left(0.36 - \frac{2}{15}\right) = 0.2125$	0
capital gains	$(0.5)(0.75)(1.5)(0.36) = 0.2025$	0
	$\$0.775$	$\$0.54$

5.

Table 4

Case	(1) Corporate Tax	(2) Cash Flow to Investor	(3) Federal Personal Tax	(4) Provincial Personal Tax	(5) Net Cash Flow (2 − 3 − 4)
a (bond)	0	1,000	0	0	1,000
a (equity)	360	640	− 106.67	− 53.33	800
b, c (bond)	0	1,000	170	85	745
b (equity)	360	640	0	0	596
c, d (equity)	360	640	0	0	640
d, e (bond)	0	1,000	260	130	610
e (equity)	360	640	101.33	50.67	488
f, g (bond)	0	1,000	290	145	565
f (equity)	360	640	125.33	62.67	452
g (equity)	360	640	139.20	69.60	431.20

Bond income is preferred in cases a, b, c, e, f, g and equity income is preferred in case d.

3. (b) Total tax on equity = $0.5275 per dollar of gross income. Tax on debt remains at $0.54.

4. (a) Aggregate supply of debt falls. Only investors with tax rates below 24% will now prefer debt.
   (b) Once new equilibrium is established, no single firm can gain an advantage by changing its capital structure.

6. A firm with no taxable income saves no taxes by borrowing and paying interest. The interest payments would simply add to its tax-loss carry-forwards. Such a firm would have little tax incentive to borrow.

7. (a) Stockholders win. Bond value falls, since the value of assets securing the bond has fallen.
   (b) Bondholder wins if we assume the cash is left invested in Treasury bills. The bondholder is sure to get $26 plus interest. Stock value is zero, because there is no chance that firm value can rise above $50.
   (c) The bondholders lose. The firm adds assets worth $10 and debt worth $10. This would increase Circular's debt ratio, leaving the old bondholders more exposed. The old bondholders' loss is the stockholders' gain.
   (d) Both bondholders and stockholders win. They share the (net) increase in firm value. The bondholders' position is not eroded by the issue of a junior security. (We assume that the preferred does not lead to still more game playing, and that the new investment does not make the firm's *assets* safer or riskier.)
   (e) Bondholders lose because they are at risk for longer. Stockholders win.

8. Specialized, intangible assets such as growth opportunities are most likely to lose value in financial distress. Safe, tangible assets with good secondhand markets are least likely to lose value. Costs of financial distress are thus likely to be less for, say, real estate firms or trucking companies than for advertising firms or high-tech growth companies.

9. More profitable firms have more taxable income to shield and are less likely to incur the costs of distress. Therefore the trade-off theory predicts high debt ratios. In practice the more profitable companies borrow least.

10. Firms have a pecking order of preference for new finance. Internal finance is preferred, followed by debt and then external equity. Each firm's observed debt ratio reflects its cumulative requirements for external finance. The more profitable companies borrow least because they have sufficient internal finance.

CHAPTER 19

1. APV = base − case NPV ± PV financing side effects
   (a) APV = 0 − 0.15(500,000)
       = −75,000
   (b) APV = 0 + 175,000
       = +175,000
   (c) APV = 0 + 76,000
       = +76,000
   (d) APV = 0 − 0.15(500,000)
       + 76,000
       = +1,000

2. PV tax shield = (0.10/0.36)
   × 592,000 = 164,400.
   APV = +170,000 + 144,000
   = 314,000.

3. APV = base case NPV + PV tax shield $= \dfrac{C_1}{1+r} - I +$

$\dfrac{r_D LT^* (APV + I)}{1 + r_D}$,

where I = investment

$= \dfrac{1{,}200}{1.20} - 1{,}000 +$

$\dfrac{0.10 \times 0.30 \times 0.20(APV + 1{,}000)}{1.1}$

APV $= +5.48$

4. (a) $r^* = r(1 - T^*L)$
   $= 0.20(1 - 0.20 \times 0.30)$
   $= 0.188$

   (b) $r^* = r - L r_D T^* \left(\dfrac{1+r}{1+r_D}\right)$

   $= 0.20 - 0.30 \times 0.10$

   $\times 0.20 \left(\dfrac{1.2}{1.1}\right)$

   $= 0.1935$

   (c) NPV (@ $r^* = 0.188$)

   $= \dfrac{1{,}200}{1.188} - 1{,}000$

   $= +10.10$

   NPV (@ $r^* = 0.1935$)

   $= \dfrac{1{,}200}{1.1935} - 1{,}000$

   $= +5.48$

   Note: The Miles-Ezzell formula gives the correct NPV for a company that borrows 30% of project *value*, i.e., initial investment plus PV tax shield. To check this, we recalculate APV as follows:

   APV = base-case NPV
   + PV tax shield

   $= 0 + \dfrac{0.1 \times 0.2 \times 0.3 \,(1{,}005.48)}{1.10}$

   $= +5.48$

5. $D = 75 \times 0.9 = \$67.5$ million
   $E = 42 \times 2.5 = \$105$ million
   $V = D + E = \$172.5$ million
   $r^* = (1 - T_C) r_D \, D/V + r_E \, E/V$
   $= (1 - 0.23)0.16(67.5/172.5)$
   $+ 0.25(105/172.5)$
   $= 0.20$ or 20%

6. MM: $r^* = 0.20(1 - 0.25 \times 0.40)$
   $= 0.180$
   Miles-Ezzell:
   $r^* = 0.20 - 0.4 \times 0.09$
   $\times 0.25 \times 1.20/1.09$
   $= 0.190$
   Sick: $r^* = 0.20 - 0.4 \times 0.08$
   $\times 0.25 \times 1.20/1.06$
   $= 0.191$

7. No. The more debt you use, the higher rate of return equity investors will require. (Lenders may demand more also.) Thus there is a hidden cost of the "cheap" debt: It makes equity more expensive.

8. PV lease
   $= \displaystyle\sum_{t=0}^{5} \dfrac{(1 - 0.36)\,100{,}000}{[1 + (1 - 0.36)0.09]^t}$
   $= \$335{,}361$

CHAPTER 20

1. Call; exercise; put; exercise; European; call; assets; bondholders (lenders); assets; promised payment to bondholders.

2. (a) Call
   (b) Put
   (c) Call
   (d) Call
   (e) Put
   (f) Call
   (g) Call
   (h) Put

3. Figure 20-11(a) represents a call seller; Figure 20-11(b) represents a call buyer.

4. (a) The exercise price of the put option (i.e., you'd sell stock for the exercise price).
   (b) The value of the stock (i.e., you would throw away the put and keep the stock).

5. Buy a call and lend the present value of the exercise price.

6. The lower bound is the option's value if it expired immediately:

either zero or the stock price less the exercise price, whichever is larger. The upper bound is the stock price.

7. (a) Zero
   (b) Stock price less the present value of the exercise price.

8. The call price
   (a) Increases
   (b) Decreases
   (c) Increases
   (d) Increases
   (e) Decreases
   (f) Decreases

9. True. The beta and standard deviation of an option always exceeds its stock's. The risk of an option decreases as the stockprice increases.
   First, estimating expected cash flows from an option is difficult, although not impossible. Second, the risk of an option changes every time the stock price changes, so there is no single, well-defined risk-adjusted discount rate.

10. With an exercise price of 60,
    $\sigma \times \sqrt{t} = 0.06 \times \sqrt{3} = 0.10$
    $P/PV(EX) = 60/(60/1.03) = 1.03$
    (a) Call price = approximately
    $$0.056 \times 60$$
    $$= 3.4$$
    Put price = call price
    $$+ PV(EX)$$
    $$- \text{stock price}$$
    $$= 3.4 + 58.23$$
    $$- 60$$
    $$= 1.6 \text{ (approx.)}$$
    (b) From Appendix Table 7 call option delta = 0.6. Thus replicating portfolio is 0.6 shares (cost = $0.6 \times 60 =$ $36) and borrow balance (36 − 3.4 = $32.6).
    Put option delta = 0.6 − 1 = −0.4. Replicating portfolio is *sell* 0.4 shares (cash inflow = $0.4 \times 60 = \$24$) and lend balance (24 + 1.6 = $25.6).

11. (a)

Payoffs	Stock Price = \$50	Stock Price = \$200
A. 1 call	\$ 0	\$ 90
B. 1 share	\$50	\$200
borrow		
PV (50)	− 50	− 50
	\$ 0	\$150

Value of 1.67 calls
= share price − loan
∴ Value of 1 call
$$= \frac{100 - 45.45}{1.67} = \$32.73$$

(b) $p(100) + (1 - p)(-50)$
$$= 10$$
$$\therefore p = 0.4$$
Value of call
$$= \frac{(0.4 \times 90) + (0.6 \times 0)}{1.10}$$
$$= \$32.73$$
Wider range of stock prices does not increase loss to option holder if stock price falls, but it does increase gain if stock price rises.

CHAPTER 21

1. (a) Backwoods has an in-the-money call option on expansion.
   (b) Project provides call option on further projects.
   (c) Standard equipment contains valuable abandonment (put) option.

2. (a) Using risk-neutral method
   $(p \times 20) + (1 - p)(-16.7)$
   $$= 1$$
   $$p = 0.48$$
   Value of call
   $$= \frac{(0.48 \times 8) + (0.52 \times 0)}{1.01}$$
   $$= 3.8$$
   (b) Delta
   $$= \frac{\text{spread of option prices}}{\text{spread of stock prices}}$$
   $$= \frac{8}{14.7} = 0.544$$

(c)

	Current Cash Flow	Possible Future Cash Flows	
Buy call *equals*	−3.8	0	+8.0
Buy 0.544 shares	−21.8	+18.2	+26.2
Borrow 18.0	+18.0	−18.2	−18.2
	−3.8	0	+8.0

(d) Possible stock prices with call option prices in brackets:

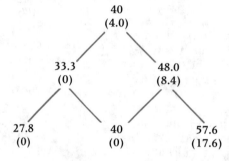

Option prices were calculated as follows:

Month 1:

(i) $\dfrac{(0.48 \times 0) + (0.52 \times 0)}{1.01}$

   $= 0$

(ii) $\dfrac{(0.48 \times 17.6) + (0.52 \times 0)}{1.01}$

   $= 8.4$

Month 0:

$\dfrac{(0.48 \times 8.4) + (0.52 \times 0)}{1.01}$

   $= 4.0$

(e) Delta

$= \dfrac{\text{spread of option prices}}{\text{spread of stock prices}}$

$= \dfrac{8.4}{14.7} = 0.57$

3. The period to expiration is subdivided into an indefinitely large number of subperiods (and when there is no incentive to early exercise).

4. (a) Yes (earn interest on exercise money)

(b) No (dividend gain is less than loss of interest)

(c) Yes (if the dividend becomes sufficiently larger than loss of interest to justify killing the option)

5. (a) $(p \times 15) + (1 - p)(-13)$
   $= 10$
   $p = 0.82$
   Put value if exercised now =
   EX − 60
   Put value if not exercised now =
   $\dfrac{(0.82 \times 0) + 0.18(\text{EX} - 52.2)}{1.1}$
   ∴ You are indifferent if EX
   $= 61.5$

(b) Higher interest rate reduces break-even exercise price (i.e., the benefit of the higher interest rate offsets the disadvantage of the lower exercise price).

6. (i) Keep gold stocks and buy put option with exercise "price" of £500,000.

(ii) Sell gold stocks, invest £472,000 in 6-month time deposit, and use balance of £128,000 to buy call option on gold stocks with exercise price of £500,000.

CHAPTER 22

1. (a) (i) 0
   (ii) 0
   (iii) 0
   (iv) $10
   (v) $20

(b)
Theoretical
value of warrant
(coloured line)

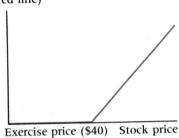

Exercise price ($40)   Stock price

(c) Buy the warrant and exercise, then sell the stock.
Net gain = −5 − 40 + 60
= +$15.

2. (a) No
(b) No
(c) 1/5 × $25 = $5
(d) No
(e) No
(f) No
(g) (i) less; (ii) less; (iii) more; (iv) more; (v) more
(h) When the share price is no longer less than the warrant price plus the exercise price.

This will occur when the dividends on the stock outweigh the interest on the exercise price.

3. (a) EPS = $2.00
(b) Diluted EPS = $1.33

4. (a) 1,000/47 = 21.28
(b) 1,000/50 = $20.00
(c) 21.28 × 41.50 = $883.12, or 88.31%
(d) 650/21.28 = $30.55
(e) No (not if the investor is free to convert immediately)
(f) $12.22, i.e., (910 − 650)/ 21.28
(g) (47/41.50) − 1 = 0.13, or 13%
(h) When the price reaches 102.75

CHAPTER 23

1. (a) Figure 4 shows that an increase in the demand for capital increases investment and savings. The rate of interest also rises.

Percent

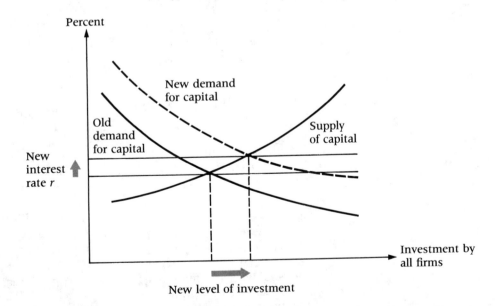

New demand
for capital

Old
demand
for capital

Supply
of capital

New
interest
rate *r*

Investment by
all firms

New level of investment

Figure 4   Chapter 23, Quiz question 1 (a).

Percent

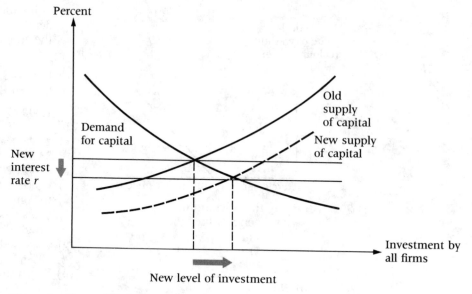

Figure 5   Chapter 23, Quiz question 1 (b).

(b) Figure 5 shows that an increase in the supply of capital also increases investment and savings. The rate of interest falls.

2. (a) $PV = \dfrac{50}{1 + r_1} + \dfrac{1{,}050}{(1 + r_2)^2}$

   (b) $PV = \dfrac{50}{1 + y} + \dfrac{1{,}050}{(1 + y)^2}$

   (c) Less (it is between the one-year and two-year spot rates)

   (d) Yield to maturity; spot rate

3. (a) Fall

   (b) Less than 100

   (c) Less than the coupon

   (d) Higher prices, other things equal

4. (a) 12%

   (b) 70.88

   (c) We know the bond is worth 71.33 now, and will be worth 73.51 after two years, when the bond will have ten years to maturity. Interpolating, the price six months from now should be approximately 71.88. Total return is

$$\frac{71.88 - 71.33 + 4.5}{71} = 0.071$$

or 7.1%

5. (a) $(1 + r_2)^2 = (1 + r_1)(1 + f_2)$
       $1.03^2 = 1.01 \times (1 + f_2)$
       $f_2 = 0.05$, or 5%

   (b) The expected one-year spot rate at time 1, $E({}_1r_2)$, equals the forward rate f_2.

   (c) Against (unless one believes that investors have generally expected interest rates to rise).

   (d) The forward rate equals the expected spot rate *plus* a liquidity premium.

   (e) Long-term bonds.

   (f) Short-term bonds.

   (g) The forward rate equals the expected spot rate plus a premium for the inflation risk.

6. (a) A + +, A +, A, and B + +

   (b) (i) Increase

       (ii) Increase

       (iii) Increase (that is, value of default-free bond decreases; also, value of default option decreases)

       (iv) Increase

7. (a) Value of guarantee = value of put (that is, shareholders' option to put the company to the bondholders for the face value of the bond)
   (b) Put option; exercise price is face value of bond.

CHAPTER 24

1. (a) High-grade utility bonds
   (b) Short-dated notes
   (c) Industrial holding companies
   (d) Industrial bonds
   (e) Railroads

2. (a) Noncallable bonds (callable bonds neither rise nor fall as much in price).
   (b) They will disappear (each side should exercise its option at 100).

3. Sinking fund c (an optional sinking fund reduces bond value; a sinking fund that gives the firm the option to purchase in the market may decrease bond value).

4. (a) You would like an issue of junior debt.
   (b) You prefer it not to do so (unless it is also junior debt). The existing property may not be sufficient to pay off your debt.

5. (a) Wood Gundy Inc.
   (b) Montreal Trust Company of Canada
   (c) 98.85% of face value
   (d) Bearer
   (e) 4%
   (f) 105.60 on or before November 15th; 104.90 after
   (g) No

6. (a) 100 plus 2/6 of 6.35 = 102.12
   (b) May 1985; 6.35%
   (c) November 15, 2004; 32% of the initial issue
   (d) It should call all bonds in just after November 15, 2000.

CHAPTER 25

1. (a) True
   (b) True
   (c) False (depends on coupon)
   (d) False
   (e) False
   (f) False
   (g) True

2. See short $1.2 million of the market portfolio. In practice rather than "sell the market" you would sell futures on $1.2 million of the market index.

3.

	Year	C_t	$PV(C_t)$	Proportion of Total Value	Proportion × Time
Security A	1	40	37.04	0.359	0.359
	2	40	34.29	0.333	0.666
	3	40	31.75	0.308	0.924
		V =	103.08	1.0	
					Duration = 1.949 years
Security B	1	20	18.52	0.141	0.141
	2	20	17.15	0.131	0.262
	3	120	95.26	0.728	2.184
		V =	130.93	1.0	
					Duration = 2.587 years
Security C	1	10	9.26	0.088	0.088
	2	10	8.57	0.082	0.164
	3	110	87.32	0.830	2.490
		V =	105.15	1.0	
					Duration = 2.742 years

Volatilities: A, 1.80; B, 2.40; C, 2.49.

4. Buy $\dfrac{100 \times 3}{1.949}$ = \$154 of security

A (i.e., $\dfrac{154}{103.08}$ = 1.49 units)

or $\dfrac{100 \times 3}{2.587}$ = \$116 of security B

(i.e., $\dfrac{116}{130.93}$ = 0.89 units)

or $\dfrac{100 \times 3}{2.742}$ = \$109 of security C

(i.e., $\dfrac{109}{105.15}$ = 1.04 units)

N.B. (i) To create a zero-value hedge, balance position with short-term borrowing (i.e., duration of zero). For example, if you buy security A, you would need to borrow PV(A) − PV(liability)

$$= 154 - \dfrac{100}{1.08^3} = \$75 \text{ to}$$

create zero-value hedge.

(ii) To retain hedge, investments should be adjusted as time passes or interest rates change.

5. $\dfrac{\text{Value of future}}{1.049}$ = 95 − 4

∴ Value of future = 95.46

6. $\dfrac{2,408}{1.12}$ = 2,550 + 110 − PV (convenience yield)

∴ PV (convenience yield) = \$500

7. (i) A promise to make a series of payments in one currency in exchange for receiving a series of payments in another currency.

(ii) A promise to make a series of fixed-rate payments in exchange for receiving a series of floating-rate payments (or vice versa). Also exchange of floating-rate payments linked to different reference rates (e.g., LIBOR and commercial paper rate).

Swaps may be used because a company believes it has an advantage in borrowing in a particular market or in order to change structure of existing liabilities.

CHAPTER 26

1. A, C; B, D or I; C, B or E; D, F; E, A; F, H; G, G

2. a, b, d, f, and h (though there may be other ways to reduce AMT).

3. (a) True
   (b) True
   (c) True
   (d) True
   (e) True
   (f) True
   (g) True

4. (a) \$60,442, the present value of the lease cash flows from $t = 1$ to $t = 3$, discounted at $r(1 - T_c) = 0.10(1 - 0.46) = 0.054$.
   (b) \$62,000 − 60,442 = 1,558.
   (c) It should not invest. The lease's value of +1,558 does not offset the machine's negative NPV. It would be happy to sign the same lease on a more attractive asset.

CHAPTER 27

1. (a) 0.22
   (b) 1.39
   (c) 0.36
   (d) 0.07
   (e) 4.37
   (f) 0.18
   (g) 0.23

2. The illogical ratios are a, b, c, f, and i. The correct definitions are:

$$\text{Debt-equity ratio} = \frac{\text{long-term debt} + \text{value of leases}}{\text{equity}}$$

$$\text{Return on equity} = \frac{\text{earnings available for common}}{\text{average equity}}$$

$$\frac{\text{Payout}}{\text{ratio}} = \frac{\text{dividend}}{\text{earnings per share}}$$

$$\frac{\text{Current}}{\text{ratio}} = \frac{\text{current assets}}{\text{current liabilities}}$$

$$\frac{\text{Average}}{\text{collection}} = \frac{\text{sales}}{\text{average receivables} \div 365}$$
$$\text{period}$$

3. (a) False
   (b) True
   (c) False
   (d) False
   (e) True (as a general rule)
   (f) True
   (g) False
   (h) False
   (i) False—it will tend to increase the price-earnings multiple.

4. (a) Shipping company
   (b) United Foods
   (c) Paper mill
   (d) Mail order company
   (e) Fledgling Electronics
   (f) Pharmaceutical company

CHAPTER 28

1. (a) False (it is a process of deciding which risks to take).
   (b) False (financial planning is concerned with possible surprises as well as expected outcomes).
   (c) True (financial planning considers both the investment and financing decisions).
   (d) False (a typical horizon for long-term planning is five years).
   (e) True (investments are usually broken down by category).

(f) True (perfect accuracy is unlikely to be obtainable, but the firm needs to produce the best possible consistent forecasts).
(g) False (excessive detail distracts attention from the crucial decisions).

2. Pro forma financial statements (balance sheets, income statements, and sources and uses of cash); description of planned capital expenditure, and a summary of planned financing.

3. Most financial models are designed to forecast acccounting statements. They do not focus on the factors that directly determine firm value, such as incremental cash flow or risk.

CHAPTER 29

1. See Table 2, below.

2. Month 3: 18 + (0.5 × 90) + (0.3 × 120) + (0.2 × 100) = $119,000
   Month 4: 14 + (0.5 × 70) + (0.3 × 90) + (0.2 × 120) = $100,000

Table 2
Chapter 29, Quiz question 1.

	Cash	Working Capital
1.	$2 million decline	$2 million decline
2.	$2,500 increase	Unchanged
3.	$5,000 decline	Unchanged
4.	Unchanged	$1 million increase
5.	Unchanged	Unchanged
6.	$5 million increase	Unchanged

3. (a) Long-term financing, cumu-lative capital requirement, marketable securities
   (b) Cash, cash, cash balance, marketable securities
   (c) Trial, error, financial models

4. (a) Inventories go up (use).
   (b) Accounts receivable go up (use).
   (c) No change shown on the firm's books.
   (d) Decrease in assets (source).
   (e) Net worth declines (use).
   (f) Retained earnings fall (use).
   (g) Long-term debt increases (source), short-term debt falls (use).

CHAPTER 30

1. (a) 1% of $1000 = $10
   (b) 1% for 30 days = 12% per annum simple interest or 12.7% compound interest.
   (c) (i) Shorter
      (ii) Longer
      (iii) Shorter

2. (a) Due lag decreases, therefore pay lag decreases.
   (b) Due lag increases, therefore pay lag increases.
   (c) Terms lag increases, therefore pay lag increases.

3. Open account, promissory note, commercial draft, shipping documents, trade acceptance, the customer's, bankers' acceptance, letter of credit, the customer's, his or her own, letter of credit, shipping documents, shipping documents

4. Reject becaue PV of Q's order
$$= \frac{0.75 \times 50}{1.10^{1/2}} - 40$$
$$= -\$4.25 \text{ per iron, or } -\$4,250 \text{ in total}$$

5. (a) Expected profit =
$$p(1,200 - 1,050) - 1,050$$
$$(1 - p) = 0$$
$$p = 0.875$$

Therefore, grant credit if probability of payment exceeds 87.5%.

   (b) Expected profit from selling to slow payer: $0.8(150) - 0.2(1,050) = -90$. Break-even point for credit check: $(0.05 \times 90 \times \text{units}) - 12 = 0$. Units $= 2.67$.

6. Total expected profit on initial order = $-40 +$
$$\frac{0.8[(p_2 \times 200) - 1,000(1 - p_2)]}{1.2}$$
$$= 0$$
$$p_2 = 0.88, \text{ or } 88\%$$

7. (a) False
   (b) True
   (c) False
   (d) False—should be collection agency or attorney.
   (e) True

8. (a) True
   (b) False
   (c) False
   (d) True
   (e) False. Tax loss carry-forwards are extinguished by liquidation.

CHAPTER 31

1. (a) Carrying cost per book/2 = $1
   (b) $(200 \times 2)/Q^2 = 1$
      $Q = \sqrt{400} = 20$ books
   (c) $200/20 = 10$ orders
   (d) $Q/2 = 10$ books.

2. (a) Carrying cost/2 = $0.01
   (b) $(20,000 \times 2)/Q^2 = \$0.01$
      $Q = \sqrt{4,000,000} = \$2,000$
   (c) $20,000/2,000 = 10$ orders
   (d) $Q/2 = \$1,000$

3. (a) Interest rate, cost of each transaction, and variability of cash balance.
   (b) It should restore it to one-third of the distance between the lower and upper limits.

(c) By holding a lower cash balance, the firm increases the transaction frequency but earns more interest.

4. (a) Less
   (b) Less
   (c) Invest the same amount
   (d) More

5. (a) Payment float = $25,000. Availability float = $75,000
   (b) It can earn interest on these funds.
   (c) Payment float increases. The bank's gross ledger balance and available balance increase by the same amount.

6. (a) The $0.40 per cheque fee is cheaper at 300 × 0.40 = $120 per day. The cost of putting up $800,000 of compensating balances is 0.09 × 800,000 = $72,000 per year, or 72,000/365 = $197 per day.
   (b) The lock-box system costs $120 per day, or $43,800 per year. You would need $487,000 additional cash to generate this much interest. Thus, the lock-box system must generate at least this much cash. The cash flow is 300 × 1,500 = $450,000 per day. Thus the lock box must speed up average collection time by 487,000/450,000 = 1.08 days.

7. Because the bank can forecast early in the day how much money will be paid out, the company does not need to keep extra cash in the account to cover contingencies. Also, since zero-balance accounts are not held in a major banking centre, the company gains several days of additional float.

8. Payment float; availability float; net float; concentration banking; wire transfer; depository transfer cheque; lock-box banking.

CHAPTER 32

1. (a) Repurchase agreements
   (b) Swapped deposits
   (c) Certificates of deposit
   (d) Treasury bills
   (e) Treasury bills
   (f) Banker's acceptances
   (g) Treasury bills

2. (a) $97.71
   (b) 9.75%
   (c) 9.16%

3. Line of credit; clean-up provision; prime rate; compensating balance; commercial paper; floating lien; collateral; with recourse; public warehouse; field warehouse; warehouse receipt; trust receipt; floor planning

4. None of the floating-rate preferred dividend is taxed versus 100% of bond interest. The fixed-dividend preferred shares this tax advantage but its price fluctuates more than the floating rate preferred's.

CHAPTER 33

1. (a) Horizontal
   (b) Conglomerate
   (c) Vertical
   (d) Conglomerate

2. (a) $5 million (We assume that the $500,000 saving is an after-tax figure.)
   (b) $4 million
   (c) $7.5 million
   (d) +$1 million
   (e) −$2.5 million

3. a, b, d

4. (a) True
   (b) False
   (c) False
   (d) True

(e) False (They may produce gains, but "substantial" is stretching it.)

(f) False

(g) True (assuming that the purchase price exceeds the value of the tangible assets acquired)

(h) False

(i) True

5. a and d; c can also make sense, although merging is not the only way to redeploy excess cash.

6. • LBO—buyout by private investors

 • Master limited partnership—partnership "units" traded

 • Poison pill—shareholders issued rights . . .

 • Tender offer—offer to buy shares directly from stockholders

 • Greenmail—target buys out shareholders threatening takeover

 • Golden parachute—payment to target firm's managers

 • Proxy fight—attempt to gain control by winning stockholders' votes

CHAPTER 34

1. (a) 2.0052 $/£

 (b) 1.9856 $/£

 (c) Premium (so the pound is at a *discount* on the Canadian dollar)

 (d) $2 \times \dfrac{1.9856 - 2.0052}{2.0052} =$
 -0.020 or a discount of 2%.

(e) $\dfrac{(1 + r_\$)^{1/2}}{(1 + r_£)^{1/2}} = \dfrac{f_{\$/£}}{S_{\$/£}}$

 $\dfrac{(1.10875)^{1/2}}{(1 + r_£)^{1/2}} = \dfrac{1.9856}{2.0052}$

 $r_£ = 13.1\%$

(f) 1.9856 $/£

(g) $\dfrac{E(1 + i_\$)}{E(1 + i_£)} = \dfrac{f_{\$/£}}{S_{\$/£}} = \dfrac{1.9856}{2.0052}$
 $= 0.9902.$

 That is, the 6-month inflation in Britain is expected to be 1% higher than that in Canada.

2. (a) The interest rate differential equals the forward premium or discount, i.e.,

 $\dfrac{1 + r_\$}{1 + r_{ItL}} = \dfrac{f_{\$/ItL}}{S_{\$/ItL}}.$

 (b) The expected change in the spot rate equals the forward premium or discount, i.e.,

 $\dfrac{E(S_{\$/ItL})}{S_{\$/ItL}} = \dfrac{f_{\$/ItL}}{S_{\$/ItL}}.$

 (c) Prices of goods in different countries are equal when measured in terms of the same currency. It follows that the expected change in the spot rate equals the expected inflation differential, i.e.,

 $\dfrac{E(S_{\$/ItL})}{S_{\$/ItL}} = \dfrac{E(1 + i_\$)}{E(1 + i_{ItL})}.$

 (d) Expected real interest rates in different countries are equal. i.e.,

 $\dfrac{1 + r_\$}{1 + r_{ItL}} = \dfrac{E(1 + i_\$)}{E(1 + i_{ItL})}.$

4. (b)

5. Zero of course. You don't need to do any calculations.

3.

	3 Months	6 Months	1 Year
Eurodollar interest rate (%)	11.5	12.25	12.5
Eurofranc interest rate (%)	19.5	19.7	20
Forward francs per dollar	7.17	7.28	7.52
Forward discount on franc, percent per year	− 6.7	− 6.3	− 6.3

Note: Spot dollars per franc = 1/7.0500 − 0.1418

6. It can borrow the present value of 1 million DM, sell the Deutschemarks in the spot market, and invest the proceeds in an 8-year dollar loan.

7. (a) Foreign inflation rates to produce cash-flow forecasts
Future exchange rates to convert cash flows into domestic currency

Domestic interest rate to discount domestic currency cash flows

(b) Foreign inflation rates to produce cash-flow forecasts
Foreign interest rate to discount foreign currency cash flows

8. (a)

Country	X	Y
Profits before tax	100.00	100.00
Foreign income tax	50.00	20.00
Net foreign profits	50.00	80.00
Withholding tax	15% of 50 = 7.50	15% of 80 = 12.00
Received in Canada	42.50	78.00
Canadian tax payable	0.00	0.00
Available for dividend	42.50	78.00

(b)

Country	X	Y
Profits before tax	100.00	100.00
Management fee	100.00	100.00
Net foreign profits	0.00	0.00
Withholding tax	15.00	15.00
Fee received in Canada	85.00	85.00
Canadian tax payable	32.30	32.30
Available for dividend	52.70	52.70

CHAPTER 35

1. (a) True
   (b) False
   (c) True
   (d) True
   (e) True, although "final salary" may mean an average over the last few years before retirement.
   (f) True

2. (a) See Table 5.

(b) The published balance sheet would show $1,000 million less cash. The augmented balance sheet would show this fall in cash, but an offsetting increase in the pension fund.

(c) The published balance sheet would not change. In the augmented balance sheet, the pension fund and equity would both fall by $2,000 million.

Table 5

Current assets	$10,770	Current liabilities	$ 9,940
Pension fund	6,830	Debt and other liabilities	5,719
Plant, equipment		Pension liabilities	6,830
and other assets	12,844	Equity	7,362
Total assets	$29,851	Total liabilities	$29,851

3. (a) Pension fund
   (b) Expected benefits for past service
   (c) Expected future service costs
   (d) Future normal costs
   (e) Expected benefits (that is, total liabilities)
   (f) Deficit

4. (a) Pension fund = investments held in trust for plan members
   Future normal costs = contributions to cover future service
   Unamortized experience losses = losses that result from difference between expectations and experience
   Unamortized supplemental liabilities = liability from improved pension benefits
   Losses from changes in actuarial assumptions = for example, effect of change in assumed discount rate
   Vested accrued benefits = benefits that would need to be paid if employees left firm immediately
   Unvested accrued benefits = benefits that have accrued but will be paid only if employment continues
   Expected future service costs = expected benefits to be paid for future service
   (i) $540 - 720 = -\$180$ million (that is, vested benefits are fully funded)
   (ii) $760 - 720 = \$40$ million
   (iii) $720/760 = 0.95$
   (iv) $720/540 = 1.33$

   (c) (i) Pension fund = 670
       Experience losses = 140
       (ii) Supplemental liabilities = 180
       Total assets = 1,740

5. Greater

6. (a) $r - r_f = 6\%$
   (b) $(r - r_f) - \beta(r_m - r_f) = 3\%$
   (c) $(r - r_f) - (\sigma/\sigma_m)(r_m - r_f) = 2\%$

7. (a) 80%
   (b) 72.5%
   (c) The time-weighted rate of return would not change.
   (d) The dollar-weighted rate of return would decrease.

INDEX

accounting. *See* Accounting
rate of return
book. *See* Book rate of return
debt policy and, on levered
equity, 439-41
discounted cash flow as
internal. *See* Discounted
cash flow
dollar-weighted, 939
internal, 52, 83-91, 596
multiple, 86-87
time-weighted, 939-40
Rate-of-return rule, 15, 20
Ratios. *See* Financial performance
analysis: financial ratios in
Ravenscroft, D.J., 889
Raviv, A., 578*n*
Reagan, P., 935*n*
Real assets, 3
Real interest rates, 102, 103, 592
Real options, 746
Recaptured depreciation, 106, 107,
129-30
Receipt for final prospectus, 366*n*
Receivables, loans secured by,
845-46
Receiver in bankruptcy, 805
Receivership, 805
Receiving order, 806
Recourse, loan with, 845
Red herring, 365
Redeemable preferred shares, 342
Registered bond, 631
Registrar, 366
Registration statement, 365*n*
Regular cash dividends, 395
Regulation of issues, 365*n*
Reinhardt, U.E., 101*n*, 247, 619*n*
Rental lease, 690
Reorganization, 808-809
Repayment provisions:
of bonds, 633-36
debt, 340
Repeat orders, credit decisions
with, 799-801
Repos, 841*n*
Repurchase agreements, 841
Repurchase, stock, 395-96
and dividend policy, 402, 407
Residual risk, 151*n*
Residual standard deviation, 208
Resources, mergers to combine
complementary, 861
Restrictive covenants, 636-39
Retractable bond, 635, 636
Retrenchment plan, 742
Returns. *See also* Rate of return

debt policy and effect of
leverage on, 434-37
effect of changing capital
structure on, 212-14
effect of inflation on book,
731-32
on equity, 57
example estimating
expected return, 216-18
risk and, 177-81
on total assets, 721-22
Reverse floaters, 640*n*
Revolving credit, 848
Rhee, S.G., 223*n*
Rice, E.M., 958*n*
Riehl, G.W., 875*n*
Riehl, I.G., 875*n*
Rightists, dividend policy as
viewed by, 402-405
Rights certificates, 377
Rights issue, 376-79
choice between cash offer
and, 378-79
effects of, on stock price,
377-78
rights exercise and irrelevance
of issue price in, 378
workings of, 376-77
Riley, R.E., 744*n*
Risk, 141-64, 171-93, 199-230. *See
also* Portfolio risk
Boyle, Panjer and Sharp
study on, 142-44, 145,
148, 149
calculating portfolio risk,
151-56
and the capital asset pricing
model. *See* Capital asset
pricing model
capital budgeting and,
199-229
cost of capital and, 212-14
and debt-equity ratio, 479
debt policy and shifting, 472-73
default risk, grading, 341
discounted cash flow and,
224-28. *See also* Discounted
cash flow
diversification, value additivity and, 162-63
diversification reducing,
149-51
dividend policy and, 403-404
effect of individual securities
on, 156-62
financing deals to reduce
political, 921-23

Ibbotson Associates study on,
142-44, 145-46, 148, 149
in managing pension fund,
935-36
market, 151, 156-57
Markowitz, portfolio theory
and, 171-77
borrowing and lending,
176-77
combining stock into
portfolios, 173-75
limits to diversification,
162-63
measuring portfolio, 144-51
and present value, 13-14
relationship between return
and, 177-81
unique, 151
and validity and role of capital
asset pricing model, 181,
183-86. *See also* Capital
asset pricing model
Risk-adjusted discount rate, 224,
225
unusable, for long-lived
assets, 227-28
Risk arbitrage, 880*n*
Risk-free rate discounting in
Monte Carlo simulation, 252
Risk-free rate of interest, in calculating value of European
options, 520*n*, 521*n*
Risk indexes, 794-97
Risk premium, 144
Risky-debt valuing, 591-621
allowing for risk of default,
612-20
and classical theory of interest, 592-95
duration and volatility in,
669-72
term structure and. *See* Term
structure
yield to maturity and. *See*
Yield to maturity
Ritter, Joy, 367
Roberts, H.V., 315*n*, 319
Robinson, C.M., 339*n*
Robinson, M.J., 183*n*, 191*n*, 330*n*
Rock, K., 367*n*
Rockley, L.E., 290*n*
Roll, R., 183*n*, 185, 191, 319*n*,
325*n*, 326, 327, 328, 593*n*,
606*n*, 889*n*, 908, 958*n*
Rorke, C.H., 210*n*, 211, 212
Rosenberg, B., 414, 734
Ross, I., 827*n*

STUDENT REPLY CARD

In order to improve future editions, we are seeking your comments on *Principles of Corporate Finance,* Second Canadian Edition, by Brealey/Myers/Sick/Giammarino.
   After you have read this text, please answer the following questions and return this form via Business Reply Mail.   *Thanks in advance for your feedback!*

1. Name of your college or university: _____

2. Major program of study: _____

3. Your instructor for this course: _____

4. Were any chapters or sections of this text *not* assigned as course reading? _____
   If so, please specify those chapters or sections:

5. How would you rate the overall accessibility of the content? Please feel free to comment on reading level, writing style, terminology, layout and design features, and such learning aids as chapter objectives, summaries, and appendices.

6. What did you like *best* about this book?

7. What did you like *least?*

If you would like to say more, we'd love to hear from you. Please write to us at the address shown on the reverse of this card.

- - - CUT HERE - - -

CUT HERE

SOME USEFUL FORMULAS

(The section number indicates the principal reference in the text.)

Perpetuity (3-2)

The value of a perpetuity of $1 per year is:

$$PV = \frac{1}{r}$$

Annuity (3-2)

The value of annuity of $1 per period for t years (t-year annuity factor) is:

$$PV = \frac{1}{r} - \frac{1}{r(1 + r)^t}$$

A Growing Perpetuity (the "Gordon" model) (3-2)

If the initial cash flow is $1 at year 1 and if cash flows thereafter grow at a constant rate of g in perpetuity,

$$PV = \frac{1}{r - g}$$

Continuous Compounding (3-3)

If r is the continuously compounded rate of interest, the present value of $1 received in year t is:

$$PV = \frac{1}{e^{rt}}$$

Capital Cost Allowance (6-2)

The undepreciated capital cost left at the end of year t for an asset with CCA rate d and capital cost C is:

$$UCC_t = C(1 - d)^t$$

The CCA tax shield for year t is:

$$CCA = CdT_c(1 - d)^{t-1}$$

The present value of the perpetual CCA tax shield is:

$$PV = \frac{CdT_c}{r + d}$$

Equivalent Annual Cost (6-3)

If an asset has a life of t years, the equivalent annual cost is:

$$\frac{PV\ (costs)}{t\text{-year annuity factor}}$$

Measures of Risk (7-2 to 7-4)

Variance of returns

$= \sigma^2$

$= $ expected value of $(\tilde{r} - r)^2$

Standard deviation of returns

$= \sqrt{\text{variance}} = \sigma$

Covariance between returns of stocks 1 and 2 $= \sigma_{12}$

$= $ expected value of

$[(\tilde{r}_1 - r_1)(\tilde{r}_2 - r_2)]$

Correlation between returns of stocks

1 and 2 $= \rho_{12} = \dfrac{\sigma_{12}}{\sigma_1 \sigma_2}$

Beta of stock $i = \beta_i = \dfrac{\sigma_{im}}{\sigma_m^2}$

Variance of Portfolio Returns (7-3)

The variance of returns on a portfolio with proportion x_i invested in stock i is:

$$\sum_{i=1}^{N} \sum_{j=1}^{N} x_i x_j \sigma_{ij}$$

Capital Asset Pricing Model (8-2)

The expected risk premium on a risky investment is:

$$r - r_f = \beta(r_m - r_f)$$

Capital Asset Pricing Model (Certainty-Equivalent Form)

(Chapter 9 Appendix)

The present value of a one-period risky investment is:

$$PV = \frac{C_t - \lambda \text{Cov}(\tilde{C}_1, \tilde{r}_m)}{1 + r_f}$$

where

$$\lambda = \frac{r_m - r_f}{\sigma_m^2}$$

Value of Right and Ex-Rights Price (Chapter 15, Appendix 15-1)

If N is the number of rights required to buy 1 share, the value of a right is:

$$\frac{\text{Rights-on price} - \text{issue price}}{N + 1}$$

$$= \frac{\text{ex-rights price} - \text{issue price}}{N}$$

The ex-rights price is:

$$\frac{1}{N + 1}(N \times \text{rights-on price} + \text{issue price})$$